Understanding A Course In Miracles Workbook Lessons

How to End Blame, Shame, Guilt and Fear With Love and Forgiveness

Author: Thomas Wakechild

Copyright 2014 by Thomas Wakechild

Published by Bay West Centre LLC

Copyright 2014 by Thomas Wakechild

My gift to you.

Get your free report and learn how to better manage your fears.
Does fear dominate your life? If you re to manage, control and eventually eliminate fear, you first need to understand what fear is and the root cause of your fears. In this free introductory guidebook you will discover: · What fear is · The two questions that if answered incorrectly will trap you in fear. · The interrelationship between stress and fear · Three common fears · Two emotions and two thought systems that control your state of mind · Proven solutions to control, manager and eliminate your fears. Click the following link to download your free report and guide book now.

Download Free Report

If above link is not live, use URL address: https://landing.mailerlite.com/webforms/landing/q2i0p0

Table of Contents

Forward by Jon Mundy: Why Study the Workbook of A Course in Miracles?

One of the things that makes <u>A Course in Miracles</u> unique among spiritual disciplines is its Workbook with its 365 lessons, or exercises. If the Course consisted of only the Text, it would not have become as important as it has. It would still be an interesting book. We could discuss the depth, and the height of the ideas, but we would be missing out on the practical application.

"Do you believe that guilt is hell? If you did, you would see at once how direct and simple the text is, and you would not need a workbook at all. No one needs practice to gain what is already his."W-39.2:4-6

On three separate occasions the Course says, "Guilt is hell." Being separated from God is hell. The ego tries to convince us that we are not a part of God and this leads us to sorrow and sadness. The purpose of <u>A Course in Miracles</u> is to help us remember what we are. Spirit, our true identity, need not be taught because it is changeless and eternal. Our "real thoughts" are the thoughts we think with God.

The ego thought system, however, having been learned must now be "unlearned," in order for us to find our way Home. We have been taught that we are mortal bodies trapped in an ego ridden mind. In truth, you are not an ego and you are not a body. No one is. How could a fantasy be true? The "work" of the Course involves our unlearning what we are not so that we might re-member, or better "re-cognize," the truth of who we already are.

In the first chapter of the Course, it says that it is "a course in mind training." All real learning necessarily involves attention and study and we have a number of "lessons" we need to learn. The more the Course is studied and the principles applied, the more "miracles" happen and things work out naturally, for the good, "the way they are supposed to."

"Miracles are natural, when they don't happen something has gone wrong." T-1.I.6

Helen Schucman, the scribe of the Course, was an academician; thus the Course includes a Textbook, a Workbook, a Teacher's Manual, and two pamphlets. If we read the Text over and again, we will gain a lot of very helpful information. However, in order to really learn and absorb the content of the Course, we must do what it asks us to do. We need to "work" the Workbook in order for the Holy Spirit to find a way to work with and through us, helping us awaken to the memory of who we already are. When Helen complained: "this Course isn't working." Jesus said, "Why don't you do what I'm asking you to do so you can hear my voice even better?"

The Workbook lessons start off with a bang. It pulls no punches. Right away we are thrown into the river of Truth, and we must learn to swim — learn to see things differently.

Look at the first two lessons:

1. Nothing I see means anything.

2. I have given everything I see, all the meaning that it has for me.

Initially, the first lesson in and of itself doesn't seem to make sense. However, by the second lesson, we already understand that whatever we see is total our responsibility. The reason "nothing I see means anything" is because whatever meaning I perceive, is the meaning I have chosen to give it. The Lessons begin by helping us to let go of the old ways of seeing thus helping us to purify and clear the mind of ego thoughts. The ego-mind is projective, lazy, irresponsible, captious and faultfinding. We need, therefore, to do these Workbook "exercises" as we have to "undoing" the ego's lies, in order to make room for the Truth. As soon as the lies are gone, the truth floods in to take its place.

Principle No. 7 of the 50 Miracles Principles says, "Miracles are everyone's right but purification is necessary first." First, we have to clean house: "If you are feeling depressed, start cleaning." There is something about setting our world in order that helps to bring the mind in order. We start in the simplest way then by "undoing" or "unwinding" the mind from its tangle of fear-based misperceptions.

Ultimately, the whole purpose of a miracle is the undoing of fear. Fear drives us into fragmentation and separation from each other and ever deeper into insanity which, in terms of the Course, can be understood as separation from God. Thus, the Workbook lessons are designed to help us undo fear, by learning how to forgive and how to listen more consistently to the Holy Spirit — the Voice for God.

Loving Unconditionally

A student came to one of my ongoing classes looking for something more than he was able to find in traditional Christianity. He was finding some of his relationships disturbing to his peace of mind. His best friends, he said, were two dogs that he knew loved him unconditionally. He kept asking about forgiveness. "Yes," he would say, "but how do you do it?" I told him that if he really wanted to learn the Course, he would have to do the Workbook lessons. The Text he enjoyed, but the Workbook looked too much like "work." Finally, he quit the class saying that the Course was not working for him. As we begin to do this work, we will encounter strong resistance. Once we've misidentified with the ego—thinking it's who we are—it takes a lot of willingness to let it go.

There is only one rule in the whole Course. "Do not undertake to do more than one set of exercises a day." (W-in.2:6) You can spend more than one day on one lesson. You can go slower than one lesson per day, just don't try to do it faster. The ego has been eons in the making, and it will not come undone in a day. We need to be patient with ourselves. The body is "a learning device." Time is a "learning device," and we are here in these bodies, in time, in order to learn a lesson — to heal the illusion of separation. So it is that we must work things out in the mind and then also through these bodies, in our relationship, in this world, and in time. The good news is that the Course is steadily leading us to the memory of God and thus to Heaven.

Re-learning

One of Freud's greatest discoveries was the amazing depth of the unconscious mind and the tremendous fear and anxieties we keep hidden. The ego's game is all about repression, denial, and projection. "Whatever you do, don't look within," or so says the ego. The Course, on the other hand, is about looking past the ego to the real truth buried deep within. Five-hundred and thirty-eight times the Course asks us to "look." Look at our projections; look beyond the obvious; look upon the world as a means of healing the separation; and look with Love upon all things.

We are literally retraining our minds to see differently – to come to a more peaceful and accepting point of view. In order to do so, we not only need to exercise, we also need to exorcise all the false beliefs we hold about ourselves so that we are able to remember the Truth. We need the help of the Holy Spirit, who shines the light that exposes the ego's hidden, fear-based error. We have a great deal of work to do to undo illusion, and we must explore the depth of our illusion before we can let illusion go.

"You want salvation. You want to be happy. You want peace. You do not have them now, because your mind is totally undisciplined, and you cannot distinguish between joy and sorrow, pleasure and pain, love and fear. You are now learning how to tell them apart. And great indeed will be your reward." W-20.2:5-8

Discipline and the Mind

The word "discipline" comes from the word disciple. A disciple is a follower of a teacher or a teaching. The teacher, be it a book or a person, brings a teaching. The unhealed mind is totally undisciplined. Being undisciplined, we have work to do, which requires time and effort, before we can be healed and whole. We have to purify our perception to remove fear. Einstein said that a wastebasket was a scientist's most important tool. In a similar way a lot of illusory thoughts have to be tossed away before we get to the one truth that endures forever.

How much time do we give to compulsions or hungers of the body we "seem" unable to control? And who is the "we" who cannot control them? When we compulsively follow the ego thought system, we dissociate (separate from Truth) and get caught in a projection of our misperceptions. Or, we become side-tracked by some habituated activity, and we do not even attempt to try to control our minds. An addict does not attempt to control a craving. The addiction has won.

We've all heard the truism about how to get to Carnegie Hall — practice, practice, practice. In order for any serious spiritual discipline to work, it must be practiced. In the practice is the learning. Learning the Course is like learning how to play a musical instrument or learning how to speak a foreign language. There is a lot to learn. Developing fluency or learning how to play an instrument well is oh so rewarding. Keep it up and one might even become a maestro. It may look tough, but doing this work is ultimately "oh, so rewarding." Once the "seeming" battle with the ego is over, we get to go Home.

Practical Suggestions

The Workbook provides "practical instruction" and every-day advice for an entire year. Begin and end the day with the Workbook. You might want to get an extra copy and place it on the nightstand by your bed or in your bathroom. Of course, now you always can find a copy on your I Pad or your phone.

In Lesson 94, we are asked to remind ourselves hourly: "I am as God created me. I am His Son eternally." When the lessons are this intense, it's helpful to have some "device" to help you remember. The daily lesson could work like a mantra. Do the lesson first thing in the morning. Some folks keep the Course in the bathroom next to the toilet where they begin the day in contemplation. See if you can remember the lesson while you are in the shower, see if you can remember the lesson while driving to work.

In order not to lose it, write the lesson for the day on a post-it note and paste it on the side of your computer screen, put it in your wallet or on the dashboard of your car or on the mirror in your bathroom. You can also listen to the daily lesson on the computer, perhaps while doing your yoga. Or you can listen to the lesson on your headphones while taking a walk.

As a single footstep will not make a path on the earth, so a single thought will not make a pathway in the mind. To make a deep physical path, we walk again and again. To make a deep mental path, we must think over and over the kind of thoughts we wish to dominate our lives. – American Transcendentalist Henry David Thoreau (1817-1862)

Doing It Again

After you've finished the Workbook once, there is nothing that says you have to go back and do it again, but folks who do it again find it ever more deeply helpful. Things they had missed the first time now become clearer. It is inevitable that if you do it a second or third time through, it will take you deeper. One day, one of my students said, "I'm just beginning to realize how incredible deep this is." And I said, "Oh yes, incredibly deep. It just keeps getting deeper and clearer. It is after all going all the way Home."

We are all going to the same Home, and we need mental discipline to get back to the Truth which, paradoxically, we never left. We are going to Heaven, and the way to get there is to do what Jesus did, to have the clarity of vision to see what He and Buddha and all the other enlightened ones have seen. Our goal is enlightenment and our real home is Heaven. It is not a place. Heaven is merely an awareness of perfect oneness (T-18.VI.1:5-6). In Lesson 49, God's Voice speaks to me all through the day we read.

"You do not live here. We are trying to reach your real home. We are trying to reach the place where you are truly welcome. We are trying to reach God." W-49.4:508

As we do the lessons in the Workbook, they become more and more gentle and trusting. As we come to know and understand what we are doing, we move ever deeper into the Knowledge of who we already are. The final lesson ends with,

"This holy instant would I give to You. Be You in charge. For I would follow You, certain that Your direction brings me peace." W-365

Lovingly,

Jon Mundy of www.miraclesmagazine.org

Preface

~~ Now Available On-Line ~~

Audio Edition of Understanding A Course In Miracles Workbook Lessons

Get the convenience, flexibility and freedom that comes from lifetime access to the audio version of Understanding A Course In Miracles Workbook Lessons. For a small one-time investment of only $47 USA*, you can listen to any of the 365 daily lessons and notes on demand without the normal physical reading restrictions. You can now go about your busy day knowing you can reconnect with each lesson whenever the need or opportunity arises. To enroll or get more information visit our website at: https://endingfear.org/ You can directly enroll by using URL address shown below: https://endingfear.org/funnel/acim-workbook-class/udb-cl-1-sales-pg/ *Prices subject to change. $47 fee was the current price at the time of this edition.

IMPORTANT NOTE: Understanding A Course In Miracles Workbook was originally published and titled as part of the A Course In Miracles - Dummies Series. This Workbook was Vol III of the series. Except for the title and some editing corrections these two book's contents are identical.

Preface: Would you like to stop blame, shame, guilt and fear from controlling your life? Must your happiness wait for a future fantasyland that never comes? These are questions that demand an immediate answer. After all, if your spiritual practice cannot bring you peace, joy and happiness today, what good is it?

You deserve better. At least I think so and so does Jesus as he states in A Course in Miracles. Your spirituality should teach you how to **respond appropriately to circumstances in your life without compromising your spiritual values or losing your inner peace.** Understanding A Course In Miracles Workbook Lesson is a practical manual that helps you live a happy, self-fulfilled life today. It cuts through the mystery of the Course's esoteric Text and makes Jesus' message understandable to the ordinary reader.

Often, ACIM's promise of inner peace and joy remains an unfulfilled promise. Why? Because most people never take the time to complete the Workbook Lessons. Instead, their ego traps them into trying to decipher the complex ACIM Text. The ACIM Workbook Lessons are designed to bypass the egoic mind and open your heart to the truth. Yet, most students either ignore, struggle or fail to grasp the true meaning and value of these lessons but now you can change that.

ACIM uses a unique terminology that references two different levels of being that are dominated by two opposing thought systems. This book demystifies the lessons by clarifying the appropriate level associated with each passage. Each lesson is specially formatted to replace any unclear references and pronouns with their proper antecedents. Any substitutions are clearly shown in **bold print** for easy reference to the original ACIM 2nd edition.

Each lesson is then followed by an explanatory note to aid in your intellectual understanding of that day's lesson. With this modified format, these lessons become the vehicle for ending the blame, shame and guilt games that once dominated your life. The richness of these lessons now becomes apparent, understandable but more importantly, practical. You now have the tools you need to be the agent for change in your life. You no longer have any excuse not to complete these daily lessons and gain the insight that they provide.

This book's focus is on you. Therefore, it provides the numerous tools you need to help uncover the blocks that are preventing the flow of love into your daily life. By completing the workbook lessons, your heart will be open through an experiential learning process. This knowing will allow you to automatically begin implementing the principles of ACIM into your daily life.

ACIM states that we are all going to make it. But aren't you sick and tired of being sick and tired? You deserve better. To live in fear is not to live. This is not God's Will for you. Change is only one choice away. This is your time to choose again. To reawaken to the truth of who you really are. The <Now> is the only time in which a different choice is possible. The past is over and the future a mere fantasy. Only in the present can you make a different choice.

Let's go on this journey of reawakening together. This material can help you just like it has helped many others to take control of their own lives. This world can become your playschool. It can become the place that you visited to learn, grow and have fun. Life does not have to be a life-and-death struggle. So as you use this book to reawaken to the truth, let's have some fun discovering who you really are.

Note: Understanding A Course In Miracles Text is a companion in this series and covers the entire ACIM Text of 31 chapters.

Introduction to ACIM's Workbook for Students

Introduction

W-in.1.A theoretical foundation such as the **ACIM** text provides is necessary as a framework to make the exercises in this workbook meaningful. 2 Yet it is doing the exercises that will make the goal of the course possible. 3 An untrained mind can accomplish nothing. 4 It is the purpose of this workbook to train your mind to think along the lines the **ACIM** text sets forth.

W-in.2.The exercises are very simple. 2 **The exercises** do not require a great deal of time, and it does not matter where you do **the exercises**. 3 **The exercises** need no preparation. 4 The training period is one year. 5 The exercises are numbered from 1 to 365. 6 Do not undertake to do more than one set of exercises a day.

W-in.3.The workbook is divided into two main sections, the first **part** dealing with the undoing of the way you see now, and the second **part deals** with the acquisition of true perception. 2 With the exception of the review periods, each day's exercises are planned around one central idea, which is stated first. 3 This is followed by a description of the specific procedures by which the idea for the day is to be applied.

W-in.4.The purpose of the workbook is to train your mind in a systematic way to a different perception of everyone and everything in the world. 2 The exercises are planned to help you generalize the lessons, so that you will understand that each of **the lessons are** equally applicable to everyone and everything you see.

W-in.5.Transfer of training in true perception does not proceed as does transfer of the training of the world. 2 If true perception has been achieved in connection with any person, situation or event, total transfer to everyone and everything is certain. 3 On the other hand, one exception held apart from true perception makes **the** accomplishments **of true perception** anywhere impossible.

W-in.6.The only general rules to be observed throughout, then, are: First, that the exercises be practiced with great specificity, as will be indicated. 2 This **specificity** will help you to generalize the ideas involved to every situation in which you find yourself, and to everyone and everything in **that situation**. 3 Second, be sure that you do not decide for yourself that there are some people, situations or things to which the ideas are inapplicable. 4 This **claim that there are exceptions to the general application** will interfere with transfer of training. 5 The very nature of true perception is that **true perception** has no limits **and thus, has no exceptions**. 6 **True perception** is the opposite of the way you see now.

W-in.7.The overall aim of the exercises is to increase your ability to extend the ideas you will be practicing to include everything. 2 This **ability to extend the ideas to include everything** will require no effort on your part. 3 The exercises themselves meet the conditions necessary for this kind of transfer.

W-in.8.Some of the ideas the workbook presents you will find hard to believe, and others **ideas** may seem to be quite startling. 2 This does not matter. 3 You are merely asked to apply the ideas as you are directed to do. 4 You are not asked to judge **the ideas** at all. 5 You are asked only to use **the ideas**. 6 It is their use **of the ideas** that will give **the ideas** meaning to you, and will show you that **these ideas** are true.

W-in.9.Remember only **to apply the ideas**; you need not believe the ideas, you need not accept them, and you need not even welcome **the ideas**. 2 Some of **the ideas** you may actively resist. 3 None of this will matter, or decrease **the ideas'** efficacy. 4 But do not allow yourself to make exceptions in applying the ideas the workbook contains, and whatever your reactions to the ideas may be, use **the ideas**. 5 Nothing more than using **these ideas** is required.

Notes to the Introduction to ACIM's Workbook for Students

For students that have never completed the entire 365 days of ACIM's workbook lessons, your goal should be to get through the lessons rather than linger on one lesson in hopes of doing that lesson perfectly. You do not need to achieve some specific result from a prior lesson before you can proceed to the next lesson. These lessons are designed to bypass the head and enter your heart. They provide an experiential learning process. You can only gain that experience by doing the lessons. Often the question that puzzles you now will be answered by completing a future lesson.

Once you have accomplished getting through the entire workbook, you can always go back and spend as much time as you feel you need on any particular lesson. The only original stipulation is that you do not attempt to complete more than one lesson per day since each is designed to provide an experience that will form the foundation for future lessons. Experiences require time to be assimilated into your consciousness.

An exception to this rule of only one lesson per day might be if you are trying to keep up with a class or group. If you missed a day, I would suggest you just read all prior missed lessons and get back on track with your group. If you are doing these lessons on your own and you miss a few days, I would suggest that you simply reread the last completed lesson and then proceed to do the next new lesson on that same day. This will get you moving forward again.

Do not backtrack or start from the beginning even if there is a large gap between your prior lessons. The objective is to complete the entire workbook once. You can always go back at a later date. Many students, including myself, will repeat these lessons on an annual basis. Once again, perfection is not required. Do not allow missing a day, month or even a year to be the excuse for not resuming where you left off.

Although you may wish to read the entire book without doing the actual lessons, this practice will circumvent the experiential learning process that the exercises were designed to teach. Although your intellectual understanding will be enhanced, your learning will be incomplete. To know and not to be, is not to know. If you choose to read the entire contents of this book in full first, don't shortchange yourself by not actually taking the time to do these lessons on a daily basis.

With that said, let us begin.

LESSON 1.

Nothing I see in this room [on this street, from this window, in this place] means anything.

W-1.1.Now look slowly around you, and practice applying this idea **that nothing I see means anything** very specifically to whatever you see:
2 This table does not mean anything.
3 This chair does not mean anything.
4 This hand does not mean anything.
5 This foot does not mean anything.
6 This pen does not mean anything.

W-1.2.Then look farther away from your immediate area, and apply the idea to a wider range:
2 That door does not mean anything.
3 That body does not mean anything.
4 That lamp does not mean anything.
5 That sign does not mean anything.
6 That shadow does not mean anything

W-1.3.Notice that these statements, **nothing I see means anything,** are not arranged in any order, and **that these statements** make no allowance for differences in the kinds of things to which they are applied. 2 That is the purpose of the exercise. 3 The statement, **nothing I see means anything,** should merely be applied to anything you see. 4 As you practice the idea for the day, use **this idea that nothing I see means anything** totally indiscriminately. 5 Do not attempt to apply **the statement that nothing I see means anything** to everything you see, for these exercises should not become ritualistic. 6 Only be sure that nothing you see is specifically excluded. 7 One thing is like another as far as the application of the idea is concerned.

W-1.4.Each of the first three lessons should not be done more than twice a day each, preferably morning and evening. 2 Nor should **the first three lessons** be attempted for more than a minute or so, unless that entails a sense of hurry. 3 A comfortable sense of leisure is essential.

Notes to Lesson # 1

Nothing I see in this room [on this street, from this window, in this place] means anything.

Do this exercise and notice your reaction to this idea.

Did certain items invoke different reactions?

Was it easy or did some objects create a state of tension or disbelief?

Just note your response and move on to the next item.

Have fun with the experience and stop judging whether you are doing it right and getting the "right" answer. It is being and having the experience that we are after.

Some students may find the notion that nothing you see means anything to be very upsetting. You see a picture of a loved one and emotions well up. How can that picture be meaningless? Yet, if someone else observed that same picture, they would have an entirely different reaction. The picture is the same, so why the different reaction?

Why, because each observer has a different interrelationship with that picture in question. It is the observer's own mind that gives the meaning to the picture, not the item itself.

The world you observe is a world of perception, not one of physical reality.

Perception requires the belief in separation. Perception implies both an observer and something to observe. This duality and separation is an underlying assumption with all things you see. If there was nothing outside yourself to observe, what would there be to see?

When we realize this, we should recognize the fact that an item by itself means nothing unless you are there to observe it. Without your awareness of the item at hand, it would not appear on your radar screen. It is your mind that empowers the object with any meaning you give it.

This is similar to the question, "If a tree falls and there is nothing to hear it, does not make a sound?" The answer is no. You need the interaction of the vibrating air current with an eardrum to make a sound.

It is your interaction with your perceived world that gives an item meaning to you. A rock can have existed for millions of years but until you choose to place your conscious attention upon it and observe it, the million year old rock means nothing to you. It only becomes meaningful to you when you have developed some relationship with it.

Question: Who is really in control over the meaning of what is observed?

Question: In this world of private individual perception, is it the object or the observer that gives the object the meaning that the observer holds to be true?

Question: Must both the object and the observer agree with whatever meaning each perceives to be true or can they differ?

I have given everything I see in this room [on this street, from this window, in this place] all the meaning that it has for me.

W-2.1.The exercises with this idea, **I have given everything I see all the meaning that it has for me,** are the same as those for the first one, which was **nothing I see means anything.** 2 Begin with the things that are near you, and apply the idea to whatever your glance rests on. 3 Then increase the range outward. 4 Turn your head so that you include whatever is on either side. 5 If possible, turn around and apply the idea, **I have given everything I see all the meaning that it has for me,** to what was behind you. 6 Remain as indiscriminate as possible in selecting subjects for the idea, **I have given everything I see all the meaning that it has for me, in this** application. Do not concentrate on anything in particular, and do not attempt to include everything you see in a given area, or you will introduce strain.

W-2.2.Merely glance easily and fairly quickly around you, trying to avoid selection by size, brightness, color, material, or relative importance to you. 2 Take the subjects simply as you see them. 3 Try to apply the exercise with equal ease to a body or a button, a fly or a floor, an arm or an apple. 4 The sole criterion for applying the idea **that I have given everything I see all the meaning that it has for me** to anything **you see** is merely that your eyes have lighted on **that object**. 5 Make no attempt to include anything particular, but be sure that nothing is specifically excluded.

Notes to Lesson # 2

Lesson # 2: I have given what I see all the meaning it has for me.

As stated in the previous exercise, the world that we claim to physically observe is actually a world of individual perception. In this case, the perception always comes from the unique viewpoint of the observer. This means that the observer has the ability to color or interpret what the eyes physically see. Your mind determines the meaning that you place on everything you see. It is your own mind that places value to what you perceive. Normally, these perceptions are drawn from past relationships that the perceiver has had with the object. Physiologists tell us that physical sight is not like a camera lens. A camera lens takes in the entire area within the range of its lens. Unlike an objective camera, our mind actually has to make a subjective choice upon what it chooses to focus. It is this subjective choice that brings the object into our awareness. Because of this, individual perception differs based on each party's past interrelationships and beliefs that they have had with the object in question. The notion of good or bad are relative concepts and not fixed since each perceiver will color their own world based on their past relationships and viewpoints.

In doing this exercise, perhaps you focused on something that was unfamiliar to you. For example, while I was doing this exercise my eyes focused upon something that was hanging from a lamp. It was what I would call a trinket. It's a decorative item that my wife places on various objects for aesthetic purposes. These trinkets have no real purpose other than perhaps to bring beauty or add a decorative element to the object it adorns. When I spotted this trinket, it really had little or no meaning for me since I really lacked any relationship with it. As such, it was of questionable value or purpose. I was unable to name the object in question, and therefore, it had little or no meaning to me.

When you name something, you define it. When you define it, you limit it. You have now assigned a specific purpose or function and from that moment on, that is how you will generally perceive it. You have pigeonholed the object's function and purpose by the name that you assign. Due to the limitation placed on the object through your naming it, you can no longer see that it could have multiple functions and purposes.

Question: Have you ever come across some object that you had no past relationship with?

Question: When confronted with some object that you are unfamiliar with, do you approach that unknown object with caution, curiosity, avoidance or fear?

Question: How do you approach people that you are unfamiliar with?

LESSON 3

I do not understand anything I see in this room [on this street, from this window, in this place].

W-3.1.Apply this idea, **I do not understand anything I see,** in the same way as the previous ones, without making distinctions of any kind. **The previous idea from lesson #1 was: Nothing I see in_____ means anything and from Lesson #2: I have given everything I see all the meaning that it has for me.** 2 Whatever you see becomes a proper subject for applying the idea. 3 Be sure that you do not question the suitability of anything for application of the idea, **which is I do not understand anything I see.**. 4 These are not exercises in judgment. 5 Anything is suitable if you see it. 6 Some of the things you see may have emotionally charged meaning for you. 7 **If the item has an emotionally charged meaning for you**, try to lay such feelings aside, and merely use these things exactly as you would anything else.

W-3.2.The point of the exercises is to help you clear your mind of all past associations, to see things exactly as they appear to you now, and to realize how little you really understand about **the item in question**. 2 It is therefore essential that you keep a perfectly open mind, unhampered by judgment, in selecting the things to which the idea for the day, **I do not understand anything I see,** is to be applied. 3 For this purpose one thing is like another; equally suitable and therefore equally useful.

Notes to Lesson #3

I do not understand anything I see.

Question: Have you ever not been able to see the forest through the trees?

Physiologists tell us that our physical seeing is not similar to what is observed through a camera lens. Physical eyesight is a rather complicated process that only takes in a very small percentage of what we normally would call our full field of vision. What we actually observe are small portions of the total field that is observable with large gaps in the full field left unaccounted. Our mind then filters that limited visual stimulus and fills in the gaps with what the mind believes should be out there based on prior experiences. Both physiologists and psychologists tell us that what we claim we objectively see tends to be a predetermined thought confirmation process that confirms our mind's preconceived notions and beliefs. Eyesight is not the objective reality that we claim it to be. This is why criminologists tell us eyewitness testimony is highly inaccurate. This inaccuracy is due to the mind's prejudicial beliefs and the physical senses' inability to accurately report historical data. This is why criminologists discount subjective eyewitness reports and instead look for objective non-human evidence.

The physical senses actually have a very limited range and focus. The focus is determined by what the mind has chosen to place its awareness upon. Although we like to believe that our mind has the ability to multitask, this capability is highly overrated.

Example: In clinical research, when a test subject was given an assignment to observe a particular activity that was taking place in a room, over 60% failed to observe the entrance and exit of a man dressed in a gorilla suit walking through that same room. The observer's mind was laser focused on the assigned tasks and failed to observe the obvious gorilla in the room. The test subjects were unaware of the big picture and, therefore, they were not privy to what was actually happening in the entire room.

Because of our limited focus, we do not truly understand the multiple faceted interrelationships or big picture that is actually unfolding before us. This lack of big picture perspective limits our understanding of what is actually taking place.

Note: It is important to note that when A Course in Miracles uses the term "seeing," it is different than the term vision. In every day usage, the terms seeing and vision would be interchangeable, but this is not the case for A Course in Miracles' purpose. When ACIM uses the term seeing, it is referencing the subjective physical sight process with all the subjective filtering that has occurred through the perceiver's egoic mind. Because of this filtering, what we refer to as seeing is actually a process in which the egoic mind has predetermined what it expects to observe outside itself. The egoic mind then assigns to the physical senses the task of looking outside itself to find something that will confirm that its predetermined beliefs are correct. Thus, the physical senses ignore any contradictory evidence and only report back information that supports its preconceived belief. The physical senses are not objective but rather they are thought confirmation devices.

The term vision, unlike seeing, involves the objective verification of reality. In this case, it would be more like a camera lens that captures the entire picture without preconceived notions or limitations. It does not go through the filtering process of the egoic mind. No subjective, made up, egoic story colors the observation.

For our purposes, I have used the term egoic mind so let me explain what I mean by that. The egoic mind comes from the belief that separation is both a physical, mental and spiritual reality. It is predicated on the belief that you are the body and the body is you. It claims that you are a limited ego body in competition with other limited ego bodies struggling for the limited resources that each needs to survive. This limited belief of who you are is the root cause of fear-based thinking.

Question: Have you ever judged something incorrectly because you failed to have the big picture?

Question: Can you correctly judge based on only one person's side of the story?

Note: Although the physiology behind physical sight is beyond the scope of this class, a more detailed explanation of the mental process involved with physical seeing is detailed in my <u>Uncovering Your Default Beliefs</u> class.

LESSON 4

These thoughts do not mean anything. They are like the things I see in this room [on this street, from this window, in this place].

W-4.1.Unlike the preceding Lessons # 1-3, these exercises do not begin with the idea for the day. 2 In these practice periods **for Lesson #4**, begin with noting the thoughts that are crossing your mind for about a minute. 3 Then apply the idea **that these thoughts do not mean anything** to those same thoughts that were previously crossing your mind. 4 If you are already aware of unhappy thoughts, use **those unhappy thoughts** as subjects for the idea **that these thoughts do not mean anything**. 5 Do not, however, select only the thoughts you think are "bad." 6 You will find, if you train yourself to look at your thoughts, that your thoughts represent such a mixture that, in a sense, none of your thoughts can be called "good" or "bad." 7 This is why your thoughts do not mean anything.

W-4.2.In selecting the subjects for the application of today's idea, the usual specificity is required. 2 Do not be afraid to use "good" thoughts as well as "bad" **thought**s. 3 None of **your thoughts that are crossing your mind** represents your real thoughts. **Your real thoughts** are being covered up by the **thoughts that are crossing your mind.** 4 The "good" **thoughts** are but shadows of what lies beyond, and shadows make sight difficult. 5 The "bad" **thoughts** are blocks to sight, and make seeing impossible. 6 You do not want either **the thoughts that you have judged as either good or bad**.

W-4.3.**Lesson #4, these thoughts do not mean anything and that these thoughts are like the things I see,** is a major exercise, and will be repeated from time to time in somewhat different form. 2 The aim here is to train you in the first steps toward the goal of separating the meaningless from the meaningful. 3 **Lesson #4** is a first attempt in the long-range purpose of learning to see the meaningless as outside you, and the meaningful within you. 4 **Lesson #4** is also the beginning of training your mind to recognize what is the same and what is different.

W-4.4.In using your thoughts for application of **today's idea, these thoughts do not mean anything and that these thoughts are like the things I see,** identify each thought by the central figure or event **that thought** contains; for example:
2 This thought about ___ does not mean anything.
3 It is like the things I see in this room [on this street, and so on].

W-4.5.You can also use the idea for a particular thought that you recognize as harmful. 2 This practice **of focusing on a particular thought that you recognize as harmful** is useful, but is not a substitute for the more random procedures to be followed for the exercises. 3 Do not, however, examine your mind for more than a minute or so. 4 You are too inexperienced as yet to avoid a tendency to become pointlessly preoccupied.

W-4.6.Further, since these exercises are the first of their kind, you may find the suspension of judgment in connection with thoughts particularly difficult. 2 Do not repeat these exercises more than three or four times during the day. 3 We will return **to these exercises** later.

Notes to Lesson # 4

These thoughts do not mean anything. They are like the things I see in this room [on this street, from this window, in this place].

Thoughts by themselves do not mean anything. They have no ability to change the truth of what is really there. They are like passing clouds that come and go. These clouds can appear to block the true vision of the sun beaming down in the sky but they have no ability to stop the sun from shining. Thoughts have no true power to change reality. Yet, in your world of private individual perception, thoughts raised to the level of beliefs do have the ability to temporarily impact the viewpoint of the thinker. Perception is impacted by the beliefs that are held by the observer. Yet, a passing thought that has not been judged as either good or bad has not been raised to the level of the belief and, therefore, has no impact on the mind of the perceiver. A passing thought may distract the person from observing or being aware of what is happening but it does not modify the event itself. When you place your attention on a passing thought, it is merely a distraction, a loss or change in focus.

Contrast an idle thought that has not been judged as either good or bad, with a thought that has been previously determined to have either a negative or positive impact. Note that we only perceive something as good or bad when we believe that it has some ability to change our world. When something has been judged, it has been raised to the level of belief within the egoic mind. When a thought has been elevated to the level of a belief, it takes on a power of its own. To the perceiver, this belief is the truth about how his world operates. Psychologists now tell us that the belief will have the ability to impact how the observer chooses to interpret their world. Physiologists tell us that the process of seeing will now be adjusted within the mind of the perceiver to fit his new preconceived reality. This is why, when you did the exercise, you may have found it difficult to accept the idea that your thoughts did not mean anything when you actually believed that a thought was either good or bad. It was no longer just a thought. Instead, due to your ego's judgment, this passing thought had been transformed into a belief and that was what made the exercise difficult to accept.

Passing thoughts are mere fantasies and any resemblance to the truth is accidental at best. Thoughts lack certainty because they lack all the facts. As new facts come to light, new thoughts arise which demonstrate the plasticity of thoughts. Yet, the egoic mind is quick to judge a thought based on incomplete evidence. It is your egoic mind's judgment that transforms an idle thought to the level of a belief. Since the belief is held to be true within your mind, your belief will have the ability to affect your individual perception. When you change your judgment, your perception must realign to fit your new perceived reality. Obviously, it would be beneficial to be able to rely on someone or something that was privy to all the facts and knew the real truth before your egoic mind's rush to judgment. False judgments lead to false perceptions which generate false realities. Perception masquerades as your own private reality. Perception is pliable and is easily manipulated.

Example:

First Look at your useful helpful hand.

Next: Look at your old lifeless hand.

Question: Was the observation the same or did your hand transform based on the adjectives used to describe it?

This little example demonstrates how your physical senses are easily manipulated to focus on different aspects of the same thing. It is your mind that told your physical senses what it was supposed to find outside itself. Now the task of the physical senses is merely to confirm what your mind has predetermined is correct. This process cannot be truly considered objective sight since the goal is simply subjective thought confirmation.

Question: What would happen if you consciously decided to change or reframe how you interpreted some past negative event and instead freely chose to view the event as a valuable learning experience that you needed for your own personal growth?

LESSON 5

I am never upset for the reason I think

W-5.1.   This idea, **I am never upset for the reason I think,** like the preceding one, **these thoughts do not mean anything as these thoughts are like the things I see,** can be used with any person, situation or event you think is causing you pain. 2 Apply **this idea that I am never upset for the reason I think,** specifically to whatever you believe is the cause of your upset, using the description of the feeling in whatever term seems accurate to you. 3 The upset may seem to be fear, worry, depression, anxiety, anger, hatred, jealousy or any number of forms, all of which will be perceived as different. 4 This is not **true that these upsets which you perceived as different do not have a common cause. The form that the upset takes may differ but the true cause is the same.** 5 However, until you learn that form does not matter, each form becomes a proper subject for the exercises for the day, **which is I am never upset for the reason I think**. 6 Applying the same idea to each of **the various upsets** separately is the first step in ultimately recognizing **that all forms of upset**s are all the same.

W-5.2.   When using the idea for today for a specific perceived cause of an upset in any form, use both the name of the form in which you see the upset, and the cause which you ascribe to **the upset**. 2 For example:
3 I am not angry at ___ for the reason I think. 4 I am not afraid of ___ for the reason I think.

W-5.3.   But again, this should not be substituted for practice periods in which you first search your mind for "sources" of upset in which you believe, and forms of upset which you think result.

W-5.4.   In these exercises, more than in the preceding ones, you may find it hard to be indiscriminate, and to avoid giving greater weight to some subjects than to others. 2 It might help to precede the exercises with the statement:
3 There are no small upsets. 4 **All upsets are** equally disturbing to my peace of mind.

W-5.5.   Then examine your mind for whatever is distressing you, regardless of how much or how little **distress** you think **the item is causing or is** doing **to your mind**.

W-5.6.   You may also find yourself less willing to apply today's idea to some perceived sources of upset than to other **sources of upset**. 2 If this occurs, think first of this:
3 I cannot keep this form of upset and let the others go. 4 For the purposes of these exercises **including Exercise #4 , I am never upset for the reason I think**, I will regard **all forms of upset** as the same.

W-5.7.   Then search your mind for no more than a minute or so, and try to identify a number of different forms of upset that are disturbing you, regardless of the relative importance you may give **the upset**. 2 Apply the idea for today **that I am never upset for the reason I think,** to each of **these upsets**, using the name of both the source of the upset as you perceive it, and of the feeling as you experience it. 3 Further examples are:
4 I am not worried about ___ for the reason I think. 5 I am not depressed about ___ for the reason I think.
6 Three or four times during the day is enough.

Notes to Lesson # 5

I am never upset for the reason I think.

The world we live in is a world of individual perception colored by our beliefs. Our physical senses are not objective but rather are thought confirmation devices that are processed through our egoic belief filters. We already acknowledged that it is difficult, if not impossible, to judge correctly when we are not privy to all the facts. Exercise #5 follows that reasoning to its logical conclusion. If you lack all the facts about a given situation, if you fail to understand the big picture, there is a high probability that you might judge your situation incorrectly. When you judge incorrectly, your conclusions are very likely to be flawed and your plan to resolve the problem is likely to be wrong.

If you fail to accurately assess the cause of the problem, resolving the problem will be highly unlikely. Eventually, you might get lucky and stumble upon the solution. But it will only be through a process of trial and error, luck and great effort on your part. Only if you are able to identify the true source of the problem, can you focus your energy and full resources on eliminating the root cause. When you solve the problem at its true source, all the negative effects that manifested from the root cause must also disappear.

Occasionally, I still do private coaching and mentoring for people who are either serious about their personal growth or in a great deal of pain. Most have been struggling for years trying to resolve chronic problems with little success. Yet, when we work together, they quickly have quantum breakthroughs. Why? Because we find the real root cause for their issues.

It is amazing to see how quickly long-term problems are resolved when you can focus on the real problem. When you do not know the true cause of the problem, you can only try to minimize, manage and control the effects of the problem. The root cause was never addressed and so the problem persisted. You resolved one form of the problem only to have the problem reappear in another form. The form of the problem may change, but the root cause continues to grow and fester.

When the ACIM speaks of the form that the upset takes, you need to realize that it is really talking about the physical manifestation that is an effect of some underlying root cause. The form can manifest in various shapes and sizes, but all the effects are the result of some underlying cause. Often we tend to focus on the effect of the problem because that is what is easiest to identify. We manage effects and fail to correct the source.

Example: If I am in an abusive situation, I may believe that my boyfriend Johnny, who has anger management issues, is the problem. Believing that the problem is Johnny, I decide to get rid of Johnny and start a new relationship with Joe. Unfortunately, a few months later, I find myself being physically abused because Joe also has those same anger management issues. On the surface, I think my boyfriend is the problem. Yet perhaps the problem is that I am choosing to date people with anger management issues. This would be a helpful insight. But, what if the true root cause of the problem was my own low self-esteem? I did not believe I deserved better.

Would that change my focus and lead to a major breakthrough? You bet it would! Great changes are possible only when you identify the true source of the problem. Until that discovery, you can only attempt to control the damage which is the effect, not the cause, of the problem. When you are wrong about the true source of the upset, you can never resolve the true cause of the problem. You will constantly look for the answer where it can never be found.

I am upset because I see something that is not there.

W-6.1.This exercise **#6** with **its** idea **that you are upset because you see something that is not there** are very similar to the preceding ones, **Exercises #1-5**. 2 Again, it is necessary to name both the form of upset (anger, fear, worry, depression and so on) and the perceived source very specifically for any application of the idea. 3 For example:
4 I am angry at ___ because I see something that is not there.
5 I am worried about ___ because I see something that is not there.

W-6.2.Today's idea **that you are upset because you see something that is not there** is useful for application to anything that seems to upset you, and can profitably be used throughout the day for that purpose. 2 However, the three or four practice periods which are required should be preceded by a minute or so of mind searching, as before, and the application of the idea to each upsetting thought uncovered in the search.

W-6.3.Again, if you resist applying the idea to some upsetting thoughts more than to others, remind yourself of the two cautions stated in the previous lesson: **These two cautions were #1** 2 There are no small upsets. 3 **All upsets** are all equally disturbing to my peace of mind.
4 And **caution #2**:
5 I cannot keep this form of upset and let **the other forms of upset** go. 6 For the purposes of these exercises, then, I will regard **all forms of ups**ets as the same.

Notes to Lesson # 6

I am upset because I see something that is not there.

Question: Have you ever perceived yourself to be mistreated while others who witnessed that same event seem oblivious to the injustice and your pain?

Have you ever asked how could this be?

The answer is simple. We live in a world of perception and perception is based on the viewpoint of each individual perceiver. As such, it is not the objective reality that we claim it to be. It is our own individual subjective reality. Thus, each individual perceiver colors the same events differently based on their own viewpoint, focus and past perspective. This transformation of objective events into subjective interpretation is then mistaken for a common shared reality that all should agree upon. Yet, each has their own unique viewpoint and, therefore, experiences that same event differently. Each starts arguing for the rightness of their interpretation of the event in question. Each privately experienced reality is a natural outcome of perception and becomes each person's own world of private individuated perception.

It is private because it is only held within the mind of each individual perceiver. This means that each person's interpretation of the events will not necessarily be exactly the same or even similar to another observer's retelling of the tale. It is individuated because it has been created within the mind of each individual. Each is the creator of their own personal reality. It is perception because it does not necessarily represent the facts, but rather is someone's story or interpretation of what happened. This means that the story cannot be safely relied upon to represent objective reality.

The story has become what I would refer to as that person's provisional reality. It is provisional because it is subject to change. As a person's interpretation or recall of the story changes, the actual events themselves seem to become metamorphic. The events transform with each embellishment to better conform to each revision of the storyline. Yet, within the person's mind, the story is now viewed as their actual reality. This is because when you believe your own story, your mind reframes and re-creates the events so that the story will confirm what you currently believe. Thus, within your mind, it is your true reality until you make a conscious decision to modify your story. When you do so, however, you have consciously chosen to create a new provisional reality from which your mind will operate in the future. Your mind will now be able to utilize this new viewpoint to interpret past, current and future events. When you consciously choose to reinterpret past events differently, you give your mind the permission and opportunity to rewrite your past history and change current and future events to support your new provisional reality.

When we say, "I am upset because I see something that is not there," we need to realize that although we need to minimize any damage that the event might currently be causing, we ultimately need to discover the true cause of the problem. All too often, we hope to change the results, without addressing the cause of the problem. When you fail to eliminate the cause of the problem, you should not be surprised when that same problem reappears in your future. When you become caught up in the drama of your own story, you become fixated on its effect. You lose your ability to move past the story's injustice and address the cause of the problem. You get stuck in your past story. You start arguing for the rightness of your story as opposed to how you can take future action to prevent it from reoccurring in the future. You remain trapped in victim consciousness. This arguing for your rightness disempowers you since you remain focused on some past event that cannot be changed. When you focus on your past stories, you are unable to place your attention on the current moment. Yet, it is only in the current moment that you have any power to act. Your past story is no longer part of this current moment unless you choose to drag it with you into the present.

Question: When you are in victim consciousness, is your focus on the past, the present or the future?

Question: In what time frame, past, present or future, does action take place?

Question: In what time frame, past, present or future, does change take place?

A Course in Miracles is black and white. It is impossible to be a little pregnant. You either are pregnant or you are not. For ACIM purposes, you are either at peace or you are not at peace. You cannot find true, lasting inner peace if there is one small war still raging within you. This is why there are no small upsets. They are all equally disturbing to your inner peace. The ultimate goal is to achieve the lasting, permanent inner peace that you seek. Since ACIM's workbook lessons are designed to be practical, their goal is to meet you where you are. Only then can ACIM take you where you need to go.

For all practical purposes, in our world of private individuated perception, the concept of "gray" or "sometimes" does appear to exist. Your world of perception is a sometimes world. Sometimes you are happy. Sometimes you are sad. Your morning may be peaceful. Yet at dinnertime, you may become upset. Don't be too hard on yourself. This is a learning process and often learning involves trial and error. The important thing is that you learn from your experiences so that you can make more appropriate choices in the future. Over this next year, you will be involved in transforming how you perceive yourself. This is a process and change often requires time and nurturing. Often it is necessary to baby step your way forward towards your new goals. You need to learn to crawl before you can walk. You need to walk before you can run. Enjoy the process and realize that the prize you seek is obtainable to you when you trust the process and complete the lessons.

So don't be too hard on yourself. Be open to a new way of thinking. Enjoy the process of reawakening by giving yourself permission to create the new you that you desire and deserve.

Question: Have you ever wasted a lot of time trying to solve a particular problem only to discover that you had failed to take the time to first identify and then properly address the true source of the problem?

Let us learn to be more like firemen. When a fire breaks out, the firemen first rush to the scene to minimize the damage the fire would cause if left unchecked. Next, they go to great lengths to find out the true source of the fire. Once the true cause has been discovered, they try to educate themselves and others so that the source of the problem is eliminated. By following this process, they help minimize the likelihood that a similar fire will reappear somewhere else.

LESSON 7

I see only the past.

W-7.1.This idea **that you see only the past** is particularly difficult to believe at first. 2 Yet **this idea that you see only the past** is the rationale for all of the preceding **six exercises.**
3 **The idea that you see only the past** is the reason why nothing that you see means anything.
4 **The idea that you see only the past** is the reason why you have given everything you see all the meaning that **what you see** has for you.
5 **The idea that you see only the past** is the reason why you do not understand anything you see.
6 **The idea that you see only the past** is the reason why your thoughts do not mean anything, and why **your thoughts** are like the things you see.
7 **The idea that you see only the past** is the reason why you are never upset for the reason you think.
8 **The idea that you see only the past** is the reason why you are upset because you see something that is not there **because you are still carrying your past beliefs into the present.**

W-7.2.Old ideas about time are very difficult to change, because everything you believe is rooted in time, and depends on your not learning these new ideas about **time.** 2 Yet that is precisely why you need new ideas about time. 3 This first time idea **that you see only the past** is not really **as** strange as it may sound at first.

W-7.3.Look at a cup, for example. 2 Do you see a cup, or are you merely reviewing your past experiences of picking up a cup, being thirsty, drinking from a cup, feeling the rim of a cup against your lips, having breakfast and so on? 3 Are not your aesthetic reactions to the cup, too, based on past experiences? 4 How else would you know whether or not this kind of cup will break if you drop **this cup**? 5 What do you know about this cup except what you learned **about cups** in the past? 6 You would have no idea what this cup is, except for your past learning. 7 Do you, then, really see **this item as it is or do you see this item colored by your past beliefs or a story about what a cup should be based upon your perceptions?**

W-7.4.Look about you. 2 **The idea that you see only the past** is equally true of whatever you look at. **All that you see is colored by your past beliefs, perceptions or stories**. 3 Acknowledge **that all you see is colored by your past beliefs, perceptions or stories** by applying the idea for today indiscriminately to whatever catches your eye. 4 For example:
5 I see only the past in this pencil.
6 I see only the past in this shoe.
7 I see only the past in this hand.
8 I see only the past in that body.
9 I see only the past in that face.

W-7.5.Do not linger over any one thing in particular, but remember to omit nothing specifically. 2 Glance briefly at each subject, and then move on to the next. 3 Three or four practice periods, each to last a minute or so, will be enough.

Notes to Lesson # 7

I see only the past.

This idea, I see only the past, is the logical consequence that your experience reflects your perception and not necessarily reality. Rarely will anyone enter into an entirely new experience without some preconceived notions of what the experience will entail. Of course, most of what is happening in our lives is not new, but rather a reoccurrence or continuation of events that are based on our past. They often are not viewed as something new, but merely as a continuation of a long series of interrelated events that are built upon the past. Yet, from where do these preconceived notions of how a current event should play out come?

Obviously, they come from judgments we have made about our past. These past experiences and judgments may be direct or indirect. They are direct when you were personally involved in the experience. They are indirect when you were told about the event by another party. It is interesting that most court systems would view these indirect reports as hearsay and, therefore, inadmissible in a court of law. Still other beliefs about an experience come indirectly through our observation of a similar event. This too is second hand information. Often these preconceived beliefs about an event come from your upbringing, parents, society, educational system or peers. Beliefs, whether directly arrived at or received through indoctrination from third-party sources, are powerful filters placed around your current experiences. Your current experiences do not exist in a vacuum. Instead, you relate your current and future experiences based upon your past. This was demonstrated in this lesson by the example of a cup.

Your egoic mind uses its past beliefs and experiences to create the expectations for your current experience. All too often, you blindly follow your old patterns and your past becomes your current provisional reality. Rather than see each moment as a new opportunity for achieving something bold and new, you choose to bring your past prejudices forward and limit your current possibilities. Your present becomes a replay of your past.

When you view your current situation as merely a continuation of some previous event, you limit your mind's ability to make exciting new quantum breakthroughs. Because you have artificially coupled the present to some past story, your mind must now limit what it believes is possible. This results in your mind's belief that you can only baby step your way to change. Instead of making a clean break from these old stories of dubious origins, your mind sees limitations where possibilities actually exist. These judgmental stories prevent your mind from making a clean break from your past and fast forwarding to the radically different future that you desire and deserve.

When you argue for your limitations, you get to keep them. Change now becomes a struggle and a long drawn out process. Don't you want a better plan?

Question;   Do you often find yourself having the same negative experiences with the same person?

If so, have you come to expect that is the experience you will have again?

Question;   Do you often find yourself in the same or similar negative experience with many different people?

If so, what is the common element that all those experiences share?

LESSON 8

My mind is preoccupied with past thoughts.

W-8.1.This idea, **my egoic mind is preoccupied with past thoughts** is, of course, the reason why you see only the past. 2 No one really sees anything. 3 He sees only his thoughts projected outward. 4 The **egoic** mind's preoccupation with the past is the cause of the misconception about time from which your seeing suffers. 5 **Because of your egoic mind's preoccupation with the past**, your **egoic** mind cannot grasp the present, which is the only time there is. 6 **Your egoic mind** therefore cannot understand time, and y**our egoic mind** cannot, in fact, understand anything.

W-8.2.The one wholly true thought one can hold about the past is that **the past** is not here. 2 To think about **the past** at all is therefore to think about illusions. 3 Very few **people** have realized what is actually entailed in picturing the past or in anticipating the future. 4 The **egoic** mind is actually blank when **the egoic mind is thinking of the past**, because **the egoic mind** is not really thinking about anything.

W-8.3.The purpose of the exercises for today is to begin to train your **egoic** mind to recognize when **your egoic mind is** not really thinking at all. 2 While thoughtless ideas preoccupy your **egoic** mind, the truth is blocked. 3 Recognizing that your **egoic** mind has been merely blank, rather than believing that **your egoic mind** is filled with real ideas, is the first step to opening the way to vision.

W-8.4.The exercises for today should be done with eyes closed. 2 This is because you actually cannot see anything **as it truly is with your physical eyes because your physical senses are filtered through your egoic mind**, and it is easier to recognize that no matter how vividly you may picture a thought **with your physical eyes since these thoughts are then filtered by your egoic mind**, you are not seeing anything. 3 With as little investment as possible, search your **egoic** mind for the usual minute or so, merely noting the thoughts you find there. 4 Name each one by the central figure or theme **that thought** contains, and pass on to the next **thought**. 5 Introduce the practice period by saying:
6 **My egoic mind** seems to be thinking about ___.

W-8.5.Then name each of your thoughts specifically, for example:
2 **My egoic mind** seems to be thinking about [name of a person], about [name of an object], about [name of an emotion], and so on, concluding at the end of the mind-searching period with:
3 But my **egoic** mind is preoccupied with past thoughts.

W-8.6.This can be done four or five times during the day, unless you find it irritates you. 2 If you find it trying, three or four times is sufficient. 3 You might find it helpful, however, to include your irritation, or any emotion that the idea for today may induce, in the mind searching itself.

Notes to Lesson # 8

My mind is preoccupied with past thoughts.

Lesson 8 continues the idea that what you perceive as your current reality is based on your past. It also introduces the idea that how we perceive time may also be incorrect.

Both physiologists and psychologists tell us that our physical senses are not the objective cameras to the world that we have been led to believe. Instead, your five senses are subjective thought confirmation devices. Your senses are designed to prove that what your mind originally holds to be true is verified by your senses and continues to remain your own individuated private provisional reality.

Lesson 8 states that no one really sees anything. Instead, you only see your own thoughts that you have projected outward. Psychologists will call this phenomenon projection. Projection relates to your mind's ability to project its own thoughts, fears and guilt outside its own personage and see those same items reflected in your external world. Each person's past is utilized to judge their own current experiences. Rather than objectively observing what is happening in the present moment, your mind is filtering all activities based on its prior preconceived beliefs and judgments. This preoccupation with your egoic past is impacting how the current situation is perceived. Instead of being in a state of objective openness, you are in a constant state of egoic judgment.

The egoic mind is one perpetual judging machine. These judgments that you carry from your past beliefs then color your current experiences so that the current events are interpreted to reconfirm the original judgment's correctness. Your egoic mind is determined to be right. As strange as it sounds, your ego would prefer to be right than happy. Because of this phenomenon, your present experiences tend to be replays of the past and any favorable modification tends to occur in small baby steps because our egoic mind is incapable of accepting the fact that its prior beliefs may be totally wrong. We will be discussing the psychological concept of projection in greater depth as we proceed in these workbook lessons.

This workbook lesson makes the bold statement that our mind cannot grasp the present, which it then claims is the only time there is. It also claims that our egoic mind cannot understand time and because of that fact, our egoic mind is incapable of understand anything. It states that the only true thought we could hold about the past is that it is not here.

The past is not here because by definition it is something that is over. It can only be brought forward into what we might call the present awareness by your own desire to do so. The past cannot be happening in the present or it would not be your past. Yet, when your egoic mind is preoccupied with the past, your mind chooses to bring its past beliefs into the present moment.

As an analogy, suppose you had only 100 energy circuits available to access anything that your mind wished to place its attention upon. In this analogy each energy circuit is only capable of handling one small item at any given moment. Let's also assume it requires all 100 circuits to be able to completely and correctly observe your current environment.

When these energy circuits are preoccupied by past beliefs and judgments, you no longer have the full complement of 100 circuits available to observe your current environment. If 40 of these circuits are dedicated to preserving or bringing your past egoic beliefs into your current consciousness, that leaves only 60 available for current observation. In this simple analogy, your current environment becomes a combination of 40% past beliefs and 60% current events. If this is the case, how much of your present environment would you physically observe objectively and what percentage would be filled in by your past?

 In order to be in what I will call the <now>, you need all 100 circuits to be focused on your current environment without any preconceived beliefs brought forward to color your physical reality. These 40 energy circuits that are focused on the past, distort, embellish and misrepresent what is actually taking place in the <now>. The <now> instead becomes what we commonly refer to as the present. What you refer to as the present merely represents a combination or blend of current and past beliefs and experiences.

Time has many definitions. One of the definitions of time that I'd like you to consider is the idea that time is the measure of change. As you experience more rapidity of change in your life, time appears to speed up. When there is little or no change taking place, time appears to be slowing down or totally stagnant. The notion that time is a measure of change helps move our understanding away from time being a constantly paced linear progression in one direction from past, present to future. We will be discussing time and its various meanings and definitions as we proceed in these lessons.

Question: What would happen if 90% of all your current available energy circuits were dedicated to preserving the rightness of your past egoic judgments and beliefs ?

Question: If 90% of your energy circuits were dedicated to maintaining your past egoic beliefs, how would that impact your ability to be objectively aware of what is taking place in the present moment?

Question: Assuming this 90/10 split, how likely would it be that you could be objective or in the <now>?

LESSON 9

I see nothing as it is now.

W-9.1.This idea, **I see nothing as it is now,** obviously follows from the two preceding ones. **Lesson #7 was I see only the past and Lesson #8 was my mind is preoccupied with past thoughts.** 2 But while you may be able to accept **this idea that I see nothing as it is now** intellectually, it is unlikely that **this idea that I see nothing as it is now** will mean anything to you as yet. 3 However, understanding is not necessary at this point **in these workbook lessons.** 4 In fact, the recognition that you do not understand is a prerequisite for undoing your false ideas. 5 These exercises are concerned with practice, not with understanding. 6 You do not need to practice what you already understand. 7 It would indeed be circular to aim at understanding, and assume that you have **understood** it already.

W-9.2.It is difficult for the untrained **egoic** mind to believe that what **the untrained egoic mind** seems to picture is not there. 2 This idea **that what the untrained egoic mind seems to picture is not there** can be quite disturbing, and may meet with active resistance in any number of forms. 3 Yet that does not preclude applying **this idea that what the untrained egoic mind seems to picture is not there.** 4 No more than applying **the idea that what the untrained egoic mind seems to picture is not there** is required for these or any other exercises. **Your faith or belief in the idea is not required** 5 Each small step will clear a little of the darkness away, and understanding will finally come to lighten every corner of the **egoic** mind that has been cleared of the debris that darkens it.

W-9.3.These exercises, for which three or four practice periods are sufficient, involve looking about you and applying the idea for the day to whatever you see, remembering the need for **each idea's** indiscriminate application, and the essential rule of excluding nothing. 2 For example:
3 **My egoic mind** does not see this typewriter as it is now.
4 **My egoic mind** does not see this telephone as it is now.
5 **My egoic mind** does not see this arm as it is now.

W-9.4.Begin with things that are nearest you, and then extend the range outward:
2 **My egoic mind** does not see that coat rack as it is now.
3 **My egoic mind** does not see that door as it is now.
4 **My egoic mind** does not see that face as it is now.

W-9.5.It is emphasized again that while complete inclusion should not be attempted, specific exclusion must be avoided. 2 Be sure you are honest with yourself in making this distinction. 3 **Your egoic mind** may be tempted to obscure **this distinction and thus, specifically excluded some items.**

Notes to Lesson # 9

I see nothing as it is now.

The idea that you see nothing as it is now is the logical consequence of the previous two lessons. Lesson 7 stated that you only see the past and Lesson 8 expanded and reconfirmed this idea by stating that your mind is preoccupied with past thoughts. No further explanation will be offered at this time. Just remember that your world is a world of perception. It is not a world of objective physical reality that we were led to believe.

The focus of the lesson's narrative is on the idea that although you may not agree with or understand these statements, your belief in the validity of these statements is not required in order for you to benefit from these exercises. You gain the benefits simply by doing these exercises indiscriminately without excluding anything. These exercises are the start of retraining your mind.

Your mind has been indoctrinated into a fear-based thought system that it now assumes to be correct. Because of this assumption, your present thought system and beliefs are never seriously questioned or challenged. You never ask yourself if your present thought system is serving you or is holding you back from achieving your goals. Is your life better or worse because of the current thought system that you are operating under? Do your beliefs support or hinder happiness?

By doing these exercises, you are beginning the process of opening your mind to a new way of thinking. These exercises will challenge your present thought system. They will provide different experiences that will justify your questioning the validity of your present thought system.

New thinking can lead to new possibilities. When you remain open to change, time speeds up. Your new thinking will challenge your egoic mind's preoccupation with your past and call forth new experience to support those new ideas. When you are open to questioning the validity of your past beliefs, you increase the probability for change to occur.

Question: If you refuse to question your current beliefs, how likely will those beliefs change?

Question: Has your current belief system made you happy or is it dominated by blame, shame, guilt and fear?

<u>Question</u>: Do you believe you can be really happy without changing your current belief system?

LESSON 10

My thoughts do not mean anything.

W-10.1.This idea, **my thoughts do not mean anything,** applies to all the thoughts of which you are aware, or become aware in the practice periods. 2 The reason the idea, m**y thoughts do not mean anything,** is applicable to all of **your thoughts** is that **your thoughts** are not your real thoughts. **These thoughts are thoughts of your egoic mind that does not understand all the facts or have the big picture.** 3 We have made this distinction before that t**hese thoughts are thoughts of your egoic mind that does not understand all the facts or have the big picture**, and **we** will do so again. 4 You have no basis for comparison as yet **between your egoic thoughts and your real thoughts.** 5 When you do, you will have no doubt that what you once believed were your thoughts did not mean anything. **Your real thoughts are based upon all the facts. They come from knowledge, not perception. Your real thoughts are based upon the big picture and therefore represent the truth. Your egoic thoughts do not represent the truth and lack knowledge of the big picture. Therefore, your egoic mind filters all information based on wrong assumptions and therefore, must distort true reality.**

W-10.2.This is the second time we have used this kind of idea **that thoughts do not mean anything. It was originally introduced in exercise #4 which was, these thoughts do not mean anything.** 2 The form is only slightly different. 3 This time the idea is introduced with "My thoughts" instead of "These thoughts," and no link is made overtly with the things around you. 4 The emphasis is now on the lack of reality of what you think you think. **Your egoic mind does not understand all the facts or know the big picture. Therefore, your egoic mind's thoughts are meaningless because they distort reality and are incorrect perceptions.**

W-10.3.This aspect of the correction process began with the idea that the **egoic** thoughts of which you are aware are meaningless, outside rather than within; and then **the egoic mind's filtering process** stresses their past rather than their present status. 2 Now we are emphasizing that the presence of these **distorted past focused** "thoughts" means that you are not thinking. 3 This is merely another way of repeating our earlier statement that your mind is really a blank. 4 To recognize **that your mind is really blank** is to recognize nothingness when you think you see **your distorted perception of reality.** 5 As such, **realizing your egoic mind distorts the truth and replaces the truth with false perception** is the prerequisite for vision.

W-10.4.Close your eyes for these exercises, and introduce **this exercise** by repeating the idea, for today, **my egoic thoughts do not mean anything,** quite slowly to yourself. 2 Then add:
3 This idea **that my egoic thoughts do not mean anything** will help to release me from all that I now believe.
4 The exercises consist, as before, in searching your mind for all the thoughts that are available to you, without selection or judgment. 5 Try to avoid classification of any kind. 6 In fact, if you find it helpful to do so, you might imagine that you are watching an oddly assorted procession going by, which has little if any personal meaning to you. 7 As each one crosses your mind, say:
8 My **egoic** thought about ___ does not mean anything.
9 My **egoic** thought about ___ does not mean anything.

W-10.5.Today's thought can obviously serve for any thought that distresses you at any time. 2 In addition, five practice periods are recommended, each involving no more than a minute or so of mind searching. 3 It is not recommended that this time period be extended, and **this time period** should be reduced to half a minute or less if you experience discomfort. 4 Remember, however, to repeat the idea **that my egoic thoughts do not mean anything** slowly before applying it specifically, and also to add:
5 This idea **that my egoic thoughts do not mean anything** will help to release me from all that I now believe.

Notes to Lesson # 10

My thoughts do not mean anything.

The reason that your thoughts do not mean anything is that your thoughts are from your egoic mind. Your ego is preoccupied with past beliefs. These beliefs do not represent the truth of what is truly out there. What you think you see outside is merely a reflection of your mind's limiting beliefs about what it expects your world to be. Your ego is not objective. Your ego is a big judging machine that argues for its rightness at the cost of your happiness.

Real thoughts would have to be based upon all the facts and represent the truth. Real thoughts come from knowledge, not perception. Your egoic mind filters all information based on its wrong assumptions and therefore, must distort true reality.

It is important to realize that a thought that is incorrect has no ability to change the ultimate reality of truth. Egoic thoughts do, however, have the ability to distort what someone believes is the truth, but this distortion cannot change the truth. This is an important distinction. If your thoughts have no ability to change the truth of reality, do they really mean anything?

If something that you believe is a causative has no ability to affect anything, is it really a cause?

A cause is not a cause if it has no effect on reality. Your erroneous belief that something does affect reality does not change the fact that it is truly impotent. Truth just is. When ACIM uses the word truth, it is talking about the changeless. Truth does not require you to believe it is true.

Yet, in our world of perception, beliefs do have the ability to impact the provisional reality of the holder of the belief. This is why we are focused on the idea that your world is a world of perception, not one based on fact. Real facts must support the real truth. Just because the general population believes something to be true, does not make it true. At one time, the general population believed that the earth was flat. This was believed to be common knowledge and so the population operated as if the world was truly flat. But that common belief did not change the physical shape of the earth. What was called common knowledge eventually was proven to be common misperception.

When ACIM says, my thoughts do not mean anything, we need to remember that even common misperception has no ability to change the truth. If your egoic thoughts do not align with the truth, they have no ability to actually change the truth. If a thought has no ability to change the truth of reality, does it really mean anything? In regards to truth, the thought really is irrelevant and meaningless. Yet, this thought does have the ability to impact your beliefs about what you perceive to be the truth. In your world of perception, it is your beliefs, not the truth, which will determine how you interact with your world. This is why it is important to realize that your egoic thoughts are ultimately meaningless. Not only do they not represent truth due to your lack of knowledge but your thoughts are also meaningless because they lack the ability to change the truth. Truth does not need you to agree with it.

By the same token, if your egoic thoughts did accidentally align with the truth, does your agreement with truth change the truth or makes it truer than it was before you agreed it was correct? Truth just is. Your thoughts are meaningless because they have no ability to change the reality of truth. Your meaningless thoughts only have power within the mind that believes the thought to be true. In your world of perception, only when your meaningless thoughts are raised to the level of a belief, do they appear to take on the power to affect your world of perception.

This one idea, if properly understood and implemented, has the power to totally change how you view your world.

Question: If someone believed they were a dog, would their belief change their true reality and transform them into a dog?

Question: If someone believed they were a dog, would that belief impact how they interacted with their world?

LESSON 11

My meaningless thoughts are showing me a meaningless world.

W-11.1.**My meaningless thoughts are showing me a meaningless world** is the first idea we have had that is related to a major phase of the correction process; the reversal of the **egoic** thinking of the world. 2 It seems as if the world determines what you perceive. 3 Today's idea introduces the concept that your thoughts determine the world you see. 4 Be glad indeed to practice the idea **that my meaningless thoughts are showing me a meaningless world** in its initial form, for in this idea is your release made sure. 5 The key to forgiveness lies in **the idea that my meaningless thoughts are showing me a meaningless world**.

W-11.2.The practice periods for today's idea are to be undertaken somewhat differently from the previous ones. 2 Begin with your eyes closed, and repeat the idea **that my meaningless thoughts are showing me a meaningless world** slowly to yourself. 3 Then open your eyes and look about, near and far, up and down,–anywhere. 4 During the minute or so to be spent in using the idea **that my meaningless thoughts are showing me a meaningless world** merely repeat it to yourself, being sure to do so without haste, and with no sense of urgency or effort.

W-11.3.To do these exercises for maximum benefit, the eyes should move from one thing to another fairly rapidly, since **the eyes** should not linger on anything in particular. 2 The words **that my meaningless thoughts are showing me a meaningless world**, however, should be used in an unhurried, even leisurely fashion. 3 The introduction to this idea **that my meaningless thoughts are showing me a meaningless world** in particular, should be practiced as casually as possible. 4 **This idea that my meaningless thoughts are showing me a meaningless world** contains the foundation for the peace, relaxation and freedom from worry that we are trying to achieve. 5 On concluding the exercises, close your eyes and repeat the idea **that my meaningless thoughts are showing me a meaningless world** once more slowly to yourself.

W-11.4.Three practice periods today will probably be sufficient. 2 However, if there is little or no uneasiness and an inclination to do more, as many as five may be undertaken. 3 More than **five** is not recommended.

Notes to Lesson # 11

My meaningless thoughts are showing me a meaningless world.

Lesson 11, my meaningless thoughts are showing me a meaningless world, is a continuation of the previous ideas and a logical progression from the previous lessons. If our thoughts do not mean anything, they have no power to change the truth. Having no effect on the truth, they are meaningless. If they are meaningless, anything that your meaningless thoughts appear to envision must also be meaningless. If like begets like, meaning cannot arise from your meaningless thoughts.

What is more important, however, is the introduction of the idea that your thoughts determine what you see. Although we have previously discussed this idea based on physiological and psychological research on perception, this is the first clear reference to that idea in these ACIM workbook lessons.

We have been raised under a thought system that assumes your experiences are the direct result of outside forces that are beyond your control. This thought system assumes that these outside forces generate your present experiences This fear-based thought system claims that we are not the true cause of our experiences but mere victims that must react to circumstances that are generated outside of ourselves and beyond our control. Our mind then draws logical conclusions based on these experiences as to how we should react to our outside world. Because of the belief that there are outside forces that determine our experiences, we have limited options as to how we can respond to this outside world. We are not causative, but rather reactive agents in our world. We are not the driving force that controls our world. The best we can hope for is to manage these outside powers so that we minimize their negative effects and maximize any positive results. Under this thought system, you will always lack the creative power to handle a given situation since your fate is ultimately controlled by arbitrary and capricious outside forces that are beyond your direct control.

But what if this teaching is actually wrong? What if we actually did have some causative power to impact what we experience in our world?

We already know that psychologists tell us that although you may not be in total control of your circumstances, you are in control of how you choose to interpret your circumstances. Based on that interpretation, your mind will then determine what it perceives is possible. This, in turn, limits the response options that you perceive are available to choose from.

This is just an introduction to the idea that your thoughts may have some causative power to affect what you perceive. You are not asked or required to believe this idea is true. You are merely asked to continue to do the exercises as prescribed.

Question: How much power do you have to control the events in your life?

Question: What area in your life do you feel you have the most control over?

Question: What area of your life do you feel you have the least control over?

I am upset because I see a meaningless world.

W-12.1.The importance of this idea **that I am upset because I see a meaningless world** lies in the fact that it contains a correction for a major perceptual distortion. 2 You think that what upsets you is a frightening world, or a sad world, or a violent world, or an insane world. 3 All these attributes are given **to the world** by you. 4 **Without these egoic judgments,** the world is meaningless in itself.

W-12.2.These exercises are done with eyes open. 2 Look around you, this time quite slowly. 3 Try to pace yourself so that the slow shifting of your glance from one thing to another involves a fairly constant time interval. 4 Do not allow the time of the shift to become markedly longer or shorter, but try, instead, to keep a measured, even tempo throughout. 5 What you see does not matter. 6 You teach yourself this as you give whatever your glance rests on equal attention and equal time. 7 This is a beginning step in learning to give **whatever your glance rests on** all equal value.

W-12.3.As you look about you, say to yourself:
2 I think I see a fearful world, a dangerous world, a hostile world, a sad world, a wicked world, a crazy world, and so on, using whatever descriptive terms happen to occur to you. 3 If terms which seem positive rather than negative occur to you, include them. 4 For example, you might think of "a good world," or "a satisfying world." 5 If such **"good"** terms occur to you, use them along with the rest. 6 You may not yet understand why these "nice" adjectives belong in these exercises but remember that a "good world" implies a "bad" one, and a "satisfying world" implies an "unsatisfying" one. 7 All terms which cross your mind are suitable subjects for today's exercises. 8 Their seeming quality **of either good or bad** does not matter.

W-12.4.Be sure that you do not alter the time intervals between applying today's idea **that I am upset because I see a meaningless world** to what you think is pleasant and what you think is unpleasant. 2 For the purposes of these exercises, there is no difference between **what you think is pleasant versus unpleasant.** 3 At the end of the practice period, add:
4 But I am upset because I see a meaningless world.

W-12.5.What is meaningless is neither good nor bad. 2 Why, then, should a meaningless world upset you? 3 If you could accept the world as meaningless **and therefore as neither good nor bad,** and let the truth be written upon **a meaningless world** for you, **the truth** would make you indescribably happy. 4 But because **the world** is meaningless, **your egoic mind** is impelled to write upon **the meaningless world** what you would have **your world** be. 5 **What your egoic mind would have your world be** is **what** you see in **this meaningless world.** 6 It is **this false perception that your egoic mind perceives** that is meaningless in truth. 7 Beneath your words is written the Word of God. 8 The truth upsets you now, but when your **egoic** words have been erased, you will see **God's Word.** 9 That is the ultimate purpose of these exercises.

W-12.6.Three or four times is enough for practicing the idea for today. 2 Nor should the practice periods exceed a minute. 3 You may find even this too long. 4 Terminate the exercises whenever you experience a sense of strain.

Notes to Lesson 12

I am upset because I see a meaningless world.

Lesson 11 stated that it is your meaningless thoughts that are showing you a meaningless world. Lesson 12 states that you are upset because you see a meaningless world. Yet, if both are true, your thoughts are the true cause of what is upsetting you, not what you see.

This idea aligns with what psychologists tell us about how your egoic mind works. Your mind places the interpretation or judgment on all events that you see. In your world of perception, your egoic mind judges something as either good or bad. This judgment that you place on the event either upsets or pleases you. You also know from personal experience that when you see something as bad, often another party will see that same event as helpful to their side. Since the event is the same, how can this be?

This is because each person is looking at the event from their perspective and judging that event based on its impact on what they choose to value. If the same event can be experienced as either joyful or frightening, does the event itself have some inherent good or bad attributes?

<OR>

Is it your own interpretation that generates the emotions that you feel that color a neutral event as either good or bad?

This lesson, I am upset because I see a meaningless world, corrects a major perceptual distortion. Lesson 12 states that all the attributes you give to any event come from your own judgmental mind. Without those judgments, the event itself would be meaningless or neutral.

Previously, we said that something is meaningless when it has no ability in and of itself to impact or change something else. In our language, we would say that something is neutral when it has no ability in and of itself to impact or change something else. Meaningless and neutral are synonymous in that neither has the ability to change something else. In both Lesson 11 and 12, we are told that it is our egoic thoughts or judgments that place meaning on something that is actually meaningless. When we substitute the word neutral for meaningless, we more clearly recognize the fact that something that is neutral is neither good nor bad.

All agree that you cannot judge properly if you do not have all the facts or understand the big picture. If this is the case, why would you let your egoic mind that lacks this information judge what is either good or bad? Doesn't it make more sense whenever possible to seek the guidance of someone who has the big picture and all the facts to guide and help you with that decision?

If you are incapable of judging correctly, perhaps you should not be so adamant in arguing for the correctness of what you judged to be either good or bad. When you understand that your erroneous judgments are upsetting, you will be more willing to relinquish those past judgments and be more receptive to the guidance of someone who is more knowledgeable on the subject.

Lesson 12 also makes the point that what is meaningless or neutral is neither good nor bad. In your egoic judgmental world, you have a tendency to perceive something as either good or bad based on some predetermined result. You seek the good and try to avoid the bad. Yet, it is your judgment that gives the event itself the good or bad qualities that you have attributed to it. ACIM points out that when you see something as either good or bad, that item takes on a fearful quality within your mind. You believe that there is something outside yourself that you need to make you happy. Since the source of your happiness is perceived to be outside of you, even when that item is obtained, it still remains a source for fear. Since the power of good or bad is attributed to something outside your mind, you do not control it and therefore, it could be lost. If something can be lost, it will be perceived as a source of fear. If it is your own mind's thinking that endows the object with the attributes you claim it possesses, this means your mind is the true source of the object's power. You are the one in control.

What are your judgments based on?

Judgments are based on what you value and why.

Most people value this world because they believe the world is either

1) a place to get their needs met
2) a place to earn love
3) or a place to earn the good life or some preferred afterlife.

When you value something because you believe it has some inherent ability to make you either happy or sad, you become very judgmental. Since your focus is on the predetermined results, you cannot enjoy the current moment within that journey. When your focus is on earning some particular result, the journey or process becomes an actual source of fear. When your focus is on learning, the process becomes an exciting adventure. Earning is always perceived as a struggle while learning can be a fun puzzle.

Question: What do you value in this world and why?

Question: Do you view your life as an earning or a learning process?

A meaningless world engenders fear.

W-13.1.Today's idea, **a meaningless world engenders fear,** is really another form of the preceding one which was **I am upset because I see a meaningless world,** except that it is more specific as to the emotion aroused **which is fear**. 2 Actually, a meaningless world is impossible. 3 Nothing without meaning exists. 4 However, it does not follow that **your egoic mind** will not think you perceive something that has no meaning. 5 On the contrary, **your egoic mind** will be particularly likely to think you do perceive **a meaningless world that your egoic mind has now given meaning to**.

W-13.2.Recognition of meaninglessness arouses intense anxiety in all the separated ones, **which are represented by the egoic mind**. 2 **Meaninglessness** represents a situation in which God and the ego "challenge" each other as to whose meaning is to be written in the empty space that meaninglessness provides. 3 The ego rushes in frantically to establish its own **egoic** ideas **on the meaninglessness,** fearful that the void may otherwise be used to demonstrate **the egoic mind's** own impotence and unreality. 4 And on this alone, **the egoic mind's own impotence and unreality,** is **the egoic mind** correct.

W-13.3.It is essential, therefore, that you learn to recognize the meaningless, and accept **the meaningless** without fear. 2 If you are fearful, it is certain that you will endow the world with attributes that **the world** does not possess, and crowd **the world** with images that do not exist. 3 To the ego illusions are safety devices, as illusions must also be to you who equate yourself with the ego.

W-13.4.The exercises for today, which should be done about three or four times for not more than a minute or so at most each time, are to be practiced in a somewhat different way from the preceding ones. 2 With eyes closed, repeat today's idea to yourself. 3 Then open your eyes, and look about you slowly, saying:
4 I am looking at a meaningless world.
5 Repeat this statement to yourself as you look about. 6 Then close your eyes, and conclude with:
7 A meaningless world engenders fear because I think I am in competition with God.

W-13.5.You may find it difficult to avoid resistance, in one form or another, to this concluding statement **that a meaningless world engenders fear because I think I am in competition with God**. 2 Whatever form such resistance may take, remind yourself that you are really afraid of such a thought because of the "vengeance" of the "enemy." 3 You are not expected to believe the statement **that a meaningless world engenders fear because I think I am in competition with God** at this point, and will probably dismiss **this statement** as preposterous. 4 Note carefully, however, any signs of overt or covert fear which **this statement that a meaningless world engenders fear because I think I am in competition with God** may arouse.

W-13.6.This is our first attempt at stating an explicit cause and effect relationship of a kind which you are very inexperienced in recognizing. 2 Do not dwell on the concluding statement, and try not even to think of **the concluding statement** except during the practice periods. 3 That will suffice at present.

Notes to Lesson 13

A meaningless world engenders fear.

Lesson13 begins with three interesting ideas. The first is the idea that a meaningless world engenders fear. This is the actual title of this lesson. This is the first time that the ACIM workbook lesson is attempting to state an explicit cause and effect relationship. It is stating that a meaningless world causes fear. Yet, the next statement says that a meaningless world is impossible. This is followed up with the statement that nothing without meaning exists.

How can all these three statements be reconciled?

If a meaningless world engenders fear but a meaningless world is impossible, how can fear result or even exist? But you have to agree that fear dominates this world.

If nothing without meaning exists, then a meaningless world cannot exist but then what are we standing on?

If lack of meaning causes fear, yet nothing is meaningless, what are we frightened about?

If lack of meaning has no ability to change reality, why should something that has no ability to change what you are, frighten you? Yet, most people live in fear.

Whenever you are studying A Course in Miracles and you read statements that appear to be contradictory statements, bells and whistles should go off. This is a warning that there is a divergence with language, perception and reality. What you perceive to be common understanding is actually common misperception. What you are assuming to be reality is actually some false understanding of what is really out there. We must realize that the world of private individuated perception is not the same as the real world which is represented by truth with a capital T.

Your world of private individuated perception, which represents your personal provisional reality, is not the same as the truth that is represented by the reality of the real world. When what you believe does not coincide with the truth, your egoic mind still operates under these false assumptions. What the ego believes becomes its provisional reality or false illusionary world that it perceives to be real. The ego then argues for its rightness. Because the ego believes its artificial world has some power to change reality, the ego must judge what it perceives to be separate as either good, bad or indifferent. Yet, what you claim is true has no ability to make truth with a capital T either more true or less true. What your ego perceives to be the truth is irrelevant since your opinion has no ability to change the reality of what the real truth is. Truth just is. Truth does not require your personal confirmation to make it true. Since your ego believes that its misperceptions are true reality, it continuously argues for the correctness of its own erroneous beliefs. The egoic mind sees itself separate and distinct from all. Believing it is in competition with its outside world, the ego argues for the correctness of its own misperception. The ego sees itself in competition with others to determine what is the "correct" truth. The ego understands that there can only be one truth and therefore, it argues for its own exclusive version of the truth.

Truth has no competition since it is fixed and changeless. Misperceptions cannot change it. Truth does not fear the false. Truth remains unchangeable and invulnerable to false misperceptions. Truth does not need or seek revenge for someone's error in thinking. Truth just remains the truth. Truth knows that your mind's misperceptions are meaningless since the false has no ability to change the truth.

Although we have made no attempt to define the term God, one of the attributes of God must be truth with a capital T. Since your egoic mind perceives itself to be separate from God, it argues for the correctness of its own meaningless thoughts. Your ego judges the world incorrectly and then argues for its rightness even at the cost of your happiness.

Because the ego thinks that its powerless thoughts are not meaningless, the ego creates its own meaningless world of provisional reality. This false world exists only in the mind of the thinker. The ego then gives meaning to that private world of individuated perception. It is this false private world of individuated perception that engenders fear. Because the ego believes its false beliefs to be true, these misperceptions become the false private world you see and relate to. It is this meaningless world that your ego creates within your own mind that engenders all the fear you feel.

Question: What do you fear the most in your world?

Question: Why do you find that item or items so fearful?

LESSON 14

God did not create a meaningless world.

W-14.1.The idea for today **that God did not create a meaningless world** is, of course, the reason why a meaningless world is impossible. 2 What God did not create does not exist. 3 And everything that does exist exists as **God** created it. 4 The world you see has nothing to do with reality. 5 It is of your own **egoic mind's** making, and **therefore, the world you egoically think you see is false perception and** does not exist.

W-14.2.The exercises for today are to be practiced with eyes closed throughout. 2 The mind-searching period should be short, a minute at most. 3 Do not have more than three practice periods with today's idea unless you find **the practice periods** comfortable. 4 If you do **find the practice periods comfortable**, it will be because you really understand what they are for.

W-14.3.The idea for today is another step in learning to let go the **egoic** thoughts that you have written on the world, and see the Word of God in place **of your egoic thoughts.** 2 This exchange **of seeing the Word of God in place of your egoic thoughts** can truly be called salvation. The **early steps** in this exchange **of seeing the Word of God in place of your egoic thoughts** can be quite difficult and even quite painful. 3 Some of the early steps will lead you directly into fear. 4 You will not be left there **in your fear.** 5 You will go far beyond **your fear.** 6 Our direction **that you will be moving** toward is perfect safety and perfect peace.

W-14.4.With eyes closed, think of all the horrors in the world that cross your mind. 2 Name each one **of these horrors** as it occurs to you, and then deny **the** reality **of these horrors.** 3 God did not create **these horrors**, and so **these horrors** are not real. 4 Say, for example:
5 God did not create that war, and so **that war** is not real.
6 God did not create that airplane crash, and so **that airplane crash** is not real.
7 God did not create that disaster [specify], and so **that disaster [specify],** is not real.

W-14.5.Suitable subjects for the application of today's idea also include anything you are afraid might happen to you, or to anyone about whom you are concerned. 2 In each case, name the "disaster" quite specifically. 3 Do not use general terms. 4 For example, do not say, "God did not create illness," but, "God did not create cancer," or heart attacks, or whatever may arouse fear in you.

W-14.6.This is your personal repertory of horrors at which you are looking. 2 These things are part of the world you see. 3 Some **of your personal repertory of horrors** are shared illusions, and others are part of your personal hell. 4 It does not matter **if they are shared with others or are private.** 5 What God did not create can only be in your own **egoic** mind apart from **God's.** 6 Therefore, it has no meaning. 7 In recognition of this fact, conclude the practice periods by repeating today's idea:
8 God did not create a meaningless world.

W-14.7.The idea for today can, of course, be applied to anything that disturbs you during the day, aside from the practice periods. 2 Be very specific in applying **today's idea that God did not create a meaningless world.** 3 Say:
4 God did not create a meaningless world. 5 **God** did not create [specify the situation which is disturbing you], and so **[specify the situation which is disturbing you]** is not real.

Notes to Lesson 14

God did not create a meaningless world.

Lesson 14 is a logical conclusion that arises from an idea in Lesson 13 that nothing without meaning exists. If the world you perceive is meaningless, God could not have created it since nothing without meaning exists. Instead, the world that you claim to you see has nothing to do with reality since it only appears real within your own egoic mind. It is your own private world of provisional reality and is shared with no one.

From the beginning of these lessons, I have tried to emphasize the idea that perception is not the same as reality. Our world is a world of perception that we judge to be either good or bad. It is our own private hell with some illusions being shared with others on a collective basis. Because we have been indoctrinated into a similar fear-based thought system, our seemingly separate minds often reach the same conclusions about this world that we call planet earth. On planet earth, we are taught that we live and share one common world. Yet, when we examine how each person views his world, we see a great divergence of opinion. Each person is viewing this supposedly same shared world differently.

You and I do not live in the same world. Instead, each person actually lives in their own private world of individuated perception. It is a world created in the mind of the beholder. To the degree that each person's belief systems and experiences are similar, there will appear to be some common overlap. The more common your beliefs, experiences and thought systems are with another person, the more similar each person's provisional reality will appear to be. People raised in the same households will have a greater likelihood to view a world that appears to hold many similar attributes. Similarly, two people who have been raised in different societies with different values, different cultural experiences and different class and health issues will perceive their worlds with less overlap.

This lesson states that the only thing that is truly real is what God created, as God created it. What is real is changeless truth. If we lack the big picture or all the facts, we will choose to misperceive what God created. Yet, our erroneous judgments have no ability to alter the truth. Only within one's own delusional mind does their misrepresentation appear to exist. Someone's delusional state has no ability to change what God created, as God created it. Our delusion is impotent and meaningless since it has no effect on anything outside the mind that made up the story in the first place.

We will revisit and expand this idea that God did not create a meaningless world in future lessons because it is an important concept to understand if you are to eliminate fear-based thinking. Today, I would rather address a common misperception that arises from this idea.

Often, I hear ACIM teachers and students state that this world is not real and therefore, we need not be concerned with how we relate to this illusionary world. Although on a theoretical level that may be a correct, it fails to help someone on a practical level. I said that if your spiritual practice does not help you live a fuller, richer, happier life today what good is it? I contend it is no good. There must be a better way. Your spiritual practice should provide practical guidance that helps you live in this world today. It should not be only for some future fantasy land. You are a spiritual being that has chosen to have an earthly experience. To deny the learning lessons that this dimension of time and space provides is to ignore why you chose to come here in the first place.

Let me assure you that if you continue with this class, before the year is over, you will understand that <u>A Course in Miracles</u> has a practical plan that provides step-by-step guidance to help you live a fuller, richer, joyful human life today. You can drop the blame, shame and guilt that are associated with being in this fear-based world. Fear does not have to dominate your life and I will not leave you with the simplistic, yet impractical idea that since this world is an illusion or not real, that it should be ignored or looked upon with disdain.

So keep doing these workbook lessons even though your egoic mind would like to dismiss, ignore and or ridicule these ideas as impractical, illogical or useless. The ego does not know who you really are. Why listen to a voice that has failed to bring the happiness, love, joy and peace that you seek and that it has promised to deliver. Your ego's plan does not work! It hasn't worked in the past. Why should you believe your ego's plan will work in the future? Isn't that the definition of insanity?

365 days is a small commitment for the long-term benefits that this course will provide. Your ego will tell you these classes are too hard or too long.

Don't you listen to your ego and don't you give up! Ask yourself how much long-term happiness and inner peace has come from following your current belief system. It is a bankrupt system that will never take you to the Promised Land.

There has never been anything wrong with you but there has been something wrong with your plan. You need a new plan. Together, we will get that new plan. It will be a plan that is both practical and delivers results.

Question: What are the odds of escaping blame, shame, guilt and fear within a thought system that was designed to generate and perpetuate the blame, shame, guilt and fear that you are trying to avoid?

Question: If you seek change in your life, doesn't it make sense to try a new plan?

LESSON 15

My thoughts are images that I have made.

W-15.1.It is because the thoughts you think you think appear as images that you do not recognize **these images** as nothing. 2 You think you think **the thoughts you imagine** and so you think you see **the thoughts you think as images**. 3 This is how your "seeing" was made. 4 This **seeing the thoughts you think as images** is the function you have given your body's eyes. 5 **Seeing the thoughts you think as images** is not seeing. 6 **Seeing the thoughts you think as images** is image making. 7 **Seeing the thoughts you think as images** takes the place of seeing, replacing vision with illusions.

W-15.2.This introductory idea to the process of image making that you call seeing will not have much meaning for you. 2 You will begin to understand **the process of image making** when you have seen little edges of light around the same familiar objects which you see now. 3 **Seeing little edges of light around familiar objects** is the beginning of real vision. 4 You can be certain that real vision will come quickly when **after seeing little edges of light around the same familiar objects** has occurred.

W-15.3.As we go along, you may have many "light episodes." 2 **These "light episodes" may** take many different forms, some of **these "light episodes "are** quite unexpected. 3 Do not be afraid of **these "light episodes."** 4 **These episodes** are signs that you are opening your eyes at last. 5 **These "light episodes"** will not persist, because **the light** merely symbolize true perception, and **these "light episodes"** are not related to knowledge. 6 These exercises will not reveal knowledge to you. 7 But **these exercises** will prepare the way to **these "light episodes."**

W-15.4.In practicing the idea for today, repeat **the idea, my thoughts are images that I have made,** first to yourself, and then apply **the idea** to whatever you see around you, using the name of **whatever you see** and letting your eyes rest on **the subject** as you say:
2 This ___ is an image that I have made.
3 That ___ is an image that I have made.
4 It is not necessary to include a large number of specific subjects for the application of today's idea. 5 It is necessary, however, to continue to look at each subject while you repeat the idea to yourself. 6 The idea should be repeated quite slowly each time.

W-15.5.Although you will obviously not be able to apply the idea, **my thoughts are images that I have made** to very many things during the minute or so of practice that is recommended, try to make the selection as random as possible. 2 Less than a minute will do for the practice periods, if you begin to feel uneasy. 3 Do not have more than three application periods for today's idea unless you feel completely comfortable with **this exercise** and do not exceed four. 4 However, the idea, **my thoughts are images that I have made,** can be applied as needed throughout the day.

Notes to Lesson # 15

My thoughts are images that I have made.

Lesson 15 states that my thoughts are images that I have made. This lesson describes why this is the case. When you think something, you imagine its appearance within your own mind. Because your thought has been converted into an image within your own mind, you believe that these images must really exist outside your mind. This image within your own mind is what your physical senses are designed to report upon. Paragraph #1 of Lesson 15 concludes that what we call seeing is really a process of observing the thoughts you think as images within your mind and making those same images appear to be outside your mind. Physical seeing is actually image making. This is why I said earlier that your physical senses are actually thought confirmation devices. They are not like a camera lens. The senses are not the objective, observing mechanisms that we have been taught.

This idea that seeing is actually image making is the logical conclusion of two ideas that we previously discussed. These ideas are the concept of projection and that of seeing. For A Course in Miracles' purposes, the term seeing is understood to be quite different than the common understanding of that term. In the note for Lesson 3, we stated that it was important to realize that when A Course in Miracles uses the term seeing, it is different from the term vision.

In every day usage, the terms seeing and vision would be interchangeable, but this is not the case for the purpose of A Course in Miracles. When ACIM uses the term seeing, it is referencing the subjective physical sight process with all the subjective filtering that has occurred through the perceiver's egoic mind. Because of this filtering, what we refer to as seeing is actually a process in which the egoic mind has predetermined what it expects to observe outside itself. The egoic mind then assigns to the physical senses the task of looking outside itself to find something that will confirm that its predetermined beliefs are correct. Thus, the physical senses ignore any contradictory evidence and only report back information that supports its preconceived belief. The physical senses are not objective but rather they are thought confirmation devices.

The term vision, unlike seeing, involves the objective verification of reality. In this case, it would be more like a camera lens that captures the entire picture without preconceived notions or limitations. It does not go through the filtering process of the egoic mind. No subjective, made up, egoic story colors the observation.

For our purposes, I have used the term egoic mind so let me explain again what I mean by that. The egoic mind comes from the belief that separation is both a physical, mental and spiritual reality. It is predicated on the belief that you are the body and the body is you. It claims that you are a limited ego body in competition with other limited ego bodies struggling for the limited resources that each need to survive. This limited belief of who you are is the root cause of fear-based thinking.

In the note for Lesson 8, projection and the meaning of that psychological term was discussed. We stated that no one really sees anything. Instead, you only see your own thoughts which you have projected outward. Psychologists will call this phenomenon projection. Projection relates to your mind's ability to project its own thoughts, fears and guilt outside its own personage and see those same items reflected in your external world. Each person's past is utilized to judge their own current experiences. Rather than objectively observing what is happening in the present moment, your mind is filtering all activities based on its prior preconceived beliefs and judgments. This preoccupation with your egoic past is impacting how each current situation is perceived. Instead of being in a state of objective openness, you are in a constant state of egoic judgment.

The egoic mind is one perpetual judging machine. These judgments that you carry from your past beliefs then color your current experiences so that the current events are interpreted to reconfirm the original judgment's correctness. Your egoic mind is determined to be right. As strange as it sounds, your ego would prefer to be right than happy. Because of this phenomenon, your present experiences tend to be replays of the past and any favorable modification tends to occur in small baby steps because our egoic mind is incapable of accepting the fact that its prior beliefs may be totally wrong. We will continue to discuss the psychological concept of projection in greater depth as we proceed in these workbook lessons.

The final item that I'd like to discuss from this lesson is the idea of "light episodes." In our language, light episodes might also be called the parapsychological phenomena of seeing an aura. The aura is considered to be an energy field emanating from the object being observed. Often this energy field is observed as light emanating from the body itself. The typical assumption, however, is that the source of the energy field is the physical body that is being observed. But what if this assumption was wrong?

Most are probably familiar with the full eclipse of the sun. This galactic phenomenon occurs when the moon passes between the earth and the sun. When this event occurs, the moon blocks the full sun itself and we are able to observe the sun's solar flares. We realize that it is the sun, not the moon that is the source for these solar flares. Yet, if you were only given a photograph of a full solar eclipse, you would draw the conclusion that it was the moon that was the source of the solar flares. This would be a logical conclusion but a wrong misperception of reality. You would be wrong because you lacked the big picture of what was really taking place. What really occurred was that the moon blocked the sun from your field of vision. It was the sun you could not see, not the moon that you saw, that was the true source. Because of this temporary blockage, you observe the effects of the sun's true power.

When you have these light episodes, do not assume that the source of the light is an actual physical body. Instead, consider the idea that the body is actually blocking the true source of the light.

Question: If the physical body was actually blocking the source of the aura, what could the true source be?

Question: Would you like to have the blockages removed from your vision so that you could recognize what is behind the blockage?

LESSON 16

I have no neutral thoughts.

W-16.1.The idea for today, **I have no neutral thoughts**, is a beginning step in dispelling the belief that your thoughts have no effect. 2 Everything you see is the result of your thoughts. 3 There is no exception to this **fact that everything you see is the result of your thoughts.**. 4 Thoughts are not big or little; powerful or weak. 5 **Thoughts** are merely true or false. 6 Those **thoughts** that are true create their own likeness. 7 Those **thoughts** that are false make **in** their **own likeness**.

W-16.2.There is no more self-contradictory concept than that of "idle thoughts." 2 **Thoughts are** what gives rise to the perception of a whole world can hardly be called idle. 3 Every thought you have contributes to truth or to illusion; either **your thought** extends the truth or **your thought** multiplies illusions. 4 You can indeed multiply nothing, but you will not extend **anything** by doing so.

W-16.3.Besides your recognizing that thoughts are never idle, salvation requires that you also recognize that every thought you have brings either peace or war; either love or fear. 2 A neutral result is impossible because a neutral thought is impossible. 3 There is such a temptation to dismiss fear thoughts as unimportant, trivial and not worth bothering about that it is essential you recognize **fear thoughts** all as equally destructive, but equally unreal. 4 We will practice this idea **that you have no neutral thoughts** in many forms before you really understand it.

W-16.4.In applying the idea for today **that you have no neutral thoughts** search your mind for a minute or so with eyes closed, and actively seek not to overlook any "little" thought that may tend to elude the search. 2 This is quite difficult until you get used to **not overlooking any "little" thought**. 3 You will find that it is still hard for you not to make artificial distinctions. 4 Every thought that occurs to you, regardless of the qualities that you assign to **that thought** is a suitable subject for applying today's idea **that you have no neutral thoughts**.

W-16.5.In the practice periods, first repeat the idea **that you have no neutral thoughts** to yourself, and then as each **thought** crosses your mind hold **that thought** in **your** awareness while you tell yourself:
2 This thought about ___ is not a neutral thought.
3 That thought about ___ is not a neutral thought.
4 As usual, use today's idea **that you have no neutral thoughts** whenever you are aware of a particular thought that arouses uneasiness. 5 The following form is suggested for this purpose:
6 This thought about ___ is not a neutral thought, because I have no neutral thoughts.

W-16.6.Four or five practice periods are recommended, if you find **the practice periods** relatively effortless. 2 If strain is experienced, three will be enough. 3 The length of the exercise period should also be reduced if there is discomfort.

Notes to Lesson # 16

I have no neutral thoughts.

Lesson 16 states that you have no neutral thoughts. The idea that you have no neutral thoughts is the first step in correcting the erroneous belief that your thoughts have no effect on what you experience. In truth, your thoughts become your experiences. This is what the world of perception is all about. There are no idle thoughts since your thoughts become your provisional reality.

In Lesson 15, my thoughts are the images that I have made, we stated that what we call seeing is actually image making. The thoughts you are thinking appear first as images within your mind. Your mind then directs your physical senses to confirm the reality of those images outside your mind which had originally created them. Your mind, not some outside force, is the true source of these perceived images. Therefore, your thoughts create everything you see. Each thought has its own effect. All thoughts are equally powerful although you may not be consciously aware of this fact.

This lesson points out that your thoughts have the power to generate a myriad of experiences that range from peace or war, love or fear.

Although thoughts all possess equal power to generate new experiences, there are only two types of thoughts. A thought is either true or it is false. Each thought will create or bear witness for either a correct representation of the truth or it will bear witness to a false image of reality.

A false thought has no ability to change the truth of reality. Although you can choose to believe something that is not true, this belief has no ability to change the truth. In regard to the big picture which is represented by truth with a capital the T, a false thought is meaningless since it cannot change the Truth.

Since your world is a world of perception, not fact, your thoughts are experienced as your private world of provisional reality. It is important to realize that any fear-based thoughts, whether large or small, will be equally powerful in its ability to destroy your inner peace.

48

Previously, I stated that thoughts have no ability to impact you and that they were like the passing clouds. So why is Lesson 16 saying that you have no neutral thoughts? Certainly, if something is not neutral, that does mean it has the ability to impact you. Are these two ideas contradictory?

You wake up in the morning. You look out your window and you see a wisp of a cirrus cloud. You think nothing of it and go about your day. Contrast this to seeing a huge thunderhead approaching your area. You instantly think you better move your picnic inside your house.

What I actually said was that thoughts have no ability to impact you. This is true. Yet, thoughts raised to the level of beliefs do have that ability to impact how you relate to your world. The real crux of the issue is whether or not you actually have some thought that is not actually based on a belief. Lesson 7 stated that you see only your past. From your past, you judge and filter your current thoughts. Because you view your thoughts from the prison of your past beliefs, your current thoughts actually represent your beliefs. They are not the innocent thoughts you claim them to be.

The example of the cirrus cloud that seemed to mean nothing to you was actually based on your prior beliefs that such a cloud was not threatening to your day's activities. Yet, the thunderhead was perceived as a source for rain. Your egoic mind is always thinking based on your past beliefs.

Your egoic mind is one big judging machine. Its judgments are based on its past beliefs. Because this is how perception works, you have no idle thoughts. All your thoughts have already been transformed into some representation of your beliefs. Although your false beliefs have no ability to change the truth. they will affect how you interact with your world of perception.

Question: On a believability scale of 0 to 10, with 10 being absolutely true, please rate the following statements,

A) My thoughts become my experiences.
B) My experiences become my thoughts.

Question: If you believed that your thoughts became your future reality, would you be more leery of your idle thoughts?

LESSON 17

I see no neutral things.

W-17.1.This idea **that I see no neutral things** is another step in the direction of identifying cause and effect as **cause and effect** really operates in the world. 2 You see no neutral things because you have no neutral thoughts. 3 It is always the thought that comes first, despite the temptation to believe that it is the other way around. **Common belief is that there is something outside of you that is first observed and that this observation causes you to have thoughts about the subject. This is not truly the case.** 4 This **understanding that thought comes first** is not the way the world thinks, but you must learn that it is the **actual** way you think. **ACIM is saying that your thoughts always come before you perceive anything.** 5 If it were not so **that your thought comes first**, perception would have no cause, and, **perception** would itself be the cause of reality. 6 In view of **perception's** highly variable nature, this is hardly likely **that perception would have no cause**.

W-17.2.In applying today's idea **that I see no neutral things** say to yourself, with eyes open:
2 I see no neutral things because I have no neutral thoughts.
3 Then look about you, resting your glance on each thing you note long enough to say:
4 I do not see a neutral ___, because my thoughts about ___ are not neutral.
5 For example, you might say:
6 I do not see a neutral wall, because my thoughts about walls are not neutral.
7 I do not see a neutral body, because my thoughts about bodies are not neutral.

W-17.3.As usual, it is essential to make no distinctions between what you believe to be animate or inanimate; pleasant or unpleasant. 2 Regardless of what you may believe, you do not see anything that is really alive or really joyous. 3 **You do not see anything that is really alive or really joyous** because you are unaware as yet of any thought that is really true, and therefore really happy.

W-17.4.Three or four specific practice periods are recommended, and no less than three are required for maximum benefit, even if you experience resistance. 2 However, if you do **experience resistance**, the length of the practice period may be reduced to less than the minute or so that is otherwise recommended.

Notes to Lesson # 17

I see no neutral things.

Lesson 17 is a logical consequence of the previous lesson. If everything is the result of your thoughts and you have no neutral thoughts, then obviously there can be no neutral things. Once again, it is important to remember that you live in a world of perception, not one based on actual fact. ACIM points out that in your world of provisional reality, thoughts always come first, despite the typical world view that experiences are the source or cause of your thoughts.

Based on physiological and psychological research, our physical senses operate out of your prior beliefs system. Physiologists tell us that the physical senses are incapable of observing the whole and therefore, large gaps exist in our power of observation. These gaps are then filled in by our mind's past beliefs. The mind is always coloring your present perception and therefore, distorting objective reality by what it expects to observe based on its past beliefs. It is always your thoughts that generate your perception. Thoughts must be present and are causative since without thoughts, perception would not exist. Perception, by definition, always comes from the viewpoint of the perceiver. Perception never comes from the viewpoint of the item being observed.

Lesson 16 was I have no neutral thoughts. The note points out that all your current thoughts are filtered based on your past beliefs. This filtering process actually transforms any potential thought into a representation of a prior existing belief. Thoughts raised to the level of a belief are empowered by your mind to impact your perceived reality. Your mind's beliefs determine how you will interact with your outside world.

At this time, it is not necessary for you to believe with 100% certainty that your thoughts are the precursors of your tomorrow. The idea that thoughts are the cause of all your experiences seems counterintuitive and is not the general consensus within our society. Our society teaches that there are outside forces beyond our control. Society then claims that your job is to manage, mitigate and manipulate these outside forces as best you can. You are relegated to the management of effects, instead of causing those effects. Such a belief system supports a worldview of disempowerment and victimization. It is difficult to escape fear-based thinking when you are indoctrinated into the belief that outside forces are in control of your destiny.

Whether you believe your experiences or thoughts come first, all must agree that at this point in your life you have had both experiences and thoughts. The bird is already out of its cage and therefore, arguing over how it originally escaped will not return the bird to its cage.

You currently find yourself in the middle of what I call the creation cycle. This self-supporting creation cycle revolves around both beliefs and experiences. Your experiences confirm your beliefs and your beliefs are reconfirmed by your experiences. Both support and reinforce each other in an endless cycle. Without any change in your beliefs or your experiences, your future will continue to be a replay of your past. Since each one of us already has a past, arguing about which came first, the belief or the experience does not change the fact that you are already in the middle of that self-fulfilling cycle.

We will discuss both the creation cycle and the causative power of your beliefs in greater depth in future lessons. Right now I only ask you to consider the possibility that your thoughts, or more accurately stated your beliefs, impact how you relate to your private world of individuated perception.

Yesterday I asked you to rate the credibility of the following statements on the following believability scale.

Question from Lesson 16: On a believability scale of 0 to 10, with 10 being absolutely true, please rate the following statements,

A) My thoughts become my experiences.
B) My experiences become my thoughts

How did you do?

For most people, the answer to these statements would not be a 10 or a 0. It would be somewhere in between. Most people do not feel they are totally powerless or in total control of their world.

Question: How much control do you believe you have in changing planet earth?

Question: How much control do you believe you have in changing your perception about how you view planet earth?

LESSON 18

I am not alone in experiencing the effects of my seeing.

W-18.1.The idea for today that I am not alone in experiencing the effects of my seeing is another step in learning that the thoughts which give rise to what you see are never neutral or unimportant. 2 This idea that I am not alone in experiencing the effects of my seeing also emphasizes the idea that minds are joined, which will be given increasing stress later on.

W-18.2.Today's idea that I am not alone in experiencing the effects of my seeing does not refer to what you see as much as to how you see it, which is a part of perception. 2 Therefore, the exercises for today emphasize how you really observe something which is an aspect of your perception. 3 The three or four practice periods which are recommended should be done as follows:

W-18.3.Look about you, selecting subjects for the application of today's idea that I am not alone in experiencing the effects of my seeing as randomly as possible, and keeping your eyes on each one long enough to say:
2 I am not alone in experiencing the effects of how I see ___ .
3 Conclude each practice period by repeating the more general statement:
4 I am not alone in experiencing the effects of my seeing.
5 A minute or so, or even less, will be sufficient for each practice period.

Notes to Lesson # 18

I am not alone in experiencing the effects of my seeing.

Today's idea that I am not alone in experiencing the effects of my seeing reinforces the idea that you have no neutral or unimportant thoughts or beliefs. It also introduces the idea that at some level, minds are joined or interrelated. We will discuss in more detail this joining or interaction between minds in later lessons.

Today's idea is not referring so much as to what you see but how you see it. We have stressed the idea that your thoughts are not innocent but rather quite judgmental. The egoic mind comes from the viewpoint of separation. The ego believes that it is in competition with others for the limited resources that it needs for its survival. Your egoic mind has to determine whether something that it perceives outside itself is either helpful or harmful to its long-term survival.

Based on its prejudicial prior judgments, your mind will then determine how it chooses to interact with the object at hand. The interaction will not be based on the objective circumstances of the moment, but rather on the subjective opinions of the egoic mind. Thus, your mind is constantly bringing forward its past beliefs into the present.

This distorted viewpoint limits what you perceive to be available options for your present experiences. This subjectivity on your part, of course, effects the possible reactions available to the other player in the relationship game. In essence, each player feeds off the limiting beliefs of the other party.

We will be discussing this interaction between the various players of any shared common experience in greater depth. When you understand this simple interaction, you will be able to greatly improve your interpersonal relationships.

Question: When you anticipate that you will have a future negative experience, do you enter that experience with an open mind or rather with a sense of dread?

Question: Do you believe this prior anticipation will have some impact on how you choose to enter into and relate to that future anticipated event?

Question: Will your preconceived notion of this event limit what is possible for you to experience from that future event?

LESSON 19

I am not alone in experiencing the effects of my thoughts.

W-19.1.The idea for today **which is I am not alone in experiencing the effects of my thoughts,** is obviously the reason why your seeing does not affect you alone. 2 You will notice that at times the ideas related to thinking precede those related to perceiving, while at other times the order is reversed **so that the ideas related to perceiving come before the ideas related to thinking**. 3 The reason is that the order does not matter. 4 Thinking and **thinking's** results, **which is perceiving,** are really simultaneous, for cause and effect are never separate.

W-19.2.Today we are again emphasizing the fact that minds are joined. 2 **The fact that minds are joined** is rarely a wholly welcome idea at first, since **the fact that minds are joined** seems to carry with it an enormous sense of responsibility, and may even be regarded as an "invasion of privacy." 3 Yet it is a fact that **minds are joined and that** there are no private thoughts. 4 Despite your initial resistance to this idea **that minds are joined and that there are no private thoughts,** you will yet understand that **this joining** must be true if salvation is possible at all. 5 And salvation must be possible because **salvation** is the Will of God.

W-19.3.The minute or so of mind searching which today's exercises require is to be undertaken with eyes closed. 2 The idea for today **that I am not alone in experiencing the effects of my thoughts** is to be repeated first, and then the mind should be carefully searched for the thoughts **the mind** contains at that time. 3 As you consider each **thought,** name **the thought** in terms of the central person or theme **the thought** contains, and holding **the thought** in your mind as you do so, say:
4 I am not alone in experiencing the effects of this thought about ___.

W-19.4.The requirement of as much indiscriminateness as possible in selecting subjects for the practice periods should be quite familiar to you by now, and will no longer be repeated each day, although **the mention of random selection** will occasionally be included as a reminder. 2 Do not forget, however, that random selection of subjects for all practice periods remains essential throughout. 3 Lack of order in this connection will ultimately make the recognition of lack of order in miracles meaningful to you.

W-19.5.Apart from the "as needed" application of today's idea **that I am not alone in experiencing the effects of my thoughts**, at least three practice periods are required, shortening the length of time involved, if necessary. 2 Do not attempt more than four.

Notes to Lesson # 19

I am not alone in experiencing the effects of my thoughts.

Lesson 18 and 19 are very similar. Lesson 18 focused on the effects of your seeing while this lesson says you are not alone in experiencing the effects of your thoughts. The interrelationship with thoughts, beliefs and seeing have already been discussed. This lesson points out that thinking and its results really are simultaneous and that cause and effect are never separate.

In regard to perception, we can easily understand that both observer and something to observe is needed. Also, the idea that a cause must have an effect or it is not a cause is obvious. Both cause and effect give rise to the existence of the other half. Without both, you would have neither. Cause and effect are two sides of one inseparable coin. In our world of perception, however, we view each part of the one continuous coin to be separate. There is no line of demarcation that separates a cause from its effect.

Earlier, I said that time was the measure of change. Time is also the belief that there is a gap between cause and effect. ACIM states that thinking and thinking's results are actually simultaneous. Yet, in our world of time and space, we believe that there is a gap between thinking and the results of thinking.

If the anticipated change in our beliefs is great, we believe a long time interval will be required before our mind will allow the effect of our new thinking to manifest on the experiential level. Often, our mind will require that we baby step our way slowly towards that change. The time interval that is required before we allow change to physically take place is contingent on our beliefs and the strength in which they are held. As the believability in a new belief increases, the rapidity of experiences that support that new belief will also increase.

The idea that you are not alone in experiencing the effects of your thoughts or your seeing implies that there is an interconnection between seemingly separate minds. Whether you believe that minds are interconnected or not, we all realize in a world of perception, no man is an island, separate and distinct. Instead, the object and the observer are interconnected. Each is dependent on the other for their seemingly private existence. Neither operates in a vacuum. Although we each live in our own private world of individuated perception, both object and perceiver share some common overlap in each other's world. This shared overlapping is the beginning of a larger collective consciousness within the group itself. The more uniform the beliefs and experiences within a given group, the more stable and similar is that group's provisional reality.

This idea that minds are connected may depress some since they may feel that this places a tremendous burden upon their shoulders. They may believe that they alone are responsible for all events that take place on this planet called earth. If this were true, this would be a tremendous burden to place on anyone. Let me assure you that as the workbook lessons unfold, this false sense of burden will be lifted. You are not responsible for everything that takes place on planet earth. But you are responsible for your own world of perception. You can live in your own peaceful world and yet, reside on a warring planet.

Question: Do you live in a peaceful world?

ACIM says if you want peace, be peace. If you want love, be love.

Or as Gandhi said," Be the Change you wish to see in the world!"

LESSON 20

I am determined to see.

W-20.1.We have been quite casual about our practice periods thus far. 2 There has been virtually no attempt to direct the time for undertaking **your practice periods**, minimal effort has been required, and not even active cooperation and interest have been asked **for during your practice periods**. 3 This approach of **lack of restrictive directions** has been intentional, and very carefully planned. 4 We have not lost sight of the crucial importance of the reversal of your thinking. 5 The salvation of the world depends on **the reversal of your thinking**. 6 Yet you will not see **and reverse your thinking** if you regard yourself as being coerced, and if you give in to resentment and opposition.

W-20.2.This is our first attempt to introduce structure. 2 Do not misconstrue **the introduction of structure** as an effort to exert force or pressure. 3 You want salvation. 4 You want to be happy. 5 You want peace. 6 You do not have **salvation, happiness or peace** now, because your mind is totally undisciplined, and you cannot distinguish between joy and sorrow, pleasure and pain, love and fear. 7 You are now learning how to tell **joy and sorrow, pleasure and pain, love and fear** apart. 8 And great indeed will be your reward.

W-20.3.Your decision to see is all that vision requires. 2 What you want is yours. 3 Do not mistake the little effort that is asked of you for an indication that our goal is of little worth. 4 Can the salvation of the world be a trivial purpose? 5 And can the world be saved if you are not **saved**? 6 God has one Son, and he, **God's one Son,** is the resurrection and the life. 7 **Your** will is done because all power is given **God's one Son** in Heaven and on earth. 8 In your determination to see is vision given you.

W-20.4.The exercises for today consist in reminding yourself throughout the day that you want to see. 2 Today's idea **that I am determined to see** also tacitly implies the recognition that you do not see now. 3 Therefore, as you repeat the idea **that you are determined to see**, you are stating that you are determined to change your present state for a better one, and **the one state** you really want.

W-20.5.Repeat today's idea slowly and positively at least twice an hour today, attempting to do so every half hour. 2 Do not be distressed if you forget to do so, but make a real effort to remember. 3 The extra repetitions **that you are determined to see** should be applied to any situation, person or event that upsets you. 4 You can see **any situation** differently, and you will. 5 What you desire you will see. 6 Such is the real law of cause and effect as it operates in the world.

Important: Please read carefully: The real Law of Cause and Effect as it operates in your world of individuate perception, which is your provisional reality, is that what you desire you will see.

Notes to Lesson # 20

I am determined to see.

Lesson 20 reveals the true goal of these workbook lessons.

These workbook lessons are really designed to train your undisciplined mind to a new way of viewing your world. The ego does not know who you are and yet you rely on your ego to advise you on how you should live your life. This is the classic example of the blind leading the blind. However, in your case, you are not truly blind. Instead, you are refusing to utilize and trust your inner guidance system that represents your Higher Self and knows the truth about who you really are. Would you rather listen to someone who argues for your limitations or someone that encourages you to fulfill your destiny and embrace your true magnificence?

I am determined to see implies that what your ego currently believes to be your only provisional reality may not be the only option available.

Instead, your ego's plan may be the source for distortion of the truth that leads to a life dominated by fear, struggle and pain. There must be another plan.

A Course in Miracles realizes that it has to meet you where you are. In these early lessons, ACIM did not attempt to impose any strict structure realizing that an undisciplined mind would oppose such an approach. Instead, ACIM only asked your willingness to be open and to do the exercises. As you proceed with these exercises, your mind is becoming more disciplined and it is opening up to new possibilities. Continue with these lessons without being overly critical if you fail to meet the suggested time intervals. Simply resume the schedule as best you can.

In this lesson, it is suggested that you repeat today's idea that you are determined to see at least twice an hour. Some people actually set their clock to beep as a reminder. In my case, I preferred to write down the lesson and place it in my pocket or someplace where I would come across it during the day. Use any aid that may help you in remembering the schedule. Do not allow failure to comply with each appointed time as an excuse to become discouraged and discontinue the lessons. Our goal this year is to get through the lessons. Perfection is not required or demanded. Don't be too hard on yourself.

As a final note, Lesson 20 casually mentions the idea that "What you want is yours." It also states that "What you desire you will see. Such is the real law of cause and effect as it operates in the world." This Law of Cause and Effect operates currently and continuously in your world of perception. Although hard to believe, it rules your world of provisional reality. This is an important concept that we will be discussing in great depth in the near future.

Question: If someone does not know the truth about themselves, will they know what is in their own best interest?

Question: Have you ever desired something, only to realize when you achieve it that item failed to make you happy?

Question: Have you ever failed to get what you wanted, only to realize that if you had gotten what you wanted, it would have brought you pain and sorrow?

LESSON 21

I am determined to see things differently.

W-21.1.The idea for today **that I am determined to see things differently** is obviously a continuation and extension of the preceding one, **which was I am determined to see.** 2 This time, however, specific mind-searching periods are necessary, in addition to applying the idea **that you are determined to see things differently** to particular situations as **these situations** may arise. 3 Five practice periods are urged, allowing a full minute for each.

W-21.2.In the practice periods, begin by repeating the idea today **that I am determined to see things differently** to yourself. 2 Then close your eyes and search your mind carefully for situations past, present or anticipated that arouse anger in you. 3 The anger may take the form of any reaction ranging from mild irritation to rage. 4 The degree of the emotion you experience does not matter. 5 You will become increasingly aware that a slight twinge of annoyance is nothing but a veil drawn over intense fury.

W-21.3.Try, therefore, not to let the "little" thoughts of anger escape you in the practice periods. 2 Remember that you do not really recognize what arouses anger in you, and nothing that you believe **about what arouses anger** in this connection means anything. 3 You will probably be tempted to dwell more on some situations or persons than on others, on the fallacious grounds that **these situations** are more "obvious." 4 This is not so. **"Little" thoughts of anger as well as more obvious ones all result in the loss of your inner peace.** 5 It is merely an example of the belief that some forms of attack are more justified than others.

W-21.4.As you search your mind for all the forms in which attack thoughts present themselves, hold each **attack thought** in mind while you tell yourself:
2 I am determined to see ___ [name of person] differently.
3 I am determined to see ___ [specify the situation] differently.

W-21.5.Try to be as specific as possible. 2 You may, for example, focus your anger on a particular attribute of a particular person, believing that the anger is limited to this **one particular** aspect. 3 If your perception is suffering from this form of distortion **involving one specific attribute of a particular person** say:
4 I am determined to see ___ [specify the attribute] in ___ [name of person] differently.
Example: I am determined to see ___the lack of punctuality___ in__Mary__ differently.

Notes to Lesson # 21

I am determined to see things differently.

Lesson 21 is both a continuation and an extension of the previous idea. Rather than just be determined to see, it asks that you be determined to see things differently. Seeing and vision, as we have indicated before, are not synonymous for ACIM purposes. Your real goal is not to see, but instead, to perceive things correctly.

Perception revolves around beliefs. As long as your beliefs are misaligned with the truth, you will not be able to achieve real vision. What you seek is not merely a different false story that becomes your provisional reality. Instead, you want to utilize correct vision while you are interacting with your perceived world. Correct vision would align and bear witness to the truth. This is Truth with a capital T. It is not another egoic story built around limitation and fear-based thinking.

The ego does not know the big picture and therefore, is unable to properly advise you. Lacking knowledge of who you really are, your egoic mind fails to realize what will truly make you happy. Your egoic mind has been indoctrinated into a fear-based thought system. It believes you are the physical body and that the body is you. Believing itself to be separate, the ego sees itself in competition for the limited resources that it needs to survive. Identifying itself with the body, the ego must assume the limitations that come with a physical body that it claims as its home. The ego fails to understand that your consciousness and spiritual essence is not limited by this physical dimension.

I would suggest that if you are determined to see things differently, you should consider major, not minor shifts, in your thinking. You can baby step your way towards a new vision or you can decide to be open and explore a thought system based on a new paradigm. Aren't you really after a big shift? Quantum breakthroughs occur when you are willing to change course, move out of your comfort zone and onto a different direction.

You have been indoctrinated into a fear-based thought system. You can never find the joy, happiness and inner peace that you seek and deserve within that same fear-based thought system. It is impossible! Joy, happiness and inner peace are incompatible with fear. You need a new vision. You need a new plan.

In order to entertain a different vision, you need to first know what your current vision **is.**

Question How do you currently see yourself?

What are your 3 greatest strengths?

What are your 3 greatest weaknesses?

List 3 single word character traits that describe your personality.

These traits could be considered positive or negative or both.

For example, your 3 traits could be unreliable, sympathetic and tenacious.

Question: Are you satisfied with your current vision?

If not, write down a different vision of who you would like to become.

List three single word character traits that such a person would have to possess.

Note: I would strongly suggest you write down your answers

If you desire to make quantum leaps, you need to honestly assess both where you currently are and where you want to go.

,

LESSON 22

What I see is a form of vengeance.

W-22.1.Today's idea **that what I see is a form of vengeance** accurately describes the way anyone who holds attack thoughts in his mind must see the world. 2 Having projected his anger onto the world, he sees vengeance about to strike at him. 3 His own attack is thus perceived as self defense. 4 This **cycle of holding thoughts of attack and counter-attack and projecting them upon the world that he sees** becomes an increasingly vicious circle until he is willing to change how he sees **his world**. 5 Otherwise, thoughts of attack and counter-attack will preoccupy him and people his entire world. 6 What peace of mind is possible to **him when this cycle of holding thoughts of attack and counter-attack preoccupy his mind**?

W-22.2.It is from this savage fantasy **which is this vicious cycle of holding thoughts of attack and counter-attack** that you want to escape. **This vicious cycle of projecting your angry thoughts upon the world you see is why you perceive a vengeful world**. 2 Is it not joyous news to hear that **the world you see as a form of vengeance** is not real? 3 Is it not a happy discovery to find that you can escape **your vengeful world that you perceive you see?** 4 **By this cycle of holding thoughts of attack and counter-attack,** you made what you would destroy. **By this cycle of holding attack and counter-attack thoughts, you made** everything that you hate and would attack and kill. 5 All that you fear does not exist **because it was from your own egoic mind that you projected your attack thoughts upon the world you perceived you saw**.

W-22.3.Look at the world about you at least five times today, for at least a minute each time. 2 As your eyes move slowly from one object to another, from one body to another, say to yourself:
3 I see only the perishable.
4 I see nothing that will last.
5 What I see is not real.
6 What I see is a form of vengeance.
7 At the end of each practice period, ask yourself:
8 Is this the world I really want to see?
9 The answer is surely obvious.

Notes to Lesson # 22

What I see is a form of vengeance

Lesson 22 is what I see is a form of vengeance. This is a logical consequence of two previously discussed factors. The first is how perception works and the second is based on your ego's limiting beliefs about yourself and your world.

The law of perception basically states that you will see what you believe. This is what psychological and physiological research shows us. Our physical senses are not objective but rather thought confirmation devices. Your senses are designed to confirm what your mind expects your outside world should be. You project your own beliefs outside your mind and your senses then confirm these predetermined beliefs to be true. Believe you will be attacked and your physical senses will find some experience to confirm that preexisting belief.

The second factor is based on your thought system's beliefs. To your ego, you are your body and the body is you. Your ego believes that you are a limited ego body in competition with other ego bodies for the limited resources that both need for their survival. Believing itself to be separate, the ego must see outside forces operating in its world that can impact the ego's very survival. The ego sets out to manipulate its perceived outside world in order to ensure its survival needs are met. The ego develops a plan to do this manipulation. Any deviation from the ego's plan is seen as a direct attack coming from the offending party.

If I believe that I need a parking spot close to the door of the grocery store, I will see other drivers entering the same parking lot as competition for my needed spot. I may attempt to race through the lot so that I can arrive at my predesignated parking spot before another driver arrives. In this simple example, my ego would prejudge the other driver as competition. The driver's actions would be seen as an attack against my needs. My ego would claim any anger or resentment that I might feel from this encounter would be justified. My action of racing through the parking lot to claim my spot would be viewed as a justified act of self-defense, not an attack on the other party. To my ego, the best defense is a good offense. My ego calls my actions a preemptive strike while the other party sees himself as an innocent victim and me as an aggressive foe.

On a more subtle level, if my survival plan requires that Jim give me his paycheck at the end of the week, Jim's failure to do so will be perceived as an attack on my very survival. In order to insure Jim's future compliance with my ego's plan, I may agree to make Jim dinner and wash his clothes. Rather than my actions of cooking and cleaning for Jim being performed out of love, these actions are part of my ego's self-defense plan to manipulate outside forces to provide the limited resources that I perceive I need for my survival. If I do not receive my expected payback, which is Jim's paycheck at the end of the week, my ego will believe I have been attacked. My ego may also view myself as a failure for not procuring its needs.

<u>Question:</u> How do you react when people fail to meet your expectations?

Do you adjust and go with the flow or do you blame the other party, become angry, hurt, or lose your inner peace?

Question: What are some of your favorite self-defense mechanisms to manipulate others to comply with your ego's plan of action?

LESSON 23.

I can escape from the world I see by giving up attack thoughts.

W-23.1.The idea for today **that I can escape from the world I see by giving up attack thoughts** contains the only way out of fear that will ever succeed. 2 **Since** nothing else will work, everything else is meaningless. 3 But this way **that I can escape from the world I see by giving up attack thoughts** cannot fail. 4 Every thought you have makes up some segment of the world you see. 5 It is with your thoughts, then, that we must work, if your perception of the world is to be changed.

W-23.2.If the cause of the world you see is **your** attack thoughts, you must learn that it is these thoughts which you do not want. 2 There is no point in lamenting the world **that you perceive**. 3 There is no point in trying to change the world **that you perceive**. 4 **The world that you perceive** is incapable of change because **the world that you perceive** is merely an effect **of your attack thoughts**. 5 But there is indeed a point in changing your **attack** thoughts about the world. 6 Here you are changing the cause **of the world that you perceive which is your attack thoughts.** 7 The effect, **which is your vengeful world that you perceive,** will change automatically.

W-23.3.The world you see is a vengeful world, and everything in it is a symbol of vengeance. 2 Each of your perceptions of "external reality" is a pictorial representation of your own attack thoughts. 3 One can well ask if this **perception of "external reality "which is the result of your mind's own pictorial representation of your own attack thoughts** can be called seeing. 4 Is not fantasy a better word for such a process **of projecting your own attack thoughts outside your mind,** and hallucination a more appropriate term for the result **of a vengeful world that you perceive you see**?

W-23.4.You see the world that you have made, but you do not see yourself as the image maker. 2 You cannot be saved from the world **you perceive,** but you can escape from **your perceived world's** cause **which is your egoic mind's attack thoughts. Your mind's attack thoughts are the real image maker**. 3 This is what salvation means, for where is the world you see when its cause, **which is your attack thoughts,** is gone? 4 Vision already holds a replacement for everything you think you see now. 5 Loveliness can light your images, and so transform **your images** that you will love them, even though **your images** were made of hate. 6 For you will not be making **your images** alone.

W-23.5.The idea for today **that I can escape from the world I see by giving up attack thoughts** introduces the thought that you are not trapped in the world you see, **because your perceived world's** cause can be changed. 2 This change requires, first, that the cause, **which is your attack thoughts,** be identified and **then the second step is** to let go, so that **your attack thought**s can be replaced. 3 The first two steps in this process,(**identifying the cause and then letting it go),** require your cooperation. 4 The final one, **which is the images you perceive,** does not. 5 Your images **you perceive** have already been replaced. 6 By taking the first two steps, you will see that this is so and **that the images you had perceived have already been replaced**.

W-23.6.Besides using **the idea that I can escape from the world I see by giving up attack thoughts** throughout the day as the need arises, five **separate** practice periods are required in applying today's idea. 2 As you look about you, repeat the idea **that I can escape from the world I see by giving up attack thoughts** slowly to yourself first, and then close your eyes and devote about a minute to searching your mind for as many attack thoughts as occur to you. 3 As each **attack thought** crosses your mind say:
4 I can escape from the world I see by giving up attack thoughts about ___ .
5 Hold each attack thought in mind as you say this, and then dismiss that **attack** thought and go on to the next.

W-23.7.In the practice periods, be sure to include both your thoughts of attacking and of being attacked. 2 Their effects are exactly the same because **your thoughts of attacking and of being attacked** are exactly the same. 3 You do not recognize this **similarity** as yet, and you are asked at this time only to treat **your thoughts of attacking and of being attacked** as the same in today's practice periods. 4 We are still at the stage of identifying the cause of the world you see. 5 When you finally learn that thoughts of attack and of being attacked are not different, you will be ready to let the cause go.

Notes to Lesson # 23

I can escape from the world I see by giving up attack thoughts.

Lesson 23 is a very important lesson. It contains many rich concepts that lie at the foundation of A Course in Miracles. It states that the world you see is an effect of your thoughts. Your thoughts spring forth from the thought system upon which you place your allegiance. The ego believes that you are a limited separate ego-body that is struggling to get its needs met. This belief lays the foundation of a fear-based thought system that generates the fearful world you perceive as your provisional reality.

ACIM states that you will never be able to escape the source of fear within a thought system that is based upon fear. Your current thought system was designed to protect, support and bear witness for your ego's belief in limitation and separation. In order to eliminate fear from dominating your life, you need to move out of this fear-based thought system. You need a new plan based on a new paradigm of thinking. As we proceed in these ACIM Workbook Lessons a new plan that will work will be provided.

61

There are only two plans or thought systems available from which to choose. One is based on the truth, with a capital T. The other is based on the false. Although there appears to be many variations of other plans, all these false plans arise from fear-based thinking. Your egoic mind does not know who you really are and therefore, has allied itself with one of the myriad of false fear-based plans. This is why all egoic plans for your salvation are incapable of bringing true happiness and lasting peace.

Because these egoic plans all arise from fear-based thinking, they are doomed to fail. These false plans cannot change the truth of who you really are. Yet, your fear-based thought system does create within its own egoic mind images that support its erroneous beliefs of separation and limitation. Your ego's own fear-based thinking supports and generates the images you perceive to be your own private world of provisional reality. These images are meaningless. A fantasy, no matter how strongly you cling to it, cannot change the truth. These false images have no ability to change the true reality of what God created. Although fantasies cannot change the truth, they can affect the actions of the believer and terrorize any delusional mind that holds those fantasies to be real. Only a thought system that supports and bears witnesses to truth with a capital T will work. Only the Truth can bring you the lasting happiness, joy, and peace that you seek.

The world you see is a world of perception. As such, it is an effect of your thoughts. The only way to change your perception of your world is to change the way you think about it. Your thoughts are the cause of your world; not the other way around. Coming from a fear-based thought system, your ego's plan, as pointed out in   Lesson 22, is a perpetual cycle of attack and counterattack. Such a thought system only protects and perpetuates your belief in a fearful world.

Lesson 23 also provides a three-step process to escape from the cause of a revengeful world, which are your own fear-based attack thoughts.

The first step in this plan is to identify the true cause of the problem, which, of course, is your own egoic thinking. The second step is to let go or change your thinking, which is the true source of your perception.

The third step occurs automatically and is the effect of completing steps one and two. By changing your thinking, the cause of what you perceive dissolves and a new vision that aligns with the truth reappears. The first two steps in this process remove the blocks your egoic mind has placed to obscure true vision. Once these blocks have been dissolved, thoughts that align with the truth come into your awareness.

These first two steps require your cooperation because your egoic mind is the source of the fear that you perceive in your world in the first place. The third step, however, is an automatic result or effect of the prior two. It requires no conscious effort on your part. This is why A Course in Miracles says, do not try and change your world. Rather change how you view your world. When you do, the world that you perceive must automatically realign to support your new viewpoint. This new alignment will produce new experiences that support and confirm the correctness of that new belief. By changing your viewpoint, your life will automatically change directions. Quantum changes will occur.

This lesson also provides a definition of salvation. Salvation means that you cannot be saved from the world, but you can escape from its cause. This is an interesting definition because it does not agree with how most people would define salvation. It states that you cannot be saved from the world. How can you be saved from a world that arises from the beliefs of your own mind? Only by eliminating the cause, does its effect disappear. It is your mind's fear-based thought system, not the world that you perceive, that is the cause of all your misery and suffering. Salvation does however offer you the ability to escape from the fear-based thought system that produces the world that you fear. Salvation states that you are not trapped in the world as you perceive it, because its cause, which is your mind, can be changed. Your mind is under your control.

This lesson also states that the images that you see can be transformed to support a new way of viewing your world. Yet, your viewpoint will not necessarily transform the collective consciousness of planet earth. Although you control your own private world of perception, the world as a whole is not made by you alone. Every thought you have makes up some segment of the world. Yet so do the thoughts of others contribute to this dimension of time and space. It is the composite of our group thinking that provides the mass collective consciousness for the overlapping world each see as their own provisional reality.

In time and space, you do not operate in a vacuum for minds are joined at some level. Although you cannot control all the circumstances that generate your experiences, you are in control of the interpretation that you place on those circumstances. You are in charge of how you choose to respond. Will you respond with fear or love?

Salvation means that you take responsibility for your own attack thoughts and change them. You cannot save the world since it is an effect of the mass collective consciousness of a fear-based thought system. But you can escape from the cause of the revengeful world you perceive by changing your thoughts about your world of provisional reality.

Salvation offers an alternative to the fear-based thought system that created this fearful world. Fear cannot and will not work to change what it alone created. Only salvation's plan, which leads to the truth, will work.

Question: If you have a religious background, how does your religion define salvation?

Question: How does ACIM definition of salvation differ?

Question: What is your understanding of salvation?

LESSON 24.

I do not perceive my own best interests.

W-24.1.In no situation that arises do you realize the outcome that would make you happy. 2 Therefore, **since you do not realize the outcome that would make you happy,** you have no guide to appropriate action, and no way of judging the result. 3 What you do is determined by your perception of the situation, and that perception is wrong. 4 **Since your perception is wrong,** it is inevitable, then, that you will not serve your own best interests. 5 Yet **your own best interests** are your only goal in any situation which is correctly perceived. 6 Otherwise, **since you do not perceive your own best interests and your perception is wrong,** you will not recognize what **your own best interests** are.

W-24.2.If you realized that you do not perceive your own best interests, you could be taught what **your own best interests** are. 2 But in the presence of your conviction that you do know what **your own best interests** are, you cannot learn **what they really are**. 3 The idea for today **that I do not perceive my own best interests** is a step toward opening your mind so that learning can begin.

W-24.3.The exercises for today require much more honesty than you are accustomed to using. 2 A few subjects, honestly and carefully considered in each of the five practice periods which should be undertaken today, will be more helpful than a more cursory examination of a large number. 3 Two minutes are suggested for each of the mind-searching periods which the exercises involve.

W-24.4.The practice periods should begin with repeating today's idea **that I do not perceive my own best interests**, followed by searching the mind, with closed eyes, for unresolved situations about which you are currently concerned. 2 The emphasis should be on uncovering the outcome you want. 3 You will quickly realize that you have a number of goals in mind as part of the desired outcome, and also that these goals are on different levels and often conflict.

W-24.5.In applying the idea for today **that I do not perceive my own best interests**, name each situation that occurs to you, and then enumerate carefully as many goals as possible that you would like to be met in its resolution. 2 The form of each application should be roughly as follows:
3 In the situation involving ___, I would like ___ to happen, and ___ to happen,
and so on. 4 Try to cover as many different kinds of outcomes as may honestly occur to you, even if some of **different kinds of outcomes** do not appear to be directly related to the situation, or even to be inherent in **the situation** at all.

W-24.6.If these exercises are done properly, you will quickly recognize that you are making a large number of demands of the situation which have nothing to do with **the situation**. 2 You will also recognize that many of your goals are contradictory, that you have no unified outcome in mind **for your goals**, and that you must experience disappointment in connection with some of your goals, however the situation turns out.

W-24.7.After covering the list of as many hoped-for goals as possible, for each unresolved situation that crosses your mind say to yourself:
2 I do not perceive my own best interests in this situation,
and go on to the next **situation**.

Notes to Lesson # 24

I do not perceive my own best interests.

If you believed you were a dog instead of a human being, would you handle a given situation differently?

What you do is determined by your perception of the situation. If you believe you are a dog, you will react to any given situation in a dog-like manner. If you do not know who you are, you will fail to realize the full range of possible options available to you. You will react based on your fundamental erroneous beliefs. You will limit yourself and what you believe is possible for your world.

We've already stated that beliefs determine how you perceive your world. If you have no idea of all the facts or how each experience relates to the big picture, you will be unable to judge correctly what is in your best interests.

Your ego does not know who you are, therefore, how could it know what is in your best interest?

Without this basic knowledge of who you are, your ego is incapable of providing the proper guidance you need to appropriately respond to any given situation. Since your ego's actions are based on its underlying belief in separation, limitation and lack, your ego is incapable of correctly assessing any given situation and determining what will be in your best interest. Not knowing who you are, your ego does not know what actions are required to make you happy.

If someone is offering you advice and you realize that they did not know what was in your best interest, would you agree to follow their advice? You would dismiss their advice as irrelevant to your situation and seek a better guide.

The information provided by the fool is indeed foolish. Yet, if you failed to realize the incompetence of your teacher, instead, mistaking him for a wise sage, you might follow that person's advice blindly. You would fail to realize that this trusted advisor was clueless and incapable of developing a plan that would insure your long-term happiness. Yet, this is precisely the situation you are in when you do not question your ego's guidance.

When you do this workbook exercise, you will recognize that you are making a large number of demands on each particular situation that has nothing to do with the situation.

Also you will find that many of your goals surrounding the situation are contradictory. You want to buy a new computer but you do not want to spend any money. You have conflicting goals because you do not have one overriding unified outcome that you wish to achieve. To buy, you must be willing to spend.

Often, you have different and conflicting long-term and short-term goals. You want to complete your college degree but you want to relax and watch televisions today. This lesson points out that when you lack that one common overriding unified outcome, your various egoic goals will conflict and you will be disappointed with your results. You need to actually know where your true happiness resides in order to chart the right path to achieve it.

Having a single unifying goal or criteria helps you decide what course of action you should take in any given situation. For example, in my case as a young child, I was very clear as to what my one goal or purpose was. I did not want to ever have to return to this hellish world again. This single mindedness reduces internal conflict and stress while increasing clarity.

Question: Do you have one common purpose or unifying goal for your life that you wish to achieve?

Question: If so, has that unifying goal remained constant or has it changed over this lifetime?

Question: What is the one unifying goal that would bring you lasting joy, peace and happiness?

I do not know what anything is for.

W-25.1.Purpose is meaning. 2 Today's idea **that I do not know what anything is for** explains why nothing you see means anything. 3 You do not know what **anything you see** is for. 4 Therefore, **anything you see** is meaningless to you. 5 Everything is for your own best interests. 6 **Your own best interest** is what **everything** is for; that is **what everything's** purpose **is**; that is what **everything** means. 7 It is in recognizing **everything is for your own best interests** that your goals become unified. 8 It is in recognizing **everything is for your own best interests** that what you see is given meaning.

W-25.2.You perceive the world and everything **in your perceived world** as meaningful in terms of ego goals. 2 These **ego** goals have nothing to do with your own best interests, because the ego is not you. 3 This false identification **that the ego is you** makes you incapable of understanding what anything is for. 4 As a result, you are bound to misuse **this false identification that the ego is you.** 5 When you believe **that the ego is not you,** you will try to withdraw the **ego's** goals you have assigned to the world, instead of attempting to reinforce **the ego's goals that you have assigned to the world.**

W-25.3.Another way of describing the goals you now perceive is to say that **the goals you now perceive** are all concerned with "personal" **ego** interests. 2 Since you have no **real** personal **ego** interests, your **egoic** goals are really concerned with nothing. 3 In cherishing **your egoic goals,** therefore, you have no goals at all. 4 And thus **since you cherish your egoic goals,** you do not know what anything is for.

W-25.4.Before you can make any sense out of the exercises for today, one more thought is necessary. 2 At the most superficial levels, you do recognize **"personal" egoic** purpose. 3 Yet purpose cannot be understood at these **egoic** levels. 4 For example, you do understand that a telephone is for the purpose of talking to someone who is not physically in your immediate vicinity. 5 What you do not understand is what you want to reach him for. 6 And **what you want to reach him for** is **what** makes your contact with him meaningful or not.

W-25.5.It is crucial to your learning to be willing to give up the **egoic** goals you have established for everything. 2 The recognition that **the egoic goals you have established for everything** are meaningless, rather than "good" or "bad," is the only way to accomplish this. 3 The idea for today **that I do not know what anything is for** is a step in this direction.

W-25.6.Six practice periods, each of two-minutes duration, are required. 2 Each practice period should begin with a slow repetition of the idea for today **that I do not know what anything is for** followed by looking about you and letting your glance rest on whatever happens to catch your eye, near or far, "important" or "unimportant," "human" or "nonhuman." 3 With your eyes resting on each subject you so select, say, for example:
4 I do not know what this chair is for.
5 I do not know what this pencil is for.
6 I do not know what this hand is for.
7 Say **that I do not know what anything is for** quite slowly, without shifting your eyes from the subject until you have completed the statement about **that subject.** 8 Then move on to the next subject, and apply today's idea **that I do not know what anything is for** as before.

Notes to Lesson # 25

I do not know what anything is for.

You do not understand what anything is for because you do not understand an item's true purpose. Your purpose gives something the meaning you assign to it. The true meaning of an item is different from a definition or name that you have assigned to that given object. When you name something, you define and limit it. Your definition of any object must come from your current belief system. We have been brought up in a fear-based thought system that believes you are a separate ego-body. It believes in limitation and lack. Because of your ego's basic misunderstanding of whom and what you are, its fear-based thought system has failed to understand your true purpose.

Your ego represents your current false beliefs about whom and what you really are. Your ego is how you define yourself. Your ego becomes your thought system which is based upon your belief in limitation, lack and separation. It is the embodiment of your fears. From this erroneous thought system, you attempt to give meaning to your perceived world of provisional reality. Since the ego perceives itself to be the body, it imagines a world whose purpose is to support and provide evidence that separation, limitation, and lack really exist in your world. The ego argues for its rightness, not your happiness.

Your false identification with your ego's goals leads to the misalignment of your world with the real purpose of the world. Your world is your own playschool for you to learn, grow, enjoy and be. It is a place where you can be what you are or pretend to be something you are not. In this dimension, you get to demonstrate and experience who you really believe you currently are. Time is the place in which beliefs can be tested and changed. This fascinates the learning process. Your egoic belief system, however, has turned your world into a place where it believes you must struggle for the limited resources that it needs to survive. Your ego believes that you must earn whatever it needs or your ego will die with the body that it perceives to be its home.

It is on the physical or bodily level, that your ego understands and defines your world of perception. Your ego identifies its very existence with your body and therefore, its viewpoint is focused on the body's needs. The ego accepts the body's limitations as its own. It defines everything as a separate physical autonomous entity. It adopts a fear-based worldview that if it is to survive, you must earn the ego's share of the limited resources that it needs. Your ego's world becomes a place of struggle and conflict, in which you must earn the limited resources that your ego believes it needs for its survival. To your ego, your worth is determined by your ability to obtain what the ego needs to survive. If you fail to provide for your ego's needs, your ego will try to blame, shame and guilt trip you into doing its bidding.

Believing itself to be separate, your ego believes that your world is a place to prove you too are separate. It is your decision to accept this belief in separation and limitation that prevents you from realizing that you alone are the creator of the world you perceive. When you accept your ego's belief in limitation and separateness, the source of your world is now perceived to be external and no longer internally powered by your own mind. Therefore, you must now earn your worth to access the limited resources that you now also perceive you need to survive. Your world view now is that you too must earn your keep. It is from this perspective of lack, limitation and separation that your egoic mind assigned all purpose or meaning to its world.

But what if you made a conscious decision to change the purpose of this world from earning, to learning? When you change the purpose of something, you also change the very meaning, or the why, of its existence. It is this why, or purpose, that gives meaning to your world.

When you believe you are the body and the body is you, the world becomes a place of conflict where you must struggle to earn the limited resources that you need to survive. If you were to change your world view from one of earning to learning, your world would become a place where you would get to learn, grow and have fun while you discover who and what you really are.

Earning is results oriented. Learning is process oriented.

When earning is your purpose, you need to get a specific result. When your focus is on some future result, a great deal of internal pressure, fear and stress is engendered. Your happiness must be deferred since it is to be determined based on some future event. Your happiness is contingent on external factors. You are in a constant state of judgment. Each step is determined to be either good or bad with fearful consequence administrated for any failure during this process. When you have an earning mindset, is it any wonder why you would approach an experience with fear and dread?

When you view this world as a place of learning, each experience becomes part of the process. It no longer is a required destination. You can enjoy the journey knowing that each part is a needed and beneficial step. When your focus is on learning, instead of earning, each moment becomes the perfect time and place that is needed for your continued forward progression towards your learning goals. Mistakes now become a feedback mechanism allowing you to make a mid-course correction so that you can get back on track. Learning becomes a process or journey that can be enjoyed.

Earning is a struggle while learning can be a fun puzzle.

When you make that conscious decision to change your purpose from earning to learning, it is easy to understand that everything is always in your best interest. What the ego calls a punishable mistake, is now seen as a simple error that requires a mid-course correction. Rather than some bad or negative experience, a "mistake" is just another forward step in the learning process.

When your world is seen as a place for earning, you become goal oriented with an external focus geared toward a result. Results can be either external or internal. Earning is typically associated with obtaining a specific reward only upon successful completion of the entire task. Being perceived as something outside of you, the reward must be fully earned. A reward is a destination, not a process.

Typically learning is associated with a skill that is acquired over time and becomes part of your being. Learning goals are typically character traits. Character traits are part of your "beingness." You are a helpful person or a loving person. A character trait is something that you demonstrate by being that trait. It becomes a part of you. As such, once learned, the trait cannot be lost. You can choose not to access that skill but that skill remains part of your knowledge base. It remains part of who you are.

Rather than earn an external reward that can be lost, make your goals character traits that are learned and become part of your very being. Rather than seeking results that are perceived to be external from you, choose inner goals that support your long-term growth. Go within and develop an internal focus rather than an exterior one.

The purpose of everything is to aid in your reawakening to the truth of who you are. Who you are is at the very core of your beingness. Each moment is the perfect time and place for your own personal journey of reawakening.

When you make a conscious decision to exchange earning for learning, your world becomes your playschool for your growth. Instead of fearing each outcome, you can sit back and enjoy the journey.

Your ego believes that you are a separate limited ego body in competition with other ego bodies for the limited resources that you both need for your survival. It is predicated on the idea that life is a zero sum game. If I am to win, someone else must lose. Winners are rewarded and losers are punished. Your worth as a person is determined based on your latest results. Since your beliefs determined your perception, the purpose of your egoic world is to prove the correctness of your ego's belief in lack, limitation and separation.

Would you expect such a thought system to create the type of world that would support the joy, happiness and inner peace that you seek? If not, you need a new plan.

Question: If you change the purpose of your world from earning an external reward to learning who you really are, how would your relationship with your world change?

Question: This lesson states that everything is always for your own best interest. If this is truly the case, how would this fact change your story about how you are a victim of your world?

Question: Can you still be a victim if everything has always been for your own best interest?

LESSON 26.

My attack thoughts are attacking my invulnerability.

W-26.1.It is surely obvious that if you can be attacked you are not invulnerable. 2 You see attack as a real threat. 3 **You see attack as a real threat** because you believe that you can really attack. 4 And what would have effects through you, **your belief you can attack others,** must also have effects on you **that you can be attacked.** 5 It is this law that **what would have effects through you must also have effects on you** that will ultimately save you, but you are misusing **this law** now. 6 You must therefore learn how **this law that what would have effects through you must also have effects on you** can be used for your own best interests, rather than against **your own best interests**.

W-26.2.Because your attack thoughts will be projected, you will fear attack. 2 And if you fear attack, you must believe that you are not invulnerable. 3 Attack thoughts therefore make you vulnerable in your own mind, which is where the attack thoughts are. 4 Attack thoughts and invulnerability cannot be accepted together. 5 **Attack thoughts and invulnerability** contradict each other.

W-26.3.The idea for today **that my attack thoughts are attacking my invulnerability** introduces the thought that you always attack yourself first. 2 If attack thoughts must entail the belief that you are vulnerable, **those same attack thought's** effect is to weaken you in your own eyes. 3 Thus **those same attack thoughts** have attacked your perception of yourself. 4 And because you believe **in your attack thoughts' ability to attack another,** you can no longer believe in your own **invulnerability.** 5 A false image of your **egoic** self has come to take the place of what you are, **which is really invulnerable spirit.**

W-26.4.Practice with today's idea **that my attack thoughts are attacking my invulnerability** will help you to understand that vulnerability or invulnerability is the result of your own thoughts. 2 Nothing except your thoughts can attack you. 3 Nothing except your thoughts can make you think you are vulnerable. 4 And nothing except your thoughts can prove to you this **perceived vulnerability** is not so.

W-26.5.Six practice periods are required in applying today's idea **that my attack thoughts are attacking my invulnerability.** 2 A full two minutes should be attempted for each of **the practice periods**, although the time may be reduced to a minute if the discomfort is too great. 3 Do not reduce **these practice periods** further.

W-26.6.The practice period should begin with repeating the idea for today **that my attack thoughts are attacking my invulnerability**, then closing your eyes and reviewing the unresolved questions whose outcomes are causing you concern. 2 The concern may take the form of depression, worry, anger, a sense of imposition, fear, foreboding or preoccupation. 3 Any problem as yet unsettled that tends to recur in your thoughts during the day is a suitable subject. 4 You will not be able to use very many **concerns** for any one practice period, because a longer time than usual should be spent with each **concern**. 5 Today's idea **that my attack thoughts are attacking my invulnerability** should be applied as follows:

W-26.7.First, name the situation:
2 I am concerned about ___.
3 Then go over every possible outcome that has occurred to you in that connection and which has caused you concern, referring to each one quite specifically, saying:
4 I am afraid ___ will happen.

W-26.8.If you are doing the exercises properly, you should have some five or six distressing possibilities available for each situation you use, and quite possibly more. 2 It is much more helpful to cover a few situations thoroughly than to touch on a larger number. 3 As the list of anticipated outcomes for each situation continues, you will probably find some of **the anticipated outcomes**, especially those that occur to you toward the end, less acceptable to you. 4 Try, however, to treat all **of the anticipated outcomes** alike to whatever extent you can.

W-26.9.After you have named each outcome of which you are afraid, tell yourself:
2 That thought is an attack upon myself.
3 Conclude each practice period by repeating today's idea **that my attack thoughts are attacking my invulnerability** to yourself once more.

Notes to Lesson # 26

My attack thoughts are attacking my invulnerability.

Lesson 26, my attack thoughts are attacking my invulnerability, is an important lesson. It is actually a statement of the obvious yet something that we do not think about. The only reason you would attack another is because you must believe that they have the ability to affect you in some way. If you did not believe that they possess this ability, why would you be concerned about them at all? Only if you felt their actions could have some positive or negative consequences on your world, would you feel compelled to attempt to control their actions. If you were invulnerable, their actions would be of no consequence to you.

Invulnerability means no outside force could change you against your will.

You believe that you must change, fix or control another's actions because you need to ensure their proper compliance with your ego's worldview and plan. When you believe that you could affect them, you must believe that by your actions you can impact their behavior. This belief that your actions can impact another person's behavior has made the belief of individual vulnerability real within your own mind.

As previously stated, perception always is colored by your beliefs. Thoughts always precede your actions. Your senses confirm your beliefs that you have projected into your world from your own mind. When you believe another is vulnerable, it must mean that your mind has first accepted the idea of your own vulnerability. To attack another, therefore, means you must first attack yourself.

The idea that you can change another confirms your belief that they can change you. Your belief that you are vulnerable to outside forces is the source of your fearful world. Yet, this belief in your vulnerability comes from your own mind. Nothing except your thoughts can attack you. Therefore, by the same token, nothing except your own thoughts can prove that you are actually invulnerable.

The law of perception tells us that what you believe would have effects through you must also have effects upon you. This is why there are no powerless or meaningless thoughts. Because your ego is one big judging machine, any thoughts of limitation that you would attempt to impose upon another must always attack your own invulnerability first. You fail to recognize the true power of your own beliefs. Therefore, you fail to realize that what has effects through you must also have effects upon you.

When you properly understand how perception works, you will realize that what you give you must also receive. To believe another is not perfect, whole and complete is to believe that you are not perfect, whole and complete. When you argue for another's limitations, you are actually arguing for your own. It is this belief that binds you to your fearful world of provisional reality.

Failing to recognize the true power of your beliefs, you misuse this law about perception. You think you can attack another and that your attack actually protects you. Once this law is properly understood, you will realize that when you attack another, you are attacking yourself. With this new found knowledge you can utilize that same law for our own best interest.

Question: The law of perception tells us that what you believe would have effects through you must also have effects upon you. How could you use this law so that it would help you achieve your own goals?

Question: Based on this law what would happen if you decided to believe that everyone was perfect, whole and complete?

69

LESSON 27

Above all else I want to see.

W-27.1.Today's idea **that above all else I want to see** expresses something stronger than mere determination. 2 **The idea that above all else I want to see** gives vision priority among your desires. 3 You may feel hesitant about using the idea **that above all else I want to see**, on the grounds that you are not sure you really mean **that you really want to replace egoic seeing with true vision**. 4 This does not matter **that you are unsure**. 5 The purpose of today's exercises is to bring the time when the idea **that you really want to replace egoic seeing with true vision** will be wholly true a little nearer.

W-27.2.There may be a great temptation to believe that some sort of sacrifice is being asked of you when you say you want to see above all else. 2 If you become uneasy about the lack of reservation involved, add:
3 Vision has no cost to anyone.
4 If fear of loss still persists, add further:
5 **Vision** can only bless.

W-27.3.The idea for today **that above all else I want to see** needs many repetitions for maximum benefit. 2 **The idea for today that above all else I want to see** should be used at least every half hour, and more if possible. 3 You might try for every fifteen or twenty minutes. 4 It is recommended that you set a definite time interval for using the idea when you wake or shortly afterwards, and attempt to adhere **to that definite time interval** throughout the day. 5 It will not be difficult to **adhere to that definite time interval**, even if you are engaged in conversation, or otherwise occupied at the time. 6 You can still repeat one short sentence **that above all else I want to see** to yourself without disturbing anything.

W-27.4.The real question is, how often will you remember **to repeat this sentence that above all else I want to see to yourself during your day**? 2 How much do you want today's idea **that above all else I want to see** to be true? 3 Answer one of these questions, and you have answered the other. 4 You will probably miss several applications, and perhaps quite a number. 5 Do not be disturbed by this **missing of several applications**, but do try to keep on your schedule from then on. 6 If only once during the day you feel that you were perfectly sincere while you were repeating today's idea **that above all else I want to see**, you can be sure that you have saved yourself many years of effort.

Notes to Lesson # 27

Above all else I want to see.

Lesson 27, above all else I want to see, is fairly straightforward.

First, realize that what you want is vision that witnesses for the truth, not misperception that is based on your belief in separation, limitation and the belief that you are the body and the body is you. When ACIM uses the term seeing, it is actually referencing the image making process that produces the distorted world of private individuated perception. This type of seeing is merely designed to confirm your ego's beliefs about your world. This is why ACIM refers to seeing as image making. Seeing is a thought confirmation device that utilizes your physical senses to merely agree with what your ego believes already exists outside your mind.

The next idea of importance is that in order to obtain correct vision, you need to have that as a priority. In an earlier lesson, we spoke of the need to have one unifying common purpose or goal. When rediscovering the truth of who you really are becomes your number one priority, the means to obtaining that goal will be made available. Clarity of purpose needs to be obtained. Only when you know where you want to go, does the decision of which direction to take become important. Prior to that decision, any direction is as good as another.

The third interesting point is the idea that multiple repetitions of a new idea is helpful when you are attempting to establish a new direction. When you are first attempting to change a previous pattern or belief, your believability in the new idea will not be total. You will have questions. You will have doubts. Yet, by simply repeating an affirmation about that desired new belief, that repetition will be helpful in creating that change in your life. By doing this you are at least bringing it into your conscious awareness. You are telling your mind that this new thought is something you desire your mind to move towards. Total belief or full desire is not required to begin the process for change. Sometimes you need to fake it until you make it.

When it comes to affirmations, repeating the idea within your mind is helpful, saying it out loud is better, and writing it down while you repeat it out loud is best.

Research on goal setting clearly indicates that written goals are clearly superior to oral ones. When a goal is in writing, it becomes your commitment toward change and achievement. Your mind sits up and takes note. When a goal is only oral, it remains an idle wish.

Question: If above all else you want to see, what is it that you desire to see with true vision?

LESSON 28

Above all else I want to see things differently.

W-28.1.Today we are really giving specific application to the idea for yesterday **which was above all else I want to see**. 2 In these practice periods, you will be making a series of definite commitments. 3 The question of whether you will keep **these definite commitments** in the future is not our concern here. 4 If you are willing at least to make **these definite commitments** now, you have started on the way to keeping **these commitments**. 5 And we are still at the beginning.

W-28.2.You may wonder why it is important to say, for example, "Above all else I want to see this table differently." 2 In itself it is not important at all. 3 Yet what is by itself? 4 And what does "in itself" mean? 5 You see a lot of separate things about you, which really means you are not seeing at all. 6 You either see or not. **Egoic seeing is not the same as true vision.** 7 When you have seen one thing differently **with true vision,** you will see all things differently **with true vision,**. 8 The light you will see in any one of them is the same light you will see in them all.

W-28.3.When you say, "Above all else I want to see this table differently," you are making a commitment to withdraw your preconceived ideas about the table, and open your mind to what **the table** is, and what **the table** is for. 2 You are not defining **the table** in past terms. 3 You are asking what **the table** is, rather than telling **the table** what it is. 4 You are not binding **the table's** meaning to your tiny experience of tables, nor are you limiting **the table's** purpose to your little personal thoughts.

W-28.4.You will not question what you have already defined. 2 And the purpose of these exercises is to ask questions and receive the answers. 3 In saying, "Above all else I want to see this table differently," you are committing yourself to **seeing with true vision**. 4 **This commitment that above all else I want to see differently** is not an exclusive commitment. 5 It is a commitment that applies to the table just as much as to anything else, neither more nor less.

W-28.5.You could, in fact, gain vision from just that table, if you would withdraw all your own ideas from **the table**, and look upon **the table** with a completely open mind. 2 **The table** has something to show you; something beautiful and clean and of infinite value, full of happiness and hope. 3 Hidden under all your ideas about **the table** is its real purpose, the purpose **the table** shares with all the universe.

W-28.6.In using the table as a subject for applying the idea for today, you are therefore really asking to see the purpose of the universe. 2 You will be making this same request of each subject that you use in the practice periods. 3 And you are making a commitment to each of them to let its **true** purpose be revealed to you, instead of placing your own judgment upon **the item**.

W-28.7.We will have six two-minute practice periods today, in which the idea for the day **that above all else I want to see things differently,** is stated first, and then applied to whatever you see about you. 2 Not only should the subjects be chosen randomly, but each **subject** should be accorded equal sincerity as today's idea **that above all else I want to see things differently,** is applied to **each subject**, in an attempt to acknowledge the equal value of **each subject** in their contribution to your seeing.

W-28.8.As usual, the applications should include the name of the subject your eyes happen to light on, and you should rest your eyes on it while saying:
2 Above all else I want to see this ___ differently.
3 Each application should be made quite slowly, and as thoughtfully as possible. 4 There is no hurry.

Notes to Lesson # 28

Above all else I want to see things differently.

In Lesson 28, you are asked to make a decision as to what you wish to see differently. Since your current perception is based on your past beliefs, in order for you to be able to see something differently, you must be willing to, at least temporarily, suspend those beliefs. If you fail to do this, your present perception of the new event will simply be a replay of your past beliefs about that subject.

When you say that you want to see things differently, you are committing to dropping your past preconceived ideas about the current event. With open-minded focus on what is presently occurring, you are allowing your mind to give new purpose and meaning to the event.

Lesson 24 stated that the purpose of everything is for your own best interest. When your current experience seems to be a replay from your past, this means that the previous experience had some learning lesson that you refused to acknowledge and absorb. You are allowing your old beliefs to cloud your vision and dictate the current event's purpose. Because of your insistence on maintaining your past belief about the old experience, you are unable and unwilling to absorb the learning lesson that the experience was designed to teach. Until you are willing to see a similar situation in a new way, you will remain stuck arguing for the correctness of your ego's past interpretation for the event. Your ego's need to be right will always trump your desire to be happy. The pearls of wisdom that the event was designed to teach remains unseen.

ACIM states that we are all going to reawaken to the truth of who we really are. We always remain as God created us. Your ego's current fantasy about who you are cannot change the Truth. This being the case, if someone decides to repeat the same learning lesson 1000 times before they fully comprehend that lesson, there is nothing wrong with their decision. Each of those supposedly 999 prior failures were actually needed for comprehending that lesson. Rather than judge those prior 999 experiences as failures, you need to develop the attitude of Thomas Edison.

It took Edison over 7000 attempts before he successfully invented the electric light bulb. When asked about what the world viewed as his many failures, Edison would state that he never failed. Edison viewed each unsuccessful attempt as simply one small baby step forward that moved him closer to finding the one way that would work. What was different about Edison, however, is that with each successful failure, he modified his approach and tried something different. He was willing to learn from his mistakes. He was constantly open-minded and saw each unsuccessful attempt as merely a warning sign that some mid-course correction was required. Edison failed his way to success. Yet, with that approach, Edison became the most prolific inventor the world had ever known.

If everything is for your best interest, this means that every moment is perfectly designed to provide the learning opportunity that you need for your growth and happiness. When you believe your purpose is earning, instead of learning, life becomes a struggle. Your current belief system is focused on earning some specific external result that will make you happy. The system has never worked in the past. Why should you expect it to work in the future? Such a thought system will always leave you in fear while preventing your enjoyment of the present moment.

You need a new plan. You need to see things differently.

Question: When similar negative experiences keep occurring in your life, your universe or your Higher Self is trying to tell you that your current beliefs are no longer serving your best interest. How many times do you need to repeat the same negative experience over again until you are willing to try a different approach?

LESSON 29

God is in everything I see.

W-29.1.The idea for today **that God is in everything I see** explains why you can see all purpose in everything. 2 **This idea that God is in everything I see** explains why nothing is separate, by itself or in itself. 3 And **this idea that God is in everything I see** explains why nothing you see means anything. 4 In fact, **this idea that God is in everything I see** explains every idea we have used thus far, and all subsequent ones as well. 5 Today's idea **that God is in everything I see** is the whole basis for vision.

W-29.2.You will probably find this idea **that God is in everything I see** very difficult to grasp at this point. 2 You may find **this idea that God is in everything I see** silly, irreverent, senseless, funny and even objectionable. 3 Certainly God is not in a table, for example, as you see **the table**. 4 Yet we emphasized yesterday that a table shares the purpose of the universe. 5 And what shares the purpose of the universe shares the purpose of its Creator.

W-29.3.Try then, today, to begin to learn how to look on all things with love, appreciation and open-mindedness. 2 You do not see **all things with love, appreciation and open-mindedness** now. 3 Would you know what is in **all things**? 4 Nothing is as it appears to you. 5 **Everything's** holy purpose stands beyond your little range. 6 When vision has shown you the holiness that lights up the world, you will understand today's idea **that God is in everything I see** perfectly. 7 And you will not understand how you could ever have found **this idea that God is in everything I see** difficult.

W-29.4.Our six two-minute practice periods for today should follow a now familiar pattern: Begin with repeating the idea **that God is in everything I see** to yourself, and then apply it to randomly chosen subjects about you, naming each one specifically. 2 Try to avoid the tendency toward self-directed selection, which may be particularly tempting in connection with today's idea **that God is in everything I see** because **of the idea's** wholly alien nature. 3 Remember that any order you impose is equally alien to reality.

W-29.5.Your list of subjects should therefore be as free of self-selection as possible. 2 For example, a suitable list might include:
3 God is in this coat hanger.
4 God is in this magazine.
5 God is in this finger.
6 God is in this lamp.
7 God is in that body.
8 God is in that door.
9 God is in that waste basket.
10 In addition to the assigned practice periods, repeat the idea **that God is in everything I see** for today at least once an hour, looking slowly about you as you say the words unhurriedly to yourself. 11 At least once or twice, you should experience a sense of restfulness as you do this.

Notes to Lesson # 29

God is in everything I see.

The idea that God is in everything I see is a common idea yet, it is difficult to grasp on the concrete level of physical form. Most religions state that God is everywhere and in everything. Yet, due to our belief in separation, we find it difficult to apply that same concept to concrete objects that appear all around us. Certainly, this lesson is asking us to look beyond the world of physical form and search for a deeper meaning or essence.

This idea may also be a frightening one. If God is in everything I see and what I see is a warring planet, is it safe to assume that God must be a God of war and not a God of peace and love?

It also leads to the question that if God is in everything I see, why does evil appear to exist in our world?

The world that we experience and see with our physical eyes is not the real world as God created it. Instead it is a myriad of false images that bear witness to our erroneous fear-based belief system. If God is in everything I see and I am failing to see God in my world, this implies that my perception is in error. True reality is not what you perceive. It must lie beyond the physical form that you claim as your reality.

The world you perceive is based on your ego's beliefs in separation, limitation and lack. Your egoic mind filters everything that you perceive based on those beliefs. This viewpoint distorts and provides false images to support your ego's beliefs about its world. When you choose to follow a different belief system, you will see a different world.

Today you are asked to look at all things with love, appreciation and open-mindedness. This is a radically different mindset than your ego's beliefs system. You are asked to look beyond mere form, beyond the past stories and abandon your previous judgments about your world. You are asked to see a different purpose for your world.

Can you look upon your world with a single yet different purpose and realize that everything you survey is there for your own best interest?

Or will you choose to perceive yourself in competition with your world?

Can you look upon all things with love and appreciation or will you see a world of struggle, conflict and fear? The choice is determined by the thought system that you choose to follow.

Mother Teresa was once asked how she was able to cope with the misery, sickness and poverty of the people of her world while still maintaining her good spirits. Her reply was a simple one. She was not administering to some unknown physical body, instead she was administering to her beloved Jesus. Mother Theresa saw the face of Christ in all. It was Jesus that peopled her world. Others saw the sick, helpless and infirmed while Mother Teresa chose to see God in everything.

Question: How easy or difficult is it for you to look past an object's physical form and see it in a larger context with appreciation and love?

Question: When you change the purpose of the object in question, is it easier to see that same object in a different mindset?

LESSON 30

God is in everything I see because God is in my mind.

W-30.1.The idea for today **that God is in everything I see because God is in my mind** is the springboard for vision. 2 From this idea **that God is in everything I see because God is in my mind** will the world open up before you, and you will look upon **the world** and see in **the world** what you have never seen before. 3 Nor will what you saw before be even faintly visible to you.

W-30.2.Today we are trying to use a new kind of "projection." 2 We are not attempting to get rid of what we do not like by seeing **what we do not like** outside **our mind**. 3 Instead, we are trying to see in the world what is in our minds, and what we want to recognize is there **in our mind**. 4 Thus, we are trying to join with what we see, rather than keeping **what we see** apart from us. 5 **Joining with what you see** is the fundamental difference between vision and the way you see.

W-30.3.Today's idea should be applied as often as possible throughout the day. 2 Whenever you have a moment or so, repeat **the idea that God is in everything I see because God is in my mind** to yourself slowly, looking about you, and trying to realize that the idea applies to everything you do see now, or could see now if **everything** were within the range of your sight.

W-30.4.Real vision is not limited to concepts such as "near" and "far." 2 To help you begin to get used to this idea **that God is in everything I see because God is in my mind** try to think of things beyond your present range as well as those you can actually see, as you apply today's idea.

W-30.5.Real vision is not only unlimited by space and distance, but **real vision** does not depend on the body's eyes at all. 2 The mind is **real vision's** only source. 3 To aid in helping you to become more accustomed to this idea **that God is in everything I see because God is in my mind also** devote several practice periods to applying today's idea with your eyes closed, using whatever subjects come to mind, and looking within rather than without. 4 Today's idea **that God is in everything I see because God is in my mind** applies equally to both **what you see and your thoughts within your own mind**.

Notes to Lesson # 30

God is in everything I see because God is in my mind.

This lesson clearly states the idea what we have mentioned in most of the previous lessons. Your mind is the power source for vision and the world that you perceive. What you perceive to be your outer world is actually a reflection of your mind's inner state. Real vision is not limited by space, distance or the body's eyes. The mind is the only source for true vision. This is why you are asked to devote several practice periods applying today's idea that God is in everything I see because God is in my mind with eyes closed. If God is everywhere, as stated in lesson 29, God must be within your mind.

We are all familiar with the idea of an inner guide. Some inner voice within you that tells you what is right or wrong. It is a voice that holds you to a higher, nobler standard and represents your better half. Some might call it your conscience, others intuition, inner guide, the Holy Spirit, your Higher Self, a guardian angel or the Voice for God. Regardless of what you call it, that inner voice always seems to represent and know your true best interest. This inner voice guides, directs and moves you towards a higher and nobler vision of who you really are. Whether or not we follow that inner guidance, we have all felt its presence.

This inner voice represents a thought system that is based on a totally different belief system. It understands the big picture and knows the truth of who you really are. It recognizes that you are not a body but rather spirit. It knows and can relate current events to the big picture. It seeks to join, not separate you from another. It understands the interrelationship of all the parts to the whole and your role in that relationship.

In this dimension of time and space, your inner guide utilizes a big picture thought system that is based on love and forgiveness. It knows that you are a spiritual being having a human experience. Its mission is to help you live in this fear-based world without being a source for that fear-based world. Rather than argue for your ego's limitations, it calls for you to reclaim your spiritual magnificence.

The fundamental difference between seeing and vision is separation versus joining. Vision supports oneness and the interconnectedness of all. Seeing supports your ego's belief that it is a separate autonomous entity in competition for the limited resources that your ego believes it needs to survive. The ego looks upon a fearful unsupportive universe because it believes in a zero-sum game. If someone is to win, someone else must lose. Lack, struggle and competition are at the foundation of the ego's world that arises from its fear-based thought system.

This lesson also talks about a different type of projection. Psychologists often refer to our mind's ability to transfer its own negative thoughts from our own mind and see those negative thoughts reflected in our outside world. This is a coping mechanism that we use in order to live with our "evil" side, so to speak. Instead of seeing a negative trait within ourselves, our mind now sees that same trait in another. Since the trait is recognized by your mind to be outside of you, you are no longer responsible for it. You do not have to deal with correcting your own mind. You get to blame another and claim that it's not your fault.

ACIM states that by projecting or transferring your negative fear-based thinking from your egoic mind, you create your own fear-based world. You get to claim that you are an innocent victim of the world you created.

Question: Typically, projection is used to transfer your negative fear-based thinking to your outside world. But what if you chose to transfer thoughts of love and appreciation from inside your mind and project them into your outer world? Would your world now reflect your new mindset and become a more peaceful and loving world?

LESSON 31

I am not the victim of the world I see.

W-31.1.Today's idea **that I am not the victim of the world I see** is the introduction to your declaration of release. 2 Again, the idea **that I am not the victim of the world I see** should be applied to both the world you see without and the world you see within **your mind**. 3 In applying the idea **that I am not the victim of the world I see**, we will use a form of practice which will be used more and more, with changes as indicated. 4 Generally speaking, the form **of practice** includes two aspects, one in which you apply the idea on a more sustained basis, and the other consisting of frequent applications of the idea **that I am not the victim of the world I see** throughout the day.

W-31.2.Two longer periods of practice with the idea **that I am not the victim of the world I see** for today are needed, one in the morning and one at night. 2 Three to five minutes for each of these **practice periods** are recommended. 3 During that time, look about you slowly while repeating the idea **that I am not the victim of the world I see** two or three times. 4 Then close your eyes, and apply the same idea **that I am not the victim of the world I see** to your inner world. 5 You will escape from both **the inner and outer world** together, for the inner is the cause of the outer **world**.

W-31.3.As you survey your inner world **of your egoic mind**, merely let whatever thoughts cross your mind come into your awareness, each **item that crosses your mind** to be considered for a moment, and then replaced by the next **item that crosses your mind**. 2 Try not to establish any kind of hierarchy among **the items that cross your mind**. 3 Watch **the items that cross your mind** come and go as dispassionately as possible. 4 Do not dwell on any one **item that crosses your mind** in particular, but try to let the stream move on evenly and calmly, without any special investment on your part. 5 As you sit and quietly watch your thoughts, repeat today's idea **that I am not the victim of the world I see** to yourself as often as you care to, but with no sense of hurry.

W-31.4.In addition, repeat the idea for today **that I am not the victim of the world I see** as often as possible during the day. 2 Remind yourself that you are making a declaration of independence in the name of your own freedom. 3 And in your freedom lies the freedom of the world.

W-31.5.The idea for today **that I am not the victim of the world I see** is also a particularly useful one to use as a response to any form of temptation that may arise. 2 **This idea that I am not the victim of the world I see** is a declaration that you will not yield to **the world you see**, and put yourself in bondage **to the world you see**.

Notes to Lesson # 31

I am not the victim of the world I see.

Although people try to make A Course in Miracles complicated, it is actually a very simple philosophy. This is because everything is always either black or white. For example, you are either a victim of the world you see, or you are not a victim of the world you see.

At any given moment, you only have two possible options on how you view your world. ACIM also recognizes the fact that within your mind, you have the power to decide which of the two possible options you will choose to follow at any given moment. ACIM's goal is for you to be able to make that decision, consciously and deliberately. This decision should not be made by default.

Your current fear-based thought system does not serve you or help you cope with your world. These workbook lessons will help you realize that within your mind, you possess the power to make a different choice. You alone have the power to decide what thought system you will follow. One thought system is based on lack, conflict, revenge, fear and separation. The other thought system is based on abundance, support, forgiveness, love and oneness.

The next question is a simple one. Which of the two possible thought systems is most likely to empower you?

When you are empowered you become a proactive agent for change. This enhances your ability to cope with or handle any given situation.

How does the idea that you are a victim of the world you see, help you handle a given situation?

It doesn't! You can only conclude such a belief is not in your best interest. It disempowers, paralyzes and limits your possible options in dealing with any situation.

Whether you choose to believe that you are the creator of every situation or not, you must agree that you are in control of how you choose to interpret your circumstances. This in turn, determines to a large degree how you will respond to those circumstances.

The focus of A Course in Miracles is on retraining your mind so that you recover your ability to make decisions. You need a thought system that helps and supports you. Your current fear-based thought system hinders and limits you. It does not serve you.

Let's review some of these ideas based on that simple criteria of does a particular belief help or hinder your ability to handle a given situation.

We previously stated that everything I see is for my best interest.

Does this idea help or hinder you? Do you somehow feel better when you believe that your world actually opposes your best interest?

Albert Einstein was considered the most intelligent person of his time. Einstein was asked, what is the most important thing for a person to determine about their world? The questioner was surprised by Einstein's answer. Einstein did not respond with E equals MC squared. Instead, his answer was simple: To decide for yourself whether you believe your universe is a friendly or unfriendly place. Why? Because based on that one belief, it will determine how you view your entire world. You will either be an optimist or a pessimist and that one decision will make all the difference in your life.

Your inner world is the cause of the outer world that you perceive. You have within you the power to decide how you will choose to interpret any given experience.

You can change your purpose from earning to learning. You get to decide if a belief serves your best interest. If a belief no longer serves your best interest, you can decide to change it.

Your best interests are served when you move away from victim consciousness and into a belief system that supports your becoming a proactive agent for the change you seek in your life and world.

Question: If you believe that the purpose of the world is to support your best interest, how can you be a victim of that world?

LESSON 32

I have invented the world I see.

W-32.1.Today we are continuing to develop the theme of cause and effect. 2 You are not the victim of the world you see because you invented **the world you see**. 3 You can give up **the world you see** as easily as you made up **the world you see**. 4 You will see **the world you made up** or not see **the world you made up,** as you wish. 5 While you want **to see the world you made up,** you will see it; when you no longer want **to see the world you made up**, that **world you made up** will not be there for you to see.

W-32.2.The idea for today **that I have invented the world I see**, like the preceding ones, applies to your inner and outer worlds, which are actually the same **world**. 2 However, since you see **your inner and outer worlds** as different, the practice periods for today will again include two phases, one involving the world you see outside you, and the other the world you see in your mind. 3 In today's exercises, try to introduce the thought that both **your inner and outer worlds** are in your own imagination.

W-32.3.Again we will begin the practice periods for the morning and evening by repeating the idea for today **that I have invented the world I see** two or three times while looking around at the world you see as outside yourself. 2 Then close your eyes and look around your inner world. 3 Try to treat **your inner and outer worlds** both as equally as possible. 4 Repeat the idea for today **that I have invented the world I see** unhurriedly and as often as you wish, as you watch the images your imagination presents to your awareness.

W-32.4.For the two longer practice periods three to five minutes are recommended, with not less than three **minutes** required. 2 More than five **minutes** can be utilized if you find the exercise restful. 3 To facilitate this, select a time when few distractions are anticipated, and when you yourself feel reasonably ready.

W-32.5.These exercises are also to be continued during the day, as often as possible. 2 The shorter applications consist of repeating the idea **that I have invented the world I see** slowly, as you survey either your inner or outer world. 3 It does not matter which you choose.

W-32.6.The idea for today **that I have invented the world I see** should also be applied immediately to any situation that may distress you. 2 Apply the idea **that I have invented the world I see** by telling yourself:
3 I have invented this situation as I see **this situation**.

Notes to Lesson # 32

I have invented the world I see.

This idea that I have invented the world I see is a continuation of the development of the theme of cause and effect. Yet, it challenges the very core beliefs that our egoic fear-based thought system rests upon. It questions what the real cause is and what is the real effect.

Most have been taught and believe that we are not the creator of the outside world that we perceive. We believe there is a separate world that exists outside of our minds and that this outside world was created prior to our existence. We have been indoctrinated to assume that there are outside forces that are beyond our control and that these forces have the ability to impact our behavior and our thinking.

Our ego tells us that we are not causative of our world and therefore, the best we can hope for is to react to this separate outside world in such a way as to mitigate the negative effects that these outside forces would impose upon us. This belief that we are not a causative agent for our world leads us towards a mindset that supports the idea that we are an innocent victim of this outside world. Such a thought system is fear-based and disempowering. This mindset fails to empower or encourage the holder of those beliefs to be proactive in their life. You can only react therefore, you must be a victim.

It is difficult to be the agent for change when you are told you are victim of circumstances and forces that are beyond your control. As surprising as it may sound, your ego has a vested interest in keeping you in a state of victim consciousness. This will sound counter-intuitive to you because of your deep identification with your ego. You believe that your ego is you, but this is not your true reality. We will discuss the many benefits the ego derives from the belief in victims and victimizers in greater depth as we proceed in these lessons.

Today's exercise also introduces the thought that both your outer and inner worlds are a product of your own mind's imagination. Coming from the same source, both your inner and outer worlds are the same. Yet, your imagination is different than true reality.

By now you should be well acquainted with the idea that the world you perceive is your private world of individuated perception. It is your provisional reality because you believe it to be so. Thoughts raised to the level of belief are endowed by your mind's creative force to create your inner world that is then reflected in your outer world.

Thoughts raised to the level of beliefs become the provisional reality of any mind that holds those same beliefs. Such imaginings or fantasies only cloud the mind of the believer. They have no ability to change the truth of who that person really is. You cannot be a victim of the world because your own mind invented the world that you see. Being your own world's cause, it is impossible for you to be its victim. Any wound or suffering must be self-inflicted.

Physiologists and psychologists tell us that our beliefs are pivotal to how we interrelate to our outside world. When you understand how perception works, it is easy to understand how we have invented the world we see. Our world is a storybook created from our own mind's beliefs in which we are the star, director and playwright.

We all appear to be legends within our own mind, yet relatively unknown in the history books of this world. Our mind creates its own story or narrative about our life in which we are the hero and that is how we perceive it to actually be. Yet, a third-party observer would tell a much different story. But does our mind actually have the ability to invent the physical world that we see?

Although our mind's ability to create physicality from thought is beyond the scope of this class, it is not as far-fetched as we have been led to believe. Quantum physicists have determined that human consciousness is pivotal in physical observation. The Heisenberg Uncertainty Principle tells us that human consciousness is the determining factor for what someone will observe in the so-called physical realm. Physicality appears to be quite pliable and not as fixed and solid as we have been led to believe.

String theorists tell us that whole galaxies exist merely because somewhere at some time, some astronomer desired to observe that galaxy. If an astronomer is responsible for the creation of entire galaxies, the idea that you have some small part to play in the creation of your physical world should not be dismissed by your egoic mind as impossible. Quantum physicists and quantum biologists have proven that our thoughts impact the very fabric of our physical world.

This lesson states that you will see the world that you made up as long as you wish to see it. When you no longer wish to see it, it will no longer be there for you to observe. This idea mirrors what the Heisenberg Uncertainty Principle tells us.

Question: Are you currently happy with your world as you see it?

Question: If not, what type of world would you prefer to see?

Question: What type of beliefs would be needed to support your new world vision?

Note: A detailed discussion of the large body of the scientific evidence that supports the power of our mind's thoughts to impact physical reality is beyond the scope of this class. This information is covered in greater depth in my Uncovering Your Default Beliefs Class.

LESSON 33

There is another way of looking at the world.

W-33.1.Today's idea **that there is another way of looking at the world** is an attempt to recognize that you can shift your perception of the world in both its outer and inner aspects. 2 A full five minutes should be devoted to the morning and evening applications. 3 In these practice periods, the idea **that there is another way of looking at the world** should be repeated as often as you find comfortable, though unhurried applications are essential. 4 Alternate between surveying your outer and inner perceptions, but without an abrupt sense of shifting **between the two**.

W-33.2.Merely glance casually around the world you perceive as outside yourself, then close your eyes and survey your inner thoughts with equal casualness. 2 Try to remain equally uninvolved in both **the outside or inside world you perceive** and to maintain this detachment as you repeat the idea **that there is another way of looking at the world** throughout the day.

W-33.3.The shorter exercise periods should be as frequent as possible. 2 Specific applications of today's idea **that there is another way of looking at the world** should also be made immediately, when any situation arises which tempts you to become disturbed. 3 For these applications, say:
4 There is another way of looking at this.

W-33.4.Remember to apply today's idea **that there is another way of looking at the world** the instant you are aware of distress. 2 It may be necessary to take a minute or so to sit quietly and repeat the idea **that there is another way of looking at the world** to yourself several times. 3 Closing your eyes will probably help in this form of application.

Notes to Lesson # 33

There is another way of looking at the world.

Lesson 33, there is another way of looking at the world, is an obvious consequence of the previous lessons. It is also a logical conclusion of what physiologists and psychologists tell us about perception.

Your perception is based on your beliefs. Perception makes and colors your world so that you observe only what confirms your pre-existing beliefs about your outer world. How you perceive the world, therefore, is a reflection of your current beliefs about your world. When you change your perception, your view of your world must automatically change to realign with those new beliefs. Change your beliefs and the color of your world must change. This is the true reality of how perception works.

Earlier we suggested that you adopt the mindset that the purpose of your existence in this current time space continuum is for learning. We advocated that you change your prior indoctrination about your life's purpose from earning to learning. The focus of earning is on future external results, whereas learning is involved with the internal process of becoming and fulfilling your destiny.

By making this shift from earning to learning, your world can become your playschool that is designed to support your best interest. A playschool is a school that allows you to interact with others while you learn and have fun in a safe environment. This environment promotes your best interest by combining fun with the learning process.

What are you here to learn in this playschool?

Ultimately, you must rediscover and then reclaim the truth about who you really are. You have come here to know and actually be or demonstrate what your true essence really is. You have come here to reclaim your destiny.

You are not a limited ego body in competition with other ego bodies for the limited resources that your ego claims it needs to survive. Instead, you are unlimited spirit that has freely embarked upon a journey of discovery to know your true spiritual magnificence. You remain as God created you. God doesn't make any junk. Your playschool is the place where you get to learn who you really are and reclaim your divine birthright in perfect safety. A fantasy cannot change reality. You remain as God created you, perfect, whole and complete.

In this playschool of time and space, you get to rediscover that you are the deliberate creator of your own experiences. I said earlier that time is the measure of change. In time, we can change our beliefs about who we really are. Change those beliefs and your experiences realign to support those new beliefs.

In space, we get to experience the illusion of separation. The experience of separation is a useful tool that allows for differentiation. Differentiation is needed if learning is to take place. It is impossible to fully comprehend the concept of white, without being able to compare white with its opposite, the color black. In order for one to really know and experience light, it is important to have experienced darkness. By the same token, it is beneficial to be able to compare the truth against the false.

Space allows us to temporarily experience differentiation which provides us the opportunity to actually be or know a particular aspect of the whole. As we move through space, we learn about particular aspects of the whole. This learning process allows us to make mid-course corrections about our beliefs. As our beliefs change, we experience the passing of time which is the measure of change.

You have been indoctrinated to believe that the time-space continuum is a place where you need to get a particular specific result if you are to survive and prosper. Coming from this belief in lack, limitation and needs, such a thought system is based on external rewards. It engenders a great deal of fear, stress, competition and conflict in your life. You are constantly being judged and are forced to argue for the rightness of your choices.

Question: If you viewed this dimension of time and space to be a playschool for the sole purpose of your learning and having fun in a totally safe environment, how would your relationship to your world change?

LESSON 34

I could see peace instead of this.

W-34.1.The idea for today **that I could see peace instead of this** begins to describe the conditions that prevail in the other way of seeing, **which would be to utilize inner vision that aligns with Truth**. 2 Peace of mind is clearly an internal matter. 3 **Peace of mind** must begin with your own thoughts, and then **peace will** extend outward. 4 It is from your peace of mind that a peaceful perception of the world arises.

W-34.2.Three longer practice periods are required for today's exercises. 2 One in the morning and one in the evening are advised, with an additional one to be undertaken at any time in between that seems most conducive to readiness. 3 All applications should be done with your eyes closed. 4 It is your inner world to which the applications of today's idea **that I could see peace instead of this** should be made.

W-34.3.Some five minutes of mind searching are required for each of the longer practice periods. 2 Search your mind for fear thoughts, anxiety-provoking situations, "offending" personalities or events, or anything else about which you are harboring unloving thoughts. 3 Note **these fearful and unloving thoughts** all casually, repeating the idea for today **that I could see peace instead of this** slowly as you watch **these fearful and unloving thoughts** arise in your mind, and let each **unloving thought** go, to be replaced by the next **unloving thought**.

W-34.4.If you begin to experience difficulty in thinking of specific subjects, continue to repeat the idea **that I could see peace instead of this** to yourself in an unhurried manner, without applying **this idea** to anything in particular. 2 Be sure, however, not to make any specific exclusions **to this idea that I could see peace instead of this.**

W-34.5.The shorter applications are to be frequent, and made whenever you feel your peace of mind is threatened in any way. 2 The purpose **of these shorter applications** is to protect yourself from temptation throughout the day. 3 If a specific form of temptation arises in your awareness, the exercise should take this form:
4 I could see peace in this situation instead of what I now see in **this situation.**

W-34.6.If the inroads on your peace of mind take the form of more generalized adverse emotions, such as depression, anxiety or worry, use the idea **that I could see peace instead of this** in its original form. 2 If you find you need more than one application of today's idea to help you change your mind in any specific context, try to take several minutes and devote **these minutes** to repeating the idea **that I could see peace instead of this** until you feel some sense of relief. 3 It will help you if you tell yourself specifically:
4 I can replace my feelings of depression, anxiety or worry [or my thoughts about this situation, personality or event] with peace.

Notes to Lesson # 34

I could see peace instead of this.

A Course in Miracles says that if you want peace, be peace. If you want love, be love. Gandhi put it this way, "Be the change you wish to see in the world!"

Peace of mind is an internal matter. Peace must begin with your own thoughts and then extend outward. From your own peaceful mind, you will create a peaceful world for yourself.

It is possible to be in a peaceful world and yet live on a warring planet. Your private world of individuated perception will be a reflection of your inner belief system. When you choose to follow a fear-based thought system rooted in the belief in lack, limitation, struggle and separation, you will perceive a world of conflict and fear. Choose instead, a thought system based on love and forgiveness and you will see a world full of mercy, caring and peace.

If your experiences are full of conflict, struggle and strife, first examine your own thoughts before you believe something outside of you is the cause for your own loss of inner peace. Your thoughts raised to the level of beliefs determine how you will color your world.

You may not believe that you are in total control of all the circumstances in your life but you are in control of the interpretation, purpose and the meaning that you give to those events. It is your interpretation of those events that will resonate within your mind and manifest outwardly as your story of your unique world of provisional reality.

Question: Do you live in a peaceful world?

LESSON 35

My mind is part of God's. I am very holy.

W-35.1.Today's idea **that my mind is part of God's Mind. I am very holy** does not describe the way you see yourself now. 2 **Today's idea that my mind is part of God's Mind and I am very holy** does, however, describe what vision will show you. 3 It is difficult for anyone who thinks he is in this world to believe this **idea that his mind is part of God's Mind and I am very holy** of himself. 4 Yet the reason he thinks he is in this world is because he does not believe **that his mind is part of God's Mind and that he is very holy.**

W-35.2.You will believe that you are part of where you think you are. 2 **You will believe that you are part of where you think you are** because you surround yourself with the environment you want. 3 And you want **the environment that you surrounded yourself with** to protect the image of yourself that you have made. 4 The image **that you made for yourself** is part of this environment **that you surround yourself with to protect that illusion or story about yourself.** 5 What you see while you believe you are in the **environment that you created to support your own viewpoint or story** is seen through the eyes of the image. 6 This **seeing what you believe** is not vision. 7 Images cannot see.

W-35.3.The idea for today **that my mind is part of God's Mind and I am very holy** presents a very different view of yourself. 2 By establishing your Source, **which is God's Mind, this idea** establishes your **true** Identity, and **this idea that my mind is part of God's Mind and I am very holy** describes you as you must really be in truth. 3 We will use a somewhat different kind of application for today's idea **that my mind is part of God's Mind and I am very holy** because the emphasis for today is on the perceiver, rather than on what he perceives.

W-35.4.For each of the three five-minute practice periods today, begin by repeating today's idea **that your mind is part of God's Mind and you are very holy** to yourself, and then close your eyes and search your mind for the various kinds of descriptive terms in which you see yourself. 2 Include all the ego-based attributes which you ascribe to yourself, positive or negative, desirable or undesirable, grandiose or debased. 3 All of **these ego-based attributes** are equally unreal, because you do not look upon yourself through the eyes of holiness.

W-35.5.In the earlier part of the mind-searching period, you will probably emphasize what you consider to be the more negative aspects of your perception of yourself. 2 Toward the latter part of the exercise period, however, more self-inflating descriptive terms may well cross your mind. 3 Try to recognize that the direction of your fantasies about yourself does not matter. 4 Illusions have no direction in reality. 5 **Both negative and positive** illusion are merely not true.

W-35.6.A suitable unselected list for applying the idea for today might be as follows:
2 I see myself as imposed on.
3 I see myself as depressed.
4 I see myself as failing.
5 I see myself as endangered.
6 I see myself as helpless.
7 I see myself as victorious.
8 I see myself as losing out.
9 I see myself as charitable.
10 I see myself as virtuous.

W-35.7.You should not think of these terms in an abstract way. 2 **These terms** will occur to you as various situations, personalities and events in which you figure cross your mind. 3 Pick up any specific situation that occurs to you, identify the descriptive term or terms you feel are applicable to your reactions to that situation, and use **these terms and situations** in applying today's idea **that your mind is part of God's Mind and you are very holy.** 4 After you have named each one, add:
5 But my mind is part of God's **Mind.** 6 I am very holy.

W-35.8.During the longer exercise periods, there will probably be intervals in which nothing specific occurs to you. 2 Do not strain to think up specific things to fill the interval, but merely relax and repeat today's idea **that my mind is part of God's Mind and I am very holy** slowly until something occurs to you. 3 Although nothing that does occur should be omitted from the exercises, nothing should be "dug out" with effort. 4 Neither force nor discrimination should be used.

W-35.9.As often as possible during the day, pick up a specific attribute or attributes you are ascribing to yourself at the time and apply the idea for today **that my mind is part of God's Mind and I am very holy** to **those attributes** adding the idea in the form stated above to each of **those attributes.** 2 If nothing particular occurs to you, merely repeat the idea **that my mind is part of God's Mind and I am very holy** to yourself, with closed eyes.

Notes to Lesson # 35

My mind is part of God's. I am very holy.

84

I stated earlier that <u>A Course in Miracles</u> is simple because it is always black or white. There is no gray. Something is either true or it is not true. However, it is possible for someone to believe, imagine or perceive that the false is true and the true is actually false. This erroneous belief has no ability to change the reality of the truth. It only appears in the imagination of the deluded mind of the thinker until he or she rediscovers the truth. Your provisional reality is the result of your current beliefs. Within time you can change your erroneous beliefs to align with Truth with a capital T.

Today's idea that my mind is part of God's Mind and that I am very holy is not how our fear-based thought system chooses to describe us. Since everything ultimately is either true or false, we can state the opposite of today's idea and we will have correctly described the ego's interpretation of who you are. Your ego believes the following. My mind is separate from God's Mind and I am very unholy.

Although you have been brought up to identify your existence as your ego, this is not the case. Your ego is your current beliefs about yourself. It is not your existence. Your beliefs can be and are radically different from your true reality. Yet, your beliefs cannot change the truth that you remain as God created you.

The truth remains that your mind is part of God's Mind and therefore, you must be very holy. To be holy is to be whole. You are part of the Oneness that is the Mind of God. Your belief that somehow your mind is separate from the Mind of God and that you are very unholy, colors your imagination and projects an environment that supports your ego's worldview of limitation, lack, struggle, conflict and fear.

When you identify and believe that you are a limited separate ego-body, your egoic mind imagines a world that supports your belief in separation. This image includes the physical world, your physical body and its physical senses through which you interact with this outside world. You claim to see the separate autonomous world that your mind has surrounded itself with. This imagined outer world was created to support your ego's inner vision of who you are. The source of these images must come from your mind yet, you perceive these images to actually be real and separate from your mind. Your egoic mind is the power source that imagines them in the first place.

Because you believe you are where you think you are, this imagined world becomes your provisional reality. Your egoic mind believes that your mind is separate from the Mind of God and you are very unholy. Your ego will argue for the reality of its delusional world vision. Your ego would rather claim it is right, even when it is proven wrong. The ego's insane need to be right comes at the cost of your happiness.

Your Higher Self or inner guide knows the truth that your mind is part of God's Mind and you are very holy. Your Higher Self does not need to argue for the truth, since truth just is. The false cannot change truth's reality. Truth is invulnerable.

Your ego is not who you are. Your ego is not your friend. Your egoic mind argues for the rightness of its own current belief system. To your ego, it is more important to argue for the correctness of its beliefs rather than seek the truth. Your ego prefers to cling to its erroneous beliefs rather than admit that it is wrong. Your ego's need to be right even when its plan is obviously not working is more important than your happiness. Your ego will argue for the rightness of its plan at the cost of both your happiness and the truth. What type of friend is so closed minded that they would refuse to consider other plans when they know that their current plan has only produced misery and suffering for their partner?

Question: Would a true friend argue for the rightness of their failed and bankrupt plan when it is continually costing you your happiness?

Question: Is the above person someone you should trust with your happiness?

Question: Do they have your best interests at heart?

LESSON 36

My holiness envelops everything I see.

W-36.1.Today's idea **that my holiness envelops everything I see** extends the idea for yesterday, which was m**y mind is part of God's Mind and I am very holy,** from the perceiver to the perceived.

2 You are holy because your mind is part of God's **Mind**. 3 And because you are holy, your sight must be holy as well. 4 "Sinless" means without sin. 5 You cannot be without sin a little. 6 You are sinless or not **sinless**. **You cannot be both**. 7 If your mind is part of God's you must be sinless, or a part of **God's** Mind would be sinful. 8 Your sight is related to **God's** Holiness, not to your ego**'s belief in your unholiness**, and therefore not to your body**'s sight**.

W-36.2.Four three-to-five-minute practice periods are required for today. 2 Try to distribute **these practice periods** fairly evenly, and make the shorter applications frequently, to protect your protection throughout the day. 3 The longer practice periods should take this form:

W-36.3.First, close your eyes and repeat the idea **that my holiness envelops everything I see** for today several times, slowly. 2 Then open your eyes and look quite slowly about you, applying the idea **that my holiness envelops everything I see** specifically to whatever you note in your casual survey. 3 Say, for example:
4 My holiness envelops that rug.
5 My holiness envelops that wall.
6 My holiness envelops these fingers.
7 My holiness envelops that chair.
8 My holiness envelops that body.
9 My holiness envelops this pen.
10 Several times during these practice periods close your eyes and repeat the idea **that my holiness envelops everything I see** to yourself. 11 Then open your eyes, and continue as before.

W-36.4.For the shorter exercise periods, close your eyes and repeat the idea **that my holiness envelops everything I see**; look about you as you repeat **that my holiness envelops everything I see** again; and conclude with one more repetition with your eyes closed. 2 All applications should, of course, be made quite slowly, as effortlessly and unhurriedly as possible.

Notes to Lesson # 36

My holiness envelops everything I see.

Lesson 36 extends the idea that you are holy from just yourself, the perceiver, to all that you perceive. Since your mind is part of God's Mind, you are holy and everything that you look upon must be holy as well. This idea that if the perceiver is holy what the perceiver sees must be holy may seem strange at first. This lesson also goes on to say that since your mind is part of God's Mind, you must be sinless or else part of God's Mind would be sinful.

Both these ideas are not what we have been taught and need to be explored further.

The first of these two ideas is that because you are holy all that you perceive must be holy. The first thing to realize is that when ACIM uses the term holy, its meaning is different from the typical dictionary definition.

Webster defines holy as:

1) Dedicated to religious use; belonging to or coming from God

2) Spiritually, perfect or purer; untainted by evil or sin; sinless: saintly

3) Regarded with or deserving deep respect, awe, reverence or adoration

Although some of these definitions are somewhat compatible, for ACIM purposes, holy means to be whole. Your mind is part of God's Mind because there is only one mind, which is God's Mind. You are part of that whole that is the Oneness of All That Is. Being an inseparable part of the whole, you also must be perfect, whole and complete. There is nothing outside of this Oneness and therefore, there can be no separation. A Oneness of All That Is can have no needs since It is complete and whole by definition. There is nothing that exists apart or outside of A Oneness of All That Is.

For ACIM purposes, when you see the term holy, you can substitute the phrase perfect, whole and complete in place of the term holy.

Of course, we do not see ourselves as holy nor perfect, whole and complete. The ego tells us that we are a separate ego-body and not perfect, not whole and very incomplete. The thought system of the ego is based on the belief in separation. The belief in separation engenders fear. Your inner guide or the Holy Spirit knows that God is your Source and that you remain part of God's Mind. You remain holy. The false imaginings of the ego have no power to change this truth.

The second idea that is challenging is that because you are holy, you must be sinless. Obviously, if you have been raised in the Western religious traditions of Judaism, Christianity or Islam, this is not what you have been taught. We have been taught that we are all sinners. So the idea that you are sinless will come as quite a surprise. How can we explain this obvious contradiction with our world religious view that we are all sinners? Again, the answer lies partially in how ACIM defines sin.

Webster defines sin as:

(1) Breaking of religious law, or moral principle, especially through a willful act

(2) Any offense, misdemeanor or fault

Based on Webster's definition of sin, it would certainly seem that we are all sinners. But how does A Course in Miracles define sin?

Sin is defined as lack. Yet, how can A Oneness of All That Is lack anything? Such a Oneness is perfect, whole and complete and there can be no lack.

Your egoic mind can and does believe that lack exists. The belief in lack is a direct result in the ego's belief in separation. It is your belief in lack that results in your belief that there is sin and you are a sinner. But once again your egoic misperceptions have no ability to change the reality of truth. Just like a boy pretending to be a dog, that pretense does not change the truth so the boy remains human. Your ego can claim that you are not perfect, whole and complete, that you lack, are separate and sinful, but this false claim has no ability to change how God created you.

In order to see yourself and your brother as holy, you need to drop your allegiance to your ego's fear-based thought system and accept the guidance of your inner Voice for God. Your true sight, which is Vision, is recovered by following your inner voice for God which knows your spiritual magnificence. You will never escape your belief in sin and unholiness as long as you choose to follow the ego's voice for limitation, separation and fear.

Since your perception of your outer world reflects your inner world, you cannot perceive yourself perfect, whole and complete if you see sin or lack in any brother or sister.

Question: Our western religious traditions claim we are all sinners that have somehow offended or hurt God. How could you hurt something as invulnerable as God?

Note: The Western religious traditions all have their origins with the Book of Genesis and its creation story with Adam and Eve and original sin. This story has been misinterpreted to give rise to a judgmental and vengeful God. There is, however, a mystical interpretation that is discussed in my Uncovering Your Default Beliefs Class that gives an alternative explanation of the Genesis story which aligns perfectly with A Course in Miracles teachings.

My holiness blesses the world.

W-37.1.This idea **that my holiness blesses the world** contains the first glimmerings of your true function in the world, or why you are here. 2 Your purpose is to see the world through your own holiness. 3 Thus are you and the world blessed together. 4 **When your purpose is to see the world through your own holiness,** no one loses; nothing is taken away from anyone; everyone gains through your holy vision **because you and the world are blessed together.** 5 **When your purpose is to see the world through your own holiness,** it signifies the end of sacrifice because **your own holiness** offers everyone his full due. 6 And he is entitled to everything because **the holiness of everything** is his birthright as a Son of God.

W-37.2.**Because you and the world are blessed together when you see the world through your own holiness,** there is no other way in which the idea of sacrifice can be removed from the world's thinking. **Seeing the world through your own holiness is the only way that will work.** 2 Any other way of seeing will inevitably demand payment of someone or something. 3 As a result, the perceiver will lose **something.** 4 Nor will **the perceiver** have any idea why **the perceiver** is losing **something.** 5 Yet is **the perceiver's** wholeness restored to **the perceiver's** awareness through your vision. 6 Your holiness blesses **the perceiver** by asking nothing of **the perceiver.** 7 Those who see themselves as whole make no demands.

W-37.3.Your holiness is the salvation of the world. 2 **Your holiness** lets you teach the world that **the world** is one with you, not by preaching to **the world** , not by telling **the world** anything, but merely by your quiet recognition that in your holiness are all things blessed along with you.

W-37.4.Today's four longer exercise periods, each to involve three to five minutes of practice, begin with the repetition of the idea for today **that my holiness blesses the world,** followed by a minute or so of looking about you as you apply the idea to whatever you see:
2 My holiness blesses this chair.
3 My holiness blesses that window.
4 My holiness blesses this body.
5 Then close your eyes and apply the idea **that my holiness blesses the world** to any person who occurs to you, using his name and saying:
6 My holiness blesses you, [name].

W-37.5.You may continue the practice period with your eyes closed; you may open your eyes again and apply the idea for today **that my holiness blesses the world** to your outer world if you so desire; you may alternate between applying the idea **that my holiness blesses the world** to what you see around you and to those who are in your thoughts; or you may use any combination of these two phases of application that you prefer. 2 The practice period should conclude with a repetition of the idea **that my holiness blesses the world** with your eyes closed, and another, following immediately, with your eyes open.

W-37.6.The shorter exercises consist of repeating the idea **that my holiness blesses the world** as often as you can. 2 It is particularly helpful to apply **the idea that my holiness blesses the world** silently to anyone you meet, using his name as you do so. 3 It is essential to use the idea **that my holiness blesses the world** if anyone seems to cause an adverse reaction in you. 4 Offer him the blessing of your holiness immediately that you may learn to keep **your holiness** in your own awareness.

Notes to Lesson # 37

My holiness blesses the world.

In order to give, you must possess what you intend to give away.

If your outer world is a reflection of your mind's inner world, you must first possess the trait before you can help another obtain that same trait or item.

To be holy is to see yourself perfect, whole and complete. This lesson points out that only when you know yourself as whole, will you be free from making counter-demands from another for the gifts you claim to provide.

When you fail to see both parties in the relationship as perfect whole and complete, you are perceiving lack in both your inner and outer worlds. Lack, as mentioned in yesterday's note, is ACIM's definition for sin. Because of the ego's belief in lack, the ego's world of perception is seen as both a sinful and fearful place.

As long as you perceive that you are not whole, you will perceive needs in both your inner and outer world. When you associate yourself with the body, this world becomes a very needy place. The world of physicality is utilized by your ego to prove its belief in separation, lack and fear. The ego uses the world of form to support its belief that you are not whole, not perfect, and very incomplete.

Even when your physical needs have been met, your ego perceives that any gift to another requires a sacrifice on your part. This belief in sacrifice follows from the ego's belief in lack. Because the ego perceives the giver and the receiver to be separate autonomous parties, the ego's world is a zero-sum game. If the receiver is to gain, the giver must lose. To the ego, giving always involves sacrifice. Because the ego believes it has needs, the ego only gives to get. The ego always wants a good deal. It expects some type of payback for any gift that it would give to another.

Only when you see yourself as whole and having no needs, will you be willing to bless your world without asking for some type of past, current or future payback in return. You are not blessing another if you expect something in return for your blessing or supposed gift.

Your Higher Self knows that to give is to receive. To the Holy Spirit, your purpose is to bless your world with your holiness. When you realize you are perfect, whole and complete, you understand that true giving requires no sacrifice. No one loses and everyone can gain their divine inheritance. Both giver and receiver are seen as perfect, whole and complete. This signifies the end of your ego's belief in lack, needs, sacrifice and separation. Each is free to reclaim their divine birthright.

Those that see themselves as holy or whole make no demands and require no payback from another. They realize that being holy, they can bless their world without any sacrifice on their part. They understand that when you are part of an indivisible Oneness of All That Is that to give is to receive.

When you bless the world with your holiness, you no longer have to fix, change, control, protect or impress another. Since they are perfect, whole and complete like yourself, you now can love them unconditionally.

Question: If you love someone, should you be allowed or perhaps even required, to fix, change, control, protect or impress the other party because you love them?

Question: How would you define unconditional love?

There is nothing my holiness cannot do.

W-38.1.Your holiness reverses all the laws of the world. 2 **Your holiness** is beyond every restriction of time, space, distance and limits of any kind. 3 Your holiness is totally unlimited in its power because **your holiness** establishes you as a Son of God, at one with the Mind of **the Son's** Creator, **which is God.**

W-38.2.Through your holiness the power of God is made manifest. 2 Through your holiness the power of God is made available. 3 And there is nothing the power of God cannot do. 4 Your holiness, then, can remove all pain, can end all sorrow, and can solve all problems. 5 **Your holiness** can do so in connection with yourself and with anyone else. 6 **Your holiness** is equal in its power to help anyone because **your holiness** is equal in its power to save anyone.

W-38.3.If you are holy, so is everything God created. 2 You are holy because all things **God** created are holy. 3 And all things **God** created are holy because you are **holy.** 4 In today's exercises, we will apply the power of your holiness to all problems, difficulties or suffering in any form that you happen to think of, in yourself or in someone else. 5 We will make no distinctions **between problems** because there are no distinctions. **Your holiness can solve all problems.**

W-38.4.In the four longer practice periods, each preferably to last a full five minutes, repeat the idea for today **that there is nothing my holiness cannot do,** close your eyes, and then search your mind for any sense of loss or unhappiness of any kind as you see **that loss.** 2 Try to make as little distinction as possible between a situation that is difficult for you, and one that is difficult for someone else. 3 Identify the situation specifically, and also the name of the person concerned. 4 Use this form in applying the idea for today **that there is nothing my holiness cannot do**:
5 In the situation involving ___ in which I see myself, there is nothing that my holiness cannot do.
6 In the situation involving ___ in which ___ sees himself, there is nothing my holiness cannot do.

W-38.5.From time to time you may want to vary this procedure, and add some relevant thoughts of your own. 2 You might like, for example, to include **relevant** thoughts such as:
3 There is nothing my holiness cannot do because the power of God lies in **my holiness.**
4 Introduce whatever variations appeal to you, but keep the exercises focused on the theme, "There is nothing my holiness cannot do." 5 The purpose of today's exercises is to begin to instill in you a sense that you have dominion over all things because of what you are **which is a holy Son of God.**

W-38.6.In the frequent shorter applications, apply the idea **that there is nothing my holiness cannot do** in its original form unless a specific problem concerning you or someone else arises, or comes to mind. 2 In that event, use the more specific form in applying the idea to **that event.**

Notes to Lesson # 38

There is nothing my holiness cannot do.

Argue for your limitations and you get to keep them.

Because you are perfect, whole and complete, this holiness reverses all laws of the world. You are beyond any restrictions of time and space. Your holiness is unlimited because your holiness is your divine birthright. Your mind is an extension of the Mind of God, your Creator. God being unlimited can only extend that same unlimitedness. For like begets like.

So what are these laws of this world that your holiness reverses?

The laws of the world are the beliefs in the fear-based thought system which dominates the mass collective consciousness of the world that you perceive. The laws of the world are based on the mistaken belief in separation, lack, limitation and fear.

Your world is controlled by how you define yourself. You have been indoctrinated and have accepted the world view that you are the body and the body is you. Your ego argues for your limitations. It claims that you are a limited ego-body in competition with other ego-bodies for the limited resources that you both need to survive. As such, it is rooted in a fear-based thought system of lack.

Fear dictates the rules of this world. Fear is false evidence appearing real. Your fear-based thought system is your private world of individuated perception that becomes your provisional reality.

Your holiness changes your erroneous beliefs about yourself. Since your world is a world of perception and not reality, the laws of perception currently govern your egoic world. The law of perception states that what you believe, you will perceive. Thoughts raised to the level of beliefs become the experiences that you call into your awareness.

Your beliefs become your provisional reality. Your provisional reality will change when you are willing to change those beliefs about who you really are.

You are holy because your mind is part of God's Mind. You are not the victim of the world you see because you have invented the world you perceive. When you realize that you are unlimited spirit and not some game token that you call the body, you will cease arguing for your limitations. When those beliefs change, those same limitations must disappear. Your beliefs are the cause and its effect is the world you perceive.

There is nothing that your holiness cannot do because by dropping your false beliefs about who you really are, you reclaim the truth of your divine birthright. All problems, difficulties or suffering, no matter what their apparent form is, are the same because they all arise from your erroneous beliefs about who you are. Accept your holiness and realize that your fantasies cannot change the truth. You and all you perceive remain as God created you, perfect, whole and complete.

Question: If you are not the body, but a spiritual essence, do the laws of physicality apply to your spiritual essence?

Question: How would your mindset differ if you knew you were a spiritual being having a bodily experience compared to believing you are a body having a spiritual experience?

Question: Which is your true reality?

LESSON 39

My holiness is my salvation.

W-39.1.If guilt is hell, what is **hell's** opposite? 2 Like the text for which this workbook was written, the ideas used for the exercises are very simple, very clear and totally unambiguous. 3 We are not concerned with intellectual feats nor logical toys. 4 We are dealing only in the very obvious, which has been overlooked in the clouds of complexity in which you think you think.

W-39.2.If guilt is hell, what is **hell's** opposite? 2 This is not difficult, surely. 3 The hesitation you may feel in answering is not due to the ambiguity of the question. 4 But do you believe that guilt is hell? 5 If you did **believe that guilt is hell**, you would see at once how direct and simple the text is, and you would not need a workbook at all. **You would know that hell's opposite is salvation.** 6 No one needs practice to gain what is already his. **Your salvation is already yours because you are holy.**

W-39.3.We have already said that your holiness is the salvation of the world. 2 What about your own salvation? 3 You cannot give what you do not have. 4 A savior must be saved. 5 How else can **a savior** teach salvation? 6 Today's exercises will apply to you, recognizing that your salvation is crucial to the salvation of the world. 7 As you apply the exercises **that my holiness is my salvation** to your world, the whole world stands to benefit.

W-39.4.Your holiness is the answer to every question that was ever asked, is being asked now, or will be asked in the future. 2 Your holiness means the end of guilt, and therefore the end of hell. 3 Your holiness is the salvation of the world, and your own **salvation**. 4 How could you to whom your holiness belongs be excluded from **your holiness**? 5 God does not know unholiness. 6 Can it be **God** does not know His Son?

W-39.5.A full five minutes are urged for the four longer practice periods for today, and longer and more frequent practice sessions are encouraged. 2 If you want to exceed the minimum requirements, more rather than longer sessions are recommended, although both are suggested.

W-39.6.Begin the practice periods as usual, by repeating today's idea **that my holiness is my salvation** to yourself. 2 Then, with closed eyes, search out your unloving thoughts in whatever form **your unloving thoughts** appear; uneasiness, depression, anger, fear, worry, attack, insecurity and so on. 3 Whatever form **your unloving thoughts** take, they are unloving and therefore fearful. 4 And so it is from **your unloving thoughts** that you need to be saved.

W-39.7.Specific situations, events or personalities you associate with unloving thoughts of any kind are suitable subjects for today's exercises. 2 It is imperative for your salvation that you see **your unloving thoughts** differently. 3 And it is your blessing on **your unloving thoughts** that will save you and give you vision.

W-39.8.Slowly, without conscious selection and without undue emphasis on any one **of your unloving thoughts** in particular, search your mind for every **unloving** thought that stands between you and your salvation. 2 Apply the idea for today **that my holiness is my salvation** to each of **your unloving thoughts** in this way:
3 My unloving thoughts about ___ are keeping me in hell.
4 My holiness is my salvation.

W-39.9.You may find these practice periods easier if you intersperse them with several short periods during which you merely repeat today's idea **that my holiness is my salvation** to yourself slowly a few times. 2 You may also find it helpful to include a few short intervals in which you just relax and do not seem to be thinking of anything. 3 Sustained concentration is very difficult at first. 4 **Sustained concentration** will become much easier as your mind becomes more disciplined and less distractible.

W-39.10.Meanwhile, you should feel free to introduce variety into the exercise periods in whatever form appeals to you. 2 Do not, however, change the idea itself **that my holiness is my salvation** as you vary the method of applying **the idea**. 3 However you elect to use **the idea**, the idea should be stated so that its meaning is the fact that your holiness is your salvation. 4 End each practice period by repeating the idea **that my holiness is my salvation** in its original form once more, and adding:
5 If guilt is hell, what is its opposite?

W-39.11.In the shorter applications, which should be made some three or four times an hour and more if possible, you may ask yourself this question. **If guilt is hell, what is its opposite? Then** repeat today's idea **that my holiness is my salvation.** Preferably do both **the question and the answer.** 2 If temptations arise, a particularly helpful form of the idea is:
3 My holiness is my salvation from this.

Notes to Lesson # 39

My holiness is my salvation.

Lesson 39 asks a question, if guilt is hell what is its opposite? Hell's opposite must be salvation or in religious terminology, heaven. Your holiness is your salvation. But what does this really mean? How can you escape from hell?

This lesson clearly states that the source of hell is your own unloving thoughts. Since your mind is the source of these thoughts, this means that you have the power within you to change them. Your own unloving thoughts must be seen differently if salvation is to be obtained.

We said that thoughts are meaningless and have no ability to impact the truth. So, how can your unloving thoughts create a living hell?

Although thoughts themselves are powerless, thoughts raised to the level of beliefs do have the power to impact your provisional reality and how you relate to your private world of individuated perception.

How do meaningless thoughts become the beliefs?

When you judge a simple thought as either good or bad, you raise that thought to the level of a belief. Beliefs are empowered with your own mind's creative energy. Your mind's beliefs can either align with the truth or the false. False beliefs have no power to change reality but they do impact the delusional mind of the holder of that belief. False beliefs generate the fearful world that becomes the believer's own private hell.

Lesson 37 stated that your holiness blesses the world. You can only bless the world when you see yourself as whole. Without this belief in your holiness or wholeness, you will make additional demands upon any situation. You will only give to get. These counter demands are made to fulfill your perceived needs. When you make demands, your focus is on some anticipated results. Believing you must earn some reward, you are constantly judging each moment as either good or bad.

Your ego is a big judging machine. Egoic judgments raise innocent thoughts to the level of powerful beliefs. When you judge something as good or bad, that moment becomes a source for guilt, blame and fear. You become a guilt thrower or a guilt catcher. Blame another and you merely project your guilt upon them while pretending to be an innocent victim. Yet, even innocent victims must feel guilty about allowing themselves to be victimized. Guilt is hell.

When you are not whole, you perceive outside forces that can rob you of your peace and happiness. You do not perceive yourself as a learner nor is everything for your best interest. Your egoic belief in victims and victimizers spawns your unloving thoughts. Because of your belief system, you judge and your outer world becomes a reflection of your inner mind's guilt.

Salvation means that you must escape from your own unloving thoughts. You cannot do this within the fear-based thought system that generated these thoughts in the first place. You need a new plan. You need a thought system based on the opposite of fear and guilt which is love and forgiveness.

Question: If you adopted the attitude of a continuous learner and realized everything is in your best interest, what or who would there be to blame or make guilty?

LESSON 40

I am blessed as a Son of God.

W-40.1.Today we will begin to assert some of the happy things to which you are entitled, being what you are **which is a holy Son of God**. 2 No long practice periods are required today, but very frequent short ones are necessary. 3 Once every ten minutes would be highly desirable, and you are urged to attempt this schedule and to adhere to **this ten minute schedule** whenever possible. 4 If you forget, try again. 5 If there are long interruptions, try again. 6 Whenever you remember, try again.

W-40.2.You need not close your eyes for the exercise periods, although you will probably find it more helpful if you do **close your eyes.** 2 However, you may be in a number of situations during the day when closing your eyes would not be feasible. 3 Do not miss a practice period because of this. 4 You can practice quite well under any circumstances, if you really want to.

W-40.3.Today's exercises take little time and no effort. 2 Repeat the idea for today **that I am blessed as a Son of God**, and then add several of the attributes you associate with being a Son of God, applying **those attributes** to yourself. 3 One practice period might, for example, consist of the following:
4 I am blessed as a Son of God.
5 I am happy, peaceful, loving and contented.
6 Another might take this form:
7 I am blessed as a Son of God.
8 I am calm, quiet, assured and confident.
9 If only a brief period is available, merely telling yourself that you are blessed as a Son of God will do.

Notes to Lesson # 40

I am blessed as a Son of God.

To bless means that the other party makes no demands upon the receiver of the blessing. Only those who see themselves as whole or holy are able to do this. When you realize that you are already perfect, whole and complete, you can give that same blessing to another party. Neither party will perceive that someone must lose or is required to make a payment for the gift received. This is an acknowledgment of the truth that you remain as God created you. There is nothing either party lacks in their core being.

This lesson asks you to realize that you are actually God's beloved Child with whom God is well pleased. Since like begets like, you are created in God's image and are part of the Mind of God. You are very holy and blessed by God, your Source.

Isn't it time to drop your ego's belief in limitation, lack and separation and reclaim your divine birthright?

Question: Since blessed means that the giver of the blessing makes no demands upon the receiver of the blessing, what demands does God make upon you, His Son?

LESSON 41

God goes with me wherever I go.

W-41.1.Today's idea **that God goes with me wherever I go** will eventually overcome completely the sense of loneliness and abandonment all the separated ones experience. 2 Depression is an inevitable consequence of separation. 3 So are anxiety, worry, a deep sense of helplessness, misery, suffering and intense fear of loss **the inevitable consequences of separation.**

W-41.2.The separated ones have invented many **egoic "cures"** for what **the separated ones** believe to be "the ills of the world." 2 But the one thing **the separated ones** do not do is to question the reality of the problem **which is their belief in separation.** 3 Yet **the belief in separation's** effects cannot be cured because the problem **of separation** is not real. 4 The idea for today **that God goes with me wherever I go** has the power to end all this foolishness **in the belief in separation** forever. 5 And foolishness it is, despite the serious and tragic forms **the belief in separation** may take.

W-41.3.Deep within you is everything that is perfect, ready to radiate through you and out into the world. 2 **Your holiness deep within you** will cure all sorrow and pain and fear and loss because **your holiness** will heal the mind that thought these things **of separation** were real. And y**our holiness will cure the effects of the belief in separation, which are the sorrow, pain, fear and loss, you** suffer out of **your mind's** allegiance to **the ego's belief in separation itself.**

W-41.4.You can never be deprived of your perfect holiness because **holiness's** Source, **which is God,** goes with you wherever you go. 2 You can never suffer because the Source of all joy**, which is God,** goes with you wherever you go. 3 You can never be alone because the Source of all life**, which is God,** goes with you wherever you go. 4 Nothing can destroy your peace of mind because God goes with you wherever you go.

W-41.5.We understand that you do not believe all this **idea that God goes with me wherever I go**. 2 How could you, when the truth **that God goes with me wherever I go** is hidden deep within, under a heavy cloud of insane thoughts, dense and obscuring, yet representing all you see? 3 Today we will make our first real attempt to get past this dark and heavy cloud, and to go through **this dark and heavy cloud of insane thoughts** to the light beyond.

W-41.6.There will be only one long practice period today. 2 In the morning, as soon as you get up if possible, sit quietly for some three to five minutes, with your eyes closed. 3 At the beginning of the practice period, repeat today's idea **that God goes with me wherever I go** very slowly. 4 Then make no effort to think of anything. 5 Try, instead, to get a sense of turning inward, past all the idle thoughts of the world. 6 Try to enter very deeply into your own mind, keeping **your mind** clear of any thoughts that might divert your attention.

W-41.7.From time to time, you may repeat the idea **that God goes with me wherever I go** if you find it helpful. 2 But most of all, try to sink down and inward, away from the world and all the foolish thoughts of the world. 3 You are trying to reach past all these things. 4 You are trying to leave appearances and approach reality.

W-41.8.It is quite possible to reach God. 2 In fact it is very easy, because **to reach God** is the most natural thing in the world. 3 You might even say **to reach God** is the only natural thing in the world. 4 The way will open, if you believe that it is possible **to reach God in the world.** 5 This exercise can bring very startling results even the first time **this exercise** is attempted, and sooner or later **this exercise to reach God in the world** is always successful. 6 We will go into more detail about this kind of practice as we go along. 7 But **this exercise to reach God in the world** will never fail completely, and instant success is possible.

W-41.9.Throughout the day use today's idea **that God goes with me wherever I go** often, repeating it very slowly, preferably with eyes closed. 2 Think of what you are saying; what the words mean. 3 Concentrate on the holiness that **the words** imply about you; on the unfailing companionship that is yours; on the complete protection that surrounds you.

W-41.10.You can indeed afford to laugh at fear thoughts, remembering that God goes with you wherever you go.

Notes to Lesson # 41

God goes with me wherever I go.

Lesson 41 introduces the term <u>separated ones.</u> We need to understand what is meant by that strange terminology.

Time and space is a dimension of perception. Your perception can either align with the truth of who you are or bear witness to the false belief that you are separate from The Oneness of All That Is. Although separation is impossible since your mind is an inseparable part of the Mind of God, it is possible to believe that you are separate from that One Self. Whenever you believe that you are separate from God, your Source, you are following the false, fear-based belief system of the ego. This thought system distorts the truth and attempts to replace the truth with an imagined world that supports the ego's belief that it is a separate autonomous entity.

Another term for <u>separated ones </u>would be the split minded. When someone is split minded, their mind's allegiance vacillates between two possible thought systems. One thought system is based on the belief of separation, limitation, lack and fear. This is the thought system of your ego. When you mind is listening to the voice of the ego, you perceive yourself as a separate autonomous ego-body in competition with other ego-bodies for the limited resources that you perceive are needed for survival.

Most of us blindly follow the egoic thought system into which we were previously indoctrinated. Yet, even when you are following your ego's fear-based thought system, there is another part of your mind that knows the truth of who you are. This is why the separated ones are also referred to as the split minded. We could call this part of your mind your intuition, your Higher Self, the Holy Spirit or the Voice for God. This is that inner guide that we previously spoke about which represents your higher ideals and supports your reawakening to your spiritual magnificence as a Child of God. This inner guide represents a thought system that is based on unconditional love, forgiveness, unity and the truth of who you really are.

Regardless of your current allegiance to your egoic belief in separation, this inner guide remains part of your mind. Its guidance cannot be lost but you can fail to access your inner guide. Ultimately however, since it represents the Voice for Truth, you will eventually reawaken to follow its guidance.

This Voice for God is always available and resides within your mind. This inner voice waits patiently within the mind of all who perceive themselves to be separate. It is waiting for you to realize that there must be a better plan. When you choose to silence your ego, ask your inner guide for help and then stop and listen, the answers that you seek will be provided. This Voice for God represents a thought system of abundance, joy, peace, happiness, love, forgiveness and unity. It is a thought system based on the truth that you are God's beloved child with whom He is well pleased. This Inner Voice or Holy Spirit is always with you because it is part of your mind.

Our belief in separation is the cause of all depression, suffering, abandonment and loneliness. The ego's fear-based thought system is the cause of the worry, anxiety, misery and all the suffering that you experience. Perceiving itself to be an innocent victim of outside forces that are beyond its control, your ego develops numerous plans which are aimed at curing the ill effects of its belief in separation.

Because your ego believes happiness to be something that comes from outside you, it develops numerous plans to make you happy. Your ego believes that since you are incomplete and not whole that there is something outside yourself that can make you happy and whole. Your ego's plans for your happiness typically revolve around you gaining wealth, fame, health, power or sex.

For example, your ego tells you that you will be happy when you can move out on your own. When you move out and are not happy, it tells you that you will be happy when you get married. When you get married, it tells you that you will be happy when you have kids. When you have them, it claims you will be happy when your children are grown. Whenever each goal is achieved but happiness is not obtained or sustained, your ego adopts a new plan. All your egoic plans for your happiness are doomed to fail.

Why?

Because all the ego's plans fail to address the true source of the problem. Your happiness was lost when you chose to follow the ego's voice for fear, limitation and lack. Your ego can never fix the problem because your ego's thought system is the problem. You are attempting to solve the problem of separation while maintaining your belief in separation. This is impossible.

This problem cannot be fixed on the outside. The problem resides within your split mind. The only way to correct the problem is at the source of the problem which is your allegiance to the ego's fear-based thought system. Your problems remain unsolvable because you are attempting to minimize its effect rather than eliminate the problem's cause. The problem itself is not real but you still must correct the false belief that created the fear-based delusional world you perceive. Your split mind is the problem. Choose to follow the Voice for Oneness. Accept the truth that God is within you and the illusion of separation, with all its ill effects, must disappear.

Question: All your life you have been following your ego's fear-based thought system. By following your ego's plan, have you obtained the lasting peace, joy, happiness, love and abundance that you seek and deserve?

Question: Do you believe you can escape the negative effects of a fear-based thought system by following that same thought system that was designed to create and perpetuate fear in the first place?

Question: Isn't it time that you get a new plan that is not based on the fear, lack and limitation that you are trying to avoid?

LESSON 42

God is my strength. Vision is His gift.

W-42.1.The idea for today **that God is my strength and Vision is God's gift** combines two very powerful thoughts, both of major importance. 2 **The idea for today that God is my strength and Vision is God's gift** also sets forth a cause and effect relationship that explains why you cannot fail in your efforts to achieve the goal of the course **which is true Vision.** 3 You will see because **Vision** is the Will of God. 4 It is **God's** strength **that gives you power. It is** not your own **ego's erroneous belief in separation that gives** you power. 5 And it is **God's** gift **of Vision,** rather than your own **ego's false perception that is mirrored in physical sight** that offers vision to you.

W-42.2.God is indeed your strength, and what **God** gives **which is Vision** is truly given. 2 This means that you can receive **Vision** anytime and anywhere, wherever you are, and in whatever circumstance you find yourself. 3 Your passage through time and space is not at random. 4 You cannot but be in the right place at the right time. **You are always in the right place and time for your reawakening to the truth about your holiness. Everything is for your best interest.** 5 Such is the strength of God. 6 Such are **God's** gifts.

W-42.3.We will have two three-to-five-minute practice periods today, one as soon as possible after you wake, and another as close as possible to the time you go to sleep. 2 It is better, however, to wait until you can sit quietly by yourself, at a time when you feel ready, than it is to be concerned with the time **of the practice periods.**

W-42.4.Begin these practice periods by repeating the idea for today **that God is my strength and Vision is God's gift** slowly, with your eyes open, looking about you. 2 Then close your eyes and repeat the idea **that God is my strength and Vision is God's gift** again, even slower than before. 3 After this, try to think of nothing except thoughts that occur to you in relation to the idea for the day **that God is my strength and Vision is God's gift.** 4 You might think, for example:
5 Vision must be possible. 6 God gives truly,
or:
7 God's gifts to me must be mine, because **God** gave them to me.

W-42.5.Any thought that is clearly related to the idea for today **that God is my strength and Vision is God's gift** is suitable. 2 You may, in fact, be astonished at the amount of course-related understanding some of your thoughts contain. 3 Let **these course-related thoughts** come without censoring unless you find your mind is merely wandering, and you have let obviously irrelevant thoughts intrude. 4 You may also reach a point where no thoughts at all seem to come to mind. 5 If such interferences occur, open your eyes and repeat the thought **that God is my strength and Vision is God's gift** once more while looking slowly about; close your eyes, repeat the idea **that God is my strength and Vision is God's gift** once more, and then continue to look for related thoughts in your mind.

W-42.6.Remember, however, that active searching for relevant thoughts is not appropriate for today's exercises. 2 Try merely to step back and let the **relevant** thoughts come. 3 If you find this difficult, it is better to spend the practice period alternating between slow repetitions of the idea **that God is my strength and Vision is God's gift** with eyes open, then with eyes closed, than it is to strain to find suitable thoughts.

W-42.7.There is no limit on the number of short practice periods that would be beneficial today. 2 The idea for the day **that God is my strength and Vision is God's gift** is a beginning step in bringing thoughts together, and teaching you that you are studying a unified thought system in which nothing is lacking that is needed, and nothing is included that is contradictory or irrelevant to **that unified thought system.**

W-42.8.The more often you repeat the idea **that God is my strength and Vision is God's gift** during the day, the more often you will be reminding yourself that the goal of the course is important to you, and that you have not forgotten **the goal of the course which is Vision and the salvation that it brings.**

Notes to Lesson # 42

God is my strength. Vision is His gift.

Lesson 42 is interesting for a number of reasons. It clearly states what A Course in Miracles actually is. You are studying a unified thought system in which nothing is lacking that is needed and nothing is included that is contradictory or irrelevant.

This is why I said that ACIM is actually quite simple to understand. The reason most people struggle with ACIM is because it represents an entirely different thought system that reaches logical, comprehensive solutions that contradict their present thought system. They wish to cling to their old indoctrinated beliefs that they have been following their entire life. Because ACIM's conclusions conflict with their present thought system, they struggle against accepting the ideas and logic of ACIM's philosophy. Their egos argues for its egoic rightness at the cost of their happiness.

A syllogism is a tool in logic. It is a string of statements or premises that lead to a logical conclusion. If the premises are all correct, the conclusion that is drawn must also be correct. If any premise is wrong, the correctness of the conclusions drawn from that premise will not necessarily be valid.

The ego's thought system is wrong because it gets the first premise wrong. It does not know who you really are. Making this initial yet monumental mistake, every conclusion that follows is wrong. Its entire fear-based thought system collapses.

When you examine other religious philosophies, you often see that their logic also breaks down. They often make obvious contradictory statements. For example, they will state that God is all-powerful yet claim that God's Will can be disobeyed. That God is only good yet evil appears to exist. That God is only love and then say that this loving God condemned His own innocent Son to a cruel death so that those who had sinned could go free.

I was brought up as a Catholic, and often would question my teachers about these apparent contradictions. In Catholicism, their answer was a simple but unsatisfying one. "It's a mystery," was their answer. Anything that was unexplainable was a mystery that was to be taken on faith. This is why ACIM is so simple. There are no mysteries. ACIM is a unified thought system which is complete without any internal contradictions.

Lesson 42 is God is my strength and Vision is God's gift. This idea combines two powerful major tenants of ACIM. It sets forth a cause and effect relationship that explains why you must succeed with your efforts of reawakening to the truth of who you really are.

When we observe an effect, it is helpful to know the effect's cause. The effect should be the logical consequence or embody similar attributes of its cause. In nature, like begets like. We look at the attributes of the cause and expect the effects to have similar attributes. If God created all things, we would expect to observe similar attributes in God's creations.

One of the attributes of God is Truth, with a capital T. God is cause and Truth is God's effect. Truth just is. Truth does not require someone's agreement to make it true. The false has no power to change the reality of what is true. Your belief that something false is true cannot make it so. Erroneous thinking has no ability to change the Truth. Truth remains steadfast and is invulnerable to anyone's beliefs about Truth's validity.

ACIM is black and white. It states that there are only two possible thought systems, or philosophies that can be followed. One is based on the truth. The second is based on the false. Although one can follow a false thought system, your allegiance to that thought system has no ability to change the truth. A fantasy cannot change reality.

Because God is cause and truth is God's effect, it is this relationship that is your strength. Truth remains invulnerable to your ego's false beliefs. What you believe yourself to be cannot be the truth. You perceive yourself to be unlike God, your Creator. If like begets like, how can that be? You perceive lack, limitation and separation. What you perceive cannot be the true reality for God knows no lack, limitation or separation.

Because God is Cause and Truth is God's Effect, your false beliefs can have no ability to change this cause and effect relationship. Truth remains invulnerable to the ego's false fantasies. Fantasies can be imagined, but cannot change the truth. Ultimately, everyone's fantasies must end and truth be recognized.

Time and space are the playschool for your fantasies. In time and space, your desire to learn about your true nature can be explored in perfect safety. Just like a dream, these false images have no ability to change your true reality. The split minded can pretend that they are separate, limited and lacking but their pretense cannot make it so. Their illusions cannot change God's Truth.

Within the minds of those that perceive themselves to be separate or split minded, there is an inner voice that God has given them. This Voice for God which resides within your mind is God's gift to you and cannot be lost or stolen. This Voice of the Holy Spirit guarantees that Vision will be returned to all who once perceived themselves to be different or separate from God, their Source.

In time and space, everything that you experience is happening so that God's sleeping Son will awaken. You are always in the right place and time for your reawakening to the truth about your holiness. Everything is always for your best interest.

Your strength comes from God, your Source. Vision represents the thought system for this Truth, with a capital T. Your reawakening is guaranteed by your divine birthright. Your inner guide, the Holy Spirit, will gently reawaken God's sleeping Son to the truth of who you really are.

In this playschool of time and space, you have simply chosen to explore a thought system based on the false premise of separation. Rather than making yourself wrong for that decision, realize that this choice to explore the concept of separation provides a learning opportunity that allows you to know, demonstrate and be what you truly are.

We said earlier that contrast and comparison help the learning process. Differentiation is needed to be able to demonstrate the various aspects of your being. Darkness helps one better appreciate the Light. Time and space is your playschool. God is your strength and reawakening to the truth of your divine birthright is your destiny. It is guaranteed because   your Inner Voice has not forgotten the Truth about God's Son. Vision or Truth must and will be restored since your mind is part of God's Mind and you are very holy.

Question: Do you find it hard to understand and reconcile the idea of an all-powerful God of Love condemning His creations to hell?

LESSON 43

God is my Source. I cannot see apart from Him.

W-43.1.Perception is not an attribute of God. 2 **An attribute of God** is the realm of knowledge. 3 Yet **God** has created the Holy Spirit as the Mediator between perception and knowledge. 4 Without **the Holy Spirit as** this link with God, perception would have replaced knowledge forever in your mind. 5 With **the Holy Spirit as** this link with God, perception will become so changed and purified that **perception** will lead to knowledge. 6 **Your return to knowledge** is **perception's** function as the Holy Spirit sees **perception**. 7 Therefore, **your return to knowledge** is **perception's** function in truth.

W-43.2.In God you cannot see. 2 Perception has no function in God, and **perception** does not exist **in God**. 3 Yet in salvation, which is the undoing of what never was, perception has a mighty purpose. 4 P**erception was** made by the Son of God for an unholy purpose. **Perception** must become the means for the restoration of **the Son of God's** holiness to **the Son of God's** awareness. 5 Perception has no meaning. 6 Yet does the Holy Spirit give **perception** a meaning very close to God's knowledge. 7 Healed perception becomes the means by which the Son of God forgives his brother, and thus forgives himself.

W-43.3.You cannot see apart from God because you cannot be apart from God. 2 Whatever you do you do in **God**, because whatever you think, you think with **God's** Mind. 3 If vision is real, and **vision** is real to the extent to which **vision** shares the Holy Spirit's purpose, then you cannot see apart from God.

W-43.4.Three five-minute practice periods are required today, one as early and one as late as possible in the day. 2 The third **practice period** may be undertaken at the most convenient and suitable time that circumstances and readiness permit. 3 At the beginning of these practice periods, repeat the idea for today **that God is my Source and I cannot see apart from God** to yourself with eyes open. 4 Then glance around you for a short time, applying the idea **that God is my Source and I cannot see apart from God** specifically to what you see. 5 Four or five subjects for this phase of the practice period are sufficient. 6 You might say, for example:
7 God is my Source. 8 I cannot see this desk apart from **God.**
9 God is my Source. 10 I cannot see that picture apart from **God**.

W-43.5.Although this part of the exercise period should be relatively short, be sure that you select the subjects for this phase of practice indiscriminately, without self-directed inclusion or exclusion. 2 For the second and longer phase, close your eyes, repeat today's idea **that God is my Source and I cannot see apart from God** again, and then let whatever relevant thoughts occur to you add to the idea **that God is my Source and I cannot see apart from God** in your own personal way. 3 Thoughts such as:
4 I see through the eyes of forgiveness.
5 I see the world as blessed.
6 The world can show me myself.
7 I see my own thoughts, which are like God's.
8 Any thought related more or less directly to today's idea **that God is my Source and I cannot see apart from God** is suitable. 9 The thoughts need not bear any obvious relationship to the idea **that God is my Source and I cannot see apart from God**, but they should not be in opposition to it.

W-43.6.If you find your mind wandering; if you begin to be aware of thoughts which are clearly out of accord with today's idea **that God is my Source and I cannot see apart from God**, or if you seem to be unable to think of anything, open your eyes, repeat the first phase of the exercise period, and then attempt the second phase again.

Note: The first phase was applying the idea that God is my Source and I cannot see apart from God specifically to what you see. The second phase was applying the idea that God is my Source and I cannot see apart from God to whatever relevant thoughts occur to you in your own personal way.

2 Do not allow any protracted period to occur in which you become preoccupied with irrelevant thoughts. 3 Return to the first phase of the exercises as often as necessary to prevent this **preoccupation with irrelevant thoughts**.

W-43.7.In applying today's idea **that God is my Source and I cannot see apart from God** in the shorter practice periods, the form may vary according to the circumstances and situations in which you find yourself during the day. 2 When you are with someone else, for example, try to remember to tell him silently:
3 God is my Source. 4 I cannot see you apart from **God.**
5 This form is equally applicable to strangers as it is to those you think are closer to you. 6 In fact, try not to make distinctions of this kind at all.

W-43.8.Today's idea **that God is my Source and I cannot see apart from God** should also be applied throughout the day to various situations and events that may occur, particularly to those which seem to distress you in any way. 2 For this purpose, apply the idea in this form:
3 God is my Source. 4 I cannot see this apart from God.

W-43.9.If no particular subject presents itself to your awareness at the time, merely repeat the idea **that God is my Source and I cannot see apart from God** in its original form. 2 Try today not to allow any long periods of time to slip by without remembering today's idea **that God is my Source and I cannot see apart from God**, and thus remembering your function.

Notes to Lesson # 43

God is my Source. I cannot see apart from Him.

Lesson 43 introduces and clarifies two ideas. The first is that knowledge is not the same as perception. Perception is not an attribute of God because the realm of God is that of knowledge or truth. It also introduces the idea of the Holy Spirit. The Holy Spirit is a mediator between perception and knowledge. So let's explore these two ideas.

Knowledge and perception are the basis for two different and opposite worlds. Knowledge represents truth. Truth alone is real. The realm of God is the realm of Truth or knowledge. Truth just is.

The realm of God or knowledge is the truth that there is only A Oneness of All That Is. There is no separation. Since there is no separation, there is nothing outside the One Self to observe. God only knows the truth that all God created must remain as God created it. God is Cause. Truth, with a capital T, is God's Effect. Cause and Effect are two inseparable sides of One Self. Cause and It's Effect comprise the Oneness of All That Is. This One Self is the realm of knowledge and truth. The real world is all God created as God created it. It remains perfect, whole and complete.

The world of perception is based on the false idea that separation exists. This false belief is a fantasy that has no consequence on the truth. Perception, being false, is therefore, unknown to the truth. Since God's realm is knowledge or truth, any misperceptions that the split minded may have about their own perceived reality is a fantasy and of no consequence to God. Since truth is invulnerable to your fantasies or misperceptions, your misperceptions have no ability to change or impact God in any way. God or Truth just is and always remains so. It is impossible for your fantasies to hurt or harm God. An effect cannot change its cause. An effect, however, can be a cause of some later effect, but that has no ability to change its original cause.

Perception requires both a perceiver and something to perceive. In A Oneness of All That Is, there is nothing outside the One Self that could be perceived. The world of perception is based on the misperception that we could be separate from God, our Source. This is impossible in truth since we remain as God created us.

Yet, one can imagine something that is not true. One can imagine a dream in which the dreamer believes he or she is awake. In this case, the dreamer would be unaware of their sleeping state until they reawakened. Once they realized they had been dreaming, they would also realize that whatever they had imagined during their dream state had never taken place. Fantasies or dreams have no ability to change reality.

The world of perception is a fantasy world based on the belief in separation. It is an effect of a misperception of who the Son of God really is. The split minded believe that they are separate autonomous beings that have lost their divine birthright. Their divine birthright is the truth that they remain part of that One Self, perfect, whole and complete.

Although our fantasies cannot change reality, thoughts raised to the level of beliefs do have the ability to create a fantasy world that becomes the believers own provisional reality. Within the mind of those who perceive themselves to be separate, their provisional reality becomes their world of perception. There now appears within their delusional mind to be both a perceiver and something outside themselves to perceive. This fantasy dream world of perception has been born only within the sleeping minds of those who have forgotten the truth of who they really are. Their make-believe world has now become their perceived or provisional reality.

The Holy Spirit is the Mediator between perception and knowledge.

The Holy Spirit knows both the truth that you are God's Son and the delusion that your sleeping mind actually believes you are separate from the One Self.

The Holy Spirit is your inner guide for the Truth. The Holy Spirit's purpose is to take your misperceptions and reinterpret them so that the new interpretation better aligns with the truth. Its task is to gently reawaken your sleeping mind to the truth so that you can reclaim your divine birthright. Your divine birthright is the truth that you remain part of the inseparable One Self. Your Oneness can never be lost, but you can forget it belongs to you. One can dream that they are separate but that dream cannot change their true reality.

Question: The Holy Spirit knows both the truth of who you really are and your misperceptions about yourself. The ego only believes its own misperceptions of who you are. When it comes to your best interest, who is most likely to be the better advisor?

LESSON 44

God is the Light in which I see.

W-44.1.Today we are continuing the idea for yesterday **which was that God is my Source and I cannot see apart from God**, adding another dimension to it. 2 You cannot see in darkness, and you cannot make light. 3 You can make darkness and then think you see in **darkness**, but light reflects life, and is therefore an aspect of creation. 4 Creation and darkness cannot coexist, but light and life must go together, being but different aspects of creation.

W-44.2.In order to see **with true vision**, you must recognize that light is within, not without. 2 You do not see **with true vision** outside yourself, nor is the equipment for seeing **with true vision** outside you. 3 An essential part of this equipment is the light that makes seeing **with true vision** possible. 4 **This Light** is with you always, making vision possible in every circumstance.

W-44.3.Today we are going to attempt to reach that light. 2 For this purpose, we will use a form of exercise which has been suggested before, and which we will utilize increasingly. 3 It is a particularly difficult form for the undisciplined mind, and represents a major goal of mind training. 4 **This form of exercise** requires precisely what the untrained mind lacks. 5 Yet this training must be accomplished if you are to see **with true vision**.

W-44.4.Have at least three practice periods today, each lasting three to five minutes. 2 A longer time is highly recommended, but only if you find the time slipping by with little or no sense of strain. 3 The form of practice we will use today is the most natural and easy one in the world for the trained mind, just as **this form of practice** seems to be the most unnatural and difficult for the untrained mind.

W-44.5.Your mind is no longer wholly untrained. 2 You are quite ready to learn the form of exercise we will use today, but you may find that you will encounter strong resistance. 3 The reason **for strong resistance** is very simple. 4 While you practice in this way, you leave behind everything that you now believe, and all the thoughts that you have made up. 5 Properly speaking, this is the release from hell. 6 Yet perceived through the ego's eyes, **this leaving behind everything that you now believe** is a loss of identity and a descent into hell.

W-44.6.If you can stand aside from the ego by ever so little, you will have no difficulty in recognizing that **the ego's** opposition and **the ego's** fears are meaningless. 2 You might find it helpful to remind yourself, from time to time, that to reach light is to escape from darkness, whatever you may believe to the contrary. 3 God is the light in which you see. 4 You are attempting to reach **God.**

W-44.7.Begin the practice period by repeating today's idea **that God is the Light in which I see** with your eyes open, and close them slowly, repeating the idea **that God is the Light in which I see** several times more. 2 Then try to sink into your mind, letting go every kind of interference and intrusion by quietly sinking past **any interference and intrusion.** 3 Your mind cannot be stopped in this unless you choose to stop **your mind.** 4 **Your mind** is merely taking its natural course **in reaching for the Light.** 5 Try to observe your passing thoughts without involvement, and slip quietly by **those passing thoughts**.

W-44.8.While no particular approach is advocated for this form of exercise, what is needful is a sense of the importance of what you are doing; **this exercise's** inestimable value to you, and an awareness that you are attempting something very holy. 2 Salvation is your happiest accomplishment. 3 **Salvation** is also the only one that has any meaning, because **salvation** is the only one that has any real use to you at all.

W-44.9.If resistance rises in any form, pause long enough to repeat today's idea **that God is the Light in which I see**, keeping your eyes closed unless you are aware of fear. 2 In that case, you will probably find it more reassuring to open your eyes briefly. 3 Try, however, to return to the exercises with eyes closed as soon as possible.

W-44.10.If you are doing the exercises correctly, you should experience some sense of relaxation, and even a feeling that you are approaching, if not actually entering into light. 2 Try to think of light, formless and without limit, as you pass by the thoughts of this world. 3 And do not forget that **the thoughts of this world** cannot hold you to the world unless you give **the thoughts of this world** the power to do so.

W-44.11.Throughout the day repeat the idea **that God is the Light in which I see** often, with eyes open or closed as seems better to you at the time. 2 But do not forget **the idea that God is the Light in which I see**. 3 Above all, be determined not to forget today.

Notes to Lesson # 44

God is the Light in which I see.

God is Cause and Creation is God's Effect. Two aspects of creation are light and life. God is your Source and is the Light within you. You cannot see in darkness and you cannot make Light because you are Light. The Source of all Light is God. Light reflects Life and is an aspect of Creation.

Being Light, you can only extend the Light that is within you. Creation is the extension of what you truly are. When God creates, God extends the totality of what God is. Nothing is held back. God being Light can only extend what God is, which is Light. Cause and Effect are actually two sides of one whole. The whole is Creation, which is all God created as God created it.

Life reflects the Truth and should not be confused with what we perceive to be the physical life associated with the physical body. Life is truth and death is the false or an illusion. Just like the false cannot be real, its counterpart, which is death, cannot be real. Both the false and death appear to exist only within the sleeping minds of the split minded who perceive themselves to be separate and different from their true Source.

ACIM makes a distinction between creation and making. Both creating and making are empowered by mind. Only mind, not some outside force beyond our control, is the power source for both creating and making.

Creation is the extension of the Oneness of All That Is. It is an expansion of the totality. When God creates, He extends or gives all to all. There is no separation. Instead, there is merely an expansion of the One Self. Creation is real.

Making arises from the egoic belief in separation and, therefore, is based on lack and limitation. Since lack and limitation cannot exist within the Mind of God, making is not real. Making is merely a delusional fantasy of the split minded. Within the egoic mind that believes in limitation, lack and separation, those beliefs are empowered by your mind to make up the false world of individuated private perception. That misperception becomes the provisional reality of the split minded. Change those beliefs and what you perceive as your provisional reality must also change accordingly.

Just as both the true and false cannot coexist, light and darkness cannot coexist. Yet, because of the creative power of mind, your egoic beliefs can imagine darkness and then pretend that you can see in it. Such images are your mind's imagination and are not your true reality. These images that you see with the egoic eyes are not real.

Because beliefs are empowered by the holder's mind to make images that appear as the holder's provisional reality, the split minded mistake these non-real images to be their personal reality. The split minded identify themselves with their ego's beliefs in limitation, lack and separation. Because of this erroneous identification, you perceive that any abandonment of those erroneous beliefs would result in a loss of your own identity. In actuality, abandoning those erroneous beliefs is the reclaiming of your divine birthright.

To the ego that perceives itself to be a limited body that is not whole, perfect and complete, the loss of this false identity is equivalent to the death of the ego. The ego perceives any challenge to its belief in separation to be an assault on its very existence and therefore, argues for the rightness of its erroneous beliefs. To the split minded, your decision to accept the truth that you are perfect, whole and complete is the death of the ego. Therefore, your ego argues for its rightness at the cost of your happiness.

Remember that the thoughts of this world of time and space cannot bind you to this world unless you give those thoughts the power to do so. Thoughts have no power to change reality. Only your beliefs become your make-believe world of provisional reality.

To have true vision, you must recognize that the light is within and not without. Since Light comes from your Source which is within you, this makes vision possible regardless of the circumstances that your egoic mind has imagined. Vision is the release from your split minded identification with limitation, lack and separation. It is your release from your private hell and the reawakening of the Son of God.

You remain as God created you, perfect, whole and complete. You are part of the indivisible Oneness of All That Is.

Question: The ego argues for the rightness of its belief in lack, limitation and separation. This false belief in egoic autonomy costs you your happiness and brings conflict, struggle and suffering. You as the commander of your own mind must decide what is more important to you. Would you rather be miserable or happy?

LESSON 45

God is the Mind with which I think.

W-45.1.Today's idea **that God is the Mind with which I think** holds the key to what your real thoughts are. 2 **Your real thoughts** are nothing that you think you think, just as nothing that you think you see is related to vision in any way. 3 There is no relationship between what is real and what you think is real. 4 Nothing that you think are your real thoughts resemble your real thoughts in any respect. 5 Nothing that you think you see bears any resemblance to what vision will show you.

W-45.2.You think with the Mind of God. 2 Therefore you share your **real** thoughts with **God**, as **God** shares His **real thoughts** with you. 3 **Real thoughts** are the same thoughts, because **real thoughts** are thought by the same Mind. 4 To share is to make alike, or to make one. 5 Nor do the **real** thoughts you think with the Mind of God leave your mind, because thoughts do not leave their source. 6 Therefore, your **real** thoughts are in the Mind of God, as you are **in the Mind of God**. 7 **Your real thoughts** are in your mind as well, where **God** is **in your mind**. 8 As you are part of **God's** Mind, so are your **real** thoughts part of **God's** Mind.

W-45.3.Where, then, are your real thoughts? 2 Today we will attempt to reach **your real thoughts**. 3 We will have to look for **your real thoughts** in your mind, because that is where **your real thoughts** are. 4 **Your real thoughts** must still be there **in your mind**, because **your real thoughts** cannot have left their source **which is your shared mind with God's Mind.** 5 What is thought by the Mind of God is eternal, being part of creation.

W-45.4.Our three five-minute practice periods for today will take the same general form that we used in applying yesterday's idea **that God is the light in which I see.** 2 We will attempt to leave the unreal and seek for the real. 3 We will deny the world in favor of truth. 4 We will not let the thoughts of the world hold us back. 5 We will not let the beliefs of the world tell us that what God would have us do is impossible. 6 Instead, we will try to recognize that only what God would have us do is possible.

W-45.5.We will also try to understand that only what God would have us do is what we want to do. 2 And we will also try to remember that we cannot fail in doing what **God** would have us do. 3 There is every reason to feel confident that we will succeed today. 4 It is the Will of God.

W-45.6.Begin the exercises for today by repeating the idea **that God is the Mind with which I think** to yourself, closing your eyes as you do so. 2 Then spend a fairly short period in thinking a few relevant thoughts of your own, keeping the idea **that God is the Mind with which I think** in mind. 3 After you have added some four or five thoughts of your own to the idea, repeat **that God is the Mind with which I think** again and tell yourself gently:
4 My real thoughts are in my mind. 5 I would like to find **my real thoughts**.
6 Then try to go past all the unreal thoughts that cover the truth in your mind, and reach to the eternal.

W-45.7.Under all the senseless thoughts and mad ideas with which you have cluttered up your mind are the **real** thoughts that you thought with God in the beginning. 2 **These real thoughts** are there in your mind now, completely unchanged. 3 **These real thoughts** will always be in your mind, exactly as **these real thoughts** always were **in your mind from the beginning.** 4 **All the senseless thoughts and mad ideas** you have thought since **your belief in separation** will change, but the Foundation on which **thoughts** rest, **which are the real thoughts that you thought with God in the beginning** are wholly changeless.

W-45.8.**These real thoughts** are this Foundation toward which the exercises for today are directed. 2 Here is your mind joined with the Mind of God. 3 Here are your **real** thoughts one with **God's thoughts.** 4 For this kind of practice only one thing is necessary; approach **the practice** as you would an altar dedicated in Heaven to God the Father and to God the Son. 5 For such is the place you are trying to reach. 6 You will probably be unable as yet to realize how high you are trying to go. 7 Yet even with the little understanding you have already gained, you should be able to remind yourself that this is no idle game, but an exercise in holiness and an attempt to reach the Kingdom of Heaven.

W-45.9.In the shorter exercise periods for today, try to remember how important it is to you to understand the holiness of the mind that thinks with God. 2 Take a minute or two, as you repeat the idea **that God is the Mind with which I think** throughout the day, to appreciate your mind's holiness. 3 Stand aside, however briefly, from all thoughts that are unworthy of **God** Whose host you are. 4 And thank **God** for the Thoughts **God** is thinking with you.

Notes to Lesson # 45

God is the Mind with which I think.

Lesson 45 states that God is the Mind with which I think. This lesson teaches us about real thoughts and the sharing of them. It tells us that thoughts of our egoic mind are not real thoughts. Real thoughts are thoughts shared with the Mind of God. It states that God shares His real thoughts with us and we share our real thoughts with God, because they are thoughts from the same Mind. It defines sharing as to make alike or to make one. It also says that thoughts do not leave their source. If the thoughts you are normally thinking are not real, what does this all mean?

It is important to note that Mind is spelled with a capital M. Anytime you see the capitalization of a word that is not the first word in the sentence, bells and whistles should go off. This capitalization signifies that ACIM is referencing the real world or Truth and not the world of perception.

God is Cause. We are God's Effect. Two sides of one inseparable coin.

A cause must have an effect and an effect must have a cause or neither exists. The existence of both halves confirms the existence of the whole. Without both, the One Self would not exist.

Although an effect cannot change its cause, an effect can be the cause of its own effects that precede itself. A child can have children of its own but cannot give birth to its own parent. This is a fundamental principle of the law of cause and effect.

In a previous note, we discussed a syllogism as a tool in logic. A syllogism is a series of statements that lead to a logical conclusion. As long as all the statements are correct, the conclusion also must be correct. If any of the preceding statements or premises are false, the conclusion is probably wrong.

In logic, once a false premise has been introduced, everything that follows may be false. The Mind, with a capital M, and real thoughts are what we share with God. These are all the thoughts that came before the introduction of any false beliefs about Truth with a capital T. Once the idea of separation was raised to the level of a belief, a false premise had been introduced into the logic. There was now a line of demarcation between guaranteed truth and the possible true or false thoughts that followed after the introduction of the erroneous premise or belief.

The real mind only knows the truth which is represented by real thoughts. With the split minded, part of their mind knows and remembers the truth while the other part has forgotten the truth and now believes that the false can be true and the truth can be false. This split mind is an effect of the erroneous thinking of the child, not the parent. The parent's mind remains whole and is not changed by the child's misperception.

All thoughts that came before this belief in separation are real, represent the truth and are part of the shared Mind of God.

All thoughts that follow the belief in separation cannot be assumed to be true, real or part of the shared Mind of God.

The source of these non-real thoughts comes from the child's mind that believed itself to be separate. Since these secondary thoughts come from the child which was an effect of God, these thoughts have no ability to change the Mind of God.

Since to share is to make alike, or to make one, the only possible way for the split minded to return to the Mind of God is to drop their belief in separation. They must return to the point before this error in their thinking occurred. By dropping the thought system of the ego, your false thoughts of separation disappear and only your real thoughts which are your mind's true foundation remain.

Our mind's return to the Mind of God is guaranteed because God's Foundation is wholly changeless. God never shared our ego's belief that we were anything other than as He created us, perfect, whole and complete. Therefore, the only way to be made alike or to make one is for the split minded to return to the Truth that is the Mind of God.

Question: Can you think of anything that you could share with another that would not require some type of sacrifice on your part?

LESSON 46

God is the Love in which I forgive.

W-46.1.God does not forgive because **God** has never condemned. 2 And there must be condemnation before forgiveness is necessary. 3 Forgiveness is the great need of this world **of perception**, but that is because **this world of perception** is a world of illusions. 4 Those who forgive are thus releasing themselves from illusions, while those who withhold forgiveness are binding themselves to **illusions.** 5 As you condemn only yourself, so do you forgive only yourself.

W-46.2.Yet although God does not forgive, **God's** Love is nevertheless the basis of forgiveness. 2 Fear condemns and love forgives. 3 Forgiveness thus undoes what fear has produced, returning the mind to the awareness of God. 4 For this reason, forgiveness can truly be called salvation. 5 **Forgiveness** is the means by which illusions disappear.

W-46.3.Today's exercises require at least three full five-minute practice periods, and as many shorter ones as possible. 2 Begin the longer practice periods by repeating today's idea **that God is the Love in which I forgive** to yourself, as usual. 3 Close your eyes as you do so, and spend a minute or two in searching your mind for those whom you have not forgiven. 4 It does not matter "how much" you have not forgiven them. 5 You have forgiven them entirely or not at all.

W-46.4.If you are doing the exercises well you should have no difficulty in finding a number of people you have not forgiven. 2 It is a safe rule that anyone you do not like is a suitable subject. 3 Mention each one by name, and say:
4 God is the Love in which I forgive you, [name].

W-46.5.The purpose of the first phase of today's practice periods is to put you in a position to forgive yourself. 2 After you have applied the idea to all those who have come to mind, tell yourself:
3 God is the Love in which I forgive myself.
4 Then devote the remainder of the practice period to adding related ideas such as:
5 God is the Love with which I love myself.
6 God is the Love in which I am blessed.

W-46.6.The form of the application may vary considerably, but the central idea **that God is the Love in which I forgive** should not be lost sight of. 2 You might say, for example:
3 I cannot be guilty because I am a Son of God.
4 I have already been forgiven.
5 No fear is possible in a mind beloved of God.
6 There is no need to attack because love has forgiven me.
7 The practice period should end, however, with a repetition of today's idea **that God is the Love in which I forgive** as originally stated.

W-46.7.The shorter practice periods may consist either of a repetition of the idea for today **that God is the Love in which I forgive** in the original or in a related form, as you prefer. 2 Be sure, however, to make more specific applications if they are needed. 3 **More specific applications** will be needed at any time during the day when you become aware of any kind of negative reaction to anyone, present or not. 4 In that event, tell him silently:
5 God is the Love in which I forgive you.

Notes to Lesson # 46

God is the Love in which I forgive.

Lesson 46 is God is the love in which I forgive. This lesson is interesting in that the focus is on the giver, not the receiver of forgiveness.

The first thing to realize is that although we perceive ourselves to be sinners that have offended God, God does not have to forgive us for our supposed sins. The reason for this is simple. God does not forgive sins because God has never condemned. Only those who have condemned perceive something to forgive.

Since the realm of God is knowledge which is based on the truth, God knows that within A Oneness of All That Is there could never be something outside the One Self to condemn. God knows that creation is the extension of the One Self. Everything remains as God created it, perfect, whole and complete. God is Cause and God's creation is Its Effect. Together, two sides of one indivisible Mind.

Although God knows His Son to be part of God's Mind, those who believe in separation have forgotten the truth of their divine birthright.

They perceive themselves as limited, separate, vulnerable beings that can attack and be attacked. They perceive themselves to be sinners that have been harmed and have harmed others as well as God.

How could God, being first cause, be harmed by one of His own effects? To sin or harm the invulnerable is impossible in Truth. Sin only appears to exist within the delusional mind that perceives separation and believes their mind's imaginings are real.

Forgiveness is needed in this world because our erroneous beliefs have made a false world with victims and victimizers. Perceiving ourselves to be a limited ego body, we also believe that we can attack and be attacked by others. This belief in the vulnerability of the Son of God is what needs correction. We need to be willing to forgive ourselves from our own mind's delusional belief system.

Although this exercise starts by asking you to forgive others, ultimately, it is only you who needs your own forgiveness. By forgiving, you free your mind from its egoic belief that there are outside forces that can harm you. Since your mind is the source of all your perceptions, you only condemn or forgive yourself. A thought system based on limitation and fear can only condemn. Only a thought system based on love and truth can forgive.

Forgiveness dissolves the illusions of your provisional reality and returns your split mind to the awareness of God. Forgiveness is salvation since it is the means that leads to the reawakening of the split minded to the truth that they alone are the maker of the provisional reality that they perceive.

Although God does not forgive, God's Love is nevertheless the basis for true forgiveness. It is God's Love that keeps us safe from our own denial of our divine inheritance. This truth that you share the one Mind of God cannot be lost, only temporarily forgotten. Your ego's belief in fantasies cannot change your holiness. God's love protects you from your ego's fantasies becoming real. You remain as God created you, perfect, whole and complete. God's sleeping Son needs only to forgive his belief in lack, limitation and separation.

Forgiveness is the dropping of your fear-based thought system and your acceptance of the thought system for the Voice for God. The Holy Spirit is God's loving gift to you. It protects all who perceive themselves to be weak, lonely or separate from those dreams becoming true. The Holy Spirit's presence within your split mind guarantees your reawakening from your perceived nightmare and your return to the Truth in perfect safety.

Question: Why must you ultimately forgive yourself when you perceive that someone else has wronged you?

LESSON 47

God is the strength in which I trust.

W-47.1.If you are trusting in your own **ego's** strength, you have every reason to be apprehensive, anxious and fearful. 2 What can **your own egoic mind** predict or control? 3 What is there in you that can be counted on? 4 What would give you the ability to be aware of all the facets of any problem, and to resolve **any problem** in such a way that only good can come of **any problem**? 5 What is there in you that gives you the recognition of the right solution, and the guarantee that **the right solution** will be accomplished?

W-47.2.Of your **egoic** self you can do none of these things. 2 To believe that **your egoic mind** can **do these things** is to put your trust where trust is unwarranted, and to justify fear, anxiety, depression, anger and sorrow. 3 Who can put his faith in **the** weakness **of your egoic mind** and feel safe? 4 Yet who can put his faith in strength **that comes from God** and feel weak?

W-47.3.God is your safety in every circumstance. 2 **God's** Voice, **the Holy Spirit**, speaks for **God** in all situations and in every aspect of all situations, telling you exactly what to do to call upon **God's** strength and **God's** protection. 3 There are no exceptions because God has no exceptions. 4 And the Voice which speaks for **God, which is the Holy Spirit**, thinks as **God** does.

W-47.4.Today we will try to reach past your own **egoic mind's** weakness to the Source of real strength, **which is God**. 2 Four five-minute practice periods are necessary today, and longer and more frequent ones are urged. 3 Close your eyes and begin, as usual, by repeating the idea for the day **that God is the strength in which I trust**. 4 Then spend a minute or two in searching for situations in your life which you have invested with fear, dismissing each **fearful situation** by telling yourself: 5 God is the strength in which I trust.

W-47.5.Now try to slip past all concerns related to your own sense of inadequacy. 2 It is obvious that any situation that causes you concern is associated with feelings of inadequacy, for otherwise you would believe that you could deal with the situation successfully. 3 It is not by trusting your **egoic** self that you will gain confidence. 4 But the strength of God in you is successful in all things.

W-47.6.The recognition of your own frailty is a necessary step in the correction of your **egoic mind's** errors, but **the recognition of your own ego's frailty** is hardly a sufficient **step** in giving you the confidence which you need, and to which you are entitled. 2 You must also gain an awareness that confidence in your real strength **which comes from God** is fully justified in every respect and in all circumstances.

W-47.7.In the latter phase of the practice period, try to reach down into your mind to a place of real safety. 2 You will recognize that you have reached **a place of real safety** if you feel a sense of deep peace, however briefly. 3 Let go all the trivial things that churn and bubble on the surface of your mind, and reach down and below **these trivial thoughts** to the Kingdom of Heaven. 4 There is a place in you where there is perfect peace. 5 There is a place in you where nothing is impossible. 6 There is a place in you where the strength of God abides.

W-47.8.During the day, repeat the idea **that God is the strength in which I trust** often. 2 Use **that idea that God is the strength in which I trust** as your answer to any disturbance. 3 Remember that peace is your right, because you are giving your trust to the strength of God.

Notes to Lesson # 47

God is the strength in which I trust.

Fear arises any time you believe that you lack the creative ability to handle a given situation. Whether you actually do have the ability to handle the situation or you do not have the ability that truth is irrelevant. Your beliefs, not the truth will determine when fear arises within your egoic mind.

You as decision-maker must decide which thought system you will follow. Each thought system is based on a different understanding of who you really are.

The ego's thought system is based on the belief in limitation, lack and separation. This thought system is the source of all fear. Accept your ego's belief that you are the body and you must accept the limitations that come with that body. When you believe in your limitations, you have every reason to be apprehensive, anxious and fearful.

The second thought system is represented by your inner guide or the Holy Spirit. It is based on the belief that you are unlimited spirit, part of the Mind of a God. In this thought system for truth with a capital T, love and forgiveness rule. You remain as God created you, perfect, whole and complete. Your strength comes from your Source which is the Mind of God Itself.

Your ego does not know who you truly are. Because its beliefs about you are wrong, your ego's fear-based thought system will always leave you in a state of fear. To escape fear you must place your trust in the Holy Spirit who knows that you are God's beloved Son.

When you place your trust in the strength from God, you are safe from your ego's belief in limitation. The laws of perception have no ability to bind a Son of God unless you decide to abdicate your own power and argue for your own limitations.

Your own egoic belief in your inadequacy is the source of all fears. Your acceptance and trust in the Holy Spirit is your salvation. The strength of God is your source for your inner peace that is your destiny.

The advice of the Holy Spirit protects you from all egoic misperceptions. Provisional reality has no power to change the Truth. You remain as God created you, perfect, whole and complete.

Question: Can you ever escape your fear of inadequacy if you believe that you are the body and the body is you?

LESSON 48

There is nothing to fear.

W-48.1.The idea for today **that there is nothing to fear** simply states a fact. 2 **The idea for today that there is nothing to fear** is not a fact to those who believe in illusions, but illusions are not facts. 3 In truth there is nothing to fear. 4 It is very easy to recognize this **idea for today that there is nothing to fear**. 5 But it is very difficult to recognize **that there is nothing to fear** for those who want illusions to be true.

W-48.2.Today's practice periods will be very short, very simple and very frequent. 2 Merely repeat the idea **that there is nothing to fear** as often as possible. 3 You can use **this idea that there is nothing to fear** with your eyes open at any time and in any situation. 4 It is strongly recommended, however, that you take a minute or so whenever possible to close your eyes and repeat the idea **that there is nothing to fear** slowly to yourself several times. 5 It is particularly important that you use the idea **that there is nothing to fear** immediately, should anything disturb your peace of mind.

W-48.3.The presence of fear is a sure sign that you are trusting in your own **egoic mind's** strength. 2 The awareness that there is nothing to fear shows that somewhere in your mind, though not necessarily in a place you recognize as yet, you have remembered God, and let **God's** strength take the place of your **own egoic mind's** weakness. 3 The instant you are willing to do this **and let God's strength take the place of your own egoic mind's weakness, you will realize that** there is indeed nothing to fear.

Notes to Lesson # 48

There is nothing to fear.

There is nothing to fear since fear is false evidence appearing real. The source of fear is your own mind's misunderstanding of who you really are. You have placed your trust in your ego's plan. Your ego believes that you are a limited ego-body in competition with other ego-bodies for the limited resources that each needs to survive.

This is not the truth of who you really are. You are God's beloved Child with whom He is well pleased.

Whenever you are in fear, you have placed your trust in your ego's plan for protection rather than the Holy Spirit's plan which rests upon the strength of God. You have accepted the belief that your perceived world of limitation, lack and separation is your true reality. You have denied your spiritual essence and forgotten your divine birthright.

Your ego has failed to realize that you are an unlimited spiritual essence having an earthly experience. Your ego has failed to realize that time and space are just a playschool in which you have fun, learn and rediscover your spiritual magnificence. In time and space, you get to demonstrate that nothing outside of your mind can rob you of your inner peace.

When you are in fear, your egoic mind has made the illusion of separation appear real. Your ego's perception of your world is now believed to be true. The Mind you share with God seems forgotten and unreal. Fear is your belief that your false thoughts are real. You have forgotten that your real thoughts are the thoughts you have shared with the Mind of God from the beginning. You have forgotten the truth of your divine inheritance.

When you believe that your ego and not God is the true source for strength, it does seem like you have something to fear.

Question: Since your body's physical reaction to both a fearful and an exciting event is exactly the same, who or what decides if your mind will interpret that event as either fearful or exciting?

God's Voice speaks to me all through the day.

W-49.1.It is quite possible to listen to God's Voice, **which is the Holy Spirit**, all through the day without interrupting your regular activities in any way. 2 The part of your **split** mind in which truth abides is in constant communication with God, whether you are aware of **this constant communication with God** or not. 3 It is the other part of your mind **that represents your ego's thought system** that functions in the world and obeys the world's laws. 4 It is this part **that represents your egoic mind** that is constantly distracted, disorganized and highly uncertain.

W-49.2.The part that is listening to the Voice for God is calm, always at rest and wholly certain. 2 **The part of your split mind that is listening to the Voice for God** is really the only **real** part there is. 3 The other part **that represents your fearful egoic mind's thought system** is a wild illusion, frantic and distraught, but without reality of any kind. 4 Try today not to listen to **your egoic mind**. 5 Try to identify with the part of your **split** mind where stillness and peace reign forever **which is the Voice for God**. 6 Try to hear God's Voice call to you lovingly, reminding you that your Creator has not forgotten His Son.

W-49.3.We will need at least four five-minute practice periods today, and more if possible. 2 We will try actually to hear God's Voice reminding you of **God** and of your **real Big "S"** Self. 3 We will approach this happiest and holiest of thoughts with confidence, knowing that in doing so we are joining our will with the Will of God. 4 **God** wants you to hear **God's** Voice. 5 **God** gave **the Holy Spirit** to you to be heard.

W-49.4.Listen in deep silence. 2 Be very still and open your mind. 3 Go past all the raucous shrieks and sick imaginings that cover your real thoughts and obscure your eternal link with God. 4 Sink deep into the peace that waits for you beyond the frantic, riotous thoughts and sights and sounds of this insane **egoic** world **of individuated perception**. 5 You do not live here **in this insane egoic world of individuated perception**. 6 We are trying to reach your real home **which is not your insane egoic world of individuated perception.** 7 We are trying to reach the place where you are truly welcome. 8 We are trying to reach God.

W-49.5.Do not forget to repeat today's idea **that God's Voice speaks to me all through the day** very frequently. 2 Do so with your eyes open when necessary, but closed when possible. 3 And be sure to sit quietly and repeat the idea for today **that God's Voice speaks to me all through the day** whenever you can, closing your eyes on the world, and realizing that you are inviting God's Voice, **the Holy Spirit**, to speak to you.

Notes to Lesson # 49

God's Voice speaks to me all through the day.

The mind that perceives itself to be separate from its Source, the Mind of God, is split minded. The goal of these workbook lessons is to retrain your mind so that you can recover your ability to hear and follow your inner guide which is the Voice for God.

In the world of perception, you perceive that there are two possible choices from which to choose. You believe that both the false and the true are viable options. These two possible choices are represented by opposite thought systems. One is the false, fear-based thought system of the ego. The other is the thought system for love and forgiveness that represents the Truth.

Your decision-maker decides which thought system will control your private world of provisional reality. Your decision maker can vacillate between either fearful or loving thoughts. But only one thought system is followed at any given time.

The advice from both thought systems are available throughout your day. Yet, we have been conditioned to hear only the voice for fear. This is because we have been indoctrinated into the idea that our ego is our true self and therefore, must know our best interest. This is not the case. Your ego does not know anything about Truth with a capital T.

The ego is a part of the split mind that has identified itself with the illusion of separation. It argues for the correctness of its belief in separation at the cost of your happiness. The ego claims that the fearful world of time and space is your reality and your body is your home. Because of the fear that is generated by a thought system based on lack, limitation and separation, the ego is always arguing for the correctness of its own survival plans.

When you seek guidance within, it will be the voice of your ego that will always respond first and loudest. Your ego must argue for the correctness of its judgments and why you were justified in responding to any situation in a fear-based manner. The ego follows the rules of this fear-based planet. It believes that there are victims and victimizers and therefore, you must attack first or you will be attacked.

Yet, if you silence this voice for fear, stop your ego's mind chatter and refuse to slip into judgment or argue for the rightness of your attack thoughts, you will hear the Voice for God. The Voice for God is calm, always at rest and wholly certain. It can be certain because it comes from God. It knows the truth that God's Son sleeps but must and will reawaken to the truth. The

Holy Spirit knows the big picture. It understands that the purpose of this world of perception is merely to provide a safe playschool for your fun and learning while you explore the process of reawakening to the truth of your spiritual magnificence.

Because the ego is uncertain, frantic and distraught, its voice appears loudest. This is only because the ego must argue for its rightness at the cost of your inner peace. You are retraining your mind so that you can go within, move past the shouts of the ego and listen to the Voice for God that resides deep within all minds that misperceive themselves to be separate from the Mind of God. This Inner Voice knows this planet is not your home and that your destiny is the peace of God.

Follow the Voice of the Holy Spirit and it will take you home.

The ego's frantic shouts will fade away as your decision-maker decides to shift its allegiance from the ego's fear-based thought system to the thought system for truth, love and forgiveness.

Question Has your ego's plans brought you the long-term, joy, peace and happiness that you want, seek and deserve?

If not, perhaps your decision-maker should stop listening to your ego and get a new advisor.

LESSON 50

I am sustained by the Love of God

W-50.1.**I am sustained by the Love of God** is the answer to every problem that will confront you, today and tomorrow and throughout time. 2 In this world **of perception**, you believe you are sustained by everything but God. 3 Your faith is placed in the most trivial and insane symbols; pills, money, "protective" clothing, influence, prestige, being liked, knowing the "right" people, and an endless list of forms of nothingness that you endow with magical powers.

W-50.2.All these **things that you endow with magical powers** are your replacements for the Love of God. 2 All these things **that you endow with magical powers** are cherished to ensure a body identification. 3 **All these things that you endow with magical powers** are songs of praise to the ego. 4 Do not put your faith in the worthless. 5 **The worthless things that you endow with magical powers** will not sustain you.

W-50.3.Only the Love of God will protect you in all circumstances. 2 **The Love of God** will lift you out of every trial, and raise you high above all the perceived dangers of this world into a climate of perfect peace and safety. 3 **The Love of God** will transport you into a state of mind that nothing can threaten, nothing can disturb, and where nothing can intrude upon the eternal calm of the Son of God.

W-50.4.Put not your faith in illusions. 2 **These egoic illusions that you endow with magical powers** will fail you. 3 Put all your faith in the Love of God within you; eternal, changeless and forever unfailing. 4 **Putting all your faith in the Love of God that is within you to protect you** is the answer to whatever confronts you today. 5 Through the Love of God within you, you can resolve all seeming difficulties without effort and in sure confidence. 6 Tell yourself **that I am sustained by the Love of God** often today. 7 **I am sustained by the Love of God** is a declaration of release from the belief in idols. 8 **The idea that I am sustained by the Love of God** is your acknowledgment of the truth about yourself.

W-50.5.For ten minutes, twice today, morning and evening, let the idea for today **that I am sustained by the Love of God** sink deep into your consciousness. 2 Repeat **the idea that I am sustained by the Love of God**, think about it, let related thoughts come to help you recognize **this idea's** truth, and allow peace to flow over you like a blanket of protection and surety. 3 Let no idle and foolish thoughts enter to disturb the holy mind of the Son of God. 4 Such is the Kingdom of Heaven. 5 Such is the resting place where your Father has placed you forever.

Notes to Lesson # 50

I am sustained by the Love of God

Lesson 50 states that you are sustained by the Love of God. It does not claim you are sustained by the love of the ego or your love for the ego.

Why is this?

Because the ego is neither your friend nor is the ego you.

We often make the mistake of identifying ourselves with our egoic mind and therefore, assume that our ego must have our best interest at heart. We fail to understand that the ego is just our false belief about who we really are. It is a belief system and not a reality or entity that has its own separate autonomous existence. Any apparent power your ego and its imagined world have over you comes from your own decision to abdicate your mind's creative power to the fear-based thought system of your ego.

Your mind's beliefs generate your outside world. Your ego is merely a reflection of your belief that you possess an autonomous existence outside and apart from the Mind of God.

This belief in separation and individual autonomy results in your mind perceiving itself as separate from God. This gives rise to the two opposing thought systems of the split mind. One is based on truth while the other is based on this false notion of separation.

Because of this belief that you are a separate autonomous entity, your ego must argue for the rightness and the correctness of its worldview. Your ego's existence hangs in the balance. To your ego, it is better to be separate and miserable than united and happy. It wants you to believe you are separate and apart from God, since its existence is contingent on your continued denial of your divine birthright. Your ego perceives being part of the shared mind of God as its own death.

In this regard, your ego is correct. If your mind, which is the power behind all thought, rejected the ego's fear-based thought system, the ego and its imagined world would disappear. Because of this, your ego feels safest when you associate yourself as being a physical body. Your ego argues that your body is your home and that you reside on this fear-based planet. To the ego, your limitation is its strength and safety.

Your provisional reality is centered around a physical body that supports and proves the lack, limitation and separation that you would expect if you were not sustained by the Love of God. Believing itself to be limited, the ego teaches that you have a precarious existence, are alone and reside on a warring planet in which attacking and being attacked rules the day. You must struggle for the limited resources you need to exist. Your world is a zero-sum game of survival of the fittest.

Perceiving yourself to be a victim of outside forces that are beyond your mind's control, the ego develops various plans that are designed to manage, mitigate and limit the damage from these outside forces. The ego seeks to replace the Love of God with the worship of false idols that it claims you need to survive and make you happy.

These false plans for your happiness take various forms. They normally revolve around the obtaining of power, money, sex and good health. The ego tells you that you will be happy when you obtain one or all of these false idols that this fear-based world worships. These egoic idols are a panacea for all suffering and unhappiness. Unfortunately, all the ego's plans are doomed to fail because they all rest on the false belief in limitation. There is nothing outside of you that has the power to make you happy.

In reality, the only thing that has the power to make you unhappy is the false, fear-based thought system of your ego. The denial of the truth that you are sustained by the Love of God is the source of your unhappiness, conflict and struggles.

Only your own mind's belief that you are a victim gives your idols any power they appear to possess over your happiness and inner peace. Your mind, not some magical external powerhouse, still remains the creator of your private world of individuated perception.

All the plans of the split minded to acquire and possess the false idols of this world only ensure your unhappiness. Seek within you for the true source of your happiness. God is inside you. Drop your egoic fear-based plans and stop arguing for your limitations.

Reclaim your divine birthright and realize the answer to every problem that confronts you now or in the future is resolved when you realize that God's Love for you is changeless, eternal , unfailing and resides within you.

Being a part of you, God's Love cannot be lost but only temporarily denied by your refusal to acknowledge the truth of who you really are.

Question: Your ego's fear-based thought system is based on your continued belief in lack, limitation and separation. Can you now understand why your ego would argue for your limitations instead of your happiness?

Introduction

W-rI.in.1.Beginning with today we will have a series of review periods. 2 Each of the **review periods** will cover five of the ideas already presented, starting with the first and ending with the fiftieth **lesson**. 3 There will be a few short comments after each of the ideas, which you should consider in your review. 4 In the practice periods, the exercises should be done as follows:

W-rI.in.2.Begin the day by reading the five ideas, with the comments included. 2 Thereafter, it is not necessary to follow any particular order in considering the five ideas, though each one **of the five ideas** should be practiced at least once. 3 Devote two minutes or more to each practice period, thinking about the idea and the related comments after reading them over. 4 Do this as often as possible during the day. 5 If any one of the five ideas appeals to you more than the others, concentrate on that one **idea**. 6 At the end of the day, however, be sure to review all of **the five ideas** once more.

W-rI.in.3.It is not necessary to cover the comments that follow each idea either literally or thoroughly in the practice periods. 2 Try, rather, to emphasize the central point, and think **about the central point** as part of your review of the idea to which **the central point** relates. 3 After you have read the idea and the related comments, the exercises should be done with your eyes closed and when you are alone in a quiet place, if possible.

W-rI.in.4.**Having your eyes closed and being in a quiet place** is emphasized for practice periods at your stage of learning. 2 It will be necessary, however, that you learn to require no special settings in which to apply what you have learned. 3 You will need your learning most in situations that appear to be upsetting, rather than in those that already seem to be calm and quiet. 4 The purpose of your learning is to enable you to bring the quiet with you, and to heal distress and turmoil. 5 **Learning how to bring the quiet with you** is not done by avoiding **distress and turmoil** and seeking a haven of isolation for yourself.

W-rI.in.5.You will yet learn that peace is part of you, and **that peace** requires only that you be there to embrace any situation in which you are. 2 And finally you will learn that there is no limit to where you are, so that your peace is everywhere, as you are **everywhere**.

W-rI.in.6.You will note that, for review purposes, some of the ideas are not given in quite their original **lesson** form. 2 Use **the ideas** as they are given here. 3 It is not necessary to return to the original statements, nor to apply the ideas as was suggested then **in the original lesson**. 4 We are now emphasizing the relationships among the first fifty of the ideas we have covered, and the cohesiveness of the thought system to which **the first fifty of the ideas** are leading you.

LESSON 51

LESSON SUMMARY #1-5

The review for today covers the following ideas **from Lessons # 1-5:**

W-51.1 <u>**Review of Lesson #1: Nothing I see means anything.**</u>
2 The reason **that nothing I see means anything** is so, is that I see nothing, and nothing has no meaning. 3 It is necessary that I recognize **I see nothing and nothing has no meaning, so that** I may learn to see **with true vision.** 4 What I think I see now is taking the place of **true** vision. 5 I must let go **of what I think I see now** by realizing **that what I think I egoically see now** has no meaning, so that **true** vision may take **the** place **of what I see with my ego's judgmental sight.**

W-51.2 <u>**Review of Lesson #2: I have given what I see all the meaning it has for me.**</u>
2 I have judged everything I look upon, and it is this **judgment** and only this **judgment that** I see. 3 This **egoic judgment** is not vision. 4 **This egoic judgment** is merely an illusion of reality, because my judgments have been made quite apart from reality. 5 I am willing to recognize the lack of validity in my judgments, because I want to see. 6 My judgments have hurt me, and I do not want to see according to **my egoic judgments**.

W-51.3. <u>**Review of Lesson #3: I do not understand anything I see.**</u>
2 How could I understand what I see when I have judged **what I see** amiss? 3 What I see is the projection of my own errors of thought. 4 I do not understand what I see because **the projections of my own errors of thought are** not understandable. 5 There is no sense in trying to understand **the projection of my own errors of thought.** 6 But there is every reason to let **go of what I egoically see** and make room for what can be seen and understood and loved. 7 I can exchange what I see now for **what can be seen and understood and loved,** merely by being willing to do so **and drop my judgments.** 8 Is not this **exchange to see with understanding and love** a better choice than the one I made before **which was based on projecting my own errors and judgments**?

W-51.4. <u>**Review of Lesson #4: These thoughts do not mean anything.**</u>
2 The thoughts of which I am aware do not mean anything because I am trying to think without God. 3 What I call "my" thoughts are not my real thoughts. 4 My real thoughts are the thoughts I think with God. 5 I am not aware of **my real thoughts, which are my thoughts that I think with God,** because I have made my **egoic judgmental** thoughts to take **the** place **of my real thoughts that I think with God.** 6 I am willing to recognize that my **egoic judgmental** thoughts do not mean anything, and to let **my judgmental thoughts** go. 7 I choose to have **my egoic judgmental thoughts** be replaced by what they were intended to replace, **which are my real thoughts that I think with God.** 8 My **egoic judgmental** thoughts are meaningless, but all creation lies in the **real** thoughts I think with God.

W-51.5. <u>**Review of Lesson #5: I am never upset for the reason I think.**</u>
2 I am never upset for the reason I think because I am constantly trying to justify my **egoic** thoughts. 3 I am constantly trying to make **my egoic thoughts** true. 4 I make all things my enemies, so that my anger is justified and my attacks are warranted. 5 I have not realized how much I have misused everything I see by assigning this role **of enemies** to **everything I see.** 6 I have done this **role of assigning enemies to everything I see** to defend **the ego's** thought system that has hurt me, and that I no longer want. 7 I am willing to let the ego's thought system go.

Notes to Lesson # 51

Notes on Summary Lesson #51 – Review of Lessons #1-5

Lesson #1: Nothing I see means anything.

Lesson #2: I have given what I see all the meaning it has for me.

Lesson #3: I do not understand anything I see.

Lesson #4: These thoughts do not mean anything.

Lesson #5: I am never upset for the reason I think.

1) ACIM does not consider the world of perception to be real since the world of perception is subject to change. What you choose to perceive changes as your beliefs change. This shifting viewpoint becomes your private world of "provisional reality."

Provisional reality is your private illusionary world of time and space. Our "dream world" appears real only to those who hold that same particular perception or belief. The more uniform your beliefs are with others, the more your provisional realities will appear to agree.

Because the Mind of God is based on knowledge, rather than perception, the real world of Truth with a capital T, is eternal and never changing. Because the real world of Truth is all God created, it is real. It is the Mind of God. The real world of Truth is a Oneness of Everything because the Mind of God is everything, perfect, whole and complete. Based on ACIM terminology, the world of perception and time and space is not real since each is subject to change. Truth is real because it is changeless. Truth is all God created as God created it.

2) Everything I "see" in my world of provisional reality is something I made up based on my own perception. My perception invariably leads to judgment. Seeing is not the same as vision.

3) Judgments further color my dream world of provisional reality. Each person has their own unique provisional reality, which is based on their own perceptions and judgments. It is your perceptions and judgments that you "see." No two people's worlds are exactly alike, but there may be large areas of overlap in their individual worlds when they share common beliefs.

4) ACIM does not consider seeing and vision to be the same. Seeing is looking through the thought system of the ego. Vision is following the thought system of the Holy Spirit. Seeing is based on perception. Vision is ultimately based on the knowledge of the Holy Spirit.

5) The thought system of the Holy Spirit is based on the knowledge that you are a Child of God, perfect, whole, and complete. The Holy Spirit understands that God's Children have fallen asleep and have dreamed that they are separated from God, their Creator. Sleeping children believe they are something that they are not. The Holy Spirit's thought system is designed to gently reawaken each child to remember and reclaim their divine birthright. Once remembered, each will recall that as God's Child, we all share the Oneness of the holographic Mind of God.

6) The thought system of the ego is based on the belief that we are separate from the Mind of God and not part of a Oneness of All That Is. To our ego, we are separate, limited yet autonomous beings. The ego's fearful thought system is based on perception, rather than knowledge. It is the perception of separateness that spawns our world of provisional reality.

The ego's thought system is designed to convince our mind that this perceived dream world is real so that we will forget to claim our divine birthright. Limitation, separateness, and individuality are the cornerstones of the egoic world of provisional reality. Your ego's goal is to convince the decision-making part of your split mind that you are not unlimited spirit, but rather a limited, vulnerable ego-body powerless to change your fate. Your ego gains strength whenever you accept victim consciousness as your own perceived reality.

7) The ego's thought system is based on attack. When you attack or believe that you can be attacked, you confirm your belief that you are your body. The body is the ego's best proof that you are suffering from lack and are not part of the Oneness of All That Is. If you were a Oneness, what would there be for you to attack? We all attack to defend the "correctness" of our egoic belief in lack, limitation and separations.

LESSON 52

LESSON SUMMARY #6-10

Today's review covers these ideas **from Lessons # 6-10:**

W-52.1. Review of Lesson #6: I am upset because I see what is not there.
2 Reality **which are my real thoughts that I think with God** is never frightening. 3 It is impossible that **reality** could upset me. 4 Reality brings only perfect peace. 5 When I am upset, it is always because I have replaced reality with **judgmental egoic** illusions I made up. 6 The **judgmental egoic** illusions are upsetting because I have given **the illusions** reality, and thus regard reality, **which are my real thoughts that I think with God,** as an illusion. 7 Nothing in God's creation is affected in any way by this confusion of mine **of giving the illusion reality, and thus regarding reality, which are my real thoughts that I think with God, as an illusion.** 8 I am always upset by nothing.

W-52.2. Review of Lesson #7: I see only the past.
2 As I look about, I condemn the world I look upon. 3 I call this **condemning of the world I look upon, as** seeing. 4 I hold the past against everyone and everything, making them my enemies. 5 When I have forgiven myself and remembered Who I am, I will bless everyone and everything I see. 6 **When I have forgiven myself,** there will be no past, and therefore no enemies. 7 And **when I have forgiven myself,** I will look with love on all that I failed to see before.

W-52.3. Review of Lesson #8: My mind is preoccupied with past thoughts.
2 I see only my own thoughts, and my mind is preoccupied with the past. 3 What, then, can I see as it **really** is **without my past egoic judgments**? 4 Let me remember that I look on the past **egoic judgments** to prevent the present from dawning on my mind. 5 Let me understand that I am trying to use time against God. 6 Let me learn to give the past **egoic judgments** away, realizing that **in giving away the past,** I am giving up nothing.

W-52.4. Review of Lesson #9: I see nothing as it is now.
2 If I see nothing as it is now, it can truly be said that I see nothing. 3 I can see **with true vision** only what is now. 4 The choice is not whether to see the past or the present; the choice is merely whether to see **with true vision** or not. 5 What I have chosen to see **has been my mind's preoccupation with the past and this preoccupation** has cost me vision. 6 Now I would choose again, that I may see **with true vision.**

W-52.5. Review of Lesson #10: My thoughts do not mean anything.
I have no private thoughts. 3 Yet it is only private thoughts **which are not real or shared with the Mind of God** of which I am aware. 4 What can these **private** thoughts mean? 5 **These private thoughts** do not exist **in the Mind of God,** and so **these private thoughts** mean nothing. 6 Yet my mind is part of creation and part of its Creator. 7 Would I not rather join the **real** thinking of the universe **that is part of the Mind of its Creator** than to obscure all that is really mine with my pitiful and meaningless "private" thoughts?

Notes to Lesson # 52

Notes on Summary Lesson #52 – Review of Lessons #6-10

Lesson #6: I am upset because I see what is not there.

Lesson #7: I see only the past.

Lesson #8: My mind is preoccupied with past thoughts.

Lesson #9: I see nothing as it is now.

Lesson #10: My thoughts do not mean anything.

1) If I am upset, it is because I have forgotten what I really am. I am a beloved Child of God. I am caught up in my dream world of provisional reality and mistook the game of separation for my reality and the truth. I have forgotten that my current lifetime is part of my learning experience. My experiences are designed to help reawaken my mind to its ability as a decision-maker to choose a different plan.

The next time, I can choose for the guidance of the Holy Spirit's thought system. I am upset because I believe the movie that I have chosen to play in is my true reality. I have forgotten that there are no outside forces that can harm me. As spirit, I am invulnerable. It can only be my own mind's beliefs in limitation that I am currently experiencing.

I have forgotten my purpose, which is to remember what I truly am. I have forgotten that this dream of mine can be utilized by the Holy Spirit to help me remember what I am if I ask for His guidance.

2) As long as I am upset, I give credence to the ego's belief that I am a separate, limited ego-body. This upset helps keep me trapped in the ego's fear-based thought system and away from my own mind's authority to follow a different thought system.

When I am upset, I have accepted the role of a victim. Victims claim to be powerless to change their circumstances. This failing to reclaim my ability to choose differently is exactly what my ego wants me to believe about myself. My ego is arguing for its rightness at the cost of my happiness.

3) Your provisional world is a world based on your perceptions. Your current perceptions are clouded and colored by your past experiences. You utilize your past experiences to form your current belief system. From this belief system, which is based on your past, you project from your mind, what you wish to "see" and "experience."

You project out into your dream world of provisional reality thoughts that will confirm your present belief system. It is this predetermined thought projection that your senses pick up and perceive. Your preoccupation with the past helps insure that your future will be similarly perceived and confirm your current belief system. Your future becomes a replay of your past. This is the basis for the saying, "whether you think you can or you think you can't, your right."

4) Your preoccupation with your perceived dream world of provisional reality prevents you from "living in the now." In the Mind of God, all things are eternal and there is no time and space; there is only a Oneness. Since you "live" in your own private world of provisional reality, you need to at least try to live in the "now" of time and space, instead of its past.

Through forgiveness for both our brother and ourselves, we regain consciousness and slowly reawaken to the truth of what we really are. Forgiveness releases our mind's preoccupation with the past and allows us to reclaim our lost awareness of current events. Forgiveness allows us to drop our judgmental stories and focus on the present, which more clearly resembles the now.

5) Our provisional reality is based on our own private perceptions. This private world based on our individual viewpoint is not shared with others nor, more importantly, is not shared with the Mind of God. Because perception is based on individuality and separateness, it cannot be shared. The Mind of God is a Oneness and is shared by all that God created because it is the truth of all reality.

Creation is a sharing or an extension of what its creator truly is. The only "real" thoughts that a Son of God can have are thoughts shared with His Creator about what he truly is. Non-real thoughts that arise from the ego's erroneous belief of separation, lack and limitation are not how God created His Son. These private thoughts of the split mind are under the guidance of the ego's fear based thought system. They have no basis in reality since they are not part of the shared Mind of God.

Provisional reality appears to be real only in the mind of the perceiver. Change your perception and you change your provisional reality. You are asked by the Holy Spirit to choose again. Forgiveness is the means by which we reclaim our ability to choose differently.

LESSON 53

LESSON SUMMARY #11-15

Today we will review the following **Lessons # 11-15:**

W-53.1. <u>Review of Lesson #11: My meaningless thoughts are showing me a meaningless world.</u>
2 Since the thoughts of which I am aware do not mean anything, the world that pictures **my meaningless thoughts** can have no meaning. 3 **My meaningless thoughts which are** what is producing this world **are** insane, and so is what it produces. 4 Reality is not insane, and I have real thoughts **that are shared with the Mind of God** as well as insane **thoughts that are not shared with the Mind of God**. 5 I can therefore see a real world, if I look to my real thoughts **that are shared with God** as my guide for seeing **with true vision**.

W-53.2. <u>Review of Lesson #12: I am upset because I see a meaningless world.</u>
2 Insane thoughts are upsetting. 3 **Insane thoughts** produce a world in which there is no order anywhere. 4 Only chaos rules a world that represents **the** chaotic thinking **of insane thoughts**, and chaos has no laws. 5 I cannot live in peace in such a **chaotic** world **that is based on insane thoughts**. 6 I am grateful that this **chaotic** world is not real, and that I need not see **this chaotic world that is based on insane thoughts** at all unless I choose to value **my insane thoughts that produce this chaotic world** . 7 And I do not choose to value what is totally insane and has no meaning.

W-53.3. <u>Review of Lesson #13: A meaningless world engenders fear.</u>
2 The totally insane engenders fear because **what is insane** is completely undependable, and offers no grounds for trust. 3 Nothing in madness is dependable. 4 **What is insane** holds out no safety and no hope. 5 But such an **insane fearful** world is not real **since it is not shared with the Mind of God**. 6 I have given **an insane fearful world** the illusion of reality, and have suffered from my belief in **an insane fearful world**. 7 Now I choose to withdraw this belief **in an insane fearful world**, and place my trust in reality **which is my thoughts shared with the Mind of God**. 8 In choosing this reality **of my shared thoughts with the Mind of God**, I will escape all the effects of the world of fear, because I am acknowledging that **fear and the insane world fear imagined** does not exist.

W-53.4. <u>Review of Lesson #14: God did not create a meaningless world.</u>
2 How can a meaningless world exist if God did not create **the insane meaningless world fear imagined**? 3 **God** is the Source of all meaning, and everything that is real is in **God's** Mind. 4 **Everything that has meaning and is real** is in my **split** mind too, because **God** created it with me. 5 Why should I continue to suffer from the effects of my own insane thoughts, when the perfection of creation is my home? 6 Let me remember the power of my decision, and recognize where I really abide **in truth which is the perfection of creation that is shared with the Mind of God**.

W-53.5. <u>Review of Lesson #15: My thoughts are images that I have made.</u>
2 Whatever I see reflects my thoughts **of my split mind**. 3 It is my thoughts that tell me where I am and what I am. 4 The fact that I see a world in which there is suffering and loss and death shows me that I am seeing only the representation of my insane **egoic fear-based** thoughts, and am not allowing my real thoughts to cast their beneficent light on what I see. 5 Yet God's way is sure. 6 The images **that represent my insane fearful thoughts that** I have made cannot prevail against **God** because it is not my will that they do so. 7 My will is **God's Will**, and I will place no other gods before **God**.

Notes to Lesson # 53

Notes on Summary Lesson #53 – Review of Lessons #11-15

Lesson #11: My meaningless thoughts are showing me a meaningless world.

Lesson #12: I am upset because I see a meaningless world.

Lesson #13: A meaningless world engenders fear.

Lesson #14: God did not create a meaningless world.

Lesson #15: My thoughts are images that I have made.

1) Our provisional reality is based on our own private perceptions. This private world is based on our individual viewpoint or perception. It is not shared with others and more importantly, it is not shared with the Mind of God. Because perception is based on individuality and separateness, it cannot be shared.

The Mind of God is a Oneness. It is shared by all that God created. Because the real world is Truth with a capital T, it is the only true reality. Creation is sharing or an extension of what its Creator truly is.

The only "real" thoughts that a Son of God can have are those thoughts shared with His Father. These thoughts are based on the Son knowing the oneness of what he truly is. Thoughts that arise from the erroneous belief of separation, lack and limitation are not known to God. These non-real thoughts cannot be shared with the Mind of God since God only knows the Truth. These false private thoughts of the split mind are under the guidance of the ego's fear-based thought system. They have no basis in reality since they are not part of the Mind of God.

Provisional reality appears to be real only in the mind of the perceiver. Change your perception and you change your provisional reality. You are asked by the Holy Spirit to choose differently. Forgiveness is the means for retraining and reclaiming the power of your mind to act as a decision-maker who freely follows the Voice for God.

2) The world we "see," our provisional reality, is really a thought projection. Our thoughts come first. Thoughts, which are based on our individual beliefs, are the cause. What we "see" is their effect. What we claim to "see" is really thought images that we project into our dream world of provisional reality. Our senses are utilized as thought confirmation devices for our projected thoughts. Our projected thoughts are reflected back to us when our senses find something that fits the predetermined objective they were told to confirm.

Because of our ability to make a physical world based on our view of separation and limitation, our senses will always discover a false witness to confirm our projected thought. We create our perceived world of provisional reality. Thoughts are things and the thought, which always comes first, is the cause of what we perceive. Thoughts that are judged and raised to the level of beliefs become our world that we perceive. Thoughts are cause and experiences are their effect.

Under the ego's thought system, we falsely assume that what is outside our mind came first and that the outside is the cause of our thoughts. This erroneous thinking helps insure that we will continue to believe that we are powerless victims and not the controllers of our own provisional reality.

3) Our world of provisional reality is a neutral learning device. It is neither good nor bad until we choose to judge it so. Only our judgmental thoughts give any experience that we perceive its characteristically good or bad nature. Whether we perceive something as good or bad, both serve to confirm the ego's goal of proving that we are separate and limited.

Any perception implies that we are not a Oneness. False perception belongs to the thought system of the ego. Since we have forgotten our divine birthright, we are incapable of judging what we perceive correctly.

Correct perception is only recovered when we choose to follow the thought system of the Holy Spirit. The thought system of the Holy Spirit has the ability to reinterpret our perceived experiences by utilizing the neutral learning device of provisional reality as a tool that will correct our wrong perception. Correct perception supports and aligns with the reawakening process. Forgiveness is the correcting device used by the Holy Spirit to return us to right-mindedness again.

4) The ego wants us to place meaning, either good or bad, on our meaningless dream world. This placing of meaning on the dream by the dreamer, gives the imaged thought the appearance of being real. If we buy into the belief that our dream is real, it becomes so in our mind's imagination. It becomes our world of provisional reality. This world seems real only to the dreamer. It remains unknown in the Mind of God. God does not make dreams or fantasies. God creates only by extending the Truth of the One Self. Truth is the Will of God.

5) If I am upset, it is because I have forgotten what I really am. I am a Child of God. I am caught up in my dream world of provisional reality and mistook the dream for reality and truth. I have forgotten that my current lifetime is part of my learning experience that is designed to help reawaken my mind to its ability to choose differently. I can choose to follow the guidance of the Holy Spirit.

I am upset because I believe that the story I made up in my mind is real. I have forgotten my purpose, which is to remember what I truly am. I have forgotten that this dream of mine can be utilized by the Holy Spirit to help me remember what I am if I only ask for His guidance. In time and space, I can experience and actually be a differentiated aspect of the One Self. Through the game of separation, the abstract One Self can both know and demonstrate Its Beingness.

6) As long as I am upset, I am giving credence to the ego's belief that I am a separate, limited ego-body. This upset helps keep me trapped in victim consciousness and away from reclaiming my authority as decision-maker for my own world. When I am upset, I have accepted the role of a victim. Victims claim to be powerless to change their circumstances. This inability to act as both the creator and decision-maker of my own world is exactly what my ego wants me to believe.

7) Projection is image making. First we have a "private" thought. This thought is judged based on our belief system. Our beliefs then determine what we expect to see. Then we project or send out that prejudged thought into the "outside world" as an image. Our senses then "find" or "make" the outside image that conforms to the projected and expected image. This is then reflected back with the senses to "confirm" the preconceived image as real and being outside the perceiver's own mind. Thus, the ego "confirms" its belief in separation through the use of false witnesses that appear to be outside and beyond the control of our mind.

LESSON 54

LESSON SUMMARY #16-20

These are the review ideas for today **from Lessons # 16-20:**

W-54.1. <u>Review of Lesson #16: I have no neutral thoughts</u>.
2 Neutral thoughts are impossible because all thoughts have power **to create and extend the truth or imagine and make the false.** 3 **Thoughts** will either make a false world or lead me to the real one **based on love and unity.** 4 But thoughts cannot be without effects. 5 As the world I see arises from my **ego's** thinking errors, so will the real world rise before my eyes as I let my **egoic** errors be corrected. 6 My thoughts cannot be neither true nor false. 7 They must be **either true** or **my thoughts are false.** 8 What I see shows me which they are. If I see a **fearful insane** world, **my thoughts are false because they are not shared with the Mind of God.**

W-54.2. <u>Review of Lesson #17: I see no neutral things</u>.
2 What I see witnesses to what I think. 3 If I did not think I would not exist, because life is thought. 4 Let me look on the world I see as the representation of my own **inner** state of mind. **If I see a fearful world, my thoughts are representing my ego's fear based thought system** 5 I know that my state of mind can change. **I can choose to follow a different non fear-based thought system.** 6 And so I also know the world I see can change as well.

W-54.3. <u>Review of Lesson #18: I am not alone in experiencing the effects of my seeing</u>.
2 If I have no private thoughts, I cannot see a private world. 3 Even the mad idea of separation had to be shared **with other split minds who believe the separation to be real** before it could form the basis of the **fearful and meaningless** world I **egoically** see. 4 Yet that sharing **of non-real thoughts** was a sharing of nothing. 5 I can also call upon my real thoughts, which share everything with everyone. 6 As my thoughts of separation call to the separation thoughts of others, so my real thoughts awaken the real thoughts in **the split minded who have perceived themselves to be separate from their Source.** 7 And the **fearless** world my real thoughts show me will dawn on their sight as well as mine.

W-54.4. <u>Review of Lesson #19: I am not alone in experiencing the effects of my thoughts</u>.
2 I am alone in nothing. 3 Everything I think or say or do teaches all the universe. 4 A Son of God cannot think or speak or act in vain. 5 **A Son of God** cannot be alone in anything **because the separation is not real.** 6 **Since everything I think or say or do teaches all the universe,** it is therefore in my power to change every mind along with mine, for mine is the power of God.

W-54.5. <u>Review of Lesson #20: I am determined to see</u>.
2 Recognizing the shared nature of my thoughts, I am determined to see **with true vision.** 3 I would look upon the witnesses **for a thought system based on love** that shows me the thinking of the **fearful egoic** world has been changed. 4 I would behold the proof that what has been done through me has enabled love to replace fear, laughter to replace tears, and abundance to replace loss. 5 I would look upon the real world, and let **the real world of love, laughter and abundance** teach me that my will and the Will of God are one **Will.**

Notes to Lesson # 54

Notes on Summary Lesson #54 – Review of Lessons #16-20

Lesson #16: I have no neutral thoughts.

Lesson #17: I see no neutral things.

Lesson #18: I am not alone in experiencing the effects of my seeing.

Lesson #19: I am not alone in experiencing the effects of my thoughts.

Lesson #20: I am determined to see.

1) Life is thought. Thoughts, raised to the level of a belief, are always the cause and what results or "manifests" is the effect. By the use of projection, the ego's thought system entraps the mind into believing that what is outside the mind is the cause and that the mind is an innocent victim of the outside world.

The goal of the ego is to maintain your belief that your mind is powerless and is not the source of all you perceive. The Holy Spirit's goal is to reawaken the decision making part of your mind to decide differently and freely choose to follow the thought system of the Holy Spirit. The thought system of the Holy Spirit is based on love and forgiveness.

2) The egoic world that we "see" is really a thought projection. Our thoughts come first. Thoughts, which are based on our individual beliefs, are the cause and what we believe we "see" is their effect. What we claim to "see" are really thought images that we project into our dream world of provisional reality.

Our senses are utilized as verifying devices for our projected thoughts. Our projected thoughts are reflected back to us when our senses find something that fits the predetermined goal. Because of our ability to make a physical world based on our view of separation and limitation, our senses will always discover some false witness to confirm our projected thought. Our senses ignore any witness that does not support its story. This is how we make our perceived world of provisional reality.

Thoughts are things. The thought always comes first. It is the cause of what we perceive. What we perceive is the effect on that judged thought. When thoughts are judged, they are raised to the level of a belief. Your mind then endows that thought with the power to impact how you relate to your world.

Under the ego's thought system, we falsely are led to believe that what is outside of us comes first and is the cause for our thoughts. This helps insure that we will continue to believe that we are innocent victims that lack the creative power to handle a given situation. This induces fear and results in our belief that we are not the causative agent of our world. We can only react to outside forces that are beyond our control. Rather than you being the writer, director, star and editor for your story, you are reduced to a mere actor in your own stage play.

3) Our world of provisional reality is a neutral learning device. It is neither good nor bad. Our thoughts give what we perceive, its characteristic of good or bad. Whether we perceive something as good or bad, it serves to confirm the ego's goal of "proving" that we are separate.

Perception requires duality. It needs both a perceiver and something to perceive. It means that we are not a Oneness. Perception belongs to the thought system of the ego. Since we have forgotten our divine birthright, we are incapable of correctly judging what we perceive.

Correct perception is only recovered when we choose to follow the thought system of the Holy Spirit. The thought system of the Holy Spirit has the ability to reinterpret our perceived reality by utilizing our experiences as neutral learning devices. Our experiences are reinterpreted with love and forgiveness and now become the tool that is used to correct our wrong perception. Forgiveness is the correcting device used by the Holy Spirit to return us to right-mindedness.

4) Fantasies have no ability to change the truth. Truth just is. Truth does not need your agreement to make it true. The ego wants us to place meaning, either good or bad, on our meaningless dream world. This placing of meaning on the dream by the dreamer gives the imagined thought the appearance of being real.

If we buy into the belief that our dream is real, it appears so within our mind. It becomes our world of provisional reality. This imagined inner world seems real to the dreamer but remains unknown in the Mind of God. God does not deal in dreams. Truth or reality is the only realm of God.

5) Because our minds are truly connected as a oneness, we cannot be alone in Truth. Truth is the sharing of all that God created, as God created it. Truth is the basis for real thoughts which are the thoughts we share with the Mind of God. Our non-real thoughts are not shared with the Mind of God. Our non-real thoughts are only shared with other delusional minds who believe that separation, lack and limitation are real.

Your non-real thoughts that you perceive to be private thoughts make your dream world of provisional reality. Yet, even in these private thoughts, you are never alone since there is always the requirement of a perceiver and something to perceive. Private thoughts always require the duality of at least two "items."

Projection, which is the tool that we use to "make" our provisional reality, requires something outside of itself so that its projected thought can be reflected back to the perceiver and thus "confirmed" by the senses as "real." This allows the projected thought to appear as if it were coming from outside the mind of the perceiver.

Even the belief of separation is a shared experience. Due to the connection and oneness of minds, whether my thoughts are under the influence of the ego or the Holy Spirit, the effects of my thoughts are shared with my brother.

6) Projection is image making. First, we have a "private" thought. This thought is judged and raised to the level of a belief. We then send out or project that prejudged thought into the "outside world" as an image. This image then "finds" or "makes" the outside image that conforms to the projected image. This is then reflected back to the senses that "confirm" the preconceived image as real and being outside of the perceiver. Projection is perception's tool that your mind utilizes to "confirm" its preconceived notion of reality. Your ego first makes up these false witnesses and then claims these images prove the reality of separation.

7) Since we are split-minded, we need to request guidance from the Holy Spirit if we are to see with true vision. When asked, the Holy Spirit will reinterpret what we erroneously perceive through the ego's eyes of fear. False perception will be transformed into correct perception. Inspired by the Holy Spirit, we will replace "false seeing" with the Vision of Truth or Christ. Forgiveness is the tool utilized by the Holy Spirit's thought system to help us reestablish our true Self. It is this Big "S" Self that is shared with our brothers and sisters.

LESSON 55

LESSON SUMMARY #21-25

Today's review includes the following **ideas from Lessons 21-25.**

W-55.1. <u>**Review of Lesson #21: I am determined to see things differently.**</u>
2 What I **egoically** see now **without true vision** are but signs of disease, disaster and death. 3 This cannot be what God created for His beloved Son. 4 The very fact that I **egoically** see such **fear-based** things is proof that I do not understand God. 5 Therefore I also do not understand **God's** Son. 6 What I **egoically** see **which is a fear-based world,** tells me that I do not know who I am. 7 I am determined to see the witnesses to the truth in me, rather than those **witnesses** which show me a **separate fear-based** illusion of myself.

W-55.2. <u>**Review of Lesson #22: What I see is a form of vengeance.**</u>
2 The **fearful and meaningless** world I see is hardly the representation of loving thoughts. 3 **This fearful world** is a picture of attack on everything by everything. 4 **This fearful world** is anything but a reflection of the Love of God and the Love of His Son. 5 **This fearful world** is my own attack thoughts that give rise to this picture **of an attacking world.** 6 My loving thoughts will save me from this perception of **a fearful attacking** world, and give me the peace God intended me to have.

W-55.3. <u>**Review of Lesson #23: I can escape from this world by giving up attack thoughts.**</u>
2 **By giving up my attack thoughts** herein lies salvation, and nowhere else. 3 Without attack thoughts I could not see a world of attack. 4 As forgiveness allows love to return to my awareness, I will see a world of peace and safety and joy. 5 And it is this **world of peace, safety and joy that** I choose to see, in place **of a fearful attacking world that** I look on now.

W-55.4. <u>**Review of Lesson #24: I do not perceive my own best interests.**</u>
2 How could I recognize my own best interests when I do not know who I am? 3 What I **mistakenly** think are my best interests would merely bind me closer to **this fearful attacking** world of illusions. 4 I am willing to follow the Guide God has given me to find out what my own **true** best interests are, recognizing that I cannot perceive **what my own true best interests are** by myself.

W-55.5. <u>**Review of Lesson #25: I do not know what anything is for**</u>.
2 To me, the purpose of everything is to prove that my illusions about myself are real. 3 It is for this purpose **of proving that my illusions about myself are real** that I attempt to use everyone and everything. 4 It is for this **proving that my illusions about myself are real** that I believe the world is for. 5 Therefore I do not recognize **the world's** real purpose. 6 The purpose I have given the world has led to a frightening picture of **the world.** 7 Let me open my mind to the world's real purpose by withdrawing the **false purpose** I have given the world **which is that of proving that my illusions about myself are real** and **instead** learning the truth about **the world and myself.**

Notes to Lesson # 55

Notes on Summary Lesson #55 – Review of Lessons #21-25

Lesson #21: I am determined to see things differently.

Lesson #22: What I see is a form of vengeance.

Lesson #23: I can escape from this world by giving up attack thoughts.

Lesson #24: I do not perceive my own best interests.

Lesson #25: I do not know what anything is for.

1) Everything I "see" is a false witness for the ego's thought system. I only "see" my dream world of provisional reality. This world has already been prejudged so I only look for selective items that support my current belief system. This is not vision, but rather image making.

2) This world and my body have a common purpose under the thought system of the ego. They were both made up to convince me that I am a separate individual and that my dream world is real. They are designed to help me forget what I truly am. This world and all its trappings are a device to sustain my false belief in separate egoic autonomy. It is this belief in separation that has cost me my happiness.

Our purpose in this lifetime must be to determine if we are still willing to pay that price. Will I remain in victim consciousness or reclaim my divine birthright?

3) God is unconditional love. To think a God of Love would require His Children to live in this world would contradict everything God stands for. We must be insane to believe God created this world that we perceive. God did not create this world. We did.

4) The backbone of the ego's thought system is to attack and defend against attack. Both "prove" that we are separate. If we were a Oneness of All That Is, what would be outside ourselves to attack? I can only be attacking myself.

5) If we don't remember who we are, how can we know what is in our best interest? If we suffer from amnesia, we can easily be manipulated by a new belief system and become a "new" person. The goal of the Holy Spirit is to help us remember what we truly are.

6) Life is thought. Thought always is the cause and what results from the thought, or "manifests," is its effect. By the use of projection, the ego's thought system entraps the mind into believing that what is outside the mind is the cause and the mind is an innocent victim of the outside world.

The goal of the ego is to maintain your belief that your mind is powerless and is not the source of all you perceive. This costs you your happiness while you get to falsely claim it is not your fault.

The Holy Spirit's goal is to reawaken the decision making part of your split mind so that you can then choose a different plan. This time choose the thought system of the Voice for God. When you do so, you become the causative agent of your perceived world. You now are capable, empowered and responsible for your own happiness and inner peace.

7) Something is meaningless when it has no ability to change your true reality. God created you as part of the One Self. Your big "S" Self remains perfect, whole and complete. Your denial of your birthright has no ability to change the Truth of who created you. Only within the delusional mind of the temporally insane does the nightmare appear real.

The ego wants us to place meaning, either good or bad, on our meaningless dream world. This placement of meaning on the dream by the dreamer gives the imaged thought the appearance of being real. If we buy into the belief that our dream is real, it becomes so in our mind. It becomes our world of provisional reality. This world seems real to the dreamer but remains unknown in the Mind of God. God does not create dreams. God's Will only extends the Truth of the One Self.

8) The world we see as our provisional reality is really a thought projection. Our thoughts come first. Thoughts that are based on our individual beliefs are the cause. What we "see" is their effect. What we claim to "see" are really thought images that we project into our dream world of provisional reality. Our senses are utilized as thought confirmation devices for our projected thoughts. Our projected thoughts are reflected back to us when our senses find something that fits the predetermined objective they were told to confirm.

Because of our ability to make a physical world based on our view of separation and limitation, our senses will always discover a false witness to confirm our projected thoughts. We create our perceived world of provisional reality. Thoughts are things and the thought, which always comes first, is the cause of what we perceive. Thoughts that are judged and raised to the level of beliefs become our world that we perceive. Thoughts are cause and experiences are their effect.

Under the ego's thought system, we falsely assume that what is outside our mind came first and that the outside is the cause of our thoughts. This erroneous thinking helps insure that we will continue to believe that we are powerless victims and not the controllers of our own provisional reality.

Only the Holy Spirit knows both the truth of who you are and your false beliefs about yourself. Because of this, only the Holy Spirit has the correct plan to bring you home. This Inner Guide was placed within your mind where it can never be lost. This gift from God guarantees your safe return to knowledge. You remain part of the inseparable holographic Mind of God. You are perfectly safe. So sit back, laugh a lot and enjoy the return flight home.

LESSON 56

LESSON SUMMARY #26-30

Our review for today covers the following **ideas from Lessons 26-30.**

W-56.1. <u>Review of Lesson #26: My attack thoughts are attacking my invulnerability.</u>
2 How can I know who I am when I see myself as under constant attack **from my ego's fear-based thought system**? 3 Pain, illness, loss, age and death seem to threaten me. 4 All my hopes and wishes and plans appear to be at the mercy of a **fearful** world I cannot control. 5 Yet perfect security and complete fulfillment are my **divine** inheritance. 6 I have tried to give my **divine** inheritance away in exchange for the world I see **through my ego's fear-based thought system**. 7 But God has kept my **divine** inheritance safe for me. 8 My own real thoughts will teach me what **my divine inheritance really** is.

W-56.2. <u>Review of Lesson #27: Above all else I want to see.</u>
2 Recognizing that what I see reflects what I think I am, I realize that **true** vision is my greatest need. 3 The world I see attests to the fearful nature of the **egoic separate** self-image I have made. 4 If I would remember who I am, it is essential that I let this **separate, limited and fearful self**-image of myself go. 5 As **this separate, limited and fearful self-image of myself** is replaced by truth, **true** vision will surely be given me. 6 And with this **true** vision, I will look upon the world and on myself with charity and love.

W-56.3. <u>Review of Lesson #28: Above all else I want to see differently.</u>
2 The **fearful egoic** world I see holds my fearful self-image in place, and guarantees **the** continuance **of my fearful self-image**. 3 While I see the world as I see it now **through the eyes of my ego's fear-based thought system**, truth cannot enter my awareness. 4 I would let the door behind this **fearful egoic** world be opened for me that I may look past **my fear-based thought system** to the world that reflects the Love of God.

W-56.4. <u>Review of Lesson #29: God is in everything I see.</u>
2 Behind every **egoic fear-based image** I have made, the truth remains unchanged. 3 Behind every veil I have drawn across the face of love, **truth and love's** light remains undimmed. 4 Beyond all my insane wishes is my will, united with the Will of my Father. 5 God is still everywhere and in everything forever. 6 And we who are part of **the Mind of God** will yet look past all **egoic** appearances, and recognize the truth beyond all **the false images of separation and fear.**

W-56.5. <u>Review of Lesson #30: God is in everything I see because God is in my mind.</u>
<u>2</u> In my own **split** mind, behind all my insane thoughts of separation and attack, is the knowledge that all is one forever. 3 I have not lost the knowledge of Who I am because I have forgotten **my divine inheritance**. 4 **My divine inheritance** has been kept for me in the Mind of God, Who has not left His Thoughts. 5 And I, who am among **God's Thoughts**, am one with **God's Thoughts** and one with **God.**

Notes to Lesson # 56

Notes on Summary Lesson #56 – Review of Lessons #26-30

Lesson #26: My attack thoughts are attacking my invulnerability.

Lesson #27: Above all else I want to see.

Lesson #28: Above all else I want to see differently.

Lesson #29: God is in everything I see.

Lesson #30: God is in everything I see because God is in my mind.

1) How can my thoughts mean anything when they are all based on the misperception of what I am? My ego does not know who I am. My past and current erroneous beliefs are preventing me from seeing with true vision.

2) The meaningless has no ability to change the truth. My ego does not know what is real and therefore, has taught me to value the meaningless. Its belief system has limitations that are not worthy of a Son of God. I am not limited, suffering from lack or alone. I have never left my Source. It is this fear-based thought system that engenders the fear I experience. My ego is constantly arguing that my mind lacks the creative ability to handle a given situation. I need a new guide to reclaim my divine birthright. My strength comes from God and I am very holy.

3) My thoughts that are shared with God's Mind are thoughts that co-create and transform an egoic meaningless world into a meaningful world where the abstract can demonstrate specific concrete examples of being love in form. God did not create a meaningless world.

On a mass collective consciousness basis, the world of perception has been made into a place to prove and support my ego's belief in separation, sin, guilt and fear. With the Holy Spirit's guidance, I can change the purpose for my world of perception. I can replace my egoic eyes of fear with the true vision of Christ.

With the Holy Spirit's guidance, I can use and share my loving thoughts to transform the meaningless world into a place to demonstrate love and forgiveness. In time and space, I can demonstrate and be love in form. If I follow the Voice for God that is within me, my world can be used to bear witness for the truth.

4) Life is thought. There is no neutral thought. Thoughts are either true or false. Since minds are joined, we either share truth or share illusion. Our thoughts attract like-minded thoughts in others. When you change your thoughts and beliefs, you attract new thoughts in others.

What you think, say or do is shared with the universe today. Be determined to share the truth. Replace fear with love. Let God's Will be your will. God's Will is that you be happy. Know that you remain perfect, whole and complete. You remain as God created you, invulnerable and sinless. You are part of the inseparable holographic Mind of God.

5) The ego argues for the correctness of its belief in separation. To the ego, the purpose of everything is to convince your decision-maker that you are a separate yet autonomous entity that exists apart from the Mind of God. You are a victim of outside forces that are beyond your control. Your ego claims that it alone has the best plan to keep you safe from the inevitable attack from others and a revengeful God. The ego wants you to believe it has your best interest at heart because it is you.

The Holy Spirit's purpose is to utilize your experience in time and space to prove that illusions cannot change what you truly are. You remain as God created you. Nothing can rob you of your inner peace unless you choose to allow it. When asked, the Holy Spirit will reframe and reinterpret your fearful experiences through the eyes of love and forgiveness. This reframing will allow you to regain your inner peace and provide proof that you alone are the source of your inner peace. When peace abides within your mind, you will see a world full of mercy and love. If you seek peace, be peace.

6) You must change your belief of who you are if you are to change the images you see and experience. You cannot maintain the belief that you are a limited ego body in competition with other ego bodies and at the same time claim you are God's beloved Child. These beliefs are mutually exclusive. Realize that you are unlimited spirit and that you remain part of the indivisible holographic mind of God. Accept your divine inheritance and allow God to live through you. Only your attack thoughts are maintaining your image of limitation, lack and separation.

Quiet your egoic mind, and ask for the guidance of the Holy Spirit. By replacing your fear-based thought system with the thought system for love and forgiveness, your world must realign to your new beliefs. Your world is a reflection of your beliefs.

Question: What eyes will you see with today, the eyes of love or the eyes of fear?

It is your decision.

LESSON SUMMARY #31-35

Today let us review these ideas **from Lessons # 31-35:**

W-57.1. <u>Review of Lesson #31: I am not the victim of the world I see.</u>
2 How can I be the victim of a world that can be completely undone if I so choose **to undo that world**? 3 My chains are loosened **when I choose to undo that world**. 4 I can drop off **my chains** merely by desiring to do so. 5 The prison door is open. 6 I can leave **the prison** simply by walking out. 7 Nothing holds me in this world. 8 Only my wish to stay **in this world** keeps me a prisoner. 9 I would give up my insane wishes **to be a prisoner in this world** and walk into the sunlight at last.

W-57.2<u>. Review of Lesson #32: I have invented the world I see.</u>
2 I made up the prison in which I see myself. 3 All I need do is recognize **that I made up** this **prison in which I see myself** and I am free. 4 I have deluded myself into believing it is possible to imprison the Son of God. 5 I was bitterly mistaken in this belief **that I could imprison the Son of God**, which I no longer want. 6 The Son of God must be forever free. 7 **The Son of God** is as God created him, and not what I would make of **the Son of God**. 8 **The Son of God** is where God would have him be, and not where I thought to hold **the Son of God a** prisoner **in my world that I see myself.**

W-57.3. <u>Review of Lesson #33: There is another way of looking at the world.</u>
2 Since the purpose of the world is not the one I ascribed to **the world**, there must be another way of looking at **the world**. 3 I see everything upside down, and my thoughts are the opposite of truth. 4 I see the world as a prison for God's Son. 5 It must be, then, that the world is really a place where **the Son of God** can be set free. 6 I would look upon the world as it is, and see **the world** as a place where the Son of God finds his freedom.

W-57.4<u>. Review of Lesson #34: I could see peace instead of this.</u>
2 When I see the world as a place of freedom, I realize that **the world** reflects the laws of God instead of **the ego's rules I** made up for **the world** to obey. 3 I will understand that peace, not war, abides in **the world**. 4 And I will perceive that peace also abides in the hearts of all who share this place **in the world** with me.

W-57.5. <u>Review of Lesson #35: My mind is part of God's. I am very holy.</u>
3 As I share the peace of the world with my brothers, I begin to understand that this peace **of the world** comes from deep within myself. 4 The world I look upon has taken on the light of my forgiveness, and **this peaceful world** shines forgiveness back at me. 5 In this light **of my forgiveness,** I begin to see what my **egoic** illusions about myself kept hidden. 6 I begin to understand the holiness of all living things, including **the holiness of** myself, and **the** oneness **of all living things** with me.

Notes to Lesson # 57

Notes on Summary Lesson #57 – Review of Lessons #31-35

Lesson #31: I am not the victim of the world I see.

Lesson #32: I have invented the world I see.

Lesson #33: There is another way of looking at the world.

Lesson #34: I could see peace instead of this.

Lesson #35: My mind is part of God's Mind. I am very holy.

1) Lesson #31 states that I am not the victim of the world I see. In this lesson, we are talking about the world of perception and saying that as a decision-maker, we have some control and input over how we view our world. If I control how I view my world, how can I be a victim of the world I see? The world I see is based on my own thought projections.

2) Lesson #32 states I have invented the world I see. In this case, ACIM is saying that I am source of my perceived world. My decision-maker is free to choose again if I do not like the world I am creating for myself. Ultimately, my dreams cannot change or alter what God has created. <u>A Course in Miracles</u> makes a distinct point that God did not create our world of provisional reality, we did.

On a collective consciousness level, we desire to experience being something other than God and to be separate from the Oneness of All That Is. We used our imagination to create a world in which we could keep God's Love out and pretend we were something other than as God created us, perfect, whole and complete. We imagined that we were not holy. To be holy is to be whole, part of the Oneness of All That Is.

The world that we imagined was based on our desire to be a separate autonomous entity. We wanted to be special. Since God created us perfect, whole and complete, to be something other than as we were created is impossible. Being part of the holographic Mind of God, separation and differentiation could never become our true reality. An indivisible Oneness of All That Is cannot be separate from Itself.

How could we experience being special if there is just the One Self?

We could only pretend or imagine that we were not perfect, not whole and very incomplete. Our quest to experience being special gave rise to our illusionary world of perception based on our belief in limitation, lack and fear. When we forgot to laugh, we made the imagined game of separation appear real. To the split minded that perceived that they were different from their Source, the quest to be special could only be played out on the game board of one's own imagination. When we forgot our world of private individuated perception was not real, our provisional reality became a fearful and frightening place.

3) Lesson 33 states there is another way of looking at this world. This lesson basically says that I as the decision-maker must decide how I choose to view the world that I perceive. I can view the world as a neutral learning device or a playschool in which I relearn who I really am.

If that is the case, this world is no longer a place to be feared. Instead, this world is a place where I can learn forgiveness. It does not have to be a prison that prevents me from recalling who I am. If this world is given over to the Holy Spirit, it can actually become the means for remembering the truth of who I am. God is abstract and formless, but I have the opportunity as His Child to have the experience of being Love in Form.

4) Lesson 34 states that I could see peace instead of this. We need to realize that the main principal of God is that of extension or creation. This is the expansion of the Oneness. God gives all because He is all. So God's Law of Creation is to be all, give all, to all.

If I asked the Holy Spirit to reinterpret my misperception, then I can learn that my misperceptions are not my true reality. I can then learn forgiveness for my brothers but more importantly, for myself. I can choose peace instead of the conflict by asking for inner guidance. When I follow the Holy Spirit's reinterpretation of the event through Its eyes of forgiveness, I will ultimately recover my inner peace. When I listen to the Voice for God, the peace of God will be my destiny.

5) The final lesson in this summary states that my mind is part of God's Mind and I am very holy. This lesson asks us to remember that there is just a Oneness and if there is only a Oneness then what I give, I also receive.

To receive forgiveness, I must give forgiveness. By seeing the Oneness in my brother, I reawaken to my own Oneness. I always was, am and will be perfect, whole and complete, just as God created me. This is both my own freely chosen will and God's Will.

Both my will and God's Will is that I be happy. My problem is that when I do not realize what I truly am, I do not have the ability to judge correctly what my true happiness is. It is this misperception about what I truly am that prevents me from knowing where my true happiness lies. My will and God's Will are the same. God, my brother and I are all One.

This recalling that my mind is part of God's Mind is the ultimate goal of A Course in Miracles. When we share our real thoughts with the Mind of God, we will recognize the real world that was hidden behind the facade of the game of separation.

LESSON 58

LESSON SUMMARY #36-40

These ideas are for review today **from Lessons # 36-40:**

W-58.1. <u>Review of Lesson #36: My holiness envelops everything I see.</u>

2 From my holiness does the perception of the real world come. 3 Having forgiven **my world of egoic perception**, I no longer see myself as guilty. 4 I can accept the innocence that is the truth about me. 5 Seen through understanding eyes **of my big "S" Self**, the holiness of the world is all I see, for I can picture only the **forgiving and holy** thoughts I hold about myself.

W-58.2. <u>Review of Lesson #37: My holiness blesses the world.</u>

2 The perception of my holiness does not bless me alone. 3 Everyone and everything I see in **my holy** light shares in the joy **my holiness** brings to me. 4 There is nothing that is apart from this joy **of my holiness**, because there is nothing that does not share my holiness. 5 As I recognize my holiness, so does the holiness of the world shine forth for everyone to see.

W-58.3. <u>Review of Lesson #38: There is nothing my holiness cannot do.</u>

2 My holiness is unlimited in its power to heal, because **my holiness** is unlimited in its power to save. 3 What is there to be saved from except illusions? 4 And what are all illusions except false ideas about myself? 5 My holiness undoes all **illusions** by asserting the truth about me. 6 In the presence of my holiness, which I share with God Himself, all idols vanish.

W-58.4. <u>Review of Lesson #39: My holiness is my salvation.</u>

2 Since my holiness saves me from all guilt, recognizing my holiness is recognizing my salvation. 3 **Recognizing my holiness** is also recognizing the salvation of the world. 4 Once I have accepted my holiness, nothing can make me afraid. 5 And because I am unafraid, everyone must share in my understanding, which is the gift of God to me and to the world.

W-58.5. <u>Review of Lesson #40: I am blessed as a Son of God.</u>

2 **Because I am blessed as a Son of God**, herein lies my claim to all good and only good. 3 I am blessed as a Son of God. 4 All good things are mine, because God intended **all good things** for me. 5 I cannot suffer any loss or deprivation or pain because of Who I am **as God's blessed Son**. 6 My Father supports me, protects me, and directs me in all things. 7 **My Father's** care for me is infinite, and is with me forever. 8 I am eternally blessed as **My Father's** Son.

Notes to Lesson # 58

Notes on Summary Lesson #58 – Review of Lessons #36-40

Lesson #36: My holiness envelops everything I see.

Lesson #37: My holiness blesses the world.

Lesson #38: There is nothing my holiness cannot do.

Lesson #39: My holiness is my salvation.

Lesson #40: I am blessed as a Son of God.

1) Lesson 58 is once again a summary lesson. It covers ACIM workbook lessons #36 through 40 that were discussed a few weeks prior.

Rather than just discuss these various lessons, I'd like to first go over some of the terminology that is used in these lesson summaries. Often common words are used that have a specific meaning for ACIM purposes. This terminology needs to trigger within your mind a much broader concept than the commonly understood definition. With that in mind, the following ideas may be helpful as you try to decipher the concepts behind these lessons.

Holy is actually to make whole. It is the knowing that you are part of the inseparable Oneness of All That Is.

Holiness is equivalent to the Oneness that you share and really are. When we speak of your holiness, we are talking about your big "S" Self. This is not the part of your split mind that perceives itself to be separate autonomous being. Your little "s" self follows the ego's thought system based on its belief in sin, guilt and fear.

The Sonship is all God created as God created it. The Sonship is holiness itself. Its holiness remains unaffected by your denial of your divine birthright. The Sonship is a synonym for the Son of God.

The real world is heaven or the Kingdom. This reflects creation, which is all God created as God created it. The real world is a reflection of the Truth of God.

Innocence is the truth about your true nature. This innocence comes from the Oneness that we really are. We share God's innocence. We do not realize that one of the qualities of God is innocence. God is innocent because God is only aware of the Truth with a capital T. God does not know the false world that our egos imagine. Since God only knows the Truth, God does not judge or condemn what the ego perceives.

The split minded actually perceive the false due to their belief in separation. Yet, our perception is not based on truth. Perception differs from knowledge because perception requires thinking due to our uncertainty. Thinking is really in the realm of judgment. Our ego is a big judging machine.

Understanding eyes represent the vision of Christ. The vision of Christ represents seeing through the thought system of the Holy Spirit.

Light is equivalent to understanding the truth. It is the realization of the truth of our being part of this Oneness.

Salvation would be equivalent to the healing of the separation. Salvation comes from your own forgiveness. Forgiveness is the healing of our sense of guilt that arose from our belief in separation. It is the reclaiming of our sense of oneness.

2) We previously stated that A Course in Miracles used the term forgiveness in a special way. In order to forgive, we need to recognize that what we thought our brother did to us never actually occurred.

Why?

Because it is just part of our own egoic projection, part of our misperception and part of our own dreaming mind. Therefore, our dream has no ability to impact the truth of what we really are. We said earlier that if something has no ability to change reality, it is not a cause. It is merely a fantasy that appears to impact the delusional mind that perceives the event to be real. Our brother is merely an actor in our screenplay. The screenplay is designed to help us learn the lessons needed to reclaim our divine birthright. As such, they are really blessings.

The gift of God is equivalent to God's Will for the Sonship, which is the peace of God. God wants us only to be happy. We reclaim our happiness when we accept the Atonement for ourselves. Although we haven't talked much about the atonement, the atonement stands for the At-One-Ment of All. When you accept the Atonement for yourself, you reject the belief in lack, limitation and separation. You accept the truth of your unity with this Oneness.

The innocent have no concept of guilt, fear or sin. They are not held accountable for their actions because they do not judge things as right or wrong. They are not judging, but rather merely seeking new experiences from which to enjoy and learn. They are curious and do not have an ulterior motive or are not trying to hurt another. Instead, they only desire to experience and be with the event itself.

We are all sharing and playing in the game of separation. We desire to learn the truth about ourselves and actually be that truth. Within this playschool of time and space, the game of separation has no power to hurt a Child of God unless one chooses to believe they can be hurt. The game has no effect on our reality but it does provide opportunities to demonstrate who and what you believe you are.

To bless is to offer good and only good. God blesses me since God intends all good things to be mine. God supports me, protects me and directs me in all things. I merely need to silence the voice for fear and follow the Holy Spirit's guidance.

My world is a reflection of me. My strength, power and safety come from God, my Source, which is unlimited. I can only appear limited in my own mind's imagination. Yet, my delusional mind has no ability to change the truth.

LESSON 59

LESSON SUMMARY #41-45

The following ideas are for review today **from Lessons # 41-45:**

W-59.1. Review of Lesson #41: God goes with me wherever I go.

2 How can I be alone when God always goes with me? 3 How can I be doubtful and unsure of myself when perfect certainty abides in **God**? 4 How can I be disturbed by anything when **God** rests in me in absolute peace? 5 How can I suffer when love and joy surround me through **God**? 6 Let me not cherish illusions about myself. 7 I am perfect because God goes with me wherever I go.

W-59.2. Review of Lesson #42: God is my strength. 2 Vision is God's gift.

3 Let me not look to my own **egoic** eyes to see today. 4 Let me be willing to exchange my pitiful illusion of **egoic** seeing for the **true** vision **of Christ** that is given by God. 5 Christ's vision is **God's** gift, and **God** has given **the true vision of Christ** to me. 6 Let me call upon this gift **of the true vision of Christ** today, so that this day may help me to understand eternity.

W-59.3. Review of Lesson #43: God is my Source. 2 I cannot see apart from God.

3 I can see **with the true vision of Christ** what God wants me to see. 4 I cannot see anything else **but what God wants me to see with the true vision of Christ**. 5 Beyond **God's** Will lie only illusions. 6 It is these **illusions** I choose when I think I can see apart from **God**. 7 It is these **illusions** I choose when I try to see through the body's eyes. 8 Yet the vision of Christ has been given me to replace **the body's eyes**. 9 It is through this vision **of Christ** that I choose to see.

W-59.4. Review of Lesson #44: God is the light in which I see.

2 I cannot see in darkness. 3 God is the only light. 4 Therefore, if I am to see **the light**, it must be through **God**. 5 **My ego** has tried to define what seeing is, and I have been wrong. 6 Now it is given me to understand that God is the light in which I see. 7 Let me welcome **the** vision **of Christ** and the happy world **the light of God** will show me.

W-59.5. Review of Lesson #45: God is the Mind with which I think.

2 I have no thoughts I do not share with God. 3 I have no thoughts apart from **God,** because I have no mind apart from **God's Mind**. 4 As part of **God's** Mind, my thoughts are **God's Thoughts** and **God's** Thoughts are mine.

Notes to Lesson # 59

Notes on Summary Lesson #59 – Review of Lessons #41-45

Lesson #41: God goes with me wherever I go.

Lesson #42: God is my strength. Vision is His gift.

Lesson #43: God is my Source. I cannot see apart from Him.

Lesson #44: God is the light in which I see.

Lesson #45: God is the Mind with which I think.

1) Lesson 59 is again a summary lesson. It covers ACIM workbook lessons #40 through 45. These 5 lessons are teaching about the idea that God is always with us. In reality, the truth is that there is only a Oneness.

A Course in Miracles tries to meet us where we are. We perceive ourselves to be separate. Therefore, ACIM uses dualistic language to aid in our retraining. There is just a Oneness in which the Father is Cause, we His Effect. These are two sides that form one inseparable coin. Yet, that is not how we perceive ourselves. So to help improve our comprehension of the fact that there is just One Self, ACIM utilizes dualistic language. It speaks of reality as being comprised of three separate parts. The Father, the Sonship and the Holy Spirit are introduced as being separate yet in reality, all three are indivisible components of the One Self. They are part of the Holy Trinity that remains a Oneness and that is the eternal truth.

Lesson 41 says, God goes with me wherever I go. God does not share our illusion about ourselves. In the real world, God never leaves us. The Holy Spirit or Voice for God always abides within us.

ACIM talks about our mind as being split into two separate and opposing halves. There are two voices within any mind that perceives itself to be separate from the Mind of God. The Christ consciousness or big "S" Self is aware of the truth and is the home of God. It is also the home of the Holy Spirit. God is our Source that resides within our Christ consciousness and is the basis for our invulnerability. We are unlimited Spirit.

Yet, there is a second voice within the split minded. Part of our mind believes that the game of separation is real. It has allowed fear to replace the truth. This part of our mind perceives itself to be separate from God. It perceives sin, guilt and fear to be its reality. This belief in the fantasy of separation results in the denial of the truth. But our denial cannot change Truth's reality. We cannot be apart from our Source.

Although we are two sides of one inseparable coin, in our private world of individuated provisional reality, we have a different view of reality. God understands that His Child is merely playing. God understands that we are trying to know, demonstrate and be an individuated aspect of love. The game of separation provides the experiences of differentiation which are needed to experience the different aspects of being love in form.

But for the child who perceives himself to be separate, this misperception has transformed the game of separation into a life-and-death struggle. The child has forgotten to laugh, took the game seriously and made fear appear real.

Fear is false evidence appearing real. There is a disconnect within the child's mind between fantasy and reality. The child is like the boy who pretended he was a dog until that illusion became the boy's apparent reality.

God knows the truth that the child is merely caught up enjoying the game and that the game has no ability to change God's Child. The Father knows that separation is impossible because that is not God's Will. The Holy Spirit is the bridge between the two.

The Holy Spirit is aware that the child has accepted the false belief in separation and hence forgotten the truth about itself. It is the task of the Holy Spirit to gently reawaken the child to the truth of the child's spiritual magnificence. The Holy Spirit uses the playschool of time and space to provide the learning lessons that we desire to bring us back home to the truth of who we really are.

2) Lesson 42 is God is my strength. Vision is His gift. We believe that what we see with the physical eyes represents reality. But this is not the case. The images that we perceive with our physical senses represent our dream world of our provisional reality.

With Christ vision, you see your brother and yourself as you truly are. You look past the form to the content of your spiritual essence and now accept the vision of Christ to be your true reality. You realize there is a much bigger picture than what your egoic eyes perceive. The ego's eyes only observe your mind's own projected images that support its preconceived beliefs about the world. They trap you in victim consciousness.

God is really a synonym for Truth with a Capital T. My strength lies in God because that is my reality. I am a spiritual essence with a divine birthright that makes me invulnerable because I share the same invulnerability as my Source.

3) Lesson 43 is God is my Source. I cannot see apart from Him. There is nothing beyond the Will of God but illusion. Illusion is a fantasy and therefore, there is nothing to see. It's just in your imagination, your own misperception.

Your decision-maker must decide which thought system you will utilize to view your world. Will it be with the vision of Christ that looks past the form to see the truth?

Will you realize that we are just actors on a learning stage for the purpose of demonstrating what we currently believe about ourselves?

Christ's vision will see everything as either a cry for love or an act of love. If it hears a cry for love, it will respond in an appropriate and loving way.

The ego is under the illusion that this fantasy has become your true reality. In truth, the false has no ability to impact your reality. Yet to the ego, the false has replaced the truth. A fantasy is causeless and without an effect. Therefore, it is nothing.

4) Lesson 44 is God is the light in which I see. The ego's thought system is darkness. It blocks reality by projecting our egoic mind's inner misperceptions into our outer world. These projections become the images that our physical senses confirm. Our physical senses are thought confirmation devices that provide the illusion of third-party objectivity. These illusions become what we perceive to be our provisional reality.

Thinking is a loss of certainty. When we abandoned knowledge, we decided to judge. Thinking revolves around the possibility that there could be something other than just the truth. Because of this, our egoic mind becomes a big judging machine. Because we perceive things to be outside of ourselves, our ego needs to judge something to be either good, bad or neutral. When we perceive ourselves to be separate, we lack the certainty that comes from knowledge.

The Holy Spirit is the bridge that will lead us back to the knowledge that we eternally remain a shared Oneness of the Mind of God. The Holy Spirit will help you reframe your misperceptions into correct perception. Correct perception provides the learning lessons that realign your split mind with the truth. This Inner Voice is the Voice for the remembrance of the Truth. It is the Voice for God.

5) Lesson 45 is God is the mind in which I think. There is nothing outside the Mind of God. God's Mind and His thoughts are shared and thus, real. Our mind, which is represented by our Christ consciousness or big "S" Self, is part of the shared Mind of God. We are a Oneness with our Creator.

We need to change our misperception to correct perception or right mindedness. Right mindedness is the healing of the split mind itself. By following the Holy Spirit's guidance, this healing will be achieved.

133

LESSON 60

LESSON SUMMARY #46-50

These ideas are for today's review **of Lessons # 46-50:**

W-60.1. <u>**Review of Lesson #46: God is the Love in which I forgive.**</u>
2 God does not forgive because **God** has never condemned. 3 The blameless cannot blame, and those who have accepted their innocence see nothing to forgive. 4 Yet forgiveness is the means by which I will recognize my innocence. 5 **Forgiveness** is the reflection of God's Love on earth. 6 **Forgiveness** will bring me near enough to Heaven that the Love of God can reach down to me and raise me up to **God.**

W-60.2. <u>**Review of Lesson #47: God is the strength in which I trust.**</u>
2 It is not my own strength through which I forgive. 3 It is through the strength of God in me, which I am remembering as I forgive. 4 As I begin to see, I recognize **God's** reflection on earth. 5 I forgive all things because I feel the stirring of **God's** strength in me. 6 And I begin to remember **God's** Love **that** I chose to forget, but which has not forgotten me.

W-60.3. <u>**Review of Lesson #48: There is nothing to fear.**</u>
2 How safe the world will look to me when I can see **the world with the vision of Christ**! 3 **The world** will not look anything like what I **egoically** imagine I see now. 4 Everyone and everything I see **with the vision of Christ** will lean toward me to bless me. 5 I will recognize in everyone my dearest Friend. 6 What could there be to fear in a world that I have forgiven, and that has forgiven me?

W-60.4. <u>**Review of Lesson #49: God's Voice speaks to me all through the day.**</u>
2 There is not a moment in which God's Voice ceases to call on my forgiveness to save me. 3 There is not a moment in which **God's** Voice fails to direct my thoughts, guide my actions and lead my feet. 4 I am walking steadily on toward truth. 5 There is nowhere else I can go **but toward truth**, because God's Voice is the only Voice and the only Guide that has been given to **God's** Son.

W-60.5. <u>**Review of Lesson #50: I am sustained by the Love of God.**</u>
2 As I listen to God's Voice, I am sustained by **God's** Love. 3 As I open my eyes, **God's** Love lights up the world for me to see **with the vision of Christ**. 4 As I forgive, **God's** Love reminds me that **God's** Son is sinless. 5 And as I look upon the world with the vision **of Christ that God** has given me, I remember that I am **God's** Son.

Notes to Lesson # 60

Notes on Summary Lesson #60 – Review of Lessons #46-50

Lesson #46: God is the Love in which I forgive.

Lesson #47: God is the strength in which I trust.

Lesson #48: There is nothing to fear.

Lesson #49: God's Voice speaks to me all through the day.

Lesson #50: I am sustained by the Love of God.

1) Lesson 60 is the final summary lesson of this series. It covers ACIM workbook lessons #46 through 50.

Lesson 46 is God is the Love in which I forgive. We are a Oneness with God. Our forgiveness reflects God's mercy on earth.

In time and space, forgiveness is the closest that we can come to unconditional love. God never forgives because God never judges. We, unlike God, have judged. When we forgive, we let our past judgments go. We grant our brothers and sisters the freedom to be or imagine anything that they want without making them wrong or demanding retribution for their choices. By granting our neighbors the freedom to be or imagine anything they want on their own perfect learning experience, we also gain that same freedom.

If we wish to be free, we need to open the doors of the prison of our mind and let all our brothers and sisters go free. This is because until we have forgiven, we, the warden of our own mind's prison, must guard all prisoners to insure no one can escape our justice. We, their jailer, remain trapped within that prison until we are willing to forgive all. Until that moment, your mind can never forgive itself for your own perceived failures, limitations and imperfections.

2) Lesson 47 is God is the strength in which I trust. All God's power is available to me whenever I accept my true nature. I remain as God created me. My mind is the power source for all I choose to experience. What we fail to realize is our mind is so powerful that whether we think we can or we think we cannot, our mind has the power to make that into our provisional reality.

Provisional reality is how we perceive our world to be. It appears true to the dreamer. Other people who do not share that same dream see a different world. We all live in our own private world because our mind has the power to make our dreams appear real. If the mind chooses the thought system of love rather than the thought system for fear, that same mind can co-create with God and his brother. Anytime we come from limitation and fear, we make. Whenever we come from love, abundance, peace and unity, we create with the shared Mind of God. God creates, because God, being all, gives all to all. Nothing is held back.

Love is extension, whereas making involves contraction. Making is the mind's confirmation that we or the other party lack something that prevents both from being perfect, whole and complete. Making confirms the separation within our own split mind and makes the separation appear real. In both extension and making, our mind is the creative powerhouse behind the events we experience. It is this power that we need to recognize. There are no victims or victimizers. We are all willing participants on this game board of time and space.

3) Lesson 48 states there is nothing to fear. Fear arises when you follow the ego's plan for salvation. You need to choose a different plan if you are to rediscover the vision of Christ that remains hidden deep inside of you. You need to reawaken your decision-maker and follow the thought system of the Holy Spirit.

Realize that you are not trapped in the dead-end thought system of victim consciousness. The thought system of the ego is fear-based. You can never escape fear within a thought system that was designed to create and perpetuate that fear in the first place. You need to reclaim your power as the creator of your experiences and make a different choice. When you forgive yourself for your past choices and erroneous beliefs, you can hear a different voice and simply choose again. When you make different choices, you get different experiences.

Realize that God has not judged us. He has never made us wrong for our desire to be and experience the various individuated aspects of love. Differentiation was needed for us to gain that experience. God merely lets His Children play safely in the illusion of time and space. When you are satisfied that you have gained all the learning experiences that the game of separation can provide, you are then free to drop your belief in lack, limitation, guilt and fear and reclaim your divine birthright. This playschool of time and space provides the opportunity to make different choices. Only here do our false beliefs appear to be real.

Your ability to choose again is simply the acceptance of the Atonement for yourself. You accept the truth that all remain as God created them, perfect, whole and complete.

4) Lesson 49 is God's Voice speaks to me all through the day. In my big "S" Self lives the Christ consciousness which is also the home of the Holy Spirit. The Holy Spirit's thought system is my guide. We have never lost knowledge. Instead, we have simply denied that we have knowledge within us. The Christ consciousness part of our split mind has always been aware of the truth of who we really are. The certainty has not been lost. The Holy Spirit has been placed within our split minds to ensure that we remember the Truth with a capital T. The Christ consciousness part of our split mind is the seat for right mindedness. We will eventually decide to put away our toys of separation and listen to the Voice for God.

5) Lesson 50 is I am sustained by the Love of God. The Holy Spirit's thought system will reawaken my sleeping mind to the Thoughts of God. God's Love flows constantly. I can deny it, but I cannot stop that endless flow. I am sustained by this constant flow of God's Love and cannot be separate from my Source. My denial cannot change the truth of what I am. I remain part of the Oneness of All That Is. It is this One Self that is the real world because there is only that One Self.

There is nobody to fix. There is nobody to change. There is nobody to control. There is nobody to protect. There is nobody to impress. There is nobody. God is and you are that One. This is the message of the At- One-Ment.

LESSON 61

I am the light of the world.

W-61.1.Who is the light of the world except God's Son? 2 **I am the light of the world** then is merely a statement of the truth about yourself. 3 **I am the light of the world** is the opposite of a statement of pride, of arrogance, or of self-deception. 4 **I am the light of the world** does not describe the self-concept you have **egoically** made. 5 **I am the light of the world** does not refer to any of the characteristics with which you have endowed your **ego's** idols. 6 **I am the light of the world** refers to you as you were created by God. 7 **I am the light of the world** simply states the truth.

W-61.2.To the ego, today's idea **that you are the light of the world** is the epitome of self-glorification. 2 But the ego does not understand humility, mistaking **humility** for self-debasement. 3 Humility consists of accepting your role in salvation and in taking no other **egoic role**. 4 It is not humility to insist you cannot be the light of the world if **being the light of the world is the function God assigned to you**. 5 It is only arrogance that would assert this function **of being the light of the world** cannot be for you, and arrogance is always of the ego.

W-61.3.True humility requires that you accept today's idea **that you are the light of the world** because it is God's Voice which tells you **today's idea** is true. 2 **Your acceptance of today's idea that you are the light of the world** is a beginning step in accepting your real function on earth. 3 **Your acceptance of today's idea that you are the light of the world** is a giant stride toward taking your rightful place in salvation. 4 **Your acceptance of today's idea that you are the light of the world** is a positive assertion of your right to be saved, and an acknowledgment of the power that is given you to save others.

W-61.4.You will want to think about this idea **that you are the light of the world** as often as possible today. 2 **I am the light of the world** is the perfect answer to all illusions, and therefore to all temptation. 3 **This idea that you are the light of the world** brings all the images you have made about your **egoic** self to the truth, and helps you depart in peace, unburdened and certain of your **real** purpose.

W-61.5.As many practice periods as possible should be undertaken today, although each one need not exceed a minute or two. 2 **These practice periods** should begin with telling yourself:
3 I am the light of the world. 4 That is my only function. 5 That is why I am here.
6 Then think about these statements **that I am the light of the world** for a short while, preferably with your eyes closed if the situation permits. 7 Let a few related thoughts come to you, and repeat the idea **that I am the light of the world** to yourself if your mind wanders away from the central thought.

W-61.6.Be sure both to begin and end the day with a practice period. 2 Thus you will awaken with an acknowledgment of the truth about yourself, reinforce **the truth that you are the light of the world** throughout the day, and turn to sleep as you reaffirm your function and your only purpose here **which is to be the light of the world**. 3 These two practice periods may be longer than the rest if you find them helpful and want to extend **these practice periods.**

W-61.7.Today's idea **that I am the light of the world** goes far beyond the ego's petty views of what you are and what your purpose is. 2 As a bringer of salvation, this is obviously necessary. 3 This is the first of a number of giant steps we will take in the next few weeks. 4 Try today to begin to build a firm foundation for these advances. 5 You are the light of the world. 6 God has built **God's** plan for the salvation of **God's** Son on you.

Notes to Lesson # 61

I am the light of the world.

Lesson 61, I am the light of the world, is an important lesson as it lays the foundation on which salvation is based. It also clearly points out the importance of answering the first question correctly. This question is, who am I?

How you choose to answer this first question will determine what thought system, you will follow. It will determine if the major premise of the entire thought system is based on the truth or the false. Each thought system promises happiness, but only one can deliver on that promise. True happiness can only rest on the knowledge that you are perfect, whole and complete. Without that knowledge, any happiness that you experience will only be temporary. Eventually, fear will reappear and claim dominion over your life.

Because your ego is based on the belief in lack, limitation and fear, your ego is forced to argue for the limitations that come with the game token we call the body. Your ego cannot acknowledge the true power of your mind that is shared with God's Mind. Failing to recognize that your strength comes from God Itself, your ego is forced to argue that you are not perfect, whole and complete. It argues that you are separate from the One Self; that you are a sinner who has lost your divine inheritance. Your ego claims that God is not a God of Love but a vulnerable, petty God that has been hurt and now seeks revenge.

Because the ego has created a false image of God, the thought that you are part of that One Self seems to epitomize self-glorification. If someone were to say that I am God, our egoic world would deem this to be the height of arrogance. Many religions would view this as blasphemous and demand that person's crucifixion.

ACIM points out that true humility consists of accepting the truth about yourself. Not overstating or understating the facts. When you answer the initial question of "Who am I?" correctly, what the ego mistakes as arrogance is simply the acceptance of the truth of the At-One-Ment of the Mind of God.

When you argue for your limitations, you are claiming that you, an Effect of God, have the power to change God's Will. This is the height of egoic arrogance.

In typical upside down logic, your ego has mistaken its arrogance for humility. Due to your ego's claim that you are limited, it believes you are being humble when your ego is actually arguing for the reality of its belief in separation, lack, guilt and fear.

God has never judged you wanting and only sees you perfect, whole and complete. You are an extension of God Himself. You have freely chosen to experience the illusion of differentiation so that the abstract One Self can be love in form. By your being the light of the world, you experience an aspect of love that comprises part of the Mind of God. Through you, God, the abstract One Self, not only knows Itself but experiences an individuated aspect of that One Self on the concrete level.

True humility is accepting your role in God's plan for the healing of the split minded. Do not accept any role that your ego has assigned for your happiness. Your ego has judged wrongly and fails to understand who you truly are. Your only function is to be a witness for the truth. That is where your happiness lies. This is the role God has given you. You are to be a "way-shower" for those who once perceived themselves to be separate from their Source.

 In time and space, forgiveness is the tool for reawakening sleeping minds to the truth of who they really are. By following the Holy Spirit's guidance, you will light your world with the truth of God's Love.

Question: Who is more likely to be right about who you really are, God or your ego?

LESSON 62

Forgiveness is my function as the light of the world.

W-62.1.It is your forgiveness that will bring the world of darkness to the light. 2 It is your forgiveness that lets you recognize the light in which you see **with the vision of Christ**. 3 Forgiveness is the demonstration that you are the light of the world. 4 Through your forgiveness does the truth about yourself return to your memory. 5 Therefore, in your forgiveness lies your salvation.

W-62.2.Illusions about yourself and **illusions about** the world are one. 2 **Because illusions about yourself and the world are one** this is why all forgiveness is a gift to yourself. 3 Your goal is to find out who you are, having denied your Identity **as a Son of God** by attacking creation and **God**, its Creator. 4 Now you are learning how to remember the truth. 5 For this attack **on creation and God** must be replaced by forgiveness, so that thoughts of life may replace **your ego's** thoughts of death.

W-62.3.Remember that in every attack you call upon your own weakness, while each time you forgive you call upon the strength of Christ in you. 2 Do you not then begin to understand what forgiveness will do for you? 3 **Since each time you forgive you call upon the strength of Christ in you, your forgiveness** will remove all sense of weakness, strain and fatigue from your mind. 4 **Your forgiveness** will take away all fear and guilt and pain. 5 **Your forgiveness** will restore the invulnerability and power God gave His Son to your awareness.

W-62.4.Let us be glad to begin and end this day by practicing today's idea **that forgiveness is my function as the light of the world** and to use **today's idea** as frequently as possible throughout the day. 2 **Today's idea that forgiveness is my function as the light of the world** will help to make the day as happy for you as God wants you to be **happy**. 3 And **today's idea that forgiveness is my function as the light of the world** will help those around you, as well as those who seem to be far away in space and time, to share this happiness with you.

W-62.5.As often as you can, closing your eyes if possible, say to yourself today:
2 Forgiveness is my function as the light of the world. 3 I would fulfill my function that I may be happy.
4 Then devote a minute or two to considering your function and the happiness and release **your function** will bring you. 5 Let related thoughts come freely, for your heart will recognize these words, and in your mind is the awareness **that these words that forgiveness is your function as the light of the world** are true. 6 Should your attention wander, repeat the idea **that forgiveness is my function as the light of the world** and add:
7 I would remember this because I want to be happy.

Notes to Lesson # 62

Forgiveness is my function as the light of the world.

Remember that it is only yourself that you attack. When you attack, you confirm your own belief in your vulnerability. To the ego, attacking is a form of self-defense. When you forgive, you confirm your true strength lies in God and that you realize that you are part of the Oneness of the shared Mind of God. Lesson 62 states that illusions about yourself and the world are one and the same.

We need to discuss further what ACIM actually means by forgiveness. We have indicated that the world of perception is not real. It is really a figment of your mind's imagination because it is not part of the shared Mind of God. Because of this, there is a great deal of confusion about what ACIM means by the term forgiveness. Forgiveness is defined as forgiving my brother for all the wrongs that I believe he did to me that never really occurred. This definition involves a big picture concept that our egoic mind has difficulty comprehending. It references the fact that your world of perception is not the real world. Yet, to the egoic mind the events of this world are real. Are we then being asked to pretend that what my brother actually did to me in time and space has never occurred?

Actually, forgiveness revolves around your story about the event, how it took place and the purpose for the event. When you forgive, you are reframing your ego's interpretation about the events so that they more clearly align with the truth of who you really are. There are no victims and there are no victimizers. In time and space, there are only willing participants each desiring to be and experience various lessons so they and others can reawaken to the truth that no one can steal your own inner peace from you unless you choose to allow that to happen.

Forgiveness does not change past events. Instead, forgiveness does change how you interpret those events. Forgiveness is still a story. It is not reality. But forgiveness's story ends the need for any additional stories. Your ego loves to create additional stories to rationalize its belief in victims and victimizers. Your ego constantly attempts to justify what you did and why. Forgiveness merely accepts the truth that you are a spiritual being, having an earthly experience. You volunteered to be here because you sought the learning lessons that this dimension of time and space provides. The purpose for the event, not the event itself, has been changed. With this change, your inner peace is restored. That is the end of the story.

Time and space allow for the appearance of separation, differentiation and individuation. It provides a means for us to determine and demonstrate what we value and why. In time and space, we learn the following lesson.

I am not a body. I am free. I am still as God created me. Nothing sources my experience but me and nothing has the ability to rob me of my inner peace unless I choose to allow it.

When you realize this lesson, you understand that all illusions arise from your limiting beliefs about yourself and your world. Having the same cause, all illusions are one grand fantasy. You realize that when you give the gift of forgiveness to your brother, you give that same forgiveness to yourself. Through your forgiveness, you reclaim the truth of who you are. You are free to drop your belief in victims and victimizers. Forgiveness empowers you as the controlling force in your world and allows you to reclaim your divine birthright.

You realize that your world is a reflection of you. Your apparent vulnerability to the laws of time and space no longer apply to someone whose strength comes from God.

God's Law states that to give is to receive. If you seek a world at peace, be the peace that you seek in your world. Forgiveness allows the Holy Spirit to reinterpret your ego's stories. The events may or may not change. But what will change is the dropping of your belief in victim consciousness and becoming the master of your own inner peace.

Question: Although you may not be in total control of all the circumstances that surround you, you are in control of how you choose to interpret those events. Does your belief that you are a victim help or rob you of your inner peace?

LESSON 63

The light of the world brings peace to every mind through my forgiveness.

W-63.1.How holy are you who have the power to bring peace to every mind! 2 How blessed are you who can learn to recognize the means for letting this be done through you, **which is by your forgiveness**! 3 What purpose could you have that would bring you greater happiness **then to bring peace to every mind**?

W-63.2.You are indeed the light of the world with such a function **of bringing peace to every mind through your forgiveness**. 2 The Son of God looks to you for his redemption. 3 **The Son of God's redemption** is yours to give him, for **peace and redemption** belongs to you. 4 Accept no trivial purpose or meaningless desire in **redemption's** place, or you will forget your function **of bringing peace to every mind through your forgiveness** and leave the Son of God in hell. 5 **Your function of bringing peace to every mind through your forgiveness** is no idle request that is being asked of you. 6 You are being asked to accept salvation that **salvation** may be yours to give.

W-63.3.Recognizing the importance of this function **of our accepting salvation so that salvation may be ours to give and** we will be happy to remember **this function** very often today. 2 We will begin the day by acknowledging that **the light of the world brings peace to every mind through my forgiveness,** and close the day with the **same** thought **that the light of the world brings peace to every mind through my forgiveness** in our awareness. 3 And throughout the day we will repeat this **idea that the light of the world brings peace to every mind through my forgiveness** as often as we can:
4 The light of the world brings peace to every mind through my forgiveness. 5 I am the means God has appointed for the salvation of the world.

W-63.4.If you close your eyes, you will probably find it easier to let the related thoughts come to you in the minute or two that you should devote to considering this **idea that the light of the world brings peace to every mind through my forgiveness**. 2 Do not, however, wait for such an opportunity. 3 No chance should be lost for reinforcing today's idea **that the light of the world brings peace to every mind through my forgiveness**. 4 Remember that God's Son looks to you for his salvation. 5 And Who but your **big "S" Self** must be **God's** Son?

Notes to Lesson # 63

The light of the world brings peace to every mind through my forgiveness.

Lesson 63, the light of the world brings peace to every mind through my forgiveness, states how important your function is to the Sonship.

ACIM uses the term Sonship or the Son of God to represent all God created as God created it. Being a shared oneness with the Mind of God, we are all joined. Yet, in our egoic world of individuated private perception, we do not feel joined. We feel very distinct and apart from the rest of what we experience through this medium of time and space.

This makes sense since we have been brought up to believe that we are in competition with our neighbors for the limited resources that we all need to survive. Our society fosters a fear-based thought system in which the strong take from the weak. If you are to win, someone else must lose.

This thought system makes it nearly impossible for anyone to truly believe another would love them unconditionally. Most perceive that the other party must have an ulterior motive or agenda for any act of kindness that they bestow upon another. In a fear-based thought system, each party is always seeking to make a good trade. Each seeks to gain as much as possible with minimal loss of their precious resources. We are consciously or subconsciously bartering to get our perceived needs met.

When you are on your deathbed and you look back at the quality of your life, you will not measure your success or failure by how many things you have accumulated. Instead, the quality of your life will be contingent on the quality of your relationships with others. Were your relationships built on love or fear?

When we believe that we are a limited ego body in competition with other limited ego bodies for the precious resources that we both need to survive, we are incapable of giving or receiving unconditional love. In the world of the split minded, the closest you can come to unconditional love is true forgiveness.

Earlier it was stated that God cannot forgive us because God has never condemned us. The only one who can forgive us is someone that has first condemned us. Because we have falsely judged and condemned both others and ourselves as guilty sinners, we, not God, have the ability to forgive.

In time and space, true forgiveness is the realization that what I thought my brother did to harm me never took place. Being an invulnerable Child of God, I could never be harmed by another since I am protected by the Love of God.

Time and space is our playschool where we can be or imagine anything we want to experience in perfect safety. We are safe because a fantasy has no ability to change the Truth that is the Will of God. It is a dimension in which you can pretend that you are vulnerable to outside forces that are beyond your control. If you forget that you are the creator of your provisional reality, it is easy to slip into fear. Fear is False Evidence Appearing Real. When you do so, you make this false world that you imagined appear real. You now believe yourself to be a victim of the provisional reality that you created. You now believe you are separate, that you can attack and be attacked.

The vast majority follow the thought system of fear. They really believe they can harm you. Therefore, when they believe they have done so, it generates a great deal of internal blame, shame and guilt about the incident within their own mind. They seek your forgiveness because they find it difficult, if not impossible, to forgive themselves. They fear retribution and punishment for their actions.

Because they follow the ego's fear-based thought system, your willingness to forgive them for what they perceive to be the harm they have done to you is of great benefit to them. Ultimately, only they can forgive themselves for they have only attacked themselves. They hold their own karmic keys of forgiveness. But when they perceive that you have forgiven them, they are often empowered to forgive themselves.

You cannot force someone to accept the At-One-Ment for themselves. Just because you know that they are innocent of any real crime or sin, they will not necessarily believe that about themselves. But by your act of forgiveness, you open their mind to the possibility of their acceptance of your higher vision about who they really are.

When you forgive another, you accept the other without judgment or conditions. You give them the freedom to do whatever they perceive to be in their best interest without making them wrong or guilty for their decisions. You do not necessarily have to agree with their decisions. Nor is it your responsibility to prevent the other party from suffering the natural consequences of their actions on this planet. But it is important to distinguish between someone's actions carried out on the game board of time and space and the truth of who they really are.

In time and space, people make inappropriate decisions that you would not choose to follow, but their decisions to experience something different does not make them a bad person. We are all on our own perfect path. Honor and allow them to follow their path without judgment and dismiss your egoic need to make another wrong. When you do, you will be demonstrating what we have all come here to experience and learn. You will be love in form and your forgiveness will light your world.

It is easy to be a holy man on a mountain. But the real trick is learning how to accept the Love of God in a world of seeming hate and fear. That is what we are here to learn. When you forgive, you accept another without judgment or conditions. When you forgive, you demonstrate unconditional love. Through your forgiveness you illuminate someone else's dark world of perception. You help lift them to the light.

Question: When did you feel you were most loved?

Was it when you received an unexpected gift from another or was it when you felt accepted by another just the way you are without any judgment or conditions?

LESSON 64

Let me not forget my function.

W-64.1.Today's idea, **let me not forget my function,** is merely another way of saying "Let me not wander into temptation." 2 The purpose of the world you see is to obscure your function of forgiveness, and provide you with a justification for forgetting **your function of forgiveness.** 3 **The world you see through the body's eyes** is the temptation to abandon or **be separate from** God and His Son by taking on a physical appearance. **The purpose of the physical world and the body form you see is to tempt and provide evidence that justifies the ego's belief that you are separate from God and His Son.** 4 It is this **temptation of form** that the body's eyes look upon.

W-64.2.Nothing the body's eyes seem to see can be anything but a form of temptation, since this **illusion of separation from God and His Son** was the purpose of the body itself. 2 Yet we have learned that the Holy Spirit has another use for all the illusions **of separation** you have made, and therefore **the Holy Spirit** sees another purpose in **the illusion of physical appearances.** 3 To the Holy Spirit, the world is a place where you learn to forgive yourself what you think of as your sins. **Your perceived sins are based on your belief of separation and that you are not holy or whole.** 4 In this **new** perception **which follows the Holy Spirit's thought system,** the physical appearance of temptation becomes the spiritual recognition of salvation.

W-64.3.To review our last few lessons, your function here **in the illusion of physical appearances** is to be the light of the world, a function given you by God. 2 It is only the arrogance of the ego that leads you to question **your function as the light of the world,** and only the fear of the ego that induces you to regard yourself as unworthy of the task assigned to you **of being the light of the world** by God Himself. 3 The world's salvation awaits your forgiveness, because through **your forgiveness** does the Son of God escape from all illusions, and thus **escape** from all temptation. 4 The Son of God is you.

W-64.4.Only by fulfilling the function given you by God **of being the light of the world through your forgiveness** will you be happy. 2 That is because your function is to be happy by using the means by which happiness becomes inevitable **which is through your forgiveness.** 3 There is no other way **to be the light of the world except through your forgiveness.** 4 Therefore, every time you choose whether or not to fulfill your function **through forgiveness,** you are really choosing whether or not to be happy.

W-64.5.Let us remember this today **that your forgiveness lights the world and is your function and your happiness.** 2 Let us remind ourselves of **our function of being the light of the world through our forgiveness** in the morning and again at night, and all through the day as well. 3 Prepare yourself in advance for all the decisions you will make today by remembering **all your decisions about forgiveness** are all really very simple. 4 Each **decision about forgiveness** will lead to happiness or unhappiness. 5 Can such a simple decision **for forgiveness and happiness** really be difficult to make? 6 Let not the form of the decision **about forgiveness** deceive you. 7 Complexity of form does not imply complexity of content. 8 It is impossible that any decision on earth can have a content different from just this one simple choice **for forgiveness and thus, your happiness.** 9 That **this choice for forgiveness and thus, your happiness** is the only choice the Holy Spirit sees. 10 Therefore, **the choice for forgiveness and your happiness** is the only choice there is.

W-64.6.Today, then, let us practice with these thoughts:
2 Let me not forget my function **of forgiveness and thus, my happiness.**
3 Let me not try to substitute **my ego's plan of happiness** for God's **Plan.**
4 Let me forgive and be happy.
5 At least once devote ten or fifteen minutes today to reflecting on this **idea that my function of forgiveness and happiness are the same** with closed eyes. 6 Related thoughts will come to help you if you remember the crucial importance of your function **of forgiveness** to you and to the world.

W-64.7.In the frequent applications of today's idea **of not forgetting your function of forgiveness** throughout the day, devote several minutes to reviewing these thoughts, and then thinking about **not forgetting your function of forgiveness** and about nothing else. 2 This will be difficult, at first particularly, since you are not proficient in the mind discipline that **this singular focused attention** requires. 3 You may need to repeat "Let me not forget my function" quite often to help you concentrate.

W-64.8.Two forms of shorter practice periods are required. 2 At times, do the exercises with your eyes closed, trying to concentrate on the thoughts you are using. 3 At other times, keep your eyes open after reviewing the thoughts, and then look slowly and unselectively around you, telling yourself:
4 This is the world it is my function to save **through my forgiveness.**

Let me not forget my function.

Have you ever known how and what you have to do and yet, when the moment arises for you to perform, you forget what you were supposed to do?

I'm sure we have all had that experience. After the experience, we wonder how we could have been so stupid to have forgotten what we had originally intended to do in the first place. We allowed fear to take over and failed to perform as we had hoped.

You can let fear defeat you or you can see that experience as a learning lesson that tells you that additional practice is needed if you are to perform up to expectations in the future.

There is a difference between intellectually knowing what to do and actually performing those acts in a real-life situation. We admire the person who can perform under pressure and still put on a great performance completing the task at hand.

Book learning and having the actual experience of doing it are two different things. We value the actual experience of doing the task and until we have had that experience of the actual doing, there is always some uncertainty in our minds as to how we might actually perform.

In time and space, our function is forgiveness, our purposes love and our destiny is the peace of God. Lesson 64 asks that you do not forget your function of forgiveness. What will happen when you actually have an opportunity to experience a situation that requires a specific response? Will you respond with love or fear?

In time and space, you always have a choice between two thought systems. Time and space are the places where the rubber meets the road. It is where you are actually given an experience that will test whether or not you will respond with love and forgiveness or fear, judgment and anger. When you are sitting on the sidelines, you know internally what the correct response should be. We should respond with love but the real question is when the pressure is on will you be able to act lovingly, or will you slip into fear?

There is nothing wrong with playing on the game board of separation. It provides rich opportunities for us to test how we will perform in concrete situations. Time and space provides a playschool for us to actually experience being love in form in perfect safety. In this playschool, if additional time is needed to learn or have fun with a particular lesson, you simply repeat the exercise again.

You are not a bad person because you failed to perform as you had originally hoped. Your actions and choices may not have been appropriate but there was nothing wrong with you. You simply need to do it again and make different choices. In this way, you get to baby step your way up the ladder of learning. Each is on their own perfect path and each will learn the lessons needed for their reawakening in their own perfect time.

Temptation is the wish to make the illusion real. Time and space provides the opportunity to actually experience in concrete form what we know is the truth of who we are. It allows the abstract to experience being individual aspects of Itself.

The purpose of the world is to obscure your remembrance of who you are so you can test and actually experience being what you are. It provides a pressure cooker atmosphere in which you get to perform under different conditions and circumstances. It gives you better insight on what you value and why. You get to test whether you have really integrated abstract knowledge into specific performance.

When we wander into temptation, we make the illusion appear real. We forget who we really are and slip into egoic fear-based thinking. We forget that time and space is simply a game board for fun and learning and mistake the game token we call the body for ourselves.

When we make the illusion appear real, we assume the limitations of the body to be our own limits as a spiritual essence. Mistaking the body to be itself, the ego sees the purpose of the world as providing a backdrop for proving and justifying the ego's belief in sin. Sin is the belief in lack, limitation and separation. The body proves that you are limited and have needs and can be hurt. The body needs to be protected and therefore, you have a reason not to fulfill your function of forgiveness.

Forgiveness is the recognition that the illusion of sin is not real. The physical world obscures the fact that the separation is not real. This creates difficulty in remembering that this world is merely a playschool designed to allow you to test how well you have learned that you are only love.

When you are a spiritual essence having an earthly experience, you take on the appearance of a physical body. There is a great temptation to identify with that body and to believe that you are separate from God and His Son. This is why ACIM says that the purpose of the world you see is to obscure your function of forgiveness. If you knew it was merely an illusion, you would not know that you had actually absorbed the lesson of being an aspect of love in the concrete example before you.

To your big "S" Self and the Holy Spirit, the world's purpose is to allow you to test your knowledge of who you really are and really awaken to the truth. In this world, you get to learn to forgive yourself for what you think are your sins. Your sins occur anytime you buy into temptation, slip into fear and make the illusion seem real. You have raised the illusion of lack and limitation to become your provisional reality. Your function is to forgive yourself and realize that time and space have no ability to change the truth of who you are. Rather than beat yourself up, you forgive yourself. You realize it is a learning lesson and now you can simply make a different choice and listen to the Voice for Love.

In time and space, we have come to test and experience the truth of who we really are. Forgiveness reverses our temporary insanity that mistook an illusion and allowed it to become our provisional reality. In forgiveness, we dismiss the egoic story of lack, limitation, guilt and fear and replace it with love and forgiveness.

Since the purpose of time and space is to provide the learning opportunities of being individuated aspects of love in form, when we forgive, we fulfill our function. We are happy whenever we are fulfilling our function because it is the purpose of why we came here. When we forgive, we dismiss illusions and accept the truth of who we really are.

Question: Is playing a video game, the same as physically performing that same adventure in real life?

If you did not realize that it was merely a video game, but actually believed it had real life and death consequences, wouldn't that be a greater test of your abilities?

Time and space is like the second situation. You believe it has consequences and therefore, the adrenaline is flowing. Yet, in actuality, you remain perfectly safe since it is merely a game that you do not realize you are playing. You have mistaken the game to be your reality and therefore, it now becomes a real test of your ability to control your fear. How will you respond to the game of physical appearance, with love or will you forget and slip into fear?

LESSON 65

My only function is the one God gave me.

W-65.1.The idea for today **that my only function is the one God gave me** reaffirms your commitment to salvation. 2 **The idea for today that my only function is the one God gave me** also reminds you that you have no function other than that **of forgiveness and thus, your happiness**. 3 Both these **two** thoughts **that your function is forgiveness and that forgiveness is your only function** are obviously necessary for a total commitment. 4 Salvation cannot be the only purpose you hold while you still cherish other **purposes and goals**. 5 The full acceptance of salvation as your only function necessarily entails two phases. **The first is** the recognition of salvation as your function, and **the second is** the relinquishment of all the other goals you have invented for yourself.

W-65.2.This **single purpose and recognition that salvation through your forgiveness** is the only way in which you can take your rightful place among the saviors of the world. 2 This **single purpose and recognition** is the only way in which you can say and mean, "My only function is the one God gave me." 3 This **single purpose and recognition that forgiveness is your function and thus, your happiness,** is the only way in which you can find peace of mind.

W-65.3.Today, and for a number of days to follow, set aside ten to fifteen minutes for a more sustained practice period, in which you try to understand and accept what the idea for the day **that my only function is the one God gave me** really means. 2 Today's idea **that my only function is forgiveness and is the key to my happiness** offers you escape from all your perceived difficulties. 3 **Having this single purpose and recognition that salvation through your forgiveness is your happiness** places the key to the door of peace, which you have closed upon yourself, in your own hands. 4 **Having this single purpose and recognition that your forgiveness is the key to your happiness** gives you the answer to all the searching you have done since time began.

W-65.4.Try, if possible, to undertake the daily extended practice periods at approximately the same time each day. 2 Try, also, to determine this time in advance, and then adhere to **that time** as closely as possible. 3 The purpose of this **adherence to that time** is to arrange your day so that you have set apart the time for God, as well as **time** for all the trivial purposes and goals you will pursue. 4 This is part of the long-range disciplinary training your mind needs, so that the Holy Spirit can use **your mind** consistently for the purpose **the Holy Spirit** shares with you, **which is the salvation or the healing of the split minded to the truth that separation is not real and you are holy.**

W-65.5.For the longer practice period, begin by reviewing the idea for the day **that the function of forgiveness is the only function God gave me**. 2 Then close your eyes, repeat the idea **that the function of forgiveness is the only function God gave me** to yourself once again, and watch your mind carefully to catch whatever thoughts cross **your mind**. 3 At first, make no attempt to concentrate only on thoughts related to the idea for the day. 4 Rather, try to uncover each thought that arises to interfere with **the idea that the function of forgiveness is the only function God gave me**. 5 Note each **interfering thought** as it comes to you, with as little involvement or concern as possible, dismissing each **interfering thought** by telling yourself:
6 This thought reflects an **egoic fear-based** goal that is preventing me from accepting my only function.

W-65.6.After a while, interfering thoughts will become harder to find. 2 Try, however, to continue a minute or so longer, attempting to catch a few of the idle **egoic fear-based** thoughts that escaped your attention before, but do not strain or make undue effort in doing this. 3 Then tell yourself:
4 On this clean slate let my true function be written for me.
5 You need not use these exact words, but try to get the sense of being willing to have your illusions of purpose be replaced by **the** truth **of the purpose you share with the Holy Spirit. Remember that to the Holy Spirit, the world is a place where you learn to forgive yourself for what you think of as your sins. Your perceived sins are based on your belief in separation and that you are not holy or whole.**

W-65.7.Finally, repeat the idea for today **that my only function is the one God gave me** once more, and devote the rest of the practice period to trying to focus on **the** importance **of forgiveness** to you. **Focus on** the relief **that your** acceptance **of you having a single function of forgiveness** will bring you. **This having a single purpose can** resolve your conflicts once and for all. **Focus on** the extent to which you really want salvation in spite of your own foolish **egoic fear-based** ideas to the contrary.

W-65.8.In the shorter practice periods, which should be undertaken at least once an hour, use this form in applying today's idea:
2 My only function is the one God gave me. 3 I want no other **function** and I have no other **function**.
4 Sometimes close your eyes as you practice this, and sometimes keep them open and look about you. 5 It is what you see now **with the eyes of your ego** that will be totally changed when you accept today's idea completely **that your function of forgiveness is the only function God gave you.**

Notes to Lesson # 65

145

My only function is the one God gave me.

Have you ever found yourself in a stressful situation? Often stress arises when we have conflicting goals or different desired outcomes for a particular event. Goals that conflict or are mutually exclusive create stress because we cannot get everything that we believe we need and want. We need to make choices but what is the best criterion to arrive at that choice?

Lesson 65 provides some simple yet practical guidelines for your decision-maker to follow. If implemented in your life, these guidelines will clarify your mission and simplify the decision-making process while maximizing the benefits.

The first criterion is to have a single purpose. When you have a single purpose, you develop a laser focus. Your decisions and actions are based on this simple question. Will making a particular choice move me forward towards my single purpose?

Of course, in time and space we often have multiple goals in mind for each day in our lives. In this case, it is important to prioritize your goals. For example, if we were to categorize our activities, they would fit into one of three categories.

Category A is working directly on the accomplishment of a number 1 priority that aligns with our single purpose.

Category B items are needed before we can move onto a Category A item. They support or are necessary steps towards the completion of a Category A item.

Category C items may be fun and enjoyable, but these items do not support or move you closer to the completion of either a Category A or B item.

In what category do you spend most of your time?

Lesson 65 says that your real function is your reawakening to the truth of who you really are. You are God's beloved child. We need to recognize and accept this fact. We are spiritual beings having an earthly experience. Therefore, our function in time and space is to recognize that salvation is our only function. We want to end or save our world from the illusion of separation and fear.

Illusions, or the taking on of the physical appearance, have no ability to change who you really are. Your goal is to reawaken sleeping minds to the truth of who they really are. You fulfill that function through the act of forgiveness. In time and space, your function is forgiveness. Salvation will arrive when you are willing to release all from the prison of your mind and accept the At-One-Ment for yourself. When you do that, you save your world.

Lesson 65 states that once you recognize that salvation or forgiveness is the only function given to you by God, you can proceed to the next step. This second step is the relinquishment of all other goals that your ego has invented for your accomplishment. Since the ego does not know who you are, the ego is incapable of developing any plan that can achieve salvation for your world. When you realize that your function has been provided by God, the goals that your ego has invented to fix, change, protect, impress or correct can easily be dismissed.

To be the salvation for your world, you need to recognize the correct and only function you have is the one God has given you. Then you need to drop any allegiance to your ego's thought system and follow exclusively the thought system of love and forgiveness. You need to follow the Holy Spirit's Plan for salvation.

Only by doing both, can you reclaim your divine birthright as savior of your world and obtainer of the Peace of God. That is your destiny because it is the Will of God. God's Will and your will must join in that single purpose.

Question: Have you ever noticed how stressful an event becomes when you have multiple or conflicting goals for that event itself?

What criteria did you use to resolve those conflicts?

LESSON 66

My happiness and my function are one.

W-66.1.You have surely noticed an emphasis throughout our recent lessons on the connection between fulfilling your function **of forgiveness** and achieving happiness. 2 This **emphasis** is because you do not really see the connection **between your happiness and your function of forgiveness**. 3 Yet there is more than just a connection between **your happiness and your function of forgiveness**; they are the same. 4 Their forms are different, but their content is completely one.

W-66.2.The ego does constant battle with the Holy Spirit on the fundamental question of what your function is. 2 So does **the ego** do constant battle with the Holy Spirit about what your happiness is. 3 It is not a two-way battle. 4 The ego attacks and the Holy Spirit does not respond. 5 **The Holy Spirit** knows what your function is. 6 **The Holy Spirit** knows that **your function** is your happiness.

W-66.3.Today we will try to go past this wholly meaningless battle and arrive at the truth about your function. 2 We will not engage in senseless arguments about what **your function** is. 3 We will not become hopelessly involved in defining happiness and determining the means for achieving **happiness**. 4 We will not indulge the ego by listening to **the ego's** attacks on truth. 5 We will merely be glad that we can find out what truth is.

W-66.4.Our longer practice period today has as its purpose your acceptance of the fact that not only is there a very real connection between the function **of forgiveness that** God gave you and your happiness, but that **the function of forgiveness and your happiness** are actually identical. 2 God gives you only happiness. 3 Therefore, the function **God** gave you must be happiness, even if **the function of forgiveness** appears to be different. 4 Today's exercises are an attempt to go beyond these differences in appearance, and recognize a common content where **a common content** exists in truth between **happiness and forgiveness.**

W-66.5.Begin the ten-to-fifteen-minute practice period by reviewing these thoughts:
2 God gives me only happiness.
3 **God** has given my function **of forgiveness** to me.
4 Therefore my function **of forgiveness** must be happiness.
5 Try to see the logic in this sequence, even if you do not yet accept the conclusion. 6 It is only if the first two thoughts are wrong that the conclusion could be false. **The first premise is God gives me only happiness and the second premise is God has given my function to me.** 7 Let us, then, think about the **two** premises for a while, as we are practicing.

W-66.6.The first premise is that God gives you only happiness. 2 This could be false, of course, but in order **for the first premise that God gives you only happiness to be false**, it is necessary to define God as something **God** is not. 3 Love cannot give evil, and what is not happiness is evil. 4 God cannot give what **God** does not have, and **God** cannot have what **God** is not. 5 Unless God gives you only happiness, **God** must be evil. 6 And it is this definition of **God as being evil** you are believing if you do not accept the first premise **that God gives you only happiness.**

W-66.7.The second premise is that God has given you your function. 2 We have seen that there are only two parts of your **split** mind. 3 One **part of your mind** is ruled by the ego, and is made up of illusions. 4 The other **part of your mind** is the home of the Holy Spirit, where truth abides. 5 There are no other guides but **the ego and the Holy Spirit** to choose between, and no other outcomes possible as a result of your choice but the fear that the ego always engenders, and the love that the Holy Spirit always offers to replace **the fear-based thought system of the ego.**

W-66.8.Thus, it must be that your function is established by God through His Voice **which is the Holy Spirit**, or **your function** is made by the ego which you have made to replace **the Holy Spirit** 2 Which is true? 3 Unless God gave your function to you, **your function** must be the gift of the ego. 4 Does the ego really have gifts to give, being itself an illusion and offering only the illusion of gifts?

W-66.9.Think about this during the longer practice period today. **Can an illusionary ego offer anything except illusionary gifts?** 2 Think also about the many forms the illusion of your function has taken in your mind, and the many ways in which you tried to find salvation under the ego's guidance. 3 Did you find **salvation or lasting happiness**? 4 Were you happy? 5 Did **your ego's plan for salvation and happiness** bring you peace? 6 We need great honesty today. 7 Remember the outcomes fairly, and consider also whether it was ever reasonable to expect happiness from anything the ego ever proposed. 8 Yet the ego is the only alternative to the Holy Spirit's Voice.

W-66.10.You will listen to **the** madness **of your ego** or hear the truth **of the Holy Spirit**. 2 Try to make this choice **between egoic madness and the truth of the Holy Spirit** as you think about the premises on which our conclusion rests. 3 We can share in this conclusion, but in no other. **The conclusion is that my function must be my happiness.**

4 For God Himself shares **the function of your happiness** with us. 5 Today's idea **that my happiness and my function are one** is another giant stride in the perception of the same as the same, and the different as different. 6 On **the** side **of the fear-based thought system of the ego** stand all illusions. 7 All truth stands on the other side **with the Holy Spirit**. 8 Let us try today to realize that only the truth **of the Voice for God** is true.

W-66.11.In the shorter practice periods, which would be most helpful today if undertaken twice an hour, this form of the application is suggested:

2 My happiness and function are one, because God has given me both **my happiness and function**.

3 It will not take more than a minute, and probably less, to repeat these words **that my happiness and my function are the same** slowly and think about them a little while as you say them.

Notes to Lesson # 66

My happiness and my function are one.

Lesson 66 makes a distinction between content and form. I'd like to go over why ACIM wants you to become aware of the difference.

Form is the condition or circumstance that we see as the event itself. Form is used by the ego to confuse and prevent your decision-maker from realizing that two seemingly different events are actually the same reoccurring event. Because the specific conditions or people involved have changed, we do not associate the two events to actually contain the same content. They appear to be unrelated and therefore, you do not associate these apparent unrelated forms as the same events. Yet, they share the same cause.

For example: Your ego can blame Mary instead of John for failing to meet your needs while the real cause of the problem is your ego's belief that you are not worthy to be loved. Since the characters and conditions appear different, you confuse the cause to be Mary or John instead of being within your own mind and its fear-based thought system.

Content has to do with the underlying purpose or thought that created the form in the first place. It is why the event occurs. Is the purpose seen through the eyes of love or fear? The content or purpose that you assign to the form is always from either the fear-based thought system of the ego or the Holy Spirit's thought system based on love and forgiveness. The content either witnesses to the truth or the false.

Physical appearances are designed to obscure or confuse your decision-maker's ability to distinguish between form and content. It tries to transform a black and white situation into numerous shades of gray. Certainty is lost when we lose sight of the content or purpose and get caught up with the drama of the form.

My happiness and my function are one because they are the same. They are different forms but the content is the same. Forgiveness recognizes my sinlessness and supports the truth of who I am. My happiness comes from recognizing and being who I truly am. I am happy when I am fulfilling my function. Both my happiness and forgiveness, witness for the truth of who I am.

God being only love gives me only happiness. The content for truth is that my will and God's Will are the same. The content for the false is that my will and God's Will are not the same.

My ego confuses a form, the physical body, for the content of who I really am. Since the ego believes my will is different from God's Will yet God's Will is only my happiness, is it any wonder why the ego does not know what will make me happy?

Question: God's Will is for you to be happy. Would God have created you a sinner?

Or,

Would God have created you, perfect, whole and complete?

Remember: Sin is the belief in lack, limitation and fear.

Question: Your ego confuses form, the physical body, with content, which is your spiritual essence. Mistaking form for content, is it any wonder that all your ego's plans for your happiness fail**?**

LESSON 67

Love created me like itself.

W-67.1.Today's idea **that Love created me like Itself** is a complete and accurate statement of what you are **which is only Love**. 2 This **idea that Love created you like Itself** is why you are the light of the world. 3 This **idea that Love created you like Itself** is why God appointed you as the world's savior. 4 This is why the Son of God looks to you for his salvation. 5 **The Son of God** is saved by what you are **which is only Love**. 6 We will make every effort today to reach this truth about you, and to realize fully, if only for a moment, that **Love created you like Itself** is the truth.

W-67.2.In the longer practice period, we will think about your reality **that Love created you like Itself** and **Love's** wholly unchanged and unchangeable nature. 2 We will begin by repeating this truth about you **that Love created you like Itself** and then spend a few minutes adding some relevant thoughts, such as:

3 Holiness created me holy.

4 Kindness created me kind.

5 Helpfulness created me helpful.

6 Perfection created me perfect.

7 Any attribute which is in accord with **a God of Love** as **God** defines Himself is appropriate for use. 8 We are trying today to undo your **ego's fear-based** definition of God and replace **the ego's false fearful god of judgment** with **God's** Own **definition of Itself which is only Love**. 9 We are also trying to emphasize that you are part of **a Loving God's** definition of Himself.

W-67.3.After you have gone over several such related thoughts, try to let all thoughts drop away for a brief preparatory interval, and then try to reach past all your images and preconceptions about yourself to the truth in you **that God created you like Itself**. 2 If love created you like itself, this **big "S"** Self must be in you. 3 And somewhere in your mind **this big "S" Self** is there for you to find.

W-67.4.You may find it necessary to repeat the idea for today **that Love created you like Itself** from time to time to replace distracting thoughts. 2 You may also find that this is not sufficient, and that you need to continue adding other thoughts related to the truth about yourself **being created only with the attributes of love, itself**. 3 Yet perhaps you will succeed in going past that, and through the interval of thoughtlessness to the awareness of a blazing light in which you recognize yourself as love created you. 4 Be confident that you will do much today to bring that awareness nearer, whether you feel you have succeeded or not.

W-67.5.It will be particularly helpful today to practice the idea for the day **that Love created you like Itself** as often as you can. 2 You need to hear the truth about yourself as frequently as possible, because your mind is so preoccupied with false **egoic fear-based** self-images. 3 Four or five times an hour, and perhaps even more, it would be most beneficial to remind yourself that love created you like itself. 4 Hear the truth about yourself in this **statement that Love created you like Itself**.

W-67.6.Try to realize in the shorter practice periods that this is not your tiny, solitary voice that tells you **that Love created you like Itself**. 2 This is the Voice for God, reminding you of your Father and of your **big "S"** Self. 3 This is the Voice of truth, **the Holy Spirit**, replacing everything that the ego tells you about yourself with the simple truth about the Son of God. 4 You were created by Love like Itself.

Notes to Lesson # 67

Love created me like itself.

The physical world was designed to confuse us. It presents false evidence that we assume to be true. In the physical world, we have two different parents and the children are not carbon copies of their parents.

Therefore, one might question the idea that like begets like. Yet, even in the physical world where there is only one parent, like does appear to produce like. When the sheep Dolly was cloned, all Dolly's offspring appeared to be replicas of their single-parent, Dolly.

ACIM states that God is only unconditional Love. Unconditional love does not hold anything back. When God creates, God being all, gives all to all. Creation is the extension of the Oneness of All That Is. There is no separation. There remains one holographic Mind of God.

A hologram is unlike a photograph. If you cut a photograph into two parts, each part would only represent half of the original picture. Contrast this with a hologram of a rose. If you were to cut the hologram into numerous parts and shine a laser beam through any part, the image of the whole rose would appear. In a true hologram, all parts contain the whole and the whole is contained in each part. The Mind of God is holographic in nature and cannot be separated into parts. It is an indivisible One Self.

God being love can only extend love. Separation can only appear to be real within the imagination of the deluded mind that perceives itself to be separate and different from its source. The ego is such a delusional mind.

A previous lesson stated that you cannot conceive of your creator being different than yourself. Because of this, your ego has created a false God in its own distorted egoic image.

Because the ego believes that giving requires sacrifice, the ego does not believe God would give all to us. The ego believes that if God were like itself, God would hold something back. This is basically due to the ego's belief in separation. The ego denies that Love or God created you like itself because your ego lives in fear.

Fear is love's opposite. They cannot coexist. The ego's thought system is fear-based. Because the ego only gives to get, it cannot conceive of a creator different from itself. Your ego denies your divine birthright. Due to its belief in separation, your ego must argue that either a God of Love does not exist or did not create you like Itself. The third alternative is that you had offended God and lost your divine birthright.

Because your ego projects its own fear-based thoughts outside its own mind, it perceives a God in its own fear-based image. The real God of Love is transformed into a petty egoic judgmental god that can be hurt and seek revenge. The ego fears this god of wrath and, therefore, has imagined a world where it can hide from this god's punishment.

Because the ego believes God is something to be feared, it argues for the need to keep the child separate from its father. It argues for the rightness in its belief that God cannot be only love at the cost of your happiness. To the ego, your safety is contingent on maintaining your distance from the god that your ego fears.

Question: Many religions including the Western religions of Judaism, Christianity and Islam all support the idea that God should be feared. You need to be aware of this fact and challenge that viewpoint.

Did a Loving God create you or did your ego create a fearful God?

LESSON 68

Love holds no grievances.

W-68.1.You who were created by love like itself can hold no grievances and know your **true big "S" Self**. 2 To hold a grievance is to forget who you **really** are. 3 To hold a grievance is to see yourself as a body. 4 To hold a grievance is to let the ego rule your mind and to condemn the body to death. 5 Perhaps you do not yet fully realize just what holding grievances does to your mind. 6 **Holding grievances** seems to split you off from your Source and make you unlike **God, your Source**. 7 **Holding grievances** makes you believe that **God** is like what you **egoically** think you have become, for no one can conceive of his Creator as unlike himself.

W-68.2.Shut off from your **big "S" Self**, which remains aware of Its likeness to Its Creator, your **big "S"** Self seems to sleep. While **your big "S" Self seems to sleep, it is** the egoic part of your **split** mind that weaves illusions in **your mind's** sleep **so that your egoic mind** appears to be awake. 2 Can all this **misperception** arise from holding grievances? 3 Oh, yes! 4 For he who holds grievances denies he was created by love. And **one who denies he was created by love holds grievances against** his Creator, **Who** has become fearful in his **ego's** dream of hate. 5 Who can dream of hatred and not fear God?

W-68.3.It is as sure that those who hold grievances will redefine God in their own **ego's** image **of lack, limitation, judgment and separation,** as it is certain that God created **His Children** like Himself, and defined **His Children as** part of **God, their Creator.** 2 It is as sure that those who hold grievances will suffer guilt, as it is certain that those who forgive will find peace. 3 It is as sure that those who hold grievances will forget who they are, as it is certain that those who forgive will remember **who they really are.**

W-68.4.Would you not be willing to relinquish your grievances if you believed all this were so? 2 Perhaps you do not think you can let your grievances go. 3 **Your ability to let your grievances go,** however, is simply a matter of motivation. 4 Today we will try to find out how you would feel without **your grievances.** 5 If you succeed even by ever so little **in letting your grievances go**, there will never be a problem in **lack of** motivation **to forgive** ever again.

W-68.5.Begin today's extended practice period by searching your mind for those against whom you hold what you regard as major grievances. 2 Some of these major grievances will be quite easy to find. 3 Then think of the seemingly minor grievances you hold against those you like and even think you love. 4 It will quickly become apparent that there is no one against whom you do not cherish grievances of some sort. 5 This **holding of grievances** has left you alone in all the universe in your perception of yourself.

W-68.6.Determine now to see all these people **that you held a grievance against** as friends. 2 Say to them all, thinking of each one in turn as you do so:
3 I would see you **who I held a grievance against** as my friend, that I may remember you are part of me and come to know my **big "S"** Self.
4 Spend the remainder of the practice period trying to think of yourself as completely at peace with everyone and everything, safe in a world that protects you and loves you, and that you love in return. 5 Try to feel safety surrounding you, hovering over you and holding you up. 6 Try to believe, however briefly, that nothing can harm you in any way. 7 At the end of the practice period tell yourself:
8 Love holds no grievances. 9 When I let all my grievances go I will know I am perfectly safe.

W-68.7.The short practice periods should include a quick application of today's idea **that love holds no grievances** in this form, whenever any thought of grievance arises against anyone, physically present or not:
2 Love holds no grievances. 3 Let me not betray my **big "S"** Self.
4 In addition, repeat the idea **that love holds no grievances** several times an hour in this form:
5 Love holds no grievances. 6 I would wake to my **big "S"** Self by laying all my grievances aside and wakening in **God.**

Notes to Lesson # 68

Love holds no grievances.

Lesson 68, love holds no grievances, is a contradiction of almost everything we have been taught about love through our ego's fear-based thought system. The ego does not know what love is and therefore, most of our beliefs about love are upside down.

Your ego believes you are the body and the body is you. Believing the separation is a fact, it sees the world full of lack. To the ego, you are a limited ego body in competition with other limited ego bodies. Life is a zero-sum game. For every winner, there must be a loser. You need to take from someone in order to get what you want. This is the dog eat dog world of our fear-based society.

Because of this, it becomes imperative for you to form alliances with others so that working together, the group will have a better chance at obtaining the limited resources that each needs for their survival. You are the body and the body is you and with that belief you must accept all limitations that come with the game token you call your physical body. Your world is a fearful place.

But this belief has strange consequences when it comes to love. Rather than unconditional love, egoic love becomes conditional love at its best. I will love you as long as you fulfill your part of the bargain. Each party is seeking a good trade. You wish to maximize what you gain from the relationship while minimize its costs. Because love is conditional, it gives you the right to make demands on the other party.

Egoic love says that you have the right, need and even perhaps the duty to fix, change, control, protect and impress the other party because you love them. If they fail to perform to your conditions, you can withdraw your love, punish them or demand that they fulfill their contract. If all the above fail, you have the right to leave and seek a better deal. This is all done in the name of love because you know what is really in the other party's best interests and they are too stupid to see things your way.

Our ego even teaches that if you love someone, you may be required to hate some third party that you have never known because that is what love does. We are taught that we are to love our friends and hate their enemies.

Because of our ego's belief in separation, our fear-based thought system teaches that you can hold a grievance against one party and that your hatred does not spillover into your other relationship or how you treat yourself. You are told each person is autonomous and therefore, you can pick and choose who is the recipient of your wrath.

This could not be further from the truth. When you attack another, you attack yourself. Only those who assume that they are separate bodies and vulnerable to attack believe that they can harm another. Yet, by doing so, they admit, at least subconsciously, that they are vulnerable and can be hurt. The invulnerable have no need to defend themselves nor to attack another.

All grievances are based on the belief in separation. If you believed you were the shared Oneness of All That Is, what could there be outside of yourself to attack? You cannot hold a grievance against another and still hold that you are part of that One Self. These concepts are mutually exclusive. When you hold a grievance against any person, place or thing, you are secretly holding a grievance against your Creator. You cannot claim God is only love and hate one of God's creations. As long as you believe that something has harmed you, which is why you are holding the grievance in the first place, you will believe even a God of only love has let you down.

You cannot conceive of a God being unlike yourself. The world you see is a world of perception, not a fact. Your world is a reflection of your state of mind. If you see yourself as limited and vulnerable, you will be a big egoic judging machine. Being judgmental, you will redefine your God to fit your ego's fearful image.

When you hold a grievance, you have allowed your ego to rule your world. You have accepted your ego's belief that you are a separate vulnerable body. You believe the game of separation to be your reality and therefore, it does become your provisional reality. To hold a grievance means that you are denying you are created by a God of Love. Since your own belief in limitation has transformed a God of Love into your ego's image, your world, your God and your life will all mirror the fear and hate you harbor within your own split mind.

Question: When you hold a grievance against somebody, do you really believe it has no impact on your own inner peace?

LESSON 69

My grievances hide the light of the world in me.

W-69.1.No one can look upon what your grievances conceal. 2 Because your grievances are hiding the light of the world in you, everyone stands in darkness, and you **stand** beside **your brother in darkness**. 3 But as the veil of your grievances is lifted, you are released with **your brother**. 4 Share your salvation now with **your brother** who stood beside you when you were in hell. 5 He is your brother in the light of the world that saves you both.

W-69.2.Today let us make another real attempt to reach the light in you. 2 Before we undertake this **attempt to reach the light in you** in our more extended practice period, let us devote several minutes to thinking about what we are trying to do. 3 We are literally attempting to get in touch with the salvation of the world. 4 We are trying to see past the veil of darkness that keeps **the salvation of the world** concealed. 5 We are trying to let the veil **of darkness** be lifted, and to see the tears of God's Son disappear in the sunlight.

W-69.3.Let us begin our longer practice period today with the full realization that this **idea that my grievances hide the light of the world in me** is so, and with real determination to reach what is dearer to us than all else. 2 Salvation is our only need. 3 There is no other purpose here, and no other function to fulfill **but salvation**. 4 Learning salvation is our only goal. 5 Let us end the ancient search **for salvation** today by finding the light in us, and holding **the light in us** up for everyone who searches with us to look upon and rejoice.

W-69.4.Very quietly now, with your eyes closed, try to let go of all the **egoic** content that generally occupies your consciousness. 2 Think of your mind as a vast circle, surrounded by a layer of heavy, dark clouds. 3 You can see only the clouds because you seem to be standing outside the circle and quite apart from **the circle**.

W-69.5.From where you stand, you can see no reason to believe there is a brilliant light hidden by the clouds. 2 The clouds seem to be the only reality. 3 They seem to be all there is to see. 4 Therefore, you do not attempt to go through **the clouds** and past them, which is the only way in which you would be really convinced of their lack of substance. 5 We will make this attempt **to go through and past the clouds** today.

W-69.6.After you have thought about the importance of what you are trying to do for yourself and the world, try to settle down in perfect stillness, remembering only how much you want to reach the light in you today,–now! 2 Determine to go past the clouds. 3 Reach out and touch **the clouds** in your mind. 4 Brush **the clouds** aside with your hand; feel **the clouds** resting on your cheeks and forehead and eyelids as you go through **the clouds**. 5 Go on; clouds cannot stop you.

W-69.7.If you are doing the exercises properly, you will begin to feel a sense of being lifted up and carried ahead. 2 Your little effort and small determination call on the power of the universe to help you, and God Himself will raise you from darkness into light. 3 You are in accord with **God's** Will. 4 You cannot fail because your will is **God's** Will.

W-69.8.Have confidence in your Father today, and be certain that **God** has heard you and answered you. 2 You may not recognize **God's** answer yet, but you can indeed be sure that **God's answer** is given you and you will yet receive **God's answer**. 3 Try, as you attempt to go through the clouds to the light, to hold this confidence in your mind **that God's answer is given you.** 4 Try to remember that you are at last joining your will to God's **Will.** 5 Try to keep the thought clearly in mind that what you undertake with God must succeed. 6 Then let the power of God work in you and through you, that **God's** Will and your **will** be done.

W-69.9.In the shorter practice periods, which you will want to do as often as possible in view of the importance of today's idea to you and your happiness, remind yourself that your grievances are hiding the light of the world from your awareness. 2 Remind yourself also that you are not searching for **the light** alone, and that you do know where to look for **the light is within you**. 3 Say, then:
4 My grievances hide the light of the world in me. 5 I cannot see what I have hidden. 6 Yet I want to let **what I have hidden** be revealed to me, for my salvation and the salvation of the world.
7 Also, be sure to tell yourself:
8 If I hold this grievance the light of the world will be hidden from me,
if you are tempted to hold anything against anyone today.

Notes to Lesson # 69

My grievances hide the light of the world in me.

Lesson 69 states, my grievances hide the light of the world in me. At this time, I would like to also call your attention to the last few lines of this same lesson which says that if I hold this grievance, the light of the world will be hidden from me.

The difference between these two lines is subtle. One is referencing that grievances hide the truth of your big" "S" Self from being seen by your outer world. The second, references the fact that when you hold a grievance, you will not be able to see or recognize the light that is actually shining from your outer world upon you.

The 20th century has been called the age of Freud. It was in the 20th century that science actually started to explore in depth the inner workings of the human mind. Although much of Freud's work has been discredited, Freud did discover the psychological coping strategy of projection.

When the human mind is overloaded with blame, shame and guilt, our mind attempts to get rid of this guilt by projecting its own internal guilt, blame and shame into its external world. In this way, the human mind hopes to rid itself of the problem. It now sees its external world as the source of the problem and therefore, it is better able to cope with its own internal blame, shame and guilt that still remain hidden deep within its subconscious mind.

In a less extreme example of projection, we see people blaming others for the poor results that they experience in their lives. They claim they are victims of outside forces that are beyond their control. Projection allows them to claim it is not their fault. They no longer have to take responsibility for the perceived failures in their own lives.

Projection actually forms the basis for our world of perception. This is why both physiologists and psychologists tell us that our physical senses are not objective cameras to our world. Instead, our senses are subjective thought confirmation devices for our inner mind's beliefs.

Psychologists now realize that projection is not only involved with negative emotions but also with positive ones. I am sure there are some people you like to be around because they seem to give off positive vibrations. There are others you prefer to avoid because they seem to drain your energy and bring you down.

Your world is a reflection of your own inner mind. This is why Einstein said the most important thing for a person to determine for himself is whether the universe is a supportive or non-supportive place. Depending upon their answer, Einstein said, they would either be optimistic or pessimistic and that would make all the difference in their life.

The world you see outside of you is a projection of your inner beliefs. The law of perception that rules our mental world states the following.

If fear holds a place in your heart, you will look upon a world full of conflict, struggle, fear and hate. If love only rules your heart, you will see a world full of mercy, love and forgiveness.

Your grievances block others from recognizing the truth of your big "S" Self. Instead, what others see is a projection of your ego's little "s" self. Perceiving yourself to be not perfect, whole and complete, your egoic mind projects its own self-image of lack, limitation and fear into its outer world. Naturally, lack, limitation and fear are what you see in your world and what your world sees coming from you.

When you recognize the truth of your big "S" Self, your mind will project that new positive self-image and your world will reflect back the positive qualities of love, forgiveness and allowance that flow from your true loving nature.

The outer world is a reflection of your inner mind. Do not let your grievances hide your light from the world. Do not let your grievances prevent you from seeing the love of God flowing from your outer world into your inner being.

Your grievances are illusionary clouds that are blocking the light from within and without. In the real world, there is only light. Darkness is the illusion. Your grievances are the darkness that prevents you from recognizing that the real world is only love's light.

Question: Do you know people that you feel energized by and others that seem to bring you down?

Question: Are these same people holding an optimistic or pessimistic view of their world?

Question: When people have been around you, do they feel uplifted and energized by your presence or are they drained?

LESSON 70

My salvation comes from me.

W-70.1.All temptation is nothing more than some form of the basic temptation not to believe the idea for today **that my salvation comes from me.** 2 Salvation seems to come from anywhere except from you. 3 So, too, does the source of guilt **seem to come from anywhere except from you.** 4 You see neither guilt nor salvation as in your own **split** mind and nowhere else. 5 When you realize that all guilt is solely an invention of your **own egoic** mind, you also realize that guilt and salvation must be in the same place. 6 In understanding **that the source of both guilt and salvation must be in your own mind,** you are saved.

W-70.2.The seeming cost of accepting today's idea **that your salvation comes from you** is this: It means that nothing outside yourself can save you; nothing outside yourself can give you peace. 2 But **today's idea that your salvation comes from you** also means that nothing outside yourself can hurt you, or disturb your peace or upset you in any way. 3 Today's idea **that your salvation comes from you** places you in charge of the universe, where you belong because of what you are **which is God's beloved Child.** 4 **Being God's beloved Child** is not a role that can be partially accepted. 5 And you must surely begin to see that accepting **today's idea that your salvation comes from you** is **your** salvation **because you are God's beloved Child.**

W-70.3.It may not, however, be clear to you why the recognition that guilt is in your own mind entails the realization that salvation is there **in your own mind** as well. 2 God would not have put the remedy for the sickness **of guilt** where **the remedy** cannot help. 3 **Placing the remedy where it cannot be found** is the way your **egoic** mind has worked, but hardly **the way God's loving Mind works.** 4 **God** wants you to be healed, so **God** has kept the Source of healing where the need for healing lies. **Your own mind needs to be healed because that is the source for all guilt.**

W-70.4.You have tried to do just the opposite, making every attempt, however distorted and fantastic it might be, to separate healing from the sickness for which **healing** was intended, and thus keep the sickness. 2 Your purpose was to ensure that healing did not occur. 3 God's purpose was to ensure that **healing** did **occur.**

W-70.5.Today we practice realizing that God's Will and our **will** are really the same in this **desire to have yourself be healed.** 2 God wants us to be healed, and we do not really want to be sick, because **sickness** makes us unhappy. 3 Therefore, in accepting the idea for today **that my salvation comes from me**, we are really in agreement with God. 4 **God** does not want us to be sick. 5 Neither do we **want to be sick.** 6 **God** wants us to be healed. 7 So do we **want to be healed.**

W-70.6.We are ready for two longer practice periods today, each of which should last some ten to fifteen minutes. 2 We will, however, still let you decide when to undertake **these two practice periods.** 3 We will follow this practice for a number of lessons, and it would again be well to decide in advance when would be a good time to lay aside for each of **these two practice periods**, and then adhering to your own decisions as closely as possible.

W-70.7.Begin these practice periods by repeating the idea for today **that my salvation comes from me**, adding a statement signifying your recognition that salvation comes from nothing outside of you. 2 You might put it this way:
3 My salvation comes from me. 4 **My salvation** cannot come from anywhere else.
5 Then devote a few minutes, with your eyes closed, to reviewing some of the external places where you have looked for salvation in **your egoic** past;–in other people, in possessions, in various situations and events, and in self-concepts that **your ego** sought to make real. 6 Recognize that **your salvation** is not there **outside of you,** and tell yourself:
7 My salvation cannot come from any of these things. 8 My salvation comes from me and only from me.

W-70.8.Now we will try again to reach the light in you, which is where your salvation is. 2 You cannot find **the light** in the clouds that surround the light, and it is in **the clouds** you have been looking for **your salvation.** 3 **The light that is your salvation** is not there. 4 **Your salvation** is past the clouds and in the light beyond. 5 Remember that you will have to go through the clouds before you can reach the light. 6 But remember also that you have never found anything in the cloud patterns **your egoic split mind** imagined that endured, or that you **really** wanted.

W-70.9.Since all **of the ego's** illusions of salvation have failed you, surely you do not want to remain in the clouds, looking vainly for idols there, when you could so easily walk on into the light of real salvation. 2 Try to pass the clouds by whatever means appeals to you. 3 If it helps you, think of me, **Jesus, or the Christ consciousness within you,** holding your hand and leading you. 4 And I assure you this will be no idle fantasy.

W-70.10.For the short and frequent practice periods today, remind yourself that your salvation comes from you, and nothing but your own **egoic** thoughts can hamper your progress. 2 You are free from all external interference. 3 You are in charge of your salvation. 4 You are in charge of the salvation of the world. 5 Say, then:
6 My salvation comes from me. 7 Nothing outside of me can hold me back. 8 Within me is the world's salvation and my own **salvation.**

Notes to Lesson # 70

My salvation comes from me.

Lesson 70, my salvation comes from me, is a pivotal lesson in this course. I would like to draw your attention to the second paragraph, which I will quote below based upon the dummies format previously discussed. The second paragraph states the following:

W-70.2.The seeming cost of accepting today's idea **that your salvation comes from you** is this: It means that nothing outside yourself can save you; nothing outside yourself can give you peace. 2 But **today's idea that your salvation comes from you** also means that nothing outside yourself can hurt you, or disturb your peace or upset you in any way. 3 Today's idea **that your salvation comes from you** places you in charge of the universe, where you belong because of what you are **which is God's beloved Child**. 4 **Being God's beloved Child** is not a role that can be partially accepted. 5 And you must surely begin to see that accepting **today's idea that your salvation comes from you** is **your** salvation **because you are God's beloved Child.**

It is only from your own split mind's misperceptions that you need to be saved. Your split mind is the source for all the sin, guilt and fear that seems to torment you. Since the source of the problem is your own split mind, the healing must take place within your own mind's belief system.

Due to your ego's belief in separation, your split mind perceives that both the source of your guilt and your salvation must be somewhere outside of your own mind. This is because the ego believes that Love did not create you like Itself. Thus, you are not perfect, not whole and very incomplete. You are justified in holding grievances against God and His world.

Your ego perceives a world of victims and victimizers. It teaches that there are outside forces that are beyond your control. Because of this, your ego is reactive rather than proactive. The ego's focus is fear-based and concentrates on resisting what it perceives to be the negative forces of God's world. Your ego refuses to take responsibility for the world it made up to support its own beliefs. Your ego projects its own guilt upon God and blames God for the mess it made.

Lack rules your egoic thoughts. Your egoic mind does not want to be sick and therefore, its focus is on resisting illness. Yet, the laws of the universe state that what you resist persists. By focusing on the negative, our egoic mind actually attracts the very item that it is trying to avoid. Now, your ego must battle against the negative forces that its negative thinking actually attracts into its world.

Because our egoic thought system is fear-based, our egoic mind's focus is on resisting the things it does not want. Rather than placing its attention on being healthy, the ego does not want to be sick. The universe does not understand the negation of an idea. When you understand how the laws of the universe work, you will realize that your ego's fear-based thinking can only result in you experiencing poor health.

Due to the scope of this class, we cannot go into detail about the law of attraction that was the focus of the movie and book called "the Secret." However, why the law of attraction does not work is covered in great detail in my course on beliefs, the creation cycle and the law of deliberate creation.

I would also like to call your attention to the fact that Lesson 70 specifically states that my salvation comes from me. Note that it does not say my brother's salvation or all salvation comes from me. There are a number of reasons for this.

On a theoretical level, the idea of separation is not real and therefore, no one needs to be saved because no one was ever lost. Your divine inheritance's existence can be denied but it cannot be lost. Therefore, there is nobody to save. Since there is no separation, there really is nobody. There is only the One Self.

But on a more practical level, the reason that you cannot save your brother is because that would mean that your brother is not the controller of his own mind. It would give rise to the belief that a Son of God is limited. There would have to be forces that are beyond his control and that would make the separation real. This can never be the case. We share the holographic Mind of God.

Since a fantasy has no ability to change reality, your ego's misperceptions only need to be corrected in the delusional mind that was the source for the misperception to begin with. Since your mind is the source, your split mind is where the healing must take place.

All temptation comes from the belief that your salvation can be found somewhere outside your mind. This is impossible since your own split mind is the source for both your salvation and your guilt. Your big "S" Self or the Holy Spirit has been placed within your mind by God's Will. The Holy Spirit will insure that this healing takes place.

The ego tells us to look everywhere but where the problem and answer resides. Both the problem and answer can only be found within the mind that thought it. The Holy Spirit knows the answer and resides within our own mind. This answer cannot be lost, but merely not recognized.

When you go within and silence the voice for fear, you will realize that guilt is solely an invention of your fear-based thought system. You will also realize that you alone hold the key to your salvation. Since your sleeping mind invented the illusion of sin, guilt and fear, you merely need to wake up and follow your inner Voice for God and your illusions will dissolve before the truth of who you really are. You merely reclaim your divine inheritance and accept the At-One-Ment for yourself.

Question: Today's idea states that nothing outside yourself can hurt you or disturb your peace or upset you in any way. This idea places you in charge of your universe where you belong. You alone decide which thought system you will follow. Based on that choice, your inner world will generate the outer world you perceive.

Does your outer world reflect an inner world of peace, allowance, love and forgiveness?

If not, you are following the voice for fear. You need to listen to the Voice for Truth that resides within your own split mind.

LESSON 71

Only God's plan for salvation will work.

W-71.1.You may not realize that the ego has set up a plan for salvation in opposition to God's **plan for salvation**. 2 It is **the ego's** plan **for salvation** in which you believe. 3 Since **the ego's** plan **for salvation** is the opposite of God's plan **for salvation**, you also believe that to accept God's **plan** in place of the ego's **plan** is to be damned. 4 This sounds preposterous, of course. 5 Yet after we have considered just what the ego's plan **for salvation** is, perhaps you will realize that, however preposterous it may be, you do believe **the ego's plan for salvation will work and that God's plan for salvation would result in your damnation.**

W-71.2.The ego's plan for salvation centers around holding grievances. 2 **The ego's plan for salvation** maintains that, if someone else spoke or acted differently, if some external circumstance or event were changed, you would be saved. 3 Thus, **according to the ego's plan for salvation** the source of salvation is constantly perceived as outside yourself. 4 Each grievance you hold is a declaration, and an assertion in which you believe, that says, "If this were different, I would be saved." 5 **According to the ego's plan for salvation,** the change of mind necessary for salvation is thus demanded of everyone and everything except yourself.

W-71.3.The role assigned to your own mind in **the ego's** plan **for salvation**, then, is simply to determine what, other than **the ego** itself, must change if you are to be saved. 2 According to this insane **ego's** plan, any perceived source of salvation is acceptable provided that it will not work. 3 This ensures that the fruitless search will continue, for the illusion persists that, although this hope **of looking for the source of salvation outside of you own mind where it cannot be found** has always failed, there is still grounds for hope in other places and in other things that the ego **has not yet tried**. 4 **According to the ego,** another person will yet serve better; another situation will yet offer success. **Your ego continues to insist that there is something outside your own mind that is the source for your salvation. Therefore, you do not have to change.**

W-71.4.Such is the ego's plan for your salvation. 2 Surely you can see how **insisting that there is something outside your own mind that must change for your salvation** is in strict accord with the ego's basic doctrine, "Seek but do not find." 3 For what could more surely guarantee that you will not find salvation than to channelize all your efforts in searching for **salvation outside your own mind** where **salvation** is not?

W-71.5.God's plan for salvation works simply because, by following **God's** direction, you seek for salvation **within your own mind** where **salvation** is **to be found**. 2 But if you are to succeed, as God promises you will, you must be willing to seek only **within your own mind where salvation can be found**. 3 Otherwise **if you also attempt to follow the ego's plan of seeking salvation outside of your mind where it cannot be found**, your purpose is divided and you will attempt to follow two plans for salvation that are diametrically opposed in all ways. 4 The result **of trying to follow two opposing plans for your salvation** can only bring confusion, misery and a deep sense of failure and despair.

W-71.6.How can you escape all this **confusion of trying to follow two opposing plans for your salvation**? 2 Very simply. 3 The idea for today **that only God's plan for salvation will work** is the answer. 4 Only God's plan for salvation will work. 5 There can be no real conflict about this, because there is no possible alternative to God's plan that will save you. 6 **God's plan for salvation** is the only plan that is certain in its outcome. 7 **God's plan for salvation** is the only plan that must succeed.

W-71.7.Let us practice recognizing this certainty **that only God's plan for salvation will work** today. 2 And let us rejoice that there is an answer to what seems to be a conflict with no resolution possible. 3 All things are possible to God. 4 Salvation must be yours because of **God's** plan **for your salvation** which cannot fail.

W-71.8.Begin the two longer practice periods for today by thinking about today's idea **that only God's plan for salvation will work**, and realizing that it contains two parts, each making equal contribution to the whole. 2 **The first part is** God's plan for your salvation will work, and **the second part is** other plans will not **work**. 3 Do not allow yourself to become depressed or angry at the second part **that your ego's plans will not work for** it is inherent in the first **part that states only God's plan will work**. 4 And in the first **part that states only God's plan will work** is your full release from all your own ego's insane attempts and mad proposals to free yourself. 5 **All the ego's plans for salvation** have led to depression and anger; but God's plan will succeed. 6 **God's plan** will lead to release and joy.

W-71.9.Remembering this **that only God's plan for salvation will work.** Let us devote the remainder of the extended practice periods to asking God to reveal His plan to us. 2 Ask **God** very specifically:
3 What would You have me do?
4 Where would You have me go?
5 What would You have me say, and to whom?
6 Give **God** full charge of the rest of the practice period, and let **God** tell you what needs to be done by you in **God's** plan for your salvation. 7 **God** will answer in proportion to your willingness to hear **God's** Voice. 8 Refuse not to hear **God's Voice which is the Holy Spirit inside your mind.** 9 The very fact that you are doing the exercises proves that you have some willingness to listen. 10 This **willingness to listen** is enough to establish your claim to God's answer **from the Holy Spirit.**

W-71.10.In the shorter practice periods, tell yourself often that God's plan for salvation, and only **God's plan** will work. 2 Be alert to all temptation to hold grievances today, and respond to **all grievances** with this form of today's idea:
3 Holding grievances is the opposite of God's plan for salvation. 4 And only **God's** plan will work.
5 Try to remember today's idea **that only God's plan for salvation will work** some six or seven times an hour. 6 There could be no better way to spend a half minute or less than to remember the Source of your salvation, and to see **God, your Source** where It is **which is inside your mind that you share with God, your Source.**

Notes to Lesson # 71

Only God's plan for salvation will work.

Lesson 71, only God's plan for salvation will work, is a simple yet powerful lesson. This lesson has two basic components. The first is the idea that only God's plan for salvation will work. This means that if we are to achieve salvation, we are only required to follow God's plan and our salvation is guaranteed.

The second component of this lesson is that God's plan is exclusive and therefore, all other plans will not work. God's plan is based on the truth of who you really are. Any other plan must be based on the false. False plans are useless and doomed to fail.

God's plan is simple. It calls for you to accept the truth of your divine birthright or the At-One-Ment for yourself. This is the simple truth that God created you like Itself. Since God is only love, you must also be only love. God created you, perfect, whole and complete. God is the One Self and you are part of that shared Mind of God.

The second component to this idea is that no other plan will work. To follow both a false and a true plan is foolish. The two plans are opposites. They are in conflict and will only lead to confusion and a sense of failure and despair. When you realize that God's plan is based on the truth and all other plans are based on the false notion of who you are, it is easy to understand why trying to follow another plan is a waste of your energy and time.

The ego does not know who you are. All the plans of your split mind are based on the fantasy that you are something that you are not. The ego claims that you are a limited ego body in competition with other ego bodies for the limited resources that it believes you both need to survive. Your ego's plans are based on the belief in lack, limitation, fear and separation.

The unifying principal behind all the ego's plans for your happiness is that you are not perfect, whole and complete. God's plan is the opposite. It knows the truth that you are as God created you, perfect, whole and complete. It is obvious that these two plans are polar opposites. You cannot be both holy and not whole. These two plans are incompatible and mutually exclusive.

The ego's plan for salvation centers around holding grievances. A grievance is based on the idea that something outside your own mind must do something to make you happy or save you. When that someone, something or God fails to meet your ego's expectations, a grievance is born. Your ego now states that you will be happy or saved only when that outside force acts differently and follows your ego's plan for your happiness and salvation.

According to the ego your happiness is contingent on some power that is outside your mind that must meet your needs. If they fail, you are justified in holding a grievance against that party because he has hurt you and robbed you of your happiness.

Both God's plan and the ego's plan claim to be based on love. God's plan is simply based on the idea that love created you like Itself. Being part of that One Self, God's plan only asks that you recognize and reclaim the truth of your divine birthright. There is nothing outside yourself that you need to fix, control, change, impress or protect because there is nothing outside your mind. There is just the One Self of the shared Mind of God. God is, and you are that One. We are merely asked to reawaken to the truth of the At- One-Ment.

The ego believes that separation is real so according to your ego, you are not holy or whole. Your ego claims that if something outside your own mind was different, you would be saved. When someone fails to perform as your ego requires, you are justified in holding a grievance against the other party until they conform to your ego's plan. The ego's plan centers around holding these grievances until the outside offending party corrects their behavior so that you can be made happy or saved by their actions. God has failed to give you the power to save yourself and therefore, you are a victim.

Your ego's plan is designed to help you manage, control, manipulate and minimize the damage that these outside forces impose upon your happiness. Your ego claims that by holding grievances against them, perhaps they will behave and do your bidding so that you can be happy. The ego believes that if they loved you, they would behave, you would get your needs met and you would be happy or saved.

Because the ego does not believe that to give is to receive, the ego does not understand what true love is. Love must be unconditional. The ego's fear-based thought system makes unconditional love impossible. To the ego, love is not freely given. Love must be earned and is to be withdrawn whenever the other party fails to perform adequately or a better deal is available.

Because of the ego's warped notion of love, the ego's plan revolves around changing, fixing, controlling and manipulating others so that your perceived needs are met. Whenever another fails to perform, the ego believes you have been harmed and are justified and entitled to hold a grievance against the offending party. When you hold a grievance, you are also justified in attacking the other by withdrawing your conditional love. As a punishment for their wrongdoing, holding grievances becomes the essential tool in the ego's arsenal of manipulation of the world it perceives to be outside its own mind.

The ego's plans for salvation always assume that some outside force is the problem and not its own erroneous thinking. Since the real problem is the ego's erroneous belief in lack, limitation and separation, the ego's plans are doomed to fail. The problem always resides within the mind that thinks and believes those erroneous ideas in the first place.

The problem is your ego's thought system, not the outside world that this split mind perceives. The ego's plan would have you seek for salvation outside your own mind where the problem can never be found or resolved. Only God's plan works because only God's plan heals the split mind that believes it is separate, not perfect, not whole and very incomplete.

Question: Does your ego's belief that love gives you the right to fix, control, change, impress or protect another actually empower you or does it disempower both parties and justify your ego's right to hold grievances?

LESSON 72

Holding grievances is an attack on God's plan for salvation.

W-72.1.While we have recognized that the ego's plan for salvation is the opposite of God's, we have not yet emphasized that **the ego's plan for salvation** is an active attack on **God's** plan, and a deliberate attempt to destroy **God's plan**. 2 In the **ego's** attack, God is assigned the attributes which are actually associated with the ego, while the ego appears to take on the attributes of **a** God **of love**.

W-72.2.The ego's fundamental wish is to replace God. 2 In fact, the ego is the physical embodiment of that wish **to replace God**. 3 For it is that **egoic** wish **to replace God** that seems to surround the mind with a body, keeping **the mind** separate and alone, and unable to reach other minds except through the body that was made to imprison **the mind**. 4 The limit on communication cannot be the best means to expand communication. 5 Yet the ego would have you believe that **limiting communication by imprisoning the mind within the body** is **the best means to expand communication.**

W-72.3.Although the attempt to keep the limitations that a body would impose **on the mind** is obvious here, it is perhaps not so apparent why holding grievances is an attack on God's plan for salvation. 2 But let us consider the kinds of things you are apt to hold grievances for. 3 Are they not always associated with something a body does? 4 A person says something you do not like. 5 **A person** does something that displeases you. 6 **A person** "betrays" his hostile thoughts in his **body's** behavior.

W-72.4.You are not dealing here with what the person is **which is God's Son**. 2 On the contrary, you are exclusively concerned with what **the person** does in a body. 3 You are doing more than failing to help in freeing **the person** from the body's limitations. 4 You are actively trying to hold **the person** to **the body's limitations** by confusing **the body** with **the person**, and judging **the person and the body** as one. 5 Herein is God attacked, for if **God's** Son is only a body, so must **God** be **a body** as well. 6 A creator wholly unlike his creation is inconceivable.

W-72.5.If God is a body, what must **God's** plan for salvation be? 2 What could **God's plan for salvation** be but death? 3 In trying to present Himself as the Author of life and not of death, **this God the ego imagines** is a liar and a deceiver, full of false promises and offering illusions in place of truth. 4 The body's apparent reality makes this view of **the** God **the ego imagines** quite convincing. 5 In fact, if the body were real, it would be difficult indeed to escape this conclusion **that God must be a body**. 6 And every grievance that you hold insists that the body is real. 7 **Every grievance** overlooks entirely what your brother is. 8 **Every grievance** reinforces your belief that **God's Son** is a body, and condemns him for **being that body**. 9 And **every grievance** asserts that **the Son of God's** salvation must be death, projecting this attack onto God, and holding **God** responsible for **the death of the body that the ego misperceives to be God's Son.**

W-72.6.To this carefully prepared arena **of egoic distortion that imagines both God and His Son to be bodies is** where angry animals seek for prey and mercy cannot enter. **Into this arena,** the ego comes to save you. 2 **The ego says.** God made you a body. 3 Very well. 4 **The ego says.** Let us accept **that you are a body** and be glad. 5 **The ego says.** As a body, do not let yourself be deprived of what the body offers. 6-7 **The ego says.** Take the little you can get **from being a body since God** gave you nothing. 8-9 **The ego claims that** the body is your only savior and **that the body** is the death of God and your salvation.

W-72.7.This **belief that the body is your only savior** is the universal belief of the world you see. 2 Some hate the body, and try to hurt and humiliate **the body**. 3 Others love the body, and try to glorify and exalt **the body**. 4 But while the body stands at the center of your concept of yourself, you are attacking God's plan for salvation. **You are** holding your grievances against **God** and **God's** creation, that you may not hear the Voice of Truth and welcome **the Voice of Truth** as **your** Friend. 5 Your **ego's** chosen savior, **the body,** takes **the Voice for Truth's** place instead. 6 **The ego says that the body** is your friend **and the Voice of Truth, which is the Holy Spirit,** is your enemy.

W-72.8.We will try today to stop these senseless attacks **by your ego** on **God's plan for your** salvation. 2 We will try to welcome **God's plan for your salvation** instead. 3 Your **ego's** upside-down perception has been ruinous to your peace of mind. 4 **By following your ego's plan,** you have seen yourself in a body and the truth outside you, locked away from your awareness by the body's limitations. 5 Now we are going to try to see this differently.

W-72.9.The light of truth is in us, where **the Voice of Holy Spirit** was placed by God. 2 It is the body that is outside us, and **the body** is not our concern. 3 To be without a body is to be in our natural state. 4 To recognize the light of truth in us is to recognize ourselves as we are **which is without a body.** 5 To see our **big "S"** Self as separate from the body is to end the attack on God's plan for salvation, and to accept **God's plan for salvation** instead. 6 And wherever **God's** plan is accepted, **God's plan for salvation** is accomplished already.

W-72.10.Our goal in the longer practice periods today is to become aware that God's plan for salvation has already been accomplished in us. 2 To achieve this goal **of the awareness that God's plan for salvation has already been accomplished in us,** we must replace attack with acceptance. 3 As long as we attack **God's plan**, we cannot understand what God's plan for us is. 4 We are therefore attacking what we do not recognize. 5 Now we are going to try to lay **egoic** judgment aside, and ask what God's plan for us is:

6 What is salvation, Father? 7 I do not know. 8 Tell me, that I may understand.
9 Then we will wait in quiet for **God's** answer. 10 We have attacked God's plan for salvation without waiting to hear what **God's plan for salvation** is. 11 We have shouted our **ego's** grievances so loudly that we have not listened to **God's** Voice **for Truth**. 12 We have used our **ego's** grievances to close our eyes and stop our ears.

W-72.11.Now we would see and hear and learn. 2 "What is salvation, Father?" 3 Ask and you will be answered. 4 Seek and you will find. 5 We are no longer asking the ego what salvation is and where to find **salvation**. 6 We are asking **the Voice** for Truth **what salvation is and where to find it.** 7 Be certain, then, that the answer will be true because of Whom you **are** asking which **is the Holy Spirit.**

W-72.12.Whenever you feel your confidence wane and your hope of success flicker and go out, repeat your question and your request, remembering that you are asking of the infinite Creator of infinity, Who created you like Himself:
2 What is salvation, Father? 3 I do not know. 4 Tell me, that I may understand.
5 **God** will answer. 6 Be determined to hear.

W-72.13.One or perhaps two shorter practice periods an hour will be enough for today, since the **practice periods** will be somewhat longer than usual. 2 These exercises should begin with this:
3 Holding grievances is an attack on God's plan for salvation. 4 Let me accept **God's plan for salvation** instead. 5 What is salvation, Father?
6 Then wait a minute or so in silence, preferably with your eyes closed, and listen for **God's** answer.

Notes to Lesson # 72

Holding grievances is an attack on God's plan for salvation.

In Lesson 71, we stated that only God's plan for salvation will work and that God's plan was exclusive. We should follow no other plan since any other plan would only confuse us and would represent a false belief about what we are.

God's plan is simple. It calls for you to accept the truth of your divine birthright for yourself. This is the simple truth that God created you like Itself. Since God is only love, you must also be only love. But that is not how your ego defines who you are. To the ego, you and your world is ruled by a God of death. How can this strange transformation have taken place?

The ego believes that separation is real. According to your ego, you are not holy or whole. Instead, you are a limited physical body. Your ego's plan for your happiness is designed to protect the imperfect physical body that it perceives to be you.

By following the ego's plan, you hope to become less incomplete and obtain some temporary happiness. The ego's plan for salvation centers around your ability to hold grievances against God and others. Grievances always require the use of bodies since only bodies can attack or be harmed. Holding grievances becomes the essential tool in the ego's plan for your salvation since grievances are used to manipulate other bodies into helping your ego getting its needs met.

Your ego claims that if something outside your own mind was different, you would be happy. When someone fails to perform as your ego's plan requires, you are justified in holding a grievance against the other party until they conform to your ego's wishes. The ego's plan for getting its own way is centered around holding these grievances until the outside offending party corrects their behavior and complies with your plan. If they do not do so, additional punitive actions are justified until you get your way.

This is how your ego's plan for your happiness works. It is based on manipulation, reward and punishment.

A grievance is based on the idea that something outside your own mind must do something to make you happy or save you. Why does your ego believe that there is something outside your mind?

Well, obviously, because the ego believes that you are a separate autonomous being. The ego's proof for the reality of the separation is the appearance of the physical world, but more importantly your physical body. To the ego, the body is you and you are the body. We identify ourselves as being our body and therefore, the ego offers this false identification with our body as proof that the separation is real.

Your true nature is to be without a body. You are a spiritual being having a fleeting human experience. Your body is merely a neutral game token that allows you to play on the game board of time and space. But when you see yourself as the body, you see yourself as separate and apart from God, your Source. Since a creation cannot conceive of itself different than its creator, this egoic belief that you are your body implies that your creator must also be a body.

Only bodies can attack. Only bodies appear to be harmed. Bodies have needs and bodies die. When we accept the belief that we are the body, we must accept the limitations that come with that body. Our egoic world of perception becomes a place of struggle in which we compete for the limited resources that we all need for our survival.

When you perceive yourself to be a limited ego body, it is logical to conclude that God has failed to adequately provide for your needs. God has failed to give you the power to save yourself and therefore, you are a victim of outside forces that are beyond your control. If you are your body, your creator did not do a very good job.

Your body is incapable of sustaining life. You need help from other bodies if you are to survive. Yet, these bodies often attack rather than submit to your wishes. What better proof does your ego need to convince your decision-maker that God, your creator, must be either limited, like yourself, or certainly not a God of love?

The ego takes the image of the body and projects those same qualities upon God. To the ego, God gave you an imperfect body that must suffer and die. Any plan that God has for you must end in your death because death is God's creation. If the body is the best that God can do, God's plan for salvation is your ultimate death and that cannot be something you would want.

The ego advises that if you are a body, you should follow the ego's plan for only the ego's plan is designed to protect the survival of the body against the ego's god of death. Eventually, the ego's god of death will kill you, but until that time, it is your ego's plan that will best protect your body that your ego perceives to be you.

The ego's plan is to replace the true God of love with itself. Within your split mind, a God of love has now been replaced by the petty, fear-based god of death that mimics your ego's image of who you are. Your ego made this false god in its own fear-based image. Your ego has successfully replaced the God of love with itself.

This new false idol was created through your misguided belief that you could hold a grievance against somebody and that the grievance has no power to change your own perception of yourself. When you believe the Son of God is a body, your split mind transforms your creator into a god of death. When you believe yourself to be the body, you really do have something to fear from the idols of this world.

Question: If you were perfect, whole and complete, what would you need from another to make you happy?

LESSON 73

I will there be light.

W-73.1.Today we are considering the will you share with God. 2 This is not the same as the ego's idle wishes, out of which darkness and nothingness arise. 3 The will you share with God has all the power of creation in it. 4 The ego's idle wishes are unshared, and therefore have no power at all. 5 **The ego's** wishes are not idle in the sense that they can make a world of illusions in which your belief can be very strong. 6 But **the ego's wishes** are idle indeed in terms of creation. 7 **The ego's wishes** make nothing that is real.

W-73.2.**The ego's** idle wishes and grievances are partners or co-makers in picturing the world you see. 2 The wishes of the ego gave rise to **the world you see**, and the ego's need for grievances, which are necessary to maintain **the world you see**, peoples **the world you see** with figures that seem to attack you and call for "righteous" judgment. 3 These figures become the middlemen the ego employs to traffic in grievances. 4 **These figures that people your ego's world seem to attack you and** stand between your awareness and your brothers' reality. 5 **Because you** behold **and judge these figures that seem to attack you**, you do not know your brothers or your **big "S"** Self's **reality.**

W-73.3.Your **shared** will **with God** is lost to you in this strange bartering, in which **egoic** guilt is traded back and forth, and grievances increase with each exchange. 2 Can such a world have been created by the Will the Son of God shares with his Father? 3 Did God create disaster for His Son? 4 Creation is the **shared** Will of Both **the Father and God's Son** together. 5 Would God create a world that kills Himself?

W-73.4.Today we will try once more to reach the world that is in accordance with your **real** will **that is shared with God's Will**. 2 The light is in **the world** because **your shared will** does not oppose the Will of God. 3 **The world we attempt to reach** is not Heaven, but the light of Heaven shines on it. 4 Darkness has vanished. 5 The ego's idle wishes have been withdrawn. 6 Yet the light that shines upon this world reflects your will, and so **light** must be in you that we will look for **that light that reflects the will you share with God's Will.**

W-73.5.Your picture of the world can only mirror what is within **your mind**. 2 The source of neither light nor darkness can be found **outside your mind**. 3 Grievances darken your mind, and you look out on a darkened world. 4 Forgiveness lifts the darkness, reasserts your will, and lets you look upon a world of light. 5 We have repeatedly emphasized that the barrier of grievances is easily passed, and cannot stand between you and your salvation. 6 The reason is very simple. 7 Do you really want to be in hell? 8 Do you really want to weep and suffer and die?

W-73.6.Forget the ego's arguments which seek to prove all this **dark grievance filled world** is really Heaven. 2 You know **this dark grievance filled world** is not **Heaven**. 3 You cannot want this **dark grievance filled world** for yourself. 4 There is a point beyond which illusions cannot go. 5 Suffering is not happiness, and it is happiness you really want. 6 Such is your will in truth. **Your shared will with God is to be happy.** 7 And so salvation is your will as well. 8 You want to succeed in what we are trying to do today. 9 We undertake it with your blessing and your glad accord.

W-73.7.We will succeed today if you remember that you want salvation **and happiness** for yourself. 2 You want to accept God's plan because you share in **God's plan**. 3 You have no will that can really oppose **God's plan for happiness** and you do not want to do so. 4 Salvation is for you. 5 Above all else, you want the freedom to remember Who you really are. 6 Today it is the ego that stands powerless before your **shared** will **with God**. 7 Your will is free, and nothing can prevail against **your will that you share with God.**

W-73.8.Therefore, we undertake the exercises for today in happy confidence, certain that we will find what it is your will to find, and remember what it is your will to remember. 2 No idle wishes **of the ego** can detain us, nor deceive us with an illusion of strength. 3 Today let your **shared** will be done, and end forever the insane **egoic** belief that **God's plan for salvation** is hell in place of Heaven that you choose.

W-73.9.We will begin our longer practice periods with the recognition that God's plan for salvation, and only **God's plan**, is wholly in accord with your will **that you share with God**. 2 It is not the purpose of an alien power, thrust upon you unwillingly. 3 **God's plan for salvation** is the one purpose here on which you and your Father are in perfect accord. 4 You will succeed today, the time appointed for the release of the Son of God from hell and from all idle wishes. 5 **The Son's** will is now restored to his awareness. 6 **The Son** is willing this very day to look upon the light in **himself** and be saved.

W-73.10.After reminding yourself of **your willingness to be restored to the light of truth** and determining to keep your **shared** will clearly in mind, tell yourself with gentle firmness and quiet certainty:
2 I will there be light. 3 Let me behold the light that reflects God's Will and mine.
4 Then let your **shared** will assert itself, joined with the power of God and united with your **big "S"** Self. 5 Put the rest of the practice period under Their **joined** guidance. 6 Join with God and your **big "S"** Self as They lead the way.

W-73.11.In the shorter practice periods, again make a declaration of what you really want. 2 Say:
3 I will there be light. 4 Darkness is not my will.
5 This should be repeated several times an hour. 6 It is most important, however, to apply today's idea in this form

immediately **when** you are tempted to hold a grievance of any kind. **Say, I will there be light. Darkness is not my will 7** This will help you let your grievances go, instead of cherishing **your grievances** and hiding **your grievances** in darkness.

Notes to Lesson # 73

I will there be light.

Lesson 73, I will there be light, is a classic example of a seemingly innocent statement that has profound consequences when properly understood.

We stated that if God made this world, He would be cruel. Lesson 72 said that holding grievances is an attack on God's plan for salvation and that if the body is our reality, then God would not only be cruel, but also be a god of death. No one could believe that a God of love would create such a flawed replica like your body and claim it is representative of a loving God's best efforts. If like begets like, your body witnesses for a different version of God.

This lesson actually discusses how a delusional mind made the physical world that we perceive with the body's eyes. It also explains why God does not share that same false vision. Truth is eternal and changeless. Knowledge must be true and is part of Truth with a capital T.

Time belongs in the realm of perception, not knowledge. Time provides a medium in which an individuated aspect of the One Self can experience, learn and know various aspects of the abstract totality. It allows for the imagined experience of differentiation. Differentiation aids in understanding since it is difficult to understand the concept of white without its opposite, the color black.

Differentiation provides concrete examples of the specific aspects that comprise the loving nature of the Mind of God. Differentiation allows the indivisible abstract One Self to have specific experiences in concrete form that demonstrate various aspects of love. Through differentiation, the abstract One Self, not only knows Itself, but can actually be or experience the various aspects of Itself.

Time and space provide a game board in which the Son of God can witness for the truth or imagine the false. Both options are available, although both take place only in the playschool of our split mind's imaginings. In time and space, we learn who we really are. Whether we choose to witness for the truth or imagine the false, either simulated experience is not real since it takes place in time.

Time is the measure of change and is part of the realm of perception. In ACIM's unique terminology, time is not real but is experienced within the mind of the beholder to be their private individuated provisional reality.

Previously, we stated that in time and space, there are two thought systems vying for the attention of your decision-maker. Just as there are two thought systems, there are only two emotions. In time and space, both the emotions of love and loves opposite, which is fear, appear to be viable choices. In truth, only love is real since that is what God is. Fear is merely false evidence appearing real. The false cannot be shared with the Mind of God because the Will of God does not create what is not true.

Time is experienced in the imaginings of the individuated aspects of the indivisible One Self that desires to know its true spiritual magnificence. For simplicity purposes, we will call that learning and experiencing aspect of the One Self to be the Son of God. We, God's Son is Spirit, or Mind, not a bodily form. As God's Child, we possess the creative power of the Mind of God.

Manifestation, whether real or imagined, occurs when two minds are joined in a common desire that they wish to experience. When individuated aspects of mind share either loving or fear-based thoughts, manifestation occurs in the illusionary game board of time and space.

The thoughts you share with God are real. Yet you can only share loving thoughts with God because God is only love. Since love knows no opposites, the split minded cannot share fear-based thoughts with the shared Mind of God. The false can only be an illusion that has no reality in Truth. The Truth only reflects God's Will. God is only love and therefore, God's Will is Love. When you share your true will with God's Will, you co-create with God because your real will is the same as God's Will which is only love.

When the split minded attempt to share their fear-based thoughts, these thoughts cannot be shared with the Mind of God. They can only be shared with other split minds that perceive both love and fear to be available choices for the learning lessons they desire to experience. Only on the game board of time and space does differentiation appear possible.

Your split mind's imaginings do have the power to manifest as illusions that appear as our physical world in time and space. These shared wishes become our provisional reality that allow us to test what we truly value and why. They provide the valuable experiences that we desire in order to know our spiritual magnificence as that One Self. In time and space, we get to hone our skills as love in form. We are given specific situations in which we can ask ourselves what would love have me do? We then get to respond and see how we did. In time and space, we get to choose between fear or love. This is part of the growing process of learning who you really are.

There was nothing wrong with wanting to participate in the game of separation. You do not have to feel guilt or blame yourself for your involvement in this game. It provides a wonderful opportunity to demonstrate what you truly are. It allows you to experience being a special or separate aspect of love, which is the only nature of the One Self. In time, the illusion of differentiation can be experienced in a totally safe environment. As long as each participant remembers that differentiation is not real, no judgment is involved with this game.

Yet, when the split minded forget to remember that the game of separation is merely a game, they slip into judgment. Judgment leads to fear. When you judge something is either good, bad or indifferent, you make the game of separation appear real. The game now seems to have real consequences. You now believe that there is something outside of you that has the ability to change the truth of who you really are. You believe you are a separate vulnerable ego body that has needs, can attack and be hurt. Your judgment forms the basis for your attack thoughts and the grievances that must follow.

It is your ego's decision to judge that turned the innocent game of separation into your provisional reality of imagined conflict, struggle, and pain that ends with the death of the body. It is your grievances against your brother, yourself and God that prevent the remembrance that separation is merely an illusion.

We have only begun to lay the foundation for the continued exploration of how our mass collective consciousness works. It is our collective fear-based thought system that continues to make and maintains the physical world that we perceive.

Question: The picture of your world can only mirror what is within your own mind and is shared with other split minds. The individual world you see will either reflect the light of love or the darkness of fear. Will you choose to share the light of love or the darkness of fear?

The choice is mutually exclusive but it is your choice.

LESSON 74

There is no will but God's Will.

W-74.1.The idea for today **that there is no will but God's Will** can be regarded as the central thought toward which all our exercises are directed. 2 God's **Will** is the only Will. 3 When you have recognized **that God's Will is the only Will**, you have recognized that your will is **God's Will.** 4 The belief that conflict is possible has gone. 5 Peace has replaced the strange idea that you are torn by conflicting goals. 6 As an expression of the Will of God, you have no goal but **God's Will.**

W-74.2.There is great peace in today's idea **that there is no will but God's Will** and the exercises for today are directed towards finding **God's Will.** 2 The idea **that there is no will but God's Will** is wholly true. 3 Therefore, **the idea that there is no will but God's Will** cannot give rise to illusions. 4 Without illusions conflict is impossible. 5 Let us try to recognize today **that without illusions conflicts are impossible**, and experience the peace this recognition brings.

W-74.3.Begin the longer practice periods by repeating these thoughts **that there is no will but God's and that without illusions conflicts are impossible** several times, slowly and with firm determination to understand what they mean, and to hold them in mind:
2 There is no will but God's. 3 I cannot be in conflict.
4 Then spend several minutes in adding some related thoughts, such as:
5 I am at peace.
6 Nothing can disturb me. 7 My will is God's.
8 My will and God's are one.
9 God wills peace for His Son.
10 During this introductory phase, be sure to deal quickly with any conflict thoughts that may cross your mind. 11 Tell yourself immediately:
12 There is no will but God's. 13 These conflict thoughts are meaningless.

W-74.4.If there is one conflict area that seems particularly difficult to resolve, single **that one difficult area** out for special consideration. 2 Think about **that one difficult area of conflict** briefly but very specifically, identify the particular person or persons and the situation or situations involved, and tell yourself:
3 There is no will but God's. 4 I share **my will** with **God's Will**. 5 My conflicts about ___ cannot be real.

W-74.5.After you have cleared your mind in this way, close your eyes and try to experience the peace to which your reality entitles you. 2 Sink into **the peace your reality entitles you** and feel it closing around you. 3 There may be some temptation to mistake these attempts for withdrawal, but the difference is easily detected. 4 If you are succeeding, you will feel a deep sense of joy and an increased alertness, rather than a feeling of drowsiness and enervation.

W-74.6.Joy characterizes peace. 2 By this experience **of joy** will you recognize that you have reached **the peace your reality entitles you.** 3 If you feel yourself slipping off into withdrawal, quickly repeat the idea for today **that there is no will but God's Will** and try again. 4 Do this as often as necessary. 5 There is definite gain in refusing to allow retreat into withdrawal, even if you do not experience the peace you seek.

W-74.7.In the shorter periods, which should be undertaken at regular and predetermined intervals today, say to yourself:
2 There is no will but God's. 3 I seek His peace today.
4 Then try to find **the peace of God that** you are seeking. 5 A minute or two every half an hour, with eyes closed if possible, would be well spent on this today.

Notes to Lesson # 74

There is no will but God's Will.

Lesson 74 states that there is no will but God's Will. One of the goals of A Course in Miracles is to help you realize that you are an expression of God's Will. There is no will but God's Will and so you have no goals but God's goals. When you realize this, there can be no conflict because there is a single purpose that you share with your Creator. Only when you have conflicting goals do you have conflict. The peace of God will be yours when you realize that your will and God's Will are the same.

Yet, once again, that is not how we perceive ourselves. The split minded believe that they do have a will that is different than God's. Yesterday we mentioned that your ego's idle wishes are unshared with the Mind of God. Therefore, these egoic fear-based thoughts have no power to create what is real.

But your ego's wishes are not idle in the sense that they create an illusion that appears so real it actually becomes your provisional reality. Your egoic illusions result in the conflict that you experience in this lifetime. If you knew that you really were God's beloved child with whom God is well pleased, conflict would be impossible. Instead, you believe you are unholy and not whole. If you would listen to the Voice for God, you would realize that your wish to be happy and God's Will are the same. Both are in perfect alignment. Being of one Mind, fulfilling the function assigned to you by God's plan is your happiness.

But the split mind sees things differently. Your split mind sees conflict where there is none because you believe in the reality of your ego's illusions. So how do your ego's illusions become your provisional reality?

Time is the game board for your split mind's imagination. Being a Son of God, your mind has the power to co-create with God by using loving thoughts that are shared with the Mind of God. Being shared with God's Mind, these thoughts are real and are the extension of the Mind of God.

But we cannot share false or fear-based thoughts with God for God only knows the Truth. In order to make illusions manifest in time and space and appear real, our split minds must share these wishes, desires or thoughts with other split minds that also wish to explore the game of separation.

Manifestation, whether real or imagined, occurs when two minds are joined in a common desire that they wish to experience. When individuated aspects of mind share either their loving or fear-based thoughts, manifestation occurs in the illusionary game board of time and space.

There is nothing wrong with wanting to participate in the game of separation. You do not have to feel guilt or blame yourself for your involvement in this game. It provides a wonderful opportunity to demonstrate what you truly are. You get to really test what you currently value in the pressure cooker we call your earthly experience. That is why the game of separation could be called the journey of awakening. It allows you to experience, learn and be a special or separate aspect of love. Love is the only nature of the One Self. But love has numerous aspects that comprise it. In time, the illusion of differentiation can be experienced in a totally safe environment. As long as each participant remembers that differentiation is not real, no judgment is involved with this game.

Yet when the split minded forget to remember that the game of separation is merely a game, they slip into judgment, which leads to fear. When you judge something is either good, bad or indifferent, you make the game of separation appear real. The game now seems to have real consequences.

You now believe that there is something outside of you that has the ability to change the truth of who you really are. You believe you are a separate vulnerable ego body that has needs, can attack and be attacked. Your judgment forms the basis for your attack thoughts and your grievances. These judgments, attack thoughts and grievances make your ego's illusions appear real and conflict possible.

There are no private thoughts. In order for an illusion to manifest as someone's provisional reality, it must be shared with another mind. There are no victims and there are no victimizers. This means that it is impossible for you to force your thoughts upon another.

An analogy may be useful in helping to explain how illusions are shared with others and manifest as someone's personal experience.

All events that manifest in time and space are actually neutral. They have no inherent ability to make you happy or make you sad. Only your mind determines how you will interpret the neutral events. It is your judgment that colors the event as either good or bad. These neutral events provide the requested and needed learning lessons in our journey of reawakening. They are your proving grounds for learning.

The world of time and space is a world of perception, not of fact. Based on your beliefs which are derived from your past, your egoic mind creates an image of an event that it would like to experience. Like a radio tower, your mind broadcasts its desired thought pattern out into its surrounding environment as a specific frequency. If another mind is tuned in to that frequency, the message is received and shared with the other party who returns a confirmation message indicating the party's willingness to participate in the event.

If someone is not looking for that event frequency, the vibration simply is unnoticed and continues to be broadcast from the sender's radio tower. If no one is willing to receive that frequency, manifestation will not occur for that event.

The mind's broadcast tower only transmits specific frequencies for desired experiences. It has no ability to broadcast the negation of an idea. For example: It can broadcast either a request for health or sickness. It lacks the ability to broadcast your desire to experience the event of not being sick. If your mind is focused on resisting sickness, the frequency is tuned to sickness and that is what will be broadcasted and experienced.

Event frequencies are neither good nor bad. They are merely neutral events that are desired to be experienced by the sender. The manifestation of the event has no inherent ability to cause the recipient to respond with either fear or love. They merely broadcast to the world that you are interested in having a particular experience.

What you choose to do with that experience is up to you. You can choose to see the experience as an attack or a cry for love. In this regard, the event or experience still remains neutral. Your mind only decides how you wish to interpret the neutral event. In time and space, the choice is always between fear or love.

168

Although no one has the ability to cause you to lose your inner peace, how you choose to interpret the events of your world can influence the other party. Your interpretation of the event becomes your broadcast signal to your outer world. If one party chooses to view the event through the eyes of love and forgiveness, that frequency of love and acceptance will be available for the other party to tune into and perhaps change their own broadcast signal to align with the other party's viewpoint. Neither party can force the other side to modify their frequency against their will. But you can provide a frequency that previously was unavailable so they can then choose a different path.

In time and space, your function is forgiveness, your purpose is love and your destiny is the peace of God. When you are willing to be a radio tower for only the Will of God, you will be broadcasting on the frequency of love and forgiveness. You will signal a different vision for your world and attract experiences that align with that new vision.

When you realize that your will is the same as God's Will, all your egoic illusions will be dismissed as meaningless by your healed mind. Conflict will be impossible and your inner peace will be restored.

Question: Time and space provides us with an opportunity to grow, learn and experience various aspects of love. God does not blame you for participating in the game of separation. Do you feel guilty or believe you are being punished for your participation in the game of separation?

Guilt keeps you bound to your past and keeps you trapped in your past. Does the game of separation have negative connotations for you?

If so, reframe the game and call it your journey of reawakening or discovery. This game we call life can be a fun and exciting adventure. It does not have to be a source of guilt or punishment.

LESSON 75

The light has come.

W-75.1.The light has come. 2 You are healed and you can heal. 3 The light has come. 4 You are saved and you can save. 5 You are at peace, and you bring peace with you wherever you go. 6 Darkness and turmoil and death have disappeared. 7 The light has come.

W-75.2.Today we celebrate the happy ending to your long dream of disaster. 2 There are no dark dreams now. 3 The light has come. 4 Today the time of light begins for you and everyone. 5 **Today** is a new era, in which a new world is born. 6 The old **era of darkness, turmoil and death** has left no trace upon **the new era of light** in **the** passing **of the old era of darkness.** 7 Today we see a different world, because the light has come.

W-75.3.Our exercises for today will be happy ones, in which we offer thanks for the passing of the **old era of darkness** and the beginning of the new **era of the light of forgiveness.** 2 No shadows from the past remain to darken our sight and hide the world forgiveness offers us. 3 Today we will accept the new world **of light and forgiveness** as what we want to see. 4 We will be given what we desire. 5 We will to see the light; the light has come.

W-75.4.Our longer practice periods will be devoted to looking at the world that our forgiveness shows us. 2 **A forgiven world** is what we want to see, and only this. 3 Our single purpose makes our goal inevitable. 4 Today the real world **of forgiveness** rises before us in gladness, to be seen at last. 5 Sight, **which is the vision of Christ,** has been given us now that the light has come.

W-75.5.We do not want to see the ego's shadow on the world today. 2 We see the light, and in **the light** we see Heaven's reflection lie across the **forgiven** world. 3 Begin the longer practice periods by telling yourself the glad tidings of your release:
4 The light has come. 5 I have forgiven the world.

W-75.6.Dwell not upon the past today. 2 Keep a completely open mind, washed of all past **egoic** ideas and clean of every concept your **ego** has made. 3 You have forgiven the world today. 4 You can look upon **a forgiven world** now as if you never saw **the world** before. 5 You do not know yet what **a forgiven world** looks like. 6 You merely wait to have **a forgiven world** shown to you. 7 While you wait, repeat several times, slowly and in complete patience:
8 The light has come. 9 I have forgiven the world.

W-75.7.Realize that your forgiveness entitles you to **the** vision **of Christ.** 2 Understand that the Holy Spirit never fails to give the gift of **the vision of Christ** to the forgiving. 3 Believe **the Holy Spirit** will not fail you now. 4 You have forgiven the world. 5 **The Holy Spirit** will be with you as you watch and wait. 6 **The Holy Spirit** will show you what true vision sees. 7 It is **the Holy Spirit's** Will, and you have joined with **the Holy Spirit.** 8 Wait patiently for **the Holy Spirit.** 9 **The Holy Spirit** will be there. 10 The light has come. 11 You have forgiven the world.

W-75.8.Tell **the Holy Spirit** you know you cannot fail because you trust in **the Holy Spirit.** 2 And tell yourself you wait in certainty to look upon the world **the Holy Spirit** promised you. 3 From this time forth you will see differently **with the forgiving eyes what the vision of Christ brings.** 4 Today the light has come. 5 And you will see the **real** world that has been promised you since time began, and in which is the end of time ensured.

W-75.9.The shorter practice periods, too, will be joyful reminders of your release. 2 Remind yourself every quarter of an hour or so that today is a time for special celebration. 3 Give thanks for mercy and the Love of God. 4 Rejoice in the power of forgiveness to heal your sight completely. 5 Be confident that on this day there is a new beginning. 6 Without the darkness of the past upon your eyes, you cannot fail to see today **with the forgiving eyes what the vision of Christ brings.** 7 And what you see will be so welcome that you will gladly extend today forever.

W-75.10.Say, then:
2 The light has come. 3 I have forgiven the world.
4 Should you be tempted, say to anyone who seems to pull you back into darkness:
5 The light has come. 6 I have forgiven you.

W-75.11.We dedicate this day to the serenity in which God would have you be. 2 Keep **the serenity** in your awareness of yourself and see **the serenity in which God would have you be** everywhere today, as we celebrate the beginning of your vision **of Christ** and the sight of the real world, which has come to replace the unforgiven world your **ego** thought was real.

Notes to Lesson # 75

170

The light has come.

Lesson 75 is the light has come. Light is a symbol that you have accepted God's Will as your will. The light was always there. God's Will has never changed, just as God's love for His creations flows continuously. We can deny that flow but we cannot stop it.

We deny God's Will and refuse to accept God's love when we allow our mind to slip into fear and hold grievances. Our grievances become the dark clouds that block the light that is God's Will from our split minds.

Grievances arise from our split mind's belief that someone or something outside of our own mind has the ability to make us happy or save us. Our ego holds grievances whenever someone fails to follow our ego's plan for our happiness. When this happens, our ego uses the blame, shame and guilt game to try to coerce the other party to change their behavior and adopt our plan.

Our grievances come from our belief that somebody should have done something differently and therefore, failed to meet our needs. If somebody had acted differently, we would be happy. Grievances focus on past actions and rob us of our ability to be in the present moment. We bring our past to the present and continue to allow these past grievances to impact how we react in the present time.

You need to forgive your past for the past cannot harm you. It is over if you choose to drop your grievances that bind you to the past. If you ask the Holy Spirit, the Holy Spirit will not fail to help you reframe your story about a past event so that it can be viewed as a beneficial learning lesson that was required so that you could continue on your journey of reawakening.

You will not be able to see the light as long as you continue to hold grievances and fail to forgive your past.

Lesson 73 was I will there be light. I would like to go back to that lesson and discuss it in reference to grievances and forgiving your world. Below is a passage from that lesson that I would like to now address.

W-73.2.**The ego's** idle wishes and grievances are partners or co-makers in picturing the world you see. 2 The wishes of the ego gave rise to **the world you see**, and the ego's need for grievances, which are necessary to maintain **the world you see**, peoples **the world you see** with figures that seem to attack you and call for "righteous" judgment. 3 These figures become the middlemen the ego employs to traffic in grievances. 4 **These figures that people your ego's world seem to attack you and** stand between your awareness and your brothers' reality. 5 **Because you** behold **and judge these figures that seem to attack you**, you do not know your brothers or your big "S" Self's **reality.**

W-73.3.Your **shared** will **with God** is lost to you in this strange bartering, in which **egoic** guilt is traded back and forth, and grievances increase with each exchange. 2 Can such a world have been created by the Will the Son of God shares with his Father? 3 Did God create disaster for His Son? 4 Creation is the **shared** Will of Both **the Father and God's Son** together. 5 Would God create a world that kills Himself?

Because we are the Son of God, we have the ability to call into our awareness the events we wish to experience. As discussed in yesterday's lesson, your mind is a broadcast tower that signals to your world what your ego expects to see and what it desires to experience. Although you do not control every detail of the circumstances and conditions that surround you, you do control the purpose that you assign to those events and how you choose to interpret them as your story.

Your beliefs about your story, not the actual objective retelling of all the facts and circumstances surrounding the event, become the history lesson that your egoic mind carries into the present moment. It is these beliefs from your past that your ego references to ensure that its past beliefs continue to influence and color current events. The present becomes a replay of your past.

We have been indoctrinated into a fear-based thought system that tells us we are a body and that outside forces impact our life. These forces are beyond our control. This belief that we are all separate limited ego-bodies gives rise to our ego's plan for our happiness and salvation.

The ego's plan revolves around influencing these outside forces so that it minimizes the negative effects and maximizes the potential benefits. The ego's plan tries to manipulate these outside powers so that we can manage and when necessary mitigate the influence of these powers over our lives and still get our needs met.

Since we are victims to the whims of these outside forces that are beyond our control, we cannot eliminate them from impacting our lives. Our ego's plan, therefore, centers on manipulating these forces so that they favorably follow our ego's plan for our body's safety.

Since the ego's world is based on its belief in lack, limitation and fear, this fearful world is a zero-sum game. In order to get your needs met, you must take from somebody else. There are always winners and losers in this game of deal making.

The ego's plan for your salvation always entails making a good deal. If you are to get your needs met, your ego must barter and make the best deal possible. You must sacrifice something to get something of equal or greater value. The goal for all your ego's plans is to always make the best deal possible. It seeks to sacrifice the least and gain the most.

Your ego does not believe that to give is to receive. Instead, your ego operates under the fear-based belief that you give only to get. To the ego, your salvation is contingent upon its ability to constantly make a good deal to insure your continued survival.

The ego enters into special relationships with other people and things in an attempt to insure that your needs are met. In the special relationship, each party agrees to exchange some of their limited resources if the other party surrenders something that the other perceives to be of equal or greater value. These special relationships are what your ego says you need to make you happy or safe. Your ego's plan is designed to insure that the body's perceived needs are met at the lowest cost to your own limited resources.

The ego believes its job is to constantly monitor and judge these special relationships to insure that they are paying off as expected. The ego expects a good return on its investment. This is why our egos are big judging machines. When another party fails to perform as anticipated, the ego files a grievance. It is a complaint against the other party for their breach of this unwritten contract.

It is interesting to note that the agreement between the two parties was not necessarily openly negotiated or even known to both sides. In each relationship, each party has their own specific and secret agenda. This agenda is adjusted and modified by our egos as we move through time.

Our egos are always seeking to renegotiate the contract or find a better deal elsewhere. These secret agendas and one-sided deals tend to make these relationships unstable as each party actively seeks to find better deals elsewhere.

Because you believe that the body is you and you are the body, you perceive lack in your world. You believe your ego has the plan that best insures that your needs are met. When these other parties fail to perform up to your ego's expectations, a grievance is filed against the offending party.

The grievance can be disclosed to the other party or just your secret. Full disclosure or fairness is of no concern to your ego's kangaroo court. Your ego then judges them guilty and punishes them for their supposed crime against you. If your ego is to forgive the offending party, some type of apology or retribution is expected in exchange for your forgiveness. This is not true forgiveness. It is merely another example of your ego playing let's make a deal.

It is your ego's belief in the illusion of separation that creates the conflict that you perceive in your world. Your ego's plan seeks to minimize the negative consequences from the illusions that time and space provide. But the ego's secret agenda is to never allow your decision-maker to rediscover that the illusions are not real. Your ego's plan coupled with your grievances block the light which is God's Will from your sight. They make the illusion appear real.

True forgiveness is different from your ego's definition of forgiveness.

True forgiveness comes from following the thought system of the Holy Spirit. True forgiveness, not the forgiveness offered by your ego, is what is needed, if you are to see the light in your world.

Question: If you demand some type of apology or payoff for forgiving another, is that really forgiveness or just another special deal?

LESSON 76

I am under no laws but God's.

W-76.1.We have observed before how many senseless things have seemed to you to be salvation. 2 Each **egoic plan for your salvation** has imprisoned you with laws as senseless as **the ego** itself. 3 You are not bound by **the senseless laws of your ego's world**. 4 Yet to understand that **the senseless laws of your ego's world no longer apply to you and that** this is so, you must first realize salvation lies not **in your ego's unforgiven world of grievances and illusions**. 5 While you would seek for **salvation** in things that have no meaning, you bind yourself to **the ego's** laws that make no sense. 6 Thus do you seek to prove salvation is where **salvation** is not. **Salvation cannot be found in the ego's false and illusionary world of individuated perception. It will only be found in the forgiven world that utilizes the vision of Christ and that follows the Voice for God.**

W-76.2.Today we will be glad **that your ego** cannot prove **that salvation can be found where salvation is not**. 2 For if **your ego could prove that salvation could be found where it is not**, you would forever seek salvation where it is not, and never find **salvation**. 3 The idea for today **that you are under no laws but God's laws** tells you once again how simple is salvation. 4 Look for **salvation** where **salvation** waits for you, and there **salvation** will be found. 5 Look nowhere else, for **salvation** is nowhere else. **You are under no laws but God's laws or God's plan for your salvation.**

W-76.3.Think of the freedom in the recognition that you are not bound by all the strange and twisted laws **your ego** has set up to save you. 2 You really think that you would starve unless you have stacks of green paper strips and piles of metal discs **that your egoic world calls money**. 3 You really think a small round pellet or some fluid pushed into your veins through a sharpened needle will ward off disease and death. 4 You really think you are alone unless another body is with you.

W-76.4.It is insanity that thinks these things. 2 You call them laws, and put **those false egoic beliefs** under different names in a long catalogue of rituals that have no use and serve no purpose. 3 You think you must obey the "laws" of medicine, of economics and of health. 4 **Your ego's laws tell you to** protect the body, and you will be saved.

W-76.5.These are not laws, but **the** madness **of the ego**. 2 The body is endangered by the **split egoic** mind that hurts itself. 3 The body suffers just in order that the **split** mind will fail to see **that the mind** is the victim of itself. 4 The body's suffering is a mask the mind holds up to hide what really suffers **which is your mind**. 5 **Your split mind** would not understand **that your mind** is its own enemy; that **your egoic mind** attacks itself and wants to die. 6 It is from **your ego's own madness that** your **ego's** "laws" would save the body. 7 It is for this **madness** you think you are a body.

W-76.6.There are no laws except the laws of God. 2 This needs repeating, over and over, until you realize it applies to everything that you**r ego** has made in opposition to God's Will. 3 Your **ego's** magic has no meaning. 4 What **your ego's magic** is meant to save does not exist. 5 Only what **your ego's magic** is meant to hide will save you **which are the laws of God and God's plan for salvation.**

W-76.7.The laws of God can never be replaced. 2 We will devote today to rejoicing that **the laws of God can never be replaced is true**. 3 **That the laws of God can never be replaced** is no longer a truth that we would hide. 4 We realize instead it is a truth that keeps us free forever. 5 Magic imprisons, but the laws of God make free. 6 The light has come because there are no laws but **God's laws.**

W-76.8.We will begin the longer practice periods today with a short review of the different kinds of "laws" **of the ego's world that** we have believed we must obey. 2 These **"laws" of the ego's world** would include, for example, the "laws" of nutrition, of immunization, of medication, and of the body's protection in innumerable ways. 3 Think further; you believe in the **ego's** "laws" of friendship, of "good" relationships and reciprocity. 4 Perhaps you even think that there are laws which set forth what is God's and what is yours. 5 Many "religions" have been based on this. 6 **Many "religions"** would not save but damn in Heaven's name. 7 Yet **many religious laws** are no more strange than other "laws" you hold must be obeyed to make you safe.

W-76.9.There are no laws but God's. 2 Dismiss all foolish magical beliefs today, and hold your mind in silent readiness to hear the Voice that speaks the truth to you. 3 You will be listening to **the Voice for Truth** Who says there is no loss under the laws of God. 4 Payment is neither given nor received. 5 Exchange cannot be made; there are no substitutes; and nothing is replaced by something else. 6 God's laws forever give and never take.

W-76.10.Hear **the Voice for Truth** Who tells you **that God's laws forever give and never take** and realize how foolish are the ego's "laws" you thought upheld the world you thought you saw **based on your ego's belief of lack, limitation, fear and separation**. 2 Then listen further. 3 **The Holy Spirit** will tell you more. 4 About the Love your Father has for you. 5 About the endless joy **God** offers you. 6 About **God's** yearning for **God's** only Son, created as **God's** channel for creation; denied to **God** by his **split minded son's egoic** belief in hell.

W-76.11.Let us today open God's channels to **the Holy Spirit**, and let **God's** Will extend through us to **God's Son**. 2 Thus is creation endlessly increased. 3 **God's** Voice will speak of this to us, as well as of the joys of Heaven which **God's** laws keep limitless forever. 4 We will repeat today's idea **that I am under no laws but God's** until we have listened and understood there are no laws but God's. 5 Then we will tell ourselves, as a dedication with which the practice period concludes: 6 I am under no laws but God's.

W-76.12.We will repeat this dedication **that I am under no laws but God's** as often as possible today; at least four or five times an hour, as well as in response to any temptation to experience ourselves as subject to other laws **of the egoic world** throughout the day. 2 **I am under no laws but God's** is our statement of freedom from all danger and all tyranny. 3 **I am under no laws but God's** is our acknowledgment that God is our Father, and that **God's** Son is saved.

Notes to Lesson # 76

I am under no laws but God's.

Lesson 76 is I am under no laws but God's laws. This lesson is again a simple statement of fact. If there is no will but God's Will, certainly only God's laws must apply. God's laws would be administered through that single Will and would apply to all of creation. Yet, once again, that is not how we perceive our current circumstances.

Earlier, we stated that illusions, not reality, are the source for all conflicts. When you believe your salvation is found in the fear-based world of individual perception, you bind yourself to the laws that apply to that illusion.

If you seek things that have no value or meaning, you bind yourself to laws that conflict and are opposites to the laws of God. Illusions have no ability to change reality and the laws that appear to apply to illusions are meaningless.

Your ego is under the illusion that you are the body and the body is you. Therefore, the laws of this physical planet are designed to apply to the body that you perceive yourself to be. When you accept the limiting beliefs of the ego's fear-based thought system, you bind yourself to the laws of that thought system.

It is your mind that empowers and enforces these beliefs upon the world that you perceive to be your own provisional reality. This is another example of the validity of the statement that when you argue for your limitations you get to keep them.

Since your decision-maker has accepted the thought system of fear, your ego's beliefs rule your world of provisional reality. Your ego's beliefs are designed to provide false confirmation that the separation is real and that your mind is a victim of outside forces that are beyond its control. Your ego does not want your decision-maker to realize that your mind is the source for all illusion and you have the power to awaken.

Your ego needs the body to suffer to prove that your mind is not the controller of its own fate. Yet, it is your split mind that powers that illusion and makes them appear real. Your mind is the creator of your own private world of provisional reality. It is your mind's desires and beliefs that bind you to the laws of this world.

On the practical side, the general rules that are applicable on the game board in time and space help insure a more uniform experience for their participants. They allow experiences to unfold in an orderly and logical fashion. The rules provide general guidelines for the game to proceed. In time and space, the physical rules of cause and effect seem to apply. We will discuss cause-and-effect in greater detail in the tomorrow's lesson.

It is important for you to realize that you are a spiritual being that has chosen to have a human experience. You have chosen to play on this game board of time and space. Your physical body is the game token that holds a space for you on that board. This game token allows you to have the human experience that you desire.

This token is not you. It is important that you do not get so caught up in the game that you forget you are not your body. If you do, that is all right too, since it makes the experience seem more real and provides an excellent test for learning what you currently value and why. It is a part of human experience that you desired.

Although the body is not you, it should not be treated with disrespect.

Your body is like a car. If you want your car to have a long service life and provide you with years of dependable transportation, it is prudent to service and maintain that car on a regular basis. If you refuse to have your car serviced and maintained, it may not be available to perform as you desire when you need it.

Eventually, even with a well-maintained car, there comes a time when it is no longer serviceable. When that is the case, you decide to trade it in for a new model. The body is just like that car. Don't mistake the body for who you really are or you will be afraid to trade it in when it no longer is capable of providing the experiences you desire.

Question: How well do you maintain your car?

Question: Do you treat your car better than you treat your body?

LESSON 77

I am entitled to miracles.

W-77.1.You are entitled to miracles because of what you are **which is God's beloved Son**. 2 You will receive miracles because of what God is. 3 And you will offer miracles because you, **God's Son,** are one with God. 4 Again, how simple is salvation! 5 **Salvation** is merely a statement of your true Identity **that you are one with God**. 6 **Your true Identity as God's Son is that you are one with God and** that is what we will celebrate today.

W-77.2.Your claim to miracles does not lie in your **ego's** illusions about yourself. 2 **Your claim to miracles** does not depend on any magical powers you have **egoically** ascribed to yourself, nor on any of the rituals your **ego** has devised. 3 **Your claim to miracles** is inherent in the truth of what you are **as God's Son**. 4 **Your claim to miracles** is implicit in what God your Father is **which is only love**. 5 **Your claim to miracles** was ensured in your creation, and guaranteed by the laws of God.

W-77.3.Today we will claim the miracles which are your right since **miracles** belong to you. 2 You have been promised full release from the **egoic** world **of separation and limitation** you made. 3 You have been assured that the Kingdom of God is within you, and **that the Kingdom of God** can never be lost. 4 We ask no more than what belongs to us in truth. 5 Today, however, we will also make sure that we will not content ourselves with less **than the Kingdom of God that is our birthright in truth**.

W-77.4.Begin the longer practice periods by telling yourself quite confidently that you are entitled to miracles. 2 Closing your eyes, remind yourself that you are asking only for what is rightfully yours. 3 Remind yourself also that miracles are never taken from one and given to another, and that in asking for your right **to miracles**, you are upholding the rights **to miracles for** everyone. 4 Miracles do not obey the laws of this world. 5 **Miracles** merely follow from the laws of God.

W-77.5.After this brief introductory phase, wait quietly for the assurance that your request is granted. 2 You have asked for the salvation of the world, and for your own **salvation**. 3 You have requested that you be given the means by which **miracles and salvation are** accomplished. 4 You cannot fail to be assured in this. 5 You are but asking that the Will of God be done.

W-77.6.In **asking that the Will of God be done**, you do not really ask for anything. 2 You state a fact that cannot be denied. 3 The Holy Spirit cannot but assure you that your request is granted. 4 The fact that you accepted must be so. **There can be no doubt that the Will of God is done** 5 There is no room for doubt and uncertainty today. 6 We are asking a real question at last. 7 The answer is a simple statement of a simple fact **that the Will of God must be done**. 8 You will receive the assurance that you seek.

W-77.7.Our shorter practice periods will be frequent, and will also be devoted to a reminder of a simple fact. 2 Tell yourself often today:
3 I am entitled to miracles.
4 Ask for **miracles** whenever a situation arises in which **miracles** are called for. 5 You will recognize these situations **in which miracles are called for.** 6 And since you are not relying on your **ego's little "s"** self to find the miracle, you are fully entitled to receive **the miracle** whenever you ask.

W-77.8.Remember, too, not to be satisfied with less than the perfect answer. 2 Be quick to tell yourself, should you be tempted:
3 I will not trade miracles for grievances. 4 I want only what belongs to me. 5 God has established miracles as my right.

Notes to Lesson # 77

I am entitled to miracles.

Lesson77 is I am entitled to miracles. So let's all meet at the swimming pool and practice walking on water. Is that what this lesson is really telling us?

You are entitled to miracles because of what you are. What you are in truth is a Child of God.

You will receive miracles because of what God is. What is God? God is only love. God is only Truth with a capital T.

You will offer miracles because you are one with God which means you also are only love and that only Truth with a capital T is real.

In regard to miracles, it says that miracles do not obey the laws of this world. Miracles merely follow the laws of God.

So what is a miracle for ACIM purposes?

It is not the ability to walk on water or change water into wine. A miracle has nothing to do with the physical world. Instead, a miracle is simply a change in your perception.

A miracle occurs whenever there is a shift within someone's mind from fear-based thinking to the thought system of love and forgiveness. When someone reacts with fear and you are able to respond with love, a miracle occurs. To an outside observer, there may or may not be any visible change in the physical world. Yet, there always is a change within the mind of the receiver.

When you ask for guidance, you will see things differently. The Holy Spirit will change false perception into correct perception. Correct perception reflects the truth of who you really are. You reinterpret the event through the eyes of love and forgiveness and drop the ego's fear-based story.

This reinterpretation is basically a reframing of the story. Rather than follow the fearful thought system of the ego, you choose to follow the thought system of the Holy Spirit. Instead of misinterpreting what happened through your ego's beliefs, you correctly apply the laws of God to the event with the help of the Holy Spirit. By correctly applying God's laws to the event, instead of holding a grievance, you gain a miracle. You have correctly applied the laws of God by utilizing the vision of Christ. You are choosing to see through the eyes of forgiveness and love.

In time and space, the laws of cause and effect appear to control destiny. There is first a cause which is then followed by a reaction or effect. Science says that for every action, there is an equal and corresponding reaction. All the great religions also reference this law of cause and effect. Some of our most popular sayings mirror this idea.

What you reap, you will sow.

An eye for an eye, a tooth for a tooth.

Do onto others what you would have them do onto you.

Like begets like.

Hinduism calls the law of cause and effect simply karma. In the West, karma has been misunderstood by many to mean that if I harm somebody that other person will eventually harm me. Certainly in this world, revenge is used as an excuse for many people's inappropriate actions. But is this how it really works? If I harm my brother, am I doomed to suffer the same negative consequences from the hands of my brother?

Lesson 76 says, I am under no laws but God's. Although we have not discussed what God's laws are, even in time and space, God's laws do apply. We just fail to understand them and misapply them to what we experience. This misapplication occurs when we follow the thought system of fear.

The thought system of fear teaches that our experiences come from outside our mind and our thoughts are the result of those outside experiences. God's law tells us that our mind's thoughts or beliefs are the cause and that the experiences that follow are the effect of our mind.

Your own mind is always the cause, not some outside power that is beyond your control. The fear-based thought system realizes that experiences come from someplace, but it misassigns where the responsibility lies and fails to recognize the true cause.

Grievances arise from the idea that someone needs to do something to make you happy or save you. It misassigns the cause of your happiness to your outside world rather than your own mind. A miracle simply applies the laws of God to your ego's story and correctly applies those laws to align with the truth.

In this world of time and space, there are no victims nor victimizers, only willing participants. No one has the ability to rob you of your inner peace unless you choose to allow it. Although you may not be in 100% control of all the circumstances that occur in your life, you are always in control of how you choose to interpret your events. You get to write the story. You also have the ability to edit the script. In a miracle, you allow the Holy Spirit to re-cut the film to correctly reflect the laws of God to the event itself.

A foundational law of God is that to give is to receive.

Our ego fails to understand how God's law applies and instead believes that you only give to get. The ego believes that when you give something, you can get something that is different from what you gave. But in time and space, the laws of God still apply. You cannot receive something different from what you are giving. But your ego misunderstands what you are really giving.

The ego believes that if you give a big enough diamond ring, you can buy someone's affection or loyalty. In this example, the ego mistakes what you are giving. It mistakes form for content. What you are giving is your fear-based belief that love can be earned or bought. What you receive back is that same belief that love can be earned or bought. You give a form of fear that we call conditional love and in return you receive that same fear-based love back.

In the physical world, we believe that the laws of God do not apply because we mistake form for content. The laws of God always apply but we just fail to understand or misapply them. Once again, let's look at God's law that to give is to receive.

When you give your fearful thoughts to the world, your fearful thoughts are reflected back to you as a fearful world.

When you give an illusion, you receive an illusion.

When you attack another, you attack yourself.

When you forgive another, you forgive yourself.

When you see another as a body, you see yourself as a body.

A miracle simply corrects the ego's misperception of the laws of God. It takes the ego story and re-edits the story so that it properly aligns with the laws of God.

The miracle allows the Holy Spirit to take a dream that was seen through fearful eyes and view that same dream through the eyes of love and forgiveness.

What the Holy Spirit's reframing does is break the cycle of giving and receiving the illusion of fear. Remember, fear is false evidence appearing real. The Holy Spirit knows that all illusions have no ability to change the truth of who you are. It takes an illusion of fear and gives back an illusion of love and forgiveness. The miracle breaks the cycle of fear-based thinking.

The miracle or the Holy Spirit's story is still a story. It is part of the dream of reawakening and therefore, is not real. But it does lead to the reawakening of sleeping minds. It still belongs in the world of perception but now misperception has been changed to correct perception. Correct perception aligns with the truth and that leads to the end of fear and the reawakening to the truth.

A miracle occurs when you choose to exchange a grievance for true forgiveness.

Remember that a grievance arises when you believe that someone's actions are needed to save or make you happy. When they fail to perform according to your ego's plan, a grievance is born.

Question: A miracle is simply a change in your perception from fear to love. It occurs within the mind and is not necessarily observable in the physical world.

How does that definition compare to your previous understanding of what a miracle is?

Question: Does this new definition help explain why you are entitled to miracles?

Let miracles replace all grievances.

W-78.1.Perhaps it is not yet quite clear to you that each decision that you make is **a decision** between a grievance and a miracle. 2 Each grievance stands like a dark shield of hate before the miracle **the grievance** would conceal. 3 And as you raise **each grievance** up before your eyes, you will not see the miracle beyond. 4 Yet all the while **the miracle beyond the grievance** waits for you in light, but you behold your grievances instead.

W-78.2.Today we go beyond the grievances, to look upon the miracle instead. 2 We will reverse the way you see by not allowing sight to stop **at the grievance** before it sees **the miracle beyond**. 3 We will not wait before the **grievance's** shield of hate, but lay **the shield of hate** down and gently lift our eyes in silence to behold the Son of God.

W-78.3.**The Son of God** waits for you behind your grievances, and as you lay **your grievances** down he will appear in shining light where each **grievance** stood before. 2 For every grievance is a block to sight, and as **your grievance** lifts you see the Son of God where **the Son of God** has always been. 3 **The Son of God** stands in light, but you were in the dark. 4 Each grievance made the darkness deeper, and you could not see **the light**.

W-78.4.Today we will attempt to see God's Son. 2 We will not let ourselves be blind to **the Son of God**; we will not look upon our grievances. 3 So is the seeing of the world reversed, as we look out toward truth, away from fear **that your grievances hold**. 4 We will select one person you have used as target for your grievances, and lay the grievances aside and look at **that person**. 5 Someone, perhaps, you fear and even hate; someone you think you love who angered you; someone you call a friend, but whom you see as difficult at times or hard to please, demanding, irritating or untrue to the ideal **that person** should accept as his, according to the role you set for **that person**.

W-78.5.You know the one to choose; his name has crossed your mind already. 2 **That person that you hold grievances against** will be the one of whom we ask God's Son be shown to you. 3 Through seeing **him as God's Son** behind the grievances that you have held against **that person**, you will learn that **his light that** lay hidden while you saw him not **as God's Son** is there in everyone, and can be seen. 4 **That person that you held grievances against** who was **your** enemy is more than **your** friend when he is freed to take the holy role the Holy Spirit has assigned to him. 5 Let **that person that you hold grievances against** be savior unto you today. 6 Such is **that person's holy role that the Holy Spirit has assigned to him as your savior** in God, your Father's plan.

W-78.6.Our longer practice periods today will see **that person** in this role **that the Holy Spirit has assigned to him as your savior**. 2 You will attempt to hold **that person** in your mind, first as you now consider him. 3 You will review **that person's** faults, the difficulties you have had with him, the pain **that person** caused you, his neglect, and all the little and the larger hurts he gave. 4 You will regard **that person's** body with its flaws and better points as well, and you will think of **that person's** mistakes and even of his "sins."

W-78.7.Then let us ask of **the Holy Spirit** Who knows this Son of God in his reality and truth, that we may look on **that person in** a different way, and see our savior shining in the light of true forgiveness, given unto us. 2 We ask **the Holy Spirit** in the holy Name of God and of His Son, as holy as Himself:
3 Let me behold my savior in this **person that** You, **the Holy Spirit,** have appointed as the one for me to ask to lead me to the holy light in which **this person** stands, that I may join with **this person that You, the Holy Spirit has assigned to me as my savior**.
4 The body's eyes are closed, and as you think of **this person** who grieved you, let your mind be shown the light in **this person** beyond your grievances.

W-78.8.What you have asked for, **to be shown the light in this person beyond your grievances,** cannot be denied. 2 **This person**, your savior, has been waiting long for this. 3 **This person that you held a grievance against** would be free, and make his freedom yours. 4 The Holy Spirit leans from **this person that you held a grievance against** to you, seeing no separation in God's Son. 5 And what you see through **the Holy Spirit** will free you both. 6 Be very quiet now, and look upon your shining savior. 7 No dark grievances obscure the sight of **this person that you held a grievance against**. 8 You have allowed the Holy Spirit to express through **this person that you held a grievance against** the role God gave Him, **the Holy Spirit,** that you might be saved.

W-78.9.God thanks you for these quiet times today in which you laid your images aside, and looked upon the miracle of love the Holy Spirit showed you in **the** place **of your ego's images**. 2 The world and Heaven join in thanking you, for not one Thought of God but must rejoice as you are saved, and all the world with you.

W-78.10.We will remember this throughout the day, and take the role assigned to us as part of God's salvation plan, and not our own **ego's plan for salvation**. 2 Temptation falls away when we allow each one we meet to save us, and refuse to hide **each person's** light behind our grievances. 3 To everyone you meet, and to the ones you think of or remember from the past, allow the role of savior to be given, that you may share **the role of savior** with **everyone**. 4 For you **and that person that**

you held a grievance against and all the sightless ones as well, we pray:
5 Let miracles replace all grievances.

Notes to Lesson # 78

Let miracles replace all grievances.

Lesson 78, let miracles replace all grievances, addresses your decision-maker. Within your split mind, you have the ability to choose between which two thought systems you will follow. Will it be the thought system for love and forgiveness or the thought system for fear?

This is always the decision that you are asked to make. Based on that decision, you will give and receive either a grievance or a miracle. You can only choose one as each is mutually exclusive.

In time and space, your life unfolds before you as a series of cause and effect relationships surrounded by conditions. The cause for all experiences is your own mind. Your world of perception reflects your own thoughts and beliefs. The experiences that follow are the effect of your mind's thinking.

The mass collective consciousness of our world is fear-based. Because of this, the provisional reality of most people is frightening. Their world reflects their ego's belief that they are a limited ego body in competition with other limited ego bodies for the limited resources both need to survive.

Your ego has developed a plan for your survival. The ego's plan says that something outside your mind must act in a certain way for you to get your needs met. This belief lays the foundation for grievances which are the primary weapon that our ego uses to manipulate its outer world in an attempt to get its way.

Another part of your ego's plan for your happiness entails entering into special relationships with other parties to help insure that your needs will be met. In the special relationship, each party surrenders some of their limited resources in exchange for the resources of the other party. When someone fails to perform according to your ego's plan, a grievance is formed and you are justified in demanding some type of satisfaction. Your ego's ability to survive revolves around you holding grievances against your neighbor.

Your ego uses these grievances to manipulate the person in hopes of getting its own way. These grievances are really your egoic mind's justification for your attack against the other. Your ego's world reflects the grievances that you hold because your outer world is merely a reflection of your inner world.

Egoic grievances are reflected in each person's actions as each attempts to manipulate the other party to get their way. Most people realize they are being manipulated and therefore, they counterattack with their own brand of the manipulation. Egoic relationships become a series of attacks and counter attacks with each party determined to get the best deal and to prove they are right.

Actually grievances are an attack on both party's abilities to be the creator of their own experience. Holding grievances helps maintain the cycle of attack and counterattack. Grievances reinforce the ego's belief that there are outside forces that must act in a certain way if you are to be happy. Grievances declare that you are an innocent victim. When you choose to let a miracle replace the attack and counterattack relationship, you break that fear-based cycle.

Your decision-maker has a choice over how you will decide to react to the egoic projections and actions of your brothers and sisters. You can choose to perceive another's actions through the eyes of fear. If so, their actions will be perceived as an attack and manipulation. This is how most people choose to react. This justifies additional grievances on both sides.

Or

You can break from tradition and choose to view their actions as a cry for love and to respond appropriately. When you choose to follow the thought system of the Holy Spirit, you obtain the vision of love and forgiveness. When you see another's actions as a cry for love, rather than an attack, you have decided that your inner peace is more important than holding a grievance against the other party.

Your choice for a miracle, instead of a grievance, breaks the fear-based cycle within your own mind and perhaps that same cycle for all parties involved. You have decided not to project back the illusion of fear into your outer world. Instead, your story reinterprets your brother's action as a cry for love and you respond with love and forgiveness. The cycle of fear has been broken and your world becomes a more peaceful place.

Question: What is more important, your right to blame another for failing to make you happy or your own inner peace?

LESSON 79

Let me recognize the problem so it can be solved.

W-79.1.A problem cannot be solved if you do not know what **the problem** is. 2 Even if **the problem** is really solved already you will still have the problem, because you will not recognize that **the problem** has been solved. 3 This is the situation of the world. 4 The problem of separation, which is really the only problem, has already been solved. 5 Yet the solution is not recognized because the problem **of separation** is not recognized.

W-79.2.Everyone in this world seems to have his own special problems. 2 Yet **everyone's special problems** are all the same **problem**, and must be recognized as one **problem** if the one solution that solves **everyone's problems** is to be accepted. 3 Who can see that a problem has been solved if he thinks the problem is something else? 4 Even if he is given the answer **to his real problem**, he cannot see the **answer's** relevance.

W-79.3.That is the position in which you find yourself now. 2 You have the answer, but you are still uncertain about what the problem is. 3 A long series of different problems seems to confront you, and as one **problem** is settled the next **problem** and the next arise. 4 There seems to be no end to **the different problems that confront you**. 5 There is no time in which you feel completely free of problems and at peace.

W-79.4.The temptation to regard problems as many is the temptation to keep the problem of separation unsolved. 2 The world seems to present you with a vast number of problems, each requiring a different answer. 3 This perception **of multiple problems requiring different answers** places you in a position in which your problem solving must be inadequate, and failure is inevitable.

W-79.5.No one could solve all the problems the world appears to hold. 2 **The world's problems** seem to be on so many levels, in such varying forms and with such varied content, that they confront you with an impossible situation. 3 Dismay and depression are inevitable as you regard **the world's problems**. 4 Some **problems** spring up unexpectedly, just as you think you have resolved the previous **problem**. 5 Other **problems** remain unsolved under a cloud of denial, and rise to haunt you from time to time, only to be hidden again but still unsolved.

W-79.6.All this complexity is but a desperate attempt not to recognize the problem **of separation**, and therefore not to let **the problem of separation** be resolved. 2 If you could recognize that your only problem is separation, no matter what form **the problem of separation** takes, you could accept the answer because you would see **the answer's** relevance **to all your problems**. 3 Perceiving the underlying constancy in all the problems that seem to confront you, you would understand that you have the means to solve all **the various forms that the problem of separation appears to take**. 4 And you would use the means, because you recognize the problem **as a form of the real problem, which is the ego's belief of separation.**

W-79.7.In our longer practice periods today we will ask what the problem is, and what is the answer to **the problem**. 2 We will not assume that we already know **what the problem and answer is**. 3 We will try to free our minds of all the many different kinds of problems we think we have. 4 We will try to realize that we have only one problem, which we have failed to recognize. 5 We will ask what **that one problem** is, and wait for the answer. 6 We will be told **what that one problem is**. 7 Then we will ask for the solution to **that one problem**. 8 And we will be told **the solution to that one problem**.

W-79.8.The exercises for today will be successful to the extent to which you do not insist on defining the problem. 2 Perhaps you will not succeed in letting all your preconceived notions go **about what your problems are**, but that is not necessary. 3 All that is necessary is to entertain some doubt about the reality of your **ego's** version of what your problems are. 4 You are trying to recognize that you have been given the answer by recognizing the problem, so that the problem and the answer can be brought together and you can be at peace.

W-79.9.The shorter practice periods for today will not be set by time, but by need. 2 You will see many problems today, each **problem** calling for an answer. 3 Our efforts will be directed toward recognizing that there is only one problem and one answer. 4 In this recognition **that there is only one problem and one answer** are all problems resolved. 5 In this recognition **that there is only one problem and one answer** there is peace.

W-79.10.Be not deceived by the form of problems today. 2 Whenever any difficulty seems to rise, tell yourself quickly:
3 Let me recognize this problem so **this problem** can be solved.
4 Then try to suspend all **your ego's** judgment about what the problem is. 5 If possible, close your eyes for a moment and ask what **this problem** is. 6 You will be heard **by the Holy Spirit** and you will be answered **by the Holy Spirit**.

Notes to Lesson # 79

Let me recognize the problem so it can be solved.

Lesson 79 is let me recognize the problem, so it can be solved. If you do not know what the problem is, you will not be able to solve the problem. Before any problem can be resolved, you must first correctly identify the problem. Without that correct identification, you will mistake the effects of the problem for the cause. Perceiving the effect of a problem to be the cause will result in you attempting to reduce, manage or mitigate the negative consequences rather than addressing the root cause of the problem at its source.

The identification of the problem is critical if you are to correct the problem at its source. Unless you address the root cause of the problem, your attempts to manage the effects of the problem will ultimately fail. You will manage one effect or form of the problem and a new form of the problem will reappear in another area of your life.

Yet, if you do not even realize you have a problem, you will not even attempt to solve the problem. This is the situation that we often find ourselves in.

This lesson says the only problem is our belief in separation. If we understood this to be the root cause of all problems in our lives, we would finally be able to focus our attention on addressing the source of the problem. Once correctly identified, the problem can be solved.

If you realize that all your problems arose from your belief in separation, you would quickly realize that the solution to the problem would be to end your belief in separation. But the world is designed to provide proof that the separation is real and make differentiation seem possible. Because of this, there is a tendency for our mind to either

1) Fail to identify the problem of separation as a problem. We like the idea that we are special or separate with our own autonomous existence.
2) Recognize the separation as a problem but feel powerless to change it because that is just the reality of our universe.

In either case, we will not attempt to correct the problem at its source. Instead, we will focus our attention on managing, controlling and mitigating the negative consequences that our belief in separation has upon our world.

Everyone seems to have their own unique problems and multiple problems abound in this world. It only seems we have multiple problems because we confuse the numerous forms of the same problem to actually be different problems. The form is different but the cause is the same. If the root cause is the same, all problems are the same.

We mistake the multiple consequences of the single problem of separation to be unrelated problems with different root causes. We fail to see that all our problems arise from one core misperception. Correct that misperception and all our numerous forms of the problem disappear because they all trace their origins back to our belief in separation.

For example, our belief in separation means the following:

You are no longer part of the Oneness of All That Is.

You cannot be perfect, whole and complete.

You must have needs.

There is something outside of you to fear.

You need to judge our world.

Your happiness is contingent on outside forces.

You are justified in holding grievances.

You must be limited.

You must lack something.

You must be a victim.

The list goes on and on. When you believe you are separate, you develop a warped sense of what real love is. You believe that love would require you to fix, change, control, protect or impress another because you love them. You would mistake the game token that is the body to be the reality of who they are and who you really are.

Question: Do you like the idea of being different or special from others?

Question: Can you see why you might not perceive separation to be a problem when you value being different?

Let me recognize my problems have been solved.

W-80.1.If you are willing to recognize your problems, you will recognize that you have no problems. 2 Your one central problem has been answered, and you have no other **problem**. 3 Therefore, you must be at peace. 4 Salvation thus depends on recognizing this one problem **of separation,** and understanding that **this one problem of separation** has been solved. 5 One problem, one solution. 6 Salvation is accomplished. 7 Freedom from conflict has been given you. 8 Accept that fact **the one problem of separation has been solved**, and you are ready to take your rightful place in God's plan for salvation.

W-80.2.Your only problem **which is the problem of separation** has been solved! 2 Repeat this over and over to yourself today **that your only problem has been solved** with gratitude and conviction. 3 You have recognized your only problem **is your belief in separation**, opening the way for the Holy Spirit to give you God's answer. 4 You have laid **your ego's** deception aside, and seen the light of truth **through the aid of the Holy Spirit**. 5 You have accepted salvation for yourself by bringing the problem to the answer. 6 And you can recognize the answer, because the problem **of separation** has been identified.

W-80.3.You are entitled to peace today. 2 A problem that has been resolved cannot trouble you. 3 Only be certain you do not forget that all problems are the same. 4 Their many forms will not deceive you while you remember **that all problems are the same**. 5 One problem, one solution. 6 Accept the peace this simple statement brings **that there is only one problem and one solution**.

W-80.4.In our longer practice periods today, we will claim the peace that must be ours when the problem **of separation** and the answer have been brought together. 2 The problem must be gone, because God's answer cannot fail. 3 Having recognized **the problem of separation**, you have recognized **the answer to the problem of separation.** 4 The solution is inherent in the problem. 5 You are answered, and have accepted the answer. 6 You are saved.

W-80.5.Now let the peace that your acceptance brings be given you. 2 Close your eyes, and receive your reward. 3 Recognize that your problems have been solved. 4 Recognize that you are out of conflict; free and at peace. 5 Above all, remember that you have one problem, **your belief in separation**, and that the problem has one solution. 6 It is in this one problem, one solution that the simplicity of salvation lies. 7 It is because of **the simplicity of salvation** that **the solution** is guaranteed to work.

W-80.6.Assure yourself often today that your problems have been solved. 2 Repeat the idea **to let me recognize my problems have been solved,** with deep conviction, as frequently as possible. 3 And be particularly sure to apply the idea for today to l**et me recognize my problems have been solved** to any specific problem that may arise. 4 Say quickly:
5 Let me recognize this problem has been solved.

W-80.7.Let us be determined not to collect grievances today. 2 Let us be determined to be free of problems that do not exist. 3 The means is simple honesty. 4 Do not deceive yourself about what the problem is, and you must recognize **the problem** has been solved.

Notes to Lesson # 80

Let me recognize my problems have been solved.

Lesson 80 is let me recognize that my problems have been solved. This is a follow-up to yesterday's lesson that asked you to recognize the problem so that it could be solved.

Yesterday's lesson said that we have only one problem and that is our belief in separation. When you recognize what the real problem is, you can seek a solution for the real problem. Without that identification, you wander aimlessly about with no direction or purpose. You attempt to bandage over the effects of the problem rather than addressing the true cause. When we realize that our grievances are maintaining the problem, we realize that we need to stop holding those grievances. Yet, our grievances stem from our erroneous belief about our world and who we really are.

When we recognize that we have only one problem, it becomes obvious that there is only one solution that will work. If there is only one problem and one solution, pursuing different plans that fail to address or recognize the real problem is a waste of time since they cannot work. Since your ego does not recognize what your happiness is, your ego's plans for your happiness are not a viable solution. Instead, your ego's plans are the problem.

Although we stated that our problem is separation, we need to clarify what that problem really is. The problem is not our participation in the game of separation. The problem is that we forgot it is a fantasy. We forget to laugh and made the game real within our own mind's imagination. We made fear into our provisional reality and heard the voice for that fear. Our mind now appears to be split with two possible voices to be heard; the voice for fear and the Voice for Love. One voice represents the false and is the problem. The other Voice represents the Truth and is the solution.

We have forgotten that time and space is merely a game board to allow inquisitive individuated aspects of the One Self to demonstrate, know and be that One Self. When we forgot, we transformed the exciting and fun journey of reawakening into a struggle to recover the paradise we thought we had lost. We came here to be, know and demonstrate the individuated aspects of love in form.

When we mistook the game board for our reality, the journey became a fearful struggle to earn back our divine inheritance that we really believed we had lost. Rather than simply explore the various aspects of being love in form in a safe environment, our ego believed we were separate from our source, had something to fear, and that love had to be earned if we were to get our needs met.

We had forgotten who we truly are. Our belief that we could be something we are not is really the problem of separation. Being an indivisible, individuated aspect of the One Self, we slipped into fear, forgot the true purpose of the game, and made the false evidence that appeared as our imagination's game board into our provisional reality. The game board was designed so that the child could learn, grow and have fun while exploring the various aspects of itself in perfect safety. The game board is incapable of changing the truth of who we are.

A wise parent allows their children to go to school. The purpose of the school is to provide a good education in a safe environment so that the child can realize their true potential and be all that it is capable of being as an adult. Children start off in kindergarten and progress as they continue to hone their skills and transform potential talent into real, usable skills. Children should not feel guilty about being in school or not being able to demonstrate all the skills that they will eventually develop and possess when they graduate.

It's all right to be in elementary school since were all guaranteed to graduate. You are exactly where you need to be in the journey of rediscovery. Don't make yourself wrong because of the grade you are in. Instead, enjoy the journey of being in elementary school so that you can continue to grow and learn.

When the journey of reawakening was judged to be a separation from our divine birthright, we transformed a fun learning experience into a battle to recover what we feared we had lost. We forgot that the game board was not our true reality. An individuated aspect of the One Self could never be separate from Itself. We forgot the truth that we remain as God created us, perfect whole and complete. We forgot who we truly are. We mistook the voice for fear, lack, limitation and separation to be our reality.

Your ego is your false belief that you could be, not perfect, not whole and not complete. Your ego is the embodiment of your belief in separation. Your ego is the false notion of who you are.

You are an individuated aspect of consciousness. In time and space, you are a feedback loop that allows you to recognize the effects of the decisions that you are currently making. You get to modify those decisions as needed as you hone your skills. This leads to your rediscovery of your true spiritual magnificence.

Your ego is the embodiment of fear. Fear is false evidence appearing real. When you realize that your problem is your belief in your ego's fear-based thought system, you can solve the problem at its source. You can decide to stop listening to the voice for fear.

Your ego is the problem. It is foolish to expect the problem to solve itself. Instead, you need to remove yourself from the problem and listen to the Voice for Truth that knows who you really are.

The Holy Spirit is within you. Therefore, you have never been separated from God. The Holy Spirit is God's Voice and the bridge that connects the Father to the Son.

There is only one problem and one solution.

Your ego is the problem. Therefore, your ego cannot be the solution.

The solution has already been provided within your mind. All you need to do is to listen to that Voice for God within and you will realize that paradise was never lost, only forgotten. Listen exclusively to the Holy Spirit and It will bring you home.

Question: Does Jesus have an ego?

REVIEW #2

Introduction

Lessons 81-90 are a review of Workbook Lessons 61- 80

W-rII.in.1.We are now ready for another review. 2 We will begin where our last review left off, and cover two ideas each day. 3 The earlier part of each day will be devoted to one of these **two** ideas, and the latter part of the day to the other **idea**. 4 We will have one longer exercise period, and frequent shorter ones in which we practice each of **the two ideas.**

W-rII.in.2.The longer practice periods will follow this general form: Take about fifteen minutes for each of **the longer practice periods**, and begin by thinking about the ideas for the day, and the comments that are included in the assignments. 2 Devote some three or four minutes to reading over slowly **the ideas for the day and the comments that are included in the assignments**, several times if you wish, and then close your eyes and listen.

W-rII.in.3.If you find your mind wandering, repeat the first phase of the exercise period **by reading the ideas for the day and the comments**, but try to spend the major part of the time listening quietly but attentively. 2 There is a message waiting for you. 3 Be confident that you will receive **a message from the Holy Spirit**. 4 Remember that **the message from the Holy Spirit** belongs to you, and that you want **the message from the Holy Spirit**.

W-rII.in.4.Do not allow your intent to waver in the face of distracting thoughts. 2 Realize that, whatever form such **distracting** thoughts may take, **distracting thoughts** have no meaning and no power. 3 Replace **these distracting thoughts** with your determination to succeed. 4 Do not forget that your will has power over all fantasies and dreams. 5 Trust **your will** to see you through, and carry you beyond all **distracting thoughts**.

W-rII.in.5.Regard these practice periods as dedications to the way, the truth and the life. 2 Refuse to be sidetracked into detours, illusions and thoughts of death. 3 You are dedicated to salvation. 4 Be determined each day not to leave your function **of forgiveness and salvation** unfulfilled.

W-rII.in.6.Reaffirm your determination in the shorter practice periods as well, using the original form of the idea for general applications, and more specific forms when needed. 2 Some specific forms are included in the comments which follow the statement of the ideas. 3 These **specific forms,** however, are merely suggestions. 4 It is not the particular words you use that matter.

Notes to Review #2

Introduction

Lessons #81-90 are a review of Workbook Lessons #61- 80

The next 10 lessons are actually a review of the previous 20. Each day you will be asked to review two of the previous lessons with an emphasis on one of the prior lessons in either your morning or evening sessions. I will not be providing any additional notes regarding these review lessons since they are brief, self-explanatory and designed for the inner contemplation of those prior lessons.

I would suggest that you review the notes that were given for each original lesson that you are focusing on during each session. For example, lesson 81 covers lesson 61 and 62. Assuming your morning session will focus on lesson 61, I would suggest you review the notes for session 61 along with a reading of lesson 81. In your evening session you would review the notes for lesson 62 along with a reading of lesson 81 again.

You will be amazed at the new insight that each review will provide. What seemed obscure a few days ago may now appear obvious. Enjoy these reviews and honor the journey of rediscovering who you really are.

LESSON SUMMARY #61-62

Our ideas for review today are:

Lesson # 61: I am the light of the world.

Lesson # 62: Forgiveness is my function as the light of the world.

W-81.1. <u>**Review of Lesson # 61: I am the light of the world.**</u>
2 How holy am I, who have been given the function of lighting up the world! 3 Let me be still before my holiness. 4 In **my holy** calm light let all my conflicts disappear. 5 In **my holy** peace let me remember Who I am. **I am God's beloved Child with whom God is well pleased.**

W-81.2.Some specific forms for applying this idea **that I am the light of the world** when special difficulties seem to arise might be:
2 Let **my ego** not obscure the light of the world in me.
3 Let the light of the world shine through this appearance.
4 This shadow will vanish before the light.

W-81.3.<u>**Review of Lesson # 62: Forgiveness is my function as the light of the world.**</u>
2 It is through accepting my function **of forgiveness** that I will see the light in me. 3 And in this light **in me** will my function **of forgiveness** stand clear and perfectly unambiguous before my sight. 4 My acceptance **of my function** does not depend on my recognizing what my function is, for I do not yet understand forgiveness. 5 Yet I will trust that, in the light, I will see **forgiveness** as **forgiveness** is.

W-81.4.Specific forms for using this idea **that forgiveness is my function as the light of the world** might include:
2 Let this help me learn what forgiveness means.
3 Let me not separate my function **of forgiveness** from my will.
4 I will not use this for an alien **egoic** purpose.

LESSON 82.

LESSON SUMMARY #63-64

We will review these ideas today:

Lesson # 63: The light of the world brings peace to every mind through my forgiveness.

Lesson # 64: Let me not forget my function.

W-82.1. **Review of Lesson # 63: The light of the world brings peace to every mind through my forgiveness.**
2 My forgiveness is the means by which the light of the world finds expression through me. 3 My forgiveness is the means by which I become aware of the light of the world in me. 4 My forgiveness is the means by which the world is healed, together with my **little "s"** self. 5 Let me, then, forgive the world, that **the world** may be healed along with me.

W-82.2. Suggestions for specific forms for applying this idea **that the light of the world brings peace to every mind through my forgiveness** are:
2 Let peace extend from my mind to yours, [name].
3 I share the light of the world with you, [name].
4 Through my forgiveness I can see this as it is.

W-82.3. **Review of Lesson # 64: Let me not forget my function.**
2 I would not forget my function **of forgiveness**, because I would remember my **big "S" Self**. 3 I cannot fulfill my function **of forgiveness** if I forget **my function**. 4 And unless I fulfill my function **of forgiveness**, I will not experience the joy that God intends for me.

W-82.4. Suitable specific forms of this idea **of let me not forget my function of forgiveness includes**:
2 Let **my ego** not use this to hide my function **of forgiveness** from me.
3 I would use this as an opportunity to fulfill my function **of forgiveness**.
4 This may threaten my ego, but cannot change my function **of forgiveness** in any way.

LESSON 83.

LESSON SUMMARY #65-66

Today let us review these ideas:

Lesson # 65: My only function is the one God gave me.

Lesson # 66: My happiness and my function are one.

W-83.1. <u>**Review of Lesson # 65: My only function is the one God gave me.**</u>
2 I have no function but the one God gave me **which is the function of forgiveness**. 3 This recognition **that my only function is from God** releases me from all conflict, because it means I cannot have conflicting **egoic** goals. 4 With one purpose only, **which is forgiveness,** I am always certain what to do, what to say and what to think. 5 All **my ego's** doubts must disappear as I acknowledge that my only function **of forgiveness** is the one God gave me.

W-83.2. More specific applications of this idea **that my only function is the one God gave me** might take these forms:
2 My **ego's** perception of this does not change my function **of forgiveness**.
3 This does not give me a function other than the one God gave me **which is forgiveness**.
4 Let **my ego** not use this to justify a function God did not give me.

W-83.3. <u>**Review of Lesson # 66: My happiness and my function are one.**</u>
2 All things that come from God are one. 3 **All things** come from Oneness, and must be received as one. 4 Fulfilling my function **of forgiveness** is my happiness because both **my function of forgiveness and my happiness** come from the same Source. 5 And I must learn to recognize what makes me happy if I would find happiness.

W-83.4. Some useful forms for specific applications of this idea **that my happiness and my function of forgiveness are one** are:
2 This cannot separate my happiness from my function **of forgiveness**.
3 The oneness of my happiness and my function **of forgiveness** remains wholly unaffected by this.
4 Nothing, including this, can justify the illusion of happiness apart from my function **of forgiveness**.

LESSON 84.

LESSON SUMMARY #67-68

These are the ideas for today's review:

Lesson # 67: Love created me like Itself.

Lesson # 68: Love holds no grievances.

W-84.1. **Review of Lesson # 67: Love created me like Itself.**
2 I am in the likeness of my Creator. 3 **Like my Creator,** I cannot suffer, I cannot experience loss and I cannot die. 4 **Like my Creator,** I am not a body. 5 I would recognize my reality today. 6 I will worship no idols, nor raise my own **egoic little "s"** self-concept to replace my **big "S"** Self. 7 I am in the likeness of my Creator. 8 Love created me like Itself.

W-84.2.You might find these specific forms helpful in applying the idea **that Love created me like Itself:**
2 Let **my ego** not see an illusion of my **little "s"** self in this.
3 As I look on this, let me remember my Creator **Who created me like Itself.**
4 My Creator did not create this as **my ego** sees it.

W-84.3. **Review of Lesson # 68: Love holds no grievances.**
2 Grievances are completely alien to love. 3 Grievances attack love and keep **love's** light obscure. 4 If I hold grievances I am attacking love, and therefore attacking my **big "S"** Self. 5 My **big "S"** Self thus becomes alien to me. 6 I am determined not to attack my **big "S"** Self today, so that I can remember Who I am, **which is God's beloved Child with whom God is well pleased.**

W-84.4.These specific forms for applying this idea **that Love holds no grievances** would be helpful:
2 This is no justification for denying my **big "S"** Self.
3 I will not use this to attack love.
4 Let this not tempt **my ego** to attack my **big "S"** Self.

LESSON SUMMARY #69-70

Today's review will cover these ideas:

Lesson #69: My grievances hide the light of the world in me.

Lesson # 70: My salvation comes from me.

W-85.1.<u>Review of Lesson # 69: My grievances hide the light of the world in me.</u>

2 My grievances show me what is not there, and hide from me what I would see. 3 Recognizing **that my grievances show me what is not there and hide from me what I would see,** what do I want my grievances for? 4 **My grievances** keep me in darkness and hide the light. 5 Grievances and light cannot go together, but light and vision must be joined for me to see. 6 To see, I must lay grievances aside. 7 I want to see, and **the laying of my grievances aside** will be the means by which I will succeed.

W-85.2.Specific applications for this idea **that my grievances hide the light of the world in me** might be made in these forms:
2 Let me not use this as a block to sight.
3 The light of the world will shine all this away.
4 I have no need for this. 5 I want to see.

W-85.3. <u>Review of Lesson # 70: My salvation comes from me.</u>

2 Today I will recognize where my salvation is. 3 **My salvation** is in me because **the Source of my salvation** is there **in me.** 4 **My salvation** has not left its Source, and so **my salvation** cannot have left my mind. 5 I will not look for **my salvation** outside myself. 6 **My salvation** is not found outside and then brought in. 7 But from within me, **my salvation** will reach beyond **me,** and everything I see will but reflect the light that shines in me and in itself.

W-85.4.These forms of the idea that **my salvation comes from me** are suitable for more specific applications:
2 Let this not tempt me to look away from me for my salvation.
3 I will not let this interfere with my awareness of the Source of my salvation.
4 This has no power to remove salvation from me.

LESSON SUMMARY #71-72

Today's review will cover these ideas:

Lesson #71: Only God's plan for salvation will work.

Lesson # 72: Holding grievances is an attack on God's plan for salvation.

These ideas are for review today:

W-86.1. <u>**Review of Lesson # 71: Only God's plan for salvation will work.**</u>
2 It is senseless for me to search wildly about for salvation. 3 I have seen **egoic salvation** in many people and in many things, but when I reached for **true salvation**, it was not there. 4 **My ego** was mistaken about where **true salvation** is. 5 **My ego** was mistaken about what **true salvation** is. 6 I will undertake no more idle seeking **by following my ego's plan for my salvation**. 7 Only God's plan for salvation will work. 8 And I will rejoice because **God's** plan can never fail.

W-86.2.These are some suggested forms for applying this idea **that only God's plan for salvation will work to some** specific **applications**:
2 God's plan for salvation will save me from my perception of this.
3 This is no exception in God's plan for my salvation.
4 Let me perceive this only in the light of God's plan for salvation.

W-86.3. <u>**Review of Lesson # 72: Holding grievances is an attack on God's plan for salvation.**</u>
2 Holding grievances is an attempt to prove that God's plan for salvation will not work. 3 Yet only **God's** plan will work. 4 By holding grievances, I am therefore excluding my only hope of salvation from my awareness **that only God's plan will work**. 5 I would no longer defeat my own best interests in this insane way **by holding grievances**. 6 I would accept God's plan for salvation, and be happy.

W-86.4.Specific applications for this idea **that holding grievances is an attack on God's plan for salvation** might be in these forms:
2 I am choosing between misperception and salvation as I look on this.
3 If I see grounds for grievances in this, I will not see the grounds for my salvation.
4 This calls for salvation, not attack.

LESSON 87.

LESSON SUMMARY #73-74

Today's review will cover these ideas:

Lesson #73: <u>I will there be light.</u>

Lesson # 74: <u>There is no will but God's.</u>

These ideas are for review today:

W-87.1. <u>**Review of Lesson # 73: I will there be light.**</u>
2 I will use the power of my **true** will today. 3 It is not my **true** will to grope about in darkness, fearful of shadows and afraid of things unseen and unreal. 4 Light shall be my guide today. 5 I will follow **the light of my true will** where it leads me, and I will look only on what **the light of my true will** shows me. 6 This day I will experience the peace of true perception.

W-87.2.These forms of this idea **that I will there be light** would be helpful for specific applications:
2 This cannot hide the light I will to see.
3 You stand with me in light, [name].
4 In the light this will look different.

W-87.3. <u>**Review of Lesson # 74: There is no will but God's.**</u>
2 I am safe today because there is no will but God's **Will**. 3 I can become afraid only when I believe there is another will. 4 I try to attack only when I am afraid **and think there is another will besides God's Will.** And only when I try to attack can I believe that my eternal safety is threatened. 5 Today I will recognize that all **my imagined threats to my safety** have not occurred. 6 I am safe because there is no will but God's.

W-87.4.These are some useful forms of this idea **that there is no will but God's Will** for **your** specific applications:
2 Let me perceive this in accordance with the Will of God.
3 It is God's Will you are His Son, [name], and **it is my will** as well.
4 This is part of God's Will for me, however I may see it.

LESSON 88.

LESSON SUMMARY #75-76

Today's review will cover these ideas:

Lesson #75: The light has come.

Lesson # 76: I am under no laws but God's laws.

W-88.1. <u>Review of Lesson # 75 The light has come.</u>
2 In choosing salvation rather than attack, I merely choose to recognize what is already there **by utilizing the vision of Christ**. 3 Salvation is a decision made already. 4 **When I use the vision of Christ,** attack and grievances are not there to choose. 5 That is why I always choose between truth and illusion; between what is there and what is not. 6 The light has come. 7 I can but choose the light, for **the light of true vision** has no alternative. 8 **Light** has replaced the darkness, and the darkness has gone.

W-88.2.These would prove useful forms for specific applications of this idea that **the light has come**:
2 This cannot show me darkness, for the light has come.
3 The light in you is all that I would see, [name].
4 I would see in this only what is there.

W-88.3. <u>Review of Lesson # 76: I am under no laws but God's.</u>
2 **I am under no laws but God's laws** is the perfect statement of my freedom. 3 I am under no laws but God's laws. 4 I am constantly tempted to make up other **egoic** laws and give **these laws of the ego** power over me. 5 I suffer only because of my belief in **the laws of the ego**. 6 **These laws of the ego** have no real effect on me at all. 7 I am perfectly free of the effects of all laws save God's **laws**. 8 And **God's laws** are the laws of freedom.

W-88.4.For specific forms in applying this idea **that I am under no laws but God's laws the following suggestions** would be useful:
2 My perception of this shows me I believe in **egoic** laws that do not exist.
3 I see only the laws of God at work in this.
4 Let me allow God's laws to work in this, and not my own **ego's laws**.

LESSON SUMMARY #77-78

Today's review will cover these ideas:

Lesson #77: I am entitled to miracles.

Lesson # 78: Let miracles replace all grievances.

W-89.1.. <u>Review of Lesson # 77: I am entitled to miracles.</u>

2 I am entitled to miracles because I am under no laws but God's **laws**. 3 **God's** laws release me from all grievances, and replace **all grievances** with miracles. 4 And I would accept the miracles in place of the grievances, which are but illusions that hide the miracles beyond. 5 Now I would accept only what the laws of God entitle me to have, that I may use **miracles** on behalf of the function **of forgiveness that God** has given me.

W-89.2.You might use these suggestions for specific applications of this idea **that I am entitled to miracles**:
2 Behind this is a miracle to which I am entitled.
3 Let me not hold a grievance against you, [name], but offer you the miracle that belongs to you instead.
4 Seen truly, this offers me a miracle.

W-89.3. <u>Review of Lesson # 78: Let miracles replace all grievances.</u>

2 By this idea **of letting miracles replace all grievances** do I unite my will with the Holy Spirit's, and perceive **both the Holy Spirit and my will** as one. 3 By this idea **of letting miracles replace all grievances** do I accept my release from hell. 4 By this idea **of letting miracles replace all grievances** do I express my willingness to have all my illusions be replaced with truth, according to God's plan for my salvation. 5 I would make no exceptions and no substitutes. 6 I want all of Heaven and only Heaven, as God wills me to have.

W-89.4.Useful specific forms for applying this idea **of letting miracles replace all grievances** would be:
2 I would not hold this grievance apart from my salvation.
3 Let our grievances be replaced by miracles, [name].
4 Beyond this is the miracle by which all my grievances are replaced.

LESSON 90.

LESSON SUMMARY #79-80

Today's review will cover these ideas:

Lesson #79: Let me recognize the problem so it can be solved.

Lesson # 80: Let me recognize my problems have been solved.

W-90.1. <u>**Review of Lesson # 79: Let me recognize the problem so the problem can be solved.**</u>
2 Let me realize today that the problem is always some form of grievance that I would cherish. 3 Let me also understand that the solution is always a miracle with which I let the grievance be replaced. 4 Today I would remember the simplicity of salvation by reinforcing the lesson that there is one problem and one solution. 5 The problem is a grievance; the solution is a miracle. 6 And I invite the solution **of a miracle** to come to me through my forgiveness of the grievance, and my welcome of the miracle that takes **the grievance's** place.

W-90.2.Specific applications of this idea **of letting me recognize the problem so the problem can be solved** might be in these forms:
2 This presents a problem to me which I would have resolved.
3 The miracle behind this grievance will resolve **this grievance** for me.
4 The answer to this problem is the miracle that **the problem** conceals.

W-90.3. <u>**Review of Lesson # 80: Let me recognize my problems have been solved.**</u>
2 I seem to have problems only because I am misusing time. 3 I believe that the problem comes first, and time must elapse before **the problem** can be worked out. 4 I do not see the problem and the answer as simultaneous in their occurrence. 5 That is because I do not yet realize that God has placed the answer together with the problem, so that **the answer and the problem** cannot be separated by time. 6 The Holy Spirit will teach me **that God has placed the answer and the problem together so that they cannot be separated by time** if I will let **the Holy Spirit**. 7 And I will understand it is impossible that I could have a problem which has not been solved already.

W-90.4.These forms of the idea **of letting me recognize my problems have been solved** will be useful for specific applications:
2 I need not wait for this to be resolved.
3 The answer to this problem is already given me, if I will accept **the answer**.
4 Time cannot separate this problem from **the problem's** solution.

LESSON 91

Miracles are seen in light.

W-91.1.It is important to remember that miracles and vision necessarily go together. 2 **That miracles and vision necessarily go together** needs repeating, and frequent repeating. 3 **That miracles and vision go together** is a central idea in your new thought system, and the perception that **your new thought system** produces. 4 The miracle is always there. 5 **The miracle's** presence is not caused by your vision; **the miracle's** absence is not the result of your failure to see. 6 It is only your awareness of miracles that is affected. 7 You will see **miracles** in the light; you will not see **miracles** in the dark.

W-91.2.To you, then, light is crucial. 2 While you remain in darkness, the miracle remains unseen. 3 Thus you are convinced **the miracle** is not there. 4 This follows from the premises from which the darkness comes. 5 Denial of light leads to failure to perceive **the light**. 6 Failure to perceive light is to perceive darkness. 7 The light is useless to you then, even though **the light** is there. 8 You cannot use **the light** because **the light's** presence is unknown to you. 9 And the seeming reality of the darkness makes the idea of light meaningless.

W-91.3.To be told that what you do not see is **actually** there sounds like insanity. 2 It is very difficult to become convinced that it is insanity not to see what is there, and to see what is not there instead. 3 You do not doubt that the body's eyes can see. 4 You do not doubt the images **the body's eyes** show you are reality. 5 Your faith lies in the darkness, not the light. 6 How can this **faith in the darkness** be reversed? 7 For **your little "s" self the reversing of your faith in darkness** is impossible, but you are not alone **in your attempt to reverse your faith in darkness.**

W-91.4.Your efforts **in reversing your faith in darkness**, however little **your efforts** may be, have strong support **from the Holy Spirit**. 2 Did you but realize how great this strength **of the Holy Spirit is**, your doubts would vanish **about your ability to reverse your faith in darkness**. 3 Today we will devote ourselves to the attempt to let you feel this strength **of the Holy Spirit**. 4 When you have felt the strength **of the Holy Spirit** in you, which makes all miracles within your easy reach, you will not doubt. 5 The miracles your sense of weakness hides will leap into awareness as you feel the strength **of the Holy Spirit** in you.

W-91.5.Three times today, set aside about ten minutes for a quiet time in which you try to leave your weakness behind. 2 **Leaving your weakness behind** is accomplished very simply, as you instruct yourself that you are not a body. 3 Faith goes to what you want, and you instruct your mind accordingly. 4 Your will remains your teacher, and your will has all the strength to do what **your will** desires. 5 You can escape the body if you choose. 6 You can experience the strength **of the Holy Spirit** in you.

W-91.6.Begin the longer practice periods with this statement of true cause and effect relationships:
2 Miracles are seen in light.
3 The body's eyes do not perceive the light.
4 But I am not a body. 5 What am I?
6 The question with which this statement ends **which is, what am I,** is needed for our exercises today. 7 What you think you are, **which is your body**, is a belief to be undone. 8 But what you really are must be revealed to you. 9 The belief you are a body calls for correction, being a mistake. 10 The truth of what you are calls on the strength **of the Holy Spirit** in you to bring to your awareness what the mistake **that you are a body** conceals.

W-91.7.If you are not a body, what are you? 2 You need to be aware of what the Holy Spirit uses to replace the image of a body in your mind. 3 You need to feel something **that replaces the image of a body** to put your faith in, as you lift **that essence** from the body. 4 You need a real experience of something else **as your essence**, something more solid and more sure; more worthy of your faith, and really there.

W-91.8.If you are not a body, what are you? 2 Ask this in honesty, and then devote several minutes to allowing your mistaken thoughts about your attributes **of what you are** to be corrected, and their opposites to take their place. 3 Say, for example:
4 I am not weak, but strong.
5 I am not helpless, but all powerful.
6 I am not limited, but unlimited.
7 I am not doubtful, but certain.
8 I am not an illusion, but a reality.
9 I cannot see in darkness, but in light.

W-91.9.In the second phase of the exercise period, try to experience these truths about yourself. 2 Concentrate particularly on the experience of strength. 3 Remember that all sense of weakness is associated with the belief you are a body. **The belief that you are a body** is mistaken and deserves no faith. 4 Try to remove your faith from **the belief that you are a body**, if only for a moment. 5 You will be accustomed to keeping faith with the more worthy in you, **your big "S" Self,** as we go along.

W-91.10.Relax for the rest of the practice period, confident that your efforts, however meager, are fully supported by the strength of God and all **God's** Thoughts. 2 It is from **all God's Thoughts** that your strength will come. 3 It is through **the strong support of all God's Thoughts** that you will feel the strength **of the Holy Spirit** in you. 4 **The Holy Spirit and God's Thoughts** are united with you in this practice period, in which you share a purpose like Their Own. 5 **The Holy Spirit and God's Thoughts are** the light in which you will see miracles, because Their strength is yours. 6 **God's Thoughts and the Holy Spirit's** strength becomes your eyes, that you may see.

W-91.11.Five or six times an hour, at reasonably regular intervals, remind yourself that miracles are seen in light. 2 Also, be sure to meet temptation with today's idea **that miracles are seen in light**. 3 This form would be helpful for this special purpose:
4 Miracles are seen in light. 5 Let me not close my eyes because of this.

Notes to Lesson # 91

Miracles are seen in light.

Lesson 91 is miracles are seen in light.

Words are symbols. When we fail to understand what these symbols mean, they obscure the message that the words are trying to convey. Let us look at the words and symbols behind this lesson to help reveal the message they are trying to convey.

A miracle is simply a change from your fear-based thought system to the thought system of love and forgiveness. It is a change in perception. In a miracle, you exchange a grievance for forgiveness.

A grievance is an attack on another for their failure to follow your ego's plans. Forgiveness rejects your ego's belief that something outside of you is needed to save or make you happy. When you forgive, you accept the responsibility of being the source for your own inner peace.

Whether you believe you are forgiving yourself or another, it doesn't matter since to give is to receive. You cannot be free from the prison of your grievance if you must stand guard over your prisoner. Both the jailer and the jailed are in the same prison of your hate and fear.

Light is a symbol for following the thought system of the Holy Spirit. Light is a symbol for love and forgiveness. In time and space, the thought system of the Holy Spirit stands for love and forgiveness. The vision of Christ is the application of the thought system of the Holy Spirit in time and space. When you utilize the vision of Christ, you look through the eyes of love and forgiveness and see the light. You look beyond the physical form to the essence that the physical form was meant to hide.

When we replace the symbols with a correct understanding of the true meaning of the symbols, the message becomes clearer if not obvious. For example:

Miracles are seen in the light.

Exchanging a grievance for a miracle allows you to see the light.

Exchanging a grievance for a miracle is seeing with the vision of Christ.

The vision of Christ comes from following the thought system of the Holy Spirit.

The thought system of the Holy Spirit is based on love and forgiveness.

Miracles are seen through the eyes of love and forgiveness.

Light is the embodiment of love and forgiveness.

Miracles are seen when you follow the thought system of the Holy Spirit.

The Holy Spirit is a symbol for your higher self or what I have referred to as your big "S" Self.

Your big "S" Self is always within your mind but you choose to deny its existence.

When you choose to listen to the thought system for fear, you place your faith in your ego's little "s" self.

When you follow the laws of the ego, you perceive a world of darkness.

You will become aware of miracles when you choose to follow the voice for love.

Miracles are always there but you fail to see them because you fail to follow the thought system of love and forgiveness.

This idea that miracles are always there but you fail to see them is another example of how perception works.

When you judge a neutral thought as either good or bad, you are placing value upon a thought that is meaningless. The thought had no power to impact your reality. When you judge the thought as something you value, your mind is placing value on the meaningless and raising that thought to a desire and belief.

The law of perception states that you will see what you want to see. You will see what you put your faith upon. Put your faith in the meaningless and you will see the meaningless. If you value the body, you will believe you are a body. Your faith that you are a body will provide the evidence you seek to confirm that belief. What you believe you will perceive. What you expect to see, your physical eyes will confirm. What you believe will become your provisional reality.

All weaknesses that you experience are associated with your belief that you are a body. This mistake that you are a body needs correction. A mistake is not a sin. You are not required to make amends or be punished. You merely need to correct the mistake and move forward.

The body is more than just flesh and bones. The body is a symbol for your ego's fear-based thought system. The body is the embodiment of your ego's belief in lack, limitation and separation. When you believe that you are the body, you are placing your faith in the thought system of your ego. You are placing your faith in fear.

You will value what you believe you are. Believe that you are the body and you will believe that you can attack and be attacked. Believe that you are the body and you will value your right to hold grievances. When you believe you are the body, you deny your divine birthright and your spiritual essence. Your denial blocks your awareness of your big "S" Self and the Voice for God within you.

Light is a symbol for following the thought system of the Holy Spirit. Light can only be seen through the eyes of love and forgiveness. Darkness is a symbol for following the thought system of the ego. Miracles are always present but without the vision of Christ the miracle's existence is blocked by the darkness. This darkness comes from your desire to maintain or hold grievances.

Placing your faith in the ego's fear-based thought system, you will believe darkness to be real. Darkness will become your provisional reality. When you believe that you are not the body and you place your faith in the thought system for love and forgiveness, the light will become your provisional reality. Faith goes to whatever you want it to. What you want becomes your provisional reality because that is what you value.

You are not asked to blindly believe that you are not the body. Instead, this lesson asks that you open your mind up to the possibility that the body is not you. When you do this, new evidence will be presented to support that new possibility. Your faith goes to wherever you direct it to go. Place your faith in your higher big "S" Self and the Holy Spirit will provide evidence to support that faith.

Question: What is the difference between believing the body is you, versus the belief that the body is merely a game token that allows your spiritual essence a place on the game board of time and space?

Question: Which concept of the body is more likely to support love and which fear?

LESSON 92.

Miracles are seen in light, and light and strength are one.

W-92.1. The idea for today **that miracles are seen in light, and light and strength are one** is an extension of the previous **lesson, miracles are seen in light.** 2 You do not think of light in terms of strength, and darkness in terms of weakness. 3 That is because your idea of what seeing means is tied up with the body and **the body's** eyes and brain. 4 Thus you believe that you can change what you see by putting little bits of glass before your eyes. 5 **Wearing glasses** is among the many magical beliefs that come from the conviction you are a body, and the body's eyes can see.

W-92.2. You also believe the body's brain can think. 2 If you but understood the nature of thought, you could but laugh at this insane idea **that the body's brain can think.** 3 It is as if you thought you held the match that lights the sun and gives **the sun** all **the sun's** warmth; or that you held the world within your hand, securely bound until you let **the world** go. 4 Yet this **idea that a match heats the sun or you hold the world in your hand** is no more foolish than to believe the body's eyes can see **and** the brain can think.

W-92.3. It is God's strength in you that is the light in which you see, as it is **God's** Mind with which you think. 2 **God's** strength denies your weakness. 3 It is your **ego's** weakness that sees through the body's eyes, peering about in darkness to behold the likeness of its **egoic s**elf; the small, the weak, the sickly and the dying, those in need, the helpless and afraid, the sad, the poor, the starving and the joyless. 4 These **helpless, poor, and joyless bodies** are seen through **the ego's** eyes that cannot see and cannot bless.

W-92.4. Strength overlooks these things by seeing past appearances. 2 **Strength** keeps its steady gaze upon the light that lies beyond **appearances.** 3 **Strength** unites with light, of which **strength** is a part. 4 **Strength** sees itself. 5 **Strength** brings the light in which your **big "S"** Self appears. 6 In darkness you perceive an **egoic little "s"** self that is not there. 7 Strength is the truth about you **as your big "S" Self**; weakness is an idol **of the ego** falsely worshipped and adored that strength may be dispelled, and darkness rule where God appointed that there should be light.

W-92.5. Strength, **your big "S" Self,** comes from truth, and shines with **the** light **God,** its Source, has given **your big "S"** Self. Weakness reflects the darkness of its **egoic** maker. 2 **The maker of weakness, the little "s"** self is sick and looks on sickness, which is like itself. 3 Truth is a savior and can only will for happiness and peace for everyone. 4 **Truth** gives **truth's** strength to everyone who asks, in limitless supply. 5 **Truth** sees that lack in anyone would be a lack in all. 6 And so **truth** gives **truth's** light that all may see and benefit as one. 7 **Truth's** strength is shared, that **truth's strength** may bring to all the miracle in which **all** will unite in purpose and forgiveness and in love.

W-92.6. Weakness, which looks in darkness, cannot see a purpose in forgiveness and in love. 2 **Weakness, your little "s" self,** sees all others different from itself, and nothing in the world that **your little "s" self** would share. 3 **Weakness** judges and condemns, but **weakness, your little "s" self,** does not love. 4 In darkness **weakness** remains to hide **its little "s" self** and dreams that **its little "s" self** is strong and conquering, a victor over limitations that but grow in darkness to enormous size.

W-92.7. **Weakness** fears and **weakness** attacks and hates **its little "s" self,** and darkness covers everything **the little "s" self** sees, leaving **weakness'** dreams as fearful as **the ego** itself. 2 No miracles are here **in darkness,** but only hate. 3 **Weakness, the little "s" self,** separates itself from what **the ego** sees, while **in contrast,** light and strength perceive themselves as one. 4 The light of strength is not the **physical** light you see. 5 **The light of strength** does not change and flicker and go out. 6 **The light of strength** does not shift from night to day, and back to darkness till the morning comes again.

W-92.8. The light of strength is constant, sure as love, forever glad to give itself away, because **the light of strength** cannot give but to itself. 2 No one can ask in vain to share **strength's** sight, **which is the vision of Christ,** and none who enters **strength's** abode can leave without a miracle before his eyes, and strength and light abiding in his heart.

W-92.9. The strength in you will offer you the light, and guide your seeing so you do not dwell on idle shadows that the body's **egoic** eyes provide for self-deception. 2 Strength and light unite in you, and where **strength and light** meet, your **big "S"** Self stands ready to embrace you as **God's** Own Son. 3 Such is the meeting place we try today to find and rest in, for the peace of God is where your **big "S"** Self, **God's** Son, is waiting now to meet Itself again, and be as One.

W-92.10. Let us give twenty minutes twice today to join this meeting **with your Big "S" Self.** 2 Let yourself be brought unto your **big "S"** Self. 3 **Your big "S" Self's** strength will be the light in which the gift of sight, **which is Christ's vision,** is given you. 4 Leave, then, the dark a little while today, and we will practice seeing in the light, closing the body's eyes **of your ego's little "s" self** and asking truth to show us how to find the meeting place of self and your **big "S"** Self, where light and strength are one.

W-92.11. Morning and evening we will practice thus. 2 After the morning meeting, we will use the day in preparation for the time at night when we will meet again in trust. 3 Let us repeat as often as we can the idea for today **that miracles are seen in light, and light and strength are one,** and recognize that we are being introduced to sight, **which is Christ's vision,** and led away from **egoic** darkness to the light where only miracles can be perceived.

Miracles are seen in light, and light and strength are one.

Lesson 92 is an extension of the previous lesson which stated that miracles are seen in light. This lesson adds the idea that light and strength are the same. Let's quickly review what a miracle is and what light symbolizes.

A miracle is simply a change from your fear-based thought system to the thought system of love and forgiveness. It is a change in perception. In a miracle, you exchange a grievance for forgiveness.

Light is a symbol for following the thought system of the Holy Spirit. Light is a symbol for love and forgiveness. In time and space, the thought system of the Holy Spirit stands for love and forgiveness. The vision of Christ is the application of the thought system of the Holy Spirit in time and space. When you utilize the vision of Christ, you look through the eyes of love and forgiveness and see the light. You look beyond the physical form to the essence that the physical form was meant to hide.

The focus of this lesson is the idea that strength and light are one. In this case, strength is derived from our Source and our Source is God. It is God's strength that resides in you that is the light in which you see with the Vision of Christ. It is from the Mind of God which resides in you, your big "S" Self, that your real thoughts are derived.

You as decision-maker must decide who created you? Did God create you or are you self-created? Is your birthright derived from the strength of God or does your inheritance come from your physical being or body?

Are you a spiritual essence having an earthly experience as a human being?

Or

Are you a physical being that is occasionally having an illusionary spiritual experience?

Based on your decision of who you are, two entirely different thought systems arise. One is based on the belief your inheritance comes from the strength of God. God being love, gives all to all. In this thought system, you are an extension of God, Itself. This is an empowering thought system.

The other thought system will believe your birthright dooms you to a life of pain, suffering, struggle and eventually death. In this second thought system, you are not created in God's likeness. You are victim and second-class citizen. Your birthright dooms you to a life of suffering and ultimate failure.

God is the source for strength, light, love and truth. When you believe that you are created by God, you accept the unity of that Oneness of All That Is. Strength knows Its oneness and therefore, shares all with all who ask. Sharing and being love is your natural birthright and is derived from the strength of your source which is God, Itself.

When you believe you are separate from God, you believe that you are not as God created you, perfect, whole and complete. Instead, you perceive yourself to be limited, sinful and weak. Your ego's misperception of who you are is the source for all weakness, darkness and fear.

All weaknesses that you experience are associated with your ego's belief that you are a body. This mistake that you are a body needs correction. A mistake is not a sin. You are not required to make amends or be punished. You merely need to correct the mistake and move forward.

Weakness sees separation and difference in all that it perceives. It judges, condemns and attacks. Weakness does not share or love for weakness sees this world as a zero-sum game. In the ego's fear-based world, if you are to win, someone else must lose.

In the fear-based thought system of the ego, the body is more than just flesh and bones. The body is a symbol for your ego's fear-based thought system. The body is the embodiment of your ego's belief in lack, limitation and separation. When you believe that you are the body, you are placing your faith in the thought system of your ego. You are placing your faith in fear.

It is you, as the decision-maker, who chooses what created you. You get to decide who you would prefer to have as your parent and what your inheritance should be. You, as the decision-maker, make this choice on a daily basis when you determine which thought system you will give your allegiance to.

Will you choose the weakness of your ego's fear-based thought system that condemns you to a life of fear, struggle and separation?

Or,

Will you give your allegiance to the strength of God?

Question: There are two thoughts systems. One is based on the belief that you are strong and the other that you are weak. Which is most likely to serve you in helping you to achieve your goal of being happy and not living in the shadows of fear?

LESSON 93.

Light and joy and peace abide in me.

W-93.1.You think **your split mind** is the home of evil, darkness and sin. 2 You think if anyone could see the truth about you, he would be repelled, recoiling from you as if from a poisonous snake. 3 You think if what is true about you were revealed to you, you would be struck with horror so intense that you would rush to death by your own hand, living on after seeing this **evil vision of yourself** being impossible.

W-93.2.These **evil visions of yourself** are beliefs so firmly fixed **in your split mind** that it is difficult to help you see that **these evil visions of yourself** are based on nothing. 2 That **your split mind** has made mistakes is obvious. 3 That **by following your ego's plan** you have sought salvation in strange ways; have been deceived, deceiving and afraid of foolish fantasies and savage dreams; and have bowed down to **your ego's** idols **that are** made of dust,–all this is true by what **your split mind** now believes.

W-93.3.Today we question this **evil egoic vision of yourself**, not from the point of view of what you think, but from a very different reference point. From **the reference** point that such idle thoughts are meaningless. 2 These **idle and meaningless** thoughts are not according to God's Will. 3 These weird beliefs **about yourself God** does not share with **your egoic mind**. 4 This is enough to prove that **your ego's beliefs about you** are wrong, but you do not perceive this is so **that God does not share your ego's beliefs**.

W-93.4.Why would you not be overjoyed to be assured that all the evil that you think you did was never done, that all your sins are nothing. **Why would you not be overjoyed to be assured** that you are as pure and holy as you were created, and that light and joy and peace abide in you? 2 Your **ego's** image of yourself cannot withstand the Will of God. 3 You think that **not being able to withstand the Will of God** is death, but it is life. 4 You think you are destroyed **if you cannot withstand the Will of God**, but you are saved.

W-93.5.The ego's little "s" self **your split mind** made is not the Son of God. 2 Therefore, this **little "s"** self does not exist at all. 3 And anything **this little "s"** self seems to do and think means nothing. 4 **What this little "s" self seems to do** is neither bad nor good. 5 **What this little "s" self seems to do** is unreal, and nothing more than that. 6 **This little "s" self** does not battle with the Son of God. 7 **This little "s" self** does not hurt **the Son of God**, nor attack **the Son of God's** peace. 8 **What this little "s" self seems to do** has not changed creation, nor reduced eternal sinlessness to sin, and love to hate. 9 What power can this **little "s"** self **that your split mind** made possess, when **what this little "s" self seems to do** would contradict the Will of God?

W-93.6.Your sinlessness is guaranteed by God. 2 Over and over this must be repeated, until **the idea that your sinlessness is guaranteed by God** is accepted. 3 **The idea that your sinlessness is guaranteed by God** is true. 4 Your sinlessness is guaranteed by God. 5 Nothing can touch **your sinlessness**, or change what God created as eternal. 6 The **little "s"** self **your split mind** made, evil and full of sin, is meaningless. 7 Your sinlessness is guaranteed by God, and light and joy and peace abide in you, **your Big "S" Self**.

W-93.7.Salvation requires the acceptance of but one thought;–you are as God created you, not what **your ego believes** you made of yourself. 2 Whatever evil **your split mind** may think you did, you are as God created you. 3 Whatever mistakes **your split mind** made, the truth about you is unchanged. 4 Creation is eternal and unalterable. 5 Your sinlessness is guaranteed by God. 6 You are and will forever be exactly as you were created. 7 Light and joy and peace abide in you because God put **light, joy and peace within you**.

W-93.8.In our longer exercise periods today, which would be most profitable if done for the first five minutes of every waking hour, begin by stating the truth about your creation **as God's beloved Child.**
2 Light and joy and peace abide in me.
3 My sinlessness is guaranteed by God.
4 Then put away your foolish **little "s"** self-images, and spend the rest of the practice period in trying to experience what God has given you, **your big "S" Self**, in place of what **your ego has** decreed for yourself.

W-93.9.You are what God created or what **your ego** made. 2 One **big "S"** Self is true; the other, **your little "s" self**, is not there. 3 Try to experience the unity of your one **big "S"** Self. 4 Try to appreciate **your big "S" Self's** Holiness and the love from which **your big "S" Self** was created. 5 Try not to interfere with **your big "S"** Self which God created as you, by hiding **your big "S" Self's** majesty behind the tiny idols of evil and sinfulness **your ego** has made to replace **your big "S" Self**. 6 Let **your big "S" Self** come into Its Own **as God's beloved Child**. 7 Here you are; This is You. 8 And light and joy and peace abide in you because **you remain as God created you**.

W-93.10.You may not be willing or even able to use the first five minutes of each hour for these exercises. 2 Try, however, **to use the first five minutes of each hour for these exercises** when you can. 3 At least remember to repeat these thoughts each hour:
4 Light and joy and peace abide in me.

5 My sinlessness is guaranteed by God.
6 Then try to devote at least a minute or so to closing your eyes and realizing that this statement **that light, joy and peace abide in me and that my sinlessness is guaranteed by God** is the truth about you.

W-93.11.If a situation arises that seems to be disturbing, quickly dispel the illusion of fear by repeating these thoughts again **that light, joy and peace abide in me and that my sinlessness is guaranteed by God**. 2 Should you be tempted to become angry with someone, tell him silently:
3 Light and joy and peace abide in you.
4 Your sinlessness is guaranteed by God.
5 You can do much for the world's salvation today. 6 You can do much today to bring you closer to the part in salvation that God has assigned to you. 7 And you can do much today to bring the conviction to your mind that the idea for the day **that light, joy and peace abide in me and that my sinlessness is guaranteed by God** is true indeed.

Notes to Lesson # 93

Light and joy and peace abide in me.

Lesson 93, light and joy and peace abide in me, is interesting from the standpoint of how ACIM approaches the subject. Rather than question your own egoic beliefs about yourself and try to convince you that these beliefs are incorrect, ACIM ignores your negative beliefs about yourself entirely.

Instead, ACIM approaches this topic from a very different reference point. They simply state that since your beliefs about yourself are not in accordance with God's Will, they are meaningless.

God only knows us as He created us, perfect, whole and complete. We are the Son of God, our big "S" Self and part of the unity of the One Self. Our egoic fantasies about ourselves are meaningless because they have no ability to change the truth about how God created us or God's Will for us. Although we can deny our divine inheritance, our denial cannot change the truth that we remain as God created us. Our denial creates an illusionary world of provisional reality in which our egoic little "s" self pretends he is something he is not.

The ego argues for our limitations claiming that we are the separate and different from our Creator. It denies our true big "S" Self and argues for our littleness. This delusional little "s" self that we have created within our own mind is not how God knows His creation. Instead, it is merely an illusion within our own split mind.

It is interesting that the image of our little "s" self is neither good nor bad. It is simply unreal and nothing more than that. It has no ability to change the truth of who we are. It has no ability to affect anything that is real and therefore, like all egoic thinking, it is meaningless.

Egoic thinking is based on uncertainty and requires judgment. It is based on perception, not reality. Knowledge is certain and real because it is shared with the Mind of God. The Will of God is our true reality. We remain God's beloved child with whom He is well pleased. Our egoic thinking has no ability to impact our big "S" Self since our sinlessness is guaranteed by God and there is nothing that our ego can do to change that reality.

We have mistakenly followed the fear-based thought system of the ego. This is obviously a mistake but not a sin. An illusion cannot harm truth for truth just is. Unlike a sin, which would require punishment, a mistake only requires correction. Correction only asks that you accept the truth that you remain as God created you. To correct your mistakes, the Holy Spirit merely advises that you accept the At-One-Ment for yourself.

Question: Who is more likely to be right, God or your ego?

LESSON 94.

I am as God created me.

W-94.1.Today we continue with the one idea which brings complete salvation; the one statement **that I am as God created me** which makes all forms of temptation powerless; the one thought **that I am as God created me** which renders the ego silent and entirely undone. 2 You are as God created you. 3 The sounds of this **fear-based** world are still, the sights of this **fear-based** world disappear, and all the thoughts that this **fear-based** world ever held are wiped away forever by this one idea **that I am as God created me**. 4 Here is salvation accomplished. 5 Here is sanity restored.

W-94.2.True light is strength, and strength is sinlessness. 2 If you remain as God created you, you must be strong and light must be in you. 3 **God,** Who ensured your sinlessness must be the guarantee of strength and light as well. 4 You are as God created you. 5 Darkness cannot obscure the glory of God's Son. 6 You stand in light, strong in the sinlessness in which you were created, and in which you will remain throughout eternity.

W-94.3.Today we will again devote the first five minutes of each waking hour to the attempt to feel the truth in you. 2 Begin these times of searching **and connecting with your big "S" Self** with these words:
3 I am as God created me.
4 I am **God's** Son eternally.
5 Now try to reach the Son of God in you. 6 This is **your big "S"** Self that never sinned, nor made an **egoic fear-based** image to replace reality. 7 This is **your big "S"** Self that never left Its home in God to walk the **fear-based egoic** world **of** uncertainty. 8 This is **your big "S"** Self that knows no fear, nor could conceive of loss or suffering or death.

W-94.4.Nothing is required of you to reach this goal except to lay all **your ego's** idols and **little "s"** self-images aside; go past the list of attributes, both good and bad, you have ascribed to your **little "s"** self; and wait in silent expectancy for the truth. 2 God has Himself promised that the **truth** will be revealed to all who ask for **the truth**. 3 You are asking now **for the truth**. 4 You cannot fail because **God** cannot fail.

W-94.5.If you do not meet the requirement of practicing for the first five minutes of every hour, at least remind yourself hourly:
2 I am as God created me.
3 I am **God's** Son eternally.
4 Tell yourself frequently today that you are as God created you. 5 And be sure to respond to anyone who seems to irritate you with these words:
6 You are as God created you.
7 You are **God's** Son eternally.
8 Make every effort to do the hourly exercises today. 9 Each **hourly exercise** you do will be a giant stride toward your release, and a milestone in learning the thought system **of love and forgiveness** which this course sets forth.

Notes to Lesson # 94

I am as God created me.

Lesson 94, I am as God created me, is the one statement that the ego does not want to hear and a statement the ego does not want you to believe. This is because this statement renders the ego powerless for it is the one statement that guarantees your salvation.

Your salvation is guaranteed through your divine inheritance. It is not predicated on what you do to earn God's love. God has created you as a light which is strength and strength is your sinlessness. The dark images of your little "s" self that your ego has created are meaningless and have no effect on who you really are. You remain as God created you.

Your big "S" Self is the home of the Holy Spirit. God resides in you and you reside in God. Your big "S" Self knows no fear, nor could conceive of loss, suffering or death. Your big "S" Self knows separation is not real and you remain part of the Oneness of All That Is.

This lesson also asks that you lay aside all your ego's idols and self-images which your ego has determined are necessary for your salvation. You are to drop your ego's plan and go past all beliefs that your ego has prescribed to you. This includes characteristics that we would generally consider both "good" and "bad" traits.

Although the need to drop negative fear-based beliefs about yourself is obvious, it may not seem as relevant that you drop your ego's positive images of who a Child of God should be.

The ego does not know who you are nor does it understand the big picture nor how each experience fits into God's plan for reawakening the sleeping Child. Instead, the ego uses its past beliefs to interpret how you should respond to any current event. These past egoic beliefs, both positive and negative, prevent you from being able to respond without any preconceived notions of what love would have you do. Thus, you are unable to go with the flow.

Rather than ask for guidance from the Holy Spirit, your ego claims it already knows what you should do and how you should react to a particular situation since you are a spiritual "person." The spiritual life is the last stand of your ego. Beware because your ego will develop a plan as to how a spiritual person should behave.

For example: Perhaps you meet a homeless man on the street. You check with your inner guide, ask what love would have you do and you are directed by the Holy Spirit to feed and clothe that person. You do this and everything seems to work out perfectly. Miracles occur.

Your ego takes that inspired experience in which you followed your inner guide, and now determines that is how a spiritual person should respond to any homeless man scenario.

The next time you meet a homeless man, rather than checking with your inner guide, your ego runs its homeless man program. You stop to pick up the man only to discover that man is not homeless but rather a thief. You are beaten, robbed and your car stolen. Things do not seem to work out so perfectly this time. Why? Because you followed your ego's plan rather than asking your big "S" Self for guidance.

It is important for you to lay aside all idols and self-images, because your ego lacks knowledge and does not know the big picture. The ego sees separation in all things and therefore, brings that belief to all situations that it encounters. The ego's plans for salvation always revolve around the idea that you must do something to earn your salvation or that another needs you to save them because they are too stupid or imperfect to save themselves. The ego does not understand that both you and your brothers and sisters are perfect, whole and complete. Your ego's plan for salvation denies that you each remain as God created you.

Rather than follow the ego's plan that includes your ego's image of what the spiritual life should be, follow your inner guide. Allow the Holy Spirit to make your life your spiritual practice.

Question: Why is it necessary to drop even your "good" egoic imaginings of what you would be if you were perfect, whole and complete?

LESSON 95.

I am one Self, united with my Creator.

W-95.1.Today's idea **that I am one Self, united with my Creator** accurately describes you as God created you. 2 You are one within your **big "S" Self**, and one with **your Creator**. 3 Your **big "S" Self** is the unity of all creation. 4 Your perfect unity makes change in you impossible. 5 You do not accept **that change in you is impossible**, and you fail to realize **that change in you is impossible and that this** must be so. **You do not accept that change in you is impossible** only because you believe that you have changed yourself already **and become a sinful little "s" self**.

W-95.2.You see your **little "s"** self as a ridiculous parody on God's creation; weak, vicious, ugly and sinful, miserable and beset with pain. 2 Such is your **ego's fear-based version** of your **little "s"** self. **Your split mind perceives** a self divided into many warring parts, separate from God, and tenuously held together by its erratic and capricious maker, to which you pray. 3 **The ego's false god of fear** does not hear your prayers, for it is deaf. 4 **The ego's false god of fear** does not see the oneness in you, for it is blind. 5 **The ego's false god of fear** does not understand you are the Son of God, for it is senseless and understands nothing.

W-95.3.We will attempt today to be aware only of what can hear and see, and what makes perfect sense. 2 We will again direct our exercises towards reaching your one **big "S" Self**, which is united with Its Creator. 3 In patience and in hope we try again today.

W-95.4.The use of the first five minutes of every waking hour for practicing the idea for the day **that I am one Self, united with my Creator** has special advantages at the stage of learning in which you are at present. 2 It is difficult at this point not to allow your mind to wander if **your mind** undertakes extended practice. 3 You have surely realized this by now. 4 You have seen the extent of your lack of mental discipline, and of your need for mind training. 5 It is necessary that you be aware of **your need for mind training**, for **this lack of discipline** is indeed a hindrance to your advance.

W-95.5.Frequent but shorter practice periods have other advantages for you at this time. 2 In addition to recognizing your difficulties with sustained attention, you must also have noticed that, unless you are reminded of your purpose frequently, you tend to forget about **your purpose** for long periods of time. 3 You often fail to remember the short applications of the idea for the day, and you have not yet formed the habit of using the idea as an automatic response to temptation.

W-95.6.Structure, then, is necessary for you at this time, planned to include frequent reminders of your goal and regular attempts to reach **your goal and purpose.** 2 Regularity in terms of time is not the ideal requirement for the most beneficial form of practice in salvation. 3 **Regularity in terms of time to practice** is advantageous, however, for those whose motivation is inconsistent, and who remain heavily defended against learning.

W-95.7.We will, therefore, keep to the five-minutes-an-hour practice periods for a while, and urge you to omit as few as possible. 2 Using the first five minutes of the hour will be particularly helpful since **regularity in terms of time** imposes firmer structure. 3 Do not, however, use your lapses from this schedule as an excuse not to return to **this schedule** again as soon as you can. 4 There may well be a temptation to regard the day as lost because you have already failed to do what is required. 5 **Your failure to follow the schedule** should, however, merely be recognized as what it is; a refusal to let your mistake be corrected, and an unwillingness to try again.

W-95.8.The Holy Spirit is not delayed in **the Holy Spirit's** teaching by your mistakes. 2 **The Holy Spirit** can be held back only by your unwillingness to let **your mistake** go. 3 Let us therefore be determined, particularly for the next week or so, to be willing to forgive ourselves for our lapses in diligence, and our failures to follow the instructions for practicing the day's idea. 4 This tolerance for weakness will enable us to overlook **weakness**, rather than give **weakness the** power to delay our learning. 5 If we give **weakness the** power to **delay our learning**, we are regarding **weakness** as strength, and are confusing strength with weakness.

W-95.9.When you fail to comply with the requirements of this course, you have merely made a mistake. 2 This calls for correction, and for nothing else. 3 To allow a mistake to continue is to make additional mistakes, based on the first and reinforcing **the original mistake.** 4 It is this process **of allowing a mistake to continue** that must be laid aside, for **your delay to correct a mistake** is but another way in which you would defend illusions against the truth.

W-95.10.Let all these errors go by recognizing these **errors** for what they are. 2 **These errors** are attempts to keep you unaware you are one **big "S" Self**, united with your Creator, at one with every aspect of creation, and limitless in power and in peace. 3 This is the truth **for you are one Self, united with your Creator**, and nothing else is true. 4 Today we will affirm this truth again **that you are one Self, united with your Creator**, and try to reach the place in you in which there is no doubt that only this **unity** is true.

W-95.11.Begin the practice periods today with this assurance **that you are one Self, united with your Creator**, offered to your mind with all the certainty that you can give:
2 I am one Self, united with my Creator, at one with every aspect of creation, and limitless in power and in peace.
3 Then close your eyes and tell yourself again, slowly and thoughtfully, attempting to allow the meaning of the words to sink

into your mind, replacing false **egoic** ideas:
4 I am one Self.
5 Repeat this several times, and then attempt to feel the meaning that the words convey.

W-95.12.You are one Self, united and secure in light and joy and peace. 2 You are God's Son, one Self, with one Creator and one goal; to bring awareness of this oneness to all minds, that true creation may extend the allness and the unity of God. 3 You are one Self, complete and healed and whole, with power to lift the veil of darkness from the **fear-based** world, and let the light in you come through to teach the **fear-based** world the truth about your **big "S'** Self.

W-95.13.You are one Self, in perfect harmony with all there is, and all that there will be. 2 You are one Self, the holy Son of God, united with your brothers in that **big "S"** Self; united with your Father in His Will. 3 Feel this one Self in you, and let **that big "S" Self** shine away all your **ego's** illusions and your **ego's** doubts. 4 This is your **big "S"** Self, the Son of God Himself, sinless as Its Creator, with **God's** strength within you and **God's** Love forever yours. 5 You are one Self, and it is given you to feel this Self within you, and to cast all your **ego's** illusions out of the one Mind that is this **big "S"** Self, the holy truth in you.

W-95.14.Do not forget today. 2 We need your help; your little part in bringing happiness to all the world. 3 And Heaven looks to you in confidence that you will try today. 4 Share, then, **Heaven's** surety, for **Heaven's surety** is yours. 5 Be vigilant. 6 Do not forget today. 7 Throughout the day do not forget your goal. 8 Repeat today's idea **that you are one Self, united with your Creator** as frequently as possible, and understand each time you do so, someone hears the voice of hope, the stirring of the truth within his mind, the gentle rustling of the wings of peace.

W-95.15.Your own acknowledgment you are one Self, united with your Father, is a call to all the world to be at one with you. 2 To everyone you meet today, be sure to give the promise of today's idea and tell him this:
3 You are one Self with me, united with our Creator in this **big "S"** Self. 4 I honor you because of What I am, and What **our Creator** is, Who loves us both as One.

Notes to Lesson # 95

I am one Self, united with my Creator.

Lesson 95, I am one Self, united with my Creator, explains why ACIM is total mind retraining. We have been brought up to believe that we are separate, limited, sinful beings and that our existence revolves around suffering, conflict, pain and ultimately death.

This is the image our collective consciousness has engendered as we perceive ourselves to be divided into many parts. Each part has its own special interests, needs and goals, and must attempt to control, manipulate and change others if its needs are to be met.

From this belief in separation and limitation, it is logical for us to perceive a judgmental, wrathful and petty God. We believe that God's Will can be opposed and that evil exists. The god that our ego has dreamed up is capricious, erratic and has a will that is both pliable and unreliable. Sometimes we can pray to this god of fear and he will answer. Other times, our prayers seem to be unheard and go unanswered.

With this belief about yourself and your god of fear, it is understandable that you would seek an alternative advisor to guide your every move. Your decision-maker turns to this warped belief system and follows the ego's voice for fear.

Our mind has been trained to accept the ego's thought system as its savior and guide. Since perception flows from our beliefs, our senses bear witness to the belief that we are the body and the body is us. Sin, guilt and fear rule our split mind's world.

From this backdrop, we seek a totally new mindset. We need a new plan with a new thought system. For this mind training to be successful, it only requires the recognition of the truth. You need only to control your fear and follow the thought system of the Holy Spirit.

When we silence our egoic mind, we will hear the Voice for Truth. We will begin to see witnesses for that truth that we alone give meaning to our experiences. No one sources your experiences but you and no one can rob you of your inner peace unless you choose to allow this to be so. You control how you choose to interpret all your experiences. You can either interpret them through the eyes of love or the voice for fear.

You are not a little "s" self as your ego claims. Instead, you are the Christ, your big "S" Self, united with your Creator. You are God's Son, the One Self, who has one Creator and one goal. This goal is to bring the oneness and the unity to all split minds and recognize the fact that you remain as God created you. Your strength and sinlessness comes from your Creator and you share the one Will of the Mind of God.

This mind training asks you to realize that you are the One Self. This training is given so that you can feel this big "S" Self within you and replace your belief in sin, guilt, fear, limitation and separation with the holy truth of who you really are. You are holy and blessed. You are as God created you, perfect, whole and complete.

Your detour into fear was merely a mistake that requires correction. It is your own self-condemnation which makes your egoic fear-based world continue to appear real to you. This mistake does not prevent the Holy Spirit from retraining your mind to the truth of who you are. Only your unwillingness to let your erroneous beliefs go keeps your nightmare of littleness alive within your split mind.

When you condemn yourself for your perceived weaknesses, you are reinforcing your belief in your ego's viewpoint for your littleness. Your ego has developed its own plan for your salvation. This plan revolves around your need to earn freedom and to accept your punishment for your perceived sins. Today, your ego's plan may revolve around your ability to do the ACIM workbook lessons perfectly. When you fail to comply perfectly, your ego claims you are a failure, incapable of following the plan and advises that you should give up and follow a different plan.

ACIM warns that this is the voice of your ego and not the Holy Spirit speaking. Instead, ACIM suggests that you should tolerate what your ego claims to be your weakness and instead overlook your mistake. Your tolerance of your failure to fully comply now becomes a strength rather than the weakness that your ego proclaimed. Realize that your failure to comply with the exact suggestions of each workbook lesson is merely a mistake that calls for correction and nothing else.

The ego will tell you that the program is too hard and based on the original mistake, you should give up. When you choose to follow your ego's advice, you compound the error. Your choice to berate yourself is a continual reinforcement of your ego's plan that makes fear real and defends illusions against the truth.

Recognize your inability to complete the workbook lesson perfectly but realize that this is simply an error that cannot delay the Holy Spirit's teachings. These mistakes are your ego's attempt to keep you unaware that you are the One Self, united with your Creator, at one with every aspect of creation and limitless in power and in peace.

This is the truth, and nothing else is true. This is the certainty of the Will of God and the Voice for the Holy Spirit and the reality of your big "S" Self.

Question: How does your failure to forgive yourself for not doing the workbook lessons "perfectly" actually strengthen your ego's thought system of sin, guilt and fear?

Question: Why does ACIM state that you should tolerate your mistakes, overlook them and simply realize that they are errors, not sins that need correction, not self-degradation?

Salvation comes from my one Self.

W-96.1.Although you are one Self, you, **the spilt minded,** experience yourself as two; as both good and evil, loving and hating, mind and body. 2 This sense of being split into opposites induces feelings of acute and constant conflict, and leads to frantic attempts to reconcile the contradictory aspects of this **spilt minded** self-perception. 3 You have sought many such solutions, and none of **your ego's plans** has worked. 4 The opposites **like good and evil that** you see in **your split mind** will never be compatible. 5 But **only** one exists **and the other is unreal, a product of your false beliefs**.

W-96.2.The fact that truth and illusion cannot be reconciled, no matter how you try, what means you use and where you see the problem, must be accepted if you would be saved. 2 Until you have accepted this **fact that truth and illusion cannot be reconciled, your ego** will attempt an endless list of **irreconcilable** goals you cannot reach; a senseless series of expenditures of time and effort, hopefulness and doubt, each **egoic plan** as futile as the **egoic plan you tried** before, and failing as the next **egoic plan** surely will **fail**.

W-96.3.Problems that have no meaning cannot be resolved within the framework **of the same thought system the problems** are set **in**. 2 Two selves in conflict could not be resolved, and good and evil have no meeting place. 3 The **ego's little "s"** self **that your split mind** made can never be your **true big "S" Self**, nor can your **true big "S"** Self be split in two, and still be what **your true big "S"** Self is and must forever be **as God created His Son**. 4 A mind and body cannot both exist. 5 Make no attempt to reconcile the **mind and the body**, for one denies the other can be real. 6 If you are physical, your mind is gone from your self-concept, for **your mind, which is different from the brain,** has no place in which **the mind** could be really part of you **if you are the body**. 7 If you are spirit, then the body must be meaningless to your reality, **which is your big "S" Self as God create you.**

W-96.4.Spirit makes use of mind as means to find its **big "S"** Self's expression. 2 And the mind which serves the spirit is at peace and filled with joy. 3 **The mind that serves spirit** power comes from spirit, and **the mind that serves spirit** is fulfilling happily its function **of forgiveness** here **in time and space**. 4 Yet **a split** mind can also see itself divorced from spirit, and perceive **a mind** within a body **that the split minded** confuses with itself. 5 Without its function **of forgiveness** then **a split mind that sees itself divorced from spirit** has no peace, and happiness is alien to its **egoic fear-based** thoughts.

W-96.5.Yet mind apart from spirit cannot think. 2 **Mind apart from spirit** has denied its Source of strength, and sees its **little "s"** self as helpless, limited and weak. 3 **A mind apart from spirit** is dissociated from its function **of forgiveness** now. **The split mind** thinks it is alone and separate, attacked by armies massed against its **little "s"** self and hiding in the body's frail support. 4 Now must **a mind that sees itself apart from spirit** reconcile unlike with like, for this is what **the split mind** thinks that its **egoic mind** is for.

W-96.6.Waste no more time on this **egoic attempt to reconcile like with unlike and the true with the false**. 2 Who can resolve the senseless conflicts which an **egoic** dream presents? 3 What could the resolution **of conflicts within a dream** mean in truth? 4 What purpose could **the resolution of conflicts within a dream** serve? 5 What is **the resolution of conflicts within a dream** for? 6 Salvation cannot make illusions real, nor solve a problem that does not exist. 7 Perhaps you hope **that salvation** can **make an illusion real**. 8 Yet would you have God's plan for the release of **God's** dear Son bring pain to **God's Son**, and fail to set **God's Son** free?

W-96.7.Your **big "S"** Self retains Its **real** Thoughts **that it shares with the Mind of God**, and **these real Thoughts** remain within your mind and in the Mind of God. 2 The Holy Spirit holds salvation in your mind, and offers **your split mind** the way to peace. 3 Salvation is a thought you share with God, because **God's** Voice, **the Holy Spirit**, accepted **God's plan for salvation** for you and answered in your name that **God's plan for salvation** was done. 4 Thus is salvation kept among the **real** Thoughts your **big "S"** Self holds dear and cherishes for you.

W-96.8.We will attempt today to find this thought **that salvation comes from my one Self. This thought's** presence in your mind is guaranteed by **the Holy Spirit** Who speaks to you from your one **big "S"** Self. 2 Our hourly five-minute practicing will be a search for **the Holy Spirit** within your mind. 3 Salvation comes from this one Self through **the Holy Spirit** Who is the Bridge between your **split** mind and your **big "S"** Self. 4 Wait patiently, and let **the Holy Spirit** speak to **your split mind** about your **big "S"** Self, and what your **healed** mind can do **once** restored to **your big "S" Self** and what your healed mind can do when free to serve **your big "S" Self's** Will.

W-96.9.Begin with saying this:
2 Salvation comes from my one Self. 3 **My big "S" Self's** Thoughts are mine to use.
4 Then seek **your big "S" Self's** Thoughts, and claim **these real Thoughts** as your own. 5 These are your own real thoughts your split mind have denied, and let your **egoic** mind go wandering in a **fearful** world of dreams, to find illusions in the place **of these real Thoughts**. 6 Here are your **real** thoughts, the only ones you have **and share with the Mind of God**. 7 Salvation is among **your real thoughts**; find **God's plan for your salvation** there.

W-96.10.If you succeed, the thoughts that come to you will tell you you are saved, and that your **split** mind has found the function **of forgiveness** that **your split mind originally** sought to lose. 2 Your **big "S"** Self will welcome **your split mind** and give **your split mind** peace. 3 Restored in strength, **your healed split mind** will again flow out from spirit to the spirit in all things created by the Spirit as Itself. 4 Your **healed split** mind will bless all things. 5 Confusion done, **your healed split mind** is restored, for you have found your **big "S"** Self.

W-96.11.Your **big "S"** Self knows that you cannot fail today. 2 Perhaps your **egoic** mind remains uncertain yet a little while. 3 Be not dismayed by this. 4 The joy your **big "S"** Self experiences It will save for **your split mind,** and **this joy your big "S" Self experiences** will yet be yours in full awareness **when your split mind is healed from its uncertainty.** 5 Every time you spend five minutes of the hour seeking **the Holy Spirit** Who joins your **split** mind and **your big "S"** Self, you offer **the Holy Spirit** another treasure to be kept for you.

W-96.12.Each time today you tell your frantic **egoic** mind salvation comes from your one **big "S"** Self, you lay another treasure in your growing store. 2 And all of **your treasure** is given everyone who asks for **your treasure** and will accept the gift **of salvation**. 3 Think, then, how much is given unto you to give this day, that **the treasure of salvation** be given you!

Notes to Lesson # 96

Salvation comes from my one Self.

Lesson 96, salvation comes from my one Self, explains why A Course in Miracles is a simple course. There are no shades of gray in A Course in Miracles. Everything is either black or white. You either look through the eyes of love or the eyes of fear.

Although there is just the one Self, you experience yourself as two distinct parts. You believe you are split minded and separate from your Source. The ego's world is a complex world because black and white do not exist. Instead, there are only various shades of gray. Thus, uncertainty rules the egoic fear-based world.

The ego attempts to make the false real and the true false. In the upside down world of the ego, both good and evil, love and hate, mind and body exist. This sense of split mindedness is the source of constant conflict, fear and struggle. Only one side can be true, for opposites are never compatible. Yet, the ego attempts to resolve that perceived conflict and reconcile the false with the true.

Truth and illusion cannot be reconciled. Remember that mind, which is an expression of spirit, is different from the physical organ we call the brain. The body and the mind cannot both exist. You cannot reconcile the physical world with mind since you are only spirit.

Spirit uses mind as a means for its self-expression as your big "S" Self. If your mind perceives itself as a body, the mind becomes confused with who and what you really are and you lose your peace of mind. When your mind perceives itself as separate from spirit, it fails to think the shared thoughts of the Mind of God. Instead, it perceives itself as limited.

Salvation cannot make illusions real nor solve problems that do not exist. Salvation reawakens your big "S" Self to its real thoughts that it shares with the Mind of God. Salvation comes from the thoughts of your big "S" Self. The Holy Spirit is the bridge between mind and your big "S" Self.

When allowed, the Holy Spirit will reinterpret the ego's fear-based stories and realign those same experiences to support and bear witness for your reawakening to the truth. The opposites that the ego imagines such as love and hate, good and evil, mind and body cannot be reconciled. Instead, the illusion of opposites will dissolve before the truth of your big "S" Self. Only love, good and mind will remain.

The collective consciousness has taught us that our world, like our mind, is split into a battleground between good and evil and that both exist. This is not true. We are only one loving big "S" Self.

Allow the Holy Spirit to make use of the mind as a means for your big "S" Self's expression that bears witness only to the truth. A mind that serves your big "S" Self is at peace and joy. Salvation cannot make illusions real or solve problems that do not exist.

The ego's problems are meaningless. They are not real. They are based on fear, which is false evidence appearing real. You can never resolve the problem of separation within the thought system that was designed to support and make the illusion appear real. Dream problems cannot be resolved if you refuse to remember that you are the dreamer.

Salvation comes from your One Self. Decide today to wake up to the truth that only your big "S" Self is real. Follow the voice of the Holy Spirit and make a conscious decision to wake up to the fact that you are not a limited ego body. Then watch as your little "s" self dissolves with the meaningless egoic thought system that created it.

Question: Do you find that when you have more choices, the decision-making process becomes more complex?

In reality, how you choose to react to all your experiences is a simple choice between fear and love.

LESSON 97.

I am spirit.

W-97.1.Today's idea, **I am spirit,** identifies you with your one **big "S" Self**. 2 **Today's idea, I am spirit,** accepts no split identity, nor tries to weave opposing factors into unity. 3 **Today's idea, I am spirit,** simply states the truth. 4 Practice this truth today **that you are spirit** as often as you can, for **today's idea that you are spirit** will bring your **split** mind from conflict to the quiet fields of peace. 5 No chill of fear can enter, for your **split** mind has been absolved from madness, letting go **your ego's** illusions of a split identity.

W-97.2.We state again the truth about your **big "S" Self**, the holy Son of God Who rests in you; whose **split** mind has been restored to sanity. 2 You are the spirit lovingly endowed with all your Father's Love and peace and joy. 3 You are the spirit which completes **God,** Himself, and shares **God's** function as Creator. 4 **God** is with you always, as you are with **God.**

W-97.3.Today we try to bring reality still closer to your **split** mind. 2 Each time you practice, awareness is brought a little nearer at least; sometimes a thousand years or more are saved. 3 The minutes which you give are multiplied over and over, for the miracle makes use of time, but is not ruled by **time.** 4 Salvation is a miracle. **Salvation is** the first and last **miracle. Salvation is** the first **miracle** that is the last **miracle,** for **Salvation** and **the miracle are** one.

W-97.4.You are the spirit in whose mind abides the miracle **of salvation** in which all time stands still; the miracle **of salvation** in which a minute spent in using these ideas **that I am spirit** becomes a time that has no limit and that has no end. 2 Give, then, these minutes **to using these ideas that I am spirit** willingly, and count on **the Holy Spirit** Who promised to lay timelessness beside **these minutes that you give to the Holy Spirit.** 3 **The Holy Spirit** will offer all His strength to every little effort that you make. 4 Give **the Holy Spirit** the minutes which He needs today, to help **your split mind** understand with **the Holy Spirit's guidance that** you are the spirit that abides in **the Holy Spirit,** and that **you** call through **the Holy Spirit's** Voice to every living thing; **That you** offer **the Holy Spirit's** sight to everyone who asks: **That you through the Holy Spirit** replace error with the simple truth.

W-97.5.The Holy Spirit will be glad to take five minutes of each hour from your hands **in which you spend using these ideas that I am spirit,** and carry **those ideas that I am spirit** around this aching world where pain and misery appear to rule. 2 **The Holy Spirit** will not overlook one open mind that will accept the healing gifts **your ideas that I am spirit** bring, and **the Holy Spirit** will lay them everywhere **the Holy Spirit** knows **your ideas that I am spirit** will be welcome. 3 And **your ideas that I am spirit** will increase in healing power each time someone accepts them as his own **split mind's** thoughts, and uses **your ideas that I am spirit** to heal **his split mind.**

W-97.6.Thus will each gift to **the Holy Spirit** be multiplied a thousandfold and tens of thousands more. 2 And when **the gift that you are spirit** is returned to you, it will surpass in might the little gift you gave as much as does the radiance of the sun outshine the tiny gleam a firefly makes an uncertain moment and goes out. 3 The steady brilliance of this light remains and leads you out of darkness, nor will you be able to forget the way **of this light** again.

W-97.7.Begin these happy exercises with the words the Holy Spirit speaks to you, and let **these words, I am spirit,** echo round the world through **the Holy Spirit.**
2 Spirit am I, a holy Son of God, free of all limits, safe and healed and whole, free to forgive, and free to save the world.
3 **With these words that you are spirit** expressed through you, the Holy Spirit will accept this gift that you received of **the Holy Spirit and** increase **this gift's healing** power and give **this gift's healing power** back to you.

W-97.8.Offer each practice period today gladly to **the Holy Spirit.** 2 And **the Holy Spirit** will speak to you, reminding you that you are spirit, one with **the Holy Spirit** and God, your brothers and your **big "S" Self**. 3 Listen for **the Holy Spirit's** assurance every time you speak the words **the Holy Spirit** offers you today, and let **the Holy Spirit** tell your mind that **the words the Holy Spirit gives you** are true. 4 Use **the words the Holy Spirit gives you** against temptation, and escape **temptation's** sorry consequences if you yield to the **ego's** belief that you are something else **than spirit.** 5 The Holy Spirit gives you peace today. 6 Receive **the Holy Spirit's** words, and offer **the words the Holy Spirit gives to you back** to the **Holy Spirit.**

Notes to Lesson # 97

I am spirit.

Lesson 97, I am spirit, states the simple fact that you do not have a choice of who you are. You are spirit and remain as God created you. This makes your decision a simple one. You do not have a choice between good and evil since only one exists. Truth is the only choice that you are given.

Your denial of the truth is not a viable option. Your refusal to accept the fact that you are spirit is simply your decision-maker's refusal to make a decision and to delay the ending of time. It is your ego's belief that the false is an actual, meaningful choice. Your egoic world is meaningless since it has no effect on truth. The truth is that only love is real and you are that One. This is the only choice you are asked to make. There is only one problem, one choice and one answer.

Time is the belief that opposites exist. Time will end when you realize that all fear-based illusions are not real and you simply freely decide to accept the At-One-Ment for yourself. The atonement is the realization that you are now and forever will be that big "S" Self. With that realization, time, which is the measure of change, ends. Time has fulfilled its purpose of healing the split mind of its belief in separation. Sleeping minds have now reawakened to the changelessness of eternity and that they are united as that One Self.

You are spirit. In time, your choice is simply to accept the truth that you remain perfect, whole and complete or attempt to deny that truth. Reject all egoic attempts to argue for your littleness.

I am spirit is simply a statement of fact. You complete God and are sharing God's function as Creator. When you help others reawaken to the truth of who they are, you are involved in the creative process of extending the good, the holy and the beautiful. You are co-creating with God.

In time, love is the creative process in which time is utilized to reawaken sleeping minds to their spiritual magnificence as the Christ, their big "S" Self. As spirit, you are endowed with God's love, peace and joy. As a miracle worker, you look past the illusions that plague the minds of those who perceive themselves to be separate from their Source. You are an instrument that the Holy Spirit utilizes to bear witness for the truth of who your brothers, sisters and you really are.

A miracle is a change in perception. It is the exchange of the ego's fear-based thought system for the thought system of love and forgiveness. The miracle maker uses time to reframe the fear-based interpretation given to an experience in time. A miracle is not ruled by the laws of time. Rather, the miracle supersedes the fear-based laws of this world.

Salvation is the miracle of reawakening to the truth. It is the first and last miracle for it is an acceptance that you are that One Self, united with your Creator. Salvation is the first and last miracle since it ends the illusion of fear, which itself was never real.

Question: There are only two possible choices. You are either spirit, perfect, whole and complete or you are a body, not perfect, not whole and very incomplete. Given those two choices why would you argue for your littleness?

LESSON 98.

I will accept my part in God's plan for salvation.

W-98.1.Today is a day of special dedication **to accept your part in God's plan for salvation.** 2 We take a stand on but one side today. 3 We side with truth and let illusions go. 4 We will not vacillate between **truth and illusions**, but take a firm position with the One **of Truth.** 5 We dedicate ourselves to truth today, and to salvation as God planned **truth and salvation to** be. 6 We will not argue **salvation** is something else **different from God's plan.** 7 We will not seek for **salvation** where **salvation** is not. 8 In gladness we accept **salvation** as **God's plan** is, and take the part assigned to us by God.

W-98.2.How happy to be certain! 2 All our doubts we lay aside today, and take our stand with certainty of purpose, and with thanks that doubt is gone and surety has come. 3 We have a mighty purpose to fulfill **in God's plan for salvation**, and have been given everything we need with which to reach the goal **of salvation.** 4 Not one mistake stands in our way. 5 For we have been absolved from errors. 6 All our sins are washed away by realizing **what we perceive to be sin**s were but mistakes.

W-98.3.The guiltless have no fear, for **the guiltless** are safe and recognize their safety. 2 **The guiltless** do not appeal to magic, nor invent escapes from fancied threats **that are** without reality. 3 T**he guiltless** rest in quiet certainty that they will do what it is given **the guiltless** to do. 4 T**he guiltless** do not doubt their own ability because **the guiltless** know their function will be filled completely in the perfect time and place. 5 T**he guiltless** took the stand **to accept their part in God's plan for salvation** which we will **also** take today. **We accept our part in God's plan so** that we may share **the** certainty **of the guiltless** and thus increase **their certainty** by accepting **that same certainty for** ourselves.

W-98.4.The guiltless will be with us; all who took the stand we take today **to accept our part in God's plan** will gladly offer us all that **the guiltless** learned and every gain they made. 2 Those still uncertain, too, will join with us, and, borrowing our certainty, will make **our certainty** stronger still. 3 While those as yet unborn will hear the call we heard, and answer **the call we heard** when they have come to make their choice again. 4 We do not choose but for ourselves today.

W-98.5.Is it not worth five minutes of your time each hour to be able to accept the happiness that God has given you? 2 Is it not worth five minutes hourly to recognize your special function **of forgiveness** here? 3 Is not five minutes but a small request to make in terms of gaining a reward so great **for salvation's reward** has no measure? 4 You have made a thousand losing bargains at the least **by following the ego's plan for salvation**.

W-98.6.**To accept your part in God's plan for salvation** is an offer guaranteeing you your full release from pain of every kind, and joy the world does not contain. 2 You can exchange a little of your time for peace of mind and certainty of purpose, with the promise of complete success. 3 And since time has no meaning, you are being asked for nothing in return for **salvation which is** everything. 4 **Exchanging time for accepting your part in God's plan for salvation** is a bargain that you cannot lose. 5 And what you gain, **salvation's truth of who you really are,** is limitless indeed!

W-98.7.Each hour today give **the Holy Spirit** your tiny gift of but five minutes. 2 T**he Holy Spirit** will give the words you use in practicing today's idea **that you will accept your part in God's plan for salvation** the deep conviction and the certainty you lack. 3 **The Holy Spirit's** words will join with your **words** and make each repetition of today's idea **that you will accept your part in God's plan for salvation** a total dedication, made in faith as perfect and as sure as **the Holy Spirit's faith** in you. 4 T**he Holy Spirit's** confidence in you will bring the light to all the words you say, and you will go beyond their sound to what **the words** really mean. 5 Today you practice with **the Holy Spirit**, as you say:
6 I will accept my part in God's plan for salvation.

W-98.8.In each five minutes that you spend with **the Holy Spirit, the Holy Spirit** will accept your words and give **your words** back to you all bright with faith and confidence so strong and steady **that your words** will light the world with hope and gladness. 2 Do not lose one chance to be the glad receiver of **the Holy Spirit's** gifts, that you may give **the Holy Spirit's gifts** to the world today.

W-98.9.Give **the Holy Spirit** the words, and **the Holy Spirit** will do the rest. 2 T**he Holy Spirit** will enable you to understand your special function **of forgiveness.** 3 T**he Holy Spirit** will open up the way to happiness, and peace and trust will be **the Holy Spirit's** gifts. **Happiness, peace and trust will be the Holy Spirit's** answer to your words. 4 T**he Holy Spirit** will respond with all **the Holy Spirit's** faith and joy and certainty that what you say is true. 5 And you will have conviction then of **the Holy Spirit** Who knows the function that you have on earth as well as Heaven. 6 T**he Holy Spirit** will be with you each practice period you share with t**he Holy Spirit** exchanging every instant of the time you offer **the Holy Spirit** for timelessness and peace.

W-98.10.Throughout the hour, let your time be spent in happy preparation for the next five minutes you will spend again with **the Holy Spirit**. 2 Repeat today's idea **that you will accept your part in God's plan for salvation** while you wait for the glad time to come to you again. 3 Repeat **today's idea that you will accept your part in God's plan for salvation** often, and do not forget each time you do so, you have let your mind be readied for the happy time to come.

W-98.11.And when the hour goes and **the Holy Spirit** is there once more to spend a little time with you, be thankful and lay down all earthly tasks, all little thoughts and limited **egoic** ideas, and spend a happy time again with **the Holy Spirit**. 2 Tell

the Holy Spirit once more that you accept the part that **the Holy Spirit** would have you take and help you fill, and **the Holy Spirit** will make you sure you want this choice, which **the Holy Spirit** has made with you and you with **the Holy Spirit**.

Notes to Lesson # 98

I will accept my part in God's plan for salvation.

Today, you are asked to choose the truth that you are spirit and proclaim that you remain as God created you. This acceptance of your role in God's plan for salvation hastens the return to knowledge of all who believe the separation to be their reality.

Today, you are asked to dedicate yourself to the truth and let all egoic illusions of separation go. When you accept your part in God's plan for salvation, you give up your ego's plans. Your ego's plans revolve around suffering and earning back something that was never lost. You understand that God's love is not earned. Instead, it is freely given and you accept God's unconditional love that your ego would have you deny.

You realize that what your ego calls sins are only mistakes that require correction, not punishment. You accept the fact that God is your strength and sinlessness comes from God. You follow the guidance of the Holy Spirit and therefore, are certain that your role in God's plan will be fulfilled and the Holy Spirit's mission of healing the split mind will be accomplished.

Your part in God's plan is to accept the truth and let all egoic illusions go. This means that you are certain that all are sinless and therefore, guiltless. The guiltless have no fear since they know and recognize that their safety is insured by their divine inheritance. The guiltless do not engage in magic in an attempt to control outside powers since they realize that there is nothing outside their own minds that can rob them of their own inner peace.

Only the guilty make up stories, believe they are victims and hold grievances against God and their brothers. In their attempt to escape from their own guilt, the guilty project their blame, guilt and fears upon their outer world. They claim to be victims of outside forces that are beyond their control. They deny that their outer world is merely a reflection of their inner mind's fears.

Your part in God's plan for salvation involves your acceptance of the atonement for yourself. You are not asked to correct attack or convince another that they are wrong when they argue for their littleness. Instead, you are only asked to hold the truth that they, like yourself, remain as God created them. With the vision of Christ, you can see them in the light. You can look past the body and behold their big "S" Self that remains united with your Creator.

As Jesus said about his role in God's plan, "If you wish to be like me, knowing that we are the same, I will help you. If you want to be different, I will wait until you change your mind." Note that Jesus does not make anyone wrong for their decision to argue for their littleness.

Unconditional love accepts and allows. It does not judge or increase another's fear. Unconditional love accepts you just the way you are. Your role is to accept the truth that you are God's beloved Child and to hold that truth even while another argues for their own littleness. Rather than judge and condemn, wait patiently and offer a helping hand when they decide to change their mind and drop their fear-based thinking.

Your role in God's plan for salvation does not require that you fix, change, control, protect or impress another. By your mere acceptance of the truth of who you really are, you are helping all hold that same truth about themselves. When you relinquish your fear-based egoic judgments and follow the guidance of the Holy Spirit, you will be fulfilling your function.

Question: Why doesn't God's plan for salvation require you to fix, change, control, impress or protect another so that they can be saved?

When you perceive another as a victim, you disempower not only them but also yourself.

LESSON 99

Salvation is my only function here.

W-99.1.Salvation and forgiveness are the same. 2 **Salvation and forgiveness** both imply that something has gone wrong; something to be saved from, forgiven for; something amiss that needs corrective change; something apart or different from the Will of God. 3 Thus do both **salvation and forgiveness** imply a thing impossible but yet which has occurred, resulting in a state of conflict seen between what is and what could never be.

W-99.2.**In your egoic world of perception,** truth and illusions both are equal now, for both have **been perceived to have really** happened. 2 The impossible becomes the thing you need forgiveness for. **The impossible becomes the thing you need** salvation from. 3 Salvation now becomes the borderland between the truth and the illusion. 4 **Salvation** reflects the truth because **salvation** is the means by which you can escape illusions. 5 Yet **salvation** is not yet the truth because **salvation** undoes what was never done. This is also the case regarding forgiveness. **Forgiveness reflects the truth because forgiveness is the means by which you can escape illusions. 5 Yet forgiveness is not yet the truth because forgiveness undoes what was never done.**

W-99.3.How could there be a meeting place at all where earth and Heaven can be reconciled within a **split** mind where both **truth and illusions are believed to both** exist? 2 The **split** mind that sees illusions thinks **illusions are** real. 3 **Illusions** have existence in that **illusions** are **egoic** fear-**based** thoughts. 4 And yet **illusions** are not real, because the **split** mind that thinks these thoughts is separate from God **and these thoughts are not shared with the Mind of God.**

W-99.4.What joins the separated **split** mind and thoughts with Mind and Thought which are forever One? 2 What plan could hold the truth inviolate, yet recognize the need illusions bring, and offer means by which **illusions** are undone without attack and with no touch of pain? 3 What but a Thought of God could be this plan, by which the never done is overlooked, and sins forgotten which were never real?

W-99.5.The Holy Spirit holds this plan of God **that undoes illusion without attack** exactly as **God's plan** was received of **the Holy Spirit** within the Mind of God and in your own **big "S" Self's mind.** 2 **This plan that undoes illusion without attack** is apart from time in that its Source, **which is God,** is timeless. 3 Yet **this plan of God that undoes illusion without attack** operates in time, because of your belief that time is real. 4 Unshaken does the Holy Spirit look on what you see; on sin and pain and death, on grief and separation and on loss. 5 Yet does **the Holy Spirit** know one thing must still be true; God is still Love, and this **egoic world you perceive** is not **God's** Will.

W-99.6.**God is Love and the egoic world you perceive is not God's Will** is the Thought that brings illusions to the truth, and sees **illusions** as appearances behind which is the changeless and the sure. 2 **God is Love and the egoic world you perceive is not God's Will** is the Thought that saves and that forgives, because **this thought** lays no faith in what is not created by the only Source **real thought** knows. 3 **God is Love and the egoic world you perceive is not God's Will** is the Thought whose function is to save by giving you **this thought's** function as your own **function of forgiveness and salvation.** 4 Salvation is your function, with the **Holy Spirit** to Whom the plan was given. 5 Now **is your big "S" Self** entrusted with **God's** plan **for salvation,** along with **the Holy Spirit.** 6 The Holy Spirit has one answer to appearances; regardless of their form, their size, their depth or any attribute **the misperceptions** seem to have:
7 Salvation is my only function here.
8 God still is Love, and this **perceived egoic illusion** is not **God's** Will.

W-99.7.You who will yet work miracles, be sure you practice well the idea for today **that salvation is your only function here.** 2 Try to perceive the strength in what you say, for these are words in which your freedom lies. 3 Your Father loves you. 4 All the world of pain is not **God's** Will. 5 Forgive yourself the thought **that God** wanted this **perceived egoic illusion** for you. 6 Then let the Thought with which **the Holy Spirit** has replaced all your **ego's** mistakes enter the darkened places of your **split** mind that thought the **unreal** thoughts that never were **God's** Will.

W-99.8.This part **of your mind that appears to be split from God's Mind** belongs to God, as does the rest. 2 **Your mind that appears to be split from God's Mind** does not think its solitary thoughts, and make **the ego's unreal** thoughts real by hiding them from **God.** 3 Let in the light **of the Holy Spirit** and you will look upon no obstacle to what **God** wills for you. 4 Open your secrets to **the Holy Spirit's** kindly light, and see how bright this light still shines in you.

W-99.9.Practice **the Holy Spirit's** Thought today **that God is still Love, and this egoic world you perceive is not God's Will,** and let **the Holy Spirit's** light seek out and lighten up all darkened spots **of your little "s" self's mind,** and shine through **these unreal egoic thoughts** to join **the healed little "s" self** to the rest **of your big "S" Self.** 2 It is God's Will your mind be one with **God's Mind.** 3 It is God's Will that **God** has but one Son. 4 It is God's Will that **God's** one Son is you. 5 Think of these things in practicing today, and start the lesson that we learn today, **that salvation is your only function here,** with this instruction in the way of truth:
6 Salvation is my only function here.
7 Salvation and forgiveness are the same.

8 Then turn to **the Holy Spirit** Who shares your function here **of salvation and forgiveness**, and let **the Holy Spirit** teach you what you need to learn to lay all fear aside, and know your **big "S" Self** as Love which has no opposite in you.

W-99.10.Forgive all thoughts which would oppose the truth of your completion, unity and peace. 2 You cannot lose the gifts your Father gave. 3 You do not want to be another **little "s" self** that opposes the truth of your completion, unity and **peace**. 4 You have no function that is not of God. 5 Forgive yourself the **egoic function** you think you made **that opposes the truth of your completion, unity and peace.** 6 Forgiveness and salvation are the same. 7 Forgive what you have made **with your split mind** and you are saved.

W-99.11.There is a special message for today which has the power to remove all forms of doubt and fear forever from your mind. 2 If you are tempted to believe **any form of doubt and fear to be** true, remember that appearances cannot withstand the truth these mighty words contain:
3 Salvation is my only function here.
4 God still is Love, and this is not **God's** Will.

W-99.12.Your only function tells you you are one **with the shared Mind of God**. 2 Remind yourself of this **oneness** between the times you give five minutes to be shared with **the Holy Spirit** Who shares God's plan with you. 3 Remind yourself:
4 Salvation is my only function here.
5 Thus do you lay forgiveness on your mind and let all your **split mind's** fear be gently laid aside, that love may find its rightful place in **your healed mind** and show you that you are the Son of God.

Notes to Lesson #99

Salvation is my only function here.

Last night, I dreamed I was a dog and that I had bitten the mailman. What must I do to correct the harm that I did to the mailman?

The answer should be obvious. I need to wake up from the dream and realize that what I thought had happened had never occurred. I would not have to be punished for my actions nor would I have to ask for the mailman's forgiveness. The belief that I was a dog was incorrect since it was a dream. In actuality, nothing had happened to impact or change my outer world. There was no wrongdoing on my part and there was no harm done to the mailman.

Because I was born a human being, my dream had no ability to change my true nature. I could imagine I was a dog and even believe it to be true but that dream would not change my reality. The dream would have no real effects or consequences upon the outer world. Yet, it could impact my mind's inner world.

The dream would only appear to impact how I behaved and reacted in my world as long as my mind was under the delusion that the dream was my reality and that I was actually a dog. Once, however, I realized that I was the dreamer of the dream, my mind would quickly realize that nothing had really occurred. The dream would fade from my consciousness and I would merely resume the knowledge of my true identity.

The mailman would be totally unaware that such a dream had occurred and would not demand an apology. The only person that would be aware that the dream had ever occurred would be myself or anyone that I chose to share my story with. Since my own mind was the source of the dream, I could relate the story in one of two ways. The first is to acknowledge that I was dreaming. The second is to fail to mention that it was a dream.

Depending on how I chose to tell the story, the listener would either think that I had harmed the mailman or merely dismiss the story as inconsequential or perhaps amusing. If I told him that the dream was a punishable offense, the listener would realize that there had never been any crime and that no punishment should be imposed upon an imaginary dog nor forgiveness asked from the mailman.

But what if I, the dreamer, failed to recognize that the story of my being the dog and biting the mailman was really a dream? If that was the case, my mind would be delusional and I would think that I had wronged the mailman. I would believe that forgiveness and punishment were warranted. I would feel guilty and expect to suffer the consequences from my actions. All of these fear-based thoughts arose because I failed to recognize the events were not real.

This is the situation that you currently find yourselves in. You believe that time has somehow changed who you really are. You have mistaken the game token that you call the body to be your true reality. You have forgotten that you are a spiritual being having an earthly experience. The differentiation that this world provides is designed to offer the rich, fun learning experiences that you desire. It is your misguided belief that the game is real that has transformed these experiences into a source for sin, guilt and fear. You remain an individuated aspect of the One Self.

You have come here to demonstrate your true spiritual magnificence. If a mistake in judgment happens in this playschool, no crime has occurred and no punishment is required. If you believe a mistake has occurred, only correction is requested from yourself. If you believe forgiveness is required, you have merely forgotten that in this playschool of time and space, nothing has really happened that can affect the Mind of God.

Your salvation and freedom lie in the fact that God is only love. This world of sin, pain and suffering that you imagine is not God's Will. You need to forgive yourself for your belief that God would want this for his beloved child. Ask the Holy Spirit for guidance and forgive yourself. Your egoic thoughts have never had any reality because they are not shared with the Mind of God.

Instead, accept the truth of God's plan for your reawakening. Set aside all fears and know that love has no opposites. Drop your egoic belief that you could have another alternate reality. You remain as God created you. Forgive and forget what your egoic mind has made and imagines. Accept the truth and you are saved.

Salvation and forgiveness are the same. They are the borderland between truth and illusion. They reflect truth because it is the means to escape from illusion. Yet, it is not the truth because forgiveness or salvation undoes what was never done since you only imagined your sins to be real. Time and space is your playschool for reawakening.

You do not have to feel guilty because you chose to play the game of separation and reawakening. When you ask the Holy Spirit, you are given God's plan of forgiveness and salvation. The Holy Spirit reframes your ego's delusional thoughts of sin, guilt and fear while recognizing the effect that these illusions have upon your split mind.

These illusions infest your sick mind with a great deal of blame, shame and guilt. God's plan ends your participation in the blame shame and guilt game of your ego's world. God's plan offers the means by which illusions are undone without any punishment or sacrifice and therefore, without any pain.

The Holy Spirit's unique understanding of forgiveness allows the reconciliation of your delusional egoic thoughts and the truth with God's love. No punishment is required and yet justice is served. God's plan for your salvation is apart from time since its source, which is God Itself, is timeless. Yet, God's plan operates in time because you believe that time, which is the measure of change, is real.

The Holy Spirit knows one thing must be eternally true. God is still love and therefore, all your egoic imaginings of pain and suffering are not God's Will. The Holy Spirit knows the truth about you and therefore, only asks what love would have you do. Salvation, which is the act of forgiving yourself for your ego's misperceptions, is your only function in time. Accept the truth or the At-One-Ment for yourself.

God is still love and your egoic imaginings are not God's Will. Salvation is your reawakening from the dream of separation. In time, forgiving yourself for following your ego's fear-based thought system is your only function.

Question: In my dream of being a dog that bites the mailman, why is it unnecessary for me to ask forgiveness from the mailman?

Question: Who and what is the source for any blame, shame and guilt that this dream imposes on the dreamer's mind?

LESSON 100

My part is essential to God's plan for salvation.

W-100.1.Just as God's Son completes his Father, so your part in **God's plan for salvation** completes your Father's plan. 2 Salvation must reverse the mad belief in separate thoughts and separate bodies, which lead separate lives and go their separate ways. 3 One function shared by separate minds unites them in one purpose, for each one of **the mad beliefs of separate thoughts and separate bodies** is equally essential to all **beliefs in separation.**

W-100.2.God's Will for you is perfect happiness. 2 Why should you choose to go against **God's** Will **when God's Will for you is perfect happiness**? 3 The part that **God** has saved for you to take in working out **God's** plan is given you that you might be restored to what **God** wills **which is your perfect happiness.** 4 This part **you play in God's plan for salvation** is as essential to **God's** plan **as it is** to your happiness. 5 Your joy must be complete to let **God's** plan be understood by those to whom **God** sends you. 6 **Those to whom God sends you** will see their function **of perfect happiness** in your shining face, and hear God calling to **those you interact with** in your happy laugh.

W-100.3.You are indeed essential to God's plan. 2 Without your joy, **God's** joy is incomplete. 3 Without your smile, the world cannot be saved. 4 While you are sad, the light that God Himself appointed as the means to save the world is dim and lusterless, and no one laughs because all laughter can but echo your **laughter.**

W-100.4.You are indeed essential to God's plan. 2 Just as your light increases every light that shines in Heaven, so your joy on earth calls to all minds to let their sorrows go, and take their **joyous** place beside you in God's plan. 3 God's messengers are joyous, and **God's messenger's** joy heals sorrow and despair. 4 **God's joyous messengers** are the proof that God wills perfect happiness for all who will accept their Father's gifts **which are perfect happiness** as their **own birthright.**

W-100.5.We will not let ourselves be sad today. 2 For if we do **let ourselves be sad**, we fail to take the part **of being perfectly happy** that is essential to God's plan, as well as **being essential** to our vision **of our big "S" Self.** 3 Sadness is the sign that you would play another part **based on your ego's belief in separation**, instead of what has been assigned to you by God. 4 Thus do you fail to show the world how great the happiness **God** wills for you. 5 And so you do not recognize that **happiness** is yours.

W-100.6.Today we will attempt to understand joy is our function here. 2 If you are sad, your part **in God's plan for salvation** is unfulfilled, and all the world is thus deprived of joy, along with you. 3 God asks you to be happy, so the world can see how much **God** loves His Son, and wills no sorrow rises to abate **the Son of God's** joy; no fear besets **God's Son** to disturb **the Son of God's** peace. 4 You are God's messenger today. 5 You bring **God's** happiness to all you look upon. **You bring God's** peace to everyone who looks on you and sees **God's** message in your happy face.

W-100.7.We will prepare ourselves for **bringing God's happiness to all we look upon today**, in our five-minute practice periods, by feeling happiness arise in us according to our Father's Will and **according to** our **real will that we share with God.** 2 Begin the exercises with the thought today's idea contains **that your part is essential to God's plan for salvation.** 3 Then realize your part **in God's plan** is to be happy. 4 Only **happiness** is asked of you or anyone who wants to take his place among God's messengers. 5 Think what this means **that only happiness is asked of you.** 6 You have indeed been wrong in your **ego's** belief that sacrifice is asked **if you are to be saved.** 7 You but receive according to God's plan, and never lose or sacrifice or die.

W-100.8.Now let us try to find that joy that proves to us and all the world God's Will for us **is only perfect happiness.** 2 It is your function that you find **only perfect happiness** here, and that you find **only perfect happiness** now. 3 For this **function that you find only perfect happiness is what** you came **here to experience.** 4 Let this one **moment** be the day that you succeed! 5 Look deep within you, undismayed by all the little **"s" self's** thoughts and foolish **egoic** goals you pass as you ascend to meet the Christ in you.

W-100.9.**Christ, your big "S" Self,** will be there. 2 And you can reach **the Christ in you** now. 3 What could you rather look upon in place of **the Christ in you** Who waits that you may look on **your big "S" Self**? 4 What little **"s" self's** thought has power to hold you back? 5 What foolish **egoic** goal can keep you from success when **the Christ in you** Who calls to you is God Himself?

W-100.10.**The Voice for God, the Christ in you,** will be there. 2 You are essential to **God's** plan **for salvation.** 3 You are **God's** messenger today. 4 And you must find what **God** would have you give **which is only perfect happiness.** 5 Do not forget the idea for today **that your part is essential to God's plan for salvation** between your hourly practice periods. 6 It is your **Big "S" Self, the Christ in you,** Who calls to you today. 7 And it is **your Big "S" Self** you answer, every time you tell yourself you are essential to God's plan for the salvation of the world.

Notes to Lesson #100

My part is essential to God's plan for salvation.

Salvation reverses the mad idea of separation and the belief that you are your body. It is impossible to be separate from the One Self. God as the Father is Cause. <u>God as the Son is Its Effect</u>. Father and Son are two sides of one indivisible coin called God. Each side completing the other is the unity of that One Self. Therefore, each side is indispensable and completes the other. Both Father and Son must play their role in God's plan for salvation.

This lesson states that your part is essential to God's plan for salvation. God's Will for you is perfect happiness. Because of this, your part in God's plan for salvation is for you to be happy. Your function is to find the joy that proves to the entire world that God's Will is for all to be happy. By being joyous and accepting this role, you help heal the world of the split minded that perceive themselves to be separate from God's love.

Joy was the prize that we desired to experience when we first enrolled in the game of separation or reawakening. We felt that differentiation was required to experience being the various aspects of love in form. True happiness comes from being what you truly are which is only love. Joy comes from fulfilling your function or purpose for being. When we experience this joy of being love in form, we complete God.

Our joy is complete when we know God's Will for us is our perfect happiness. Sadness shows that you fail to recognize that happiness is your divine birthright and that your part in God's plan is to be perfectly happy. When you are sad, you demonstrate that you have chosen to play a different role within God's plan. You have slipped into egoic thinking and believe that God is not unconditional love. You are perceiving yourself to be separate and therefore something less than perfect, whole and complete.

You believe that you are a sinner and have lost your divine birthright. Perceiving yourself to be a sinner, your ego now believes that you must do something to earn God's love. This leads to the ego's belief that you need to make some sort of sacrifice to earn your inheritance back.

The ego does not comprehend unconditional love. The ego believes that love has to be earned. Therefore, sacrifice, pain and suffering are required on your part to atone for your past wrongdoing.

God's love, being unconditional makes no demands on the recipient of that love. The recipient can refuse or accept the love, but the love flows continuously. When you accept that God's love is unconditional, you understand that God's Will for His Son is only your perfect happiness.

In the Bible there is the parable of the prodigal son. In this story, a wealthy father has two sons, both of which he showers with his affection. One day, one of his sons requests from the father his inheritance so that the son can do with it what he wants. The son believes this will make him happy and the father complies with the son's wishes. This son goes off and quickly spends his entire inheritance. Having lost his inheritance, the prodigal son must now work if he is to eat. He finds that life is a hard struggle.

Eventually, the son decides that even his father's servants have a better lifestyle than what he has created for himself. The prodigal son vows to return to his father's home with the hope of at least being given a job. This son longs for the quality of life that his father's servants enjoy. Yet, this son realizes that he alone has squandered his inheritance and has no expectation of being treated any better than a common servant. Upon the son's return, the father orders a great feast and restores the prodigal son to his full birthright.

This parable is difficult for the egoic mind to grasp. Although one can perhaps understand the joy that the father felt for the return of his long-lost son, what about the good son that had stayed at home and obeyed his father's wishes?

To the ego, it seems unjust that the prodigal son should regain the inheritance that he had already squandered. It seems that the father is being unfair to the good son. The good son is being asked to surrender or sacrifice part of his future inheritance so that the prodigal son can be restored to his former glory.

To the ego, this seems to be a great injustice. We will discuss the various aspects of this parable of the prodigal son in the ongoing lessons. But today I would like to focus on the father's reaction to the prodigal son's return.

To the father, the son was his treasure. The father only wanted his son to be happy. The son's happiness, not the father's wealth, was what the father valued. The prodigal son felt that if he received his full inheritance, it would make him happier. Therefore, when the prodigal son asked to receive his inheritance early, the father granted that wish. The father did not necessarily want his son to leave his home, but valued the son's happiness more. To be happy, the son felt he needed to be free to explore the world on his terms.

Love does not bind but instead offers freedom to the recipient. Unconditional love makes no demands upon the recipient of that love. To the giver of unconditional love, happiness comes from the giving of that love and the happiness that giving brings to the recipient. It expects nothing in return for to give is to receive.

The prodigal son's choice to freely return to his father's house signaled to the father that his treasure was back home where he belonged. The father could once again directly shower that child with his love and see the joy in his son's face. The father's joy was complete in knowing that his son was once again happy, safe and comfortable in his home.

You are God's treasure. Rather than try to earn God's love through your ego's plan that requires atoning for your perceived sins, merely accept your role in God's plan for salvation. That role is only to be perfectly happy and return to the truth that your divine inheritance has never been lost, only forgotten. When you realize that God's Will is your perfect happiness, it is easy to accept God's plan for your salvation. It is easy to say that God's Will and your will are the same.

Question: Do you see yourself as God's treasure or God's mistake?

LESSON 101

God's Will for me is perfect happiness.

W-101.1.Today we will continue with the theme of happiness. 2 This **theme of happiness** is a key idea in understanding what salvation means. 3 You still believe **salvation** asks for suffering as penance for your "sins." 4 This is not so. 5 Yet you must think **salvation asks for suffering as penance for your "sins"** so **long as** you believe that sin is real, and that God's Son can sin.

W-101.2.If sin is real, then punishment is just and **punishment** cannot be escaped. 2 **If sin is real**, salvation thus cannot be purchased but through suffering. 3 If sin is real, then happiness must be illusion, for **sin and happiness** cannot both be true. 4 The sinful warrant only death and pain, and it is this **suffering that those who believe they have sinned** ask for. 5 For **the sinful** know **death and pain** waits for them, and **death and pain** will seek **the sinful** out and find them somewhere, sometime, in some form that evens the account they owe **to their god of judgment**. 6 **The sinful** would escape **this god of judgment** in their fear. 7 And yet **this god of judgment** will pursue, and **the sinful** cannot escape **from the ego's god of punishment**.

W-101.3.If sin is real, salvation must be pain. 2 Pain is the cost of sin, and suffering can never be escaped, if sin is real. 3 **If sin is real**, salvation must be feared, for **salvation** will kill, but slowly, taking everything away before **salvation** grants the welcome boon of death to victims who are little more than bones before salvation is appeased. 4 **If sin is real, this god of judgment's** wrath is boundless, merciless, but wholly just.

W-101.4.**If sin is real,** who would seek out such savage punishment? 2 **If sin is real**, who would not flee salvation, and attempt in every way he can to drown the Voice which offers **such savage punishment as salvation** to **those who believe they have sinned**? 3 Why would **those who believe they have sinned** try to listen and accept **this god of judgment's** offering **of suffering and death**? 4 If sin is real, **salvation's** offering is death, and meted out in cruel form to match the vicious wishes in which sin is born. 5 If sin is real, salvation has become your bitter enemy, the curse of God upon you who have crucified **God's** Son.

W-101.5.You need the practice periods today. 2 The exercises that **God's Will for me is perfect happiness** teach sin is not real, and all that you believe must come from sin will never happen, for **these imagined effects of sin are not real since they have** no cause. 3 Accept Atonement with an open mind, which cherishes no lingering belief that you have made a devil of God's Son. 4 There is no sin. 5 We practice with this thought **that there is no sin** as often as we can today, because **this thought that there is no sin** is the basis for today's idea **that God's Will for me is perfect happiness.**

W-101.6.God's Will for you is perfect happiness because there is no sin, and suffering is causeless. 2 Joy is just, and pain is but the sign **your split minds** have misunderstood yourself **to be a sinner**. 3 Fear not the Will of God. 4 But turn to **the Will of God** in confidence that **the Will of God** will set you free from all the consequences sin has wrought in **your ego's** feverish imagination. 5 Say:
6 God's Will for me is perfect happiness.
7 There is no sin. **Therefore, sin** has no consequence.
8 So should you start your practice periods, and then attempt again to find the joy these thoughts **that God's Will for me is perfect happiness and there is no sin** will introduce into your mind.

W-101.7.Give these five minutes gladly, to remove the heavy load **of guilt** you lay upon yourself with the insane belief that sin is real. 2 Today escape from **the** madness **that sin is real**. 3 You are set on freedom's road, and now today's idea **that God's Will for me is perfect happiness** brings wings to speed you on, and hope to go still faster to the waiting goal of peace. 4 There is no sin. 5 Remember this today **that there is no sin**, and tell yourself as often as you can:
6 God's Will for me is perfect happiness.
7 This is the truth, because there is no sin.

Notes to Lesson #101

God's Will for me is perfect happiness.

Yesterday we asked the question, do you see yourself as God's treasure or God's mistake?

In the parable about the prodigal son, the son saw himself as a sinner. He perceived that by taking his inheritance and wasting it, he had wronged his father and therefore, was ashamed and feared to return to his father's home. He believed he had to struggle and suffer in the world as penance for his decision to waste his inheritance on wine, women and song. In an effort to obtain happiness outside himself, he ultimately realized he had been happiest when he freely followed his father's will.

His father's will had only been that his son be happy. All the lavish gifts that his father had bestowed upon that son when he had been living in his father's home was his father's unconditional love which was the prodigal son's true inheritance.

The purchases that the money had bought the prodigal son were fleeting and did not bring the son the happiness he had envisioned. They were external and did not last or replace the happiness that unconditional love brings. With his inheritance spent, the son was forced to struggle to earn his livelihood.

Eventually he made a wise decision to return home rather than continue to live the life he had created for himself. Separated from his father, the life the boy had created was a world that only brought him pain, misery, conflict and suffering. By returning to his father's home, the boy hoped to at least obtain a job in his father's household. The boy realized that even the least of his father's servants had a richer lifestyle than the life the prodigal son had self-created.

The boy felt he had no right or expectation to be restored to his former glory. He also realized that he had self-created a mess for himself and only had himself to blame for his misadventure. The boy was stunned to find that upon his return, his father held a great feast in the son's honor and even restored the child's inheritance that had been foolishly wasted. The son finally realized that he was his father's treasure.

The father was overjoyed when his son returned to his household. The father's will had only and always been that his children be happy. The father felt complete in his children's presence. Only when his children were by his side and he could see their smiling faces as he lavishly bestowed all he had upon his children was he happy.

The father loved his children unconditionally. The prodigal son did not have to earn his father's love again. Nor did the prodigal son have to suffer the consequences of his bad decisions to waste his inheritance on the worthless transitory things of this egoic world. The boy merely had to forgive himself for his misdeeds and return to his father's home. There, in his father's home, he once again accepted the gifts that only his father's unconditional love could provide.

The son saw himself as a sinner who had wasted his inheritance. The father saw the son as an explorer who had sought new adventures that would help the boy reawaken to the truth of who he really was. When the boy realized he was not of this egoic world, the father had gained a wiser son. The boy had learned the lesson of unconditional love which is that to give is to receive. The boy forgave himself and was richly blessed with the return of his divine inheritance. He was not treated as a servant for his inheritance could never be lost, only denied by the son alone. The prodigal son always remained his father's beloved son with whom the father was well pleased.

In our egoic world, we believe that we can harm another. When you harm another, your ego says that you have wronged them and have sinned against that person. Your ego believes that the other party is entitled to some type of revenge and that they require that you suffer and do some type of penance in order to be forgiven for your sins.

The ego does not realize that when you attack another, you only attack yourself. Because your ego does not realize what you are, it perceives that there are outside forces that can steal your happiness. The ego fails to realize that your divine inheritance insures that nothing sources your experiences but you and that nothing can rob you of your inner peace unless you choose to allow it to do so.

A fantasy has no ability to change reality. Your sins cannot be real if they have no ability to actually harm another. If you dreamed you killed someone as the dreamer, you merely need to wake up to the fact that your dream was only an illusion. Upon this realization, the suffering and punishment that you believed to be the logical consequences of your fantasy will cease to terrorize your deluded mind. You can forgive yourself and reawaken to the truth of who you really are.

Because the ego believes sin is real, it also believes that salvation requires sacrifice since a just God would require sinners to be punished. Because of this, the ego tells us that we should fear, hide and try to avoid God's justice which the ego believes to be our suffering and ultimate death.

Since sin is not real, the suffering that your ego calls for is meaningless. The ego does not want you to realize that what you perceive as an attack upon another harms no one but yourself. There is no sin and therefore, there are no consequences to fear as long as you accept the truth about yourself and see all as sinless. You are God's beloved child.

In time, A Course in Miracles defines sin as your ego's belief in lack. This belief in lack leads to your egoic belief that there are outside forces that can impact or change what you really are. Because the ego believes that sin is real, it also maintains that there are victims and victimizers. This is not the case. We are all willing volunteers. You are like the prodigal son that wishes to have experiences so that you can ultimately rediscover the truth of who you really are and reclaim your divine inheritance.

Question: When you believe you have wronged someone, does the other party's reaction to that event impact your ability to forgive yourself and then move on with your life?

LESSON 102

I share God's Will for happiness for me.

W-102.1.You do not want to suffer. 2 You may think **suffering** buys you something, and may still believe a little that **suffering** buys you what you want. 3 Yet this belief **that suffering buys you something** is surely shaken now, at least enough to let you question it and to suspect **that the belief that suffering buys you something** really makes no sense. 4 **The belief that suffering buys you something** has not gone as yet, but lacks the roots that once secured **this belief in suffering** tightly to the dark and hidden secret places of your mind.

W-102.2.Today we try to loose **the belief that suffering buys you something and** weakened **its** hold still further, and to realize that pain is purposeless, without a cause and with no power to accomplish anything. 2 **Pain and suffering** cannot purchase anything at all. 3 **Pain** offers nothing, and does not exist. 4 And everything you think **pain and suffering** offers you is lacking in existence, like **pain,** itself. 5 You have been slave to nothing. 6 Be you free today to join the happy Will of God.

W-102.3.For several days we will continue to devote our periods of practicing to exercises planned to help you reach the happiness God's Will has placed in you. 2 **Your happiness that is God's Will** is your home, and here your safety is. 3 **Your happiness that is God's Will** is your peace, and here there is no fear. 4 **Your happiness that is God's Will** is salvation. 5 Here is rest at last.

W-102.4.Begin your practice periods today with this acceptance of God's Will for you:
2 I share God's Will for happiness for me, and I accept it as my function now.
3 Then seek this function **of happiness** deep within your mind, for **your happiness that is God's Will** is there, awaiting but your choice. 4 You cannot fail to find **your happiness that is God's Will** when you learn it is your choice, and that you share God's Will.

W-102.5.Be happy, for your only function here is happiness. 2 You have no need to be less loving to God's Son than **God** Whose Love created him as loving as **God,** Himself. 3 Besides these hourly five-minute rests, pause frequently today, to tell yourself that you have now accepted happiness as your one function. 4 And be sure that you are joining with God's Will in doing this.

Notes to Lesson #102

I share God's Will for happiness for me.

Lesson 102**,** I share God's Will for happiness for me, continues the theme that God's Will is that you be happy. It even goes so far as to state that your real function is to be happy. This makes sense when you realize that God is not the judgmental, wrathful god your ego imagines but rather only unconditional love. Being unconditional love, God would want Its creation to be happy.

You share God's Will for you since you also desire to be happy. You do not desire, pain, suffering and sacrifice, but being split minded, you mistakenly believe you have sinned so your future happiness must be earned. The ego's erroneous thought system believes that you are a limited separate ego body struggling to survive in a world of sin, guilt and fear. To escape this egoic nightmare, your ego demands that you suffer and do penance for your sins if you are ever to be forgiven and granted any happiness in this or future worlds.

In contrast, the Holy Spirit knows that you remain as God created you perfect, whole and complete. You are an individuated aspect of the One Self. You remain part of the holographic Mind of God. As an indivisible aspect of that One Mind, you are on a quest of being and demonstrating various aspects of love.

The Holy Spirit realizes that you desire to understand, know and be your spiritual magnificence. As such, your decision to participate in the game of separation, or preferably the journey of reawakening, is not a sin but merely an exercise in learning, understanding, demonstrating and ultimately reawakening to the truth of who you really are. Through this adventure, the abstract One Self knows Itself in specific contexts.

The ego has mistaken the journey of awakening as a detour into fear. Fear is false evidence appearing real. The ego believes that you have sinned against your Creator. Therefore, punishment and penance must be performed if you are ever to be forgiven for your past sins.

Your ego's plan for salvation revolves around the idea that you must suffer in order to earn your salvation. It has transformed a God of unconditional love into a God of judgment, punishment and something to fear.

This is your ego story, not God's Truth. Where the ego sees a sinner, the Holy Spirit recognizes that God's sleeping child does not need to earn God's forgiveness for there is nothing to forgive. You remain sinless. Your ego's false belief that you are separate from the One Self is a mistake that only needs correction, not punishment or sacrifice.

Your ego's plan that calls for sacrifice, pain and suffering can earn you nothing. Your divine birthright has never been lost, but it has been denied by your ego. Your ego's plan for your salvation requires you to suffer in the hopes of buying back your happiness, but instead it only buys fear. Sacrifice is a useless journey. Instead, follow the Holy Spirit's plan to reclaim your inheritance and recall that God's Will is that you be happy. Your happiness is your ultimate function for you are your Creator's treasure.

Yesterday we asked the following question. When you believe you have wronged someone, does the other party's reaction to that event impact your ability to forgive yourself and then move on with your life?

In the story of the prodigal son, it was the father's knowledge that his son's happiness was his treasure that allowed the prodigal son to forgive himself and reclaim his inheritance. The son's plan called for the acceptance of the son's erroneous belief that he had wronged his father and had lost his inheritance forever. But that was not his father's will. His father only wanted his son by his side so that he could see his son's happy face. The father knew that through the experience of separation his son had gained wisdom about himself. It was his father's will that made it easy for the son to forgive himself and reclaim his inheritance.

God, being unconditional love, only wants you to be happy. Drop your ego's useless plan to re-earn something that was never lost. Instead, follow the Holy Spirit's plan for your gentle reawakening to the truth. Your Creator awaits the return of Its beloved child and the reclaiming of your divine inheritance.

Question: Your ego believes you have sinned and must do penance. The Holy Spirit knows you to be sinless and that your ego's beliefs are mistakes that only need correction, not punishment. Just like the prodigal son in regard to forgiving yourself for your past choices, isn't it beneficial to know that God's Will is that you be happy?

God, being Love, is also happiness.

W-103.1.Happiness is an attribute of love. 2 Happiness cannot be apart from **love**. 3 Nor can **happiness** be experienced where love is not. 4 Love has no limits, being everywhere. 5 And therefore joy is everywhere as well. 6 Yet can the mind deny **the belief** that **love has no limits** is so, believing there are gaps in love where sin can enter, bringing pain instead of joy. 7 This strange belief **that love has limits and is not everywhere** would limit happiness by redefining love as limited, and introducing opposition in what has no limit and no opposite.

W-103.2.**When one holds the false belief that love has limits and is not everywhere,** fear is associated then with love, and **this false belief in fear's** results become the heritage of minds that think what **the split minded** have made **and imagined as fear's effects are** real. 2 These **fear-based** images, with no reality in truth, bear witness to the fear of God, forgetting **that God,** being **only** Love, **God** must **also** be joy. 3 This basic error **that love has limits and is not everywhere** we will try again to bring to truth today, and teach ourselves:
4 God, being Love, is also happiness.
5 To fear **God** is to be afraid of joy.
6 Begin your periods of practicing today with this association **that God, being Love, is also happiness and to fear God is to be afraid of joy, for this** corrects the false belief that God is fear. 7 **This association that God, being Love, is also happiness and to fear God is to be afraid of joy** also emphasizes happiness belongs to you, because of what **God** is.

W-103.3.Allow this one correction **that God, being Love, is also happiness and that to fear God is to be afraid of joy** to be placed within your mind each waking hour today. 2 Then welcome all the happiness **this one correction** brings as truth replaces fear, and joy becomes what you expect to take the place of pain. 3 God, being Love, **joy** will be given you. 4 Bolster this expectation **that God, being Love, will give you joy,** frequently throughout the day, and quiet all your fears with this assurance, kind and wholly true:
5 God, being Love, is also happiness.
6 And it is happiness I seek today.
7 I cannot fail, because I seek the truth.

Notes to Lesson #103

God, being Love, is also happiness.

For this lesson to be a believable, it is helpful to revisit the ancient philosophical question that if God is only love and is all powerful, all knowing, everywhere and every when, why does evil exist?

Note: Evil is the belief that there is something that can harm you.

Religious traditions have wrestled with this question about the apparent existence of evil over millenniums. This is especially a problem for the Western traditional religions of Islam, Judaism and Christianity. Religious traditions have attempted to explain this through the use of free will but the existence of evil ultimately leads to the belief in a judgmental God in which salvation must be earned and not freely given to all.

The belief in evil result is a God of unconditional love being transformed into a God to be feared. Rather than unconditional love, we now have what the ego calls conditional love. Conditional love claims that love is limited and has an opposite. To the ego, love's opposite is fear. Hate is merely an extreme form of focused fear. The ego believes that both love and fear are possible and both are real and have the ability to change what you really are.

ACIM's answer to the question of the apparent existence of evil is a simple one. Evil cannot come from God and therefore, evil can only appear to exist in the imagination of the split minded who believe themselves to be separate from the Mind of God. Evil cannot be real but can be imagined. Imagination has no ability to change the truth that love has no limits and has no opposites. Yet, your ego's denial of love's unlimited nature makes a distorted fear-based world that masquerades as your provisional reality.

Time provides a playschool in which the split minded can be or imagine anything in perfect safety. The ego forgets the fact that this playschool is not real and that your safety is not threatened.

In time, opposites are imagined to exist to provide contrast or differentiation for individuated learning experiences. Without this differentiation, the various experiences needed for experiential learning to take place would be missing. It would be like a chemistry class without the hands-on experience provided by doing the lab work. We value the hands-on experience rather than just information read from a book. Through this imagined differentiation, we are able to learn, know, demonstrate and be various aspects of love in form.

Yet, in truth, love is not limited. Time is merely a playschool for fun and learning. In the real world, the shared Mind of God, there are no opposites for only love is real. When your ego denies the truth that love is unlimited and has no opposites, your ego believes that there are gaps in love in which evil can exist. Evil results in sin and leads to pain and suffering and ultimately to a judgmental God to be feared.

When you believe in the reality of evil, your egoic mind associates fear with love. The ego has redefined true love into false, conditional love which must be earned and can be lost. Rather than see all as perfect, whole and complete, part of the Oneness of All That Is, your ego imagines sin, guilt and fear to be real and separation to be your provisional reality.

Because the ego believes that fear, love's opposite, is real, egoic love is now fear-based. Since the ego believes that evil is a real threat to your existence, its warped notion of love gives you the right to change, fix, control, impress and protect another because you love them. God created them too stupid and limited to know what is best for themselves. To your ego, if God allows evil to exist, God himself must be limited and feared for he could not be a God of unconditional love.

Evil only appears to exist within the split mind that chooses to follow a fear-based thought system. Follow the Voice for God and change your thought system to love and your provisional reality will change.

The fear-based world that your ego made is a fantasy land that has no ability to change the truth of who you really are. Love has no opposites and cannot be limited by these misperceptions of who you are.

Happiness is an attribute of love and happiness and joy cannot be experienced apart from love. God being love is also happiness. Do not allow your ego's false fantasies to transform a God of unconditional love into a judgmental God to be feared. To be afraid of God is to be afraid of the joy that God's unconditional love alone brings.

Question: God is only love and love has no limits or opposites. Why is a fear-based thought system so incompatible with that truth?

You can never escape fear within the same thought system that was designed to create and perpetuate fear in the first place.

LESSON 104

I seek but what belongs to me in truth.

W-104.1.Today's idea **that I seek but what belongs to me in truth** continues with the thought that joy and peace are not but idle dreams. 2 **Joy and peace** are your right, because of what you are **as God's Son.** 3 **Joy and peace** come to you from God, Who cannot fail to give you what **God** wills. 4 Yet must there be a place made ready to receive **God's** gifts. 5 **Joy and peace** are not welcomed gladly by **an egoic split** mind that has instead received the gifts **the egoic split mind** made where **God's gifts** belong, as substitutes for **joy and peace**.

W-104.2.Today we would remove all meaningless and self-made gifts **made by our fear-based thought system** which we have placed upon the holy altar where God's gifts **of joy and peace** belong. 2 **God's gifts** are the gifts that are our own in truth. 3 **God's gifts** are the gifts that we inherited before time was, and that will still be ours when time has passed into eternity. 4 **God's gifts** are the gifts that are within us now, for **God's gifts** are timeless. 5 And we need not wait to have **God's gifts**. 6 **God's gifts** belong to us today. **God's gifts are our divine inheritance.**

W-104.3.Therefore, we choose to have **God's gifts** now, and know, in choosing **God's gifts** in place of what we made **with our fear-based thought system**, we but unite our will with what God wills, and recognize the same **wills** as being one. 2 Our longer practice periods today, the hourly five minutes given truth for your salvation, should begin with this:

3 I seek but what belongs to me in truth, and joy and peace are my inheritance.

4 Then lay aside the conflicts of the **ego's fear-based** world that offer other gifts and other goals made of illusions **based on the ego's belief in lack, limitation and separation**, witnessed to **by the appearance of a body**, and sought for only in a world of **egoic dreams based on separation.**

W-104.4.**All these conflicts and beliefs that arise from the ego's fear-based thought system** we lay aside, and seek instead that which is truly ours, as we ask to recognize what God has given us. 2 We clear a holy place within our **split** minds before **God's** altar, where **God's** gifts of peace and joy are welcome, and to which we come to find what has been given us by **God.** 3 We come in confidence today, aware that what belongs to us in truth is what **God** gives. 4 And we would wish for nothing else, for nothing else belongs to us in truth.

W-104.5.So do we clear the way for **God** today by simply recognizing that **God's** Will is done already, and that joy and peace belong to us as **God's** eternal gifts. 2 We will not let ourselves lose sight of **God's eternal gifts of joy and peace** between the times we come to seek for **God's gifts and** where God has laid them **which is within our Christ consciousness of our big "S" Self.** 3 This reminder will we bring to mind as often as we can:
4 I seek but what belongs to me in truth.
5 God's gifts of joy and peace are all I want.

Notes to Lesson #104

I seek but what belongs to me in truth.

This lesson asks that you seek what belongs to you in truth rather than seek to acquire the false egoic gifts of the physical world. This is an ongoing and continuing problem that needs to be addressed and resolved.

If your ego does not know who you truly are, it will be unable to realize what will make you happy or recognize when you are truly happy. The ego will mistake pain for happiness and value conflict over peace. It will value the transient over the eternal. Since your ego perceives yourself to be your body, it will value what it believes will make your body safe.

The ego believes that you are limited, suffer from lack and are incapable of surviving unless you are taking what you need from others. It sees the world as a zero-sum game. If you are to win, someone must lose. Because of this, your ego perceives a fear-based world in which attack is a useful tool in helping you obtain the limited resources that the ego believes it needs to survive.

Your ego's world is seen as a place of struggle, conflict, pain and suffering. Therefore, joy and happiness are not highly valued. Instead, manipulation, control, attack, and your ability to hold grievances are deemed more important for your survival.

If you are your body and the body is you, the body's self-defense and maintenance is fundamental to what your ego's thought system most highly values. Coming from this misperception that you are limited and lacking, your ego develops its own plan for your safety. The task of your ego is to argue for its plan's rightness rather than your happiness.

Your ego claims you are not the source of your own experiences, but rather a victim of outside forces that are beyond your control. Your ego's plan seeks to manage and manipulate these outside forces so that you can obtain the necessary things you need for its survival. Blame shame, guilt, plus your ability to attack and hold grievances are all highly valued as weapons for manipulation, getting your own way and proving your ego is right.

Because your ego believes you are victim of outside forces that are beyond your control, it places a high value on obtaining gifts from outside forces. Your ego is constantly seeking a good deal and values obtaining the items that it believes it needs for as low a price as possible.

Unfortunately, when you follow your ego's plan, you are seeking happiness, joy and love in all the wrong places. You need a new plan that will value your happiness over your ego's need to be right.

Joy, peace and happiness are your divine birthright because they are God's gifts to His creation. These gifts are freely given and are constantly available to all but must be freely accept by the recipient. Unconditional love does not force you to accept these gifts. Instead, unconditional love waits patiently until you are willing to receive the joy, peace and happiness that flow from your Source.

Stop valuing your ego's false plans for your happiness and start listening to the Voice for Truth that God has placed within you. The Holy Spirit will lead you to the joy, happiness, love and peace that you seek since that is God's Will for you.

In this playschool of time and space, your function is forgiveness, your purpose is love and your destiny is the peace of God. Follow the Holy Spirit's guidance and reclaim the joy, happiness, love and peace that is your destiny.

Question: When you mistake the game token of the body to be who you really are, your ability to attack and be attacked becomes the focus of your ego's attention. Coming from this viewpoint, can you see why a friend's ability to attack and hold grievances against your enemy would be a precious gift that your ego would highly value?

LESSON 105

God's peace and joy are mine.

W-105.1.God's peace and joy are yours. 2 Today we will accept **God's peace and joy**, knowing **God's gifts** belong to us. 3 And we will try to understand these gifts increase as we receive **God's gifts**. 4 P**eace and joy** are not **to be likened** to the gifts the world can give, in which the giver loses as he gives the gift; the taker is the richer by **the giver's** loss. 5 Such **fear-based egoic gifts of the world** are not gifts, but bargains made with guilt. 6 The truly given gift entails no loss. 7 It is impossible that one can gain because another loses. 8 This **egoic belief that one can gain because another loses** implies a limit and an insufficiency.

W-105.2.No **true** gift is given thus **when one believes that one can gain because another loses**. 2 Such egoic "gifts" are but a bid for a more valuable return; a loan with interest to be paid in full; a temporary lending, meant to be a pledge of debt to be repaid with more than was received by the **recipient** who took the gift. 3 This strange distortion of what giving means pervades all levels of the world you see. **This strange distortion of what giving is requires some sort of current or future payback in exchange for the supposed "gift."** 4 This strange distortion strips all meaning from the gifts you give, and leaves you nothing in the **gifts** you take **or receive since you will have to repay the "gift" in full with interest.**

W-105.3.A major learning goal this course has set is to reverse your view of giving, so you can receive. 2 For giving has become a source of fear **since you believe sacrifice is required by the giver**, and so you would avoid **giving which is** the only means by which you can receive. 3 Accept God's peace and joy, and you will learn a different way of looking at a gift. 4 God's gifts will never lessen when **God's gifts of peace and joy are given away**. 5 **God's gifts** but increase thereby **when God's gifts are given away.**

W-105.4.As Heaven's peace and joy intensify when you accept **Heaven's peace and joy** as God's gift to you, so does the joy of your Creator grow when you accept **God's** joy and peace as yours. 2 True giving is creation. 3 **True giving** extends the limitless to the unlimited, eternity to timelessness, and love unto itself. 4 **True giving** adds to all that is complete already, not in simple terms of adding more, for that implies **that the recipient of the gift** was less before. 5 **True giving** adds by letting what cannot contain itself fulfill its **creative** aim of giving everything it has away, securing **everything** forever for itself.

W-105.5.Today accept God's peace and joy as yours. 2 Let **God** complete Himself as **God** defines completion. 3 You will understand that what completes **God** must complete **God's** Son as well. 4 **God** cannot give through loss. 5 No more can you **give through loss.** 6 Receive **God's** gift of joy and peace today, and **God** will thank you for your gift to **God of joy and peace.**

W-105.6.Today our practice periods will start a little differently. 2 Begin today by thinking of those brothers who have been denied by you the peace and joy that are their right under the equal laws of God. 3 **By denying your brother God's gifts,** you denied **that same peace and joy** to yourself. 4 And here **to those brothers whom you have denied God's peace and joy**, you must return. **If you are** to claim **and regain the peace and joy** as your own, **you must be willing to drop your grievance and forgive your brother.**

W-105.7.Think of your "enemies" a little while, and tell each **of your "enemies"** as he occurs to you:
2 My brother, peace and joy I offer you, That I may have God's peace and joy as mine.
3 Thus you prepare yourself to recognize God's gifts to you, and let your **split** mind be free of all **your ego's beliefs that** would prevent success today. 4 Now are you ready to accept the gift of peace and joy that God has given you. 5 Now are you ready to experience the joy and peace you have denied yourself. 6 Now you can say, "God's peace and joy are mine," for you have given **God's peace and joy to your brother and so** what you would receive **is that same peace and joy returned back to you**.

W-105.8.You must succeed today **in receiving God's peace and joy** if you prepare your mind as we suggest. 2 For **through your forgiveness** you have let all bars to peace and joy be lifted up, and what is your **inheritance** can come to you at last. 3 So tell yourself, "God's peace and joy are mine," and close your eyes a while, and let **the Holy Spirit's** Voice assure you that the words you speak are true.

W-105.9.Spend your five minutes thus with **the Holy Spirit** each time you can today, but do not think that less is worthless when you cannot give **the Holy Spirit** more. 2 At least remember hourly to say the words which call to **the Holy Spirit** to give you what **God** wills to give, and **God** wills you to receive. 3 Determine not to interfere today with what **God** wills. 4 And if a brother seems to tempt you to deny God's gift to **that brother**, see **this perceived attempt** as but another chance to let yourself receive the gifts of God as yours. 5 Then bless your brother thankfully, and say:
6 My brother, peace and joy I offer you, That I may have God's peace and joy as mine.

Notes to Lesson #105

God's peace and joy are mine.

This lesson states that God's peace and joy are yours whenever you accept them and realize they belong to you. God's peace and joy are your birthright because God is your source. When God creates, God gives all to all. Nothing is held back. Yet, if you are to reclaim the peace and joy that is your divine birthright, you must understand that giving and receiving are the same.

The fundamental law of God states that to give is to receive. This differs radically from the ego's belief that you only give in order to get. Giving is a source of fear to the ego because giving involves the relinquishment of something that once belonged to the giver.

In this world of form, when giving something to another, you lose that item. Form cannot be shared. The receiver is the benefactor and the giver loses what has been given. This egoic mindset that surrounds the act of giving reinforces both parties belief in lack, limitation, fear and separation. One party is perceived as being in need of something outside itself to make them happy or reduce their suffering. The other is asked to sacrifice the little that they have to reduce their guilt about having too much.

The ego only gives to get. Because of this, the gift is not given without some expectation of repayment or future gain. To the ego, this is not a gift. Instead, it is an advanced payment for something that our ego values more. It is an IOU to be repaid in full. The repayment may not be immediate, but repayment is expected at some later date. The gift may eventually be redeemed for some reward in heaven but the supposed gift is anticipated to be repaid in full.

Often we give to relieve our own sense of guilt for being more fortunate than another. With egoic gifts there is always the expectation that your good deed will be repaid in time. Charitable organizations often use guilt as a chief motivating factor in their solicitation campaigns. If they can make you feel guilty because you are more fortunate than another or make you feel sorry for another, the likelihood of you contributing to their cause is increased.

On a practical level, does this mean that you should avoid making charitable contributions because it implies and supports the belief in lack and insufficiency in this world?

Well that depends on the content rather than the form that your giving takes.

For example: Two people contribute $1000 to a particular organization.

The first party believes they are giving money to the needy, yet in reality what they are giving with their money is confirming their belief in dependency. The second party gives with the intent of giving hope to those who temporarily feel less hope. In this case, the second party's money is intended to give hope, not a misguided belief in another's inadequacy to help themselves. The external form, or means, is exactly the same, but the purpose or end for the giving is radically different.

Ideas can be shared. It is the intent behind the giving, not the form of the gift that determines what is truly given.

Are you giving due to your belief about abundance or reducing your own guilt for having too much?

Are you giving hope or confirming your belief in dependency??

Are you giving because you are guided to do so or because you will gain some reward?

You must look to why you give and not what you give. Content, not form is what matters. ACIM wants you to understand that you give so that you can receive. Ideas, unlike form, can be shared. Give God's gifts of peace and joy and they will be received by you. All benefit and no one is diminished. When you free another from the prison of your mind's own grievances and belief in lack, you free yourself from guarding that same prison.

You will never be able to reclaim God's peace and joy when you refuse to give that same peace and joy to another. Under the laws of God all are equal for each receives what they are willing to give.

Question: When you give to another, what is the intent, or purpose, behind your supposed gift?

Is your gift really a Trojan horse with some self-serving hidden agenda?

Let me be still and listen to the truth.

W-106.1.If you will lay aside the ego's voice, however loudly **your ego's voice** may seem to call; if you will not accept **your ego's** petty gifts that give you nothing that you really want; if you will listen with an open mind, that has not told you what salvation is; then you will hear the mighty Voice of truth, quiet in power, strong in stillness, and completely certain in **truth's** messages.

Note and clarification of terms: <u>The Voice of truth also could be called the Voice for God, the Holy Spirit or the voice of your big "S" Self. It is the Voice that knows and represents the truth and remembers who you really are. The voice for the ego represents the voice for the false and does not know who you really are.</u>

W-106.2.Listen, and hear your Father speak to you through **God's** appointed Voice, **the Holy Spirit,** which silences the thunder of the meaningless **voice of the ego**, and shows the way to peace to those who cannot see. 2 Be still today and listen to the truth. 3 Be not deceived by voices of the dead, which tell you they have found the source of life and offer **witnesses for the false and meaningless** to you for your belief. 4 Attend **the voices for the false** not, but listen to the truth, **the Voice of the Holy Spirit**.

W-106.3.Be not afraid today to circumvent the voices of the **egoic** world. 2 Walk lightly past **the voices for the false and their** meaningless persuasion. 3 Hear **the voices for the false** not. 4 Be still today and listen to the truth, **which is the Voice of the Holy Spirit**. 5 Go past all things which do not speak of **a God of Unconditional Love Who** holds your happiness within His Hand, held out to you in welcome and in love. 6 Hear only **the Voice for the God of Unconditional Love** today, and do not wait to reach **the God of Love any** longer. 7 Hear one Voice today, **only the Voice of the Holy Spirit.**

W-106.4.Today the promise of God's Word is kept. 2 Hear **the Voice of the Holy Spirit** and be silent. 3 **The Holy Spirit** would speak to you. 4 **The Holy Spirit** comes with miracles a thousand times as happy and as wonderful as those you ever dreamed or wished for in your **ego's** dreams. 5 **The Holy Spirit's** miracles are true. 6 **The Holy Spirit's miracles** will not fade when dreaming ends. 7 **The Holy Spirit's miracles** end the dream instead; and last forever, for **the Holy Spirit's miracles** come from God to **God's** dear Son, whose other name is you. 8 Prepare yourself for miracles today. 9 Today allow your Father's ancient pledge to you and all your brothers to be kept.

W-106.5.Hear **the Holy Spirit** today, and listen to the Word **of God** which lifts the veil that lies upon the earth, and wakes all those who sleep and cannot see. 2 God calls to **all those who sleep and cannot see** through you. 3 **The Holy Spirit** needs your voice to speak to **all those who sleep**, for who could reach God's Son except his Father, calling through your **big "S"** Self? 4 Hear **the Holy Spirit** today, and offer **the Holy Spirit** your voice to speak to all the multitude who wait to hear the Word **of God** that **the Holy Spirit** will speak today **through you**.

W-106.6.Be ready for salvation. 2 **Salvation** is here, and **salvation** will today be given unto you. 3 And you will learn your function **of salvation** from the **Holy Spirit** Who chose **salvation** in your Father's Name for you. 4 Listen today, and you will hear a Voice **of the Holy Spirit** which will resound throughout the world through you. 5 **The Holy Spirit,** the bringer of all miracles has need that you receive **the miracles** first, and thus become the joyous giver of **the miracles** you received.

W-106.7.Thus does salvation start and thus **salvation** ends; when everything is yours and everything is given away, **everything** will remain with you forever. 2 And the lesson **that giving is receiving** has been learned. 3 Today we practice giving, not the way you understand **giving** now, but **giving** as it **truly** is. **When you give, you receive. Your ego falsely believes that when you give, you lose and therefore, sacrifice is required.** 4 Each hour's exercises should begin with this request for your enlightenment:
5 I will be still and listen to the truth.
6 What does it mean to give and to receive?

W-106.8.Ask and expect an answer. 2 Your request is one whose answer has been waiting long to be received by you. 3 **The request to understand what it truly means to give and receive** will begin the ministry for which you came, and which will free the world from thinking giving is a way to lose. 4 And so the world becomes ready to understand and to receive.

W-106.9.Be still and listen to the truth today. 2 For each five minutes spent in listening, a thousand minds are opened to the truth and **these open minds** will hear the holy Word you hear. 3 And when the hour is past, you will again release a thousand more who pause to ask that truth be given them, along with you.

W-106.10.Today the holy Word of God is kept through your receiving **the holy Word of God** to give **it** away, so you can teach the world what giving means by listening and learning **what giving means from the Holy Spirit**. 2 Do not forget today to reinforce your choice to hear and to receive the Word by this reminder, given to yourself as often as is possible today:
3 Let me be still and listen to the truth.
4 I am the messenger of God today, My voice is **the Holy Spirit's Voice**, to give what I receive.

Notes to Lesson #106

Let me be still and listen to the truth.

Note and clarification of terms: The Voice of truth also could be called the Voice for God, the Holy Spirit or the Voice of your big "S" Self. It is the voice that knows and represents the truth and remembers who you really are. Some people call it their inner guide, higher self or the voice of their conscience. It represents your higher ideals rather than your baser instincts. It speaks for the thought system of love and forgiveness that supports your inner peace, happiness and unity.

The voice for your ego represents the voice for the false and does not know who you really are. It represents the fear-based thought system that supports the ego's world of lack, limitation, conflict and separation.

Lesson 106 is let me be still and listen to the truth.

Most of us are in a constant inner dialogue with our egoic mind. We may hear a voice inside our head or more likely we will be engaging in self-talk. This inner talk of the ego tends to be negative and often revolves around justifying your actions and emotions or judging another's words and deeds. Most people are in continuous communication with this judging machine that we call our ego. The ego is the voice for your littleness, arguing for its own rightness and justifying its own attack thoughts and grievances.

Most people are constantly engaged in internal egoic mind chatter. This inner dialogue prevents real communication from occurring. Most two party conversations are carried on between four voices, the two talking heads and their two egos. Mostly communication is actually taking place, not between the two talking heads, but rather between each person's body and their own egoic mind.

This inner dialogue rather than the voice of the other party is what we tend to hear. Each party is looking for any verbal pause by the other person so that they can interrupt and take over the conversation. Rather than listen to what the other party is saying, they are thinking about what they are going to say next. If they hear the other party's voice, those words are first filtered through their ego's belief system as they eagerly await their next chance to take over and allow their ego's inner voice to go public.

Before you can hope to hear the voice for your big "S" Self, you need to silence the constant mind chatter of your ego or little "s" self. This lesson suggests that you be still and listen to the truth.

Because we are so used to carrying on this inner dialogue with our ego's judging machine, most people fail to hear the voice for their higher Self .The voice for the Holy Spirit resides within your split mind and patiently waits for you to ask for its guidance. Silence your ego's voice and listen and follow this higher guidance.

ACIM cautions that your undisciplined mind must be retrained to hear that voice for your big "S" Self. Beware, for when you ask for guidance, the voice for your ego will always answer first. Your ego will argue for your rightness and justify why you are entitled to feel and react in your normal negative fear-based ways.

A Course in Miracles says you should not just blindly assume that because you have asked for inner guidance that any voice you hear is coming from the Holy Spirit. Instead, ACIM offers a test to confirm the true source of the communication.

Ask yourself this question: Does following that guidance help restore my inner peace? If it does not, you have heard the false voice for fear, littleness and your ego.

If your inner peace is not restored, you need to once again be still, silence your egoic mind chatter and ask again for guidance from the Holy Spirit. When that new guidance is received, retest that advice with that same question. Does following that guidance help restore my inner peace? Repeat the process until your inner peace has been restored.

Although it appears that the ego's voice is the loudest, it is not the strongest. Your ego's voice will not last against the Voice for Truth. The Holy Spirit will always answer your call. Your task is to be still, listen and ultimately follow the voice of your higher big "S" Self.

Remember, to constantly monitor your own inner peace. The Holy Spirit will never do anything that would increase your fear so it is no longer necessary to continue to argue for your ego's littleness. Instead, silence the ego and listen for the voice for the Holy Spirit.

Learn the truth that to give is to receive. Dismiss the voice for the egoic world that claims you are a limited ego body. Listen to the Voice for Truth and become a messenger for God.

Your world is a reflection of you. Become a witness for God and the Voice for Love. By following the Holy Spirit, you will learn that to give is to receive. You will become the peace you seek in your world and your world will reflect back that same peace that you have given. Your world can be at peace even when a fear-based world surrounds you.

Question: Is your mind constantly having an inner dialogue with your ego?

Question: Is your current inner dialogue a negative or positive influence on your life?

LESSON 107

Truth will correct all errors in my mind.

W-107.1.What can correct illusions but the truth? 2 And what are errors but illusions that remain unrecognized for what **errors** are, **which are only illusions**? 3 Where truth has entered errors disappear. 4 **Errors** merely vanish, leaving not a trace by which to be remembered. 5 **Errors** are gone because, without belief, **errors** have no life. 6 And so **errors, without the supporting underlying belief** disappear to nothingness, returning whence **to the nothingness from which the errors originally** came. 7 From dust to dust **errors** come and go, for only truth remains.

W-107.2.Can you imagine what a state of mind without illusions is? 2 How it would feel **to have your split mind healed from its belief in separation**? 3 Try to remember when there was a time,–perhaps a minute, maybe even less–when nothing came to interrupt your peace; when you were certain you were loved and safe. 4 Then try to picture what it would be like to have that moment **of peace, love and safety** be extended to the end of time and to eternity. 5 Then let the sense of quiet that you felt be multiplied a hundred times, and then be multiplied another hundred more.

W-107.3.And now you have a hint, not more than just the faintest intimation of the state your mind will rest in when the truth has come **and your split mind is healed from its belief in separation**. 2 Without illusions there could be no fear, no doubt and no attack. 3 When truth has come all pain is over, for there is no room for transitory thoughts and dead ideas to linger in your mind. 4 **When truth has come**, truth occupies your mind completely, liberating you from all beliefs in the ephemeral. 5 **Fear, doubt and attack** have no place because the truth has come, and **illusions** are nowhere. 6 **Fear, doubt and attack** cannot be found, for truth is everywhere forever, now. **All misperceptions that arose from your erroneous beliefs have been corrected and your illusions have disappeared into the nothingness from which they arose.**

W-107.4.When truth has come **truth** does not stay a while, to disappear or change to something else. 2 **Truth** does not shift and alter in its form, nor **does truth** come and go and go and come again. 3 **Truth** stays exactly as **truth** always was, to be depended on in every need, and trusted with a perfect trust in all the seeming difficulties and the doubts that the appearances **of** the egoic fear-based world presents **and** engender. 4 **Fear, doubt and attack** will merely blow away, when truth corrects the errors in your **split** mind.

W-107.5.When truth has come **truth** harbors in its wings the gift of perfect constancy, and love which does not falter in the face of pain, but looks beyond **the face of pain,** steadily and sure. 2 Here is the gift of healing, for the truth needs no defense, and therefore no attack is possible **upon the healed split mind**. 3 Illusions can be brought to truth to be corrected. 4 But the truth stands far beyond illusions, and can not be brought to **illusions** to turn **illusions** into truth.

W-107.6.Truth does not come and go nor shift nor change, in this appearance now and then in that, evading capture and escaping grasp. 2 **Truth** does not hide. 3 **Truth** stands in open light, in obvious accessibility. 4 It is impossible that anyone could seek **truth** truly, and would not succeed. 5 Today belongs to truth. 6 Give truth its due, and **truth** will give you your **truth about who you really are which is God's beloved Child**. 7 You were not meant to suffer and to die. 8 Your Father wills these **egoic fear-based** dreams be gone. 9 Let truth correct all **dreams that arose from your belief in separation.**

W-107.7.We do not ask for what we do not have. 2 We merely ask for what belongs to us **in truth**, that we may recognize **our divine inheritance** as our own. 3 Today we practice on the happy note of certainty that has been born of truth. 4 The shaky and unsteady footsteps of illusion are not our approach today. 5 We are as certain of success as we are sure we live and hope and breathe and think. 6 We do not doubt we walk with truth today, and count on **truth** to enter into all the exercises that we do this day.

W-107.8.Begin by asking **the Holy Spirit, Whose home is your big "S" Self and** Who goes with you upon this undertaking that **the Holy Spirit** be in your awareness as you go with **the Holy Spirit**. 2 You are not made of flesh and blood and bone, but were created by the selfsame Thought which gave the gift of life to **your big "S" Self** as well. 3 **Your big "S" Self** is your Brother, and so like to you your Father knows that You are both the same. 4 It is your **big "S" Self** you ask to go with you, and how could **your big "S" Self** be absent where you are?

W-107.9.Truth will correct all errors in your mind which tell you you could be apart from **the Holy Spirit, whose home is your big "S" Self**. 2 You speak to **the Holy Spirit** today, and make your pledge to let **the Holy Spirit's** function, **which is your reawakening from the illusion of separation**, be fulfilled through you. 3 To share **the Holy Spirit's** function is to share **the Holy Spirit's** joy. 4 **The Holy Spirit's** confidence is with you, as you say:
5 Truth will correct all errors in my mind, And I will rest in **the Holy Spirit** Who is my **big "S"** Self.
6 Then let **the Holy Spirit** lead you gently to the truth, which will envelop you and give you peace so deep and tranquil that you will return to the familiar **egoic fear-based** world reluctantly.

W-107.10.And yet you will be glad to look again upon this **egoic fear-based** world. 2 For you will bring with you the promise of the changes which the truth that goes with you will carry to the **egoic fear-based** world. 3 **The changes which the truth** brings **to your ego's fear based world** will increase with every gift you give of five small minutes, and the errors that surround the **fear based** world will be corrected as you let **those errors** be corrected in your **split** mind.

W-107.11.Do not forget your function for today. 2 Each time you tell yourself with confidence, "Truth will correct all errors in my mind," you speak for all the world and **the Holy Spirit, Whose home is your big "S" Self** Who would release the world, as **the Holy Spirit** would set you free.

Notes to Lesson #107

Truth will correct all errors in my mind.

Lesson 107, truth will correct all errors in my mind, presents a fundamentally different approach to the problem of how to correct erroneous thinking.

An illusion cannot be corrected by another illusion. The false cannot be made true. Erroneous thinking will continue until we recognize the error is not the changeless reality our mind originally assumed it to be. Once recognized for the illusion that it is, the source of the error, which is our erroneous belief, can then be corrected with the truth.

Errors are illusions that vanish when they are brought before the light of truth. Illusions only exist within a mind that believes the illusions to be real. Remove the belief that powers the illusion and the illusion must disappear.

All our erroneous thinking is rooted in our belief that the separation is real. Because we believe we are separate from our Source, we believe we suffer from lack, limitation and reside in a fear-based world. We believe our will is different from God's Will and that we must take what we need from others if we are to survive.

Our egoic mind has developed its own plan to handle our belief in separation. Perceiving the separation to be real, our ego's plan never questions or addresses the source of the problem. Instead, it assumes that separation is unchanging and attempts to manage and mitigate the effects that arise from that erroneous belief.

All your ego's plans for your happiness attempt to manage and mitigate fear but are incapable of eliminating fear because the ego's thought system is predicated on fear's reality. You can never escape fear within the thought system that is built to create fear in the first place.

Coming from its belief in lack, the ego's plans for your happiness revolve around its fundamental belief in separation. The ego believes that there is something outside yourself that can make you happy. The ego says that you will be happy when you acquire more power, wealth, health, sex or fame. The ego constantly worships the achievement of these external idols.

The ego claims you will be less miserable or happier when you obtain these external things. Yet, even if these idols are obtained, the ego's plan still maintains your belief in limitation, lack and separation that is the source for all your fears. If you obtain all the power, sex, wealth, health and fame that the ego claims you need to be happy, you will still be afraid you could lose them. After all, these items being external can be lost or stolen from you.

As long as you believe you are not perfect, whole and complete, fears will continue to rule your world. Your belief in lack will keep you in victim consciousness. Perceiving yourself to be the body, your life will be a constant struggle in which attack, counter attack and grievances become the tools needed to make you happy.

An illusion cannot be corrected with another illusion. All your ego's plans are different versions of the same story that keep you trapped in your belief in separation and victimization. This detour into fear is a nightmare created by your own mind's beliefs. These beliefs are not true. Truth cannot make your belief in separation real but truth does end that illusion. Place your faith in the truth and the illusion disappears.

Only when you look outside the fear-based thought system that created the illusion will you find the love, peace and safety that you seek. Since the truth states that to give is to receive, you need a new plan based on the love and forgiveness that you seek. You need guidance from someone who knows the truth.

When you listen to the Voice for Truth, you will know that you are God's beloved child. Your little "s" self will disappear along with the fear-based thought system that argues for and maintains your belief in littleness. Truth rests on certainty, not upon doubt. Truth ends your belief in separation and victim consciousness.

When you choose to follow the thought system of love and forgiveness, you will still be in time. The external fear-based world of the mass collective consciousness will not suddenly disappear. But you will realize that you are not a victim or your body. Instead, you will know you are free and still remain as God created you, perfect, whole and complete, part of the One Self. You will understand the truth that nothing sources your experiences but you and nothing can rob you of your inner peace unless you choose to allow it.

Armed with the knowledge of the truth of your big "S" Self, your external world will realign with those new beliefs. This world will no longer be something to be feared. Instead, your experiences will support and bear witness for the healing of the split mind's belief in separation. Illusions cannot harm you. Illusions disappear before the truth. Truth ends all uncertainty and doubt. Love, peace and safety are eternally yours.

Question: Why will your acceptance of the truth not end time immediately?

LESSON 108

To give and to receive are one in truth.

W-108.1.Vision depends upon today's idea **that to give and to receive are one in truth.** 2 The light is in **truth**, for **truth** reconciles all seeming opposites. 3 And what is light except the resolution, born of peace, of all your conflicts and mistaken thoughts into one concept which is wholly true? 4 Even that one **concept which is wholly true** will disappear, because the Thought behind **that one concept which is wholly true** will appear instead to take **that one concept's** place. 5 And now you are at peace forever, for the dream is over then.

W-108.2.True light that makes true vision possible is not the light the body's eyes behold. 2 **True light that makes true vision possible** is a state of mind that has become so unified that darkness cannot be perceived at all. 3 And thus what is the same, **which is the true light**, is seen as one, while what is not the same, **which is darkness**, remains unnoticed, for **darkness** is not there.

W-108.3.This is the **true** light that shows no opposites, and vision, being healed, has power to heal. 2 This is the **true** light that brings your peace of mind to other minds, to share **that peace with others** and **so they are** glad that they are one with you and with themselves. 3 This is the **true** light that heals because **this true light** brings single perception, based upon one frame of reference, from which one meaning comes.

W-108.4.Here are both giving and receiving seen as different aspects of one Thought whose truth does not depend on which is seen as first, nor which appears to be in second place. 2 Here it is understood that both **giving and receiving** occur together, that the Thought remain complete. 3 And in this understanding **that giving and receiving** are **different aspects of one Thought** is the base on which all opposites are reconciled, because **all opposites** are perceived from the same frame of reference which unifies this Thought.

W-108.5.One thought, completely unified, will serve to unify all thought. 2 This is the same as saying one correction will suffice for all correction, or that to forgive one brother wholly is enough to bring salvation to all minds. 3 For these are but some special cases of one **unifying** law which holds for every kind of learning, if it be directed by the One, **the Holy Spirit**, Who knows the truth.

W-108.6.To learn that giving and receiving are the same has special usefulness, because **giving and receiving are the same** can be tried so easily and seen as true. 2 And when this special case has proved **that to give is to receive and it** always works, in every circumstance where it is tried, the thought behind **that giving and receiving are the same** can be generalized to other areas of doubt and double vision. 3 And from there **that general thought that to give is to receive** will extend, and finally arrive at the one Thought which underlies all **special or specific cases**.

W-108.7.Today we practice with the special case of giving and receiving. 2 We will use this simple lesson in the obvious because **the special case of giving and receiving are the same** has results we cannot miss. 3 To give is to receive. 4 Today we will attempt to offer peace to everyone, and see how quickly peace returns to us. 5 Light is tranquility, and in that peace is vision given us, and we can see.

W-108.8.So we begin the practice periods with the instruction for today, and say:
2 To give and to receive are one in truth.
3 I will receive what I am giving now.
4 Then close your eyes, and for five minutes think of what you would hold out to everyone **as your gift you give**, to have **that same item be** yours **to receive in return**. 5 You might, for instance, say:
6 To everyone I offer quietness.
7 To everyone I offer peace of mind.
8 To everyone I offer gentleness.

W-108.9.Say each one slowly and then pause a while, expecting to receive the gift you gave. 2 And **the gift you give** will come to you in the amount in which you gave **the gift.** 3 You will find you have exact return, for that is what you asked. 4 It might be helpful, too, to think of one to whom to give your gifts. 5 He represents the others, and through him you give to all.

W-108.10.Our very simple lesson for today **that to give and to receive are one in truth** will teach you much. 2 Effect and cause will be far better understood from this time on, and we will make much faster progress now. 3 Think of the exercises for today as quick advances in your learning, made still faster and more sure each time you say, "To give and to receive are one in truth."

Notes to Lesson #108

To give and to receive are one in truth.

Lesson 108 states that to give and to receive are one in truth. Because your ego believes that the separation is real, the idea that to give and receive are one in truth is vehemently denied by your ego. Your ego's belief in separation results in a corresponding belief in lack. Because your ego mistakes your body for your essence, it concludes that you must struggle to obtain the limited resources that you need to survive. This ultimately leads to the ego's belief that you should only give when there is an equal or greater corresponding benefit that you will receive.

The ego is always interested in obtaining a good deal. It wishes to obtain as much of the resources that it perceives it needs with a minimal loss to your own precious resources. The idea that you only give to get is directly related to your ego's belief that this world is a zero-sum game. There are limited resources available and each party must struggle to insure that they receive their fair share.

The ego realizes that form cannot be shared and therefore, it associates giving with loss and sacrifice. This belief in sacrifice and loss reinforces the ego's fear-based thought system. Lack, limitation, conflict and struggle continue to rule the world of the split minded who perceive themselves separate from their unlimited Creator.

The Law of God states that to give is to receive. On a theoretical basis, this idea is easy to explain since there is just the One Self. No separation is possible within the shared Mind of God. If there is only one, obviously, you can only give to yourself. But this is not the only explanation offered for this idea. ACIM offers an additional explanation as to why to give and to receive are one in truth.

We have been taught that our experiences come first and that our thoughts and beliefs are the result of those experiences. We believe that in time there is a gap between cause and effect. This gap results in our belief that cause and effect are two separate items. Therefore, we perceive giving and receiving as two separate and distinct events.

A Course in Miracles states that your thought is the powerhouse behind all that you experience. Thoughts come first and your physical experiences follow. But how can you have the thought of giving if you do not simultaneously also have the thought of receiving? Giving and receiving are actually two aspects of one thought. Without both simultaneous concepts, the other would cease to exist.

Just like a cause needs its effect or it is not a cause, so too does the thought of giving require the simultaneous thought of receiving. This idea that giving and receiving are different aspects of one thought is true and does not depend on which aspect seems to appear first. Giving and receiving are inseparable and simultaneous. Each requires the other component and therefore, they occur together and cannot be separated. You need both for either giving or receiving to take place and be true.

Because our ego confuses form with content, we failed to understand that the relinquishing of a specific form does not mean that the giver has not received something back of equal value. When you move past form to the content or purpose behind the giving and receiving, you understand that what is given or received is always returned in full. No sacrifice is required by either party. There are no victims and there are no victimizers. Each receives in direct proportion to what they give.

The idea that to give is to receive is the only thought that you need to unify all supposed opposites that the egoic mind perceives. The recognition that to give and to receive are one in truth brings salvation and healing to all that would perceive themselves as separate and split minded. When asked, the Holy Spirit will utilize this truth to reframe and correct your ego's belief in lack, limitation and separation.

In today's workbook lesson, you are given an exercise that allows you to confirm the statement that to give and to receive are one in truth. This thought holds the power to correct all errors. The specific form that the problem may appear in may be different but the correction is the same. Realize that to give is to receive and the error is undone.

If you want peace, give peace and you will receive the peace that you seek and desire.

Question: While doing today's exercise, did you find that the gift you offered your brother was also received by you in kind?

Question: When you offered peaceful, loving thoughts to another, did your own mind benefit from those same thoughts?

LESSON 109

I rest in God.

W-109.1.We ask for rest today, and quietness unshaken by the **egoic** world's appearances. 2 We ask for peace and stillness, in the midst of all the turmoil born of clashing **egoic** dreams. 3 We ask for safety and for happiness, although we seem to look on danger and on sorrow. 4 And we have the thought, **I rest in God**, that will answer our asking with what we request.

W-109.2."I rest in God." 2 This thought **that you rest in God** will bring to you the rest and quiet, peace and stillness, and the safety and the happiness you seek. 3 "I rest in God." 4 This thought **that you rest in God** has power to wake the sleeping truth in you, whose vision **of Christ** sees beyond appearances to that same truth in everyone and everything there is. 5 **I rest in God** is the end of suffering for all the world, and everyone who ever came and yet will come to linger for a while **in this world**. 6 **I rest in God** is the thought in which the Son of God is born again, to recognize himself.

W-109.3."I rest in God." 2 Completely undismayed, this thought **that you rest in God** will carry you through storms and strife, past misery and pain, past loss and death, and onward to the certainty of God. 3 There is no suffering **this thought that you rest in God** cannot heal. 4 There is no problem that **this thought that you rest in God** cannot solve. 5 And no appearance but will turn to truth before the eyes of you who rest in God.

W-109.4.This is the day of peace. 2 You rest in God, and while the **egoic** world is torn by winds of hate your rest remains completely undisturbed. 3 Yours is the rest of truth. 4 Appearances cannot intrude on you. 5 You call to all to join you in your rest, and they will hear and come to you because you rest in God. 6 **All that join you** will not hear another voice than yours because you gave your voice to God, and now you rest in **God** and let **the Holy Spirit** speak through you.

W-109.5.In **the Holy Spirit** you have no cares and no concerns, no burdens, no anxiety, no pain, no fear of future and no past regrets. 2 In timelessness you rest, while time goes by without **time's** touch upon you, for your rest **in God** can never change in any way at all. 3 You rest today **in God**. 4 And as you close your eyes, sink into stillness. 5 Let these periods of rest and respite reassure your mind that all its frantic **fear-based egoic** fantasies were but the dreams of fever that has passed away. 6 Let **your egoic mind** be still and thankfully accept **your ego's** healing. 7 No more fearful **egoic** dreams will come, now that you rest in God. 8 Take time today to slip away from **fearful egoic** dreams and into **the peace of God.**

W-109.6.Each hour that you take your rest **in God** today, a tired **split** mind is suddenly made glad, a bird with broken wings begins to sing, a stream long dry begins to flow again. 2 The world is born again each time you rest **in God**, and hourly remember that you came to bring the peace of God into the world, that **the world** might take its rest **in God** along with you.

W-109.7.With each five minutes that you rest **in God** today, the world is nearer waking. 2 And the time when rest **in God** will be the only thing there is comes closer to all worn and tired **split** minds, too weary now to go their way alone. 3 And **the tired split minds** will hear the bird begin to sing and see the stream begin to flow again, with hope reborn and energy restored to walk with lightened steps along the road that suddenly seems easy as they go.

W-109.8.You rest within the peace of God today, and call upon your brothers from your rest **in God** to draw **your brothers** to their rest **in God**, along with you. 2 You will be faithful to your trust today, forgetting no one, bringing everyone into the boundless circle of your peace **in God**, the holy sanctuary where you rest **in God**. 3 Open the temple doors and let **all** come from far across the world, and near as well; your distant brothers and your closest friends; bid them all enter here and rest **in God** with you.

W-109.9.You rest within the peace of God today, quiet and unafraid. 2 Each brother comes to take his rest **in God**, and offer **his rest in God** to you. 3 We rest together here, for thus our rest is made complete, and what we give today we have received already. 4 Time is not the guardian of what we give today. 5 We give to those unborn and those passed by, to every Thought of God, and to the Mind in which these Thoughts were born and where **these Thoughts** rest. 6 And we remind **all** of their resting place each time we tell ourselves, "I rest in God."

Notes to Lesson #109

I rest in God.

I rest in God is what we have actually come here to experience in this fear-based world that the collective consciousness of the egoic mind has created.

I rest in God has the power to restore your inner peace. This is the one thought in which the Son of God is born again to recognize himself as the big "S" Self. This world of conflict, struggle and egoic striving gives way to the realization that you remain God's beloved Child and nothing can rob you of your inner peace. You rest in the strength and certainty that God's plan is the perfect path for all.

You accept God's Will as your will. Happiness and the peace of God are both your divine birthright and your destiny. You no longer are concerned with your ego's plans that dictate you must obtain a certain result to gain salvation. Instead, you realize that everyone's salvation is guaranteed by God and that each is on their own perfect path of reawakening. Tolerance, allowance and acceptance have replaced striving, correcting and arguing for the rightness of your ego's plan for salvation.

When you rest in God, calmness and peace abide in you. You accept the grace of God. Grace is the acceptance of the love of God in a world of seeming hate and fear. Note this definition. Grace does not mean that the mass collective consciousness that created this world of egoic form will suddenly become all peaceful and loving. Everyone will not share your vision of Christ and fear will not disappear from this planet. Instead, it will mean that the illusion of fear and hatred will no longer find a place in your heart. You will not allow your inner peace to be subservient to the drama that this fear-based world seems to relish.

To the outside observer, the world may continue to be full of hate and fear. But this illusion no longer is something you need fear. Illusions cannot shake your certainty in the truth of what you are. When you rest in God, you have given yourself the right to drop your ego's plan to save the world. You have given yourself permission to allow and go with the flow that is God's plan.

The ego's plan envisions some predetermined results that must be obtained. It dictates a particular plan that you must follow to get the predetermined results. This engenders a great deal of stress and prevents you from being in the moment.

When you rest in God, you can enjoy everyone's journey resting in the certainty that each is exactly where they want to be and need to be in their own journey of rediscovery. You can observe another's journey that seems full of turmoil and drama and simply marvel at their creation. You do not make them wrong for choosing a different perfect path from your own. You have surrendered your ego's will to the Will of God. You feel safe and confident in asking and following the guidance of the Holy Spirit.

You are a spiritual being having an earthly experience and can enjoy the journey. You no longer have to save, fix, control, change, impress or protect another. Instead, you accept, allow and simply ask the Holy Spirit what love would have you do. You follow your inner guidance system that monitors your inner peace and go in that direction.

This does not mean that you will automatically comply with another party's plans because you rest in God. Rather, it means you are free from being manipulated by the blame, shame, and guilt games of this world. It is no longer necessary for you to follow anyone's egoic plans for their salvation and happiness. You rest in the certainty that the Voice for God is within you and is the only plan to be followed.

This means that discernment has replaced egoic judgment. You will still be able to observe events as they unfold in time and space and realize that you would not choose that experience for yourself nor respond to those circumstances in the same way. But you will no longer have to make the other party wrong for their decision. Allowance and tolerance will replace your need to judge and be right. This change in perception arises from the knowledge that each is on their own perfect path.

This change in how you perceive time grants you the calmness and inner peace that allows you to accept the love of God in a world of seeming fear and hate. Nothing can rob you of your own inner peace. You realize that you do not know the big picture but your strength rests in the certainty that only God's plan will work and you become a willing and active witness for that plan.

Question: On the practical level, if you rest in God, does that mean that you will become a passive observer and not an active participant on this game board of time and space?

Meditate and contemplate that question and we will discuss this question more in future lessons.

LESSON 110

I am as God created me.

W-110.1.We will repeat today's idea **that I am as God created me** from time to time. 2 For this one thought **that I am as God created me** would be enough to save you and the **egoic** world, if you believed that it is true. 3 Its truth **that you are as God created you** would mean that **you believe that your egoic split mind has** made no changes in yourself that have reality, nor changed the universe so that what God created was replaced by fear and evil, misery and death. 4 If you remain as God created you fear has no meaning, evil is not real, and misery and death do not exist.

W-110.2.Today's idea **that you are as God created you** is therefore all you need to let complete correction heal your **split** mind, and give you perfect vision **of Christ** that will heal all the mistakes that any mind **that perceives separation to be real** has made at any time or place. 2 **Today's idea that you are as God created you** is enough to heal the past and make the future free. 3 **Today's idea that you are as God created you** is enough to let the present be accepted as **the present actually is without your past egoic misperceptions and beliefs that distort what you currently perceive.** 4 **Today's idea that you are as God created you** is enough to let time be the means for all the **egoic fear-based** world to learn escape from time, and **to escape from** every **fear-based** change that time appears to bring in passing by.

W-110.3.If you remain as God created you, appearances cannot replace the truth, health cannot turn to sickness, nor can death be substitute for life, or fear for love. 2 All **these errors that appear to be real to the split mind have** not occurred, if you remain as God created you. 3 You need no thought but just this one **that you are as God created you**, to let redemption come to light the world and free **the egoic world** from the past.

W-110.4.In this one thought **that you are as God created you** is all the past undone; the present saved to quietly extend into a timeless future. 2 If you are as God created you, then there has been no separation of your mind from **God's Mind**, no split between your mind and other minds, and only unity within your own **healed split mind.**

W-110.5.The healing power of today's idea **that you are as God created you** is limitless. 2 **The idea that you are as God created you** is the birthplace of all miracles, the great restorer of the truth to the awareness of the **egoic fear-based** world **you imagined**. 3 Practice today's idea **that you are as God created you** with gratitude. 4 **The idea that you are as God created you** is the truth that comes to set you free. 5 **The idea that you are as God created you** is the truth that God has promised you. 6 **The idea that you are as God created you** is the Word in which all sorrow ends.

W-110.6.For your five-minute practice periods, begin with this quotation from the text:
2 I am as God created me. 3 **God's** Son can suffer nothing.
4 And I am **God's** Son.

W-110.7.Then, with this statement **that I am as God created me, God's Son can suffer nothing and I am God's Son** firmly in your mind, try to discover in your mind the **big "S"** Self Who is the holy Son of God Himself.

W-110.8.Seek **your big "S" Self** within you Who is Christ in you, the Son of God and brother to the world; the Savior Who has been forever saved, with power to save whoever touches **your big "S" Self**, however lightly, asking for the Word that tells him **who perceive they are separate that** he is brother unto **your big "S" Self.**

W-110.9.You are as God created you. 2 Today honor your **big "S"** Self. 3 Let **the** graven images **of idols that your ego** made to **replace** the Son of God instead of **your big "S" Self** not be worshipped today. 4 Deep in your **split** mind the holy Christ in you is waiting your acknowledgment as you. 5 And you are lost and do not know yourself while **your big "S" Self, the holy Christ in you,** is unacknowledged and unknown.

W-110.10.Seek **your big "S" Self, the holy Christ in you** today, and find **your big "S" Self.** 2 **Your big "S" Self, the holy Christ in you** will be your Savior from all **egoic** idols you have made. 3 For when you find **your big "S" Self**, you will understand how worthless are your **ego's** idols, and how false the images which you believed were you **as your ego's little "s" self**. 4 Today we make a great advance to truth by letting **all egoic** idols go, and opening our hands and hearts and minds to God today.

W-110.11.We will remember **your big "S" Self, the holy Christ in you,** throughout the day with thankful hearts and loving thoughts for all who meet with us today. 2 For it is thus that we remember **the holy Christ in you**. 3 And we will say, that we may be reminded of **God's** Son, our holy **big "S"** Self, the Christ in each of us:
4 I am as God created me.
5 Let us declare this truth **that I am as God created me** as often as we can. 6 **I am as God created me** is the Word of God that sets you free. 7 **I am as God created me** is the key that opens up the gate of Heaven, and that lets you enter in the peace of God and **your big "S" Self's** eternity.

Notes to Lesson #110

I am as God created me.

Lesson 110 is one of my favorite lessons because it is such a liberating idea. Liberation from what? Well, in my case it was liberating from my own negative image of who I was. When I was younger, I was in such a dark place. I hated myself and my life. I was mean spirited and hateful to myself and others. I certainly was not Mr. Sunshine. I felt that I deserved to be punished and have bad things happen because I was really such a bad person.

As a youth, I did not have A Course in Miracles or anyone else who would argue for my big "S" Self. I had nothing to counterbalance or dispute my own negative self-talk and destructive opinions that I received from others. No one claimed that although my actions were inappropriate that I myself was not evil. Instead, I was told and believed myself to be a sinful, evil person that no one could ever love. So I grew up hating the world that hated me. It took years of struggle and inner work before I was able to slowly dig out of that black hole I had created for myself.

If I knew what I know now, this idea would have saved me years of pain, suffering and conflict. Of course, if I had actually been introduced to that idea as a youth, it would have frightened me. I would have believed that any egoic god of fear had intentionally made me evil. Therefore, I would have remained stuck in that black hole of despair. This is why it is important to understand that everyone is on their own perfect path and not to judge or compare where you are on your journey of reawakening to anyone else.

We do not understand the big picture. God's plan always provides the necessary learning lessons that are needed for your rapid progression towards your reawakening. Each desires these learning experiences for their own personal growth. We volunteered so that our decision-maker could understand, learn and demonstrate the power behind the thought system of love and forgiveness. When you silence the egoic mind, ask, listen and follow the Holy Spirit's guidance, you gently reawaken to a new world. Your old fear-based world becomes a bright and joyful place.

This one thought that I am as God created me, if accepted, holds the power to heal your split mind and your world. It heals all the blame, shame and guilt that you bear against yourself and your world. When you realize that the past has no ability to change what a God of unconditional love created, the experiences of struggle, conflict, sickness, evil, death and suffering are recognized as items that you once required but no longer value since they are meaningless. You realize that nothing you have imagined can change what God created.

This idea heals the past and corrects all mistakes that your split mind has made at any time or place. You can lighten up and forgive yourself for you alone are the keeper of your own karmic keys. God has never condemned anyone.

This thought that you remain as God created you allows for you to accept the present just as it is. Rather than being a slave to time, time is now the means to escape from time itself. Every change that time appeared to bring has never occurred. Time, which is the measure of change, has lost its old egoic purpose since illusions have no ability to change what God created.

Your ego, like time itself, has no ability to change God's reality. God's Will remains unaltered by your ego's fantasy world of fear, evil, misery and death. Fear has no meaning and does not exist. Appearances cannot replace the truth. The past is undone along with time because only the changeless that God created is real. You remain part of the unity of all and recognize that you are the Christ, the big "S" Self, home to the Holy Spirit and God, Itself.

The realization that you remain as God created you is the idea that births all miracles and restores the truth to your world's awareness. It ends your frantic search for the false idols that your ego believes you need to make you happy. Instead, you rest in God.

Question: How comforting is it to know that both God and the Holy Spirit are defending your spiritual magnificence against your ego's beliefs in your littleness?

Introduction

W-rIII.in.1.Our next review begins today. 2 We will review two recent lessons every day for ten successive days of practicing. 3 We will observe a special format for these practice periods, that you are urged to follow just as closely as you can.

W-rIII.in.2.We understand, of course, that it may be impossible for you to undertake what is suggested here as optimal each day and every hour of the day. 2 Learning will not be hampered when you miss a practice period because **a practice period** is impossible at the appointed time. 3 Nor is it necessary that you make excessive efforts to be sure that you catch up in terms of numbers. 4 Rituals are not our aim, and **rituals** would defeat our goal.

W-rIII.in.3.But learning will be hampered when you skip a practice period because you are unwilling to devote the time to **a practice period** that you are asked to give. 2 Do not deceive yourself in this. 3 Unwillingness **to do a practice period** can be most carefully concealed behind a cloak of situations you cannot control. 4 Learn to distinguish situations that are poorly suited to your practicing from those that you establish to uphold a camouflage for your unwillingness **to do a practice period**.

W-rIII.in.4.Those practice periods that you have lost because you did not want to do **a practice period**, for whatever reason, should be done as soon as you have changed your mind about your goal. 2 You are unwilling to cooperate in practicing salvation only if **a practice period** interferes with goals you hold more dear. 3 When you withdraw the value given **to other goals**, allow your practice periods to be replacements for your litanies to **those other goals**. 4 **Those other goals** gave you nothing. 5 But your practicing can offer everything to you. 6 And so accept **a practice period's** offering and be at peace.

W-rIII.in.5.The format you should use for these reviews is this: Devote five minutes twice a day, or longer if you would prefer it, to considering the thoughts that are assigned. 2 Read over the ideas and comments that are written down for each day's exercise. 3 And then begin to think about **those ideas and comments**, while letting your mind relate **those ideas and comments** to your needs, your seeming problems and all your concerns.

W-rIII.in.6.Place the ideas **and comments** within your mind, and let **your big "S" Self's mind** use **those ideas and comments** as **your mind** chooses. 2 Give **your mind** faith that **your big "S" Self** will use **those ideas and comments** wisely, being helped in **your minds** decisions by the **Holy Spirit**, Who gave the thoughts to you. 3 What can you trust but what is in your **big "S" Self's** mind? 4 Have faith, in these reviews, the means the Holy Spirit uses will not fail. 5 The wisdom of your **big "S" Self's** mind will come to your assistance. 6 Give direction at the outset; then lean back in quiet faith, and let the **big "S" Self's** mind employ the thoughts you gave as these **thoughts** were given you for **your big "S" Self** to use.

W-rIII.in.7.You have been given **these ideas and comments** in perfect trust; in perfect confidence that you would use **these ideas and comments** well; in perfect faith that you would see **these ideas'** messages and use **these messages** for yourself. 2 Offer **these messages** to your mind in that same trust and confidence and faith. 3 **Your big "S" Self's mind** will not fail. 4 **Your big "S" Self's mind** is the Holy Spirit's chosen means for your salvation. 5 Since **your big "S" Self's mind** has **the Holy Spirit's** trust, **the Holy Spirit's** means must surely merit your **trust** as well.

W-rIII.in.8.We emphasize the benefits to you if you devote the first five minutes of the day to your reviews, and also give the last five minutes of your waking day to **your review**. 2 If this **first and last five minutes of the day for review** cannot be done, at least try to divide **your review** so you undertake one **review** in the morning, and the other **review** in the hour just before you go to sleep.

W-rIII.in.9.The exercises to be done throughout the day are equally important, and perhaps of even greater value. 2 You have been inclined to practice only at appointed times, and then go on your way to other things, without applying what you learned to **the other events of your day**. 3 As a result, you have gained little reinforcement, and have not given your learning a fair chance to prove how great are **these new learnings'** potential gifts to you **are**. 4 Here is another chance to use **these new learnings** well.

W-rIII.in.10.In these reviews, we stress the need to let your learning not lie idly by between your longer practice periods. 2 Attempt to give your daily two ideas a brief but serious review each hour. 3 Use one **idea** on the hour, and the other **idea** a half an hour later. 4 You need not give more than just a moment to each **idea**. 5 Repeat **the idea**, and allow your mind to rest a little time in silence and in peace. 6 Then turn to other things, but try to keep the thought with you, and let **the idea** serve to help you keep your peace throughout the day as well.

W-rIII.in.11.If you are shaken, think of **the idea** again. 2 These practice periods are planned to help you form the habit of applying what you learn each day to everything you do. 3 Do not repeat the thought and lay **the idea** down. 4 **The idea's** usefulness is limitless to you. 5 And **the idea** is meant to serve you in all ways, all times and places, and whenever you need help of any kind. 6 Try, then, to take **the idea** with you in the business of the day and make **the day** holy, worthy of God's Son, acceptable to God and to your **big "S" Self**.

W-rIII.in.12.Each day's review assignments will conclude with a restatement of the thought to use each hour, and the **thought** to be applied on each half hour as well. 2 Forget **these thoughts** not. 3 This second chance with each of these ideas will bring such large advances that we come from these reviews with learning gains so great we will continue on more solid ground, with firmer footsteps and with stronger faith.

W-rIII.in.13.Do not forget how little you have learned.
2 Do not forget how much you can learn now.
3 Do not forget your Father's need of you,
As you review these thoughts **the Holy Spirit** gave to you.

Notes to Review #3

Introduction

Lessons 111-120 are a review of Workbook Lessons #90-110

The next 10 lessons are actually a review of the previous 20. Each day you will be asked to review two of the previous lessons with an emphasis on one of the prior lessons in either your morning or evening sessions. I will not be providing any additional notes regarding these review lessons since they are brief, self-explanatory and designed for the inner contemplation of those prior lessons.

I would suggest that you review the notes that were given for each original lesson that you are focusing on during each session. For example, lesson 111 covers lesson 91 and 92. Assuming your morning session will focus on lesson 91, I would suggest you review the notes for session 91 along with a reading of lesson 111. In your evening session you would review the notes for lesson 92 along with a reading of lesson 111.

You will be amazed at the new insight that each review will provide. What seemed obscure a few days ago may now appear obvious. Enjoy these reviews and honor the journey of rediscovering who you really are.

LESSON 111.

LESSON SUMMARY #91-92

For morning and evening review:

Lesson # 91: Miracles are seen in light

Lesson # 92: Miracles are seen in light, and light and strength are one.

W-111.1. <u>**Review of Lesson # 91 Miracles are seen in light.**</u>
2 I cannot see in darkness. 3 Let the light of holiness and truth light up my mind, and let me see the innocence within **my mind**.

W-111.2. <u>**Review of Lesson # 92 Miracles are seen in light, and light and strength are one.**</u>
2 I see through strength **and strength is** the gift of God to me. 3 My weakness is the dark **God's** gift **of strength** dispels, by giving me **God's** strength to take **the** place **of my ego's weakness**.

W-111.3.On the hour:
2 Miracles are seen in light.
3 On the half hour:
4 Miracles are seen in light, and light and strength are one.

LESSON 112.

LESSON SUMMARY #93-94

For morning and evening review:

Lesson # 93: Light and joy and peace abide in me.

Lesson # 94: I am as God created me

W-112.1. <u>**Review of Lesson # 93: Light and joy and peace abide in me.**</u>
2 I am the home of light and joy and peace. 3 I welcome **light, joy and peace** into the home I share with God, because I am a part of **God**.

W-112.2. <u>**Review of Lesson # 94: I am as God created me.**</u>
2 I will remain forever as I was, created by the Changeless like **God,** Himself. 3 And I am one with **God,** and **God is one** with me.

W-112.3.On the hour:
2 Light and joy and peace abide in me.
3 On the half hour:
4 I am as God created me.

LESSON 113.

LESSON SUMMARY #95-96

For morning and evening review:

Lesson # 95: I am one Self, united with my Creator.

Lesson # 96: Salvation comes from my one Self.

W-113.1.(95) I am one **big "S"** Self, united with my Creator.
2 Serenity and perfect peace are mine, because I am one **big "S"** Self, completely whole, at one with all creation and with God.

W-113.2.(96) Salvation comes from my one **big "S"** Self.
2 From my one **big "S"** Self, Whose knowledge still remains within my **split** mind, I see God's perfect plan for my salvation perfectly fulfilled.

W-113.3.On the hour:
2 I am one Self, united with my Creator.
3 On the half hour:
4 Salvation comes from my one Self.

LESSON 114.

LESSON SUMMARY #97-98

For morning and evening review:

Lesson # 97: I am spirit.

Lesson # 98: I will accept my part in God's plan for salvation.

W-114.1.(97) I am spirit.
2 I am the Son of God. 3 No body can contain my spirit, nor impose on me a limitation God created not.

W-114.2.(98) I will accept my part in God's plan for salvation.
2 What can my function be but to accept the Word of God, Who has created me for what I am and will forever be?

W-114.3.On the hour:
2 I am spirit.
3 On the half hour:
4 I will accept my part in God's plan for salvation.

LESSON 115.

LESSON SUMMARY #99-100

For morning and evening review:

Lesson # 99: Salvation is my only function here.

Lesson # 100: My part is essential to God's plan for salvation.

W-115.1.(99) Salvation is my only function here **in time**.
2 My function here **in time** is to forgive the world for all the errors I have made **with my split mind**. 3 For thus am I released from **all errors I have made along** with all the world.

W-115.2.(100) My part is essential to God's plan for salvation.
2 I am essential to the plan of God for the salvation of the world. 3 For **God** gave me His plan that I might save the world.

W-115.3.On the hour:
2 Salvation is my only function here.
3 On the half hour:
4 My part is essential to God's plan for salvation.

LESSON 116.

LESSON SUMMARY #101-102

For morning and evening review:

Lesson # 101: God's Will for me is perfect happiness.

Lesson # 102: I share God's Will for happiness for me.

W-116.1.(101) God's Will for me is perfect happiness.
2 God's Will is perfect happiness for me. 3 And I can suffer but from the **ego's** belief there is another will apart from **God's Will**.

W-116.2.(102) I share God's Will for happiness for me.
2 I share my Father's Will for me, His Son. **God's will for me is perfect happiness.** 3 What **God** has given me is all I want. 4 What **God** has given me is all there is.

W-116.3.On the hour:
2 God's Will for me is perfect happiness.
3 On the half hour:
4 I share God's Will for happiness for me.

LESSON 117.

LESSON SUMMARY #103-104

For morning and evening review:

Lesson # 103: God, being Love, is also happiness.

Lesson # 104: I seek but what belongs to me in truth.

W-117.1.(103) God, being Love, is also happiness.
2 Let me remember love is happiness, and nothing else brings joy. 3 And so I choose to entertain no **egoic** substitutes for love.

W-117.2.(104) I seek but what belongs to me in truth.
2 Love is my heritage, and with it joy. 3 **Love and joy** are the gifts my Father gave to me. 4 I would accept all that is mine in truth.

W-117.3.On the hour:
2 God, being Love, is also happiness.
3 On the half hour:
4 I seek but what belongs to me in truth.

LESSON 118.

LESSON SUMMARY #105-106

For morning and evening review:

Lesson # 105: God's peace and joy are mine.

Lesson # 106: Let me be still and listen to the truth.

W-118.1.(105) God's peace and joy are mine.
2 Today I will accept God's peace and joy, in glad exchange for all the **egoic** substitutes that I have made for happiness and peace.

W-118.2.(106) Let me be still and listen to the truth.
2 Let my own **ego's** feeble voice **for my littleness** be still, and let me hear the mighty Voice for Truth Itself assure me that I am God's perfect Son.

W-118.3.On the hour:
2 God's peace and joy are mine.
3 On the half hour:
4 Let me be still and listen to the truth.

LESSON 119.

LESSON SUMMARY #107-108

For morning and evening review:

Lesson # 107: Truth will correct all errors in my mind.

Lesson # 108: To give and to receive are one in truth.

W-119.1.(107) Truth will correct all errors in my **egoic split** mind.
2 I am mistaken when I think I can be hurt in any way. 3 I am God's Son, whose **big "S"** Self rests safely in the Mind of God.

W-119.2.(108) To give and to receive are one in truth.
2 I will forgive all things today, that I may learn how to accept the truth in me, and come to recognize my sinlessness.

W-119.3.On the hour:
2 Truth will correct all errors in my mind.
3 On the half hour:
4 To give and to receive are one in truth.

LESSON 120.

LESSON SUMMARY #109-110

For morning and evening review:

Lesson # 109: I rest in God.

Lesson # 110: I am as God created me.

W-120.1.(109) I rest in God.
2 I rest in God today, and let **God** work in me and through me, while I rest in **God** in quiet and in perfect certainty.

W-120.2.(110) I am as God created me.
2 I am God's Son. 3 Today I lay aside all sick illusions of my **little "s"** self, and let my Father tell me Who I really am.

W-120.3.On the hour:
2 I rest in God.
3 On the half hour:
4 I am as God created me.

LESSON 121

Forgiveness is the key to happiness.

W-121.1.Here **in the statement, forgiveness is the key to happiness,** is the answer to your search for peace. 2 Here **in forgiveness** is the key to meaning in a world that seems to make no sense. 3 Here **in forgiveness** is the way to safety in apparent dangers that appear to threaten you at every turn, and bring uncertainty to all your hopes of ever finding quietness and peace. 4 Here **in forgiveness** are all questions answered; here **in forgiveness** the end of all uncertainty **is** ensured at last.

W-121.2.The unforgiving mind is full of fear, and offers love no room to be itself; no place where **love** can spread its wings in peace and soar above the turmoil of the **egoic fear-based** world. 2 The unforgiving mind is sad, without the hope of respite and release from pain. 3 **The unforgiving mind** suffers and abides in misery, peering about in darkness, seeing not, yet certain of the danger lurking there.

W-121.3.The unforgiving mind is torn with doubt, confused about itself and all **an unforgiving mind** sees. **The unforgiving mind is** afraid and angry, weak and blustering, afraid to go ahead, afraid to stay. **The unforgiving mind is** afraid to waken or to go to sleep. **The unforgiving mind is** afraid of every sound, yet more afraid of stillness. **The unforgiving mind is** terrified of darkness, yet more terrified at the approach of light. 2 What can the unforgiving mind perceive but its **own** damnation? 3 What can **an unforgiving mind** behold except the proof that all its sins are real?

W-121.4.The unforgiving mind sees no mistakes, but only sins. 2 **The unforgiving mind** looks upon the world with sightless eyes, and shrieks as **the unforgiving mind** beholds its own projections rising to attack **the unforgiving mind's own** miserable parody of life. 3 **The unforgiving mind** wants to live, yet wishes it were dead. 4 **The unforgiving mind** wants forgiveness, yet it sees no hope. 5 **The unforgiving mind** wants escape, yet can conceive of none because **the unforgiving mind** sees the sinful everywhere.

W-121.5.The unforgiving mind is in despair, without the prospect of a future which can offer anything but more despair. 2 Yet **the unforgiving mind** regards its judgment of the world as irreversible, and does not see **the unforgiving mind** has condemned itself to this despair. 3 **The unforgiving mind** thinks it cannot change, for what **the unforgiving mind** sees bears witness that **the unforgiving mind's own** judgment is correct. 4 **The unforgiving mind** does not ask, because **the unforgiving mind** thinks it knows. 5 **The unforgiving mind** does not question, certain it is right.

W-121.6.Forgiveness is acquired. 2 **Forgiveness** is not inherent in the mind, which cannot sin. 3 As sin is an idea you taught your **egoic little "s" self,** forgiveness must be learned by you as well, but from a Teacher other than your **egoic little "s" self. This Teacher of forgiveness is the Holy Spirit,** Who represents the other **big "S"** Self in **your split mind.** 4 Through **this Teacher, the Holy Spirit,** you learn how to forgive the **little "s"** self you think you made, and let **your little "s" self you imagined** disappear. 5 Thus you return your **healed** mind as one to Him Who is your **big "S"** Self, and Who can never sin.

W-121.7.Each unforgiving mind presents you with an opportunity to teach your own **split mind** how to forgive itself. 2 Each one, **who perceives themselves separate,** awaits release from hell through you, and turns to **your big "S" Self** imploringly for Heaven here and now. 3 **Each one, who perceives themselves separate,** has no hope, but you become its hope. 4 And as **you are the** hope **of those who perceive themselves as separate, so** do you become your own **hope.** 5 The unforgiving mind must learn through your forgiveness that **the unforgiving mind** has been saved from hell. 6 And as you teach salvation **to the unforgiving mind,** you will learn **salvation.** 7 Yet all your teaching and your learning will be not of **your egoic little "s" self,** but of the Teacher, **the Holy Spirit,** Who was given **to** you **by God** to show the way to you.

W-121.8.Today we practice learning to forgive. 2 If you are willing, you can learn today to take **forgiveness which is** the key to happiness, and use **forgiveness** on your own behalf. 3 We will devote ten minutes in the morning, and at night another ten, to learning how to give forgiveness and receive forgiveness, too.

W-121.9.The unforgiving mind does not believe that giving and receiving are the same. 2 Yet we will try to learn today that **giving and receiving** are one through practicing forgiveness toward one whom you think of as an enemy, and one whom you consider as a friend. 3 And as you learn to see both **enemy and friend** as one, we will extend the lesson to yourself, and see that their escape included your **escape through your forgiveness**.

W-121.10.Begin the longer practice periods by thinking of someone you do not like, who seems to irritate you, or to cause regret in you if you should meet him; **Think of someone** you actively despise, or merely try to overlook. 2 It does not matter what the form your anger takes. 3 You probably have chosen him already. 4 He will do.

W-121.11.Now close your eyes and see **that person you dislike** in your mind, and look at him a while. 2 Try to perceive some light in **that person you dislike** somewhere; a little gleam which you had never noticed. 3 Try to find some little spark of brightness shining through the ugly picture that you hold of **that person you dislike.** 4 Look at this picture till you see a light somewhere within **that person you dislike,** and then try to let this light extend until **the light** covers **that person you dislike,** and makes the picture beautiful and good.

W-121.12.Look at this changed perception **of that person you formerly disliked** for a while, and turn your mind to one you call a friend. 2 Try to transfer the light you learned to see around your former "enemy" to **your friend**. 3 Perceive **your former "enemy"** now as more than friend to you, for in that light **your former enemy's** holiness shows you your savior, saved and saving, healed and whole.

W-121.13.Then let **your former "enemy"** offer you the light you see in **your friend**, and let your "enemy" and friend unite in blessing you with what you gave **which was also this light of forgiveness**. 2 Now are you one with them, and they **one** with you. 3 Now have you been forgiven by yourself. 4 Do not forget, throughout the day, the role forgiveness plays in bringing happiness to every unforgiving mind, with your **little "s" egoic mind** among them. 5 Every hour tell yourself: 6 Forgiveness is the key to happiness. 7 I will awaken from the **egoic** dream that I am mortal, fallible and full of sin, and know I am the perfect Son of God.

Notes to Lesson #121

Forgiveness is the key to happiness.

Lesson 121, forgiveness is the key to my happiness, is a very important lesson. What true forgiveness involves will be a main topic in the next 20 workbook lessons.

Although this lesson states that forgiveness is the key to your happiness, it fails to define what true forgiveness is. Instead, it states that forgiveness is an acquired talent. It is not something that is a natural part of the shared Mind of God that cannot sin. Since sin is an idea that arose within the split mind that believed itself to be separate from the One Self, sin, itself, is an illusion.

Since we taught ourselves that sin was real by arguing for a little "s" self, forgiveness must be learned by ourselves as well. Forgiveness undoes our belief in our little "s" self. True forgiveness is the key to happiness since it alleviates the natural negative consequences that plague the mind that suffers from its belief in the reality of sin.

The ego is incapable of teaching us how to forgive anyone, including ourselves, since the ego's thought system is based on the false belief that sin or lack is the reality of our world. Believing lack to be real, your ego will never question the reality of its belief in sin. Sin sits at the foundation of the ego's fear-based thought system. It is impossible to escape your belief in lack, limitation and sin within the same fear-based thought system whose sole purpose is to provide false evidence to perpetuate the myth about your existence as a separate limited being.

ACIM states that if one is to understand true forgiveness, one needs to seek a different teacher who knows the truth of who you really are. Only the Holy Spirit understands that you remain as God created you, perfect, whole and complete. This Voice for God and your big "S" Self both understand that your ego's imaginings that arose from your belief in separation are not real and have no ability to change the truth of who you really are.

Only the split minded need to learn what true forgiveness involves. Because your ego believes that sin is real, your ego is constantly arguing for the rightness of its own erroneous beliefs rather than for your happiness.

The ego's thought system is based on the belief that there are outside forces that need to behave in a certain way in order for you to be happy. A grievance arises anytime someone or something fails to perform according to your ego's plan for your happiness. Your ego then judges the other party as having wronged you and then argues for the rightness of its own judgment that condemns that party. While arguing for the rightness of its own plan, your ego attempts to manipulate or punish the offending party in order to get its own way. Your ego's need to be right trumps your desire to be happy.

The ego fails to realize that when you imprison another, you too, as their jailer, must remain in that same prison to insure the perpetrator does not escape from your justice. Both remain caged in the prison of your own unforgiving mind.

An unforgiving mind does not question because it knows it is right. An unforgiving mind is full of fear and trapped within a thought system that prevents love from entering. An unforgiving mind is sad, suffers and abides in misery, doubt, anger and constant fear. Because it believes sin to be real, an unforgiving mind demands punishment, penance and retribution for those wrongs.

Since an unforgiving mind perceives sin instead of error, sin requires punishment and damnation rather than just correction as an error would require. The unforgiving mind never questions the correctness of its own judgment. Your physical senses are told to seek and find evidence that confirms your ego's belief that this is a sinful world. This evidence is then used to perpetuate your ego's belief and viewpoint that its sinful outside world is correct, irreversible and unchangeable and reflects a sinful you. You remain a victim of powers that are beyond your control.

In the lessons ahead, we will continue to discover what true forgiveness entails and why it is the key to true happiness.

As a side note: Is forgiveness an attribute of God?

Forgiveness is not an attribute of God because in order to forgive, you first must have condemned. Since God has never condemned anyone, forgiveness is not an attribute within the Mind of God. This is why we stated earlier that forgiveness is not a natural attribute in the mind that understands it is perfect, whole and complete.

Question: This lesson ends with the request that every hour you tell yourself the following message:

"Forgiveness is the key to happiness. I will awaken from the egoic dream that I am mortal, fallible and full of sin, and know I am the perfect Son of God."

Why is the focus of the above statement on your image of your little "s" self rather than on the "wrong" you suffered at the hands of another?

LESSON 122

Forgiveness offers everything I want.

W-122.1.What could you want forgiveness cannot give? 2 Do you want peace? 3 **True** forgiveness offers **peace**. 4 Do you want happiness, a quiet mind, a certainty of purpose, and a sense of worth and beauty that transcends the world? 5 Do you want care and safety, and the warmth of sure protection always? 6 Do you want a quietness that cannot be disturbed, a gentleness that never can be hurt, a deep, abiding comfort, and a rest so perfect **your rest** can never be upset?

W-122.2.All **these attributes** forgiveness offers you, and more. 2 **True forgiveness** sparkles on your eyes as you awake, and gives you joy with which to meet the day. 3 **True forgiveness** soothes your forehead while you sleep, and rests upon your eyelids so you see no dreams of fear and evil, malice and attack. 4 And when you wake again, **forgiveness** offers you another day of happiness and peace. 5 All this forgiveness offers you, and more.

W-122.3.**True** forgiveness lets the veil be lifted up that hides the face of Christ from those who look with unforgiving eyes upon the world. 2 **True forgiveness** lets you recognize the Son of God, and clears your memory of all dead thoughts so that remembrance of your Father can arise across the threshold of your **split** mind. 3 What would you want **true** forgiveness cannot give? 4 What gifts but these are worthy to be sought? 5 What fancied value, trivial effect or transient **egoic** promise, never to be kept, can hold more hope than what **true** forgiveness brings?

W-122.4.Why would you seek an answer other than **forgiveness,** the answer that will answer everything? 2 **True forgiveness** is the perfect answer, given to imperfect questions, meaningless requests, halfhearted willingness to hear, and less than halfway diligence and partial trust. 3 **True forgiveness** is the answer! 4 Seek for **your ego's answer for happiness** no more. 5 You will not find another **answer** instead **of what true forgiveness offers**.

W-122.5.God's plan for your salvation cannot change, nor can **God's plan for your salvation** fail. 2 Be thankful **God's plan for your salvation** remains exactly as **God** planned it. 3 Changelessly **God's plan for your salvation** stands before you like an open door, with warmth and welcome calling from beyond the doorway, bidding you to enter in and make yourself at home, where you belong.

W-122.6.**God's plan for your salvation** is the answer! 2 Would you stand outside while all of Heaven waits for you within? 3 Forgive and be forgiven. 4 As you give you will receive. 5 There is no plan but **true forgiveness** for the salvation of the Son of God. 6 Let us today rejoice that **God's plan for your salvation through true forgiveness** is so, for here we have an answer **for your salvation**, clear and plain, beyond deceit in **the** simplicity **of God's plan**. 7 All the complexities the **fear-based egoic** world has spun of fragile cobwebs disappear before the power and the majesty of this extremely simple statement of the truth **that as you give you will receive. Therefore, forgive and be forgiven.**

W-122.7.Here is the answer **that true forgiveness gives! As you give you will receive. Therefore, forgive and be forgiven**. 2 Do not turn away in **egoic** aimless wandering again. 3 Accept salvation now. 4 **Salvation's plan that as you give you will receive** is the gift of God**'s plan**, and not **your ego's fear-based** world. 5 The **ego's** world can give no gifts of any value to a **healed** mind that has received what God has given as **your healed mind's** own. 6 God wills salvation be received today, and that the intricacies of your **split mind's** dreams no longer hide their nothingness from you.

W-122.8.Open your eyes today and look upon a happy world of safety and of peace. 2 Forgiveness is the means by which **a happy world of safety and of peace** comes to take the place of **your ego's** hell. 3 In quietness **a happy world of safety and of peace** rises up to greet your open eyes, and fill your heart with deep tranquility as ancient truths, forever newly born, arise in your awareness. 4 What you will remember then can never be described. 5 Yet your **true** forgiveness offers **a happy world of safety and of peace** to you.

W-122.9.Remembering the gifts **true** forgiveness gives, we undertake our practicing today with hope and faith that this will be the day salvation will be ours. 2 Earnestly and gladly will we seek for **salvation** today, aware we hold the key **that true forgiveness offers** within our hands, accepting Heaven's answer to the hell we made, but where we would remain no more.

W-122.10.Morning and evening do we gladly give a quarter of an hour to the search in which the end of hell is guaranteed. 2 Begin in hopefulness, for we have reached the turning point at which the road becomes far easier. 3 And now the way **to salvation** is short that yet we travel. 4 We are close indeed to the appointed ending of the **egoic** dream **of separation**.

W-122.11.Sink into happiness as you begin these practice periods, for **these practice periods** hold out the sure rewards of questions answered and what your acceptance of the answer brings. 2 Today it will be given you to feel the peace **true** forgiveness offers, and the joy the lifting of the veil holds out to you.

W-122.12.Before the light you will receive today the world will fade until **your ego's fear-based world** disappears, and you will see another world arise you have no words to picture. 2 Now we walk directly into light, and we receive the gifts that have been held in store for us since time began, kept waiting for today.

W-122.13.**True** forgiveness offers everything you want. 2 Today all things you want are given you. 3 Let not your gifts recede throughout the day, as you return again to meet an **egoic** world of shifting change and bleak appearances. 4 Retain your gifts **that true forgiveness brings** in clear awareness as you see the changeless in the heart of change; the light of truth behind **egoic** appearances.

W-122.14.Be tempted not to let your gifts **that true forgiveness brings** slip by and drift into forgetfulness, but hold **your gifts that true forgiveness brings** firmly in your mind by your attempts to think of **these gifts** at least a minute as each quarter of an hour passes by. 2 Remind yourself how precious are these gifts **that true forgiveness brings** with this reminder, which has power to hold your gifts in your awareness through the day:
3 Forgiveness offers everything I want.
4 Today I have accepted this as true.
5 Today I have received the gifts of God.

Notes to Lesson #122

Forgiveness offers everything I want.

Lesson 122 continues with the theme of forgiveness stating that true forgiveness offers everything you want. Forgiveness brings peace, happiness and certainty of purpose allowing you to transcend the fear-based thought system that creates your current provisional reality.

Forgiveness lifts the veil that your body's senses and the physical world were designed to hide. It brings the illusions of sin, lack and limitation before the truth of who you really are. This allows the fearful illusions of inadequacy and separation to be reframed into a happy dream that empowers and leads you to the reclamation of your divine birthright.

This lesson does not define what true forgiveness entails. Yet, it does provide some clues.

In paragraph W – 122.4, we are told that, "Forgiveness is the perfect answer, given to imperfect questions, meaningless requests, halfhearted willingness to hear, and less than halfway diligence and partial trust." But what does that mean?

An imperfect question is a question that cannot be answered in a simple way because it has internal flaws within the logic of the question itself or places unfair limitations upon the answer. The question often contains embedded assumptions that are assumed to be true but are actually false.

For example: an imperfect question might take the following form: Please answer this question with a simple yes or no. In the last 6 months have you finally stopped beating your spouse?

The question assumes that you previously were beating your spouse. It then places unreasonable restrictions on how you may reply. Whether you answer yes or no, you are damned.

The ego is a master of asking imperfect questions. It also is a master at making meaningless requests.

For example: Your ego may tell you that you need a diamond ring, so that you can be happy. This is a typical meaningless request since nothing outside yourself has the ability to make you happy.

Because the ego's thought system is based on its belief in lack, limitation and separation, your ego's plan for your happiness implies something outside of your own mind has the power to make you happy or sad. It is this false belief that births all the grievances that you hold.

No one has the power to rob you of your inner peace unless you choose to allow it. Yet, all grievances are predicated on the belief that you are a victim of outside forces that are beyond your control. Your ego's plan for your happiness always rests on your mind's inability to be the source of your own happiness.

Since forgiveness is the perfect answer to imperfect questions and meaningless requests, true forgiveness must have the ability to address, reframe and correct the erroneous logic that the question itself entails. It must have the ability to reframe or transform a fearful dream into a non-frightening or happy dream. True forgiveness must address the fact that the source of all fearful experiences is your mind's belief in its own littleness. True forgiveness must correct your ego's belief that you are a victim of outside forces that are beyond your control.

This lesson does not state what God's exact plan for your salvation is but it does state that God's plan is changeless and cannot fail. We are all guaranteed to reawaken to the truth of who we really are. This lesson does state that even in time and space, God's laws apply. God's primary law is that to give is to receive. Because God's law applies even in the illusionary world of provisional reality, when we forgive, we are forgiven.

The overall plan for the salvation of the Son of God is as follows:

Forgive and be forgiven for as you give you will receive. This is a clear plan whose simplicity is beyond deceit. Yet, God's plan awaits your decision to drop your allegiance to your fear-based thought system and follow the Voice for God.

Before you decide which voice you will choose to follow today, remember that only true forgiveness offers everything you want.

Question: Because God never condemned you, God cannot forgive you for there is nothing for God to forgive. Yet we are told "Forgive and be forgiven for as you give you will receive." Who or what are we to forgive and who or what is to forgive us?

I thank my Father for His gifts to me.

W-123.1.Today let us be thankful. 2 We have come to gentler pathways and to smoother roads. 3 There is no thought of turning back, and no implacable resistance to the truth. 4 A bit of wavering remains, some small objections and a little hesitance, but you can well be grateful for your gains **towards healing your split mind**, which are far greater than you realize.

W-123.2.A day devoted now to gratitude will add the benefit of some insight into the real extent of all the gains **towards healing your split mind** which you have made; the gifts **from God** you have received. 2 Be glad today, in loving thankfulness, your Father has not left you to yourself, nor let you wander in the dark alone. 3 Be grateful **your Father** has saved you from the **ego's small "s"** self you thought you made to take the place of **your Father** and **your Father's** creation, **the Sonship**. 4 Give **your Father** thanks today.

W-123.3.Give thanks that **your Father** has not abandoned you, and that **your Father's** Love forever will remain shining on you, forever without change. 2 Give thanks as well that you are changeless, for the Son **your Father** loves is changeless as **God,** Himself. 3 Be grateful you are saved. 4 Be glad you have a function in salvation to fulfill. 5 Be thankful that your value far transcends your **ego's** meager gifts and petty judgments of the one whom God established as **God's** Son.

W-123.4.Today in gratitude we lift our hearts above despair, and raise our thankful eyes, no longer looking downward to the dust. 2 We sing the song of thankfulness today, in honor of the **big "S" Self** that God has willed to be our true Identity in **God**. 3 Today we smile on everyone we see, and walk with lightened footsteps as we go to do what is appointed us to do.

W-123.5.We do not go alone. 2 And we give thanks that in our solitude a Friend**, the Holy Spirit**, has come to speak the saving Word of God to us. 3 And thanks to you for listening to **the Holy Spirit**. 4 **The Holy Spirit's** Word is soundless if **the Holy Spirit's Words** be not heard. 5 In thanking **the Holy Spirit** the thanks are yours as well. 6 An unheard message will not save the world, however mighty be the Voice **for God** that speaks, however loving may the message be.

W-123.6.Thanks be to you who heard, for you become the messenger who brings **the Holy Spirit's** Voice with you, and lets **the Holy Spirit's Voice** echo round and round the world. 2 Receive the thanks of God today, as you give thanks to **the Holy Spirit**. 3 For **the Holy Spirit** would offer you the thanks you give, since **the Holy Spirit** receives your gifts in loving gratitude, and gives **your gift of gratitude** back a thousand and a hundred thousand more than **your gifts** were given. 4 **The Holy Spirit** will bless your gifts by sharing **your gifts** with you. 5 And so **your gifts of gratitude grow** in power and in strength, until **your gifts** fill the world with gladness and with gratitude.

W-123.7.Receive **the Holy Spirit's** thanks and offer **your thanks** to **the Holy Spirit** for fifteen minutes twice today. 2 And you will realize to Whom you offer thanks, and Whom **the Holy Spirit** thanks, **which is your big "S" Self,** as you are thanking **the Holy Spirit**. 3 This holy half an hour given **the Holy Spirit** will be returned to you in terms of years for every second; power to save the world eons more quickly for your thanks to **the Holy Spirit**.

W-123.8.Receive **the Holy Spirit's** thanks, and you will understand how lovingly **your Father and the Holy Spirit** hold you in **Their** Mind, how deep and limitless **your Father and the Holy Spirit's** care for you, how perfect is **Their** gratitude to you. 2 Remember hourly to think of **your Father and the Holy Spirit**, and give **your Father** thanks for everything **your Father** gave His Son, that **the split minded** might rise above the **fear-based** world **of the egoic little "s" self**, remembering his Father and his **big "S"** Self.

Notes to Lesson #123

I thank my Father for His gifts to me.

Today we are asked to give thanks for the gifts that we have received from Our Creator. Gratitude and thankfulness is an acknowledgment that you have received the gifts that have been offered. When you acknowledge the receipt of these gifts through your gratitude, you actually assert your right to claim those gifts as your own.

The gifts we have received from our Creator are too numerous to mention. After all, when God creates, He gives all to all. Nothing is held back. We are an extension of the Oneness of All That Is. This is a true indication of God's unconditional love for His Creation.

Although we cannot define what God is since to define would be to limit, we can recognize the effects of the energy of God, which is only unconditional love. We can and should be grateful for the constant and endless flow of God's love upon all of creation. We can deny the existence of this flows but our denial cannot stop the flow. This loving energy's mission is to reawaken us to the truth of who we are.

One of God's greatest gifts to ourselves is God's Will. God's Will remains changeless and unaffected by your ego's dream of separation. This changelessness of God's Will guarantees that you will reawaken to the truth that you are not the body but are free and remain as God created you. This freedom allows you to temporarily deny your divine birthright. Yet, your denial cannot change the fact that you remain God's beloved child with whom He is well pleased. Your divine inheritance is unaffected by what your ego imagines you have become.

We had a wish to not only be a recipient of God's unconditional love but to co-creator with God and be and demonstrate love in specific examples. In our desire to better know ourselves, we felt we needed to experience differentiation. Differentiation does not mean that you are different. Instead, it only means you are aware of various different aspects of the One Self. When the ego mistook differentiation for differences, it made the separation appear real. This error birthed the ego's fear-based thought system.

Truth just is and does not reawaken. Truth does not pretend it is something it is not. The Father, being Truth with a capital T, could not join us on our imagined journey of being something we are not. But God did not abandon us when we chose to embark on this detour into fear. Instead, God guaranteed our safe return by placing within our split mind, the Holy Spirit.

It is the Holy Spirit's mission to bring us safely home by healing our ego's split mind. Our ego's belief in separation and littleness must end. The Holy Spirit's guidance will return us to the remembrance of our big "S" Self and the Truth. God's gift of the Holy Spirit guarantees our homecoming while allowing us the perfect freedom to be or imagine anything we want in total safety.

Although we speak as if the Holy Spirit is different and separate from God and our big "S" Self, the indivisible nature of the One Self needs to be mentioned. Our ego believes the separation to be real and ACIM attempts to meet the student where they currently are. Therefore, ACIM uses dualistic language for the ease of understanding by speaking of the One Self as if there are three separate parts.

The Father or Creator is Cause. The Father's creation, which is all He created as He created it, is the Son or the Effect. Together they form two sides of one inseparable coin. The Holy Spirit is the bridge that joins the two sides as One Self. In the dream of separation, the Holy Spirit is aware of the Son's dream of separation yet, also remembers the truth. The Holy Spirit's task is to lovingly reawaken the sleeping egoic mind from its dream of separation. Together, all three parts form an indivisible Trinity that we would call God. Each part appears to have its own separate mission yet, each is dependent on the other parts for its existence.

Question: If a tree falls and no one is there to hear it, does it make a sound?

The answer is no. You need both the vibration from the fallen tree and an eardrum to hear the sound. We are like the eardrum of the Holy Spirit. Without our big "S" Self hearing the Voice for God that Voice would fail to be heard around your world. When you silence your ego, go within and hear the Voice for God, you become the messenger for the Holy Spirit that saves your world. Both parts are needed and become inseparable for the message to be heard. The Holy Spirit and your big "S" Self are connected. Each component completes and shares each other's function. Each part displays differentiation but there is no difference. They remain connected and are one.

LESSON 124

Let me remember I am one with God.

W-124.1.Today we will again give thanks for our Identity in God. 2 **Because of our Identity in God,** our home is safe, protection guaranteed in all we do, power and strength available to us in all our undertakings. 3 **Because of our Identity in God,** we can fail in nothing. 4 **Because of our Identity in God,** everything we touch takes on a shining light that blesses and that heals. 5 At one with God and with the universe we go our way rejoicing, with the thought that God Himself goes everywhere with us.

W-124.2.**Because of our Identity in God,** how holy are our minds! 2 And everything we see reflects the holiness within the mind at one with God and with itself. 3 **Because of our Identity in God,** how easily do errors disappear, and death give place to everlasting life. 4 Our shining footprints point the way to truth, for God is our Companion as we walk the world a little while. 5 And **because of our Identity in God,** those who come to follow us will recognize the way because the light we carry stays behind, yet still remains with us as we walk on.

W-124.3.**Because of our Identity in God,** what we receive is our eternal gift to those who follow after, and to those who went before or stayed with us a while. 2 And God, Who loves us with the equal love in which we were created, smiles on us and offers us the happiness we gave.

W-124.4.Today we will not doubt **God's** Love for us, nor question **God's** protection and **God's** care. 2 No meaningless anxieties **of the ego** can come between our faith and our awareness of **God's** Presence. 3 We are one with **God** today in recognition and remembrance. 4 We feel **God** in our hearts. 5 Our minds contain **God's** Thoughts; our eyes behold **God's** loveliness in all we look upon. 6 Today we see only the loving and the lovable.

W-124.5.We see **only the loving and the lovable** in appearances of pain, and pain gives way to peace. 2 We see **only the loving and the lovable** in the frantic, in the sad and the distressed, the lonely and afraid, who are restored to the tranquility and peace of mind in which they were created. 3 And we see **only the loving and the lovable** in the dying and the dead as well, restoring them to life. 4 All this we see because we saw it first within our **big "S" Selves.**

W-124.6.No miracle can ever be denied to those who know that they are one with God. 2 No thought of **those who know that they are one with God** but has the power to heal all forms of suffering in anyone, in times gone by and times as yet to come, as easily as in the **split-minded** ones who walk beside them now. 3 **The** thoughts **of those who know that they are one with God** are timeless, and apart from distance as apart from time.

W-124.7.We join in this awareness **that the thoughts of those who know that they are one with God are timeless** as we say that we are one with God. 2 For in these words **that we are one with God,** we say as well that we are saved and healed; that we can save and heal accordingly. 3 We have accepted, and we now would give. 4 For we would keep the gifts our Father gave **by giving those same gifts to others.** 5 Today we would experience ourselves at one with **God,** so that the world may share our recognition of reality. 6 In our experience **that we are one with God** the world is freed. 7 As we deny our separation from our Father, **our ego's belief in separation** is healed along with us.

W-124.8.Peace be to you today. 2 Secure your peace by practicing awareness you are one with your Creator, as **God** is **one** with you. 3 Sometime today, whenever it seems best, devote a half an hour to the thought that you are one with God. 4 This is our first attempt at an extended period for which we give no rules nor special words to guide your meditation. 5 We will trust God's Voice to speak **as the Holy Spirit** sees fit today, certain **the Holy Spirit** will not fail. 6 Abide with **the Holy Spirit** this half an hour. 7 **The Holy Spirit** will do the rest.

W-124.9.Your benefit will not be less if you believe that nothing happens. 2 You may not be ready to accept the gain today. 3 Yet sometime, somewhere, **the gain** will come to you, nor will you fail to recognize **the benefit** when **the gain** dawns with certainty upon your mind. 4 This half an hour will be framed in gold, with every minute like a diamond set around the mirror that this exercise will offer you. 5 And you will see Christ's face upon **your mind's inner mirror,** in reflection of your own **big "S" Self.**

W-124.10.Perhaps today, perhaps tomorrow, you will see your own transfiguration in the glass this holy half an hour will hold out to you, to look upon **your big "S" Self, your own face of Christ.** 2 When you are ready you will find **your own face of Christ** there, within your mind and waiting to be found. 3 You will remember then the thought **that we are one with God** to which you gave this half an hour, thankfully aware no time was ever better spent.

W-124.11.Perhaps today, perhaps tomorrow, you will look into this glass, **the mirror within your inner mind,** and understand the sinless light you see belongs to you, **your big "S" Self.** The loveliness you look on is your own **true big "S" Self.** 2 Count this half hour as your gift to God, in certainty that **God's** return will be a sense of love you cannot understand, a joy too deep for you to comprehend, a sight too holy for the body's eyes to see. 3 And yet you can be sure someday, perhaps today, perhaps tomorrow, you will understand and comprehend and see.

W-124.12.Add further jewels to the golden frame that holds the mirror **the Holy Spirit** offered you today, by hourly repeating to yourself:

2 Let me remember I am one with God, at one with all my brothers and my **big "S"** Self, in everlasting holiness and peace.

Notes to Lesson #124

Let me remember I am one with God.

This lesson has a simple yet powerful call to action. It asks you to remember that you are one with God. Your identity with God, your Creator, is the source of your strength, power and ultimate recovery of your divine birthright. When you are one with God, you acknowledge that you rest in the safe, loving arms of a God of unconditional love and that your return home is guaranteed.

This lesson asks you to simply acknowledge that when you follow your ego's thought system, you remain trapped in your belief in littleness. The ego's false image of who you are condemns you to a constant state of conflict, fear and struggle. Your ego's plan is doomed to fail. You need a new plan that provides a new paradigm that encompasses your true spiritual magnificence. When you follow the Holy Spirit's advice and identify your reality with God, you cannot fail. This lesson simply asks you to remember that fact.

When you are one with God, your big "S" Self sees only love and the lovable. This vision of Christ allows you to look past the outward appearances of form to the content or purpose of the experiences you call into your awareness. No miracle can ever be denied to those who know they are one with God. This is why the appearance of pain gives way to peace and the dying are restored to life.

Does this mean that the game token we call the body will not physically die?

Of course not. A miracle takes place in the mind of the beholder. It is a state of mind, not a bodily phenomenon. There may or may not be an actual observable change in physiology. A miracle is simply a change in perception. It is a recovery of your own inner peace.

The miracle is the acknowledgment that nothing can rob you of your own inner peace unless you allow it. In the miracle, you merely reclaim the power to be the controller of your own inner peace. The miracle transforms your ego's story of your littleness and recognizes the strength of your big "S" Self. It is the remembrance and recognition that your true reality is one with God.

When you identify with your egoic little "s" self, life is a struggle. When you identify with God, life becomes an interesting, exciting adventurous puzzle. When you are one with God, the puzzle of your ego's erroneous belief in separation is one mystery you cannot fail to solve.

Question: Why are you asked at the end of today's lesson to not only repeat that you are one with God, but also one with all your brothers and your big "S" Self?

Question: Is it possible to be one with God and yet separate from another?

LESSON 125

In quiet I receive God's Word today.

W-125.1.Let this day be a day of stillness and of quiet listening. 2 Your Father wills you hear **God's** Word today. 3 **Your Father** calls to you from deep within your **big "S' Self's** mind where **your Father** abides. 4 Hear **your Father's Word** today. 5 No peace is possible until **God's** Word is heard around the world; until your mind, in quiet listening, accepts the message that the world must hear to usher in the quiet time of peace.

W-125.2.This world will change through you. 2 No other means can save **this world**, for God's plan is simply this: The Son of God is free to save himself, given the Word of God, **the Holy Spirit,** to be his Guide, forever in **the son's split** mind and at **the son's** side to lead **the son** surely to his Father's house by **the son's split mind's** own will, forever free as God's **Will**. 3 **The Son of God** is not led by force, but only love. 4 **The Son of God** is not judged, but only sanctified.

W-125.3.In stillness we will hear God's Voice today without intrusion of our petty **egoic** thoughts, without our personal **egoic** desires, and without all judgment of **God's** holy Word. 2 We will not judge ourselves today, for what we are, **our big "S" Selves and God's Son,** cannot be judged. 3 We stand apart from all the **egoic** judgments which the **fear-based** world **of the ego** has laid upon the Son of God. 4 **The fear-based** world **of the ego** knows **the Son of God** not. 5 Today we will not listen to the **fear-based** world **of the ego**, but wait in silence for the Word of God.

W-125.4.Hear, holy Son of God, your Father speak. 2 Your Father's Voice, **the Holy Spirit** would give to you **God's** holy Word, to spread across the world the tidings of salvation and the holy time of peace. 3 We gather at the throne of God today, the quiet place within the **big "S" Self's** mind where **God** abides forever, in the holiness that **your Father** created and will never leave.

W-125.5.**Your Father** has not waited until you return your **healed** mind to **your Father** to give **God's** Word to you. 2 **Your Father** has not hid Himself from you, while **your egoic little "s" self's split mind** has wandered off a little while from **your Father**. 3 **Your Father** does not cherish the **egoic** illusions **of littleness** which you hold about yourself **as separate from the One Self**. 4 **Your Father** knows His Son, and wills that **His Son** remain as part of **the One Self** regardless of **the ego's** dreams **of littleness**; regardless of **your ego's split-minded** madness that **your ego's** will is not **your ego's** own **will**.

W-125.6.Today **your Father, through the Holy Spirit** speaks to you. 2 **God's** Voice awaits your silence, for **the Holy Spirit's** Word cannot be heard until your mind is quiet for a while, and meaningless **egoic** desires have been stilled. 3 Await **the Holy Spirit's** Word in quiet. 4 There is peace within you to be called upon today, to help make ready your most holy **big "S" Self's** mind to hear the Voice for its Creator speak.

W-125.7.Three times today, at times most suitable for silence, give ten minutes set apart from listening to the **fear-based** world **of your ego**, and choose instead a gentle listening to the Word of God. 2 **The Holy Spirit** speaks from nearer than your heart to you. 3 **The Holy Spirit's** Voice is closer than your hand. 4 **The Holy Spirit's** Love is everything you are and that **the Holy Spirit** is. **The Holy Spirit is** the same as you**, your big "S" Self** and **your big "S" Self is** the same as **the Holy Spirit**.

W-125.8.It is your **big "S" Self's** voice to which you listen as **the Holy Spirit** speaks to you. 2 It is your **big "S" Self's** word **the Holy Spirit** speaks. 3 It is the Word of freedom and of peace, of unity of will and purpose, with no separation nor division in the single Mind of Father and of Son. 4 In quiet listen to your **big "S"** Self today, and let **the Holy Spirit** tell you God has never left His Son, and you have never left your **big "S"** Self.

W-125.9.Only be quiet. 2 You will need no rule but this **quietness** to let your practicing today lift you above the thinking of the **fear-based** world **of your ego**, and free your **Christ** vision from the body's eyes. 3 Only be still and listen. 4 You will hear the Word in which the Will of God the Son joins in his Father's Will, at one with **his Father's Will**, with no illusions interposed between the wholly indivisible and true **Will of the One Self**. 5 As every hour passes by today, be still a moment and remind yourself you have a special purpose for this day; in quiet to receive the Word of God.

Notes to Lesson #125

In quiet I receive God's Word today.

In your split mind, there are two voices seeking to advise your decision-maker. The ego is the voice that seems to shout the loudest and argues for your littleness and a fear-based belief system based upon lack, limitation and separation. The ego is the voice for fear and represents your little "s" self.

Although the Holy Spirit's voice seems quiet, it is a quietness that comes from strength. It is the voice for love that speaks on behalf your big "S" Self. The Holy Spirit's task is to heal your split mind and end the nightmare of the belief that the separation is real. The Holy Spirit represents and follows God's plan for your salvation.

But what is God's plan for your salvation?

In lesson 122, we stated that God's law applies to both reality and your ego's illusionary worlds. God's laws supersede the laws of the ego that encase this world in fear. Because of this, the previous lesson advised us to, "forgive and be forgiven for as you give you receive." But this law is not God's plan for the healing of the fear-based world that your split mind perceives.

God's plan for salvation is stated in the second paragraph of lesson 125. It states:

W-125.2.This world will change through you. 2 No other means can save **this world**, for God's plan is simply this: The Son of God is free to save himself, given the Word of God, **the Holy Spirit,** to be his Guide, forever in **the son's split** mind and at **the son's** side to lead **the son** surely to his Father's house by **the son's split mind's** own will, forever free as God's **Will**. 3 **The Son of God** is not led by force, but only love. 4 **The Son of God** is not judged, but only sanctified.

Your world is a reflection of you. It mirrors the thought system you have chosen to follow. Your ego's plan can never end this fear-based world because it is the thought system that created the fear in the first place. Your world of provisional reality will change through you only when you decide to freely follow the voice for love.

God's plan is simple. You are always free to save yourself and have the power to do so. Within your mind, God has placed a homing device, your personal GPS system that will lead you back to your Father's house, your true home. This voice of the Holy Spirit resides within your big S Self's mind and cannot be lost. It is your decision-maker who is constantly free to choose which channel you will access and follow.

God, being unconditional love, does not force you to follow your big "S' Self's internal guidance system. Instead, this guidance system only leads through love. God does not judge your path or your decisions to play on the game board of egoic illusions. Instead, God only sanctifies, protects and blesses your journey. You are always free to return to your rightful home whenever you decide to do so based upon your own free will.

What prevents you from making such a simple and seemingly obvious decision? It is your belief that your ego's plans for your happiness and its judgments about your littleness are correct. If you are to hear the Voice for God's Word today, you need to silence the voice that argues for its rightness over your happiness.

Your ego is a big judging machine. It is your ego's judgments about you and your brother's imperfections that hide and prevents you from seeking the truth about your big "S" Self. Your ego justifies your need to continue to hold grievances against your brother and yourself. This prevents you from forgiving and being forgiven for your ego does not believe that what you give, you will receive.

If your world of provisional reality is to change, you must stop judging and start listening to the voice for the Holy Spirit which is also the voice for God and your big "S" Self. They are the only voice for freedom and the peace that you seek. They are united in will and purpose with no separation nor division in the single Mind of the Father and the Son.

Question: What is the biggest obstacle that stops you from following God's plan for your salvation?

LESSON 126

All that I give is given to myself.

W-126.1.Today's idea **that all that I give is given to myself is** completely alien to the ego and the thinking of the **fear-based** world **of the ego**. Today's idea **that all that I give is given to myself** is crucial to the thought reversal that this course will bring about. 2 If you believed this statement **that all that I give is given to myself is true**, there would be no problem in complete forgiveness, certainty of goal, and sure direction. 3 **If you believed this statement that all that I give is given to myself is true**, you would understand the means by which salvation comes to you, and would not hesitate to use **this statement as the means for your salvation** now.

W-126.2.Let us consider what you do believe, in place of this idea **that all that I give is given to myself**. 2 It seems to you that other people are apart from you, and able to behave in ways which have no bearing on your thoughts, nor **your behavior has any bearing** on their **thoughts**. 3 Therefore, your attitudes have no effect on them, and their appeals for help are not in any way related to your own **appeals for help**. 4 You further think that they can sin without affecting your perception of yourself, while you can judge their sin, and yet remain apart from **your ego's** condemnation **of them** and at peace **with yourself**.

W-126.3.**Your ego currently believes that** when you "forgive" a sin, there is no gain to you directly. 2 You give charity to one unworthy, merely to point out that you are better, on a higher plane than he whom you forgive. 3 He **whom you forgive** has not earned your charitable tolerance, which you bestow on one unworthy of the gift, because his sins have lowered him **whom you forgive** beneath a true equality with you. 4 He **whom you forgive** has no claim on your forgiveness. 5 **Your forgiveness** holds out a gift to him, but hardly **a gift** to yourself.

W-126.4.Thus **your ego currently believes that** forgiveness is basically unsound; a charitable whim, benevolent yet undeserved, a gift bestowed at times, at other times withheld. 2 **Your ego currently believes that forgiveness is** unmerited **and that** withholding **forgiveness** is just; nor **does your ego believe it** is fair that you should suffer when **forgiveness** is withheld. 3 **Your ego currently believes that** the sin that you forgive is not your own. 4 Someone apart from you committed **the sin**. 5 And if you then are gracious unto him **who sinned** by giving him **your forgiveness that** he does not deserve, the gift is no more yours than was his sin.

W-126.5.If **what your ego believes is** true, forgiveness has no grounds on which to rest dependably and sure. 2 **Egoic forgiveness** is an eccentricity, in which you sometimes choose to give indulgently **to** an undeserved reprieve. 3 Yet **with egoic forgiveness, it** remains your right to let the sinner not escape the justified repayment for his sin. 4 Think you the Lord of Heaven would allow the world's salvation to depend on this **eccentricity and your ego's whim**? 5 Would not **the Lord of Heaven's** care for you be small indeed, if your salvation rested on a whim?

W-126.6.You do not **currently** understand **true** forgiveness. 2 As you **currently see egoic forgiveness,** it is but a check upon overt attack, without requiring correction in your mind. 3 **As you currently see egoic forgiveness,** it cannot give you peace as you perceive **peace**. 4 **As you currently see egoic forgiveness,** it is not a means for your release from what you see in someone other than yourself. 5 **As you currently see egoic forgiveness,** it has no power to restore your unity with him **whom your ego believes has sinned** to your awareness **of his and your big "S" Self**. 6 **Egoic forgiveness** is not what God intended **true forgiveness** to be for you.

W-126.7.Not having given **God's Son** the gift He asks of you, you cannot recognize **God's Son's** gifts, and think He has not given **the gift of salvation back** to you. 2 Yet would **God's Son** ask you for a gift unless **the gift** was for you? 3 Could **God's Son** be satisfied with empty gestures, and evaluate such petty gifts as worthy of **God's** Son? 4 Salvation is a better gift than this. 5 And true forgiveness, as the means by which **salvation** is attained. **True forgiveness** must heal the **split** mind that gives **true forgiveness**, for giving is receiving. 6 What remains as unreceived has not been given, but what has been given must have been received.

W-126.8.Today we try to understand the truth that giver and receiver are the same. 2 You will need help to make this meaningful, because **the truth that giver and receiver are the same** is so alien to the **ego's thought system** to which you are accustomed. 3 But the Help you need **from the Holy Spirit** is there. 4 Give **the Holy Spirit** your faith today, and ask **the Holy Spirit** that He share your practicing in truth today **that giver and receiver are the same**. 5 And if you only catch a tiny glimpse of the release that lies in the idea we practice for today **that giver and receiver are the same and therefore, all that you give is given to yourself**, this is a day of glory for the world.

W-126.9.Give fifteen minutes twice today to the attempt to understand today's idea **that all that you give is given to yourself**. 2 **That all that I give is given to myself** is the thought by which forgiveness takes its proper place in your priorities. 3 **That giver and receiver are the same and therefore, all that you give is given to yourself** is the thought that will release your mind from every bar to what **true** forgiveness means, and let you realize **true forgiveness's** worth to you.

W-126.10.In silence, close your eyes upon the world that does not understand **true** forgiveness, and seek sanctuary in the quiet place where thoughts are changed and false beliefs laid by. 2 Repeat today's idea **that all I give is given to myself**, and ask for help in understanding what **true forgiveness** really means. 3 Be willing to be taught. 4 Be glad to hear the Voice of truth and healing speak to you, and you will understand the words **the Holy Spirit** speaks, and recognize **the Holy Spirit** speaks your words **of your big "S" Self** to you.

W-126.11.As often as you can, remind yourself you have a goal today **to understand that all you give is given to yourself** ; an aim which makes this day of special value to yourself and all your brothers. 2 Do not let your mind forget this goal **of understanding that all you give is given to yourself** for long, but tell yourself:
3 All that I give is given to myself. 4 The Help I need to learn that this is true is with me now. 5 And I will trust in **the Holy Spirit.**
6 Then spend a quiet moment, opening your mind to **the Holy Spirit's** correction and **the Holy Spirit's** Love. 7 And what you hear of **the Holy Spirit** you will believe, for what **the Holy Spirit** gives will be received by you.

Notes to Lesson #126

All that I give is given to myself.

Yesterday, we ended the session by asking you this question, what is your biggest obstacle that stops you from following God's plan for your salvation?

Today's workbook lesson provides what ACIM describes as a critical idea to accept if you are to escape the grip of the ego's fear-based thought system.

The idea that all that I give is given to myself is so alien to the thinking of both our ego and the fear-based world that we tend to dismiss this idea as a fallacy. Yet we are told that the acceptance of this idea is critical if we are to end the nightmare that results from our split mind's belief that minds are not joined but instead separate.

We are taught that our world is not a reflection of our thinking. We have been brought up to believe that our experiences are the result of outside forces and that our beliefs follow logically from those experiences.

The first fifty workbook lessons were designed to chip away at our belief that what our physical senses observe is the proper interpretation of reality. Instead, our physical senses are mere thought confirmation devices for our existing beliefs.

Our mind and its thoughts are the source of all our experiences. This idea that the world is our own private world of individuated perception differs radically from what the mass collective consciousness of this planet believes and teaches. Both psychologists and physiologists are confirming through scientific research that what we perceive to be objective reality is actually a pliable canvas that reflects our mind's viewpoint. It is our beliefs that color our world.

Your world is a world of perception, not of fact or reality. It only appears real to the mind of the perceiver. Change your beliefs and you change your world. This is why ACIM advises that you do not try to change your world. Instead, it suggests that you should change how you view your world and your world will automatically realign to your new way of thinking. God's plan for your salvation states that the world will change through you as you reject fear and adopt the thought system for only love. Only God's plan will work. There is no other means that can save the world except through a change in your own thinking.

Because the ego believes that we have separate minds, it teaches that another person's sin or thinking has no effect on your own mind and character. Our thoughts and our attitudes are perceived to behave independently from each other and that one party's perceptions, whether they be negative or positive thoughts, have no impact on the other party. Because of this belief in separation, our ego claims we can judge and condemn another without our actions affecting our own inner peace or how we perceive ourselves.

Because the ego does not believe that what you give is given to yourself, the ego's understanding of forgiveness is diametrically opposed to what true forgiveness is. Again, this lesson does not attempt to define what true forgiveness is. Instead, it explains why our egoic beliefs about forgiveness must be corrected if forgiveness is to become the means to bring salvation for yourself and your world.

Because the ego does not believe that giver and receiver are the same and therefore, that all you give is given to yourself, egoic forgiveness is believed to be a charitable gift that is neither earned nor deserved by the offending party. The giver receives nothing of value in return.

Egoic forgiveness is based on the idea that there are victims and victimizers and that being a body, you can attack and be attacked. Egoic forgiveness can only be bestowed by the victim of the crime. The victim has the right to grant or withhold forgiveness or demand retribution at their own discretion. Egoic forgiveness is based on the whim of the victim and we are taught that the withholding or the granting of forgiveness has no impact on the victim's own inner peace. This is because according to the ego, the giver and receiver are separate and minds are not related.

Since egoic forgiveness is charity and not deserved, you have the right to withhold forgiveness. If you do decide to grant forgiveness to the offending party, it is a demonstration of your moral superiority and actually proves and confirms the inequality that you believe exists between the parties involved. Because the ego believes that giver and receiver are separate, it claims that there is no benefit to you, the giver. Whether you choose to condemn or forgive another, your decision has no impact on your own inner peace.

Obviously, if giver and receiver are the same, the logical consequence of that fact would be that what you give would be truly given to yourself.

Earlier, we were told that the laws of God operate even in the world of egoic illusions; that when you forgive, you are forgiven for as you give you will receive.

Today's lesson that all that I give is given to myself reinforces God's Law and is instrumental in the thought reversal that this course is bringing about. Our ego cannot help us bring about this new paradigm for it is our ego that is the guardian of our fear-based thought system. This is why we need the help of the Holy Spirit to learn the truth that all that I give is given to myself. Ask for that help today and it will be given to you.

Question: Although true forgiveness has still not been defined, what do you believe true forgiveness must entail?

Question: If there are no victims and victimizers, what could true forgiveness be addressing or forgiving?

LESSON 127

There is no love but God's.

W-127.1.Perhaps you think that different kinds of love are possible. 2 Perhaps you think there is a kind of love for this, a kind **of love** for that; a way of loving one, another way of loving still another. 3 Love is one. 4 **Love** has no separate parts and no degrees; no kinds nor levels, no divergencies and no distinctions. 5 **Love** is like itself, unchanged throughout. 6 **Love** never alters with a person or a circumstance. 7 **Love** is the Heart of God, and also Love is **the Heart of God's** Son.

W-127.2.Love's meaning is obscure to anyone who thinks that love can change. 2 He **who does not understand that love is changeless** does not see that changing love must be impossible. 3 And thus he thinks that he can love at times, and hate at other times. 4 He **who does not understand that love is changeless** also thinks that love can be bestowed on one, and yet remain itself although **love** is withheld from others. 5 To believe these things of love is not to understand **love**. 6 If **love** could make such distinctions, **love** would have to judge between the righteous and the sinner, and perceive the Son of God in separate parts.

W-127.3.Love cannot judge. 2 As **love** is one itself, **love** looks on all as one. 3 **Love's** meaning lies in oneness. 4 And **love's meaning** must elude the mind that thinks of **love** as partial or in part. 5 There is no love but God's **love**, and all of love is **God's love**. 6 There is no other principle that rules where love is not. 7 Love is a law without an opposite. 8 **Love's** wholeness is the power holding everything as one. **Love is** the link between the Father and the Son. **It is love** which holds **the Father and the Son** both forever as the same.

W-127.4.No course whose purpose is to teach you to remember what you really are could fail to emphasize that there can never be a difference in what you really are **which is your big "S" Self** and what love is. 2 Love's meaning is your own **meaning**, and shared by God Himself. 3 For what you are, **which is only love,** is what God is. 4 There is no love but **God's love**, and what **God** is, is everything there is. 5 There is no limit placed upon **God,** Himself, and so are you, **your big "S" Self,** unlimited as well.

W-127.5.No law the **fear-based egoic** world obeys can help you grasp love's meaning. 2 **The laws that seem to govern this world are** what the world believes **and were** made **by the ego** to hide love's meaning, and to keep **the love of God** dark and secret. 3 There is not one principle the **fear-based egoic** world upholds but violates the truth of what **God's** love is, and what you, **your big "S" Self is** as well.

W-127.6.Seek not within the **fear-based egoic** world to find your **big "S"** Self. 2 Love is not found in darkness and in death. 3 Yet **love** is perfectly apparent to the eyes that see and ears that hear love's Voice. 4 Today we practice making free your mind of all the laws **of the egoic world that your split mind** thinks you must obey; of all the limits under which you live, and all the changes that you think are part of human destiny. 5 Today we take the largest single step this course requests in your advance towards **this course's** established goal **of reawakening you to the truth of your big "S" Self**.

W-127.7.If you achieve the faintest glimmering of what love means today, you have advanced in distance without measure and in time beyond the count of years to your release. 2 Let us together, then, be glad to give some time to God today, and understand there is no better use for time than **discovering what God's love means**.

W-127.8.For fifteen minutes twice today escape from every law **of your ego's world** in which you now believe. 2 Open your mind and rest. 3 The world that seems to hold you prisoner can be escaped by anyone who does not hold **the world of your ego** dear. 4 Withdraw all value you have placed upon **the world of your ego's** meager offerings and senseless gifts, and let the gift of God replace them all.

W-127.9.Call to your Father, certain that His Voice, **the Holy Spirit**, will answer. 2 **Your Father,** Himself has promised this **answer**. 3 And **Your Father,** Himself will place a spark of truth within your **big "S" Self's** mind wherever you give up a false belief, a dark illusion of your own **little "s" self's** reality and what love means **according to your ego**. 4 **The Holy Spirit** will shine through your **ego's** idle thoughts today, and help you understand the truth of **God's** love. 5 In loving gentleness **your Father** will abide with you, as you allow **God's** Voice to teach love's meaning to your clean and open mind. 6 And **the Holy Spirit** will bless the lesson with **God's** Love.

W-127.10.Today the legion of the future years of waiting for salvation disappears before the timelessness of what you learn. 2 Let us give thanks today that we are spared a future like the **fear-based** past. 3 Today we leave the **fear-based** past behind us, nevermore to be remembered. 4 And we raise our eyes upon a different present, where a future dawns unlike the **fear-based** past in every attribute.

W-127.11.The world in infancy is newly born. 2 And we will watch a **new loving world** grow in health and strength, to shed its blessing upon all who come to learn to cast aside the **fear-based** world they thought was made in hate to be love's enemy. 3 Now are they all made free, along with us. 4 Now are they all our brothers in God's Love.

W-127.12.We will remember **all our brothers** throughout the day, because we cannot leave a part of us outside our love if we would know our **big "S"** Self. 2 At least three times an hour think of **a brother or sister** who makes the journey with you, and who came to learn what you must learn. 3 And as he **or she** comes to mind, give **them** this message from your **big "S' Self:**

4 I bless you, brother, with the Love of God, which I would share with you. 5 For I would learn the joyous lesson that there is no love but God's and yours and mine and everyone's love.

Notes to Lesson #127

There is no love but God's.

This idea that there is no love but God's love is a difficult concept to grasp because it conflicts with traditional thought. We have been taught that there are numerous forms of love. Our philosophies abound about the many different types and stages of the human experience that our world refers to as love.

In the fear-based world of the ego, love is constantly changing. You can love someone today and hate them tomorrow or you can love someone and then withhold your love from another. Love appears to be in a constant state of flux. Ebbing and flowing with each emotional swing and change in our circumstance.

In the world of time and space, both change and opposites appear to exist and be the reality of our world. After all, time is the measure of change and the ego tells us that opposites are required if we are to learn through the process of differentiation. If there was only one uniform substance of which we were all part, what would there be for us to learn? We would be that one and to be is to know.

The world we perceive was not created by God. Rather, it is the product of our mind's own inner imagination. Our mind's belief system colors the world that we observe with our physical senses. Our physical senses are mere thought confirmation devices to prove the correctness of our mind's point of view.

This world is the product of our egoic fear-based belief system. It is based on the ego's belief in lack, limitation and separation. All the laws of this world are based on the belief in separation. Separation implies there is something you are not and differences and opposites now become our provisional reality.

Because of this belief in separation, there is not one principle or law that our fear-based world follows that does not violate the truth of what God's love is. This belief in separation hides the truth of our big "S" Self. Our current world reflects the mass collective consciousness of the split mind that believes in lack, limitation and separation. Our belief in separation is the source of all fear in this world.

In this world, there appears to be two emotions, love and its opposite, fear. Fear is false evidence appearing real. Fear arises out of our ego's belief that we are separate and different from our Source. Although we are only love, we cannot expect to find our big "S" Self in a world that arose from our belief in separation.

Because we believe that we are separate autonomous beings, we believe that our continued survival is contingent on obtaining the limited resources that we perceive to be outside our mind's control. We value these outside resources as something that we need for our survival. It is this valuing and acquiring of these supposed limited resources that imprison us in our fear-based thought system and hide the unlimited nature of our big "S" Self. The transient things of this world become our ego's idols that replace God's love.

The ego believes that those who give us what we need love us and those who fail to comply with our ego's plans for our happiness hate us. It is important to note that when you follow the laws of this world, you will be incapable of recognizing what true love is. Due to your belief in separation, you will always question the motives of others.

Since our egoic world teaches that you only give to get, each party believes everyone must also be following that same principle. Because of this limiting belief, even if you were the recipient of true unconditional love, you would fail to perceive its presence. Because of this world's law that each only gives to get, we believe love's flow is contingent upon the good will of the giver or the recipient's ability to earn love.

When you believe love can change, you become incapable of accepting the flow of the God's unconditional love into your life. Within your own mind, you replace God's unconditional love with the notion that love must be earned. A God of conditional love must be a judgmental god. Egoic conditional love is based on fear and is not real love. It was made to replace God's unconditional love with fear and specialness.

Conditional love is based on a special bartering relationship between two parties. Each gives to the other with the expectation of some equivalent or greater return. Each is seeking a good deal. The special relationship is the embodiment of the give to get principle that rules the world. Being separate from God, our Source, our ego tells us that we need special alliances with other vulnerable parties if we are to survive.

Yet, God's love never alters based on the person or circumstance. It is changeless and does not judge. God's love flows endlessly and is never withheld from anyone. The Oneness of God knows everything is perfect, whole and complete. A Oneness of All That Is has no opposites. God's love is the only law. In the real world there are no alternate realities since all egoic fantasies are equally unreal. There is no difference between what you are and God is since only love is real for love is everything.

In the next few lessons, we will continue to explore the interconnection between love, the egoic world of provisional reality and forgiveness.

Question: If you believed love could be earned, how would you ever be sure you were the giver or recipient of unconditional love?

The world I see holds nothing that I want.

W-128.1.The **ego's fear-based** world you see holds nothing that you need to offer you; nothing that you can use in any way, nor anything at all that serves to give you joy. 2 Believe this thought **that the world I see holds nothing that I want,** and you are saved from years of misery, from countless disappointments, and from hopes that turn to bitter ashes of despair. 3 No one but must accept this thought **that the world I see holds nothing that I want** as true if he would leave the **ego's fear-based** world behind and soar beyond this world's petty scope and little ways.

W-128.2.Each thing you value here is but a chain that binds you to the **ego's fear-based** world, and each thing you value of this world will serve no other end but **to bind you to** this world. 2 For everything must serve the purpose you have given it, until you see a different purpose there. 3 The only purpose worthy of your mind this world contains is that you pass **this world** by and **place no value upon this world. By not valuing this world, you will not be** delaying **your journey of reawakening due to erroneously** perceiving some hope where there is none. 4 Be you deceived no more **by the promises of your ego's plan for your salvation and happiness.** 5 The **ego's fear-based** world you see holds nothing that you want.

W-128.3.Escape today the chains you place upon your **split** mind when you perceive salvation here **in this world**. 2 For what you value you make part of you as you perceive yourself. 3 All things **your ego** seeks to make your value greater in your sight limits you further, hides your worth **of your big "S" Self** from you, and adds another bar across the door that leads to true awareness of your **big "S"** Self.

W-128.4.Let nothing that relates to body thoughts delay your progress to salvation, nor permit temptation to believe the world holds anything you want to hold you back. 2 Nothing is here **in this world** to cherish. 3 Nothing here **in this world** is worth one instant of delay and pain; **nothing here is worth** one moment of uncertainty and doubt. 4 The worthless offer nothing. 5 Certainty of worth cannot be found in worthlessness.

W-128.5.Today we practice letting go all thought of values we have given to the world **of the ego**. 2 We leave **the world of the ego** free of the purposes we gave its aspects and its phases and its dreams. 3 We hold **the world of the ego** purposeless within our minds, and loosen **this world** from all we wish it were. 4 Thus do we lift the chains that bar the door to freedom from the world, and go beyond all little values and diminished goals **that the ego has placed upon this world.**

W-128.6.Pause and be still a little while, and see how far you rise above the world, when you release your mind from chains and let **your mind** seek the level where it finds itself at home **as your big "S" Self** . 2 **Your big "S" Self's mind** will be grateful to be free a while. 3 **Your big "S" Self's mind** knows where it belongs. 4 But free its wings, and **your big "S" Self's mind** will fly in sureness and in joy to join its holy purpose. 5 Let **your big "S" Self's mind** rest in its Creator, there to be restored to sanity, to freedom and to love.

W-128.7.Give **your big "S" Self's mind** ten minutes rest three times today. 2 And when your eyes are opened afterwards, you will not value anything you see as much as when you looked at **those things** before. 3 Your whole perspective on the world will shift by just a little, every time you let your mind escape its chains **of valuing the worthless**. 4 The world is not where it belongs. 5 And you, **your big "S" Self,** belong where **the real world** would be, and where **the real world** goes to rest when you release **the real world** from the world **of your ego's erroneous beliefs and values**. 6 Your Guide, **the Holy Spirit**, is sure. 7 Open your mind to **the Holy Spirit**. 8 Be still and rest.

W-128.8.Protect your mind throughout the day as well. 2 And when you think you see some value in an aspect or an image of the **egoic** world, refuse to lay this chain **of limitation** upon your mind, but tell yourself with quiet certainty:
3 This **item of the world that my ego values** will not tempt me to delay myself **in my journey of reawakening to my big "S" Self.** 4 The **ego's** world I see holds nothing that I want.

Notes to Lesson #128

The world I see holds nothing that I want.

It is important to realize that the world you see holds nothing that is of any value for your current or future happiness or inner peace. This world provides nothing that can make you joyous or happy since your mind, not the outside world, is the source of your experiences. By the same token, this world should not be valued as a place that allows you to earn some future reward.

But this is far from what we have been taught to expect from this world.

Instead, we have generally been taught either one of two viewpoints.

One prevalent viewpoint is that happiness is something that comes from outside us. Most have been taught that there is something outside yourself that you need to make you happy. This belief leads to a great deal of conflict, struggle and pain as members argue over the correctness of their own ego's plan for world happiness.

Grievances arise any time another fails to comply with someone's predetermined performance standards that were supposedly required to make the world happy. Each party is in a constant battle for the rightness of their plan in their quests to manipulate the outside forces that they perceive are needed to make them safe and happy.

This viewpoint binds us to the belief that something outside ourselves is responsible for our happiness. Happiness is something that happens to us, rather than through us. This viewpoint disempowers us while supporting our ego's belief in lack, limitation and separation. Our ego's plan fails to recognize that our mind is the source for our happiness. We are told to seek for happiness, love and peace where it cannot be found. We fail to realize our world is a mere reflection of the values of our own mind.

This world was designed to provide false evidence to support your ego's belief in your littleness. When you value the things of this world, you bind yourself to your belief that you are your body. You accept the limitations that come with the physical body and argue for your own littleness. The body is a neutral communication device that holds a place on the game board of time and space. It is not who you are. By identifying with the body's needs as if they were your own needs, you hide and obscure your true big "S" Self's identity.

The second viewpoint that is prevalent in our society is that this world is a place where we come to suffer, do penance, be judged and perhaps earn our way to heaven or some future reward. In this case, it would seem as if the world would not be something that you would value or want. But that is not really the case. In this warped view of reality, your ego has transformed a God of unconditional love into a judgmental God.

The world of the ego now becomes a proving ground in which you need to do something to earn God's favorable judgment so that you can be happy. In this case, your future happiness rests on your ability to change your world to comply with how your ego believes God would want the world to be. Correcting the world becomes your function and your duty. This duty gives you the right to impose your will upon another in an effort to fix, change, control, protect and impress in the name of both God and love. We value the world as a place where we can earn God's love back.

The second viewpoint reinforces the erroneous belief that God's love is something that must be earned and can be lost. It maintains our ego's belief in sin, guilt and separation. But most of all, it confirms that our ego is right and that God's love is not unconditional and that our fear of God is justified, warranted and real.

This viewpoint that love can or must be earned is a major barrier in our willingness to accept God's plan for salvation. We see God as someone to fear. This fear becomes a major stumbling block in our willingness to accept the simplicity of God's plan for salvation. God's plan states that our egos need do nothing to earn our divine inheritance. It was freely given and never could be lost. We simply are asked to freely accept the At-One-Ment, or truth about ourselves. But accepting this truth is impossible as long as you believe this world could be either the source for your happiness or the place where you earn your happiness.

This world is not a place that can make you happy or rob you of your inner peace. It is not a place where you come to do penance, earn some heavenly reward or make God love you. This world is not a place. It is an illusion that only appears to exist within your own state of mind. When you no longer value this world, the illusion will also disappear.

Question : Although valuing the things of this world is often seen as an impediment to spiritual growth, can you understand that your belief that the world is a place where you earn some reward actually chains you to your fear-based thought system and the belief that God's love is not unconditional?

Beyond this world there is a world I want.

W-129.1.Beyond this world there is a world I want **is the thought that follows from the one we practiced yesterday. Yesterday's lesson was the world I see holds nothing that I want. 2** You cannot stop with the idea the world **you see** is worthless, for unless you see that there is something else to hope for, you will only be depressed **by the idea of a worthless world. 3** Our emphasis is not on giving up the world, but on exchanging **a worthless world** for **a world that** is far more satisfying, filled with joy, and capable of offering you peace. 4 Think you this world **created from a fear-based thought system** can offer that **peace** to you?

W-129.2.It might be worth a little time to think once more about the value of this world. 2 Perhaps you will concede there is no loss in letting go all thought of value here. 3 The world you see **that was created from a fear-based thought system** is merciless indeed, unstable, cruel, unconcerned with you, quick to avenge and pitiless with hate. 4 **The world the ego envisions** gives but to rescind, and takes away all things that you have cherished for a while. 5 No lasting love is found, for none is here **in the world of separation that the ego envisions.** 6 This is the world of time, where all things end.

W-129.3.Is it a loss to find a world instead where losing is impossible; where love endures forever, hate cannot exist and vengeance has no meaning? 2 Is it loss to find all things you really want, and know **that all you really want** has no ending and they will remain exactly as you want them throughout time? 3 Yet even **all you perceive to be what you really want** will be exchanged at last for what we cannot speak of, for you go from there to where words fail entirely, into a silence where the language is unspoken and yet surely understood.

W-129.4.Communication, unambiguous and plain as day, remains unlimited for all eternity. 2 And God Himself speaks to His Son, as His Son speaks to **God**. 3 Their language has no words, for what **God and Son** say cannot be symbolized. 4 Their knowledge is direct and wholly shared and wholly one. 5 How far away from this are you **and your little "s" self** who stay bound to this world **of lack, limitation and fear.** 6 And yet how near are you, when you exchange **the world of your little "s" self** for the world **that your big "S" Self really** wants.

W-129.5.Now is the last step certain; now you stand an instant's space away from timelessness. 2 Here can you but look forward, never back to see again the **fear-based** world **of your little "s" self that** you do not want. 3 Here is the **real** world that comes to take its place, as you unbind your **once split** mind from **valuing** the little things the **fear-based** world **of your ego** set forth to keep you prisoner. 4 Value not **anything from your ego's world** and **these valueless things** will disappear. 5 Esteem **something from your ego's world**, and **those things** will seem real to you.

W-129.6.Such is the choice. **You get to decide what you will value.** 2 What loss can be for you in choosing not to value nothingness? 3 This **fear-based** world **of your ego** holds nothing that you really want, but what you choose instead **your big "S" Self** wants indeed! 4 Let **what your big "S" Self wants** be given you today. 5 **The real world** waits but for your choosing it, to take the place of all the things **your ego** seeks but **your big "S" Self** does not want.

W-129.7.Practice your willingness to make this change **in what you value for** ten minutes in the morning and at night, and once more in between. 2 Begin with this:
3 Beyond this world there is a world I want. 4 I choose to see that world instead of this **world of egoic littleness**, for here **in this false world of the ego** is nothing that I really want.
5 Then close your eyes upon the **ego's** world you see, and in the silent darkness watch the lights that are not of this world light one by one, until where one begins another ends loses all meaning as **the lights of Heaven** blend in one.

W-129.8.Today the lights of Heaven bend to you, to shine upon your eyelids as you rest beyond the world of darkness. 2 Here is light your eyes can not behold. 3 And yet your mind can see **the lights of Heaven** plainly, and can understand. 4 A day of grace is given you today, and we give thanks. 5 This day we realize that **the ego's world that** you feared to lose was **valueless and** only loss.

W-129.9.Now do we understand there is no loss **in giving up the ego's world born from the belief in separation.** 2 For we have seen its opposite at last, and we are grateful that the choice is made **for seeing that new world with the vision of Christ.** 3 Remember your decision hourly, and take a moment to confirm your choice by laying by whatever **egoic** thoughts you have, and dwelling briefly only upon this:
4 The **ego's** world I see holds nothing that I want.
5 Beyond this **false** world **of separation** there is a **real** world I want.

Notes to Lesson #129

Beyond this world there is a world I want.

It is important to realize that beyond the fear-based world that is your current provisional reality, there is a world that your big "S" Self truly wants. This is a world that your big "S" Self would recognize as a more appropriate home for the Son of God.

If our current world holds nothing that you currently want and there was no hope of a better tomorrow, how would that help your present state of mind?

Unless there was a better alternative or some hope looming on the horizon, such a realization that this world offers nothing that you want would only leave you depressed. You would be forever trapped in a meaninglessness world within an unhappy existence. This idea would not serve to encourage, empower or advance your pursuit of a new paradigm of who you really are.

Today's lesson offers us the promise of a better future. You need this second idea to encourage you to pursue a new course of action, to question the validity of your old fear-based thought system and to adopt a new plan.

Beyond this world there is a world I want, encourages you to reframe the purpose of what this world is for. Instead of your world being a place to earn God's love or postpone God's judgment, it can become your playschool for learning, remembering, demonstrating and accepting the truth about who you really are.

Your provisional reality can become a place in which you exchange time for eternity. While yesterday's idea, this world holds nothing that you want, by itself may be seen as depressing, today's idea that there is something better is a source for hope and inspiration. The emphasis now shifts from no longer having to give up the little this world offers but rather exchange your world of provisional reality to better align with a real world that does provide joy, satisfaction, happiness and peace.

What you value, you make real. When you follow the egoic thought system of lack, limitation and separation, you are actually making a choice to value fear. The result is the fear-based world that you currently perceive becomes your provisional reality. But what thought system you choose to follow is a choice.

When you follow the guidance of the Holy Spirit, you value the choice for love. When you stop valuing your egoic need to judge this world, you give up nothing but the fear that arose from your belief in lack, limitation and separation. These items are not anything that you really want.

Fear offers nothing to be prized. By valuing forgiveness, love, oneness and unity, you replace your egoic fear-based world with a world that better aligns with the truth. You start becoming a co-creator with God.

Beyond this world of separation is the real world that you share with the Mind of God. That is the world that you want.

Question: When you follow the thought system of the Holy Spirit, are you experiencing the real world or just a happier dream that better aligns with the truth?

LESSON 130

It is impossible to see two worlds.

W-130.1.Perception is consistent. 2 What you see reflects your thinking. 3 And your thinking but reflects your choice of what you want to see. 4 Your values are determiners of **what you want to see,** for what you value you must want to see, believing what you see is really there. 5 No one can see a world his mind has not accorded value. 6 And no one can fail to look upon what he believes he wants **and therefore what he values**.

W-130.2.Yet who can really hate and love at once? 2 Who can desire what he does not want to have reality? 3 And who can choose to see a **loving** world of which he is afraid? 4 Fear must make blind, for **fear's** weapon is: That which you fear to see you cannot see. 5 Love and perception thus go hand in hand, but fear obscures in darkness what is there **which is only love**.

W-130.3.What, then, can fear project upon the world? 2 What can be seen in darkness that is real? 3 **The** truth **of love's reality** is eclipsed by fear, and what remains is but imagined **by the fears of the split mind**. 4 Yet what can be real in blind imaginings of panic born **out of fear? Fear's imaginings are unreal.** 5 What would you want that **fear's images are** shown to you? 6 What would you wish to keep in such a **fearful** dream **that is unreal**?

W-130.4.Fear has made everything you think you see. 2 **Fear has made** all separation, all distinctions, and the multitude of differences you believe make up the **fear-based** world **you perceive as your reality.** 3 **Separation, distinction and difference** are not there. 4 Love's enemy, **fear,** has made **these illusions** up. 5 Yet love can have no enemy, and **so these illusions that your split mind falsely perceives to be real** have no cause, no being and no consequence. 6 **These illusions that your split mind falsely perceives** can be valued, but remain unreal. 7 **These illusions that your split mind falsely perceives** can be sought, but they cannot be found. 8 Today we will not seek for **these illusions that your split mind falsely perceives,** nor waste this day in seeking what cannot be found.

W-130.5.It is impossible to see two worlds which have no overlap of any kind. 2 Seek for the **unreal fearful world and** the other, **a real loving world** disappears. 3 But **only** one **world** remains. 4 **An unreal fearful world or loving real world** are the range of choice beyond which your decision cannot go. 5 The real and the unreal are all there are to choose between, and nothing more than these.

W-130.6.Today we will attempt no compromise where none is possible. 2 The world you see is proof you have already made a choice as all-embracing as its opposite **choice.** 3 What we would learn today is more than just the lesson that you cannot see two worlds. 4 It also teaches that the **fearful or loving world** you see is quite consistent from the point of view from which you see **the world, either from fear or love.** 5 It is all **one** piece because **what you see** stems from one emotion, either **love or fear,** and **what you see** reflects **the one emotion that is the source** in everything you see.

W-130.7.Six times today, in thanks and gratitude, we gladly give five minutes to the thought that **it is impossible to see two worlds** which ends all compromise and doubt, and goes beyond them all as one. 2 We will not make a thousand meaningless distinctions, nor attempt to bring with us a little part of unreality, as we devote our minds to finding only what is real.

W-130.8.Begin your searching for the **real** world **of love** by asking for a strength beyond your own **little "s" self,** and recognizing what it is you seek. 2 You do not want illusions. 3 And you come to these five minutes emptying your hands of all the petty treasures of this **fearful unreal** world. 4 You wait for God to help you, as you say:
5 It is impossible to see two worlds. 6 Let me accept the strength God offers me and see no value in this **unreal** world, that I may find my freedom and deliverance **from my fears.**

W-130.9.God will be there. 2 For you have called upon the great unfailing power which will take this giant step with you in gratitude. 3 Nor will you fail to see **God's** thanks expressed in tangible perception and in truth. 4 You will not doubt what you will look upon, for though **what you will look upon** is perception, it is not the kind of seeing that your eyes alone have ever seen before. 5 And you will know God's strength upheld you as you made this choice.

W-130.10.Dismiss temptation easily today whenever **temptations** arise, merely by remembering the limits of your choice. 2 The unreal or the real, the false or true is what you see and only what you see. 3 Perception is consistent with your choice, and hell or Heaven comes to you as one.

W-130.11.Accept a little part of hell as real, and you have damned your eyes and cursed your sight, and what you will behold is hell indeed. 2 Yet the release of Heaven still remains within your range of choice, to take the place of everything that hell would show to you. 3 All you need say to any part of hell, whatever form **hell** takes, is simply this:
4 It is impossible to see two worlds. 5 I seek my freedom and deliverance, and this is not a part of what I want.

Notes to Lesson #130

It is impossible to see two worlds.

This lesson is talking about the realm of perception, not knowledge. Time belongs to the realm of perception. Time is the measure of change and perception is the world of the changeable. As your beliefs about your world change your perception or how you see your world must adjust to support those new beliefs.

Time is also a world of individuated private perception. Each person lives in their own private world that reflects their own unique set of beliefs. Based on the similarity of each party's beliefs, the world that each perceives will have some common overlap.

In the world of perception, differentiation is apparent. There appears to be an observer and something outside itself to observe. In the world of perception, differentiation is normally understood to imply separation, rather than various aspects of one unified whole. The world of knowledge is beyond the illusion of time and is changeless and therefore, real. The world of knowledge is the ultimate reality but is beyond the scope of this lesson. This lesson deals with perception and the world you perceive that surrounds you.

The laws of perception are stable. What you see is a reflection of your thinking and your values. What you see reflects the choices that you make within your own mind. What you value determines what you will call into your conscious awareness. It is this awareness that you will believe to be the reality of your world. No one sees a world that is misaligned with what he values and no one can fail to look upon what he wants.

In this world of perception there are two emotions, love and fear. Each emotion generates a world that can be observed within the mind. Love's world supports the return to knowledge. Fear blocks and obscures what would be observed through the eyes of love. Perception is consistent and follows the laws related to valuing. Because of this, you cannot see what you fear. Fear blinds you to the reality of love's presence and obscures and hides the light with fear's darkness.

Fear is false evidence appearing real. Fear is the tool that our ego uses to project its judgments upon the world. Fear's projections block the truth of love's presence. Fear has made everything you think you see. All thoughts of separation, all distinctions and the billions of differences that you believe make up the world are projected from those fears. These projections are not real but do appear to exist within the mind of the dreamer who believes that God judges them and that love must be earned.

These fear-based egoic distinctions and differences are illusions that block the truth from being recognized by your own mind. Love has no opposites and no enemies. Yet, these fear based beliefs can be valued even though they have no effect upon the truth that they obscure. As long as you value those fear-based beliefs, they will continue to block the truth that only love is real.

The egoic world of lack, limitation and separation is consistent with the ego's fear-based point of view that you are limited, God's love is conditional, and that love must be earned. The ego does not understand what true love is and therefore argues that you should fear God. The law of valuing states that what you fear, you cannot see. When you fear God, you will value the fear-based world that you perceive.

The world is a product of your mind and the thought system that you choose to value and follow. Fear and love are opposites and are incompatible. You cannot be under the control of both emotions at the same time. From each thought system you will observe a different world. When you follow the thought system for love, you will perceive a world that aligns with the truth that only love is real. When you follow the thought system for fear, you will observe an unreal world that obscures the truth of who you, God and the world really are.

Question: Perception is based on the law of valuing and fear blinding your mind. What you fear, you cannot see. If you have been brainwashed into believing you are a sinner, that God is something to fear, that love is conditional or must be earned, can you understand why you would value the ego's illusion of lack, limitation and separation?

Since it is impossible to see two worlds, you must change your beliefs about yourself, God and what love is if your ego's fear-based world is to disappear.

LESSON 131

No one can fail who seeks to reach the truth.

W-131.1.Failure is all about you while you seek for **your ego's** goals that cannot be achieved. 2 You look for permanence in the impermanent, for love where there is none, for safety in the midst of danger; immortality within the darkness of the dream of death. 3 Who could succeed where contradiction is the setting of his searching, and the **unreal the** place to which he comes to find stability?

W-131.2.Goals that are meaningless are not attained. 2 There is no way to reach **meaningless goals**, for the means by which you strive for **meaningless goals** are meaningless as the **egoic goals** are. 3 Who can use such senseless means, and hope through **those senseless means** to gain in anything? 4 Where can **senseless means** lead? 5 And what could **senseless means** achieve that offers any hope of being real? 6 Pursuit of the imagined leads to death because it is the search for nothingness, and while **your ego claims to** seek for life you ask for death. 7 You look for safety and security, while in your heart you **actually** pray for danger and protection for the **ego's** little dream you made.

W-131.3.Yet searching is inevitable here **in the unreal world of time and space**. 2 For this **searching is what** you came **for**, and you will surely do the thing you came for. 3 But the world cannot dictate the goal for which you search unless you give **the world of your imagination the** power to do so. 4 Otherwise, you still are free to choose a goal that lies beyond the world **you imagine** and every worldly thought **of your little "s" self**. And **you still are free to choose a goal** that comes to you from an idea relinquished yet remembered **by your big "S" Self. An idea** old yet new; an echo of a heritage forgot, yet holding everything you really want.

W-131.4.Be glad that search you must. 2 Be glad as well to learn you search for Heaven, and must find the goal **of Heaven that** you really want. 3 No one can fail to want this goal **of Heaven and not** reach it in the end. 4 God's Son cannot seek vainly **for Heaven**, though **the split minded Son can** try to force, delay **and** deceive himself and think that it is hell **that the split minded** seek. 5 When **the split minded Son** is wrong, he finds correction. 6 When **the split minded Son** wanders off, he is led back to his appointed task **of remembering and finding Heaven.**

W-131.5.No one remains in hell, for no one can abandon his Creator, nor affect His **Creator's** perfect, timeless and unchanging Love. 2 You will find Heaven. 3 Everything you seek but **Heaven** will fall away. 4 Yet not because **the unreal egoic world of time has** been taken from you. 5 It will go because you do not want **the dream of separation.** 6 You will reach the goal **of Heaven that** you really want as certainly as God created you in sinlessness.

W-131.6.Why wait for Heaven? 2 **Heaven** is here today. 3 Time is the great illusion **that Heaven is in the** past or in the future. 4 Yet this **illusion that Heaven is not here in the present** cannot be if **Heaven** is where God wills His Son to be. 5 How could the Will of God be in the past, or yet to happen? 6 What **God** wills is now, without a past and wholly futureless. 7 **What God wills** is as far removed from time as is a tiny candle from a distant star, or what **your split mind's little "s' self** chose from what you, **your big "S" Self**, really want.

W-131.7.Heaven remains your one alternative to this strange **egoic** world you made and all its ways; its shifting patterns and uncertain goals, its painful pleasures and **the** tragic joys **your ego imagines this world offers.** 2 God made no contradictions **to Heaven**. 3 What denies its own **true** existence, **which is your split mind**, and attacks itself is not of **God**. 4 **God** did not make two minds, with Heaven as the glad effect of **your big "S" Self**, and earth **the little "s" self's** sorry outcome which is Heaven's opposite in every way.

W-131.8.God does not suffer conflict. 2 Nor is **God's** creation split in two. 3 How could it be **God's** Son could be in hell, when God Himself established **His Son** in Heaven? 4 Could **God's Son** lose what the Eternal Will **of God** has given **His Son** to be the **Son's** home forever? 5 Let us not try longer to impose an alien will upon God's single purpose. 6 **God's Son** is here **in Heaven** because **God** wills **it** to be, and what **God** wills is present now, beyond the reach of time.

W-131.9.Today we will not choose a paradox **of time** in place of truth. 2 How could the Son of God make time to take away the Will of God? 3 **With the illusion of time, God's Son** thus denies himself, and contradicts what has no opposite. 4 **God's Son** thinks he made a hell opposing Heaven, and believes that he abides in **the illusion of time that** does not exist, while Heaven is the place he cannot find.

W-131.10.Leave foolish thoughts like these **egoic illusions that you can change God's Will** behind today, and turn your mind to true ideas instead. 2 No one can fail who seeks to reach the truth, and it is truth we seek to reach today. 3 Three times today, we will devote ten minutes to this goal **of seeking the truth** and we will ask to see the rising of the real world to replace the foolish images that **our little "s" self** holds dear, with true ideas arising in the place of **egoic** thoughts that have no meaning, no effect, and neither source nor substance in the truth.

W-131.11.**The idea that no one can fail who seeks to reach the truth is what** we acknowledge as we start upon our practice periods. 2 Begin with this:
3 I ask to see a different world, and think a different kind of thought from those **my split egoic mind** made. 4 The world **of Heaven that** I seek I did not make alone, the **real** thoughts I want to think are not my own **thoughts of my little "s" self but**

rather the shared thoughts I think with the Mind of God.

5 For several minutes watch your mind and see, although your eyes are closed, the **ego's** senseless world you think is real. 6 Review the thoughts as well which are compatible with such **an unreal egoic** world, and which you think are true. 7 Then let **your egoic thoughts** go, and sink below them to the holy place where they can enter not. 8 There is a door beneath them in your mind, which you could not completely lock to hide what lies beyond **your egoic thoughts**.

W-131.12.Seek for that door **that lies beyond your egoic thoughts** and find it. 2 But before you try to open **that door that leads to truth**, remind yourself no one can fail who seeks to reach the truth. 3 And it is this request **that no one can fail who seeks to reach the truth** you make today. 4 Nothing but this has any meaning now; no other goal is valued now nor sought, nothing before this door you really want, and only **the truth that** lies past **your egoic thoughts** do you seek.

W-131.13.Put out your hand, and see how easily the door **for truth** swings open with your one intent to go beyond **your egoic thoughts and find that truth**. 2 Angels light the way, so that all darkness vanishes, and you are standing in a light so bright and clear that you can understand all things you see. 3 A tiny moment of surprise, perhaps, will make you pause before you realize the world you see before you in the light reflects the truth you knew, and did not quite forget in wandering away in egoic dreams **of lack, limitation and separation**.

W-131.14.You cannot fail today. 2 There walks with you the **Holy** Spirit Heaven sent you, that you might approach this door **to truth** some day, and through **the Holy Spirit's** aid slip effortlessly past **your egoic thoughts**, to the light. 3 Today that day has come. 4 Today God keeps His ancient promise to His holy Son, as does His Son remember his **promise to return** to **God, the Father**. 5 This is a day of gladness, for we come to the appointed time and place where you will find the goal of all your searching here, and all the seeking of the world, which end together as you pass beyond the door **to Truth**.

W-131.15.Remember often that today should be a time of special gladness, and refrain from dismal thoughts and meaningless **egoic** laments. 2 Salvation's time has come. 3 Today is set by Heaven itself to be a time of grace for you and for the world. 4 If you forget this happy fact, remind yourself with this:
5 Today I seek and find all that I want.
6 My single purpose **of finding the truth** offers **all that I want** to me.
7 No one can fail who seeks to reach the truth.

Notes to Lesson #131

No one can fail who seeks to reach the truth.

No one can fail who seeks to reach the truth but does the ego's thought system actually seek the truth?

The ego is the master of the imperfect question. Remember the example of the imperfect question:

Please answer this question with either yes or no. In the last 6 months have you finally stopped beating your spouse?

Either answer will result in your damnation.

Your ego does not seek the truth. Instead, your ego seeks proof that its false beliefs about God, you and love are real. The ego, then asks you to correct a problem that never existed. False assumptions cannot be made true so that your ego can solve a problem that never existed in the first place. The problem is a creation of your ego's own imagination. Yet, this is the goal your ego created for this world to solve.

The ego seeks to solve a problem that never existed by first making the problem real so that the ego can solve the fictitious problem. The ego's plan is insane. Why not correct the false assumptions and allow the fictitious problem to disappear into the nothingness from which it arose?

The Holy Spirit has a different approach to solving fictitious problems.

The Holy Spirit's plan simply questions the false assumptions and lets the truth reappear. The false problems that your ego's world was designed to solve now become the means for learning and accepting the truth about God, you and love.

The ego's goal of making the false true is useless and meaningless. Such a goal is impossible to achieve. By following your ego's wishes, you only delay, deceive and prevent your mind from seeking the correct solution that can recover the happiness and peace that is your true reality.

When you believe that the ego's plan can actually work, you mistake activity for progress towards your goal. You fail to realize that you are seeking happiness in a dream of separation that is an effect of the problem. By refusing to question the assumptions that your ego's dream rests upon, you remain trapped seeking answers within the dream of separation itself.

The dreamer's beliefs are the source of the problem. Correct the mind of the dreamer and the problem of the dream automatically fades away. You cannot solve the problem within the dream itself. Instead, go to the source of the problem which is your allegiance to your ego's thought system.

Time is the measure of change. But what is the egoic thought system trying to change?

The ego believes that paradise has been lost and needs to be recovered. The ego insists that Heaven is something that belongs in your past or in your future but is not obtainable based on your current state of affairs. Happiness or Heaven belong to those who are either perfect, whole and complete, or have earned their redemption and the ego does not see you in this light at all. Time is the grand illusion of the ego's mind. Time is an invention of the split mind and was designed to hide the reality that Heaven is the eternal and therefore is accessible here and now.

Your ego believes that God is not a God of unconditional love; that God did not create you, perfect, whole and complete; that you have sinned; that God has condemned you and now you must do penance to earn salvation back.

Because of this, the world your ego imagines is either a refuge from God's vengeance or a place in which you can earn your redemption in the future. Either viewpoint prevents you from the truth that God is unconditional love and has never judged you.

The truth is that you remain as God created you, perfect, whole and complete. God's Will is changeless and is unaffected by your ego's belief in lack, limitation and separation. No one can fail who seeks to reach the truth that you are the Effect of a God of unconditional love. Heaven is only one decision away.

Failure can only occur when you seek answers to the imperfect questions that your ego asks. It is impossible to make the false real. Your ego's goal is to seek and never find. Change your goal from seeking to make egoic illusions true to accepting God's Will of Heaven for you. God's Will is now without the past and wholly futureless. Time is a great illusion that Heaven belongs in your past or in the future and therefore, cannot be obtained in the now.

This is not the case. The ego and its dream world that attack and deny the true nature of God is not real. God did not create the dream of separation, your fears did.

God is only love and like begets like. You remain sinless as God created you. Your ego's belief that you have somehow lost your divine inheritance or changed God's will is impossible. Drop your egoic thought system and accept the Holy Spirit's thought system and you cannot fail. It is impossible to make the false true. It is equally impossible to make the true false. Seek only the truth and you cannot fail.

Question: Were you taught or do you believe that heaven belongs either to your past or future?

It is this belief that heaven does not belong in your now that prevents you from exchanging time for eternity.

LESSON 132

I loose the world from all I thought it was.

W-132.1.What keeps the world in chains but your **ego's** beliefs? 2 And what can save the world except your **big "S" Self**? 3 Belief is powerful indeed. 4 The thoughts you hold are mighty, and illusions are as strong in their effects as is the truth. 5 A madman thinks the world he sees is real, and does not doubt **his false vision of reality**. 6 Nor can he be swayed by questioning his **mad** thoughts' effects. 7 It is but when **the source for his mad thoughts which is his mind** is raised to question that the hope of freedom comes to him at last.

W-132.2.Yet is salvation easily achieved, for anyone is free to change his mind, and all his thoughts change with **his mind**. 2 Now the source of thought has shifted, for to change your mind means you have changed the source of all ideas you think or ever thought or yet will think. 3 **When you change your mind,** you free the past from what you thought before. 4 **When you change your mind,** you free the future from all ancient thoughts of seeking what you do not want to find.

W-132.3.**When you change your mind,** the present now remains the only time. 2 Here in the present is the world set free. 3 For as you let the past be lifted and release the future from your ancient fears, you find escape and give **that same escape from your past fears** to the world. 4 You have enslaved the world with all your fears, your doubts and miseries, your pain and tears; and all your sorrows press on **the world**, and keep the world a prisoner to your beliefs. 5 Death strikes **the world** everywhere because you hold the bitter thoughts of death within your mind.

W-132.4.The world is nothing in itself. 2 Your mind must give **the world** meaning. 3 And what you behold upon **the world** are your wishes, acted out so you can look on **your wishes** and think them real. 4 Perhaps you think you did not make the world, but came unwillingly to **a world that** was made already **and** hardly waiting for your thoughts to give **that world** meaning. 5 Yet in truth you found exactly what you looked for when you came **to this world**.

W-132.5.There is no world apart from what you wish, and herein lies your ultimate release. 2 Change but your mind on what you want to see, and all the world must change accordingly. 3 Ideas leave not their source **which is your mind**. 4 This central theme **that ideas do not leave their source** is often stated in the text, and must be borne in mind if you would understand the lesson for today **that you can free the world from all you thought it was by changing your mind.** 5 It is not pride which tells you that you made the world you see, and that **the world you see** changes as you change your mind.

W-132.6.But it is pride that argues you have come into a world **that is** quite separate from yourself, impervious to what you think, and quite apart from what you chance to think **your world** is. 2 There is no world! 3 **That there is no world that exists outside your own mind** is the central thought the course attempts to teach. 4 Not everyone is ready to accept **the idea that there is no world that exists outside your own mind** and each one must go as far as he can let himself be led along the road to **that** truth. 5 He will return and go still farther, or perhaps step back a while and then return again **but the truth remains that there is no world that exists outside your own mind**.

W-132.7.But healing is the gift of those who are prepared to learn there is no world **that exists outside your own mind**, and can accept the lesson **that there is no world** now. 2 Their readiness will bring the lesson **that there is no world** to them in some form which they can understand and recognize. 3 Some see **that there is no world** suddenly on point of death, and rise to teach **that this world is unreal**. 4 Others find **that this world is unreal** in experiences that are not of this world, which shows them that the world does not exist because what they behold must be the truth, and yet **these experiences** clearly contradict the world.

W-132.8.And some will find **this world is unreal from** this course, and in the exercises that we do today. 2 Today's idea **this world is unreal and that there is no world that exists outside your own mind** is true because the world does not exist. 3 And if **the world** is indeed your own imagining, then you can loose **or free the world you imagine** from all things you ever thought **your world** was by merely changing all the thoughts that gave **your world** these appearances. 4 The sick are healed as you let go all thoughts of sickness, and the dead arise when you let thoughts of life replace all thoughts you ever held of death.

W-132.9.A lesson earlier repeated once must now be stressed again, for it contains the firm foundation for today's idea **that you can loose or free the world from all you thought it was.** 2 You are as God created you. 3 There is no place where you can suffer, and no time that can bring change to your eternal state. 4 How can a world of time and place exist, if you remain as God created you?

W-132.10.What is the lesson for today except another way of saying that to know your **big "S"** Self is the salvation of the world? 2 To free the world from every kind of pain is but to change your mind about **the ideas you hold about** yourself. **You must choose between your ego's beliefs about your little "s" self or the Holy Spirit's truth about your big "S" Self.** 3 There is no world apart from your ideas **about yourself** because ideas leave not their source, and you maintain the world within your mind in thought.

W-132.11.Yet if you are as God created you, you cannot think apart from **God**, nor make what does not share **God's** timelessness and Love. 2 **Is God's timelessness and Love** inherent in the world you see? 3 Does **your mind** create like

God? 4 Unless **your mind creates like God's Mind** does, **what your mind imagines** is not real, and cannot be at all. 5 If **your Big "S" Self is** real, the world you see is false, for God's creation is unlike the world **your ego sees** in every way. 6 And as it was **God's** Thought by which you were created, so it is your thoughts **of your little "s" self that made your egoic world** and **it is your mind that** must set **your world** free, that you may know the Thoughts **of your big "S" Self that** you share with God.

W-132.12.Release the world! 2 Your real creations wait for this release to give you fatherhood, not of illusions, but as God in truth. 3 God shares His Fatherhood with you, **your big "S" Self**, who are His Son, for **God** makes no distinctions in what is Himself and what is still Himself. 4 What **God** creates is not apart from **God**, and nowhere does the Father end, the Son begin as something separate from **God**.

W-132.13.There is no world because it is a thought apart from God, and made to separate the Father and the Son, and break away a part of God Himself and thus destroy **God's** Wholeness. 2 Can a world which comes from this idea **of separation and destroying God's Wholeness** be real? 3 Can **separation** be anywhere? 4 Deny **the** illusions **of separation**, but accept the truth **of oneness**. 5 Deny you are a shadow briefly laid upon a dying world. 6 Release your mind **from your belief in separation** and you will look upon a world released.

W-132.14.Today our purpose is to free the world from all the idle thoughts we ever held about **the world within our egoic mind**, and about all living things we see upon **our world**. 2 They cannot be there. 3 No more can we **exist in an unreal world**. 4 For we are in the home our Father set for us, along with **all God created**. 5 And we who are as **God** created us would loose the world this day from every one of our **ego's** illusions, that we may be free.

W-132.15.Begin the fifteen-minute periods in which we practice twice today with this:
2 I who remain as God created me would loose **or free** the world from all I thought it was. 3 For I am real because the world **my little "s"** self imagined is not **real**, and I would know my own reality **as God created me, my big "S" Self.**
4 Then merely rest, alert but with no strain, and let your mind in quietness be changed so that the world is freed, along with you.

W-132.16.You need not realize that healing comes to many brothers far across the world, as well as to the ones you see nearby, as you send out these thoughts **you share with the Mind of God** to bless the world. 2 But you will sense your own release, although you may not fully understand as yet that you could never be released alone.

W-132.17.Throughout the day, increase the freedom sent through your ideas to all the world, and say whenever you are tempted to deny the power of your simple change of mind:
2 I loose the world from all I thought it was, and choose my own reality **as my big "S" Self** instead.

Notes to Lesson #132

I loose the world from all I thought it was.

This lesson, I loose, or free, the world from all I thought it was is a key lesson and a major tenant that the Course in Miracles is attempting to impart upon your conscious mind.

We have been taught that our beliefs are of little consequence in regard to our outside world. We are mere specks of dust in the cosmic scheme of things, and that our existence is of little or no consequence. Yet, this lesson tells us that it is our mind that gives the world all the meaning that it holds.

This idea has often been eluded to in the past. It follows logically from understanding how human perception works. It is our mind's beliefs that color all that we perceive. This is not a shocker as we have previously stated that our mind acts as a filter for our experiences and interprets our outside world to align with our current belief system.

But this lesson is saying a great deal more. The world is nothing in itself. There is no world apart from what you wish. There is no outside world that exists outside your own mind. It is your mind that creates and calls into your awareness all that you perceive as experiences. It all happens within, not outside, your own mind.

We have often mentioned that your world is a reflection of you. But this lesson unambiguously states that there is no world apart from what your mind chooses to experience. If you do not like what you see, your mind can create an alternate reality. When you change what you value your world will change.

This is why the Course in Miracles suggests that you do not try to change your world. Instead, change your mind about your world and your world must realign to fit your new beliefs and viewpoint. We are advised to fix the problem at its source rather than tinker with its effects. What you value is what you want and what you want is what you will experience.

Your mind is the source of your world. Ideas never leave their source and therefore, your world resides within your mind. Because of this, you have the ability to change your world by changing what you believe and value. This idea, if understood, accepted and implemented, offers the ultimate release from all pain, suffering and misery that you perceive in your world.

It is only your belief in lack, limitation and separation that keeps you chained to your fear-based world. Your mind's beliefs keep re-creating your past. The world is a reflection of you, but that reflection is simply the window that describes what you secretly value. Your mind is the powerhouse behind your world and illusions are as strong in their effect as is the truth. Your mind, not some illusionary outside world, is the source of your experiences. Although it is difficult to accept, your mind created and continues to create the world you claim you despise. The truth is that your ego would rather rule in hell than serve in heaven.

You are not a victim of outside forces that are beyond your control. You can pretend you are but there are no victims and there are no victimizers. Your mind is the master of your own disaster and therefore, the source for all hope and change for your world. This world is not real and is not part of the shared Mind of God. It exists only within the split mind that dreamed it.

Your mind is the script writer, director, editor and star of your own play. Time and space are products of your own imagination. It is your playhouse for what you value and why.

It is not pride to think that you created the world you perceive. Rather, it is pride and arrogance to think that you are separate and that your thoughts do not impact your world. Change your thoughts and your world must change accordingly.

You can either continue to let your egoic small "s" self pretend you are a powerless victim of your own dream or you could choose to reawaken the dreamer to the truth about your big "S" Self. As decision-maker, you can accept the truth of the power of your own mind, reclaim your divine inheritance and become the deliberate creator of your world.

Which will you choose?

Note: Although the idea that there is no world that exists outside your mind seems hard to believe, this is exactly what science currently declares to be the truth about our physical world.

Physiologists and brain research confirm that your mind is constantly creating the world that you see. The Heisenberg uncertainty principle states that human consciousness is needed to fix observable reality. Quantum physicists and string theorists assert that entire galaxies exist only because somewhere, at some time, some astronomer wanted to observe that galaxy.

If an astronomer's wish can create entire galaxies, is it that far-fetched to believe that there is no world that exists outside your own mind?

I will not value what is valueless.

W-133.1.Sometimes in teaching there is benefit, particularly after you have gone through what seems theoretical and far from what the student has already learned, to bring him back to practical concerns. 2 This we will do today. 3 We will not speak of lofty, world-encompassing ideas, but dwell instead on **practical** benefits to you.

W-133.2.You do not ask too much of life, but far too little. 2 When you let your mind be drawn to bodily concerns, to things you buy, to eminence as valued by the world, you ask for sorrow, not for happiness. 3 This course does not attempt to take from you the little that you have. 4 **This course** does not try to substitute utopian ideas for satisfactions which the world contains. 5 There are no satisfactions in the world **your little "s" self imagines**.

W-133.3.Today we list the real criteria by which to test all things you think you want. 2 Unless they meet these sound requirements, **all things you think you want** are not worth desiring at all, for they can but replace what offers more. 3 The laws that govern choice you cannot make, no more than you can make alternatives from which to choose. 4 The choosing you can do; indeed, you must. 5 But it is wise to learn the laws you set in motion when you choose, and what alternatives you choose between.

W-133.4.We have already stressed there are but two **choices**, however many there **may** appear to be. 2 The range **between real or unreal and fear or love** is set, and this we cannot change **for these are the only two options that are available to choose**. 3 It would be most ungenerous to you to let alternatives be limitless, and thus delay your final choice until you had considered all of **the variations of the choice for the unreal that appear to exist** in time; and **with such numerous additional false options you would** not **have** been brought so clearly to the place where there is but one choice that must be made.

W-133.5.Another kindly and related law is that there is no compromise in what your choice must bring. 2 **Your choice** cannot give you just a little, for there is no in between. 3 Each choice you make brings everything to you or nothing. 4 Therefore, if you learn the tests by which you can distinguish everything from nothing, you will make the better choice.

W-133.6.First, if you choose a thing that will not last forever, what you chose is valueless. 2 A temporary value is without all value. 3 Time can never take away a value that is real. 4 What fades and dies **in time** was never there, and makes no offering to him who chooses **what does not last forever**. 5 He is deceived by nothing in a form he thinks he likes.

W-133.7.Next, if you choose to take a thing away from someone else, you will have nothing left. 2 This is because, when you deny **someone's** right to everything, you have denied your own **right to everything**. 3 You therefore will not recognize the things you really have, denying **the things you really have** are there. 4 Who seeks to take away has been deceived by the illusion loss can offer gain. 5 Yet loss must offer loss, and nothing more.

W-133.8.Your next consideration is the one on which the others rest. 2 Why is the choice you make of value to you? 3 What attracts your mind to **valuing that choice**? 4 What purpose does **that choice** serve? 5 Here it is easiest of all to be deceived. 6 For what the ego wants **the ego** fails to recognize. 7 **The ego** does not even tell the truth as it perceives **truth**, for **the ego** needs to keep the halo which it uses to protect **the ego's** goals from tarnish and from rust, that you may see how "innocent" **the ego's goals are**.

W-133.9.Yet is **the ego's** camouflage a thin veneer, which could deceive but those who are content to be deceived. 2 **The ego's** goals are obvious to anyone who cares to look for them. 3 Here is deception doubled, for the one who is deceived will not perceive that he has merely failed to gain **the ego's promised goals**. 4 He will believe that he has served the ego's hidden goals **which is to reinforce your belief in lack, limitation and separation**.

W-133.10.Yet though he tries to keep **the ego's** halo clear within his vision, still must he perceive **the ego's** tarnished edges and its rusted core. 2 His ineffectual mistakes appear as sins to him, because he looks upon the tarnish as his own; the rust a sign of deep unworthiness within himself. 3 He who would still preserve the ego's goals and serve **the goals of the ego** as his own **goals** makes no mistakes, according to the dictates of his guide **which is the ego**. 4 **The ego's** guidance teaches it is error to believe that sins are but mistakes, for who would suffer for his sins if this were so? **For if sin were viewed as a mere mistake, correction, not punishment, would only be required.**

W-133.11.And so we come to the criterion for choice that is the hardest to believe, because **this criterion's** obviousness is overlaid with many levels of obscurity. 2 If you feel any guilt about your choice, you have allowed the ego's goals to come between the real alternatives. 3 And thus **because you have allowed your ego's goals to cloud the two choices,** you do not realize there are but two **choices**, and the alternative you think you chose seems fearful, and too dangerous to be the nothingness it actually is.

W-133.12.All things are valuable or valueless, worthy or not of being sought at all, entirely desirable or not worth the slightest effort to obtain. 2 Choosing is easy just because of this **black and white two choice dichotomy**. 3 Complexity is nothing but a screen of smoke, which hides the very simple fact that no decision can be difficult. 4 What is the gain to you in learning **the real criteria by which to test all things you think you want?** 5 It is far more than merely letting you make choices easily and without pain.

W-133.13.Heaven itself is reached with empty hands and open minds, which come with nothing to find everything and claim **everything** as their own. 2 We will attempt to reach this state **of empty yet open mindedness** today, with **egoic** self-deception laid aside, and with an honest willingness to value but the truly valuable and the real. 3 Our two extended practice periods of fifteen minutes each begin with this:
4 I will not value what is valueless, and only what has value do I seek, for only **what has value** do I desire to find.

W-133.14.And then receive what waits for everyone who reaches, unencumbered, to the gate of Heaven, which swings open as he comes. 2 Should you begin to let yourself collect some needless burdens, or believe you see some difficult decisions facing you, be quick to answer with this simple thought:
3 I will not value what is valueless, for what is valuable belongs to me.

Notes to Lesson #133

I will not value what is valueless.

We do not ask too much from life but far too little. Often we are asking for things that are of no value or have any long-term benefits. This lesson offers the real criteria that you should utilize to test all things you think you want for the value they offer you.

Based on this four part test, you can determine what has real value and what is worthless. In this test, nothing is determined to be of partial value. Something is either of value or valueless. There are no shades of gray.

When your mind is drawn to bodily concerns, you are often valuing the worthless but this is not necessarily the case. It is not the intent of this course to take away the few things of this world that you possess. We are not trying to substitute some grand plan or utopian ideas so that this world can make you happy or satisfy your needs. Instead, this lesson says that there is no satisfaction in the egoic world. The things of this world do not last and therefore, they cannot bring the lasting happiness, love and inner peace that are your divine birthright.

In the twelfth paragraph of this lesson it states:

W-133.12.All things are valuable or valueless, worthy or not of being sought at all, entirely desirable or not worth the slightest effort to obtain. 2 Choosing is easy just because of this.

Does this mean that certain things or experiences are always valueless and other items or experiences are always to be valued?

Let's look at the four part test or criteria for determining the value of all things you think you want.

1) Does it last forever? If you choose something that will not last forever, you have chosen the valueless. Time can never take away a value that is real. If something fades and dies in time, what you have chosen is valueless.

2) Does the choice take away from another? If it does, it also is valueless because when you deny another's right to everything, you have denied your own right to everything. To give is to receive and loss can only offer loss in return.

3) Why is the choice you make of value to you? What purpose does it serve? It is this third criterion in which the other three actually rest. In time, all events are actually neutral. Without your judgment, an experience has no ability to increase or decrease your joy, happiness or inner peace. Only your mind has that power. Nothing can rob you of your own inner peace unless you choose to allow it.

All things become either valuable or worthless based on the purpose that your mind assigns to that item. Your mind often assigns value to the worthless and disregards priceless wealth. In this regard, there are only two choices to choose from. The purpose that you assign to an item is contingent upon which thought system you are following. Either you will value that item out of fear or love.

Because there are only two thought systems, fear or love, you only have two choices. You will ask yourself, what would love have me do or what would fear have me do. Whichever voice you choose to follow, will determine whether or not the item is of value and will last forever or is valueless.

For example, someone decides to give a contribution of one million dollars to a hurricane relief fund. Is this something of value or is it valueless? Just because it deals with the temporal does not mean it is valueless. Instead, we must look past the form to content or the purpose for the giving. If the person is making the contribution out of fear-based thinking, it will fail this test. If the person has asked and is following what love would have him do, it, the content, not the form, is something that will last and is of real value.

I use this example of a contribution because it clearly demonstrates that context behind the gift's purpose is the determining factor for valuing anything. The actual form that the experience is delivered is a meaningless part of the equation. Mother

Teresa did not administer to the sick in Calcutta to earn some heavenly reward. She did it out of love for her beloved Jesus, who she saw in the faces of all her patients.

If I make a contribution because I believe that it will earn some future reward or get my name recognized as a good person, I am valuing the worthless. If I make a contribution because I see someone as a victim, I am supporting the belief that there are outside forces that can rob me of my own inner peace. If I choose to contribute out of love, I do not judge the event. Instead, I realize that each is on their own perfect path and I followed my inner guide. I can give and share my hope, love and encouragement rather than my fears with another.

With each circumstance in time, you have a decision to make. What value will I place on that experience? What was that experience meant to teach me? What was the purpose I will choose to give it?

When you value this world as a place to make you happy or hide from God's judgment or perhaps earn another's love, you are making the experience worthless. When you value that same experience for the learning lessons it provides or the opportunity to demonstrate being love in form, that same event becomes a means for reawakening. The form of the event is the same but the context or purpose is different.

4) The fourth and final criterion is, does it leave you feeling guilty? If so, it is a choice that was made out of fear and supports your ego's belief in lack, limitation and separation. In regard to this final test, if the reason you do something is to avoid feeling guilty, you also have reinforced your belief in lack, limitation and separation.

When you understand that all remain as God created them, perfect, whole and complete, you realize that each is on their own perfect path and this gives you the freedom to look beyond any circumstance and simply ask your inner guide, the Holy Spirit, what would love have me do. When you follow that guidance, you will be co-creating something of value that will last forever.

Question: Based on this four-part test for determining the value of anything that you want, please answer this question about yourself for each of these four categories in your life.

Do you want

1) good health?
2) abundance?
3) loving relationships?
4) fame?

All four categories are things of this world that will not last forever but does that automatically mean that you are valuing the worthless?

Let me perceive forgiveness as it is.

W-134.1.Let us review the meaning of "forgive," for **forgive** is apt to be distorted and to be perceived **by your ego** as something that entails an unfair sacrifice of righteous wrath, a gift unjustified and undeserved, and a complete denial of the truth. 2 In such a view, forgiveness must be seen **by the ego** as mere eccentric folly, and this course appear to rest salvation on a whim **of egoic forgiveness.**

W-134.2.**Your ego sees forgiveness as an unfair sacrifice of righteous wrath, a gift unjustified and undeserved, and a complete denial of the truth. It is** this twisted view of what forgiveness means **that** is easily corrected, when you can accept the fact that pardon is not asked for what is true. 2 **Pardon** must be limited to what is false. 3 **Pardon** is irrelevant to everything except illusions. 4 Truth is God's creation, and to pardon **truth** is meaningless. 5 All truth belongs to **God**, reflects **God's** laws and radiates **God's** Love. 6 Does **truth and God's love** need pardon? 7 How can you forgive the sinless and eternally benign?

W-134.3.The major difficulty that you find in genuine forgiveness on your part is that you still believe you must forgive the truth, and not illusions. 2 You conceive of pardon as a vain attempt to look past what is there; to overlook the truth, in an unfounded effort to deceive yourself by making an illusion true. 3 This twisted **egoic** viewpoint but reflects the hold that the idea of sin retains as yet upon your **split** mind, as you **still** regard yourself **as a sinful little "s" self.**

W-134.4.Because **your little "s" self** thinks your sins are real, you look on pardon as deception. 2 For it is impossible to think of sin as true and not believe forgiveness, **as the ego understands it,** is a lie. 3 Thus is forgiveness **as seen by the ego's fear-based thought system** really but a sin, like all the rest. 4 **The ego's view of forgiveness** says the truth is false, and smiles on **what the ego falsely judges to be** the corrupt **sinner** as if **the sinner** were as blameless as the grass; as white as snow. 5 **To the ego, forgiveness** is delusional in what it thinks **forgiveness** can accomplish. 6 **To the ego, forgiveness** would see as right the plainly wrong; the loathsome as the good.

W-134.5.Pardon is no escape in such a view **that sin is real.** 2 **Pardon** merely is a further sign that sin is unforgivable, at best to be concealed, denied or called another name, for pardon is a treachery to truth. 3 Guilt cannot be forgiven. 4 If you sin, your guilt is everlasting. 5 Those who are forgiven from the view their sins are real are pitifully mocked and twice condemned. **Those who believe their sins are real are** first **condemned** by themselves for what **sins** they think they did, and once again by those who pardon them **for their fictitious sins**.

W-134.6.It is sin's unreality that makes **true** forgiveness natural and wholly sane, a deep relief to those who offer **true forgiveness, due to sin's unreality**; a quiet blessing where **forgiveness** is received. 2 **Due to sin's unreality, true forgiveness** does not countenance illusions, but collects **illusions** lightly, with a little laugh, and gently lays **the illusions** at the feet of truth. 3 And there **before the truth, the illusions** disappear entirely.

W-134.7.Forgiveness is the only thing that stands for truth in the illusions of the world. 2 **Due to sin's unreality, true forgiveness** sees **the illusion's** nothingness, and looks straight through the thousand forms in which **illusions** may appear. 3 **Due to sin's unreality, true forgiveness,** looks on lies, but **forgiveness** is not deceived **by illusion's lies.** 4 **Due to sin's unreality, true forgiveness** does not heed the self-accusing shrieks of sinners mad with guilt. 5 **Due to** sin's **unreality, true forgiveness** looks on **those who believe they are sinners** with quiet eyes, and merely says to them, "My brother, what you think is not the truth. **You have not sinned."**

W-134.8.The strength of pardon is **pardon's** honesty, which is so uncorrupted that **pardon** sees illusions as illusions, not as truth. 2 It is **because pardon does not mistake the illusion of sin for the truth** that **pardon** becomes the undeceiver in the face of lies; the great restorer of the simple truth. 3 By **pardon's** ability to overlook what is not there, **pardon** opens up the way to truth, which has been blocked by dreams of guilt. 4 Now are you free to follow in the way your true forgiveness opens up to you. **You are able to ask your big "S" Self what it would have you do.** 5 For if one brother has received this gift of **ending his guilt by true forgiveness through** you, the door **of true forgiveness that ends guilt** is open to yourself **also.**

W-134.9.There is a very simple way to find the door to true forgiveness, and perceive **the door of true forgiveness** open wide in welcome. 2 When you feel that you are tempted to accuse someone of sin in any form, do not allow your **egoic** mind to dwell on what you think he did, for that is **egoic** self-deception. 3 Ask instead, "Would I accuse myself of doing this?"

W-134.10.Thus will you see alternatives for choice in terms that render choosing meaningful, and keep your mind as free of guilt and pain as God Himself intended **your mind** to be **free of guilt and pain,** and as **your big "S" Self** is in truth. 2 It is but lies that would condemn. 3 In truth is innocence the only thing there is. 4 **Due to sin's unreality, true** forgiveness stands between illusions and the truth. **Due to sin's unreality, true forgiveness stands** between the world you see **through your ego's viewpoint** and that which lies beyond. **True forgiveness stands** between the hell of guilt and Heaven's gate.

W-134.11.Across this bridge **of true forgiveness,** as powerful as love which laid **love's** blessing on **true forgiveness,** are all dreams of evil and of hatred and attack brought silently to truth. 2 **All dreams of evil and attack** are not kept to swell and bluster, and to terrify the foolish dreamer who believes in **these false dreams.** 3 He, **who once believed the dreams of sin**

and attack were real has been gently wakened from his dream by understanding what he thought he **egoically** saw was never there. 4 And now he, **who once believed the dreams of sin were real,** cannot feel that all escape has been denied to him.

W-134.12.He, **who once believed the dreams of sin and attack were real,** does not have to fight to save himself. 2 He, **who once believed his dreams of sin were real,** does not have to kill the dragons which he thought pursued him **in those dreams**. 3 Nor need he erect the heavy walls of stone and iron doors he thought would make him safe **from those dreams of sin**. 4 He, **who once believed his dreams of sin were real,** can remove the ponderous and useless armor made to chain his mind to fear and misery. 5 His step is light, and as he lifts his foot to stride ahead a star is left behind, to point the way to those who follow him **to the truth that sin is unreal**.

W-134.13.**True** forgiveness must be practiced, for the world cannot perceive **the meaning of true forgiveness**, nor provide a guide to teach you **the beneficence of true forgiveness**. 2 There is no thought in all the world that leads to any understanding of the laws **true forgiveness** follows, nor the Thought, **due to sin's unreality** that **true forgiveness** reflects. 3 **The thought of what true forgiveness means** is as alien to the world as is your own reality, **which is your sinlessness**. 4 And yet **the thought of what true forgiveness means** joins your mind with the reality in you, **your big "S" Self**.

W-134.14.Today we practice true forgiveness, that the time of joining be no more delayed. 2 For we would meet with our **big "S" Self's** reality in freedom and in peace. 3 Our practicing becomes the footsteps lighting up the way for all our brothers, who will follow us to the reality we share with them **as big "S" Selves**. 4 That this may be accomplished, let us give a quarter of an hour twice today, and spend **that time** with the Guide, **the Holy Spirit,** Who understands the meaning of **true** forgiveness and was sent to us to teach **true forgiveness and sin's unreality**. 5 Let us ask of **the Holy Spirit**:
6 Let me perceive **true** forgiveness as it is.

W-134.15.Then choose one brother as **the Holy Spirit** will direct, and catalogue **your brother's** "sins," as one by one they cross your mind. 2 Be certain not to dwell on any one of **your brother's "sins",** but realize that you are using his "offenses" but to save the world from all ideas of sin. 3 Briefly consider all the evil things you thought of **your brother**, and each time ask yourself, "Would I condemn myself for doing this?"

W-134.16.Let **your brother** be freed from all the thoughts you had of sin in him. 2 And now you are prepared for freedom. 3 If you have been practicing thus far in willingness and honesty, you will begin to sense a lifting up, a lightening of weight across your chest, a deep and certain feeling of relief. 4 The time remaining should be given to experiencing the escape from all the heavy chains you sought to lay upon your brother, but were laid upon yourself.

W-134.17.**True** forgiveness should be practiced through the day, for there will still be many times when you forget **the** meaning **of true forgiveness** and attack yourself **as a sinner**. 2 When this **belief in sin's reality** occurs, allow your mind to see through this illusion as you tell yourself:
3 Let me perceive **true** forgiveness as it is. 4 Would I accuse myself of doing this? 5 I will not lay this chain upon myself.
6 In everything you do remember this:
7 No one is crucified alone, and yet no one can enter Heaven by himself.

Notes to Lesson #134

Let me perceive forgiveness as it is.

This lesson asks that we perceive forgiveness as it is. My question to you is the following:

Why is the goal of this lesson to perceive forgiveness as it is, rather than know forgiveness?

The concept of forgiveness can only exist in the world of perception. In the real world, which is the Mind of God, forgiveness makes no sense and is a meaningless term.

As strange as it may sound, forgiveness is not an attribute of God. You would think that if God is only love, forgiveness would be an attribute of a loving God. Yet, in order to forgive, one must first have condemned. God does not forgive, because God has never condemned anything. God's love is freely given and there is nothing you can do to stop the flow of that unconditional love.

Another reason why forgiveness does not exist in the real world or Mind of God is because in order to forgive, one party must have harmed another. This implies two things that are impossible in the real world.

The first is that in A Oneness of All That Is, there is nothing outside the Oneness and therefore, the concept of two separate autonomous beings is impossible. The other reason is that A Oneness of All That Is is invulnerable and therefore, cannot be harmed.

Being unlimited spirit, no one can harm you or rob you of your inner peace unless you choose to allow it. If it is your own choice to allow something to interfere with your own inner peace, this means that it was your decision and you cannot be a victim of outside forces that are beyond your control.

The concept of forgiveness belongs in the realm of perception because perception deals with illusions, not reality. Because of this, this lesson's goal is to help us perceive forgiveness as it is in relationship to this fear-based world. When we utilize true forgiveness in the world of perception, our reframed story will more clearly align with the truth of what we really are in the real world of the Mind of God.

Although in the world of time and space, it appears that the laws of love have been superseded by the laws of fear, this is not actually the case. The Laws of God supersede our ego's laws even in our fear-based dream world. We just fail to recognize this fact because of our allegiance to the ego's thought system of lack, limitation and separation.

We confuse form with content or purpose. Form is an illusion and of no meaning. The purpose or content is the why behind your wanting to have that experience. The content is what gives value to the experience. Even in the illusion of time, the content always follows the laws of God.

For example, we do not believe that to give is to receive. This world teaches that when you give you lose what you once had. The laws of the world see giving as a sacrifice and so the ego says that you should only give to get. Although our egoic world operates from this framework, when we examine the facts, we realize that what we give we ultimately do receive. Our ego confuses and mistakes form with content. When you give fear, you get fear. The laws of God deal with content, not illusionary form.

Surprisingly, this lesson says that sin does require condemnation. With sin comes guilt and that guilt cannot be forgiven. This lesson says if you commit a sin, your guilt is everlasting. Pardon or forgiveness is not appropriate, justifiable or even possible to be received or given if sin is involved.

But didn't an earlier lesson say that forgiveness is the key to happiness and that forgiveness offers everything I want? How can these statements be reconciled with the fact that sin cannot be forgiven?

In the egoic world, we understand the word forgiveness to be defined as the suspension of righteous wrath or the giving up the right to retribution that an injured party is entitled to receive from the wrongdoer. The party that has been wronged is entitled to retribution but may occasionally decline to exercise those rights to the full extent that justice would allow. In this case, the victim would be sacrificing their right to retribution and would in essence be giving a gift that was unjustified and undeserved to the party who had committed the punishable act.

In our egoic world, forgiveness rests on the whim of the victim. The offending party is not entitled to nor has any right to demand that the gift of forgiveness be granted. The only thing the offending party is entitled to is the everlasting guilt associated with his harming another.

Forgiveness cannot take away his guilt nor wipe the slate clean. The offering of penance or the paying of retribution may balance the scales between the two parties but that balancing only results in both parties harboring everlasting guilt for wronging each other. In this case, the victim's retribution may be viewed by the outside world as justified but it still involves the taking or harming of the original perpetrator of the crime. This taking from another, regardless of the ego's justification, results in feelings of guilt associated with the restitution the victim received. This balancing of the scale continues to perceive that the guilt associated with the sins of each party are real and everlasting.

This lesson asks us to perceive the term forgiveness in a different light that more properly aligns with the truth that no one can rob you of your inner peace unless you allow it. You are not the body and the world of perception is played on the game board of time. Time is a medium that gives us the opportunity to experience what we desire in perfect safety and without any adverse consequences that would affect or change what we truly are. Events in this world have no ability to change the truth that we remain as God created us, perfect, whole and complete. We remain part of The Oneness of All That Is.

What ACIM calls forgiveness would perhaps be more appropriately identified with the concept that if there is no harm there is no foul. Because of the inability of experiences on the game board of time and space to change what you are, these experiences cannot harm you or another. Experiences are merely tests or learning lessons to provide feedback as to what you truly value and why.

If a cause does not have an effect, it is not a cause. Sin is the harming of yourself or another. A sin, without a harmful effect or victim, cannot be a sin. Without sin, there is no harm and nothing to condemn. Without condemnation there is nothing to forgive.

The major difficulty that the world and our egos have with genuine forgiveness is our ego's belief that we must forgive the truth that harm was actually inflicted on you or another.

The ego believes you are the body and the body is you. Only bodies can attack and be harmed. The body is actually a neutral communication device that demonstrates what your mind values. The body is a mere game token that holds a place on the game board of planet earth. The ego does not believe that this playschool of time and space is not real and only a game board for fun and learning. In the world of perception, we are actually asked to forgive the illusion that provided the appearance that someone's game token was actually harmed by another or themselves.

Earlier, I asked the question, what the definition of true forgiveness is as understood by A Course in Miracles. I would like to offer you a definition to utilize when you see the term forgiveness referenced in these lessons. True forgiveness does not follow the typical definition since it acknowledges the unreality of the idea of sin and harm. After all, how can learning the truth be harmful?

In time and space, forgiveness could be described as follows.

I forgive my brother for all the wrongs that I thought he did to me that never really occurred.

This is the recognition that there are no victims and there are no victimizers. Instead, there are only willing volunteers on the game board of rediscovering who they really are. It acknowledges the world of perception as a means for learning and reawakening rather than a place of punishment or earning your salvation.

If sin were real, it would mean that there is some outside force that could harm or rob you of your inner peace. If sin were real, you would no longer be unlimited and part of the shared Mind of God. You would be changed and no longer as God created you. This would change God's Will and change God. Separation would be real. If sin were possible, sin could not be forgiven and if you sinned your guilt would be everlasting.

But sin is not real. Sin is impossible. This is why we are asked to only perceive forgiveness as it is. For in the Mind of God, the real world, forgiveness is meaningless and serves no purpose.

Question: If tomorrow, you are walking down the street and someone for no apparent reason kicks you in the teeth and you forgive that person, does that mean that the event never occurred?

Remember my definition of forgiveness. Forgiveness means I forgive my brother for all the wrongs that I thought he did to me that never really occurred.

If you forgave him, does that mean he never kicked you in the teeth?

Or,

Since he really did kick you in the teeth and there are witnesses who will testify on the truth of your story, is forgiveness impossible?

LESSON 135

If I defend myself I am attacked.

W-135.1.Who would defend himself unless he thought he were attacked, that the attack were real, and that his own **egoic** defense could save himself **from the perceived attack**? 2 And herein lies the folly of defense; for **your defense** gives **the** illusion **that you are vulnerable to attack** full reality, and then attempts to handle **the illusion of attack** as real. 3 **Your defense** adds illusions to **the illusions of attack and vulnerability,** thus making correction doubly difficult. 4 And it is this **doubling of illusions that** you do when you attempt to plan the future, activate the past, or organize the present as **your ego's** wish.

W-135.2.You operate from the belief you must protect yourself from what is happening because **what is happening outside your mind** must contain what threatens you. 2 A sense of threat is an acknowledgment of an inherent weakness **in yourself**; a belief that there is **a** danger **outside your mind** which has power to call on you to make appropriate defense. 3 The world is based on this insane belief **that there are outside forces that can attack you.** 4 And all **the world's** structures, all **the world's** thoughts and doubts, its penalties and heavy armaments, **the world's** legal definitions and its codes, **the world's** ethics and its leaders and **the world's** gods, all serve but to preserve **the world's** sense of threat **to your vulnerability**. 5 For no one walks the world in armature but must have terror striking at his heart.

W-135.3.Defense is frightening. 2 **Defense** stems from fear **and** increasing fear as each defense is made. 3 You think **defense** offers safety. 4 Yet **defense** speaks of fear made real and terror justified. 5 Is it not strange you do not pause to ask, as you elaborate your ego's plans and make your armor thicker and your locks more tight, what you defend, and how, and against what?

W-135.4.Let us consider first what you defend. 2 **What you defend** must be something that is very weak and easily assaulted. 3 **What you defend** must be something made easy prey, unable to protect itself and needing your defense. 4 What but the body has such frailty that constant care and watchful, deep concern are needful to protect **the body's** little life? 5 What but the body falters and must fail to serve the Son of God as worthy host?

W-135.5.Yet it is not the body that can fear, nor be a thing of fear. 2 **The body** has no needs but those which **your mind** assigns to **the body**. 3 **The body** needs no complicated structures of defense, no health-inducing medicine, no care and no concern at all. 4 Defend **the body's** life, or give **the body's** gifts to make it beautiful or walls to make **the body** safe, and you but say your home is open to the thief of time, corruptible and crumbling, so unsafe **that the body that your ego perceives to be your reality** must be guarded with your very life.

W-135.6.Is not this picture **that you are your body** fearful? 2 Can you be at peace with such a concept of your home **being your body**? 3 Yet what endowed the body with the right to serve you thus except your own **mind's** belief? 4 It is your mind which gave the body all the functions that you see in **the body**, and set **the body's** value far beyond a little pile of dust and water. 5 Who would make defense of something that he recognized as **a little pile of dust and water**?

W-135.7.The body is in need of no defense. 2 This cannot be too often emphasized. 3 **The body** will be strong and healthy if the mind does not abuse **the body** by assigning **the body** to roles **the body** cannot fill, to purposes beyond **the body's** scope, and to exalted aims which **the body** cannot accomplish. 4 Such attempts **by your mind of assigning to the body roles** ridiculous yet deeply cherished **that the body cannot fill**, are the sources for the many mad attacks you make upon **the body**. 5 For **the body** seems to fail your hopes, your needs, your values and your dreams.

W-135.8.The **ego's little "s" "self"** that needs protection is not real. 2 The body, valueless and hardly worth the least defense, need merely be perceived as quite apart from you, and **the body** becomes a healthy, serviceable instrument through which the mind can operate until **the body's** usefulness is over. 3 Who would want to keep **the body** when **the body's** usefulness is done?

W-135.9.Defend the body and you have attacked your mind. 2 For you have seen in **your mind** the faults, the weaknesses, the limits and the lacks from which you think the body must be saved. 3 You will not see the mind as separate from bodily conditions. 4 And you will impose upon the body all the pain that comes from the conception of the mind as limited and fragile, and apart from other minds and separate from its Source, **which is the Mind of God**.

W-135.10.These are the **ego's thoughts of lack, limitation and separation** in need of healing, and the body will respond with health when **these erroneous thoughts** have been corrected and replaced with truth. 2 **The correction of erroneous thought with the truth** is the body's only real defense. 3 Yet is this **correcting of your mind's thinking** where you look for **the body's** defense? 4 You offer **the body** protection of a kind from which **the body** gains no benefit at all, but merely adds to your distress of mind. 5 You do not heal **the body**, but merely take away the hope of healing, for you fail to see where hope must lie if **healing is to** be meaningful **which is in the healing of the mind's** erroneous beliefs.

W-135.11.A healed mind does not plan. 2 **A healed mind** carries out the plans that **the mind** receives through listening to wisdom that is not its own **but from the wisdom of the Holy Spirit**. 3 **A healed mind** waits until it has been taught what should be done, and then proceeds to do it. 4 **A healed mind** does not depend upon **the egoic little "s" self** for anything except its adequacy to fulfill the plans assigned to **you from the Holy Spirit**. 5 **A healed mind** is secure in certainty that obstacles cannot impede **your big "S" Self's** progress to accomplishment of any goal that serves the greater plan established for the good of everyone **by the Holy Spirit**.

W-135.12.A healed mind is relieved of the belief that **the mind** must plan, although **an egoic mind** cannot know the outcome which is best, the means by which **the favorable outcome** is achieved, nor how to recognize the problem that the plan is made to solve. 2 **The egoic mind** must misuse the body in its plans until **your mind** recognizes this is so **and realizes that your mind does know the big picture and therefore, must not plan but instead follow the guidance of the Holy Spirit**. 3 But when **your mind** has accepted this as true, then is **your mind** healed, and lets the body go.

W-135.13.Enslavement of the body to the plans the unhealed **egoic** mind sets up to save itself must make the body sick. 2 **The body** is not free to be the means of helping in a plan which far exceeds **the body's** own protection. And **the Holy Spirit's plan** needs **the body's** service for a little while **in order to complete the Holy Spirit's plan**. 3 In this capacity **by following the Holy Spirit's plan** is health assured. 4 For everything the mind employs for this **completion of the Holy Spirit's plan** will function flawlessly, and with the strength that has been given **the mind** and cannot fail.

W-135.14.It is, perhaps, not easy to perceive that self-initiated plans **made by your ego** are but defenses, with the purpose all of them were made to realize. 2 **Self-initiated plans made by your ego** are the means by which a frightened mind would undertake its own protection, at the cost of truth. 3 This is not difficult to realize in some forms which these self-deceptions take, where the denial of reality is very obvious. 4 Yet planning **itself** is not often recognized as a defense **against the truth**.

W-135.15.The mind engaged in planning for itself is occupied in setting up control of future happenings. 2 **The mind engaged in planning for itself** does not think that it will be provided for, unless **the egoic mind** makes its own provisions. 3 Time becomes a future emphasis, to be controlled by learning and experience obtained from past events and previous beliefs. 4 **The mind engaged in planning for itself** overlooks the present, for **the egoic mind** rests on the idea the past has taught enough to let the **egoic** mind direct its future course.

W-135.16.The mind that plans is thus refusing to allow for change. 2 What **the egoic mind** has learned before **from its past** becomes the basis for **the ego's** future goals. 3 **The ego's** past experience directs **the ego's** choice of what will happen. 4 And **the egoic mind** does not see that here and now is everything **the healed mind** needs to guarantee a future quite unlike the past, without a continuity of any old **egoic** ideas and sick beliefs. 5 Anticipation **or planning** plays no part at all **in the here and now**, for present confidence directs the way **and the healed mind follows the guidance of the Holy Spirit.**

W-135.17.Defenses are the plans you undertake to make against the truth. 2 **The aim of your ego's plans for your defense** is to select what you approve, and disregard what you consider incompatible with your beliefs of your reality **as a little "s" self**. 3 Yet what remains is meaningless indeed. 4 For it is your reality **as your big "S" Self** that is the "threat" which your defenses would attack, obscure, and take apart and crucify.

W-135.18.What could you not accept, if you but knew that everything that happens, all events, past, present and to come, are gently planned by **the Holy Spirit** Whose only purpose is your good? 2 Perhaps you have misunderstood **the Holy Spirit's** plan, for **the Holy Spirit** would never offer pain to you. 3 But your **ego's** defenses did not let you see **the Holy Spirit's** loving blessing shine in every step you ever took. 4 While you made plans for death, **the Holy Spirit** led you gently to eternal life.

W-135.19.Your present trust in **the Holy Spirit** is the defense that promises a future undisturbed, without a trace of sorrow, and with joy that constantly increases, as this life becomes a holy instant, set in time, but heeding only immortality. 2 Let no defenses but your present trust **in the Holy Spirit** direct the future, and this life becomes a meaningful encounter with the truth that only your **ego's** defenses would conceal.

W-135.20.Without **your ego's** defenses, you become a light which Heaven gratefully acknowledges to be **Heaven's** own **light**. 2 And **this light** will lead you on in ways appointed for your happiness according to the ancient plan, begun when time was born. 3 Your followers will join their light with yours, and it will be increased until the world is lighted up with joy. 4 And gladly will our brothers lay aside their cumbersome **egoic** defenses, which availed them nothing and could only terrify.

W-135.21.We will anticipate that time **of reawakening to the truth** today with present confidence, for this is part of what was planned for us. 2 We will be sure that everything we need is given us for our accomplishment of this today. 3 We make no **egoic** plans for how **reawakening to the truth** will be done, but realize that our defenselessness is all that is required for the truth to dawn upon our minds with certainty.

W-135.22.For fifteen minutes twice today we rest from senseless **egoic** planning, and from every thought that blocks the truth from entering our minds. 2 Today we will receive **the truth from guidance** instead of plan **with our egoic mind** that we may give instead of organize. 3 And we are given truly, as we say:
4 If I defend myself I am attacked. 5 But in defenselessness I will be strong, and I will learn what my defenses hide.

W-135.23.Nothing but that. 2 If there are plans to make, you will be told of **those plans**. 3 **These plans** may not be the plans **your ego** thought were needed, nor indeed **are these plans** the answers to the problems which **your ego** thought confronted you. 4 But **these plans** are answers to another kind of question, which remains unanswered yet in need of answering until the Answer **of the truth** comes to you at last.

W-135.24.All your **ego's** defenses have been aimed at not receiving what you will receive today **which is the guidance of the Holy Spirit Who knows the big picture and the truth**. 2 And in the light and joy of simple trust, you will but wonder why you ever thought that you must be defended from release **that the truth about your big "S" Self brings**. 3 Heaven asks nothing. 4 It is hell that makes extravagant demands for sacrifice. 5 You give up nothing in these times today when, undefended, you present yourself to your Creator as you, **your big "S" Self**, really are.

W-135.25.**Your Creator** has remembered you. 2 Today we will remember **our Creator**. 3 For this is Eastertime in your salvation. 4 And you rise again from what was seeming death and hopelessness. 5 Now is the light of hope reborn in you, for now you come without **your ego's** defense, to learn the part for you, **your big "S" Self**, within the plan of God. 6 What little **egoic** plans or magical beliefs can still have value, when you have received your function from the Voice for God Himself?

W-135.26.Try not to shape this day as **your ego** believes would benefit you most. 2 For you cannot conceive of all the happiness that comes to you without your **ego's** planning. 3 Learn today. 4 And all the world will take this giant stride, and celebrate your Eastertime with you. 5 Throughout the day, as foolish little things appear to raise defensiveness in you and tempt you to engage in weaving **egoic** plans, remind yourself this is a special day for learning, and acknowledge it with this: 6 This is my Eastertime. 7 And I would keep **my Eastertime** holy. 8 I will not defend myself, because the Son of God needs no defense against the truth of his reality **as his big "S" Self**.

Notes to Lesson #135

If I defend myself I am attacked.

Yesterday we asked the following question.

If tomorrow, you are walking down the street and someone for no apparent reason kicks you in the teeth and you forgive that person, does that mean that the event never occurred?

Remember my definition of forgiveness. Forgiveness means I forgive my brother for all the wrongs that I thought he did to me that never really occurred.

If you forgave him, does that mean he never kicked you in the teeth?

Or,

Since he really did kick you in the teeth and there are witnesses that will testify to the truth of your story, is forgiveness impossible?

In this world of time, circumstances do occur in your life in which there appear to be victims and victimizers. But this occurs because we are not privy to the big picture. We fail to understand the learning lesson or desired experience that each party requires on their own perfect path to reawakening to the truth of who they are.

We confuse the form with the content or purpose of the event. If you turn the event over to the Holy Spirit and ask for guidance, the Holy Spirit will reframe the event to align with the truth. Form will be bypassed and content or purpose will be the focus of the reframed experience. The purpose of the event will be seen through the eyes of love rather than fear. The event will now be viewed as a learning or teaching experience.

The context of the event will now focus on the learning lesson and the feedback that the experience provided. The facts and circumstances of the prior event, the form, will not necessarily change but the purpose for the event will transform from your being a victim or victimizer to becoming an active learner or teacher.

Events now become the proving grounds where you can test and demonstrate what you truly value and why. When viewed from this big picture perspective, all participants are mere actors whose presence is required so that you can have the learning lesson you desired on your own perfect path. Instead of condemning some actors for the role they were assigned, you should thank them for the supporting role they performed in your play on the stage of time and space.

Since to give is to receive, you never condemn another without crucifying yourself. By the same token, you never forgive another without forgiving yourself. Ultimately, since no one can rob you of your own inner peace, you are the only person you need to forgive when you realize you have lost your own inner peace.

Lesson 135 is that if I defend myself, I am attacked. Only those who believe that there are outside forces that can rob them of their own inner peace believe attack is possible. When you seek to defend yourself, you are accepting the ego's belief that you can be attacked and are not invulnerable spirit.

You are operating from the belief that you must protect yourself from what is happening because it must contain what threatens you. Your belief that you could be threatened is an acknowledgment of your own inherent weakness and a confirmation that you do not perceive yourself as perfect, whole and complete.

The egoic world revolves around the belief in lack, limitation and separation. In the ego's world, you are the body and the body is you. This lesson asks you to consider what you are defending. When you understand what you are defending, you will also understand that your defenses are attacking the truth of who you really are.

Defenses are the plans your ego undertakes to make the truth appear false and the false appear real. Your ego's defenses are designed to protect the ego's image of you as a little "s" self. Your ego believes you are a limited being in competition with other limited beings struggling for the limited resources that both need to survive and prosper. To the ego, defending the body becomes necessary if you are to survive and prosper.

When you associate your essence, which is mind or spirit, with the body, you accept the limitations that come with the body. The body is merely a game token that holds a place on the game board of time. The body needs no defenses. The body will prove to be a serviceable instrument as long as your mind, which gives all purpose to the body, does not abuse the body by assigning roles that the body is incapable of fulfilling.

When you see the body as separate from your essence, the body becomes a useful communication device through which the mind can operate until the body's usefulness is over. When the body's usefulness is over, the game token can be discarded as you continue on your perfect path to reawakening.

If your ego does not know what you are, how can your ego properly identify any potential problems and successfully chart a course to avoid and defend you against those problems?

The ego believes that Paradise has been lost. It perceives you to be a sinner who must now either do penance for past sins or earn back salvation in the future through your actions and good deeds.

Because of this belief that heaven belongs to your past and must be earned if it is to ever reappear in your future, your ego becomes both a judging and planning machine. Lacking the big picture, your ego falsely judges what the problem is. This judging makes the problem appear real within your mind. Then the ego sets forth to solve the fictitious problem that only exists within your own imagination. Identifying your essence to be your little "s" self, all egoic defenses are plans that attack your big "S" Self's reality in the present moment.

It is your ego's erroneous belief about what you are that is the problem. The ego has been caught up in the illusion of the dream of separation and forgotten that your mind is the source of the dream itself. Only the Holy Spirit is aware that you have forgotten to laugh and made the game of separation into a real nightmare that has become your provisional reality.

The Holy Spirit is aware that God's sleeping Son has forgotten that you are the script writer, director, editor and actor in your own dream of separation; that this dream has no ability to change the truth that you remain as God created you. Only the Holy Spirit has the big picture and knows all the parts of the puzzle and how all the players fit into God's plan for your return to knowledge.

Your ego fails to realize that God has already devised the perfect plan for your reawakening. Everything is already designed to support your needs and you need do nothing but simply follow the Voice for Truth that God has placed within your mind.

Your ego does not trust that God has already provided the answer to your ego's fictitious problem that you could be something other than as God created you. Perceiving yourself to be limited and sinful, your ego thinks it knows what the problem is and that you need a plan that will earn God's love back. The ego is working on a solution for a fictitious problem. We are not sinners and God's love can never be lost or earned. God's love was, is and always will be always freely given. Our ego's false belief about God, you and your world is the problem.

Your decision-maker must realize that your ego is incapable of judging anything correctly and your ego's fallacious judgments are the source for all the problems that you imagine. You need to follow God's plan. You must trust a new guide who knows the real problem, has the big picture, and has the right plan.

The Holy Spirit is the guide you seek and must trust. When you follow the guidance of the Holy Spirit, the body will always be capable of fulfilling its proper role in God's plan. The body's role is to act as a neutral communication device and game token that allows our mind to gather feedback on what you currently value and why. Based on that feedback, your mind learns and makes mid-course corrections that keep you progressing on your journey of reawakening.

Question: Defenses acknowledge your ego's belief that you are the body. Defenses are plans you undertake to make your illusions appear real against the truth.

Since you are not your body, should you allow another to harm your game token that you call your body?

Or

Are you required to simply turn the other cheek?

LESSON 136

Sickness is a defense against the truth.

W-136.1.No one can heal unless he understands what purpose sickness seems to serve. 2 For then he understands as well **the purpose of sickness** has no meaning. 3 Being causeless and without a meaningful intent of any kind, **sickness** cannot be at all. 4 When **sickness** is seen **as causeless and meaningless**, healing is automatic. 5 **Healing** dispels this meaningless illusion by the same approach that carries all **illusions** to truth, and merely leaves **the illusions** there to disappear.

W-136.2.Sickness is not an accident. 2 Like all defenses, it is an insane device for self-deception. 3 And like all the rest **the purpose of sickness** is to hide reality, attack it, change **reality**, render it inept, distort **reality**, twist it, or reduce **reality** to a little pile of unassembled parts. 4 The aim of all defenses is to keep the truth from being whole. 5 The parts **of the indivisible whole** are seen as if each one were whole within itself.

W-136.3.Defenses are not unintentional, nor are **defenses** made without **conscious** awareness. 2 **Defenses** are secret, magic wands you wave when truth appears to threaten what you would believe **about lack, limitation and separateness.** 3 **Defenses** seem to be unconscious but **only** because of the rapidity with which you choose to use **a defense**. 4 In that second, even less, in which the choice is made **to use a defense**, you recognize exactly what you would attempt to do, and then proceed to think that **the defense** is done.

W-136.4.Who but yourself evaluates a threat, decides escape is necessary, and sets up a series of defenses to reduce the **fictitious** threat that **your mind** has been judged as real? 2 All this **evaluating and planning** cannot be done unconsciously. 3 But afterwards, your **ego's plan for your own self-deception** requires that you must forget you made **a conscious decision to use a plan for defense**, so **the plan** seems to be external to your own **mind's** intent; a happening beyond your state of mind, an **external** outcome with a real effect on you, instead of **an internal outcome** effected **only** by **the mind of** yourself.

W-136.5.It is this quick forgetting of the part **your decision-maker** plays in making your "reality" that makes defenses seem to be beyond your own **mind's** control. 2 But what you have forgot can be remembered, given willingness to reconsider the decision which is doubly shielded by oblivion. 3 Your not remembering is but the sign that this **conscious** decision **of your mind** still remains in force, as far as your desires are concerned. 4 Mistake not **your decision to defend your false little "s" self's beliefs** for fact. 5 Defenses must make facts unrecognizable. 6 **All defenses** aim at **making the facts unrecognizable**, and **making the fact unrecognizable** is **what defenses** do.

W-136.6.Every defense takes fragments of the whole, assembles **these fragments** without regard to all their true relationships, and thus constructs illusions of a whole that is not there. 2 It is this **defense** process **that attempts to falsely fragment the indivisible whole into autonomous parts** that imposes threat, and not whatever outcome may result. 3 When parts are wrested from the whole and seen as separate and wholes within themselves, **the parts** become symbols standing for attack upon the whole. **This attack by the ego upon the whole is** successful in effect, and **the whole is** never to be seen as whole again. 4 And yet you have forgotten that **the attack you made of these parts against the indivisible whole** stand but for your own **ego's** decision of what should be real, to take the place of what is real.

W-136.7.Sickness is a decision. 2 **Sickness** is not a thing that happens to you, quite unsought, which makes you weak and brings you suffering. 3 **Sickness** is a choice you make, a plan you lay, when for an instant truth arises in your own deluded mind, and all your world **and the false beliefs it is based upon** appears to totter and prepare to fall. 4 Now are you sick, that truth may go away and threaten your establishments **as a little "s" self** no more.

W-136.8.How do you think that sickness can succeed in shielding you from truth **of your big "S" Self**? 2 Because **sickness** proves the body is not separate from you, and so you must be separate from the truth. 3 You suffer pain because the body does, and in this pain are you made one with **the body**. 4 Thus is your "true" identity **as the body** preserved, and the strange, haunting thought that you might be something beyond this little pile of dust silenced and stilled. 5 For see, this dust can make you suffer, twist your limbs and stop your heart, commanding you to die and cease to be **and therefore, the ego claims you must be the body.**

W-136.9.**According to your ego** thus is the body stronger than the truth. **For the truth** asks you live, but **the truth** cannot overcome your **ego's** choice to die. 2 And so the body is more powerful than everlasting life, Heaven more frail than hell, and God's design for the salvation of **God's** Son opposed by **an ego's** decision **that appears** stronger than **God's** Will. 3 **God's** Son is dust, the Father incomplete, and chaos sits in triumph on **God's** throne.

W-136.10.Such is your **ego's** planning for your own defense. 2 And you believe that Heaven quails before such mad attacks as these, with God made blind by your **ego's** illusions, truth turned into lies, and all the universe made slave to laws which your **egoic** defenses would impose on **the truth**. 3 Yet who believes illusions but the one who made **the illusion** up? 4 Who else can see **the illusion** and react to **the illusion** as if **the illusion** were the truth?

W-136.11.God knows not of your plans to change **God's** Will. 2 The universe remains unheeding of the laws **of lack, limitation and separation** by which **your ego** thought to govern **the universe**. 3 And Heaven has not bowed to hell, nor life to death. 4 You can but choose to think you die, or suffer sickness or distort the truth in any way. 5 What is created is apart from all of this **ego's mad illusions**. 6 Defenses are plans to defeat what cannot be attacked **which is the truth of the indivisible wholeness of the One Self.** 7 What is unalterable, **which is God's Will,** cannot change. 8 And what is wholly sinless, **which is God's Son,** cannot sin.

W-136.12.Such is the simple truth. 2 **Truth** does not make appeal to might nor triumph. 3 **Truth** does not command obedience, nor seek to prove how pitiful and futile your attempts to plan defenses that would alter **the truth.** 4 Truth merely wants to give you happiness, for such **truth's** purpose is. 5 Perhaps **truth** sighs a little when you throw away its gifts, and yet **truth** knows, with perfect certainty, that what God wills for you must be received.

W-136.13.It is this fact **that what God wills for you must be received** that demonstrates that time is an illusion. 2 For time lets you think what God has given you is not the truth right now, as **truth** must be. 3 The Thoughts of God are quite apart from time. 4 For time is but another meaningless defense you made against the truth. 5 Yet what **God** wills is here, and you remain as **God** created you.

W-136.14.Truth has a power far beyond defense, for no illusions can remain where truth has been allowed to enter. 2 And **truth** comes to any mind that would lay down its **ego's** arms, and cease to play with **the folly of the ego's thought system.** 3 **Truth** is found at any time; today if you will choose to practice giving welcome to the truth.

W-136.15.**Giving welcome to the truth** is our aim today. 2 And we will give a quarter of an hour twice to ask the truth to come to us and set us free. 3 And truth will come, for **truth** has never been apart from us. 4 **Truth** merely waits for just this invitation which we give today. 5 We introduce **truth** with a healing prayer, to help us rise above **the ego's** defensiveness, and let truth be as **truth** has always been:
6 Sickness is an **ego's** defense against the truth. 7 I will accept the truth of what I am, **my big "S" Self,** and let my **split** mind be wholly healed today.

W-136.16.Healing will flash across your open mind, as peace and truth arise to take the place of war and vain imaginings. 2 There will be no dark corners sickness can conceal, and keep defended from the light of truth. 3 There will be no dim figures from your dreams, nor their obscure and meaningless pursuits with double purposes insanely sought, remaining in your mind. 4 **Your split mind** will be healed of all the sickly wishes that **your egoic mind** tried to authorize the body to obey.

W-136.17.Now is the body healed because the source of sickness, **which is your mind,** has been opened to relief. 2 And you will recognize you practiced well by this: The body should not feel at all. 3 If you have been successful, there will be no sense of feeling ill or feeling well, of pain or pleasure. 4 No response at all is in the mind to what the body does. 5 **The body's** usefulness remains and nothing more.

W-136.18.Perhaps you do not realize that this removes the limits you had placed upon the body by the purposes you gave to **the body.** 2 As these **limits and purpose you placed upon the body** are laid aside, the strength the body has will always be enough to serve all truly useful purposes. 3 The body's health is fully guaranteed, because **the body's health** is not limited by time, by weather or fatigue, by food and drink, or any laws you made **the body to** serve before. 4 You need do nothing now to make **the body** well, for sickness has become impossible.

W-136.19.Yet this protection needs to be preserved by careful watching **to avoid following your old egoic thought system based upon lack, limitation and separation.** 2 If you let your mind harbor attack thoughts, yield to judgment or make plans against uncertainties to come, you have again misplaced yourself, and made a bodily identity which will attack the body, for the mind is sick.

W-136.20.Give instant remedy, should this occur, by not allowing your **ego's** defensiveness to hurt you longer. 2 Do not be confused about what must be healed, **which is your mind's limiting beliefs about who you really are,** but tell yourself:
3 I have forgotten what I really am, for I mistook my body for myself. 4 Sickness is an **egoic** defense against the truth. 5 But I am not a body. 6 And my mind cannot attack. 7 So I cannot be sick.

Notes to Lesson #136

Sickness is a defense against the truth.

Yesterday we mentioned that defenses are plans that you make against the truth. They are designed to support your belief that you are a little "s" self and not part of the shared Mind of God.

Every defense attempts to disassemble and separate the various aspects of an indivisible whole into numerous autonomous parts and then reassembles some of those aspects of the whole without regard to their true relationship to the whole. Defenses are designed to create the illusion that there are numerous autonomous separate entities that exist apart from each other and are different from what comprised the original whole. The true interrelationship and interconnectedness is disregarded and ignored.

A whole is indivisible and cannot be subdivided into smaller units or autonomous parts that have their own separate existence. A whole is not the sum of its parts because the relationships create something greater than the indivisible parts. When indivisible aspects are segregated from the whole and seen as separate and autonomous by themselves, they become an attack against the whole.

On a grand scale, we can see how this defense was utilized to attack the truth of the One Self. God cannot be defined because God is unlimited. To define is to limit. Yet, this is what we have attempted to do with that One Self. We speak of God the Father being Cause and the Son being the Effect. Yet, Father and Son are two aspects of one indivisible force that we call God. Each aspect is needed to complete the other. A cause without its effect is not a cause. An effect needs its cause for without it, the effect would cease to exist. Both cause and effect are dependent upon the other for their existence and form one indivisible whole. Without their true interrelationship and interconnectedness there would be no whole or separate parts. There would be nothing. Different aspects of one whole cannot have their own separate existences. The true relationship is that there is only the one. When we perceive any aspect to be autonomous from the whole, we have attacked the oneness of the shared Mind of God. Unless we are willing to drop our defenses which fragment the whole, we will never see our mind as part of the whole again.

Sickness is the ego's proof that you are the body and the body is you. You suffer pain because you believe your body does and in this suffering, you associate your mind as belonging to your body. Your mind becomes synonymous with the brain. When you believe your mind is just another body part, your mind must also accept the limitations that come with the physical body.

The ego utilizes sickness whenever the truth of your big "S" Self threatens to overcome your ego's belief in your littleness. A sick body is used to prove that the mind is part of and under the control of the body.

Yet, sickness is really your mind's decision to support your ego's belief in lack, limitation and separation. Sickness is not something that happens to you because you are an innocent victim of outside forces that are beyond your control. Both sickness and the death of the body create illusions that support the accuracy of the ego's belief in lack, limitation and separation. Sickness is a uniquely personal experience that cannot be shared with others since the sick person alone feels the direct effect of the pain.

Sickness is a decision of your mind and is not an accident. The idea that you would decide to be sick is often challenged. People invariably say that they did not want to be sick. Although on the surface this may appear to be true, there are numerous benefits that your egoic mind derives from sickness.

To your ego, sickness provides proof that you truly suffer from lack and limitation and are separate. Sickness reinforces the ego's claim that you are an innocent victim of outside forces that are beyond your control; that your mind is not the powerhouse behind your world. Being insignificant, you cannot be responsible for your world. Sickness proves that your ego's story about your littleness is right. You can now confidently declare that you are not responsible for your world and that the numerous negative experiences you encounter in your life are not your fault. You get to be irresponsible and yet claim you are a victim.

Question: Popular among New Age thought is the idea that sickness is the result of your mind's improper thinking. This belief often becomes the source of a great deal of guilt when "spiritual types" suffer a devastating illness to their own body. This often happens late in their life and leads these individuals to question the validity of their spiritual practices. They cannot see how their own thinking brought about the cancer, stroke, heart attack or other disease from which they suffer. This generates a crisis in their faith.

Can you see how sickness can be used by the ego to effectively attack your belief that your mind is the source for your experience?

If your physical body is sick, does that mean your mind must also be sick?

LESSON 137

When I am healed I am not healed alone.

W-137.1.Today's idea **that when I am healed I am not healed alone** remains the central thought on which salvation rests. 2 For healing is the opposite of all the world's ideas which dwell on sickness and on separate states. 3 Sickness is a retreat from others, and a shutting off of joining. 4 **Sickness** becomes a door that closes on a separate **little "s"** self, and keeps **the self** isolated and alone.

W-137.2.Sickness is isolation. 2 For **isolation** seems to keep one self apart from all the rest, to suffer what the others do not feel. 3 **Sickness** gives the body final power to make the separation real, and keep the mind in solitary prison, split apart and held in pieces by a solid wall of sickened flesh, which **the mind** cannot surmount.

W-137.3.The world obeys the laws that sickness serves, but healing operates apart from **the world's laws**. 2 It is impossible that anyone be healed alone. 3 In sickness must he be apart and separate. 4 But healing is his own **mind's** decision to be one again, and to accept his **big "S"** Self with all Its parts intact and unassailed. 5 In sickness does his **big "S"** Self appear to be dismembered, and without the unity that gives **the big "S" Self** life. 6 But healing is accomplished as he sees the body has no power to attack the universal Oneness of God's Son.

W-137.4.Sickness would prove that lies must be the truth. 2 But healing demonstrates that truth is true. 3 The separation sickness would impose has never really happened. 4 To be healed is merely to accept what always was the simple truth, and always will remain exactly as **the truth** has forever been. 5 Yet eyes accustomed to illusions must be shown that what **the eyes** look upon is false. 6 So healing, never needed by the truth, must demonstrate that sickness is not real.

W-137.5.Healing might thus be called a counter-dream, which cancels out the dream of sickness in the name of truth, but not in truth itself. 2 Just as forgiveness overlooks all sins that never were accomplished, healing but removes **the illusions of sickness** that have not occurred. 3 Just as the real world will arise to take the place of what has never been at all, healing but offers restitution for imagined states and false ideas which dreams embroider into **false** pictures of the truth.

W-137.6.Yet think not healing is unworthy of your function here. 2 For anti-Christ, **the belief that you are the body**, becomes more powerful than Christ to those who dream the world is real. 3 The body seems to be more solid and more stable than the mind. 4 And love becomes a dream, while fear remains the one reality that can be seen and justified and fully understood.

W-137.7.Just as forgiveness shines away all sin and the real world will occupy the place of what you made, so healing must replace the fantasies of sickness which you hold before the simple truth **that you are not a body but remain as God created you.** 2 When sickness has been seen to disappear in spite of all the laws that hold **that sickness** cannot but be real, then questions have been answered. 3 And the laws **sickness follows** can be no longer cherished nor obeyed.

W-137.8.Healing is freedom. 2 For **healing** demonstrates that dreams will not prevail against the truth. 3 Healing is shared. 4 And by this attribute **of sharing, healing** proves that **the laws of forgiveness, love and oneness,** unlike the **egoic laws of lack, limitation and separation** which hold that sickness is inevitable are more potent than their sickly **fear-based egoic** opposites. 5 Healing is strength. 6 For by **healing's** gentle hand is weakness overcome, and minds that were walled off within a body free to join with other minds, to be forever strong.

W-137.9.Healing, forgiveness, and the glad exchange of all the world of sorrow for a world where sadness cannot enter, are the means by which the Holy Spirit urges you to follow Him. 2 **The Holy Spirit's** gentle lessons teach how easily salvation can be yours; how little practice you need undertake to let **the Holy Spirit's** laws replace the **laws your ego** made to hold yourself a prisoner to death. 3 **The Holy Spirit's** life becomes your own, as you extend the little help **the Holy Spirit** asks in freeing you from **every egoic thought** that ever caused you pain.

W-137.10.And as you let yourself be healed, you see all those around you, or who cross your mind, or whom you touch or those who seem to have no contact with you, healed along with you. 2 Perhaps you will not recognize all **that your healing touches,** nor realize how great your offering **of healing is** to all the world, when you let healing come to you. 3 But you are never healed alone. 4 And legions upon legions will receive the gift of **healing** that you receive when you are healed.

W-137.11.Those who are healed become the instruments of healing. 2 Nor does time elapse between the instant **those who are healed** are healed, and all the grace of healing it is given **those who are healed** to give. 3 What is opposed to God does not exist, and who accepts not **what is opposed to God** within his mind becomes a haven where the weary can remain to rest. 4 For here **in the healed mind** is truth bestowed, and here are all illusions brought to truth.

W-137.12.Would you not offer shelter to God's Will? 2 You but invite your **big "S"** Self to be at home. 3 And can this invitation **to be in your true big "S" Self's home that you never left** be refused? 4 Ask the inevitable to occur, and you will never fail. 5 The other choice is but to ask what cannot be to be, and this cannot succeed. 6 Today we ask that only truth will occupy our minds; that thoughts of healing will this day go forth from what is healed to what must yet be healed, aware that **healed minds** will both occur as one **for when you are healed you are not healed alone.**

W-137.13.We will remember, as the hour strikes, our function is to let our minds be healed, that we may carry healing to the world, exchanging curse for blessing, pain for joy, and separation for the peace of God. 2 Is not a minute of the hour worth the giving to receive a gift like **healing**? 3 Is not a little time a small expense to offer for the gift of everything **that healing offers for when you are healed you are not healed alone?**

W-137.14.Yet must we be prepared for such a gift **of healing**. 2 And so we will begin the day with this, and give ten minutes to these thoughts with which we will conclude today at night as well:
3 When I am healed I am not healed alone. 4 And I would share my healing with the world, that sickness may be banished from the mind of God's one Son, Who is my only "**big "S" Self**.

W-137.15.Let healing be through you this very day. 2 And as you rest in quiet, be prepared to give **healing** as you receive **healing**, to hold but what you give, and to receive the Word of God to take the place of all the foolish **egoic** thoughts that ever were imagined. 3 Now we come together to make well all that was sick, and offer blessing where there was attack. 4 Nor will we let this function **of healing** be forgot as every hour of the day slips by, remembering our purpose **of healing** with this thought:
5 When I am healed I am not healed alone. 6 And I would bless my brothers, for I would be healed with **my brothers**, as **my brothers** are healed with me.

Notes to Lesson #137

When I am healed I am not healed alone.

Just as sickness is a defense against the truth of your big "S" Self's reality, healing is the acceptance of the truth that your body and your ego's little "s" self is the real illusion.

Sickness is isolation or retreat from others. It is the opposite of joining and is optimized by the sickness of the physical body. When you are physically sick, the body seems to have the power to make the separation appear real. When sick, you are alone, separate and apart from the rest. You suffer what the others do not feel because they are not your body. The bodily suffering seems to confirm that your ego was right and that you are the body and the body is you.

As sickness is a decision to be separate and isolated, healing is a decision to be one again, join and accept the truth that your big S Self remains as God created it, perfect, whole and complete. Healing is the acceptance that nothing can attack the universal truth and oneness that you share with the Mind of God.

While sickness is the belief that the mind is trapped, separate and isolated in the body, healing is the counter dream that cancels out the dream of sickness in the name of truth, but not in truth itself. Similar to forgiveness, which overlooks all sins that never took place but were only imagined, so does healing remove the illusion of sickness that had never occurred. Both sickness and sin have no reality, but only appear to exist within the delusional mind that argues for your littleness.

Healing is freedom because it demonstrates that dreams cannot prevail against the truth. Both sickness and healing are your own mind's decision. The decision for sickness supports the illusion of separation and the limitations that come with the body. The decision to be healed simply accepts the truth of your big "S" Self and joins in the sharing of that truth. Just like with forgiveness, when illusions are brought before the truth, the illusion of sickness disappears from the mind of the dreamer.

Healing is accomplished when one realizes that the body has no power over your big "S" Self. Healing proves truth is true and the false is false. Healing overlooks the illusion of sickness and overturns the limitations that your ego would place upon your mind.

Healing takes place at the level of mind. Your mind's limiting beliefs are the source of sickness and it is the mind that is healed from those beliefs. Just like a miracle which also takes place at the level of mind, an observable physical change in the body's condition may or may not occur. Do not mistake the physical appearance of the game token we call the body with the healing that actually takes place at the level of mind.

Forgiveness and healing are two tools that the Holy Spirit utilizes to reawaken us to the truth. Forgiveness addresses the illusion that you are a sinner. Healing corrects the illusion that you are the body. Our function is to let our split minds be healed, so we can carry that truth to the rest of the world.

By following the guidance of the Holy Spirit, we exchange pain and separation for joining and sharing. When truth is shared everyone gains and no one is diminished. Because healing is the joining and the sharing of the truth of our divine birthright, we are never healed alone.

<u>Question</u>: If the mind is healed from its limiting beliefs, why does that not automatically translate into a physical healing of the body?

Heaven is the decision I must make.

W-138.1.In this world **of perception,** Heaven is a choice, because here **in time** we believe there are alternatives to choose between. 2 We think **in time** that all things have an opposite, and what we want we choose. 3 If Heaven exists there must be hell as well, for contradiction is the way we make what we perceive, and what we think is real.

W-138.2.Creation knows no opposite. 2 But here **in the world of time and space** is opposition part of being "real." 3 It is this strange perception of the truth that makes the choice of Heaven seem to be the same as the relinquishment of hell. 4 It is not really thus **since hell is not real and Heaven has no opposite.** 5 Yet what is true in God's creation cannot enter here **in the world of perception** until **what is true in God's creation** is reflected in some form the world can understand. 6 Truth cannot come where **truth** could only be perceived with fear. 7 For this would be the error truth can be brought to illusions. 8 Opposition makes the truth unwelcome, and **truth** cannot come **where truth is unwelcomed, feared and not understood.**

W-138.3.Choice is the obvious escape from what appears as opposites. 2 Decision lets one of conflicting goals become the aim of effort and expenditure of time. 3 Without decision, time is but a waste and effort dissipated. 4 **Without decision, time** is spent for nothing in return, and time goes by without results. 5 **Without decision,** there is no sense of gain, for nothing is accomplished; nothing learned.

W-138.4.You need to be reminded that you think a thousand choices are confronting you, when there is really only one **choice** to make, **which is the choice for truth.** 2 And even this but seems to be a choice. 3 Do not confuse yourself with all the doubts that myriad decisions would induce. 4 You make but one. 5 And when that one is made, you will perceive **that the choice for truth** was no choice at all. 6 For truth is true, and nothing else is true. 7 There is no opposite to choose instead. 8 There is no contradiction to the truth. **The choice for the false is not a choice since it is unreal.**

W-138.5.Choosing depends on learning. 2 And the truth cannot be learned, but only recognized. 3 In recognition **truth's** acceptance lies, and as **truth** is accepted **truth** is known. 4 But knowledge is beyond the goals we seek to teach within the framework of this course. 5 Ours are teaching goals, to be attained through learning how to reach **the goals,** what **the goals** are, and what **the goals** offer you. 6 Decisions are the outcome of your learning, for **decisions** rest on what you have accepted as the truth of what you are, and what your needs must be.

W-138.6.In this insanely complicated world, Heaven appears to take the form of choice, rather than merely being what **Heaven** is. 2 Of all the choices you have tried to make this **choice for Heaven** is the simplest, most definitive and prototype of all the rest, the one **choice** which settles all decisions. 3 If you could decide the rest, this **choice for Heaven** remains unsolved. 4 But when you solve **the choice for Heaven,** the other **choices** are resolved with **the choice for Heaven,** for all decisions but conceal this one **decision for Heaven** by taking different forms. 5 Here **in the choice for Heaven** is the final and the only choice in which is truth accepted or denied.

W-138.7.So we begin today considering the choice **for Heaven** that time was made to help us make. 2 Such is **time's** holy purpose, now transformed from the intent **your ego's** gave **time, which was** that **time was to** be a means for demonstrating hell is real, hope changes to despair, and life itself must in the end be overcome by death. 3 **To the ego,** in death alone are opposites resolved, for ending opposition is to die. 4 And thus, **to the ego,** salvation must be seen as death, for life is seen as conflict. 5 **To the ego,** to resolve the conflict is to end your life as well.

W-138.8.These mad beliefs **of the ego like the idea that death is salvation** can gain unconscious hold of great intensity, and grip the mind with terror and anxiety so strong that **the egoic mind** will not relinquish its ideas about **the ego's** own protection. 2 **To the ego, the mind** must be saved from salvation, threatened to be safe, and magically armored against truth. 3 And these **fear-based egoic** decisions **that you must be saved from salvation and the truth** are made unaware, to keep **these egoic decisions** safely undisturbed; apart from **your decision-maker's** question and from reason and from doubt.

W-138.9.Heaven is chosen consciously. 2 The choice **for Heaven** cannot be made until alternatives are accurately seen and understood. 3 All **the ego's beliefs** that are veiled in shadows must be raised to understanding, to be judged again, this time with Heaven's help. 4 And all mistakes in judgment that the **split** mind had made before are open to correction, as the truth dismisses **the mistakes in egoic judgment** as causeless. 5 Now are **the mistakes in judgment recognized as** without **any** effects. 6 **The mistakes in judgment** cannot be concealed, because their nothingness is recognized.

W-138.10.The conscious choice of Heaven is as sure as is the ending of the fear of hell, when **the choice for Heaven** is raised from **the ego's unconscious** protective shield of unawareness, and is brought to **the decision-maker's** light. 2 Who can decide between the clearly seen and the unrecognized? 3 Yet who can fail to make a choice between alternatives when only one, **the choice for Heaven,** is seen as valuable; the other as a wholly worthless thing, a but imagined source of guilt and pain? 4 Who hesitates to make a choice like this? 5 And shall we hesitate to choose **Heaven** today?

W-138.11.We make the choice for Heaven as we wake, and spend five minutes making sure that we have made the one decision, **the choice for Heaven,** that is sane. 2 We recognize we make a conscious choice between what has existence, **which is Heaven,** and what has nothing but an appearance of the truth, **which is the ego's illusion of separation.** 3 The ego's pseudo-being brought to what is real, is flimsy and transparent in the light. 4 **The ego's pseudo-being** holds no terror now, for what was made enormous, vengeful, pitiless with hate, demands obscurity for fear to be invested there. 5 Now **your ego's belief system** is recognized as but a foolish, trivial mistake.

W-138.12.Before we close our eyes in sleep tonight, we reaffirm the choice **for Heaven** that we have made each hour in between. 2 And now we give the last five minutes of our waking day to the decision **for Heaven** with which we awoke. 3 As every hour passed, we have declared our choice **for Heaven** again, in a brief quiet time devoted to maintaining sanity. 4 And finally, we close the day with this, acknowledging we chose but what we want:
5 Heaven is the decision I must make. 6 I make **the choice for Heaven** now, and will not change my mind, because **Heaven** is the only thing I want.

Notes to Lesson #138

Heaven is the decision I must make.

This lesson says that heaven is a decision I must make. But what is heaven?

Heaven is not a place. It is a state of mind. Heaven is a symbol for the truth. Since God is only love, our acceptance of that truth would be heaven. Ultimately, you do not decide for heaven, instead you make a conscious decision for the truth.

Truth just is. There is no opposite to the truth.

Love is truth and has no opposites.

God is only love and has no opposite.

In truth, there is only Heaven which is God's love and has no opposite.

In the world of knowledge, only truth exists because only truth is real. There is nothing that exists outside of truth. Since there is no real opposite to truth, there is no alternative to choose but the truth.

The terms called God, love, truth, heaven, the real world and knowledge all become synonyms that stand for the Oneness of All That Is. They are all indivisible aspects of the One Self. Where one aspect exists, all the other aspects must also be there. These aspects are indivisible. Anything that exists must share these same characteristics since like begets like. There can be nothing outside the truth that is real. This One Self represents all that God created as God created it as an extension of the One Self. The terms represent what is real, eternal and changeless. They are the Oneness of All That Is and there is nothing else.

Yet, in the world of perception, which is the world of illusion, heaven, truth, love and God all appear to have opposites. In perception there appears to be heaven and hell; the true and the false; love and fear; and a God of love versus a God of fear. The world of perception is the world of imagination in which both the real and unreal can appear side by side in the same fantasy called time. In the illusion of time, opposites are what make your dream world of provisional reality appear to be real since change seems to happen. Change occurs in the dreamer's provisional reality whenever different decisions or choices are made within the mind of the dreamer.

Time is the measure of change. Time provides a game board in which one can imagine and pretend what it would be like to be something other than what they are. While playing on time's game board, each participant remains perfect, whole and complete, a part of the indivisible One Self. Yet, while playing, each temporarily forgets their oneness. Due to this temporary suspension of the knowledge of what they are, the participants can have a simulated experience that most clearly replicates reality, without any real consequence.

Without this amnesia or forgetfulness, the game of "What am I" would not be much fun or a challenge. It would be like playing tic tac toe. Once you have played the game a few times, you quickly realize that unless someone purposely tries to lose, the game will end in a draw. The game has so few options, it quickly becomes boring. The game of tic tac toe offers so few learning lessons that you quickly become a master of the game. Because of this, no one really wants to play it as an adult.

To hold your attention a game needs to have one of two elements. It needs to be fun or it needs to teach you something. The game of time offers both. A third component that makes for a good game is that it should be safe.

You would not want your children playing a game of cops and robbers with real loaded guns. Again, the illusion of time protects the participants from any real damage. They may appear to get bloody and even die but it has no actual effect. In the next moment, they always spring back to life for another go at the game. Each is happy to have had the experience and just a little wiser because of it. They now are a better player that has honed their skills in their quest to become a grand master of the game of "What am I."

Time allows for learning. Learning takes place when there appears to be conflicting choices. We learn through comparison and contrast. Without conflicting choices that allow for contrast and comparison, choice becomes more difficult. Black and white decisions are easier to make and provide better feedback. Shades of gray clutter and delay the decision-making process.

When you make a choice you get an experience. This experience provides the feedback or consequences that help you learn the effect of the choices that you have made. Decisions allow you to choose between conflicting goals. When you make a decision, you eliminate one of the goals which help you narrow the playing field of possibilities. Decisions are needed to advance toward the more desirable goal that you value and seek.

As you continue you make more decisions, you gain additional experiences that provide better feedback so that you can decide if you need to make any mid-course corrections to stay on target with your goals. Over time, as you learn more about the game of "What am I," you will focus your attention on one single goal. You will decide you want to only know the truth and be that truth.

In time, you think you have a choice. Yet, the choice for the false really is no choice. When you choose the false, you simply deny the truth but the truth still is the only thing that is real. Truth cannot be learned but only recognized.

In the world of perception, truth must be first understood to be an available alternative. Truth cannot come where truth is not welcomed or viewed with fear. One of the laws of perception states that what you fear, you cannot see. As long as you argue for your littleness, you will fear the truth of your Big "S" Self. You will not understand that your big "S" Self is a viable option. As long as you believe that this world provides something of value, whether it be hiding from a wrathful God or doing penance to earn some future reward, the choice for the truth will appear frightening.

Hell is the denial of the truth and the belief in the false. It is your own belief in the reality of your little "s" self. Your beliefs in the false are often held unconsciously so that they are never questioned. Because of these false beliefs, the truth can be made to appear frightening when you claim you do not know the truth of who you really are.

To the ego, the purpose of time is to keep you afraid of the truth of who you are. As long as you perceive yourself to be a sinner, you will fear leaving this world that you think protects you from a wrathful god. As long as you perceive you have sinned, you will value this world as a place in which you can earn back the love of your fearful god. To the Holy Spirit, the purpose of time is to restore your awareness to the truth. Once recognized, you can accept the truth and come home.

When you fail to make a decision, either one way or the other, you waste time. Decisions are needed to facilitate the learning process. Decisions are based on your beliefs about what you really are. The only decision that we came here to learn is that we only want the truth. When you choose the truth, all other decisions you had made become irrelevant because the truth was always the only viable choice. You realize the choice for the false is meaningless and offers nothing that you could want or value. It is the choice for nothing.

The choice for truth must be made consciously and freely. This choice for truth cannot be made in time until the alternatives are accurately seen, understood, questioned and then the decision to choose differently is made. The only alternatives are the true or the false. You are perfect, whole and complete or you are not. With the feedback that is derived from making decisions based on fear, we learn that there must be a better way.

You will choose to follow the Voice for Love. The choice was always between the acceptance of the truth of who you are or the denial of that truth. Eventually, we will all freely choose the choice for heaven. Heaven is the only real choice possible because truth, heaven, love and God have no opposites. There is only the One Self and you are an indivisible aspect of that One.

Question: Why do you think your ego would not want you to realize that you have the option of choosing the truth that you are your big "S" Self?

Question: If given the simple choice between being your ego's little "s" self or your big "S" Self, would it be a difficult decision?

LESSON 139

I will accept Atonement for myself.

W-139.1.**I will accept Atonement for myself** is the end of choice. 2 For **when we accept Atonement for ourselves,** we come to a decision to accept ourselves as God created us. 3 And what is choice except uncertainty of what we are? 4 There is no doubt **that** is not rooted here **in the uncertainty of what we are.** 5 There is no question but reflects this one **question about what you are.** 6 There is no conflict that does not entail the single, simple question, "What am I?"

W-139.2.Yet who could ask this question **of "What am I?"** except one who has refused to recognize himself? 2 Only refusal to accept yourself could make the question **of "What am I?"** seem to be sincere. 3 The only thing that can be surely known by any living thing is what it is. 4 From this one point of certainty **of what it is**, it looks on other things as certain as itself.

W-139.3.Uncertainty about what you must be is self-deception on a scale so vast, **the** magnitude **of the self-deception** can hardly be conceived. 2 To be alive and not to know yourself is to believe that you are really dead. 3 For what is life except to be yourself, and what but you can be alive instead? 4 Who is the doubter? 5 What is it he doubts? 6 Whom does he question? 7 Who can answer him **who claims he does not know himself**?

W-139.4.He, **who claims he does not know himself,** merely states that he is not himself, and therefore, being something else, becomes a questioner of what that something **else** is. 2 Yet he, **who claims he does not know himself,** could never be alive at all unless he knew the answer **of who he was.** 3 If he asks as if he does not know **who he is**, it merely shows he does not want to be the thing he is. 4 He has accepted **being the thing he is** because he lives. **He** has judged against **what he is** and denied **the** worth **of being what he is**, and has **then** decided that he does not know the only certainty by which he lives.

W-139.5.Thus he **who claims he does not know himself** becomes uncertain of his life, for what **his life** is has been denied by him. 2 It is for this denial **of what your life is** that you need Atonement. 3 Your denial **of what your life is** made no change in what you are. 4 But you have split your mind into what knows **the truth, your big "S" Self,** and does not know the truth, **your little "s" self.** 5 You are yourself. 6 There is no doubt of this. 7 And yet you doubt **you are yourself, your big "S" Self.** 8 But you do not ask what part of you can really doubt yourself. 9 **Your ego, your little "s" self,** cannot really be a part of you that asks this question. 10 For **your ego** asks of one, **your big "S" Self,** who knows the answer. 11 Were **your ego** a part of you, then certainty would be impossible **for your ego would not know the answer of what you are**.

W-139.6.Atonement remedies the strange idea that it is possible to doubt yourself, and be unsure of what you really are. 2 This **belief of the ego that you can be unsure of what you really are** is the depth of madness. 3 Yet **"What am I?"** is the universal question of the world. 4 What does this mean except the world is mad? 5 Why share **the world's** madness in the sad belief that what is universal here, **which is the claim each does not know what they are**, is true?

W-139.7.Nothing the world believes is true. 2 **The world** is a place whose purpose is to be a home where those who claim they do not know themselves can come to question what it is they are. 3 And **those who claim they do not know themselves** will come again until the time Atonement is accepted. And **those who claim they do not know themselves will come again to this world until they** learn it is impossible to doubt yourself, and not to be aware of what you are.

W-139.8.Only acceptance can be asked of you, for what you are, **your big "S" Self,** is certain. 2 **What you are** is set forever in the holy Mind of God, and in your own **mind of your big "S" Self.** 3 **What you are** is so far beyond all doubt and question that to ask what must be **obvious to your big "S" Self** is all the proof you need to show that you believe the contradiction that you know not what you cannot fail to know, **which is to know what you are.** 4 Is **what am I** a question or a statement which denies itself in **the** statement? 5 Let us not allow our holy minds to occupy themselves with senseless musings **and egoic imperfect questions** such as this.

W-139.9.We have a mission here **in this world**. 2 We did not come to reinforce the madness that we once believed in **that we are a little "s" self.** 3 Let us not forget the goal that we accepted **which is to end the mad claim of not knowing what you are.** 4 It is more than just our happiness alone we came to gain. 5 What we accept as what we are, **our big "S" Self,** proclaims what everyone must be, along with us. 6 Fail not your brothers, or you fail **your big "S" Self.** 7 Look lovingly on **your brothers,** that **your brothers** may know that they are part of you, and you **a part** of **your brothers' big "S" Self.**

W-139.10.This **Oneness** does Atonement teach. And **Atonement** demonstrates the Oneness of God's Son is unassailed by his **ego's mad** belief he knows not what he is. 2 Today accept Atonement, not to change reality, but merely to accept the truth about **what you are, your big "S" Self,** and go your way rejoicing in the endless Love of God. 3 It is but **to accept Atonement for yourself** that we are asked to do. 4 It is but **to accept Atonement for yourself** that we will do today.

W-139.11.Five minutes in the morning and at night we will devote to dedicate our minds to our assignment **of the acceptance of the Atonement for ourselves** for today. 2 We start with this review of what our mission is:
3 I will accept Atonement for myself, For I remain as God created me.
4 We have not lost the knowledge that God gave to us when **God** created us like **God, Himself.** 5 We can remember **this knowledge that we remain as God created us** for everyone, for in creation are all minds as one. 6 And in our memory is the

recall how dear our brothers are to us in truth, how much a part of us is every mind, how faithful **our brothers** have really been to us, and how our Father's Love contains them all.

W-139.12.In thanks for all creation, in the Name of its Creator and **God's** Oneness with all aspects of creation, we repeat our dedication to our cause today each hour, as we lay aside all thoughts that would distract us from our holy aim **of accepting Atonement for ourselves.** 2 For several minutes let your mind be cleared of all the foolish cobwebs which the world would weave around the holy Son of God. 3 And learn the fragile nature of the **ego's** chains that seem to keep the knowledge of **your big "S" Self** apart from your awareness, as you say:
4 I will accept Atonement for myself, For I remain as God created me.

Notes to Lesson #139

I will accept Atonement for myself.

The purpose of this world is to be a home for those who claim they do not know themselves. A place where the split minded can come to question what it is they really are. As long as they continue to claim that they do not know what they are, the split minded will continue coming here until they learn it is impossible to doubt oneself and not be aware of what you are.

This world will be the split minded's playschool where they can pretend they are a little "s" self until the time they remember and freely accept the truth of their big "S" Self. This world is a place where anyone can play the game of "What am I?" in perfect safety. By playing the game, you learn what you are not so that you can remember what you are.

In the real world, which is the world of knowledge, there is no uncertainty. If we were to describe our state of mind in the world of knowledge, it would be the "I Am" state. In creation, all minds are one mind and are part of that "I Am" state.

The separation is the mad idea that you could not know what you are. The world of perception was birthed out of doubt or uncertainty. Uncertainty and self-doubt about who you are would be described as the "What am I?" state of mind. In time, which is in the world of perception, we seem to have choice only because we claim to be uncertain about what we are. All conflict arises out of the question of "What am I?"

Uncertainty about what you are is a massive self-deception. This deception is on so large a scale that on a mass collective consciousness basis, we birthed a world in which the entire planet goes around asking the question "What am I?"

What is life accept to be yourself. It is impossible to not know and be yourself. Even when pretending, you are still you. In order to play the game of "What am I?" within your own mind, you need to split off a part of your mind that can claim it does not know itself from the part of your mind that does know the truth. Throughout this course, these parts have been referred to as your little "s" self and your big "S" Self.

The world of time and space is the game board upon which the game of "What I am?" is played out. The game always ends with each participant reawakening and remembering the truth of who they are. This is the acceptance of Atonement for themselves.

The Atonement is the acceptance of who you really are, your big "S" Self. It is the realization that you remain as God created you. The Atonement is the At-One-Ment or knowledge that the separation is not real. Atonement teaches and demonstrates that the oneness of God's Son is unaffected by our split mind's belief that you do not know what you are.

The Atonement is the end of choice for it is our decision to accept ourselves as God created us. Change is not required since it is only the acceptance of the truth that we remain forever in the Mind of God as God created us, perfect, whole and complete.

Question: Why does the lesson ask that you only accept Atonement for yourself? Shouldn't you be accepting it for everyone?

LESSON 140

Only salvation can be said to cure.

W-140.1."Cure" is a word that cannot be applied to any **egoic** remedy the world accepts as beneficial. 2 What the world perceives as therapeutic is but what will make the body "better." 3 When **the egoic world** tries to heal the mind, **it** sees no separation **of the mind** from the body. **In the egoic world, the body's brain is where it** thinks the mind exists. 4 **Since the mind is not the brain, this world's** forms of healing thus must substitute illusion for illusion. 5 One belief in sickness takes another form, and so the patient now perceives himself as well.

W-140.2.**The patient** is not healed. 2 **The patient** merely had a dream that he was sick, and in the dream he found a magic formula to make him well. 3 Yet **the patient** has not awakened from the dream **that he is not the body**, and so his **delusional** mind remains exactly as it was before. 4 He has not seen the light that would awaken him and end the dream **of pretending to not know what he is**. 5 What difference does the content of a dream make in reality? 6 One either sleeps or wakens **to the truth that your big "S" Self is what you are**. 7 There is nothing in between.

W-140.3.The happy dreams the Holy Spirit brings are different from the dreaming of the world, where one can merely dream he is awake. 2 The dreams forgiveness lets the mind perceive do not induce another form of sleep, so that the dreamer dreams another dream. 3 **The Holy Spirit's** happy dreams **of forgiveness** are heralds of the dawn of truth upon the mind. 4 **The Holy Spirit's happy dreams of forgiveness** lead from sleep to gentle waking, so that dreams are gone. 5 And thus **the patient's sick mind is** cure for all eternity.

W-140.4.Atonement heals with certainty, and cures all sickness. 2 For the mind which understands that sickness can be nothing but a dream is not deceived by the **physical and nonphysical** forms the dream may take. 3 Sickness where guilt is absent cannot come, for **sickness** is but another form of guilt. 4 Atonement does not heal the sick, for that is not a cure. 5 **Atonement** takes away the guilt that makes the sickness possible. 6 And that **taking away of the guilt that makes sickness possible** is cure indeed. 7 For sickness now is gone, with no **guilt** left to which **sickness** can return.

W-140.5.Peace be to you who have been cured in God, and not in idle dreams. **You have accepted the At-One-Ment for yourself.**2 For cure, **which is the removal of guilt,** must come from holiness, and holiness cannot be found **in illusions of this world** where sin is cherished. 3 God abides in holy temples. 4 **God** is barred where sin has entered. 5 Yet there is no place where **God** is not **since sin is not real**. 6 And therefore sin can have no home in which to hide from **God's** beneficence. 7 There is no place where holiness is not, and nowhere sin and sickness can abide.

W-140.6.**There is no place where holiness is not, and nowhere sin and sickness can abide** is the thought that cures. **This is the truth of the Atonement.** 2 **This thought that cures** does not make distinctions among unrealities. 3 Nor does **this thought that cures** seek to heal what is not sick, unmindful where the need for healing is **which is the mind's erroneous beliefs about what you are** . 4 This is no magic. 5 **This thought that cures, which is that there is no place where holiness is not, and nowhere sin and sickness can abide,** is merely an appeal to truth, which cannot fail to heal and heal forever. 6 **That there is no place where holiness is not, and nowhere sin and sickness can abide,** is not a thought that judges an illusion by its size, its seeming gravity, or anything that is related to the form **the illusion** takes. 7 **This thought that cures** merely focuses on **the truth of** what it is, and knows that no illusion can be real.

W-140.7.Let us not try today to seek to cure what cannot suffer sickness. **The mind's beliefs, not the body is sick.** 2 Healing must be sought but where it is **needed, which is the sick mind**, and then applied to what is sick, so that **what is sick** can be cured. 3 There is no remedy the world provides that can effect a change in anything. 4 The mind that brings illusions to the truth is really changed. 5 There is no change **that can heal** but **the bringing of the mind's illusions to the truth.** 6 For how can one illusion differ from another **illusion** but in attributes that have no substance, no reality, no core, and nothing that is truly different?

W-140.8.Today we seek to change our minds about the source of sickness, **which is our mind's beliefs about what we are**, for we seek a cure for all illusions, not another shift among **illusions**. 2 We will try today to find the source of healing, which is in our minds because our Father placed **the Holy Spirit, the source of healing** there for us **within our big "S" Self**. 3 **The source of healing** is not farther from us than **our big "S" Selves**. 4 **The Holy Spirit** is as near to us as our own thoughts; so close **that the source of healing** is impossible to lose. 5 We need but seek **the Holy Spirit** and **the source of healing** must be found.

W-140.9.We will not be misled today by what appears to us as sick **which is merely the form**. 2 We go beyond **all illusions and bodily** appearances today and reach the source of healing, from which nothing is exempt. 3 We will succeed to the extent to which we realize that there can never be a meaningful distinction made between what is untrue and equally untrue. 4 Here, **in illusions** there are no degrees, and no beliefs that what does not exist is truer in some forms **of illusions** than other **illusionary forms**. 5 All of the forms **that illusions take** are **equally** false, and can be cured because **all illusions** are not true.

W-140.10.So do we lay aside our amulets, our charms and medicines, our chants and bits of magic in whatever form they take. 2 We will be still and listen for the Voice of healing, which will cure all ills as one, restoring saneness to the Son of God. 3 No voice but **the Holy Spirit's** can cure. 4 Today we hear a single Voice **of the Holy Spirit** which speaks to us of truth, where all illusions end, and peace returns to the eternal, quiet home of God.

W-140.11.We waken hearing **the Holy Spirit**, and let **the Holy Spirit** speak to us five minutes as the day begins, and end the day by listening again five minutes more before we go to sleep. 2 Our only preparation is to let our interfering thoughts be laid aside, not separately, but all of **our interfering thoughts** as one. 3 **All our interfering thoughts** are the same. 4 We have no need to make **our interfering thoughts** different, and thus delay the time when we can hear our Father speak to us. 5 We hear **our Father** now. 6 We come to **our Father** today.

W-140.12.With nothing in our hands to which we cling, with lifted hearts and listening minds we pray:
2 Only salvation can be said to cure.
3 Speak to us, Father, that we may be healed.
4 And we will feel salvation cover us with soft protection, and with peace so deep that no illusion can disturb our minds, nor offer proof to us that **an illusion** is real. 5 This will we learn today **that only salvation can be said to cure.** 6 And we will say our prayer for healing hourly, and take a minute as the hour strikes, to hear the answer to our prayer be given us as we attend in silence and in joy. 7 This is the day when healing comes to us **for only salvation can be said to cure**. 8 This is the day when separation ends, and we remember Who we really are.

Notes to Lesson #140

Only salvation can be said to cure.

What are you?

Are you a spiritual being having an earthly experience?

Or

Are you your body?

All our problems come from our failure to get the first question right. There is no conflict that does not involve the question of, What am I. When you answer this question correctly, all your problems fade away. When you claim you do not know what you are, your mind becomes clouded with uncertainties. Your mind is now sick.

Sickness as defined in this class is a mind that does not know itself.

It is the mind that is sick and not the game token we call the body. All healing takes place at the level of mind because mind is the source for all sickness. The mind's beliefs about what is true must be corrected.

If you are playing a game that utilizes a game board, does it really matter what the game token that holds your place on the board looks like? If you are to advance four spaces, are you prevented from moving on the board because you are using a paperclip instead of a game token that looks like a race car?

Since the world believes that you are the physical body, egoic healing revolves around administering to the body. Even mental illness is seen as a problem within your physical brain. The medical community looks at the physical and mental health of their patient, but is silent about their spiritual health. If you are a spiritual being, your spiritual health is the criteria for determining good health.

Egoic healing assumes the mind is a body part, and merely substitutes one illusion for another. It mistakes the body for you, gives you a diagnosis that your game token looks bad, gives the game token a facelift and then pronounces you healed. Egoic healing maintains the charade that you are the game token. But you are not the body.

The physical body has nothing to do with your spiritual health which centers around your own self-image of what you are. You can get a facelift, take some wonder drug or other magical formula that administers to the game token but you will still suffer from a poor self-image. The illusion that you are a sick body has changed to the illusion that your body is in good health, but your mind's identification with the body has not changed. Your mind is still sick because you still do not recognize the reality of your big "S" Self.

The healing of the Holy Spirit corrects the delusional mind's belief in its existence as a little "s" self. True healing reawakens your mind to the reality of your big "S" Self by correcting the uncertainty of what you are. Healing is the replacement of your ego's belief in lack, limitation and separation with the truth that you remain as God created you.

Sin is your belief in lack. Sin is your belief that you are not as God created you, perfect, whole and complete. Sin is uncertainty about the truth of who you really are. This "What am I?" state of mind generates a great deal of guilt. Sin, guilt and fear are at the core of your ego's thought system. Sickness needs guilt and is just another physical manifestation of guilt in this world. An ill body is only an effect of a guilty mind.

If true healing is to take place, the mind's belief about what it is needs to be corrected. The source of guilt that manifests as sickness in the body needs to be removed. It is your ego's belief in your littleness that is the source of your guilt and needs to be removed.

Atonement, which is the acceptance of the truth about what you are, does not heal the sick. Instead, the Atonement takes away guilt that has made sickness possible. Atonement merely brings illusions to the truth and the mind is healed. The separation and identification with the body is recognized as not real. With the source of the guilt removed, true healing can occur.

The Holy Spirit uses forgiveness to eliminate the guilt which causes sickness. Healing comes from the holiness of what you are. To be holy is to make whole. By following the guidance of the Holy Spirit, you can see all as equally sinless. Atonement focuses on the acceptance of the truth of what is.

When you accept Atonement for yourself, you know that no illusion is real and therefore, all dreams of guilt disappear. There are no degrees of difficulty when it comes to healing. Atonement heals all illusions about what you really are. The dream that you have cancer or the dream that you have the flu is recognized as the same dream. Both are equally not true.

Important Note: You should not feel guilty because you have chosen to play on time's game board of "What am I?" This game board is simply a playschool in which you can have fun while you learn and demonstrate the truth that the separation is not real.

If a boy wants to pretend he is a dog, there is nothing wrong with playing that game. The game itself can be fun and a source for learning. A problem only arises when the boy forgets who he is and identifies himself as a dog. Now his mind is sick and needs to be healed.

On the game board of time, the goal is to accept Atonement for yourself. That is how the game must end. When you accept Atonement for yourself, it is the reawakening to the truth that you are God's beloved child and are no longer bound by the rules of a fear-based world.

It does not mean that you no longer can play on the game board of time. It merely means you will realize the truth that you remain as God created you. You have simply decided to use the freedom that love grants you to participate on the game board of "What am I? No sin has been committed and no guilt need be involved. Instead, you have chosen to demonstrate being love in form. Through you, the abstract One Self gets to demonstrate and be a specific aspect of Itself.

In time, love is the creative process in which time is utilized to reawaken sleeping minds to their spiritual magnificence that they are the Christ. In the world of perception, you can choose to play the role that aligns with the truth of your big "S" Self. When you make that choice, you dismiss the voice for littleness and follow the guidance of the Holy Spirit. You simply ask what would love have me do. Then silence your ego and follow the Voice for Truth.

Question: What is the interrelationship between Truth, Atonement, Salvation and Time?

Hint: Truth just is. Truth is real and timeless. Truth has no opposites. Truth is beyond time. Both the Atonement and Salvation are relevant only in the illusionary realm of time because only in time is the game of separation played out. Salvation and the Atonement belong in our mind's imagination that believes sin to be real.

In time, the Atonement is the acceptance of the truth. It becomes the means for the removal of guilt that arises from your uncertainty of not knowing who you are. Atonement is the healing of your split mind.

Salvation is the knowing of Truth. Salvation is the end of both perception and time and the return to knowledge. Salvation is the recognition that your split mind is healed.

Atonement is the means and salvation is the end. The game of uncertainty and the belief in separation is over.

REVIEW #4

Introduction

Review of Workbook Lessons 121-140

W-rIV.in.1.Now we review again, this time aware we are preparing for the second part of learning how the truth can be applied. 2 Today we will begin to concentrate on readiness for what will follow next. 3 **Your readiness for the lessons that will follow** is our aim for this review, and for the lessons following. 4 Thus, we review the recent lessons and their central thoughts in such a way as will facilitate the readiness that we would now achieve.

W-rIV.in.2.There is a central theme that unifies each step in the review we undertake, which can be simply stated in these words:
2 My mind holds only what I think with God.
3 That **my mind holds only what I think with God** is a fact, and represents the truth of What you are and What your Father is. 4 It is this thought **that my mind holds only what I think with God** by which the Father gave creation to the Son, establishing the Son as co-creator with Himself. 5 It is this thought **that my mind holds only what I think with God** that fully guarantees salvation to the Son. 6 For in **the Son's** mind no thoughts can dwell but those his Father shares. 7 Lack of forgiveness blocks this thought **that my mind holds only what I think with God** from **the Son's** awareness. 8 Yet **this thought that my mind holds only what I think with God** is forever true.

W-rIV.in.3.Let us begin our preparation with some understanding of the many forms in which the lack of true forgiveness may be carefully concealed. 2 Because **these blocks to forgiveness** are illusions, **these blocks to forgiveness** are not perceived to be but what they are; defenses that protect your unforgiving thoughts from being seen and recognized. 3 **The purpose of these blocks to forgiveness** is to show you something else, and hold correction off through self-deceptions made to take **true forgiveness'** place.

W-rIV.in.4.And yet, your mind holds only what you think with God. 2 Your self-deceptions cannot take the place of truth. 3 No more than can a child who throws a stick into the ocean change the coming and the going of the tides, the warming of the water by the sun, the silver of the moon on **the ocean** by night. 4 So do we start each practice period in this review with readying our minds to understand the lessons that we read, and see the meaning that **those lessons** offer us.

W-rIV.in.5.Begin each day with time devoted to the preparation of your mind to learn what each idea you will review that day can offer you in freedom and in peace. 2 Open your mind, and clear **your mind** of all thoughts that would deceive, and let this thought **that my mind holds only what I think with God** alone engage **your mind** fully, and remove the rest:
3 My mind holds only what I think with God.
4 Five minutes with this thought **that my mind holds only what I think with God** will be enough to set the day along the lines which God appointed, and to place **God's** Mind in charge of all the thoughts you will receive that day.

W-rIV.in.6.**All the thoughts you will receive that day** will not come from you alone, for **those thoughts** will all be shared with **God**. 2 And so each **thought** will bring the message of **God's** Love to you, returning messages of your **love** to God. 3 So will communion with the Lord of Hosts be yours, as **God** Himself has willed **communion to** be between **Father and Son**. 4 And as **God's** Own completion, **which is you**, joins with **God**, so will **God's completion** join with you who are complete as you unite with **God** and **God** with you.

W-rIV.in.7.After your preparation, merely read each of the two ideas assigned to you to be reviewed that day. 2 Then close your eyes, and say **the two ideas assigned for your review** slowly to yourself. 3 There is no hurry now, for you are using time for **time's** intended purpose, **which is your reawakening**. 4 Let each word shine with the meaning God has given it, as **each word** was given to you through **God's** Voice. 5 Let each idea which you review that day give you the gift that **God** has laid in **each idea** for you to have of **God**. 6 And we will use no format for our practicing but this:

W-rIV.in.8.Each hour of the day, bring to your mind the thought with which the day began **that my mind holds only what I think with God**, and spend a quiet moment with **that thought**. 2 Then repeat the two ideas you practice for the day unhurriedly, with time enough to see the gifts that **the two ideas for the day** contain for you, and let **the gifts** be received where **the gifts** were meant to be.

W-rIV.in.9.We add no other thoughts, but let these be the messages **that these two ideas for the day** are. 2 We need no more than **these two** ideas for the day to give us happiness and rest, and endless quiet, perfect certainty, and all our Father wills that we receive as the inheritance we have of **our Father**. 3 Each day of practicing, as we review, we close as we began, repeating first the thought **that my mind holds only what I think with God which** made the day a special time of blessing and of happiness for us; and through our faithfulness restored the world from darkness to the light, from grief to joy, from pain to peace, from sin to holiness.

W-rIV.in.10.God offers thanks to you who practice thus the keeping of **God's** Word. 2 And as you give your mind to the ideas for the day again before you sleep, **God's** gratitude surrounds you in the peace wherein **God** wills you be forever, and are learning now to claim **that peace** again as your **divine** inheritance.

Review of Workbook Lessons 121-140

Introduction

Lessons 141-150 are a review of Workbook Lessons #121-140

The next 10 lessons are actually a review of the previous 20. Each day you will be asked to review two of the previous lessons with an emphasis on one of the prior lessons in either your morning or evening sessions. I will not be providing any additional notes regarding these review lessons since they are brief, self-explanatory and designed for the inner contemplation of those prior lessons to prepare you for the lessons that will follow.

I would suggest that you review the notes that were given for each original lesson that you are focusing on during each session. For example, lesson 141 covers lesson 121 and 122. Assuming your morning session will focus on lesson 121, I would suggest you review the notes for session 121 along with a reading of the main idea of lesson 122. In your evening session you would review the notes for lesson 122 along with a reading of the main idea of lesson 121. Remember to begin each session with the thought that my mind holds only what I think with God.

You will be amazed at the new insight that each review will provide. What seemed obscure a few days ago may now appear obvious. Enjoy these reviews and honor the journey of rediscovering who you really are.

LESSON 141.

LESSON SUMMARY #121-122

My mind holds only what I think with God

W-141.1.(121) Forgiveness is the key to happiness.

W-141.2.(122) Forgiveness offers everything I want.

General instruction:

Begin each session with time devoted to preparing your mind to learn what each of today's review lessons will offer you in freedom and in peace. Open and clear your mind of all thoughts that would block your communion with God. Let this thought that
My mind holds only what I think with God
engage your mind fully. After your preparation, merely read each of the two ideas assigned today for your review. Then close your eyes, and say the two ideas for review slowly to yourself.

Forgiveness is the key to happiness.

Forgiveness offers everything I want.

There is no hurry. Let each idea which you review today give you the gifts that the Holy Spirit has prepared for you. This is the only format for your practice periods. Once again begin with the thought that
My mind holds only what I think with God.
Followed by

Forgiveness is the key to happiness.

Forgiveness offers everything I want.

LESSON 142.

LESSON SUMMARY #123-124

My mind holds only what I think with God.

W-142.1.(123) I thank my Father for His gifts to me.

W-142.2.(124) Let me remember I am one with God.

General instruction:

Begin each session with time devoted to preparing your mind to learn what each of today's review lessons will offer you in freedom and in peace. Open and clear your mind of all thoughts that would block your communion with God. Let this thought that
My mind holds only what I think with God
engage your mind fully. After your preparation, merely read each of the two ideas assigned today for your review. Then close your eyes, and say the two ideas for review slowly to yourself.
I thank my Father for His gifts to me.

Let me remember I am one with God.

There is no hurry. Let each idea which you review today give you the gifts that the Holy Spirit has prepared for you. This is the only format for your practice periods. Once again begin with the thought that
My mind holds only what I think with God.
Followed by

I thank my Father for His gifts to me.

Let me remember I am one with God.

LESSON 143.

LESSON SUMMARY #125-126

My mind holds only what I think with God.

W-143.1.(125) In quiet I receive God's Word today.

W-143.2.(126) All that I give is given to myself.

General instruction:

Begin each session with time devoted to preparing your mind to learn what each of today's review lessons will offer you in freedom and in peace. Open and clear your mind of all thoughts that would block your communion with God. Let this thought that
My mind holds only what I think with God
engage your mind fully. After your preparation, merely read each of the two ideas assigned today for your review. Then close your eyes, and say the two ideas for review slowly to yourself.
In quiet I receive God's Word today.

All that I give is given to myself.

There is no hurry. Let each idea which you review today give you the gifts that the Holy Spirit has prepared for you. This is the only format for your practice periods. Once again begin with the thought that
My mind holds only what I think with God.
Followed by

In quiet I receive God's Word today.

All that I give is given to myself.

LESSON 144.

LESSON SUMMARY #127-128

My mind holds only what I think with God.

W-144.1.(127) There is no love but God's.

W-144.2.(128) The world I see holds nothing that I want.

General instruction:

Begin each session with time devoted to preparing your mind to learn what each of today's review lessons will offer you in freedom and in peace. Open and clear your mind of all thoughts that would block your communion with God. Let this thought that
My mind holds only what I think with God
engage your mind fully. After your preparation, merely read each of the two ideas assigned today for your review. Then close your eyes, and say the two ideas for review slowly to yourself.
There is no love but God's.

The world I see holds nothing that I want.

There is no hurry. Let each idea which you review today give you the gifts that the Holy Spirit has prepared for you. This is the only format for your practice periods. Once again begin with the thought that
My mind holds only what I think with God.
Followed by

There is no love but God's.

The world I see holds nothing that I want.

LESSON 145.

LESSON SUMMARY #129-130

My mind holds only what I think with God.

W-145.1.(129) Beyond this world there is a world I want.

W-145.2.(130) It is impossible to see two worlds.

General instruction:

Begin each session with time devoted to preparing your mind to learn what each of today's review lessons will offer you in freedom and in peace. Open and clear your mind of all thoughts that would block your communion with God. Let this thought that
My mind holds only what I think with God
engage your mind fully. After your preparation, merely read each of the two ideas assigned today for your review. Then close your eyes, and say the two ideas for review slowly to yourself.
Beyond this world there is a world I want.

It is impossible to see two worlds.

There is no hurry. Let each idea which you review today give you the gifts that the Holy Spirit has prepared for you. This is the only format for your practice periods. Once again begin with the thought that
My mind holds only what I think with God.
Followed by

Beyond this world there is a world I want.

It is impossible to see two worlds.

LESSON 146.

LESSON SUMMARY #131-132

My mind holds only what I think with God.

W-146.1.(131) No one can fail who seeks to reach the truth.

W-146.2.(132) I loose the world from all I thought it was.

General instruction:

Begin each session with time devoted to preparing your mind to learn what each of today's review lessons will offer you in freedom and in peace. Open and clear your mind of all thoughts that would block your communion with God. Let this thought that
My mind holds only what I think with God
engage your mind fully. After your preparation, merely read each of the two ideas assigned today for your review. Then close your eyes, and say the two ideas for review slowly to yourself.
No one can fail who seeks to reach the truth.

I loose the world from all I thought it was.

There is no hurry. Let each idea which you review today give you the gifts that the Holy Spirit has prepared for you. This is the only format for your practice periods. Once again begin with the thought that
My mind holds only what I think with God.
Followed by

No one can fail who seeks to reach the truth.

I loose the world from all I thought it was.

LESSON 147.

LESSON SUMMARY #133-134

My mind holds only what I think with God.

W-147.1.(133) I will not value what is valueless.

W-147.2.(134) Let me perceive forgiveness as it is.

General instruction:

Begin each session with time devoted to preparing your mind to learn what each of today's review lessons will offer you in freedom and in peace. Open and clear your mind of all thoughts that would block your communion with God. Let this thought that
My mind holds only what I think with God
engage your mind fully. After your preparation, merely read each of the two ideas assigned today for your review. Then close your eyes, and say the two ideas for review slowly to yourself.
I will not value what is valueless.

Let me perceive forgiveness as it is.

There is no hurry. Let each idea which you review today give you the gifts that the Holy Spirit has prepared for you. This is the only format for your practice periods. Once again begin with the thought that
My mind holds only what I think with God.
Followed by

I will not value what is valueless.

Let me perceive forgiveness as it is.

LESSON 148.

LESSON SUMMARY #135-136

My mind holds only what I think with God.

W-148.1.(135) If I defend myself I am attacked.

W-148.2.(136) Sickness is a defense against the truth.

General instruction:

Begin each session with time devoted to preparing your mind to learn what each of today's review lessons will offer you in freedom and in peace. Open and clear your mind of all thoughts that would block your communion with God. Let this thought that
My mind holds only what I think with God
engage your mind fully. After your preparation, merely read each of the two ideas assigned today for your review. Then close your eyes, and say the two ideas for review slowly to yourself.
If I defend myself I am attacked.

Sickness is a defense against the truth.

Forgiveness offers everything I want.

There is no hurry. Let each idea which you review today give you the gifts that the Holy Spirit has prepared for you. This is the only format for your practice periods. Once again begin with the thought that
My mind holds only what I think with God.
Followed by

If I defend myself I am attacked.

Sickness is a defense against the truth.

LESSON SUMMARY #137-138

My mind holds only what I think with God.

W-149.1.(137) When I am healed I am not healed alone.

W-149.2.(138) Heaven is the decision I must make.

<u>General instruction</u>:

Begin each session with time devoted to preparing your mind to learn what each of today's review lessons will offer you in freedom and in peace. Open and clear your mind of all thoughts that would block your communion with God. Let this thought that
My mind holds only what I think with God
engage your mind fully. After your preparation, merely read each of the two ideas assigned today for your review. Then close your eyes, and say the two ideas for review slowly to yourself.
When I am healed I am not healed alone.

Heaven is the decision I must make.

There is no hurry. Let each idea which you review today give you the gifts that the Holy Spirit has prepared for you. This is the only format for your practice periods. Once again begin with the thought that
My mind holds only what I think with God.
Followed by

When I am healed I am not healed alone.

Heaven is the decision I must make.

LESSON SUMMARY #139-140

My mind holds only what I think with God.

W-150.1.(139) I will accept Atonement for myself.

W-150.2.(140) Only salvation can be said to cure.

<u>General instruction</u>:

Begin each session with time devoted to preparing your mind to learn what each of today's review lessons will offer you in freedom and in peace. Open and clear your mind of all thoughts that would block your communion with God. Let this thought that
My mind holds only what I think with God
engage your mind fully. After your preparation, merely read each of the two ideas assigned today for your review. Then close your eyes, and say the two ideas for review slowly to yourself.
I will accept Atonement for myself.

Only salvation can be said to cure.

There is no hurry. Let each idea which you review today give you the gifts that the Holy Spirit has prepared for you. This is the only format for your practice periods. Once again begin with the thought that
My mind holds only what I think with God.
Followed by

I will accept Atonement for myself.

Only salvation can be said to cure.

LESSON 151

All things are echoes of the Voice for God.

W-151.1.No one can judge on partial evidence. 2 **To judge on partial evidence** is not judgment. 3 **To judge on partial evidence** is merely an opinion based on ignorance and doubt. 4 **Judgment based on partial evidence's** seeming certainty is but a cloak for the uncertainty **that the opinion** would conceal. 5 **Judgment based on partial evidence** needs irrational defense because **the judgment's opinion** is irrational. 6 And **a** defense **based on partial evidence** seems strong, convincing, and without a doubt because of all the doubting underneath **that judgment's opinion.**

W-151.2.You do not seem to doubt the world you see. 2 You do not really question what is shown you through the body's eyes. 3 Nor do you ask why you believe **what is shown you through the body's eyes**, even though you learned a long while since your senses do deceive **you**. 4 That you believe **your senses** to the last detail **about that** which **your senses** report is even stranger, when you pause to recollect how frequently **your senses** have been faulty witnesses indeed! 5 Why would you trust **your senses** so implicitly? 6 Why but because of underlying doubt **about your judgment**, which you would hide with **a** show of **egoic** certainty?

W-151.3.How can you judge? 2 Your judgment rests upon the witness that your senses offer you. 3 Yet witness never falser was than **your senses**. 4 But how else do you judge the world you see? 5 You place pathetic faith in what your eyes and ears report. 6 You think your fingers touch reality, and close upon the truth. 7 This **sensory information filtered by your ego** is **an** awareness that you understand, and think more real than what is witnessed to by the eternal Voice for God Himself.

W-151.4.Can this be judgment? 2 You have often been urged to refrain from judging, not because **judgment** is a right to be withheld from you. 3 You cannot judge. 4 You merely can believe the ego's judgments, all of which are false. 5 **Your ego** guides your senses carefully, to prove how weak you are; how helpless and afraid, how apprehensive of just punishment, how black with sin, how wretched in your guilt.

W-151.5.This **weak and sinful little "s"** thing **your ego** speaks of, and would yet defend, **your ego** tells you is **your real self.** 2 And you believe that your ego's **little "s" image of yourself** is so with stubborn certainty. 3 Yet underneath remains the hidden doubt that what **your ego** shows you as reality with such conviction, **your ego** does not believe **to be really true**. 4 It is **the ego,** itself, alone that **your ego** condemns. 5 It is within **the ego,** itself, **that your ego** sees the guilt. 6 It is **the ego's** own despair **that your ego** sees **and claims is** in you.

W-151.6.Hear not **your ego's** voice. 2 The witnesses **that your ego** sends to prove to you **that the ego's** evil is your own are false, and **the ego's witnesses including your senses** speak with certainty of what **these false witnesses and your ego** do not know. 3 Your faith in **your ego's false witnesses** is blind because you would not share the doubts their lord, **your ego,** cannot completely vanquish. 4 You believe to doubt **the ego's** vassals **including the physical senses** is to doubt yourself.

W-151.7.Yet you must learn to doubt **the false** evidence **that the ego's witness bring because it** will clear the way to recognize **your big S" Self,** and let the Voice for God alone be Judge of what is worthy of your own belief. 2 **The Holy Spirit** will not tell you that your brother should be judged by what your eyes behold in him, nor what **your brother's** body's mouth says to your ears, nor **that you should judge your brother by** what your fingers' touch reports of him. 3 **The Holy Spirit** passes by such idle witnesses **like the physical senses** which merely bear false witness to God's Son. 4 **The Holy Spirit** recognizes only what God loves, and in the holy light of what **the Holy Spirit** sees do all the ego's dreams of what you are vanish before the splendor **the Holy Spirit** beholds.

W-151.8.Let **the Holy Spirit** be Judge of what you are, for **the Holy Spirit** has certainty in which there is no doubt, because **the Holy Spirit's judgment** rests on Certainty so great that doubt is meaningless before Its face. 2 Christ cannot doubt Himself. 3 The Voice for God can only honor **Christ, your big "S" Self,** rejoicing in **Christ's** perfect, everlasting sinlessness. 4 Whom **the Holy Spirit** has judged can only laugh at guilt, unwilling now to play with toys of sin; unheeding of the body's witnesses before the rapture of Christ's holy face.

W-151.9.And thus **the Holy Spirit** judges you **as the face of Christ**. 2 Accept **the Holy Spirit's** Word for what you are, **the Christ, your big "S" Self,** for **the Holy Spirit** bears witness to your beautiful creation, and the Mind **of God** Whose Thought created your reality. 3 What can the body mean to **the Holy Spirit** Who knows the glory of the Father and the Son? 4 What whispers of the ego can **the Holy Spirit** hear? 5 What could convince **the Holy Spirit** that your sins are real? 6 Let **the Holy Spirit** be Judge as well of everything that seems to happen to you in this world. 7 **The Holy Spirit's** lessons will enable you to bridge the gap between illusions and the truth.

W-151.10.**The Holy Spirit** will remove all faith that you have placed in pain, disaster, suffering and loss. 2 **The Holy Spirit** gives you **the** vision **of Christ** which can look beyond these grim appearances, and can behold the gentle face of Christ in all of them. 3 You will no longer doubt that only good can come to you who are beloved of God, for **the Holy Spirit** will judge all happenings, and teach the single lesson that **your experiences** all contain.

W-151.11.**The Holy Spirit** will select the elements in **your experiences** which represent the truth, and disregard those aspects which reflect but idle dreams **of your ego's belief in lack and separation**. 2 And **the Holy Spirit** will reinterpret all you see, and all occurrences, each circumstance, and every happening that seems to touch on you in any way from **the Holy Spirit's** one frame of reference, wholly unified and sure. 3 And **with the Holy Spirit's reinterpretation** you will see the love beyond the hate, the constancy in change, the pure in sin, and only Heaven's blessing on the world.

W-151.12.Such is your resurrection, for your life is not a part of anything you see. 2 **Your real life** stands beyond the body and the world, past every witness for unholiness, within the Holy, holy as Itself. 3 In everyone and everything **the Holy Spirit's** Voice would speak to you of nothing but your **big "S" Self** and your Creator, Who is One with **your big "S" Self**. 4 So will you see the holy face of Christ in everything, and hear in everything no sound except the echo of God's Voice.

W-151.13.We practice wordlessly today, except at the beginning of the time we spend with God. 2 We introduce these times with but a single, slow repeating of the thought with which the day begins **which is all things are echoes of the Voice for God**. 3 And then we watch our thoughts, appealing silently to **the Holy Spirit** Who sees the elements of truth in **our thoughts**. 4 Let **the Holy Spirit** evaluate each thought that comes to mind, remove the elements of dreams, and give **the reinterpreted thoughts** back again as clean ideas that do not contradict the Will of God.

W-151.14.Give **the Holy Spirit** your thoughts, and **the Holy Spirit** will give **your thoughts** back as miracles which joyously proclaim the wholeness and the happiness God wills His Son, as proof of God's eternal Love. 2 And as each thought is thus transformed, **the transformed thought** takes on healing power from the **shared** Mind **of God** which saw the truth in **the thought**, and failed to be deceived by what was falsely added **by your ego**. 3 All the threads of **egoic** fantasy are gone **from the thought**. 4 And what remains is unified into a perfect Thought that offers **the transformed thought's** perfection everywhere.

W-151.15.Spend fifteen minutes thus when you awake, and gladly give another fifteen more before you go to sleep. 2 Your ministry begins as all your **egoic** thoughts are purified. 3 So are you taught to teach the Son of God the holy lesson of **you and your brother's** sanctity **as the big "S" Self**. 4 No one can fail to listen, when you hear the Voice for God give honor to God's Son. 5 And everyone will share the thoughts with you which **the Holy Spirit** has retranslated in your mind.

W-151.16.Such is your Eastertide. 2 And so you lay the gift of snow-white lilies on the world, replacing witnesses to sin and death. 3 Through your transfiguration **from a little "s" self to your big "S" Self** is the world redeemed, and joyfully released from guilt. 4 Now do we lift our resurrected minds in gladness and in gratitude to **the Holy Spirit** Who has restored our sanity **of our big "S" Self** to us.

W-151.17.And we will hourly remember **the Holy Spirit** Who is salvation and deliverance. 2 As we give thanks, the world unites with us and happily accepts our holy thoughts, which Heaven has corrected and made pure. 3 Now has our ministry begun at last, to carry round the world the joyous news that truth has no illusions, and the peace of God, through us, belongs to everyone.

Notes to Lesson #151

All things are echoes of the Voice for God.

This lesson repeats the often mentioned fact that our physical senses are not the objective confirmation devices that we have been led to believe. Physiologists tell us that our physical senses are rather poor indicators of reality. The senses are subjective thought confirmation devices, rather than objective cameras to our world.

This subjectivity occurs because our mind's beliefs are utilized to fill in the large gaps that our physical senses miss and are incapable of accurately observing. Our mind selectively processes the sensory input. It modifies, discards and focuses on limited aspects of the data while ignoring other conflicting reports to provide a distorted picture that replicates what our mind expects, anticipates and believes should be observed in its world.

This lesson also talks about judgment and why it is foolish to believe that we could accurately judge our world based on the limited information and data that we receive from our senses.

We previously talked about our inability to judge correctly when we do not have all the facts and circumstances about a particular event. To claim with certainty the correctness of your judgments based on incomplete and erroneous data is foolish. Yet, this is what we consistently do. This error is compounded by the fact that we lack an accurate vision of our future to be able to understand how the current experience fits into a much larger picture.

We all have been in this situation where we have judged incorrectly because we lacked all the information. We have also been in a situation where we have judge something as good or bad today, only to find out based on future events that the previous experience had favorable or unfavorable repercussions that we had originally failed to foresee.

Your ego is incapable of judging anything correctly because your ego does not know what you are. It perceives you as a physical body and the world of time and space as your true and only reality. Your ego believes that your survival depends on your ability to manipulate the outside forces of this world to attain the limited resources that you need for your survival and happiness.

The ego fails to understand that you are a spiritual being having an earthly experience and that time is the playfield of your own mind's imagination. Time is designed to provide a medium in which you can pretend you are something you are not so that you can rediscover the truth of what you really are.

When properly understood, time becomes a game board that facilitates fun and learning. You came here to enjoy and learn while you honed your skills in a world where opposites appear to thrive. Time is your playschool to enjoy the learning tools of contrast, differentiation and change to demonstrate the various aspects of love in specific forms.

Your ego believes that the game of reawakening is really the nightmare of lack, limitation and separation. Your ego has turned a fun learning experience into a fearful place with dreadful consequences. Whenever you fail to achieve the predetermined results that your ego has judged to be needed for its survival, you get a good dose of guilt, blame, shame and pain.

The ego believes that sin, guilt and fear are real and that this world is a place where you can hide from a wrathful God or earn your salvation through your ego's plan for your safety and happiness. Your ego's plan is always based on fear and the erroneous idea that love can be earned and that you can make someone love you through your actions.

Your ego fails to understand that God is only love and that the ego's belief in sin, guilt and fear are all fallacious judgments. Because the ego's judgments are incorrect, any of your ego's numerous plans for your happiness are based on erroneous assumptions and are guaranteed to disappoint.

Because you remain as God created you, perfect, whole and complete, you cannot be satisfied with your ego's insistence on your littleness. Your ego's plan revolves around your little "s" self and how to make you feel a little better about yourself. Because your ego believes the separation is real, it fails to recognize that you have the power as the dreamer to simply choose to awaken.

In the world of perception, we are incapable of knowing all the facts and being privy to the big picture. We do not know what we are, the true purpose of this world of perception and what our numerous experiences are really for. We need the guidance of someone who does know all the facts and can judge correctly. We need to turn to the Holy Spirit.

The Holy Spirit knows the truth of what we really are, how all the parts in God's plan for reawakening fit together and what our own split mind believes and misperceives. Unlike the ego that misperceives the world to be a place to either hide from God's wrath or try to earn love, the Holy Spirit knows paradise has never been lost. The Holy Spirit knows that God is only love, God's love cannot be earned, it is freely given to all and there is nothing that can stop that flow of love. To the Holy Spirit, this world is a playschool that allows us to learn the various aspects of love and allow the abstract One Self to know Itself in specific form.

When you stop judging and start listening to the Holy Spirit, your worldview will change. When the purpose of your world changes from earning to learning, your experiences will be seen differently. Instead of being focused on obtaining a particular result so that you can earn some future reward or avoid some pain, you will understand that it is the actual doing and the feedback the learning lesson provides that are what you value.

Any experience provides an opportunity to demonstrate and learn what you value and why. Each event becomes a feedback mechanism for your learning, growth and enjoyment. You no longer have to constantly judge your progress against some artificial, predetermined specific result. You can go with the flow by simply asking what would love have me do. Then you follow that guidance. The Holy Spirit will take any experience you give It and reframe the event through the eyes of love, not fear. This reframing allows us to enjoy the journey and absorb the learning lessons that we need for our reawakening to the truth of what we really are.

Listen to the Holy Spirit Who knows with certainty that you are God's beloved Child with whom He is well pleased. The Holy Spirit only sees the Christ in you and your brothers and frames every experience around the single purpose of your reawakening to the truth.

When you set aside your ego's judgments and misperceptions and follow the guidance of the Holy Spirit, all things become witnesses for the truth. Rather than your world being a place of egoic struggle where you must suffer to earn love, the playschool of the Holy Spirit becomes a fun and exciting learning puzzle for your enjoyment.

Question: How does changing how you define yourself impact your judgment about an event?

Question: How does changing the event's purpose effect how you view the experience?

The power of decision is my own.

W-152.1.No one can suffer loss unless it be his own decision **to suffer loss**. 2 No one suffers pain except his choice elects this state **of pain** for **himself**. 3 No one can grieve nor fear nor think him sick unless these are the outcomes that he wants. 4 And no one dies without his own consent **to die**. 5 Nothing occurs but represents your wish, and nothing is omitted that you choose. 6 Here **in your own wishes and decisions** is your world, complete in all details. 7 Here **in your own wishes and decisions** is **your world's** whole reality for you. 8 And it is only here **in your own wishes and decisions** salvation is.

W-152.2.You may believe that this position **that in your own wishes and decisions** is **your world's** whole reality is extreme, and too inclusive to be true. 2 Yet can truth have exceptions? 3 If you have the gift of everything, can loss be real? 4 Can pain be part of peace, or grief of joy? 5 Can fear and sickness enter in a mind where love and perfect holiness abide? 6 Truth must be all-inclusive, if **truth is to** be the truth at all. 7 Accept no opposites and no exceptions **to truth**, for to do so is to contradict the truth entirely.

W-152.3.Salvation is the recognition that the truth is true, and nothing else is true. 2 **The statement that the truth is true, and nothing else is true** you have heard before, but may not yet accept both parts of **that statement**. 3 Without the first **part that the truth is true**, the second **part that nothing else is true** has no meaning. 4 But without the second **part that nothing else is true**, is the first **part about truth** no longer true. 5 Truth cannot have an opposite. 6 **That truth cannot have an opposite** cannot be too often said and thought about. 7 For if what is not true is true as well as what is true, then part of truth is false. 8 And **if truth can have an opposite and the false be true,** truth has lost its meaning. 9 Nothing but the truth is true, and what is false is false.

W-152.4.**The idea that truth can have no opposites** is the simplest of distinctions, yet the most obscure. 2 But not because **the idea that truth can have no opposites** is a difficult distinction to perceive. 3 **The idea that truth can have no opposites** is concealed behind a vast array of choices that do not appear to be entirely your own. 4 And thus the truth appears to have some aspects that belie consistency, but do not seem to be but contradictions introduced by **your own egoic mind**.

W-152.5.As God created you, you must remain unchangeable, with transitory states by definition false. 2 And **these false transitory states** include all shifts in feeling, alterations in conditions of the body and the mind; in all awareness and in all response. 3 This is the all-inclusiveness **definition of truth** which sets the truth apart from falsehood, and the false kept separate from the truth, as what **truth** is.

W-152.6.Is it not strange that you believe to think you made the world you see is arrogance? 2 God made not **the world you see**. 3 Of this **that God did not create the world you see** you can be sure. 4 What can **God** know of the ephemeral, the sinful and the guilty, the afraid, the suffering and lonely, and the mind that lives within a body that must die? 5 You but accuse **God** of insanity, to think **God** made a world where such things **like sin, guilt, separation and fear** seem to have reality. 6 **God** is not mad. 7 Yet only madness makes a world like this **that you perceive to be your provisional reality**.

W-152.7.To think that God made chaos, contradicts **God's own** Will, invented opposites to truth, and suffers death to triumph over life; all this is arrogance. 2 Humility would see at once these things **like suffering pain and death** are not of **God**. 3 And can you see what God created not? 4 To think you can **see what God did not create** is merely to believe you can perceive what God willed not to be. 5 And what could be more arrogant than **to believe you can perceive what God willed not to be?**

W-152.8.Let us today be truly humble, and accept what we have made as what it is **which is a false world that arose from our own false perception and decisions**. 2 The power of decision is our own. 3 Decide but to accept your rightful place as co-creator of the universe, and all you think **your ego's little "s" self's decisions** made will disappear. 4 What rises to awareness then will be all that there ever was, eternally as it is now. 5 And **the real world of your big "S" Self** will take the place of **egoic** self-deceptions made but to usurp the altar to the Father and the Son.

W-152.9.Today we practice true humility, abandoning the false pretense by which the ego seeks to prove **truth** arrogant. 2 Only the ego can be arrogant. 3 But truth is humble in acknowledging **truth's** mightiness, **truth's** changelessness and **truth's** eternal wholeness. **Truth's humility is** all-encompassing. **Truth is** God's perfect gift to **God's** beloved Son. 4 We lay aside the **ego's** arrogance which says that we are sinners, guilty and afraid, ashamed of what we are; and lift our hearts in true humility instead to **God** Who has created us immaculate, like to **God**, Himself, in power and in love.

W-152.10.The power of decision is our own. 2 And we accept of **God** that which we are, **our big "S" Self**, and humbly recognize the Son of God. 3 To recognize God's Son implies as well that all **egoic** self-concepts **of sin, limitation, separation and fear** have been laid aside, and recognized as false. 4 **The arrogance of your ego's self-concept of your little "s" self** has been perceived. 5 And in humility the radiance of God's Son, his **big "S" Self's** gentleness, his perfect sinlessness, his Father's Love, his right to Heaven and release from hell, are joyously accepted as our own.

W-152.11.Now do we join in glad acknowledgment that lies are false, and only truth is true. 2 We think of truth alone as we arise, and spend five minutes practicing **truth's** ways, encouraging our frightened **egoic** minds with this:

3 The power of decision is my own. 4 This day I will accept myself as what my Father's Will created me to be, **my big "S" Self.**

5 Then will we wait in silence, giving up all **egoic** self-deceptions, as we humbly ask our **big "S"** Self that He reveal Himself to us. 6 And **the Holy Spirit** Who never left will come again to our awareness, grateful to restore **the Son's** home to God, as **the Son's home** was meant to be.

W-152.12.In patience wait for **the Holy Spirit** throughout the day, and hourly invite **the Holy Spirit** with the words with which the day began, **that the power of decision is my own while** concluding it with this same invitation to your **big "S"** Self. 2 God's Voice will answer, for **the Holy Spirit** speaks for you and for your Father. 3 **The Holy Spirit** will substitute the peace of God for all your frantic **egoic** thoughts, the truth of God for **your ego's** self-deceptions **of sin, limitation, separation and fear**, and God's Son for your illusions of your **ego's little "s" self.**

Notes to Lesson #152

The power of decision is my own.

This is a pivotal lesson in the course because it provides four definitions which once again are quite surprising and unusual, yet their implications are profound. These four definitions hold the key to controlling and ultimately overcoming all fears in your life. This lesson defines truth, salvation, decision and thinking.

All four words are used in our everyday language and we claim to understand what these words mean. Yet, because of their unusual definition used in this course, these four words can lead to a great deal of misunderstanding and confusion. Let's tackle all four of these key words and their meanings as defined in this lesson.

Truth is defined as what is truth is true and that nothing else is true.

On the surface, that seems like a strange yet obvious definition for truth. Everybody is well aware that what is truth is true. Yet it is the second half of this definition that states nothing else is true that we fail to realize and whose implications we choose to ignore.

The second half of the statement that nothing else is true states that truth can have no opposite. What is false cannot be true. It is our belief that what is false can be true that is the source of all our problems. Why?

Because of this error in misunderstanding what "truth" means, we confuse a make-believe world of our own mind's imagination with the reality of what God created, as God created it.

If what is not true is true as well as what is actually true, then part of truth is false. If an original statement is false and a second statement acknowledges that this first statement is not true, we assume the second statement is true. Yet, ACIM makes an important distinction that this is not the case.

When I use the words "not true," I am confusing the issue of the non-reality of the false by using imprecise language. The correct language would be to say that the first statement is false, which is the recognition that the false has no reality. We fall into the language trap that assumes the words "not true" are equivalent to the word "false." This gives rise to the idea that the false can be true and the truth can sometimes be false.

The false has no reality and therefore, how can you define what is nothing? When you define something that does not exist, you give an illusion the appearance of being real. Because of confusing the false with reality, your mind can quickly jump to the false conclusion that what appears to be real must have the ability to change what does really exist.

This belief that the false can change the truth is the source of all our fears. Our mind has made fear real and now our mind has entrapped itself into a fear-based thought system. Our mind has forgotten that the false is but an illusion that only exists within our mind's imagination. Because our mind's beliefs gave reality to the false, we are the creator of the false and therefore, our mind has the power to end the illusion by changing its beliefs that what is false can be real.

Although the law of attraction is beyond the scope of this class, this failure to understand the idea that the truth is true and nothing else is true is why so many people do not believe that the law of attraction really works.

The law of attraction says that what you place your attention on, you attract. This law claims the universe is like a genie that promptly fulfills all your wishes. This notion that you always get what you want, obviously does not appear to be correct on the surface because people claim they do not wish to be sick, have poor relationships, suffer or be in poverty.

The disbelievers of the law of attraction claim that if all their experiences were based on their own wishes and they did not want to be sick but suffered a major illness, the law of attraction must be false. And so they dismiss the law of attraction as bogus and the masses continue to believe they are victims of outside forces that are beyond their control.

The reason for the apparent failure of the law of attraction is their failure to realize that nothing else is true. They mistake the idea that placing their attention on not being sick is the same as placing their attention on being healthy. Being healthy and not being sick are not the same and involve different vibrational frequencies.

Here is an analogy to help explain this problem. First recall that time is the belief that opposites exist. Time is the game board for the belief that both love and fear are equally real. With that caveat, let's get back to the analogy.

There is a bar magnet for health and there is a bar magnet for sickness. These are two separate magnets. When you place your attention on not being sick, you have placed your attention on the bar magnet of sickness. Your mind has tuned your vibrational tuning fork to sickness and so that is what you attract. If you had understood that nothing else is true, you would have realized you needed to place your attention on health if you are to experience being healthy. In a world of opposites, good health and not being sick are not the same thing.

If nothing else is true, the "not true" cannot have any reality. The belief in the existence of the "not true," ACIM explains can only appear real within a delusional mind that believes that truth could have an opposite that is just as real as what is true.

This is impossible. The false can only appear to exist in the delusional mind that believes truth has an opposite. The "not true" is a pretend world that can only be experienced within your own mind's imagination, which becomes your own private world of individuated perception or provisional reality.

The idea that truth has an opposite can be stated as the belief that the false can be true and that the true can be false. Truth just is and nothing else is real.

This gets us to the next strange definition that is provided in this lesson.

Salvation is the recognition that the truth is true and nothing else is true.

This definition is simple yet, surprising. Normally, we would associate salvation with some type of blissful state or removal of the consequences of our sins and our return to heaven. Instead, salvation is simply defined as our recognition of the truth, which ultimately would lead us to the realization that we remain as God created us, perfect, whole and complete.

With salvation, we finally understand that the false is not real and our egoic mind cannot change what God created. Our provisional reality that we experience in the world of perception is a mere illusion that has no ability to change God's Will or God's creations. We always will remain as God created us, perfect, whole and complete, part of the One Self.

The recognition that the truth is true and nothing else is true means that this world that we perceive as our provisional reality is not real and has not been created by God. The ego's dream world of perception has no ability to change the truth that only what God created is real, changeless and eternal.

The third definition has to deal with decision.

Decision is the belief that there is something that is not true and therefore, we can experience the false. It is the belief that truth has an opposite and that the opposite of truth is as real as truth itself.

The belief that the false exists is only an illusion because truth has no opposites. In time, there is only one decision that we need to make and that is the recognition that the truth is true and nothing else is true which has been defined as salvation. This means that salvation is one decision away. Salvation is simply the acceptance of the truth or the Atonement for yourself.

The power of decision is your own because the power of decision is your belief that the false can exist and has the ability to change the truth of what God created as God created it. The power of decision only appears to exist within the delusional mind that believes the false is real.

The power of decision is not an attribute of God. God is truth and truth just is. Nothing opposes truth for nothing else is real. In time, it appears that we have a decision to make because we believe that the false is real.

In reality, a decision for the false is no decision because to choose the false is a decision to choose nothingness. Since nothingness cannot change what is real, a decision for nothingness has no effect and therefore, is ultimately no decision. There is only one choice available, which is truth because truth has no opposites.

The fourth term that is defined is thinking.

To think is to claim that you do not know. Thinking comes from the belief that there is both truth and truth's opposite. The ego is arrogant and believes that it can think because it claims it does not know the truth of who you really are. The power of decision entails thinking which is the illusion of not knowing. The power of decision is your claim that you could not know what you really are and that you could have an existence other than as God created you.

So what are the implications of these four terms and their strange definitions?

Salvation is the recognition that the truth is true and nothing else is true. Truth has no opposites. Everything you choose to perceive is because you want a certain outcome. There are no exceptions. It is your choice that is reflected in your provisional reality. Your provisional reality is the illusion that you could be something other than what God created.

Arrogance is to claim God created your provisional reality, which implies that God would have allowed evil to exist in your world. Evil contradicts God's Will and therefore, cannot be real. God did not create your world of perception, you did. Your ego's world can only be birthed by a delusional mind that believes sin, guilt and fear to be real.

Truth has no opposites. The ego tries to confuse us by claiming that there are some choices over which we have no control. The ego claims there are exception to the rule that your provisional reality reflects your own thinking. To think you see evil is to contradict God's changeless Will, which is the height of arrogance.

True humility rests on the fact that you must always remain as God created you. Your ego can deny this truth, but its denial cannot change this truth. Egoic arrogance says sin, guilt and fear are real.

Salvation is the recognition of the truth that you have the freedom to be or imagine anything that you want but that your imagination cannot change the truth or make the false real.

Question: Here is a statement I would like you to consider.

In this world, we all commit suicide but some disguise it better than others. Do you believe this is true?

Why or why not?

LESSON 153

In my defenselessness my safety lies.

W-153.1.You who feel threatened by this changing world, its twists of fortune and its bitter jests, **this changing world's** brief relationships and all the "gifts" **this changing world** merely lends to take away again; attend this lesson well **that in your defenselessness your safety lies.** 2 The world provides no safety. 3 **This changing world** is rooted in attack, and all **the changing world's** "gifts" of seeming safety are illusory deceptions. 4 **This changing world** attacks, and then attacks again. 5 No peace of mind is possible where danger threatens thus **in this world of change and attack.**

W-153.2.The world **of change and attack** gives rise but to defensiveness. 2 For threat brings anger, anger makes attack seem reasonable, honestly provoked, and righteous in the name of self-defense. 3 Yet is defensiveness a double threat. 4 For **defensiveness** attests to weakness, and sets up a system of defense that cannot work. 5 Now are the weak still further undermined, for there is treachery **perceived** without and still a greater treachery within **from your own egoic mind's beliefs.** 6 The mind **that feels threatened** is now confused, and knows not where to turn to find escape from its **own egoic mind's** imaginings.

W-153.3.It is as if a circle held **the mind that feels threatened** fast, wherein another circle bound **around the first circle** and another one in that, until escape no longer can be hoped for nor obtained **by the mind that feels threatened.** 2 Attack, defense; defense, attack, become the circles of the hours and the days that bind the mind **that feels threatened** in heavy bands of steel with iron overlaid, returning but to start again. 3 There seems to be no break nor ending in the ever-tightening grip of the imprisonment upon the mind **that feels threatened.**

W-153.4.Defenses are the costliest of all the prices which the ego would exact. 2 In **defenses** lies madness in a form so grim that hope of sanity seems but to be an idle dream, beyond the possible. 3 The sense of threat the world encourages is so much deeper, and so far beyond the frenzy and intensity of which you can conceive, that you have no idea of all the devastation **the sense of threat** has wrought.

W-153.5.You, **the little "s" self that feels threatened by this world** are slave **to your ego's defenses.** 2 You know not what you do, in fear of **attack and defense.** 3 You do not understand how much **your split minds** have been made to sacrifice, as **your split minds** feel the iron grip **of your ego's defense** upon your heart. 4 You do not realize what you have done to sabotage the holy peace of God by your **ego's** defensiveness. 5 For you behold the Son of God as **a little "s" self and** but a victim to attack by fantasies, by dreams, and by illusions **that his egoic mind** has made; yet **the little "s" self is** helpless in **the illusion's** presence, needful only of **additional egoic** defense by still more fantasies, and dreams by which illusions of his safety comfort **your little "s" self.**

W-153.6.Defenselessness is strength. 2 **Defenselessness** testifies to recognition of the Christ, **your big "S" Self,** in you. 3 Perhaps you will recall the text maintains that choice is always made between Christ's strength and your own weakness **of the little "s" self which is** seen apart from **Christ, your big "S" Self.** 4 Defenselessness can never be attacked, because **defenselessness** recognizes strength so great attack is folly, or a silly game a tired child might play, when **the child** becomes too sleepy to remember what he wants.

W-153.7.Defensiveness is weakness. 2 **Defensiveness** proclaims you have denied the Christ, **your big "S" Self,** and come to fear His Father's anger. 3 What can save you now from your delusion of an angry god, whose fearful image you believe you see at work in all the evils of the world **you made**? 4 What but illusions could defend you now, when it is but illusions **of a fearful god** that you fight?

W-153.8.We will not play such childish games today. 2 For our true purpose is to save the world, and we would not exchange for foolishness the endless joy our function **to save the world** offers us. 3 We would not let our happiness slip by because a fragment of a senseless dream happened to cross our **split** minds, and we mistook the figures in **the senseless dream** for the Son of God; **and we mistook the senseless dream's** tiny instant for eternity.

W-153.9.We look past dreams today, and recognize that we need no defense because we are created **by God and are** unassailable. **We are** without all thought or wish or dream in which attack has any meaning. 2 Now we cannot fear, for we have left all fearful thoughts behind. 3 And in defenselessness we stand secure, serenely certain of our safety now, sure of salvation; sure we will fulfill our chosen purpose **to save our world,** as our ministry extends its holy blessing through the world.

W-153.10.Be still a moment, and in silence think how holy is your purpose, how secure you rest, untouchable within **truth's** light. 2 God's ministers have chosen that the truth be with them. 3 Who is holier than **God's ministers for the truth**? 4 Who **but God's ministers for the truth** could be surer that his happiness is fully guaranteed? 5 And who **but God's ministers for the truth** could be more mightily protected? 6 What defense could possibly be needed by the ones who are among the chosen ones of God, by **God's** election and their own **decision for truth** as well?

W-153.11.It is the function of God's ministers to help their brothers choose **the truth** as **God's ministers for the truth** have done. 2 God has elected all **to know the truth,** but few have come to realize **God's** Will is but their own **will.** 3 And while you fail to teach what you have learned, salvation waits and darkness holds the world in grim imprisonment. 4 Nor will you learn that light has come to you, and your escape has been accomplished. 5 For you will not see the light, until you offer **the light of truth** to all your brothers. 6 As **your brothers** take **the light of truth** from your hands, so will you recognize **the light of truth** as your own **light**.

W-153.12.Salvation can be thought of as a game that happy children play. 2 **The game of salvation** was designed by **God** Who loves His children, and Who would replace their **ego's** fearful toys **of belief in lack, limitation and separation** with joyous games, which teach them that the game of fear is gone. 3 **God's game of salvation** instructs in happiness because there is no loser. 4 Everyone who plays **God's game of salvation** must win, and in his winning is the gain to everyone ensured. 5 The game of fear is gladly laid aside, when children come to see the benefits **God's game of** salvation brings.

W-153.13.You who have played **the ego's game of fear and separation so long** that you are lost to hope, abandoned by your Father, left alone in terror in a fearful world made mad by sin and guilt; be happy now. 2 That **the ego's** game **of fear and separation** is over. 3 Now a quiet time has come, in which we put away the toys of guilt, and lock our quaint and childish thoughts of sin forever from the pure and holy minds of Heaven's children and the Son of God.

W-153.14.We pause but for a moment more, to play our final, happy game **of salvation** upon this earth. 2 And then we go to take our rightful place where truth abides and games are meaningless. 3 So is the **ego's** story **of our little "s" self** ended. 4 Let this day bring the last chapter closer to the world, that everyone may learn the **ego's** tale he reads of terrifying destiny, defeat of all his hopes, his pitiful defense against a vengeance he cannot escape, is but his own **split mind's** deluded fantasy. 5 God's ministers **for the truth** have come to waken him from the dark dreams this story has evoked in his confused, bewildered memory of this distorted tale. 6 God's Son can smile at last, on learning that **the ego's fearful story of your lack, limitation and separation** is not true.

W-153.15.Today we practice in a form we will maintain for quite a while. 2 We will begin each day by giving our attention to the daily thought as long as possible. **Today's thought is in my defenselessness my safety lies.** 3 Five minutes now becomes the least we give to preparation for a day in which salvation is the only goal we have. 4 Ten would be better; fifteen better still. 5 And as distraction ceases to arise to turn us from our purpose **of salvation which is the acceptance that only the truth is true and nothing else is true**, we will find that half an hour is too short a time to spend with God. 6 Nor will we willingly give less at night, in gratitude and joy.

W-153.16.Each hour adds to our increasing peace, as we remember to be faithful to the Will we share with God. 2 At times, perhaps, a minute, even less, will be the most that we can offer as the hour strikes. 3 Sometimes we will forget. 4 At other times the business of the world will close on us, and we will be unable to withdraw a little while, and turn our thoughts to God.

W-153.17.Yet when we can, we will observe our trust as ministers of God, in hourly remembrance of our mission **of salvation** and **God's** Love. 2 And we will quietly sit by and wait on **the Holy Spirit** and listen to His Voice, and learn what **the Holy Spirit** would have us do the hour that is yet to come; while thanking **the Holy Spirit** for all the gifts He gave us in the one **hour** gone by.

W-153.18.In time, with practice, you will never cease to think of **the Holy Spirit** and hear **the Holy Spirit's** loving Voice guiding your footsteps into quiet ways, where you will walk in true defenselessness. 2 For you will know that Heaven goes with you. 3 Nor would you keep your mind away from **the Holy Spirit** a moment, even though your time is spent in offering salvation to the world. 4 Think you **the Holy Spirit** will not make this possible, for you who chose to carry out **God's** plan for the salvation of the world and yours?

W-153.19.Today our theme is our defenselessness. 2 We clothe ourselves in **our defenselessness**, as we prepare to meet the day. 3 We rise up strong in Christ, and let our weakness disappear, as we remember that **Christ's** strength abides in us. 4 We will remind ourselves that **Christ, our big "S" Self,** remains beside us through the day, and never leaves our weakness unsupported by **Christ's** strength. 5 We call upon **Christ's** strength each time we feel the threat of our **egoic** defenses undermine our certainty of purpose. 6 We will pause a moment, as **Christ's** tells us, "I am here."

W-153.20.Your practicing will now begin to take the earnestness of love, to help you keep your mind from wandering from its intent **of reawakening to the truth**. 2 Be not afraid nor timid. 3 There can be no doubt that you will reach your final goal **of reawakening to the truth**. 4 The ministers of God can never fail, because the love and strength and peace that shine from **the ministers of God** to all their brothers come from **God**. 5 **Love, strength and peace** are **God's** gifts to you. 6 Defenselessness is all you need to give **Christ** in return. 7 You lay aside but what was never real, to look on Christ and see **Christ's** sinlessness.

In my defenselessness my safety lies.

This lesson, in my defenselessness my safety lies, is a logical conclusion to the definition of truth. Remember that truth was defined simply as truth is true and nothing else is true. Truth does not change. Yet, your world of provisional reality is a world in which change is the norm, stability the exception and changelessness the unreal.

Because we perceive our provisional reality to have the ability to change what we truly are, this world of perception becomes a fearful place. This world arose from the split mind's belief that the false had the ability to change the changeless Mind of God. This is the belief that the false is true. The world of perception is the crystallization of our mind's belief that the game of differentiation could actually cause separation to be real and change the truth of what we really are.

This is the transformation of an innocent game of pretending that you can be something you were not, into fear. Fear is false evidence appearing real. Fear is the belief that the false can change the truth. Fear occurs whenever your mind forgets the second half of the definition of truth, which is that nothing else is true. Fear makes change appear possible.

When you no longer know yourself as perfect, whole and complete, you have accepted the ego's false belief that there is another will that can oppose God's Will. Now change has become your delusional mind's provisional reality. Your ego's world becomes a place in which opposites exist and lack, limitation, separation and fear abound. Your provisional reality is a fearful place of attack, counterattack and defenses, all built around your belief in the reality that the changeless has been changed.

Why is this world such a fearful place? Because you have forgotten that you are changeless and remain as God created you. Your belief in separation has created the illusion of the changeable world in which outside forces have the ability to rob you of your inner peace.

When you believe you are no longer perfect, whole and complete, you have accepted the idea that change is your reality. You claim you are the living proof that change exists. With change possible, your world becomes an inevitable cycle of attack and defense.

Why is this cycle of attack and defense inevitable?

Because you believe there are outside forces that have the ability to change what you really are. If you perceive that you are perfectly happy and content, you still need to build defenses to protect your happiness. If you perceive that you are not perfectly happy and content, you will believe attack is needed to make you happy. Your belief in outside forces that can make you happy or sad, leads to the vicious cycle of attack and defense. According to your ego, this cycle is required if you are to survive in this fearful world of your mind's own imagination.

Your ego's belief in defense is a double threat to your happiness. First, it accepts the idea that you must be weak and vulnerable to attack. This confirms that you are indeed your ego's little "s" self. This makes the illusion of the separation appear real.

The second threat is that your ego goes about trying to solve a problem that is not real by creating another illusion which reconfirms the reality of the first illusion. Your ego's defense plan is a counterattack against a fictitious attack that never was, is or could be real. Thus, you are twice deceived by your split mind. One illusion is piled upon another illusion and makes the truth more difficult to uncover.

Defensiveness is weakness because it denies the reality of your big "S" Self and supports the ego's notion that the world is a product of God's wrath rather than the creation of your own mind.

Defenselessness saves the world by looking past the dream that believes an illusion can change the truth. Defenselessness recognizes that we were created as invulnerable spirit and there is nothing to fear. The ego's defense against an illusion of our vulnerability only compounds the problem and makes the false appear real. Your ego's world of provisional reality can provide no safety. This world was created by the split mind for the purpose of providing a war zone where you can attack and be attacked.

Since your ego tells us that this is a fearful place, any appearance of safety within its world can only be an illusion. Your provisional reality merely confirms your ego's belief that you are weak and in need of defenses. You believe you are threatened and that your feelings of anger and injustice are appropriate and should give rise to your defensiveness.

This makes your defenses and counter attacks seem reasonable and justified. Your participation in the attack-defense cycle is a reaction provoked by outside forces that would rob you of your inner peace. Your ego says you are righteous in your self-defense which is actually a hidden attack upon your own true nature as your big "S" Self.

All defenses attest to weakness and the belief that you are a victim abandoned by an uncaring God. Defenselessness comes from your Source which is the God of unconditional love. Defenselessness rests on your strength as Christ, Who rests in you and thus, you can never be vulnerable to attack.

Salvation is like a happy game God designed out of His love to replace our ego's game of fear that arose when we failed to understand that second half of truth's definition. We failed to realize that nothing else is true. We made our illusions of sin, guilt and fear real.

In the happy dream of salvation, we accept the complete definition of truth. Our ego's fearful toys of lack, limitation and separation are replaced so that the game of fear disappears. Sin, guilt, separation and fear all give way to a new game based on forgiveness, love and oneness. The new game of reawakening teaches that fear is gone and provides instructions on happiness since there are no losers. God's game of salvation acknowledges that everyone who plays must win and in each win, everyone's gain is insured.

The ego's fearful game is hopelessness. It is based on the belief that God abandoned His Child, left the child alone with limited resources to live in terror in a fearful world made insane by sin and guilt. When you realize that the truth is true and nothing else is, you exchange the game of fear and separation for the happy dream. All games and stories about victims and victimizers end. You are able to reclaim your divine birthright. By your defenselessness, you reconfirm that you remain as God created you and claim that reality as your own.

Question: If you believed you were changeless, what could you possibly gain from either attack or defense?

Question: Can you see how your belief in change makes fear appear real?

LESSON 154

I am among the ministers of God.

W-154.1.Let us today be neither arrogant nor falsely humble. 2 We have gone beyond such foolishness. 3 We cannot judge ourselves, nor need we do so. 4 These **judgments about ourselves** are but attempts to hold decision off, and to delay commitment to our function **in God's plan for salvation.** 5 It is not our part to judge our worth, nor can we know what role is best for us; what we can do within a larger plan we cannot see in **the plan's** entirety. 6 Our part is cast in Heaven, not in the hell **of our ego's split mind.** 7 And what we think is weakness can be strength; what we believe to be our strength is often **our ego's** arrogance.

W-154.2.Whatever your appointed role may be, **your role** was selected by the Voice for God, Whose function is to speak for you as well. 2 Seeing your strengths exactly as **they** are, and equally aware of where **your strengths** can be best applied, for what, to whom and when, **the Holy Spirit** chooses and accepts your part for you. 3 **The Holy Spirit** does not work without your own consent. 4 But **the Holy Spirit** is not deceived in what **your ego thinks** you are, and listens only to **the Holy Spirit's** Voice in you **which is your big "S" Self.**

W-154.3.It is through **your big "S" Self's** ability to hear one Voice which is **the Holy Spirit's** Own **Voice** that you become aware at last there is one Voice in you **which speaks for both the Holy Spirit and your big "S" Self as one.** 2 And that one Voice **of the Holy Spirit** appoints your function, and relays **your function** to you, giving you the strength to understand **your function,** do what **your function** entails, and to succeed in everything you do that is related to **your function.** 3 God has joined His Son in this, and thus His Son becomes **God's** messenger of unity with **God.**

W-154.4.It is this joining **of God and God's Son,** through the Voice for God, of Father and of Son, **which is the Holy Spirit's Voice** that sets apart salvation from the world. 2 It is this **one** Voice **of the Holy Spirit** which speaks of laws the world does not obey; which promises salvation from all sin, with guilt abolished in the mind that God created sinless. 3 Now this **once split** mind becomes aware again of **God** Who created **this sinless mind,** and of God's lasting union with itself**, which is part of the shared Mind of God.** 4 So is its **big "S"** Self the one reality in which **the once split mind's** will and that of **God's Will** are joined.

W-154.5.A messenger is not the one who writes the message **the messenger** delivers. 2 Nor does **the messenger** question the right of him who does **write the message,** nor **does the messenger** ask why **the writer** has chosen those who will receive the message that **the messenger** brings. 3 It is enough that **the messenger** accepts **the message,** give **the message** to the ones for whom **the message** is intended, and fulfill his role in **the message's** delivery. 4 If **the messenger** determines what the messages should be, or what **the message's** purpose is, or where **the message** should be carried, **the messenger** is failing to perform **the messenger's** proper part as bringer of the Word.

W-154.6.There is one major difference in the role of Heaven's messengers, which sets **Heaven's messengers** off from those the world appoints **as messengers.** 2 The messages that **Heaven's messengers** deliver are intended first for **the messengers themselves.** 3 And it is only as **Heaven's messengers** can accept **the messages** for themselves that **Heaven's messengers** become able to bring **the messages** further, and to give **the messages** everywhere that **the messages** were meant to be. 4 Like earthly messengers, **Heaven's messengers** did not write the messages they bear, but **Heaven's messengers** become their first receivers **of the messages** in the truest sense, receiving **the messages** to prepare themselves to give **the messages.**

W-154.7.An earthly messenger fulfills his role by giving all his messages away. 2 The messengers of God perform their part by their acceptance of **God's** messages as for themselves, and show **that the messengers of God** understand the messages by giving **God's message** away. 3 **Messengers of God** choose no roles that are not given them by **God's** authority. 4 And so **messengers of God** gain by every message that they give away.

W-154.8.Would you receive the messages of God? 2 For thus do you become **God's** messenger. 3 You are appointed now **to be God's messenger.** 4 And yet you wait to give the messages you have received. 5 And so you do not know that **the messages you have received** are yours, and do not recognize **the messages of God because you have not given them away.** 6 No one can receive **the messages of God** and understand he has received **the messages of God** until he gives **the messages of God away.** 7 For in the giving **of the messages of God** is **the messenger's** own acceptance of what he received **from God which were those same messages.**

W-154.9.You who are now the messenger of God, receive **God's** messages. 2 For **the receiving of God's messages** is part of your appointed role. 3 God has not failed to offer what you need, nor has **God's offer** been left unaccepted **by the Holy Spirit on your behalf.** 4 Yet another part of your appointed task is yet to be accomplished. 5 **The Holy Spirit** Who has received for you the messages of God would have **the messages from God** be received by you as well **by you giving those same messages away.** 6 For thus do you identify with **the Holy Spirit** and claim your own **big "S" Self.**

W-154.10.It is this joining that we undertake to recognize today. 2 We will not seek to keep our minds apart from **the Holy Spirit** Who speaks for us, for it is but our voice **of our big "S" Self** we hear as we attend **the Holy Spirit.** 3 **The Holy Spirit** alone can speak to us and for us, joining in one Voice the getting and the giving of God's Word; the giving and receiving of **God's** Will.

W-154.11.We practice giving **the Holy Spirit** what **the Holy Spirit** would have, that we may recognize **the Holy Spirit's** gifts to us. 2 **The Holy Spirit** needs our voice that **the Holy Spirit** may speak through us. 3 **The Holy Spirit** needs our hands to hold **the Holy Spirit's** messages, and carry them to those whom **the Holy Spirit** appoints. 4 **The Holy Spirit** needs our feet to bring us where **the Holy Spirit** wills, that those who wait in misery may be at last delivered. 5 And **the Holy Spirit** needs our will united with **the Holy Spirit's** Own **Will**, that we may be the true receivers of the gifts **the Holy Spirit** gives.

W-154.12.Let us but learn this lesson for today: We will not recognize what we receive until we give **what we received away to another.** 2 You have heard this said a hundred ways, a hundred times, and yet belief is lacking still **that to give is to receive.** 3 But this is sure; until belief is given **to the idea that to give is to receive**, you will receive a thousand miracles and then receive a thousand more, but will not know that God Himself has left no gift beyond what you already have; nor has denied the tiniest of blessings to His Son. 4 What can **these miracles** mean to you, until you have identified with **God** and with His Own **Son and given those same miracles away**?

W-154.13.Our lesson for today is stated thus:
2 I am among the ministers of God, and I am grateful that I have the means by which to recognize that I am free.

W-154.14.The world recedes as we light up our minds, and realize these holy words are true. 2 **These holy words that you are a minister of God and grateful that you have the means by which to recognize that you are free** are the message sent to us today from our Creator. 3 Now we demonstrate how **these holy words** have changed our minds about ourselves, and what our function is **as a minister of God by giving that same message away.** 4 For as we prove that we accept no will we do not share **with God**, our many gifts from our Creator will spring to our sight and leap into our hands, and we will recognize what we received **as we share those gift with others**.

Notes to Lesson #154

I am among the ministers of God.

This lesson represents our true purpose and why we currently find ourselves on the game board of time. We have come here to bear witness for the truth of who we really are. We have come here to be a minister or messenger for God's plan for salvation that recognizes that the truth is true and nothing else is true.

It is not arrogance or false humility to recognize that the function we have all come here to fulfill in time is to be a messenger for truth. Our ego is incapable of being a messenger for truth because the ego has determined that its plan, not God's plan, is what is needed for our salvation.

This lesson cautions us that we should not question our assigned role in God's plan as a messenger for the truth. We are not aware of the big picture. Therefore, we are incapable of judging what is the most beneficial role we can play in the reawakening of sleeping minds to their spiritual magnificence as the Christ. As a messenger for God, your function is to spread the truth that all remain innocent and sinless, perfect, whole and complete, part of the shared Mind of the One Self.

Our role is to act as that messenger. Our ego believes that you should play a different and perhaps larger role. When we allow our ego to judge or determine what our role should be, what message needs to be delivered and who should be the recipient for that message, we are delaying our commitment to fulfilling our true function of being a messenger for the Voice for God.

We are all messengers for the Holy Spirit and the truth. As a messenger, we do not write, edit or determine who writes or receives the message. We merely follow the orders of the Holy Spirit Who has God's plan. We simply deliver the message as it was written to the proper recipient at the proper time. When we fail to do this, we overstep our function as a messenger and are following our ego's plan.

Unlike an earthly messenger, we must first accept the message for ourselves and understand the message before we can deliver it. Even in time, the law of God that to give is to receive still applies. You must first accept the message before you can deliver it to another. You cannot give what you do not possess.

We demonstrate our acceptance and understanding of the message through our actions. Only then can we give that same message away to another. To be a minister for God, you first need to walk the talk before you share the message. Your actions, not your words, will demonstrate the message has been understood and accepted.

A messenger for God, quiets the egoic mind chatter of the little "s" self and then listens for the guidance of the Holy Spirit. Only the Holy Spirit knows the big picture and possesses the road map that will take us home. When we listen and follow the Voice for the Holy Spirit, we are actually joining our mind with our big "S" Self and the Holy Spirit in a single purpose. With this single purpose our minds are joined as one mind and become one voice.

When minds share a single purpose of witnessing for the truth, there is a joining of those minds. With this joining with the Holy Spirit and your big "S" Self, you are freed from the split mind's belief in lack, limitation and separation. You realize that you are among the ministers of God, and you, like your brother, share in the single purpose of recognizing the truth and sharing that truth with all.

Question: If two messages were worded exactly the same, is it possible that one message is from your ego and another could be from the Holy Spirit?

Hint: Remember form is not the same as content or purpose. The message could be exactly the same but the purpose of the messenger will be the determining factor. The form that the message takes is not the determining factor. The deciding factor is always the purpose behind why the message is being delivered.

If the message is being delivered on behalf of the Holy Spirit, the purpose of the messenger will be to facilitate the joining of minds that recognizes the oneness and sinless nature of all involved.

If the message is being delivered on behalf of the ego, the messenger will actually be reinforcing the messenger's own belief in limitation, inequality and separation. The hidden purpose behind an egoic message and its messenger will be the originating belief that the there is something actually wrong that needs to be fixed. The messenger will actually believe that the message is designed to fix change, protect, impress or correct the other party in order to save that party.

The messenger will always accept the hidden belief that there is something that needs to be changed because someone is no longer perfect, whole and complete. The egoic message and its messenger always assume the illusion to be real and therefore, have failed to realize that only truth is true and nothing else is true.

LESSON 155

I will step back and let the Holy Spirit lead the way.

W-155.1.There is a way of living in the world that is not here **in the world**, although it seems to be. 2 You do not change appearance, though you smile more frequently. 3 Your forehead is serene; your eyes are quiet. 4 And the ones who walk the world **with the Holy Spirit** as you do recognize their own. 5 Yet those who have not yet perceived the way **of the Holy Spirit** will recognize you also, and believe that you are like them, as you were **before you learned to follow the guidance of the Holy Spirit.**

W-155.2.The world is an illusion. 2 Those who choose to come to **the world** are seeking for a place where they can be illusions, and avoid their own reality **of their big "S" Self.** 3 Yet when they find their own reality **of their big "S" Self** is even here, then they step back **from their ego's beliefs** and let **their big "S" Self and the Holy Spirit** lead the way. 4 What other choice is really theirs to make **but to follow the reality of truth**? 5 To let illusions walk ahead of truth is madness. 6 But to let illusion sink behind the truth and let the truth stand forth as what **the truth** is, is merely sanity.

W-155.3.This is the simple choice **for the truth of our big "S" Self that** we make today. 2 The mad illusion **of the little "s" self and its world** will remain awhile in evidence, for those to look upon who chose to come, and have not yet rejoiced to find they were mistaken in their choice **to follow the voice of the ego.** 3 They, **who perceive themselves to be the little "s" self,** cannot learn directly from the truth, because they have denied that **the truth of their big "S" Self** is so. 4 And so they, **who perceive themselves to be the little "s" self** need a Teacher , **the Holy Spirit,** Who perceives their madness, but Who still can look beyond illusion to the simple truth in them **as their big "S" Self.**

W-155.4.If truth demanded they, **who perceive themselves to be the little "s" self,** give up the world, it would appear to them as if **truth** asked the sacrifice of something that is real. 2 Many have chosen to renounce the world while still believing **the world's** reality. 3 And they, **who have chosen to renounce the world while still believing the world to be real** have suffered from a sense of loss, and have not been released accordingly. 4 Others have chosen nothing but the world, and they have suffered from a sense of loss still deeper, which they **who have chosen to value this world of illusion** do not understand.

W-155.5.Between these **two paths of renouncing or valuing the world,** there is another road that leads away from loss of every kind, for sacrifice and deprivation both are quickly left behind. 2 This is the way appointed for you now. **It is the realization that this world is not real.** 3 You walk this path as others walk **in the world**, nor do you seem to be distinct from them **who believe this world is real** although you are indeed **different since you realize the illusionary nature of this world.** 4 Thus can you serve them, **who believe this world is real,** while you serve **your big "S" Self,** and set their footsteps on the way that God has opened up to you, and them through you.

W-155.6.Illusion still appears to cling to you, that you may reach them **who believe this world is real.** 2 Yet **illusion** has stepped back. 3 And it is not illusion that they, **who believe this world is real,** hear you speak of, nor illusion that you bring their eyes to look on and their minds to grasp. 4 Nor can the truth, which walks ahead of you, speak to them, **who believe this world is real,** through illusions, for the road leads past illusion now, while on the way you call to them **who believe this world is real** that they may follow you.

W-155.7.All roads will lead to this one **road to truth** in the end. 2 For sacrifice and deprivation are paths that lead nowhere, choices for defeat, and aims that will remain impossible. 3 All **illusion** steps back as truth comes forth in you, to lead your brothers from the ways of death, and set **your brothers** on the way to happiness. 4 **Your brothers'** suffering is but illusion. 5 Yet **your brothers** need a guide to lead them out of **illusion** for **your brothers** mistake illusion for the truth.

W-155.8.Such is salvation's call to **lead the delusional to the truth**, and nothing more. 2 **Salvation** asks that you accept the truth, and let **truth** go before you, lighting up the path of ransom from illusion. 3 **Salvation** is not a ransom with a price. 4 There is no cost, but only gain **from salvation.** 5 Illusion can but seem to hold in chains the holy Son of God. 6 It is but from illusions **the holy Son of God** is saved. 7 As **illusions** step back, **the holy Son of God** finds **his big "S" Self** again.

W-155.9.Walk safely now, yet carefully, because this path **of following the guidance of the Holy Spirit** is new to you. 2 And you may find that you are tempted still to walk ahead of truth, and let illusions **and your ego** be your guide. 3 Your holy brothers have been given you, to follow in your footsteps as you walk with certainty of purpose to the truth. 4 **Truth** goes before you now, that **your brothers** may see something with which they can identify; something they understand to lead the way **to the truth of their big "S" Self.**

W-155.10.Yet at the journey's ending there will be no gap, no distance between truth and you. 2 And all illusions walking in the way you travelled will be gone from you as well, with nothing left to keep the truth apart from God's completion, holy as **God,** Himself. 3 Step back in faith and let truth lead the way. 4 You**r ego** knows not where you go. 5 But **the Holy Spirit** Who **knows where you go**, goes with you. 6 Let **the Holy Spirit lead** you with the rest **of your brothers**.

W-155.11.When dreams are over, time has closed the door on all the things that pass and miracles are purposeless, the holy Son of God will make no journeys. 2 **When dreams are over** there will be no wish to be illusion rather than the truth. 3 And we step forth **from the illusion that this world is real** toward this **desire to be your big "S" Self** as we progress along the way that truth points out to us. 4 This is our final journey **from illusions to the truth**, which we make for everyone. 5 We must not lose our way. 6 For as truth goes before us, so **truth** goes before our brothers who will follow us.

W-155.12.We walk to God. 2 Pause and reflect on this. 3 Could any way be holier, or more deserving of your effort, of your love and of your full intent **then to walk to God**? 4 What way could give you more than everything, or offer less and still content the holy Son of God? 5 We walk to God. 6 The truth that walks before us now is one with **God**, and leads us to where **God** has always been. 7 What way but this could be a path that you would choose instead?

W-155.13.Your feet are safely set upon the road that leads the world to God. 2 Look not to **the** ways **of the ego** that seem to lead you elsewhere. 3 Dreams are not a worthy guide for you who are God's Son. 4 Forget not **God** has placed His Hand in yours, and given you your **brothers' hand** in **God's** trust that you are worthy of **God's** trust in you. 5 **God** cannot be deceived. 6 **God's** trust has made your pathway certain and your goal secure. 7 You will not fail your brothers nor your **big "S"** Self.

W-155.14.And now **the Holy Spirit** asks but that you think of God a while each day, that **the Holy Spirit** may speak to you and tell you of **God's** Love, reminding you how great **God's** trust; how limitless **God's** Love. 2 In your Name and **God's** Own, which are the same, we practice gladly with this thought today:

3 I will step back and let **the Holy Spirit** lead the way, For I would walk along the road to **God**.

Notes to Lesson #155

I will step back and let the Holy Spirit lead the way.

This is one of my favorite lessons because it indicates that there are only three possible paths that a person can choose for reawakening. What is more important, only one of the three will actually work.

This world is a place where we come to pretend that we are something that we are not. Time is the tool of our mind's imagination where we can hide from the truth. But even here on planet earth, the call for truth is still strong within us. What is the truth we really seek?

Earlier, we defined truth as the following: Truth is true and nothing else is true. The truth is your remembrance of this simple fact about yourself. I am not a body. I am free. I am still as God created me. Nothing sources my experience but me and nothing has an effect upon me unless I choose to allow it. Put another way, it is the realization that this world is not real and has no ability to change what you really are.

So what are the three possible choices or paths that are available to us that attempt to end pain, suffering and conflict?

The first path is to find happiness and lasting peace within this material world. This is the path of valuing the things of this world and nothing else. This path is stubbornly followed by most people because it offers an endless variety of shapes and patterns. Put in egoic terms, it is the belief that I will be happy when… and then you get to fill in the blank. When you obtain the goal you sought and still are unhappy, you then get to substitute a new goal in place of the old and continue in a seamless endless cycle of unfulfilled promises of you will be happy when…

This first path rests on the belief that there is something magical that is outside your own mind that has the power to make you happy. This path sees the world as real and having something of value that if obtained could make you happy or safe. It rests on the belief that there are some magical items outside your own mind that if obtained have the power to save you from the pain, conflict and struggle that are the apparent realities of this world.

The second is the path of renunciation while still believing this world has power over you. It is the realization that this world cannot bring you happiness but rather is the source of your suffering and pain. When you follow the path of renunciation, you no longer value the things of this world. Yet, you still believe that this world has the power to harm or rob you of your own inner peace. Similar to the first path, the path of renunciation rests on the idea that this world is real and has the ability to change the truth of who you really are.

The third path is to be aware of the appearance of this illusionary world while you maintain your awareness of the truth while acting in the dream. The third path is the realization that you are a spiritual being having an earthly experience and that the experience has no ability to change the truth of who you really are. You are in the world but not of the world. This is the path of reawakening yourself and others to the truth.

Once a spiritually enlightened master was asked, how does your world change after enlightenment? The master answered, before enlightenment, I fetched water and chopped wood. After enlightenment, I fetch water and chop wood.

In the eyes of the world, there may not appear to be any physical difference between the two states of mind. Yet, there is a profound difference in how those same tasks are performed and the purpose that the tasks are meant to serve. Again the outward appearance or form may be the same but the content or purpose has changed radically. Now there is a realization that the outside world has no ability to rob you of your own inner peace.

Only this third path is the realization that this world is not real. Therefore, you can play in the dream world while realizing you are not of it. This allows you to be a witness for the truth. You get to serve the Holy Spirit, yourself and your brother in the process of reawakening sleeping minds to the truth.

Although there are three possible paths that you can follow, there are only two voices and two choices to choose from. You must choose between either the voice for truth or the voice for the false. The ego leads you on the first two paths and accepts the illusion of lack, limitation and separation to be your reality. The ego mistakes who you really are so following its guidance can never get you to the Promised Land.

Only someone who knows both the truth and is also aware of your misperceptions can properly guide you home. You need someone who has the big picture and understands your delusional state so that they can help you heal your split mind. By letting the Holy Spirit lead the way, you follow that guidance back to the truth and become a way shower for your brothers. No sacrifice or loss is required by anyone for there is only gain for all.

Because your brothers believe this world to be something they value, they need your help realizing they have mistaken the illusion for the truth. By stepping back and letting the Holy Spirit lead the way, you heed salvation's call to help lead the delusional minds back to the truth.

In this mission of reawakening to the truth, the Holy Spirit cannot fail because it is God's Will. When you trust in God, you have placed your faith in truth. Only God's plan will work and the Holy Spirit is the only voice for that plan. Stop following your ego's bankrupt plans for your salvation and let the Holy Spirit lead the way.

Question: Why does the path of renouncing this world fail to bring you home? After all, the plan does calls for you to stop valuing the things of this world.

LESSON 156

I walk with God in perfect holiness.

W-156.1.Today's idea **that I walk with God in perfect holiness** but states the simple truth that makes the thought of sin impossible. 2 **Today's idea that I walk with God in perfect holiness** promises there is no cause for guilt, and being causeless **guilt** does not exist. 3 **Today's idea that I walk with God in perfect holiness** follows surely from the basic thought so often mentioned in the text **that** ideas leave not their source. 4 If this be true **that ideas never leave their source**, how can you be apart from God **Who is your Source?** 5 How could you walk the world alone and separate from **God,** your Source?

W-156.2.We are not inconsistent in the thoughts that we present in our curriculum. 2 Truth must be true throughout, if **truth is to** be true. 3 **Truth** cannot contradict itself, nor be in parts uncertain and in others sure. 4 You cannot walk the world apart from God, because you could not be without **God.** 5 God is what your life is. 6 Where you are **God** is. 7 There is one life. 8 That **one** life you share with **God.** 9 Nothing can be apart from **God** and live.

W-156.3.Yet where **God** is, there must be holiness as well as life. 2 No attribute of **God** remains unshared by everything that lives. 3 What lives is holy as **God**, Himself, because what shares **God's** life is part of Holiness, and could no more be sinful than the sun could choose to be of ice; the sea elect to be apart from water, or the grass to grow with roots suspended in the air.

W-156.4.There is a light in you which cannot die; whose presence is so holy that the world is sanctified because of you **and your light.** 2 All things that live bring gifts to you, and offer **those gifts to you** in gratitude and gladness at your feet. 3 The scent of flowers is their gift to you. 4 The waves bow down before you, and the trees extend their arms to shield you from the heat, and lay their leaves before you on the ground that you may walk in softness, while the wind sinks to a whisper round your holy head.

W-156.5.The light in you is what the universe longs to behold. 2 All living things are still before you, for **all living things** recognize **that God** walks with you. 3 The light you carry is their own **light.** 4 And thus **all living things** see in you their holiness, saluting you as savior and as God. 5 Accept their reverence, for **their reverence** is due to **God's** Holiness Itself, which walks with you, transforming in **Holiness'** gentle light all things unto **Holiness'** likeness and **Holiness'** purity.

W-156.6.This is the way salvation works. 2 As you step back **from your egoic beliefs of lack, limitation and separation**, the light in you **from your big "S" Self** steps forward and encompasses the world. 3 **The light in you** heralds not the end of sin in punishment and death. 4 In lightness and in laughter is sin gone, because **sin's** quaint absurdity is seen. 5 **Sin** is a foolish thought, a silly dream, not frightening, ridiculous perhaps, but who would waste an instant in approach to God Himself for such a senseless whim?

W-156.7.Yet you have wasted many, many years on just this foolish thought **that sin, guilt and fear were real**. 2 The past is gone, with all **the ego's** fantasies **based upon the ego's belief in lack, limitation and separation gone as well**. 3 **Fantasies of sin, guilt and fear** keep you bound no longer. 4 The approach to God is near. 5 And in the little interval of doubt that still remains, you may perhaps lose sight of **God,** your Companion, and mistake **God** for the senseless, ancient dream that now is past.

W-156.8."Who walks with me?" 2 This question **of "who walks with me,"** should be asked a thousand times a day, till certainty has ended doubting and established peace. 3 Today let doubting cease. 4 God speaks for you in answering your question **of who walks with you,** with these words:
5 I walk with God in perfect holiness. 6 I light the world, I light my mind and all the minds which God created one with me.

Notes to Lesson #156

I walk with God in perfect holiness.

To make holy is to make whole.

Thoughts never leave their source.

Since we are a thought of God, we remain part of the inseparable Oneness of All That Is, the One Self.

Like begets like and being part of that Oneness, we possess all the attributes of our Source. Nothing but the attributes of our Source can be real. There can be no sin, separation or guilt because there is none in God.

God, Who is our Source, cannot be apart from us and there can be no life but the one life that we all share with God. No attribute of God remains unshared by everything that lives. God is in everything that lives and thus, God is in you. There is no life apart from God for there is nothing that could be outside or separate. God is and nothing else is.

Sin has been defined as lack. Yet, God being everything cannot lack anything that is real. Sin or lack cannot be real since there is no lack in God. When God creates, He gives all to all. Creation is an extension of that Oneness. God is life and God is what your life is.

In time, Love is the creative process in which time is utilized to reawaken sleeping minds to their spiritual magnificence as the Christ.

God or this universe is a supportive place with God's law being that to give is to receive. All things, being part of the Oneness of All That Is, look to you in gratitude and desire to behold the light in you. Each part supports the other in appreciation and gratitude for the light that shines in each. By seeing the light in you, they recognize that same light in themselves. When you realize that all are supporting you in being that light, you recognize that all are playing their part in God's plan for your reawakening to your divine inheritance. All are part of that One Self, perfect, whole and complete. All walk with God in perfect holiness.

Question: This lesson states that God is life, but it goes beyond that and says that God is what your life is. This being the case, shouldn't we all be going about "Godding," which would be the act of being only love?

Into His Presence would I enter now.

W-157.1.This is a day of silence and of trust. 2 **This day** is a special time of promise in your calendar of days. 3 **This day** is a time Heaven has set apart to shine upon, and cast a timeless light upon this day, when echoes of eternity are heard. 4 This day is holy, for **this day** ushers in a new experience; a different kind of feeling and awareness. 5 You have spent long days and nights in celebrating death. 6 Today you learn to feel the joy of life.

W-157.2.This is another crucial turning point in the curriculum. 2 We add a new dimension now; a fresh experience that sheds a light on all that we have learned already, and prepares us for what we have yet to learn. 3 **This day** brings us to the door where learning ceases, and we catch a glimpse of what lies past the highest reaches **that learning** can possibly attain. 4 **This day** leaves us here an instant, and we go beyond **the door where learning ceases**, sure of our direction and our only goal.

W-157.3.Today it will be given you to feel a touch of Heaven, though you will return to paths of learning. 2 Yet you have come far enough along the way to alter time sufficiently to rise above **time's** laws, and walk into eternity a while. 3 This you will learn to do increasingly, as every lesson, faithfully rehearsed, brings you more swiftly to this holy place and leaves you, for a moment, to your **big "S"** Self.

W-157.4.**The Holy Spirit** will direct your practicing today, for what you ask for now is what **the Holy Spirit** wills. 2 And having joined your will with **the Holy Spirit's** this day, what you are asking must be given you. 3 Nothing is needed but today's idea **that into God's Presence would I enter now** to light your mind, and let **your mind** rest in still anticipation and in quiet joy, wherein you quickly leave the **ego's** world behind.

W-157.5.From this day forth, your ministry takes on a genuine devotion, and a glow that travels from your fingertips to those you touch, and blesses those you look upon. 2 A vision reaches everyone you meet, and everyone you think of, or who thinks of you. 3 For your experience today will so transform your mind that **your mind** becomes the touchstone for the holy Thoughts of God.

W-157.6.Your body will be sanctified today, **the body's** only purpose being now to bring the vision of what you experience this day to light the world. 2 We cannot give experience like this **of being in God's presence** directly. 3 Yet **our experience of being in God's presence** leaves a vision in our eyes which we can offer everyone, that **everyone** may come the sooner to the same experience **of being in God's presence** in which the world **of the ego** is quietly forgot, and Heaven is remembered for a while.

W-157.7.As this experience **of being in God's presence** increases and all goals but this become of little worth, the world to which you will return becomes a little closer to the end of time; a little more like Heaven in its ways; a little nearer **the world's** deliverance **from your ego's purpose of being a place to keep you separate from God.** 2 And you who bring **the world** light will come to see the light more sure; the vision **of Christ** more distinct. 3 The time will come when you will not return in the same form in which you now appear, for you will have no need of **the body's form**. 4 Yet now **the body** has a purpose, and **the body** will serve **its** purpose well.

W-157.8.Today we will embark upon a course you have not dreamed of. 2 But the Holy One, **the Holy Spirit ,** the Giver of the happy dreams of life, Translator of perception into truth, the holy Guide to Heaven given you, has dreamed for you this journey which you make and start today, with the experience this day holds out to you to be your own.

W-157.9.Into Christ's Presence will we enter now, serenely unaware of everything except **Christ's** shining face and perfect Love. 2 The vision of **Christ's** face will stay with you, but there will be an instant which transcends all vision, even this, the holiest **vision of Christ**. 3 This you will never teach, for you attained **the vision of Christ** not through learning. 4 Yet the vision **of Christ** speaks of your remembrance of what you knew that instant, and will surely know again.

Notes to Lesson #157

Into His Presence would I enter now.

God is what your life is. Your life should be joyous. When you choose to live in fear, it is a celebration of death. To live in fear is to be dead to life. When you rest in God's presence, you leave this fear-based world behind. You need to learn to feel the joy of life which is why only the third path of being in this world but not of it will bring you home.

To the ego, the body's purpose is to be a concrete symbol for lack, limitation and separation. When you follow the guidance of the Holy Spirit, the purpose of the body is transformed. The body's purpose now is to bring the vision of what you experience with love to light your world.

The body is now utilized as a communication device to share that loving vision of Christ to your brother so that this fear-based world is forgotten and Heaven remembered. The body can be utilized to assist others in joining with you in that vision and reframing the experience in a different light. When you utilize the vision of Christ, you look past form, and you become unaware of anything except the shining face of Christ.

Although you can bring this vision into your brother's presence, you cannot force another to accept that vision or become "enlightened." Your mission is only to offer the truth and then allow them to exercise their own free will in accepting or denying the truth for themselves without your judgment or condemnation. You know that all are on their own perfect path. The allowance of the Holy Spirit replaces the judgment of your ego.

Your body is a communication device that acts as a witness for the truth rather than to be truth's enforcer. You realize that whether your brother accepts or denies the vision of Christ that you offer, each experience is a necessary step on his own perfect path of reawakening. You acknowledge his free will to be or imagine anything that he wants while you continue to hold this higher vision of his big "S" Self as his reality.

The presence of God is not something that is learned but rather remembered. It comes from personal revelation and is not something you can teach another due to its reliance upon personal experience. As you drop your ego's many goals, your mind focuses on the one single goal of reawakening into God's presence.

As you move closer to this one goal that you share with the Holy Spirit, you also move closer to the end of time. Having turned your experiences over to the Holy Spirit, the body now serves as that communication device for the truth. More time is spent experiencing the higher state of joining with God and being aware of your big "S" Self. Christ consciousness, like the presence of God, is not learned but only remembered.

Over the course of these lessons you have been learning to remove the blocks that you have placed before the truth of your big "S" Self. You are now on that path of remembrance and have no desire to turn back. Your ego's fearful world of sin, guilt and fear holds no appeal to you except for the fact that it can be utilized to help reawaken sleeping minds to the truth. Into God's presence will you enter now unaware of anything except Christ's shining face and God's perfect love.

Question: Why can't you just force or impose your will upon another so they can more quickly accept the truth that they too are the Christ?

Question: Isn't it in everybody's best interest that you fix their erroneous thinking right away?

LESSON 158

Today I learn to give as I receive.

W-158.1.What has been given you? 2 The knowledge that you are a mind, in Mind and purely mind, sinless forever, wholly unafraid, because you were created out of love. 3 Nor have you left your Source, remaining as you were created. 4 This was given you as knowledge **of what you truly are, your big "S" Self,** which you cannot lose. 5 **This same knowledge of what we truly are** was given as well to every living thing, for by that knowledge only do **all things** live.

W-158.2.You have received all this **knowledge of what you truly are**. 2 No one who walks the world but has received **this knowledge of what we truly are**. 3 It is not this knowledge which you give, for that is what creation gave. 4 All this **knowledge of what you truly are** cannot be learned. 5 What, then, are you to learn to give today? 6 Our lesson yesterday evoked a theme found early in the text. 7 Experience cannot be shared directly, in the way that **the** vision **of Christ** can. 8 The revelation that the Father and the Son are one will come in time to every mind. 9 Yet is that time determined by **each one's** mind itself, not taught.

W-158.3.The time is set already **for your reawakening**. 2 **This time of your reawakening** appears to be quite arbitrary. 3 Yet there is no step along the road that anyone takes but by chance. 4 **Each step** has already been taken by him, although he has not yet embarked on **that step**. 5 For time but seems to go in one direction, **from the past to the future.** 6 We but undertake a journey that is over. 7 Yet **time** seems to have a future still unknown to us.

W-158.4.Time is a trick, a sleight of hand, a vast illusion in which figures come and go as if by magic. 2 Yet there is a plan behind appearances that does not change. 3 The script is written. 4 When experience will come to end your doubting has been set. 5 For we but see the journey from the point at which **the journey of separation to reawakening** ended, looking back on **the journey**, imagining we make **the journey of separation to reawakening** once again; reviewing mentally what has gone by.

W-158.5.A teacher does not give experience, because **a teacher** did not learn **experience**. 2 **Experience** revealed itself to him at the appointed time **for the experience**. 3 But vision is **the teacher's** gift. 4 This **vision of the teacher, the Christ , your big "S" Self,** can give directly, for Christ's knowledge is not lost, because **Christ** has a vision, **Christ** can give **that vision** to anyone who asks. 5 The Father's Will and **Christ's Will** are joined in knowledge. 6 Yet there is a vision which the Holy Spirit sees because the Mind of Christ beholds **that vision** too.

W-158.6.Here **in this vision of Christ** is the joining of the world of doubt and shadows made with the intangible. 2 Here **in this vision of Christ** is a quiet place within the world made holy by forgiveness and by love. 3 Here **in this vision of Christ** are all contradictions reconciled, for here the journey ends. 4 Experience–unlearned, untaught, unseen–is merely there. 5 This is beyond our goal, for **this vision** transcends what needs to be accomplished. 6 Our concern is with Christ's vision. 7 This we can attain.

W-158.7.Christ's vision has one law. 2 **Christ's vision** does not look upon a body, and mistake **the body** for the Son whom God created. 3 **Christ's vision** beholds a light beyond the body; an idea beyond what can be touched, a purity undimmed by errors, pitiful mistakes, and fearful thoughts of guilt from dreams of sin. 4 **Christ's vision** sees no separation. 5 And **Christ's vision** looks on everyone, on every circumstance, all happenings and all events, without the slightest fading of the light **that the vision of Christ** sees.

W-158.8.**Christ's vision** can be taught; and must be taught by all who would achieve **Christ's vision.** 2 **Christ's vision** requires but the recognition that the world cannot give anything that faintly can compare with **the vision of Christ** in value; nor set up a goal that does not merely disappear when this has been perceived. 3 And this, **the vision of Christ,** you give today: See no one as a body. 4 Greet **all** as the Son of God he is, acknowledging that **your brother** is one with you in holiness.

W-158.9.Thus are **your brother's** sins forgiven him, for Christ has vision that has power to overlook all **belief in sin.** 2 In **Christ's** forgiveness are **sins** gone. 3 Unseen by **Christ, sins** merely disappear, because a vision of the holiness that lies beyond **the belief in sin** comes to take **sins'** place. 4 It matters not what form **the belief in sin** took, nor how enormous **the sin** appeared to be, nor who seemed to be hurt by **the sin.** 5 **Sins** are no more. 6 And all effects **the belief in sin** seemed to have are gone with **the sin**, undone and never to be done.

W-158.10.Thus do you learn to give as you receive. 2 And thus Christ's vision looks on you as well. 3 This lesson **that to give as you receive** is not difficult to learn, if you remember in your brother you but see yourself. 4 If **your brother** be lost in sin, so must you be **lost in sin**; if you see light in **your brother**, your sins have been forgiven by yourself. 5 Each brother whom you meet today provides another chance to let Christ's vision shine on you, and offer you the peace of God.

W-158.11.It matters not when revelation comes, for **revelation** is not of time. 2 Yet time has still one gift to give **which is the vision of Christ**, in which true knowledge is reflected in a way so accurate its image shares its unseen holiness; its likeness shines with its immortal love. 3 We practice seeing with the eyes of Christ today. 4 And by the holy gifts we give, Christ's vision looks upon ourselves as well.

Today I learn to give as I receive.

Today's lesson is I learn to give as I receive. This is an important lesson as it covers the notion of time and Christ's vision. I would also like to use this lesson to explain why we have such a difficult time with the idea that to give is to receive.

Christ vision has one law. Never look upon the body and mistake the body for the Son of God as God created him. We are to look past bodily forms and not be deceived by appearances. When you give Christ vision, you look past the body and instead, see that all are joined as one mind, perfect, whole and complete.

The gift of Christ vision is what we have received from God and that we give to another. God knows us as the Christ, part of the One Self, perfect, whole and complete. This lesson asks you to give that same vision of what you are to another.

This lesson also talks of time. In the fourth paragraph of this lesson it states.

W-158.4.Time is a trick, a sleight of hand, a vast illusion in which figures come and go as if by magic. 2 Yet there is a plan behind appearances that does not change. 3 The script is written. 4 When experience will come to end your doubting has been set. 5 For we but see the journey from the point at which **the journey of separation to reawakening** ended, looking back on **the journey**, imagining we make **the journey of separation to reawakening** once again; reviewing mentally what has gone by.

We believe time has a future unknown to us in which truth could be different than what we perceive truth to be today. We perceive that time is linear and moves in one direction from past, to present to the future. Instead, time is in a journey that is already over and we are merely looking back from the completed journey and imagining we are making the journey once again, reviewing mentally what has already gone by.

Experience is not the same as vision. We cannot share experience but we can share vision. Christ vision is the truth of our oneness, sinless and guiltless nature that all God's creations possess. Experiences provide context for content that deals with purpose that can be shared. Content, purpose and vision, all deal with the reason behind the experience.

When we utilize the vision of Christ, we are witnessing for the truth that we are mind and not a body. We are sinless, guiltless and remain as God created us. Vision is the knowledge of the truth that you are mind, in mind and purely mind, sinless forever, wholly unafraid, created out of love. With vision you know you have not left your source and you remain as God created you. This gift of vision is the knowledge that all have been given which cannot be lost. Because of this knowledge, all live and remain connected to God, their Source. Christ vision is the recognition, awareness and sharing of the knowledge of your divine birthright with others.

With that said, I'd like to discuss the law of God that states to give is to receive. If we truly understood this law, our belief in sin, guilt and fear would disappear.

In this course, we have often said that to give is to receive. Yet, most of us still believe that this is not the case. We have a problem with the idea that to give is to receive because we still perceive that giving requires sacrifice. We believe sacrifice is required because we do not understand the what, to whom, where and when that is involved during the act of giving.

A major stumbling block with God's law that to give is to receive is our confusion with what is actually being given. We believe we are giving some kind of form and not the content, purpose or what the course might refer to as vision.

What we are actually giving to another is our vision or purpose. They are free to accept or reject our vision but our vision is the real gift. The form that the actual giving encompasses is immaterial and of no consequence. Yet, most perceive the form to be most important. Most mistake the item or physical thing to be the only gift that is being given to the recipient. We ignore the giver's vision that was behind the gift.

Let's take the example of giving $10,000 to another. The question really is what is the giving for?

Are you giving $10,000 or are you giving hope?

Are you giving dependence or are you giving abundance?

Are you giving to a needy body or are you giving to Christ?

Do you perceive the other to be your equal or someone who is either beneath or above you?

Ultimately, in time, what we are really giving is either being a witness for the false or the true. We are either giving unconditional love or promoting fear.

The second problem we encounter with the idea that to give is to receive is our failure to understand to whom we are giving the gift.

God gives love because God knows that there is only One Self and therefore, God is actually giving to that One Self. God does not perceive since there is nothing separate from God and perception requires both an observer and something to observe.

We, however, have a problem with this because we perceive there is something outside of ourselves and that the separation is real. When we give love, it is conditional love because we perceive the separation to be real.

Ideas never leave their source but that is not what our split minds believe. Our split mind believes that our love leaves our mind and goes out to a separate entity and that the second entity receives and responds to our love by either accepting or rejecting our love. The recipient's response to our love is perceived by our split mind to be outside feedback that is needed to determine if we should continue our "loving actions." To the ego, we only give to get and therefore, we want some return for our investment of our so-called "loving actions."

Because we believe we are a separate body and not one shared mind, we believe that our ideas leave their source. We believe that based on the feedback we receive from the recipient of our idea that their reaction has the ability to impact our ongoing behavior. We perceive their feedback to be the mechanism that determines if we should continue to send our love to the other party. Because we believe there are outside forces that can affect how we behave, we have substituted conditional love for real love. Conditional love is fear-based. Conditional love only gives to get.

God's love is unconditional. It flows continuously. God does not require our feedback to determine whether or not God should continue to love us. God knows that to give is to receive and therefore, the joy of giving the love is completion. We, being the recipients of God's love, are God's treasures. Since ideas never leave their source, we are an indivisible part of the One Self. Unlike conditional love, God does not require our acceptance of His love to obtain the joy or satisfaction that is often associated with behaving lovingly in the realm of duality and perception.

Yet, in the world of perception, we perceive ourselves to be separate from God. We felt we were the recipient of God's love and mistook receiving and giving to be two separate autonomous events. To the split mind, giving and receiving are not considered one inseparable act. God knows that giving and receiving are instantaneous and the same thing because there is only the One Self.

In the world of duality, giving and receiving are perceived to be separate because we perceive the giver and receiver to be separate. We believe there is a cause-and-effect relationship. There are two separate happenings which create a measurable gap in time between cause and effect. We fail to perceive it as one spontaneous event.

The game of separation is birthed from our minds' failure to understand that giving and receiving are one inseparable act. We, being the recipients of God's love, felt we needed to give God our feedback. We failed to realize that just our being available to be given God's love was God's joy and treasure. Perceiving giver and receiver to be different, our now split mind felt that how the recipient received the love was important feedback to the giver. Ultimately we felt that we should reciprocate God's love with our own love to God. This desire to reciprocate led to the idea that giver and receiver were separate and that love should be earned.

God's joy was already complete just by the act of giving. Since there was only the One Self, being perfect, whole and complete, there was nothing that God needed. God did not require any response from us to "make" God happy.

Since God's love was truly unconditional and complete within itself, there was no way we could earn God's love. God does not need approval or acceptance. Yet, within our split mind, we believed that we should reciprocate God's love with our own love to God. We wanted some way to be able to earn God's love which is impossible within a Oneness of All That Is. Earned love, which would be conditional love, could only be possible in the mind that imagined the separation to be real.

Perceiving itself to be separate from its Source, our ego felt we lacked the ability to earn God's love. Only if duality existed, could the ability to earn another's favor or displeasure be possible. Because we failed to understand that to give is to receive, we felt our inability to reciprocate God's love demonstrated lack. The belief in lack, of course, has been defined as sin.

God could not understand our desire to earn God's love because the concept itself had numerous erroneous assumptions. Love could not be earned since separation is impossible and to give is to receive. This is why God's answer to the question of how we earn love is the Atonement. The Atonement is the acceptance of the At-One-Ment principle. Atonement is the acceptance of the truth that you remain as God created you, part of the indivisible One Self, perfect, whole and complete. Earned love is impossible since it contradicts what real love is.

This notion that giving and receiving are separate gives rise to the belief in sin, guilt and fear. Fear is the notion that love can be earned and that there are outside forces that can impact what you are and that by your actions you can make these outside forces love you.

This egoic world was birthed by our belief that our inability to reciprocate God's love was a sin. We felt we had sinned against God Whom we perceived to be a separate entity and the giver of the love that we received. This belief that the recipient could or should reciprocate to the giver made the separation appear real.

Conditional love was born because we believed giver and receiver were different and separate. This egoic world is a place where we can pretend that conditional love, which is love's opposite, actually exists. This world is where we believe love can be earned which is why this world seems to be such a fearful place. Conditional love requires the belief that you are needy. Conditional love perceives the recipient to be not perfect, whole and complete. The more lacking and needy one is, the better for the giver.

This belief made the separation appear real and created an opposite to God's love that is totally unconditional. Our desire to be able to earn love created conditional love which is actually a form of fear. Because we fail to understand that to give is to receive, our split mind is incapable of recognizing unconditional love. If and when unconditional love is received, our split mind will misjudge it to be conditional love.

Our third problem with the idea that to give is to receive is our confusion with where and when the giving and receiving take place. We believe giving and receiving take place in time, not eternity.

Time is the belief that there is a gap between cause and effect. The only reason that there can be a gap between cause-and-effect is because we fail to recognize cause and effect as instantaneous, being two sides of one inseparable event. Because of this gap, we believe that the cause requires the delayed feedback of the effect to determine whether or not it should continue.

We see this belief in a gap between cause-and-effect in conditional love. One person acts in a supposedly loving way and then waits upon the reaction of the recipient to determine whether or not the giver should continue to behave lovingly to the recipient. The so-called giver of the love now believes that how the receiver reacts to their love is the source for their joy, rather than their joy being instantaneous with the act of their giving. In eternity, there is no gap between cause and effect. Within the giving of the love is also the completion of the joy of love.

We can better understand our problem in recognizing that to give is to receive when we understand the difference between unconditional love and conditional love. Remember that what we call conditional love is actually the opposite of God's love and should be called fear. Love, as the ego perceives it, is a euphemism for fear. In our world, conditional love is a mask for fear and fear often manifests as and is described as hate.

Unconditional love gives to itself since it recognizes the oneness of all. Conditional love gives to another since it believes separation to be real. Unconditional love gives content or its vision. Conditional love gives form. Unconditional love recognizes that to give is to receive, whereas conditional love does not. Unconditional love is spontaneous and belongs to eternity. Conditional love takes place over time and there are gaps between giver and receiver. Unconditional love recognizes that ideas never leave their source. Conditional love believes that ideas leave their source. Unconditional love is based on oneness and unity. Conditional love is based on duality and separation.

When you realize that the joy of love is in the giving and not in the feedback, you will be on the road to exchanging time for eternity.

When you can look at another person's story and say with a sense of awe and wonderment what an interesting creation they have made for themselves, you are honoring their path. You are responding without making or judging another wrong or guilty for exercising their free will on their own perfect journey. When you can do this, you will be demonstrating that the end of time is near. You will no longer be mistaking a story and its form for the content and vision that the experience provides. You will be able to look at all with the state of awe and marvel at the creative power of mind.

When you realize that ideas never leave their source, you have the freedom to accept or reject another's vision or story for your own or you can walk away from their creation. Without judging them, you can recognize that each is the creator of their own story and you are free to write your own script and do not have to participate in their story. You are free to follow your own perfect path as you allow others that same freedom and right.

God smiled at our story that we could be something other than what we really are. God basically says what a fertile imagination and what an interesting game of make-believe. God does not choose to participate in our game of separation therefore, it is not real. God did not mistake giving as separation from receiving or that love had to be received by some outside entity or it was not love. God's love remains unchangeable, unconditional and eternal. It is not earned and our denial of its flow has no impact on God or what God created.

Question: Can you see how what we call conditional love is really a euphemism for fear and is the opposite of God's love?

LESSON 159

I give the miracles I have received.

W-159.1.No one can give what he has not received. 2 To give a thing requires first you have **the item** in your own possession. 3 Here the laws of Heaven and the world agree. 4 But here **the laws of Heaven and the world** also separate. 5 The world believes that to possess a thing, it must be kept. 6 Salvation teaches otherwise **that to possess a thing, it must be given away.** 7 To give is how to recognize you have received. 8 **To give the item away** is the proof that what you have is yours.

W-159.2.You understand that you are healed when you give healing. 2 You accept forgiveness as accomplished in yourself when you forgive. 3 You recognize your brother as yourself, and thus do you perceive that you are whole. 4 There is no miracle you cannot give, for all **miracles** are given you. 5 Receive **the miracles** now by opening the storehouse of your mind where **the miracles** are laid, and giving **those same miracles** away.

W-159.3.Christ's vision is a miracle. 2 **Christ's vision** comes from far beyond itself, for **Christ's vision** reflects eternal love and the rebirth of love which never dies, but has been kept obscure. 3 Christ's vision pictures Heaven, for **Christ's vision** sees a world so like to Heaven that what God created perfect can be mirrored there **within the now open storehouse of your mind that utilizes the vision of Christ.** 4 The darkened glass the **ego's** world presents can show but twisted images in broken parts. 5 The real world pictures Heaven's innocence.

W-159.4.Christ's vision is the miracle in which all miracles are born. 2 **Christ's vision** is **the miracle's** source, remaining with each miracle you give, and yet remaining yours. 3 **Christ's vision** is the bond by which the giver and receiver are united in extension here on earth, as **the giver and receiver** are one in Heaven. 4 Christ beholds no sin in anyone. 5 And in **Christ's** sight the sinless are as one. 6 **Everyone's sinlessness and** holiness was given by **Christ's** Father and Himself, **our big "S" Self.**

W-159.5.Christ's vision is the bridge between the worlds. 2 And in **the** power **of Christ's vision,** can you safely trust to carry you from this world **made from your ego's belief in sin, guilt and fear** into **a world** made holy by forgiveness. 3 Things which seem quite solid here are merely shadows there **in a world based upon love, forgiveness and oneness. In this new world, things which seem quite solid in the ego's world are** transparent, faintly seen, at times forgot, and never able to obscure the light that shines beyond **the shadows of this fear-based world.** 4 **In the world of Christ's vision which is based upon love, forgiveness and oneness,** holiness has been restored to vision, and the blind can see.

W-159.6.**Christ's vision** is the Holy Spirit's single gift; the treasure house to which you can appeal with perfect certainty for all the things that can contribute to your happiness. 2 All **gifts** are laid here already **in the treasure house of Christ's vision.** 3 All **things that can contribute to your happiness** can be received but for the asking. 4 Here **with the gift of Christ's vision** the door is never locked, and no one is denied his least request or his most urgent need. 5 There is no sickness not already healed, no lack unsatisfied, no need unmet within this golden treasury of Christ.

W-159.7.Here **with Christ's vision** does the world remember what was lost when **the egoic world** was made. 2 For here **with the vision of Christ the ego's world of lack, limitation and separation** is repaired, made new again, but in a different light **of forgiveness, oneness and love.** 3 What was to be the home of sin **and the split mind** becomes the center of redemption and the hearth of mercy, where the suffering are healed and welcome. 4 No one will be turned away from this new home **for redemption,** where **the split mind is healed and** his salvation waits. 5 No one is stranger to **the split mind that suffers.** 6 No one asks for anything of **the split mind** except the gift of **the split mind's** acceptance of his welcoming **into Christ's redemption center based upon forgiveness, love and oneness.**

W-159.8.Christ's vision is the holy ground in which the lilies of forgiveness set their roots. 2 **Christ's vision** is **the** home **of forgiveness that the lilies symbolize.** 3 **The lilies of forgiveness** can be brought from here back to the **ego's** world, but **the lilies of forgiveness** can never grow in **the ego's world of sin, guilt and fear for the ego's thought system is** unnourishing and **its** soil **too** shallow. 4 **The lilies of forgiveness** need the light and warmth and kindly care Christ's charity provides. 5 **The lilies of forgiveness** need the love with which **Christ** looks on **those who forgive.** 6 And **those who forgive** become **Christ's** messengers, who give **forgiveness as Christ's messengers** received **their forgiveness.**

W-159.9.Take from **Christ's** storehouse **in your mind the message of forgiveness** that **Christ's** treasures may increase. 2 **Christ's** lilies **of forgiveness** do not leave their home when **the lilies of forgiveness** are carried back into the **ego's world of sin, guilt and fear.** 3 **The lilies of forgiveness'** roots remain **within Christ's world of forgiveness, love and healing.** 4 **The lilies of forgiveness** do not leave their source, but carry **the forgiveness, love and healing of Christ's** beneficence with them, and turn the world into a garden **for redemption** like the one they came from, and to which **the lilies of forgiveness** go again with added fragrance. 5 Now are **those who forgive, Christ's messengers,** twice blessed. 6 The messages **of forgiveness, love and healing** that **those who forgive** brought from Christ have been delivered, and returned to **the messenger.** 7 And **Christ's messengers** return **the messages of forgiveness, love and healing** gladly unto **Christ.**

W-159.10.Behold the store of miracles set out for you to give. 2 Are you not worth the gift **of all miracles**, when God appointed **all miracles** be given you? 3 Judge not God's Son, but follow in the way **God** has established. 4 Christ has dreamed the dream of a forgiven world. 5 **A forgiven world** is **Christ's** gift, whereby a sweet transition can be made from death to life; from hopelessness to hope. 6 Let us an instant dream with **Christ.** 7 **Christ's happy** dream awakens us to truth. 8 **Christ** vision gives the means for a return to our unlost and everlasting sanctity in God.

Notes to Lesson #159

I give the miracles I have received.

Today, you are asked to give the miracles you have received. Throughout your life, you have asked and received numerous miracles yet, you may not realize this fact. In order to realize that you have received a miracle, you must share that miracle by giving it away. When you give something away, you prove that you possess it for you can only give what you have.

The egoic world values form over context. Because of this, the world teaches that when you give something away, you lose it for you no longer possess it. But salvation teaches that when you receive something, you need to give it away for that is how you recognize and prove that you have it in the first place.

The laws of God deal with content, not form. Thoughts can be shared with no diminishment to the giver of a thought. Vision is in the realm of thought.

To give, you must have the gift or vision in your possession. Vision is an attribute of the mind. Because vision is thought, it can be shared with no diminishment to the giver. If the second party adopts your vision and accepts it for their own, all parties gain and the vision is strengthened.

This lesson asks that you give away the miracles that you have received. But what are you really asked to give to your brothers and sisters?

Remember, a miracle is not some physical event but rather a change in your thinking. A miracle takes place at the level of mind. A miracle occurs whenever a fear-based thought is reframed by the Holy Spirit and now viewed through the eyes of love and forgiveness.

You cannot give another your experiences for your experiences are your own personal and unique perception of an event. Whenever two people witness the same event, each will have their own unique experience of the event based on their own viewpoint and perception. So, if you cannot share an experience what can you share? You can share your vision for that experience.

Just as there are two thought systems, there are two visions for this world that we can experience as our own provisional reality. The ego's vision for this world is a place of lack, limitation and separation. Sin, guilt and fear abound and it is the opposite of a loving world.

The vision of the Holy Spirit is based on forgiveness, love and oneness as it is symbolized and seen through the eyes of Christ. It is based on the truth that we are sinless and guiltless and remain as God created us.

These two thought systems create worlds that are polar opposites. Forgiveness is the bridge that connects these two visions and transports the experience of fear to fearlessness through the bridge that forgiveness brings to escape the vision of a fearful world.

The eyes of Christ see a vision of a forgiven world. This vision of a forgiven world represents a happy dream that aligns with the truth. With the vision of Christ, we see Heaven's innocence mirrored in our provisional reality.

The gift of the Holy Spirit is Christ vision. Christ vision holds all things that contribute to your happiness and is the source of all miracles. The miracle reflects eternal love and courage. Christ vision heals the world by transforming this home for sin into a center of redemption and forgiveness. Christ vision is the fertile ground in which forgiveness grows. Its roots are found and nurtured in the thought system of the Holy Spirit. The ego's thought system is incapable of nourishing and sustaining the thoughts of forgiveness and love because it was designed to grow only fear.

Christ vision is the bridge of forgiveness that spans the gulf between heaven and the world of the ego. It repairs the memory of God that we lost when we forgot to laugh and made the game of separation real within our mind. Christ's vision is grounded in forgiveness that brings your provisional reality's experiences back to the real world.

It is this vision of a forgiving world that you are asked to share. Christ vision allows you to see this happier dream and share it with your brothers. You cannot force another to accept the vision of Christ, but you can hold your brother in that light and maintain that vision for him. When you do this, you provide a different vision that your brother can claim for himself. Now he has the option to choose a different path and receive a different experience. Your brother can then share the forgiving world that Christ vision brings to all.

<u>Question</u>: Each of us is the script writer, director, editor and star of our own provisional reality show.

What is the overriding theme or vision that you want your script to demonstrate and teach to your world? As the show's director, what guiding vision will you be providing for the supporting cast in your play?

LESSON 160

I am at home. Fear is the stranger here.

W-160.1.Fear is a stranger to the ways of love. 2 Identify with fear and you will be a stranger to **your Big "S" Self**. 3 And thus **when you identify with fear, your big "S" self** is unknown to you. 4 What is your **big "S"** Self remains an alien to the part of you, **your ego's little "s" self,** which thinks that fear is real. But **your ego believes that fear is** different from **and not sourced by your ego's own mind.** 5 Who could be sane in such a circumstance? 6 Who but a madman could believe he is what he is not, and judge against his **big "S" Self**?

W-160.2.There is a stranger in our midst, **our ego,** who comes from an idea **of fear which is** so foreign to the truth, that **our ego** speaks a different language, looks upon a world truth does not know, and understands what truth regards as senseless. 2 Stranger yet, **your ego** does not recognize to whom he comes, **which is God's Son, your big "S" Self.** And yet **your ego** maintains **your big "S" Self's** home, **which is your mind,** belongs to **your ego to rule. Although the ego is the real** alien **in your mind,** now **your ego seems to be** at home **and in control of your mind. Your ego** falsely proclaims that your big **"S" Self** is the foreigner that does not belong within your mind which is now split and sick with fear. 3 And yet, how easy it would be **for you, the decision-maker and true ruler of your mind, to choose for the truth of your big "S" Self and** to say, "**The Mind I share with God** is my home. 4 Here I, **my big "S" Self,** belong, and will not leave the **Mind I share with God** because a **fearful** madman, **my ego,** says I must."

W-160.3.What reason is there for not saying this **and reclaiming your home which is the Mind you share with God**? 2 What could the reason be except that you had asked this stranger in, **which is the fear-based thought system of the ego,** to take your place, and let **you and your decision-maker** be a stranger to **the thought system for love**? 3 No one would let himself be dispossessed so needlessly, unless **you, as decision-maker for all your choices,** thought there was another home more suited to **your** tastes.

W-160.4.Who is the stranger **in the home that is the Mind you share with God**? 2 Is it fear or you, **your big "S" Self,** who are unsuited to the home which God provided for His Son? 3 Is fear **God's** Own, created in **God's** likeness? 4 Is it fear that love completes, and is **fear** completed by **love**? 5 There is no home **that** can shelter **both** love and fear. **6 Love and fear** cannot coexist. 7 If you, **being only love,** are real, then fear must be illusion. 8 And if fear is real, then you do not exist at all.

W-160.5.How simply, then, the question is resolved. 2 Who **that** fears has but denied **his big "S" Self, the Christ,** and said, "I am the stranger here **in Heaven, the home of only love.** 3 And so I leave my home **of only love** to **seek a different home based on fear that is** more like **the fearful little "s" self I** imagine myself to be rather than **my true reality as the Christ.** And **with my denial of who I really am, I** give **my ego** all I thought belonged to **my big "S" Self, including the creative power of mind."** 4 With this self-denial of his Christ nature and perceiving himself to be something he is not, now is **the split minded** exiled of necessity **since love and fear cannot coexist. The split minded,** not knowing who he is, uncertain of all things but this; that **the Son of God** is not himself, and that **the Son's** home has been denied to him.

W-160.6.What does **the split-mind** search for now? 2 What can **the split-mind** find? 3 A stranger to **the big "S" Self, the split-mind who does not know what he is** can find no home wherever he may look, for **due to fear** he has made return **to love** impossible. 4 **To he who does not know who he is,** his way is lost, except a miracle will search him out and show him that he is no stranger **to love** now **even in his self-imposed exile into fear.** 5 The miracle will come. 6 For in his **real** home, his **big "S"** Self, **the Christ,** remains. 7 **His big "S" Self** asked no stranger **of fear** in, and took no alien **egoic** thought to be **mistaken for** Itself, **the Christ.** 8 And **the Christ** will call Its Own **who do not know what they are** unto Itself in recognition of what is Its Own.

W-160.7.Who is the stranger? 2 Is **the stranger** not the **voice for fear that** your **big "S"** Self calls not? 3 You are unable now to recognize this stranger **of fear, your ego** in your midst, for you have given **your ego** your rightful place **as the decision-maker for your mind's thought system.** 4 Yet is your **big "S"** Self as certain of Its Own as God is of His Son. 5 **God** cannot be confused about creation. 6 **God** is sure of what belongs to **God.** 7 No stranger can be interposed between **God's** knowledge and His Son's reality. 8 **God** does not know of strangers. 9 **God** is certain of His Son.

W-160.8.God's certainty suffices. 2 Who **God** knows to be His Son belongs where **God** has set His Son forever. 3 **God** has answered you who ask, "Who is the stranger?" 4 Hear **the Holy Spirit's** Voice assure you, quietly and sure, that you are not a stranger to your Father, nor is your Creator **a** stranger to you **whom God created.** 5 Whom God has joined remain forever one, at home in **God,** no stranger to **God,** Himself.

W-160.9.Today we offer thanks that Christ has come to search the world for what belongs to **God.** 2 **Christ's** vision sees no strangers, but beholds **Christ's** Own and joyously unites with them. 3 **The split minded** see **Christ** as a stranger, for they do not recognize themselves **as their big "S" Selves.** 4 Yet as **the split minded** give **Christ** welcome, **the split minded are healed and** remember **who they really are.** 5 And **Christ** leads **the once split minded** gently home again, where **their healed minds** belong.

W-160.10.Not one does Christ forget. 2 Not one **Christ** fails to give you to remember, that your home may be complete and perfect as **your loving home** was established. 3 **Christ** has not forgotten you. 4 But you will not remember **Christ** until you look on all as **Christ** does. 5 Who denies his brother is denying **Christ**, and thus refusing to accept the gift of sight by which his **big "S"** Self is clearly recognized, his home remembered and salvation come.

Notes to Lesson #160

I am at home. Fear is the stranger here.

Do you live in a peaceful world or is your world full of fears?

Love has no opposites. Fear is a stranger to love. When you identify with fear, you have imagined the loss of your true identity and have denied the truth of who you really are. Your decision-maker has forgotten that truth is true and nothing else is true. You have become split minded and allowed fear to enter into a world of your mind's imagination.

Fear is unknown in the shared Mind of God. By making the false appear real, you have allowed the thought system of fear to masquerade as the ruler of your world. Your decision-maker has chosen to deny your own birthright. Your mind has been made sick with fear and now has become an alien to the truth.

God did not create fear. God's creations complete God, Himself, and are only an extension of love. Love has no opposites. Love and fear cannot coexist. A fearful world cannot be the home that God prepared for his beloved creation. If you perceive a fearful world, it is a world that only exists within your mind's imagination.

Your split mind has imagined lack, limitation and separation to exist. These beliefs have birthed a false world that is the home of the little "s" self that you imagine yourself to be. This is the home for the sin, guilt and fear that your ego perceives to be real.

Only love is real and is complete in itself for love is the Oneness of All That Is. Fear, which would have to be defined as love's opposite, cannot be real. Fear is false evidence appearing real. Fear does not complete love and can only appear real within the imaginings of a delusional mind. If you are real, fear must be an illusion. If fear is real, you do not exist at all.

If your life is full of fear, you have denied the truth of your big "S" Self. You have forgotten that you are the writer, director and star of your dream world of perception. You have invited an alien thought system to enter your mind and now that thought system rules in the place of the truth. When you believe that lack, limitation and separation are possible, you have forgotten your divine birthright. You have turned the exciting game of What am I into the bad dream of separation that you mistake to be real.

Differentiation does not mean different. Different means that there exist separate and autonomous beings. Differentiation only allows for various aspects of the One Self to experience an aspect of Itself. When we mistook the game board of differentiation to be interpreted as differences, we allowed a stranger to enter our mind. The stranger is the ego's fear-based thought system of separation.

You have forgotten that you are the creator of the game of What am I. You have allowed your mind's imagination to become the arbitrator for truth. Your mind now imagines that the false can be true and the true false. But pretense and imagination cannot change the truth of who you really are. God, the Holy Spirit and your big "S" Self all know that you remain the Christ, part of the indivisible One Self.

God knows the truth and with knowledge comes certainty. God's certainty guarantees that those who have mistaken the game of What am I to be their reality will reawaken to the truth.

Christ sees your fearful ego as the real stranger in the world of truth. Christ knows that fear cannot be real. Christ searches this dream world for what belongs to Christ. The Holy Spirit and Christ can reframe the world you perceive into a witness for that truth if you let them. The Holy Spirit recognizes your big "S" Self to be the true ruler of your mind.

When you, as decision-maker, decide to follow the thought system of the Holy Spirit, you join with them and allow them to lead you home to the recognition of the truth. Paradise was never lost. God's Son has never left his home but has merely forgotten that his mind sleeps and only needs to awaken.

You will not remember your big "S" Self until you see the Christ in all your brothers. To give is to receive. When you follow the thought system of love and forgiveness and extend that to all you touch, you recognize the truth of who you really are. Fear will dissipate before the reality of the truth. The mind you share with God is your home. Fear is a stranger here because fear does not exist within the Mind of God.

Question: Your world is a reflection of you. The thought system that you follow determines the world you perceive. You can only follow one thought system at any given moment in time. When you follow the ego's thought system, your world is perceived to be a fearful place.

How fearful is your world?

LESSON 161

Give me your blessing, holy Son of God.

W-161.1.Today we practice differently, and take a stand against our anger, that our fears may disappear and offer room to love. 2 Here is salvation in the simple words in which we practice with today's idea **to give me your blessing, holy Son of God.** 3 Here is the answer to temptation which can never fail to welcome in the Christ where fear and anger had prevailed before. 4 Here is Atonement made complete, the world passed safely by and Heaven now restored **when you see your brother as the holy Son of God.** 5 Here **by always seeing your brother's perfect holiness** is the answer of the Voice for God.

W-161.2.Complete abstraction is the natural condition of the mind. 2 But part of **your mind** is now unnatural **and split.** 3 **Your split mind** does not look on everything as one. 4 **Your split mind** sees instead but fragments of the whole, for only thus could **your mind** invent the partial world you see. 5 The purpose of all **egoic** seeing is to show you what you wish to see. 6 All hearing but brings to your mind the sounds **your split mind** wants to hear.

W-161.3.**Because your split mind sees only fragments of the whole and sees only what it wants to see,** thus were specifics made. 2 And now it is specifics we must use in practicing. 3 We give **the specifics that we perceive** to the Holy Spirit, that **the Holy Spirit** may employ **the specifics that we wanted to see** for a purpose which is different from the one we gave **originally** to **what we perceived.** 4 Yet **the Holy Spirit** can use but what we made, to teach us from a different point of view, so we can see a different use in everything.

W-161.4.One brother is all brothers. 2 Every mind contains all minds, for every mind is one. 3 Such is the truth. 4 Yet do these thoughts **of oneness** make clear the meaning of creation? 5 Do these words bring perfect clarity with **these abstract explanations** to you? 6 What can they seem to be but empty sounds; pretty, perhaps, correct in sentiment, yet fundamentally not understood nor understandable **by your mind that deals in specifics.** 7 The **split** mind that taught itself to think specifically can no longer grasp abstraction in the sense that **the abstract** is all-encompassing. 8 We need to see a little **with specific examples so** that we learn a lot.

W-161.5.It seems to be the body that we feel limits our freedom, makes us suffer, and at last puts out our life. 2 Yet bodies are but symbols for a concrete form of fear. 3 Fear without symbols calls for no response, for symbols can stand for the meaningless. 4 Love needs no symbols, being true. 5 But fear attaches to specifics, being false **and meaningless.**

W-161.6.Bodies attack, but minds do not **attack.** 2 This thought is surely reminiscent of our text, where **the need for a body for attack to be possible** is often emphasized. 3 This is the reason bodies easily become fear's symbols. 4 You have many times been urged to look beyond the body, for **the** sight **of a body** presents the symbol of love's "enemy" **that** Christ's vision does not see. 5 The body is the target for attack, for no one thinks he hates a mind. 6 Yet what but mind directs the body to attack? 7 What else could be the seat of fear except what thinks of fear **which is the split mind?**

W-161.7.Hate is specific. 2 There must be a thing to be attacked. 3 An enemy must be perceived in such a form he can be touched and seen and heard, and ultimately killed. 4 When hatred rests upon a thing, **hatred** calls for death as surely as God's Voice proclaims there is no death. 5 Fear is insatiable, consuming everything **the** eyes **of fear** behold, seeing **fear** in everything, compelled to turn upon itself and to destroy **its own mind.**

W-161.8.Who sees a brother as a body sees him as fear's symbol. 2 And he **who sees a brother as a body** will attack, because what he beholds **in his brother's body** is his own fear external to himself, poised to attack, and howling to unite with him again **and end his separate autonomous existence.** 3 Mistake not the intensity of rage projected fear must spawn. 4 **Fear** shrieks in wrath, and claws the air in frantic hope **fear's rage** can reach to its maker and devour **fear's maker which is your own mind.**

W-161.9.**A concrete symbol of fear** do the body's eyes behold in one whom Heaven cherishes, the angels love and God created perfect. 2 **The big "S" Self, not the body,** is **your brother's** reality. 3 And in Christ's vision is **your brother's** loveliness reflected in a form so holy and so beautiful that you could scarce refrain from kneeling at his feet. 4 Yet you will take his hand instead, for you are like **your brother** in the sight **of Christ** that sees **your brother** thus **as the Son of God.** 5 Attack on **your brother** is enemy to you **and an attack on yourself,** for you will not perceive that in **your brother's** hands is your salvation. 6 Ask **your brother** but for **his blessings and salvation,** and he will give **his blessings and salvation** to you. 7 Ask **your brother** not to symbolize your fear. 8 Would you request that love destroy itself? 9 Or would you have **love** be revealed to you and set you free?

W-161.10.Today we practice in a form we have attempted earlier. 2 Your readiness is closer now, and you will come today nearer Christ's vision. 3 If you are intent on reaching **Christ's vision,** you will succeed today. 4 And once you have succeeded **in reaching Christ's vision,** you will not be willing to accept the witnesses your body's eyes call forth. 5 What you will see will sing to you of ancient melodies you will remember. 6 You are not forgot in Heaven. 7 Would you not remember **the truth of your big "S" Self's oneness with all?**

W-161.11.Select one brother, symbol of the rest, and ask salvation of him. 2 See **your brother** first as clearly as you can, in that same **bodily** form to which you are accustomed. 3 See his face, his hands and feet, his clothing. 4 Watch **your brother** smile, and see familiar gestures which **your brother** makes so frequently. 5 Then think of this: What you are seeing now conceals from you the sight of one who can forgive you all your sins; whose sacred hands can take away the nails which pierce your own, and lift the crown of thorns which you have placed upon your bleeding head. 6 Ask **forgiveness and the blessings** of **your brother** that he may set you free:

7 Give me your blessing, holy Son of God. 8 I would behold you with the eyes of Christ, and see my perfect sinlessness in you.

W-161.12.And **the Holy Spirit** will answer Whom you called upon. 2 For **the Holy Spirit** will hear the Voice for God in you, and answer in your own. 3 Behold **your brother** now, whom you have seen as merely flesh and bone, and recognize that Christ has come to you. 4 Today's idea **of asking your brother's blessing as the holy Son of God** is your safe escape from anger and from fear. 5 Be sure you use **today's idea of asking your brother's blessing as the holy Son of God** instantly, should you be tempted to attack a brother and perceive in **your brother** the symbol of your fear. 6 And **in the asking** you will see **your brother** suddenly transformed from enemy to savior; from the devil into Christ.

Notes to Lesson #161

Give me your blessing, holy Son of God.

The natural state of our mind is abstract. Yet, this lesson tells us that our split mind now finds itself in an unnatural state. What do they mean by this?

The mind that we share with God is abstract. This means that everything is seen and known to be one. There are no specifics because there is no separation. The abstract knows that truth just is and nothing else is true. The abstract is all-encompassing with no exceptions for there is only the One Self.

This means that one brother is all brothers and that every mind contains all minds for every mind is one. Yet, does your split mind comprehend what this really means? The idea that one brother is actually all brothers seems incomprehensible to our thinking minds.

This is because our split mind has taught itself to thinks in specifics. Our mind is no longer able to grasp abstract concepts like the all-encompassing nature of a Oneness of All That Is. Because of this unnatural state of our split mind, we now need specifics in order to learn and remember the all-encompassing aspects of Ourselves.

To better understand what I mean by the mind being unnatural, let us quickly consider what we believe our split mind does. Our split mind allows us to think and make decisions. When we think of what our egoic mind does, we associate mind with the thinking and decision process. Yet, does the Mind of God think and make decisions?

God does not think. God knows. God does not make decisions for truth just is. God's Will is changeless so there is nothing to decide.

In Lesson 152, the power of decision and thinking were both discussed and defined. How they were defined was unusual and needs to be reviewed. Their unusual definitions help clarify why our egoic mind is in an unnatural state. Our egoic mind's function and purpose seems to center around thinking and decision-making. Yet, both thinking and decision-making are not attributes of the Mind of God.

Decision is based on the belief that there is something that is not true and therefore, we could experience the false. To think means you claim you did not know. The power of decision entails thinking which is the illusion of not knowing. The power of decision is your claim that you could not know what you really are and that you could have an existence other than as God created you.

Below is an excerpt from the notes of Lesson 152.

Decision is the belief that there is something that is not true and therefore, we can experience the false. It is the belief that truth has an opposite and that the opposite of truth is as real as truth itself.

The belief that the false exists is only an illusion because truth has no opposites. In time, there is only one decision that we need to make. This decision is the recognition that the truth is true and nothing else is true which has been defined as salvation. This means that salvation is one decision away. Salvation is simply the acceptance of the truth or the Atonement for yourself.

The power of decision is your own because the power of decision is your belief that the false can exist and has the ability to change the truth of what God created as God created it. The power of decision only appears to exist within the delusional mind that believes the false is real.

The power of decision is not an attribute of God. God is truth and truth just is. Nothing opposes truth for nothing else is real. In time, it appears that we have a decision to make because we believe that the false is real.

In reality, a decision for the false is no decision because to choose the false is a decision to choose nothingness. Since nothingness cannot change what is real, a decision for nothingness has no effect and therefore, is ultimately no decision. There is only one choice available, which is truth because truth has no opposites.

To think is to claim that you do not know. Thinking comes from the belief that there is both truth and truth's opposite. The ego is arrogant and believes that it can think because it claims it does not know the truth of who you really are. The power of decision entails thinking which is the illusion of not knowing. The power of decision is your claim that you could not know what you really are and that you could have an existence other than as God created you.

End of excerpt from the notes from lesson 152.

So how did we get into this unnatural state of mind?

The egoic mind does not look on everything as one. Instead, the egoic mind believes the separation to be real. The ego takes parts from the indivisible whole and invents a partial world that our senses currently see.

Our split mind made these specifics by perceiving the whole to be fragmented into separate autonomous parts. It then uses our senses to selectively observe the parts of the whole that it wishes to perceive as our reality. Our senses are thought confirmation devices designed to confirm only what our egos wish to see and hear.

Your ego only sees and hears a partial world and ignores the wholeness that is the truth. Because of your ego's belief that the separation is real, your split mind has lost its ability to grasp the abstract. Yet, if we choose to give the ego's specifics over to the Holy Spirit, the Holy Spirit can use those same specifics and reframe their purpose to teach us the truth. Instead of witnessing for fear, the Holy Spirit can reinterpret these events through the eyes of love.

The ego and the Holy Spirit teach from different points of view. One teaches separation and the other oneness. The Holy Spirit uses the ego's specific symbols of fear to teach oneness and that your mind is joined with all minds. Every mind is part of the shared holographic Mind of God.

Because the ego thinks in specifics, it can no longer grasp the abstract One Self. We need the help of the Holy Spirit Who knows both the abstract truth and also that our mind perceives and thinks in specifics. Having the complete picture, the Holy Spirit can change the purpose of the ego's specific events so that we can begin to remember the truth.

Fear arises out of our belief in specifics. Specifics support our belief in separation and birthed the idea that one can gain from another's loss. If there was just a oneness, your brother's loss would be your own. Without the illusion of specifics, there would be nothing to fear since there would only be the unity of the One Self.

The body symbolizes a concrete form of fear. Bodies can attack and be attacked. Without the body, which symbolizes separation, there would be nothing to attack because the natural state of mind is the abstract One Self.

Hate is specific for you must perceive something to attack. The ego projects its own fears from within its mind into an illusionary outer world of specific forms. It sees your brother's body as separate from itself and then attacks hoping to destroy your brother, which has become the symbol of the ego's own fears. The ego believes that ideas do leave their source and therefore, erroneously believes its attacks upon another are not attacks upon itself.

Do not see your brother as a symbol for your own ego's fears. Instead, use the Holy Spirit's gift of Christ vision to look past the body and behold the sinless and guiltless nature of all.

When you see your brother as the Christ, you will ask for your brother's blessing instead of using his body as a symbol for your fears. The Holy Spirit can use your brother as a specific symbol for the truth of your holiness. With the Holy Spirit's vision you can see before you a witness for forgiveness and union.

Question: Your egoic mind is engaged in thinking and decision-making. Your ego's goal is to make the false appear real and the truth appear false.

Is this the type of teacher you would freely follow?

LESSON 162

I am as God created me.

W-162.1.This single thought **that I am as God created me**, held firmly in the mind, would save the world. 2 From time to time we will repeat **this thought that I am as God created me**, as we reach another stage in learning. 3 **That you remain as God created you** will mean far more to you as you advance. 4 These words are sacred, for they are the words God gave in answer to the world **of fear that your split mind** made. 5 By **these words that I am as God created me, your ego's world** disappears, and all things seen within **the ego's** misty clouds and vaporous illusions vanish as these words are spoken. 6 For **these words that I am as God created me** come from God.

W-162.2.**This thought that I am as God created me** is the Word by which the Son became his Father's happiness, His Love and His **Father's** completion. 2 **In these words that I am as God created me,** creation is proclaimed, and honored as **creation** is. 3 There is no dream these words will not dispel; no thought of sin and no illusion which the dream contains that will not fade away before **the** might **of these words**. 4 **These words that I am as God created me** are the trumpet of awakening that sounds around the world. 5 The dead awake in answer to **the call of these words**. 6 And those who live and hear this sound will never look on death.

W-162.3.Holy indeed is he who makes these words **that I am as God created me** his own; arising with them in his mind, recalling them throughout the day, at night bringing **these words that I am as God created me** with him as he goes to sleep. 2 His dreams are happy and his rest secure, his safety certain and his body healed, because he sleeps and wakens with the truth **that I am as God created me** before him always. 3 He **that makes these words his own that I am as God created me** will save the world, because he gives the world **God's truth about creation** what he receives each time he practices the words of truth.

W-162.4.Today we practice simply. 2 For the words we use are mighty, and they need no thoughts beyond themselves to change the mind of him who uses **these words that I am as God created me**. 3 So wholly is **the mind** changed **of him who uses these words that I am as God created me** that **his healed mind** is now the treasury in which God places all His gifts and all **God's** Love, to be distributed to all the world, increased in giving; kept complete because **his healed mind's** sharing is unlimited. 4 And thus you learn to think with God. 5 Christ's vision has restored your sight by salvaging **and healing** your **once split** mind.

W-162.5.We honor you today. 2 Yours is the right to perfect holiness you now accept. 3 With this acceptance **of your perfect holiness** is salvation brought to everyone, for who could cherish sin when holiness like this has blessed the world? 4 Who could despair when perfect joy is yours, available to all as remedy for grief and misery, all sense of loss, and for complete escape from sin and guilt?

W-162.6.And who would not be brother to you now; **for** you **are your brother's** redeemer and his savior. 2 **What brother** could fail to welcome **someone like** you, **his redeemer who has accepted God's word about creation** into his heart with loving invitation, eager to unite with one like him in holiness? 3 You are as God created you. 4 These words dispel the night, and darkness is no more. 5 The light is come today to bless the world. 6 For you have recognized the Son of God, and in that recognition is the world's **recognition and transformation**.

Notes to Lesson #162

I am as God created me.

This lesson answers that obvious question that we fail to ask ourselves. Do we remain as God created us or not? Those are the only two options that are available.

Which is more likely to be correct?

Is your ego's will more powerful than God's Will?

Is it not arrogance to believe that your reality could be different from God's Will?

When you answer this question incorrectly, you create many imaginary problems and intellectual dilemmas that leave you in a constant state of fear.

When you claim you are not as God created you, you basically transform the typical understanding of what God is. Most Western religions tend to define God as an all-powerful and all-knowing being. How can this be true if you are not as God created you?

The idea that you are not as God created you also poses the dilemma of how evil came into being.

If evil is real, can God be all-powerful?

If evil is real, who created evil?

The idea that you could be different from what God declared as very good and made in God's own image has created all kinds of contradictory questions that Western religions struggle to resolve. Ultimately, the answers are convoluted and intellectually unsatisfying. Often these questions are answered by the simple statement that it is a mystery that must be taken on faith alone.

When you claim that you are not as God created you, this belief challenges and contradicts your original understanding of what a God of love is. In order to sustain your ego's belief that you are different from how God created you, your ego must transform a God of love into a God of fear.

The single thought that you remain as God created you, if believed, firmly saves you, your brother and your world from your ego's belief in lack, limitation and separation. I am as God created me is God's answer given in response to the world of illusion that our egos have created.

The fact that you remain as God created you is God's word by which the Father's creation becomes His happiness, His love and His completion. We are our Father's completion. This is how God knows Himself, Father being Cause and Son being the Effect. They comprise two sides of one single indivisible coin called God.

When you say I am as God created me, you honor and proclaim the truth about God's creation and dispel all illusions and all thoughts of sin.

When you have accepted these words to be your truth, your thinking aligns with God's knowing and Christ vision is restored. You will no longer mistake illusions for the Son of God. When you totally believe that you are as God created you, you have accepted the Atonement for yourself.

Question: Most Western religions are based on the concept of original sin. How does the idea that you remain as God created you impact this notion of original sin?

Question: Can both beliefs be correct?

There is no death. The Son of God is free.

W-163.1.Death is a thought that takes on many forms, often unrecognized. 2 **Death** may appear as sadness, fear, anxiety or doubt; as anger, faithlessness and lack of trust; concern for bodies, envy, and all forms in which the **ego's** wish to be as you are not may come to tempt you. 3 All such thoughts are but reflections of the worshipping of death as **your ego's** savior and **the worshipping of death** as **the** giver of release.

W-163.2.**Death is the** embodiment of fear. **Since death is** the host of sin, god of the guilty and the lord of all illusions and deceptions, does the thought of death seem mighty. 2 For **death** seems to hold all living things within **death's** withered hand; all hopes and wishes in **death's** blighting grasp; all goals perceived but in **death's** sightless eyes. 3 The frail, the helpless and the sick bow down before **death's** image, thinking **death** alone is real, inevitable, worthy of their trust. 4 For **death** alone will surely come.

W-163.3.All things but death are seen to be unsure, too quickly lost however hard to gain, uncertain in their outcome, apt to fail the hopes **all things** once engendered, and to leave the taste of dust and ashes in their wake, in place of aspirations and of dreams. 2 But death is counted on. 3 For **death** will come with certain footsteps when the time has come for **death's** arrival. 4 **Death** will never fail to take all life as hostage to **death**, itself.

W-163.4.Would you bow down to idols such as this? 2 **In the idol of death** is the strength and might of God Himself perceived within an idol made of dust. 3 **In the idol of death** is the opposite of God proclaimed as lord of all creation, stronger than God's Will for life, **stronger than** the endlessness of love and Heaven's perfect, changeless constancy. 4 **In the idol of death** is the Will of Father and of Son defeated finally, and laid to rest beneath the headstone death has placed upon the body of the holy Son of God.

W-163.5.Unholy in defeat, **God's seemingly dead son** has become what death would have him be, **the dead body of the ego's little self "s" self. 5** 2 **The** epitaph **for the ego-body's death**, which death itself has written, gives no name to him, for **the ego-body** has passed to dust. 3 **The epitaph** says but this: "Here lies a witness, God is dead." 4 And this **epitaph death** writes again and still again, while all the while **death's** worshippers **who perceive themselves to be a little "s" self or just a body** agree, and kneeling down with foreheads to the ground, **as the worshippers of death** whisper fearfully that **the death of the body is witness to the death of a God of love and that this belief** is so.

W-163.6.It is impossible to worship death in any form, and still select a few **of death's numerous forms that** you would not cherish and would yet avoid, while still believing in the rest **of death's numerous forms are real**. 2 For death is total. 3 Either all things die, or else **all things** live and cannot die. 4 No compromise is possible. 5 For here again we see an obvious position, which we must accept if we be sane; what contradicts one thought entirely cannot be true, unless its opposite is proven false.

W-163.7.The idea of the death of God is so preposterous that even the insane have difficulty in believing **God is dead**. 2 For **the idea that God is dead** implies that God was once alive and somehow perished; killed, apparently, by those who did not want **God** to survive. 3 **It requires that those who did not want God to survive had a** stronger will **that** could triumph over **God's Will**, and so eternal life gave way to death. 4 And with the Father's **death,** the Son **died** as well.

W-163.8.Death's worshippers may be afraid. 2 And yet, can thoughts like these be fearful? 3 If **death's worshippers** saw that it is only this **preposterous and insane idea that God is dead** which they believe, **the worshippers of death** would be instantly released. 4 And you will show **the worshippers of death** this today **that God is not dead**. 5 There is no death, and we renounce **death** now in every form for **both the worshippers of death's** salvation and our own **salvation** as well. 6 God made not death. 7 Whatever form **death** takes must therefore be **an** illusion. 8 **That death is an illusion is** the stand we take today. 9 And **the illusion of death** is given us to look past death, and see the life beyond **the death of the game token we call the body.**

W-163.9. <Our Father, bless our eyes today. 2 We are **God's** messengers, and we would look upon the glorious reflection of **God's** Love which shines in everything. 3 We live and move in **God** alone. 4 We are not separate from **God's** eternal life. 5 There is no death, for death is not **God's** Will. 6 And we abide where **God** has placed us, in the life we share with **God** and with all living things, to be like **God** and part of **God** forever. 7 We accept **God's** Thoughts as ours, and our will is one with **God's** Will eternally. 8 Amen.>

Notes to Lesson #163

There is no death. The Son of God is free.

Yesterday's lesson was I am as God created me. Would God create something that would die?

The real definition of death is not the death of the illusionary body. Instead, death is defined as any thought that claims you could be something you are not. Because of this unusual definition, death takes on many different forms in our ego's fear-based world. Death masquerades as sadness, fear, anxiety, lack of trust and ultimately as the death of the body.

When you claim you do not know what you are, you are claiming you are dead. You are living in fear. To live in fear is to be dead to the reality of God's love in the real world.

Death is the embodiment of fear. Death is the host of sin and the god of guilt. Death proclaims itself as the Lord of all illusions. The deception of death is the only certainty in this world of time and space. Thus, death appears to have power over life itself. The death of our body is the ultimate witness that our ego's will is stronger than God's Will. Death proves that the God of Love has been killed by our ego's god of fear and that fear is real.

Death is total in that either all things die or all things live for there can be no compromise with death. Death either is or it is not. God did not create death and therefore, death cannot be real. God created life for life is creation and God's completion. Life is all that is real.

The ego looks upon death as the only sure thing that we all must eventually endure. The ego holds up death to be our savior and proof that the ego's vision of our little "s" self is correct. Death proclaims that God's Will has been usurped by the ego's will and that God is dead.

Unfortunately, you cannot believe that something dies without the belief that all die. If God is dead, your death is also inevitable for death must be total with no exceptions. Death is the ego's proof that fear is both real and necessary for our daily survival. It justifies our decision to follow the ego's fear-based thought system.

To believe in death is to believe that God, the eternal, has somehow been changed by the ego. This erroneous egoic belief has transformed a God of love into a god of judgment, wrath and death. Yet, this insane transformation is only imagined and cannot be real. Death is the real illusion.

When you mistake the Son of God for the body, you have transformed the eternal into a symbol for death. We need to look past the illusion of death to the life that exists beyond the illusion. Death and life cannot both exist and when you remember who you are, you can confidently declare that death, not God, is dead.

Question: If you believed death is real, can you believe that you remain as God created you?

These ideas are mutually exclusive and cannot both be correct.

Question: Can you see why death is the ego's ultimate proof that the ego's will is stronger than God's Will?

LESSON 164

Now are we one with God Who is our Source.

W-164.1.What time but now can truth be recognized? 2 The present is the only time there is. 3 And so today, this instant, now, we come to look upon what is forever there, **which is Truth with a capital T. Truth** not in our **egoic** sight, but in the eyes of Christ. 4 **Christ** looks past time, and sees eternity as represented there. 5 **Christ** hears the sounds the senseless, busy world engenders, yet **Christ** hears them faintly. 6 For beyond them all **Christ** hears the song of Heaven, and the Voice for God more clear, more meaningful, more near.

W-164.2.The **ego's** world fades easily away before **Christ's** sight. 2 **The** sounds of **the world of the ego** grow dim. 3 A melody from far beyond the world increasingly is more and more distinct; an ancient call to which **Christ** gives an ancient answer. 4 You will recognize both **Heaven's call and Christ's answer,** for they are but your **big "S" Self's** answer to your Father's Call to you. 5 Christ answers for you, echoing your **big "S"** Self, using your voice to give **Christ's** glad consent; accepting your deliverance for you.

W-164.3.How holy is your practicing today, as Christ gives you **Christ's** sight and hears for you, and answers in your name the Call **Christ** hears! 2 How quiet is the time you give to spend with **Christ,** beyond the world. 3 How easily are all your seeming sins forgot, and all your sorrows unremembered. 4 On this day is grief laid by, for sights and sounds that come from nearer than the world are clear to you who will today accept the gifts **Christ** gives.

W-164.4.There is a silence into which the world can not intrude. 2 There is an ancient peace you carry in your heart and have not lost. 3 There is a sense of holiness in you, **your big "S" Self,** the thought of sin has never touched. 4 All this today you will remember. 5 Faithfulness in practicing today will bring rewards so great and so completely different from all things **your ego** sought before, that you will know that here your treasure is, and here your rest.

W-164.5.This is the day when vain imaginings **of your ego's little "s" self** part like a curtain, to reveal what lies beyond **the illusions of a fear-based world.** 2 Now is what is really there made visible, while all the shadows which appeared to hide **the real world** merely sink away. 3 Now is the balance righted, and the scale of judgment left to **the Holy Spirit** Who judges true. 4 And in **the Holy Spirit's** judgment will a world unfold in perfect innocence before your eyes. 5 Now will you see **an innocent world** with the eyes of Christ. 6 Now is **the** transformation **of your ego's fearful world** clear to you.

W-164.6.Brother, this day is sacred to the world. 2 Your vision **of Christ,** given you from far beyond all things within the world, looks back on **all things within the world** in a new light. 3 And what you see becomes the healing and salvation of the world. 4 The valuable and valueless are both perceived and recognized for what they are. 5 And what is worthy of your love receives your love, while nothing to be feared remains.

W-164.7.We will not judge today. 2 We will receive but what is given us from **the Holy Spirit's** judgment made beyond the world. 3 Our practicing today becomes our gift of thankfulness for our release from blindness and from misery. 4 All that we see will but increase our joy, because **the** holiness **we see in all** reflects our **own holiness.** 5 We stand forgiven in the sight of Christ, with all the world forgiven in our own **forgiveness.** 6 We bless the world, as we behold **the world** in the light in which our Savior looks on us, and offer **the world** the freedom given us through **Christ's** forgiving vision, not our own **ego's unforgiving eyes.**

W-164.8.Open the curtain in your practicing by merely letting go all things **your egoic mind** thinks you want. 2 Your **ego's** trifling treasures put away, **come to these practice periods** and leave a clean and open space within your mind where Christ can come, and offer you the treasure of salvation. 3 **The Holy Spirit** has need of your most holy mind to save the world. 4 Is not this purpose **of saving the world from your ego's belief in lack, limitation and separation** worthy to be **your own true purpose?** 5 Is not **the goal of** Christ's vision worthy to be sought above the world's unsatisfying goals?

W-164.9.Let not today slip by without the gifts **the present moment** holds for you receiving your consent and your acceptance. 2 We can change the world, if you acknowledge **God's call and accept the gifts that Christ's vision brings.** 3 You may not see the value your acceptance **of the vision of Christ** gives the world. 4 But **Christ's vision** you surely want; you can exchange all suffering for joy this very day. 5 Practice in earnest, and the gift **of Christ's vision** is yours. 6 Would God deceive you? 7 Can **God's** promise fail? 8 Can you withhold so little **as your acceptance of God's gifts,** when **God's** Hand holds out complete salvation to **God's** Son?

Notes to Lesson #164

Now are we one with God Who is our Source.

The present is the only time there is. Truth can only be recognized in the now since all decisions are made in the present. Yet, your ego uses the past to keep you unaware of an innocent world based on love and forgiveness. You fail to recognize God as your source because you choose to relive your past fears. This keeps you trapped in time and unaware that eternity can be here and now. Salvation is only one decision away.

The ego is a big judging machine. Your ego believes that your little "s" self is your reality and lives in fear because it does not understand what you really are. Your ego values the worthless idols that it believes can save you from the lack, limitation and separation that it perceives to be everywhere. Denying the unity of the One Self, the ego enters into special relationships in a vain attempt to get its fictitious needs met. It fails to realize that its own sleeping mind is the creator of those artificial needs and only needs to reawaken.

The ego uses its past judgments to determine what it will choose to value in the present. In the world of perception, we only see what we want to see. The current moment is so greatly influenced by our past beliefs that the present becomes a replay of our ego's past judgments.

When you give your ego's judgments over to the Holy Spirit, the Holy Spirit will reframe your current experiences so that they help all sleeping minds reawakening from the belief of being separate from God, your Source. Your purpose is to remember that you remain as God created you, perfect, whole and complete, part of the indivisible One Self.

The Holy Spirit utilizes the vision of Christ to look past time and see eternity as represented in the present moment. With Christ vision you still can faintly hear and see the illusion of the ego's world but you choose to follow the voice for the Holy Spirit. Christ vision does not judge but merely follows the Holy Spirit who has the big picture and knows the truth. When you follow the voice for the Holy Spirit, you accept your divine birthright and realize your true nature as your big "S" Self.

Christ vision sees an innocent, forgiven and sinless world. Christ vision simply chooses not to judge, instead opting to ignore the ego's illusionary world as unreal.

With Christ vision you realize what is valuable and what is worthless. What is worthy of your love receives your love and what is valueless fades away. With the vision of Christ, you realize that there is nothing to fear. You can forgive and forget your past egoic judgments and come with a blank and open mind to give to the Holy Spirit. Now the Holy Spirit can use your mind to save the world. This is a worthy purpose for you as the Son of God. Yet, the Holy Spirit needs your permission to be His messenger. You must learn that to give is to receive. When you give the world the gift of its own innocence and sinlessness, you have accepted your role as a messenger for the Voice for Love.

Question: Why does egoic judgment keep you stuck in the past and prevents you from recognizing the oneness that you share with all?

Let not my mind deny the Thought of God.

W-165.1.What makes this world seem real except your own denial of the truth that lies beyond **your ego's belief in lack, limitation and separation**? 2 What but your thoughts of misery and death obscure the perfect happiness and the eternal life your Father wills for you? 3 And what could hide what cannot be concealed except illusion? 4 What could keep from you what you already have except your choice to not see **what you truly have**, denying **the truth that it** is **really** there?

W-165.2.The Thought of God created you. 2 **The Thought of God** left you not, nor have you ever been apart from **the Thought of God that created you for** an instant. 3 **The Thought of God** belongs to you. 4 By **the Thought of God** you live. 5 **The Thought of God** is your Source of life, holding you one with **God's Thoughts** and everything is one with you because **the Thought of God** left you not. 6 The Thought of God protects you, cares for you, makes soft your resting place and smooth your way, lighting your mind with happiness and love. 7 Eternity and everlasting life shine in your mind, because the Thought of God has left you not, and still abides with you.

W-165.3.Who **but your ego** would deny his safety and his peace, his joy, his healing and his peace of mind, his quiet rest, his calm awakening, if he but recognized where they abide? 2 Would he not instantly prepare to go where **the peace, joy and the safety that he wants** are found, abandoning all else as worthless in comparison with them? 3 And having found **what is of true value**, would he not make sure they stay with him, and he remain with **what he truly valued**?

W-165.4.Deny not Heaven. 2 **Heaven** is yours today, but for the asking. 3 Nor need you perceive **with your egoic mind** how great the gift **of Heaven** or how changed your mind will be before **Heaven** comes to you. 4 Ask to receive **Heaven**, and **Heaven** is given you. 5 Conviction lies within **the asking.** 6 Till you welcome **Heaven** as yours, uncertainty remains. 7 Yet God is fair. 8 Sureness is not required to receive what only your acceptance can bestow.

W-165.5.Ask with desire. 2 You need not be sure that you request the only thing you want. 3 But when you have received **Heaven**, you will be sure you have the treasure you have always sought. 4 What would you then exchange for **Heaven, which comes from your acceptance of the Thought of God**? 5 What would induce you now to let **Heaven** fade away from your ecstatic vision? 6 For this sight **of Heaven** proves that you have exchanged your blindness for the seeing eyes of Christ. **This sight of Heaven proves that your split mind** has come to lay aside **its** denial **of your big "S" Self** and accept the Thought of God as your inheritance.

W-165.6.Now is all doubting past, the journey's end made certain, and salvation given you. 2 Now is Christ's power in your **healed** mind, to heal as you were healed. 3 For now you are among the saviors of the world. 4 Your destiny lies there and nowhere else. 5 Would God consent to let His Son remain forever starved by **the split mind's** denial of the nourishment he needs to live **which comes from the acceptance of the Thought of God**? 6 Abundance dwells in **your big "S" Self** and deprivation cannot cut **God's Son** off from God's sustaining Love and from his **true** home.

W-165.7.Practice today in hope. 2 For hope indeed is justified. 3 Your doubts are meaningless, for God is certain. 4 And the Thought of **God** is never absent. 5 Sureness **of the Holy Spirit** must abide within you, **your big "S" Self,** who are host to **God.** 6 This course removes all doubts which **your ego's beliefs in sin, guilt and fear have** interposed between **God** and your certainty of **God.**

W-165.8.We count on God, and not upon **our ego's little "s" self**, to give us certainty. 2 And in **God's** Name we practice as **the Holy Spirit's** Word directs we do. 3 **The Holy Spirit's** sureness lies beyond our every doubt. 4 **The Holy Spirit's** Love remains beyond our every fear. 5 The Thought of **God** is still beyond all **our ego's** dreams and in our **big "S" Self's** minds, according to **God's** Will.

Notes to Lesson #165

Let not my mind deny the Thought of God.

The Thought of God created you, sustains you and cannot be lost. The Thought of God, which is creation, has never left you and continues to protect you. The Thought of God is the source for all of life. Nothing exists without the Thought of God.

This being the case, why aren't we continuously aware of the Thought of God?

It is because we have forgotten who we are. Our split mind is in an unnatural state and thinks in specifics. Our sick mind has lost its ability to understand and know the abstract One Self. We fail to understand that we are one with everything and remain a part of the shared Mind of God. We now appear to have two choices available to us. We can either deny the Thought of God or ask to receive the Thought of God.

Our denial of the truth made and sustains the world of illusion. Our denial of the truth makes our provisional reality seem real. Our ego's belief in lack, limitation and separation obscure the happiness and peace that is our true reality. We replace Christ vision with our ego's thoughts of misery and death that block the truth that is hidden behind our misperceptions. Our denial of the truth has created an illusionary fear-based world of provisional reality that blocks our recognition of Heaven and creates uncertainty within our split mind.

Heaven will be yours when you ask for it. Ask and it is given you. But you must ask to receive. Conviction is not required to receive but only your acceptance of God's gift is needed. As long as you ask with desire, you will become aware of the Thought of God. You do not have to be sure that it is the only thing that you want. Mutual exclusivity is not required.

Yet, when you accept the gift of the Thought of God, the peace and happiness that you experience will provide specific examples so that your uncertainty about what you want will be removed. As you learn to ask for the Thought of God, you will realize that only your ego's denials have prevented your split mind from recognizing the joy, love, peace and happiness that is your divine birthright and natural state of being.

The Thought of God has never left the Christ Mind for we are the host to God and God is certain. Until you accept the Thought of God, your uncertainty remains. Sureness is not required but you must ask. Once you accept the Atonement for yourself, you will be sure that the Thought of God is what you always wanted and will always have.

God's Will for creation is happiness and eternal life. Once the thought of God is accepted, all doubting is over and you will recognize your big "S" Self. With the power of Christ, your mind will heal others as your mind is healed. Thus, you join and are counted among the saviors of the world. You fulfill your purpose as a messenger for the Thought of God.

Question: If the Thought of God is constantly flowing, why aren't we continuously aware of it?

Although the Thought of God is everywhere and sustains all life, our egoic mind has created an illusionary world of lack, limitation and separation. This world of fear obscures the real world from our vision. The goal of A Course in Miracles is not to create a world of love, peace and harmony since that real world already exists beyond the illusion. Instead it is to remove the blocks that we have placed to hide the awareness of the love, joy, peace and oneness that is our divine birthright and natural inheritance as part of the One Self.

Question: Why are we not required to exclusively only want the Thought of God to receive the Thought of God?

Because our mind can no longer understand the abstract, the Holy Spirit will take our specific requests and provide concrete examples that we can experience and baby step our way from uncertainty to certainty. If exclusivity were required, our relearning would never begin because our split mind cannot comprehend the abstract absolute.

However, as we ask and experience the benefits of the joy, love and peace that come from recognizing our big "S" Self, we learn to realize that the egoic world of our little "s" self holds nothing that we truly desire. This baby stepping our way back to remembering the truth leads us back to the realization of the abstract oneness that is our reality. When you accept the Atonement for yourself, you accept the truth that comes from certainty that is the Mind of God.

LESSON 166

I am entrusted with the gifts of God.

W-166.1.All things are given you. 2 God's trust in you is limitless. 3 **God** knows His Son. 4 **God** gives without exception, holding nothing back that can contribute to your happiness. 5 And yet, unless your will is one with **God's Will, God's** gifts are not received. 6 But what would make you think there is another will than **God's Will**?

W-166.2.**This idea of separate multiple wills** is the paradox that underlies the making of the world. 2 This world is not the Will of God, and so **this world** is not real. 3 Yet those who think **this world** real must still believe there is another will, and one that leads to opposite effects from those **God** wills. 4 Impossible indeed; but every mind that looks upon the world and judges **this world** as certain, solid, trustworthy and true believes in two creators; or in one **creator**, himself alone. 5 But **those who believe this world is real** never **believe only** in one God. **Those who believe this world is real either believe in no god or multiple gods.**

W-166.3.The gifts of God are not acceptable to anyone who holds such strange beliefs **that there is another will than God's Will**. 2 He, **who believes his will is different from God's Will,** must believe that to accept God's gifts, however evident **God's gifts** may become, however urgently he may be called to claim **God's gifts** as his own, is to be pressed to treachery against himself **and his own different will.** 3 He, **who believes that there is another will other than God's Will,** must deny **the** presence **of God's gifts**, contradict the truth, and suffer to preserve the world **that** he, **who opposes God's Will** made.

W-166.4.**The dream world of those that believe their will is different from God's Will** is the only home he thinks he knows. 2 **For one who denies God's Will to be their own, the dream world of their egoic mind** is the only safety he believes that he can find. 3 Without the world **his delusional mind** made is he an outcast; homeless and afraid. 4 He, **who believes his will is different from God's Will,** does not realize that it is here **in his ego's dream world that** he is afraid indeed, and homeless, too; an outcast wandering so far from **his real** home so long away, he does not realize he has forgotten where he came from, where he goes, and even who he really is **as God's beloved Son and part of the shared Mind of the One Self.**

W-166.5.Yet in his lonely, senseless wanderings **within his own delusional mind that believes his will is separate and different from God's Will,** God's gifts go with him, all unknown to him. 2 He **who denies his will is the same as God's Will still** cannot lose **God's gifts**. 3 But **his delusional mind** will not look at what is given him. 4 He **who denies that there is only God's Will,** wanders on, aware of the futility **of the egoic world** he sees about him everywhere, perceiving how his little lot but dwindles, as he goes ahead to nowhere. 5 Still he, **who believes his will is separate from God's Will** wanders on in misery and poverty, alone though God is with him, and **with** a treasure **from God that is** so great that everything the **ego's** world **of his dream** contains is valueless before **the** magnitude **of God's gifts.**

W-166.6.He **who denies his will is the same as God's Will** seems a sorry figure; weary, worn, in threadbare clothing, and with feet that bleed a little from the rocky road he walks. 2 No one but has identified with him, for everyone who comes here **to this fearful dream world** has pursued the path he follows, and has felt defeat and hopelessness as he is feeling **defeat**. 3 Yet is he really tragic, when you see that he, **who denies his will is the same as God's Will,** is following the way he chose, and need but realize Who walks with him **is the Holy Spirit** and **he can choose to** open up his treasures **that the Holy Spirit has kept for his split mind** to be free?

W-166.7.This is your chosen **little "s"** self, the one you made as a replacement for reality. 2 This is the **little "s"** self you savagely defend against all reason, every evidence, and all the witnesses with proof to show this **little "s"** self is not you. 3 You heed not **the evidence of your big "S" Self**. 4 You go on your appointed way, with eyes cast down lest you might catch a glimpse of truth, and be released from **your split mind's** self-deception and set free.

W-166.8.You cower fearfully lest you should feel Christ's touch upon your shoulder, and perceive **Christ's** gentle hand directing **your little "s"** self to look upon your gifts **that the Holy Spirit has kept for you**. 2 How could you then proclaim your poverty in exile? 3 **Christ and the Holy Spirit** would make you laugh at this perception of **your little "s"** self. 4 Where is self-pity then? 5 And what becomes of all the tragedy you sought to make for **your little "s"** self whom God intended only joy?

W-166.9.Your ancient fear has come upon you now, and justice has caught up with you at last. 2 Christ's hand has touched your shoulder, and you feel that you are not alone. 3 You even think the miserable **little "s"** self you thought was you may not be your Identity. 4 Perhaps God's Word is truer than your own **split mind**. 5 Perhaps **God's** gifts to you are real. 6 Perhaps **God** has not wholly been outwitted by your **split mind's** plan to keep **God's** Son in deep oblivion, and go the way you chose without your **big "S"** Self.

W-166.10.God's Will does not oppose. 2 **God's Will** merely is. 3 It is not God you have imprisoned in your plan to lose your **big "S"** Self. 4 **God** does not know about a plan so alien to **God's** Will. 5 There was a need **God** did not understand, to which **God** gave an Answer. 6 That is all. 7 And you who have this Answer given you have need no more of anything but this **answer, which is Atonement or the acceptance of the truth that you remain as God created you, perfect, whole and complete. Your will and God's Will are the same.**

W-166.11.Now do we live, for now we cannot die. 2 The wish for death is answered, and the **ego's** sight that looked upon **death** now has been replaced by **the** vision **of Christ** which perceives that you are not **the little "s" self that** you pretend to be. 3 **The Holy Spirit** walks with you Who gently answers all your fears with this one merciful reply, "It is not so." 4 **The Holy Spirit** points to all the gifts **of God** you have each time the thought of poverty oppresses you, and speaks of **the Holy Spirit's** Companionship when you perceive yourself as lonely and afraid.

W-166.12.Yet **the Holy Spirit** reminds you still of one thing more you had forgotten. 2 For **God's** touch on you has made you like **God,** Himself. 3 The gifts you have are not for you alone. 4 What **the Holy Spirit** has come to offer you, you now must learn to give. 5 This is the lesson that **the Holy Spirit's** giving holds, for **the Holy Spirit** has saved you from the solitude **of the world your ego** sought to make in which to hide from God. 6 **The Holy Spirit** has reminded you of all the gifts that God has given you. 7 **The Holy Spirit** speaks as well of what becomes your will when you accept these gifts, and recognize **God's gifts** are your own **gifts that you can now give away**.

W-166.13.**God's** gifts are yours, entrusted to your care, to give to all who chose the lonely road you have escaped. 2 They, **who believe their will is different from God's Will,** do not understand they but pursue their **own split mind's** wishes. 3 It is you who teach **the split minded** now. 4 For you have learned of Christ **that** there is another way for **the split minded** to walk. 5 Teach **the split minded** by showing them the happiness that comes to those who feel the touch of Christ, and recognize God's gifts. 6 Let sorrow not tempt you to be unfaithful to your trust **of sharing God's gift with your brother.**

W-166.14.Your sighs will now betray the hopes of those who look to you for their release. 2 Your tears are theirs **tears**. 3 If you are sick, you but withhold their healing. 4 What you fear but teaches them their fears are justified. 5 Your hand becomes the giver of Christ's touch; your change of **the healed split** mind becomes the proof that who accepts God's gifts can never suffer anything. 6 You are entrusted with the world's release from pain.

W-166.15.Betray **this trust in your healing** not. 2 Become the living proof of what Christ's touch can offer everyone. 3 God has entrusted all **God's** gifts to you. 4 Be witness in your happiness to how transformed the **healed split** mind becomes which chooses to accept **God's** gifts, and feel the touch of Christ. 5 Such is your mission now. 6 For God entrusts the giving of His gifts to all who have received **God's gifts**. 7 **God** has shared His joy with you. 8 And now you go to share **God's joy** with the world.

Notes to Lesson #166

I am entrusted with the gifts of God.

This lesson tells us that we are entrusted with the gifts of God, but what are these gifts?

All things are given to you without exception and nothing is held back that can contribute to your happiness. God's trust in you is unlimited. Yet, unless your will is one with God's Will, the gifts that you have been given will not be recognized as your own by your split mind. You must be willing to accept the gifts and claim them for your own to realize that you have received those gifts.

When we think of the many gifts God gives us, we fail to realize that perhaps the greatest gift that God has given us is the fact that there is only one will, God's Will, and that Will is changeless. God's Will is that we be happy. Since we also only want our own happiness, our wills are in perfect alignment. Yet, we fail to recognize this. When minds are joined in a single purpose, they are of one mind.

It is this denial that we share the same will as God's that created the world we perceive. God did not create a world of lack, limitation and separation. If you judge this world as real, you are saying that there is another will other than God's Will. God's Will is that you remain as He created you, perfect, whole and complete, part of The Oneness of All That Is.

This world that you perceive is the opposite of God's Will and therefore, must be unreal. It is a world of lack, limitation and separation that engenders fear which is false evidence appearing real. Your belief in the reality of this world is evidence that you are refusing to accept God's gifts that only contribute to your happiness.

Being created perfect, whole and complete, you cannot be happy with being a limited little "s" self that your ego envisions. Yet, when you believe your will is different from God's Will, your ego must argue for your littleness. Your ego values its own need to be right over your desire to be happy.

It is your belief that you have a will other than God's that dreams up your egoic world of provisional reality. Sin now appears real within your split mind. You have forgotten your true home and your Christ nature. You believe that without this fear-based world, you would be homeless.

The world you see is in your mind's imagination. Everyone who believes that their will is different from God's Will perceives an unreal world of lack, limitation and separation. What else but lack could be imagined when you already have been given all that is? Your belief that your will is different than God's Will is a decision that is your own free choice and is being made daily.

This idea that your will is separate from God's is an error that needs to be corrected. It is impossible to change God's Will. Yet, your ego has created an illusionary world and continues to argue for your ego's rightness that your provisional reality could be separate from what God created. The ego believes that by rejecting God's gifts that God's Will has been usurped.

The ego believes that you can change what is true and fights to preserve the illusion of the existence of multiple wills. Your imagination cannot change God's Will and make the false true and the truth false. The ego has created a little "s" self to replace the reality of the one mind that is the shared Mind of God. Since it is everyone's own decision to experience being something they are not that birthed this world of make believe, you cannot be a victim of your own mind's creation. Your self-pity is unwarranted.

God's Will does not oppose. It merely is the changeless eternal reality of what is. We wanted to be something other than what we were and God let us play the game of What Am I. We make our own provisional reality and play this game of differentiation in perfect safety because God's Will protects the truth that we remain as the Christ.

In the game of What Am I, there are no victims and there are no victimizers. Each participant is there of their own free choice and their own decision to experience what they want. Your world of perception is a reflection of your inner beliefs and desires. God is not imprisoned by your denial of God's Will. Only you are trapped when you deny the reality of your big "S" Self and argue for your littleness. God has provided the answer for your escape from your own self-imprisonment by merely accepting the truth.

God placed within your split mind the Holy Spirit to guide you home. When asked, the Holy Spirit will provide all God's gifts that It saved for you for what God gives must be received. Yet, only when you accept God's gifts do you recognize that they are your own and now you can freely give them away to others.

When God creates, He gives all to all. Nothing is held back. God has entrusted all his gifts to you as the Christ. Accept them and your split mind is healed. When you share God's gifts, you prove that they are yours.

Recognize that you make your own provisional reality and that God's Will protects your true reality as your big "S" Self. Your provisional reality cannot change the truth that you remain safe as God's Will created you. Allow your brothers the same right to play the game of What I Am while holding the truth about the one Will of God that we all share. Remember, God's Will is that you be happy.

God's gifts of all things have been given to you but you must accept them. If you choose to deny or reject God's gifts, you will think that you do not have them. The ego's thought system is alien to God. We had a need God did not understand. We desired to be something that we were not. This is impossible but we could experience differentiation of the various aspects of the indivisible One Self.

Differentiation does not mean separation. When we mistook differentiation to mean different, we forgot the all-inclusive nature of the Mind of God. We forgot to laugh and made the game of What Am I appear real.

God's answer for our reawakening from this mistake is the Atonement. By placing the Holy Spirit within our mind, we are guaranteed to remember the truth and end our belief that separation could be real. Imagination allows the game of What Am I to proceed. Time provides the game board but the Holy Spirit guarantees that we will reawaken to our big "S" Self. The Holy Spirit reminds you that you are not the little "s" self that you pretend to be. The Holy Spirit gently directs you to the acceptance of the Atonement for yourself.

When you accept God's gifts, your mind is healed. Share those same gifts with your brother and they are yours. By giving them away, you prove you have received God's gifts for to give is to receive. This proves that you have accepted your role as the Holy Spirit's messenger for the Truth.

Question: How does the fact that there is only one will, God's Will, protect us and guarantee the end of our belief in separation?

LESSON 167

There is one life, and that I share with God.

W-167.1.There are not different kinds of life, for life is like the truth. 2 **Life, like truth,** does not have degrees. 3 **Life** is the one condition in which all that God created share. 4 Like all **God's** Thoughts, **life** has no opposite. 5 There is no death because what God created shares **God's** life. 6 There is no death because an opposite to God does not exist. 7 There is no death because the Father and the Son are One.

W-167.2.In this world **made by the split mind**, there appears to be a state that is life's opposite. 2 You call it death. 3 Yet we have learned that the idea of death takes many forms. 4 **Death** is the one idea which underlies all feelings that are not supremely happy. 5 **Death** is the alarm to which you give response of any kind that is not perfect joy. 6 All sorrow, loss, anxiety and suffering and pain, even a little sigh of weariness, a slight discomfort or the merest frown, acknowledge death. 7 And thus deny you live.

W-167.3.You think that death is of the body. 2 Yet **death** is but an idea, irrelevant to what is seen as physical. 3 A thought is in the mind. 4 **A thought** can be then applied as mind directs **that thought**. 5 But **the thought's** origin, **which is the mind**, is where **the thought** must be changed if change occurs. 6 Ideas leave not their source. 7 The emphasis this course has placed on that idea **that ideas never leave their source** is due to **this idea's** centrality in our attempts to change your **split mind's** belief about yourself. 8 **The concept that ideas leave not their source** is the reason you can heal. 9 **This idea** is the cause of healing. 10 **Because ideas never leave their source** is why you cannot die. 11 Its truth established you as one with God **since ideas leave not their source**.

W-167.4.Death is the thought that you are separate from your Creator. 2 **Death** is the belief conditions change, emotions alternate because of causes you cannot control, you did not make, and you can never change. 3 **Death** is the fixed belief ideas can leave their source, and take on qualities the source does not contain, becoming different from their own origin, apart from **their source** in kind as well as distance, time and form.

W-167.5.Death cannot come from life. 2 Ideas remain united to their source. 3 **Ideas** can extend all that their source contains. 4 In that, **the ideas** can go far beyond themselves. 5 But **ideas** cannot give birth to what was never given **those ideas**. 6 As **ideas** are made, so will their making be. 7 As **ideas** were born, so will **those ideas** then give birth. 8 And where **ideas** come from, there will **those ideas** return.

W-167.6.The mind can think **the mind** sleeps, but that is all. 2 **The mind that thinks it sleeps** cannot change what is its waking state. 3 **The mind that thinks it sleeps** cannot make a body, nor abide within a body. 4 What is alien to the mind does not exist, because **what is alien to the mind** has no source. 5 For mind creates all things that are, and cannot give **things** attributes **the mind itself** lacks, nor change **the mind's** own eternal, mindful state. 6 **Mind, which is only spirit,** cannot make the physical. 7 What seems to die is but the sign of **a** mind **that must be** asleep.

W-167.7.The opposite of life can only be another form of life. 2 As such, **the other form of life** can be reconciled with what created **the other form of life** because **life** is not opposite in truth. 3 **Life's** form may change; **life** may appear to be what **life** is not. 4 Yet mind is mind, awake or sleeping. 5 **Mind** is not **mind's** opposite in anything created, nor in what **mind** seems to make when **mind** believes it sleeps.

W-167.8.God creates only mind awake. 2 **God** does not sleep, and **God's** creations cannot share what **God** gives not, nor make conditions which **God** does not share with **God's creations**. 3 The thought of death is not the opposite to thoughts of life. 4 Forever unopposed by opposites of any kind, the Thoughts of God remain forever changeless, with the power to extend forever changelessly, but yet within themselves, for **the Thoughts of God** are everywhere.

W-167.9.What seems to be the opposite of life is merely sleeping. 2 When the mind elects to be what **the mind** is not, and to assume an alien power which **the mind** does not have, a foreign state **the mind** cannot enter, or a false condition not within its Source, **the mind** merely seems to go to sleep a while. 3 **The sleeping mind** dreams of time; an interval in which what seems to happen never has occurred, the changes wrought are substanceless, and all events are nowhere. 4 When the mind awakes **the mind** but continues as **the mind** always was.

W-167.10.Let us today be children of the truth, and not deny our holy heritage. 2 Our life is not as we imagine it **to be for we are not our ego's little "s" self.** 3 Who changes life because he shuts his eyes, or makes himself what he is not because he sleeps, and sees in dreams an opposite to what he is? 4 We will not ask for death in any form today. 5 Nor will we let imagined opposites to life, **like our ego's little "s" self**, abide even an instant where the Thought of life eternal has been set by God Himself.

W-167.11.God's holy home we strive to keep today as **God** established it, and wills **God's home to** be forever and forever. 2 **God** is Lord of what we think today. 3 And in **God's** Thoughts, which have no opposite, we understand there is one life, and that we share **that one life** with God, with all creation, with their thoughts as well, whom **God** created in a unity of life that cannot separate in death and leave the Source of life from where it came.

W-167.12.We share one life because we have one Source, a Source from which perfection comes to us, remaining always in the holy minds which **God** created perfect. 2 As we were, so are we now and will forever be. 3 A sleeping mind must waken, as **the sleeping mind** sees its own perfection mirroring the Lord of life so perfectly **the sleeping mind** fades into what is reflected there. 4 And now **the mind** is no more a mere reflection. 5 **The mind, now awake,** becomes the thing reflected, and the light which makes reflection possible. 6 No vision now is needed. 7 For the wakened mind is one that knows its Source, its **big "S"** Self **and** its **mind's** Holiness.

Notes to Lesson #167

There is one life, and that I share with God.

If you asked people what is the opposite of life, most would reply, death. But when your body ceases to function, does your essence cease to exist?

Once again, ACIM has a rather strange definition for the term death.

W-167.4.3 **Death** is the fixed belief ideas can leave their source, and take on qualities the source does not contain, becoming different from their own origin, apart from **their source** in kind as well as distance, time and form.

This definition for death stresses the idea that you are mind and not the physical body. Death is any feeling of unhappiness. In time, death takes on many forms, such as sadness, anxiety, fear, lack of trust and what we typically associate with death as being the death of the body.

God's Will is that you be happy. When you are not happy, you have denied that you are part of the shared Mind of God. You have claimed you have a will different from God's Will. Unhappiness or death denies that you live. It claims that you are the body. It is an erroneous belief of your egoic mind.

You are a thought of God and thought is in the realm of mind. It is your mind that believes that you are a body and therefore, it is the mind's beliefs that need correction. Death is the thought that you could be separate from God and you could change and develop attributes that your Source does not possess.

Ideas remain united with their source. You can only extend what your Source contains. When your mind denies its Source, it claims it does not know itself and basically is asleep. When you sleep, you are not aware of who you really are. You fail to recognize your big "S" Self.

Mind has the power to create or imagine anything it desires. When it is awake, it creates like itself. When it sleeps, it imagines what it is not. Since you cannot be something you are not, mind cannot make the physical body. When you perceive yourself to be something that seems to die, this indicates that your mind is asleep for it has denied what it truly is.

The opposite of life must be another form of life. To live is to be aware of whom you really are. An awakened mind is one that knows it's Source, the reality as his big "S" Self and its holiness. To be holy is to be whole, which is the recognition that you are part of the indivisible One Self. Since life is the awareness of what you are, the opposite of life must be the unawareness of what you are, which the course references as a sleeping mind.

God does not sleep. Therefore, what God creates can only be an awakened mind. God's creations can neither share nor possess what God does not give nor make conditions which God does not share with them. Sleep cannot be real. Your true reality must be the mind that is awakened which your big "S" Self is. What a sleeping mind imagines cannot be real and has no ability to change the truth. When a sleeping mind awakens, it finds nothing has changed.

Yet even a sleeping mind possesses creative power to be or imagine anything that it desires. A mind that sleeps pretends it is something that it is not. A sleeping mind assumes an alien power that it does not have. It believes mind can create the physical. It believes it can be a body and create a false condition that is not an attribute of its Source. A sleeping mind mistakes differentiation for a different autonomous existence. It believes it is separate and different from its Source.

A sleeping mind dreams of the illusion of time. Time becomes the game board of the sleeping mind's imagination. Opposites appear to exist in time and take on a fearful reality of their own. Time is an interval in which what seems to happen never has occurred and the changes that took place in time are without substance and the events are nonexistent. When the mind awakens, the illusion of time disappears and the mind continues as it always was. Nothing has changed.

Life, like truth, has no opposite. Your reality cannot be a sleeping mind for God creates only awakened minds. In time, we are unaware of our big "S" Self, its holiness and unity with the One Self. When we sleep, we dream of time, believe that we are the body, that death is life's opposite, that ideas can leave their source and become something different and separate from its source.

This is not true. God's thoughts have no opposite and therefore, we remain changeless and eternal. Ideas never leave their source. We share one life because we share one Source which is the Mind of God.

Question: In time, what is the opposite of death?

352

Hint: Death is the illusion of your essence leaving a physical body. In time, birth is the illusion of your essence entering a physical body.

LESSON 168

Your grace is given me. I claim God's grace now.

W-168.1.God speaks to us. 2 Shall we not speak to **God**? 3 **God** is not distant. 4 **He** makes no attempt to hide from us. 5 We try to hide from **Him**, and suffer from deception. 6 **God** remains entirely accessible. 7 **God** loves His Son. 8 There is no certainty but this **truth that God loves His Son**, yet this **one truth** suffices. 9 **God** will love His Son forever. 10 When **His Son's** mind remains asleep, **God** loves **His Son** still. 11 And when **the Son's** mind awakes, **God** loves **His Son** with a never-changing Love.

W-168.2.If you but knew the meaning of **God's** Love, hope and despair would be impossible. 2 For hope would be forever satisfied; despair of any kind unthinkable. 3 **God's** grace is **God's** answer to all despair, for in **God's grace** lies remembrance of **God's** Love. 4 Would **God** not gladly give **grace which is** the means by which **God's** Will is recognized? 5 **God's** grace is yours by your acknowledgment **of the gift of grace**. 6 And memory of **God** awakens in the mind that asks the means of **God** whereby sleep is done **and the mind awakens. Grace is God's means for awakening a sleeping mind.**

W-168.3.Today we ask of God the gift **of grace that God** has most carefully preserved within our hearts, waiting to be acknowledged. 2 **Grace is** the gift by which God leans to us and lifts us up, taking salvation's final step Himself. 3 All steps but this we learn, instructed by **God's** Voice, **the Holy Spirit**. 4 But finally **God** comes Himself, and takes us in His Arms and sweeps away the cobwebs of our sleep. 5 **God's** gift of grace is more than just an answer. 6 **Grace** restores all memories the sleeping mind forgot. **Grace restores** all certainty of what Love's meaning is.

W-168.4.God loves His Son. 2 Request **God** now to give the means by which this world **of your sleeping mind** will disappear, and **Christ's** vision first will come, with knowledge but an instant later. 3 For in grace you see a light that covers all the world in love, and watch fear disappear from every face as hearts rise up and claim the light as theirs. 4 What now remains that Heaven be delayed an instant longer? 5 What is still undone when your forgiveness rests on everything **and is given to all**?

W-168.5.It is a new and holy day today, for we receive what has been given us. 2 Our faith lies in **God,** the Giver, not our own acceptance. 3 We acknowledge our mistakes, but **God,** to Whom all error is unknown is yet the One Who answers our mistakes by giving us the means to lay them down, and rise to **God,** in gratitude and love.

W-168.6.And **God** descends to meet us, as we come to **God**. 2 For what **God** has prepared for us **God** gives and we receive. 3 Such is **God's** Will because He loves His Son. 4 To **God** we pray today, returning but the word **God** gave to us through **God's** Own Voice, His Word, His Love:
5 Your grace is given me. 6 I claim **God's grace** now. 7 Father, I come to You. 8 And You will come to me who ask. 9 I am the Son You love.

Notes to Lesson #168

Your grace is given me. I claim God's grace now.

On the game board of time and space, we try to hide from God's love. This world of provisional reality is a place we made where we could pretend we were something we were not. We wanted to experience what it would be like to be separate and different from our true reality that is the indivisible One Self.

Yet, God's love for His Son has never changed. God continues to speak to us and has placed the Holy Spirit inside our split mind to insure we must reawaken to the truth that only God's love is real. The Holy Spirit acts as the bridge between our sleeping mind's illusions and the truth. Yet, in our world of provisional reality, we hide from God and suffer from our own self-deception.

God does not try to hide from us and waits patiently for his children to put away their fantasies of make-believe and return home. God remains entirely accessible for there is only one certainty and that is the fact that God loves His Son.

When our mind sleeps, we have denied who we really are and forgotten that God's love for us is never changing and unconditional. Our ego tells us that we are sinners, have been abandoned by God and now must either earn God's forgiveness or suffer His wrath. God knows we remain as He created us, perfect, whole and complete. God has not judged or condemned us. God's love flows eternally but our sleeping minds deny that truth.

We are the only ones that see God's Son as sinful, guilty and full of fears. We are the keepers of our own karmic keys. We will free ourselves from our belief in lack, limitation and separation when we choose to forgive ourselves. We need but to acknowledge our mistaken beliefs and freely choose the truth.

In God's grace lies the remembrance that God loves His Son unconditionally. Grace restores all our memories of our big "S" Self that our sleeping minds appear to have forgotten. When we accept God's grace, this world of fear will disappear, the vision of Christ will be restored and knowledge will follow an instant later.

When we choose to accept it, grace will cover our world with God's love and fear will be gone. When you choose to forgive yourself, God and your world, everyone will be free to reclaim their divine birthright.

God has always remained entirely accessible but we continue to want to hide from God and follow the ego's fear-based thought system. As a result, we suffer from our own ego's self-deception. God's love is unchangeable. Only when we freely choose to accept God's gift of grace, can God take the final step and reawaken us to the knowledge that we remain God's beloved child with whom He is well pleased.

Question: Why doesn't God just force our sleeping minds to wake up?

LESSON 169.

By grace I live. By grace I am released.

W-169.1.Grace is an aspect of the Love of God which is most like the state prevailing in the unity of truth. 2 **Grace** is the world's most lofty aspiration, for **grace** leads beyond the world entirely. 3 **Grace** is past learning, yet **grace is** the goal of learning, for grace cannot come until the mind prepares itself for true acceptance. 4 Grace becomes inevitable instantly in those who have prepared a table where **grace** can be gently laid and willingly received; an altar clean and holy for the gift **of grace.**

W-169.2.Grace is acceptance of the Love of God within a world of seeming hate and fear. 2 By grace alone the hate and fear are gone, for grace presents a state so opposite to everything the world **of time** contains, that those whose minds are lighted by the gift of grace cannot believe the world of fear is real.

W-169.3.Grace is not learned. 2 The final step must go beyond all learning. 3 Grace is not the goal this course aspires to attain. 4 Yet we prepare for grace in that an open mind can hear the Call to waken. 5 **An open mind** is not shut tight against God's Voice. 6 **An open mind** has become aware that there are things **the mind** does not know **in time** , and thus is ready to accept a state completely different from experience with which **the mind** is familiarly at home **in eternity**.

W-169.4.We have perhaps appeared to contradict our statement that the revelation of the Father and the Son as One has been already set. 2 But we have also said the mind determines when that time will be **when the revelation of the Father and the Son as One is made** and **mind** has determined **this**. 3 And yet we urge you to bear witness to the Word of God to hasten the experience of truth, and speed **truth's** advent into every mind that recognizes truth's effects on you.

W-169.5.Oneness is simply the idea God is. 2 And **Oneness is the idea that** in **God's** Being, **God** encompasses all things. 3 No mind holds anything but **God**. 4 We say "God is," and then we cease to speak, for in that knowledge **that "God is"** words are meaningless. 5 There are no lips to speak **the words**, and no part of mind sufficiently distinct to feel that **mind** is now aware of something not itself. 6 **All parts of mind have** united with its Source. 7 And like its Source Itself, **all parts of mind** merely are.

W-169.6.We cannot speak nor write nor even think of this **Oneness** at all. 2 **Oneness** comes to every mind when total recognition that **the mind's** will is God's **Will are one** has been completely given and received completely. 3 **This total recognition of the mind's oneness with God's Will** returns the mind into the endless present, where the past and future cannot be conceived. 4 **The awakened mind** lies beyond salvation; past all thought of time, forgiveness and the holy face of Christ. 5 The Son of God has merely disappeared into his Father, as his Father has **merely disappeared into His Son**. 6 The **egoic** world **of separation and time** has never been at all. 7 Eternity remains a constant state.

W-169.7.This is beyond experience we try to hasten. 2 Yet forgiveness, taught and learned, brings with **that forgiveness** the experiences which bear witness that the time the mind itself determined to abandon all **beliefs of separation** is now at hand. 3 We do not hasten **the time of the revelation of the Father and the Son as One**, in that what you will offer was concealed from **the Holy Spirit, the Voice for Christ and your big "S" Self,** Who teaches what forgiveness means.

W-169.8.All learning was already in **the Holy Spirit's** Mind, accomplished and complete. 2 **The Holy Spirit** recognized all that time holds, and gave **all that time holds** to all minds **that perceive separation** that each one might determine, from a point where time was ended, when **the sleeping mind** is released to revelation and eternity. 3 We have repeated several times before that you but make a journey that is done.

W-169.9.For oneness must be here **even in the dream of separation**. 2 Whatever time the mind has set for revelation is entirely irrelevant to what must be a constant state **of Oneness**, forever as **oneness** always was; forever to remain as **oneness** is now. 3 We merely take the part assigned long since, and fully recognized as perfectly fulfilled by **the Holy Spirit** Who wrote salvation's script in His Creator's Name, and in the Name of His Creator's Son.

W-169.10.There is no need to further clarify what no one in the world **of time** can understand. 2 When revelation of your oneness comes, **your oneness** will be known and fully understood. 3 Now we have work to do, for those in time can speak of things beyond **time**, and listen to words **about changeless eternity** which explain what is to come is past already. 4 Yet what meaning can the words convey to those who count the hours still, and rise and work and go to sleep by **their belief in time's reality**?

W-169.11.Suffice it, then, that you have work to do to play your part. 2 The ending must remain obscure to you until your part is done. 3 **The fact that the ending is obscure to you** does not matter. 4 For your part is still what all the rest depends on. 5 As you take the role assigned to you, salvation comes a little nearer each uncertain heart that does not beat as yet in tune with God.

W-169.12.Forgiveness is the central theme that runs throughout salvation, holding all **salvation's** parts in meaningful relationships, the course it runs directed and **salvation's** outcome sure. 2 And now we ask for grace, the final gift salvation can bestow. 3 Experience that grace provides will end in time, for grace foreshadows Heaven, yet **grace** does not replace the thought of time but for a little while.

W-169.13.The interval suffices. 2 It is here **in time** that miracles are laid; to be returned by you from holy instants you receive, through grace in your experience, to all who see the light that lingers in your face. 3 What is the face of Christ but his who went a moment into timelessness, and brought a clear reflection of the unity he felt an instant back to bless the world? 4 How could you finally attain to **this unity of the oneness of mind** forever, while a part of you remains outside, unknowing, unawakened, and in need of you as witness to the truth?

W-169.14.Be grateful to return **to time**, as you were glad to go an instant **into timelessness**, and accept the gifts that grace provided you. 2 You carry **grace's gifts** back to yourself. 3 And revelation stands not far behind. 4 **The** coming **of the revelation of the unity of the oneness of mind** is ensured. 5 We ask for grace, and for experience that comes from grace. 6 We welcome the release **grace** offers everyone. 7 We do not ask for the unaskable. 8 We do not look beyond what grace can give. 9 For this **gift of grace's release** we can give in the grace that has been given us.

W-169.15.Our learning goal today does not exceed this prayer. 2 Yet in the world **of time**, what could be more than what we ask this day of **the Christ, the Holy Spirit,** Who gives the grace we ask, as **grace** was given Him?
3 By grace I live. 4 By grace I am released.
5 By grace I give. 6 By grace I will release.

Notes to Lesson #169

By grace I live. By grace I am released.

Lesson 169 defines two key terms with which we need to become familiar. The first term is grace. Anyone who has a religious background should be familiar with the term grace. Grace has not been mentioned much throughout this course and how it is defined will provide a few surprises. The second term is a word that has been used often throughout this course. The term is Oneness.

Grace is defined as the acceptance of the love of God within a world of seeming hate and fear. Grace is an aspect of God's love that is most like the state prevailing in the unity of truth. Grace presents a state opposite to our egoic world of provisional reality and its numerous fearful experiences. When experienced, the state of grace is so prevalent that you can no longer believe that the egoic world of hate and fear is real.

Grace is not learned. By having an open mind, you realize that you do not know everything and therefore, you are willing to challenge what your ego says your fear-based experiences would teach. It is the gift of grace that the Holy Spirit utilizes to reframe our experiences to align with the truth.

It is interesting to note that grace is defined as the acceptance of the love of God within the world of seeming hate and fear. Grace is always present because it is an aspect of the love of God yet, we must accept the gift of grace to realize that we possess it.

Another interesting caveat is the idea that we accept God's love in a seeming world of hate and fear. This reference to a seeming world of hate and fear reflects the illusionary nature of the world that we perceive to be our provisional reality. Our perception does not have the ability to change the fact that all our experiences actually assist in our realignment with the truth. What we perceive to be bad or evil is merely an incorrect judgment that has no impact upon the experience's true purpose.

The second concept defined in this lesson is the idea of a Oneness. This term has been used often throughout these lessons and notes, yet it has not necessarily been defined. Oneness is simply the idea that God is and in God's being, God encompasses all things. No mind holds anything but God. God is and nothing else is. God is not aware of something that is not Itself. All is united with its Source and like its Source, It merely is.

Oneness is the total recognition that the Will of God has been completely given and received in every mind. Oneness returns the mind to the ever present. In oneness, the Son of God has returned into the Father and the Father has returned into the Son.

We say God is and we cease to speak for words would only support the idea of separation for to define is to limit. Words like the Father, God's Son, the Holy Spirit, Christ and the big "S" Self all become synonymous with God since there is only a Oneness of All That Is.

Although our split mind cannot understand the abstract idea of a Oneness, perhaps it would be helpful to look upon the Mind of God as holographic in nature. In a true hologram, all parts contain the whole and the whole is contained in all parts. This recognition of our oneness with the Mind of God will arrive when we fully accept and recognize that the Will of God is our will.

Forgiveness is the central theme in salvation and holds all the parts together in meaningful relationships. Forgiveness is in the realm of time. Time provides a game board for differentiation and separation that has become our apparent provisional reality.

It is this provisional reality that provides a seeming or illusionary world of hate and fear that will disappear with our acceptance of grace.

Earlier, we said that in time, forgiveness is the idea that I forgive my brother for all the things that I thought he had done to harm me that never really happened. This definition of forgiveness is the acknowledgment that nothing sources your experience but yourself and that nothing can rob you of your inner peace unless you choose to allow it.

Forgiveness leads to the abandonment of our belief in time as we realize that all learning has never been lost and we remain as God created us. We accept and share that realization with all minds so that each mind will be open to revelation for themselves and be released from time.

Forgiveness and grace are intertwined and lead to our acceptance that we merely make a journey in time that was already done and that oneness is our true reality.

When revelation of your oneness comes, your oneness will be known and fully understood. Until then, we must play the role assigned to us in God's plan for salvation. By playing our role, we move nearer the point when we abandon time and all minds understand, recognize and accept that God's Will has been completely given and received in every mind. By grace we live and by grace we are released from the illusion of hate and fear.

Question : The ending prayer is:

By grace I live. By grace I am released.

By grace I give. By grace, I will release.

What does grace release you from?

Hint: Remember the definition of grace. Grace is the acceptance of the love of God within a world of seeming hate and fear.

LESSON 170.

There is no cruelty in God and none in me.

W-170.1.No one attacks without intent to hurt. 2 This **idea that no one attacks without intent to hurt** can have no exception. 3 When you think that you attack in self-defense, you mean that to be cruel is protection; you are safe because of cruelty. 4 **When you think that you attack in self-defense,** you mean that you believe to hurt another brings you freedom. 5 And **when you think that you attack in self-defense,** you mean that to attack is to exchange the state in which you are for something better, safer, more secure from dangerous invasion and from fear.

W-170.2.How thoroughly insane is the idea that to defend from fear is to attack! 2 For here **in your attack** is fear begot and fed with blood, to make **fear** grow and swell and rage. 3 And thus **by your attack** is fear protected, not escaped. 4 Today we learn a lesson which can save you more delay and needless misery than you can possibly imagine. 5 **The lesson** is this: 6 You make what you defend against, and by your own defense against it is **what you made** real and inescapable. 7 Lay down your arms, and only then do you perceive **what you would defend yourself against as** false.

W-170.3.It seems to be the **external** enemy without that you attack. 2 Yet your defense sets up an enemy within **your own mind**; an alien thought at war with you, **your big "S" Self,** depriving you of peace, splitting your mind into two camps which seem wholly irreconcilable. 3 For love now has an "enemy," an opposite; and fear, the alien, now needs your defense against the threat of what you really are **which is your big "S" Self.**

W-170.4.If you consider carefully the means by which your fancied self-defense proceeds on its imagined way, you will perceive the premises on which the idea **of your self-defense** stands. 2 **When you believe attack is self-defense,** first, it is obvious **you believe** ideas must leave their source, for it is you who make attack, and must have first conceived of **attack.** 3 Yet you attack outside yourself, and separate your mind from **the other party's mind** who is to be attacked, with perfect faith the split you made **within the one shared Mind of God** is real.

W-170.5.Next, are the attributes of love bestowed upon **fear, love's** "enemy." 2 For fear becomes your safety and protector of your peace, to which you turn for solace and escape from doubts about your strength, and hope of rest in dreamless quiet. 3 And as love is shorn of what belongs to **love** and **love** alone, love is endowed with attributes of fear. 4 For love would ask you lay down all defense as merely foolish. 5 And your arms **and weapons for defense** indeed would crumble into dust. 6 For such **egoic defenses** are **foolish and useless**.

W-170.6.With love as enemy, must cruelty become a god. 2 And gods **of revenge** demand that those who worship them obey their dictates, and refuse to question **this egoic god of fear and cruelty**. 3 Harsh punishment is meted out relentlessly to those who ask if the demands **of fear** are sensible or even sane. 4 It is **the enemies of the ego's god of fear** who are unreasonable and insane, while they, **who defend themselves against their own fears by attack** are always merciful and just.

W-170.7.Today we look upon this cruel god dispassionately. 2 And we note that though **this cruel egoic god of fear's** lips are smeared with blood, and fire seems to flame from him, **this false god** is but made of stone. 3 **This cruel god of fear** can do nothing. 4 We need not defy **this false god's** power. 5 **This cruel god of fear** has none. 6 And those who see in **this imagined god of fear** their safety have no guardian, no strength to call upon in danger, and no mighty warrior to fight for them.

W-170.8.This moment can be terrible. 2 But **the moment that you realize your egoic god of fear cannot protect you** can also be the time of your release from abject slavery. 3 You make a choice, standing before this idol **of those who believe minds are separate and ideas can leave their source and see** him exactly as **the false god fear** is. 4 Will you restore to love what you have sought to wrest from **love** and lay before this mindless piece of stone? 5 Or will you make another idol to replace **ego's god of cruelty and fear**? 6 For the god of cruelty takes many forms. 7 Another **form for this false god of your little "s" self** can be found.

W-170.9.Yet do not think that fear is the escape from fear. 2 Let us remember what the text has stressed about the obstacles to peace. 3 The final **obstacles to peace**, the hardest to believe is nothing, and a seeming obstacle with the appearance of a solid block, impenetrable, fearful and beyond surmounting, is the fear of God Himself. 4 Here **in the fear of God Himself** is the basic premise which enthrones the thought of fear as god. 5 For fear is loved by those who worship **the gods of fear**, and love appears to be invested now with cruelty.

W-170.10.Where does the totally insane belief in gods of vengeance come from? 2 Love has not confused **love's** attributes with those of fear. 3 Yet must the worshippers of fear perceive their own confusion **about what love is** in fear's "enemy" **which is real love. Fear's** cruelty as now **misperceived to be** a part of love. **Because of the ego's confusion about what true love is, a God of only love has been imaged to possess attributes of fear and now has been transformed by the ego into a god of vengeance to be feared.** 4 And what becomes more fearful than the Heart of Love Itself? 5 The blood appears to be upon **the egoic version of a God of love's** Lips; the fire comes from **this imagined egoic god of vengeance.** 6 And

this God of love imaged by the ego to be a god of vengeance is terrible above all else, cruel beyond conception, striking down all who acknowledge Him to be their God.

W-170.11.The choice you make today is certain. 2 For you look for the last time upon this bit of carven stone you made, and call no longer **upon your ego's belief in a god of vengeance and fear**. 3 You have reached this place before, but you have chosen that this cruel god **your ego fears** remain with you in still another form. 4 And so the fear of God returned with you. 5 This time you leave **the fear of God** there **behind you**. 6 And you return to a new world, unburdened by **fear's** weight; beheld not in **fear's** sightless eyes, but in the **Christ** vision that your choice restored to you.

W-170.12.Now do your eyes belong to Christ, and **Christ, your big "S" Self** looks through them. 2 Now your voice belongs to God and echoes **the Holy Spirit's Voice**. 3 And now your heart remains at peace forever. 4 You have chosen **the true God of only love** in place of idols **for fear**, and your attributes **of being only love**, given by your Creator, are restored to you at last. 5 The Call for God is heard and answered. 6 Now has fear made way for love, as God Himself replaces cruelty.

W-170.13. <Father, we are like You. 2 No cruelty abides in us, for there is none in You. 3 Your peace is **our peace**. 4 And we bless the world with what we have received from You alone. 5 We choose again, and make our choice for all our brothers, knowing they are one with us. 6 We bring to **all our brothers** Your salvation as we have received **salvation** now. 7 And we give thanks for **all our brothers** who render us complete. 8 In **all our brothers** we see Your glory, and in them we find our peace. 9 Holy are we because Your Holiness has set us free. 10 And we give thanks. 11 Amen.>

Notes to Lesson #170

There is no cruelty in God and none in me.

Lesson 170 is a critical lesson because it points out a fundamental flaw in our ego's belief system. The ego claims that because you are limited, unequal and separate, it is necessary to attack another in order to obtain the limited resources that you need for your survival. Because the ego does not know who you really are, it perceives self-defense as a means to protect yourself from outside forces that can rob you of your inner peace.

Your ego does not associate your own self-defense as an attack against another. It proclaims your defenses are justifiable and are not designed to harm another. Yet, we have often heard that the best defense is a good offense. A preemptive strike against a potential enemy is perceived as justifiable and even righteous.

You always attack with the intent to harm. This is true even when we claim we are attacking in self-defense. When you defend yourself, you are claiming that your protection is dependent upon cruelty. Your ego has taught us that your ability to harm another protects you and brings you freedom and alleviates your fears. It does not. Instead, your defenses only make what you fear appear real.

Attack is based on two erroneous egoic beliefs. The first is the belief that ideas leave their source and therefore, there is something outside your own mind that is separate and can be attacked. This also means there are separate outside forces that can attack you.

The second idea is that love has an opposite. Because the ego does not know what love is, your ego confuses attributes that are associated with fear and believes they are part of love. The ego claims that love would require the giver of love to protect the object of its love from love's opposite which masquerades as various forms of fear.

"Egoic love" insists that if you loved me, you would attack and destroy my perceived enemies. "Egoic love" demands that love contain an element of cruelty. Thus, your ability to harm another in the name of love becomes a cornerstone of the ego's fear-based thought system.

God is only love and love has no opposites. Since there is no fear in God, there is nothing we should fear from God. Yet, because your ego thinks fear is real, it teaches that you can escape from fear through fear. The ego instructs that to love someone is to defend and protect another from their fears.

"Egoic love" becomes a guardian against fear. Yet, if others can be harmed in the name of love, this confirms your ego's belief that you are not unlimited spirit, but instead limited, lacking and separate. "Egoic love" proves you are vulnerable to forces that are beyond your control.

Your ego looks to God for your protection. But if God is to protect you, He must be cruel to your enemies. This results in the transformation of a God of unconditional love into an egoic god of judgment, punishment, cruelty and wrath. The ego teaches that even if God loved you, you would still need to fear His judgment.

When you follow the ego's fear-based thought system, your greatest fear is the fear of God Himself. The ego has made fear a part of love. When we co-mingle love with fear, we perceive the need to protect someone against something else. Love does not possess any attributes of fear. Yet when we assign the attribute of cruelty to love, this misclassification makes what we fear appear real.

The Holy Spirit teaches love has no opposites. It knows that ideas never leave their source and therefore, to give is to receive. When you make fear real, you split the One Self into separate parts and create a fictitious enemy where none existed. Your ego claims there is an enemy outside your mind. Whereas the truth is that the actual enemies are the beliefs held by your ego.

The ego does not believe that to give is to receive. The ego teaches that our fears protect and keep us safe from outside dangers. The ego claims that love defends and protects its loved ones. Therefore, if God loved you, God would protect you and attack your enemies. Thus, the God of love becomes a God of cruelty to your enemies. But this is a double edged sword. If you don't obey God's Will, God will punish you.

This creates the final obstacle to your own peace which is your deep seated belief that God is something you need to fear. When you believe love has an opposite that you must be protected against, your ego has transformed a God of only love into a god of judgment, punishment, cruelty and something that must be feared. The only way to correct this fundamental error is to not defend yourself against those fears.

When you stop defending yourself, you discover that your fears are powerless and simply disappear. When you defend yourself, you maintain those fears making them appear real and proclaim that God must protect you from harm. This confirms your ego's belief in separateness, lack and inequality. This leads to a need to defend and protect yourself which ultimately translates into your need to attack.

You need to decide if God is a God of unconditional love or a god to be feared. God cannot be both. When we understand that there is no cruelty in God, we will stop fearing God and stop our egoic belief that love gives us the right to change, fix, correct, impress or protect another because we love them. To do so implies that we believe that love and cruelty are synonymous and are two sides of one coin. This is impossible for love is not cruel.

Question: Historically, when hate is met with hate, does hate dissipate or does this just breed more hate?

Only when hate is met with love will hatred end.

REVIEW #5

Introduction:

Review of Workbook Lessons 151-170

W-rV.in.1.We now review again. 2 This time we are ready to give more effort and more time to what we undertake. 3 We recognize **with this review that** we are preparing for another phase of understanding. 4 We would take this step completely, that we may go on again more certain, more sincere, with faith upheld more surely. 5 Our footsteps have not been unwavering, and doubts have made us walk uncertainly and slowly on the road this course sets forth. 6 But now we hasten on, for we **approach these workbook lessons** with a greater certainty, a firmer purpose and a surer goal.

W-rV.in.2. <Steady our feet, our Father. 2 Let our doubts be quiet and our holy minds be still, and speak to us. 3 We have no words to give to You. 4 We would but listen to Your Word, and make **Your Word** ours. 5 Lead our practicing as does a father lead a little child along a way **the child** does not understand. 6 Yet does **the child** follow, sure that **the child** is safe because his father leads the way for him.>

W-rV.in.3. <So do we bring our practicing to **God with the aid of the Holy Spirit**. 2 And if we stumble, **the Holy Spirit** will raise us up. 3 If we forget the way, we count upon **the Holy Spirit's** sure remembering. 4 We wander off, but **the Holy Spirit** will not forget to call us back. 5 Quicken our footsteps now, that we may walk more certainly and quickly unto **God**. 6 And we accept the Word **that the Holy Spirit** offers us to unify our practicing, as we review the thoughts that **God** have given us.>

W-rV.in.4.This **idea that God is but Love, and therefore so am I** is the thought which should precede the thoughts that we review. 2 Each **lesson we review** but clarifies some aspect of this thought **that God is but Love, and therefore so am I** or helps **this thought** be more meaningful, more personal and true, and more descriptive of the holy **big "S"** Self we share and now prepare to know again:
3 God is but Love, and therefore so am I.
4 This **big "S"** Self alone knows Love. 5 This **big "S"** Self alone is perfectly consistent in Its Thoughts; knows Its Creator, understands Itself, is perfect in Its knowledge and Its Love, and never changes from the **big "S" Self's** constant state of union with Its Father and Itself.

W-rV.in.5.And it is this **constant state of union with your Father and your big "S" Self** that waits to meet us at the journey's ending. 2 Every step we take brings us a little nearer. 3 This review will shorten time immeasurably, if we keep in mind that this **constant state of union with your Father and your big "S" Self** remains our goal, and as we practice it is this to which we are approaching. 4 Let us raise our hearts from dust to life, as we remember this **constant state of union with your Father and your big "S" Self** is promised us, and that this course was sent to open up the path of light to us, and teach us, step by step, how to return to the eternal **big "S"** Self we thought we lost.

W-rV.in.6.I, **Jesus,** take the journey with you. 2 For I share your doubts and fears a little while, that you may come to me who recognize the road by which all fears and doubts are overcome. 3 We walk together **in the dream of lack, limitation and separation.** 4 I must understand uncertainty and pain, although I know they have no meaning. 5 Yet, **on the game board of time and belief in separation**, a savior must remain with those he teaches, seeing what they see, but still retaining in his mind the way that led him out **of the belief in separation**, and now will lead you out with him **to this constant state of union with your Father and your big "S" Self.** 6 God's Son is crucified until you walk along the road **of reawakening** with me.

W-rV.in.7.My resurrection **to the truth of what we are** comes again each time I lead a brother safely to the place at which the journey **of separation** ends and is forgot. 2 I am renewed each time a brother learns there is a way from misery and pain. 3 I am reborn each time a brother's mind turns to the light in him and looks for me. 4 I have forgotten no one. 5 Help me now to lead you back to where the journey was begun, to make another choice with me **for union with your Father and your big "S" Self.**

W-rV.in.8.Release me as you practice once again the thoughts I brought to you from **the Holy Spirit** Who sees your bitter need, and knows the answer God has given **the Holy Spirit**. 2 Together we review these thoughts. 3 Together we devote our time and effort to **the review of these thoughts.** 4 And together we will teach **these thoughts** to our brothers. 5 God would not have Heaven incomplete. 6 **Heaven** waits for you, as I do. 7 I am incomplete without your part in me. 8 And as I am made whole we go together to our ancient home, prepared for us before time was and kept unchanged by time, immaculate and safe, as **our home** will be at last when time is done.

W-rV.in.9.Let this review be then your gift to me. 2 For this alone I need; that you will hear the words I speak, and give them to the world. 3 You are my voice, my eyes, my feet, my hands through which I save the world. 4 The **big "S"** Self from which I call to you is but your own **big "S"** Self. 5 To **God, our Father,** we go together. 6 Take your brother's hand, for this is not a way we walk alone. 7 In **your brother** I walk with you, and you with me. 8 Our Father wills His Son be one with **the Father**. 9 What lives but must not then be one with you?

362

W-rV.in.10.Let this review become a time in which we share a new experience for you, yet one as old as time and older still. 2 Hallowed your Name. 3 Your glory undefiled forever. 4 And your wholeness now complete, as God established **you perfect, whole and complete**. 5 You are His Son, completing His extension in your own **extension**. 6 We practice but an ancient truth **that God is but Love, and therefore so am I that** we knew before illusion seemed to claim the world. 7 And we remind the world that it is free of all illusions every time we say:

8 God is but Love, and therefore so am I.

W-rV.in.11.With this **thought that God is but Love, and therefore so am I,** we start each day of our review. 2 With this we start and end each period of practice time. 3 And with this thought **that God is but Love, and therefore so am I,** we sleep, to waken once again with these same words upon our lips, to greet another day. 4 No thought that we review but we surround with it, and use the thoughts to hold it up before our minds, and keep **this thought that God is but Love, and therefore so am I** clear in our remembrance throughout the day. 5 And thus, when we have finished this review, we will have recognized the words we speak are true.

W-rV.in.12.Yet are the words **for our review** but aids, and to be used, except at the beginning and the end of practice periods, but to recall the mind, as needed, to its purpose. 2 We place faith in the experience that comes from practice, not the means we use. 3 We wait for the experience, and recognize that it is only here **in the actual experiences that** conviction lies. 4 We use the words, and try and try again to go beyond **the words** to their meaning, which is far beyond their sound. 5 The sound grows dim and disappears, as we approach the Source of meaning. 6 It is Here that we find rest.

Notes to Review #5

Introduction for Review Lesson 171-180

Introduction

We are now beginning our review of the last twenty lessons. Lesson 170 ended this series by revealing that the final obstacle to peace is our fear of God Himself.

We have been indoctrinated to believe that we are sinners and unworthy of God's love. Because of this fundamental error, our egoic world has transformed a God of only love into a God of punishment, judgment and fear. Your ego now believes it needs to save you from its imagined god of wrath. Your ego's defenses make the fictitious problem seem real and fear is born. Now buried deep within your conscious or subconscious mind is a deep-seated fear of God.

The central theme for this review is that God is but love and therefore, so are you and I. This idea is critical if we are to break free from our egoic fear-based thought system. The source of our fear is our belief that somehow we have lost our divine birthright and caused a God of love to mutate into a god of wrath. This egoic world of fear was made as the place to either hide from God's wrath or earn God's favor. Either idea transforms God into something to be feared.

Yet, within our split mind, there remains the remembrance of the truth that we remain as God created us and that God is only love. Our big "S" Self alone knows love and is a witness for that truth. Our big "S" Self always remains in a constant state of union with our Creator and Its Cause. This Cause and Effect relationship are two inseparable parts of one whole. Your big "S" Self, like the Holy Spirit and Jesus, knows the way home and remains within your sleeping mind to assist in your gentle reawakening.

As Jesus said in A Course in Miracles, he should be thought of as an older brother who has earned our respect because he has gone before us. Jesus has also been on the game board of time and differentiation. He has experienced the pitfalls and trappings of this world and has learned how to smooth our path and guide us home.

In time, Jesus, the Holy Spirit, our big "S" Self all journey with those who believe the game of separation is real. They travel with us to guarantee the healing of our split mind. All three names describe the same Thought of God that was placed within our delusional mind to maintain communion with God. They recognize our fears, reframe our thinking and extend a helping hand for they are one with us. We have never been alone or separate from God. Our big "S" Self, the Holy Spirit and Jesus keep all sleeping minds eternally connected to their Source.

We are God's beloved child with whom He is well pleased. God's Son is the completion and extension of God Himself. We wanted to experience the various aspects of love by experiencing differentiation. Our purpose in time is to experience and demonstrate being an aspect of the perfect love that is God. We complete God as we co-create and extend the love that we share with God.

Time provides a game board in which the abstract One Self can experience specific expressions of love. By being love in form, we remind the world that it is free of all illusions of lack, limitation and separation. We allow each to experience their desires without judging their path.

We have come here to experience the truth that nothing can rob us of our own inner peace unless we choose to allow it. As you quiet your egoic mind and go within, these review periods will provide a state of union with your Father and your big "S" Self.

As you have more of these experiences, your certainty will grow that you are not your body, that God is only love and that you have nothing to fear for you are part of that One. You will take your place among the messengers of God and experience that union with God, your brother and your big "S" Self.

Enjoy and have fun with this review section while dropping your ego's fears and experiencing the fact that God is only love and therefore, so are you.

LESSON 171

LESSON SUMMARY #151-152

Lesson # 151: All things are echoes of the Voice for God.

Lesson # 152: The power of decision is my own.

God is but Love, and therefore so am I.

W-171.1.(151) All things are echoes of the Voice for God.
2 God is but Love, and therefore so am I.

W-171.2.(152) The power of decision is my own.
2 God is but Love, and therefore so am I.

General instruction:

Lesson #171 is a review of Lessons #151 and 152.We will begin and end each session with the theme behind this review lesson which is:

God is but Love, and therefore so am I.

The central idea from Lesson 151 is

(151)All things are echoes of the Voice for God.

Consider how this lesson clarifies and enhances the theme that

God is but Love, and therefore so am I.

Next, review the central theme from Lesson 152, which is:

(152)The power of decision is my own.

How does this lesson clarify and enhance the theme that

God is but Love, and therefore so am I.

Remember to end your session by repeating the general theme that

God is but Love, and therefore so am I.

Throughout your day, remember the words but go beyond the words. Share the experience of being that love and you will create a great day for yourself and your world.

LESSON 172

LESSON SUMMARY #153-154

Lesson # 153: In my defenselessness my safety lies.

Lesson # 154: I am among the ministers of God.

God is but Love, and therefore so am I.

W-172.1.(153) In my defenselessness my safety lies.
2 God is but Love, and therefore so am I.

W-172.2.(154) I am among the ministers of God.
2 God is but Love, and therefore so am I.

General instruction:

Lesson #172 is a review of Lessons #153 and 154.We will begin and end each session with the theme behind this review lesson which is:

God is but Love, and therefore so am I.

The central idea from Lesson 153 is

(153) In my defenselessness my safety lies.

Consider how this lesson clarifies and enhances the theme that

God is but Love, and therefore so am I.

Next, review the central theme from Lesson 154, which is:

(154) I am among the ministers of God.

How does this lesson clarify and enhance the theme that

God is but Love, and therefore so am I.

Remember to end your session by repeating the general theme that

God is but Love, and therefore so am I.

Throughout your day, remember the words but go beyond the words. Share the experience of being that love and you will create a great day for yourself and your world.

LESSON 173

LESSON SUMMARY #155-156

Lesson # 155: I will step back and let **the Holy Spirit** lead the way.

Lesson # 156: I walk with God in perfect holiness.

God is but Love, and therefore so am I.

W-173.1.(155) I will step back and let **the Holy Spirit** lead the way.
2 God is but Love, and therefore so am I.

W-173.2.(156) I walk with God in perfect holiness.
2 God is but Love, and therefore so

General instruction:

Lesson #173 is a review of Lessons #155 and 156. We will begin and end each session with the theme behind this review lesson which is:

God is but Love, and therefore so am I.

The central idea from Lesson 155 is

(155) I will step back and let the Holy Spirit lead the way.

Consider how this lesson clarifies and enhances the theme that

God is but Love, and therefore so am I.

Next, review the central theme from Lesson 156, which is:

(156) I walk with God in perfect holiness.

How does this lesson clarify and enhance the theme that

God is but Love, and therefore so am I.

Remember to end your session by repeating the general theme that

God is but Love, and therefore so am I.

Throughout your day, remember the words but go beyond the words. Share the experience of being that love and you will create a great day for yourself and your world.

LESSON 174

LESSON SUMMARY #157-158

Lesson # 157: Into His Presence would I enter now.

Lesson # 158: Today I learn to give as I receive.

God is but Love, and therefore so am I.

W-174.1.(157) Into His Presence would I enter now.
2 God is but Love, and therefore so am I.

W-174.2.(158) Today I learn to give as I receive.
2 God is but Love, and therefore so am I.

General instruction:

Lesson #174 is a review of Lessons #157 and 158.We will begin and end each session with the theme behind this review lesson which is:

God is but Love, and therefore so am I.

The central idea from Lesson 157 is

(157) Into His Presence would I enter now.

Consider how this lesson clarifies and enhances the theme that

God is but Love, and therefore so am I.

Next, review the central theme from Lesson 158, which is:

(158) Today I learn to give as I receive.

How does this lesson clarify and enhance the theme that

God is but Love, and therefore so am I.

Remember to end your session by repeating the general theme that

God is but Love, and therefore so am I.

Throughout your day, remember the words but go beyond the words. Share the experience of being that love and you will create a great day for yourself and your world.

LESSON 175

LESSON SUMMARY #159-160

Lesson # 159: I give the miracles I have received.

Lesson # 160: I am at home. 2 Fear is the stranger here.

God is but Love, and therefore so am I.

W-175.1.(159) I give the miracles I have received.
2 God is but Love, and therefore so am I.

W-175.2.(160) I am at home. 2 Fear is the stranger here.
3 God is but Love, and therefore so am I.

General instruction:

Lesson #175 is a review of Lessons #159 and 160.We will begin and end each session with the theme behind this review lesson which is:

God is but Love, and therefore so am I.

The central idea from Lesson 159 is

(159) I give the miracles I have received.

Consider how this lesson clarifies and enhances the theme that

God is but Love, and therefore so am I.

Next, review the central theme from Lesson 160, which is:

(160) I am at home. 2 Fear is the stranger here.

How does this lesson clarify and enhance the theme that

God is but Love, and therefore so am I.

Remember to end your session by repeating the general theme that

God is but Love, and therefore so am I.

Throughout your day, remember the words but go beyond the words. Share the experience of being that love and you will create a great day for yourself and your world.

LESSON 176

LESSON SUMMARY #161-162

Lesson # 161: Give me your blessing, holy Son of God.

Lesson # 162: I am as God created me.

God is but Love, and therefore so am I.

W-176.1.(161) Give me your blessing, holy Son of God.
2 God is but Love, and therefore so am I.

W-176.2.(162) I am as God created me.
2 God is but Love, and therefore so am I.

General instruction:

Lesson #176 is a review of Lessons #161 and 162. We will begin and end each session with the theme behind this review lesson which is:

God is but Love, and therefore so am I.

The central idea from Lesson 161 is

(161) Give me your blessing, holy Son of God.

Consider how this lesson clarifies and enhances the theme that

God is but Love, and therefore so am I.

Next, review the central theme from Lesson 162, which is:

(162) I am as God created me.

How does this lesson clarify and enhance the theme that

God is but Love, and therefore so am I.

Remember to end your session by repeating the general theme that

God is but Love, and therefore so am I.

Throughout your day, remember the words but go beyond the words. Share the experience of being that love and you will create a great day for yourself and your world.

LESSON 177

LESSON SUMMARY #163-164

Lesson # 163: There is no death. 2 The Son of God is free.

Lesson # 164: Now are we one with **God** Who is our Source.

God is but Love, and therefore so am I.

W-177.1.(163) There is no death. 2 The Son of God is free.
3 God is but Love, and therefore so am I.

W-177.2.(164) Now are we one with **God** Who is our Source.
2 God is but Love, and therefore so am I.

General instruction:

Lesson #177 is a review of Lessons #163 and 164. We will begin and end each session with the theme behind this review lesson which is:

God is but Love, and therefore so am I.

The central idea from Lesson 163 is

(163) There is no death. 2 The Son of God is free.

Consider how this lesson clarifies and enhances the theme that

God is but Love, and therefore so am I.

Next, review the central theme from Lesson 164, which is:

(164) Now are we one with God Who is our Source.

How does this lesson clarify and enhance the theme that

God is but Love, and therefore so am I.

Remember to end your session by repeating the general theme that

God is but Love, and therefore so am I.

Throughout your day, remember the words but go beyond the words. Share the experience of being that love and you will create a great day for yourself and your world.

LESSON 178

LESSON SUMMARY #165-166

Lesson # 165: Let not my mind deny the Thought of God.

Lesson # 166: I am entrusted with the gifts of God.

God is but Love, and therefore so am I.

W-178.1.(165) Let not my mind deny the Thought of God.
2 God is but Love, and therefore so am I.

W-178.2.(166) I am entrusted with the gifts of God.
2 God is but Love, and therefore so am I.

General instruction:

Lesson #178 is a review of Lessons #165 and 166. We will begin and end each session with the theme behind this review lesson which is:

God is but Love, and therefore so am I.

The central idea from Lesson 165 is

(165) Let not my mind deny the Thought of God.

Consider how this lesson clarifies and enhances the theme that

God is but Love, and therefore so am I.

Next, review the central theme from Lesson 166, which is:

(166) I am entrusted with the gifts of God.

How does this lesson clarify and enhance the theme that

God is but Love, and therefore so am I.

Remember to end your session by repeating the general theme that

God is but Love, and therefore so am I.

Throughout your day, remember the words but go beyond the words. Share the experience of being that love and you will create a great day for yourself and your world.

LESSON 179

LESSON SUMMARY #167-168

Lesson # 167: There is one life, and that I share with God.

Lesson # 168: **God's** grace is given me. 2 I claim it now.

God is but Love, and therefore so am I.

W-179.1.(167) There is one life, and that I share with God.
2 God is but Love, and therefore so am I.

W-179.2.(168) **God's** grace is given me. 2 I claim it now.
3 God is but Love, and therefore so am I.

General instruction:

Lesson #179 is a review of Lessons #167 and 168. We will begin and end each session with the theme behind this review lesson which is:

God is but Love, and therefore so am I.

The central idea from Lesson 167 is

(167) There is one life, and that I share with God.

Consider how this lesson clarifies and enhances the theme that

God is but Love, and therefore so am I.

Next, review the central theme from Lesson 168, which is:

(168) God's grace is given me. 2 I claim it now.

How does this lesson clarify and enhance the theme that

God is but Love, and therefore so am I.

Remember to end your session by repeating the general theme that

God is but Love, and therefore so am I.

Throughout your day, remember the words but go beyond the words. Share the experience of being that love and you will create a great day for yourself and your world.

LESSON SUMMARY #169-170

Lesson # 169: By grace I live. 2 By grace I am released.

Lesson # 170: There is no cruelty in God and none in me.

God is but Love, and therefore so am I.

W-180.1.(169) By grace I live. 2 By grace I am released.
3 God is but Love, and therefore so am I.

W-180.2.(170) There is no cruelty in God and none in me.
2 God is but Love, and therefore so am I.

General instruction:

Lesson #180 is a review of Lessons #169 and 170. We will begin and end each session with the theme behind this review lesson which is:

God is but Love, and therefore so am I.

The central idea from Lesson 169 is

(169) By grace I live. 2 By grace I am released.

Consider how this lesson clarifies and enhances the theme that

God is but Love, and therefore so am I.

Next, review the central theme from Lesson 170, which is:

(170) There is no cruelty in God and none in me.

How does this lesson clarify and enhance the theme that

God is but Love, and therefore so am I.

Remember to end your session by repeating the general theme that

God is but Love, and therefore so am I.

Throughout your day, remember the words but go beyond the words. Share the experience of being that love and you will create a great day for yourself and your world.

Introduction to Lessons 181-200.

WpI.in.181-200.1.Our next few lessons make a special point of firming up your willingness to make your weak commitment strong; your scattered goals blend into one intent. 2 You are not asked for total dedication all the time as yet. 3 But you are asked to practice now in order to attain the sense of peace such unified commitment will bestow, if only intermittently. 4 It is experiencing **this sense of peace** that makes it sure that you will give your total willingness to following the way the course sets forth.

WpI.in.181-200.2.Our lessons now are geared specifically to widening horizons, and direct approaches to the special blocks that keep your vision narrow, and too limited to let you see the value of our goal. 2 We are attempting now to lift these blocks, however briefly. 3 Words alone cannot convey the sense of liberation which their lifting **of these blocks to your peace** brings. 4 But the experience of freedom and of peace that comes as you give up your tight **egoic** control of what you see speaks for itself. 5 Your motivation will be so intensified that words become of little consequence. 6 You will be sure of what you want, and what is valueless.

WpI.in.181-200.3.And so we start our journey beyond words by concentrating first on what **block** impedes your progress still. 2 Experience of what exists beyond defensiveness remains beyond achievement while **defensiveness** is denied. 3 **Defensiveness** may be there, but you cannot accept **the** presence **of defensiveness**. 4 So we now attempt to go past all defenses for a little while each day. 5 No more than this is asked, because no more than this **going past all defenses for a little while each day** is needed. 6 **This going past all defenses for a little while each day** will be enough to guarantee the rest will come.

LESSON 181.

I trust my brothers, who are one with me.

W-181.1.Trusting your brothers is essential to establishing and holding up your faith in your ability to transcend doubt and lack of sure conviction in yourself. 2 When you attack a brother, you proclaim that **your brother** is limited by what you have perceived in him. 3 You do not look beyond **your brother's** errors. 4 Rather, **your brother's errors** are magnified, becoming blocks to your awareness of the **big "S" Self** that lies beyond your own mistakes, and past **your brother's** seeming sins as well as your **own sins.**

W-181.2.Perception has a focus. 2 It is this **focus** that gives **perception the** consistency to what you see. 3 Change but this focus **of your perception**, and what you behold will change accordingly. 4 Your vision now will shift, to give support to the intent which has replaced the **intent** you held before **you changed your focus.** 5 Remove your focus on your brother's sins, and you experience the peace that comes from faith in sinlessness. 6 This faith **in sinlessness** receives its only sure support from what you see in others past their sins. 7 For their mistakes, if focused on, are witnesses to sins in you. 8 And you will not transcend their sight and see the sinlessness that lies beyond.

W-181.3.Therefore, in practicing today, we first let all such little focuses **on mistakes** give way to our great need to let our sinlessness become apparent. 2 We instruct our minds that it is this **sinlessness that** we seek, and only **sinlessness** for just a little while. 3 We do not care about our future goals. 4 And what we saw an instant previous has no concern for us within this interval of time wherein we practice changing our intent **to seeing only sinlessness.** 5 We seek for innocence and nothing else. 6 We seek for **the innocence of sinlessness** with no concern **about the past or future** but **only the present** now.

W-181.4.A major hazard to success has been involvement with your past and future goals. 2 You have been quite preoccupied with how extremely different the goals this course is advocating are from those **goals your ego** held before. 3 And you have also been dismayed by the depressing and restricting thought that, even if you should succeed **with the goals of this course**, you will inevitably lose your way again.

W-181.5.How could this **concern about losing your way in the future** matter? 2 For the past is gone; the future but imagined. 3 These concerns are but defenses against present change of focus in perception **from sin to sinlessness.** 4 Nothing more. 5 We lay these pointless limitations by a little while. 6 We do not look to past beliefs, and what we will believe **in the future** will not intrude upon us now. 7 We enter in the time of practicing with one intent; to look upon the sinlessness within.

W-181.6.We recognize that we have lost this goal **of looking upon the sinlessness within** if anger blocks our way in any form. 2 And if a brother's sins occur to us, our narrowed focus will restrict our sight, and turn our eyes upon our own mistakes, which we will magnify and call our "sins." 3 So, for a little while, without regard to past or future, should such blocks arise we will transcend **these blocks** with instructions to our minds to change their focus, as we say:
4 It is not this **mistake** that I would look upon.
5 I trust my brothers, who are one with me.

W-181.7.And we will also use this thought **that we will not focus on the mistake but rather trust our brothers, who are one with us** to keep us safe throughout the day. 2 We do not seek for long-range goals. 3 As each obstruction **from our focusing upon a mistake** seems to block the vision of our sinlessness, we seek but for surcease an instant from the misery the focus upon sin will bring, and **the misery that** will remain **if our focus on sin is left** uncorrected.

W-181.8.Nor do we ask for fantasies. 2 For what we seek to look upon, **our sinlessness** is really there. 3 And as our focus goes beyond mistakes, we will behold a wholly sinless world. 4 When seeing this **sinlessness** is all we want to see, when **sinlessness** is all we seek for in the name of true perception, are the eyes of Christ inevitably ours. 5 And the Love **Christ** feels for us becomes our own **love** as well. 6 This **love and sinlessness** will become the only thing we see reflected in the world and in ourselves.

W-181.9.The world which once proclaimed our sins becomes the proof that we are sinless. 2 And our love for everyone we look upon attests to our remembrance of the holy **big "S" Self** which knows no sin, and never could conceive of anything without Its sinlessness. 3 We seek for this remembrance **of the big "S" Self's sinlessness** as we turn our minds to practicing today. 4 We look neither ahead nor backwards. 5 We look straight into the present. 6 And we give our trust to the experience we ask for now. 7 Our sinlessness is but the Will of God. 8 This instant is our willing one with **God's Will.**

Notes to Lesson #181

I trust my brothers, who are one with me.

This lesson states what the first fifty workbook lessons were trying to demonstrate experientially. When you change your focus, you change what you call into your awareness. Your beliefs and thoughts color your world. Your physical senses are thought confirmation devices and not the objective cameras to the world as we have been taught. The job of your senses is merely to confirm what your mind already believes to be "out there."

The goal of perception is to provide witnesses that proclaim the reality of your ego's current belief system. Perception has a focus and this focus gives consistency to what we see. The focus is always to confirm what your mind wants your outside world to reflect. If you change your focus, you will become aware of items that support your new intent.

In our egoic world, our current focus is on getting our perceived needs met. Your ego's plan revolves around its belief in lack, limitation and separation. The ego has assigned roles for all parties to fulfill in its plan for its own survival. Your egoic thinking is centered on judging the performance of you and your brother.

Since you associate yourselves with your ego, whenever another has failed to fulfill the role your ego has assigned for your happiness, you see that party as a sinner. This reinforces your ego's belief that there are outside forces that can make you happy or sad.

Since you are not happy, your focus is on your brothers' mistakes that you perceive to be a sin. Therefore, your world is perceived to be a sinful place. This ongoing focus on your brother's failures to make you happy gives consistency to what you see.

Since ideas do not leave their source, the sins you see in your brother are your own beliefs in lack. Since to give is to receive, if you choose to see your brother as innocent and sinless, you give yourself that same innocence. When you consciously decide to change your focus from sin to sinlessness, the awareness you glean from each experience will reflect this new focus.

The world of perception is a vast array of endless possibilities. You get to choose what you will place your attention upon. It is this focus that determines which of the endless array of possibilities you will call into your awareness.

A major problem in changing your focus is your involvement with your past beliefs and your future goals. You cling to the past and the future and fail to be aware of the present. The present becomes a replay of your past beliefs and fears. You are not in the now. The past is gone and the future is but imagined. Your past and future concerns are mere defenses designed to block your decision to change your current focus. Only in the present can you make a different choice.

Whenever you become angry, you have lost focus on sinlessness which is not a fantasy. Yet, for sinlessness to be recognized as your true and current reality, you need to change your focus from your brother's sins to the sinlessness and innocence of all who choose to participate in the game of reawakening.

The focus of the ego's thought system is on finding sin, guilt and fear in your brother and thus, in yourself. The intention of the Holy Spirit's thought system is to see your brother and yourself as perfect, whole and complete.

When sinlessness is your only focus, you will obtain the vision of Christ and love will be all you see. Your sinless and innocent world will become proof that you remain as God created you, perfect, whole and complete.

Question: A Course in Miracles suggests that you do not try to change your world, but rather change how you view your world. When you do, your world must automatically realign to support your new viewpoint.

Have you ever had the experience of changing your focus and watching the perception of your world change?

LESSON 182.

I will be still an instant and go home.

W-182.1.This **egoic** world **of perception and time that** you seem to live in is not home to you, **your big "S" Self or your true Christ nature**. 2 And somewhere in your mind you know that this is true. 3 A memory of **your** home **in Heaven that** keeps haunting you, as if there were a place that called you to return, although you do not recognize the voice, nor what it is the voice reminds you of. 4 Yet still you feel an alien here **in this egoic world of perception and time**, from somewhere all unknown. 5 **This feeling of being an alien is** nothing so definite that you could say with certainty you are an exile here. 6 Just a persistent feeling, sometimes not more than a tiny throb, at other times hardly remembered, actively dismissed, but surely to return to mind again.

W-182.2.No one but knows **our real home** whereof we speak. 2 Yet some try to put by their suffering in games they play to occupy their time, and keep their sadness from them. 3 Others will deny that they are sad **in this egoic world of lack, limitation and separation** and do not recognize their tears at all. 4 Still others will maintain that what we speak of **as the real home or Heaven** is an illusion, not to be considered more than but a dream. 5 Yet who, in simple honesty, without defensiveness and self-deception, would deny he understands the words we speak **when we say that we do not feel this world is our true home**?

W-182.3.We speak today for everyone who walks this **egoic** world **of fear** for he is not at home. 2 He goes uncertainly about in endless search **for his true home**, seeking in darkness what he cannot find; not recognizing what it is he seeks. 3 A thousand homes he makes, yet none contents his restless mind. 4 He does not understand he builds in vain. 5 The home he seeks cannot be made by **his egoic split mind**. 6 There is no substitute for Heaven. 7 All he ever made **with his split mind** was hell.

W-182.4.Perhaps you think it is your **body's** childhood home that you would find again. 2 The childhood of your body, and its place of shelter, are a memory now so distorted that you merely hold a picture of a past that never happened. 3 Yet there is a Child in you, **your big "S" Self, the Christ**, Who seeks His Father's house, and knows that **the Christ, God's Son** is alien here. 4 This childhood is eternal, with an innocence that will endure forever. 5 Where this Child shall go is holy ground. 6 It is **the Holiness of your Christ nature** that lights up Heaven, and that brings to earth the pure reflection of the light above, wherein are earth and Heaven joined as one.

W-182.5.It is this Child in you, **your Christ nature**, your Father knows as His Own Son. 2 It is this Child, **your big "S" Self**, Who knows His Father. 3 **Your big "S" Self** desires to go home so deeply, so unceasingly, **this inner** voice cries unto **your split mind** to let **your big "S" Self** rest a while. 4 **Your Christ nature** does not ask for more than just a few instants of respite; just an interval in which **God's Son** can return to breathe again the holy air that fills His Father's house. 5 You are **Christ's** home as well. 6, **Your Christ nature** will return **to your ego's world**. 7 But give your **Christ** just a little time to be Himself **as God's Son**, within the peace that is **God's Son's** home, resting in silence and in peace and love.

W-182.6.This Child, **the Christ who is God's Son and your big "S" Self,** needs your protection. 2 **The Son of God** is far from home. 3 **This Child** is so little that **the Christ** seems so easily shut out. **Christ's** tiny voice **for truth** so readily obscured by the voice **for your ego and your little "s" self**. **Christ's** call for help **is** almost unheard amid the grating sounds and harsh and rasping noises of the **ego's** world **of fear**. 4 Yet does **God's Son** know that in **your mind** still abides His sure protection. 5 **Your mind** will fail **God's Son and your big "S" Self** not. 6 **God's Son** will go home, and you along with Him.

W-182.7.This Child is your defenselessness; your strength. 2 **Your big "S" Self** trusts in you. 3 He came **into this egoic world of time and fear** because **Christ** knew you would not fail. 4 **Your Big "S" Self** whispers of **Christ's** home unceasingly to you. 5 For **Christ** would bring you back **to Heaven** with Him, that **Christ** Himself might stay **in Heaven** and not return again where He does not belong **in your ego's illusionary world of separation**, and where **God's Son** lives **as** an outcast in a world of alien thoughts. 6 **Christ's** patience has no limits. 7 **Christ** will wait until you hear His gentle Voice **for Truth** within you, calling you to let Him go in peace, along with you, to where **Christ** is at home **in heaven** and you with Him.

W-182.8.When you are still an instant, when the **egoic** world recedes from **your mind**, when valueless ideas cease to have value in your restless **egoic** mind, then will you hear **Christ's** Voice. 2 So poignantly **Christ** calls to you that you will not resist Him longer. 3 In that instant **Christ** will take you to His home, and you will stay with **Christ** in perfect stillness, silent and at peace, beyond all words, untouched by fear and doubt, sublimely certain that you are at home.

W-182.9.Rest with **Christ** frequently today. 2 For **Christ** was willing to become a little Child that you might learn of **Christ** how strong is he who comes without defenses, offering only love's messages to those who think **Christ** is their enemy. 3 **Christ** holds the might of Heaven in His hand and calls them friend, and gives His strength to them **who thought Christ was their enemy**, that they may see **Christ** would be **a** Friend to them. 4 **Christ** asks that they **who once perceived Christ to be their enemy now** protect **Christ**, for **Christ's** home is far away, and **Christ** will not return to **His home in Heaven** alone **without them**.

W-182.10.Christ is reborn as but a little Child each time a wanderer would leave his home **in Heaven**. 2 For **the wanderer who plays the game of differentiation and separation** must learn that what he would protect is but this Child, **his true Christ nature,** Who comes defenseless and Who is protected by defenselessness. 3 Go home with **Christ who is your big "S" Self** from time to time today. 4 You are as much an alien here **in the ego's dream world of lack, limitation and separation** as **Christ who is your big "S" Self**.

W-182.11.Take time today to lay aside your shield **of defense** which profits nothing, and lay down the spear and sword you raised against an enemy without existence. 2 Christ has called you friend and brother. 3 **Christ** has even come to ask your help in letting Him go home today, completed and completely. 4 **Christ** has come as does a little child, who must beseech his father for protection and for love. 5 **Christ** rules the universe, and yet **Christ** asks unceasingly that you return with Him, and take illusions as your gods no more.

W-182.12.You have not lost your innocence. 2 It is for this **innocence that** you yearn. 3 **Innocence** is your heart's desire. 4 This is the voice you hear, and this the call which cannot be denied. 5 The holy Child remains with you. 6 **Christ's** home is yours. 7 Today **Christ** gives you His defenselessness, and you accept **Christ's defenselessness** in exchange for all the toys of battle you have made. 8 And now the way is open, and the journey has an end in sight at last. 9 Be still an instant and go home with **Christ** and be at peace a while.

Notes to Lesson #182

I will be still an instant and go home.

Where are you?

This is a basic question and yet, we fail to ask it because we believe the answer is obvious. But is it?

When asked, we typically respond in a superficial way by providing an address or specific location on planet earth which we assume to be our true reality. We fail to go beyond the superficial and ask if this world is real or is it only an illusion. If it is an illusion, it has no ability to change the truth of who we really are. If it is an illusion and we are real, it cannot be our home.

Before you can answer where you are, you need to first determine what you are. If you are unlimited spirit, part of the shared Mind of God, your home cannot be a world of lack, limitation and separation. Yet, because we fail to understand what we are, we tend to answer the question of where we are based upon our erroneous beliefs that the body is us and time and space are real.

The world we perceive is not our home and something deep inside tells us that this cannot be where we belong. God did not create the fear-based world that you perceive to be your provisional reality. If God created you, this cannot be your home. The egoic fearful world we have made and perceive to be our reality is not a worthy home for God's Son, the Christ, your big "S" Self.

Instead, this illusionary world provides the game board where we can play the game of What Am I in perfect safety. Because we have forgotten who we are, our egos have mistaken the game token of the body to be our reality. Our egos now defend this game token and in that defense make the game of What Am I appear real. Our decision-maker has chosen to follow the voice for fear and our egos have turned the game of What Am I into a detour into fear. This decision to follow the ego's fear-based thought system has turned our provisional reality into hell.

The Christ, our big "S" Self, is like an innocent child that has accompanied its parent into the movie theater. This child does not belong in a movie that represents lack, limitation and separation. Instead, this child reflects the holiness and innocence of its divine birthright as part of the indivisible One Self. We are the home of Christ for we are not of this world but rather Mind or Spirit. We too are part of the shared Mind of God.

The Christ in us remembers that the theater that we have brought this child into is not our reality. Instead, it is an illusionary world in which we decide what movie we will watch. Our decision-maker has freely decided to watch the horror show called fear.

There is nothing wrong with someone's decision to attend a horror movie. Every day many people go to our movie houses and pay for the right to be scared out of their wits. But these people realize that what they see on the movie screen is merely an illusion and is not real.

Yet, if you fail to remember where you are, it is easy to get caught up in the drama and get pulled into the story that appears upon the big screen. When you do this, the movie theater becomes a scary place. Yet, once you remember where you are, your fear quickly dissipates and you can go back to watching and enjoying the show.

The Christ asks your decision-maker to stop attending these fearful shows and to realize that the illusionary world of your provisional reality is not your real home. This child knows that the dream world of lack, limitation and separation is not real and longs to return with you to the home God created for His Son.

The Christ, your big "S" Self and the Holy Spirit ask that your decision-maker give up your dreams of sin, guilt and fear and return with them to your real home. They know that you remain as God created you, perfect, whole and complete and therefore, have never lost your innocence.

Your decision-maker must first decide what you are if it is to properly answer the question of where you are. Within each of us there is the Voice for God that knows the answer. We are aliens in this fear-based world. The Voice for Truth seems weak due to our decision-maker's habit of following the voice for fear.

When you are still and quiet the egoic mind chatter, you will hear the voice from deep within that knows that fear cannot be your home. This Inner Voice will not abandon you because you have freely chosen to attend this movie house for fear. The Voice for God trusts you because it knows what you are. This Voice will lead you back to that truth and reawaken your sleeping mind.

When you decide to stop defending yourselves against a fantasy, the illusion no longer will appear real and must disappear. Truth needs no defense. Let Christ's defenselessness be your strength.

Question: Put aside your embedded egoic beliefs that you are tethered to the body and ask yourself this question, where are you?

LESSON 183.

I call upon God's Name and on my own.

W-183.1.God's Name is holy, but no holier than **your Name**. 2 To call upon **God's** Name is but to call upon your own **Name**. 3 A father gives his son his name, and thus identifies the son with **the father**. 4 His brothers share **their father's** name, and thus are they united in a bond to which they turn for their identity. 5 Your Father's Name reminds you who you are, even within a world that does not know **that you are God's Son**; even though you have not remembered **that you and your brothers are all God's One Son.**

W-183.2.God's Name cannot be heard without response, nor said without an echo in the mind **of your big "S" Self** that calls you to remember. 2 Say **God's** Name, and you invite the angels to surround the ground on which you stand, and sing to you as **the angels** spread out their wings to keep you safe, and shelter you from every worldly thought that would intrude upon your holiness.

W-183.3.Repeat God's Name, and all the world responds by laying down illusions. 2 Every dream the world holds dear has suddenly gone by, and where **the illusion** seemed to stand, you find a star; a miracle of grace. 3 The sick arise, healed of their sickly thoughts. 4 The blind can see; the deaf can hear. 5 The sorrowful cast off their mourning and the tears of pain are dried as happy laughter comes to bless the world.

W-183.4.Repeat the Name of God, and little names have lost their meaning. 2 No temptation but becomes a nameless and unwanted thing before God's Name. 3 Repeat **God's** Name, and see how easily you will forget the names of all the gods you valued. 4 **What your ego had valued** has lost the name of god you gave them. 5 **What your ego had valued** becomes anonymous and valueless to you, although before you let the Name of God replace their little names, you stood before **what your ego valued** worshipfully, naming them as gods.

W-183.5.Repeat the Name of God, and call upon your **big "S" Self**, Whose Name is **God's Name**. 2 Repeat **God's** Name, and all the tiny, nameless things on earth slip into right perspective. 3 Those who call upon the Name of God cannot mistake the nameless for the Name, nor sin for grace, nor bodies for the holy Son of God. 4 And should you join a brother as you sit with him in silence, and repeat God's Name along with him within your quiet mind, you have established there an altar which reaches to God Himself and to His Son.

W-183.6.Practice but this today; repeat God's Name slowly again and still again. 2 Become oblivious to every name but **God's Name** 3 Hear nothing else. 4 Let all your thoughts become anchored on **God's Name**. 5 No other word we use except at the beginning, when we say today's idea **that I call upon God's Name and on my own** but once. 6 And then God's Name becomes our only thought, our only word, the only thing that occupies our minds, the only wish we have, the only sound with any meaning, and the only Name of everything that we desire to see; of everything that we would call our own.

W-183.7.**By calling upon God's Name,** thus do we give an invitation which can never be refused. 2 And God will come, and answer **your call** Himself. 3 Think not **God** hears the little prayers of those who call on **God** with names of idols cherished by the world. 4 They **who pray to the idols of the egoic world** cannot reach **God** thus. 5 **God** cannot hear requests that **God** be not Himself, or that His Son receive another name than **God's Name.**

W-183.8.Repeat God's Name, and you acknowledge **God** as sole Creator of reality. 2 And you acknowledge also that His Son is part of **God**, creating in **God's** Name. 3 Sit silently, and let **God's** Name become the all-encompassing idea that holds your mind completely. 4 Let all thoughts be still except this one **that I call upon God's Name.** 5 And to all other thoughts respond with **repeating God's Name**, and see God's Name replace the thousand little names you gave your thoughts, not realizing that there is one Name for all there is, and all that there will be **for God is the sole Creator of reality**.

W-183.9.Today you can achieve a state in which you will experience the gift of grace. 2 You can escape all bondage of the world, and give the world the same release you found. 3 You can remember what the world forgot, and offer **the world** your own remembering **that there is only God's Name for God is the sole Creator of reality**. 4 You can accept today the part you play in **the world's** salvation, and your own **salvation** as well. 5 And both can be accomplished perfectly.

W-183.10.Turn to the Name of God for your release, and **your release** is given you. 2 No prayer but **the calling upon God's Name** is necessary, for **God's Name** holds all **prayers** within it. 3 Words are insignificant, and all requests unneeded when God's Son calls on his Father's Name. 4 His Father's Thoughts become **the Son's** own **thoughts**. 5 **God's Son** makes his claim to all his Father gave, is giving still, and will forever give. 6 **God's Son** calls on **His Father** to let all things **the son** thought he **egoically** made **by his little "s" self** be nameless now, and in their place the holy Name of God becomes his judgment of their worthlessness.

W-183.11.All little things are silent. 2 Little sounds are soundless now. 3 The little things of earth **that your little "s" self imagined** have disappeared. 4 The universe consists of nothing but the Son of God, who calls upon his Father. 5 And his Father's Voice gives answer in his Father's holy Name. 6 In this eternal, still relationship, in which communication far transcends all words, and yet exceeds in depth and height whatever words could possibly convey, is peace eternal. 7 In our Father's Name, we would experience this peace today. 8 And in **God's** Name, **the peace of God** shall be given us.

I call upon God's Name and on my own.

Sanskrit is the ancient literary language of India. Sanskrit traces its origins to the 4th century BC. Sanskrit is very important in the origin and development of the comparative Indo-European languages of our time. Sanskrit has been described as the language of God because in its original form, it recognizes and acknowledges the reality of God in all things. How does Sanskrit do this?

Every word is actually a reference to or another name for God. Here is a simplified example. If we were to consider the Sanskrit word for horse, the literal translation would actually be the God nature appearing in the form of a horse. The word for running would translate into the God nature participating in the act of running. Everything references back to the idea that God is in all things, and that there is nothing that is separate or distinct from God.

Our modern language has forgotten that God is in all things. Modern language is now used to distinguish one part of the whole from another. Modern languages confirm our belief in separation ignoring the interdependence and true relationship of each part to the whole. Modern language looks upon the parts as autonomous separate entities that can change or affect another part of the whole.

In Lesson 169, we defined the term Oneness as simply the idea of God and knowing God encompasses all things and that there is nothing outside the One Self. There is no mind that is aware of anything that is not Itself and all minds have united with Its Source and are therefore, like Its Source. There is no judgment since there is nothing outside the One Self to judge.

This lesson, I call upon God's name and my own, is the recognition of that Oneness. Our name and God's name are interchangeable and the same. They are equally holy because we are inseparable from our Source.

Our Father's name reminds us of who we are. Creation is extension and the Father gives His name and identity to His Son in totality. Nothing is held back. God identifies Himself with His creations and His creations share that one common identity. The Father's name and the Son's name reflect the true nature of our big "S" Self each being equally holy since they are the same.

In time, the Father's name helps us remember our true identity. By repeating God's name, we acknowledge God as the sole creator of reality. We are part of that reality. When we call on God's name, we are co-creating with God.

Similar to ancient Sanskrit, God is the name for all things and all Thoughts for God are the One Self. When you use God's name exclusively you will see God everywhere and God will answer your call for you are only asking God to be Himself.

God's name reminds us of our true identity for God is love and truth. In God's name all illusions of egoic littleness disappear and peace is restored and given.

Question: Namaste is an Indian term that is loosely translated as the God in me recognizes the God in you. It is often used as a greeting of acknowledgment of another's presence or when leaving that person's presence.

If you were to begin or end your conversation with Namaste instead of hello or goodbye, would that term better help remind you of your connectedness to God and the Oneness of all things?

The Name of God is my inheritance.

W-184.1.You live by symbols. 2 You have made up names for everything you see. 3 Each **thing you see** becomes a separate entity, identified by its own name **or symbol**. 4 By this **naming** you carve **everything you see** out of **a unity of one**. 5 By this **carving out of parts of the whole into separate autonomous things,** you designate its special attributes, and set **the parts of the whole** off from other things by emphasizing space surrounding **each part of the whole.** 6 This space you lay between all things to which you give a different name; all happenings in terms of place and time; all bodies which are greeted by a name.

W-184.2.This space you see as setting off all things from one another is the means by which the world's perception is achieved. 2 You see something where nothing is, and see as well nothing where there is unity; a space between all things, between all things and you. 3 Thus do you think that you have given life in separation **of the whole One Self**. 4 By this **splitting out of parts of the whole into separate autonomous lives,** you think you are established as a unity which functions with an independent will.

W-184.3.What are these names by which the world becomes a series of discrete events, of things ununified, of bodies kept apart and holding bits of mind as separate awarenesses? 2 You gave these names to **these indivisible parts or attributes of the whole**, establishing perception as you wished to have perception be. 3 The nameless things were given names, and thus reality was given **the indivisible attributes** as well. 4 For what is named is given meaning and will then be seen as meaningful. **What is named will be perceived to be** a cause of true effect, with consequence inherent in itself.

W-184.4.This is the way **provisional** reality is made by partial vision, purposefully set against the given truth. 2 **Provisional reality's** enemy is wholeness. 3 **The egoic mind** conceives of little things and looks upon them **as your provisional reality that you seem to experience.** 4 And a lack of space, a sense of unity or vision that sees differently, become the threats which **the egoic mind's provisional reality** must overcome, conflict with and deny.

W-184.5.Yet does this other **partial** vision **of separate things** still remain a natural direction for the mind to channel its perception. 2 It is hard to teach the mind a thousand alien names, and thousands more. 3 Yet you believe this **teaching of fictitious alien names** is what learning means. **You believe learning names is the** one essential goal by which communication is achieved, and concepts can be meaningfully shared.

W-184.6.This **naming of indivisible attributes of the whole as separate beings** is the sum of the inheritance the **egoic world of separation** bestows. 2 And everyone who learns to think that **separation** is so accepts the signs and symbols that assert the world **of separation and perception** is real. 3 It is for this **belief in separation for which these symbols** stand. 4 **These symbols** leave no doubt that what is named is there **as a separate autonomous thing**. 5 **These symbols** can be seen, as is anticipated. 6 What denies that **these symbols of partial vision** are true is but illusion, for **what you perceive to be your provisional reality** is the ultimate reality **according to your egoic split mind**. 7 To question **perception's partial vision as your reality** is madness. To accept **the presence of perception's partial vision to be your reality** is the proof of sanity **according to the ego's fear-based thought system.**

W-184.7.Such is the teaching of the world. 2 **This naming of indivisible attributes of the whole as separate beings** is a phase of learning everyone who comes **into time** must go through. 3 But the sooner he perceives on what **the teachings of separation** rest, how questionable are **the beliefs in separation's** premises, how doubtful the results of separation, the sooner does he question **the belief in the** effects of separation. 4 Learning that stops with what the world **of separation** would teach stops short of meaning. 5 In its proper place, **the naming of indivisible attributes of the whole as separate beings** serves but as a starting point from which another kind of learning can begin, a new perception can be gained, and all the arbitrary names the world bestows can be withdrawn as **the beliefs in separate, autonomous beings** are raised to doubt.

W-184.8.Think not you made the world. 2 Think you made illusions, yes! 3 But what is true in earth and Heaven is beyond your naming. 4 When you call upon a brother, it is to his body that you make appeal. 5 **Your brother's** true Identity is hidden from you by **the body that** you believe he really is. 6 His body makes response to what you call him, for **your brother's** mind consents to take the name you give **your brother** as his own **name**. 7 And thus **your brother's** unity is twice denied, for you perceive him separate from you, and **your brother** accepts this separate name as his.

W-184.9.It would indeed be strange if you were asked to go beyond all symbols of the world, forgetting **the symbols** forever; yet were asked to take a teaching function. 2 You have need to use the symbols of the world a while **if you are to teach that separation is not real**. 3 But be you not deceived by **these symbols for separation** as well. 4 **These names and symbols of separation** do not stand for anything at all, and in your practicing it is this thought **of their unreality** that will release you from them. 5 **These names and symbols of separation** become but means by which you can communicate in ways the world can understand, but which you recognize is not the unity where true communication can be found.

W-184.10.Thus what you need are intervals each day in which the learning of the world becomes a transitory phase; a prison house from which you go into the sunlight and forget the darkness **of the ego's world of separation**. 2 Here **in the Holy**

Spirit's sunlight you understand the Word, the Name which God has given you; the one Identity which all things share; the one acknowledgment of what is true. 3 And then step back to darkness, not because you think **the ego's world of separation is** real, but only to proclaim **the** unreality **of the ego's world of separation** in terms which still have meaning in the world that darkness rules.

W-184.11.Use all the little names and symbols which delineate the world of darkness. 2 Yet accept **the names and symbols of separation** not as your reality. 3 The Holy Spirit uses all of **the symbols**, but **the Holy Spirit** does not forget creation has one Name, one meaning, and a single Source which unifies all things within **God** Itself. 4 Use all the names the world bestows on **what the world perceives to be separate from the One Self** but for convenience, yet do not forget **all** share the Name of God along with you.

W-184.12.God has no name. 2 And yet **God's** Name becomes the final lesson that all things are one, and at this lesson does all learning end. 3 All names are unified; all space is filled with truth's reflection. 4 Every gap is closed, and separation healed. 5 The Name of God is the inheritance **God** gave to those who chose the teaching of the **ego's** world of separation to take the place of Heaven. 6 In our practicing, our purpose is to let our **split** minds accept what God has given as the answer to the pitiful inheritance **your ego's belief in lack, limitation and separation** made as fitting tribute to the Son **God** loves.

W-184.13.No one can fail who seeks the meaning of the Name of God. 2 Experience must come to supplement the Word **of God**. 3 But first you must accept the Name **of God** for all reality, and realize the many names you gave its aspects have distorted what you see, but have not interfered with truth at all. 4 One Name we bring into our practicing. 5 One Name, **which is the Name of God**, we use to unify our sight.

W-184.14.And though we use a different name for each awareness of an aspect of God's Son, we understand that **all aspects of God's Son** have but one Name, which God has given them. 2 It is this **one** Name **of God** we use in practicing. 3 And through **the use of this one Name**, all foolish **egoic thoughts of** separations disappear which kept us blind. 4 And we are given strength to see beyond **egoic perception**. 5 Now our sight is blessed with blessings we can give as we receive.

W-184.15. Father, our Name is **Your Name**. 2 In **Your Name** we are united with all living things, and You Who are their one Creator. 3 What we made and call by many different names is but a shadow we have tried to cast across Your Own reality **of our Christ nature**. 4 And we are glad and thankful we were wrong **and are not our ego's little "s" self**. 5 All our mistakes we give to You, that we may be absolved from all effects our errors seemed to have. 6 And we accept the truth You give, in place of every one of **our ego's misperceptions**. 7 Your Name is our salvation and escape from **the world of perception and time that** we made. 8 Your Name unites us in the oneness which is our inheritance and peace. 9 Amen.

Notes to Lesson #184

The Name of God is my inheritance.

How you define yourself will determine what you believe is your birthright. Unless you perceive yourself to be part of the Oneness of All That Is, you will not believe that the Name of God is your divine inheritance.

In the world of time and space, we live by symbols. The names we assign to everything are the symbols that we live by. When you name something, you assign to that item certain characteristics and behavioral traits. Naming assigns a past history that limits what you believe that item is capable of doing in the future.

To name is to limit. Once named, your beliefs will limit how you perceive that item will behave in the future. Your past beliefs are symbolized and frozen in time by the name you assigned to a particular object. Those same historic beliefs will be imposed upon that item by your mind in any future interactions. This results in any future experiences becoming a replay of your past beliefs since your mind limits what interactions are acceptable encounters with that item in the future.

When you name something, you do not just define it but you also make it real. These names and definitions become the constraints of your provisional reality because when you accept the name, you also automatically accept the limitations that are associated with that name.

The goal of naming is to break up the unity of the whole by separating the whole into various specific attributes of the whole. Next, naming takes these special attributes and emphasizes the space that we perceive to exist between the parts of the whole. It then assigns special names to the indivisible parts. These names are then falsely assumed to possess separate, independent and autonomous existences. These artificial parts are then perceived to have powers that can impact and change other aspects of the whole.

When we name, we emphasize the space between what has no separate reality since there is only one whole. Naming obscures the reality of the continued indivisible existence of the whole from our vision. This partial vision creates the illusion of space and makes the separation appear real. By naming, we separate the indivisible whole into special parts. We ignore the true interrelationship and interdependence of the parts that comprise the indivisible whole.

Naming is the means that is utilized by our egos to create the world of perception and separation. What we perceive to be our provisional reality is made with partial vision which ignores the oneness of the whole. Partial vision's goal is to separate the unity and fragment the whole and thus make littleness appear real. We accept this partial vision to be our provisional reality.

Today we find ourselves in a world of time and space. It is an illusionary world that was created through our split mind's belief that lack, limitation and separation are real. If you are to teach others the truth of what they are, you must meet them where they perceive themselves to be. Most perceive separation and limitation to be their reality.

In order to communicate with them, you must use the words, symbols and dualistic language of their world of time and space. Yet, use their symbols to teach the fact that these symbols are not real. Use the language and symbols of separation to bring into their awareness the various aspects of God's Son. But also know and teach that true reality is that all aspects remain part of the indivisible shared oneness of the Mind of God. Let them know that all those attributes of God's Son also belong to them for that is their true inheritance.

God is a Oneness. God is not the sum of the parts. Although the names assigned to the whole distort what we see, these distortions cannot change the truth. The truth is that there is no name but God's Name. We say God's name and we cease to speak. Use the Name of God to unify your sight and correct the illusions of separation that were created through partial vision. Restore the vision of Christ.

Do not allow the use of separate names to obscure the awareness that each of the various aspects of God is an indivisible attribute that belongs to the whole. Names and symbols have no ability to change the totality of the One Self. There is no separation.

The only name that you should acknowledge as your own is the Christ. The Christ is your big "S" Self. The name of God and Christ are interchangeable symbols for the truth. God is and all things are God. There is nothing apart from God that is real.

You are not an individual separate autonomous being. You are a Oneness of All That Is. This reality of your oneness with what we call God is the final lesson and your inheritance. When will you cease arguing for your limitations and instead choose to reclaim your rightful place within the Mind you share with God?

Question: How you define yourself determines what you believe is your inheritance. You cannot believe you are both separate and also claim you are one with God. These ideas are mutually exclusive.

So what are you?

LESSON 185.

I want the peace of God.

W-185.1.To say these words, **I want the peace of God** is nothing. 2 But to mean these words, **I want the peace of God** is everything. 3 If you could but mean **these words** for just an instant, there would be no further sorrow possible for you in any form; in any place or time. 4 Heaven would be completely given back to full awareness, memory of God entirely restored, the resurrection of all creation fully recognized.

W-185.2.No one can mean these words **that I want the peace of God** and not be healed. 2 **One** cannot play with dreams, nor think he is himself a dream **if he only wants the peace of God**. 3 He cannot make a hell and think it real. 4 He **only** wants the peace of God, and **the peace of God** is given him. 5 For that is all he wants, and that is all he will receive. 6 Many have said these words. 7 But few indeed have meant **these words that they only want the peace of God**. 8 You have but to look upon the world you see around you to be sure how very few they are **that only want the peace of God**. 9 The world would be completely changed, should any two agree these words express the only thing they want.

W-185.3.Two minds with one intent become so strong that what **the two minds** will **together** become the Will of God. 2 For minds can only join in truth. 3 In dreams, no two **minds** can share the same intent. 4 To each, the hero of the dream is different; the outcome wanted not the same for both. 5 Loser and gainer merely shift about in changing patterns, as the ratio of gain to loss and loss to gain takes on a different aspect or another form.

W-185.4.Yet compromise alone a dream can bring. 2 Sometimes **a dream** takes the form of union, but only the form. 3 The meaning must escape the dream, for compromising is the goal of dreaming. 4 Minds cannot unite in dreams. 5 **Dreaming minds** merely bargain. 6 And what bargain can give **a sleeping mind** the peace of God? 7 Illusions come to take **God's** place. 8 And what **the Oneness of God** means is lost to sleeping minds intent on compromise, each to his gain and to another's loss.

W-185.5.To mean you want the peace of God is to renounce all dreams. 2 For no one means these words **that they only want the peace of God** who wants illusions, and who therefore seeks the means which bring illusions **about by following the voice for your ego.**3 He **who only wants the peace of God** has looked on **illusions** and found them wanting. 4 Now he seeks to go beyond **illusions,** recognizing that another dream would offer nothing more than all the others. 5 Dreams are one to him **who only wants the peace of God**. 6 And he has learned their only difference is one of form, for one **dream** will bring the same despair and misery as do the rest.

W-185.6.The mind which means that all it wants is peace must join with other minds, for that is how peace is obtained. 2 And when the wish for peace is genuine, the means for finding **peace** is given, in a form each mind that seeks for **peace** in honesty can understand. 3 Whatever form the lesson takes is planned for him in such a way that he cannot mistake **peace** if his asking is sincere. 4 But if he asks without sincerity, there is no form in which the lesson **of peace** will meet with acceptance and be truly learned.

W-185.7.Let us today devote our practicing to recognizing that we really mean the words we say. 2 We want the peace of God. 3 This is no idle wish. 4 These words **that I want the peace of God** do not request another dream be given us. 5 **These words that I want the peace of God** do not ask for compromise, nor try to make another bargain in the hope that there may yet be one **egoic plan** that can succeed where all the rest have failed. 6 To mean these words acknowledges illusions are in vain, requesting the eternal in the place of shifting dreams which seem to change in what **form the dream** offers, but are one in nothingness.

W-185.8.Today devote your practice periods to careful searching of your mind, to find the dreams you cherish still. 2 What do you ask for in your heart? 3 Forget the words you use in making your requests. 4 Consider but what you believe will comfort you, and bring you happiness. 5 But be you not dismayed by lingering illusions, for their form is not what matters now. 6 Let not some dreams be more acceptable, reserving shame and secrecy for **other dreams**. 7 **All your ego's illusions within the dream of separation** are one. 8 And being one, one question should be asked of all of **your ego's plans for your peace and happiness**, "Is this what I would have, in place of Heaven and the peace of God?"

W-185.9.This **decision between wanting your ego's plan or the peace of God** is the choice you make. 2 Be not deceived that it is otherwise. 3 No compromise is possible in this. 4 You choose God's peace, or you have asked for **your ego's** dreams. 5 And **your ego's** dreams will come as you requested them. 6 Yet will God's peace come just as certainly, and to remain with you forever. 7 **God's peace** will not be gone with every twist and turning of the road, to reappear, unrecognized, in forms which shift and change with every step you take.

W-185.10.You want the peace of God. 2 And so do all who seem to seek for dreams. 3 For **those who seem to seek for dreams** as well as for yourself, you ask but this when you make this request **for the peace of God** with deep sincerity. 4 For thus you reach to what they really want **which is the peace of God**, and join your own intent with what they seek above all things, perhaps unknown to them, but sure to you. 5 You have been weak at times, uncertain in your purpose, and unsure of what you wanted, where to look for **the peace of God**, and where to turn for help in the attempt. 6 Help has been given you. 7 And would you not avail yourself of **the help of the Holy Spirit** by sharing it?

W-185.11.No one who truly seeks the peace of God can fail to find **God's peace**. 2 For he merely asks that he deceive himself no longer by denying to **his big "S" Self** what is God's Will. 3 Who can remain unsatisfied who asks for what he, **his Christ nature,** has already? 4 Who could be unanswered who requests an answer which is his to give? 5 The peace of God is yours.

W-185.12.For you was peace created, given you by its Creator, and established as **God's** Own eternal gift. 2 How can you fail, when you but ask for what **God** wills for you? 3 And how could your request be limited to you alone? 4 No gift of God can be unshared. 5 It is this attribute **that God's gifts are shared by all** that sets the gifts of God apart from every dream that ever seemed to take the place of truth.

W-185.13.No one can lose and everyone must gain whenever any gift of God has been requested and received by anyone. 2 God gives but to unite. 3 To take away is meaningless to **God**. 4 And when **to take away** is as meaningless to you, you can be sure you share one Will with **God**, and **God's Will** with you. 5 And you will also know you share one Will with all your brothers, whose intent is yours.

W-185.14.It is this one intent **of only wanting the peace of God that** we seek today, uniting our desires with the need of every heart, the call of every mind, the hope that lies beyond despair, the love attack would hide, the brotherhood that hate has sought to sever, but which still remains as God created it, **perfect, whole and complete**. 2 With Help like this beside us, can we fail today as we request the peace of God be given us?

Notes to Lesson #185

I want the peace of God.

Everyone claims they want the peace of God, but do they?

We confuse inner peace with getting our way. Your ego values your need to be right even when it is wrong and that costs you your happiness and inner peace. You will have the peace of God only when that is what you exclusively desire. Currently, most people value their need to be right over their happiness and inner peace.

Yesterday's workbook lesson talked about naming. To name is to limit. When you name, you assign certain special characteristics that limit and separate one part of the indivisible whole from itself. Our final question for yesterday was to define what you are. How you define yourselves tells a great deal about the exclusivity of your desire for God's peace.

You cannot want the peace of God and believe in lack, limitation and separation. Although most people would argue that they do not want lack and limitation in their lives, our egos cling to our desire for separation and autonomous existence. Unfortunately, when you perceive yourself to be separate from God, your Source, this naming of what you are must include the attributes of lack and limitation.

You cannot define yourself as separate without also creating the illusion of lack and limitation in your life. Yesterday we said that naming makes your provisional reality real within your own mind. You cannot accept a special name yet deny the attributes that come with that particular name. Accept the belief in separation and you get the lack and limitation that are associated with that name or belief.

In this world of time and space, it would seem that we share the common belief in separation with our brothers and sisters. Yet, this lesson says you cannot share illusions since you can only share the truth. It also states that two minds that share one intent become the Will of God. Doesn't our egoic mind share the same intent when two parties both argue for their littleness? Shouldn't this become God's Will?

Since each party believes that they have a separate autonomous existence, how each party views a common event will differ. This means each party's intent behind their common experiences will not be the same. Although each person's story may revolve around the same set of facts, each person will be the hero of their story. The story will always be told from their own perspective based upon what they value and why. Each will always be the star and narrator of their own story.

When you perceive the separation to be real, the intent or objective of your provisional reality will be the fulfillment of your perceived personal needs. Needs are an attribute of your belief in separation. Whenever you associate yourself with being separate, special or different from the One Self, needs automatically appear.

Because we have needs, the goal of our provisional reality is not to share our abundance but rather to bargain from our belief in lack. The ego believes that sharing or giving requires sacrifice and therefore, it attempts to minimize the price you must pay to get your needs met. The ego wants a good deal.

Compromise is the goal of all the many versions of the dream of separation. All forms of the dream seek to obscure the oneness of our big "S" Self. The ego seeks to manage, control and mitigate the damage that fictitious outside forces pose to its survival.

The goal or intent of each party within the dream of separation is to sacrifice or trade something of lesser value in exchange for something of greater value.

In the dream of separation, the ego hopes to minimize or remove the illusion of lack and limitation while maintaining its belief in the illusion of separation. You cannot find the peace of God if you insist on keeping the illusions of separation. Truth and illusions cannot coexist. If you want the peace of God, you must choose exclusively for the truth of your oneness and reject your ego's belief in separation.

Peace is obtained by joining with other minds in the truth that all remain part of the indivisible One Self. The peace of God is our natural state of being since it is God's Will. It is only our desire for the illusion of specialness that keeps this truth obscured from our vision.

You cannot serve two masters nor follow two opposing thought systems. When you follow the guidance of the Holy Spirit's thought system exclusively, you will truly want God's peace. Since God's gifts have already been given, the Holy Spirit will help you remove the blocks that prevent you from recognizing that those gifts already are part of your big "S" Self.

All God's gifts are shared by all but each can choose to deny that truth. The peace of God is the realization that no one can rob you of your own inner peace unless you choose to allow it. This is the truth that we need to share with our brothers and sisters. Everybody wants this truth, but most fail to understand what it means. They prefer to argue for the rightness of their ego's belief in victims and victimizers.

All dreams are different forms of our belief in separation. As decision-maker, you only have two possible choices. Each choice is mutually exclusive. You must choose between the dream of separation or the oneness that is the peace of God. Only when you want the peace of God, for all, will it be given you. For like all of God's gifts, the peace of God must be shared with all.

As a messenger for God, you must realize that our big "S" Self already possesses the peace of God within and thus, this peace can be shared with anyone, even if their egoic mind may not realize this fact. When you only want the peace of God for all, your will and God's Will are the same. You share one intention, one purpose and are of one mind. This Mind is, of course, the shared Mind of God.

Question: Your world of provisional reality is a reflection of what you value and why. It reflects your true beliefs at any given moment in time about what you are. So how peaceful is your world?

Based on this feedback about the peace in your private world of individuated perception, how strongly do you really desire the peace of God?

Give it a percentage from 0 -100%.

Bonus Question: What actions can you take today, to improve that percentage?

More importantly, will you choose to implement these actions?

LESSON 186.

Salvation of the world depends on me.

W-186.1.**Salvation of the world depends on me** is the statement that will one day take all arrogance away from every mind. 2 **Salvation of the world depends on me** is the thought of true humility, which holds no function as your own but that which has been given you. 3 T**his thought that salvation of the world depends on me** offers your acceptance of a part assigned to you, without insisting on another role. 4 **This thought** does not judge your proper role. 5 **This statement that the salvation of the world depends on me** but acknowledges the Will of God is done on earth as well as Heaven. 6 **This statement** unites all wills on earth in Heaven's plan to save the world, restoring **the world** to Heaven's peace.

W-186.2.Let us not fight our function. 2 We did not establish **our function in God's plan for salvation**. 3 **Our role is** not our **ego's** idea. 4 The means are given us by which **our function** will be perfectly accomplished. 5 All that we are asked to do is to accept our part in genuine humility, and not deny with self-deceiving arrogance that we are worthy. 6 What is given us to do, we have the strength to do. 7 Our minds are suited perfectly to take the part assigned to us by **the Holy Spirit** Who knows us well.

W-186.3.Today's idea **that the salvation of the world depends on me** may seem quite sobering, until you see its meaning. 2 All it says is that your Father still remembers you, and offers you the perfect trust **God** holds in you who are His Son. 3 It does not ask that you be different in any way from what you are **which is your Christ nature**. 4 What could humility request but this? 5 And what could arrogance deny but this **truth that you remain as God created you**? 6 Today we will not shrink from our assignment on the specious grounds that modesty is outraged. 7 It is pride that would deny the Call for God Himself.

W-186.4.All false humility we lay aside today, that we may listen to God's Voice reveal to us what **the Holy Spirit** would have us do. 2 We do not doubt our adequacy for the function **the Holy Spirit** will offer us. 3 We will be certain only that **the Holy Spirit** knows our strengths, our wisdom and our holiness. 4 And if **the Holy Spirit** deems us worthy, so we are. 5 It is but arrogance that judges otherwise.

W-186.5.There is one way, and only one, to be released from the imprisonment your **ego's** plan to prove the false is true has brought to you. 2 Accept the plan **your ego** did not make instead. 3 Judge not your value to **God's Plan**. 4 If God's Voice assures you that salvation needs your part, and that the whole depends on you, be sure that it is so. 5 The arrogant **ego** must cling to words, afraid to go beyond **the words** to **the** experience which might affront their stance **for the ego's belief in your little "s" self.** 6 Yet are the humble free to hear the Voice **of the Holy Spirit** which tells them what they are, **which is their big "S" Self** and what to do.

W-186.6.Arrogance makes an image of yourself that is not real. 2 It is this **egoic** image **of a little "s" self** which quails and retreats in terror, as the Voice for God assures you that you have the strength, the wisdom and the holiness to go beyond all images **of lack and separation**. 3 You are not weak, as is the image of **your ego's little "s" self.** 4 You are not ignorant and helpless. 5 Sin cannot tarnish the truth in you, and misery can come not near the holy home of God, **your big "S" Self.**

W-186.7.All this the Voice for God relates to you. 2 And as **the Holy Spirit** speaks, the **ego's** image trembles and seeks to attack the threat **your ego** does not know, sensing **your ego's littleness** will basically crumble **before the Hoy Spirit's truth**. 3 Let **your ego's belief in your littleness** go. 4 Salvation of the world depends on you, and not upon this little pile of dust. 5 What can **the voice for littleness** tell the holy Son of God? 6 Why need **the holy Son of God** be concerned with **the ego's fear-based thought system** at all?

W-186.8.And so we find our peace. 2 We will accept the function God has given us, for all illusions rest upon the weird belief that we can make another **function** for ourselves. 3 Our self-made roles are shifting, and **our ego's roles and plans** seem to change from mourner to ecstatic bliss of love and loving. 4 We can laugh or weep, and greet the day with welcome or with tears. 5 Our very being seems to change as we experience a thousand shifts in mood, and our emotions raise us high indeed, or dash us to the ground in hopelessness.

W-186.9.Is this the Son of God? 2 Could **God** create such instability and call it Son? 3 **God, the Creator** Who is changeless shares His attributes with His creation. 4 All the images His **Son's egoic mind** appears to make have no effect on what he is, **his big "S" Self**. 5 **The ego's images of what he is** blow across his mind like wind-swept leaves that form a patterning an instant, break apart to group again, and scamper off. 6 Or like mirages seen above a desert, rising from the dust.

W-186.10.These egoic unsubstantial images **of your separation and littleness** will go, and leave your mind unclouded and serene, when you accept the function given you **in the Holy Spirit's plan for salvation**. 2 The images **your ego** makes give rise to but conflicting goals, impermanent and vague, uncertain and ambiguous. 3 Who could be constant in his efforts, or direct his energies and concentrated drive toward **vague ambiguous** goals like these? 4 The functions which the **fear-based** world esteems are so uncertain that **the function** changes ten times an hour at their most secure. 5 What hope of gain can rest on **shifting** goals like this?

W-186.11.In lovely contrast, certain as the sun's return each morning to dispel the night, your truly given function **of the Holy Spirit's plan** stands out clear and wholly unambiguous. 2 There is no doubt of its validity. 3 **Our function** comes from **God** Who knows no error, and **the Holy Spirit's** Voice is certain of Its messages. 4 **Our function and messages** will not change, nor be in conflict. 5 All of **the messages** point to one goal, and one **goal** you can attain. 6 Your **ego's** plan may be impossible, but God's **plan** can never fail because **God** is **the plan's** Source.

W-186.12.Do as God's Voice directs. 2 And if **the Holy Spirit** asks a thing of you which seems impossible, remember Who it is that asks, and **that it is your ego** who would make denial. 3 Then consider this; which is more likely to be right? 4 The Voice that speaks for the Creator of all things, Who knows all things exactly as they are, or a distorted **egoic** image of yourself, confused, bewildered, inconsistent and unsure of everything? 5 Let not **your ego's** voice **for your littleness** direct you. 6 Hear instead a certain Voice **of the Holy Spirit**, which tells you of a function given you by your Creator Who remembers you, and urges that you now remember **your Creator**.

W-186.13.**The Holy Spirit's** gentle Voice is calling from the known to the unknowing. 2 **The Holy Spirit** would comfort you, although **your Christ nature** knows no sorrow. 3 **The Holy Spirit** would make a restitution, though **your Christ nature** is complete; a gift **of restitution** to you, although **the Holy Spirit** knows that you have everything already. 4 **God** has Thoughts which answer every need His Son perceives, although **God** sees **these perceived needs** not. 5 For Love must give, and what is given in **God's** Name takes on the form most useful in a world of form.

W-186.14.**The gifts of God's love** are the forms which never can deceive because **the gifts of love** come from Formlessness Itself. 2 Forgiveness is an earthly form of love, which as **love** is in Heaven has no form. 3 Yet what is needed here **in the world of form** is given here as it is needed. 4 In this form **of forgiveness which is an earthly form of love,** you can fulfill your function even here, although what love will mean to you when formlessness has been restored to you is greater still. 5 Salvation of the world depends on you who can forgive. 6 Such is your function **of forgiveness** here **in the world of form**.

Notes to Lesson #186

Salvation of the world depends on me.

This lesson is enough to strike fear in the heart of anyone. It states that the salvation of the world depends upon you. This seems like a tremendous burden to place upon anyone. Surely this heavy responsibility would seem to be too much to ask of anyone, let alone you. But is this what the lesson is truly saying?

The weight of this burden will be quickly released when you realize what the definition of salvation means according to <u>A Course in Miracles</u>.

Salvation is God's promise that everyone will find their way home. Put another way, it is the promise that any mind that sleeps must wake up. It is the guarantee that all illusions made in time will end. Salvation promises that what is true is true and what is false is not true. Salvation is God's guarantee for our safe return to the truth of what we really are. No one can fail in their quest to reawakening since this is not God's Will.

Salvation is God's promise that all will find their way home but it is obvious that this promise cannot be kept unless you make the decision to wake up. No one can be left behind if God's promise is to be fulfilled. Since every sleeping mind must awaken, the success of the whole depends upon your acceptance of your role in God's plan to wake up.

Your role in God's plan is simply to drop your allegiance to your ego's plan for your salvation. Your ego's plan is an insane attempt to make the false true and the true false. Such a plan can only come from a delusional mind and will never work.

Truth just is and does not change. God's plan is simply to accept the truth that truth is true and nothing else is true. Doesn't accepting God's plan for salvation make more sense?

The idea that the salvation of the world depends on you is not arrogance but rather true humility. Humility is simply the acceptance of the role God has assigned to you in the process of reawakening. Humility requires that you accept your function without insisting upon playing a different role.

Arrogance is your denial that you are worthy and capable of fulfilling the role God has assigned to you. If God deems you worthy, so it must be. God's plan does not ask for the impossible. It only asks that you accept the truth.

It is the arrogance of your ego that insists upon playing a different role or claiming that you are unworthy of fulfilling your part in God's plan. Your ego is the height of arrogance. Arrogance makes an image of you that is not real. It claims that you are a little "s" self that is a weak sinner, who is ignorant and helpless and therefore, unworthy of being God's beloved Son.

God remembers and trusts His creations totally. We are arrogant when we claim we are not worthy of accepting what God knows to be the truth that we remain as God created us, perfect, whole and complete. Who is more likely to be right, God or your ego?

Our role is to follow the Holy Spirit's guidance and ignore the voice for fear. The Holy Spirit cannot fail in its mission of gently reawakening your sleeping mind and returning you safely home. If the Holy Spirit asked what seems to be the impossible to your egoic mind, remember Who made the request. Which is more likely to be right, **your ego or the Voice for God?**

In the world of time and space, the function that you have been assigned is forgiveness. This world's redemption depends upon those who can forgive. In time, forgiveness is an earthly form of love. In heaven, love is formless and much greater than what the experience of earthly forgiveness can impart.

In forgiveness, I forgive my brother for all the wrongs that I thought he did to me that never really occurred. It is a story that ends the need of any additional stories. It is our recognition that we have mistaken the body for the Son of God and made the illusion of separation appear real.

In our forgiveness, we give back to our brother his sinlessness and thus, we receive our own sinlessness in return. This definition of forgiveness brings about an end to a story of lack, limitation and separation. It also ends the belief that something outside ourselves has the ability to rob us of our own inner peace unless we choose to allow it to.

Your function on earth is forgiveness. When you forgive, you are accepting your role in God's plan for your own salvation. You are consciously making a decision to wake up.

Question: Salvation is defined as God's promise that all will find their way back home to God. Does this definition reduce your fear and anxiety about your ability to fulfill your part in God's plan for salvation?

LESSON 187.

I bless the world because I bless myself.

W-187.1.No one can give unless he has. 2 In fact, giving is proof of having. 3 We have made this point before **that you must have before you can give**. 4 What seems to make **this point** hard to credit is not this. 5 No one can doubt that you must first possess what you would give. 6 It is the second phase on which the world and true perception differ. 7 Having had and given, then the world asserts that you have lost what you possessed. 8 The truth maintains that giving will increase what you possess.

W-187.2.How is this possible **that giving can increase what you possess**? 2 For it is sure that if you give a finite thing away, your body's eyes will not perceive **the finite thing you give away as still** yours. 3 Yet we have learned that things but represent the thoughts that make them. 4 And you do not lack for proof that when you give ideas away, you strengthen **the ideas** in your own mind. 5 Perhaps the form in which the thought seems to appear is changed in giving. 6 Yet **the thought** must return to him who gives. 7 Nor can the form **the thought** takes be less acceptable. 8 **The thought** must be more **acceptable.**

W-187.3.Ideas must first belong to you before you give **the idea away**. 2 If you are to save the world, you first accept salvation for yourself. 3 But you will not believe that **your salvation** is done until you see the miracles **your salvation** brings to everyone you look upon. 4 Herein is the idea of giving clarified and given meaning. 5 Now you can perceive that by your giving is your store increased.

W-187.4.Protect all things you value by the act of giving them away, and you are sure that you will never lose **what you value**. 2 What you thought you did not have is thereby proven yours. 3 Yet value not its form. 4 For **the form of what you value** will change and grow unrecognizable in time, however much you try to keep **the form** safe. 5 No form endures. 6 It is the thought behind the form of things that lives unchangeable.

W-187.5.Give gladly. 2 You can only gain thereby **through your giving**. 3 The thought remains, and grows in strength as **the thought** is reinforced by giving. 4 Thoughts extend as they are shared, for **the thought** cannot be lost. 5 There is no giver and receiver in the sense the world conceives of **a giver and receiver.** 6 There is a giver who retains; another who will give as well. 7 And both must gain in this exchange, for each will have the thought in form most helpful to him. 8 What he seems to lose is always something he will value less than what will surely be returned to him.

W-187.6.Never forget you give but to yourself. 2 Who understands what giving means must laugh at the idea of sacrifice **since you only give to yourself.** 3 Nor can he **who understands what giving means** fail to recognize the many forms which sacrifice may take. 4 He **who understands what giving means** laughs as well at pain and loss, at sickness and at grief, at poverty, starvation and at death. 5 He **who understands what giving means** recognizes sacrifice remains the one idea that stands behind all **forms of suffering**, and in his gentle laughter are **the egoic ideas of lack, limitation and separation** healed.

W-187.7.Illusion recognized must disappear. 2 Accept not suffering, and you remove the thought of suffering. 3 Your blessing lies on everyone who suffers, when you choose to see all suffering **as the illusion of sacrifice that** it is. 4 The thought of sacrifice gives rise to all the forms that suffering appears to take. 5 And sacrifice is an idea so mad that sanity dismisses **the idea that giving involves sacrifice** at once.

W-187.8.Never believe that you can sacrifice. 2 There is no place for sacrifice in what has any value. 3 If the thought **that you can sacrifice** occurs, **this belief's** very presence proves that error has arisen and correction must be made **within your mind**. 4 Your blessing will correct **the thought that sacrifice is possible.** 5 **Having** given **your blessing** first to you, **your blessing** now is yours to give as well. 6 No form of sacrifice and suffering can long endure before the face of one who has forgiven and has blessed himself.

W-187.9.The lilies **of innocence and forgiveness** that your brother offers you are laid upon your altar **of your mind** with the **lilies** you offer **your brother** beside **his lilies**. 2 Who could fear to look upon such lovely holiness? 3 The great illusion of the fear of God diminishes to nothingness before the purity that you will look on here. 4 Be not afraid to look **at this altar of holiness**. 5 The blessedness you will behold will take away all thought of form, and leave instead the perfect gift forever there, forever to increase, forever yours, forever given away.

W-187.10.Now are we one in thought, for fear has gone. 2 And here, before the altar to one God, one Father, one Creator and one Thought, we stand together as one Son of God. 3 Not separate from **God** Who is our Source; not distant from one brother who is part of our one **big "S"** Self Whose innocence has joined us all as one, we stand in blessedness, and give as we receive. 4 The Name of God is on our lips. 5 And as we look within, we see the purity of Heaven shine in our reflection of our Father's Love.

W-187.11.Now are we blessed, and now we bless the world. 2 What we have looked upon we would extend, for we would see the **blessed world** everywhere. 3 We would behold **this oneness** shining with the grace of God in everyone. 4 We would not have **the blessing of grace** be withheld from anything we look upon. 5 And to ensure this holy sight **of Christ vision** is ours, we offer **the vision of Christ** to everything we see. 6 For where we see **holiness,** it will be returned to us in **the** form of lilies **of innocence and forgiveness that** we can lay upon our altar, making **the altar of your mind** a home for Innocence Itself, Who dwells in us and offers us His Holiness as our **holiness.**

Notes to Lesson #187

I bless the world because I bless myself.

This lesson asked that you bless the world because you bless yourself. Certainly if to give is to receive, when we bless another, we would receive that same blessing in return. Yet, what power do we possess that would lead us to believe that we have the authority or the right to bless the world?

Our world teaches that our experiences lead to our thoughts. We are taught that we are the product of our environment or our genetic makeup. We are brought up to believe that our mind is designed to react to outside forces and stimulus and that these external events are the original cause of our thoughts.

This leads to our belief that our mind is reactive rather than causative, and that any creative power that we possess comes from our ability to manipulate the external things in our world. External things become what we value because we assume that those things possess creative power over our thoughts.

Yet, in the world of time and space, which is the world of individuated perception, science is now in general agreement that thoughts appear to possess a creative power of their own and can even manipulate the physical world. It now appears that human consciousness or thought is the causative agent for what you call into your awareness.

This course has been attempting to demonstrate that thoughts create things. Your thoughts are the creative force behind everything you see. Things only represent the thoughts that originally made them. Thoughts come first and your experiences are the product of those thoughts.

Things are merely thought forms in slow-motion that appear temporarily frozen in time. Over time, all forms change yet, the thought that created the form remains. Because we falsely attribute creative power to the form rather than the thought that created the form, the observation that forms change over time is the source for fear.

Fear would not be possible if we did not believe that change is real. The ego's belief that form is real creates the illusion that is used by our fear-based thought system to prove that you have changed over time. This change means that you no longer remain as God created you. You no longer are perfect, whole and complete.

The world values form because it perceives form to be the reality of what you are. It fails to recognize that form is only a representation of the creative power that exists in the mind that created the form in the first place. We mistakenly believe that the form is the source behind creation.

Because of this, the world of form teaches that when you give something, you lose the creative power that the form was believed to possess. The world teaches that you now have fewer resources than you previously possessed. The egoic fear-based thought system teaches that sacrifice is required when we give something away, because it fails to recognize and acknowledge the creative power of your mind.

Both the thought systems of love and fear agree that you must possess something before you can give it away. But when you believe that form possesses its own creative power, you erroneously believe that when you give that form away, you lose that creative power. This is where the two thought systems diverge.

The thought system for love teaches that all creative power resides in the mind and therefore, when you give there is no sacrifice. When you understand that thoughts become things, you realize that the giving of form requires no sacrifice. Since thoughts never leave their source, when you give the creative power of thought to another, you strengthen that thought which remains within your own mind.

The thought is extended as it is shared but it is never lost. There is no giver or receiver with thoughts, as we traditionally associate those terms since there is no diminishment in either party. The giver of the original thought has reinforced and enhanced their idea and now there is another who can also extend that same thought. Each party benefits from the exchange of the idea and each has the thought that is most helpful to them.

When you understand the creative power of mind, you must laugh at the idea that giving requires sacrifice. Sacrifice rests on the idea in limitation. Limitation is an attribute of your belief in separation.

The world of form and the idea that you are the body are the ego's proof that the separation is real. The body is a concrete example of fear in form. The ego has erroneously assigned the creative power of the mind to a form that lacks any creative power of its own.

When you reclaim the creative power of your own mind, you reinstate the truth that your mind is the creative force that powers and generates your provisional reality. You realize that you are the dreamer and therefore, you have the power to end the dream of lack, limitation and separation.

You now realize there is no one to blame or forgive but yourself and your own past egoic beliefs. You now can become a messenger for the truth of what you really are. You can forgive yourself for your detour into fear and fear will simply dissolve away. Fear is merely false evidence appearing real.

By holding and sharing the thought of the creative power of mind with another, you open the door for another to accept their own holiness. When you look past the body and see another as part of the Oneness of All That Is, you help them heal their belief in lack, limitation and separation and their healed mind is made holy and whole. Because you realize the power of mind and what you really are, you now are in the position of blessing your world with the truth that all are part of the shared Mind of God.

When you share that thought with another, you strengthen the idea that all are unlimited spirit and as such there is no external power that can rob anyone of their divine inheritance accept themselves. When you do this, you bless the world because you bless and recognize the sinlessness and innocence of your big "S" Self, your Christ nature.

Question: If you realized that thoughts are the causative power behind all things, would you still believe that giving required sacrifice?

LESSON 188.

The peace of God is shining in me now.

W-188.1.Why wait for Heaven? 2 Those who seek the light are merely covering their eyes. 3 The light is in them now. 4 Enlightenment is but a recognition, not a change at all. 5 Light is not of the world, yet you who bear the light in you are alien **in this world** as well. 6 The light came with you from your native home, and stayed with you because it is your own **light**. 7 **Light** is the only thing you bring with you from **God** Who is your Source. 8 **Light** shines in you because it lights your home, and leads you back to **your Source** where light came from and you are at home.

W-188.2.This light cannot be lost. 2 Why wait to find **the light** in the future, or believe **the light** has been lost already, or was never there? 3 **The light** can so easily be looked upon that arguments which prove **the light** is not there become ridiculous. 4 Who can deny the presence of what he beholds in him? 5 It is not difficult to look within, for there **within your mind** all vision starts. 6 There is no sight, be it of dreams or from a truer Source, that is not but the shadow of the seen through inward vision. 7 There **through inward vision** perception starts, and there **perception** ends. 8 **Perception** has no source but this **inward vision of your mind**.

W-188.3.The peace of God is shining in you now, and from your heart extends around the world. 2 **The peace of God** pauses to caress each living thing, and leaves a blessing with it that remains forever and forever. 3 What **the peace of God** gives must be eternal. 4 **The peace of God** removes all thoughts of the ephemeral and valueless. 5 **The peace of God** brings renewal to all tired hearts, and lights all vision as it passes by. 6 All of **peace's** gifts are given everyone, and everyone unites in giving thanks to you who give, and you who have received **the peace of God**.

W-188.4.The **light** shining in your mind reminds the world of what **the world** has forgotten, and the world restores the memory **of the light** to you as well. 2 From you salvation radiates with gifts beyond all measure, given and returned. 3 To you, the giver of the gift, does God Himself give thanks. 4 And in **God's** blessing does the light in you shine brighter, adding to the gifts you have to offer to the world.

W-188.5.The peace of God can never be contained. 2 Who recognizes **the peace of God** within himself must give **the peace of God**. 3 And the means for giving **the peace of God** are in his understanding. 4 He forgives because he recognized the truth in him. 5 The peace of God is shining in you now, and in all living things. 6 In quietness is **the peace of God** acknowledged universally. 7 For what your inward vision looks upon is your perception of the universe.

W-188.6.Sit quietly and close your eyes. 2 The light within you is sufficient. 3 **The light within you** alone has power to give the gift of sight to you. 4 Exclude the outer world, and let your thoughts fly to the peace within. 5 **Your thoughts** know the way. 6 For honest thoughts, untainted by the **ego's** dream of worldly things outside yourself, become the holy messengers of God Himself.

W-188.7.These **honest** thoughts you think with **God**. 2 **The thoughts you think with God** recognize their home. 3 And **these honest thoughts** point surely to their Source, Where God the Father and the Son are One. 4 God's peace is shining on **these honest thoughts**, but they must remain with you as well, for **these honest thoughts** were born within your mind, as yours was born in God's **Mind**. 5 **These thoughts you think with God** lead you back to peace, from where **these honest thoughts** came but to remind you how you must return.

W-188.8.**These thoughts you think with God** heed your Father's Voice when you refuse to listen. 2 And **these honest thoughts** urge you gently to accept **God's** Word for what you are, instead of **your ego's** fantasies and shadows. 3 **These thoughts you think with God** remind you that you are the co-creator of all things that live. 4 For as the peace of God is shining in you, **the peace of God** must shine on **all things that live**.

W-188.9.We practice coming nearer to the light in us today. 2 We take our wandering thoughts, and gently bring **our wandering thoughts** back to where they fall in line with all the thoughts we share with God. 3 We will not let **our thoughts** stray. 4 We let the light within our minds direct **our wandering thoughts** to come home. 5 We have betrayed **our thoughts**, ordering that they depart from us. 6 But now we call **our wandering thoughts** back, and wash them clean of strange **egoic** desires and disordered wishes. 7 We restore to **our wandering thoughts** the holiness of their inheritance.

W-188.10.Thus are our minds restored with **our wandering thoughts**, and we acknowledge that the peace of God still shines in us, and from us to all living things that share our life. 2 We will forgive them all, absolving all the world from what we thought **the world** did to us. 3 For it is we who make the world as we would have **the world** be. 4 Now we choose that **the world** be innocent, devoid of sin and open to salvation. 5 And we lay our saving blessing on **the world**, as we say:
6 The peace of God is shining in me now.
7 Let all things shine upon me in that peace, And let me bless **all things** with the light in me.

Notes to Lesson #188

The peace of God is shining in me now.

Enlightenment is not a change but merely a recognition that the light is in you now. We have been taught that we are guilty sinners who have offended God, lost paradise and must perform penance to earn our way back into heaven.

In the egoic world of form, if you lose something you must seek outside yourself to recover what you lost. Because of our belief in sin, guilt and fear, our ego says that we have lost the light which represents our connection to God, our Source. The ego, however, has developed a plan to earn our enlightenment back. Our ego's plan calls for looking outside our own minds to recover what our ego perceives our minds have lost.

The ego believes there is something we must do to earn or obtain enlightenment. Therefore, we fail to look within and recognize that the light was never lost. God could never abandon His Creation. Creation is an extension of the One Self. We have just failed to remember this truth.

Instead of looking within our own mind, our ego has told us that we can recover the light that we seek by following an alien fear-based thought system. Yet, it is this same thought system that is designed to hide the truth that we are the light. When we follow the ego's plan, we are looking in the wrong place because both the light and our true big "S" Self are aliens in the ego's fearful world of perception.

Light is the peace of God. Light is the remembrance or Thoughts of God. Light is not of this world because God did not create a world of lack, limitation and separation. The world we perceive to be our provisional reality is the product of our egoic fear-based thought system.

Light comes from God, our Source, and cannot be lost. Light is the Source of all that lives. Because of this, the light or love of God is the only thing that we brought with us on our detour into fear. It is this light that we must follow to lead us back to Our Source and our true home.

In the near death experience, people speak of going into the light and following it to a world of only love, peace and oneness. God's love is our true home.

In meditation, we speak of quieting your mind and going within to find that same light. When you meditate, you will have honest thoughts which are untainted by your egoic fear-based thought system. Follow those thoughts and you will temporarily drop your mind's association with your dream world of provisional reality.

These thoughts or experiences of going into the light are thoughts you think with God. They remind us that we are co-creators with God and all things that live. We are part of that One Self.

Yesterday's lesson was the idea that in order to prove you have something, you must give it away. The light is within you and cannot be contained. It must shine and extend its true nature. Enlightenment and the peace of God cannot be obtained but only recognized. They are your natural birthright. Because of this, both enlightenment and the peace of God have already been given and are in all of us. Yet, the only way we will recognize this fact is to give them both away.

Your mind is the creative power behind what you perceive. You must decide which thought system you will follow. When fear controls your thoughts, you will fail to recognize the light within. When you go within and follow the guidance of the Holy Spirit, you will find that light. The thought system of love and forgiveness will be followed and you will co-create with God.

Light symbolizes the love of God. In this world of form, forgiveness is the form that represents this love on earth. When you forgive the world for all you thought the world did to you, you realize that you made your world. You acknowledge the truth that your world is a reflection of your thinking and that nothing can steal the peace of God from you unless you choose to allow it.

You can choose to see an innocent world, free from all thoughts of lack, limitation and separation. You can make a conscious decision to now see an innocent and sinless world. By choosing the loving and forgiving thoughts that you share with God, you can restore the world to its holiness.

Now you are co-creating with God and by this action you recognize the peace of God and your enlightenment. By giving your world your own sinlessness and innocence, you recognize and you prove that you have those same attributes.

This is the recognition of an enlightened master and that the peace of God is shining in you.

Question: What, if anything, must you to do to earn your enlightenment?

LESSON 189.

I feel the Love of God within me now.

W-189.1.There is a light in you the world cannot perceive. 2 And with **your physical** eyes you will not see this light, for you are blinded by the world. 3 Yet you have eyes to see **the light in you**. 4 **The light in you** is there for you to look upon. 5 **The light in you** was not placed in you to be kept hidden from your sight. 6 This light is a reflection of the thought we practice now. 7 To feel the Love of God within you is to see the world anew, shining in innocence, alive with hope, and blessed with perfect charity and love.

W-189.2.Who could feel fear in such a world as this **world where you feel the love of God within you**? 2 **This world that reflects God's love within you** welcomes you, rejoices that you came, and sings your praises as it keeps you safe from every form of danger and of pain. 3 **This world where you feel God's love within you** offers you a warm and gentle home in which to stay a while. 4 **This world that reflects God's love** blesses you throughout the day, and watches through the night as silent guardian of your holy sleep. 5 **This world where you feel God's love within you** sees salvation in you, and protects the light in you, in which it sees its own **light**. 6 **This world that reflects God's love** offers you its flowers and its snow, in thankfulness for your benevolence.

W-189.3.This is the world the Love of God reveals. 2 It is so different from the **egoic** world **of fear that** you see through darkened eyes of malice and of fear, that one belies the other. 3 Only one **of those two worlds** can be perceived at all. 4 The other one is wholly meaningless. 5 A world in which forgiveness shines on everything, and peace offers its gentle light to everyone, is inconceivable to those who see a world of hatred rising from attack, poised to avenge, to murder and destroy.

W-189.4.Yet is the world of hatred equally unseen and inconceivable to those who feel God's Love in them. 2 **The** world **of those who feel God's Love in them** reflects the quietness and peace that shines in them; the gentleness and innocence they see surrounding them; the joy with which they look out from the endless wells of joy within. 3 What **those who feel God's Love in them** have felt in them, they look upon, and see **God's love's** sure reflection everywhere **in their world**.

W-189.5.What **world** would you see? 2 The choice is given you. 3 But learn and do not let your mind forget this law of seeing: You will look upon that which you feel within. 4 If hatred finds a place within your heart, you will perceive a fearful world, held cruelly in death's sharp-pointed, bony fingers. 5 If you feel the Love of God within you, you will look out on a world of mercy and of love.

W-189.6.Today we pass **egoic** illusions **of lack, limitation and separation**, as we seek to reach to what is true in us, and feel **truth's** all-embracing tenderness, its Love which knows us perfect as itself, its sight which is the gift its Love bestows on us. 2 We learn the way today. 3 It is as sure as Love itself, to which it carries us. 4 For its simplicity avoids the snares the foolish convolutions of the world's apparent reasoning but serve to hide **the truth in us**.

W-189.7.Simply do this: Be still, and lay aside all thoughts of what you are and what God is; all concepts you have learned about the world; all images you hold about yourself. 2 Empty your mind of everything **your mind** thinks is either true or false, or good or bad, of every thought **your mind** judges worthy, and all the ideas of which it is ashamed. 3 Hold onto nothing. 4 Do not bring with you one thought the past has taught, nor one belief you ever learned before from anything. 5 Forget this world, forget this course, and come with wholly empty hands unto your God.

W-189.8.Is it not **God** Who knows the way to you? 2 You need not know the way to **God**. 3 Your part is simply to allow all obstacles that you have interposed between the Son and God the Father to be quietly removed forever. 4 God will do His part in joyful and immediate response. 5 Ask and receive. 6 But do not make demands, nor point the road to God by which **God** should appear to you. 7 The way to reach **God** is merely to let **God** be. 8 For in that way is your reality proclaimed as well.

W-189.9.And so today we do not choose the way in which we go to **God**. 2 But we do choose to let **God** come. 3 And with this choice we rest. 4 And in our quiet hearts and open minds, **God's** Love will blaze its pathway of itself. 5 What has not been denied is surely there, if **what has not been denied is** true, it can be surely reached. 6 God knows His Son, and knows the way to **His Son**. 7 **God** does not need His Son to show **God** how to find His **Son's** way. 8 Through every opened door **God's** Love shines outward from its home within, and lightens up the world in innocence.

W-189.10. <Father, we do not know the way to You. 2 But we have called, and You have answered us. 3 We will not interfere. 4 Salvation's ways are not our own, for **salvation's way** belongs to You. 5 And it is unto You we look for **salvation**. 6 Our hands are open to receive Your gifts. 7 We have no thoughts we think apart from You, and cherish no **egoic** beliefs of what we are, or Who created us. 8 Yours is the way that we would find and follow. 9 And we ask but that Your Will, which is our own **will** as well, be done in us and in the world, that **the world** become a part of Heaven now. 10 Amen.>

Notes to Lesson #189

I feel the Love of God within me now.

This lesson states that when you "feel the love of God within you, you will see the world anew, shining in innocence, alive with hope, and blessed with perfect charity and love."

How is such a dramatic change possible?

What we see as our outer world reflects what we feel in our inner world. We have been given a choice between two possible worlds. We either see a fearful world or a world of love and mercy. This choice is not controlled by our intellect or logical mind. Rather it is made through our feelings.

Your feelings can override your mind's logic and are the true litmus test that determines what your mind truly desires, believes and values. Even though your feelings control this choice, it is important that your logical mind remembers that you, as decision-maker, are the one freely making the choice between love and fear. This decision determines what type of world you choose to perceive.

The law of seeing states: "You will look upon that which you feel within. If hatred finds a place in your heart, you will perceive a fearful world, held cruelly by death's sharp pointed bony fingers. If you feel the love of God within you, you will look out on a world of mercy and of love."

The law of seeing confirms the idea that your world is a reflection of the creative power of your own mind. Your thoughts and feelings are causative and determine how you will view and interpret the circumstances and events that seem to swirl independently around you. You can either choose to look upon your world through the eyes of fear or the eyes of love and forgiveness.

Your thoughts are the precursors for your experience. Thoughts, raised to the level of beliefs, become your provisional reality. Thoughts always come first and are the cause for the experience that follows. The law of seeing states that your experiences merely align and conform to what you feel within.

Your ego is wrong to assert that there is some outside force that can cause you to lose your inner peace. The peace of God is your divine birthright that is given to all God created and cannot be lost. It is only your own split mind's decision to move into fear that obscures and hides this truth and prevents you from seeing this world of mercy and love.

If you wish to obtain this new vision, you need to feel the love of God within you. If you are to achieve this new worldview, you need a new plan with a new vision. You need to drop your allegiance to the ego's fear-based thought system.

This lesson asks you to be still, quiet your mind and go within. Empty your mind of all egoic thoughts and drop your ego's plans and judgments. Do not bring one thought the past has taught you or one belief you ever learned previously. You are to forget this world. Forget A Course in Miracles and come with wholly empty hands to God.

Your ego does not need to develop a plan for you to find God. God has not left or forgotten you. Your ego's plans have obscured the vision of Christ from your sight. All your egoic beliefs are obstacles that have been placed between God and yourself, His Son. When you silence the voice for fear and listen, you will hear the Voice for God.

Your ego believes this fear-based world is your home. The Holy Spirit knows your big "S" Self is an alien in the ego's world of hate and fear. Stop participating in the ego's game of hide and seek and let God find you.

Question: Does the law of seeing support your ego's belief that your outside world is a fixed and independent force that is unaffected by your own mind's thoughts and beliefs?

LESSON 190.

I choose the joy of God instead of pain.

W-190.1.Pain is a wrong perspective. 2 When **pain** is experienced in any form, **pain** is a proof of self-deception. 3 **Pain** is not a fact at all. 4 There is no form **that pain** takes that will not disappear if seen aright. 5 For pain proclaims God cruel. 6 How could **pain** be real in any form? 7 **Pain** witnesses to God the Father's hatred of His Son, the sinfulness **God** sees in **His Son**, and **the Father's** insane desire for revenge and death.

W-190.2.Can such projections **of pain** be attested to? 2 Can **these projections of pain** be anything but wholly false? 3 Pain is but witness to the Son's mistakes in what **the split-minded ego** thinks he is. 4 **Pain** is a dream of fierce retaliation for a crime **against God** that could not be committed; for **a fictitious** attack on **God Who** is wholly unassailable. 5 **Pain** is a nightmare of abandonment by an Eternal Love, which could not leave the Son whom **God** created out of love.

W-190.3.**To those who believe they are sinners,** pain is a sign illusions reign in place of truth. 2 **To the egoic mind, pain** demonstrates God is denied, confused with fear, perceived as mad, and seen as traitor to Himself. 3 If God is real, there is no pain. 4 If pain is real, there is no God. 5 For vengeance is not part of love. 6 And fear, denying love and using pain to prove that God is dead, has shown that death is victor over life. 7 The body is the Son of God, corruptible in death, as mortal as the Father **the split-minded Son imagines** he has slain.

W-190.4.Peace to such foolishness! 2 The time has come to laugh at such insane ideas **of pain's reality that would proclaim a God of Love to be cruel.** 3 There is no need to think of **these insane ideas** as savage crimes, or secret sins with weighty consequence. 4 Who but a madman could conceive of **these insane ideas** as cause of anything? 5 Their witness, pain, is mad as they **who would proclaim a God of Love to be cruel.** And **pain is** no more to be feared than the insane illusions which **pain** shields. For pain tries to demonstrate **that a God of Love when disobeyed is cruel and revengeful and that this** must still be true **because you suffer pain.**

W-190.5.It is your thoughts alone that cause you pain. 2 Nothing external to your mind can hurt or injure you in any way. 3 There is no cause beyond yourself that can reach down and bring oppression. 4 No one but yourself affects you. 5 There is nothing in the world that has the power to make you ill or sad, or weak or frail. 6 But it is you who have the power to dominate all things you see by merely recognizing what you are. 7 As you perceive the harmlessness in **all things, all things** will accept your holy will as **their will**. 8 And what was seen as fearful now becomes a source of innocence and holiness.

W-190.6.My holy brother, think of this awhile: The world you see does nothing. 2 **The world you see** has no effects at all. 3 **The world you see** merely represents your thoughts. 4 And **the world you see** will change entirely as you elect to change your mind, and choose the joy of God as what you really want. 5 Your **big "S" Self** is radiant in this holy joy, unchanged, unchanging and unchangeable, forever and forever. 6 And would you deny a little corner of your **split** mind its own **divine** inheritance, and keep **the egoic mind** as a hospital for pain; a sickly place where living things must come at last to die?

W-190.7.The world may seem to cause you pain. 2 And yet the world, as causeless, has no power to cause. 3 **The world you see** is an effect **and an effect** cannot make effects. 4 As an illusion, **the world you see** is what you wish. 5 Your idle **egoic** wishes represent **the** pains **you see in your world**. 6 Your strange desires bring evil dreams **to the world you see**. 7 Your thoughts of death envelop **the world you see** in fear, while in your kind forgiveness does **the world** live.

W-190.8.Pain is the thought of evil taking form, and working havoc in your holy mind. 2 Pain is the ransom you have gladly paid not to be free. 3 In pain is God denied the Son He loves. 4 In pain does fear appear to triumph over love, and time replace eternity and Heaven. 5 And **in pain** the world becomes a cruel and a bitter place, where sorrow rules and little joys give way before the onslaught of the savage pain that waits to end all joy in misery.

W-190.9.Lay down your arms, and come without defense into the quiet place where Heaven's peace holds all things still at last. 2 Lay down all thoughts of danger and of fear. 3 Let no attack enter with you. 4 Lay down the cruel sword of judgment that you hold against your throat, and put aside the withering assaults **of egoic misperceptions about your big "S" Self** with which **your ego** seeks to hide your **big "S" Self's** holiness.

W-190.10.Here, **when you drop all egoic thoughts of danger, fear and judgment** will you understand there is no pain. 2 Here, **in your defenselessness**, does the joy of God belong to you. 3 This is the day when it is given you to realize the lesson that contains all of salvation's power. 4 **The lesson that contains all of salvation's power** is this: Pain is illusion; joy **is** reality. 5 Pain is but sleep; joy is awakening. 6 Pain is deception; joy alone is truth.

W-190.11.And so again we make the only choice that ever can be made; we choose between illusions and the truth, or pain and joy, or hell and Heaven. 2 Let our gratitude unto our Teacher, **the Holy Spirit**, fill our hearts, as we are free to choose our joy instead of pain, our holiness in place of sin, the peace of God instead of conflict, and the light of Heaven for the darkness of the world.

Notes to Lesson #190

I choose the joy of God instead of pain.

This lesson is critical to reawakening our sleeping mind to the truth of what we are. This lesson contradicts and overturns what this world of fear and hate was designed to teach us. It states that our mind, not some external force beyond our control, is the cause of the world you perceive. This world is merely an effect of your mind's own thinking and is powerless to affect anything at all. As we have said many times in many different ways, the world is a reflection of you.

Pain is incorrect perception. When you experience pain in any form, it proves that self-deception is currently ruling your mind. Pain has no reality except in the deluded mind of the one who thinks it. To your ego, pain is the proof that you are not God's beloved Child with whom God is well pleased. Pain confirms that you do not know what you are and that your mind has accepted your ego's limiting beliefs.

Pain proclaims that God is cruel. Pain bears false witness to God's hatred for His sinful son. Pain embodies our egoic belief that the illusion of lack, limitation and separation is real and has replaced the truth. Pain is based on the belief that God is vulnerable, could be hurt and when hurt, love responds to their disobedient child with cruelty, punishment and revenge.

If a God is real, there is no pain. If pain is real, the God of love must be dead or an illusion. A God of only love and a God that would punish and inflict pain cannot both be real. For each is a contradiction of the other. Only one God can be the truth.

Your egoic thought system is based on the belief that you are a limited ego body in competition with other ego bodies. This is based on the belief that there are outside forces that are beyond your control. These outside forces are the cause of your world and you are an effect of those forces. It sees you as a victim and not the creator of your world.

This lesson states that the source of your world is your mind. That pain, like your world, is the result of your own thinking and there is nothing external that can hurt you but yourself. As a Child of God, you have been given the power to dominate all things on earth as well as Heaven by merely recognizing the truth of what you really are and reclaiming your divine inheritance.

This is a world of perception, not absolute reality. As such, it is pliable and follows your will, thoughts and beliefs. Perceive your world as harmless and holy and your world will accept your viewpoint and reflect that same harmless, innocent and holy nature you assigned to it. Your world is an effect of your thinking. An effect is neutral in that it has no causative powers of its own. Being an effect, your world has no ability to impact or create other effects.

The world you see represents your thoughts and will change only when you truly want it to change. In each moment in time, you get to decide what you will value and why. You, as decision-maker, must decide whether your world will bear witness for either fear or love. When will you decide to choose the joy of God instead of pain?

Pain is illusion, sleep and deception. The joy of God is reality and represents a mind that is awake and knows what it is. It is a choice between truth versus illusion; pain versus joy; heaven versus hell; or joining versus separation. The world reflects your mind's true beliefs, desires and wants. These beliefs are often hidden and buried deep within your mind and may not be what you consciously claim you desire. Because your mind's beliefs and desires make your world, by looking at your experiences, you can determine what you truly value, desire and want.

This lesson asks that you accept responsibility for your world of dreams. It asks you to drop your belief in victims and victimizers and lay aside all your ego's plans for your self-defense. God's Son needs no defense. Defenses make the illusion of lack, limitation, separation and pain all seem real.

Since your mind is the causative agent for your world, replace your ego's misperceptions with the truth of the thought system of the Holy Spirit. Choose to see your world as innocent and sinless. Accept the creative power of your mind and know that you make your own provisional reality. Yet, also know that in your defenselessness, God's Son is invulnerable. When you do this, the illusion of a fearful world is transformed into a world of mercy and love.

On the game board of time, you are the writer and director for all the experiences that you call into your awareness. You get to decide if you will star in comedies or tragedies.

The world you see does nothing to you and has no causative power to affect anything. Your world only reflects your mind's wants, values and desires. Nothing sources your experience but your own mind and nothing can rob you of your own peace unless you choose to write the script that way.

Question: If you seek the peace of God and are your own script writer, why are you told to lay down your weapons, defenses and judgments?

LESSON 191.

I am the holy Son of God Himself.

W-191.1.Here **in the statement, I am the holy Son of God Himself,** is your declaration of release from bondage of the world. 2 And here **in this declaration** as well is all the world released. 3 You do not see what you have done by giving to the world the role of jailer to the Son of God. 4 What could **the world that jails God's Son be** but vicious and afraid, fearful of shadows, punitive and wild, lacking all reason, blind, insane with hate?

W-191.2.What have you done that this should be your world **to fear**? 2 What have you done that this is what you see? 3 Deny your own Identity **as your big "S" Self,** and this **fearful world** is what remains. 4 You look on chaos and proclaim **this fearful identity** is yourself. 5 There is no sight that fails to witness **this false identity of your littleness** to you. 6 There is no sound that does not speak of frailty within you and without; no breath you draw that does not seem to bring you nearer death; no hope you hold but will dissolve in tears.

W-191.3.Deny your own Identity **of your big "S" Self as God's Son,** and you will not escape the madness which induced this weird, unnatural and ghostly thought that mocks creation and that laughs at God. 2 Deny your own Identity **as God's Son,** and you assail the universe alone, without a friend, a tiny particle of dust against the legions of your enemies. 3 Deny your own Identity **of your Christ nature,** and look on evil, sin and death, and watch despair snatch from your fingers every scrap of hope, leaving you nothing but the wish to die.

W-191.4.Yet what is it except a game you play in which **your true** Identity **of your big "S" Self** can be denied? 2 You are as God created you. 3 All else but this one thing **that you are as God created you** is folly to believe. 4 In this one thought **that you are as God created you** is everyone set free. 5 In this one truth **that you are as God created you** are all illusions gone. 6 In this one fact **that you are as God created you** is sinlessness proclaimed to be forever part of everything, the central core of **everything's** existence and its guarantee of immortality.

W-191.5.But let today's idea **that you are the holy Son of God Himself** find a place among your thoughts and you have risen far above the **ego's** world **of fear,** and all the worldly thoughts that hold **the world its** prisoner. 2 And from this place of safety and escape you will return and set **the ego's world of fear** free. 3 For he who can accept his true Identity **as his Christ nature** is truly saved. 4 And his salvation is the gift he **who accepts his Christ nature's identity** gives to everyone, in gratitude to **the Holy Spirit** Who pointed out the way to happiness that changed his whole perspective of the world.

W-191.6.One holy thought like this **that you are the holy Son of God** and you are free: You are the holy Son of God Himself. 2 And with this holy thought you learn as well that you have freed the world. 3 You have no need to use **the world** cruelly, and then perceive this savage need **for cruelty to belong to the world.** 4 You set **the world** free of your imprisonment. 5 You will not see a devastating image of **your little "s" self** walking the world in terror, with the world twisting in agony because your fears have laid the mark of death upon the heart of **your little "s" self.**

W-191.7.Be glad today how very easily is hell undone. 2 You need but tell yourself:
3 I am the holy Son of God Himself. 4 I, **God's holy Son** cannot suffer, cannot be in pain; I cannot suffer loss, nor fail to do all that salvation asks.
5 And in that thought **that you are the holy Son of God** is everything you look on wholly changed.

W-191.8.A miracle has lighted up all dark and ancient caverns, where the rites of death echoed since time began. 2 For time has lost its hold upon the world. 3 The Son of God has come in glory to redeem the lost, to save the helpless, and to give the world the gift of **the Son of God's** forgiveness. 4 Who could see the world as dark and sinful, when God's Son has come again at last to set **the world** free **from your ego's erroneous beliefs?**

W-191.9.You who perceive yourself as weak and frail, with futile hopes and devastated dreams, born but to die, to weep and suffer pain, hear this: All power is given unto you, **the Son of God,** in earth and Heaven. 2 **As the Son of God,** there is nothing that you cannot do. 3 You play the game of death, of being helpless, pitifully tied to dissolution in a world which shows no mercy to you. 4 Yet when you accord **the world** mercy, will **the world's** mercy shine on you.

W-191.10.Then let the Son of God awaken from his sleep, and opening his holy eyes, return again to bless the world he made. 2 In error **the world of fear** began, but **the world** will end in the reflection of **the Son of God's** holiness. 3 And **God's Son** will sleep no more and dream of death. 4 Then join with me today. 5 Your glory is the light that saves the world. 6 Do not withhold salvation longer. 7 Look about the world, and see the suffering there. 8 Is not your heart willing to bring your weary brothers rest?

W-191.11.**Your brothers** must await your own release. 2 **Your brothers** stay in chains till you are free. 3 **Your brothers** cannot see the mercy of the world until you find **mercy** in yourself. 4 **Your brothers** suffer pain until you have denied **pain's** hold on you. 5 **Your brothers** die till you accept your own eternal life. 6 You are the holy Son of God Himself. 7 Remember **that you are the holy Son of God** and all the world is free. 8 Remember **that you are the holy Son of God** and earth and Heaven are one.

I am the holy Son of God Himself.

Yesterday's lesson stated that your thoughts make the world you perceive. This ability to create your own world demonstrates how powerful your mind is.

Your world of perception is the product of your own mind's beliefs. Your mind's beliefs are reflected in the world that you see. Because of this, how you define yourself becomes critical to your world since your self-identity provides the foundation for your entire belief system.

I am the holy son of God is the declaration that will release you from your ego's beliefs in lack, limitation and separation. Because we follow our ego's thought system, we have accepted the idea that we are the product of that same lack, limitation and separation. We see ourselves as a little "s" self that is an effect of outside forces that are beyond our control. We abdicate the true creative power of our mind to a fantasy world letting this world of illusions become the prison for our mind and God's Son.

Since we are God's Son, we have been given all the power in heaven and earth. Our mind has the ability to be or imagine anything that it wants. Our mind is a creative powerhouse in our universe. When we act according to our true nature as our big "S" Self, our mind has the ability to co-create with God. In co-creation, we extend the thoughts we share with the Mind of God.

When we follow the thought system of the ego, we come from fear and make or imagine an illusionary world that does not align with the truth. Since our fearful beliefs are not part of the shared Mind of God, they are not real. Instead, these experiences are played out on the game board of time, appear real only within our own deluded split mind and become our mind's world of perception.

Because of the creative power of mind, our beliefs create the world of perception. Whether our beliefs are true or false, those beliefs become the world we perceive in time and become the provisional reality that we experience and perceive.

Because of our erroneous egoic belief in lack, limitation and separation, our mind's limiting beliefs have created a world that is an appropriate jailer for the little "s" self that our mind perceives itself to be. When you reclaim your divine birthright as God's beloved Son, you free your mind, yourself and your world from your ego's limiting beliefs about itself.

Insanity is a game we play when we deny our true identity as our big "S" Self. Since our denial cannot change the truth that we remain as God created us, this game of What Am I is played within our minds imagination upon the game board of time. The ultimate purpose of the game of What Am I is to rediscover our true identity as our big "S" Self. By accepting the belief that we remain as God created us, we are released from our ego's limiting beliefs.

When you change your beliefs about what you are, you automatically change your perception about your world. What you once perceived to be a hell that jailed your little "s" self now disappears and is replaced by a world of mercy and love.

Once you accept your own innocence and sinlessness, you are in a position to give that same message to your world. To give is to receive and by giving you prove that you have. By sharing the idea that you are the holy Son of God with your brother, that idea is extended and strengthened.

Since your world is a reflection of your beliefs, your world will also be released from your belief in lack, limitation and separation. When you believe you are God's Son and accept your own eternal life, pain, suffering and death will end.

Because your mind made the world you perceive, your mind has always possessed the creative power to grant mercy upon your world. When you reclaim your divine birthright, there is nothing you cannot do. You, your brother and your world will be set free only because you have accepted the truth of what you really are. When you remember that you are the holy Son of God, earth and heaven become one.

Question: In your world of perception, why does your brother remain in chains until you free yourself from your ego's belief in lack, limitation and separation?

LESSON 192.

I have a function God would have me fill.

W-192.1.It is your Father's holy Will that you complete Himself, and that your **big "S" Self** shall be **God's** sacred Son, forever pure as **God**, of love created and in love preserved, extending love, creating in **love's** name, forever one with God and with your **Christ nature**. 2 Yet what can such a function **of completing God** mean within a world of envy, hatred and attack?

W-192.2.Therefore, you have a function in the world in its own terms **which deal with the correction of the envy, hatred and attack that appear to exist here**. 2 For who can understand an **alien** language **of fear** far beyond his simple grasp? 3 Forgiveness represents your function here **in this world of fear**. 4 **This world of fear** is not God's creation, for **the world the ego perceives** is the means by which untruth can be undone. 5 And who would pardon Heaven? 6 Yet on earth, you need the means to let **egoic** illusions go. 7 Creation merely waits for your return **as your big "S" Self** to be acknowledged, not to be complete.

W-192.3.Creation cannot even be conceived of in the world **your ego perceives**. 2 **Creation** has no meaning here. 3 Forgiveness is the closest **that creation** can come to on earth. 4 For being Heaven-born, **creation** has no form at all. 5 Yet God created One, **the Big "S" Self,** Who has the power to translate in form the wholly formless. 6 What **the Big "S" Self** makes are dreams, but of a kind **of dream** so close to waking that the light of day already shines in **the Big "S" Self's dreams** and eyes already opening behold the joyful sights the offerings **of these dreams** contain.

W-192.4.Forgiveness gently looks upon all things unknown in Heaven **like lack, limitation, fear and separation and** sees them disappear, and leaves the world a clean and unmarked slate on which the Word of God can now replace the senseless symbols written there before. 2 Forgiveness is the means by which the fear of death is overcome, because **death** holds no fierce attraction now and guilt is gone. 3 Forgiveness lets the body be perceived as what **the body** is; a simple teaching aid. **And the body** is to be laid by when learning is complete, but hardly changing him who learns at all.

W-192.5.The mind without the body cannot make mistakes. 2 **The mind without the body** cannot think that it will die, nor be the prey of merciless attack. 3 Anger becomes impossible, and where is terror then? 4 What fears could still assail those who have lost **the body, which is** the source of all attack, the core of anguish and the seat of fear? 5 Only forgiveness can relieve the mind of thinking that the body is **the Son of God's** home. 6 Only forgiveness can restore the peace that God intended for His holy Son. 7 Only forgiveness can persuade the Son to look again upon his holiness **as his Christ nature**.

W-192.6.With anger gone, you will indeed perceive that **holiness**, for Christ's vision and the gift of sight, no sacrifice was asked, and only pain was lifted from a sick and tortured mind. 2 Is this **release from pain** unwelcome? 3 Is **this release from pain** to be feared? 4 Or is **this release from pain** to be hoped for, met with thanks and joyously accepted? 5 We are one, and therefore give up nothing. 6 But we have indeed been given everything by God.

W-192.7.Yet do we need forgiveness to perceive that this **release from pain and our oneness** is so. 2 Without the kindly light **of forgiveness** we grope in darkness, using reason but to justify our rage and our attack. 3 **Without the light of forgiveness**, our understanding is so limited that what we think we understand is but confusion born of error. 4 **Without the light of forgiveness,** we are lost in mists of shifting dreams and fearful thoughts, our eyes shut tight against the light; our minds engaged in worshipping what is not there.

W-192.8.Who can be born again in Christ but him who has forgiven everyone he sees or thinks of or imagines? 2 Who could be set free while he imprisons anyone? 3 A jailer is not free, for **the jailer** is bound together with his prisoner. 4 **The jailer** must be sure that **his prisoner** does not escape, and so **the jailer** spends his time in keeping watch on **his prisoner**. 5 The bars that limit **his prisoner** become the world in which his jailer lives, along with **his prisoner**. 6 And it is on **his prisoner's** freedom that the way to liberty depends for both of them, **jailer and prisoner.**

W-192.9.Therefore, hold no one prisoner. 2 Release instead of bind, for thus are you made free. 3 The way is simple. 4 Every time you feel a stab of anger, realize you hold a sword above your head. 5 And **the sword of anger** will fall or be averted as you choose to be condemned or free. 6 Thus does each one who seems to tempt you to be angry represent your savior from the prison house of death. 7 And so you owe **those who tempt you to be angry, your** thanks **and forgiveness** instead of pain **and condemnation.**

W-192.10.Be merciful today. 2 The Son of God deserves your mercy. 3 It is **the Son of God, your brother,** who asks that you accept the way to freedom now. 4 Deny **God's Son who is your brother** not **his freedom and your forgiveness**. 5 His Father's Love for **your brother** belongs to you. 6 Your function here on earth is only to forgive **your brother**, that you may accept **your brother** back as your **big "S" Self's** Identity **that you both share**. 7 **Your brother** is as God created him. 8 And you are what **your brother** is **which is God's One Son**. 9 Forgive **your brother** now his sins, and you will see that you are one with **your brother**.

Notes to Lesson #192

I have a function God would have me fill.

God's Will is that you complete God by being His sacred Son, forever pure, created out of love, preserved in love, extending love, creating in love's name, forever one with God and your Christ nature. Our function is to fulfill God's Will. Yet, this lesson asks what such a function can mean within this earthly world that is dominated by envy, hate and attack?

God, being A Oneness of All That Is, is abstract. God is love. Love is formless and the totality of the One Self. God's creations are an extension of Itself. We, our big "S" Self, have been given the power to translate into form the love which is wholly formless.

In time, our purpose is to demonstrate love in form. We complete God by demonstrating within the abstract One Self specific examples of various attributes of love so in this way God knows Itself. On earth, our function is to demonstrate the attribute of love we call forgiveness.

We would all agree that forgiveness is an attribute of love. Yet, God does not forgive because there is nothing outside Itself to forgive. If love is all there is, what is there to be forgiven? In heaven, the real world, there is nothing to forgive. In heaven, it is impossible for the abstract One Self to experience the characteristic of love that we call forgiveness.

Forgiveness implies a prior act that harmed another. Without a past harm, there could be nothing to forgive. An inquisitive mind might ask this question about love. How would love respond to something opposite of itself?

Since fear is false evidence appearing real, it is not an attribute of the shared Mind of God and was not created by God. Fear, if it was real, is love's opposite. We are an aspect of God that desired to demonstrate what it would be like to be love in a non-loving world.

What would a loving response be in such a fearful world?

It is easy to be "loving" to something that is nice, sweet, caring, cute, and always helpful and kind to you. But what would love do in a world of seeming hate and fear? How would love behave when confronted by fear, anger, distrust, lack, limitation and separation?

We have freely chosen to appear in this playschool called earth that is dominated by hate and fear. Our function is to demonstrate what love would do in such an alien environment.

We cannot make the false real. Fear and hate are not real and cannot be an aspect of love. We cannot magically transform fear and hatred into love, for to do so would be to make something that is false true. But we can make the dream of separation, which is the source of fear, disappear with forgiveness.

On earth, forgiveness is a worldly form of love. Forgiveness ignores the false and realizes that the illusion of hate and fear cannot change what can only be love. Forgiveness doesn't change fear into love but it does end the story that there is something outside of love that can alter love. Forgiveness makes fear disappear.

In order to demonstrate the aspect of love called forgiveness, we had to come to a place in our mind's imagination that was foreign to love. We wanted to test and hone our skills in being love in form. It is no real test to love another who is kind, considerate and loving but to love someone when they are being angry, needy and fearful is different.

Time provides the medium in which love's opposite, fear, can appear to coexist with love. Now we really have a true test that will provide the feedback that we need to learn what love would have us do in such an alien environment.

Grace is the acceptance of the love of God in a world of seeming hate and fear. When you forgive, you do not allow the drama and circumstances that surround you to rob you of your inner peace.

You do not empower an event with some imaginary powers that can effect what love would have you do. You do not respond to hatred with cruelty or raise the level of fear within yourself or another. You do not make the illusion appear real. Instead, you respond with forgiveness.

In time, forgiveness is the means to undo illusion and bring the illusion before the truth. Before the truth, fear dissolves in the realization that nothing has the power to change what God created. You remain only love and nothing can rob you of the peace of God. Forgiveness removes past beliefs of sin, shame, blame and guilt and each is free to choose differently.

Forgiveness does not judge or make another person wrong for their decisions. It merely allows and holds the truth that each remain as God created them. Each is on their own perfect path of reawakening. Your ego's plan for fixing, changing, controlling, protecting or impressing another is dropped and the guidance of the Holy Spirit is followed.

This world and the language of fear are alien to love and yourself. This is why the definitions for common words that are used both in this course and this fearful world are radically different. Words like forgiveness, salvation, sickness, death, pain, sin, guilt, lack, limitation and separation are all fear-based terms that symbolize a fearful world and do not exist in Heaven. The language of fear is far beyond the grasp of the language of love because the language of love is not spoken. Language and words are symbols that remove you from the actual experience of being. Language is not needed within the Mind of God since all minds are joined as one.

Forgiveness is unknown in heaven since separation is impossible. Yet, without the body, you could not demonstrate love in form. Bodies are needed to experience the aspect of love we call forgiveness. Without a body, mind cannot make mistakes. Only if you have a bodily form, can there appear to be the existence of something opposite to love. This is why this world is alien to our true formless nature as mind. Yet, a body does allow us to demonstrate and experience how love would react to a world of seeming hate and fear.

Creation or extension cannot be conceived of in this world of illusion. Forgiveness is the closest to creation that we can experience on earth. Since creation is born in heaven, it has no form. Yet, God created us so that we could translate into form the wholly formless. This power within our mind allows us to experience being love in form.

On earth, our function is forgiveness, our purpose is love and our destiny is the peace of God. Forgiveness relieves the mind of thinking that the body is the home of the Son of God. Only forgiveness can persuade a sleeping mind to look again upon its own holiness.

Forgiveness restores peace to your world. Forgiveness ends the story of hatred, anger and fear that must be undone before Christ vision returns. To be born in Christ is to forgive everyone you see, think of or imagine. Forgiveness is needed for another to recognize that they too are holy for love connects and joins.

Forgiveness replaces the dream of sin with the dream of sinlessness and mercy. The body is no longer seen as the home of God's Son. Instead, the body is a teaching aid to help the learning process of reawakening from your fears. When learning is complete, the body is merely put aside. Without a body, there is no anger, death or fear for a mind without a body is incapable of making any mistakes.

On earth, our function is to forgive our brother and when we do this, we both are released from our belief in sin and are joined as one. You cannot complete God while you insist upon keeping one brother in the prison of your unforgiving mind. The unforgiving mind is the jailer of your brother and yourself. Both remained imprisoned by your belief in sin, guilt and fear. The only way to escape this prison is to forgive all.

Forgiveness ends all illusions with the realization that there is nothing outside your own mind that can rob you of the peace of God. By your forgiveness of your brother, you accept your brother back as part of your big "S" Self and are joined as one mind. When you forgive, your world of hate and fear is transformed into a world of mercy and love. By your forgiveness, what once appeared as separate wills are joined in a common purpose and become of one mind.

In the world of form, forgiveness is your function and how your big "S" Self completes God. You are the God of your world of perception. Forgiveness is the act of "Godding" in this world. When you are "Godding," you are simply following the guidance you receive from the Holy Spirit to your question of, what would love have you do.

Question: Do you see yourself as God's completion or God's mistake?

You cannot be God's completion, if you see your brother as God's mistake.

LESSON 193.

All things are lessons God would have me learn.

W-193.1.God does not know of learning. 2 Yet **God's** Will extends to what **God** does not understand, in that **God** wills the happiness His Son inherited of **God** be undisturbed; eternal and forever gaining scope, eternally expanding in the joy of full creation, and eternally open and wholly limitless in **God's Son**. 3 That **happiness of His Son** is **God's** Will. 4 And thus **God's** Will provides the means to guarantee that **the happiness of the Son of God** is done.

W-193.2.God sees no contradictions. 2 Yet **God's** Son believes he sees **contradiction to his happiness**. 3 Thus **God's Son** has a need for One, **the Holy Spirit,** Who can correct **the Son of God's** erring sight, and give **the Son** vision that will lead him back to where perception ceases. 4 God does not perceive at all. 5 Yet it is **the Holy Spirit** Who gives the means by which perception is made true and beautiful enough to let the light of Heaven shine upon **the misperception of the split mind.** 6 It is **the Holy Spirit** Who answers what **God's** Son would contradict, and keeps **God's Son** sinlessness forever safe.

W-193.3.These are the lessons God would have you learn. 2 **God's** Will reflects all **the lessons God would have you learn,** and **these lessons** reflect **God's** loving kindness to the Son He loves. 3 Each lesson has a central thought, the same in all of **the lessons God would have you learn.** 4 The form **of each lesson** alone is changed, with different circumstances and events; with different characters and different themes, apparent but not real. 5 **All the lessons God would have you learn** are the same in fundamental content. 6 It is this:
7 Forgive, and you will see this differently.

W-193.4.Certain it is that all distress does not appear to be but unforgiveness. 2 Yet un**forgiveness** is the content underneath the form **of distress**. 3 It is this sameness **of the lesson's problem and the one solution** which makes learning sure, because the lesson is so simple that **its one solution** cannot be rejected in the end. 4 No one can hide forever from a truth so very obvious that **the truth** appears in countless forms, and yet is recognized as easily in all of **the forms of the problem,** if one but wants to see the simple lesson and **its solution** there.

W-193.5.<Forgive, and you will see this differently.>
2 These are the words the Holy Spirit speaks in all your tribulations, all your pain, all suffering regardless of its form. 3 **Forgive, and you will see this differently** are the words with which temptation ends, and guilt, abandoned, is revered no more. 4 These are the words which end the dream of sin, and rid the mind of fear. 5 **Forgive, and you will see this differently** are the words by which salvation comes to all the world.

W-193.6.Shall we not learn to say these words when we are tempted to believe that pain is real, and death becomes our choice instead of life? 2 Shall we not learn to say these words, **forgive, and you will see this differently** when we have understood their power to release all minds from bondage? 3 **Forgive, and you will see this differently** are words which give you power over all events that seem to have been given power over you. 4 You see **all events** rightly when you hold these words **of forgiveness, and you will see this differently** in full awareness, and do not forget these words apply to everything you see or any brother looks upon amiss.

W-193.7.How can you tell when you are seeing wrong, or someone else is failing to perceive the lesson he should learn? 2 Does pain seem real in the perception? 3 If **pain** does **seem real,** be sure the lesson is not learned. 4 And there remains an unforgiveness hiding in the mind that sees the pain through eyes the mind directs.

W-193.8.God would not have you suffer thus. 2 **The Holy Spirit** would help you forgive yourself. 3 **God's** Son does not remember who he is. 4 And God would have the **Son** not forget **God's** Love, and all the gifts **God's** Love brings with it. 5 Would you now renounce your own salvation? 6 Would you fail to learn the simple lessons Heaven's Teacher, **the Holy Spirit** sets before you that all pain may disappear and God may be remembered by His Son?

W-193.9.All things are lessons God would have you learn. 2 **The Holy Spirit** would not leave an unforgiving thought without correction, nor one thorn or nail to hurt **God's** holy Son in any way. 3 **The Holy Spirit** would ensure **the Son's** holy rest remains untroubled and serene, without a care, in an eternal home which cares for **God's Son.** 4 And **the Holy Spirit** would have all tears be wiped away, with none remaining yet unshed, and none but waiting their appointed time to fall. 5 For God has willed that laughter should replace each **tear,** and that **God's** Son be free again.

W-193.10.We will attempt today to overcome a thousand seeming obstacles to peace in just one day. 2 Let mercy come to you more quickly. 3 Do not try to hold **forgiveness and mercy** off another day, another minute or another instant. 4 Time was made for **forgiveness.** 5 Use **time** today for what **time's** purpose is **which is for forgiveness.** 6 Morning and night, devote what time you can to serve **time's** proper aim **of forgiveness,** and do not let the time be less than meets your deepest need **of forgiveness.**

W-193.11.Give all **the time** you can **to your purpose of forgiveness,** and give a little more. 2 For now we would arise in haste and go unto our Father's house. 3 We have been gone too long, and we would linger here no more. 4 And as we practice, let us think about all things **or grievances** we saved to settle by **our ego's plan** and **thus** kept apart from **true** healing. 5 Let us give all **our grievances** to **the Holy Spirit** Who knows the way to look upon them so that **all our**

grievances will disappear. 6 Truth is **the Holy Spirit's** message; truth **the Holy Spirit's** teaching is. 7 **The Holy Spirit's messages that forgive, and you will see this differently** are the lessons God would have us learn.

W-193.12.Each hour, spend a little time today, and in the days to come, in practicing the lesson in forgiveness in the form established for the day. 2 And try to give application to **the lesson in forgiveness to any of the** happenings the hour brought, so that the next one is free of **any grievance from the hour** before. 3 The chains of time are easily unloosened in this way. 4 Let no one hour cast its shadow **of unforgiveness** on the one that follows, and when that **hour** goes, let everything that happened in its course go with it. 5 Thus will you remain unbound, in peace eternal in the world of time.

W-193.13. **Forgive, and you will see this differently** is the lesson God would have you learn: There is a way to look on everything that lets **each experience** be to you another step to **God** and to salvation of the world. 2 To all that speaks of terror, answer thus:
3 I will forgive, and this will disappear.
4 To every apprehension, every care and every form of suffering, repeat these selfsame words, **I will forgive, and this will disappear.** 5 And then you hold the key that opens Heaven's gate, and brings the Love of God the Father down to earth at last, to raise **the earth** up to Heaven. 6 God will take this final step Himself. 7 Do not deny the little steps **the Voice for God, the Holy Spirit** asks you take to **God.**

Notes to Lesson #193

All things are lessons God would have me learn.

God's Will is that His Son be wholly limitless and create like God, Himself and that your happiness be undisturbed. Yet, because we have forgotten what we are, we need to remember that truth. God's Will guarantees that we will return to the knowledge of our true Identity. To ensure this result, God has given us the Holy Spirit to teach us the learning lessons that are needed for us to reawaken to our divine birthright.

Because we identify with the ego's thought system, we perceive ourselves to be a little "s" self. We believe lack, limitation and separation are our reality. We perceive that we have needs that have not been provided by our creator. Due to this erroneous belief, we believe that our happiness and God's Will are not the same.

We see contradictions where there are none. We believe that there is something outside ourselves that we need to make us happy and that our Creator has failed to provide for our needs. Our ego, however, has developed numerous plans to insure that these perceived needs of our ego are met.

When another party fails to perform according to our ego's plan, we claim to be harmed by the other party. We blame them for their failure to make us happy and hold a grievance against them. Our ego's failure to understand that our mind is the power source for all our experiences, leads us to believe that there are external forces that oppose our happiness. We believe God's plan and our plan for our happiness are in conflict.

God does not learn. God knows. Since God knows that our mind is the powerhouse behind all our experiences, God sees no contradiction between our happiness and His Will. Whenever we see a contradiction between the two plans, it is because of the ego's desire to be different and special from the One Self.

Our ego believes that its happiness lies in its belief in separation. Unfortunately, when you accept the idea of separation, you automatically inherit the attributes of lack and limitation that accompany that belief. When the ego uses the power of the mind to create, it extends its own belief in lack, limitation and separation. Being unlimited, our ego's false fantasies can only result in our unhappiness.

God allows our ego's wish to experience lack, limitation and separation, since our split mind believes it will lead to our happiness. Unfortunately for the split minded, it only leads to pain, suffering and misery. But the Holy Spirit knows that these same experiences will provide learning lessons for our return to right mindedness.

Although the form and actors within each lesson will change over time, the theme behind all these lessons is the same. The fundamental content that all lessons are designed to teach is this:

Forgive and you will see this differently.

Your ego's beliefs and desires become your experiences that provide the lessons that are needed for your decision to reclaim your true Identity. Pain provides the feedback mechanism that allows you to monitor your state of mind. If there is any pain when you experience or review an event, you are still holding grievances and have not forgiven yourself and your world.

You remain trapped within the prison of your unforgiving mind. You are still under the misperception that if something outside your mind behaved differently, you would be happy. You have failed to claim responsibility for your own thoughts and denied the creative power of your mind.

Until you are willing to forgive as defined in this course, you will experience some form of pain associated with that experience. Whenever someone perceives pain as real, the lesson the experience was designed to teach has not been learned and they still need to forgive.

When you turn that same event over to the Holy Spirit, the Holy Spirit will reframe the experience to allow you to forgive yourself. This allows you to move out of victim consciousness and recover your inner peace. You are never a victim of outside forces that are beyond your control.

Any unforgiving thought that you hold about yourself, your world and your brother will be corrected by the Holy Spirit and your mind will be freed from that grievance. The Holy Spirit teaches the truth that heals the split mind's misperception that God's Will is different from your own will.

All stress in your life is caused by your unforgiving mind and your ego's desire to hold grievances. Forgiveness removes all thoughts of sin, guilt, fear and pain that were or are associated with any event. When you forgive, you control your fear and realize that you are the causative force for your experiences. Because of this, your mind is invulnerable and cannot be affected by anything outside your mind unless you choose to allow it.

Forgiveness has the power to release all minds from the bondage of the grievances that they hold. There is a three-step process that will give you power over all events. When anything appears that would move your mind into fear, remember these three steps as you ask for guidance.

First, remember all things are lessons God would have you learn. Next, tell yourself that when you forgive, you will see this differently. Finally, affirm that you will forgive and this will disappear. When you ask for the guidance of the Holy Spirit, repeat these three thoughts and the Holy Spirit will provide the miracle that you seek. Your inner peace will be restored.

Remember that a miracle is merely a change in your own mind's perception that moves your mind from fear to love and forgiveness.

Question: The ego teaches that you must earn your way back into heaven. The Holy Spirit teaches that you learn your way. What is the difference?

I place the future in the Hands of God.

W-194.1.Today's idea **that I place the future in the Hands of God,** takes another step toward quick salvation, and a giant stride it is indeed! 2 So great the distance is that it encompasses **that the idea that I place the future in the Hands of God** sets you down just short of Heaven, with the goal in sight and obstacles behind. 3 Your foot has reached the lawns that welcome you to Heaven's gate; the quiet place of peace, where you await with certainty the final step of God **which is your return to knowledge.** 4 How far are we progressing now from earth! 5 How close are we approaching to our goal **of remembering the truth of what we are!** 6 How short the journey still to be pursued!

W-194.2.Accept today's idea **that you place the future in the Hands of God,** and you have passed all anxiety, all pits of hell, all blackness of depression, thoughts of sin, and devastation brought about by guilt. 2 Accept today's idea **that you place the future in the Hands of** the Holy Spirit, and you have released the world from all imprisonment by loosening the heavy chains that locked the door to freedom on **the world.** 3 You are saved, and your salvation thus becomes the gift you give the world, because you have received **salvation.**

W-194.3.**When you have placed the future in the Hands of God,** in no one instant is depression felt, or pain experienced or loss perceived. 2 In no one instant sorrow can be set upon a throne, and worshipped faithfully. 3 In no one instant can one even die. 4 And so each instant given unto God in passing, with the next one given **the Holy Spirit** already, is a time of your release from sadness, pain and even death itself.

W-194.4.God holds your future as **God** holds your past and present. 2 **Past, present and future** are one to **God,** and so **the past, present and future** should be one to you. 3 Yet in this world, the **time's** temporal progression still seems real. 4 And so you are not asked to understand the lack of sequence really found in time. 5 You are but asked to let the future go, and place **the future** in God's Hands. 6 And you will see by your experience that you have laid the past and present in **God's** Hands as well, because the past will punish you no more, and future dread will now be meaningless.

W-194.5.Release the future. 2 For the past is gone, and what is present, freed from **past's** bequest of grief and misery, of pain and loss, becomes the instant in which time escapes the bondage of illusions where **time** runs **time's** pitiless, inevitable course. 3 Then is each instant which was slave to time transformed into a holy instant, when the light that was kept hidden in God's Son is freed to bless the world. 4 Now is **God's Son** free, and all **the** glory **of God's Son** shines upon a world made free with him, to share **the** holiness **of God's Son.**

W-194.6.If you can see the lesson for today as the deliverance **this idea** really is, you will not hesitate to give as much consistent effort as you can, to **making the placement of the future in the Hands of God** be a part of you. 2 As **placing the future in the Hands of the Holy Spirit** becomes a thought that rules your mind, a habit in your problem-solving repertoire, a way of quick reaction to temptation, you extend your learning to the world. 3 And as you learn to see salvation in all things, so will the world perceive that **the world** is saved.

W-194.7.What worry can beset the one who gives his future to the loving Hands of God? 2 What can he suffer? 3 What can cause him pain, or bring experience of loss to him **who places his future in the Hands of God**? 4 What can he fear? 5 And what can he **who gives his future to the Hands of God** regard except with love? 6 For he who has escaped all fear of future pain has found his way to present peace, and certainty of care the world can never threaten. 7 He **who gives his future to the Hands of God** is sure that his perception may be faulty, but will never lack correction **from the Holy Spirit.** 8 He **who places his future in the Hands of God** is free to choose again when he has been deceived; to change his mind when he has made mistakes **and follow the guidance of the Holy Spirit.**

W-194.8.Place, then, your future in the Hands of God. 2 For thus you call the memory of **God** to come again, replacing all your thoughts of sin and evil with the truth of love. 3 Think you the world could fail to gain thereby, and every living creature not respond with healed perception **when you place the future in the Hands of God**? 4 Who entrusts himself to God has also placed the world within the Hands **of God** to which he has himself appealed for comfort and security. 5 He **who places his future in the Hands of God** lays aside the sick illusions of the world along with his **own illusions,** and offers peace to both **himself and the world.**

W-194.9.Now are we saved indeed **when we place the future in the Hands of God.** 2 For in God's Hands we rest untroubled, sure that only good can come to us. 3 If we forget, we will be gently reassured **by the Holy Spirit's guidance.** 4 If we accept an unforgiving thought, **the unforgiving thought** will be soon replaced by love's reflection. 5 And if we are tempted to attack, we will appeal to **the Holy Spirit** Who guards our rest to make the choice for us that leaves temptation far behind. 6 No longer is the world our enemy, for **when we place the future in the Hands of the Holy Spirit** we have chosen that we be **the world's** friend.

Notes to Lesson #194

I place the future in the Hands of God.

We believe that time is linear. Our world teaches that time is a logical progression that moves in one direction from the past to the present before we finally arrive in the future. This is not so. The past, present and future are all available within your mind since all belong to your world of illusions. To God, the past, present and future are one for God's Will is eternally the same. God's Will is that His beloved Son be happy.

When you place your future in God's hands, you are at heaven's gate. You have accepted God's plan for your salvation and realize your ego's plans will not work. Now, you can eagerly await God taking the final step in your restoration to knowledge.

By giving up your ego's plans for your salvation, you have ended your allegiance to a teacher who was always incapable of leading you to the Promised Land. It was foolish to believe that fear could be escaped within a thought system that was designed to make separation appear real. By placing your future in the hands of God, you have accepted the Holy Spirit as your guide and teacher. You now have chosen the thought system for love and forgiveness. Healing your split mind and reclaiming your divine inheritance are insured.

When you follow the Holy Spirit's guidance, there is no time for your egoic belief in sin, guilt and fear. Lack, limitation and separation fade away before the vision of Christ. You no longer have to worry about obtaining some predetermined result that your ego claims is necessary for you to earn God's love.

Now, you are free to go with the flow, realizing that this moment is exactly where you need to be. The journey of reawakening can be enjoyed, not feared. If you stumble along the way, if fear raises its ugly head or you make a mistake, the Holy Spirit will be there to correct your misperception and get you back on track.

When you place your future in God's hands, you have also placed both the past and the present there as well. By accepting God's plan, your past beliefs no longer punish you in the present. Your ego's blame, shame and guilt game has been replaced by love and forgiveness. Your fear and anxiety about your future also ceases since your safe return is guaranteed by the One who walks beside you.

With your past egoic beliefs reframed by the Holy Spirit, your karmic chains that previously bound the present to your past have been broken. Instead of the present being a replay to your past, you are now free to see each moment in the light of love and forgiveness. Your present is no longer a slave to time and fear. It has been transformed into a holy instant in which you can bless the world, your brother and yourself with love and forgiveness.

Because placing your future under the guidance of the Holy Spirit replaces all thoughts of sin and evil with the truth of love and forgiveness, this idea will become a habit. That habit will end the temptation and desire to argue for your littleness.

When you place your future under the guidance of the Holy Spirit, your world ceases to be a place of fear and dread. Because you walk with God, your fearful world has been transformed into a friendly place of love and mercy.

Question: If God is only love, why would you not want to place your future in the hands of God?

407

LESSON 195.

Love is the way I walk in gratitude.

W-195.1.Gratitude is a lesson hard to learn for those who look upon the world amiss **and perceive a world of lack, limitation, separation, misery, suffering, pain, anger and fear**. 2 The most that they **who perceive a world of hatred and fear** can do is see themselves as better off than others. 3 And they **who perceive a world of hatred and fear** try to be content because another seems to suffer more than they. 4 How pitiful and deprecating are such thoughts! 5 For who has cause for thanks while others have less cause **to be thankful**? 6 And who could suffer less because he sees another suffer more? 7 Your gratitude is due to **God** alone Who made all cause of sorrow disappear throughout the world **you perceive to be a world of lack, limitation, separation, hatred and fear**.

W-195.2.It is insane to offer thanks because of suffering. 2 But it is equally insane to fail in gratitude to **the Holy Spirit** Who offers you the certain means whereby all pain is healed, and suffering replaced with laughter and with happiness. 3 Nor could the even partly sane refuse to take the steps which **the Holy Spirit** directs, and follow in the way **the Holy Spirit** sets before them, to escape a prison that they thought contained no door to the deliverance they now perceive **to be salvation**.

W-195.3.Your brother is your "enemy" because you see in **your brother** the rival for your peace; a plunderer who takes his joy from you, and leaves you nothing but a black despair so bitter and relentless that there is no hope remaining. 2 Now is vengeance all there is to wish for **against your brother who you perceive to have robbed you of your peace and happiness**. 3 Now can you but try to bring **your brother** down to lie in death with you, as useless as yourself; as little left within his grasping fingers as in **your fingers**.

W-195.4.You do not offer God your gratitude because your brother is more slave than you, nor could you sanely be enraged if **your brother** seems freer. 2 Love makes no comparisons. 3 And gratitude can only be sincere if **gratitude** be joined to love. 4 We offer thanks to God our Father that in us all things will find their freedom. 5 It will never be that some are loosed while others still are bound. 6 For who can bargain in the name of love?

W-195.5.Therefore give thanks **to God**, but in sincerity. 2 And let your gratitude make room for all who will escape with you; the sick, the weak, the needy and afraid, and those who mourn a seeming loss or feel apparent pain, who suffer cold or hunger, or who walk the way of hatred and the path of death. 3 All these go with you **in your gratitude**. 4 Let us not compare ourselves with them, for thus we split them off from our awareness of the unity we share with **all**, as **the unity all** must share with us.

W-195.6.We thank our Father for one thing alone; that we are separate from no living thing, and therefore one with **God**. 2 And we rejoice that **there are** no exceptions **in our oneness with all that** ever can be made which would reduce our wholeness, nor impair or change our function to complete **God,** Who is Himself completion. 3 We give thanks for every living thing, for otherwise we offer thanks for nothing, and we fail to recognize the gifts of God to us.

W-195.7.Then let our brothers lean their tired heads against our shoulders as **our brothers** rest a while. 2 We offer thanks for **all our brothers**. 3 For if we can direct **our brothers** to the peace that we would find, the way is opening **to peace** at last to us. 4 An ancient door **of peace and the remembrance of God** is swinging free again; a long forgotten Word re-echoes in our memory, and gathers clarity as we are willing once again to hear **the Voice for God**.

W-195.8.Walk, then, in gratitude the way of love. 2 For hatred is forgotten when we lay comparisons aside. 3 What more remains as obstacles to peace? 4 The fear of God is now undone at last, and we forgive without comparing **and judging**. 5 Thus we cannot choose to overlook some things, and yet retain some other things still locked away as "sins." 6 When your forgiveness is complete **with all,** you will have total gratitude **for all,** for you will see that everything has earned the right to love by being loving, even as your **Christ nature has earned the right to love by being loving.**

W-195.9.Today we learn to think of gratitude in place of anger, malice and revenge. 2 We have been given everything. 3 If we refuse to recognize **everything as ours**, we are not entitled therefore to our bitterness, and to a self-perception which regards us in a place of merciless pursuit, where we are badgered ceaselessly, and pushed about without a thought or care for us or for our future. 4 Gratitude becomes the single thought we substitute for these insane perceptions **of lack limitation and separation.** 5 God has cared for us, and calls us Son. 6 Can there be more **to be grateful for** than this **divine inheritance God has given to all?**

W-195.10.Our gratitude will pave the way to **God**, and shorten our learning time by more than you could ever dream of. 2 Gratitude goes hand in hand with love, and where **either gratitude or love** is the other must be found. 3 For gratitude is but an aspect of the Love which is **God,** the Source of all creation. 4 God gives thanks to you, His Son, for being what you are **which is God's** Own completion and the Source of love, along with **God.** 5 Your gratitude to **God** is one with **God's gratitude** to you. 6 For love can walk no road except the way of gratitude, and thus **in gratitude** we go who walk the way to God.

Notes to Lesson #195

Love is the way I walk in gratitude.

In our ego's fearful world, we are told that we should be grateful because we suffer less than someone else. Because our ego sees separation everywhere, it claims we should be thankful because suffering appears to be unequal and there is always someone who suffers more than you.

Gratitude is difficult to learn when you view the world as a place of sacrifice and struggle. Our ego's belief in lack, limitation and separation requires that you must earn what you have. Because of this, we see our brother in competition for the limited resources that we both need for our survival, peace and happiness. Our brother becomes our rival and rivals become our enemies.

Love makes no comparisons and gratitude can only be sincere if it is joined with love. Our gratitude is because God's love means that all will be healed from our split mind's belief in separation. God's plan guarantees our happiness and peace. In us, all things will find the freedom that comes from right mindedness which is our return to only love.

We are grateful that we are not separate from one living thing. Therefore, we are one with all and one with God, our Source. There are no exceptions to this oneness for God is completion. We give thanks for all living things which are God's gifts to us.

Love makes no comparisons. When you compare, your egoic mind is splitting off and dividing the inseparable whole into separate autonomous parts. By comparing, our ego is breaking up the unity of the One Self that we all share.

Love makes no comparisons. Why?

Because when you compare, you separate.

When you separate, you judge.

When you judge, you make separation appear real.

When there is separation, you have competition.

When you compete, you have rivals.

When you have rivals, you believe there are outside forces that can rob you of your peace and happiness.

When there are outside forces that can affect you, you need plans for your own self- defense.

When others fail to follow your ego's plan for your happiness, grievances are sure to arise.

When grievances arise, you become trapped by your own unforgiving mind in its prison of fear and hatred.

With all these interactions, hatred is forgotten when you make no comparisons. Forgive without comparing or judging. When you follow the guidance of the Holy Spirit, you forgive all because you realize that all have earned the right to love, by being loving. This also includes yourself.

You have been given everything and if you refuse to recognize everything is yours, you are not entitled to be bitter or jealous of anyone. When you give your future over to the Holy Spirit, the Holy Spirit will replace your ego's belief in lack, limitation and separation with gratitude for God's love. You are unlimited and have been given everything. You are one with all and thus, one with God. What more could you want to be grateful for?

True gratitude can only be sincere when it is joined with love. When your forgiveness is total and complete, you will have total gratitude and the fear of God disappears. Now there is only a God of love that has given all to all. We have been given everything for we all share the Mind of God.

Where either gratitude or love is found, the other is also there for gratitude is an aspect of love. Our gratitude paves the way to God. God is completion and therefore, you must be complete. God is grateful for you for you are God's completion. You should be grateful for God for God's Will is only that you, His Child, be happy and at peace.

Question: What are you grateful for?

LESSON 196.

It can be but myself I crucify.

W-196.1.When this is firmly understood and kept in full awareness **that it can be but yourself you crucify**, you will not attempt to harm yourself, nor make your body slave to vengeance. 2 **When you understand that it can be but yourself you crucify**, you will not attack yourself, and you will realize that to attack another is but to attack yourself. 3 You will be free of the insane belief that to attack a brother saves yourself. 4 And you will understand **your brother's** safety is your own **safety**, and in **your brother's** healing you are healed.

W-196.2.Perhaps at first you will not understand how mercy, limitless and with all things held in its sure protection, can be found in the idea we practice for today **that it can be but yourself you crucify**. 2 **That it can be but yourself you crucify** may, in fact, appear **to your ego** to be a sign that punishment can never be escaped because the ego, under what **the ego** sees as threat, is quick to cite the truth to save **the ego's** lies. 3 Yet must **the ego** fail to understand the truth **the ego** uses thus **to deceive so that it teaches that you can attack another in safety**. 4 But you can learn to see these foolish applications **of the ego's thought system** and deny the meaning **the ego's false witnesses** appear to have.

W-196.3.Thus **by rejecting your ego's false witnesses and its thought system** do you also teach your mind that you are not an ego. 2 For the ways in which the ego would distort the truth will not deceive you longer. 3 You will not believe you are a body to be crucified. 4 And you will see within today's idea **that it can be but yourself you crucify,** the light of resurrection, looking past all thoughts of crucifixion and of death, to thoughts of liberation and of life.

W-196.4.Today's idea **that it can be but yourself you crucify** is one step we take in leading us from **egoic** bondage to the state of perfect freedom. 2 Let us take this step today **from egoic bondage,** that we may quickly go the way salvation shows us, taking every step in **salvation's** appointed sequence, as the mind relinquishes its **egoic blocks and** burdens one by one. 3 It is not time we need for this. 4 It is but willingness **to follow the Holy Spirit's guidance.** 5 For what would seem to need a thousand years can easily be done in just one instant by the grace of God.

W-196.5.The dreary, hopeless thought that you can make attacks on others and escape yourself has nailed you to the cross. 2 Perhaps **your ego's belief that you can attack another and still gain your freedom** seemed to be salvation. 3 Yet **your ego's belief that you can attack another and gain your freedom** merely stood for the belief the fear of God is real. 4 And what is **your ego's fear of God** but hell? 5 Who could believe his Father is his deadly enemy, separate from him, and waiting to destroy his life and blot him from the universe, without the fear of hell upon his heart?

W-196.6.**Your ego's belief that you must fear a God of only love** is the form of **egoic** madness you believe, if you accept the fearful thought you can attack another and be free yourself. 2 Until this form **of madness** is changed, there is no hope. 3 Until you see at least that this **egoic belief that by attacking another, you could gain** must be entirely impossible, how could there be escape **from the fear of God**? 4 The fear of God is real to anyone who thinks this thought **that by attacking another you could gain** is true. 5 And he will not perceive **the idea's** foolishness, or even see that **foolishness** is there, so that it would be possible to question **the foolish belief that you can attack another and gain your freedom.**

W-196.7.To question **the ego's belief that the fear of God is real** at all, **the belief's** form must first be changed at least as much as will permit fear of retaliation to abate, and the responsibility returned to some extent to you. 2 From there you can at least consider if you want to go along this painful path **of following the ego's thought system and making the fear of God appear real**. 3 Until this shift **of taking responsibility for your own mind's thinking** has been accomplished, you cannot perceive that it is but your thoughts that bring you fear, and your deliverance depends on you **taking responsibility for what your mind thinks.**

W-196.8.Our next steps will be easy, if you take this one today **of taking responsibility for what your mind thinks**. 2 From there we go ahead quite rapidly. 3 For once you understand it is impossible that you be hurt except by your own **mind's** thoughts, the fear of God must disappear. 4 You cannot then believe that fear is caused without **your mind's own thinking**. 5 And God, Whom you had thought to banish **from your mind**, can be welcomed back within the holy mind **of your big "S" Self which God** never left.

W-196.9.Salvation's song can certainly be heard in the idea we practice for today **that it can be but yourself you crucify**. 2 If it can but be you you crucify, you did not hurt the world, and need not fear **the world's** vengeance and pursuit. 3 **If it can but be yourself you crucify**, you **no longer** need **to** hide in terror from the deadly fear of God **that your ego's** projection hides behind. 4 **Your mind's decision to be responsible for your own thoughts is** the thing **your ego** dreads the most **but** is your salvation. 5 You are strong, and it is strength you want. 6 And you are free, and glad of freedom. 7 You have sought to be both weak and bound **to your ego's fear-based thought system**, because you feared your strength and freedom **of your mind and your big "S" Self**. 8 Yet salvation lies in **your mind's strength and freedom as God's Son.**

W-196.10.There is an instant in which terror seems to grip your mind so wholly that escape appears quite hopeless. 2 When you realize, once and for all, that it is you you fear, the mind perceives itself as split. 3 And this **split within your own mind** had been concealed while you believed attack could be directed outward **toward another**, and returned from outside to within **your mind**. 4 It seemed to be an enemy outside **your own mind that** you had to fear. 5 And thus a god **of fear** outside yourself became your mortal enemy; the source of fear.

W-196.11.Now, for an instant, is a murderer perceived within you, eager for your death, intent on plotting punishment for you until the time when **the enemy within your split mind** can kill **you** at last. 2 Yet in this instant is the time as well in which salvation comes. 3 For fear of God has disappeared. 4 And you can call on **the Holy Spirit** to save you from illusions by **God's** Love, calling Him Father and yourself His Son. 5 Pray that the instant may be soon,–today. 6 Step back from fear, and make advance to love.

W-196.12.There is no Thought of God that does not go with you to help you reach that instant **of fear**, and to go beyond **fear** quickly, surely and forever. 2 When the fear of God is gone, there are no obstacles that still remain between you and the holy peace of God. 3 How kind and merciful is the idea **that it can be but yourself you crucify that** we practice! 4 Give it welcome, as you should, for **in the idea that it can be but yourself you crucify** is your release. 5 It is indeed but you your mind can try to crucify. 6 Yet your redemption, too, will come from **your mind and your Christ nature.**

Notes to Lesson #196

It can be but myself I crucify.

It can be but myself I crucify is one idea that your ego vehemently opposes. For when this idea is properly understood, it marks the end of your allegiance to the ego and ultimately to its death. All of your ego's plans for your safety and salvation would become laughable and foolish.

The ego does not want you to know that you can only attack yourself since if it were known, you would quickly realize that your mind is the creative source behind your experiences. It would become obvious that your thoughts become your reality. You would realize that you alone are responsible for your own thoughts and that you could not be a victim of outside forces that are beyond your control as your ego claims.

The fear-based thought system of your ego would be uncovered as the source for all your pain, suffering and unhappiness. You would realize that your ego is not your friend, but rather the source of all your problems. You would decide to drop your allegiance to your fear- based thought system and get a new guide with a different thought system.

Your ego's thought system rests on the idea that you are a separate ego body in competition with other ego bodies. It claims that there are outside forces that are competing against you for the limited resources that you both need for your survival. If you are to survive, you must take from another for what is their loss becomes your gain.

The ego says that you are a body that can attack another without your own body being hurt. Because of this, attack becomes your ego's best form of self-defense. When you realize that you are not the body but rather mind whose thoughts never leave their source, you realize you are only crucifying yourself.

The idea that you can attack and not hurt yourself is predicated on the belief that we are each separate ego-bodies and your body is you. If you were formless mind or spirit, attack would be impossible. Mind needs a body if attack is to be possible. But if you are a body, you must fear retribution or the revenge from the other party.

You need to understand that it is but yourself you crucify, so that to attack another is to attack yourself. This idea that all attack is self-attack frees us from the bondage of the ego's belief system. When this is properly understood, it leads us to a state of perfect freedom.

Our belief that we could attack another and gain something of value while not harming ourselves has led to our own self crucifixion. When you believe that you can attack another because they have a body, you too must accept those same limitations and be vulnerable to attack yourself.

The idea that we can attack without harming ourselves leads to the belief that God also can seek revenge for our shortcomings. Thus, we transform a God of love into a God to be feared and something from which we need to hide.

If like begets like, God, like you, is vulnerable to attack and will seek revenge upon anyone who fails to fulfill God's desires. God becomes a deadly enemy and the fear of God is real to anyone who perceives God to be anything but unconditional love.

It can only be your own thoughts that create what you fear and your ego does not want you to realize this. When we understand that we can only be hurt by our own thoughts, the fear of God disappears. Our own mind and its beliefs are the cause of all that we fear. Fear cannot be caused by anything outside our mind. Fear is always an inside job, which means that all fears are totally within our mind's power to control.

If it is only our own mind that we can crucify, there is no reason to fear vengeance from any outside source since we are incapable of harming anything outside our own mind. When you realize that it is only you that you fear, you understand that your own mind has been split and that your ego's thought system has been the source for all your pain and suffering.

It is your egoic thought system that needs correction. Rather than your ego's guidance being your salvation, it has been the source of your own ruin. Because of your misplaced trust in your ego, you have forgotten your true Identity. You have allowed your ego to attack and replace your big "S" Self with its own version of a little "s" self.

This idea that it is but yourself that you crucify is the key to a resurrection of your Christ nature. When you realize that any attack is self-attack, you realize that it is your own mind that is the source of all attack thoughts. Therefore, there is nothing outside your own mind to fear. You now have identified and met the enemy and know that it is your own ego.

You no longer need to fear the world or God since you have never attacked or harmed them nor have they ever attacked or harmed you. It was only your mind's use of projection that made it appear as if there was something outside your own mind that had attack you. Now you know it was only your own split mind.

Since your own mind is the source for all you fear, your mind must also have the power to correct those thoughts and heal your split mind. You now realize the power of your own mind and can make a conscious decision to get a new plan and follow a different teacher. Let the Holy Spirit correct all your erroneous beliefs and the image of your little "s" self will disappear as you behold the Christ.

When you realize the creative power of your mind, you are in a position to take responsibility for your own thoughts and make different choices. The fear of God dissipates and you are only left with a God of love.

Your eyes are now open; your ego's fear-based thought system has been discredited. Now there is only one Voice to be heard. The only viable choice that remains is the thought system for love and forgiveness. You have no choice but to choose the truth.

Question: Who or what do you fear and why?

Question: If each can only crucify themselves, what is it that you should control?

Question: What is the true source of your fears?

LESSON 197.

It can be but my gratitude I earn.

W-197.1.Here **in the idea that it can be but my gratitude I earn** is the second step we take to free your mind from the belief in outside force pitted against your own **mind**. 2 You make attempts at kindness and forgiveness. 3 Yet you turn **your kindness and forgiveness into** attack again, unless you find external gratitude and lavish thanks **for your gifts**. 4 Your gifts must be received with honor, lest **your kindness and forgiveness** be withdrawn. 5 And so you think God's gifts are loans at best; at worst, deceptions which would cheat you of defenses, to ensure that when **God** strikes **God** will not fail to kill.

W-197.2.How easily are God and guilt confused by those who know not what their thoughts can do. 2 Deny your strength **of the power of your mind's thoughts** and weakness must become salvation to you. 3 See yourself as bound, and bars become your home. 4 Nor will you leave the prison house **of your own mind**, or claim your strength, until guilt and salvation are not seen as one and **you can only leave the prison house of your mind when** freedom and salvation are perceived as joined, with strength beside **freedom and salvation**, to be sought and claimed, and found and fully recognized.

W-197.3.The world must thank you when you offer **the world** release from your illusions. 2 Yet your thanks belong to you as well, for **the world's release** can only mirror your **release**. 3 Your **own** gratitude is all your gifts require, that **your gifts of kindness and forgiveness** be a lasting offering of a thankful heart, released from hell forever. 4 Is it this **release from hell** you would undo by taking back your gifts, because **your gifts of kindness and forgiveness** were not honored? 5 It is you who honor **your gifts of kindness and forgiveness** and give **those gifts** fitting thanks, for it is you who have received the gifts **of your own kindness and forgiveness**.

W-197.4.It does not matter if another thinks your gifts **of kindness and forgiveness are** unworthy. 2 In his mind there is a part that joins with yours in thanking you. 3 It does not matter if your gifts **of kindness and forgiveness** seem lost and ineffectual. 4 **Your gifts of kindness and forgiveness** are received where **those gifts** are given. 5 In your gratitude are **your gifts** accepted universally, and thankfully acknowledged by the Heart of God Himself. 6 And would you take **your gifts of kindness and forgiveness** back, when **God** has gratefully accepted **those gifts**?

W-197.5.God blesses every gift you give to **God**, and every gift is given **God**, because **your gifts** can be given only to yourself. 2 And what belongs to God must be **God's** Own. 3 Yet you will never realize **God's** gifts are sure, eternal, changeless, limitless, forever giving out, extending love and adding to your never-ending joy while you forgive **only to withdraw that forgiveness** but to attack again.

W-197.6.Withdraw the gifts **of kindness and forgiveness that** you give, and you will think that what is given you has been withdrawn. 2 But learn to let forgiveness take away the sins you think you see outside yourself, and you can never think the gifts of God are lent but for a little while, before **God** snatches **God's gifts** away again in death. 3 For death will have no meaning for you then **when your forgiveness has taken away your belief in sin.**

W-197.7.And with the end of this belief **in sin** is fear forever over. 2 Thank your **big "S" Self** for this **end of fear**, for He is grateful only unto God, and **God** gives thanks for you unto Himself. 3 To everyone who lives will Christ yet come, for everyone must live and move in **Christ**. 4 **Your Christ nature's** Being in His Father is secure, because Their Will is One. 5 **Your joint** gratitude to all **that your Christ nature and God** have created has no end, for gratitude remains a part of love.

W-197.8.Thanks be to you, **your big "S" Self, the Christ who is** the holy Son of God. 2 For as you were created, you contain all things within your **big "S"** Self. 3 And you are still as God created you. 4 Nor can you dim the light of your perfection. 5 In your heart the Heart of God is laid. 6 **God** holds you dear, because you are **God**, Himself. 7 All gratitude belongs to you, because of what you are, **God's holy Son**.

W-197.9.Give thanks as you receive **thanks**. 2 Be you free of all ingratitude to anyone who makes your **big "S" Self** complete. 3 And from this **big "S"** Self is no one left outside. 4 Give thanks for all the countless channels which extend this **big "S"** Self. 5 All that you do is given unto **God**. 6 All that you think can only be **God's** Thoughts, sharing with **God** the holy Thoughts of God. 7 Earn now the gratitude you have denied yourself when you forgot the function **on earth of forgiveness that** God has given you. 8 But never think that **God** has ever ceased to offer thanks to you **who complete God**.

Notes to Lesson #197

It can be but my gratitude I earn.

Your ego's favorite pastime is to attempt to split off, separate and disempower your mind from the unity it shares with the Mind of God. Because the ego does not believe that to give is to receive, it sees separation and lack everywhere. Your ego fails to see your true holiness and wholeness.

Just as the ego believes that there is such a thing as conditional love, the ego also believes that conditional forgiveness and kindness exist. By conditional, we mean that the recipient is required to behave in some predetermined way if the flow of the love, kindness or forgiveness is to continue to be sent. If the recipient fails to meet the expectations of the giver, the circuit is broken and the flow is stopped or the gifts are withdrawn. In this case, a proper response or feedback is required from the recipient to insure the continued flow of love, forgiveness, or kindness.

This egoic brand of kindness or forgiveness is not what it claims to be. It is actually a bargaining arrangement in which the giver is expecting to receive something of equal or greater value in return. If the giver's expectations are not met, this act of conditional kindness actually becomes an attack on the recipient with the withdrawal of the previous gift. What once appeared to be an act of kindness quickly becomes a grievance against the recipient.

Remember, a grievance occurs any time you believe you would be happy if someone behaved differently or, in this case, behaved up to your expected level of gratitude for your actions. You believe they have robbed you of the joy of giving because they have not displayed an adequate appreciation for your gift.

Just like love, kindness and forgiveness can impose no conditions. As long as there are conditions imposed upon either party, there is no freedom. Freedom makes no demands on the other party. The other party is free to accept, reject or reciprocate in any way they desire without the fear of any negative consequences or the withdrawal of the original gift.

When we are kind or forgiving with the expectation of receiving the recipient's gratitude, we are engaged in bargaining. If we are not properly rewarded by the recipient, we withdraw our kindness or forgiveness. Thus, this conditional act of supposed kindness actually becomes an attack upon another. It becomes a source for a future grievance.

We have actually confused and denied the power of our own thought by believing that some outside party's approval is required. For without the proper feedback response, we are forced to change our own mind's thinking and future behavior. When you attach strings to the act of giving, it means that the other party must earn the right to keep the gift and if they don't respond properly, they force you to withdraw that gift.

This egoic belief that you only give to get, disempowers the giver for now the recipient is in control of your future activities. You are claiming the recipient has the power to rob you of the happiness and joy that you would naturally feel when you are acting in a kind, forgiving and loving way.

When we think others must be grateful for our gifts, we automatically think and assume that we too are also required to be grateful for the gifts we received from God. Our ego teaches that if we fail to respond correctly to God's love, God will withdraw His love. This leads to our belief that we must continually do something to earn God's favor, love or salvation.

This belief that God's gifts can be withdrawn is the source of our fears. We have confused a God of unconditional love with our ego's warped belief of conditional love, forgiveness and kindness. We have failed to recognize the power of our own thoughts and transformed unconditional love into conditional love.

We have judged and failed to recognize that unconditional love, forgiveness or kindness makes no comparisons. When you perceive and know that God's gifts are eternal and changeless, fear disappears. There is no longer anything that we could do that would force God to withdraw His gifts.

Since there is only a Oneness, it is only your own gratitude that you can earn. To give is to receive. When your forgiveness and kindness is unconditional or total, the sins you think you see outside yourself disappear and you understand God's gifts can never be taken away from you. You see the Christ nature in all. You can now go about fulfilling your earthly function of being love in form.

You can be kind and forgiving. By such actions, you cease denying your true identity and accept your big "S" Self. You, the giver are grateful to the recipient for just being available to provide you the opportunity of demonstrating what love would have you do. Your joy comes from the act of giving; not from some external reaction from the recipient.

With this realization that it can be but your own gratitude you earn, you realize that God has never seen you without total gratitude for His holy Son, the recipient of God's unconditional love.

Question: How does what you think about others impact what you think about yourself?

LESSON 198.

Only my condemnation injures me.

W-198.1.Injury is impossible. 2 And yet illusion makes illusion. 3 If you **believe you** can condemn, you **believe you** can be injured. 4 For you have believed that you can injure, and the right **to injury that** you have established for yourself can be now used against you. **This right to injury and condemnation will appear true in your illusionary world** till you lay down **the belief that you can condemn and injure another** as valueless, unwanted and unreal. 5 Then does illusion cease to have effects, and those **effects that the illusion** seemed to have will be undone. 6 Then are you free **from the illusion,** for freedom is your gift, and you can now receive the gift you gave **of freedom from condemnation and injury**.

W-198.2.Condemn and you are made a prisoner. 2 Forgive and you are freed. 3 Such is the law that rules perception. 4 **The law of perception that condemnation imprisons you while forgiveness sets you free** is not a law that knowledge understands, for freedom is a part of knowledge. 5 To condemn is thus impossible in truth **because it would take away freedom**. 6 What seems to be **condemnation's** influence and **condemnation's** effects have not occurred at all **but in the illusions of the mind that sleeps.** 7 Yet must we deal with **condemnation's apparent influences and effects** a while as if **condemnation** had **real consequences and effects**. 8 Illusion makes illusion. 9 Except one. 10 Forgiveness is **the** illusion that is **the answer** to **end** the rest **of illusions**.

W-198.3.Forgiveness sweeps all other dreams away, and though **forgiveness** is itself a dream, **forgiveness** breeds no others **illusions**. 2 All illusions save this one **of forgiveness** must multiply a thousandfold. 3 But **forgiveness** is where illusions end. 4 Forgiveness is the end of dreams, because **forgiveness** is a dream of waking. 5 **Forgiveness** is not itself the truth. 6 Yet does **forgiveness** point to where the truth must be, and gives direction with the certainty of God Himself. 7 **Forgiveness** is a dream in which the Son of God awakens to his **big "S"** Self and to his Father, knowing **Father and Son** are One.

W-198.4.Forgiveness is the only road that leads out of disaster, past all suffering, and finally away from death. 2 How could there be another way, when this one **of forgiveness** is the plan of God Himself? 3 And why would you oppose **forgiveness,** quarrel with **God's plan,** seek to find a thousand ways in which **God's plan** must be wrong; a thousand other possibilities **so that you do not have to forgive**?

W-198.5.Is it not wiser to be glad you hold the answer to your problems in your hand? 2 Is it not more intelligent to thank the One Who gives salvation, and accept **God's** gift **of forgiveness** with gratitude? 3 And is it not a kindness to yourself to hear **the Holy Spirit's** Voice and learn the simple lessons **the Holy Spirit** would teach **that only your own condemnation injures you,** instead of trying to dismiss His words, and substitute your own in place of **the Holy Spirit's**?

W-198.6.**The Holy Spirit's** words **that only your own condemnation injures you** will work. 2 **The Holy Spirit's** words **of forgiveness** will save. 3 **The Holy Spirit's** words **that only your own condemnation injures you** contain all hope, all blessing and all joy that ever can be found upon this earth. 4 **The Holy Spirit's** words **of forgiveness** are born in God, and come to you with Heaven's love upon them. 5 Those who hear **the Holy Spirit's** words **that only your own condemnation injures you** have heard the song of Heaven. 6 For these are the words **of forgiveness** in which all merge as one at last. 7 And as **the words of forgiveness** will fade away, the Word of God will come to take **the words of forgiveness'** place, for **the Word of God** will be remembered then and loved.

W-198.7.This world has many seeming separate haunts where mercy has no meaning, and attack appears as justified. 2 Yet all **illusions of separation** are one. **They are all** a place where death is offered to God's Son and to his Father. 3 You may think They **who perceive the separation to be real** have accepted **death to be their reality.** 4 But if you will look again upon the place where you beheld Their blood, you will perceive a miracle instead. 5 How foolish to believe that They **who think the separation is real** could die! 6 How foolish to believe you can attack! 7 How mad to think that you could be condemned, and that the holy Son of God can die!

W-198.8.The stillness of your **big "S"** Self remains unmoved, untouched by thoughts like these **where attack, not forgiveness, seems justified.** And **your Christ nature is** unaware of any condemnation which could need forgiveness. 2 Dreams of any kind are strange and alien to the truth. 3 And what but truth could have a Thought which builds a bridge to **the dream** that brings illusions **of condemnation and death** to the other side **toward truth**?

W-198.9.Today we practice letting freedom come to make its home with you. 2 The truth bestows these words **about condemnation and forgiveness** upon your mind, that you may find the key to light and let the darkness end:
3 Only my condemnation injures me.
4 Only my own forgiveness sets me free.
5 Do not forget today that there can be no form of suffering that fails to hide an unforgiving thought. 6 Nor can there be a form of pain forgiveness cannot heal.

W-198.10.Accept the one illusion **of forgiveness** which proclaims there is no condemnation in God's Son, and Heaven is remembered instantly; the world forgotten, all **the ego's** weird beliefs forgotten **along** with **the world of fear** as the face of Christ appears unveiled at last in this one dream **of forgiveness.** 2 **The dream of forgiveness** is the gift the Holy Spirit holds for you from God your Father. 3 Let today be celebrated both on earth and in your holy home as well. 4 Be kind to Both **God and His Son**, as you forgive the trespasses you thought **God and His Son** guilty of, and see your innocence shining upon you from the face of Christ.

W-198.11.Now is there silence all around the world. 2 Now is there stillness where before there was a frantic rush of thoughts **of separation** that made no sense. 3 Now is there tranquil light across the face of earth, made quiet in a dreamless sleep. 4 And now the Word of God alone remains upon **the sleeping mind**. 5 Only **the Word of G**od can be perceived an instant longer. 6 Then are symbols done, and everything you ever thought you made completely vanished from the mind that God forever knows to be **God's** only Son.

W-198.12.There is no condemnation in **God's Son**. 2 **God's Son** is perfect in his holiness. 3 **God's Son** needs no thoughts of mercy. 4 Who could give **God's Son** gifts when everything is his? 5 And who could dream of offering forgiveness to the Son of Sinlessness Itself, so like to **God** Whose Son he is, that to behold the Son is to perceive no more, and only know the Father? 6 In this vision of the Son, so brief that not an instant stands between this single sight and timelessness itself, you see the vision of yourself, and then you disappear forever into God.

W-198.13.Today we come still nearer to the end of everything that yet would stand between this vision and our sight. 2 And we are glad that we have come this far, and recognize that **the Holy Spirit** Who brought us here will not forsake us now. 3 For **the Holy Spirit** would give to us the gift **of forgiveness** that God has given us through **our forgiveness of God's Son** today. 4 Now is the time for your deliverance. 5 The time has come. 6 The time has come today.

Notes to Lesson #198

Only my condemnation injures me.

Yesterday we asked the question about how your thoughts about others impact what you think about yourself. This lesson provides some additional insight about your world of perception.

Injury is impossible but illusions make illusions. In order to make the illusion of injury seem real, it is first necessary for you to identify your mind with the illusion of a body.

Our ego teaches that we have the right to judge and condemn another whenever they fail to make us happy. Because we believe we have the right to condemn, our egoic mind needs something apart from itself. Mind is truly formless, inseparable and invulnerable to attack. Yet, we have created the illusion of the body that appears to be separate and vulnerable to our attack. Unfortunately, when you give yourself the right to condemn or injure another, you automatically give that same right to your world. You believe that you too can be hurt.

We fail to recognize the creative power of our own mind. Our mind has the ability to be or imagine anything that it desires. When we imagine we are not as God created us, perfect, whole and complete, our mind makes the illusion that supports that erroneous belief. Our ego's belief makes the illusion of our little "s" self appear to be our reality.

The ego argues for the rightness of its illusions and clings to its desire to judge and compare. It creates story upon story, arguing for your littleness and your inability to be the causative agent of the world you perceive. You cannot give up the illusion that you can be hurt unless you first give up the illusion that you can condemn another.

We fail to realize that we live in a world that is the creation of our own mind's erroneous beliefs. The law of perception states: Condemn and you are made prisoner. Forgive and you are set free.

Forgiveness is the answer to all the illusions of your egoic world. Forgiveness itself is an illusion but unlike all other illusions that argue for your littleness, forgiveness is the story that argues for the truth of your big "S" Self. Forgiveness ends the need for any additional stories involving blame, shame, guilt and fear. Forgiveness is not the truth but it does point the way to truth. Forgiveness ends the dream of separation with the happy dream of reawakening to the truth that the Father, Son and your big "S" Self are One.

Truth knows nothing of forgiveness since in truth there is nothing to forgive. Yet, forgiveness recognizes the truth that we are not the body and cannot be hurt. Forgiveness is one illusion that proclaims God's Son is not condemned and that your ego's stories of lack, limitation and separation are not real.

Forgiveness is the only tool that leads out of the dream that we are separate. Forgiveness is the Holy Spirit's reframing of our story to reawaken us to the truth about ourselves. We are not the body and Mind cannot be hurt by outside forces that are beyond our control. Forgiveness is the bridge that brings illusions to the gates of Heaven.

When you understand that your mind is the source of your experiences, you realize that nothing outside your own mind has the power to harm your peace. It is only your condemnation that injures yourself. When you insist on your ego's need to judge, make comparisons and condemn, you only crucify yourself. Any form of suffering that you experience hides an unforgiving thought. Forgiveness corrects your thinking and thus heals all pain.

Forgiveness is God's plan for salvation since it states the truth of the sinlessness of all and the impossibility of condemnation. Forgiveness leads to the remembrance of Heaven and the Truth. Ultimately, you see the vision of yourself in a forgiving dream in which the illusion of your littleness disappears forever into God. Forgiveness leads to the knowledge that you remain one with the shared Mind of God.

When you condemn another, you as their jailer must remain in the prison of your unforgiving mind. Until you are willing to claim responsibility for the creative power of your own thoughts, you will continue to blame your brother for his failure to do the impossible and make you happy.

Forgive your brother for the role you required him to play in your illusion of being a victim of forces beyond your control. Accept responsibility for your own illusions and let the nightmare of separation end in the final happy dream of forgiveness.

In time, your function is forgiveness, your purpose is love and your destiny is the peace of God. Forgive and you are set free. Forgive and you can reawaken to your destiny.

Question: Is your ego's need to be right, judge and condemn so important that you would allow yourself to remain trapped in the same prison of your own unforgiving mind rather than forgive and let all, including yourself, go free?

Only your own condemnation injures you while only your forgiveness can set you free. You get to choose which it will be.

I am not a body. I am free.

W-199.1.Freedom must be impossible as long as you perceive a body as yourself. 2 The body is a limit. 3 Who would seek for freedom in a body looks for **freedom** where **freedom** cannot be found. 4 The mind can be made free when **the mind** no longer sees itself as in a body, firmly tied to **the body** and sheltered by **the body's** presence. 5 If this were the truth **that the mind is part of the body**, the mind **would be** vulnerable indeed!

W-199.2.The mind that serves the Holy Spirit is unlimited forever, in all ways, beyond the laws of time and space, unbound by any preconceptions, and with strength and power to do whatever **the mind that serves the Holy Spirit** is asked. 2 Attack thoughts cannot enter such a mind, because **the mind that serves the Holy Spirit** has been given to the Source of love, and fear can never enter in a mind that has attached itself to love. 3 **A mind that serves the Holy Spirit** rests in God. 4 And who can be afraid who lives in Innocence, and only loves?

W-199.3.It is essential for your progress in this course that you accept today's idea, and hold **the idea that I am not a body, I am free** very dear. 2 Be not concerned that to the ego **the idea that you are not a body and are free** is quite insane. 3 The ego holds the body dear because **the ego** dwells in **the body**, and lives united with the **bodily** home that **the ego** has made. 4 **The body** is a part of the illusion that has sheltered **the ego** from being found illusory itself.

W-199.4.Here does **the ego** hide, and here **the ego** can be seen as what **the ego** is. 2 Declare your innocence and you are free. 3 The body disappears, because you have no need of **the body** except the need the Holy Spirit sees. 4 For this, the body will appear as useful form for what the mind must do. 5 **The body** thus becomes a vehicle which helps forgiveness be extended to the all-inclusive goal that **forgiveness** must reach, according to God's plan.

W-199.5.Cherish today's idea **that you are not a body and are free**, and practice it today and every day. 2 Make **today's idea that you are not a body and are free** a part of every practice period you take. 3 There is no thought that will not gain thereby in power to help the world, and none which will not gain in added gifts to you as well. 4 We sound the call of freedom round the world with this idea **that you are not a body and are free**. 5 And would you be exempt from the acceptance of the gifts **of freedom** you give?

W-199.6.The Holy Spirit is the home of minds that seek for freedom. 2 In **the Holy Spirit, minds that seek for freedom** have found **the freedom that** they have sought. 3 The body's purpose now is unambiguous. 4 And **the body** becomes perfect in the ability to serve an undivided goal. 5 In conflict-free and unequivocal response to mind with but the thought of freedom as **the mind's** goal, the body serves, and serves its purpose well. 6 Without the power to enslave, **the body** is a worthy servant of the freedom which the mind within the Holy Spirit seeks.

W-199.7.Be free today. 2 And carry freedom as your gift to those who still believe they are enslaved within a body. 3 Be you free, so that the Holy Spirit can make use of your escape from bondage, to set free the many who perceive themselves as bound and helpless and afraid **within a body**. 4 Let love replace their fears through you. 5 Accept salvation now, and give your mind to **the Holy Spirit** Who calls to you to make this gift **of your mind** to **the Holy Spirit**. 6 For **the Holy Spirit** would give you perfect freedom, perfect joy, and hope that finds its full accomplishment in God.

W-199.8.You are God's Son. 2 In immortality you live forever. 3 Would you not return your mind to **this state of immortality as God's Son**? 4 Then practice well the thought **that you are not a body and are free that** the Holy Spirit gives you for today. 5 Your brothers stand released with you in **this thought**; the world is blessed along with you, God's Son will weep no more, and Heaven offers thanks for the increase of joy your practice brings even to **Heaven**. 6 And God Himself extends **God's** Love and happiness each time you say:
7 I am not a body. 8 I am free. 9 I hear the Voice that God has given me, and it is only this **Voice for God** my mind obeys.

Notes to Lesson #199

I am not a body. I am free.

Freedom implies being unlimited. You cannot be free if you are limited in any way. If your actions have ongoing consequences that effect what you will be able to do in the future, you are not free.

Time is the belief in change which time is designed to measure. Time is the belief that there is a gap between cause and effect and that actions have ongoing consequences. You cannot be free in time since time is comprised of the past, present and future. We perceive time to be one directional, a linear progression of change from past, present to the future. The past is over. Yet, the past contains a history that seems to have ongoing consequences that one is never free to escape.

The present is contingent upon your past which limits what you believe your current available options are. We perceive the future to be dependent on both the past and present. To most, the future is the natural consequence of our past because of our belief in the linear progression of change in time.

The body appears to anchor you to time. You cannot perceive yourself as a body without your belief in time. When you identify your existence with the body, you also accept the limitations that come with the body. The ego created the body to be its home. The purpose of the body is to keep you tied to time and your ego's belief in separation.

If you believe that your mind is the body part we call the brain, you must accept the limitations that come with that body. The body is a smokescreen that hides the creative power of Mind from your own awareness. By identifying Mind with the limits of the body, you fail to realize the creative power that you possess as the decision-maker for your experiences in your world. Your ego gets its way and keeps you accepting littleness as your reality.

Within your ego's thought system, the idea that you are not the body and are free to create your own reality is inconceivable. The ego sees such beliefs as total insanity for the ego's thought system is the birthplace for fear. Fear is false evidence appearing real. Your mind's identification with the body is the anchor that makes fear seem real in time.

Your mind can only be made free when you no longer believe your safety to be tied to the shelter of the body's presence. The body is not your mind's home. When your mind serves the Holy Spirit and comes from love, instead of fear, the laws of time and space no longer apply.

The mind that serves the Holy Spirit is unlimited and your ego's preconceived limits are discarded. Your mind has the power to do whatever the Holy Spirit requests and love and forgiveness replace your ego's past attack thoughts.

Your ego uses your identification with the body as protection against your ability as decision-maker to choose a different thought system. The ego's thought system is the home for all minds that seek separation and specialness. The Holy Spirit's thought system is the home for those that seek freedom.

When given over to the Holy Spirit, the body becomes a useful communication device and teaching aid for what mind must do. On earth, your mind's purpose is the extension of love and forgiveness. This purpose implies inclusion and the joining of minds. When your mind is in alignment with the Holy Spirit, it is free of conflict and the body serves the Holy Spirit and your big "S" Self's true purpose. The body no longer has any power to enslave and attack since your mind is no longer associated with being the body.

When you freely choose to follow the thought system of love, the Holy Spirit will utilize your experience to escape the ego's thought system which teaches that you are a body that attacks and is attacked. Now, the body serves as a device to communicate with your brother that he too is not a body and is free.

The mind that serves the Holy Spirit lives in innocence and only love. The body becomes a useful form for the Holy Spirit to use as a vehicle for fulfilling God's plan. On earth, the body is now the instrument that serves to fulfill your function of extending forgiveness and salvation to all.

Question: Would you rather be special or free?

Your ego's thought system sells you on the idea that you can be special or better than another. This is why the ego likes to compare and judge.

Most people like the thought of being special although they may be opposed to the idea of being separate. This is because most people associate being special as possessing some positive attributes that make them stand out from the general population. Unfortunately, you can be special by having negative attributes also. When you seek specialness, you remain trapped in your ego's desire to compare and judge.

The ego is the guide for those who seek specialness while the Holy Spirit guides those who seek freedom. Although specialness sounds good, specialness is an attribute of the belief in separation. When you desire to be special, specialness comes with the price tag of lack, limitation and separation. The choice of specialness comes at a high price and no longer is as appealing. Freedom, not specialness, is what we truly desire and what love offers to those who seek only the truth.

LESSON 200.

There is no peace except the peace of God.

W-200.1.Seek you no further. 2 You will not find peace except the peace of God. 3 Accept this fact **that peace cannot be found by following the ego's plans** and save yourself the agony of yet more bitter disappointments, bleak despair, and sense of icy hopelessness and doubt. 4 Seek you no further **to follow your ego's plans**. 5 There is nothing else for you to find except the peace of God unless you seek for misery and pain **that your ego's plans bring**.

W-200.2.This is the final point to which each one must come at last, to lay aside all hope of finding happiness where there is none; of being saved by what can only hurt; of making peace of chaos, joy of pain, and Heaven out of hell. 2 Attempt no more to win through losing, nor to die to live. 3 You cannot but be asking for defeat **when you follow your ego's plans and its thought system for fear**.

W-200.3.Yet you can ask **the Holy Spirit just** as easily for love, for happiness, and for eternal life in peace that has no ending. 2 Ask for this **peace of God**, and you can only win. 3 To ask for what you, **your big "S" Self,** have already must succeed. 4 To ask that what is false be true can only fail. 5 Forgive yourself for vain imaginings, and seek no longer what you cannot find **which is the peace of God in the ego's illusionary world of lack, limitation and separation.** 6 For what could be more foolish than to seek and seek and seek again for hell, when you have but to look with open eyes to find that Heaven lies before you, through a door that opens easily to welcome you?

W-200.4.Come home. 2 You have not found your happiness in foreign places and in alien forms that have no meaning to you, though **your split mind has** sought to make **the false alien world of form** meaningful. 3 This **alien** world **of fear** is not where you belong. 4 You are a stranger here **in the ego's world of perception**. 5 But it is given you to find the means whereby the world **of perception** no longer seems to be a prison house or jail for anyone.

W-200.5.Freedom is given you where you beheld but chains and iron doors. 2 But you must change your mind about the purpose of the world, if you would find escape **from your ego's belief in lack, limitation and separation**. 3 You will be bound till all the world is seen by you as blessed, and everyone made free of your **ego's** mistakes **in perception** and honored as **your brothers really** are **as the big "S" Self.** 4 You made **your brother** not a sinner; no more **than you made** yourself **a sinner**. 5 And as you free the one **from your belief in sin**, the other is accepted as he is **as the Christ.**

W-200.6.What does forgiveness do? 2 In truth **forgiveness** has no function, and does nothing. 3 For **forgiveness** is unknown in Heaven. 4 It is only hell where **forgiveness** is needed, and where **forgiveness** must serve a mighty function. 5 Is not the escape of God's beloved Son from evil dreams **of lack, limitation and separation** that **his split mind** imagines, yet believes are true a worthy purpose? 6 Who could hope for more, while there appears to be a choice to make between success and failure; love and fear?

W-200.7.There is no peace except the peace of God because **God** has one Son who cannot make a world **of fear** in opposition to God's Will and **in opposition** to **the Son's** own **will**, which is the same as **God's Will.** 2 What could **the split mind** hope to find in such **an illusionary** world **of lack, limitation and separation?** 3 **This false world of fear** cannot have reality, because it never was created **by God.** 4 Is it here **in this false world of fear** that he would seek for peace? 5 Or must **God's Son** see that, as he looks on **a false fearful** world, the world can but deceive? 6 Yet can he learn to look on **the egoic world of lack, limitation, separation and fear** another way, and **by following the Holy Spirit's thought system of love and forgiveness** find the peace of God.

W-200.8.Peace is the bridge that everyone will cross, to leave this **fearful** world **of egoic perception** behind. 2 But peace begins within the world perceived as different **from fear and now blessed** and leading from this fresh perception **of a world blessed by forgiveness, mercy and love is the bridge of peace that leads** to the gate of Heaven and the way beyond. 3 Peace is the answer to conflicting goals, to senseless journeys, frantic, vain pursuits, and meaningless endeavors. 4 Now the way **to freedom, salvation and truth** is easy, sloping gently toward the bridge where freedom lies within the peace of God.

W-200.9.Let us not lose our way again today. 2 We go to Heaven, and the path is straight. 3 Only if we attempt to wander **from the path of forgiveness and peace** can there be delay, and needless wasted time on thorny byways. 4 God alone is sure, and **the Holy Spirit** will guide our footsteps. 5 **The Holy Spirit** will not desert **God's** Son in need, nor let him stray forever from **the true** home **of God's Son.** 6 The Father calls; the Son will hear. 7 And that is all there is to what appears to be a **fearful** world apart from God, where bodies **appear to** have reality.

W-200.10.Now is there silence. 2 Seek no further. 3 You have come to where the road is carpeted with leaves of false desires, fallen from the trees of hopelessness **that your ego** sought before. 4 Now are **these false egoic desires** underfoot. 5 And you look up and on toward Heaven, with the body's eyes but serving for an instant longer now. 6 Peace is already recognized at last, and you can feel **peace's** soft embrace surround your heart and mind with comfort and with love.

W-200.11.Today we seek no idols. 2 Peace cannot be found in the **idols of an egoic world of fear**. 3 The peace of God is ours, and only **God's peace** will we accept and want. 4 Peace be to us today. 5 For we have found a simple, happy way to leave the **ego's** world of ambiguity, and to replace our shifting goals and solitary dreams with single purpose and companionship. 6 For peace is union, if **peace** be of God. 7 We seek no further. 8 We are close to home, and draw still nearer every time we say:

9 There is no peace except the peace of God, And I am glad and thankful it is so.

Notes to Lesson #200

There is no peace except the peace of God.

Be single-minded in purpose and have only one goal. Seek only the peace of God.

You cannot find happiness in a world that is made from your desire to imagine that you could be something other than as God created you. This lesson states a basic truth that you could never make the false become true so let's stop trying. Why would anyone not want to be perfect, whole and complete?

The ego's plans for your happiness will not work because they are all attempts to find happiness and peace within a thought system that was designed to support lack, limitation, separation, struggle, pain, conflict and fear. Your ego's plans for your happiness are based on its belief that you will be satisfied when you suffer less than someone else. This limit on your suffering is the only benefit that following your ego's plans actually offers. Isn't just the thought of such a goal depressing?

How can God's Son be happy living in a constantly changing world where blame, shame, guilt and fear appear around every corner? You cannot find happiness in such an alien world. To ask what is false to be true can only lead to failure. Instead of seeking a brief respite from the world of hate and fear, ask the Holy Spirit to lead you to true love, happiness and eternal life.

As God's beloved child these gifts of love, joy, happiness, peace and oneness are your divine birthright. You can only find happiness in the truth because only truth is real and changeless. Ask for the gifts God has bestowed upon all His Creations and you must succeed because they are already in your possession.

This fearful world you perceive is not your home. Your ego's purpose for this world is to deceive you into believing forms, such as the body, are real. These forms provide false evidence that create the illusion of lack, limitation and separation. This world is your ego's attempt to make the false appear real. The only way to free your mind from your ego's belief in your littleness is to change the purpose for your world.

You are not a victim in your world of provisional reality. Instead, your mind is the creator of it. Change how you view your world and your world will automatically realign to fit its new purpose. The law of perception states: Condemn and you are imprisoned. Forgive and you are set free.

Change the purpose of your ego's world from being a witness for fear and your littleness to a world that your big "S" Self has made and entered into to bless and see as only innocent and holy. Free everyone from your mistaken beliefs that God's Son could be sinful and limited. Honor your brother as the Christ that he is and you will receive that same freedom and blessing that is the peace of God.

In truth or Heaven, forgiveness does nothing. Forgiveness serves no function in Heaven where it is meaningless since there is nothing to forgive. But in the illusion of time, forgiveness has the mighty purpose of reawakening sleeping minds to the truth of what they are. In this world of time, forgiveness is the only illusion you want to share since it ends the need for all other illusions. Forgiveness is the escape from the dream that you could be something other than as God created you.

This world of provisional reality was not made by God but by the creative power of your mind's imagination. It is unknown to God and not God's Will. Forgiveness is God's answer to your desire to experience something you are not. Forgiveness is God's plan that guarantees His Son's safe return home to His Father. Forgiveness is the remembrance that God, your brother and your big "S" Self remain One.

There is no peace except the peace of God. Peace is the bridge everyone will cross to leave this fear-based world of illusion behind. This bridge to freedom begins in the world of perception when you choose to bless and forgive all and recognize the Christ in your brother. The peace of God is the answer to the ego's conflicting goals that are designed to experience what can only be false.

Peace will be found when the peace of God is your single purpose. Peace cannot be found in the idols of this world that attempt to hide and deceive by making form appear real. Peace of God is union with the One Self and the recognition that the truth is only true and nothing else is.

Question: When you accept the truth that you are perfect, whole and complete and part of that One Self, what more could you ask for or want?

Introduction:

Review of Workbook Lessons 181-200

W-rVI.in.1.For this review we take but one idea each day, and practice **that one idea** as often as is possible. 2 Besides the time you give morning and evening, which should not be less than fifteen minutes, and the hourly remembrances you make throughout the day, use the idea as often as you can between them. 3 Each of these ideas alone would be sufficient for salvation, if **that one idea** were learned truly. 4 Each **idea** would be enough to give release to you and to the world from every form of bondage, and invite the memory of God to come again.

W-rVI.in.2.With this in mind we start our practicing, in which we carefully review the thoughts the Holy Spirit has bestowed on us in our last twenty lessons. 2 Each **of the twenty individual thoughts from these lessons** contains the whole curriculum if understood, practiced, accepted, and applied to all the seeming happenings throughout the day. 3 One **of the twenty individual thoughts from these lessons** is enough **to release you and the world from every form of bondage**. 4 But from that one **thought**, there must be no exceptions made. 5 And so we need to use all **twenty thoughts** and let them blend as one, as each contributes to the whole we learn.

W-rVI.in.3.These practice sessions, like our last review, are centered round a central theme with which we start and end each lesson. 2 It is this:
3 I am not a body. 4 I am free.
5 For I am still as God created me.
6 The day begins and ends with this **central theme that I am not a body. I am free. For I am still as God created me**. 7 And we repeat this **central theme** every time the hour strikes, or we remember, in between, we have a function that transcends the world we see. 8 Beyond this, and a repetition of the special thought we practice for the day, no form of exercise is urged, except a deep relinquishment of everything that clutters up the mind, and makes **the mind** deaf to reason, sanity and simple truth.

W-rVI.in.4.We will attempt to get beyond all words and special forms of practicing for this review. 2 For we attempt, this time, to reach a quickened pace along a shorter path to the serenity and peace of God. 3 We merely close our eyes, and then forget all that we thought we knew and understood. 4 For thus is freedom given us from all we did not know and failed to understand.

W-rVI.in.5.There is but one exception to this lack of structuring. 2 Permit no idle thought to go unchallenged. 3 If you notice **an idle thought**, deny **the idle thought's** hold and hasten to assure your mind that this **idle thought** is not what **your Christ nature** would have **you think**. 4 Then gently let the thought which you denied be given up, in sure and quick exchange for the idea we practice for the day.

W-rVI.in.6.When you are tempted, hasten to proclaim your freedom from temptation, as you say:
2 This thought I do not want. 3 I choose instead ___.
4 And then repeat the idea for the day, and let **the idea for the day** take the place of what you thought. 5 Beyond such special applications of each day's idea, we will add but a few formal expressions or specific thoughts to aid in practicing. 6 Instead, we give these times of quiet to the Teacher, **the Holy Spirit,** Who instructs in quiet, speaks of peace, and gives our thoughts whatever meaning **those thoughts** may have.

W-rVI.in.7.To **the Holy Spirit**, I offer this review for you. 2 I place you in **the Holy Spirit's** charge, and let **the Holy Spirit** teach you what to do and say and think, each time you turn to **the Holy Spirit**. 3 **The Holy Spirit** will not fail to be available to you, each time you call to **the Holy Spirit** to help you. 4 Let us offer **the Holy Spirit** the whole review we now begin, and let us also not forget to Whom **this review** has been given, as we practice day by day, advancing toward the goal **the Holy Spirit** set for us; allowing **the Holy Spirit** to teach us how to go, and trusting **the Holy Spirit** completely for the way each practice period can best become a loving gift of freedom to the world.

Notes to Review #6

Introduction for Review Lesson 201-220

Introduction

We are now beginning our review of the last twenty ACIM workbook lessons which ended with Lesson 200. Each of these last 20 lessons contains the whole curriculum and if understood and completely accepted, would lead to salvation. Each lesson is enough but only if you make no exceptions.

No unloving thought can be allowed to fester unchallenged by any one of these ideas. When any egoic thought arises, challenge it as soon as possible by repeating just one of these ideas. You will be granted the miracle and be able to see the event differently through the eyes of love and forgiveness.

Lessons 196-200 actually comprise a five-step process that you can utilize to free yourself from the idea that there are outside forces that are competing against you. You might wish to repeat these five steps to yourself as you begin or end your day or whenever you find yourself in a challenging situation. Each step comes from one of these last five lessons and is referenced in the list below.

1) It can be but myself I crucify. (From Lesson196)
2) It can be but my gratitude I earn. (From Lesson197)
3) Only my condemnation injures me. Only my own forgiveness sets me free. (From Lesson198)
4) I am not a body. I am free. I hear and obey the Voice God has given me. (From Lesson199)
5) There is no peace except the peace of God. I seek only this truth. I no longer seek to make the false true. This is the peace of God. (From Lesson200)

When you repeat these five statements to yourself, you are commanding your mind to replace egoic misperceptions with correct perceptions. The truth is that you have always been free and that nothing robs you of your own inner peace unless you choose to allow it. You alone are responsible for your mind's thoughts and your thoughts determine your perception.

Your egoic beliefs and thoughts are not an effect of outside forces that are beyond your control. Instead, your egoic beliefs keep you trapped in the cycle of victim consciousness. Until you understand the creative power of your own mind and accept responsibility for your own beliefs and thoughts, you will perceive that there are outside forces that can cause you to lose your own inner peace. This has never been the case!

You are the keeper of your own thoughts. No one is responsible but you. When you are tempted by thoughts of lack, limitation and fear, proclaim your freedom by being totally responsible for your own thinking. Whether or not you are willing to accept the belief that you control all the circumstances in your life, we can all agree that you are in control of how you choose to respond to those events.

When your egoic mind wishes to compare, judge and have non-loving thoughts, you can take control of the situation by saying this to yourself:

"This thought I do not want. I choose instead…

And then repeat the idea from one of these 20 lessons or perhaps simply the theme of this review set, which is:

"I am not a body. I am free. I am still as God created me."

By following this advice, you will find that the Holy Spirit will come to your aid and it will be easy for you to drop your egoic thinking. By following the guidance of the Holy Spirit, your inner peace will be restored.

The ego's thought system is designed to draw your attention back to bodily thoughts that are alien to your true nature. Your ego's goal is to have you accept the body as your home. When you do this, you must also accept the limitations that come with the body.

Your ego's desire to be special always comes with the attributes of lack, limitation and separation. Your ego's desire to be something other than as God created you is the source of your fears and costs you your happiness, oneness and inner peace. Permit no fearful or unloving thoughts to go unchallenged by remembering this truth:

"I am not a body. I am free. For I am still as God created me."

You will now be in the proper mindset to accept the peace of God. The Holy Spirit will not fail you in your request for Its help for that is the Holy Spirit's mission and your destiny.

In time, your function is forgiveness, your purpose is love and your destiny is the peace of God.

The God in me recognizes the God in you.

Namaste

LESSON 201

Review of #181:

I trust my brothers, who are one with me.

General instruction:

Lesson #201 is a review of Lesson #181. We will begin and end each session with the theme behind this review lesson which is:

I am not a body. I am free. For I am still as God created me.

LESSON 201.

I am not a body. I am free. For I am still as God created me.

W-201.1.(181) I trust my brothers, who are one with me.
2 No one but is my brother. 3 I am blessed with oneness with the universe and God, my Father, one Creator of the whole that is my **big "S"** Self, forever One with me.
4 I am not a body. 5 I am free.
6 For I am still as God created me.

LESSON 202

Review of #182:

I will be still an instant and go home.

General instruction:

Lesson #202 is a review of Lesson #182. We will begin and end each session with the theme behind this review lesson which is:

I am not a body. I am free. For I am still as God created me.

LESSON 202.

I am not a body. I am free. For I am still as God created me.

W-202.1.(182) I will be still an instant and go home.
2 Why would I choose to stay an instant more where I do not belong, when God Himself has given me His Voice to call me home?
3 I am not a body. 4 I am free.
5 For I am still as God created me.

LESSON 203

Review of #183:

I call upon God's Name and on my own.

General instruction:

Lesson #203 is a review of Lesson #183. We will begin and end each session with the theme behind this review lesson which is:

I am not a body. I am free. For I am still as God created me.

LESSON 203.

I am not a body. I am free. For I am still as God created me.

W-203.1.(183) I call upon God's Name and on my own.
2 The Name of God is my deliverance from every thought of evil and of sin, because **the Name of God** is my own **name** as well as God's.
3 I am not a body. 4 I am free.
5 For I am still as God created me.

LESSON 204

Review of #184:

The Name of God is my inheritance.

General instruction:

Lesson #204 is a review of Lesson #184. We will begin and end each session with the theme behind this review lesson which is:

I am not a body. I am free. For I am still as God created me.

LESSON 204.

I am not a body. I am free. For I am still as God created me.

W-204.1.(184) The Name of God is my inheritance.
2 God's Name reminds me that I am His Son, not slave to time, unbound by laws which rule the world of sick illusions. **God's Name reminds me that I am** free in God, forever and forever one with **God**.
3 I am not a body. 4 I am free.
5 For I am still as God created me.

LESSON 205

Review of #185:

I want the peace of God.

General instruction:

Lesson #205 is a review of Lesson #185. We will begin and end each session with the theme behind this review lesson which is:

I am not a body. I am free. For I am still as God created me.

LESSON 205.

I am not a body. I am free. For I am still as God created me.

W-205.1.(185) I want the peace of God.
2 The peace of God is everything I want. 3 The peace of God is my one goal; the aim of all my living here. **The peace of God is** the end I seek, my purpose and my function and my life, while I abide where I am not at home **in this illusionary world of perception**.
4 I am not a body. 5 I am free.
6 For I am still as God created me.

LESSON 206

Review of #186:

Salvation of the world depends on me.

General instruction:

Lesson #206 is a review of Lesson #186. We will begin and end each session with the theme behind this review lesson which is:

I am not a body. I am free. For I am still as God created me.

LESSON 206.

I am not a body. I am free. For I am still as God created me.

W-206.1.(186) Salvation of the world depends on me.
2 I am entrusted with the gifts of God, because I am God's Son. 3 And I would give **God's** gifts where **God** intended **His gifts** to be.
4 I am not a body. 5 I am free.
6 For I am still as God created me.

LESSON 207

Review of #187:

I bless the world because I bless myself.

General instruction:

Lesson #207 is a review of Lesson #187. We will begin and end each session with the theme behind this review lesson which is:

I am not a body. I am free. For I am still as God created me.

LESSON 207.

I am not a body. I am free. For I am still as God created me.

W-207.1.(187) I bless the world because I bless myself.
2 God's blessing shines upon me from within my heart, where **God** abides. 3 I need but turn to **God**, and every sorrow melts away, as I accept **God's** boundless Love for me.
4 I am not a body. 5 I am free.
6 For I am still as God created me.

LESSON 208

Review of #188:

The peace of God is shining in me now.

General instruction:

Lesson #208 is a review of Lesson #188. We will begin and end each session with the theme behind this review lesson which is:

I am not a body. I am free. For I am still as God created me.

LESSON 208.

I am not a body. I am free. For I am still as God created me.

W-208.1.(188) The peace of God is shining in me now.
2 I will be still, and let the earth be still along with me. 3 And in that stillness **my world and I** will find the peace of God. 4 **The peace of God** is within my heart, which witnesses to God Himself.
5 I am not a body. 6 I am free.
7 For I am still as God created me.

LESSON 209

Review of #189:

I feel the Love of God within me now.

General instruction:

Lesson #209 is a review of Lesson #189. We will begin and end each session with the theme behind this review lesson which is:

I am not a body. I am free. For I am still as God created me.

LESSON 209.

I am not a body. I am free. For I am still as God created me.

W-209.1.(189) I feel the Love of God within me now.
2 The Love of God is what created me. 3 The Love of God is everything I am. 4 The Love of God proclaimed me as **God's** Son. 5 The Love of God within me sets me free.
6 I am not a body. 7 I am free.
8 For I am still as God created me.

LESSON 210

Review of #190:

I choose the joy of God instead of pain.

General instruction:

Lesson #210 is a review of Lesson #190. We will begin and end each session with the theme behind this review lesson which is:

I am not a body. I am free. For I am still as God created me.

LESSON 210.

I am not a body. I am free. For I am still as God created me.

W-210.1.(190) I choose the joy of God instead of pain.
2 Pain is my own **ego's** idea. 3 **Pain** is not a Thought of God, but one I thought apart from **God** and from **God's** Will. 4 **God's** Will is joy, and only joy for **God's** beloved Son. 5 And that **joy of God** I choose, instead of **the pain my egoic thoughts** made.
6 I am not a body. 7 I am free.
8 For I am still as God created me.

LESSON 211

Review of #191:

I am the holy Son of God Himself.

General instruction:

Lesson #211 is a review of Lesson #191. We will begin and end each session with the theme behind this review lesson which is:

I am not a body. I am free. For I am still as God created me.

LESSON 211.

I am not a body. I am free. For I am still as God created me.

W-211.1.(191) I am the holy Son of God Himself.
2 In silence and in true humility I seek God's glory. **I seek** to behold **God's glory** in the Son whom **God** created as my **big "S"** Self.
3 I am not a body. 4 I am free.
5 For I am still as God created me.

LESSON 212

Review of #192:

I have a function of forgiveness God would have me fill.

General instruction:

Lesson #212 is a review of Lesson #192. We will begin and end each session with the theme behind this review lesson which is:

I am not a body. I am free. For I am still as God created me.

LESSON 212.

I am not a body. I am free. For I am still as God created me.

W-212.1.(192) I have a function **of forgiveness** God would have me fill.
2 I seek the function **of forgiveness** that would set me free from all the vain illusions of the world. 3 Only the function **of forgiveness that** God has given me can offer freedom. 4 Only **the function of forgiveness** I seek, and only **forgiveness** will I accept as **my function.**
5 I am not a body. 6 I am free.
7 For I am still as God created me.

LESSON 213

Review of #193:

All things are lessons God would have me learn.

<u>General instruction</u>:

Lesson #213 is a review of Lesson #193.We will begin and end each session with the theme behind this review lesson which is:

I am not a body. I am free. For I am still as God created me.

LESSON 213.

I am not a body. I am free. For I am still as God created me.

W-213.1.(193) All things are lessons God would have me learn.
2 A lesson is a miracle which God offers to me, in place of **my egoic** thoughts I made that hurt me. 3 What I learn **from the Holy Spirit** becomes the way I am set free. 4 And so I choose to learn **the Holy Spirit's lessons** and forget my own **ego's false teaching**.
5 I am not a body. 6 I am free.
7 For I am still as God created me.

LESSON 214

Review of #194:

I place the future in the Hands of God.

<u>General instruction</u>:

Lesson #214 is a review of Lesson #194.We will begin and end each session with the theme behind this review lesson which is:

I am not a body. I am free. For I am still as God created me.

LESSON 214.

I am not a body. I am free. For I am still as God created me.

W-214.1.(194) I place the future in the Hands of God.
2 The past is gone; the future is not yet. 3 Now am I freed from both **the past and future**. 4 For what God gives can only be for good. 5 And I accept but what **God** gives as what belongs to me.
6 I am not a body. 7 I am free.
8 For I am still as God created me.

LESSON 215

Review of #195:

Love is the way I walk in gratitude.

<u>General instruction</u>:

Lesson #215 is a review of Lesson #195.We will begin and end each session with the theme behind this review lesson which is:

I am not a body. I am free. For I am still as God created me.

LESSON 215.

I am not a body. I am free. For I am still as God created me.

W-215.1.(195) Love is the way I walk in gratitude.
2 The Holy Spirit is my only Guide. 3 **The Holy Spirit** walks with me in love. 4 And I give thanks to **the Holy Spirit** for showing me the way to go.
5 I am not a body. 6 I am free.
7 For I am still as God created me.

LESSON 216

Review of #196:

It can be but myself I crucify.

<u>**General instruction**</u>:

Lesson #216 is a review of Lesson #196.We will begin and end each session with the theme behind this review lesson which is:

I am not a body. I am free. For I am still as God created me.

LESSON 216.

I am not a body. I am free. For I am still as God created me.

W-216.1.(196) It can be but myself I crucify.
2 All that I do I do unto myself. 3 If I attack, I suffer. 4 But if I forgive, salvation will be given me.
5 I am not a body. 6 I am free.
7 For I am still as God created me.

LESSON 217

Review of #197:

It can be but my gratitude I earn.

<u>**General instruction**</u>:

Lesson #217 is a review of Lesson #197.We will begin and end each session with the theme behind this review lesson which is:

I am not a body. I am free. For I am still as God created me.

LESSON 217.

I am not a body. I am free. For I am still as God created me.

W-217.1.(197) It can be but my gratitude I earn.
2 Who should give thanks for my salvation but myself? 3 And how but through salvation can I find the **big "S"** Self to Whom my thanks are due?
4 I am not a body. 5 I am free.
6 For I am still as God created me.

LESSON 218

Review of #198:

Only my condemnation injures me.

<u>**General instruction**</u>:

Lesson #218 is a review of Lesson #198.We will begin and end each session with the theme behind this review lesson which is:

I am not a body. I am free. For I am still as God created me.

LESSON 218.

I am not a body. I am free. For I am still as God created me.

W-218.1.(198) Only my condemnation injures me.
2 My condemnation keeps my vision dark, and through my **ego's** sightless eyes I cannot see the vision of my glory. 3 Yet today I, **my big "S" Self**, can behold this glory **of my Christ nature** and be glad.
4 I am not a body. 5 I am free.
6 For I am still as God created me.

LESSON 219

Review of #199:

I am not a body. I am free.

General instruction:

Lesson #219 is a review of Lesson #199. We will begin and end each session with the theme behind this review lesson which is:

I am not a body. I am free. For I am still as God created me.

LESSON 219.

I am not a body. I am free. For I am still as God created me.

W-219.1.(199) I am not a body. 2 I am free.
3 I am God's Son. 4 Be still, my mind, and think a moment upon this **that I am God's Son**. 5 And then return to earth, without confusion as to what my Father loves forever as His Son.
6 I am not a body. 7 I am free.
8 For I am still as God created me.

LESSON 220

Review of #200:

There is no peace except the peace of God.

General instruction:

Lesson #220 is a review of Lesson #200. We will begin and end each session with the theme behind this review lesson which is:

I am not a body. I am free. For I am still as God created me.

LESSON 220.

I am not a body. I am free. For I am still as God created me.

W-220.1.(200) There is no peace except the peace of God.
2 Let me not wander from the way of peace, for I am lost on other roads than this **path of peace**. 3 But let me follow **the Holy Spirit** Who leads me home, and peace is certain as the Love of God.
4 I am not a body. 5 I am free.
6 For I am still as God created me.

Introduction to Part 2 of the ACIM Workbook

Part 2 covers Lessons 221- 365

Part 2 Introduction

W-pII.in.1.Words will mean little now. 2 We use **words** but as guides on which we do not now depend. 3 For now we seek direct experience of truth alone. 4 The lessons that remain are merely introductions to the times in which we leave the world of pain, and go to enter peace. 5 Now we begin to reach the goal **of the peace of God that** this course has set, and find the end toward which our practicing was always geared.

W-pII.in.2.Now we attempt to let the exercise be merely a beginning. 2 For we wait in quiet expectation for our God and Father. 3 **God** has promised He will take the final step Himself. 4 And we are sure **God's** promises are kept. 5 We have come far along the road, and now we wait for **God**. 6 We will continue spending time with **God** each morning and at night, as long as makes us happy. 7 We will not consider time a matter of duration now. 8 We use as much **time** as we will need for the result that we desire. 9 Nor will we forget our hourly remembrance in between, calling to God when we have need of **the Holy Spirit** as we are tempted to forget our goal.

W-pII.in.3.We will continue with a central thought for all the days to come, and we will use that **central** thought to introduce our times of rest, and calm our minds at need. 2 Yet we will not content ourselves with simple practicing in the remaining holy instants which conclude the year that we have given God. 3 We say some simple words of welcome, and expect our Father to reveal Himself, as **God** has promised. 4 We have called on **God,** and **God** has promised that His Son will not remain unanswered when **His Son** calls **God's** Name.

W-pII.in.4.Now do we come to **God** with but **God's** Word upon our minds and hearts, and wait for **God** to take the step to us that He has told us, through **the Holy Spirit's** Voice, **God** would not fail to take **the final step** when we invited Him. 2 **God** has not left His Son in all his **son's** madness, nor betrayed **the son's** trust in **God.** 3 Has not **God's** faithfulness earned **God** the invitation that **God** seeks to make us happy? 4 We will offer **the invitation for God to make us happy**, and **the invitation** will be accepted. 5 So our times with **God** will now be spent. 6 We say the words of invitation that **the Holy Spirit's** Voice suggests, and then we wait for **God** to come to us.

W-pII.in.5.Now is the time of prophecy fulfilled. 2 Now are all ancient promises upheld and fully kept. 3 No step remains for time to separate **God's promise** from **the prophecy's** accomplishment. 4 For now we cannot fail. 5 Sit silently and wait upon your Father. 6 **God** has willed to come to you when you have recognized it is your will **that God** do so. 7 And you could have never come this far unless you saw, however dimly, that it is your will **to return to God.**

W-pII.in.6.I, **Jesus,** am so close to you **that together** we cannot fail. 2 Father, we give these holy times to You, in gratitude to **the Holy Spirit** Who taught us how to leave the world of sorrow in exchange for its replacement **of a forgiven world that has been** given us by You. 3 We look not backward now. 4 We look ahead, and fix our eyes upon the journey's end. 5 Accept these little gifts of thanks from us, as through Christ's vision we behold a world beyond the **ego's world** we made, and take that **forgiven** world to be the full replacement of our own **egoic world of fear and sorrow**.

W-pII.in.7.And now we wait in silence, unafraid and certain of **God's** coming. 2 We have sought to find our way by following **the Holy Spirit,** the Guide **God** sent to us. 3 We did not know the way, but **God** did not forget us. 4 And we know that You will not forget us now. 5 We ask but that Your ancient promises be kept which are Your Will to keep. 6 We will with **God's Will** in asking this. 7 The Father and the Son, Whose holy Will created all that is, can fail in nothing. 8 In this certainty, we undertake these last few steps to You, and rest in confidence upon Your Love, which will not fail the Son who calls to You, **His Father.**

W-pII.in.8.And so we start upon the final part of this one holy year, which we have spent together in the search for truth and God, Who is **Truth's** one Creator. 2 We have found the way **God** chose for us, and made the choice to follow **the way** as **God** would have us go. 3 **God's** Hand has held us up. 4 **God's** Thoughts have lit the darkness of our minds. 5 **God's** Love has called to us unceasingly since time began.

W-pII.in.9.We had a wish that God would fail to have the Son whom **God** created for Himself. 2 We wanted God to change Himself, and be what we would make of **God**. 3 And we believed that our insane desires were the truth. 4 Now we are glad **that this wish that we could be different than how God created us** is all undone, and we no longer think illusions true. 5 The memory of God is shimmering across the wide horizons of our minds. 6 A moment more, and **the memory of God** will rise again. 7 A moment more, and we who are God's Sons are safely home, where **God** would have us be.

W-pII.in.10.Now is the need for practice almost done. 2 For in this final section, we will come to understand that we need only call to God, and all temptations disappear. 3 Instead of words, we need but feel **God's** Love. 4 Instead of prayers, we need but call **God's** Name. 5 Instead of judging, we need but be still and let all things be healed. 6 We will accept the way

God's plan will end, as we received the way **God's plan** started. 7 Now **God's plan** is complete. 8 This year has brought us to eternity.

W-pII.in.11.One further use for words we still retain. 2 From time to time, instructions on a theme of special relevance will intersperse our daily lessons and the periods of wordless, deep experience which should come afterwards. 3 These special thoughts should be reviewed each day, each one of **these special themes** to be continued till the next **theme** is given you. 4 These special thoughts **like the following thought about what is forgiveness** should be slowly read and thought about a little while, preceding one of the holy and blessed instants in the day. 5 We give the first of these instructions now **about what is forgiveness**.

Part 2 of ACIM Workbook

Notes to Introduction to Part 2 of the Workbook Lessons 221- 365

Notes to Introduction

We have now entered Part Two of these workbook lessons. Part Two consists of a series of brief introductions to a central theme. Each theme is then followed by ten workbook lessons that support and provide additional time to integrate the central theme into your daily life.

Over the next 10 day, each of the daily lessons that follow each theme consist of a supporting idea which is typically followed by a prayer and one paragraph about that day's idea. The course also suggests that before you begin your study of the new supporting idea of the day, you first review the central theme for that ten session set.

I would recommend that you follow the course's suggestion and do not skip the daily review of the central theme. Reviewing the central theme of each section is a critical component for understanding the entire course. The explanation tends to clarify and redefine the meaning of that key word that is often referenced throughout this course. Understanding these unique definitions is critical to clearly understanding and adopting the teachings of this course into your life.

With this daily review of the unique meanings of each central theme, you will start reprogramming your conscious and subconscious mind. Currently your mind associates the definitions of these words as automatically supporting your ego's fear-based thought system. Words like forgiveness, salvation, the world, sin and the body all are examples of words that are commonly used in our everyday language. Yet, the use of those words with their typical definitions automatically induces a state of fear within your split mind.

This is because these common words all have embedded assumptions that support the ego's belief in lack, limitation and separation. Without your ability to consciously and eventually automatically redefine these terms within your own mind, your normal conversations will have a tendency to ignite the fearful subconscious assumptions that are embedded in the use of these words within our language itself.

Because of this language problem, Part Two will try to avoid the use of words whenever possible. Instead, it will rely upon you quieting your egoic mind and listening for the guidance of the Holy Spirit. By quieting the mind, you will experience personal revelations and insights coming directly to you. Drop all your judgments and come with an empty and open mind to these daily sessions.

Ask, expect and anticipate that your role in God's plan will be revealed to you. Be thankful that God's Will cannot be changed by our ego's plans for your littleness. You are and always will be God's beloved Child with whom He is well pleased. Look forward to accepting God's Will as your will and you will become a messenger for the Holy Spirit and a witness for the Truth you seek.

What Is Forgiveness?

Covers ACIM Workbook Lessons 221-230

1. What Is Forgiveness?

W-pII.1.1.Forgiveness recognizes what you thought your brother did to you has not occurred. 2 **Forgiveness** does not pardon sins and make **sins** real. 3 **Forgiveness** sees there was no sin. 4 And in that view **that there are no sins** are all your sins forgiven. 5 What is sin, except a false idea about God's Son? 6 Forgiveness merely sees **the** falsity **that God's Son could sin**, and therefore lets **the belief in sin's reality** go. 7 What then is free to take **the place of the ego's erroneous belief in sins** is now **forgiveness which follows** the Will of God.

W-pII.1.2.An unforgiving thought is one which makes a judgment that **the mind** will not raise to doubt, although **the judgment** is not true. 2 The mind is closed, and will not be released **from the mind's unforgiving judgment**. 3 The thought protects projection, tightening **the unforgiving thought's** chains, so that distortions are more veiled and more obscure; less easily accessible to doubt, and further kept from reason. 4 What can come between a fixed projection and the aim that **the mind** has chosen as **the** wanted goal **of the unforgiving thought**?

W-pII.1.3.An unforgiving thought does many things. 2 In frantic action **an unforgiving thought** pursues **the mind's** goal, twisting and overturning what **the mind** sees as interfering with **the unforgiving thought's** chosen path **and story**. 3 Distortion is **an unforgiving thought's** purpose, and the means by which **the mind** would accomplish its **distortion** as well. 4 **An unforgiving thought** sets about **the mind's** furious attempts to smash reality **by creating a false narrative or story about the event**, without concern for anything that would appear to pose a contradiction to **the erroneous** point of view **of the unforgiving thought and mind.**

W-pII.1.4.Forgiveness, on the other hand, is still, and quietly does nothing. 2 **Forgiveness** offends no aspect of reality, nor seeks to twist **aspects of reality** to appearances **forgiveness** likes. 3 **Forgiveness** merely looks, and waits, and judges not. 4 He who would not forgive must judge, for he **who refuses to forgive** must justify his failure to forgive. 5 But he who would forgive himself must learn to welcome truth exactly as **truth** is.

W-pII.1.5.Do nothing, then, and let forgiveness show you what to do, through **the Holy Spirit** Who is your Guide, your Savior and Protector, strong in hope, and certain of your ultimate success. 2 **The Holy Spirit** has forgiven you already, for such is **the Holy Spirit's** function, given **to the Holy Spirit** by God. 3 Now must you share **the Holy Spirit**'s function, and forgive whom **the Holy Spirit** has saved, whose sinlessness **the Holy Spirit** sees, and whom **the Holy Spirit** honors as the Son of God.

Notes to Special Theme #1: What Is Forgiveness?

Covers ACIM Workbook Lessons 221-230

What is forgiveness?

Central Theme for Lessons 221 to 230

In time, your function is forgiveness, your purpose is love and your destiny is the peace of God. Since forgiveness is your function, it is important to know what forgiveness really entails.

True forgiveness recognizes that what you thought your brother did to you has not occurred. It does not pardon sin and make sin real. Forgiveness sees that there is no sin.

Sin is the false idea about God's Son. Sin assumes God's Son could be different from what God created as your big "S" Self, your Christ nature. Forgiveness merely sees the falsity of the erroneous beliefs your ego has assigned to God's Son and lets those beliefs dissipate. Forgiveness drops the ego's belief that the body is your home and protector. What remains to take the place of these false ideas is the truth that reflects the Will of God.

The key distinction between what the world sees as forgiveness and how forgiveness is defined in this course revolves around the reality of the experience itself. ACIM's viewpoint about forgiveness recognizes that what you thought your brother did to you has not occurred as you perceive it. The ego disagrees and assumes its interpretation of the event is correct and that someone has been wronged by another.

The idea in A Course in Miracles is that in forgiveness you are to recognize that what you thought your brother did to you has not occurred. This is the source of confusion and triggers our egoic mind into justifying why its story and judgment about the event is correct. Anyone who perceives the events of this world to be real will have a difficult time accepting ACIM's definition of forgiveness.

Perhaps an example would best illustrate the difference between the two definitions of forgiveness. Here are the events. You are walking down the street and a man approaches you with a gun and robs you taking your purse or wallet. Your money, credit cards and some personal items have been stolen.

Does this mean that the event never took place and the man did not take your money?

No. Both agree that in time, the events seem to have taken place. But the question surrounding forgiveness really becomes the interpretation that you assign to the event's purpose, its cause and its effect.

In time, the event or experience did take place. Your story or recollection about the event may not depict exactly what took place but your story has some basis in the historical fact that you were physically robbed at some point in time and space. ACIM does not ask that you deny the occurrence of the physical robbery. Instead, it asks that you reframe your narrative about what the event's purpose, cause and effects actually were.

In our fear-based world, the need for forgiveness rests upon the belief that there are actual victims and victimizers. It claims that the events in this world can change what your true nature actually is.

Our ego's main purpose is to confirm its belief in separation. Our ego's primary function revolves around subdividing the whole into imaginary autonomous entities and falsely assigning causative powers to those parts that can then change the reality of the whole. The role of the ego is to determine when these outside forces have changed another and to judge the impact of that influence as either good or bad.

Our egos are big judging machines designed to assign blame, shame and guilt based on its own internal view of justice. Our ego then argues for the correctness of its viewpoint and demands justice be served through a system of rewards and punishments administered to the supposed causative agent.

In the world of the ego, there are real victims and victimizers and the ego's function is to determine between the two. Your ego is the sole judge, jury and prosecutor of its world. Your ego claims to be the ultimate arbitrator of truth. It judges events and circumstances as it sees fit and then insists that its interpretation is correct.

An unforgiving thought makes a judgment that it will not raise to doubt although the judgment is not true. The mind is closed and will not re-examine its previous judgment. Instead, the unforgiving mind chooses to project its previous belief out into the world to provide new evidence that confirms its own current beliefs. Your senses are assigned the task of gathering additional incriminating evidence to reconfirm the ego's previous beliefs. Your mind discards and ignores any evidence that does not support its past judgments and beliefs.

To your ego, the purpose of the world is to provide supporting evidence that bears false witness that your unforgiving thought is correct. Your egoic mind projects out its fixed beliefs into this pliable world for the sole purpose of reconfirming past judgments made by your ego. These fixed projections serve your egoic mind's predetermined goals and provides stability for your pre-existing world view.

On the mass collective consciousness basis, our earth is a fixed projection of our joint beliefs in lack, limitation, separation, sin, guilt, shame and fear. In time, planet Earth is a warring planet whose egoic purpose is to provide physical evidence to support our belief that there are outside forces that can rob us of our happiness and peace.

Your egoic world was designed to prove that there are real victims and victimizers and that your mind lacks the creative power to protect you from these outside forces. Both your happiness and suffering are the result of these outside forces that are the cause of your experiences. Thus, these outside forces are attributed with artificial powers to make you happy or sad. A grievance occurs whenever these outside forces fail to fulfill the role assigned to them by your ego to make you happy.

In egoic forgiveness, you first accept the erroneous belief that some outside force could make you happy. When they fail to do so, they have wronged you. A real crime or sin against your happiness has been committed by the offending party. Egoic forgiveness then suspends the victim's right to future retribution from the offending party.

Egoic forgiveness always insists that the crime was real. Because of this belief in the reality of sin, an unforgiving mind never questions the validity of the ego's major premise that there are outside forces that can harm you against your will. This false belief that you can be harmed disempowers you as God's Son and is the source for fear.

In order for A Course in Miracles' definition of forgiveness to make sense, you need to understand the world's purpose as understood by the Holy Spirit. The Holy Spirit takes the ego's world that was made to support our belief in lack, limitation and separation and changes its purpose. To the Holy Spirit, the purpose of this world is to teach one lesson and thus, reawaken sleeping minds to the truth of who they really are.

The Holy Spirit uses this world to teach us this lesson.

You are not a body. You are free. You are still as God created you. In time, nothing sources your experience but yourself and nothing can affect you unless you choose to allow it.

ACIM's definition of forgiveness aligns with the Holy Spirit's purpose for this world. It acknowledges the fact that you are not the body and that nothing in the world of our imagination has any ability to change the truth that we remain as God created us.

ACIM's definition of forgiveness recognizes that you are free. Freedom allows us the option to be what we really are or pretend we are something we are not. Freedom allows us to imagine anything we want in perfect safety. Although the illusions appear real to the dreaming mind, our fantasies have no ability to change our reality. The dream of sin has no lasting consequences. Awaken from the dream of separation and you remember your sinless nature and reconnect to the One Self.

The illusion of time and space provides the game board for our minds' imagination. In time, we imagine an event that we desire and gain the experience and learning lessons that we wished the event to provide. Yet being a playschool, these events have no permanent consequences that could change the truth of what we really are. They only are designed to reawaken us to the truth.

This world of form provides a game board in which we can have specific examples which help us demonstrate what love would have us do in a world of seeming hate and fear. We get to hone our skills and learn about an attribute of love called forgiveness. In Heaven, you could not learn about or practice forgiveness since there is nothing that would require your forgiveness.

In Heaven, forgiveness serves no function and the term itself becomes meaningless. If you want to learn or practice the attribute of love called forgiveness, you need to find a practice field where hate and fear seem real. This fear-based world provides that playschool for forgiveness.

In time, we get to demonstrate that illusions cannot change the truth about God's Son, our big "S" Self. Although our mind's imagination can deny our divine birthright, it has no ability to change that fact that we remain as God created us. You are not a body but you are Mind or Spirit. Being a Child of God, you are endowed with the creative power of Mind.

ACIM's definition of forgiveness reflects the truth that your mind is the creative source for your experiences. There are no outside forces that can steal your peace or make you unhappy. Your grievances are predicated upon your ego's erroneous beliefs that you are limited and another could harm you or make you happy.

Everything you experience in time is sourced by your mind's own fertile imagination. Nothing happens without your secret wish to experience that event. We seek problems because we need the pearls of wisdom that those experiences are designed to teach.

True forgiveness recognizes that there are no victims or victimizers. We are all willing participants on this game board of time and space. True forgiveness reestablishes the causative nature of your own mind and reestablishes the truth that you, as the dreamer, are 100% responsible for your own dreams.

You are the script writer, director and editor of your own plays. You should not blame another for being an actor in a play of your own creation. You wanted that particular scene in your play for the important lesson that it was designed to provide. True forgiveness recognizes this fact.

When asked, the Holy Spirit uses your experiences to reawaken you to this fundamental truth.

You are not a body. You are free. You are still as God created you. In time, nothing sources your experience but yourself and nothing can affect you unless you choose to allow it to.

When you forgive your world, you acknowledge the truth of the above statement and reaffirm the sinlessness of God's Son.

Forgiveness does nothing. It does not judge. Instead, it lets the Holy Spirit guide you to what love would have you do. Since to give is to receive, when you drop your ego's grievances against your brother, you empower your mind, acknowledge responsibility for your thoughts and reclaim your sinless nature as God's beloved Son.

Additional action step to take: In order for you to better grasp what true forgiveness is, repeat the following affirmation at the beginning and end of each day and whenever needed throughout your day.

I am not a body. I am free. I am still as God created me. Nothing sources my experiences but me and nothing can affect me unless I choose to allow it.

This affirmation reflects the truth of what you have come here to learn and why forgiveness is your function in this world of form.

Question: How does the above truth change what forgiveness is all about?

Question: You can never escape fear within a thought system that defines forgiveness as a relationship between a victim and its victimizer. Why is this the case?

Peace to my mind. Let all my thoughts be still.

W-221.1. <Father, I come to You today to seek the peace that You alone can give. 2 I come in silence. 3 In the quiet of my heart, the deep recesses of my mind, I wait and listen for Your Voice. 4 My Father, speak to me today. 5 I come to hear Your Voice in silence and in certainty and love, sure You will hear my call and answer me.>

W-221.2.Now do we wait in quiet. 2 God is here, because we wait together. 3 I, **Jesus**, am sure that **God** will speak to you, and you will hear. 4 Accept my confidence, for **Jesus' confidence** is yours. 5 Our minds are joined. 6 We wait with one intent; to hear our Father's answer to our call, to let our **egoic** thoughts be still and find **God's** peace, to hear **God** speak to us of what we are, and to reveal Himself unto His Son.

Notes to Lesson #221

Peace to my mind. Let all my thoughts be still.

<u>**Comment**</u>: When you silence the voice for your ego's fear-based thought system, you will hear the Voice for God. By quieting your egoic mind and going within, you join with Jesus and the Holy Spirit in the single purpose of remembering God. Minds are joined. Your true thoughts are the thoughts you share with the Mind of God.

LESSON 222

God is with me. I live and move in Him.

W-222.1.God is with me. 2 **God** is my Source of life, the life within, the air I breathe, the food by which I am sustained, the water which renews and cleanses me. 3 **God** is my home, wherein I live and move; the Spirit which directs my actions, offers me **God's** Thoughts, and guarantees my safety from all pain. 4 **God** covers me with kindness and with care, and holds in love the Son **God** shines upon, who also shines on **God**. 5 How still is he who knows the truth of what **God** speaks today!

W-222.2. <Father, we have no words except Your Name upon our lips and in our minds, as we come quietly into Your Presence now, and ask to rest with You in peace a while.>

Notes to Lesson #222

God is with me. I live and move in Him.

<u>**Comment**</u>: When you silence the voice for your ego's fear-based thought system, you will hear the Voice for God. By quieting your egoic mind and going within, you join with Jesus and the Holy Spirit in the single purpose of remembering God. Minds are joined. Your true thoughts are the thoughts you share with the Mind of God.

God is my life. I have no life but God's.

W-223.1.I was mistaken when I thought I lived apart from God, a separate entity that moved in isolation, unattached, and housed within a body. 2 Now I know my life is God's, I have no other home, and I do not exist apart from **God.** 3 **God** has no Thoughts that are not part of me, and I have none but those which are of **God.**

W-223.2. <Our Father, let us see the face of Christ instead of our mistakes. 2 For we who are Your holy Son are sinless. 3 We would look upon our sinlessness, for guilt proclaims that we are not Your Son. 4 And we would not forget You longer. 5 We are lonely here **in the illusion of time and separation**, and long for Heaven, where we are at home. 6 Today we would return **to Heaven**. 7 Our Name is Yours, and we acknowledge that we are Your Son.>

Notes to Lesson #223

God is my life. I have no life but God's.

Comment: There is only the One Self. My true thoughts are the thoughts I share with the Mind of God. I was mistaken to believe God's beloved Child could be limited and separate from my Source. I and my Father are One. I claim my divine birthright for I have no existence apart from God, my Source.

LESSON 224

God is my Father, and God loves His Son.

W-224.1.My true Identity , **my big "S" Self,** is so secure, so lofty, sinless, glorious and great, wholly beneficent and free from guilt, that Heaven looks to **my true Identity** to give **Heaven** light. 2 **My true Identity** lights the world as well. 3 **My true Identity** is the gift my Father gave to me; the one as well I give the world. 4 There is no gift but **my true Identity** that can be either given or received. 5 **My true Identity** is reality, and only this. 6 **My true Identity** is illusion's end. 7 **My true Identity** is the truth.

W-224.2. <My Name, O Father, still is known to You. 2 I have forgotten **my true Identity**, and do not know where I am going, who I am, or what it is I do. 3 Remind me, Father, now, for I am weary of the **egoic** world **of fear** I see. 4 Reveal what You would have me see instead.>

Notes to Lesson #224

God is my Father, and God loves His Son.

Comment: Because God is my Father and loves me unconditionally, I cannot fail to reawaken to the truth of what I am. The Holy Spirit resides within me and guides me to the truth that light is my true Identity. This fear-based world is not my home. I will let the Holy Spirit lead me home and reclaim my divine inheritance.

God is my Father, and His Son loves Him.

W-225.1. <Father, I must return Your Love for me, for giving and receiving are the same, and You have given all Your Love to me. 2 I must return **Your Love for me** for I want it mine, in full awareness, blazing in my mind and keeping **my mind** within **the** kindly light **of Your Love**, inviolate, beloved, with fear behind and only peace ahead. 3 How still the way Your loving Son is led along to You!>

W-225.2.Brother, we find that stillness now. 2 The way is open. 3 Now we follow **the way to God** in peace together. 4 You have reached your hand to me, and **I, Jesus**, will never leave you. 5 We are one, and it is but this oneness that we seek, as we accomplish these few final steps which end a journey that was not begun.

Notes to Lesson #225

God is my Father, and His Son loves Him.

Comment: God is living in us. Accept and extend the love of God to all by sharing your Christ nature. To give is to receive. It is only by being a conduit for God's love do you realize that you possess the love of God. By sharing the thought of God with your brother, you strengthen that thought within both minds. Together, as one mind united in a common goal, we advance towards the peace of God that is our destiny.

LESSON 226

My home awaits me. I will hasten there.

W-226.1.If I so choose, I can depart this **egoic** world **of misperception** entirely. 2 It is not death which makes **departing this egoic world** possible, but it is change of mind about the purpose of the world. 3 If I believe **this egoic world of perception** has a value as I see it now, so will **this world** still remain for me. 4 But if I see no value in the **egoic world** as I behold it, nothing that I want to keep as mine or search for as a goal, **the world as I previously perceived it** will depart from me. 5 For I have not sought for illusions to replace the truth.

W-226.2. <Father, my home awaits my glad return. 2 Your Arms are open and I hear Your Voice. 3 What need have I to linger in a place of vain desires and of shattered dreams, when Heaven can so easily be mine?>

Notes to Lesson #226

My home awaits me. I will hasten there.

Comment: Value truth, not illusions. To escape this world, you do not have to die. You merely have to change your mind about your world's purpose.

Your ego believes that you are not perfect, whole or complete. It believes a little "s" self has replaced God's beloved Son. Because of this, your ego values the world as an outside power that can fulfill your needs and provide some limited safety or happiness.

Your mind is the true creative power behind your world. Change how you define yourself. You are as God created you, perfect, whole and complete. There is nothing outside your own mind that can make you happy or cause you to lose your inner peace.

The idols of your egoic world possess no creative power. When you stop valuing the things of this world, the world you perceive must change to align with your new viewpoint. This world's purpose can either be to confirm your belief in your littleness as an ego-body or your spiritual magnificence as the Christ. You get to choose which it will be.

LESSON 227

This is my holy instant of release.

W-227.1. <Father, it is today that I am free, because my will is Your **Will**. 2 I thought to make another will. 3 Yet nothing that I thought apart from You exists. 4 And I am free because I was mistaken, and did not affect my own reality at all by my illusions. 5 Now I give **my illusion of lack, limitation and separation** up, and lay them down before the feet of truth, to be removed forever from my mind. 6 This is my holy instant of release. 7 Father, I know my will is one with Your Will.>

W-227.2. And so today we find our glad return to Heaven, which we never really left. 2 The Son of God this day lays down his dreams **of sin, guilt and fear.** 3 The Son of God this day comes home again, released from sin and clad in holiness, with his right mind, **his Christ nature,** restored to him at last.

Notes to Lesson #227

This is my holy instant of release.

Comment: Your illusions cannot change the truth that you remain as God created you. Your fantasies cannot change a God of love into a God of fear. Give up your illusions of sin, guilt and fear and accept the truth that you are God's beloved child and reclaim your divine birthright that was never lost, but merely forgotten.

LESSON 228

God has condemned me not. No more do I.

W-228.1. My Father knows my holiness. **My ego denies my holiness.** 2 Shall I deny **God's** knowledge, and believe in what **God's** knowledge makes impossible? 3 Shall I accept as true what **God** proclaims as false? 4 Or shall I take **God's** Word for what I am, since **God** is my Creator, and the One Who knows the true condition of His Son?

W-228.2. <Father, I was mistaken in myself **by following the thought system of my ego**, because I failed to realize **You alone are** the Source from which I came. 2 I have not left **God, my** Source, to enter in a body and to die. 3 My holiness remains a part of me, as I am part of **God, my Source.** 4 And my mistakes about myself are dreams. 5 I let **my mistakes and egoic misperceptions** go today. 6 And I stand ready to receive Your Word alone for what I really am.>

Notes to Lesson #228

God has condemned me not. No more do I.

Comment: Like begets like. God is your Source and thus, you must be holy. God knows that you remain part of the One Self. God has never condemned His Creation, so why would you? Your ego denies your holiness and claims its egoic fantasies have changed God's reality.

Who is more likely to be right, God or your ego? Today, let us not question or doubt God's knowledge and authority.

LESSON 229

Love, which created me, is what I am.

W-229.1.I seek my own Identity, and find **my Identity** in these words: "Love, which created me, is what I am." 2 Now need I seek no more **for I know what I am.** 3 Love has prevailed. 4 So still **my Identity as Love** waited for my coming home, that I will turn away no longer from the holy face of Christ. 5 And what I look upon attests **to the truth that my** Identity **as being only love remains although** I sought to lose **it,** but my Father has kept **my true Identity** safe for me.

W-229.2. <Father, my thanks to You for what I am; for keeping my Identity **as my big "S" Self** untouched and sinless, in the midst of all the thoughts of sin my foolish **egoic** mind made up. 2 And thanks to You for saving me from **all my ego's thoughts of sin, guilt, fear, lack, limitation and separation.** 3 Amen.>

Notes to Lesson #229

Love, which created me, is what I am.

Comment: God's love always protects your true Identity which is your Christ nature. We remain only love. Because like begets like, we cannot be anything but love. By removing your ego's belief in lack, limitation and separation, you remove the blocks that hide your true identity from your awareness.

As these blocks are removed, your true identity reappears. Your goal is not to become love for that is what you already are. Instead, your goal is merely to remove the erroneous beliefs about what you are and then the light of who you are will shine forth and illuminate your world.

LESSON 230

Now will I seek and find the peace of God.

W-230.1.In peace I was created. 2 And in peace do I remain. 3 It is not given me to change my **big "S" Self.** 4 How merciful is God my Father, that when He created me **God** gave me peace forever. 5 Now I ask but to be what I am, **my Christ nature which is only love.** 6 And can **my Christ nature which is only love** be denied me, when **what God created** is forever true?

W-230.2. <Father, I seek the peace You gave as mine in my creation. 2 **The peace that** was given then must be here now, for my creation was apart from time, and still remains beyond all change. 3 The peace in which Your Son was born into Your Mind is shining there unchanged. 4 I am as You created me. 5 I need but call on You to find the peace You gave. 6 It is Your Will that gave **eternal peace** to Your Son.>

Notes to Lesson #230

Now will I seek and find the peace of God.

Comment: You are part of the shared Mind of God and remain holy and sinless as God created you. Your denial of that truth cannot change your inheritance. Yet, it can prevent you from realizing the gifts that you have been given.

Forgive yourself, your world and God. When you do so, you reclaim your divine birthright. God has never condemned you. It is only your own mind's unforgiving thoughts that crucify yourself. Unlock the prison doors of your unforgiving mind and allow all, including yourself, to go free.

What Is Salvation?

Covers ACIM Workbook Lessons 231-240

2. What Is Salvation?

W-pII.2.1.Salvation is a promise, made by God, that you would find your way to **God** at last. 2 **The promise of salvation and your return to God** cannot but be kept. 3 **Salvation** guarantees that time will have an end, and all the **fear-based** thoughts **of lack, limitation and separation** that have been born in time will end as well. 4 God's Word is given every mind which thinks that **its split mind** has separate thoughts, and will replace these thoughts of conflict with the Thought of peace.

W-pII.2.2.The Thought of peace was given to God's Son the instant that his **split** mind had thought of war. 2 There was no need for such a Thought before, for peace was given without opposite, and merely was. 3 But when the mind is split there is a need of healing. 4 So the Thought **of peace and forgiveness** that has the power to heal the split became a part of every fragment of the mind that still was one, but failed to recognize its oneness **and believed itself to be separate from its Source.** 5 Now **the split mind** did not know **its Big "S" Self**, and thought its own Identity **as God's beloved Son** was lost.

W-pII.2.3.Salvation is undoing in the sense that **salvation** does nothing, failing to support the world of dreams and malice. 2 Thus **salvation** lets illusions go. 3 By not supporting **the split mind's illusions of lack, limitation and separation, salvation** merely lets **the illusions** quietly go down to dust. 4 And what **the illusions** hid is now revealed. **Hidden behind the illusion is** an altar to the holy Name of God whereon **God's** Word is written, with the gifts of your forgiveness laid before **the altar to God**, and the memory of God not far behind.

W-pII.2.4.Let us come daily to this holy place, and spend a while together. 2 Here we share our final dream. 3 **Our final dream** is a dream in which there is no sorrow, for **this final happy dream** holds a hint of all the glory given us by God. 4 The grass is pushing through the soil, the trees are budding now, and birds have come to live within their branches. 5 Earth is being born again in new perspective. 6 Night has gone, and we have come together in the light.

W-pII.2.5.From **this final happy dream** we give salvation to the world, for it is here salvation was received. 2 The song of our rejoicing is the call to all the world that freedom is returned, that time is almost over, and God's Son has but an instant more to wait until his Father is remembered, dreams are done, eternity has shined away the world, and only Heaven now exists at all.

Notes to Special Theme #2: What Is Salvation?

Covers ACIM Workbook Lessons 231-240

What Is Salvation?

Central Theme for Lessons 231 to 240

Salvation is a promise, made by God, that you would find your way to **God** at last. God is Truth with a capital T. By substituting the word truth for God, salvation now becomes a promise made by God, that you would find your way to Truth at last.

Since truth is true and what is false is not true, truth must become our reality. Salvation guarantees that time will end and with it, all egoic illusions of lack, limitation and separation will dissolve and only the truth of the unity and love of the One Self will remain.

God knows what He is. The natural state of mind is to know itself. A mind that claims it does not know itself is a mind that is asleep. A mind that is awake knows what it is and has no identity crisis.

It is impossible to not be what you are. An example of Mr. Smith might best illustrate this point.

Mr. Smith can only be Mr. Smith. He cannot be a dog. Mr. Smith can pretend he is a dog, but his pretense does not transform him magically into becoming a dog. Mr. Smith remains a man pretending he is a dog. He retains his true reality as a human being called Mr. Smith. Mr. Smith's denial of who he is does not change the truth that he still is Mr. Smith.

Similarly we are God's beloved child with whom God is well pleased. We remain as God created us. Like Mr. Smith, we can deny the truth and pretend we do not know what we are. Yet, we still remain God's beloved Child pretending to be something he is not.

The Child's mind is asleep and needs to wake up. Once awake, the mind remembers what it truly is and that nothing has changed. The mind returns to its natural state and joins with the shared Mind of God. The dream of separation had no ability to change the reality of what the sleeping Mind truly is.

According to ACIM, salvation does nothing. Salvation is merely the undoing in the sense that your mind simply stops supporting your dream world of anger and fear. Salvation lets illusions go by no longer supporting them. The illusion that you could be something other than as God created you simply disappears. What the illusion hid is now revealed and you reawaken to the truth that you remain as God created you.

Salvation is the happy dream of reawakening to that Truth. Salvation is the final dream with a different purpose and viewpoint. Therefore, salvation fosters a new perspective for your world based on the idea of love, forgiveness and oneness. The world you perceive is transformed from a world of hate and fear to a world of mercy and love. This is the same shift in purpose for your world that was discussed in the forgiveness section that we just completed.

In this final dream, our purpose is to give to the world its salvation rather than our condemnation. By granting salvation to all, we receive and acknowledge our own salvation. Time is almost over and the return to the remembrance of God is only an instant away. We are at Heaven's Gate where all illusions disappear and only Heaven will remain.

Your mind needs healing when you claim you are not your big "S" Self. Salvation is the healing of the split mind. A mind that fails to recognize its true identity is delusional. Just like Mr. Smith who has forgotten that he is merely a human pretending to be a dog, our insane mind needs to remember our true Identity as our big "S" Self. Healing restores the split mind by remembering its true and eternal nature as Christ.

The peace of God was given to God's Son the instant the split mind thought of war. What is war but an attack upon your own Identity as God's Creation. A split mind is a sleeping mind that makes war upon your Christ nature based upon your ego's misperceptions about what you are.

Salvation is the healing or awakening of the sleeping mind to the truth that it has only been dreaming. Forgiveness brings about healing because it is the recognition of the truth that we remain God's beloved Child even when we sleep.

When asked, people often reply that they feel the most loved when they are accepted just the way they are. Love is the acceptance of another without judgment and thus, love has no need to change, control or fix another. Love allows and holds the truth for another without egoic conditions. Love may or may not perform the role another ego-body had hoped it would play because love simply follows the guidance of the Holy Spirit. Love does not follow the voice for fear.

In our world of time and space, the term salvation is associated with the idea of being saved. Typically in salvation, you are brought from a state of sin, conflict and unhappiness into a new state of joy and redemption. Religious salvation assumes that someone has sinned and that retribution needs to be made if heaven is to be obtained or regained.

Salvation is another example of a common word that subconsciously engenders fear since it assumes that Paradise has been lost. The common definition of salvation supports the idea of sin, guilt and fear that is associated with the ego's belief in lack, limitation and separation.

Salvation, like forgiveness, is an aspect of love that we could not experience in Heaven since there is no one to be saved. Paradise was never lost. Only in the illusion of time could the need for salvation exist because time is the illusion of pretending you are something you are not. In time, our egos can pretend we or someone else needs to be saved. Only in the illusion of time could a sleeping mind fail to realize its unity with the One Self or that it is the dreamer of the dream of lack, limitation and separation.

In the world of form, salvation or the saving of another is a specific example of helping. Salvation or being helpful is an attribute of love, yet it is something that cannot be experienced in Heaven. To be helpful requires someone to pretend that they truly need help. To save another requires someone to erroneously believe they have sinned or could die.

For you to experience the attribute of love that we call helpfulness or saving another from their troubles, you need someone who is willing to play the role of requiring your help. Our desire to participate in the game of separation has never been a problem. The game of separation allows us to demonstrate in the world of form, aspects of love that cannot be experienced in Heaven.

In Heaven, these attributes and terms are meaningless due to our true reality as part of the One Self. Due to the abstract nature of a Oneness of All That Is, these terms have no function or purpose in Truth. Differentiation is needed, if one is to simulate the experience of the specific aspects of love that we call forgiveness or salvation.

Like Mr. Smith, our problem with the game of separation is not the fact that we wanted to pretend we were something we are not. Our problem only arose when we failed to remember that we are merely playing a game and that the game has no ability to change what we are. When we forgot to laugh and mistook the game as having real life and death consequences, fear was born within the minds of the players. Within our confused mind, the game now took on a reality of its own and became our provisional reality.

The game of What Am I was designed to provide simulated experiences that we desired and were impossible to experience within the truth of the abstract One Self. We desire to be love not just to know that we are love. We wanted to demonstrate the various aspects of love and differentiation is required for that experience to be possible.

By being love in form, we complete God and the abstract One Self knows Itself. Remember, differentiation does not mean different. Differentiation just allows us to be aware of various aspects of Itself, which is only Love.

In time, salvation is the realization that nobody needs salvation. This is why salvation does nothing. It merely is the ending of our ego's belief that we could be something other than as God created us, perfect, whole and complete, part of the inseparable Oneness of All That Is.

The final happy dream that brings salvation to your world is your sharing of the truth that sin, lack, limitation and separation are not real. Your brothers and sisters are innocent and sinless. There is no one to save for salvation is guaranteed by God and was never lost, only momentarily forgotten. Each is on their own perfect path and exactly where they need to be in their reawakening to the truth according to God's plan.

In the dream of salvation, you need do nothing to fix, change, control, protect or impress another. You merely hold the truth that sleeping minds have temporarily forgotten what they are. The happy dream of salvation is similar to what Jesus said that he does. From A Course in Miracles Jesus says, "If you want to be like me, I will help you knowing that we are the same. If you want to be different, I will wait until you change your mind."

In the happy dream of salvation, our egoic mind needs to do nothing. We do not judge another or make them wrong for where they are in their journey of awakening. We merely hold the truth for all, and when guided, extend a helping hand. We rest in the knowledge that only God's plan guarantees all will find their way home and that the remembrance of God will heal the split mind. We trust the guidance of the Holy Spirit as we ask and follow what love would have us do.

Salvation is the happy dream in which you realize that your egoic mind has nothing to do. You can drop all your ego's plans for your salvation since salvation cannot be earned. God wills that your divine inheritance was never lost. You share the truth that all rest safely in God's love. With this granting of the truth of your brother's salvation, you receive your own salvation. You now rest in the peace of God.

Father, I will but to remember You.

W-231.1. <What can I seek for, Father, but Your Love? 2 Perhaps I think I seek for something else **other than Your Love**; a something I have called by many **egoic** names. 3 Yet is Your Love the only thing I seek, or ever sought. 4 For there is nothing else that I could ever really want to find **but Your Love.** 5 Let me remember You. 6 What else could I desire but the truth about myself?>

W-231.2.**The desire to remember God and know the truth about your big "S" Self** is your will, my brother. 2 And you share this will **of being only Love** with me, and with **God** as well Who is our Father. 3 To remember **God** is Heaven. 4 **It is** this **remembrance and Love of God** we seek. 5 And only **God's Love** is what it will be given us to find.

Notes to Lesson #231

Father, I will but to remember You.

Comment: The remembrance of God is to know the truth about your big "S" Self, your Christ nature. Seek only the love of God and all is given you. There is nothing outside to seek for love knows no opposites. God, your brother and you are only love for all are part of that One Self.

LESSON 232

Be in my mind, my Father, through the day.

W-232.1. <Be in my mind, my Father, when I wake, and shine on me throughout the day today. 2 Let every minute be a time in which I dwell with You. 3 And let me not forget my hourly thanksgiving that You have remained with me, and **the Holy Spirit** always will be there to hear my call to You and **the Holy Spirit will** answer me. 4 As evening comes, let all my thoughts be still of You and of Your Love. 5 And let me sleep sure of my safety, certain of Your care, and happily aware I am Your Son.>

W-232.2.This is as every day should be. 2 Today, **you** practice the end of fear. 3 **Today, you** have faith in **God** Who is your Father. 4 **Today, you** trust all things to **the Holy Spirit.** 5 Let **the Holy Spirit** reveal all things to you, and be you undismayed because you are **God's** Son.

Notes to Lesson #232

Be in my mind, my Father, through the day.

Comment: Place your faith in God and fear will end. You will realize that you are always safe in God's hands. Today be willing to forgive yourself for allowing fear to hide the reality of your Christ nature. Deny your ego's vision of God's Son being a sinful, powerless victim that lives in fear. Give your day over to the Holy Spirit and follow the Voice for God's love and fear will no longer rule your day.

LESSON 233

I give my life to God to guide today.

W-233.1. <Father, I give You all my thoughts today. 2 I would have none of **my ego's thoughts of littleness, lack, separation and fear.** 3 In place of **my fear-based thoughts**, give me Your Own **Thoughts.** 4 I give You all my acts as well, that I may do Your Will instead of seeking **the** goals **of my ego** which cannot be obtained, and wasting time in vain **egoic** imaginings. 5 Today I come to You. 6 I will step back and merely follow **the guidance of the Holy** Spirit. 7 **I allow the Holy Spirit to** be **my** Guide, and I the follower who questions not the wisdom of the Infinite, nor Love whose tenderness I cannot comprehend, but which is yet Your perfect gift to me.>

W-233.2. Today we have one Guide, **the Holy Spirit,** to lead us on. 2 And as we walk together, we will give this day to **the Holy Spirit** with no reserve at all. 3 This is **the Holy Spirit's** day. 4 And so it is a day of countless gifts and mercies unto us.

Notes to Lesson #233

I give my life to God to guide today.

Comment: Give up your allegiance to your ego's fear-based thought system. You can never escape fear within a thought system that is based upon the ego's belief in lack, limitation and separation.

Instead, drop your ego's plans and give your thoughts, deeds and actions over to the Holy Spirit's guidance. By following the Voice for God, you become a messenger for the Holy Spirit and fulfill your role in God's plan for the reawakening of our sleeping minds to their spiritual magnificence.

LESSON 234

Father, today I am Your Son again.

W-234.1. Today we will anticipate the time when dreams of sin and guilt are gone, and we have reached the holy peace we never left. 2 Merely a tiny instant has elapsed between eternity and timelessness. 3 So brief the interval **between eternity and timelessness that** there was no lapse in continuity, nor break in thoughts which are forever unified as one **thought of the shared Mind of God.** 4 Nothing has ever happened to disturb the peace of God the Father and the Son. 5 This **eternal peace that we share with God as His Son** we accept as wholly true today.

W-234.2. <We thank You, Father, that we cannot lose the memory of You and of Your Love. 2 We recognize our safety, and give thanks for all the gifts You have bestowed on us, for all the loving help we have received, for Your eternal patience, and the Word which You have given us that we are saved.>

Notes to Lesson #234

Father, today I am Your Son again.

Comment: Time is like the blink of your eye. In eternity and timelessness, the illusion of time is over as soon as it is begun. In reference to the big picture, our dreams of separation are brief and our reawakening is guaranteed since we never truly forgot or lost the memory of God or the truth of what we are.

God in His mercy wills that I be saved.

W-235.1.I need but look upon all things that seem to hurt me, and with perfect certainty assure myself, "God wills that I be saved from this **egoic belief that I could be hurt**," and merely watch **the belief** disappear. 2 I need but keep in mind my Father's Will for me is only happiness, to find that only happiness has come to me. 3 And I need but remember that God's Love surrounds His Son and keeps his sinlessness forever perfect, to be sure that I am saved and safe forever in **God's** Arms. 4 I am the Son **God** loves. 5 And I am saved because God in His mercy wills **my perfect sinlessness is** so.

W-235.2. <Father, Your Holiness is mine. 2 Your Love created me, and made my sinlessness forever part of You. 3 I have no guilt nor sin in me, for there is none in You.>

Notes to Lesson #235

God in His mercy wills that I be saved.

Comment: God's Will is that you remain safe from all things that could hurt you. The only thing that can appear to harm you is your own ego's beliefs in lack, limitation and separation. These illusions are your own mind's making yet leave you in a state of fear. Turn your egoic thoughts over to the Holy Spirit and learn to accept the truth about yourself.

God's Will for you is only your happiness and God protects you from your own mind's misperceptions. You remain guiltless and sinless. Your illusions cannot change what God has created. God's Will keeps you safe from your own ego's belief in sin, guilt and fear guaranteeing your reawakening to the truth. You remain guiltless and sinless and are God's beloved Son with whom He is well pleased.

LESSON 236

I rule my mind, which I alone must rule.

W-236.1.I have a kingdom I must rule **which is my mind**. 2 At times, it does not seem I am **my mind's** king at all. 3 **My egoic mind** seems to triumph over me, and tell me what to think, and what to do and feel. 4 And yet **my mind** has been given me to serve whatever purpose I perceive in **my mind.** 5 My mind can only serve. 6 Today I give **my mind's** service to the Holy Spirit to employ as **the Holy Spirit** sees fit. 7 I thus direct my mind, which I alone can rule. 8 And thus I set **my mind** free to do the Will of God.

W-236.2. <Father, my mind is open to Your Thoughts, and closed today to every thought but **Your Thoughts**. 2 I rule my mind, and offer **my mind** to You. 3 Accept my gift, for **my mind** is **Your gift** to me.>

Notes to Lesson #236

I rule my mind, which I alone must rule.

Comment: Your mind is your own domain to rule and control. The world you see is merely a reflection of your mind's thoughts and beliefs. You are the decision-maker who decides which thought system you will choose to follow. You must choose between fear or love and forgiveness.

As the ruler of your mind, freely choose to follow the thought system of the Holy Spirit and turn everything over to It. When you do your mind is now free to follow and serve God's Will. By doing so, you receive God's gifts which are His Thoughts for your happiness. Your mind now will serve the purpose of love and forgiveness instead of conflict and fear. By following God's plan, you will look upon a world of mercy and love. Rule your mind with love and forgiveness and the Holy Spirit will see that your world reflects that same viewpoint.

LESSON 237

Now would I be as God created me.

W-237.1.Today I will accept the truth about myself. 2 I will arise in glory, and allow the light in me to shine upon the world throughout the day. 3 I bring the world the tidings of salvation which I hear as God my Father speaks to me. 4 And I behold the world that Christ would have me see, aware **Christ vision** ends the bitter dream of death; aware **the tidings of salvation** are my Father's Call to me.

W-237.2. <Christ is my eyes today, and **Christ** the ears that listen to the Voice for God today. 2 Father, I come to You through **Christ** Who is Your Son, and my true **big "S" Self** as well. 3 Amen.>

Notes to Lesson #237

Now would I be as God created me.

Comment: Accept the truth of your big "S" Self and embrace your divine inheritance. Allow the Holy Spirit to direct your thoughts and the vision of Christ will be granted. The law of Christ vision says, never to mistake the body for the Son of God. Accept the Atonement or Oneness for yourself. When you do, since to give is to receive, you will be giving that same truth to all.

LESSON 238

On my decision all salvation rests.

W-238.1. <Father, Your trust in me has been so great, I must be worthy. 2 You created me, and know me as I am. 3 And yet You placed Your Son's salvation in my hands, and let **Your Son's salvation** rest on my decision. 4 I must be beloved of You indeed. 5 And I must be steadfast in holiness as well, that You would give Your Son to me in certainty that **Your Son** is safe Who still is part of You, and yet is mine, because **Your Son** is my **big "S" Self**.>

W-238.2.And so, again today, we pause to think how much our Father loves us. 2 And how dear **God's** Son, created by **God's** Love, remains to **God** Whose Love is made complete in **God's Son**.

Notes to Lesson #238

On my decision all salvation rests.

Comment: God's love is made complete in us. God loves and trusts us to be able to take our egoic illusions and allow the Holy Spirit to reframe those illusions to support the truth of the oneness of the whole.

Salvation rests on your decision to abandon fear and accept the truth of who you are. God trusts us to demonstrate in this world of form the specific attributes of love called forgiveness and helpfulness. By demonstrating these attributes of love in your world, you heal the split mind and complete God's Will.

When you live in fear, your ego believes that you must do something to save yourself, your brother and your world. Instead, drop your ego's fear based plans for salvation and follow the guidance of the Holy Spirit. Only God's plan will work and is guaranteed to reclaim your divine inheritance.

Rather than perceive your world as a fearful place, see it as a playschool for reawakening to the truth. Each is the creator of their own experiences and all are on the perfect path of reawakening. Rule your mind and be vigilant only for God. When your sole purpose is only to follow God's plan, your course of action becomes clear. By following the Holy Spirit's guidance, conflicts and stress fade away since the outcome is guaranteed by God's Will.

Now you can drop all your ego's plans to fix, change, control, impress, protect or save another. Your ego does not understand who and what God's creations are. When you accept the truth for yourself that all remain innocent and sinless as God created them, there is no one to save. God has never condemned anyone and neither will you. All are free to take their rightful place as God's beloved Child. You have saved your world from your own ego. You are now free to go home.

LESSON 239

The glory of my Father is my own.

The glory of my Father is my own.

W-239.1.Let not the truth about ourselves today be hidden by a false humility. 2 Let us instead be thankful for the gifts our Father gave us. 3 Can we see in **God's Son** with whom **God** shares His glory any trace of sin and guilt? 4 And can it be that we are not among **God's Children**, when He loves His Son forever and with perfect constancy, knowing **God's Son** is as **God** created him?

W-239.2. <We thank You, Father, for the light that shines forever in us, **Your Son**. 2 And we honor **the light** because You share **the light** with us. 3 We are one, united in this light and one with You, at peace with all creation and ourselves.>

Notes to Lesson #239

The glory of my Father is my own.

Comment: Arrogance is the claim that you are less than what God knows you to be. God knows that you are part of the indivisible One Self. Do not be arrogant. Instead, accept your divine birthright.

God has extended Himself in all of us. We are expressions of God. On earth, our function is forgiveness which is a demonstration of being love in form. You glorify God when you accept and extend the truth that you, like your Source, are only love.

LESSON 240

Fear is not justified in any form.

Fear is not justified in any form.

W-240.1.Fear is deception. 2 **Fear** attests that you have seen yourself as you could never be, and therefore look upon a world **of egoic misperception** which is impossible. 3 Not one thing in this world is true. 4 It does not matter what the form in which **the things of this world of perception** may appear. 5 **All things you perceive are** witnesses but to your own illusions of yourself. 6 Let us not be deceived today. 7 We are the Sons of God. 8 There is no fear in us, for we are each a part of Love Itself.

W-240.2. <How foolish are our fears! 2 Would **God** allow **His** Son to suffer? 3 Give us faith today to recognize **God's** Son **in our brother**, and set **God's Son** free. 4 Let us forgive **our brother, God's Son,** in **God's** Name, that we may understand **the** holiness **of God's Son** and feel the love for **God's Son** which is **God's** Own **love** as well.>

Notes to Lesson #240

Fear is not justified in any form.

Comment: If you are in fear, it means that you have forgotten that you are God's beloved Child with whom He is well pleased. You have allowed body thoughts to rise to the level of mind and made the belief that you are the body into your provisional reality.

Fear is false evidence appearing real. Fear is the deception that you could be something other than as God created you. There is not one thing in this world that your ego perceives correctly. By allowing yourself to be vulnerable, you teach yourself that you are actually invulnerable unlimited spirit and not some game token that we call the body. As mind or spirit, there are no outside forces that can rob you of your inner peace unless your mind allows it.

What Is the World?

Covers ACIM Workbook Lessons 241-250

3. What Is the World?

W-pII.3.1.The world is false perception. 2 **The world** is born of error, and **the world** has not left its source **which is the mind that thought in error**. 3 **The world of false perception** will remain no longer than the **erroneous** thought that gave it birth is cherished. 4 When the thought of separation has been changed to one of true forgiveness, will the world be seen in quite another light; and one which leads to truth, where all the world **of false perception** must disappear and all its errors vanish. 5 Now its source, **the mind's false beliefs and thoughts** have gone, and **the** effects **of the mind's erroneous beliefs** are gone as well.

W-pII.3.2.The **false** world **of separation** was made as an attack on God. 2 **The false world of separation** symbolizes fear. 3 And what is fear except love's absence? 4 Thus the world **of false perception** was meant to be a place where God could enter not, and where **God's** Son could be apart from **God**. 5 Here **in the false belief that God's Son could be separated from God, his Source,** was perception born, for knowledge could not cause such insane thoughts. 6 But with **perception,** eyes deceive, and ears hear falsely. 7 Now, **in the world of perception,** mistakes become quite possible, for **the** certainty **of knowledge** has gone.

W-pII.3.3.The **split egoic mind with its physical senses are the** mechanisms of illusions **that** have been born instead **of Truth, with a capital T.** 2 And now **the senses** go to find **the illusions that have** been given **to the senses** to seek **by the split mind's erroneous belief in separation**. 3 **The** aim **of perception and its senses are** to fulfill the **egoic** purpose which the world was made to witness **which is the false belief in separation** and make **the separation appear** real. 4 **The senses** see in **the split mind's** illusions but a solid base where truth exists, upheld apart from lies. 5 Yet everything that **the senses** report is but illusion which is kept apart from truth.

W-pII.3.4.As sight was made to lead away from truth, **sight** can be redirected. 2 **When redirected by the Holy Spirit** sounds become the call for God, and all perception can be given a new purpose by the One Whom God appointed Savior to the world. 3 Follow **the Holy Spirit's** light, and see the world as **the Holy Spirit** beholds it. 4 Hear **the Holy Spirit's** Voice alone in all that speaks to you. 5 And let **the Holy Spirit** give you peace and certainty, which you have thrown away, but Heaven has preserved for you in **the Holy Spirit**.

W-pII.3.5.Let us not rest content until the world has joined our changed perception. 2 Let us not be satisfied until forgiveness has been made complete. 3 And let us not attempt to change our function **of forgiveness**. 4 We must save the world **of false perception that arose from the split mind's belief in separation**. 5 For we who made **the false world of separation** must behold **perception** through the eyes of Christ, that what was made **by our split mind** to die can be restored to everlasting life.

Notes to Special Theme #3: What Is the World?

Covers ACIM Workbook Lessons 241-250

What Is the World?

Central Theme for Lessons 241 to 250

The world as we know it is a world of false perception. The world was born out of the idea of separation and will continue to remain as our provisional reality as long as the mind that birthed the world continues to value the thought of separation. When the thought of separation has been changed to the thought of true forgiveness, the world as you perceive it will be seen differently by your mind.

The new viewpoint for seeing your world will lead to the truth that the separation is not real. By changing the thoughts that the mind values, the belief and effects of the thought of separation and its related world will disappear. All errors that arose from those thoughts will also vanish. The thought of separation is the powerhouse that made the world of false perception seem real. When this thought is gone, the effects of the belief in separation are also gone.

The world of false perception is an attack on God. This world symbolizes fear and what is fear but the absence of love. This world was perceived to be a place where God's love could not enter. It was a place where we could imagine that we had been exiled from the safety and protection of a God of only love. It becomes a place where sinners can either hide from or be punished by a judgmental god of wrath. Here, in the world of perception, we can pretend that we are separate from God's love, separate from God and separate from our Source.

This world is a place where we can pretend we do not know what we are. We have lost the knowledge of our true Identity. This loss of certainty with our connection to our Source provides the mechanism for illusions to arise. Knowledge is based on certainty. Perception is based on uncertainty.

Perception is someone's judgment or opinion, not necessarily the facts. With the loss of certainty, mistakes become possible. Our senses were born to verify our ego's belief that its judgments were correct. Both our senses and the world of form are designed to prove that the separation is real.

So what does this all mean anyway?

A Course in Miracles says that this world is not real. This seems to contradict our senses and leads to an argument over whether the non-reality of this world is true. It also leads to the idea that if the world is not real, it is of no consequence. If so, what we do within this illusionary world is of no concern. If you kill, hate, steal, love, forgive or help another, it would not matter since the world is not real. No matter what you did, it would have no consequences since it would not change the truth of what you really are and you would always remain perfect, whole and complete.

If there are no real consequences to our actions in the form of a reward or punishment, what does it matter how we behave towards one another?

Our physical senses are designed to confuse form for content or purpose. We look at the form as something that we value rather than the purpose behind the thought-form.

ACIM states that the world is false perception born from the thought of separation. But what does separation really mean?

When most people talk about separation, they mean that there is a space or gap between two parties and they are not one. This is a proper interpretation based on form but not based on content or purpose. The senses and the world your senses observe deal with the form but not the thought that caused the manifestation of that thought to appear as some physical form or object.

The thought that birthed the form is what we need to focus on. When we mistake the form as separate from the thought that manifested it, we fail to realize the causative nature of our own mind. It now appears as if there are outside forces that create your world and that your mind is not the causative power behind your world.

The thought of separation is not the idea that you are physically separate from God. The thought of separation is the idea that there are outside forces that can rob you of your inner peace or make you happy. The thought of separation is the belief that you are not perfect, whole and complete as God created you and therefore, this imperfect creation has needs that must be met by outside forces that you do not directly control.

You may have some limited ability to indirectly influence these outside forces so that you can partially control, manage and mitigate the effects of their independent actions. Yet, your belief in separation asserts that these forces have some ability to oppose your will and that opposition to your desires can affect your own state of being. Separation is the belief that you are at least partially a victim of these outside forces and your happiness can be impacted by them. The implication is that you are flawed in some way.

A Course in Miracles states that rather than attempt to change your world, you should change how you view your world. When you change the purpose for your world, your world will automatically realign to support that new viewpoint or purpose. In our previous discussions, we have cloaked this idea with the terminology of our purpose being either love or fear. In the world of form, forgiveness represents acting in a loving manner and is fears opposite.

Fear arises any time you believe you lack the creative power to handle a given situation. Fear is really the belief that there are outside forces that can affect your state of being. ACIM is really asking that you change, not the form of your world, but rather the purpose that your world serves. Surprisingly, a world of seeming hate and fear does not have to support your mind's belief in separation. Currently, the purpose of this fearful world is to prove that your mind is an effect and not the cause of your experiences. Yet, you can reverse that thinking.

Your world currently acts as your mind's proving grounds to confirm that there are outside forces that can make you happy or sad. Perceiving ourselves as separate, we believe we are not totally responsible for our own happiness. We value the things of the world because we believe something outside ourselves can make us happy or sad.

It is important to note that our belief in separation supports the idea that outside forces can make us either happy or sad. Many spiritual types do not value this world as a source for their happiness. Instead, they view it as the cause that prevents them from being happy. Many spiritual types believe that only by departing from this world through physical death or renunciation can they escape to the Promised Land. This belief supports the thought that there are outside forces that can either make you happy or prevent your happiness. Both beliefs are equally disempowering and support and reaffirm your ego's belief in separation.

Grace is the acceptance of the love of God in a world of seeming hate and fear. Grace is accepting the power of your mind to interpret the events that swirl around your consciousness in a way that empowers your mind and supports your inner peace.

Grace is the acceptance that God has given you the gift of Mind. Your Mind is the source for your experiences. Because you have been given the gift of Mind, there is nothing outside your own mind that can rob you of your own inner peace or happiness. The Holy Spirit uses this world's belief in separation to teach that lesson.

Within the control of your mind is the power of interpretation. You get to give meaning to all that comes into your awareness. You can either choose to interpret the events and circumstances with fear or with love and forgiveness. Remember, forgiveness acknowledges and rests upon the fact that your own mind, not your brother, has the sole power to affect your inner peace.

If you choose to interpret this world of perception through the eyes of fear, you will be confirming your belief that there are outside forces that can rob you of your inner peace. You will be reaffirming your belief in separation. You will continue to hold grievances against these outside forces for not behaving in a manner conducive to your ego's plan for your happiness.

If you choose to interpret your world of perception through the eyes of love, you will confirm your belief that there are no outside forces that can make you happy or sad. You will realize that nothing can rob you of your own inner peace because your mind is the sole interpreter for all the meaning you assign to your world. When you forget that fact and a grievance arises, remember the truth and you will be able to forgive all and reinterpret your own thoughts with loving eyes thus reclaiming the creative power of your own mind. You will not attribute a thought-form with any creative power to impact your reality.

When you give your day over to the Holy Spirit, you are actually asking the Holy Spirit to teach you that there are no external forces outside your own mind that can make you happy or sad. You are not asking that all the events that transpire within your day be pleasant. Instead, you are asking that all events be seen through the prism of true reality that nothing outside your mind has any power over you.

You are asking the Holy Spirit's guidance in properly interpreting all events to support the causative nature of your own mind. In the world of form, you may still be physically robbed but you will know that no one can rob you of your mind's power of interpretation. You alone determine what meaning you will assign to that event. When you associate yourself as Mind and not the game token called the body, you no longer believe your safety rests in the preservation of the body or the things of this world.

The mind that knows that it alone is responsible for its own happiness is not affected by a world of seeming hate and fear. A mind that values this world as the source for its own happiness or sadness disempowers itself. It makes the world support its belief in separation and makes the world of seeming hate and fear real. Perceiving itself to lack the creative ability to handle the situations in its world, fear becomes that mind's provisional reality.

You save your world when you stop blaming the world for the loss of your inner peace and joy. Your world is an effect of your own mind's causative powers of thought. Being an effect, your world has no creative power to change the mind that thought it.

When you accept this principle of the creative power of your own mind, you drop the blame, shame and guilt game that keeps you trapped within the world of time. By claiming responsibility for your own thinking, you free yourself from the thought system of fear that was originally designed to support your ego's belief in lack, limitation and separation.

In eternity, your world remains exactly as it behaved in time. Your world has always been changeless; not in its appearance as form but rather in its inability to change the creative power of your own mind. The mind that transports its world from time to eternity knows this truth. You are not a body, you are free. You are still as God created you. Nothing sources your experience but you and nothing can affect you unless you choose to allow it within your own mind.

LESSON 241

This holy instant is salvation come.

W-241.1.What joy there is today! 2 It is a time of special celebration. 3 For today holds out the instant to the darkened world **of false perception** where **the world's** release is set. 4 The day has come when sorrows pass away and pain is gone. 5 The glory of salvation dawns today upon a world set free. 6 This is the time of hope for countless millions. 7 They will be united now, as you forgive them all. 8 For I will be forgiven by you today.

W-241.2. <We have forgiven one another now, and so we come at last to **God** again. 2 Father, Your Son, who never left, returns to Heaven and his home. 3 How glad are we to have our sanity restored to us, and to remember that we all are one.>

Notes to Lesson #241

This holy instant is salvation come.

Comment: Before you can forgive, you need to be willing to drop all your ego's judgments. Your ego cannot judge anything correctly for it fails to recognize that your mind is the true creative power behind your experiences. Your ego's fallacious judgments turn into grievances against your brother.

Give this day over to the Holy Spirit and allow the Holy Spirit to reframe your egoic judgments. Your condemnation of your brother only condemns yourself. Forgive and you will see things differently. Forgive and you are set free from your ego's belief in lack, limitation and separation.

LESSON 242

This day is God's. It is my gift to Him.

This day is God's. **This day** is my gift to Him.

W-242.1.I will not lead my life alone today. 2 I do not understand the world **of perception**, and so to try to lead my life alone must be but foolishness. 3 But there is One, **the Holy Spirit,** Who knows all that is best for me. 4 And, **the Holy Spirit** is glad to make no choices for me but the ones that lead to God. 5 I give this day to **the Holy Spirit**, for I would not delay my coming home, and it is **the Holy Spirit** Who knows the way to God.

W-242.2. <And so we give today to **God.** 2 We come with wholly open minds. 3 We do not ask for anything that **our egoic mind** may think we want. 4 Give us what You would have received by us. 5 You know all our desires and our wants. 6 And You will give us everything we need in helping us to find the way to You.>

Notes to Lesson #242

This day is God's. It is my gift to Him.

Comment: Since your ego does not know what you are, you cannot trust your ego's judgments or advice. Instead, follow the Voice for God, the Holy Spirit, who knows the truth and the way home. Surrender your egoic will to God's Will and be an expression of the love of God in form.

LESSON 243

Today I will judge nothing that occurs.

W-243.1.I will be honest with myself today. 2 I will not think that I already know what must remain beyond my present grasp. 3 I will not think I understand the whole from bits of my perception, which are all that I can see. 4 Today I recognize that this is so **and that I lack the complete picture.** 5 And so I am relieved of judgments that I cannot make **correctly.** 6 Thus do I free myself and what I **erroneously** look upon, to be in peace as God created us.

W-243.2. <Father, today I leave creation free to be itself. 2 I honor all **Creations'** parts, in which I am included. 3 We are one because each part contains Your memory, and truth must shine in all of us as one.>

Notes to Lesson #243

Today I will judge nothing that occurs.

Comment: Because we fail to understand the big picture, we cannot judge anything correctly. We do not have all the facts and therefore, are not asked or required by God to make any judgments. This is a good thing because we are incapable of judging correctly. When we judge another, we crucify and imprison ourselves.

All our ego's judgments are based on partial evidence that is designed to distort and falsely confirm our ego's belief in lack, limitation and separation.

Follow the guidance of the Holy Spirit, Who understands the big picture. If allowed, the Holy Spirit will reinterpret your experiences to honor the truth of who you really are. We are all part of the whole and each part contains the memory of our oneness with God. All minds are joined and all share in that remembrance of God, Who is our Source.

LESSON 244

I am in danger nowhere in the world.

W-244.1. <Your Son is safe wherever he may be, for You are there with him. 2 **Your Son** need but call upon **God's** Name, and **Your Son** will recollect his safety and Your Love, for **safety and love** are one. 3 How can **Your Son** fear or doubt or fail to know he cannot suffer, be endangered, or experience unhappiness, when **Your Son** belongs to You, beloved and loving, in the safety of Your Fatherly embrace?>

W-244.2.And there we are in truth. 2 No storms can come into the hallowed haven of our home. 3 In God we are secure. 4 For what can come to threaten God Himself, or make afraid what will forever be a part of **God**?

Notes to Lesson #244

I am in danger nowhere in the world.

Comment: Your world of perception has no ability to change the truth that you remain part of the shared oneness of the Mind of God. Illusions have no power to change what God has created eternally safe and loved. You are an extension of God and the illusion of separation has no power to harm you. You are not the body. You are free. You still remain as God created you.

Your peace is with me, Father. I am safe.

W-245.1. <Your peace surrounds me, Father. 2 Where I go, Your peace goes there with me. 3 **God's peace** sheds its light on everyone I meet. 4 I bring **God's peace** to the desolate and lonely and afraid. 5 I give Your peace to those who suffer pain, or grieve for loss, or think they are bereft of hope and happiness. 6 Send them to me, my Father. 7 Let me bring **God's** peace with me. 8 For I would save Your Son, as is Your Will, that I may come to recognize my **big "S" Self**.>

W-245.2.And so we go in **God's** peace. 2 To all the world we give the message that we have received. 3 And thus we come to hear the Voice for God, Who speaks to us as we relate **God's** Word; Whose Love we recognize because we share the Word that **God** has given unto us.

Notes to Lesson #245

Your peace is with me, Father. I am safe.

Comment: To receive the peace of God, you need to give the peace of God to all. Only by our giving peace, do we prove and acknowledge that we possess the peace of God.

Peace belongs to the mind that joins with all in forgiveness. An unforgiving mind is the mind at war with itself and its world. In time, your function is forgiveness, your purpose is love and your destiny is the peace of God.

LESSON 246

To love my Father is to love His Son.

W-246.1.Let me not think that I can find the way to God if I have hatred in my heart. 2 Let me not try to hurt God's Son, and think that I can know his Father or my **big "S" Self**. 3 Let me not fail to recognize **my big "S" Self**, and still believe that my awareness can contain my Father, or my mind conceive of all the love my Father has for me, and all the love which I return to **God, my Father**.

W-246.2. <I will accept the way You choose for me to come to You, my Father. 2 For in **accepting the way God chose for me to come to God** will I succeed, because it is **God's** Will. 3 And I would recognize that what You will is what I will as well, and only that. 4 And so I choose to love Your Son. 5 Amen.>

Notes to Lesson #246

To love my Father is to love His Son.

Comment: God, my brother and myself all share the one Mind of God. Because minds are joined, I cannot withhold love from one component of the whole without withholding that love from all, including myself. There is only one will and that is the love I share with the Mind of God.

LESSON 247

Without forgiveness I will still be blind.

W-247.1.Sin is the symbol of attack. 2 Behold **sin** anywhere, and I will suffer. 3 For forgiveness is the only means whereby Christ's vision comes to me. 4 Let me accept what **Christ's** sight shows me as the simple truth, and I am healed completely. 5 Brother, come and let me look on you. 6 Your loveliness reflects my own. 7 Your sinlessness is mine. 8 You stand forgiven, and I stand with you.

W-247.2. <So would I look on everyone today. 2 My brothers are Your Sons. 3 Your Fatherhood created **my brothers**, and gave them all to me as part of You, and my own **big "S" Self** as well. 4 Today I honor You through **my brothers**, and thus I hope this day to recognize my **big "S" Self**.>

Notes to Lesson #247

Without forgiveness I will still be blind.

Comment: Sin is a symbol of attack thoughts. When you perceive yourself or another as a sinner, you perceive that party to be something less than perfect, whole and complete. You have accepted the belief in the vulnerability of the body and your egoic little "s" self.

Forgiveness leads to the Christ vision where you look beyond the world of form to the purpose behind the thought form. The law of Christ vision says, never mistake the body for the Son of God. Forgiveness recognizes that your mind is the creative power behind your world. There are no external forces that can rob you of your own inner peace.

Since to give is to receive, when you forgive your brother for his failure to do the impossible, which was to make you happy, you recognize his guiltless nature. He was merely an actor in a story of your own mind's making. Your mind can now reclaim its power of interpretation and assign a different narrative and purpose for that event. You can choose to reframe the story to support the truth.

LESSON 248

Whatever suffers is not part of me.

W-248.1.I have disowned the truth. 2 Now let me be as faithful in disowning falsity. 3 Whatever suffers is not part of me. 4 What grieves is not myself. 5 What is in pain is but illusion in my mind. 6 What dies was never living in reality, and did but mock the truth about **my big "S" Self**. 7 Now I disown **egoic** self-concepts and deceits and lies about the holy Son of God. 8 Now am I ready to accept **God's Son and my big "S" Self** back as God created him, and as **God's Son** is.

W-248.2. <Father, my ancient love for You returns, and lets me love Your Son again as well. 2 Father, I am as You created me. 3 Now is Your Love remembered, and my own **love**. 4 Now do I understand that **God's Love and my love** are one.>

Notes to Lesson #248

Whatever suffers is not part of me.

Comment: What you truly are is unlimited spirit or Mind. Spirit cannot be hurt, suffer or die. What is pain can only be an illusion within your own mind that perceives itself to be the body. You are not the body.

It is only your mind's false identification with the game token called the body that causes you pain. When you consider your body to be your home, your mind must accept the limitations that come with the body to be its own limitations.

Forgiveness ends all suffering and loss.

W-249.1.Forgiveness paints a picture of a world where suffering is over, loss becomes impossible and anger makes no sense. 2 **Forgiveness paints a picture of a world where** attack is gone, and madness has an end. 3 **In a forgiven world,** what suffering is now conceivable? 4 **In a forgiven world,** what loss can be sustained? 5 The world becomes a place of joy, abundance, charity and endless giving. 6 **A forgiven world** is now so like to Heaven that **a forgiven world** quickly is transformed into the light that it reflects. 7 And so the journey which the Son of God began has ended in the light from which **the Son of God** came.

W-249.2. <Father, we would return our minds to You. 2 We have betrayed **our minds**, held them in a vise of bitterness, and frightened **our minds** with thoughts of violence and death. 3 Now would we rest again in You, as You created us.>

Notes to Lesson #249

Forgiveness ends all suffering and loss.

Comment: Forgiveness transforms your world from a place of attack to a place where you can extend only love. On earth, forgiveness is an expression of being love in form. Forgiveness is the realization that when you condemn another, you only crucify yourself. True forgiveness acknowledges the fact that your mind alone is the creative source of your world. Your mind provides all the meaning that you give to your world.

When you forgive, you change your world's purpose from your egoic belief that there are outside forces beyond your control that can affect your inner peace or make you happy. Forgiveness allows you to reclaim your divine birthright as the source for your experiences. Forgiveness allows you to move from victim consciousness to responsibility consciousness. You are now free to accept the truth about yourself, your brother and your world.

LESSON 250

Let me not see myself as limited.

W-250.1.Let me behold **my big "S" Self,** the Son of God today, and witness to **the glory of God's Son.** 2 Let me not try to obscure the holy light in **my big "S" Self,** and see **the** strength **of God's Son** diminished and reduced to frailty; nor perceive the lacks in him with which I would attack **the sovereignty of my big 'S' Self that is God's Son.**

W-250.2. <My big "S" Self is Your Son, my Father. 2 And today I would behold **the gentleness of the Son of God** instead of my **egoic** illusions of **a little "s" self**. 3 **The Son of God** is what I am, and as I see **God's creations,** so I see myself. 4 Today I would see truly **with the vision of Christ** that this day I may at last identify with **my big "S" Self, God's Son.**>

Notes to Lesson #250

Let me not see myself as limited.

Comment: Accept the truth that you are Mind and not the body. With the gift of Mind, God has given you the creative power to source your own experiences. Your mind can co-create with God and extend the love that you are or it can sleep and make a fantasy world in which you let your ego argue for your littleness.

Stop arguing for your littleness. Accept the truth that you remain as God created you. Get a new guide, and follow the Holy Spirit Who knows the truth. Use the vision of Christ to look past the body and behold the guiltless and sinless Son of God. Embrace your big "S" Self today!

What Is Sin?

Covers ACIM Workbook Lessons 251-260

4. What Is Sin?

W-pII.4.1.Sin is insanity. 2 **Sin** is the means by which the mind is driven mad, and seeks to let illusions take the place of truth. 3 And being mad, **the insane split mind** sees illusions where the truth should be, and where **truth** really is. 4 Sin gave the body eyes, for what is there the sinless would behold? 5 What need have t**he sinless** of sights or sounds or touch? 6 What would **the sinless** hear or reach to grasp? 7 What would t**he sinless** sense at all? 8 To sense is not to know. 9 And truth can be but filled with knowledge, and with nothing else.

W-pII.4.2.The body is the instrument the mind made in its efforts to deceive itself. 2 **The body's** purpose is to strive. 3 Yet can the goal of striving change. 4 And now the body serves a different aim for striving. 5 What **the body** seeks for now is chosen by the aim the mind has taken as replacement for the goal of **egoic** self-deception. 6 Truth can be **the body's** aim as well as lies. 7 The senses then will seek instead for witnesses to what is true.

W-pII.4.3.Sin is the home of all illusions, which but stand for things imagined. **These illusions** are issuing from thoughts that are untrue. 2 **The illusions of sin** are the **imaginary** "proof" that what has no reality is real. 3 Sin **falsely** "proves" God's Son is evil; timelessness must have an end; eternal life must die. 4 And **the illusions of sin** are the **false** "proof" that God Himself has lost the Son **God** loves, with but corruption to complete Himself, **God's** Will forever overcome by death, love slain by hate, and peace to be no more.

W-pII.4.4.A madman's dreams are frightening, and sin appears indeed to terrify. 2 And yet what sin perceives is but a childish game. 3 The Son of God may play he has become a body, prey to evil and to guilt, with but a little life that ends in death. 4 But all the while his Father shines on **the child at play**, and **God** loves **His Child** with an everlasting Love which **the playing child's** pretenses cannot change at all.

W-pII.4.5.How long, O Son of God, will you maintain the game of sin? 2 Shall we not put away these sharp-edged children's toys? 3 How soon will you be ready to come home? 4 Perhaps today? 5 There is no sin. 6 Creation is unchanged. 7 Would you still hold return to Heaven back? 8 How long, O holy Son of God, how long?

Notes to Special Theme #4: What Is Sin?

What Is Sin?

Central Theme for Lessons 251 to 260

Sin is the means that allows illusions to take the place of truth. Sin is insanity. Sin is a childish game that the Son of God plays to pretend he is something other than as God created him. Unfortunately for us, we have forgotten that it is a game of make-believe and now perceive the illusion of lack, limitation and separation to be real.

Due to our belief that sin is real, we have become split minded. Our split mind is delusional and insane. We have become unable to differentiate between make believe and our true identity as our big "S" Self.

Sin is the home of all illusions. Sin is the proof that illusions are real and that God's Son is no longer perfect, whole and complete. Sin is the means for insane minds to let illusions replace the truth.

The body is an instrument the split mind made for the purpose of self-deception. Your ego claims the physical body is your home and that the brain is your Mind. The ego uses the game token we call the body as its tool to prove that your safety and existence is contingent upon the well-being of the body. The ego claims that you are the body and the body is you. When you accept this erroneous belief, you also must accept the limitations that come with the body.

The goal of the body's physical senses is to confirm and bear false witness that the illusions of lack, limitation and separation are real. To sense is to not know. Physiologists explain that the physical senses are designed to confirm what your mind already believes to be true. The physical senses are not objective cameras to the world. Instead, they are merely thought confirmation devices. Your senses only confirm your mind's beliefs and ignore any evidence that would be contradictory. Thus, the senses fulfill their purpose of providing false evidence that supports your ego's erroneous beliefs about you, your world and God.

S-I-N is Self-Inflicted Nonsense. Sin is the belief in lack. When you believe that you are not perfect, whole and complete, you automatically accept the idea that you are missing something to make you whole. You accept the idea that you have needs that must be met if you are to be safe, happy and survive. This belief implies that there is something outside your own mind that has power over you. Sin is your acceptance of the ego's belief in lack, limitation and separation.

The ego uses the body as the means to make it appear there are outside forces beyond your control that can make you happy or sad. The body proves you are not Mind and can be hurt. To the ego, the purpose of the world is to bear false witness that your mind is not the source of your experiences. If your ego can prove that your mind has needs and lacks the creative ability to keep you safe, your decision-maker will accept and follow your ego's plan for its own survival.

The purpose of the body is to provide a vehicle the ego can use to fulfill the ego's plans for its protection, safety and continued insanity. The body's purpose is to strive and the ego's aim for striving is to make the false true and the true false. The body provides the means for the ego to argue for its rightness over your happiness. The body falsely "proves" that your ego's little "s" self is your reality and the big "S" Self that God created is the illusion.

Sin, guilt and fear are interrelated. Sin, guilt and fear comprise the unholy trinity of your egoic thought system. When you find one, you will find the other two beliefs. Sin is the belief in lack and lack engenders fear. In the egoic world when you commit a sin, you are coming from fear and trying to reduce or minimize the fear that you are currently feeling.

Yet, the only reason you are in fear is because you believe in lack. Fear and sin, which is your belief in lack, are always coupled together. Guilt is always associated with lack in your world. All three beliefs occur in unison. You cannot escape the experience of sin, guilt and fear without removing and healing all three of these erroneous beliefs from your delusional mind.

Your ego has developed its own survival plan to insure that its needs are met. The ego never questions its own belief in lack, limitation and separation that is the true source of this fictitious problem. Instead, the ego's plan always starts with the confirmation that lack is real and that there are outside forces that can directly affect your inner peace.

The ego does not know who you are. The ego fails to recognize the truth that your big "S" Self has no needs. Therefore, the ego always assumes sin (lack) is real and is the problem. The ego, then attempts to solve the fictitious problem of needs that only exist within the delusional mind that believes sin could be real. Assuming sin to be real, the ego's plans center around one of two possible solutions to the fictitious problems of needs and lack.

The first solution is simply to take from another what you perceive you need. The attack may be direct or indirect but the solution will entail some form of taking. This is based on the ego's belief that someone's loss can be another's gain. This first solution reinforces your ego's belief in separation and the reality of form. This solution embodies the belief that life is a zero-sum game. If I am to win, someone else must lose. It also flames feelings of guilt.

The second solution rests upon the special relationship. A special relationship is a bartering transaction between two or more parties. Each seeks to trade some of their limited resources in exchange for something they perceive they need which is of equal or greater value. The goal of the special relationship is to get a good deal. You want to give up as little as possible while maximizing the return on your investment.

The special relationship also assumes that sin or lack is the reality of the world and that both parties have needs that cannot be fulfilled solely by the creative power of each party's own mind. To insure one gets their way, guilt becomes the favorite tool of manipulation in the special relationship.

We have all experienced manipulating and being manipulated by guilt. Our ego uses the blame, shame and guilt game very effectively to obtain its own way. Projecting guilt is often used in the special relationship as each party attempts to make the other party feel guilty for any shortcomings in the relationship. In this world of special relationships, we often vacillate between being an active guilt catcher or guilt thrower. Often, we take turns and switch roles as each ego struggles for the rightness of its own plan.

Most of you are probably familiar with the religious concept of sin. The common definition of sin would be to commit an offense or fault of any kind. Depending on the religion, it may involve the breaking of religious laws or moral principles typically through a willful act. This notion of sin implies that there is both a wrongdoer and something that has been wronged.

When we look at the two solutions offered by your ego to obtain its needs, the first plan that involves the taking from another would be the sin of stealing. Yet, the second plan of entering into a special relationship would be seen as an act of cooperation and not a sin.

Yet, both solutions are the ego's attempt to make the illusion of bodily needs become your reality. Therefore, both would meet ACIM's definition of a sin.

ACIM defines sin as a means of seeking to replace truth with an illusion. Sin is your belief in lack, limitation and separation. It is your belief that you could be something other than as God created you. Sin is your belief that your Mind is not the creative power behind your experiences and that there are outside forces that can rob you of your inner peace and happiness.

Earlier I stated that sin, guilt and fear are interrelated and occur simultaneously as one grouping. You can't have one without the other two occurring. Most can easily relate to the idea of guilt being associated with the common definition of sin that involves the wrongful taking from another. Yet, guilt is not necessarily associated with the special relationship. Most perceive a special relationship to be a mutually agreeable transaction with each party gaining from the interrelationship. So why would I say that a special relationship automatically engenders guilt within the mind of each party?

On the conscious or subconscious level, when you believe that you have needs, you are admitting that you are incapable of being self-sufficient. A lot of guilt is self-guilt and is not directed at another party.

You believe that there is something wrong with you because you are not perfect, whole and complete. Perhaps, there is something wrong with you because you allowed someone to abuse you. Guilt is a natural result from these feelings of inadequacy. You either feel guilty for your inability to provide for yourself or you project that guilt upon another for their failure to provide for your needs.

Many religions have the idea of original sin or the idea that we have offended God and therefore, are being punished and must earn our salvation. Often we blame God for what we perceive to be God's failure to create us properly or take into consideration our special needs. Your ego tells you that if God would have done His job properly when He created you, you would be happy or would not have messed things up later. It is God, not you, who is to blame. Your own self perceived inadequacies now become God's fault. Your ego has transformed an all-powerful God of only love into a limited God of lack, stupidity, imperfection and whim.

According to our ego, if God made us imperfect, we cannot trust God's plan for our happiness. God showed that He was incompetent when He created us. If we believe we have offended or sinned against God, God cannot be pure Love. Because of our ego's erroneous belief in a judgmental god, we must now fear God's retribution, do our penance or somehow earn our redemption. A God that is only Love has been transformed by our egoic mind into something to hide from and fear.

When the ego plans for our salvation, it is based on the idea that God's Son must earn his way back into Heaven through penance or good deeds. It assumes we are sinners and that Paradise is lost. This belief that we have lost our divine birthright leads to our ego's plan to earn back God's love by our actions.

With this idea that God's love can be earned, our ego has once again transformed a God of unlimited love and abundance into a god of judgment and conditional love. This is an egoic god whose conditional love and gifts can be purchased and acquired through bribes, negotiations, prayers and good deeds. The ego's plan requires us to earn or purchase our way back into heaven.

When properly understood and if true, the ego's belief that we can do something to earn God's love would also be a sin. This is because such a belief implies that we could earn something that God has already given us and never taken away. When you believe that God's love can be earned, you are trying to make the illusion of lack, limitation and separation real.

Be aware that all plans that suggest you can earn your way into heaven are fear-based and keep you trapped in fear. Guard against plans that claim you can be saved or save another through good deeds or by second party surrogates for these plans disempower all involved.

Your ego's plans for your salvation only keep you trapped within the belief that Paradise has been lost and sin is real. They all strive to use the body as the tool to make amends for your assumed failure as God's sinful son. Only God's plan for our salvation will work because only God's plan accepts the innocence, guiltless and sinless nature of God and His Creations.

Good people end up in their own hell because they refuse to forgive themselves for their own perceived failure to save or make another happy. This was always an impossible task. No one has the power to make someone else happy. To do so would deny them their freedom to use the creative power of their own mind as they desired.

You and your ego believe that they are too stupid to know what their own perfect plan for their reawakening should be. That only your plan, not God's plan, will work. This belief would also deny and prevent you from exercising that same freedom. Each mind alone has the power of interpretation for their own experiences. That is why they created the experience in the first place. Each one's own mind assigns all meaning that each gives to any experience.

Free yourself from your ego's belief in lack and the sin, guilt and fear that lack engenders will cease. There is no sin. Sin is self-inflected nonsense. There is no lack in God and there is none in you. Your denial of your divine birthright cannot make the illusion of lack, limitation and fear real.

Egoically you need do nothing. Drop your egoic plans that insist on making the illusion of sin real and accept this fact. You remain as God created you. Deny your ego's belief in sin and reclaim your divine inheritance.

LESSON 251

I am in need of nothing but the truth.

W-251.1.I sought for many things, and found despair. 2 Now do I seek but one, **which is the truth,** for in that one is all I need, and only what I need. 3 All that I sought before I needed not, and did not even want. 4 My only need **which was the truth,** I did not recognize. 5 But now I see that I need only truth. 6 In **the truth** all needs are satisfied all cravings end, all hopes are finally fulfilled and dreams are gone. 7 Now **with the truth** have I everything that I could need. 8 Now have I everything that I could want. 9 And now at last **with the truth** I find myself at peace.

W-251.2. <And for that peace **which comes from the truth,** our Father, we give thanks. 2 **The truth that** we denied ourselves You have restored, and only **the truth** is what we really want.>

Notes to Lesson #251

I am in need of nothing but the truth.

Comment: Like begets like. You were created perfect, whole and complete. You cannot be happy being anything less than what God created you to be. Your egoic illusions only bring pain and struggle. Truth offers you the release from all the illusions of lack, limitation and separation. It is this truth that will set you free.

LESSON 252

The Son of God is my Identity.

W-252.1.My **big "S" Self** is holy beyond all the thoughts of holiness of which I now conceive. 2 **My big "S" Self's** shimmering and perfect purity is far more brilliant than is any light that I have ever looked upon. 3 **My big "S" Self's** love is limitless, with an intensity that holds all things within it, in the calm of quiet certainty. 4 **My big "S" Self's** strength comes not from burning impulses which move the world, but from the boundless Love of God Himself. 5 How far beyond this world my **big "S"** Self must be, and yet how near to me and close to God!

W-252.2. <Father, You know my true Identity, **my big "S" Self**. 2 Reveal **my true Identity** now to me who am Your Son, that I may waken to the truth in You, and know that Heaven is restored to me.>

Notes to Lesson #252

The Son of God is my Identity.

Comment: You can only be what you truly are. You cannot be anything other than as God created you. You can attempt to deny that truth, but your denial can never change the truth that you are God's beloved Child with whom He is well pleased. You are your big "S" Self. You are the Christ.

LESSON 253

My Self is ruler of the universe.

My **big "S"** Self is ruler of the universe.

W-253.1.It is impossible that anything should come to me unbidden by myself. 2 Even in this world, it is I who rule my destiny. 3 What happens is what I desire. 4 What does not occur is what I do not want to happen. 5 This must I accept that **nothing comes into my awareness unless I desire it**. 6 For thus am I led past this world to my **true** creations, children of my **true** will **that I share with God's Will**, in Heaven where my holy **big "S"** Self abides with **my true creations** and **God** Who has created me.

W-253.2. <You are the **big "S"** Self Whom **God** created. **You are God's Son** creating like **God, Itself** and One with You, **your higher Self.** 2 My **big "S"** Self, which rules the universe, is but **God's** Will in perfect union with my own **will**, which can but offer glad assent to **God's Will,** that it may be extended to Itself.>

Notes to Lesson #253

My Self is ruler of the universe.

Comment: You must accept the fact that your experiences are what your own mind desires. Your own mind rules what you call into your awareness. Your experiences are only what you desire and want. There are no victims. You must decide whether love or fear will rule your world of provisional reality.

Your ego rules a world of fear, sin, conflict and pain designed to support its illusion of separation. Your ego's goal is to make the illusion of lack, limitation and separation appear real. Your ego secretly strives to create experiences that witness for your own self-deception. The ego's goal is to make you believe that you are the body, a little "s" self which is not the source of your world.

As decision-maker, you rule your mind and can decide which thought system you will choose to follow. You can choose the thought system of the Holy Spirit and your big "S" Self that represents love and forgiveness. When you do, your fearful world will become a world of mercy and love. You are the source of your own experiences and nothing sources your world but your own mind's desires, thoughts, beliefs and decisions.

LESSON 254

Let every voice but God's be still in me.

W-254.1. <Father, today I would but hear Your Voice. 2 In deepest silence I would come to You, to hear Your Voice and to receive Your Word. 3 I have no prayer but this: I come to You to ask You for the truth. 4 And truth is but Your Will, which I would share with You today.>

W-254.2.Today we let no ego thoughts direct our words or actions. 2 When such thoughts **of our ego** occur, we quietly step back and look at **those egoic thoughts** and then we let them go. 3 We do not want what **those egoic thoughts** would bring with them **which are the fearful illusions of lack, limitation and separation.** 4 And so we do not choose to keep **those egoic thoughts**. 5 **Those egoic thoughts** are silent now. 6 And in the stillness, hallowed by **God's** Love, God speaks to us and tells us of our will, as we have chosen to remember **God**.

Notes to Lesson #254

Let every voice but God's be still in me.

Comment: Stop following the voice for fear. Drop your allegiance to all egoic thinking for it offers nothing that you want. Your ego argues for the correctness of its misperceptions and for your littleness. Your ego's beliefs only bring you pain, disappointment and suffering while keeping you trapped in fear.

Instead, ask for the guidance of the Holy Spirit Who knows the truth of what you are. Follow the Voice for God and the peace, love and unity that you seek will be yours.

LESSON 255

This day I choose to spend in perfect peace.

This day I choose to spend in perfect peace.

W-255.1.It does not seem to **my egoic mind** that I can choose to have but peace today. 2 And yet, my God assures me that His Son is like **God,** Himself. 3 Let me this day have faith in **God** Who says I am God's Son. 4 And let the peace I choose be mine today bear witness to the truth of what **God** says. 5 God's Son can have no cares, and must remain forever in the peace of Heaven. 6 In **God's** Name, I give today to finding what my Father wills for me, accepting **God's Will** as mine, and giving **God's Will and peace** to all my Father's Sons, along with me.

W-255.2. <And so, my Father, would I pass this day with You. 2 Your Son has not forgotten You. 3 The peace You gave **God's Son** still is in his **big "S" Self's** mind, and it is there I choose to spend today.>

Notes to Lesson #255

This day I choose to spend in perfect peace.

<u>Comment:</u> God's Son is created like God, Himself. Therefore, you are entitled to the peace of God. When you accept and choose to follow God's plan, not your ego's plan, the pain, sin, guilt and fear that you are currently experiencing will disappear.

Your life's experiences are the fulfillment of your own choices based upon what you value, want and desire. Your world is a reflection of the thought system you have chosen to follow. You can choose peace instead of war, love rather than fear, allowance to replace judgment, and forgiveness over condemnation.

LESSON 256

God is the only goal I have today.

W-256.1.The way to God is through forgiveness here **on earth**. 2 There is no other way **to God but through forgiveness**. 3 If sin had not been cherished by the **egoic** mind, what need would there have been to find the way to where you **truly** are? 4 Who would still be uncertain **of where you are**? 5 Who could be unsure of **the Identity of** who he is? 6 And who would yet remain asleep, in heavy clouds of doubt about the holiness of **himself, God's Son** whom God created sinless? 7 Here **with a mind that sleeps** we can but dream. 8 But we can dream we have forgiven him in whom all sin remains impossible, and it is this we choose to dream today. 9 God is our goal; forgiveness is the means by which our **sleeping** minds return to God at last.

W-256.2. <And so, our Father, would we come to You in Your appointed way **and follow the guidance of the Holy Spirit**. 2 We have no goal except to hear Your Voice, and find the way Your sacred Word has pointed out to us.>

Notes to Lesson #256

God is the only goal I have today.

<u>Comment:</u>

Because your ego prefers its rightness over your happiness, it values its belief in sin. Sin keeps you trapped in fear and lack. The only way to shed your ego's belief in sin and recover the remembrance of God is through forgiveness. Forgiveness removes the illusion of sin.

The ego is uncertain about who you are and thinks that your true home is the ego's dream world of lack, limitation and separation. You have allowed your ego's dream to become your provisional reality. Forgiveness is the means to end the dream of sin forever. Forgiveness removes the uncertainty of where you truly belong and returns you to the truth.

Knowledge is the certainty of who you really are. Follow the guidance of the Holy Spirit, Who has that knowledge. Be vigilant only for the remembrance of God.

LESSON 257

Let me remember what my purpose is.

W-257.1.If I forget my goal I can be but confused, unsure of what I am, and thus conflicted in my actions. 2 No one can serve contradicting goals and serve **those conflicting goals** well. 3 Nor can he function without deep distress and great depression **when you are pursuing conflicting goals**. 4 Let us therefore be determined to remember what we want today, that we may unify our thoughts and actions meaningfully, and achieve only what God would have us do this day.

W-257.2. <Father, forgiveness is Your chosen means for our salvation. 2 Let us not forget today that we can have no will but **Your Will**. 3 And thus our **single** purpose must be Yours as well if we would reach the peace You will for us.>

Notes to Lesson #257

Let me remember what my purpose is.

Comment: When you forget that your sole goal is the remembrance of God, your mind becomes confused, unsure and conflicted. When you are attempting to serve conflicting goals, you will experience a great deal of stress in your life. It is impossible to serve two thought systems at the same time since each thought system will have different goals.

When you know what your primary goal is, decisions become clear and easy. When you have only one overriding goal, you develop a single purpose and your thoughts and actions align with that single goal and you get meaningful results. Remember that your true goal is the peace of God.

On earth, your function is forgiveness, your purpose is love and your destiny is the peace of God.

LESSON 258

Let me remember that my goal is God.

W-258.1.All that is needful is to train our minds to overlook all little senseless **egoic** aims, and to remember that our goal is God. 2 **God's** memory is hidden in our **big "S" Selves'** minds, obscured but by our pointless little **egoic** goals which offer nothing, and do not exist. 3 Shall we continue to allow God's grace to shine in unawareness, while the toys and trinkets of the **egoic** world are sought instead? 4 God is our only goal, our only Love. 5 We have no aim but to remember **God**.

W-258.2. <Our goal is but to follow **the guidance of the Holy Spirit** in the way that leads to You. 2 We have no goal but this. 3 What could we want but to remember You? 4 What could we seek but our Identity **as our Big "S" Self and Your Son**?>

Notes to Lesson #258

Let me remember that my goal is God.

Comment: Your ego's priorities conflict with the goal of remembering God. The ego's goals are the pursuit of making the illusions of sin, lack, limitation and separation seem more bearable. Your ego attempts to do this through special relationships that it claims have the power to make you happy or safe. The pursuits of such egoic goals only lead to pain and disappointment. Pursuing these goals makes fear and separation appear real.

The idols of the ego only sidetrack us from our true purpose and function. Our goal is the acceptance of the truth that we remain as God created us and are part of the indivisible One Self. Our priority is to reawaken to this truth.

The goal of remembering God has always remained within our mind and is kept alive by the Holy Spirit. Your reawakening is guaranteed by God Himself. When your reawakening to the truth is your only priority, your focus will be clear and you will drop all your egoic goals and useless plans. The stress and striving you felt when you were in pursuit of your ego's meaningless goals will disappear.

LESSON 259

Let me remember that there is no sin.

W-259.1.Sin is the only thought that makes the goal of God seem unattainable. 2 What else **but our ego's belief in sin** could blind us to the obvious, and make the strange and the distorted seem more clear **than the remembrance of God**? 3 What else but sin engenders our attacks? 4 What else but sin could be the source of guilt, demanding punishment and suffering? 5 And what but sin could be the source of fear, obscuring God's creation; giving love the attributes of fear and of attack?

W-259.2. <Father, I would not be insane today. 2 I would not be afraid of love, nor seek for refuge in its opposite **which is fear**. 3 For love can have no opposite. **Fear cannot be real.** 4 You are the Source of everything there is. 5 And everything that is remains with You, and You with it.>

Notes to Lesson #259

Let me remember that there is no sin.

Comment: Sin is the source of guilt and demands punishment and suffering. Sin is the only thought that makes the goal of the remembrance of God seem unobtainable for we believe that we have lost Paradise. Sin makes fear, guilt, suffering and punishment appear to be God's Will. Sin assigns the attributes of fear and attack to love and God, Himself. Our ego's belief in sin transforms a God of love into a God of judgment, wrath and vengeance.

Love can have no opposites. Since God is only love, fear cannot be real. Sin, like fear itself, is false evidence appearing real. Sin is self-inflicted nonsense. Sin is your own self-condemnation for God has never condemned His Son. Sin is our ego's attempt to condemn God's beloved Child with whom God is well pleased. Your belief in sin condemns and crucifies yourself. Sin is not real. Stop condemning your world and allow all, including yourself, to escape the prison of your unforgiving mind.

Do not allow your ego's belief about sins reality to keep you trapped in the thought system of fear. There is no sin in God's Son and therefore, there is nothing to fear.

LESSON 260

Let me remember God created me.

W-260.1. <Father, I did not make myself, although in my **ego's** insanity I thought I did. 2 Yet, as **God's** Thought, I have not left my Source, remaining part of **God** Who created me. 3 Your Son, my Father, calls on You today. 4 Let me remember You created me. 5 Let me remember my Identity **as my big "S" Self**. 6 And let my sinlessness arise again before Christ's vision, through which I would look upon my brothers and myself today.>

W-260.2.Now is our Source remembered, and Therein we find our true Identity **as our big "S" Self** at last. 2 Holy indeed are we, because **God,** our Source can know no sin. 3 And we who are **God's** Sons are like each other, and alike to **God**.

Notes to Lesson #260

Let me remember God created me.

Comment: We are a thought of God. From God's Thoughts all Creation arose. Since like begets like, we must be like our Creator. Since there is no sin in God, there cannot be sin in His Creations.

With your brother and through him, you get to fulfill your purpose. On earth, your function is forgiveness, which is an attribute of love. Your forgiveness is an act of love in this egoic world of seeming hate and fear.

God created you to be a conduit for love. In time, love is the creative process used to awaken sleeping minds to their magnificence as the Christ. Today remember God and be that conduit. Be love in form.

What Is the Body?

Covers ACIM Workbook Lessons 261-270

5. What Is the Body?

W-pII.5.1.The body is a fence the Son of God imagines he has built, to separate parts of his **big "S"** Self from other parts. 2 It is within this fence **called the body** he thinks he lives, to die as **the body** decays and crumbles. 3 For within this fence **called the body** he thinks that he is safe from love. 4 Identifying with his safety, he regards himself as what his safety is **which he believes to be his body**. 5 How else could he be certain he remains within the body, keeping love outside **if he failed to identify himself as his body**?

W-pII.5.2.The body will not stay. 2 Yet this **the egoic mind** sees as double safety. 3 For the Son of God's impermanence is "proof" his fences work, and do the task his **egoic** mind assigns to them **which is to separate the parts from the whole**. 4 For if his oneness still remained untouched, who could attack and who could be attacked? 5 **For if his oneness still remained** who could be victor? 6 Who could be his prey? 7 Who could be victim **if oneness still remained**? 8 Who the murderer? 9 And if he did not die, what "proof" is there that God's eternal Son can be destroyed?

W-pII.5.3.The body is a dream. 2 Like other dreams it sometimes seems to picture happiness, but can quite suddenly revert to fear, where every dream is born. 3 For only love creates in truth, and truth can never fear. 4 Made to be fearful, must the body serve the purpose given **the body by your mind**. 5 But we can change the purpose that the body will obey by changing what we think that **the body** is for.

W-pII.5.4.The body is the means by which God's Son returns to sanity. 2 Though **the body** was made to fence **God's Son** into hell without escape, yet has the goal of Heaven been exchanged for the pursuit of hell. 3 The Son of God extends his hand to reach his brother, and to help **his brother** walk along the road with him. 4 Now is the body holy. 5 Now **the body** serves to heal the mind that **the body** was made to kill.

W-pII.5.5.You will identify with what you think will make you safe. 2 Whatever it may be **that you think makes you safe**, you will believe that it is one with you. 3 Your safety lies in truth, and not in lies. 4 Love is your safety. 5 Fear does not exist. 6 Identify with love, and you are safe. 7 Identify with love, and you are home. 8 Identify with love, and find your **big "S"** Self.

Notes to Special Theme #5: What Is the Body?

5. What Is the Body?

Central Theme for Lessons 261 to 270

The body is a barrier that you imagine keeps you separate from your oneness. The body is the means your ego uses to prove that you are not the eternal Son of God but rather something separate from God, your Source. As long as you identify with the body, the body proves that your ego was right and that you are not perfect, whole and complete.

The body serves as physical proof that lack, limitation and separation are the reality of your world and your being. The body was made to support your ego's belief that you are an autonomous being that exists independently from God and are not part of the Oneness of All That Is. The body becomes a symbol for a concrete form of fear.

The body is the servant for the mind, supporting the goals that the mind assigns to the body. You can change the goal of the body from supporting your ego's belief in fear and separation to become a means for awakening to the truth. When you do so, the body will serve that new purpose. The body can now become the means to reawaken your sleeping mind to the truth of who you really are.

We identify with what we think makes us safe. Our ego believes that our fears make us safe and protect us from circumstances that endanger our existence. Therefore, the body becomes an instrument for those egoic fears. Believing the body to be your home, you perceive that your safety lies in the maintenance, protection and survival of your body.

The ego teaches that the body has the ability to make us happy and also to protect us from outside forces that could harm us. Only bodies are vulnerable, need defenses and can attack. Perceiving ourselves to be the body, we believe that we can be hurt and harm others. The body now becomes something that we value for its ability to defend us by attacking our opponents.

Thus, the body keeps us safe within our fear-based thought system. The body is our ego's instrument to control and influence outside forces to comply with our ego's plans for our happiness. The purpose of our body is to protect and defend our ego's separate autonomous existence by enforcing our ego's wishes. The body is a fence that separates us from love.

When you follow the thought system of the Holy Spirit, you automatically change the purpose that the body is meant to serve. When you identify yourself with love and forgiveness, love becomes your safety and your home. The body can become the means to heal sick minds by returning them to the sanity of their Christ nature. Rather than a vehicle for attack, the body becomes a useful tool to help sleeping minds awaken to the truth.

In time and space, the body is like a game token that holds a place on the game board of reawakening to the truth. When you mistake the game token for what you truly are, the protection of the body becomes your main focus and a source of fear. When you realize that the body is merely a place holder on your journey of rediscovery, the body becomes a neutral communication device to be discarded when it is time to move on.

You get to decide how you will utilize the body in communications to other players on this game board of learning. Will you choose to communicate love or fear? The body becomes part of a feedback mechanism to aid in your learning about yourself. The body provides specific experiences which you utilize to learn, hone your skills and demonstrate what you truly value and why.

In my earlier years, I studied the Rosicrucian philosophy. The Rosicrucians have a motto, "As above, so below." What this means is that the highest truth, God, would be reflected in His Creations below. Since like begets like, the truth of our lower world must reflect the truth of God or Heaven above.

In the upside down world of the ego, the ego's motto is, "As below, so above." If the ego knew the truth that God was only love, this inversion of the motto would not be a problem. If "as above, so below" is true, it implies that "as below, so above" must also be true. Unfortunately, in this role reversal, your ego, not God, becomes the source for your perception. God's Knowledge has been replaced by the uncertainty of the ego's misperceptions and erroneous judgments.

"As above, so below" is based on God's knowledge and truth. "As below, so above" is based on the ego's efforts to make the false appear true. "As below, so above" allows your ego to make a false world based on its erroneous belief in lack, limitation and separation. The ego, then uses this imagined world of fear and projects its limiting beliefs above to the heavens and ultimately upon God, Himself. Your ego's projections change a God of Love into a God of lack, limitation and separation.

The ego has taken differentiation within the One Self to mean differences. The ego, then judges these differences to be separate, autonomous beings, independent from the One Self.

Differentiation does not mean different. Time provides a game board for differentiation. Time provides a playschool for fun and learning in which various aspects of love can be demonstrated. Our ego has mistaken what differentiation entails. It assumes differentiation requires separation and individual autonomy. To our ego, differentiation means different and different means separate. Our egos assume separation to be the reality between God and His Creation.

This is not the case. Differentiation only allows specific attributes to be displayed within the inseparable Mind of God. Because the world we perceive is dualistic in nature, this concept of differentiation and difference is difficult to understand. Perhaps an example in biology will help clarify why differentiation does not mean different or separate.

Your human body is comprised of trillions of individual cells. Yet, when you think of your body, you perceive the body as one whole. You do not attribute each cell with its own individual autonomous conscious existence. Nor, do you consider yourself to be trillions of separate autonomous cells.

You understand the big picture and the interrelationship of the parts with the whole. You recognize the parts as one indivisible whole that comprises your body. According to biologists, each cell could be considered a separate autonomous life form even though its survival is contingent on its connection to the whole.

Yet, when scientists examine each cell, they find that each cell contains the entire blueprint or working knowledge of the whole contained in each cell's own DNA. Although each cell contains the ability to replicate the entire whole, each cell chooses through the process of differentiation to only access the part of the blueprint that it needs to fulfill its own function within the context of the whole.

For example, a blood cell will access only that portion of the DNA that it needs to fulfill its function as a blood cell. Each cell has access to all the information to replicate the whole, yet it differentiates itself. Each cell recognizes that it is part of the much larger whole. It allows other cells to access that same DNA to generate other parts of the whole. The cells work in unison with that one DNA blueprint to create one autonomous being. That being is a mass of differentiated cells that comprise the various organs and body parts that come together in one common purpose and unite as one indivisible whole.

Stem cell research is based on the idea of each cell having this ability to replicate any part of the whole within itself. Scientific research centers on how to turn on and off the various parts of the DNA blueprint that contain the whole. Scientists recognize that the cells and DNA are holographic in nature.

Although each part can appear to be separate and different, each part contains the whole and the whole is contained in each part. Each part appears different but is following the same blueprint. There is no real difference except that each is exercising the cell or mind's power of choice.

Your mind and the Mind of God share that holographic quality for they are of One Mind. Creation is the extension of that One Mind. Unlike the physical birthing process, creation does not involve the extrusion of some part of God that then becomes separate from its source. Extension maintains the Oneness and holographic nature of Mind. There is no separation. You can experience differentiation yet, there are no differences for all have access to the totality of All That Is.

Time provides a game board in which differentiation can appear to be real. Differentiation provides an opportunity to learn, demonstrate and be a certain aspect of love that cannot be experienced in the oneness of Heaven. Time provides a medium for the various aspects of love to appear as separate components so that the abstract One Self can know, demonstrate and be all the attributes of love.

The body makes the appearance of lack, limitation and separation seem real and provides the medium whereby individual aspects of love like forgiveness and helpfulness can be demonstrated in concrete and specific forms. God is living us and we are the various aspects of love in which the abstract One Self can know and be those specific attributes through our differentiation.

On earth, the body provides the means by which the mind can pursue an aspect of love called forgiveness. The body can be used to communicate and teach that nothing causes you to lose your inner peace unless your mind chooses to allow it. The body can be the instrument to teach that fear is not real and that you are the source for your experiences.

The body can be used to demonstrate and help others realize that love is the creative process in which time is utilized to reawaken sleeping minds to their true magnificence as the Christ. The body can teach that you are a spiritual being having an earthly experience and that your true reality is the holographic Mind of your big "S" Self which you share with God.

You are not the body. You are an infinite focus of consciousness. You are a feedback loop that allows you to witness the effects of the choices you are making in the depth of your mind that rests along the Mind of God. Each thought is the vibration of creation which you use to communicate to the world in an attempt to experience communion with all of life.

You are part of the shared Mind of God. You are pure spirit, unaffected by anything. You have been given the power to choose and therefore, you create your own experiences as you would have them be. Do not choose and accept your ego's little "s" self as your reality. You are not the egoic part of the mind that claims to be affected by outside forces that are beyond your control. Instead, you are the creator of your world and are 100% responsible for your feelings and interpretations.

The body is a neutral communication device. Communication is your attempt to rest in communion with your Source and all of creation. On earth, what you choose to perceive, believe and accept as your truth is what you will radiate through your communication device called the body.

Your body is also a teaching and learning device. What you communicate and teach is what you have allowed inside your consciousness. You teach what you believe and your beliefs reflect what you value. Your mind does not reside in the body but the body is within the field of your mind. The mind's thoughts are the creative force that powers your experiences.

Your body allows you to communicate to others what you value and why. Will you choose to communicate your ego's belief in lack, limitation, separation and fear?

< Or >

Will you choose to communicate love, forgiveness and the joining of all minds in communion with each other as One?

Allow the body to communicate and reveal the truth of your big "S" Self, your Christ nature, to your world and your brother.

LESSON 261

God is my refuge and security.

W-261.1.I will identify with what I think is refuge and security. 2 I will behold myself where I perceive my strength, and think I live within the citadel where I am safe and cannot be attacked. 3 Let me today seek not security in danger, nor attempt to find my peace in murderous attack **by identifying myself with the body**. 4 I live in God. 5 In **God** I find my refuge and my strength. 6 In **God** is my Identity **as my big "S" Self**. 7 In **God** is everlasting peace. 8 And only there **in the shared Mind of God** will I remember Who I really am.

W-261.2. <Let me not seek for idols. 2 I would come, my Father, home to You today. 3 I choose to be as You created me, and find the Son whom You created as my **big "S" Self**.>

Notes to Lesson #261

God is my refuge and security.

Comment: We identify with what we think makes us safe. Because we associate ourselves with the body, we believe our safety lies with the protection and maintenance of that body. The body will not last and is yet another egoic illusion. The body was made to serve the ego's purpose of bearing false witness for the illusion of lack, limitation and separation.

Your true reality is that you live in God for you are God's Son. Identify with your Source for that is where your true safety lies. You are invulnerable for you share the Mind of God. God is at home in your big "S" Self for both are of one Mind.

LESSON 262

Let me perceive no differences today.

W-262.1. <Father, You have one Son. 2 And it is **Your one Son** that I would look upon today. 3 **Your one Son** is Your one creation. 4 Why should I perceive a thousand forms in what remains as one? 5 Why should I give **God's** one **Son** a thousand names, when only one suffices? 6 For Your Son must bear **God's** Name, for You created him. 7 Let me not see **Your one Son** as a stranger to his Father, nor as stranger to **my big "S" Self**. 8 For he is part of me and I of him, and we are part of You Who are our Source, eternally united in Your Love; eternally the holy Son of God.>

W-262.2.We who are one would recognize this day the truth about ourselves **and the oneness that is the shared Mind of God**. 2 We would come home, and rest in unity **as that One Self**. 3 For there is peace, and nowhere else can peace be sought and found.

Notes to Lesson #262

Let me perceive no differences today.

Comment: All Creation is part of the shared Mind of God. Nothing is real outside the Mind of God. If you see differences you have made the separation appear real only within your own split mind. Your imaginings have no power to change the truth.

Your egoic judgments have transformed the playschool of differentiation into a nightmare of perceived differences. When you see differences, your split mind has mistaken form for content. Your insane mind will perceive a fearful world that supports your ego's belief in lack, limitation and separation.

Differentiation does not mean different. Only your erroneous judgment makes it appear so. There is only one Son and all of creation is part of that One Self. See your brother and yourself as the Christ, the big "S" Self that is one with the Mind of God.

LESSON 263

My holy vision sees all things as pure.

W-263.1. <Father, Your Mind created all that is, Your Spirit entered into **all creation**, Your Love gave life to **all creation**. 2 And would I look upon what You created as if **creation** could be made sinful? 3 I would not perceive such dark and fearful images. 4 A madman's dream is hardly fit to be my choice, instead of all the loveliness with which You blessed creation; all **creation's** purity, its joy, and **creation's** eternal, quiet home in You.>

W-263.2.And while we still remain outside the gate of Heaven, let us look on all we see through holy vision and the eyes of Christ. 2 Let all appearances seem pure to us, that we may pass **all appearances** by in innocence, and walk together to our Father's house as brothers and the holy Sons of God.

Notes to Lesson #263

My holy vision sees all things as pure.

Comment: God didn't create any junk. When God creates, God extends all that He is to all. All are perfect, whole and complete, part of the unity that comprises the One Self.

See everything with Christ vision. Do not allow egoic judgments to blur your true vision. Your ego does not know what God's Son is. Therefore, your ego cannot judge anything correctly. Today let us not mistake the body for the Son of God.

Instead, ask the Holy Spirit to guide your vision past the form and see your brother's innocence and sinless nature. In time, we need our brother's help so that we can fulfill our purpose of awakening our sleeping mind to its true magnificence as the Christ.

LESSON 264

I am surrounded by the Love of God.

W-264.1. <Father, You stand before me and behind, beside me, in the place I see myself, and everywhere I go. 2 You are in all the things I look upon, the sounds I hear, and every hand that reaches for my own. 3 In You time disappears, and place becomes a meaningless **egoic** belief. 4 For what surrounds Your Son and keeps **God's Son** safe is Love itself. 5 There is no source but **God's Love**, and nothing is that does not share **Love's** holiness. **There is nothing** that stands beyond Your one creation, or without the Love which holds all things within itself. 6 Father, Your Son is like Yourself, **only Love**. 7 We come to You in Your Own Name today, to be at peace within **God's** everlasting Love.>

W-264.2.My brothers, join with me in this today. 2 This is salvation's prayer. 3 Must we not join in what will save the world, along with us?

Notes to Lesson #264

I am surrounded by the Love of God.

Comment: God is only Love. Love has no opposites for fear is not real. Love keeps all creation safe. We are an expression of that Love. In time, love is the creative process in which time is utilized to reawaken sleeping minds to their true magnificence as the Christ.

LESSON 265

Creation's gentleness is all I see.

W-265.1.I have indeed misunderstood the world because I laid my sins on **the world** and saw **my sins** looking back at me. 2 How fierce **my sins reflected back to me** seemed! 3 And how deceived was I to think that what I feared was in the world, instead of in my mind alone. 4 Today I see the world in the celestial gentleness with which **God's** creation shines. 5 There is no fear in **a world of God's creation**. 6 Let no appearance of my sins obscure the light of Heaven shining on the world. 7 What is reflected there is in God's Mind. 8 The **egoic** images I see reflect my **egoic** thoughts. 9 Yet is my mind at one with God's **Mind**. 10 And so I can perceive creation's gentleness **through the mind of my big S" Self that is part of the shared Mind of God**.

W-265.2. <In quiet would I look upon the world, which but reflects Your Thoughts, and mine as well. 2 Let me remember that **these thoughts** are the same, and I will see creation's gentleness.>

Notes to Lesson #265

Creation's gentleness is all I see.

Comment: You project your beliefs out upon your world and it is merely the reflection of those beliefs that you perceive. If you believe in lack, you will see a world of lack. If you believe you are not good enough, you will see a world that reflects your belief in limitation.

The world is a reflection of your own thought projections and a product of your own thinking. Nothing sources what you call into your awareness but your own mind. The sin that you perceive in your world resides within your own mind. Sin is your belief in lack. Your true will and God's will are the same for creation is the extension of the Mind of God.

The law of seeing states that if fear holds a place in your heart, you will look upon a world of anger and fear. If love and forgiveness is only found within you, you will behold a world of love and mercy. The power of your interpretation resides solely within your own mind. Which type of world will you choose to see today?

LESSON 266

My holy Self abides in you, God's Son.

My holy **big "S"** Self abides in you, God's Son.

W-266.1. <Father, You gave me all Your Sons, to be my saviors and my counselors in sight; the bearers of Your holy Voice to me. 2 In **all Your Sons** are You reflected, and in **all Your Sons** does Christ look back upon me from my **big "S"** Self. 3 Let not Your Son forget Your holy Name. 4 Let not Your Son forget **God,** his holy Source. 5 Let not Your Son forget his Name is Yours.>

W-266.2.This day we enter into Paradise, calling upon God's Name and on our own, acknowledging our **big "S"** Self in each of us; united in the holy Love of God. 2 How many saviors God has given us! 3 How can we lose the way to **God**, when **God** has filled the world with those who point to **God**, and given us the sight **of Christ** to look on **our saviors**?

Notes to Lesson #266

My holy Self abides in you, God's Son.

Comment: All of creation acts as your counselor for your reawakening to the truth. Your ego sees everything through the prism of lack, limitation and separation. If allowed, the Holy Spirit can reframe all your egoic judgments so that those same experiences can align with the truth and bring you home.

God is in all. Choose to see God in your brothers and you will see God in yourself. Your big "S" Self abides in all of creation. You are definitely not your body or your ego. You are the shared Mind of God. Your true Self, like your brother, is the Christ. There is no separation. You are that One.

My heart is beating in the peace of God.

W-267.1.Surrounding me is all the life that God created in **God's** Love. 2 **God's Love** calls to me in every heartbeat and in every breath; in every action and in every thought. 3 Peace fills my heart, and floods my body with the purpose of forgiveness. 4 Now my mind is healed, and all I need to save the world is given me. 5 Each heartbeat brings me peace; each breath infuses me with strength. 6 I am a messenger of God, directed by **God's** Voice, sustained by **God** in love, and held forever quiet and at peace within **God's** loving Arms. 7 Each heartbeat calls **God's** Name, and every one is answered by **God's** Voice, assuring me I am at home in **God**.

W-267.2. <Let me attend **God's** Answer, not my own. 2 Father, my heart is beating in the peace the Heart of Love created. 3 It is there and only there **in the peace of God** that I can be at home.>

Notes to Lesson #267

My heart is beating in the peace of God.

<u>**Comment**</u>: You are a messenger for God and a conduit for love. Surrounding you is all the life that God's Love has created. Will you view it with a loving and forgiving heart or one that beats in fear and anger?

On earth, your purpose is forgiveness for your world, your brother and also, for yourself. Forgiveness stems from recognizing that your mind gives all the meaning your experiences have and there is nothing outside of you that can rob you of your inner peace.

You have been given the freedom to interpret all the events you call into your awareness. Your mind determines what effect if any, these neutral events will have upon your consciousness.

Forgive your world for your erroneous belief that something outside your own mind had the power to make you happy or sad. You alone control your inner peace for you are the ruler of your mind.

You are free as God created you to be or imagine anything you desire. Choose to be the truth and accept your role in the oneness that is the shared Mind of God. Accept the Atonement for yourself and allow your mind to rest in the peace of God.

LESSON 268

Let all things be exactly as they are.

W-268.1. <Let me not be Your critic, Lord, today, and judge against You. 2 Let me not attempt to interfere with Your creation, and distort **God's creation** into sickly forms. 3 Let me be willing to withdraw my **ego's** wishes from **creation's** unity, and thus to let **God's creation** be as You created it. 4 For thus will I be able, too, to recognize my **big "S"** Self as You created me. 5 In love was I created, and in love will I remain forever. 6 What can frighten me, when I let all things be exactly as **God's creations** are?>

W-268.2.Let not our sight be blasphemous today, nor let our ears attend to lying tongues. 2 Only reality is free of pain. 3 Only reality is free of loss. 4 Only reality is wholly safe. 5 And it is only **reality as God created** we seek today.

Notes to Lesson #268

Let all things be exactly as they are.

<u>**Comment**</u>: Accept the truth of your divine birthright and your oneness with the One Self. Drop all egoic plans for they are a distraction and hide the truth of your true Identity. Do not allow your ego to judge against God or your Christ nature. You remain as God created you. Love created you and therefore, you are love.

All things are neutral learning devices that help you reawaken to the truth of who you are. Any belief that you are not exactly where you need to be on your own perfect path to reawakening is your ego talking. Any perceived failure along the journey can only be your ego's erroneous judgment.

Your ego is clueless and has the wrong road map. Do not listen to your ego that fails to grasp the big picture. Instead, follow the guidance of the Holy Spirit who has the correct plan. Only God's plan will work. God's plan is guaranteed to bring you home. You are exactly where you need to be.

LESSON 269

My sight goes forth to look upon Christ's face.

W-269.1. <I ask Your blessing on my sight today. 2 **The Holy Spirit's blessing of my sight** is the means which You have chosen to become the way to show me my mistakes, and look beyond **my mistakes**. 3 **Christ vision** is given me to find a new perception through the Guide, **the Holy Spirit, that** You gave to me, and through **the** lessons **of the Holy Spirit** to surpass perception and return to truth. 4 I ask for the **grand** illusion **of forgiveness** which transcends all **egoic illusions** I made. 5 Today I choose to see a world forgiven, in which everyone shows me the face of Christ, and teaches me that what I look upon belongs to me; that nothing is, except Your holy Son.>

W-269.2.Today our sight is blessed indeed. 2 We share one vision, as we look upon the face of **Christ** Whose **big "S"** Self is our **big "S" Self**. 3 We are one because of **Christ** Who is the Son of God; of **Christ** Who is our own Identity **as our big 'S'** Self.

Notes to Lesson #269

My sight goes forth to look upon Christ's face.

Comment: The power of your mind rests in its ability to interpret all events as you would have them be. The grand illusion is your decision to interpret all events with forgiving eyes. ACIM's forgiveness proves that no matter what you look upon, you alone are the source for any effect that an event has on your well-being.

All events are neutral. You alone choose how you will interpret each event. The choice is always between the eyes of love and forgiveness or fear and hate. The grand illusion of forgiveness corrects all misperception and returns it to the truth.

Your physical senses were designed to hide the truth. If asked, the Holy Spirit will provide a new way to view your world. With Christ vision, you look upon a forgiven world and see the face of Christ in all. Ask the Holy Spirit to provide the grand illusion that transcends all your ego's illusions that attempt to make the false true.

Forgiveness is the grand illusion for it alone ends the need to create additional stories that support your ego's belief in lack, limitation and separation. As decision-maker, allow your mind to become the source to reclaim the oneness that you share with all as God's Son.

LESSON 270

I will not use the body's eyes today.

W-270.1. <Father, Christ's vision is Your gift to me, and **Christ's vision** has power to translate all that the body's eyes behold into the sight of a forgiven world. 2 How glorious and gracious is this **forgiven** world **when viewed with the vision of Christ.** 3 Yet how much more will I perceive in **this forgiven world** than sight can give. 4 The world forgiven signifies **God's** Son acknowledges his Father, lets his **egoic** dreams be brought to truth, and waits expectantly the one remaining instant more of time which ends forever, as **God's** memory returns to him. 5 And now **the Son's** will is one with **God's Will**. 6 **The Son's** function now is but **God's Own function of being Love**, and every thought except **God's** Own **Thought** is gone.>

W-270.2.The quiet of today will bless our hearts, and through **our blessed hearts** peace will come to everyone. 2 Christ is our eyes today. 3 And through **Christ's** sight we offer healing to the world through **Christ**, the holy Son whom God created whole; the holy Son whom God created One.

Notes to Lesson #270

I will not use the body's eyes today.

Comment: Your physical senses were designed to hide the truth and deceive you. They merely confirm what your mind desires to observe in its world. With Christ vision you will see with forgiving eyes. The law of Christ vision states that you should never mistake the body for the Son of God.

Give all your ego's thoughts over to the Holy Spirit for reinterpretation. Be still, listen and trust in the guidance of the Holy Spirit. You have placed the Holy Spirit in charge and He will not fail you. Use the vision of Christ that the Holy Spirit grants and you will look upon a healed and forgiven world.

Special Theme #6: What Is the Christ?

What Is the Christ?

Covers ACIM Workbook Lessons 271-280

6. What Is the Christ?

W-pII.6.1.Christ is God's Son as **God** created **His Son.** 2 **Christ** is the **big "S"** Self we share, uniting us with one another, and with God as well. 3 **Christ** is the Thought which still abides within the Mind **of God** that is **Christ's** Source. 4 **Christ** has not left His holy home, nor lost the innocence in which **Christ** was created. 5 **Christ** abides unchanged forever in the Mind of God.

W-pII.6.2.Christ is the link that keeps you one with God, and guarantees that separation is no more than an **egoic** illusion of despair, for hope forever will abide in **Christ.** 2 Your mind is part of **Christ's Mind,** and **Christ's Mind is part** of yours. 3 **Christ's Mind** is the part in which God's Answer lies; where all decisions are already made, and dreams are over. 4 **Christ's Mind** remains untouched by anything the body's eyes perceive. 5 For though in **God,** His Father placed the means for your salvation, yet does **Christ** remain the **big "S"** Self Who, like His Father, knows no sin.

W-pII.6.3.Home of the Holy Spirit, and at home in God alone, does Christ remain at peace within the Heaven of your holy mind. 2 **Christ's Mind, your Big "S" Self,** is the only part of you that has reality in truth. 3 The rest is **egoic** dreams. 4 Yet will these **egoic** dreams **of lack, limitation and separation** be given unto Christ, to fade before **Christ's** glory and reveal your holy **big "S"** Self, the Christ, to you at last.

W-pII.6.4.The Holy Spirit reaches from the Christ in you to all your dreams **of lack, limitation and separation,** and bids **these fearful dreams** come to **the Holy Spirit** to be translated into truth. 2 **The Holy Spirit** will exchange **all our ego's dreams** for the final dream **of forgiveness** which God appointed as the end of dreams. 3 For when forgiveness rests upon the world and peace has come to every Son of God, what could there be to keep things separate, for what remains to see except Christ's face?

W-pII.6.5.And how long will this holy face **of Christ** be seen, when **seeing the face of Christ** is but the symbol that the time for learning now is over, and the goal of the Atonement **which is the accepting of the Truth for yourself** has been reached at last? 2 So therefore let us seek to find Christ's face and look on nothing else. 3 As we behold **Christ's** glory, will we know we have no need of learning or perception or of time, or anything except the holy **big "S"** Self, the Christ Whom God created as His Son.

Notes to Special Theme #6: What Is the Christ?

Covers ACIM Workbook Lessons 271-280

6. What Is the Christ?

Central Theme for Lessons 271 to 280

Christ is God's Son, as God created Him. Christ is the thought that still abides within the Mind that is God, your Source. Christ abides and is at home in God alone. The Christ is the home of the Holy Spirit and is the only part of you that has reality in Truth.

Throughout this course, I have often referred to the Christ under a synonym of your big "S" Self. Christ is your true big "S" Self and is part of the shared Mind of God. In the world of perception, we appear to be split minded. Part of our mind appears to be separate from the Mind of God and would be referred to as our egoic mind or little "s" self.

Our egoic mind perceives and believes lack, limitation and separation to be real. It is the part of our mind that we typically identify with and is how we define ourselves. The ego is closely associated with the body and looks to the body for its own safety and protection.

Our egoic mind uses the physical senses to navigate and negotiate in this world of form. Most people associate themselves with their ego and it appears to be the only voice they hear and follow. The ego is associated with the thinking mind and is constantly judging its world. It argues for the correctness of its judgments at the cost of your happiness.

The ego follows a fear-based thought system which rests upon its belief in the reality of sin, guilt and fear. This unholy trinity of sin, guilt and fear are the pillars that support and bear false witness to an egoic world of misperception. Your world of perception supports your ego's belief in lack, limitation and separation. We identify ourselves as separate autonomous beings and associate our existence and safety with the body. Your body becomes your ego's perceived home.

We have said that our mind is the source for our experiences. Our experiences are based on what we desire and value. Most people would take exception to the belief that their mind is the source of their experiences. They would site as proof their past negative experiences as events they did not want to happen.

They all claim that no one in their right mind would desire to experience the sickness, pain, struggle and conflict that they have suffered. If their mind was the source of their experiences, they would have chosen happiness, abundance, good health, peace and love. Because their life is so different, they claim that this is positive proof that their mind is not the causative power behind their experiences. This, of course, assumes that they are in their right mind. Perhaps, in truth, it means they are actually insane.

While it is true that most people would not consciously claim that they value and desire sin, guilt and fear, it does not follow that those items will not be experienced in their life. People fail to realize that the choice they make is not between sin versus sinlessness, guilt versus innocence or fear versus love. Instead it is a choice between what is true and what is false.

What we fail to realize is that what the ego values is its separate autonomous existence. The ego wants to be special or different. Unfortunately, since God created you perfect, whole and complete, the only way to experience being special or different is to value being flawed, not whole and incomplete.

When the ego values specialness over oneness, it automatically gets the attributes that come with specialness. To the ego, specialness requires separation and being different. Since God created you sinless, guiltless and only love, being different means believing you have some attributes of sin, guilt and fear. It is not that we value fear over love. Instead, what we value is being special instead of being equal. Our ego prefers to pretend to be special over being an equal and inseparable part of the Oneness of All That Is.

Differentiation allows for the experience of specialness while maintaining the equality of all the inseparable parts. Through differentiation, we experience accessing various attributes of the whole while maintaining our connection with the whole. We recognize the inseparable nature of the parts to the whole and that all parts contain the whole and the whole is contained in all parts. This is the realization of the holographic nature of Mind.

When our split minds mistook differentiation for different, it made the separation appear real. Our egoic mind is the part of our mind that believes the separation to be its reality and argues for the correctness of that belief. It misunderstood differentiation to require being different. Because the egoic mind values specialness for its reality, it automatically gets the attributes that support its belief in being different.

Because God created us perfect, whole and complete, our desire to be different means our ego must now value the false over the true. The ego argues for the rightness of its belief that separation is real. With that original decision, we automatically get the attributes that logically follow from that first erroneous belief. Our ego's desire to make the false replace the truth creates a false world based on the attributes of separation. Some of the negative attributes of separation include sin, guilt, fear, lack, limitation and the special relationships. Our ego argues for and chooses its rightness over our happiness.

The Christ part of the mind knows that differentiation does not mean different. That the separation is not real and that our illusions cannot change the truth of what we really are. That beneath any perceived differences is the reality of our true equality and indivisibility that we share with the Mind of God.

The Christ is that part of the mind that is the home of the Holy Spirit and the thought system for love and forgiveness. This thought system rests on the truth that you remain as God created you, a part of that indivisible One Self. Because you are Mind, you are free to be or imagine anything that you want and desire in perfect safety. Your egoic imaginings cannot change or shatter the peace of God that is your destiny and reality.

The Christ, your big "S" Self and the Holy Spirit all are closely related and synonymous. The line of demarcation between these terms is blurred and often they are used interchangeably because they all reference our direct connection to the Mind of God, which is our Source. Ultimately, there is only the Mind of God and names themselves are meaningless. Names are only utilized due to the dualistic nature of language as a means for communication in the world of form.

This class has often referenced the vision of Christ. Christ vision allows one to look past the form to the essence, content or purpose behind the thought form. The law of Christ vision says to never mistake the body for the Son of God.

Our physical senses are made to deceive because they mistake the cloak of form to be the essence of our reality. The senses are confirmation devices for our ego's belief and desire to experience specialness and the separation that must logically follow.

The vision of Christ can be experienced in many different ways. When you are aware of the bodily form yet, can look past what is happening on the physical plane and see in the other party their higher self, you are utilizing the vision of Christ. Anytime you are viewing your world through the eyes of love and forgiveness, you are accessing that vision. The vision of Christ does not necessarily mean you will physically see the object differently, but it does mean you will not view it through the eyes of fear and judgment.

For some, the vision of Christ may include the actual physical seeing of an aura or energy field surrounding the form itself. Observing this energy field does not necessarily mean you are employing Christ vision. Christ vision revolves around the interpretation or meaning assigned to the experience.

I have known some who see auras and recognize the Christ nature in all that they observe. They are seeing through the eyes of forgiveness and love. To them, this helps them remember what we really are and they look upon their world with mercy and love. Others see auras and utilize those experiences to reinforce their ego's judgments and beliefs in specialness and separation. While they may both be having the same physical light experience, they are not both seeing with the eyes of Christ.

As an extreme example of Christ vision, let me offer you this personal experience. In this case, I had been involved in some intensive spiritual practices that were centered on the discreation of any belief that no longer served me. I had basically discreated most of my beliefs when I realized that my belief that I was separate no longer served me. I attempted to discreate all my beliefs about separation and join the Oneness of the Mind of God. I cannot say I was totally successful for there was still something conscious that was experiencing and observing but I did not feel apart from anything.

All forms and distinct shapes that might imply separation had disappeared. There were no objects. All was vibrating in a kaleidoscope of light patterns of varying colors that was extraordinarily beautiful. There was no separation between the patterns as each blended and emanated from a common source. I could perceive no point where one ended and another began. They were all pulsating as one indivisible whole. I was in the state of ecstasy, bliss and awe at the wonderment that surrounded, pulsated and was part of me. I felt only love, peace and the oneness of connection. All words lost their meaning, for I could no longer discern any separation or differentiation between a table and a chair because there was no table or chair. I had lost all past beliefs that had once distinguished one item from another. All were one pulsating vibrating light and energy pattern that could not be separate or apart from itself.

This was not some drug-induced state, out of body experience or dream vision. I was seeing with my own eyes and could be taken to various places and would observe different light patterns but no separation.

Based on what physiologists tell us about physical sight, our mind actually acts as a filter and fills in gaps that exist in our observations. Our normal sight can only pick up visible light, which is a very tiny part of the electromagnetic spectrum. Perhaps, in my discreation, I had discreated some of my egoic filters that block what the mind normally allows the physical senses to report. Or perhaps, our physical senses are actually capable of observing more than just the physical light spectrum, but our egoic mind blocks that capability. In any case, what I observed was real and not something of my mind's imagination.

Although this state of oneness was measured in days and lasted less than one week, it did leave a lasting impression on what true vision entails. Before I returned to the world of form and differentiation, all names had lost their meaning. I was incapable of identifying any specific object. All was one indivisible part of the whole. All were pulsating vibrational light and energy patterns that could not be separate from each other. I felt no fear for only love, harmony and peace remained within that state of oneness. I had no desire to leave and it was interesting how my handlers reintegrated me back into the world of form.

I mention that this was what I would describe as an extreme example of Christ vision. I use the term extreme because in that state, I would not have been able to function in the world of form. I had no need for and had lost my bodily connection to this world. Part of the reintegration process was the reconnecting of my consciousness to a physical body. Without the ability to distinguish any separation between forms, this world had lost its purpose. If on earth our purpose is forgiveness, in this extreme state, there was nothing that could possibly require forgiveness or anything outside the beauty and wonder of that one creation.

In order to once again become functional in this world of form, it was necessary to reestablish some of those egoic filters so I could once again "see" the forms that blocked our true essence. It became necessary for me to create artificial boundaries within that oneness and apply names to those boundaries that would define and limit what my mind would allow them to do. I had to take the differentiation within the One Self and pretend that differentiation actually meant separate and different autonomous entities.

This is why I say that if you are to function in this world of form, the vision of Christ allows you to be aware of the form so that you can respond appropriately to the events in this world while recognizing the illusionary nature of the event. You realize the event itself has no ability to change the oneness of what you truly are. You no longer need to run what the physical senses observe through all your ego's filters of past beliefs and judgments.

This experience was more than adequate evidence to realize that my true happiness is in being in a state of oneness and connection. With this example of vision that was given to me, I know that we cannot be satisfied with what our ego offers when this higher state of joy, bliss, awe, ecstasy and oneness is our divine birthright.

Words cannot describe the experience that revelation brings. Revelation is a personal experience that loses its meaning when translated into words. You really have to be there in the experience. I only share this experience with the hope that it will open new possibilities for how you may choose to view your world. But one thing is certain. You are definitely not your body. In this world of form, your function is forgiveness, your purpose is love and your destiny is that peace of God.

LESSON 271

Christ's is the vision I will use today.

W-271.1.Each day, each hour, every instant, I am choosing what I want to look upon, the sounds I want to hear, the witnesses to what I want to be the truth for me. 2 Today I choose to look upon what Christ would have me see, to listen to God's Voice, and seek the witnesses to what is true in God's creation. 3 In Christ's sight, the world and God's creation meet, and as they come together all **egoic** perception **of lack, limitation and separation** disappears. 4 **Christ's** kindly sight redeems the world from death, for nothing that **Christ** looks on but must live, remembering the Father and the Son; Creator and creation unified.

W-271.2. <Father, Christ's vision is the way to You. 2 What **Christ** beholds invites Your memory to be restored to me. 3 And this I choose, to be what I would look upon today.>

Notes to Lesson #271

Christ's is the vision I will use today.

Comment: You, as the ruler of your mind, get to choose what you will call into your awareness. You determine how you will interpret all events that you experience. As the decision-maker for your mind, you can choose between utilizing the body's eyes or Christ vision. The Law of Christ Vision says, do not mistake the body for the Son of God.

With Christ vision, the world, God and all of creation meet and come together. As they are joined as one, perception disappears.

LESSON 272

How can illusions satisfy God's Son?

W-272.1. <Father, the truth belongs to me. 2 My home is set in Heaven by Your Will and mine. 3 Can **egoic** dreams **that always end in lack, limitation and separation** content me? 4 Can illusions bring me happiness? 5 What but Your memory can satisfy Your Son? 6 I will accept no less than You have given me. 7 I am surrounded by Your Love, forever still, forever gentle and forever safe. 8 God's Son must be as You created him.>

W-272.2.Today we pass illusions by. 2 And if we hear temptation call to us to stay and linger in an **egoic** dream **of separation**, we turn aside and ask ourselves if we, the Sons of God, could be content with dreams, when Heaven can be chosen just as easily as hell, and love will happily replace all fear.

Notes to Lesson #272

How can illusions satisfy God's Son?

Comment: Awakening is one decision away. Accept the At-One-Ment or Truth for yourself. Your mind has the freedom and power of choice and interpretation. You can choose truth over illusion; love over fear; Heaven over hell. Why pretend you are limited when God created you, perfect, whole and complete?

The ego does not have a plan that can ever end in your happiness. All your ego's plans ultimately leave you trapped in fear. All your ego's plans support your ego's belief in lack, limitation and separation. They all end badly for God's Son.

The Holy Spirit and your big "S" Self know what God's Will is. Accept the Atonement for yourself. God's Will is that you be happy. Therefore, as ruler of your own mind, make the choice for truth over illusions.

Paradise was never lost. Decide today to reclaim your divine birthright. With that single purpose, you cannot fail for that is God's Will for all of creation.

The stillness of the peace of God is mine.

W-273.1.Perhaps we are now ready for a day of undisturbed tranquility. 2 If **a day of undisturbed tranquility** is not yet feasible, we are content and even more than satisfied to learn how such a day can be achieved. 3 If we give way to a disturbance, let us learn how to dismiss **that disturbance** and return to peace. 4 We need but tell our minds, with certainty, "The stillness of the peace of God is mine," and nothing can intrude upon the peace that God Himself has given to His Son.

W-273.2. <Father, Your peace is mine. 2 What need have I to fear that anything can rob me of **the peace that God** would have me keep? 3 I cannot lose Your gifts **of peace that You gave** to me. 4 And so the peace You gave Your Son is with me still, in quietness and in my own eternal love for You.>

Notes to Lesson #273

The stillness of the peace of God is mine.

Comment: As the decision-maker and ruler of your mind, you can reclaim your peace at any time you desire. Your own mind has the power of interpretation and controls your inner peace. Nothing outside your mind has the power to rob you of your well-being unless you choose to allow it.

You have freely chosen to come here onto a planet of seeming hate and fear to learn this lesson about the creative power of your mind.

You are not a body. You are free. You remain as God created you. Nothing sources your experience but your own mind and nothing has the power to rob you of your own inner peace unless you choose to allow it.

The peace of God is your inheritance and nothing can intrude upon the peace that God has given you. Your task is to quiet the chatter of your egoic mind, to stop judging and go within to find the peace of God that is your destiny.

LESSON 274

Today belongs to love. Let me not fear.

W-274.1. <Father, today I would let all things be as You created them, and give Your Son the honor due **the Son**'s sinlessness; the love of brother to his brother and his Friend. 2 Through **love and by letting all things be as You created them** I am redeemed. 3 Through **love and by letting all things be as You created them** as well, the truth will enter where illusions were, light will replace all darkness, and Your Son will know he is as You created him.>

W-274.2.A special blessing comes to us today, from **God** Who is our Father. 2 Give this day to **God** and there will be no fear today, because the day is given unto love.

Notes to Lesson #274

Today belongs to love. Let me not fear.

Comment: What kind of a day do you want? If you want peace and love, give the day over to the Holy Spirit. When you follow the guidance of the Holy Spirit, no fear will stop you. You will be able to walk through any ring of fear with the Holy Spirit and Christ being with you.

LESSON 275

God's healing Voice protects all things today.

W-275.1.Let us today attend the Voice for God, **the Holy Spirit,** which speaks an ancient lesson, no more true today than any other day. 2 Yet has this day been chosen as the time when we will seek and hear and learn and understand. 3 Join me in hearing **these lessons.** 4 For the Voice for God tells us of things we cannot understand alone, nor learn apart. 5 It is in **the Holy Spirit's understanding and interpretation** that all things are protected. 6 And in this **understanding of these lessons** the healing of the Voice for God is found.

W-275.2. <Your healing Voice protects all things today, and so I leave all things to You. 2 I need be anxious over nothing. 3 For **the Holy Spirit** will tell me what to do and where to go; to whom to speak and what to say to him, what thoughts to think, what words to give the world. 4 The safety that I bring is given me. 5 Father, Your Voice, **the Holy Spirit,** protects all things through me.>

Notes to Lesson #275

God's healing Voice protects all things today.

Comment: God's love protects all things. We are joined together by God's love. God's plan for your reawakening protects His Son's true Identity and guarantees the reawakening to the Truth. The Holy Spirit has been placed in your mind to bring you home. In this task, it cannot fail.

The ego knows nothing and can only hinder your progress. Ask and follow the thought system of the Holy Spirit. The Holy Spirit will reframe your egoic thoughts to align with the truth and protect the sinless nature of God's creation. Use the vision of Christ to see that all remain perfect, whole and complete as God created us.

LESSON 276

The Word of God is given me to speak.

W-276.1.What is the Word of God? 2 "My Son is pure and holy as Myself." 3 And thus did God become the Father of the Son He loves, for thus was **the Son** created. 4 This the Word **God's** Son did not create with **God** because in this **God's** Son was born. 5 Let us accept **God's** Fatherhood, and all is given us. 6 Deny we were created in **God's** Love and we deny our **big "S" Self. When we deny we were created in God's Love, we become** unsure of Who we are, of Who our Father is, and for what purpose we have come. 7 And yet, we need but to acknowledge **God** Who gave His Word to us in our creation, to remember **God** and so recall our **big "S" Self.**

W-276.2. <Father, Your Word is mine. 2 And it is **God's** Word that I would speak to all my brothers, who are given me to cherish as my own, as I am loved and blessed and saved by **God.**>

Notes to Lesson #276

The Word of God is given me to speak.

Comment: God is First Cause and we are God's First Effect. God created us when He said or thought. "My Son is as pure as Myself." With this Thought, God created the Son He loves. This opening thought was God's alone. The Son did not share this thought or co-create with God because in this thought the Son was created.

The Atonement is the acceptance of the truth for yourself. It is the acknowledgment that God is your Creator and you remain as God created you, part of that One Self.

Our ego is in denial of God's Fatherhood and claims that we are either not created by God in His likeness or have somehow been able to change how God created us and overcome God's Will. This belief that we could change God or be something different than as God created us is referred to in A Course in Miracles as the authority problem.

We can deny God's Fatherhood, but our denial cannot change the fact that we were created in God's love. Our true reality remains our big "S" Self that we share with the Mind of God. Our split mind's denial of this truth cannot change the truth.

You are an extension of the Oneness of All That Is. Share the Word of God that all of creation remains perfect, whole and complete, just like God. When you share the truth that God's Son is as pure and holy as God, Himself, you extend that thought to your brother and co-create with God. Your co-creations are the sharing and extension of the Thoughts and Words you think with God.

LESSON 277

Let me not bind Your Son with laws I made.

Let me not bind Your Son with laws I made.

W-277.1. <Your Son is free, my Father. 2 Let me not imagine I have bound **God's Son** with the **egoic** laws I made to rule the body. 3 **God's Son** is not subject to any laws **of my ego that** I made by which I try to make the body more secure. 4 **God's Son** is not changed by what is changeable. 5 **God's Son** is not slave to any laws of time. 6 **God's Son** is as **God** created **His Son,** because **God's Son** knows no law except the law of love.>

W-277.2.Let us not worship idols, nor believe in any law idolatry would make to hide the freedom of the Son of God. 2 **God's Son** is not bound except by his **own egoic mind's** beliefs. 3 Yet what **God's Son** is, is far beyond his faith in slavery or freedom. 4 **God's Son** is free because he is his Father's Son. 5 And **God's Son** cannot be bound unless God's truth can lie, and God can will that **God** deceive Himself.

Notes to Lesson #277

Let me not bind Your Son with laws I made.

<u>**Comment**</u>: The law of love is that to give is to receive. The law that rules this world is that you only give to get. This idea that you only give to get has replaced true love with conditional love. Conditional love is actually fear-based and an extension of your fears. Conditional love rests upon the idea that love can be earned and therefore, you only give to get.

God's love cannot be earned for it is real love which means it is unconditional. God's love flows endlessly. The recipient can deny the flow but that denial has no power to change God's Love or Will.

Because of the creative power of mind, your decision-maker is free to be or imagine anything that you desire. Idolatry is the worship of the ego's belief that something that is false can make you truly happy, perfect, whole and complete. The ego's special relationship is the embodiment of this false idea that something outside yourself has the power to make you happy.

The special relationship accepts the idea that each party is basically flawed and has needs. Using this world's give to get philosophy, the ego hopes to make you less imperfect by entering into relationships in which you exchange some of your limited resources for things of equal or greater value.

The special relationship is based on the idea that love can be earned. When you believe love can be earned, you no longer believe someone can love you unconditionally. You always live in fear that their love can be withdrawn because your ego has accepted the world's law that one only gives to get.

Your salvation is guaranteed by the truth that God created you out of love. As Christ, your big "S" Self cannot be limited by your ego's beliefs in lack, limitation and separation. These erroneous beliefs keep your split mind arguing for its limitations. It is only your own split mind's beliefs that bind you to the laws of this world.

Reject your ego's belief that you are the body and free yourself from your own unforgiving mind. The laws of your ego have no power to bind God's Son. Accept this truth and reclaim your divine birthright.

If I am bound, my Father is not free.

W-278.1.If I accept that I am prisoner within a body, in a world in which all things that seem to live appear to die, then is my Father prisoner with me. 2 And this **imprisonment of God** do I believe, when I maintain the laws the world obeys must I obey; the frailties and the sins which I perceive are real, and cannot be escaped. 3 If I am bound in any way, I do not know my Father nor my **big "S"** Self. 4 And I am lost to all reality. 5 For truth is free, and what is bound is not a part of truth.

W-278.2. <Father, I ask for nothing but the truth. 2 I have had many foolish thoughts **of lack, limitation and separation** about myself and my creation, and have brought a dream of fear into my **split** mind. 3 Today, I would not dream. 4 I choose the way to You instead of madness and instead of fear. 5 For truth is safe, and only love is sure.>

Notes to Lesson #278

If I am bound, my Father is not free.

<u>**Comment**</u>: Because of the creative power of mind, when you believe the laws of the world apply to you, they do. When you accept the belief that you are a body, you will automatically obey the laws and limitations that apply to the bodily form. You have accepted a false fear-based thought system to be your provisional reality. You will remain trapped in fear as long as you value your body as the source for your safety.

When you believe love can be earned, you bind yourself to the law of this earth that claims someone only gives to get. This belief keeps you trapped in fear. When you judge someone as either worthy or unworthy of your love, you deny your reality as the Christ.

God's Love is free. It cannot be earned. Truth is free and what appears bound by limits cannot be part of the Truth. Your safety rests in the truth that God's Love created you. Do not allow your ego's beliefs to artificially imprison God's Son in a body. You are not the body. You are free as God created you. You remain part of the indivisible Mind of God.

Fear is your mind's creation and therefore, must be corrected at its source which is your split mind's beliefs about who you are. Fear is not real. Accept the truth of God's Fatherhood and fear cannot bind you. Love has no opposites. You are the Effect of the Mind of a God of only love. As God's Effect, you cannot change your Cause. Fear cannot be real and therefore, the laws of this fear-based world cannot imprison God's Son.

Creation's freedom promises my own.

W-279.1.The end of dreams is promised me, because God's Son is not abandoned by **God's** Love. 2 Only in dreams is there a time when **God's Son** appears to be in prison, and awaits a future freedom, if **freedom** be at all. 3 Yet in reality his **egoic** dreams **of lack, limitation and separation** are gone, with truth established in their place. 4 And now is freedom his already. 5 Should I wait in chains which have been severed for release, when God is offering me freedom now?

W-279.2. <I will accept **God's** promises today, and give my faith to **God**. 2 My Father loves the Son Whom **God** created as His Own. 3 Would **God** withhold the gifts **God** gave to me?>

Notes to Lesson #279

Creation's freedom promises my own.

Comment: God's Will is that you be happy. You cannot be happy if you are not free. You are not free if your actions have consequences and could result in the withdrawal of God's love. Because of this, time provides a game board in which you are free to be or imagine in perfect safety anything that you desire.

In time, you can pretend that you have forgotten your true Identity as God's Son. Yet, your dreams cannot change the eternal truth that you remain as God created you, part of the holographic indivisible Mind of God

Only in dreams can you believe that you are not free. Being created perfect, whole and complete, you cannot find happiness in an illusion of lack, limitation and separation. Put away your childish toys of make-believe and reclaim your true Identity as your big "S" Self. Illusions cannot make you happy since your true happiness remains as God created you.

Your will and God's Will are the same. God created you like Himself, and you cannot be happy without being the expression of that love. Be the conduit for love that you came here to experience. In that love, your freedom is protected and safe. Nothing sources your experience but your own mind. Your true happiness rests in experiencing being love in form. Only with a forgiving mind can you be free to be the love that you are.

LESSON 280

What limits can I lay upon God's Son?

W-280.1.Whom God created limitless is free. 2 I can invent imprisonment for **what God created limitless and free**, but only in illusions, not in truth. 3 No Thought of God has left its Father's Mind. 4 No Thought of God is limited at all. 5 No Thought of God but is forever pure. 6 Can I lay limits on the Son of God, whose Father willed that **God's Son** be limitless, and like Himself in freedom and in love?

W-280.2. <Today let me give honor to Your Son, for **by honoring God's Son** thus alone I find the way to **God**. 2 Father, I lay no limits on the Son You love and You created limitless. 3 The honor that I give to **God's Son** is Yours, and what is Yours belongs to me as well.>

Notes to Lesson #280

What limits can I lay upon God's Son?

Comment: You are free because God created you without limits. No Thought of God can be limited nor leave the Mind of God. God's Thoughts are changeless and eternal.

Your split mind can imagine that you are limited but that can never be your true reality as the Christ. Your imagination or denial of the truth cannot change the fact that you remain free as God created you. Your ego's belief in limitation cannot bind what God has created as unlimited. No creation of God is limited. God's word has declared His Creation is pure and as holy as Himself.

Only in time can your pretense of lack, limitation and separation appear real. God does not share your misperception and therefore, your illusions are powerless to change the truth. Yet, because of the creative power of your mind, your split mind's illusions become your provisional reality as long as you value those beliefs. All your illusion will end when you stop valuing your ego's fear-based thought system.

What Is the Holy Spirit?

Covers ACIM Workbook Lessons 281-290

7. What Is the Holy Spirit?

W-pII.7.1.The Holy Spirit mediates between illusions and the truth. 2 Since **the Holy Spirit** must bridge the gap between reality and dreams, perception leads to knowledge through the grace that God has given **the Holy Spirit**, to be His gift **of grace** to everyone who turns to **the Holy Spirit** for truth. 3 Across the bridge that **the Holy Spirit** provides are dreams all carried to the truth, to be dispelled before the light of knowledge. 4 There are sights and sounds forever laid aside. 5 And where **sights and sounds** were perceived before, forgiveness has made possible perception's tranquil end **and the return toward knowledge.**

W-pII.7.2.The goal the Holy Spirit's teaching sets is just this end of dreams. 2 For sights and sounds must be translated from the witnesses of fear to those of love. 3 And when this **translation of perception from fear to love** is entirely accomplished, learning has achieved the only goal **learning** has in truth. 4 For learning, as the Holy Spirit guides it to the outcome **the Holy Spirit** perceives for **learning which is to translate perception from dreams of fear to love**, becomes the means to go beyond **the dream of perception** itself, to be replaced by the eternal truth.

W-pII.7.3.If you but knew how much your Father yearns to have you recognize your sinlessness, you would not let **the Holy Spirit's** Voice appeal in vain, nor turn away from **the Holy Spirit's** replacement for the fearful images and dreams you made. 2 The Holy Spirit understands the means **your ego** made, by which **your ego** would attain what is forever unattainable **which is to change God's sinless Son.** 3 And if you offer **your egoic illusions of lack, limitation and separation** to Him, **the Holy Spirit** will employ the means you made for exile to restore your mind to where **your mind** truly is at home.

W-pII.7.4.From knowledge, where **the Holy Spirit** has been placed by God, the Holy Spirit calls to you, to let forgiveness rest upon your **egoic** dreams, and be restored to sanity and peace of mind. 2 Without forgiveness will your **ego's** dreams remain to terrify you. 3 And the memory of all your Father's Love will not return to signify the end of dreams **of separation that** has come.

W-pII.7.5.Accept your Father's gift **of the Holy Spirit.** 2 **The Holy Spirit** is a Call from Love to Love, that **Love** be but Itself. 3 The Holy Spirit is **God's** gift, by which the quietness of Heaven is restored to God's beloved Son. 4 Would you refuse to take the function of completing God, when all **God** wills is that you be complete?

Notes to Special Theme #7: What Is the Holy Spirit?

Covers ACIM Workbook Lessons 281-290

7. What Is the Holy Spirit?

Covers ACIM Workbook Lessons 281-290

The Holy Spirit is God's gift to all of creation. The Holy Spirit has been placed within your mind to insure that you will never forget what you truly are and always return to your home and the remembrance of God.

The Holy Spirit mediates between illusion and truth to bridge the gap between reality and dreams. It takes our dream world of perception and leads us back to the knowledge of what we are. Our mind is asleep and currently dreams what it would be like to be something other than as God created us. The goal of the Holy Spirit is to end the dream of hell and reawaken our sleeping minds to the truth of Heaven.

When allowed, the Holy Spirit will translate our experiences from witnesses for fear to witnesses for love. The Holy Spirit will use the dream of separation to help gently awaken God's sleeping Son to the return to truth and ultimately knowledge. The truth is that God's Son remains perfect as God created him. The Holy Spirit will utilize our ego's dream of imperfection and fear and return our split mind to sanity. The Son's function is to complete God and God's Will is that the Son be complete. God is living in His Son and the Holy Spirit guarantees that God's Will is eternally accomplished.

Grace is the Holy Spirit's gift to anyone who asks for the healing of the split mind. Grace is the acceptance of the love of God in a world of seeming hate and fear. Your goal is not to create a new world, but rather to be only love in that world. You complete God by demonstrating being love in form.

On earth your function is forgiveness, your purpose is love and your destiny is the peace of God. In heaven, which is the abstract Oneness of All That Is, certain aspects of love like forgiveness and being helpful are meaningless and cannot be experienced. The illusion of duality with its appearance of separation and opposites are needed. By being love in form, you demonstrate an aspect of God that cannot be experienced outside the imagined world of perception.

The Holy Spirit takes perception's illusions of duality, opposites, lack, limitation and separation and utilizes those experiences to reawaken our sleeping minds to the truth. In this process, we first learn to control and manage our fears, then recognize our fears are not real. Finally, we eliminate our fears and reawaken to the truth that our fears had previously kept hidden from our awareness. All that remains is the love that you are.

Through grace and the tool of forgiveness, we reawaken to the truth that only love is real. We demonstrate love in form. In time, love is the creative process in which time is utilized to reawaken sleeping minds to their spiritual magnificence as the Christ. By being love in form, we become messengers for the Holy Spirit and help other sleeping minds accept the At- One-Ment for themselves.

The Holy Spirit represents the thought system of love and forgiveness. With this thought system for Christ vision, you can see this world of seeming hate and fear differently. The Holy Spirit's thought system is reflected in the mind of your big "S" Self. This is that part of your mind that remains in communion with God and recognizes that the game of separation is not real and you remain as God created you as an inseparable part of the One Self.

The Holy Spirit is the bridge between the Father and the Son. The Holy Spirit rests in the knowledge that we remain as God created us. Yet, It is also aware that our minds have fallen asleep and forgotten their true identity. The Holy Spirit understands our sleeping minds perceive the dream of What Am I to be real.

The Holy Spirit is in the unique position of knowing both the truth about you and your current state of misperception within the dream itself. Because of Its unique position, the Holy Spirit can take your misperceptions and reframe them to align with the truth. When coupled with forgiveness, this reinterpretation will ultimately heal your split mind and return God's Son to sanity.

The goal of the Holy Spirit is the end of dreams and the recognition that you are sinless and guiltless. The Holy Spirit knows that without forgiveness, your dreams of sin and guilt will keep you trapped in fear. The Holy Spirit is God's gift for the Son's restoration to the truth. With this restoration, we complete God by completing ourselves and being and demonstrating the aspect of love, we call forgiveness. By being love in form, we recognize that only love is real and has no opposite. By being love in form, the abstract One Self knows another aspect of Itself.

In the dream of What am I, the goal of the Holy Spirit is to teach us the following lesson.

You are not a body. You are free. You are still as God created you. Nothing sources your experiences but you and nothing can affect your peace unless you choose to allow it.

This is the lesson we have come to this world to experience and learn. Let us break down what learning that lesson means.

1) **You are not a body.** We need to learn that we are unlimited spirit. As spirit, the rules of the world of form do not apply to us. The beliefs in lack, limitation and separation are not real and have no impact on our reality or peace.
2) **You are free.** Love is freedom. Love does not punish or withdraw its love from the recipient based upon the recipient's response. God's love is given to you unconditionally. There is nothing you need to do to earn God's love, nor is it possible to lose God's love. This means that you are free to be the truth or to pretend you are something you are not. There are no punishments or rewards imposed for exercising your freedom to experience whatever you desire and want. You are truly free and safe.
3) **You are still as God created you**. Your pretense or denial of what you really are has no consequence and cannot change the truth that you remain as God created you. You remain changeless and eternally safe in the love of God. You can deny that reality, but your denial has no ability to change God's beloved Child with whom God is well pleased. Your sinless and guiltless nature is guaranteed by God. You always rest safely in the Mind of God. Paradise cannot be lost but only temporarily forgotten within your mind's imagination. Truth just is and you will eventually, freely choose to return to that truth for God's Will is that you be happy.
4) **Nothing sources your experiences but you**. You are Mind. Mind has the creative power to call into its awareness whatever it desires and wants to experience. The power of your thoughts generates the experiences that appear as your provisional reality. The world you perceive is a reflection of what you value and desire. You alone determine what you will call into your awareness.
5) **Nothing can affect your peace unless you choose to allow it.** You are not the victim of outside forces that are beyond your control. You alone have the power of interpretation. The power of interpretation assigns all meaning you give to any event that you have chosen to experience. All events are neutral learning opportunities. The event itself has no inherent good or bad qualities that can make you happy or sad. It is only your interpretation and judgment that colors an experience as either positive or negative. When you truly recognize that you are the dreamer of the dream, you realize that you have the power to write, create, edit and modify the script to support your current desires. Your experience will be based upon what you truly value and why. You will decide to value either love or fear. Regardless of the circumstances, it is always your own mind that will make this choice.

This is the lesson that you have come to this world of seeming hate and fear to discover and learn. You have come here to be and demonstrate that fear is not real and that love is the creative process of reawakening sleeping minds to the truth of their spiritual magnificence.

A sleeping mind is a mind that is trapped in fear. Just as the Holy Spirit is your guide to reawakening to your own spiritual magnificence, you too can share that same message with your brother. You can recognize that if your brother is fearful, he has forgotten his true Identity and now perceives his own dream of lack, limitation and separation to be real. With love and forgiveness, you can unite with the Holy Spirit in the single purpose of helping your brother reawaken his sleeping mind to accept the At-One-Ment for himself.

The Holy Spirit is the embodiment of love. The Holy Spirit is always with us. When we ask for guidance, the Holy Spirit will respond to us in a loving way. When we turn to the Holy Spirit for guidance, we are asking the Holy Spirit to take into consideration both our current state of being and our interpretation of some event and to respond to us in a loving way that will help reduce our fear or restore our inner peace.

Let us examine the loving response of the Holy Spirit.

The number one overriding priority of the Holy Spirit is to decrease fear. The Holy Spirit will never ask you to do something that you are incapable of handling since that would ultimately result in your fear being increased. This does not mean that you will not be asked to do some things that your ego would perceive to be fearful. But it does mean that the Holy Spirit will be there to help you reframe your ego's fears so that you can move beyond the form and glean the learning lesson that the experience was designed to provide. The Holy Spirit understands the big picture and how all experiences are baby steps to the ending of fear and the return to love.

Because love's guiding principle is never to increase your fear, this restricts the options that would be considered appropriate loving responses in any given situation. Each situation is unique which is why you should always seek the guidance of the Holy Spirit who knows the big picture. The external events may appear to be the same but each person's state of mind is in a constant state of flux due to new experiences and lessons learned. The appropriate loving response of yesterday may not be a loving response for today.

Because the Holy Spirit will never do anything that will increase your fear, the Holy Spirit will meet you where you currently are on your own perfect path. If you are currently terrified, a loving response would be to decrease the level of fear that you are currently experiencing. If you are terrified because you find yourself in in a burning building and believe your safety rests with the body, a loving response would be to direct you to the nearest safe exit.

Based on your current state of mind, it would not be appropriate for the Holy Spirit to whack you on the side of the head and tell you that you are not a body and therefore, you should just remain in the building. Why? Because that would increase your state of fear and you are not ready to take such a giant step.

By the same token, the fact that we are not the body and that each is the creator of their own world is not the message someone is always ready to hear even if it is the truth. To move someone from their long-held belief in victim consciousness to responsibility consciousness may require some intermediate steps along the way. Love would allow for this. The Holy Spirit's purpose is to gently reawaken sleeping minds to their spiritual magnificence, not have them die in fright during the process.

So let's look at how the Holy Spirit gently reawakens us to the truth.

When we are not ready or willing to hear the truth, the Holy Spirit holds that truth for us. It recognizes that we remain as God create us even when we choose to live in fear. It waits patiently until we are willing to open our minds to a new way of viewing our world. The Holy Spirit does not judge our own perfect path or question our ability to eventually arrive at the correct destination. Rather than call us stupid, It waits patiently by our side. It trusts that we will eventually lose faith in our ego's plans and seek a new guide. When we do, the Holy Spirit will be there to answer our call.

When asked, the Holy Spirit responds to our call in a way to reduce, manage and mitigate our fears and thus, ultimately gently reawaken us to the truth. It takes our current state of mind into consideration and then reframes and reinterprets the circumstances to help support our reduction of fear and restoration of peace. The Holy Spirit knows the big picture and realizes the truth that you always remain as God created you.

The Holy Spirit is there to assist and help guide you home. It realizes that we have all the time we need and that we are merely re-experiencing a journey that was over before it even began. The Holy Spirit knows that it does not have to save you from your detour into fear because you never cease to be God's beloved Son. God's holy Son has never needed to be saved for He has never sinned nor left the Mind of God.

In time, love is the creative process in which you can choose to act like the Holy Spirit for your brother and help reawaken his sleeping mind to the truth of his spiritual magnificence. On earth, you do this through forgiveness and love.

Remember that the Holy Spirit is God's representative for love Who lives in your holy mind. Act like the Holy Spirit whose home is your big "S" Self. For they, like you, are the same. As Jesus said, if you want to be like me, knowing that we are the same, I will help you. If you want to be different, I will wait until you change your mind.

Note how Jesus' response is just like the Holy Spirit's response to the question of what would love have you do. Be the Holy Spirit's messenger for your brother and mirror that mindset of being love in this world of seeming hate and fear.

I can be hurt by nothing but my thoughts.

W-281.1. <Father, Your Son is perfect. 2 When I think that I am hurt in any way, it is because I have forgotten who I am, and that I am as You created me. 3 **God's** Thoughts can only bring me happiness. 4 If ever I am sad or hurt or ill, I have forgotten what **God** thinks, and put my little meaningless **egoic** ideas in place of where **God's** Thoughts belong, and where **God's** Thoughts are. 5 I can be hurt by nothing but my thoughts. 6 The Thoughts I think with **God** can only bless. 7 The Thoughts I think with **God** alone are true.>

W-281.2. I will not hurt myself today. 2 For I am far beyond all pain. 3 My Father placed me safe in Heaven, watching over me. 4 And I would not attack the Son He loves, for what **God** loves is also mine to love.

Notes to Lesson #281

I can be hurt by nothing but my thoughts.

Comment: You are invulnerable because God made you perfect, whole and complete. Yet, you can deny that truth. You can forget what you are. Only your own belief in lack, limitation and separation causes you to behave as if you are not perfect, have needs, are the body and can suffer and die.

Only the thoughts you think with the Mind of God are true and real. Only your ego's beliefs that you are a sinner, have lost Paradise and now must earn your redemption need to be corrected. God's love is freely given and cannot be earned. Your worth and safety come from your divine birthright, not from the body and what it does. Let the Holy Spirit correct your erroneous beliefs and heal your split mind.

LESSON 282

I will not be afraid of love today.

W-282.1. If I could realize but this today **to not be afraid of love**, salvation would be reached for all the world. 2 **To not be afraid of love is** the decision not to be insane, and to accept myself as God Himself, my Father and my Source, created me. 3 **To not be afraid of love is** the determination not to be asleep in dreams of death, while truth remains forever living in the joy of love. 4 And **to not be afraid of love is** the choice to recognize the **big "S"** Self Whom God created as the Son He loves, and Who remains my one Identity.

W-282.2. <Father, Your Name is Love and so is **Love my name**. 2 Such is the truth. 3 And can the truth be changed by merely giving it another name? 4 The name of fear is simply a mistake. 5 Let me not be afraid of truth today.>

Notes to Lesson #282

I will not be afraid of love today.

Comment: Accept yourself as God created you. Be determined to not be asleep even while appearing within the ego's dreams of death and separation. To live in fear is not to live. Your fears are false evidence appearing real and keep you dead to the truth of your big "S" Self. Give your fear-based thoughts over to the Holy Spirit to be reinterpreted through the eyes of truth, love and forgiveness.

God created you as a conduit for love and an extension of Himself. When you believe love can be earned, you will always be afraid for you have mistaken God's love with earthly conditional love. What this world calls conditional love is not love but a disguised form of fear. God's love is unconditional. It cannot be earned nor lost for God's love flows unceasingly. You have nothing to fear from real love and a God of only love.

LESSON 283

My true Identity abides in You.

My true Identity abides in **God**.

W-283.1. <Father, I made an image of **a little "s" self**, and it is this **little "s" self** I call the Son of God. 2 Yet is creation as it always was, for God's creation is unchangeable. 3 Let me not worship idols. 4 I am **God's creation** my Father loves. 5 My holiness remains the light of Heaven and the Love of God. 6 Is not what is beloved of **God** secure? 7 Is not the light of Heaven infinite? 8 Is not Your Son my true Identity **as my Big "S" Self,** when **God** created everything that is?>

W-283.2.Now are we One in shared Identity, with God our Father as our only Source, and everything created part of us. 2 And so we offer blessing to all things, uniting lovingly with all the world, which our forgiveness has made one with us.

Notes to Lesson #283

My true Identity abides in You.

<u>Comment</u>: We have allowed our ego's belief in lack, limitation and separation to hide the truth of what we really are. Do not be both naïve and arrogant about your true nature. You are not the image of your ego's little "s" self but instead, remain the big "S" Self that God created. You are part of the indivisible One Self.

There is nothing outside of God and everything is God. God is only love and you are a conduit for that love and share that one Identity of only Love. The Father, the Son and the Holy Spirit are merely different aspects of the whole, for they are inseparable and of One Mind.

Your true Identity abides in God; not in your ego's illusions. God, the Father is first Cause. God, the Son, is Its Effect. They are forever joined by the Holy Spirit in one inseparable union called God or Love.

LESSON 284

I can elect to change all thoughts that hurt.

W-284.1.Loss is not loss when properly perceived. 2 Pain is impossible. 3 There is no grief with any cause at all. 4 And suffering of any kind is nothing but a dream. 5 **That I can elect to change all thoughts that hurt** is the truth, at first to be but said and then repeated many times; and next to be accepted as but partly true, with many reservations. 6 Then **the belief that I can elect to change all thoughts that hurt is** to be considered seriously more and more, and finally accepted as the truth. 7 I can elect to change all thoughts that hurt. 8 And I would go beyond these words today, and past all reservations, and arrive at full acceptance of the truth in them **that I can elect to change all thoughts that hurt.**

W-284.2. <Father, what You have given cannot hurt, so grief and pain must be impossible. 2 Let me not fail to trust in **God** today, accepting but the joyous as **God's** gifts; accepting but the joyous as the truth.>

Notes to Lesson #284

I can elect to change all thoughts that hurt.

I can elect to change all thoughts that hurt.

<u>Comment</u>: Loss only represents your belief in separation and cannot be real. Loss only appears to exist in the insane mind of the ego that perceives itself to be the body. Any suffering is a part of your dream of separation and you can choose to see that dream differently.

Your mind alone is the source for your own provisional reality and therefore, you can choose to interpret things differently. All experiences are neutral. It is only your own mind's beliefs and judgments that color an experience as either good or bad. You can elect to change all thoughts that hurt by changing your mind about what you are.

At first, you will not believe that your mind alone possesses this power to transform your experiences. Most will have to baby step their way to this belief that they alone are the source of their own experiences.

This lesson provides a progressive formula for changing your beliefs.

1) Repeat the new belief as many times as possible.

2) Accept the belief as partially true with many reservations and exceptions.

3) Consider the belief more seriously and apply that belief to those exceptions.

4) Finally accept the new belief as true, applying it to all circumstances and thus, replacing the old belief with the new.

Your mind is the source of your experience and alone has the power of interpretation. Your mind assigns any meaning to the neutral events that you have desired to experience. There is nothing outside of your own mind that can rob you of your own peace. Your mind alone sources your world.

LESSON 285

My holiness shines bright and clear today.

W-285.1.Today I wake with joy, expecting but the happy things of God to come to me. 2 I ask but **the happy things of God** to come, and realize my invitation will be answered by the thoughts to which **my invitation** has been sent by me. 3 And I will ask for only joyous things the instant I accept my holiness. 4 For what would be the use of pain to me, what purpose would my suffering fulfill, and how would grief and loss avail me if insanity departs from me today, and I accept my holiness instead?

W-285.2. <Father, my holiness is **God's holiness**. 2 Let me rejoice in **my holiness** and through forgiveness be restored to sanity. 3 Your Son is still as You created him. 4 My holiness is part of me, and also part of **God**. 5 And what can alter Holiness Itself?>

Notes to Lesson #285

My holiness shines bright and clear today.

Comment: Because of the creative power of your mind, your thoughts become your experiences. Your world is a reflection of your thoughts. When you realize that you are holy, your mind will think those types of thoughts and your world will reflect that new found holiness. If you see yourself as a separate sinner, you will be trapped within the ego's fear-based thought system. Your experiences will reflect those fears and the blame, shame and guilt game will dominate your world.

When you fail to forgive and choose to blame others for not making you happy, you bind yourself to that illusion and disempower yourself. Your belief in being a victim becomes your provisional reality. You have denied that your mind is the power source behind your experiences. You are arguing for your littleness. This reinforces your claim that you have been hurt by outside forces that are beyond your control. This is your ego's denial of your own divine birthright.

You need a new plan and a new guide. Allow the Holy Spirit to teach you what you truly are so that you can see a world that reflects your true holiness.

LESSON 286

The hush of Heaven holds my heart today.

W-286.1. <Father, how still today! 2 How quietly do all things fall in place! 3 This is the day that has been chosen as the time in which I come to understand the lesson that there is no need that **my ego** do anything. 4 In **God** is every choice already made. 5 In **God** has every conflict been resolved. 6 In **God** is everything I hope to find already given me. 7 Your peace is mine. 8 My heart is quiet, and my mind at rest. 9 Your Love is Heaven, and **God's** Love is mine.>

W-286.2.The stillness of today will give us hope that we have found the way, and travelled far along **God's path** to a wholly certain goal. 2 Today we will not doubt the end which God Himself has promised us. 3 We trust in **God**, and in our **big "S"** Self, Who still is One with **God**.

Notes to Lesson #286

The hush of Heaven holds my heart today.

Comment: Forgive your past for the past is over. Only your own unforgiving mind keeps the past alive. As an ego body, you need do nothing. No plan of your ego can earn you salvation. There is nothing that you can do in this dream of separation that can earn God's love for it was never lost.

God's love flows automatically. It is only your ego's plans that block that flow from your awareness. Your past beliefs are based on fear and do not serve you. When you are willing to drop your ego's judgments, you will realize that the past is over. When you still the mind and allow the Holy Spirit to guide you, you will align to that consciousness of love, peace and forgiveness. Simply ask the Holy Spirit what love would have you do.

God's plan is automatic. You need only to be willing to give your day over to the Holy Spirit. God's plan for salvation is guaranteed for it is God's Will and the Holy Spirit will not fail in His mission of reawakening God's sleeping Son.

God's Will is that you be happy. No sacrifice is required but merely the acceptance of the truth that you are not a body but rather unlimited spirit. You remain as God created you. Fear is not a part of a still mind. Control your fear and accept and receive the Holy Spirit's guidance. Open yourself up to the flow of God's love and it will be there for you.

LESSON 287

You are my goal, my Father. Only You.

You are my goal, my Father. Only **God.**

W-287.1.Where would I go but Heaven? 2 What could be a substitute for **Heaven's** happiness? 3 What gift could I prefer before the peace of God? 4 What treasure would I seek and find and keep that can compare with my Identity **as my big "S" Self**? 5 And would I rather live with fear than love?

W-287.2. <You are my goal, my Father. 2 What but **God** could I desire to have? 3 What way but that which leads to **God** could I desire to walk? 4 And what except the memory of **God** could signify to me the end of **egoic** dreams **of separation** and futile substitutions **of illusions** for the truth? 5 **God** is my only goal. 6 Your Son would be as **God** created him. 7 What way but this **remembrance of God** could I expect to recognize my **big "S"** Self, and be at one with my Identity?>

Notes to Lesson #287

You are my goal, my Father. Only You.

Comment: Accepting the truth about your Identity as your big "S" Self is the only thing that offers the peace of God. Your ego's illusions are mere fantasies and cannot make you happy. Even if temporarily achieved, your ego's plans always leave you in fear and fail to give you the lasting joy, love and peace that you seek and deserve.

Be vigilant only for God. In God, your true happiness rests. Let reclaiming your divine birthright be your single purpose and watch the nightmare of sin, guilt and fear fade away.

Let me forget my brother's past today.

W-288.1. < **Let me forget my brother's past** is the thought that leads the way to **God** and brings me to my goal **of remembering God**. 2 I cannot come to **God** without my brother. 3 And to know my Source, I first must recognize what **God** created one with me. 4 My brother's is the hand that leads me on the way to **God**. 5 **My brother's** sins are in the past along with **my sins**, and I am saved because the past is gone. 6 Let me not cherish **the past** within my heart, or I will lose the way to walk to **God**. 7 My brother is my savior. 8 Let me not attack the savior **God** has given me. 9 But let me honor **my brother and savior** who bears **God's** Name, and so remember that **God's Name** is my own **Name**.>

W-288.2.**Jesus says,** forgive me, then, today. 2 And you will know you have forgiven me, **Jesus,** if you behold your brother in the light of holiness. 3 **My brother** cannot be less holy than can I, **Jesus,** and you cannot be holier than **my brother**.

Notes to Lesson #288

Let me forget my brother's past today.

Comment: We are all part of the shared Mind of God. I and my brother are one. All of God's creations are one with their Source.

How you treat your brother will disclose what you truly value and why. Drop your ego's story of what your brother did to you unless you wish the present to be a replay of your past. The past will end only when you are willing to drop your prior judgments about it.

Through your brother, you get to hone and demonstrate your skills at being love in form. When you forgive your brother, you forgive yourself. If you insist on keeping your brother in the jail of your own unforgiving mind, you must also remain in that same prison as his jailer.

The past is gone. The ego's thought system wants to keep you focused on your past because the past is fear-based. Only your own unforgiving mind, not your brother, keeps the past alive. Forgive and the past will no longer bind you. Without your past beliefs, you are free to exercise your mind's power of interpretation in a new, exciting and liberating way.

You can drop your old stories which support your ego's belief in victim consciousness. You can choose to recognize your brother's holy and sinless nature. You can allow your brother the freedom to be on his own perfect path without making him wrong for not following your path.

When you free your brother from your own past judgments, you stop crucifying yourself.

The past is over. It can touch me not.

The past is over. **The past** can touch me not.

W-289.1.Unless the past is over in my mind, the real world must escape my sight. 2 For I am really looking nowhere; seeing but **the past that** is not there. 3 How can I then perceive the world forgiveness offers? 4 This **world of forgiveness is what** the past was made to hide, for this **forgiven world is** the world that can be looked on only now, **without any reference to the past**. 5 **A forgiven world** has no past. 6 For what can be forgiven but the past, and if **the past** is forgiven **the past** is gone.

W-289.2. <Father, let me not look upon a past that is not there. 2 For You have offered me Your Own replacement, in a present world the past has left untouched and free of sin. 3 Here **in a forgiven world free from the past** is the end of guilt. 4 And here **in a forgiven world** am I made ready for Your final step. 5 Shall I demand that You wait longer for Your Son to find the loveliness You planned to be the end of all his **ego's** dreams and all his pain?>

Notes to Lesson #289

The past is over. It can touch me not.

Comment: The past is your belief in sin, guilt and fear. The past is only important when you think it effects the present or the future. Yet, the past is over. It is not real and only exists in your split mind. Cause and effect are instantaneous. Yet, in time, we believe that there is a gap between cause and effect. This perceived gap allows us to believe that the past impacts our present and future.

Only your past can be forgiven. If forgiven, the past is gone and can have no impact on the present or future. With the past gone, your world is free from your beliefs in sin, guilt and fear. Your belief that the past has some ability to impact your present and future is the source that fueled your dreams of a fearful and hateful world.

This belief in your past's future effects prevents you from being in the <now> and keeps you trapped in your past fear-based thinking and judgments. It is only your unforgiving mind that keeps you trapped in fear. Forgiveness is the end of guilt. Without forgiveness, the blame shame and guilt game will dominate and rule your unforgiven world.

LESSON 290

My present happiness is all I see.

W-290.1.Unless I look upon what is not there, my present happiness is all I see. 2 Eyes that begin to open see at last. 3 And I would have Christ's vision come to me this very day. 4 What I perceive without God's Own Correction **of Christ vision** for the **ego's** sight I made is frightening and painful to behold. 5 Yet I would not allow my mind to be deceived by the belief the dream **of lack, limitation and separation that** I made is real an instant longer. 6 This the day I seek my present happiness, and look on nothing else except the thing I seek.

W-290.2. <With this resolve I come to **God** and ask **God's** strength to hold me up today, while I but seek to do **God's** Will. 2 You cannot fail to hear me, Father. 3 What I ask have You already given me. 4 And I am sure that I will see my happiness today.>

Notes to Lesson #290

My present happiness is all I see.

Comment: The world of sin, guilt and fear that your ego perceives is not real. It is the product of your own erroneous beliefs in lack, limitation and separation. Today, drop your ego's beliefs and judgments and allow the Holy Spirit to be your guide. Allow the vision of Christ to show you a world of mercy and love.

Since God's Will is that you be happy, that should be your true reality. Only your ego's judgments and beliefs block you from seeing the happy and forgiven world that you seek. Forgive and you will see differently.

What Is the Real World?

Covers ACIM Workbook Lessons 291-300

8. What Is the Real World?

W-pII.8.1.The real world is a symbol **for your beliefs and values just** like the rest of what perception offers. 2 Yet **the real world** stands for what is opposite to what you made **with your ego's desire to be different and separate.** 3 Your **ego's** world is seen through eyes of fear, and brings the witnesses of terror to your **split** mind. 4 The real world cannot be perceived except through eyes forgiveness blesses, so **forgiving eyes** see a world where terror is impossible, and witnesses to fear cannot be found.

W-pII.8.2.The real world holds a counterpart for each unhappy thought reflected in your world. **The real world holds** a sure correction for the sights of fear and sounds of battle which your world contains. 2 The real world shows a world seen differently, through quiet eyes and with a mind at peace. 3 Nothing but rest is there **in the real world.** 4 **In the real world,** there are no cries of pain and sorrow heard, for nothing there remains outside forgiveness. 5 And the sights are gentle. 6 Only happy sights and sounds can reach the mind that has forgiven itself.

W-pII.8.3.What need has such a **forgiving** mind for thoughts of death, attack and murder? 2 What can **a forgiving mind** perceive surrounding **itself** but safety, love and joy? 3 What is there **a forgiving mind** would choose to be condemned, and what is there that **a forgiving mind** would judge against? 4 The world **a forgiving mind** sees arises from a mind at peace within itself. 5 No danger lurks in anything it sees, for **a forgiving mind** is kind, and only kindness does **a forgiving mind** look upon.

W-pII.8.4.The real world is the symbol that the dream of sin and guilt is over, and God's Son no longer sleeps. 2 His waking eyes perceive the sure reflection of his Father's Love; the certain promise that **God's Son** is redeemed. 3 The real world signifies the end of time, for **the** perception **of a sinless, guiltless and forgiven world** makes time purposeless.

W-pII.8.5.The Holy Spirit has no need of time when **time** has served **the Holy Spirit's** purpose. 2 Now **the Holy Spirit** waits but that one instant more for God to take His final step, and time has disappeared, taking perception with it as **time** goes, and leaving but the truth to be itself. 3 That instant **of our return to knowledge** is our goal, for it contains the memory of God. 4 And as we look upon a world forgiven, it is **God** Who calls to us and comes to take us home, reminding us of our Identity **as our big "S" Self, the Christ,** which our forgiveness has restored to us.

Notes to Special Theme # 8: What Is the Real World?

Special Theme #8 What Is the Real World?

Covers ACIM Workbook Lessons 291-300

The real world is not a physical place. Instead, it represents a state of mind. The real world is a symbol that stands for the opposite of what you have made through your mind's belief in lack, limitation and separation. The real world is perceived through the eyes of forgiveness that bless as opposed to the eyes of fear that judge and condemn.

The real world holds a counterpart for each unhappy thought that is currently reflected in your world of provisional reality. This counterpart, being fear's opposite, offers a sure correction for your ego's misperceptions because it is based on the Holy Spirit's thought system of peace and forgiveness.

In the real world, there is no judgment, sin or guilt. Your current world of perception is built around the ego's desire to judge because it believes there are outside forces that can impact your reality. The real world recognizes that your mind is the creative power that is reflected in the world that you perceive.

The real world signifies the end of time because when your perception aligns with the truth, time becomes purposeless. The purpose of time is to allow for change and to measure it. Time allows misperception to be changed eventually into correct perception. When all your misperceptions have been replaced by correct perception, the need for change is over. Once the real world is all you perceive, time has served its purpose and is no longer needed. You no longer need to change your mind about anything since you have finally accepted the truth.

When you only perceive the real world, it signifies that all misperceptions have been changed to correct perception. God can now take the final step which is your return to knowledge. The game of What Am I is over for your identity is no longer uncertain. Both time and perception disappear and only truth remains. As we look upon our forgiven world, God can return us to our proper home.

This final step that God takes is the end of perception and our return to knowledge. We will recognize that I and my Father are One. In this truth, we will also realize that we are not the body. We are free. We are as God created us and that nothing can affect us unless we choose to allow it. The real world is a symbol that God's Son is awake.

The real world symbolizes that the dream of sin and guilt is over. It is the recognition that the Holy Spirit has used time to reawaken God's beloved Child. We had merely been asleep and now are awakened to our eternal reality that has never been lost or changed. The need for time is over and God can take the final step to remind us of our true identity as the Christ, our big "S" Self, and our oneness that we share with the Mind of God.

Question: Based on how A Course in Miracles defines real, is the real world, real?

The real world is not real for the real world is a symbol. A symbol stands for something else but is not real. A symbol represents something that may be either true or false. The real world signifies the end of time for its correct perception makes time without a purpose. In the real world, you are no longer suffering from erroneous thinking. Therefore, there is no change that needs to take place within your mind and there is no need for time. Remember, time is the measure of change. If the truth is recognized and truth does not change, there is no change for time to measure. Time itself, having lost its function, now becomes meaningless.

The real world is not real but offers a counter part to the dream of separation. For every unloving thought it provides an opposite that corrects that original thought. Your world of perception is a world in which opposites appear to exist. Fear and love both appear to exist in this physical world. A forgiving mind allows the Holy Spirit to take our misperceptions and reframe those thoughts so that they will support the truth.

Forgiveness is a counter dream to our dream that there are victims and victimizers but it is still a dream. Forgiveness is a dream that ends the need for additional egoic stories that support our belief in lack, limitation and separation. Yet, the real world still belongs to the world of perception. There appears to be both an observer and something outside the mind to observe.

The real world is not something external but rather reflects your own state of mind. Because of this, the physical world that you perceive may still be seen by another as a fearful place. Each party lives in their own world of provisional reality. You may look upon a forgiven world that your brother still views as a world of hate and fear.

All things are neutral. It is your mind that gives all the meaning you believe belongs to an item. The item itself has no power to make you happy or sad. Only your mind determines how you will interpret the events you call into your world.

The real world is a world of allowance and freedom as opposed to judgment and condemnation. The real world can be here if you let it for the real world is a world seen by a forgiving mind. This is why A Course in Miracles does not want you to ignore your experiences in this lifetime.

Just because the world of perception is not real, the world you see is a symbol for what you currently value and desire within your own mind. It is a reflection of your own thoughts. The real world is the realization that you create your own world and that you cannot be happy in a fearful world. In the real world, you have deliberately chosen to see a happy world through the eyes of love and forgiveness.

You freely chose to enter the game of What Am I to demonstrate what you truly are. You needed to pretend that you were something you were not to reawaken to the truth of what you really are. You came here to experience the learning lesson that this material world provides. The Holy Spirit uses this world to teach the truth of what you are.

You are not a body. You are free. You are still as God created you. Nothing causes your experiences but you and nothing can affect you unless you choose to allow it. That is the lesson that you desire to learn and that is why you are here in this world of seeming hate and fear.

The real world is your realization that nothing can rob you of your own inner peace and that you remain as God created you. The real world acknowledges that your mind is the source for all your experiences and your forgiving mind has chosen to look upon a happy world. Your mind has created a world without judgment, sin, guilt and fear. The real world demonstrates that your mind realizes that only love is real.

In your real world, another may observe your brother acting in a mean and fearful way. Yet, because you are coming from a forgiving mind, you will recognize your brother's actions as a cry for love. He is really asking can you love him even when he may be behaving badly and acting out of fear.

We are all teachers and we are all students. When you react lovingly to your brother's fearful state, you are teaching him that he is lovable because he is God's Son and not because of what he does. He is also trying to teach you that you alone have the power to interpret your experiences and that there is no outside power that can rob you of your own inner peace. Each is given an opportunity to learn, grow and teach.

If our purpose in this physical world is to learn forgiveness, we need our brother to behave in a way that would merit the need for someone's forgiveness. How could we demonstrate the attribute of forgiveness in a world that only reflects love, kindness, harmony and peace? How could such a loving world test our ability to demonstrate the attribute of love called forgiveness? To practice forgiveness, we need someone to think he has harmed us and is in need of our forgiveness.

In time, love is the creative process in which time is utilized to reawaken sleeping minds to their spiritual magnificence. Each party plays the role of student and teacher for each other. Even when your brother is acting in an unloving way, he is helping you realize that your mind alone is the source for your own inner peace. That is the lesson that you have come here to learn. You need your brother to test you if you are to improve and demonstrate your skills of forgiveness.

When you are the master of a forgiving mind, this fear-based world will have no purpose for you will perceive a forgiven world. Sin and guilt will not be part of your perceived world. Instead, you will see a happy and innocent world that does not judge or question your brother's own perfect path. You will honor the creative power of your brother's mind and thus, recognize your own. Perceiving a sinless and guiltless world, perception's purpose is now over and God can take the final step to your return of knowledge. Certainty about your true identity has replaced perception's once uncertain mind. You now know what you really are. The game of <u>What Am I</u> is drawing to a close.

LESSON 291

This is a day of stillness and of peace.

W-291.1.Christ's vision looks through me today. 2 **Christ's** sight shows me all things forgiven and at peace, and offers this same **Christ** vision to the world. 3 And I accept this **Christ** vision in **Christ's** name, both for myself and for the world as well. 4 What loveliness we look upon today! 5 What holiness we see surrounding us! 6 And **the world's holiness** is given us to recognize it is a holiness in which we share; it is the Holiness of God Himself.

W-291.2. <This day my mind is quiet, to receive the Thoughts **of God the Holy Spirit** offers me. 2 And I accept what comes from **God and the Holy Spirit** instead of from **my ego's little "s" self**. 3 **My ego does** not know the way to **God**. 4 But **the Holy Spirit is** wholly certain **of the way to God**. 5 Father, **let the Holy Spirit** guide Your Son along the quiet path that leads to You. 6 Let my forgiveness be complete, and let the memory of **God** return to me.>

Notes to Lesson #291

This is a day of stillness and of peace.

<u>**Comment:**</u> A still mind is a mind that does not judge. When we drop our fear-based thought system and follow the Holy Spirit's guidance, we see the world through the eyes of love and forgiveness. By dropping our ego's beliefs and judgments, we allow the vision of Christ to show us a forgiven world that is holy. To be holy is to be whole. When you are whole, there is no need to judge. A forgiven mind looks past the illusion of form and sees the holiness of God in all.

LESSON 292

A happy outcome to all things is sure.

W-292.1.God's promises make no exceptions. 2 And **God** guarantees that only joy can be the final outcome found for everything. 3 Yet it is up to us when **the joy of the final outcome** is reached. **It is up to us to decide** how long we let an **egoic** alien will appear to be opposing **God's Will**. 4 And while we think this **separate** will is real, we will not find the **joyful** end **God** has appointed as the outcome of all problems **our egos** perceive, all trials we see, and every situation that we meet. 5 Yet is the **joyful** ending certain. 6 For God's Will is done in earth and Heaven. 7 We will seek and we will find according to **God's** Will, which guarantees that our **true** will **that we share with God** is done.

W-292.2. <We thank You, Father, for Your guarantee of only happy outcomes in the end. 2 Help us not **to allow our egos to** interfere and so delay the happy endings **God has** promised us for every problem that we can perceive **and** for every trial **our egos** think we still must meet.>

Notes to Lesson #292

A happy outcome to all things is sure.

<u>**Comment:**</u> God's Will is that we be happy. Love allows and grants us the freedom to be what we are or to imagine something we are not in perfect safety. As long as your ego believes it has a better plan for your happiness, you will believe your will is different from God's Will.

Being created perfect, whole and complete, you cannot be happy following your ego's plan that demands that you be less than what you are. Ultimately, we will realize that our happiness rests in following God's plan. God's plan guarantees that joy is the final outcome for everything. Yet, because we have free will, it is up to us to determine how long it will take before we freely reject our egos' fear-based thought system and accept that God's will is our will.

Free will does not allow us to determine the curriculum. The curriculum is determined by God and thus, guarantees a joyous final outcome of reawakening our sleeping minds. Yet, free will does allow you to determine when you will take the class and when it will be concluded. You get to decide when the Will of God will be done.

All fear is past and only love is here.

W-293.1.All fear is past because fears source, **which is your mind's past** is gone, and all **your mind's past** thoughts gone with it. 2 Love remains the only present state, whose Source is here forever and forever. 3 Can the world seem bright and clear and safe and welcoming, with all my past mistakes oppressing **my current world that I perceive**, and showing me distorted forms of fear? 4 Yet in the present love is obvious, and **love's** effects apparent. 5 All the world shines in reflection of **love's** holy light, and I perceive a world forgiven at last.

W-293.2. <Father, let not Your holy world escape my sight today. 2 Nor let my ears be deaf to all the hymns of gratitude the world is singing underneath the **ego's** sounds of fear. 3 There is a real world which the present holds safe from all past mistakes **my egoic mind imagined**. 4 And I would see only this **forgiven** world before my eyes today.>

Notes to Lesson #293

All fear is past and only love is here.

Comment: Fear arises from your belief in lack, limitation and separation. Fear is embedded in your egoic thought system. Yet, the source of your fear is your past erroneous beliefs about yourself and your world. When you change your beliefs, your world reflects those new beliefs. We believe our past impacts the present and our future. This is not so. The past is over. Time has no ability to change what God created perfect.

If the past is gone and is over, it is only your egoic mind that keeps the past alive and brings it forward to distort the current moment. When you drop your judgments about the past, the past no longer binds you. Your mind now is free to be in the present moment and see the real world with Christ vision. When you drop your ego's fear-based thought system which insists that your current world must pass before the filter of the past egoic judgments and beliefs, you will be in the <now>and be able to see a real world that reflects only love.

LESSON 294

My body is a wholly neutral thing.

W-294.1.I am a Son of God. 2 And can I be another thing, **like the body** as well? 3 Did God create the mortal and corruptible? 4 What use has God's beloved Son for what must die **like the body**? 5 And yet a neutral thing **like the body** does not see death, for thoughts of fear are not invested there **in the body**, nor is a mockery of love bestowed upon **a neutral thing like the body**. 6 **The body's** neutrality protects it while **the body** has a use. 7 And afterwards, without a purpose, **the body** is laid aside. 8 **The body** is not sick nor old nor hurt. 9 **The body** is but functionless, unneeded and cast off. 10 Let me not see **the body** more than this today; of service for a while and fit to serve, to keep **the body's** usefulness while **the body** can serve, and then to be replaced for greater good.

W-294.2. <My body, Father, cannot be Your Son. 2 And what is not created cannot be sinful nor sinless; neither good nor bad. 3 Let me, then, use this dream **of the body** to help Your plan that we awaken from all dreams we made.>

Notes to Lesson #294

My body is a wholly neutral thing.

Comment: God's creations are an extension of Himself. God did not create something that is mortal and corruptible. The body, like all things our delusional mind has imagined, is neutral. Something is neutral when it has no ability to impact or change another. Only mind, not the body is endowed with creative power. Mind alone is causative.

The neutrality of an item, like the body, protects the item while it has a use or purpose. Our body is a neutral communication device. The body serves as a neutral place holder on this playschool of time and space. This game board provides experiences that demonstrate what our mind currently values and desires.

Because of the neutrality of the body, the Holy Spirit can use the body to aid in our reawakening to the truth of what we are. To our ego the body's purpose is to be a concrete form of fear. To the Holy Spirit, the body's purpose is a teaching aid to demonstrate love in form. After the body has served its purpose in the learning process, it is laid aside to be replaced for a greater good as you advance along your own perfect path to reawakening.

The body is a neutral tool that allows the abstract to know itself and be love in form. Our egoic mind erroneously bestows creative power to the body which it does not possess. Now the body appears to be a source for fear. The body is not real and has no ability to make you happy or sad. It is merely a service vehicle that eventually must be replaced when its serviceable life is over. Only your own mind has the creative power of interpretation to make a neutral item appear to steal your peace or make you happy. Your Mind, not the neutral body, sources your experiences.

LESSON 295

The Holy Spirit looks through me today.

W-295.1.Christ asks that He may use my eyes today, and thus redeem the world. 2 **Christ** asks this gift **to use my eyes today** that **Christ** may offer peace of mind to me, and take away all terror and all pain. 3 And as **my terror and pain** are removed from me, the dreams that seemed to settle on the **once fearful** world are gone. 4 Redemption must be one. 5 As I am saved, the world is saved with me. 6 For all of us must be redeemed together. 7 Fear appears in many different forms, but love is one.

W-295.2. <My Father, Christ has asked a gift of me **to use my eyes to redeem the world**, and one I give that **redemption** be given me. 2 Help me to use the eyes of Christ today, and thus allow the Holy Spirit's Love to bless all things which I may look upon, that **the Holy Spirit's** forgiving Love may rest on me.>

Notes to Lesson #295

The Holy Spirit looks through me today.

Comment: To seek happiness in your ego's world of provisional reality is to seek your happiness in an illusion. Illusions cannot make you happy or substitute for the peace of God. The ego believes that there is something outside of you that is needed to make you happy. This is the opposite of the truth and creates a world full of grievances.

When you drop your grievances and forgive your world, you receive peace. Fear makes it appear that you are separate. Forgiveness and love prove we are one. When you utilize Christ vision you do not mistake the body for the Son of God. Therefore, Christ vision takes away all terror and pain that results from your false identification with the body as your home.

To the ego, the body is a concrete form of fear that proves the separation to be real. The belief in separation is a root of fear which appears in a multiplicity of forms. Love is based on the unity and oneness of the One Self. The recognition of this truth is our one purpose and our one reality. Give your day over to the Holy Spirit and watch the vision of Christ bring forgiveness to your world and peace to you.

The Holy Spirit speaks through me today.

W-296.1. <The Holy Spirit needs my voice today, that all the world may listen to Your Voice, and hear Your Word through me. 2 I am resolved to let You speak through me, for I would use no words but Yours, and have no thoughts which are apart from Yours, for only Yours are true. 3 I would be savior to the world I made. 4 For having damned it I would set it free, that I may find escape, and hear the Word Your holy Voice will speak to me today.>

W-296.2.We teach today what we would learn, and that alone. 2 And so our learning goal becomes an unconflicted one, and possible of easy reach and quick accomplishment. 3 How gladly does the Holy Spirit come to rescue us from hell, when we allow His teaching to persuade the world, through us, to seek and find the easy path to God.

Notes to Lesson #296

The Holy Spirit speaks through me today.

Comment: Follow the Holy Spirit's thought system and think and speak only loving and forgiving thoughts today. When you hold grievances, you only crucify yourself. Your grievances create false witnesses for your belief that there are outside forces that can rob you of your inner peace. Only by forgiving your world from these disempowering thoughts can you recognize both you and your world's guiltless and sinless reality.

What you give, you receive. We teach what we would learn. Learning comes quickly when you have a single purpose. Seek and be vigilant only for the real world that offers the counterpart to your ego's fearful world that is based on lack, limitation and separation.

The Holy Spirit, your Christ consciousness and your big "S" Self are all one with you. Be the love in form you came here to demonstrate by allowing God's love to be expressed through you. Since you only give to yourself, your gift of God's love to your world is only given to yourself. Allow the Holy Spirit and God to live through you today.

LESSON 297

Forgiveness is the only gift I give.

W-297.1.Forgiveness is the only gift I give because **forgiveness** is the only gift I want. 2 And everything I give I give myself. 3 This is salvation's simple formula **that everything I give, I give to myself**. 4 And I, who would be saved, would make **salvation** mine, to be the way I live within a **fear-based** world that needs salvation, and that will be saved as I accept Atonement for myself.

W-297.2. <Father, how certain are Your ways; how sure their final outcome, and how faithfully is every step in my salvation set already, and accomplished by **God's** grace. 2 Thanks be to **God** for Your eternal gifts, and thanks to You for my Identity **as the Christ, my big "S" Self**.>

Notes to Lesson #297

Forgiveness is the only gift I give.

Comment: Since to give is to receive, salvation's formula is simple. Recognize that everything you give, you give to yourself. Because of this, forgiveness is the only thing you want to give. When you drop your grievances and forgive your world, you receive that same forgiveness.

You can forgive your brother and yourself for the desire to experience being different than as God created you. The ego promises us specialness. We fail to understand that with the desire to be special, we would have to experience the attributes of lack, limitation and separation. How could it be different when God had already created us perfect, whole and complete? When we forgot our mind was the creator of this fantasy world, we took the game of What Am I seriously. We forgot to laugh and made the game of separation real within our own split mind.

Through forgiveness, we recognize that we alone are the creator for our experiences. Since it is our dream, our mind has the power to change it by simply accepting the truth of what we are. Forgive your world and accept the At-One-Ment for yourself. Forgiveness empowers and restores the truth. This is how you will save your world.

LESSON 298

I love You, Father, and I love Your Son.

W-298.1.My gratitude permits my love to be accepted without fear. 2 And thus, **in gratitude and love** am I restored to my reality at last **as the Christ**. 3 All that intruded on my holy sight forgiveness takes away. 4 And I draw near the end of **my ego's** senseless journeys, mad careers and artificial values. 5 I accept instead what God establishes as **my divine birthright**, sure that in that alone I will be saved; sure that I go through fear to meet my Love.

W-298.2. <Father, I come to You today, because I would not follow any way but **Your plan for salvation**. 2 You are beside me. 3 Certain is Your way **and plan**. 4 And I am grateful for Your holy gifts of certain sanctuary, and escape from everything that would obscure my love for God my Father and His holy Son.>

Notes to Lesson #298

I love You, Father, and I love Your Son.

Comment: Gratitude is unconditional positive regard. Gratitude is an attribute of love. In gratitude, you appreciate and honor another. Your gratitude permits your love to be accepted without fear.

Love is the only true reality. When we drop the illusion of fear, the fearful world that we once perceived is replaced by a forgiven world. Forgiveness removes the grievances that we had placed before love's presence. When you are not in gratitude, what you perceive to be love will be manipulative, insincere and fear-based. Without gratitude, love cannot be unconditional.

Forgiveness holds the key to gratitude and love. Whereas true gratitude is unconditional positive regard for another, egoic gratitude is positive regard for what you believe another gives to make you happy. Egoic gratitude disempowers and supports our fear-based world of lack, limitation and separation. Our ego expects us to be grateful because we suffer less than another.

To love God, you must move through your ego's fear-based thought system. Forgiveness allows you to break free from your fears and accept the love of God. Salvation's formula is that everything you give, you give to yourself. Because of this, when you love your brother and God, you love yourself for they are all one.

Do not love your brother's egoic illusion of lack, limitation and separation. The false does not warrant our love. Instead, love your brother for his sinless and guiltless reality. Love your brother for the creative power of his mind. When you love your brother's true reality as the Christ, you recognize the truth and your oneness with God and all of creation.

LESSON 299

Eternal holiness abides in me.

W-299.1.My holiness is far beyond my own ability to understand or know. 2 Yet God, my Father, Who created **my holiness**, acknowledges my holiness as **God's holiness**. 3 Our Will, together, understands **our holiness**. 4 And Our Will, together, knows that **Our eternal holiness** is so.

W-299.2. <Father, my holiness is not of me. 2 **My holiness** is not mine to be destroyed by sin. 3 **My holiness** is not mine to suffer from attack. 4 Illusions can obscure **my holiness**, but cannot put out **my holiness'** radiance, nor dim its light. 5 **My holiness** stands forever perfect and untouched. 6 In **my holiness** are all things healed, for **all things** remain as **God** created them. 7 And I can know my holiness. 8 For Holiness Itself created me, and I can know my Source because it is **God's** Will that You be known.>

Notes to Lesson #299

Eternal holiness abides in me.

Comment: To be holy is to be whole. We are holy because we are one with God. Your will and God's Will are joined as one, and therefore, your holiness is God's holiness.

Your illusion about yourself can obscure your holiness from your awareness, but illusions cannot change your holiness because it comes from God. God desires that He be known. When you demonstrate forgiveness and love, you allow God's love to flow through you in this world of seeming hate and fear.

LESSON 300

Only an instant does this world endure.

Only an instant does this world endure.W-300.1.**Only an instant does this world endure** is a thought which can be used to say that death and sorrow are the certain lot of all who come here, for their joys are gone before they are possessed, or even grasped. 2 Yet this **thought that only an instant does this world endure** is also the idea that lets no false perception keep us in its hold, nor represent more than a passing cloud upon a sky eternally serene. 3 And it is this serenity **of not being trapped in a false world of perception that** we seek, unclouded, obvious and sure, today.

W-300.2. <We seek Your holy world today. 2 For we, Your loving Sons, have lost our way a while. 3 But we have listened to **the Holy Spirit's** Voice, and learned exactly what to do to be restored to Heaven and our true Identity **as our big "S" Self**. 4 And we give thanks today the **egoic** world **of perception** endures but for an instant. 5 We would go beyond that tiny instant to eternity.>

Notes to Lesson #300

Only an instant does this world endure.

Comment: This journey into the world of perception is brief and our return to knowledge is certain and quick. Illusions cannot last since illusions are not real. Our sleeping mind will awaken and sleep no more.

The illusion of separation is only a brief experience that helps us rediscover the truth about ourselves. It is a playschool that we can enjoy, learn and demonstrate love in form. Only our failure to recognize that we are the dreamer makes our journey of self-discovery appear frightening.

We desired to know what it would be like to be something other than as God created us. Since it is impossible not to be yourself, this experiment can only take place in your own mind's imagination. We appear to sleep yet our true reality still is changeless. When we claim we do not know what we are, we allow uncertainty to cloud our mind.

Knowledge is certain. All learning takes place in the world of perception. Perception provides a play field for change and uncertainty. We learn through our numerous experiences in a world that allows opposites to coexist. Time has been defined as the measure of change. In time, we are able to make different choices, create different experiences, gather feedback, change our mind about our identity and end uncertainty thus, paving the way for our return to knowledge.

The real world is the mind's counterpart to our ego's world that supports the belief in lack, limitation and separation. In time, the illusions of opposites appear to exist. You have the ability to choose between the true and the false. We can choose to experience our world through either fear or love.

When we decide to forgive, we make a choice to see things differently through the eyes of Christ vision. Ultimately, we will choose to end this game of What Am I when we decide to see a world free of sin and guilt. Until we choose to see a forgiven world, there will still be a need for time. Time will continue while the Holy Spirit waits patiently until you decide to change your mind.

When fear no longer holds a place in your heart, the need to change your ego's misperception to correct perception will be over. Time, now without a purpose, will end. The return to knowledge and certainty will be at hand. You will reawaken to the remembrance of God and recognize that your true Identity has never been lost. It had only been forgotten for a brief instant in the illusion of time.

Special Theme #9: What Is the Second Coming?

What Is the Second Coming?

Covers ACIM Workbook Lessons 301-310

9. What Is the Second Coming?

W-pII.9.1.Christ's Second Coming, which is sure as God, is merely the correction of mistakes, and the return of sanity. 2 **Christ's Second Coming** is a part of the condition that restores the never lost, and re-establishes what is forever and forever true. 3 **Christ's Second Coming** is the invitation to God's Word to take illusion's place; the willingness to let forgiveness rest upon all things without exception and without reserve.

W-pII.9.2.It is the all-inclusive nature of Christ's Second Coming that permits **the Second Coming** to embrace the world and hold you safe within its gentle advent, which encompasses all living things with you. 2 There is no end to the release the Second Coming brings, as God's creation must be limitless. 3 Forgiveness lights the Second Coming's way, because **forgiveness** shines on everything as one. 4 And thus **with the correction of all mistakes** is oneness recognized at last.

W-pII.9.3.The Second Coming ends the lessons that the Holy Spirit teaches, making way for the Last Judgment, in which learning ends in one last summary that will extend beyond **learning** itself, and reaches up to God. 2 The Second Coming is the time in which all minds are given to the hands of Christ, to be returned to spirit in the name of true creation and the Will of God.

W-pII.9.4.The Second Coming is the one event in time which time itself can not affect. 2 For every one who ever came to die, or yet will come or who is present now, is equally released from what he made **in error**. 3 In this equality **of correcting all our mistakes** is Christ restored as one Identity, in which the Sons of God acknowledge that they all are one. 4 And God the Father smiles upon His Son, **God's** one creation and **God's** only joy.

W-pII.9.5.Pray that the Second Coming will be soon, but do not rest with that **prayer.** 2 **The Second Coming** needs your eyes and ears and hands and feet. 3 **The Second Coming** needs your voice. 4 And most of all **the Second Coming** needs your willingness. 5 Let us rejoice that we can do God's Will, and join together in **God's** holy light. 6 Behold, the Son of God is one in us, and we can reach our Father's Love through **God's one indivisible Son.**

Notes to Special Theme # 9: What Is the Second Coming?

Covers ACIM Workbook Lessons 301-310

The Second Coming is the correction of mistakes to pave the way for the return to sanity and thus, the reestablishment of Truth. The Second Coming allows God's Word to take the place of egoic illusions. It marks the willingness to let forgiveness rest upon everyone without exception and without reservation.

The Second Coming is all inclusive and embraces all. It ends the lessons taught by the Holy Spirit and makes way for the Last Judgment. In the Second Coming, all minds are given to Christ and God's Will. It is the one event in which time itself cannot affect because the Second Coming releases all from all past, present or future mistakes. In this equal and complete correction, all mistakes are corrected so that all are restored to their one Identity as the Christ. All are acknowledged as an indivisible part of the shared Mind of God and of one unified Will of God.

The Second Coming reestablishes the truth that was never lost. It marks the forgiveness of all things and the return to the oneness of all minds as unlimited Spirit. The Second Coming is the end of learning that makes way for the Last Judgment that declares God's Son sinless, guiltless, innocent and of one Mind. Our true Identity as the big "S" Self is restored to all as God's one Son.

The Holy Spirit's mission is to return our sleeping minds to sanity. The Holy Spirit's core lesson is the teaching of this truth.

You are not the body. You are free. You are still as God created you. Nothing sources your experience but you and nothing has any effect upon you unless you choose to allow it to.

When this lesson is learned, the Second Coming is at hand. We have previously covered various aspects of this one learning lesson. Yet, due to our ego's belief that sin is real, we have a hard time accepting that we remain as God created us. How can we be created by God and yet be a sinner? How can we be free if sin is real?

The Second Coming is the correction of all mistakes and the return to sanity. It is important to note that it is the correction of mistakes and not the forgiveness of sins. Why the difference?

Sin is an offense in which one party has been harmed. If someone is actually harmed by another, justice requires the punishment of the offending party. If sin were real, forgiveness would not be possible. Instead, some type of penance or retribution would first be required before the offending party could be freed. But even after the offending party has been punished, he would still be known as a sinner. The taint of sin would be his eternal legacy.

Yet, if you are not your body but rather unlimited spirit, you are free and nothing can harm you unless you choose to allow it. Although you can choose to imagine that you are a body that can be hurt, due to the illusionary nature of time, the harming of another remains impossible. Our imagination has no ability to change how God created us.

Because we are free to be or imagine anything that we want, our mind chooses what we will call into our awareness. The experiences we choose cannot be sins because they have no ability to harm anyone including ourselves. Any effects we perceive are caused by our actions and only take place in our own mind's imagination.

Our ego desires to be special. Unfortunately, this desire to be special brings with it the unwanted attributes of lack, limitation and separation. To our ego, it does appear that we are the body and can be harmed or hurt another. This notion of sin is inherent in our belief that we are a body. Sin rests at the core of our ego's fear-based thought system. Our ego believes that God, like ourselves, can be harmed, and because of our sins, we have lost Paradise. Perceiving ourselves to be sinners, our ego lives in fear of God and attempts to either hide from God's punishment or earn God's love back.

Your ego is the part of your mind that is uncertain about your true identity. Perceiving itself to be at home in the body, your ego is that part of the mind that believes you have sinned and are being punished by God. The split mind fears God's retribution and hopes to earn God's love back. Your ego has transformed a God of only unconditional love into a God of judgment, revenge, reward and punishment. The false god of the ego is a god of conditional love and therefore, a god to be feared.

Because our ego fails to understand time's true purpose, it fails to recognize that time is the tool for learning. The Holy Spirit uses time to gently reawaken sleeping minds to their true magnificence as the Christ. Our egos perceive time as a place where we have been banished or hide from God's punishment and seek redemption from our sins. The ego's fear-based thought system rests on the belief that sin is real. The ego never questions sin's reality. Because of this, the ego believes time provides a medium in which a sinner can potentially earn God's love back and gain redemption.

To our ego, time is result oriented because it allows a sinner to earn their redemption or gain some temporary happiness if they follow their ego's plan. Time is the place where actions have consequences. Our actions result in some reward or punishment in the future. The ego believes that there is a gap between cause and effect but eventually the effects of our current actions and decisions will impact our future. These beliefs keep your ego in a constant state of fear. Your ego is constantly comparing where it perceives you are against where the ego believes you should be according to your ego's plan for your salvation.

The Holy Spirit knows that sin is impossible and that time provides the medium in which God's creations can pretend they are something they are not in order to better understand and be what they truly are. Time provides the game board in which we can demonstrate specific aspects of love that could not be experienced in the abstract. It is a place in which God's Son can demonstrate what it would be like to be love in form.

Time is the measure of change. The Holy Spirit uses time to teach the sleeping mind what it truly is. Time becomes a playschool of our mind's imagination. The purpose of a playschool is to provide a safe environment in which a child can have fun and learn about themselves and their world.

The Holy Spirit understands that we have come here for the experiences and learning lessons that the world of form provides. The Holy Spirit knows that when someone is learning, mistakes will happen. Those mistakes are not sins that require punishment, but rather are errors that need to be corrected. Our mistakes provide the necessary feedback that our minds need to make mid-course corrections and thus, stay on course to ultimately arrive at the proper destination.

What the ego sees as our sins that require punishment, the Holy Spirit knows to be learning lessons that help us regain our true Identity. Each error, or mistake, moves us one step closer to correctly changing our minds about what we are.

The Second Coming is the return to sanity. Our sleeping minds are insane because we fail to recognize what we truly are. Our mind is delusional and believes that our ego's little "s" self is our true reality. The insane mind fails to realize that the game token which we call our body is not our true reality. The insane mind forgets that your mind is the dreamer who believes you are a sinner. Believing sin to be real, your split mind is driven mad with guilt and fear. Yet, even on earth, we now realize that insanity requires treatment, not punishment. The insane mind cannot sin because it does not know what it is. The Holy Spirit knows that we are not in our right mind and therefore, are not sinners.

Our big "S" Self and the Holy Spirit both recognize the game of time for what it is. This game of What Am I is merely a fun and exciting learning opportunity for God's Son to reawaken to his full spiritual magnificence as the Christ. The Holy Spirit knows that we are exactly where we need to be in the game and that we have freely chosen to play the game of What Am I for the fun experiences that the learning process provides.

Heaven and hell do not hang in the balance. Everyone who plays the game is guaranteed to reawaken to the truth because Paradise was never lost. Both the Holy Spirit and big "S" Self do not judge or find fault with the game itself or with the participants. They merely enjoy the adventures the game provides knowing that all participants must win for reawakening is guaranteed by God.

Your ego believes Paradise was lost. Only your ego's judgments and dissatisfaction with where it perceives you are along your own perfect path makes you believe that you are guilty of some sin and have offended God. God realizes that His Child is an innocent who is merely playing a childish game of make-believe. Yet, your ego has mistaken the game to be real and now mistakenly believes that you are in jeopardy of eternal damnation.

Your ego believes your mistakes are sins that demand punishment instead of simple errors that require simple corrections. Whereas the Holy Spirit sees a continuous learning process ultimately culminating in your successful reawakening, your ego sees a life-and-death struggle for the reclamation of your very soul.

This second sinful will that your ego imagines appears real only within your ego's dream world that refuses to understand the learning process. Perceiving lack, limitation and separation to be punishment for your sins rather than an indispensable part of the learning process, your ego perceives a second sinful will that opposes God's Will. Evil now appears to exist.

Evil is not real but is an attribute associated with your ego's belief in sin and a second will in opposition to God's Will. It is your ego's judgment regarding where your ego believes you should be along the journey that actually keeps you in fear. When you silence the voice for your ego's fears, you will reawaken to discover that your true big "S" Self remains changeless as God created you.

The Holy Spirit knows that the insane are not sinners. Yet, the Holy Spirit also knows that we are eternally innocent for we remain as God created us. God did not create evil, so evil cannot be real. Because evil is not real, God is innocent and knows no evil for God knows that all He created is very good. We, being created like God, share His innocence.

The innocent child lacks the knowledge to correctly decipher right from wrong. The innocent child seeks new experiences and is curious about its world. This curiosity and inquisitive nature allows the child to learn about himself and his world. The child is acting without malice or evil. The child considers experiences to be learning lessons that provide additional feedback so that he can learn and be better prepared to make correct decisions in the future.

Until we know what we truly are, our interactions with this world are like that of the innocent child. Our curiosity creates desires that lead to experiences. These experiences provide the necessary feedback that becomes the learning lessons that hone our skills so that we can reawaken to the truth of what we truly are.

Our mistakes cannot be sins that require punishment because we are innocent. With the guidance of the Holy Spirit, we are healing our delusional split mind. Our errors are merely mistakes that we need to correct. Mistakes provide valuable feedback that encourages us to learn and make different decisions. Because of these mistakes, we learn to change our mind.

The Second Coming needs our willingness to let God live us. When God is living us, we are following God's plan and Will. The Second Coming requires more than just our prayers. God needs our eyes, ears, hands and feet. In this world of form, it is by our actions that we recognize and teach that we are not the body but rather unlimited spirit that is joined as the One Self.

By our actions, we recognize the innocence we share with our brother and heal the insane mind that claims it does not know what it is. Neither the innocent nor the insane can sin for they do not know what they do. The act of our forgiveness leads us to the recognition of the oneness and innocence of all living things.

Being innocent, you are sinless and guiltless. When you drop your ego's belief in sin, guilt and fear, you realize that you have nothing to fear. When you look within, you will rediscover your true Identity as the Christ. What you mistook to be your egoic will was merely a dream, an illusion that has no effect on the truth or the real world.

Illusions are fantasies that change nothing. Within you is the holiness which you share with God, your Creator. When you silence your ego and look within, you will find the Christ, which is the home to God, Himself. Sin is the illusion. Sin cannot bind you or make the false real for you remain eternally innocent as God created you. When you no longer perceive sin and guilt to be real, the Second Coming is at hand.

LESSON 301

And God Himself shall wipe away all tears.

W-301.1. <Father, unless I judge I cannot weep. 2 Nor can I suffer pain, or feel I am abandoned or unneeded in the world **unless I choose to judge**. 3 **God's world** is my home because I judge **God's world** not, and therefore is **God's world** only what God wills. 4 Let me today behold **God's world** uncondemned, through happy eyes forgiveness has released from all distortion. 5 Let me see, **God's** world instead of **my egoic world of sin, guilt and fear**. 6 And all the tears I shed will be forgotten, for their source **which are my ego's erroneous beliefs and** judgments are gone. 7 Father, I will not judge Your world today.>

W-301.2.God's world is happy. 2 Those who look on **God's world** can only add their joy to it, and bless **God's world** as a cause of further joy in them. 3 We wept because we did not understand. 4 But we have learned the **ego's** world **of sin, guilt and fear that** we saw was false, and we will look upon God's world today.

Notes to Lesson #301

And God Himself shall wipe away all tears.

Comment: It is only your ego's judgment that causes you pain. To judge is your own choice. Choose today not to judge your world and release your world from the grievances your judgments have brought upon it. Judging causes pain and supports the belief in separation. Judging disempowers you.

You only judge because you feel you are not perfect, whole and complete. You believe that there is something outside your own mind that will make you happy or sad. It is only your judgments that block you from seeing a forgiven world. All things are neutral. Do not judge and you will see a world of mercy and love.

Your ego clings to its erroneous judgments at the cost of your happiness. The Holy Spirit's thought system guards your happiness and restores your inner peace. The real world is a happy world because it is a world that is free from your ego's judgments. Give your judgments over to the Holy Spirit and let the vision of Christ be restored.

LESSON 302

Where darkness was I look upon the light.

W-302.1. <Father, our eyes are opening at last. 2 Your holy world awaits us, as our sight is finally restored and we can see **with Christ vision**. 3 We thought we suffered. 4 But we had forgot the Son, **the Christ,** whom You created **as our big "S" Self**. 5 Now we see that darkness is our own **ego's** imagining, and light is there for us to look upon. 6 Christ's vision changes darkness into light, for fear must disappear when love has come. 7 Let me forgive Your holy world today, that I may look upon **Your world's** holiness and **understand the holiness of God's world** but reflects my own **holiness**.>

W-302.2.Our Love awaits us as we go to **God**, and **the Holy Spirit** walks beside us showing us the way. 2 **The Holy Spirit** fails in nothing. 3 **God is** the End we seek, and **the Holy Spirit** the Means by which we go to **God**.

Notes to Lesson #302

Where darkness was I look upon the light.

Comment: Only our belief in specialness and separation has kept us imprisoned in the fearful dream that has become our provisional reality. Heaven is only a choice away. We need to forgive our world of misperception that we created so that we can behold the real world.

It is our lack of forgiveness that prevents us from being in the moment or the <now>. We have too many of our mind's energy circuits locked into our past beliefs and judgments. These past judgments that we carry into the present block our ability to recognize the current moment as separate, distinct and unaffected by the past.

The past is over. Be in the present moment. Your past beliefs and judgments block and hide the constant flow of love that is always present. What you give you receive. Your forgiveness of your brother, your world and yourself is the means to reach the happiness and peace that is your divine birthright.

We all desire to rediscover our true Identity. In that recognition, our true safety lies. Our salvation is certain for the truth is always true. Where separation and fear once were, through forgiveness, we can see the oneness and love that is in the real world. By rejecting your ego's fear-based thought system, you can choose to see with the vision of Christ. Decide to follow only the Holy Spirit's thought system of love and forgiveness. Only your lack of forgiveness blocks the light that symbolizes the real world.

LESSON 303

The holy Christ is born in me today.

W-303.1.Watch with me, angels, watch with me today. 2 Let all God's holy Thoughts surround me, and be still with me while Heaven's Son is born. 3 Let earthly sounds be quiet, and the **egoic** sights to which I am accustomed disappear. 4 Let Christ be welcomed where **the Christ** is at home. 5 And let **the Christ** hear the sounds **Christ** understands, and see but sights that show His Father's Love **for the Christ**. 6 Let **the Christ** no longer be a stranger here, for **Christ** is born again in me today.

W-303.2. <Your Son, **the Christ,** is welcome, Father. 2 **The Christ** has come to save me from the evil **little "s"** self I made. 3 **The Christ** is the **big "S" Self** that You have given me. 4 **The Christ, my big "S" Self,** is but what I really am in truth. 5 **The Christ** is the Son You love above all things. 6 **The Christ** is my **big "S"** Self as You created me. 7 It is not Christ that can be crucified. 8 Safe in Your Arms let me receive Your Son **who is my true reality**.>

Notes to Lesson #303

The holy Christ is born in me today.

Comment: Stop following the ego's fear-based thought system and accept the Atonement or truth for yourself. Follow the Holy Spirit who knows your true Identity as the Christ. Your split mind cannot lose the Christ consciousness that resides in you.

When you follow the thought system of the Holy Spirit, you become single-minded and aware that love is your home and your big "S" Self is your true reality. The Atonement is the acceptance that you remain as God created you. The At-One-Ment is the rejection of your ego's little "s" self for your true reality as the Christ, your big "S" Self.

LESSON 304

Let not my world obscure the sight of Christ.

W-304.1.I can obscure my holy sight if I intrude my **ego's** world upon **the vision of Christ.** 2 Nor can I behold the holy sights Christ looks upon, unless it is **Christ** vision that I use. 3 Perception is a mirror, not a fact. 4 And what I look on is my state of mind, reflected outward. 5 I would bless the world by looking on **the world** through the eyes of Christ. 6 And **with Christ vision** I will look upon the certain signs that all my sins have been forgiven me.

W-304.2. <You lead me from the darkness to the light; from sin to holiness. 2 Let me forgive, and thus receive salvation for the world. 3 **Forgiveness** is Your gift, my Father, given me to offer to Your holy Son, that he may find again the memory of You, and of Your Son as You created him, **the Christ who is the big "S" Self** .>

Notes to Lesson #304

Let not my world obscure the sight of Christ.

Comment: Your perception mirrors the thought system that you choose to follow. Follow the thought system of the Holy Spirit and you will see with Christ vision. You will look upon a forgiven world of mercy and love. Follow the ego's thought system and your world will bear witness to the sin, guilt and fear that you hold within your mind.

Whatever your mind believes, you will perceive in your outer world. What you look upon is your own state of mind projected outwardly. Thus, perception is a mirror and not a fact. Forgive all and salvation is yours for to give is to receive.

You can choose to give the gift of forgiveness and love to all you behold. These two thought systems are mutually exclusive. Your world cannot reflect both fear and love at the same moment. Which will you choose? It is your choice since your world is merely a reflection of what you truly value and desire.

There is a peace that Christ bestows on us.

W-305.1.Who uses but Christ's vision finds a peace so deep and quiet, undisturbable and wholly changeless, that the world contains no counterpart. 2 Comparisons are still before this peace. 3 And all the world **of my fears** departs in silence as this peace envelops **my ego's world**, and gently carries **the world** to truth, no more to be the home of fear. 4 For love has come, and healed the world by giving **the world** Christ's peace.

W-305.2. <Father, the peace of Christ is given us, because it is Your Will that we be saved. 2 Help us today but to accept Your gift **of the peace of Christ** and judge it not. 3 For **through Christ vision, the peace of Christ** has come to us to save us from our judgment on ourselves.>

Notes to Lesson #305

There is a peace that Christ bestows on us.

<u>Comment</u>: When you utilize Christ vision, you have the big picture and a single purpose. Forgiveness is natural and the ability to maintain the peace of God is within your power. You know that the peace of God is what you truly want.

The peace of Christ is holy, changeless and there is no counterpart to that peace in your egoic world of provisional reality. When you experience the peace of Christ, provisional reality disappears and only the real world remains. The peace of Christ removes all fear for love has healed the world. To receive the peace of Christ, you only need to accept God's gift, which is the Atonement and stop judging your world.

LESSON 306

The gift of Christ is all I seek today.

W-306.1.What but Christ's vision would I use today, when **Christ vision** can offer me a day in which I see a world so like to Heaven that an ancient memory returns to me? 2 Today I can forget the **ego's** world I made **to support my beliefs in sin, guilt and fear.** 3 Today I can go past all fear, and be restored to love and holiness and peace. 4 Today I am redeemed, and born anew into a world of mercy and of care; of loving kindness and the peace of God.

W-306.2. <And so, our Father, we return to You, remembering we never went away; remembering Your holy gifts to us. 2 In gratitude and thankfulness we come, with empty hands and open hearts and minds, asking but what **God** gives. 3 We cannot make an offering sufficient for Your Son. 4 But in Your Love the gift of Christ is **given to all God's Creation.**>

Notes to Lesson #306

The gift of Christ is all I seek today.

<u>Comment</u>: What we truly want is the vision of Christ since it prevents us from mistaking our ego's story for the reality of God's Son. Christ vision prevents us from mistaking the body for the Son of God.

Christ vision also transforms our fears into love, peace and holiness. With it, our fear-based provisional reality is reframed and reshaped into a happy dream. The ego's world that was born in fear is exchanged for the truth and the vision of the real world. Christ vision is God's gift to His Son. With it, you know and accept the truth that we are one with God Himself.

LESSON 307

Conflicting wishes cannot be my will.

W-307.1. <Father, Your Will is **my will**, and only that. 2 There is no other will for me to have. 3 Let me not try to make another will **for my split mind's ego,** for it is senseless and will cause me pain. 4 Your Will alone can bring me happiness, and only **Your Will** exists. 5 If I would have **the happiness and peace** what only You can give, I must accept Your Will for me, and enter into peace where conflict is impossible, Your Son is one with You in being and in will, and nothing contradicts the holy truth that I remain as You created me.>

W-307.2.And with this prayer we enter silently into a state where conflict cannot come, because we join our holy will with God's **Will,** in recognition that **both Wills** are the same.

Notes to Lesson #307

Conflicting wishes cannot be my will.

Comment: We experience conflict and stress due to our split mind's conflicting goals. Our ego's goals are constantly shifting and conflict with our true happiness. We have mistaken the ego's goal of specialness with our happiness. The ego's goals keep us in fear for specialness must bring with it the attributes of lack, limitation and separation.

You are in conflict because truth and illusions cannot be reconciled. Your big "S" Self yearns for your return of the truth. Yet, the ego is constantly attempting to make the false true and the true false. The ego claims that there are opposites and that gray exists.

To the ego, truth changes like the weather. Yet, God, the Holy Spirit and your big "S" Self all know that truth is true and nothing else is true. Only truth is real. Illusions cannot make you happy. The Son of God cannot be content with accepting lack, limitation and separation when he remains as God created him.

Drop your ego's thought system and follow the thought system of the Holy Spirit. When you do, you will freely accept the fact that God's Will is your will. God's Will is that His Son be happy. Accept the truth that you are an extension of Your Creator. God is living in you for there is only One Self.

When you are vigilant only for God, you are single-minded and the stress and conflict caused by the conflicting goals with your ego's thought system will be a thing of the past.

LESSON 308

This instant is the only time there is.

W-308.1.I have conceived of time in such a way that I defeat my aim. 2 If I elect to reach past time to timelessness, I must change my perception of what time is for. 3 Time's purpose cannot be to keep the past and future one. 4 The only interval in which I can be saved from time is now. 5 For in this **present** instant has forgiveness come to set me free. 6 The birth of Christ is now, without a past or future. 7 **Christ** has come to give His present blessing to the world, restoring **the world** to timelessness and love. 8 And love is ever-present, here and now.

W-308.2. <Thanks for this instant, Father. 2 It is now **in the present, not in the past or future that** I am redeemed. 3 This instant is the time You have appointed for Your Son's release, and for salvation of the world in **Your Son.**>

Notes to Lesson #308

This instant is the only time there is.

Comment: To the ego's thought system, the purpose of time is to keep the future and the present the same as the past. Your ego's goal for time is to keep you in victim consciousness. As long as you believe there are outside forces that control your fate, you will not believe your mind is the creative power behind your world.

The ego uses your past as its filters to judge your current experiences as either good or bad. These judgments keep you in fear and support your ego's belief in lack, limitation and separation. Because you are continually carrying those past egoic judgments forward, you are forcing your current and future experiences to become replays of your past.

Coming from fear, your ego relies on its past to judge current and future events in an effort to keep you safe. Because the ego believes fear is necessary to keep you safe, it does not want you to abandon your past beliefs. Maintaining your past grievances support your ego's plan that you would be happy if only someone else behaved differently.

Without a past, your ego would have no criteria to judge the present. Your mind would be forced to be in the present and consider new ways of viewing your world. With the past gone, your mind would finally be free to choose differently. To be in the <now>, you must be willing to forgive your past. The past is over and it is only your ego's need to judge that keeps the past alive within your split mind.

Time is the measure of change. Yet, the true purpose of time is to return God's Son to the truth. Truth being changeless, would mark the end of time. The Holy Spirit uses time to take your ego's illusions and reframe them to support your return to the truth.

The Christ, which is your big "S" Self, is in the <now> and looks upon a world without a past or future. The Christ does not judge and therefore, can see the presence of love in this moment. Your ego's need to judge blocks your ability to recognize love's presence in this moment.

In the holy instant there is the suspension of all judgment. The past and future are irrelevant for only the present moment exists. Without a past, you can choose differently. You can choose to see a forgiven world. You and your world's salvation can only be found in the <now>.

In the real world, there is only the eternal < now>. The past is over and the future is a mere fantasy. This moment is the only time there is and the only time that matters. In each instant, you have always been free to choose differently yet, your ego's belief in the past kept you trapped in fear.

You have always been the creator of your own experiences. You just prefer to deny that fact in order to make your brother responsible for your happiness. When you choose to drop your grievances and forgive, you are in the present moment and are freed from your past. You can choose differently and save your world.

It is interesting to note that this lesson states that the world that you will save is the world which is in you. This once again acknowledges the creative power of your mind and that your world is a projection of your own mind's thoughts. The real world is one decision away.

LESSON 309

I will not fear to look within today.

W-309.1. Within me is eternal innocence, because **eternal innocence** is God's Will that **innocence** be there forever and forever. 2 I, **God's** Son, whose will is limitless as is **God's** Own, can will no change in this **eternal innocence**. 3 For to deny my Father's Will is to deny my own **will**. 4 To look within is but to find my will as God created **my will**, and as **my will** is. 5 I fear to look within because I think I made another will that is not true, and made **this false will** real. 6 Yet **this false will** has no effects. 7 Within me is the Holiness of God. 8 Within me is the memory of **God**.

W-309.2. <The step **of looking within without fear that** I take today, my Father, is my sure release from idle dreams of sin. 2 Your altar stands serene and undefiled. 3 **Your altar** is the holy altar to my **big "S"** Self, and there I find my true Identity **as the Christ.**>

Notes to Lesson #309

I will not fear to look within today.

Comment: We are eternally innocent because this is God's Will. Our will is one and the same as God's Will. We believe that we have created a will in opposition to God's Will. We believe that we have actually harmed God, and defied God's Will.

Within the split minded who perceive lack, limitation and separation to be real, it does appear that we have a second will that can oppose God's Will. But this is not the case. Our ego's will is not real and has no ability to change the will we share with God. What we perceive to be our ego's will is actually our ego's judgments.

The ego is a judging machine. Your ego is judging where you are on God's plan for your reawakening versus where the ego believes you should be on its plan. The ego has forgotten that a journey is comprised of many steps. Instead, it is focusing on whether or not we have arrived at our ego's predetermined destination. Because the ego falsely believes Paradise has been lost, it is concerned with our redemption. Our ego is once again attempting to solve a problem that does not exist.

Our egos have made the game of What Am I into a life-and-death struggle with heaven and hell in the balance. The ego believes that we have sinned and now must earn our salvation. The ego has mistaken the game of reawakening to be our true reality and thus, made the playing of the game into a fearful process.

God created us as innocent. A child who is innocent cannot commit sins or feel guilty. The innocent child is merely curious, not malicious. The child is merely seeking new experiences so that he can learn about himself and his world.

When a child is first learning to walk, the child will stumble and fall. We do not perceive the child to be sinful or bad because he failed to walk at his first attempt. We realize that a baby must first crawl before it learns to walk. We understand that by making mistakes like stumbling and falling, the child is actually engaged in the learning process. Eventually, through trial and error, the child learns how to walk.

We are God's innocent Child learning to be love in form. In this learning process, we will stumble and fall. We will make mistakes along the way. But because of those mistakes, we will discover the correct way. Our mistakes provide valuable feedback along the journey of being love in form. When we stumble, we have not sinned. We have merely gained a valuable learning lesson that will eventually allow us to achieve our goal.

Being innocent, you are sinless and guiltless. When you drop your ego's belief in sin, guilt and fear, you realize that you have nothing to fear. When you look within, you will rediscover your true Identity as the Christ. What you mistook to be your egoic will was merely a dream, an illusion that has no effect on truth or the real world.

Illusions are fantasies that change nothing. Within you is the holiness which you share with God, your Creator. When you silence your ego and look within, you will find the Christ, which is the home to God, Himself. Sin is the illusion. Sin cannot bind you or make the false real for you remain eternally innocent as God created you. When you no longer perceive sin and guilt to be real, the Second Coming is at hand.

LESSON 310

In fearlessness and love I spend today.

W-310.1. <This day, my Father, would I spend with You, as You have chosen all my days should be. 2 And what I will experience is not of time at all. 3 The joy that comes to me from spending this day with God in fearlessness and love is not of days nor hours, for the joy comes from Heaven to Your Son. 4 This day will be God's sweet reminder to remember God. This day will be God's gracious calling to God's holy Son. This day will be the sign God's grace has come to me, and that it is God's Will I be set free today.>

W-310.2. We spend this day together, you and I, **Jesus**. 2 And all the world joins with us in our song of thankfulness and joy to **God** Who gave salvation to us, and Who set us free. 3 We are restored to peace and holiness. 4 There is no room in us for fear today, for we have welcomed love into our hearts.

Notes to Lesson #310

In fearlessness and love I spend today.

Comment: You cannot experience love when you are in fear. You cannot escape fear as long as you follow your ego's fear-based thought system. Today, accept the At-One-Ment or Truth of what you are. Today, choose love over fear.

Give your day over to the Holy Spirit and follow that voice for love and fearlessness. The Holy Spirit will not allow you to mistake form for content. See your brother's innocence and what you once perceived with fear, you will now realize was merely your brother's cry for love. Your brother was merely asking if you could look past the form and still recognize the Christ that we all are.

Our birthright has been given to us by God. It cannot be earned or lost. God's Son is eternally innocent and therefore, without guilt or sin. There is nothing to fear when you rest with God and Truth. When you rest in God's love, you know no fear, and only love remains.

What Is the Last Judgment?

Covers ACIM Workbook Lessons 311-320

10. What Is the Last Judgment?

W-pII.10.1. Christ's Second Coming gives the Son of God this gift: to hear the Voice for God proclaim that what is false is false, and what is true has never changed. 2 And **God's proclamation that what is false is false, and what is true has never changed is** the judgment in which perception ends. 3 At first you see a world that has accepted this **proclamation that what is false is false, and what is true has never changed** as true, projected from a now corrected mind. 4 And with this holy sight, perception gives a silent blessing and then **perception** disappears, its goal accomplished and **perception's** mission done, **which is our split minds return to Truth.**

W-pII.10.2. The final judgment on the world contains no condemnation. 2 For **the final judgment** sees the world as totally forgiven, without sin and wholly purposeless. 3 Without a cause, and now without a function in Christ's sight, **the world of perception** merely slips away to nothingness. 4 There **from nothingness the world of perception** was born, and there **into nothingness the world of perception** ends as well. 5 And all the figures in the dream in which the world began go with **the world of perception into nothingness**. 6 Bodies now are useless, and will therefore fade away, because the Son of God is limitless.

W-pII.10.3. You who believed that God's Last Judgment would condemn the world to hell along with you, accept this holy truth: God's Judgment is the gift of the Correction **God** bestowed on all your errors, freeing you from **all errors**, and all effects **errors** ever seemed to have. 2 To fear God's saving grace is but to fear complete release from suffering, return to peace, security and happiness, and union with your own Identity **as your big "S" Self**.

W-pII.10.4. God's Final Judgment is as merciful as every step in **God's** appointed plan to bless **God's** Son, and call **the Son** to return to the eternal peace **God** shares with **His Son**. 2 Be not afraid of love. 3 For **love** alone can heal all sorrow, wipe away all tears, and gently waken from **the ego's** dream of pain the Son whom God acknowledges as **God's Own**. 4 Be not afraid of **God's love and Final Judgment**. 5 Salvation asks you give **God's Final Judgment** welcome. 6 And the world awaits your glad acceptance **of God's Final Judgment**, which will set **the world** free.

W-pII.10.5. This is God's Final Judgment: "You are still **God's** holy Son, forever innocent, forever loving and forever loved, as limitless as your Creator, and completely changeless and forever pure. 2 Therefore awaken and return to **God**. 3 I, **God,** am your Father and you are My Son."

Notes to Special Theme # 10: What Is the Last Judgment?

Covers ACIM Workbook Lessons 311-320

God's first, last and final judgment is this, "You are still My holy Son, forever innocent, forever loving and forever loved as limitless as your Creator, and completely changeless and forever pure. Therefore, awaken and return to Me. I am your Father and you are My Son."

This being the case, why does the notion of a last and final judgment by God move us into such a state of fear?

The last judgment terrifies us because we have allowed our ego to judge ourselves to be sinners and therefore, we seem to have something to fear. We perceive God to be a God of justice rather than God of love. If we truly have offended or harmed another party, justice would demand that we be punished. If we have offended God, we believe we may have earned eternal damnation.

Yet, the final judgment that God bestows upon the world contains no condemnation. Instead, God's Final Judgment is merely the recognition that we remain as God created us perfect, whole and complete, part of the One Self. Our egoic denial of our true reality as our big "S" Self has not changed the truth of our changeless and therefore, sinless nature.

It was only our ego's judgment that we had defied God's Will that led us into fear. Fear is false evidence appearing real. Because our egos have falsely judged us to be sinners, our egos have created an illusionary world that appears separate and apart from God. In this world of perception, our egos constantly find new witnesses that confirm its false judgments of a sinful world. To our egos, this world is a place where we can either hide from the wrath of God or earn our redemption. In either case, this world is perceived to be a fearful yet safer place than having to face God's Final Judgment.

Perception follows judgment. Having first judged, we perceive and see what we have chosen to look upon. Our senses are merely tools to confirm our ego's preconceived judgments. Only our ego's condemnation of ourselves and our world traps us within a thought system that has come to fear a God of love. We judge ourselves as condemned and therefore, fear God's Judgment. Thus, we continue to cling to the dream of separation in hopes of postponing the final judgment until we can earn back God's love.

Yet, God has never condemned His Creation for their decision to participate in the game of <u>What Am I</u>. God merely waits for us to end our childish game of pretending we are something we are not and freely reclaim our divine inheritance. We wanted a playschool where the abstract One Self could demonstrate in specific form the various aspects of Itself. This world provides the experiences we desire to demonstrate what love would have us do.

God understands that during the learning process of reawakening to what we truly are, we will make mistakes along the journey home. These mistakes provide valuable feedback during the learning process. They provide necessary feedback so that the student can make mid-course corrections. These mistakes require correction, not punishment. Unfortunately, our ego has misjudged these errors to be sins that require punishment. It is only because our egos have judged and condemned our world that we fear God's Final Judgment.

Until we see both our world and ourselves as sinless, we will continue to cling to the dream of separation that prevents us from reclaiming our divine birthright. As long as we see ourselves as condemned, we will believe that our separation from God is real and actually keeps us safe from our deserved punishment. Unfortunately, by allowing your ego to falsely judge your world, you will continue to fear God's Judgment. To escape this fear, you need a new plan based on a thought system of love and forgiveness.

God has provided that plan. The curriculum for your reawakening has already been established by God and is guaranteed to work. God has placed the Holy Spirit within your big "S" Self to gently guide you back home. God's curriculum leads to the remembrance of God and the acceptance of the At-One-Ment for yourself. You reawaken to your unlimited spiritual magnificence as the shared Mind of God.

The curriculum that provides these learning lessons corrects all our past, current and future errors. It utilizes the dream of separation to find the sinlessness that God has placed in you. Thankfully, free will does not put your ego in charge of the curriculum. If it did, we would all be trapped in an endless cycle of judgment and fear. Free will only allows you to choose when you will take each part of the curriculum. This guarantees that all must reawaken to the truth yet each gets to decide their time for reawakening.

Without your ego's condemnation and judgments, your world will be seen as sinless. The need to be separate, hide from God's wrath or earn your salvation now becomes meaningless. Paradise was never lost. Sin cannot be real and a God of only love can have no wrath. Without a cause and without a function, your ego's world of separation fades into the nothingness from which it was created.

As you stop judging and instead, look through the eyes of Christ, you see God's Son as limitless, sinless and innocent. You are now ready to hear the Voice for God proclaim that what is false is false and what is true has never changed. Rather than the Last Judgment being something to dread, it is now something to be eagerly anticipated. It is your time to come home.

LESSON 311

I judge all things as I would have them be.

W-311.1. Judgment was made to be a weapon used against the truth. 2 **Judgment** separates what it is being used against, and sets it off as if **what is being judged** were a thing apart **from the judge**. 3 And then **judgment** makes of it what **the judge** would have it be. 4 **The judge** judges what it cannot understand, because **the judge** cannot see totality and therefore judges falsely. 5 Let us not use **judgment** today, but make a gift **of what we would judge** to **the Holy Spirit** Who has a different use for **judgment**. 6 **The Holy Spirit** will relieve us of the agony of all the judgments we have made against ourselves, and re-establish peace of mind by giving us God's Judgment of His Son.

W-311.2. <Father, we wait with open mind today, to hear Your Judgment of the Son You love. 2 We do not know **the truth about Your Son**, and we cannot judge. 3 And so we let Your Love decide what he whom You created as Your Son must be.>

Notes to Lesson #311

I judge all things as I would have them be.

Comment: We are incapable of judging anything correctly because we lack the knowledge of the big picture. Egoic judgment is used as a weapon against the truth. Your ego's judgments support its belief in separation by taking something that is part of the whole and seeing it as separate and divisible. It then judges that item as its beliefs would have the item in question appear to be.

The purpose of egoic judgment is to make separation appear real. Since we fail to understand what we really are, we need to stop judging and instead let the Holy Spirit reinterpret our experiences to support the truth and allow for the correction of our erroneous beliefs.

Judgment is based on your beliefs and beliefs determine what your mind will project into your universe. Your projections are confirmed by your perceptions and thus, falsely support the accuracy of your ego's judgments. Do not allow your ego's belief in lack, limitation and separation to condemn God's Son for your ego is incapable of judging anything correctly because your ego does not know what you are.

LESSON 312

I see all things as I would have them be.

W-312.1. Perception follows judgment. 2 Having judged, we therefore see what we would look upon. 3 For sight can merely serve to offer us what we would have **judged it to be**. 4 It is impossible to overlook what we would see, and fail to see what we have chosen to behold. 5 How surely, therefore, must the real world come to greet the holy sight of anyone who takes the Holy Spirit's purpose as his goal for seeing. 6 And he **who takes the Holy Spirit's purpose as his goal for seeing** cannot fail to look upon what Christ would have him see, and share Christ's Love for what he looks upon.

W-312.2. <I have no purpose for today except to look upon a liberated world, set free from all the **ego's** judgments I have made. 2 Father, this is Your Will for me today, and therefore **a world liberated and free from my ego's judgments** must be my goal as well.>

Notes to Lesson #312

I see all things as I would have them be.

Comment: Your thoughts are the causative power behind the world you perceive. Your thoughts become your experiences. It is important to realize that before you perceive anything, your mind first must judge. Perception follows judgment and therefore, what we see merely reflects our previous judgments. Our physical senses are mere thought confirmation devices. The physical senses are not the objective cameras to the world, but merely devices designed to falsely confirm our prejudged misperceptions.

We judge based on our past beliefs. Christ vision frees you from your past egoic judgments. Christ vision ends your ego's judgments that support lack, limitation and separation. When you give your experiences over to the Holy Spirit, you are dropping your ego's fear-based thought system and accepting the thought system of love and forgiveness. Since judgment precedes perception, only by dropping your ego's desire to judge another as sinful and guilty will you be able to see things differently.

When you follow the thought system of the Holy Spirit, you are changing the purpose for each experience. The purpose for each experience will now support your reawakening to the truth and thus, hasten the end of your belief in sin, guilt and fear. You will choose to extend forgiveness and love to your brother instead of your ego's judgments and condemnation.

You can only see your brother as God's perfect Son when you are willing to suspend your ego's need to judge and allow the Holy Spirit's thought system to rule your mind. Since you see all things as you would have them be, you get to choose which thought system you will follow. As you choose to see your brother, you will see yourself.

LESSON 313

Now let a new perception come to me.

W-313.1. <Father, there is a vision **of Christ** which beholds all things as sinless, so that fear has gone, and where **fear** was is love invited in. 2 And love will come wherever **love** is asked. 3 This vision **of Christ** is **God's** gift. 4 The eyes of Christ look on a world forgiven. 5 In **Christ's** sight are all **the world's** sins forgiven, for **Christ** sees no sin in anything He looks upon. 6 Now let **Christ's** true perception come to me, that I may waken from the dream of sin and look within upon my sinlessness, which **God** has kept completely undefiled upon the altar to **God's** holy Son, the **big "S"** Self with which I would identify.>

W-313.2. Let us today behold each other in the sight of Christ. 2 How beautiful we are! 3 How holy and how loving! 4 Brother, come and join with me today. 5 We save the world when we have joined. 6 For in our vision **the world** becomes as holy as the light in us.

Notes to Lesson #313

Now let a new perception come to me.

Comment: When you follow a new thought system, you will perceive your world differently. When you behold all things as sinless, fear also must depart. Where fear was previously perceived, now love has been invited in. Christ vision sees all as sinless. Fear is replaced by love and your brother and you are seen as sinless, guiltless and innocent.

Christ vision sees a forgiven world. It realizes that you and your brother are united as God's one Son. When you utilize the thought system of love and forgiveness, you will see a world of only mercy and love. What you mistook previously to be an attack will now be properly interpreted as a cry for love from your brother.

By following the thought system of the Holy Spirit, love and forgiveness will replace your past judgments that supported your ego's belief in sin, guilt and fear. A world of seeming hate and fear will be transformed into a forgiven and happy world.

LESSON 314

I seek a future different from the past.

W-314.1. From new perception of the world there comes a future very different from the past. 2 The future now is recognized as but **an** extension of the present. 3 Past mistakes can cast no shadows on **the future**, so that fear has lost its idols and its images, and being formless, **fear** has no effects. 4 Death will not claim the future now, for life is now **the future's** goal, and all the needed means **for life** are happily provided. 5 Who can grieve or suffer when the present has been freed **from fear**, extending **the present's** security and peace into a quiet future filled with joy?

W-314.2. <Father, we were mistaken in the past, and choose to use the present to be free **from the past**. 2 Now do we leave the future in Your Hands, leaving behind our past mistakes, and sure that You will keep Your present promises, and guide the future in their holy light.>

Notes to Lesson #314

I seek a future different from the past.

Comment: The past was based on your ego's belief that you could oppose God's Will. Today you can choose to have your present and future based on the idea that God is living you and that you have one will that you share with God.

When you drop your ego's judgments, the present is freed from the past and viewed differently. Previously, the present was a replay of your past egoic judgments and beliefs. As you change your beliefs, your future will no longer be bound by your egoic beliefs in sin, guilt and fear.

The Holy Spirit understands that past mistakes are not sins but merely learning lessons that require correction. They are not sins but mere errors or mistakes and therefore, you remain sinless, guiltless and innocent as God created you. When you learn that lesson, you will be freed from your ego's beliefs in lack, limitation and separation.

When you choose to follow God's plan, all past mistakes are corrected. You are now free from your egoic belief that you are a sinner who must earn God's love. Time has a different use. Time's purpose now becomes to awaken sleeping minds to their spiritual magnificence as God's beloved Child. The current and the future now have one single purpose which is to allow God to live through you. By being and demonstrating what love would have you do, you complete God.

LESSON 315.

All gifts my brothers give belong to me.

W-315.1. Each day a thousand treasures come to me with every passing moment. 2 I am blessed with gifts throughout the day, in value far beyond all things of which I can conceive. 3 A brother smiles upon another, and my heart is gladdened. 4 Someone speaks a word of gratitude or mercy, and my mind receives this gift **of gratitude or mercy** and takes it as its own. 5 And everyone who finds the way to God becomes my savior, pointing out the way to me, and giving me his certainty that what he learned **by following God's way** is surely mine as well.

W-315.2. <I thank You, Father, for the many gifts that come to me today and every day from every Son of God. 2 My brothers are unlimited in all their gifts to me. 3 Now may I offer **my brothers** my thankfulness, that gratitude to **my brothers** may lead me on to my Creator and **God's** memory.>

Notes to Lesson #315

All gifts my brothers give belong to me.

Comment: Minds are connected. To give is to receive. You receive each gift your brother gives because we are joined in the Mind of God. Being part of the One Self, you are everything. Nothing is outside of you. Only your own unforgiving split mind keeps you separate and trapped within your ego's fear-based thought system.

Your judgments keep the grievances you hold against your brother alive. When you drop your grievances against your brother, you will recognize only your brother's loving thoughts are real. You can now see your brother in a new light as your savior and teacher. You can be grateful for the role he has played in your reawakening and recognize that all the gifts you thought he gave to another were also given to you.

LESSON 316

All gifts I give my brothers are my own.

W-316.1.As every gift my brothers give is mine, so every gift I give belongs to me. 2 Each one **of the gifts** allows a past mistake to go, and leave no shadow on the holy mind my Father loves. 3 **God's** grace is given me in every gift a brother has received throughout all time, and past all time as well. 4 My treasure house is full, and angels watch **my treasure house's** open doors that not one gift is lost, and only more **gifts** are added. 5 Let me come to where my treasures are, and enter in where I am truly welcome and at home, among the gifts that God has given me.

W-316.2. <Father, I would accept Your gifts today. 2 I do not recognize **God's gifts**. 3 Yet I trust that **God** Who gave **the gifts** will provide the means by which I can behold **those gifts**, see their worth, and cherish only **those gifts** as what I want.>

Notes to Lesson #316

All gifts I give my brothers are my own.

Comment: Love and forgiveness are the gifts you give to your brother and that he gives to you. The gifts of forgiveness and love remove the past mistakes and misperceptions that you have placed upon yourself and your world.

To give is to receive. Because minds are joined, you need to realize that you have already been the everywhere and every when in the dance of separation. You can choose to forgive the past and accept the At-One-Ment for yourself. Since to give is to receive, when you accept the atonement for yourself, you accept it for all.

LESSON 317

I follow in the way appointed me.

W-317.1.I have a special place to fill **in God's plan**; a role for me alone. 2 Salvation waits until I take this part **in God's plan** as what I choose to do. 3 Until I make this choice **to fill my role in God's plan**, I am the slave of time and human destiny. 4 But when I willingly and gladly go the way my Father's plan appointed me to go, then will I recognize salvation is already here, **salvation has** already **been** given all my brothers and already mine as well.

W-317.2. <Father, Your way is what I choose today. 2 Where **God's plan** would lead me do I choose to go; what **God's plan** would have me do I choose to do. 3 **God's** way is certain, and the end secure. 4 The memory of **God** awaits me there. 5 And all my sorrows end in **God's** embrace, which You have promised to Your Son, who thought mistakenly that **God's Son** had wandered from the sure protection of **God's** loving Arms.>

Notes to Lesson #317

I follow in the way appointed me.

Comment: Only God's plan will work. Turn over your egoic judgments and perceptions to the Holy Spirit and let the Holy Spirit lead the way. The journey of reawakening is secured by God and thus, we are all guaranteed to make it home.

God's Will is that you freely choose to follow His Will or plan. When you follow the ego's thought system, you become a slave to time and human destiny. You have chosen to associate your essence with the physical body.

As unlimited spirit, we each are an individualized facet of God's Creation and have our own unique experiences in the world of form. We each have a role to play in the reawakening of God's sleeping Son to his true spiritual magnificence as the Christ. As differentiated aspects of the One Self, we each have a part to play in God's plan to teach that only love is real. Be vigilant only for God's plan and let the voice for the Holy Spirit be your guide.

LESSON 318

In me salvation's means and end are one.

W-318.1.In me, God's holy Son, are reconciled all parts of Heaven's plan to save the world. 2 What could conflict, when all the parts **of Heaven's plan to save the world** have but one purpose and one aim? 3 How could there be a single part that stands alone **from Heaven's plan to save the world,** or one of more or less importance than the rest? 4 I am the means by which God's Son is saved, because salvation's purpose is to find the sinlessness that God has placed in me. 5 I was created as the **sinless** thing I seek. 6 I am the goal **of sinlessness that** the world is searching for. 7 I am God's Son, **God's** one eternal Love. 8 I am salvation's means and end as well.

W-318.2. <Let me today, my Father, take the role **of sinlessness that** You offer me in Your request that I accept Atonement for myself. 2 For **by accepting the Atonement for myself** thus does **my sinlessness that** is thereby reconciled in me become as surely reconciled to You.>

Notes to Lesson #318

In me salvation's means and end are one.

Comment: When you only have one purpose and one aim, there is no conflict because your decisions become obvious. Multiple goals lead to conflict and stress since multiple goals cannot always be pursued simultaneously and often conflict and contradict each other.

God has a plan for you and your one purpose is to follow that plan. God has reconciled all parts of salvation's plan for the ending of your belief in separation within yourself. The purpose of the plan is to bring about the reconciliation within your split mind to the truth that God's Son is without sin.

God created you sinless and this is what we all seek to rediscover. You are both the means and the end since the sinlessness that you seek has been placed within you. Your role is to be and teach that only love is real. Thus, you accept the Truth or Atonement for yourself.

The Atonement reconciles God's Son with the truth about your big "S" Self. If the game of What Am I is to be played, the players must enter into the medium of time along with the belief in limitation. This is needed if one is to experience the illusion of being separate from the One Self. As a player in the game of separation, you are both the cause and effect of love and therefore, the means and end for love.

Each and all parts of creation are equal and each contains the whole. All parts are holographic in nature and are joined as one. In the illusion of physical form, we need each other to appear as separate so that we can experience and demonstrate love in form. Without the illusion of separation, how could the One know Itself?

LESSON 319

I came for the salvation of the world.

W-319.1.**I came here for the salvation of the world** is a thought from which all arrogance has been removed, and only truth remains. 2 For arrogance opposes truth. 3 But when there is no arrogance the truth will come immediately, and fill up the space the ego left unoccupied by lies. 4 Only the ego can be limited, and therefore **the ego** must seek for aims which are curtailed and limiting. 5 The ego thinks that what one gains, totality must lose. 6 And yet it is the Will of God I learn that what one gains is given unto all.

W-319.2. <Father, Your Will is total. 2 And the goal which stems from **God's Will** shares its totality. 3 What aim but the salvation of the world could **God** have given me? 4 And what but **the salvation of the world** could be the Will my **big "S"** Self has shared with **God's Will?**>

Notes to Lesson #319

I came for the salvation of the world.

Comment: The ego believes that if you are to win, someone else must lose. It believes in a zero-sum game. Your ego only gives to get. The Holy Spirit knows that to give is to receive. The Holy Spirit understands that in order for you to receive, you must give for what one gains is given to all. You prove that you have something when you can give it away.

This fear-based world was created out of the ego's belief in lack, limitation and separation. The ego's own belief in limitation binds your mind as a little "s" self. Yet, as an extension of God Himself, you truly must be as unlimited as your Creator.

Only the ego can be limited and therefore, your ego seeks goals that confirm its limiting beliefs about itself. The ego is arrogant since arrogance opposes the truth. The ego argues for your littleness. The Holy Spirit argues for your spiritual magnificence. You, like the Holy Spirit, are not being arrogant when you are merely stating the truth about your big S Self.

Salvation is the promise made by God that you will find your way back to the truth that you remain as God created you. You are not being arrogant when you accept the truth or At-One-Ment for yourself. Your purpose is to end your ego's false misperception and save your world. You do this by returning to the truth and reclaiming your divine inheritance which was never lost, just momentarily forgotten. Accept that you have come into time to save your world by following God's Will.

LESSON 320

My Father gives all power unto me.

W-320.1.The Son of God is limitless. 2 There are no limits on **the Son of God's** strength, his peace, his joy, nor any attributes his Father gave in **the Son's** creation. 3 What **God's Son** wills with his Creator and Redeemer must be done. 4 **God's Son's** holy will can never be denied, because his Father shines upon **the Son's** mind, and lays before **the Son's mind** all the strength and love in earth and Heaven. 5 I am **God's Son** to whom all this is given. 6 I am **God's Son** in whom the power of my Father's Will abides.

W-320.2. <**God's** Will can do all things in me, and then extend to all the world as well through me. 2 There is no limit on **God's** Will. 3 And so all power has been given to **God's** Son.>

Notes to Lesson #320

My Father gives all power unto me.

Comment: All attributes that belong to God have been given to God's Creation and therefore, you truly are unlimited. All attributes that seem to limit God's Son are the creation of the ego and only exist within the split mind that perceives itself to be separate from God, its Source.

God and my big "S" Self share one will which is God's Will. When we think the thoughts of God, we co-create with God and extend the truth that only love is real. In time, as in heaven, God's Will must be done.

You have freely chosen to let God live in you so that you can be God's powerful conduit for Christ. Through your little "s" self, you can do nothing. Yet, through your big "S" Self, God can do everything.

What Is Creation?

Covers ACIM Workbook Lessons 321-330

11. What Is Creation?

W-pII.11.1.Creation is the sum of all God's Thoughts, in number infinite, and everywhere without all limit. 2 Only love creates, and **love** only **creates** like itself. 3 There was no time when all that **God's Love** created was not there. 4 Nor will there be a time when anything that **God's Love** created suffers any loss. 5 Forever and forever are God's Thoughts exactly as they were and as **God's Thoughts** are, unchanged through time and after time is done.

W-pII.11.2.God's Thoughts are given all the power that their own Creator has. 2 For **God** would add to love by **love's** extension. 3 Thus, **God's** Son shares in creation, and **God's Son** must therefore share in power to create. 4 What God has willed to be forever One will still be One when time is over; and will not be changed throughout the course of time, remaining **forever One** as it was before the thought of time began.

W-pII.11.3.Creation is the opposite of all illusions, for creation is the truth. 2 Creation is the holy Son of God, for in creation is **God's** Will complete in every aspect, making every part container of the whole. 3 **Creation's** oneness is forever guaranteed inviolate; forever held within **God's** holy Will. **Creation's oneness is** beyond all possibility of harm, of separation, imperfection and **creation's oneness is beyond all possibility** of any spot upon **creations** sinlessness.

W-pII.11.4.We are creation; we the Sons of God. 2 We seem to be discrete, and unaware of our eternal unity with **God**. 3 Yet back of all our doubts, past all our fears, there still is certainty **of our unity with God**. 4 For love remains with all **love's** thoughts, **love's** sureness being **creation's sureness**. 5 God's memory is in our holy minds, which know their oneness and their unity with their Creator. 6 Let our function be only to let this memory **of God** return **in our holy minds**, only to let God's Will be done on earth, only to be restored to sanity, and to be but as God created us.

W-pII.11.5.Our Father calls to us. 2 We hear **God's** Voice, and we forgive creation in the Name of its Creator, Holiness Itself, Whose Holiness **God's** Own creation shares; Whose Holiness is still a part of us.

Notes to Special Theme # 11: What Is Creation?

Covers ACIM Workbook Lessons 321-330

Creation is the sum of all God's Thoughts, infinite in number and everywhere without limit. God's Thoughts are unlimited and changeless in time. There was never a time when all that God's Thoughts created were not there. Nor will there be a time when anything that was created suffers any loss. God's Thoughts are forever exactly as they were, as they are, unchanged through time and after the illusion of time will be over.

Only love creates and love creates like itself. Creation is the extension of God's Thoughts, not the extrusion or separation of the thought from the Mind of God. Creation is different than the physical birthing process in which the child is expelled and becomes separate from its mother. Extension maintains the holographic inseparable nature of mind. Every part contains the whole and the whole is contained in each part.

Creation is all inclusive. God gives all to all. There is no exclusion, inequality or separation. Each of God's Thoughts are all powerful extensions of God Himself and therefore, all creation shares in the power to create. God's creations are One with God, inseparable and are of one Mind. Creation completes God's Will for all of creation shares the same will as God, its Source. God's creations, like God Himself are limitless, and cannot be harmed; know separation, lack, sin or guilt.

The memory of God is within Creation's unified Mind. Your big "S" Self knows its oneness and unity with its Creator. Through creation, God knows Itself. God's thoughts are Cause. Creation is the Effect of God's Thoughts. Together Cause and Effect are inseparably joined as God. We are God's creations and complete God. There is only one Will, one Mind, one truth, and one eternal, changeless reality. God is and there is nothing else but God.

In time, we appear to be split minded and separate from God, our Source. Within the illusion of time, our function is to reclaim the memory of God and demonstrate that only love is real. When we recognize that our will is the same as God's Will, we will heal our split mind and restore God's creation to sanity. Illusions will end and we will recognize that we have always remained as God created us. We will return to the knowledge of what we are and accept our At-One-Ment with the One Self.

Our big "S" Self has never forgotten what it truly is. Our ego is a part of our split mind that has forgotten its true Identity and its Source. Our ego imagines that we have a will separate from God's Will and have sinned against our Creator. Our ego has created a fictitious identity crisis which A Course in Miracles calls the "authority problem." Our ego claims that we are either not created by God or that we, an Effect of God's Thoughts, have the power to change what God thought. The "authority problem" claims that an effect can change its cause.

In reality, the idea that we could be something that we are not is impossible and ridiculous. A child can pretend to be a dog but that pretense has no power to magically transform the child into a dog. Imagination is not the same as reality. Nor is perception the same as truth.

Time is the tool of the mind's imagination in which opposites appear to exist. In the illusion of time, the false can appear to be true and the true can appear to be false. The illusion of time has no ability to change the truth. The Truth does not need our agreement to become true. Truth just is.

Only within the deluded mind of the dreamer does the illusion of lack, limitation and separation appear to be real. The illusion will last only as long as the dreamer refuses to wake up and accept the truth that his mind is the creator of the dream. An illusion can appear real only within the sleeping mind of one who has temporarily forgotten the truth about God's creation.

Because of the creative power of thought, our mind has the ability to create or imagine anything it desires. Loving thoughts are shared and co-create with God and thus, are real. Fear-based thoughts are not shared with the Mind of God and therefore, are not real. Fearful thoughts manifest as illusions within the split mind of the thinker who believes the separation to be real.

Our decision to participate in the game of What Am I is not a sin against God. Time provides a game board in which we can demonstrate specific aspects of love like forgiveness and helpfulness that require the appearance of duality. We have come here to learn about ourselves, demonstrate and be love in form. By allowing God to live as us, we complete God and God completes us. We remain forever of One Mind and extend the love that is only God.

Creation is the opposite of illusion. Creation is changeless, eternal, real and true. Illusions are changeable, belong to the fantasy of time, are not real and are false. Creation, like love, has no opposite. Only in time, does the illusion of opposites appear to exist. In time, both love and fear appear to exist alongside the true and the false.

Exchange the illusion of time for the reality of eternity and reclaim your destiny. Realize that illusions are not real and therefore, sin cannot exist. The illusion of time is part of the learning process. In the learning process, we will make some mistakes. Yet, mistakes are errors that merely need to be corrected. They provide the necessary feedback we need to make mid-course corrections so that we can remember our way home. Mistakes, unlike sins, require correction not punishment.

When you are willing to forgive your split mind's mistaken belief that you are a sinner, you will see things differently. Ask and the Holy Spirit will help you correct your beliefs that you are apart from God's love. Realize that God's love does not need to be earned since God's love was never lost.

You remain God's sinless, guiltless Creation, an indivisible part of the holographic Mind of God. You will return to the truth that all share the oneness that is the eternal and indivisible Mind of God. This memory of God cannot be lost. It only needs to be remembered. Your big "S" Self has never forgotten this truth and knows that you remain holy, sinless and One with God. Your big "S" Self and the Holy Spirit eagerly await your decision to forgive your world and accept the At-One-Ment for yourself.

Father, my freedom is in You alone.

W-321.1. <I did not understand what made me free, nor what my freedom is, nor where to look to find **my freedom**. 2 Father, I have searched in vain until I heard Your Voice, **the Holy Spirit** directing me. 3 Now I would guide myself no more. 4 For I have neither made nor understood the way to find my freedom. 5 But I trust in You **and the Holy Spirit**. 6 You Who endowed me with my freedom as Your holy Son will not be lost to me. 7 **The Holy Spirit's** Voice directs me, and the way to You is opening and clear to me at last. 8 Father, my freedom is in You alone. 9 Father, it is my will that I return **to You, Who is my freedom**.>

W-321.2.Today we answer for the world, which will be freed along with us. 2 How glad are we to find our freedom through the certain way our Father has established. 3 And how sure is all the world's salvation, when we learn our freedom can be found in God alone.

Notes to Lesson #321

Father, my freedom is in You alone.

<u>Comment</u>: Since the ego does not know who you are, the ego is a poor guide or teacher. Your freedom comes from abandoning your ego's plan for your salvation and choosing a new guide. The Holy Spirit, not the ego, will guide you gently to rediscovering your true nature as the Christ, your big "S" Self.

You cannot be free when you live in fear. You cannot be free when you believe you are something other than as God created you, perfect, whole and complete, part of the Oneness of All That Is. Freedom can be found in God alone. Follow God's Will, not your ego's will, and you will be set free when you accept the At-One-Meant for yourself.

LESSON 322

I can give up but what was never real.

W-322.1.I sacrifice illusions; nothing more. 2 And as illusions go I find the gifts illusions tried to hide, awaiting me in shining welcome, and in readiness to give God's ancient messages to me. 3 **God's** memory abides in every gift that I receive of **God**. 4 And every dream serves only to conceal the **big "S"** Self which is God's only Son, the likeness of Himself, the Holy One Who still abides in **God** forever, as **God** still abides in me.

W-322.2. <Father, to You all sacrifice remains forever inconceivable. 2 And so I cannot sacrifice except in dreams. 3 As **God** created me, I can give up nothing **God** gave me. 4 What **God** did not give has no reality. 5 What loss can I anticipate except the loss of fear, and the return of love into my mind?>

Notes to Lesson #322

I can give up but what was never real.

<u>Comment</u>: What is false is false, and what is true has never changed. In this egoic world of illusion, you can only give up the false world of lack, limitation and separation which was designed to hide the truth. Illusions only conceal your true reality as your big "S" Self.

To sacrifice an illusion is to sacrifice nothing. What you actually give up when you exchange illusions for the truth, are the fears that arose from the illusion of being less than perfect, whole and complete.

When you give up fear, you return to love. Love, not fear, is what is real. You rediscover that you remain as God created you, part of the indivisible One Self. You have given up the illusion of separation for the truth that you share God's Will. You have sacrificed nothing and gained everything.

I gladly make the "sacrifice" of fear.

W-323.1. <**Fear** is the only "sacrifice" **God** asks of **His** beloved Son; **God** asks **His beloved Son** to give up all suffering, all sense of loss and sadness, all anxiety and doubt, and freely let **God's** Love come streaming in to **the Son's** awareness, healing **the Son** of pain, and giving him **God's** Own eternal joy. 2 Such is the "sacrifice" **God** asks of me, and one I gladly make; **the ending of my fear is** the only "cost" of **the** restoration of **God's** memory to me, **and** for the salvation of the world.>

W-323.2.And as we pay the debt we owe to truth,–a debt that merely is the letting go of self-deceptions and of images we worshipped falsely–truth returns to us in wholeness and in joy. 2 We are deceived no longer **by our ego's misperceptions and false beliefs**. 3 Love has now returned to our awareness. 4 And we are at peace again, for fear has gone and only love remains.

Notes to Lesson #323

I gladly make the "sacrifice" of fear.

Comment: God and the Holy Spirit ask only that you sacrifice your fears. When you give up your fears, it ends all of your egoic suffering, sense of loss, sadness, anxiety and doubt. With fear gone, you reawaken to the truth. You abandon your ego's thought system of self-deception that claims you are a limited little "s" self. Following the Holy Spirit, you cultivate self-honesty as you reawaken to the truth about your big "S" Self.

LESSON 324

I merely follow, for I would not lead.

W-324.1. <Father, You are the One Who gave the plan for my salvation to me. 2 **God has** set the way I am to go, the role to take, and every step in my appointed path. 3 I cannot lose the way. 4 I can but choose to wander off a while, and then return **to the path that God has appointed for my own salvation**. 5 Your loving Voice, **the Holy Spirit,** will always call me back **to the correct path**, and guide my feet aright. 6 My brothers all can follow in the way I lead **my brothers**. 7 Yet I merely follow in the way to **God** as You direct me and would have me go.>

W-324.2.So let us follow **the Holy Spirit** Who knows the way. 2 We need not tarry, and we cannot stray except an instant from **the Holy Spirit's** loving Hand. 3 We walk together, for we follow **the Holy Spirit**. 4 And it is **the Holy Spirit** Who makes the ending sure, and guarantees a safe returning home.

Notes to Lesson #324

I merely follow, for I would not lead.

Comment: Ultimately, we must follow God's plan for salvation. God has set the curriculum for the guaranteed remembrance of our divine inheritance. Our egos do not know the way home. God's plan for salvation is certain for it is God's Will that we all return home. We have the free will to delay our return to the truth but that delay can only postpone, not change, the final outcome of our reawakening.

The Holy Spirit has been placed within all minds that believe the separation to be real. All minds share that connection with the Holy Spirit and our collective consciousness leads to the remembrance of God. When you choose to follow the Holy Spirit, your brother can also follow you home.

Ultimately, we will all freely choose to follow the guidance of the Holy Spirit. The Holy Spirit cannot fail in Its mission because our reawakening is guaranteed by God's Will alone. We all will become the Holy Spirit's messengers who help reawaken our sleeping brothers to their spiritual magnificence as the Christ.

LESSON 325

All things I think I see reflect ideas.

W-325.1.**The thought that all things I think I see reflect ideas** is salvation's keynote: What I see reflects a process in my mind, which starts with my idea of what I want. 2 From there, the mind makes up an image of the thing the mind desires, judges valuable, and therefore seeks to find. 3 These images are then projected outward **from our own mind into our world**, looked upon, esteemed as real and guarded as one's own. 4 From insane wishes comes an insane world. 5 From judgment comes a world condemned. 6 And from forgiving thoughts a gentle world comes forth, with mercy for the holy Son of God, to offer him a kindly home where **God's holy Son** can rest a while before he journeys on, and help his brothers walk ahead with him, and find the way to Heaven and to God.

W-325.2. <Our Father, Your ideas reflect the truth, and **my ego's ideas that are thought** apart from **God's ideas** but make up **illusionary** dreams. 2 Let me behold what only **God's ideas** reflect, for **God's ideas** and **God's** alone establish truth.

Notes to Lesson #325

All things I think I see reflect ideas.

Comment: This lesson explains the step-by-step process of projection. Thoughts always come first and are the creative power behind what you perceive. Your mind creates your experiences. Your experiences do not create your thoughts.

We always start first with an idea of something that we desire to experience. Our mind then makes an image of the thing that the mind desires, judges valuable and seeks to find. These images are then projected outward and your senses are then ordered to find those projected thought forms in your outer world. The senses then report back to the mind the images they were ordered to find. Those images are then perceived to be real and are guarded as your own truth. Thus, our senses are thought confirmation devices that merely confirm our previous judgments of what we wanted to find in our private world of individuated perception.

Perception follows judgment. From our ego's insane wishes, we make an insane world. From our ego's fear-based judgments comes a world that we see as sinful and condemned. When we choose to value forgiveness and love, instead of judgment and condemnation, we will create a world that reflects only our thoughts of mercy and love. The world is a reflection of you because all things you think you see reflect your own ideas.

LESSON 326

I am forever an Effect of God.

W-326.1. <Father, I was created in Your Mind, a holy Thought **of God** that never left its home. 2 I am forever **an** Effect **of God's Thought**, and **God's Thought** forever and forever are my Cause. 3 As **God** created me I have remained. 4 Where **God** established me I still abide. 5 And all **God's** attributes abide in me, because it is **God's** Will to have a Son so like his Cause that Cause and Its Effect are indistinguishable. 6 Let me know that I am an Effect of God, and so I have the power to create like **God**. 7 And as it is in Heaven, so on earth. 8 **God's** plan I follow here **on earth**, and at the end I know that **God** will gather **His** effects into the tranquil Heaven of **God's** Love, where earth will vanish, and all separate thoughts unite in glory as the Son of God.>

W-326.2.Let us today behold earth **disappear**, at first, **our ego's world of perception is** transformed, and then, forgiven. **This now forgiven world then** fades entirely into God's holy Will.

Notes to Lesson #326

I am forever an Effect of God.

Comment: We are the Thought of God and, therefore, an Effect of God's Thought. God is Cause and we are an extension of the Mind of God. Like begets like, and therefore, we, like God, have the creative power to create as God creates. When we share the Thought of God, we co-create with God and the Effects of that co-creation are indistinguishable for we share one Will. When we are of one Mind, our ego's world of lack, limitation and fear will disappear to be replaced by the Truth of Heaven.

Although we can dream we are something we are not, our dreams cannot change the fact that we remain forever an Effect of God. God is only love and God is our Cause. When we follow God's plan, we, God's Effect, demonstrate we are also only love. Cause and Effect, both being only love are now indistinguishable as the one holy Will of God.

LESSON 327

I need but call and You will answer me.

W-327.1.I am not asked to take salvation on the basis of an unsupported faith. 2 For God has promised He will hear my call, and answer me Himself **through the Voice of the Holy Spirit**. 3 Let me but learn from my experience that this is true, and faith in **God and His Voice** must surely come to me. 4 This is the faith **in God** that will endure, and take me farther and still farther on the road that leads to **God**. 5 For thus I will be sure that **God** has not abandoned me and loves me still, awaiting but my call to give me all the help I need to come to **God through the Holy Spirit's guidance**.

W-327.2. <Father, I thank You that Your promises will never fail in my experience, if I but test **my experiences** out. 2 Let me attempt therefore to try them, and to judge **my experiences** not. 3 **The Holy Spirit's** Word is one with You. 4 You give the means **through the Holy Spirit's interpretation of my experiences** whereby conviction comes, and surety of **God's** abiding Love is gained at last.>

Notes to Lesson #327

I need but call and You will answer me.

Comment: We are not asked to take God's plan for our salvation on unsupported faith alone. Instead, we are asked to drop our egoic judgments about our experiences and turn them over to the Holy Spirit. The Holy Spirit will reinterpret those same experiences according to God's plan for your salvation. When we follow the Holy Spirit's guidance, we will see that our experiences provide the exact learning lessons we need to reawaken to the truth of our loving and sinless nature as God's beloved Child.

As you follow the guidance of the Holy Spirit and see the restoration of your inner peace and happiness, your faith and trust will grow in God's plan for your salvation. You will realize you have not been left alone.

Ask the Holy Spirit to teach you that your world is sinless, guiltless and innocent and you will soon learn that same innocence about yourself. Do not prejudge your world but instead, turn your experiences over to God's teacher and the Holy Spirit will answer and guide you home. Your world will become a happy and peaceful place that reflects God's mercy and love.

LESSON 328

I choose the second place to gain the first.

W-328.1.What seems to be the second place is first **place**, for all things we perceive **with our egos** are upside down until we listen to the **Holy Spirit, the** Voice for God. 2 It seems that we will gain autonomy but by our striving to be separate, and that our independence from the rest of God's creation is the way in which salvation is obtained. 3 Yet all we find **in our egoic desire to experience separate autonomy from the One Self** is sickness, suffering and loss and death. 4 This is not what our Father wills for us, nor is there any second **separate will** to **God's** Will. 5 To join with **God's Will** is but to find our own **true Will**. 6 And since our will is **God's Will**, it is to **God** that we must go to recognize our **true** will.

W-328.2. <There is no will but **God's Will**. 2 And I am glad that nothing **my ego** imagines contradicts what You would have me be. 3 It is Your Will that I be wholly safe, eternally at peace. 4 And happily I share that **One** Will which You, my Father, gave as part of me.>

Notes to Lesson #328

I choose the second place to gain the first.

Comment: The ego's world is upside down. The ego imagines a world that is based on its own misperception, not knowledge; its egoic fantasy instead of God's reality. The ego wants individual autonomy so that it can experience a special kind of love. Yet, God's Love is total, complete and cannot be special. God's love extends all to all. God's love cannot be unequal or different because there is only equality within the One Self. One form of love cannot be greater than another in an inseparable whole that cannot be divided into autonomous parts.

The Holy Spirit and God know that your happiness rests in your oneness and unity of the One Self. You cannot be separate or apart from God since Cause and Effect are forever joined as One. Only God's Will leads to happiness since you cannot be happy being less than what you truly are.

The ego's world, like its fear-based thought system, is opposed to truth. Your ego believes that specialness and inequality can make you happy. Yet, when you have already been created as part of the Oneness of All That Is, specialness can only bring with it the attributes of lack, limitation and separation. You truly want union, not separation. You want to return to your true home.

Because our ego believes our happiness and safety rests with the body, our ego will always be the first voice we hear. The ego will answer from fear which is based on its erroneous beliefs in lack, limitation and separation. Your ego will argue for the limitations that come with its belief in your body's reality. It will argue that there are outside forces that can harm you and rob your peace and happiness. It will claim it has a plan to keep you safe. Yet, your experiences prove that your ego's plans always end in pain, sickness, suffering, conflict, loss and death. The ego's plans offer nothing you truly want.

Do not choose to follow this voice for fear. Instead, silence your ego's voice and listened for that second voice, the voice of the Holy Spirit. Choose the second plan. If you desire to obtain the peace and happiness that you seek, choose God's plan for only that plan will work.

There is no will but God's Will. By choosing to ignore your ego and following God's plan, you will allow the Holy Spirit to transform your ego's fear-based world into a learning device for your reawakening to the truth. By choosing differently you can reclaim your divine inheritance that had never been lost but merely forgotten. The Holy Spirit will take the ego's upside down world and use it to restore the truth that brings you home.

LESSON 329

I have already chosen what You will.

W-329.1. <Father, I thought I wandered from Your Will, defied **God's Will**, broke **God's** laws, and interposed a second will more powerful than **God's Will**. 2 Yet what I am in truth is but **God's** Will, extended and extending. 3 **God's Will is what** am I, and this will never change. 4 As **God is** One, so am I one with **God**. 5 And this **being one with God** I chose in my creation, where my will became forever one with **God's Will**. 6 That choice **of being one with God and God's Will** was made for all eternity. 7 **Creation being one with God** cannot change, and be in opposition to itself. 8 Father, my will is **your Will**. 9 And I am safe, untroubled and serene, in endless joy, because it is Your Will that it be so **that I eternally remain one with God in safety and endless joy.**>

W-329.2.Today we will accept our union with each other and **God,** our Source. 2 We have no will apart from **God's Will,** and all of us are one because **God's** Will is shared by all of us. 3 Through **God's Will** we recognize that we are one. 4 Through **God's Will** we find our way at last to God.

Notes to Lesson #329

I have already chosen what You will.

Comment: God desires that He be known. We were created as an extension of only love and through God's Creation, God knows Himself. You are a conduit for love and have entered the illusion of time to remember and demonstrate what love would have you do. Allow God to live through you. You are a Thought of God to demonstrate love in form. In time, love is the creative process in which time is utilized to reawaken sleeping minds to their true magnificence as part of the indivisible One Self.

Creation is extension. Therefore, you and God are One. We are all united and of one shared Mind and Will. As a conduit for God's love, we have come to demonstrate that only love is real. Through extension, God knows Himself.

Arrogance is our egos' denial that we are of one mind and one will with God. Your ego is focused on a past that misjudges you as separate and claims you are a guilty sinner. This is not so. You remain eternally sinless, guiltless, innocent and connected to your Source. Drop your ego's focus on its fictitious past. Instead, focus on the truth of the oneness of all Creation with God as Its Source.

God is Cause and you are God's Effect. God's Will is that you be happy and in eternal joy. Listen to the Holy Spirit and follow God's plan and reawaken to the truth that there is only one Will. Being an Effect of God, we cannot change our Cause. God has already chosen that we be one with God, our Source. Therefore, our current job is only to remember that fact and be happy, safe and at peace as we extend what we truly are.

In time, your function is forgiveness, your purpose is love and your destiny is the peace of God. You have already chosen to do God's Will and fulfill your destiny so it is time to silence the false will of your ego and choose to follow the true will that you share with God.

LESSON 330

I will not hurt myself again today.

W-330.1.Let us this day accept forgiveness as our only function. 2 Why should we attack our minds, and give **our minds** images of pain? 3 Why should we teach you **our minds** are powerless, when God holds out His power and His Love, and bids **our minds** take what is already theirs? 4 The mind that is made willing to accept God's gifts has been restored to spirit, and extends **the mind's** freedom and its joy, as is the Will of God united with **the mind's** own will. 5 The **big "S" Self** which God created cannot sin, and therefore **the big "S" Self** cannot suffer. 6 Let us choose today that **our big "S" Self** be our Identity, and thus escape forever from all things the dream of fear appears to offer us.

W-330.2. <Father, Your Son can not be hurt. 2 And if we think we suffer, we but fail to know our one Identity **as our big "S" Self that** we share with You. 3 We would return to **our one Identity that we share with You** today, to be made free forever from all our mistakes, and to be saved from what we thought we were **which was our ego's erroneous image of a little "s" self.**>

Notes to Lesson #330

I will not hurt myself again today.

Comment: On earth, your function is forgiveness. When you attack another, you attack and disempower your own mind. When you condemn another, it is only your own mind that you crucify and imprison. Drop the past grievances and judgments of your ego and see your brother as sinless, guiltless and innocent. When you forgive your brother, only then are you free to vacate the prison of your own unforgiving mind.

A mind that accepts God's gifts of the power of extension is free of fear. That mind is restored to the freedom and joy that is the shared Mind of God. All the power of God flows through us. The creative power of Mind generates the images that become our experiences. When we live in fear, we fail to acknowledge the truth of what we are. We disempower our mind with images of pain, conflict and suffering. When we extend God's Will, we co-create with God and extend love and forgiveness.

Our ego believes that lack, limitation and separation are real. Our ego has imagined an image of a little "s" self that supports those erroneous beliefs. It sees a body that the ego imagines to be a sinful, guilty autonomous being that lives in fear, suffers and dies. Yet, God created us and therefore, we cannot suffer or die. As an extension of God, we are unlimited spirit. Drop your ego's fear-based beliefs and choose to remember your true Identity as your big "S" Self for you are God.

What Is the Ego?

Covers ACIM Workbook Lessons 331-340

12. What Is the Ego?

W-pII.12.1.The ego is idolatry; the sign of limited and separated self, born in a body, doomed to suffer and to end its life in death. 2. **The ego** is the "will" that sees the Will of God as enemy, and takes a form in which **the Will of God** is denied. 3 The ego is the "proof" that strength is weak and love is fearful, life is really death, and what opposes God alone is true.

W-pII.12.2.The ego is insane. 2 In fear **the ego** stands beyond the Everywhere, apart from All, in separation from the Infinite. 3 In **the ego's** insanity it thinks **it** has become a victor over God Himself. 4 And in **the ego's** terrible autonomy **the ego** "sees" the Will of God has been destroyed. 5The ego dreams of punishment, and trembles at the figures in its dreams, **the ego's** enemies, who seek to murder **the ego** before **the ego** can ensure its safety by attacking **the ego's enemies first**.

W-pII.12.3.The Son of God is egoless. 2 What can **the Son of God** know of madness and the death of God, when **the Son** abides in **God**? 3 What can **the Son of God** know of sorrow and of suffering, when **the Son** lives in eternal joy? 4 What can **the Son of God** know of fear and punishment, of sin and guilt, of hatred and attack, when all there is surrounding **the Son** is everlasting peace, forever conflict-free and undisturbed, in deepest silence and tranquility?

W-pII.12.4.To know reality is not to see the ego and **the ego's** thoughts, its works, **the ego's** acts, its laws and its beliefs. **To know reality is not to see the ego's** dreams, its hopes, **the ego's** plans for its salvation, and the cost belief in it entails. 2 In suffering, the price for faith in **the ego** is so immense that crucifixion of the Son of God is offered daily at **the ego's** darkened shrine, and blood must flow before the altar where **the ego's** sickly followers prepare to die.

W-pII.12.5.Yet will one lily of forgiveness change the darkness into light; the altar to illusions to the shrine of Life Itself. 2 And peace will be restored forever to the holy minds which God created as His Son, **God's** dwelling place, **God's** joy, **God's** love. **The Son's holy mind is** completely **God's Mind and the Son** completely one with **God**.

Notes to Special Theme # 12: What Is the Ego?

Covers ACIM Workbook Lessons 331-340

Our ego is a composite of our erroneous beliefs about ourselves, God and our world. The ego is idolatry and the belief in limitation, lack and separation. The ego is an attack on God, creation and the Truth. It is the idea of a separate autonomous little "s" self that has harmed, offended or even killed God, and therefore, must fear God's revenge. The ego lives in a delusional world of sin, guilt and fear of its own creation.

The ego believes that Paradise has been lost and that sacrifice is required for salvation to be regained. The ego's plan for our salvation revolves around crucifixion, pain and suffering instead of forgiveness, mercy and love. The ego judges us as sinners and demands our punishment. Some sacrifice must be made to atone for these past offenses. To the ego, salvation is not something God freely gives to all. Instead, salvation has been lost and now must be earned through you or another's good deeds, suffering or sacrifice. Someone must atone for our sins or there will be hell to pay.

The altar of the ego is its belief in separation. This belief that we are separate from God, our Source, envisions the world of lack, limitation, sin, guilt and fear. The ego is how we choose to define ourselves. The goal of the Holy Spirit is to help us drop our ego's judgments and misperceptions by replacing them with correct perception. With the Holy Spirit's guidance, forgiveness will replace the ego's illusions and bring us back to the Truth.

God's Son, our Christ nature, is without an ego. God's Son abides in God and is undisturbed, free of conflict and at peace. To know reality is to not see the ego and its fear-based thought system. To know reality is to not see the ego's world of lack, limitation and separation. To know the truth is to understand that the ego's laws, beliefs, hopes and dreams are not what we want and cannot bind God's Son. To reawaken to the truth is to realize that the ego's plans can never succeed and only bring failure and misery. To know reality is to realize that suffering is the price paid for our belief in our ego.

Unlike the ego that believes sacrifice is required to earn salvation, the Son of God knows forgiveness is the key to the return to Truth. The Son of God knows that sin, guilt, fear and separation are not real. Our big "S" Self knows of our oneness with God and thus, the truth about ourselves.

It is important to realize that how we choose to define ourselves becomes our provisional reality. Due to the power of your mind when you argue for your littleness, you make those limits appear real and your mind lives within those false parameters. Those limiting beliefs become your provisional reality. Until you change your beliefs, you get to keep those limitations.

Our insane ego believes that the separation is real and that we do not remain as God created us. Our ego believes that we are not perfect, whole and complete. It claims that we are separate and therefore, not part of the Mind of God. Our ego denies the creative power of our mind.

Our mind is the true creator of our experiences. We need to understand that our own mind writes an ego for everyone and everything we perceive. Because our world is a world of perception, not fact, we are actually experiencing our mind's own beliefs, judgments and projections. We are not dealing with reality.

Each person also creates an ego for everyone and everything they perceive. We believe that our experiences are the direct result of our interaction with each other. Yet, this is not the case. Our experiences are the result of our own ego's interaction with our own ego's beliefs about the other party. Each party is actually reacting to their own mind's egoic projections that each has made up about themselves and the other party. The mind of each person is judging and creating his own story rather than just observing and being in the present moment. Thus, each party's experiences become a replay of their past egoic beliefs and judgments about themselves, their brother, their world and God.

The egos we have mentally created are obscuring and restricting the creative power of our mind. The problem with the ego is not that we have imagined fictitious powers that we do not possess. Rather, the problem is that we have so little faith in the creative power of our own mind. We do not believe our mind is the power source for our experiences.

We have written an ego that asks for and envisions too little, not too much. We see ourselves as sinners that must earn our way back to heaven. Even when we see ourselves as God's beloved child with whom He is well pleased, we are still arguing for our littleness and separation. We are denying that we are one with God. We are refusing to allow God to live in us. We are denying our Source and that we are God.

Time is an illusion of our mind's making. Our mind has created an ego for time based on its beliefs about time. Because we believe I and my Father are not one, our ego's need time to allow us to re-earn our salvation and reconnect with our oneness with God sometime in the future. Time allows for our ego's false beliefs to be corrected in time. Time is a measure of that change.

Time is the belief that there is a gap between cause and effect. This gap is the separation that we perceive exists in God between the Father, as Cause, and the Son, as the Effect. The gap between Father and Son is not real but does appear to exist within our provisional reality that we perceive as time. In time, change appears real and allows the future to "catch up" with the past. Time will end when we drop our ego's belief that there is a gap between Father and Son. Eternity is the realization that there is only God and you are that One.

Perhaps one of the most important egos that we create is the ego for our own mind. Once again, we have placed restrictions that limit the creative power of mind. We have chosen to write an ego for our minds in which we claim to be victims of outside forces that are beyond our control. At best, we give our mind some limited permission to manage and mitigate the damages that these outside forces bring. Yet, most cling to the belief that their mind is not the causative power behind their experiences. As long as you believe that there are outside forces that can rob you of your own inner peace, time will continue to exist until you change those limiting beliefs.

We also write an ego for our world. Currently, due to our belief in separation, our world is a place that we have made to either hide from God's vengeance or earn our redemption. As long as we believe that we have been judged by God to be sinners, we will need this world as a place to hide from God's wrath or to redeem ourselves. When we drop our belief in sin, the egoic fear-based world will disappear.

Our mind's beliefs have also redefined what God is. The ego we have created for God has transformed a God of only love into a God of judgment. The god of our ego rewards and punishes us for our actions. Thus, a God of only love becomes a god to be feared. The ego we have created for God is that of a petty, jealous, limited god with a sadistic personality. Secretly, we realize that if God created this world of pain, suffering and conflict, such a god must be cruel. As long as our split mind believes that God created the egoic world we perceive, time will still have a purpose.

We have created two different scenarios for our brothers. Either we see a brother as a rival or sinner who is competing for the limited resources that we need for survival or happiness

<Or>

we see our brother as someone who has the ability to save us or make us happy. In either case, we are disempowering our mind and setting our brother up for failure. When our brother fails to comply with our ego's wishes, we judge and condemn our brother while holding a grievance against him. Until we are willing to forgive our brother for our belief that he could make us happy or sad, we will need time so that we can change our mind.

Based on our beliefs and desires, we each write a script or ego for all things that we perceive within our private world of provisional reality. Your mind has the power to interpret. You, as decision maker, write and create an ego for your mind, time, the world, your brothers, yourself and God.

Instead of failing to recognize our true spiritual magnificence, we can write an ego that assumes that all are united with their Source. Instead of seeing the separation as real, we can allow the game of What Am I to become a Playschool for fun and learning. Instead of seeing our brother in fear or in attack mode, we can recognize his actions are merely a cry for love. You can grant your brother mercy and forgiveness rather than judgment and condemnation. You can write an ego in which you remember your brother's true reality even when he is pretending he is something else. You can choose to see your brother as your teacher, mentor or savior if you wish.

The power of interpretation rests on your mind's ability to write an ego for anything you perceive and make that desire become your provisional reality. With the Holy Spirit's guidance, we can deliberately use this power of mind to baby step our way back home to the truth. The Holy Spirit will meet us where we are and help in this reframing of our past egoic beliefs.

For example, you may not be the able to currently recognize a terrorist suicide bomber as one with God. To do so may increase your fear about God, Himself. Yet, if allowed, the Holy Spirit may reframe your ego's belief about the terrorist into someone who is living in tremendous fear. Perhaps you would be able to forgive the terrorist for their action as merely a cry for love. Eventually, you might see the terrorist as someone who is merely asleep and does not know what they do. Eventually, you may even reach the point where you understand the terrorist is your teacher and is merely playing a role in your dream of separation. The key is to allow the Holy Spirit to take your past, present and future egoic beliefs, judgments and projections and reframe and reinterpret them in such a way to allow you to move from fear to forgiveness and love.

Because of the creative power of your mind, you, as the decision maker, can write an ego for all things that support your reawakening to this truth. You are not the body, you are free. You are still as God created you. Nothing can source your experiences but you and nothing can rob you of your own inner peace unless you choose to allow.

When you do so, you will be co-creating with God a world in which there is nobody to fix; nobody to change; nobody to control; nobody to impress; and nobody to protect for there is nobody. God is and you are that One.

LESSON 331

There is no conflict, for my will is Yours.

There is no conflict, for my will is **God's Will**.

W-331.1. <How foolish, Father, to believe Your Son could cause himself to suffer! 2 Could **the ego** make a plan for **the Son's own** damnation, and **the Son** be left without a certain way to **the Son's** release? 3 You love me, Father. 4 You could never leave me desolate, to die within **an egoic** world of pain and cruelty. 5 How could I think that Love has left Itself? 6 There is no will except the Will of Love. 7 Fear is a dream, and has no will that can conflict with **God's Will**. 8 Conflict is sleep, and peace awakening. 9 Death is illusion; life, eternal truth. 10 There is no opposition to **God's** Will. 11 There is no conflict, for my will is **God's Will**.>

W-331.2.Forgiveness shows us that God's Will is One, and that we share **that one Will with God**. 2 Let us look upon the holy sights forgiveness shows today, that we may find the peace of God. 3 Amen.

Notes to Lesson #331

There is no conflict, for my will is Yours.

Comment: Suffering arises from the ego's belief that you could be something other than God's Will. God loves you and has not abandoned His Child. You are not meant to suffer alone and die in your ego's illusionary world of fear. Use the Holy Spirit as your guide and It will correct your ego's misperceptions and judgments about yourself.

God's Will is that you only know the truth of God's unconditional love. You are a Oneness of All That Is but to realize this you need to be willing to drop your ego's fear-based thought system. The God of Love has never abandoned us for the only true Will is the Will of Love.

Fear is a dream that we have a will in conflict with God's Will. This cannot be. When you are in conflict, realize that your mind is asleep. Death is the illusion for life is eternal truth. Forgiveness shows us that we share God's Will. Since God is only love, God's Will can be only love.

LESSON 332

Fear binds the world. Forgiveness sets it free.

Fear binds the world. Forgiveness sets **the world** free.

W-332.1.The ego makes illusions. 2 Truth undoes **the ego's** evil dreams by shining **the illusions** away. 3 Truth never makes attack. 4 **Truth** merely is. 5 And by **truth's** presence is the mind recalled from fantasies, awaking to the real. 6 Forgiveness bids **the presence of truth to** enter in, and take **truth's** rightful place within the mind. 7 Without forgiveness is the mind in chains, believing in **the mind's** own futility. 8 Yet with forgiveness does the light shine through the **egoic** dream of darkness, offering **the mind** hope, and giving **the mind** the means to realize the freedom that is **the mind's own** inheritance.

W-332.2. <We would not bind the world again today. 2 Fear holds **the world** prisoner. 3 And yet **God's** Love has given us the means to set **the world** free. 4 Father, we would release **the world** now. 5 For as we offer freedom, **freedom** is given us. 6 And we would not remain as prisoners **to our ego's unforgiving mind**, while **God is** holding freedom out to us.>

Notes to Lesson #332

Fear binds the world. Forgiveness sets it free.

Comment: Both fear and forgiveness happen within your own mind. Both are the products of your mind's thought process. Fear binds the world while forgiveness sets it free.

The egoic mind makes illusions based on its belief in lack, limitation and separation. The truth undoes these illusions. Truth does not attack the illusion for truth merely is. Forgiveness allows the truth to be recalled within the split mind that was previously entrapped by fear. Forgiveness quiets the mind and lets the truth replace your egoic fear-based thought system.

Forgiveness allows the mind to only recognize the truth and thus, reawakens us to our big "S" Self. Without forgiveness, the split mind is enslaved and believes itself to be a victim to outside forces that are beyond its control. Forgiveness is the means to realize that your mind is the creator of your own experiences. Forgiveness offers hope to your split mind to heal and reclaim the freedom that is your divine inheritance.

LESSON 333

Forgiveness ends the dream of conflict here.

W-333.1.Conflict must be resolved. 2 **Conflict** cannot be evaded, set aside, denied, disguised **or** seen somewhere else. **Conflict cannot be** called by another name, or hidden by deceit of any kind, if **conflict** would be escaped. 3 **Conflict** must be seen exactly as it is, where **conflict** is thought to be. **Conflict must be seen exactly** in the reality which has been given **conflict**, and with the purpose that the **egoic** mind accorded **conflict**. 4 For only then are **conflict**'s defenses lifted, and the truth can shine upon **conflict** as it disappears.

W-333.2. <Father, forgiveness is the light You chose to shine away all conflict and all doubt, and light the way for our return to **God**. 2 No light but this **light of forgiveness** can end our evil dream. 3 No light but **forgiveness** can save the world. 4 For **forgiveness** alone will never fail in anything, **forgiveness** being Your gift to Your beloved Son.>

Notes to Lesson #333

Forgiveness ends the dream of conflict here.

<u>**Comment**</u>: Conflict must be resolved if it is to go away. Conflict cannot be denied, transferred or hidden without it remaining in your own mind. Forgiveness removes that conflict.

All conflict is between the truth and your ego's insistence on attempting to make the false into your reality. Conflict arises from your ego's belief in separation which spawns the belief that you have a will different from God's Will.

Forgiveness is based on the truth that you are not an ego body in competition with other ego bodies. Instead, you are unlimited spirit. You are not a victim of outside forces that are beyond your control since you can only be victimized by your own mind's erroneous thinking.

In forgiveness, you take responsibility for your experiences. By taking ownership for your experiences, conflict is no longer out there but rather within your own mind and always under your control. You can now use your mind to end the conflict by reframing the purpose for the experience and realigning it with the truth. When this is done, the conflict must disappear.

LESSON 334

Today I claim the gifts forgiveness gives.

W-334.1.I will not wait another day to find the treasures **of forgiveness** that my Father offers me. 2 Illusions are all vain, and dreams are gone even while they **both** are woven out of thoughts that rest on false perceptions. 3 Let me not accept such meager **illusionary** gifts **of my ego** again today. 4 God's Voice is offering the peace of God to all who hear and choose to follow **the Holy Spirit**. 5 **My decision to follow the Holy Spirit** is my choice today. 6 And so **by following the Holy Spirit** I go to find the treasures God has given me.

W-334.2. <I seek but the eternal. 2 For **God's** Son can be content with nothing less than **the eternal**. 3 What, then, can be **the Son's** solace but what **God is** offering to **His son's** bewildered **egoic** mind and frightened heart, to give **the Son** certainty and bring **God's Son** peace? 4 Today I would behold my brother sinless. 5 **2 Beholding my brother's sinlessness is God's** Will for me, for so will I behold my **own** sinlessness.>

Notes to Lesson #334

Today I claim the gifts forgiveness gives.

<u>**Comment**</u>: Illusions and dreams are worthless since both rest on false perception. You cannot be content with an illusion of lack, limitation and separation when you remain as God created you, perfect, whole and complete. When you follow the thought system of the Holy Spirit, you have chosen to follow God's Will and reclaim your divine birthright.

The Son of God knows the truth of his Christ nature and therefore, does not fear any experiences. The Son of God knows that if he chooses to participate in the game of <u>What Am I,</u> the game of make believe has no ability to change His reality. He remains eternally innocent and sinless as God wills. Forgiveness ends the illusion of sin and restores peace. When you see your brother as sinless, you see yourself in that same light.

LESSON 335

I choose to see my brother's sinlessness.

W-335.1.Forgiveness is a choice. 2 I never see my brother as he is, for that is far beyond perception. 3 What I see in **my brother** is merely what I wish to see, because **what I see in my brother** stands for what I want to be the truth. 4 It is to this **projection of my own mind's wishes** alone that I respond, however much I seem to be impelled by outside happenings. 5 I choose to see what I would look upon, and this I see, and only this **projection from my own mind's beliefs do I see**. 6 My brother's sinlessness shows me that I would look upon my own **sinlessness**. 7 And I will see **my sinlessness**, having chosen to behold my brother in **forgiveness'** holy light.

W-335.2. <What could restore **God's** memory to me, except to see my brother's sinlessness? 2 **My brother's** holiness reminds me that **my brother** was created one with me, and like myself. 3 In **my brother** I find my big "S" Self, and in **God's** Son I find the memory of **God** as well.>

Notes to Lesson #335

I choose to see my brother's sinlessness.

Comment: Our mind is the creator of our experiences. We need to understand that our own mind writes an ego for everyone and everything we perceive. Because our world is a world of perception, not fact, we are actually experiencing our mind's own beliefs, judgments and projections. We are not dealing with reality.

Our brother also creates an ego for everyone and everything he perceives. We believe that our experiences are the direct result of our interaction with each other. Yet, this is not the case. Our experiences are the result of our own ego's interaction with our own ego's beliefs about the other party. Each party is actually reacting to their own mind's egoic projections that each has created for himself and the other party. The mind of each person is judging and creating their own story rather than just observing and being in the present moment. Thus, each party's experiences become a replay of their past egoic beliefs and judgments about themselves, God, their brother and their world.

Because of this, forgiveness is a choice. When you look upon another, you only see him as you wish to see him because that stands for what you want to be the truth about your world of private individuated perception. This internal vision was generated by your beliefs and judgments to which you alone are responsible and respond to. Therefore, forgiveness is a decision that you alone make for yourself. When you decide to deliberately choose to see your brother as sinless, you will see yourself in that same way.

531

Forgiveness lets me know that minds are joined.

W-336.1.Forgiveness is the means appointed for perception's ending. 2 Knowledge is restored after perception first is changed **to correct perception through forgiveness**, and then **correct perception** gives way entirely to what remains forever past **perception's** highest reach. 3 For sights and sounds, at best, can serve but to recall the memory that lies beyond them all. 4 Forgiveness sweeps away distortions, and opens the hidden altar to the truth. 5 **The lilies of forgiveness** shine into the mind, and calls **the mind** to return and look within **itself**, to find what **the mind** has vainly sought without. 6 For **within the mind**, and only here, is peace of mind restored, for **your big "S" Self is** the dwelling place of God Himself.

W-336.2. <In quiet may forgiveness wipe away my **egoic** dreams of separation and of sin. 2 Then let me, Father, look within **my big "S" Self** and find Your promise of my sinlessness is kept; **God's** Word remains unchanged within my mind **that is my big "S" Self**, Your Love is still abiding in my heart.>

Notes to Lesson #336

Forgiveness lets me know that minds are joined.

Comment: Forgiveness is the means appointed to change misperception into correct perception. Forgiveness removes the distortions of perception that hid the truth. Forgiveness opens the mind to the hidden truth of our big "S" Self that lies within us and is the dwelling place of God, Himself.

The correct perception that forgiveness provides proves that all minds are one in truth. When you look within, you can see the sinlessness of both yourself and your brother since there is but one mind that we all share with God. Forgiveness leads to the end of perception and the restoration of knowledge to our once sleeping mind.

LESSON 337

My sinlessness protects me from all harm.

W-337.1.My sinlessness ensures me perfect peace, eternal safety, everlasting love, freedom forever from all thought of loss. **My sinlessness insures me** complete deliverance from suffering. 2 And **my sinlessness insures** only happiness can be my state, for only happiness is given me. 3 What must I do to know all this is mine **because of my sinlessness**? 4 I must accept Atonement for myself, and nothing more. 5 God has already done all things that need be done **to insure my happiness, peace and freedom**. 6 And I must learn I need do nothing of my **egoic little "s" self**, for I need but accept my **big "S" Self**, my sinlessness, created for me, now already mine, to feel God's Love protecting me from harm, to understand my Father loves His Son; to know I am the Son my Father loves.

W-337.2. <**God** Who created me in sinlessness **is** not mistaken about what I am. 2 I was mistaken when I thought I sinned, but I accept Atonement for myself. 3 Father, my dream is ended now. 4 Amen.>

Notes to Lesson #337

My sinlessness protects me from all harm.

Comment: Your sinlessness insures peace, safety, love and freedom from all loss and suffering. God's Will is that you be happy. God made, keeps and sees His Creations as sinless. This insures your perfect safety and freedom from loss since you remain eternally as God created you.

The only barrier preventing you from realizing this truth is your own refusal to accept the truth of the At-One-Ment for yourself. Atonement is merely the acceptance of the Truth for yourself. Your ego's belief in lack, limitation and separation hides the truth from your mind's remembrance. Surrender all your ego's plans for your salvation for they are all doomed to fail. Instead, accept the guidance of the Holy Spirit which God has placed within your mind to bring you home.

LESSON 338

I am affected only by my thoughts.

W-338.1.It needs but this **realization that you are affected only by your own thoughts** to let salvation come to all the world. 2 For in this single thought **that you are affected only by your own thoughts** is everyone released at last from fear. 3 Now has he learned that no one frightens him, and nothing can endanger him **since each is affected only by their own thoughts**. 4 He has no enemies, and he is safe from all external things. 5 His thoughts can frighten him, but since these thoughts belong to him alone, he has the power to change **his thoughts** and exchange each fear thought for a happy thought of love. 6 He crucified himself. 7 Yet God has planned that His beloved Son will be redeemed.

W-338.2. <**God's** plan **for His Son's redemption** is sure. My Father,–only **Your plan will work**. 2 All other plans will fail. 3 And I will have **egoic** thoughts that will frighten me, until I learn that **God has** given me the only Thought that leads me to salvation. 4 **My own egoic thoughts for my redemption** alone will fail, and lead me nowhere. 5 But the Thought **God** gave me promises to lead me home, because **the Thought God gave me** holds **God's** promise to **His** Son **for His Son's redemption**.>

Notes to Lesson #338

I am affected only by my thoughts.

Comment: Because your mind is the creator of your experiences, no outside force can threaten or frighten you. It can only be your own egoic thoughts of lack, limitation and separation that appear frightening. Yet, because it is your own mind that is the source for these fearful thoughts, you alone have within you the power to change those thoughts. Today, choose to exchange your fearful thoughts for happy, loving and forgiving thoughts.

Only your fear-based egoic thought system crucifies you. You can drop your allegiance to fear by asking for the guidance of the Holy Spirit. With this guidance, you can choose to utilize Christ vision and see things through the eyes of mercy and love.

You are the script writer of your own dreams. Realize that these dreams only crucify yourself and that no one is responsible for your loss of inner peace except you. Surrender your ego's plans and follow the guidance of the Holy Spirit which is the Voice for God.

The Holy Spirit will teach you this truth. Nothing sources your experiences but your own mind and nothing can rob you of your own inner peace unless your own mind allows it. You are affected only by your own thoughts and your world is a reflection of those thoughts.

LESSON 339

I will receive whatever I request.

W-339.1.No one desires pain. 2 But he can think that pain is pleasure. 3 No one would avoid his happiness. 4 But he can think that joy is painful, threatening and dangerous. 5 Everyone will receive what he requests. 6 But he can be confused indeed about the things he wants; the state he would attain. 7 **In such a confused state of mind,** what can he then request that he would want when he receives it? 8 **Because of his confusion,** he has asked for what will frighten him, and bring him suffering. 9 Let us resolve today to ask for what we, **our big "S" Self,** really want, and only this, that we may spend this day in fearlessness, without confusing pain with joy or fear with love.

W-339.2. <Father, this is Your day. 2 It is a day in which I would do nothing by my **egoic little "s" self,** but **instead** hear **the Holy Spirit's** Voice in everything I do; requesting only what You offer me, accepting only Thoughts You share with me.>

Notes to Lesson #339

I will receive whatever I request.

Comment: Because we do not know what we are, we fail to realize what we truly want. If you believe you are a sinner, your mind will limit what you believe are possible available options. You will no longer believe that you are sinless and innocent and thus, you will fear God's judgment and eventual punishment.

Believing sin, guilt and fear to be real, your egoic mind believes that lack, limitation and separation are your reality. Your egoic mind believes that it can only choose between differing degrees of an unfavorable option. Your egoic mind desires to manage and mitigate the lack, limitation, separation and fear that it believes it deserves and perceives in its world. It desires what it perceives to be the least unfavorable option available.

Since your ego believes you are a sinner, it believes your available choices are limited to these four unpleasant alternatives;

1) Eternal punishment in hell,
2) Hiding from God and temporarily postponing your judgment day,
3) Delaying God's final judgment until you can earn your own redemption through your current temporal suffering or good deeds, or
4) Someone else redeeming or saving you.

The idea that God knows you are sinless will not appear on the ego's radar screen as a possible viable option. Your ego's belief in sin has precluded the possibility that you could be sinless, innocent or forgiven.

It is not that your mind desires pain and suffering but it can think that pain is better than death or eternal damnation. Everyone gets what he requests but what we request is far too little because we have forgotten that God is only unconditional love. We have been requesting pain, suffering or the right to earn God's love back because our ego has mistaken the God of love to be a God of judgment and wrath.

LESSON 340

I can be free of suffering today.

W-340.1. <Father, I thank You for today, and for the freedom I am certain **today** will bring. 2 This day is holy, for today Your Son will be redeemed. 3 **The Son's** suffering is done. 4 For **God's Son** will hear **the Holy Spirit's** Voice directing him to find Christ's vision through forgiveness, and be free forever from all suffering. 5 Thanks for today, my Father. 6 I was born into this world but to achieve this day **that ends all suffering,** and **I was born for** what **this day of redemption** holds in joy and freedom for Your holy Son and for the **egoic** world **your Son** made, which is released along with **God's Son** today.>

W-340.2.Be glad today! 2 Be glad! 3 There is no room for anything but joy and thanks today. 4 Our Father has redeemed His Son this day. 5 Not one of us but will be saved today. 6 Not one who will remain in fear, and none the Father will not gather to Himself, awake in Heaven in the Heart of Love.

Notes to Lesson #340

I can be free of suffering today.

Comment: We came into this world of time and space to learn about the attribute of love that we called forgiveness. Through forgiveness, we obtain the vision of Christ and look upon a world of mercy and love. A forgiving mind sees a forgiven world.

Love allows and gives eternal freedom to the object of its love. Because we are mind, we have always had the creative ability to be or imagine anything that we desire to experience. Because our ego thought we had sinned, we argued for our limitations and made them appear real. We became confused about what we truly are. Therefore, we did not know what our true happiness is. Yet today, we can choose love and forgiveness instead of fear.

Forgiveness is a choice that each one makes on an individual basis. Forgiveness exchanges fear-based thoughts for thoughts of mercy and love. We all can be free from our egoic fear-based thought system by going within and following the guidance of the Holy Spirit. When we choose the path of love and forgiveness, we empower all with the truth that each is affected only by their own thoughts. There is no outside force that makes or requires that you suffer. Only your own unforgiving mind can crucify you.

Freedom from pain and suffering is one choice away. We are all guaranteed by our Creator to reclaim our divine birthright. Our return home is inevitable. We merely need to accept the Truth or Atonement for ourselves. Why not make that choice today?

What Is a Miracle?

Covers ACIM Workbook Lessons 341-350

13. What Is a Miracle?

W-pII.13.1.A miracle is a correction. 2 **A miracle** does not create, nor really change at all. 3 **A miracle** merely looks on devastation, and reminds the mind that what **the mind** sees is false. 4 **A miracle** undoes error, but does not attempt to go beyond perception, nor exceed the function of forgiveness. 5 Thus **a miracle** stays within time's limits. 6 Yet **a miracle** paves the way for the return of timelessness and love's awakening, for fear must slip away under the gentle remedy **a miracle** brings.

W-pII.13.2.A miracle contains the gift of grace, for **a miracle** is given and received as one. 2 And thus **a miracle** illustrates the law of truth the world does not obey, because **the world** fails entirely to understand **the miracle and the laws of truth's** ways. 3 A miracle inverts perception which was upside down before, and thus **a miracle** ends the strange distortions that were manifest. 4 Now is perception open to the truth. 5 Now is forgiveness seen as justified.

W-pII.13.3.Forgiveness is the home of miracles. 2 The eyes of Christ deliver **miracles** to all they look upon in mercy and in love. 3 Perception stands corrected in **the eyes of Christ's** sight, and what was meant to curse has come to bless. 4 Each lily of forgiveness offers all the world the silent miracle of love. 5 And each **lily of forgiveness** is laid before the Word of God, upon the universal altar to Creator and creation in the light of perfect purity and endless joy.

W-pII.13.4.The miracle is taken first on faith, because to ask for **a miracle** implies the mind has been made ready to conceive of what **the mind** cannot see and does not understand. 2 Yet faith will bring **the miracle's** witnesses to show that what **faith** rested on is really there. 3 And thus the miracle will justify your faith in **the miracle**, and show **the miracle** rested on a world more real than what you saw before; a world redeemed from what you thought was there.

W-pII.13.5.Miracles fall like drops of healing rain from Heaven on a dry and dusty world, where starved and thirsty creatures come to die. 2 Now **the starved and thirsty creatures** have water. 3 Now the world is green. 4 And everywhere the signs of life spring up, to show that what is born can never die, for what has life has immortality.

Notes to Special Theme # 13: What Is a Miracle?

Covers ACIM Workbook Lessons 341-350

A miracle is a correction. It is a change from misperception to right mindedness. With this change in thinking, forgiveness is now seen as justified. The miracle actually changes nothing that is real but merely reminds the mind that what it perceives is false and thus, undoes erroneous thinking.

Because of the miracle, our egoic thinking now gives way to the truth. A miracle does not go beyond correcting misperception and remains within the realm of time. Although the miracle's purpose is to restore your mind to right mindedness through forgiveness, it stays within time's limits. The miracle does not attempt to restore your mind to knowledge but it does pave the way to the return to knowledge and timelessness.

Forgiveness is the home of miracles. Christ vision corrects our ego's misperception so that you can view your world through the eyes of mercy, forgiveness and love. Forgiveness offers the entire world the miracle of love. No one is excluded from its reach.

Because the miracle is a change in perception, it may appear to have no effect upon the physical world to a third-party observer. The miracle happens within your own mind and does not necessarily change the outside world. This change in your own thinking does have the ability to open other minds to new possible ways of viewing their world and thus, can impact how they, in turn, view their world. Because minds are connected, a miracle that is given to one is given to all.

Because miracles belong to the realm of thought, rather than the physical world, miracles first rest upon your faith. This is because initially the split mind cannot see and understand how the miracle works. Yet, due to the miracle's result, which is the restoration of your own inner peace, you realize that your faith in miracles has not been misplaced.

When you experience the miracle's beneficial effects on your state of being, it becomes apparent that your faith in miracles has been properly placed. Miracles rest upon truth and reality, not hope and fantasy. The miracle shows that we are the source of our experiences and that nothing can rob us of our own inner peace unless we choose to allow it. The miracle acknowledges our immortality and unlimited nature as spirit or mind.

The miracle happens within your own mind and cannot be forced upon another. You can hold the truth for another, but you cannot force them to accept the truth. If you could force them to change their mind, this would mean that their mind was subservient to an outside power, in this case your mind which was beyond their control. Such a belief is disempowering and would only increase fear in both parties involved.

If you can force another to accept something against their will, it implies that you too can be manipulated by similar outside forces. A miracle allows and does not judge or condemn another for their decisions to be or imagine anything that they wish to experience. The miracle replaces judgment with forgiveness and offers allowance instead of condemnation.

The miracle changes your perception from fear-based thinking to the thought system that supports love and forgiveness. Fear arises any time we believe that we lack the creative power to handle a given situation. Whenever we fail to answer either of the follow two questions correctly, fear will raise its ugly head.

The first question is, What am I?

The second question is, What do I value and why?

The miracle temporarily corrects your ego's mistaken answers to either of these two questions. The Holy Spirit uses the miracle to reframe your misperception and move your mind out of its current fear-based thinking.

Since the next special theme will deal with the question of what am I, we will discuss the second question which is, What do you value and why? The miracle corrects your ego's answer to what you value and why. Typically what you value is not the critical issue. The problem normally revolves around why you value the item in question.

Obviously, if you perceive that you are a limited ego-body with needs, you will value something because you will believe that obtaining that item will make or improve your safety, survival or happiness. When you believe you have needs, even when you possess the item in question, you will still be in fear since the item could be consumed, lost or stolen. As long as an item is perceived to be something outside of your mind, it is not part of your beingness and will not be perceived to be under the total control of your mind's creative powers.

Although this idea of what you value is typically associated with things, it also applies to non-things like verbs or character traits.

For example, you can value the attribute of peace because your ego believes that peace can make you happy or you can value peace because that is what you are. When you value an attribute like peace because it is part of you, time and space become a playschool that allows you to be or demonstrate that attribute in specific form. You get to be the thing that you are. Being what you are does not engender fear because it is the fulfillment of your function and purpose. Only when you are being what you are, can you truly be happy for only what you are is real. Fantasies that claim you are something you are not only disappoint since they do not last and can never be real.

We could substitute the attribute of peace with love, forgiveness, or any other item in the critical question of why you value something and the answer would always revolve around the same thing. Do you value the attribute because you believe it has some magical force outside of your mind that you need to make you happy or safe?

<Or>,

Do you believe that your mind is the source of that attribute and that the experience allows you to demonstrate what you are and thus, fulfill your function and purpose?

Why do you value a particular relationship? Is it because you understand that each is perfect, whole and complete and therefore, it gives you just another opportunity to be and demonstrate love in form.

<Or?

Do you perceive lack, limitation and separation and therefore, seek a special relationship to make you happy or feel more complete?

On earth, we are here to demonstrate and be the attribute of love we call forgiveness. In heaven, forgiveness, like miracles, has no meaning for there is nothing that warrants forgiveness. On earth, we can value our experiences because they provide an opportunity to know and be ourselves. We can value our earthly experiences because of the learning lessons they provide. On earth, we need the experiences miracles provide to remember what we are.

This is different than valuing the experience because you believe the experience itself has some external magical power to make you happy or more complete. When you believe something outside yourself can make you happy, you have secretly disempowered your mind and accepted the idea that there are outside forces that can steal your inner peace or make you happy or sad. You have moved into fear and made victim consciousness your provisional reality. You have denied the creative power of your own mind.

You can value time because you believe it either keeps you safe from God's wrath or provides the time that you need to earn your redemption from your imagined sins. If so, your focus will be results oriented and time will be a place of fear.

<Or>

You can value the opportunity time provides because it allows you to demonstrate and be what you really are through specific experiences in the illusion of separation. If so, your focus will be on the process of being what you are and time will be a place of fulfillment, not fear.

<Or>

You can value time because it provides a feedback mechanism that allows you to learn what you currently value and make mid-course corrections as you hone your skills for becoming love in form. If so, your focus will be on the process of rediscovering your true big "S" Self or Christ nature and time will be a fun and exciting place of learning.

We have all come here for the learning experiences that the world of perception provides. Time and space is a means to awakening and not an end. When we value time and space as an end, we become results oriented with a focus on the future which keeps us trapped in fear.

When we value this world as a means, we realize that this is a process, not a destination. We can now enjoy the journey and be in the present moment. Instead of having to get it right and earn our salvation, the journey is a process that becomes our perfect personal path that guarantees our return to sanity. When the journey becomes a means, instead of an end, the fear of earning dissolves and the world becomes your playschool for fun and learning.

The miracle is a change in perception that allows you, at least temporarily, to change what you value and why. You no longer value an illusion; instead, you value what is real. You stop clinging to fears and start valuing forgiveness, mercy and love. You stop valuing your need to be right over your happiness. You drop your judgments and condemnation in exchange for allowance and forgiveness.

The miracle moves you out of your fear-based thought system and facilitates learning and your reawakening to the truth. Through forgiveness, the miracle allows you to change your mind's perception about itself, you, your brother, your world and your God.

I can attack but my own sinlessness,
And it is only that which keeps me safe.

I can attack but my own sinlessness, and it is only **my own sinlessness** which keeps me safe.

W-341.1. <Father, Your Son is holy. 2 I am **God's Son** on whom **God** smiles in love and tenderness so dear and deep and still the universe smiles back on **God,** and shares **God's** Holiness. 3 How pure, how safe, how holy, then, are we, abiding in **God's** Smile, with all **God's** Love bestowed upon us, living one with **God,** in brotherhood and Fatherhood complete; in sinlessness so perfect that the Lord of Sinlessness conceives us as **God's** Son, a universe of Thought completing **God.**>

W-341.2.Let us not, then, attack our sinlessness, for **our sinlessness** contains the Word of God to us. 2 And in **the** kind reflection **of our sinlessness** we are saved.

Notes to Lesson #341

I can attack but my own sinlessness,
And it is only that which keeps me safe.

Comment: God created us sinless and our sinlessness is what keeps us safe even in our ego's world of misperception. The ego perceives us to be a sinner in a sinful world. Any perceived attack on or by another or yourselves is your own ego's attack upon your own sinlessness.

You are a thought of God completing Himself. God is living us. Our safety lies in the fact that God does not judge but rather knows that we are eternally sinless and remain as God created us.

LESSON 342

I let forgiveness rest upon all things,
For thus forgiveness will be given me.

W-342.1. <I thank You, Father, for Your plan to save me from the **egoic** hell I made. 2 **The world that I made and perceive is based on my egoic fears and** is not real. 3 And **God has** given me the means to prove **the** unreality **of this illusionary world of perception** to me. 4 The key **of forgiveness** is in my hand, and I have reached the door beyond which lies the end of dreams. 5 I stand before the gate of Heaven, wondering if I should enter in and be at home. 6 Let me not wait again today. 7 Let me forgive all things, and let creation be as **God** would have **creation** be and as **creation** is. 8 Let me remember that I am **God's** Son, and opening the door at last, forget illusions in the blazing light of truth, as memory of **God** returns to me.>

W-342.2.Brother, forgive me now. 2 I come to **my brother** to take you home with me. 3 And as we go, the world goes with us on our way to God.

Notes to Lesson #342

I let forgiveness rest upon all things,
For thus forgiveness will be given me.

Comment: Forgiveness is the key that unlocks the door of illusions and allows you to enter into the light of truth. Do not fear the truth for God's Will for you is that you be happy and remember your divine inheritance.

Forgiveness is the counter dream that ends the need for all other dreams. Forgive your brother for all the things you imagined he did to you for they have never occurred except within your own mind's imagination. You must forgive all, including yourself. When you attempt to keep someone in the prison of your unforgiving mind, you, as their jailer, must remain in that same prison to guard against their escape. You are both imprisoned. Since to give is to receive, when you forgive another, together you are both free to return home.

I am not asked to make a sacrifice
To find the mercy and the peace of God.

W-343.1. <The end of suffering cannot be loss. 2 **God's** gift of everything can be but gain. 3 **God** only gives. 4 **God** never takes away. 5 And **God** created me to be like **God**, so sacrifice becomes impossible for me as well as **God**. 6 I, too, must give. 7 And so all things are given unto me forever and forever. 8 As I was created I remain. 9 **God's** Son can make no sacrifice, for **God's Son** must be complete, having the function of completing **God**. 10 I am complete because I am **God's** Son. 11 I cannot lose, for I can only give, and everything is mine eternally.>

W-343.2.The mercy and the peace of God are free. 2 Salvation has no cost. 3 **Salvation** is a gift that must be freely given and received. 4 And it is this **truth that salvation is freely given and received** that we would learn today.

Notes to Lesson #343

I am not asked to make a sacrifice
To find the mercy and the peace of God.

Comment: Your function is to complete God and, therefore, you must be complete. You cannot lose and are never asked to sacrifice anything that is real. You are only asked to surrender your ego's illusions of lack, limitation and separation. To give up illusions is to sacrifice nothing. God has given everything that is real to all and what God has given can never be taken away.

Sacrifice is impossible because we remain as God created us. The gift of salvation costs us nothing and cannot be earned for it was never lost. Instead, salvation, which is your acceptance of the Truth, must be freely given to all to be received by you. To give is to receive. By your giving forgiveness, mercy and peace to another, you recognize that you already are those attributes.

Salvation has been given eternally to us by God. Our egoic split mind can deny the receipt of God's gift of everything, but our denial has no ability to change the truth that we remain perfect, whole and complete. The mercy and peace of God is our destiny and changeless reality.

LESSON 344

Today I learn the law of love; that what
I give my brother is my gift to me.

W-344.1. <This **law that what I give my brother is my gift to me** is God's law. **It is** my **Father's** law **and not the law** my own **ego chooses to follow.** 2 I have not understood what giving means, and **my ego** thought to save what I desired for myself alone. 3 And as I looked upon the treasure that I **egoically** thought I had, I found an empty place where nothing ever was or is or will be. 4 Who can share a dream? 5 And what can an illusion offer me? 6 Yet, **my brother** whom I forgive will give me gifts beyond the worth of anything on earth. 7 Let my forgiven brothers fill my store with Heaven's treasures, which alone are real. 8 Thus is the law of love fulfilled **that what I give my brother is my gift to me.** 9 And thus Your Son arises and returns to **God**.>

W-344.2.How near we are to one another, as we go to God. 2 How near is **God** to us. 3 How close the ending of the dream of sin, and the redemption of the Son of God.

Notes to Lesson #344

Today I learn the law of love; that what
I give my brother is my gift to me.

Comment: The law of God is that to give is to receive. Therefore, this law of love states that what you give to your brother is truly a gift to yourself. The ego believes in a zero-sum game so if someone is to win, another must lose. Because of this erroneous belief, the ego only gives to get so whenever the ego gives something, it wants a good deal in return. The ego seeks to obtain something that it perceives to be of greater value than what it must relinquish in exchange.

Because of the ego's belief in lack, limitation and separation, the ego can only offer illusions in exchange for your happiness. Illusions are not real and can only bring conflict, pain and suffering to those who have forgotten their true Identity. Your big "S" Self knows that God's Son cannot be content with being anything less than as God created him, perfect, whole and complete, an indivisible part of the One Self.

LESSON 345

I offer only miracles today,
For I would have them be returned to me.

I offer only miracles today, for I would have **the miracles** be returned to me.

W-345.1. <Father, a miracle reflects **God's** gifts to me, Your Son. 2 And every **miracle** I give returns to me, reminding me the law of love, **what I give my brother is my gift to myself,** is universal. 3 Even here, **the law of love that what I give my brother is my gift to myself** takes a form which can be recognized and seen to work. 4 The miracles I give are given back in just the form I need to help me with the problems I perceive. 5 Father, in Heaven it is different, for there, there are no needs **and therefore miracles are not needed**. 6 But here on earth, the miracle is closer to Your gifts than any other gift that I can give. 7 Then let me give this gift **of the miracle** alone today, which, born of true forgiveness, lights the way that I must travel to remember **God**.>

W-345.2.Peace to all seeking hearts today. 2 The light has come to offer miracles to bless the tired world. 3 **This tired world** will find rest today, for we will offer **the world the miracles we** have received.

Notes to Lesson #345

I offer only miracles today,
For I would have them be returned to me.

Comment: On earth, in time and space, we need miracles because we have misperceptions that arise from our lack of knowledge. A miracle is a change and correction of our ego's false perception. In heaven, which is the realm of knowledge, there is no perception and nothing that needs to be corrected since truth just is.

When you give forgiveness to yourself or another, you are changing your misperception that there are outside forces that can rob you of your own inner peace or make you happy. The miracle that you give to another is returned in just the right form so that you resolve your own perceived problems which reduce your fear and restore your inner peace.

The miracle is God's gift that you can give another here on earth. The miracle offers a different way to perceive their world. God's gift of grace allows one to perceive God's love in a world of seeming hate and fear. When you give forgiveness to another, you grant them the opportunity to perceive mercy and love in a world of seeming hate and fear. The miracle of the law of love is that when you give to another, the miracle is always returned onto you.

Today the peace of God envelops me,
And I forget all things except His Love.

Today the peace of God envelops me, and I forget all things except **God's** Love.

W-346.1. <Father, I wake today with miracles correcting my **egoic** perception of all things. 2 And so begins the day I share with **God** as I will share eternity **with God**, for time has stepped aside today. 3 I do not seek the things of time, and so I will not look upon **the things time seeks**. 4 What I seek today transcends all laws of time and things perceived in time. 5 I would forget all things except **God's** Love. 6 I would abide in **God**, and know no laws except **God's** law of love **which is that what I give my brother is my gift to me**. 7 And I would find the peace which **God** created for **God's** Son, forgetting all the foolish toys I made as I behold **God's** glory and my own **glory as my true big "S" Self**.>

W-346.2.And when the evening comes today, we will remember nothing but the peace of God. 2 For we will learn today what peace is ours, when we forget all things except God's Love.

Notes to Lesson #346

Today the peace of God envelops me,
And I forget all things except His Love.

Comment: Love transcends time since only love is real. Realize that in time, the law of God that to give is to receive still applies. Remember that on earth, the law of love supersedes the ego's law that claims that when you give, you lose. The law of love disagrees and states that what you give your brother is the gift you give to yourself.

Choose to see God's love in all events. When you do, you can elect to give and share the miracle's change in perception with your brothers. God's love transcends all things, including time. Forget your ego's thought system and its belief in lack, limitation and separation. Instead, accept the love of God and experience and extend the peace of God that is your destiny.

LESSON 347

Anger must come from judgment.
Judgment is the weapon I would use against myself
To keep the miracle away from me.

W-347.1. <Father, I **egoically** want what goes against my **true** will, and **my ego does** not want what is my **true** will to have. 2 Straighten my mind, my Father. 3 **My split mind** is sick. 4 But You have offered freedom, and I choose to claim Your gift **of freedom** today. 5 And so I give all judgment to the **Holy Spirit that God** gave to me to judge for me. 6 The Holy Spirit sees what I behold, and yet **the Holy Spirit** knows the truth. 7 The Holy Spirit looks on pain, and yet **the Holy Spirit** understands **pain** is not real, and in **the Holy Spirit's** understanding **pain** is healed. 8 **The Holy Spirit** gives the miracles my **ego's** dreams would hide from my awareness. 9 Let **the Holy Spirit** judge today. 10 I do not know my **true** will, but **the Holy Spirit** is sure **my true will** is **God's** Own **Will**. 11 And **the Holy Spirit** will speak for me, and call **God's** miracles to come to me.>

W-347.2.Listen today. 2 Be very still, and hear the **Holy Spirit's** gentle Voice for God assuring you that **God** has judged you as the Son **God** loves.

Notes to Lesson #347

Anger must come from judgment.
Judgment is the weapon I would use against myself
To keep the miracle away from me.

Comment: Anger comes from judgment and your egoic judgments block the miracle from appearing within your split mind as an available option. Your ego's judgments drive you into attack mode as it proclaims that your anger and attacks are justified as an act of self-defense. When you attack another, you attack yourself. Your anger and judgments are self-crucifixion and only disempower your own mind.

Because your ego does not know your true Identity, your ego is incapable of judging anything correctly. Give all your experiences over to the Holy Spirit Who knows the truth about your real identity as your big "S" Self. Only the Holy Spirit knows the truth and has the big picture to judge correctly. The Holy Spirit knows that your true will is God's Will. God's Will proclaims His Creation to be innocent, guiltless and without sin. Trust and let the Holy Spirit be your guide and judge. The Holy Spirit cannot fail in His mission to bring you home.

LESSON 348

I have no cause for anger or for fear,
For You surround me. And in every need
That I perceive Your grace suffices me.

I have no cause for anger or for fear for **God surrounds** me. And in every need that I perceive, **God's** grace suffices me.

W-348.1. <Father, let me remember You are here, and I am not alone. 2 Surrounding me is **God's** everlasting Love. 3 I have no cause for anything except the perfect peace and joy I share with **God**. 4 What need have I for anger or for fear? 5 Surrounding me is **God's** perfect safety. 6 Can I be afraid, when **God's** eternal promise goes with me? 7 Surrounding me is perfect sinlessness. 8 What can I fear, when **God** created me in holiness as perfect as **God's** Own **Holiness**?>

W-348.2.God's grace suffices us in everything that **God** would have us do. 2 And only that we choose to be our will as well as **God's Will**.

Notes to Lesson #348

I have no cause for anger or for fear,
For You surround me. And in every need
That I perceive Your grace suffices me.

Comment: It is only your ego's judgmental mind that causes you to experience anger and fear. Turn the events of your day over to the Holy Spirit and follow Its guidance. God has never abandoned you. God's grace allows you to accept God's love in a world of seeming hate and fear. Release your ego's judgment and know that you rest in God's love.

When you allow God to live as you, you recognize that the will of your true big "S" Self is one with God's Will. God's love envelops you and all the power of the Mind of God dwells in you. When you drop your ego's plan for your salvation, you realize that God's grace provides all you need.

Egoically, you need do nothing. Your ego's plans only end in pain and can never bring you safety or happiness. Only God's plan will work. God surrounds you in perfect peace and safety and walks with you. When you drop your ego's judgments, there is nothing left to fear.

Today I let Christ's vision look upon
All things for me and judge them not, but give
Each one a miracle of love instead.

Today I let Christ's vision look upon all things for me and judge **all things** not, but give each **thing I see** a miracle of love instead.

W-349.1. <**By giving the miracle of love to all things I see,** so would I liberate all things I see, and give to **all I see** the freedom that I seek. 2 For thus **by giving the miracle of love to all things I see** do I obey the law of love, and give what I would find and make my own. 3 **The miracle** will be given me, because I have chosen **the miracle** as the gift I want to give. 4 Father, Your gifts are mine. 5 Each **of God's gifts** that I accept gives me a miracle to give. 6 And giving as I would receive, I learn **God's** healing miracles belong to me.>

W-349.2.Our Father knows our needs. 2 **God** gives us grace to meet all **our needs**. 3 And so we trust in **God** to send us miracles to bless the world, and heal our minds as we return to **God**.

Notes to Lesson #349

Today I let Christ's vision look upon
All things for me and judge them not, but give
Each one a miracle of love instead.

Comment: Christ vision does not judge but instead looks upon all through the eyes of forgiveness and love. The law of love tells us that what you seek to find is what you should give to another. Allow the Holy Spirit to reframe your ego's judgments about your world .You can deliberately choose to give the miracle of love and forgiveness instead of your ego's judgments and condemnation. When you realize that what you give, you will receive, it becomes insanity to do anything else.

LESSON 350

Miracles mirror God's eternal Love.
To offer them is to remember Him,
And through His memory to save the world.

Miracles mirror God's eternal Love. To offer **miracles** is to remember **God**, and through **God's** memory to save the world.

W-350.1. <What we forgive becomes a part of us, as we perceive ourselves **to be.** 2 The Son of God incorporates all things within himself as **God** created **the Son of God**. 3 Your memory **of God and your true Identity as your big "S" Self** depends on **the** forgiveness **you bestow upon the Son of God as you perceive him to be**. 4 What **the Son of God** is, is unaffected by his **split mind's** thoughts. 5 But what **your mind perceives and** looks upon is **the** direct result **of your mind's thoughts**. 6 Therefore, my Father, I would turn to You. 7 Only **the** memory **of God** will set me free. 8 And only my forgiveness teaches me to let **God's** memory return to me, and give **God's memory** to the world in thankfulness.>

W-350.2.And as we gather miracles from **God** we will indeed be grateful. 2 For as we remember **God, God's** Son will be restored to us in the reality of Love.

Notes to Lesson #350

Miracles mirror God's eternal Love.
To offer them is to remember Him,
And through His memory to save the world.

Comment: Your egoic mind judges and makes an ego for everything that it perceives. Because of this, your mind has created its own version of what God's Son should be. It is your ego's version, not the reality of God's Son that your mind will perceive.

Although your thoughts cannot change the reality of what God created, your ego's judgments and misperceptions act as a filter for what the mind is willing to allow you to perceive as your provisional reality. Your provisional reality belongs to the world of perception, not knowledge. Perception follows your thinking. Without forgiveness, your mind will remain stuck in your past egoic judgments and misperceptions. Forgiveness allows you to escape your past beliefs and thus, create a different future.

What we forgive becomes a part of us. When we drop our past judgments, our mind is open to a new way of thinking. When we give the miracle of corrected perception to another, we receive that same miracle. We need to realize that we have already been the everywhere and every when in the dance of separation and therefore, can now choose to be the Christ. Forgiveness allows each to be or imagine whatever they wish with the realization that each remains part of the indivisible shared Mind of God. No one is made wrong because of the part they have chosen to play in the harmless yet informative game of <u>What Am I.</u>

Our egoic judgments block the memory of God from our current awareness. These judgments block and obscure our true identity from our mind's awareness. Forgiveness restores the memory of the truth that we alone are responsible for what we choose to call into our awareness. What we are cannot be affected by our ego's misperceptions and judgments.

With Christ vision, the miracle transforms your ego's fearful misperceptions into correct perception. Forgive yourself for not knowing that it was your judgments that created the hell you perceive to be your provisional reality. You were only the victim of your own mind's imaginings. When you forgive, you empower yourself and can then stop arguing for the limitations of the little "s" self. You allow the memory of God to reawaken you to the truth and now can reclaim your divine birthright for yourself and your world.

What Am I?

Covers ACIM Workbook Lessons 351-360

14. What Am I?

W-pII.14.1. <I am God's Son, complete and healed and whole, shining in the reflection of **God's** Love. 2 In me is **God's** creation sanctified and guaranteed eternal life. 3 In me is love perfected, fear impossible, and joy established without opposite. 4 I am the holy home of God Himself. 5 I am the Heaven where **God's** Love resides. 6 I am **God's** holy Sinlessness Itself, for in my purity abides **God's** Own **purity.**>

W-pII.14.2.Our use for words is almost over now. 2 Yet in the final days of this one year we gave to God together, you and I, **Jesus** ,we found a single purpose that we shared. 3 And thus you joined with me, so what I am are you as well. 4 The truth of what we are is not for words to speak of nor describe. 5 Yet we can realize our function here, and words can speak of **our function** and teach **what we are**, too, if we exemplify the words in us.

W-pII.14.3.We are the bringers of salvation. 2 We accept our part as saviors of the world, which through our joint forgiveness **the world** is redeemed. 3 And this **joint forgiveness of our world is** our gift **and** is therefore given **back to** us. 4 We look on everyone as brother, and perceive all things as kindly and as good. 5 We do not seek a function that is past the gate of Heaven. 6 Knowledge will return when we have done our part **and forgiven our world**. 7 We are concerned only with giving welcome to the truth.

W-pII.14.4.Ours are the eyes through which Christ's vision sees a world redeemed from every thought of sin. 2 Ours are the ears that hear the **Holy Spirit, the** Voice for God, proclaim the world as sinless. 3 Ours the minds that join together as we bless the world. 4 And from the oneness that we have attained we call to all our brothers, asking **all our brothers** to share our peace and consummate our joy.

W-pII.14.5.We are the holy messengers of God who speak for **God**, and carrying **God's** Word to everyone whom **God** has sent to us, we learn that **God's word** is written on our hearts. 2 And thus our minds are changed about the aim for which we came, and which we seek to serve. 3 We bring glad tidings to the Son of God, who thought he suffered. 4 Now is **the Son of God** redeemed. 5 And as **the redeemed Son of God** sees the gate of Heaven stand open before him, **the Son of God** will enter in and disappear into the Heart of God.

Notes to Special Theme #14: What AM I?

Covers ACIM Workbook Lessons 351-360

In truth, there is just the One Self. You are an indivisible part of that One. The Father is Cause. The Son is the Father's Effect. The Holy Spirit is the link that connects the two sides of one indivisible coin called God. There is no separation for in that Trinity there is just a Oneness of All That Is.

Yet, within our split minds that perceive rather than know, we think in terms of duality and therefore, see ourselves as God's Creation, an Effect of the Thought of God. As such, you are God's Son, complete, healed and whole. You are a reflection of God's eternal love. In you, love is perfected, fear impossible and joy established without opposite. You are the completion of God.

As the Christ, you are perfect, whole and complete. You are the home of God, holy and sinless as God Himself. In time, you help the Holy Spirit reawaken sleeping minds that currently look upon a sinful world that requires redemption. Through your forgiveness, you save your world. Through your forgiveness, you reawaken sleeping minds to the truth that they, like you, are the Christ.

We are the messengers of God and speak for God with love in our hearts. We have changed our egoic mind from fear-based thinking to the realization that we are only love. Now, endowed with the vision of Christ, we see the world free of all thoughts of sin and recognize everything as kind and good. In time, we are the bringers of salvation. Yet, in Heaven, we will disappear into the heart of God and remain eternally one with the indivisible One Self.

In time, our purpose is to change our world of perception from a witness for the false to a witness for the truth. Because of our minds' erroneous beliefs about the existence of lack, limitation, sin and separation, our minds have created a false ego for everything that it envisions. Time allows us to correct those erroneous beliefs about ourselves and our world. Since time provides us the opportunity to change our minds, we can now deliberately choose to see all God's creations as innocent, sinless and forever one with God. God and the Holy Spirit know the world as sinless. Who are we to argue with God and defend our mind's belief in fear?

Fear arises any time we believe that we lack the creative power to handle a given situation. Whenever we fail to answer either of the following two questions correctly, fear will raise its ugly head.

The first question is. What am I?

The second question is. What do I value and why?

Previously, we discussed the second question. What do I value and why? We said that the miracle temporarily corrects your mind's mistaken answers to either of the two above questions. The Holy Spirit uses the miracle to reframe your misperception and move your mind from victim consciousness to responsibility consciousness and the truth.

Obviously, if you fail to see yourself as Christ, perfect, whole and complete, you have answered the first question, what am I, incorrectly. Because of this, you will find yourself in a state of constant fear.

When you perceive that you are a limited ego-body with needs, you will value something because you will believe that obtaining that item will make or improve your safety, survival or happiness. As long as an item is perceived to be something outside of your mind's control, you will continue to see yourself as a victim.

In the illusion of time, you have come here to reawaken to the truth that you are not the body but are free. You are still as God created you, part of the indivisible One Self. Nothing sources your individuated experience but you and nothing has the ability to rob you of your inner peace unless you choose to allow it. In time and space, your mind rules your world of perception.

In this playschool of time, you are an infinite focus of consciousness. You are a feedback loop that can witness the effects of the choices that you are making in the depth of your mind that rests within the Mind of God. Therefore, each thought is a vibration of creation to communicate to the world in an attempt to experience communion with all life. This feedback loop provides the learning experiences that you desire.

In reality you are perfect spirit, unaffected by anything. You have been given the full power to choose and to create your experiences as you would have them be. You are not the egoic part of your mind that perceives itself to be a little "s" self. Instead, you are 100% responsible for your feelings and all that you call into your awareness. Your mind gives all the meaning to your world through its power of interpretation.

You are the creator of your world of perception. You are the decision-maker that determines what you desire to call into your awareness. You write the mental program that determines the beliefs that will govern how you will interact with life.

You, as decision-maker, ask the question, "What am I?" You, as the decision-maker then fill in the answer. The answer to the question, "What am I?" forms the basis for your beliefs that become the thought system which governs and limits what you believe you are and how you are capable of relating to your world.

Your ego is your current answer to the question, what am I. The ego, like a computer, can only run programs. A computer has no power to write the program. Yet, when we choose to forget that our mind originally decided to write the program that became our ego, it will appear as if our mind is powerless to control our experiences.

It will seem as if you are a victim of outside powers that are beyond your mind's control. Yet, these experiences are the natural effect of which mental programs you choose to write and run. You have just failed to remember that your mind writes, holds, runs and projects the images that comprise your private world of individuated perception.

These images seem to be caused by some mysterious external force. Yet, it is your mind that is projecting these images. It is the same mind that forgot it ran the program that also made the observation. Forgetting that your mind is the computer operator, it appears that the events being viewed on the screen of consciousness have no relationship with your mind. You now believe that you can only respond to what you observe on the screen of consciousness rather than simply choosing to run a different program.

By deciding to forget that you control the mental input, your faulty memory leads you into victim consciousness. Only when you remember that you are the decision-maker can you realize that you also have the power to choose differently. You can choose differently by deciding to stop arguing for your littleness and instead follow the guidance of the Holy Spirit Who knows the correct answer to the question, what am I.

Why not make that decision today?

My sinless brother is my guide to peace.
My sinful brother is my guide to pain.
And which I choose to see I will behold.

W-351.1. <Who is my brother but **God's** holy Son? 2 And if I see **God's Son as** sinful, I proclaim myself a sinner, not a Son of God; alone and friendless in a fearful world. 3 Yet this perception is a choice I make, and can relinquish **this misperception for correct perception**. 4 I can also see my brother sinless, as **God's** holy Son. 5 And with this choice I see my sinlessness, my everlasting Comforter and Friend beside me, and my way secure and clear. 6 Choose, then, for me, my Father, through Your Voice, **the Holy Spirit**. 7 For **the Holy Spirit** alone gives judgment in **God's** Name.>

Notes to Lesson #351

My sinless brother is my guide to peace.
My sinful brother is my guide to pain.
And which I choose to see I will behold.

<u>Comment</u>: Perception is a choice, not a fact. Although your thoughts cannot change the truth, your thoughts control and affect what your mind allows your senses to observe and call into your awareness. Your thoughts are the causative power behind your perception that manifests as your experiences.

Your egoic beliefs are the filters for your split mind. What you believe and desire to observe in your outer world is a product of your own mind's projections. Through projection, you can observe whatever you wish for projection makes perception.

Since perception is your own mind's choice, you can deliberately choose to see your brother as either a sinner or a savior. Your thinking is the cause and your feelings are the effect of your own thoughts. When you are in victim consciousness, you get to blame another for how you feel and think. You get to claim that it is not your fault and that someone else has made you feel that way since you are not responsible for your world.

When you accept responsibility for your own thinking, you realize that nothing outside your own mind can make you happy or sad. This empowering thought makes your mind the ruler of your world of private individuated perception. Responsibility consciousness allows your mind to deliberately choose what you will behold.

LESSON 352

Judgment and love are opposites. From one
Come all the sorrows of the world. But from
The other comes the peace of God Himself.

Judgment and love are opposites. From **judgment** comes all the sorrows of the world. But from the other, **which is love,** comes the peace of God Himself.

W-352.1. <Forgiveness looks on sinlessness alone, and judges not. 2 Through **forgiveness** I come to **God**. 3 Judgment will bind my eyes and make me blind. 4 Yet love, reflected in forgiveness here, reminds me, **God has** given me a way to find **God's** peace again. 5 I am redeemed when I elect to follow in this way **of forgiveness**. 6 **God** has not left me comfortless. 7 I have within me both the memory of **God** and **the Holy Spirit** Who leads me to **the memory of God**. 8 Father, I would hear **the Holy Spirit's** Voice and find **God's** peace today. 9 For I would love my own Identity **as my big "S" Self**, and find in **my big "S" Self's Identity** the memory of **God**.>

Notes to Lesson #352

Judgment and love are opposites. From one
Come all the sorrows of the world. But from
The other comes the peace of God Himself.

<u>Comment</u>: Judgment and love are opposites. Judgment is thinking in fear. Forgiveness is thinking with love. Thinking is always the cause and our feelings are our thought's effect. To judge is to see sin in yourself or another. To Love is to see sinlessness.

From judgment comes all the sorrows of the world but from love comes the peace of God. Forgiveness looks upon the sinless and does not judge. Through forgiveness, Jesus comes to us. Judgment binds us to the ego's fear-based thought system and blocks our awareness of the Holy Spirit, our big "S" Self and the memory of God.

Our true reality is that we create the world of our perception. You can change the purpose of what you have come here to witness. Your ego would have you witness for the sinfulness of our brother and yourself. Yet, you can use this world to witness for God's love through your acts of forgiveness.

When we speak of forgiveness as defined by A Course in Miracles, we are really proclaiming our brother is sinless. We are accepting the fact that we are the writer and director for our own experiences. We alone have the power of interpretation for our own experiences. We are not the victims of powers beyond the control of our own mind.

Our ego's goal is to prove our brother's sinfulness. Yet, our egoic judgments only crucify us and bring us pain. Choose to drop your ego's right to judge and instead, turn all your experiences over to the Holy Spirit. Only the Holy Spirit knows the truth and has the big picture. Only the Holy Spirit can judge correctly. By following the Holy Spirit's guidance, your forgiving mind will restore your inner peace.

LESSON 353

My eyes, my tongue, my hands, my feet today
Have but one purpose; to be given Christ
To use to bless the world with miracles.

W-353.1. <Father, I give all that is mine today to Christ, to use in any way that best will serve the purpose that I share with **Christ**. 2 Nothing is mine alone, for **Christ** and I have joined in purpose. 3 Thus has learning come almost to learning's appointed end **in time**. 4 A while I work with **Christ** to serve **Christ's** purpose. 5 Then I lose myself in my **big "S" Self's** Identity, and recognize that Christ is but my **big "S"** Self.>

Notes to Lesson #353

My eyes, my tongue, my hands, my feet today
Have but one purpose; to be given Christ
To use to bless the world with miracles.

Comment: Your body is a servant of your mind. The body is a neutral communication device that responds to your thoughts. Turn over your thoughts to the Holy Spirit for your egoic mind is insane and does not know who you are. Depending on whose guidance you will follow, your thoughts will witness for either the truth or fantasy; love or fear.

Your true big "S" Self is one with Christ and the Holy Spirit. All share the one goal of seeing a sinless world and bearing witness to the truth of the Son of God's innocence and sinless reality.

Give the game token that you call your body over to the Holy Spirit to be utilized as the Holy Spirit deems fit. When you follow the Holy Spirit's thought system, your body becomes a communication device to teach love and forgiveness. Your body will now be a tool to witness for the truth. Your body will take its orders from the mind of Christ, your big "S" Self.

**We stand together, Christ and I, in peace
And certainty of purpose. And in Him
Is His Creator, as He is in me.**

We stand together, Christ and I, in peace and certainty of purpose. And in **Christ** is **God**, **Christ's** Creator, as **God** is in me.

W-354.1. <My oneness with the Christ establishes me as **God's** Son, beyond the reach of time, and wholly free of every law but **God's Law**. 2 I have no self except the Christ in me. 3 I have no purpose but **Christ's** Own **purpose**. 4 And **Christ** is like His Father. 5 Thus must I be one with **God, My Creator** as well as **one with Christ**. 6 For who is Christ except **God's** Son as **God** created **His Son**? 7 And what am I except the Christ in me?>

Notes to Lesson #354

**We stand together, Christ and I, in peace
And certainty of purpose. And in Him
Is His Creator, as He is in me.**

<u>Comment</u>: Christ, your big "S" Self, the Holy Spirit, and God, the Father, are all One. They share one indivisible mind with one purpose, which is to be only love. There is no separation but only the one indivisible Mind of God.

When you witness for the Christ, you witness for the sinlessness of God's Son. To see this world as sinless is to utilize the vision of Christ and be unconditional love which alone allows and grants freedom to all. You, as Christ, share God's purpose and goal of being and extending only love.

We are joined beyond time and rest in truth. Even in time, only God's law applies to you, God's Son. The fear-based laws of this world only seem to apply when the egoic mind denies its union with the One Self.

When you see yourself as Christ, you witness for God living you. Your true reality is that you are only Christ and therefore, you remain as God created you. Since creation is the extension of God, Itself, you are the one shared Mind of God.

LESSON 355

**There is no end to all the peace and joy,
And all the miracles that I will give,
When I accept God's Word. Why not today?**

There is no end to all the peace and joy, and all the miracles that I will give when I accept God's Word. Why not **accept God's Word** today?

W-355.1. <Why should I wait, my Father, for the joy **that God has** promised me? 2 For **God** will keep **His** Word **that God** gave **His** Son in exile. 3 I am sure my treasure waits for me, and I need but reach out my hand to find **the treasure that God has given me**. 4 Even now my fingers touch **the treasure that God has given me**. 5 **The treasure that God has given me** is very close. 6 I need not wait an instant more to be at peace forever. 7 It is **God** I choose and my Identity as my **big "S" Self** along with **God**. 8 Your Son would be **His big "S" Self** and know **God** as his Father and Creator, and his Love.>

Notes to Lesson #355

**There is no end to all the peace and joy,
And all the miracles that I will give,
When I accept God's Word. Why not today?**

<u>Comment</u>: God's Will is that you be happy but when will you accept that fact? When you freely decide that your will is the same as God's Will, you will be ready to reclaim your divine birthright.

God's law is that to give is to receive. When you give the same gift of forgiveness to your sinless brother, you will be ready to accept the At-One-Ment for yourself. The miracle of forgiveness must be shared with all.

As the Christ, miracles are your divine birthright. Give the miracle of forgiveness to your brother. Through the gift of miracles, you partake in the creative process of using time to help reawaken sleeping minds to the truth of what they really are.

Sickness is but another name for sin.
Healing is but another name for God.
The miracle is thus a call to Him.

Sickness is but another name for sin. Healing is but another name for God. The miracle is thus a call to **God.**

W-356.1. <Father, You promised **God** would never fail to answer any call **God's** Son might make to **God**. 2 It does not matter where **God's Son** is, what seems to be his problem, nor what **God's Son** believes he has become. 3 He is Your Son, and You will answer him. 4 The miracle reflects Your Love, and thus, **the miracle** answers **God's Son**. 5 **God's** Name replaces every thought of sin, and who is sinless cannot suffer pain. 6 **God's** Name gives answer to **God's** Son, because to call **God's** Name is but to call **upon the Son's** own **name.**>

Notes to Lesson #356

Sickness is but another name for sin.
Healing is but another name for God.
The miracle is thus a call to Him.

Comment: Sickness is another name for sin since both come from your belief in lack. Healing is the recognition of the Truth and thus, God and Truth are synonymous. The miracle is a call for Truth and thus, a call to God.

The laws of God rule everywhere, even in an illusion. Even if you believe that you are Adolf Hitler and in hell, if you call to God, God will answer. You can remember the truth even in the middle of a dream. All experiences are stepping stones placed by God and the Holy Spirit to bring you back to the truth of what you really are. In truth, there is no gap between God, your brother and yourself for there is only the One Self.

LESSON 357

Truth answers every call we make to God,
Responding first with miracles, and then
Returning unto us to be itself.

Truth answers every call we make to God, responding first with miracles, and then truth responds by returning unto us to be **Truth,** itself.

W-357.1. <Forgiveness, truth's reflection, tells me how to offer miracles, and thus escape the prison house in which I think I live. 2 Your holy Son is pointed out to me, first in my brother **and** then **God's holy Son is pointed out** in me. 3 Your Voice, **the Holy Spirit,** instructs me patiently to hear **God's** Word, and give as I receive. 4 And as I look upon Your Son today, I hear Your Voice instructing me to find the way to **God** as **God** appointed that the way shall be: 5 "Behold **God's Son's** sinlessness, and be you healed.">

Notes to Lesson #357

Truth answers every call we make to God,
Responding first with miracles, and then
Returning unto us to be itself.

Comment: Truth answers every call you make to God for God is Truth. In time, Truth is first reflected in miracles. A miracle is a change in your perception from fear to love and forgiveness. Forgiveness is the recognition of the sinlessness of your brother, which of course, reflects the truth.

You, as the dreamer, are the creator of your own experiences. When you recognize your brother is a mere actor in your play, you reflect the truth within your own provisional reality. Forgiveness reflects the truth and tells us how to perform miracles. With Christ vision, you can now see the sinlessness in all.

When you see your brother as sinless, you, yourself, are healed. Forgiveness is the key to escaping the illusion of your little "s" self and returning to the truth of your big "S" Self, the Christ.

**No call to God can be unheard nor left
Unanswered. And of this I can be sure;
His answer is the one I really want.**

No call to God can be unheard nor left unanswered. And of this I can be sure; **God's** answer is the one **answer** I really want.

W-358.1. <You, **the Holy Spirit,** Who remember what I really am alone remember what I really want. 2 **The Holy Spirit** speaks for God, and so **the Holy Spirit** speaks for me. 3 And what **the Holy Spirit** gives me comes from God Himself. 4 **The Holy Spirit's** Voice, my Father, then is mine as well, and all I want is what **God** offers me, in just the form **God** chooses that it be mine. 5 Let me remember all I do not know, and let my voice be still, remembering. 6 But let me not forget **God's** Love and care, keeping **God's** promise to **God's** Son in my awareness always. 7 Let me not forget **my little "s" self** is nothing, but my **big "S"** Self is all.>

Notes to Lesson #358

**No call to God can be unheard nor left
Unanswered. And of this I can be sure;
His answer is the one I really want.**

Comment: Our true nature is that of our big "S" Self. We are the Christ and therefore, we only truly want God's Will. In this single purpose of allowing God to live us, we find true peace, joy and happiness. The Holy Spirit will lead us to that realization and answer all our calls.

Our egos do not know anything and constantly mistake illusions for reality. Our egoic mind has imagined a false little "s" self that is an illusion of nothingness. Littleness cannot be what God created as His Son. God created us as an extension of Himself. Our big "S" Self, the Christ, is part of the shared Mind of God and is everything. Your ego can do nothing but your Christ nature, being of God, can do all.

LESSON 359

**God's answer is some form of peace. All pain
Is healed; all misery replaced with joy.
All prison doors are opened. And all sin
Is understood as merely a mistake.**

W-359.1. <Father, today we will forgive Your world, and let creation be **God's** Own **rather than what our egos would misperceive God's creations to be**. 2 We **with our egoic minds** have misunderstood all things. 3 But **our egoic minds** have not made sinners of the holy Sons of God. 4 What **God** created sinless so abides forever and forever. 5 Such are we, **God's sinless creation**. 6 And we rejoice to learn that we have made mistakes which have no real effects on us. 7 Sin is impossible, and on this fact **that sin is impossible** forgiveness rests upon a certain base more solid than the shadow world we see. 8 Help us forgive, for we would be redeemed. 9 Help us forgive, for we would be at peace.>

Notes to Lesson #359

**God's answer is some form of peace. All pain
Is healed; all misery replaced with joy.
All prison doors are opened. And all sin
Is understood as merely a mistake.**

Comment: No harm can result from a dream that has no ability to change reality. Mistakes are not sins that require punishment. Mistakes only call for correction. Your ego has mistaken its false imaginings to be your reality. Only within the dreamer's own mind, the illusion of separation appears to be real. Yet, what has no effect is nothing. The mind that sleeps only needs to awaken and once again remember the truth.

Our egoic mind clings to its desire to make the false appear real imagining a world based on its belief in sin, guilt and fear. It argues that we are separate from God, have sinned and have lost Paradise. This belief that sin is real keeps us trapped in the prison of our own unforgiving egoic minds.

eliefs and judgments about yourself, your brother, your world and your God are mistakes that need correction. ʾns that demand punishment and condemnation. Your ego's erroneous judgments cannot change the truth and ᵤs.

ᵤᵤ fails to understand that an unforgiving mind only crucifies yourself. When you condemn another, you, as their jailer ɾequired to remain in the prison of your mind to guard against their escape. Through forgiveness, you realize that mistakes only require correction, not punishment. You can now recognize that the game of <u>What Am I</u> is a Playschool for your reawakening to the truth of what you really are. Because of forgiveness, your split mind can now heal itself.

LESSON 360

Peace be to me, the holy Son of God.
Peace to my brother, who is one with me.
Let all the world be blessed with peace through us.

W-360.1. <Father, it is Your peace that I would give, receiving the **peace** of **God**. 2 I am Your Son, forever just as **God** created me, for the Great Rays remain forever still and undisturbed within me. 3 I would reach to **the Great Rays** in silence and in certainty, for nowhere else can certainty be found. 4 Peace be to me, and peace to all the world. 5 In holiness were we created, and in holiness do we remain. 6 Your Son is like to You in perfect sinlessness. 7 And with this thought **that Your Son is sinless like God,** we gladly say "Amen.">

Notes to Lesson #360

Peace be to me, the holy Son of God.
Peace to my brother, who is one with me.
Let all the world be blessed with peace through us.

<u>Comment</u>: Certainty lies in the fact that you remain as God created you. You are unlimited spirit. You are light, a great ray of the Mind of God. In the act of your creation, your safety, happiness, joy and peace are insured. The separation is not real for you belong to the indivisible One Self.

When you choose to deliberately see a sinless world, your world of perception will be at peace. You will be ready to remember God and go home.

Introduction to Workbook Lessons # 361 to-365

W.fl.in.1.Our final lessons will be left as free of words as possible. 2 We use **words** but at the beginning of our practicing, and only to remind us that we seek to go beyond **words**. 3 Let us turn to **the Holy Spirit** Who leads the way and makes our footsteps sure. 4 To **the Holy Spirit** we leave these lessons, as to **the Holy Spirit** we give our lives henceforth. 5 For we would not return again to the **ego's** belief in sin that made the world seem ugly and unsafe, attacking and destroying, dangerous in all **the world's fear-based** ways, and treacherous beyond the hope of trust and the escape from pain.

W.fl.in.2.**The Holy Spirit** is the only way to find the peace that God has given us. 2 It is **the Holy Spirit's** way that everyone must travel in the end **to reach the peace of God**, because it is this **peaceful** ending God Himself appointed. 3 In the dream of time **the Holy Spirit's way** seems to be far off. 4 And yet, in truth, **the Holy Spirit's way** is already here; already serving us as gracious guidance in the way to go **toward peace**. 5 Let us together follow in the way that truth points out to us. 6 And let us be the leaders of our many brothers who are seeking for the way **of the Holy Spirit**, but find it not.

W.fl.in.3.And to this purpose **of following and leading in the Holy Spirit's way** let us dedicate our minds, directing all our thoughts to serve the function of salvation. 2 Unto us the aim is given to forgive the world. 3 **Forgiveness of the world** is the goal that God has given us. 4 **Forgiveness of the world** is **God's** ending to the dream we seek, and not **the dream ending in** our own **ego's condemnation of ourselves and the world**. 5 For all that we forgive we will not fail to recognize as part of God Himself. 6 And thus **God's** memory is given back, completely and complete.

W.fl.in.4.It is our function to remember **God** on earth, as **our function** is given us to be **God's** Own completion in reality. 2 So let us not forget our goal **of completing God that** is shared, for it is that remembrance which contains the memory of God, and points the way to **God** and to the Heaven of **the peace of God**. 3 And shall we not forgive our brother, who can offer this **completion and remembrance of God** to us? 4 **Our brother** is the way, the truth and life that shows the way to us. 5 In **our brother** resides salvation. **Salvation is** offered us through our forgiveness, given unto **our brother**.

W.fl.in.5.We will not end this year without the gift our Father promised to His holy Son. 2 We are forgiven now. 3 And we are saved from all the wrath we thought belonged to God, and found **the wrath of God** was a dream. 4 We are restored to sanity, in which we understand that anger is insane, attack is mad, and vengeance merely foolish fantasy. 5 We have been saved from wrath because we learned **our egoic mind was** mistaken. 6 Nothing more than that **for mistakes are not sins**. 7 And is a father angry at his son because **the son** failed to understand the truth **about his sinless and innocent reality**?

W.fl.in.6.We come in honesty to God and say we did not understand **the truth** and ask **God** to help us to learn **God's** lessons **for truth**, through the Voice of **God's** Own Teacher, **the Holy Spirit**. 2 Would **God** hurt His Son? 3 Or would **God** rush to answer **His Son**, and say, "This is My Son, and all I have is his"? 4 Be certain **God** will answer thus, for these are **God's** Own words to you **that all God has, has been given eternally to you**. 5 And more than **the all that God has given you** can no one ever have, for in these words is all there is, and all that there will be throughout all time and in eternity.

Note to Final Lessons

Note to Introduction to Final Lessons # 361 to365

Follow the guidance of the Holy Spirit for this is the only way one can find the peace of God. Your ego is clueless as to the truth and has mistaken the dream of lack, limitation and separation to be your reality. Instead, give all your thoughts over to the Holy Spirit and focus upon the salvation of your brother. Since the Law of God states that to give is to receive, by recognizing our brother's sinless nature, we reawaken to our own true nature as our big "S" Self.

Our aim is to forgive the world that our ego imagines. In time, forgiveness is the function and goal God has given us to fulfill. All that we forgive is recognized as part of God and therefore, through our forgiveness of our world we remember God. Our function is to remember God on earth and through this remembrance complete the reality of God. Grace is the acceptance of the love of God in a world of seeming hate and fear. Through our forgiveness, we transform the fear-based world of egoic misperception into a world of forgiveness, mercy and love.

Our salvation rests in our brother's salvation. When we forgive our brother we realize that God's wrath existed only within the nightmare of our egoic mind's imagination. We have always remained as God created us, perfect, whole and complete, part of the One Self. We understand that anger is insane, attack madness and vengeance a foolish fantasy. Following our ego's fear-based thought system has only brought pain, conflict and self-condemnation. By turning our thoughts over to the Holy Spirit, we realize that our ego's misperceptions were mere mistakes that require correction, not punishment.

When we recognize sin's nonexistent, we are free to drop our allegiance to our ego's judgments and misperceptions and follow the Voice for love and forgiveness. By following the Holy Spirit's thought system, we are restored to sanity. Our split mind is healed and our big "S" Self remembered. Our ego's judgments and beliefs give way to the Holy Spirit's correct perception.

Our healed mind is now able to hear God's Voice say that we are God's one Son and all God has belongs to us, His Son. Being God's Creation, we are an inseparable extension of the Mind of God Himself. All that God is has been given unto us and thus, we can want for nothing. We accept the truth of the At-One-Ment for ourselves and are restored to sanity. Our mind is now awake and will sleep no more.

This holy instant would I give to You.
Be You in charge. For I would follow You,
Certain that Your direction gives me peace.

This holy instant would I give to **the Holy Spirit**. Be **the Holy Spirit** in charge. For I would follow **the Holy Spirit** certain that **the Holy Spirit's** direction gives me peace.

W-361-5.1.And if I need a word to help me, **the Holy Spirit** will give it to me. 2 If I need a thought, that will **the Holy Spirit** also give. 3 And if I need but stillness and a tranquil, open mind, these are the gifts I will receive of **the Holy Spirit**. 4 **The Holy Spirit** is in charge by my request. 5 And **the Holy Spirit** will hear and answer me, because **the Holy Spirit** speaks for God my Father and His holy Son.

Notes to Lesson #361 to 365

This holy instant would I give to You.
Be You in charge. For I would follow You,
Certain that Your direction gives me peace.

<u>Comment</u>: While your egoic thought system is sure to fail, the Holy Spirit's thought system is guaranteed by God to succeed. Give your day over to the Holy Spirit and you will find the peace that you seek. The Holy Spirit will take your thoughts and reframe them so that your egoic belief in lack, limitation, sin, guilt and fear is eliminated and replaced by the truth of love, forgiveness and the oneness that is the shared Mind of God.

Give your life over to God, and let God live you. Ask your inner guide for help and then be still. Silence your egoic mind chatter and listen. Follow the Voice for God and you will reawaken to the peace and truth that is your divine birthright.

Only the Holy Spirit can give you the certainty and direction to reawaken your sleeping mind to the truth of your spiritual magnificence as the Christ. As the Christ, you are home to God, the Holy Spirit and your big "S" Self, for they are all one.

Epilogue

W.ep.1.This course is a beginning, not an end. 2, Your Friend, **the Holy Spirit,** goes with you. 3 You are not alone. 4 No one who calls on **the Holy Spirit** can call in vain. 5 Whatever troubles you, be certain that **the Holy Spirit** has the answer, and will gladly give **the answer** to you if you simply turn to **the Holy Spirit** and ask it of Him. 6 **The Holy Spirit** will not withhold all answers that you need for anything that seems to trouble you. 7 **The Holy Spirit** knows the way to solve all problems, and resolve all doubts. 8 **The Holy Spirit's** certainty is your **certainty**. 9 You need but ask **for the certainty** of **the Holy Spirit** and it will be given you.

W.ep.2.You are as certain of arriving home as is the pathway of the sun laid down before **the sun** rises, after **the sun** has set, and in the half-lit hours in between. 2 Indeed, your pathway is more certain still. 3 For it cannot be possible to change the course of those whom God has called to Him. 4 Therefore obey your will, and follow **the Holy Spirit** Whom you accepted as your voice, to speak of what you really want and really need. 5 **The Holy Spirit** is the Voice for God and also your **voice**. 6 And thus **the Holy Spirit** speaks of freedom and of truth.

W.ep.3.No more specific lessons are assigned, for there is no more need of **specific lessons**. 2 Henceforth, hear but the Voice for God and for your **big "S"** Self when you retire from the world, to seek reality instead. 3 **The Holy Spirit** will direct your efforts, telling you exactly what to do, how to direct your mind, and when to come to **the Holy Spirit** in silence, asking for **the Holy Spirit's** sure direction and His certain Word. 4 **The Holy Spirit** is the Word that God has given you. 5 **The Holy Spirit** is the Word you chose to be your own **word**.

W.ep.4.And now I, **Jesus,** place you in **the Holy Spirit's** hands, to be His faithful follower, with **the Holy Spirit** as Guide through every difficulty and all pain that you may think is real. 2 Nor will **the Holy Spirit** give you pleasures that will pass away, for **the Holy Spirit** gives only the eternal and the good. 3 Let **the Holy Spirit** prepare you further. 4 **The Holy Spirit** has earned your trust by speaking daily to you of your Father and your brother and your **big "S"** Self. 5 **The Holy Spirit** will continue. 6 Now you walk with **the Holy Spirit**, as certain as is He of where you go; as sure as He of how you should proceed; as confident as He is of the goal, and of your safe arrival in the end.

W.ep.5.The end is certain, and the means as well. 2 To this we say "Amen." 3 You will be told exactly what God wills for you each time there is a choice to make. 4 And **the Holy Spirit** will speak for God and for your **big "S"** Self, thus making sure that hell will claim you not, and that each choice you make brings Heaven nearer to your reach. 5 And so we walk with **the Holy Spirit** from this time on, and turn to **the Holy Spirit** for guidance and for peace and sure direction. 6 Joy attends our way. 7 For we go homeward to an open door which God has held unclosed to welcome us.

W.ep.6.We trust our ways to **the Holy Spirit** and say "Amen." 2 In peace we will continue in **the Holy Spirit's** way, and trust all things to **the Holy Spirit**. 3 In confidence we wait **the Holy Spirit's** answers, as we ask **the Holy Spirit's** Will in everything we do. 4 **The Holy Spirit** loves God's Son as we would love **God's Son**. 5 And **the Holy Spirit** teaches us how to behold **God's Son** through **the Holy Spirit's** eyes, and love **God's Son** as **the Holy Spirit** does. 6 You do not walk alone. 7 God's angels hover near and all about. 8 **God's** Love surrounds you, and of this be sure; that I, **Jesus,** will never leave you comfortless.

Personal Note to the Epilogue to the Workbook Lessons from ACIM Miracles

The Holy Spirit is your friend, guide, confidant and teacher. The Holy Spirit is the voice of your Higher Self. The Holy Spirit will never fail you since the Holy Spirit's mission has been guarantee by God Himself.

In truth, there is just the One Self. You are an indivisible part of that One. The Father is Cause. The Son, the Father's Effect. The Holy Spirit is the link that connects the two sides of one indivisible coin called God. There is no separation for in that Trinity there is just a Oneness of All That Is.

In the illusion of time, you have come here to reawaken to the truth that you are not the body and you are free. You are still as God created you, part of the indivisible One Self. Nothing sources your individuated experience but you and nothing has the ability to rob you of your inner peace unless you choose to allow it. In time and space, your mind rules your world of perception.

In this playschool of time, you are an infinite focus of consciousness. You are a feedback loop so that you can witness the effects of the choices you are making in the depth of your mind that rests in the mind of God. Therefore, each thought is a vibration of creation to communicate to the world in an attempt to experience communion with all life.

In reality you are perfect spirit, unaffected by anything. You have been given the full power to choose and to create your experiences as you would have them be. You are not the egoic part of your mind that perceives itself to be a little "s" self. You are 100% responsible for your feelings and all that you call into your awareness. Your mind gives all the meaning to your world through its power of interpretation.

Every aspect of life is a symbol of what you have chosen to experience and convey throughout creation. You have been given the infinite and perfect freedom to choose the vibrational frequency which you desire to experience. Your world of perception is a reflection of you. What you are truly committed to, you will experience. Whatever is the focus of your intention will manifest as the fulfillment of your desires. What you are experiencing is always the effect of your own desires and thinking. There are no victims and there are no victimizers; only willing volunteers.

You can choose to cultivate the reality of your oneness within the Mind of God. Why not choose that reality today? When you follow the Holy Spirit, which is your big "S" Self, you will be in harmony with the Will of God. Minds that are joined in a single purpose are of one mind.

You are not an individual. You are oneness. As you allow God to live you, you complete God and experience that oneness. God is only love and we are here to realize that only love is real and that love has no opposite.

The truth is that unconditional love recognizes these facts.

There is nobody to fix.
There is nobody to change.
There is nobody to control.
There is nobody to protect.
There is nobody to impress.
There is nobody.
God is.
And you are that One.

You get to decide when the above truth will become your reality. Drop your allegiance to your ego's fear-based beliefs, judgments and misperceptions. Instead, turn your thoughts over to the Holy Spirit and let the Voice for Truth reawaken your sleeping mind.

This is Tom Wakechild suggesting that you create a great day for yourself and your world. In order to do this, let God, the Holy Spirit and your Christ nature lead the way for they are of one purpose and one mind. Your will is Their Will.

In time, your function is forgiveness, your purpose is love and your destiny is the peace of God. Choose to reclaim your destiny and let God live you.

Namaste

Tom Wakechild

PS: Namaste means that the God in me recognizes the God in you.

About Tom Wakechild

Tom Wakechild is a contemporary teacher who combines the scientific with the spiritual to present a practical message for self-empowerment and inner peace for this world and this time. Known as a practical mystic, Tom helps spiritual minded people escape the world's blame, shame and guilt game, thus enabling them to respond appropriately to events in their life without compromising their spiritual values or losing their inner peace.

Tom's focus has always been on living all aspects of life in balance and alignment with his higher inner values and beliefs. When your actions align with your higher values, you maintain internal integrity with who you really are. This reduces the level of stress, fear and conflict you experience in life. Everything Tom teaches is practical and geared toward transforming your life today. As the best-selling author of <u>Understanding A Course In Miracles Text</u> and <u>Understanding A Course In Miracles Workbook</u>, originally known and published as <u>A Course in Miracles For Dummies Series</u>, Tom is known as a masterful teacher who can clarify the most difficult esoteric concepts. These concepts can then be understood, absorbed and implemented to transform the lives of his students and clients.

As author, coach and mentor for <u>Ending Fear: The "7R" Formula for Fearless Awakening</u>, Tom understands that you can never escape fear within a thought system that was designed to create, maintain and perpetuate fear in the first place. To break free, you must overthrow the old and adopt a new plan. Tom has helped thousands to develop that new plan to overcome their deep seated fears while reclaiming their ability to become the proactive agent for change in their lives. Through his proven 7 Step Formula of Realize, Recognize, Relationships, Responsibility, Reinterpret, Revolt and Restructure, you too can learn to eliminate fear in your life. Grounded by his many years of owning and operating a successful business consulting firm, this formula allows you to break free from the world's negative creation cycles that short-circuit your happiness.

Our society teaches that fear keeps you safe while it actually robs you of any chance for true happiness and inner peace. To maintain power and control, our society brainwashed us as children into its fear-based thought system. It determines our identity and worth. Society utilizes this fear to impose a dependent and subservient mindset upon its members. Controlling these fears, rather than fulfilling one's destiny becomes our full-time job.

Tom's mission is to help over one million self-motivated people learn to control, manage and eliminate their fears so that they are empowered with a new creative mindset to live richer, fuller, happier, self-directed lives. Through his books, mentoring and on-line classes, this mission is rapidly being accomplished.

For more about Tom and his work visit his websites at:

endingfear.org

or

understandingACIM.org

You can also contact Tom by email at:

tom@wakechild.com

Books and Classes by Tom Wakechild

Uncovering Your Default Beliefs on-line class

On-line Class Description: What is actually running your life? Why do you keep repeating the same mistakes over and over again? What makes change seem so impossible?

This on-line class helps you uncover your personal default operating belief system that is secretly running the show. With that discovery, you will probe into those previously hidden beliefs. You will finally comprehend their devastating impact on your happiness and well-being. Until you understand the limitations of your current internal belief system, your future will be a replay of your past. Once uncovered, however, you can objectively look upon each belief and modify them as needed.

Each session will discuss one or more of the fundamental concepts that form the bedrock of your personal operating belief system. Exercises will also be provided. We will challenge both the validity and the natural consequence of your current belief system. Alternative beliefs will be provided that can generate alternate realities. Only when you realize that your current beliefs no longer serve you, will you finally decide to change them.

Thoughts, raised to the level of beliefs, become things. They are the forerunners of your tomorrows. Your beliefs are the governing factors of your life. Your beliefs determine your perception. Your perception determines your experiences. Rather than change your world, you will learn how to change how you view your world. When you change how you view your world, your world will automatically realign to your new viewpoint. Learn how to reclaim your power as the decision-maker in your own life. Stop arguing for your limitations. Instead, choose differently. Become the agent for the change that you seek in your life. This class will help you unlock your true potential and reclaim your true identity and destiny.

Decoding and Living a Course in Miracles: A 12 Session Workbook book and on-line class

Book and On-line Class Description: If your spirituality cannot bring joy, peace and happiness into your life today, what good is it? Learn how to handle life's events without sacrificing your spiritual values or losing your inner peace. Life does not have to be a struggle. This book unlocks the secrets of A Course in Miracles so you can live your life in internal integrity and escape the blame, shame and guilt game that dominates our world.

This twelve session program provides a comprehensive study guide that familiarizes the reader with the main principles, terms and concepts that are encountered in A Course In Miracles. These materials instruct and teach the core ACIM principles in a systematic, logical, and easy to follow order without you deciphering the ACIM Text. Both newcomers and long time students agree that this book builds a solid foundation for both the practical implementation of the principles and any ongoing study of the ACIM Text.

These materials are appropriate for both individual and group studies of A Course in Miracles. No previous knowledge of ACIM is required. This book can be used as a stand-alone program or part of an on-line class. Additional support materials for this book and its' on-line class are available on Tom Wakechild's website: **https://endingfear.org**. To get more information or directly enroll use the following URL Address: **https://endingfear.org/funnel/dcm-class-sales-funnel/udb-cl-1-sales-pg/**

Understanding A Course In Miracles Text

NOTE: As a paperback, this book was originally titled and published as A Course In Miracles for Dummies Vol I & II. As such, it was Vol I & II of A Course In Miracles - Dummies Series. The book and series has been retitled under the Understanding A Course In Miracles Series. The book's contents remains the same.

Book Description: The text of A Course in Miracles (ACIM) is difficult and mystifying for most readers. Both teachers and students struggle for many years with little success in unlocking the secrets to understanding this Course. They often abandon their studies and end up confused and discouraged. Understanding A Course In Miracles Text cuts through the mystery of the Course's esoteric Text and makes Jesus' message understandable to the ordinary reader. ACIM uses a unique terminology that references two different levels of being that are dominated by two opposing thought systems. This book demystifies the text by clarifying the appropriate level associated with each passage. Each Text paragraph is specially formatted to replace any unclear references and pronouns with their proper antecedents. Any substitutions are clearly shown in bold print for easy reference to the original ACIM 2nd edition.

Each text paragraph is then followed by an explanatory note to assist the reader in their own interpretation of the paragraph. These notes are designed to foster discussion and clarity, not to limit ideas and prevent individual interpretation. As such, Understanding A Course In Miracles Text can be utilized as either a primary or secondary text for independent or group study. It is known as an excellent reference tool for those who seek a practical yet deeper level of understanding of the Course's teachings.

The complete digital edition of Understanding A Course In Miracles Text covers the entire ACIM text which consists of 31 chapters. Due to its length and printing restrictions, it is published and sold as two separate paperback volumes. Understanding A Course In Miracles Text Volume #1 covers Chapters #1-15 of ACIM's text. Understanding A Course In Miracles Text Volume #2 covers Chapters #16-31 of ACIM's text.

Note: Understanding A Course In Miracles Workbook Lessons is a companion in this series and covers the 365 daily lessons found in the ACIM Workbook for Students

Understanding A Course In Miracles Workbook Lessons Book and on-line class

AUDIO EDITION NOW AVAILABLE: An on-line audio edition of Understanding A Course In Miracles Workbook Lessons is now available. To enroll or get more information visit our website at: **https://endingfear.org/**. You can directly enroll by using the URL address: **https://endingfear.org/funnel/acim-workbook-class/udb-cl-1-sales-pg/** . Prices subject to change. $47 fee was the current price at the time of this edition.

NOTE: This book was originally titled and published as A Course In Miracles Workbook for Dummies. As such it was Vol III of A Course In Miracles - Dummies Series. The book and series has been retitled under the Understanding A Course In Miracles Series. The book's contents remains the same.

Book Description: This book is part of the Understanding A Course in Miracles Series and covers the ACIM Workbook For Students. All 365 daily workbook lessons from A Course In Miracles are covered in detail by this book. Each lesson is specially formatted to replace any unclear references and pronouns with their proper antecedents. Any substitutions are clearly shown in bold print for easy reference to the original ACIM 2nd edition.

Each lesson is then followed by an explanatory note to aid in your understanding and implementation of the exercise. In this modified format, these lessons become the vehicle for ending the blame, shame and guilt games that once dominated your life. The richness of these lessons now becomes apparent, understandable but more importantly, practical. You now have the tools you need to be the agent for change in your life. You no longer have any excuse not to complete these exercises and gain the insight that they provide.

This book's focus is on you. Therefore, it provides the numerous tools you need to help uncover the blocks that are preventing the flow of love into your daily life. By completing the workbook lessons, your heart will be open through an experiential learning process. This knowing will allow you to automatically begin implementing the principles of ACIM into your daily life.

Note: Understanding A Course In Miracles Text is a companion in this series and covers the entire ACIM Text of 31 chapters.

Ending Fear: The "7 R" Formula for Fearless Awakening book and on-line class

Book Description: You can never escape fear within a thought system whose sole purpose is to create, maintain and perpetuate fear in the first place. To end fear, you must revolt against this past brainwashing. Ending Fear: The "7 R" Formula for Fearless Awakening provides the why and how steps to break free from those indoctrinated fears. It gives you permission to challenge the unchallengeable.

Our society teaches that fear keeps you safe while actually, it robs you of any chance for true happiness and inner peace. To maintain power and control, society indoctrinates its children into its fear-based thought system. It determines your identity and worth. Fear is utilized to impose a dependent and subservient mindset upon its members. Controlling these fears becomes your full-time job. Fear arises anytime you believe you lack the creative power to handle a given situation. Whenever you fail to answer either of these two questions correctly, fear will arise. The first is, what are you? The second is, what do you value and why?

Society's constant brainwashing insures that you will never answer these questions correctly. Rather than teach you how to think, it tells you what to think. Unaware of this indoctrination, you abdicate control over your identity and blindly accept a belief system that empowers your masters and hurts you.

The seven steps of Realize, Recognize, Relationships, Responsibility, Reinterpret, Revolt and Restructure allow you to break free from the world's negative creation cycles that short-circuit your happiness. Because beliefs are the limiting factors for experiences, this book combines psychological, sociological and scientific studies to support the "7 R" Formula. It defines the real problem and provides the rational to empower individuals to overthrow society's fear-based thought system.

This book approaches big ideas in simple, logical yet unusual ways. It challenges commonly held indoctrinated beliefs while exposing fatal flaws in our thought systems. Those fundamental errors disempower, insure dependency and fear while secretly undermining your happiness and inner peace. You have within you the power to reclaim your true identity and determine what principles will guide your life in the future but you need a new plan. With the "7R" Formula you can achieve the happiness and inner peace that you seek and deserve. This book will help you become the deliberate creator of the new you that has been hidden within you, waiting to emerge.

Beliefs: The True Powerhouse For Your Mind on-line class

Class Description: This Four Module class covers the importance of beliefs as the key factor in determining the quantity and quality of joy and happiness or conflict and pain that you will experience in your life. Thoughts differ from beliefs. Thoughts are neutral and have no creative power to impact your life. Yet, when your thoughts are raised to the level of a belief, they are endowed with the creative ability to transform your life. Your beliefs, not your thoughts, determine what you will experience. Conscious, and more importantly, subconscious beliefs limit what you believe is possible in your life. Unfortunately, many of your core beliefs governing your life are held at the subconscious level. Thus, it becomes very important that you know and discover what your hidden beliefs are. Beliefs, if properly utilized, can help you overcome and eliminate fear in your life.

Overcoming Adversity: 7 Step Comeback Plan on-line class

Class Description: Is your world and your spirituality in conflict?

You can really be a proactive participant in this world while maintaining your inner peace. Your life does not have to be a struggle unless you choose to make it that way. You can learn how to cope with adversity in your life so that it can become a learning experience that moves you forward instead of holding you back. That's what this short video series on problems and how to handle adversity in your life is all about. This is a 4 part training series on overcoming adversity in your life. In this four part series, you will discover the true nature of problems and how to approach problems in a new way. Develop the mindset of a winner while learning the 7 R Comeback Formula. Access both the 4 levels of learning and the 3 areas of knowledge. When you do this, great quantum leaps become possible in your life.

Made in the USA
Coppell, TX
05 November 2024

39666428R00308